PF	Present value of a one-time cash flow
PV	Present value
P/E	Price-to-earnings multiple
r	Rate of return on a security; for fixed-income securities, r may denote the rate of interest for a particular period
r_f	The risk-free rate of interest
r_M	The rate of return on the market portfolio
ROE	Return on equity, incremental economic earnings per dollar reinvested in the firm
S_p	Reward-to-volatility ratio of a portfolio, also called Sharpe's measure; the excess expected return divided by the standard deviation
S_t	Stock price at time t
t	Time
T_p	Treynor's measure for a portfolio, excess expected return divided by beta
U	Utility function
V	Intrinsic value of a firm, the present value of future dividends per share
X	Exercise price of an option
y	Yield to maturity
α	Rate of return beyond the value that would be forecast from the market's return and the systematic risk of the security
β	Systematic or market risk of a security
ρ_{ij}	Correlation coefficient between returns on securities i and j
σ	Standard deviation
σ^2	Variance
Cov(r_i, r_j)	Covariance between returns on securities i and j

INVESTMENTS

INVESTMENTS

Zvi Bodie
Boston University

Alex Kane
University of California, San Diego

Alan J. Marcus
Boston University

with **234** illustrations

1989

Homewood, IL 60430
Boston, MA 02116

Sponsoring Editors: *Denise Clinton and Mike Junior*
Developmental Editor: *Terry Eynon*
Project Manager: *Carol Sullivan Wiseman*
Production Editor: *John A. Rogers*
Design: *John Rokusek*

Compositor: *The Clarinda Company*
Illustrations: *Top Graphics*
Typeface: *10/12 Times Roman*
Display: *Meridien*
Printer: *R.R. Donnelley & Sons Company*

© RICHARD D. IRWIN, INC., 1989

Library of Congress Cataloging in Publication Data

Bodie, Zvi.
    Investments / Zvi Bodie, Alex Kane, Alan J. Marcus.
    p.   cm.
    Includes bibliographical references and index.
    ISBN 0-256-07496-8
    1. Investments. 2. Portfolio management. I. Kane, Alex.
  II. Marcus, Alan J. III. Title.
  HG4521.B564 1989
  332.63′2—dc19
                                    88−27581
                                       CIP

Printed in the United States of America

3 4 5 6 7 8 9 0 DO 6 5 4 3 2 1 0

Foreword

Along with the explosive growth in world financial markets has come an interaction between scholarly theory and day-to-day business practice that is unprecedented in the history of economics. Not only are the tools of modern finance the accepted modes of analysis for sophisticated investors and traders, they are also the sources of many of the new products that are dramatically altering the financial markets. For the teacher of investments, however, the excitement and relevance of the field are matched by its dangers. A teacher must carefully craft a course for the student that balances the ever-changing and often unsettled background of scholarly theories against the temptation to titillate with the latest fad to hit the securities markets. The only way to teach successfully in such a minefield is to take a firm grasp of what is truly fundamental and to utilize what is happening in the financial markets to illustrate the workings of these fundamentals. *Investments* accomplishes that difficult task with consummate skill.

Investments sensibly begins with an overview that lays out the workings of the securities markets in a thorough but lively fashion. After the student has been exposed to the institutional structure of the securities markets, the fundamental intuitions of the trade-off between return and risk and the role of information are developed and used to clarify the workings of the markets. The major asset-pricing models are all treated with a commendable clarity that should make teaching them a pleasure.

A central theme of the book is the investor's perspective on using securities to form portfolios. The fine treatments of the stock and fixed-income markets further this theme with their emphasis on the empirical properties of these markets, and derivative securities such as options and futures become natural topics from the perspective of how they fit into investor portfolios. A careful distinction is drawn between passive and active investment management, and this distinction is used to great advantage to deal with such troublesome matters as the reconciliation of the efficient market hypotheses with active management. As with all the material, a clear presentation of the theory is accompanied by a rich matrix of institutional material within which it is applied.

Students and teachers will welcome this thoroughly modern and well executed treatment of investments. I believe that it will become the central text in the field.

Stephen A. Ross

v

About the Authors

Zvi Bodie
Boston University

Zvi Bodie is Professor of Finance and Economics at the Boston University School of Management. He is the director of Boston University's Chartered Financial Analysts Examination Review Program and has served as a consultant to many private and governmental organizations. Professor Bodie is a research associate of the National Bureau of Economic Research, where he was director of the NBER Project on Financial Aspects of the U.S. Pension System, and he is a member of the Pension Research Council of The Wharton School. He is widely published in leading professional journals, and his previous books include *Pensions in the U.S. Economy, Issues in Pension Economics,* and *Financial Aspects of the U.S. Pension System.*

Alex Kane
University of California, San Diego

Alex Kane is Professor of Finance and Economics at the University of California, San Diego, and is a fellow of the National Bureau of Economic Research in the Financial Markets and Monetary Economics Group. The author of many articles published in finance and management journals, Professor Kane has research interests in the areas of capital market theory, corporate finance, and portfolio management.

Alan J. Marcus
Boston University

Alan Marcus is Associate Professor of Finance at Boston University. He is a research fellow of the National Bureau of Economic Research, where he participates in the Financial Markets and Monetary Economics Group. He also took part in the NBER project on pension economics. Professor Marcus has been a research fellow of the Center for the Study of Futures Markets at Columbia University. His main research interests are futures and options markets, and he has published more than 20 articles in these and related areas. Professor Marcus is currently a member of the Financial Research department at Freddie Mac, the Federal Home Loan Mortgage Corporation.

To our families with love and gratitude.

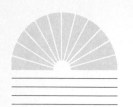

Preface

In teaching and practice, the field of investments has experienced many changes over the last 2 decades. This is due in part to an abundance of newly designed securities, in part to the creation of new trading strategies that would have been impossible without concurrent advances in computer technology, and in part to rapid advances in the theory of investments that have come out of the academic community. In no other field, perhaps, is the transmission of theory to real-world practice as rapid as is now commonplace in the financial industry. These developments place new burdens on practitioners and teachers of investments far beyond what was required only a short while ago.

Investments is intended primarily as a textbook for courses in investment analysis. Our guiding principle has been to present the material in a framework that is organized by a central core of consistent fundamental principles. We make every attempt to strip away unnecessary mathematical and technical detail, and we have concentrated on providing the intuition that may guide students and practitioners as they confront new ideas and challenges in their professional lives.

Our primary goal is to present material of practical value, but all three of us are active researchers in the science of financial economics and find virtually all of the material in this book to be of great intellectual interest. Fortunately, we think, there is no contradiction in the field of investments between the pursuit of truth and the pursuit of money. Quite the opposite. The capital asset pricing model, the arbitrage pricing model, the efficient markets hypothesis, the option pricing model, and the other centerpieces of modern financial research are as much intellectually satisfying subjects of scientific inquiry as they are of immense practical importance for the sophisticated investor.

Since 1983 we have conducted an annual review program at Boston University for candidates from all over the world preparing for the Chartered Financial Analyst examinations. From its inception in 1963 the CFA program has come to symbolize high standards of professionalism in the investment community. The CFA curriculum represents the consensus of a committee of distinguished scholars and practitioners regarding the core of knowledge required by the investment professional.

This book has benefited from our continuing CFA experience in two ways. First, we have incorporated in the text much of the content of the readings and other study materials in the official CFA curriculum. As a result, the book includes some material not found in most other investments texts. Most notably, Part VIII presents material on portfolio management principles and techniques for both the individual and institutional investor that stems largely from the CFA curriculum.

Second, we have included questions from CFA examinations in the end-of-chapter problem sets throughout the book. In every case we have indicated the year and level of the examination in which the question appeared.

Realistic Presentation of Modern Portfolio Theory

The exposition of modern portfolio theory in this text differs from its presentation in all other major investments texts in that we develop the basic model starting with a risk-free asset such as a bank certificate of deposit or a U.S. Treasury bill, and a single risky asset such as a common stock mutual fund.[1] Not until later do we add other risky assets. Other texts develop the model by first assuming that the investor has to choose from two risky assets; only later do they introduce the possibility of investing in a risk-free asset. Ultimately both approaches reach the same end point, which is a model in which there are many risky assets in addition to a risk-free asset.

We think our approach is better for two important reasons. First, it corresponds to the actual procedure that most individual investors follow. Typically, one starts with all of one's money invested in a bank account and only then considers how much to invest in something riskier that may offer the prospect of a higher expected return. The next logical step is to consider the addition of other risky assets such as real estate or gold, which requires determining whether the benefits of such increased diversification are worth the additional transaction costs involved in including them in one's portfolio.

The second advantage of our approach is that it vastly simplifies exposition of the mathematics for deriving the menu of risk-return combinations open to the investor. Portfolio optimization techniques are mathematically complex, ultimately requiring a computer. Anything that can help to simplify their presentation should thus be welcome. In short, we believe our approach is both more realistic and analytically simpler than the conventional one.

Organization and Content

The text is composed of eight sections, which are fairly independent and may be studied in a variety of sequences. Since there is enough material in the book for two

---

[1]We define and discuss mutual funds in Chapter 3. For now it is sufficient to know that a common stock mutual fund is a diversified portfolio of stocks in which an investor can invest as much money as desired.

one-semester courses, clearly a one-semester course will require the instructor to decide which parts to include and which to exclude. In the **Instructor's Manual** that accompanies the text we suggest several alternative syllabi for a one- or a two-course sequence in investments.

Part I is introductory and contains much institutional material. Chapter 1 is a description of the financial environment that contains useful background information for the student of investments.

Chapter 2 is an overview of the types of securities traded in financial markets: fixed-income, equities, options, and futures contracts. It presents a complete taxonomy of security types, describes their main features, and explains how to read security listings in the financial pages of the newspaper. The emphasis throughout the chapter is on understanding the essential features of the financial instruments without getting bogged down in unnecessary detail.

Chapter 3 explains how and where securities are traded. It starts from the issuance of new securities in the primary market, explains the securities exchanges and the over-the-counter market and how they operate, and then gives a thorough but not overly detailed presentation of the mechanics of trading. It goes through the types of orders an investor might give and explains the meaning and mechanics of buying and short-selling. It also discusses the costs of trading, how to choose a broker, and the use of mutual funds and other investment companies by the individual investor.

The material presented in Chapters 2 and 3 should make it possible for the instructor to assign term projects early in the course. These projects might require the students to analyze in detail a particular security or group of securities. Many instructors like to involve their students in some sort of investment game, which gets them to simulate the process of real-world investing. The material in these two chapters is intended to facilitate this.

Part II contains the core of modern portfolio theory as it relates to optimal portfolio selection. Chapters 4 and 5 introduce the fundamental concepts of expected return, risk, risk aversion, and diversification. Chapter 6 develops the model of portfolio optimization with a risk-free asset and a single risky asset, and Chapter 7 generalizes it to encompass many risky assets.

The level of analysis in this part of the book is as nontechnical as possible without being operationally useless. In the computer software diskette provided free to adopters of the book there is a portfolio optimization program that is quite easy to use. The student must still develop at least enough sophistication to be able to supply the inputs required and interpret the output. All of the mathematics needed to master this material is presented in the Quantitative Review at the end of the book.

Part III contains the core of modern portfolio theory as it relates to the equilibrium structure of expected rates of return on risky assets. It builds on the material in Part II, which is a prerequisite. Topics covered include the capital asset pricing model and the arbitrage pricing theory.

The last chapter in Part III, Chapter 13, treats the efficient markets hypothesis. It gives rigorous definitions of the alternative forms of the hypothesis, explains the rationale behind it, and summarizes in some detail the evidence for and against it.

Part IV, which focuses on the analysis and valuation of fixed-income securities, is the first of three parts devoted to security valuation. The other two deal with equity securities and derivative securities. For a course emphasizing security analysis and excluding portfolio theory, one may proceed directly from Part I to Part IV with no loss in continuity.

Chapter 14 introduces the fundamentals of bond pricing and yield calculations. Chapter 15 addresses the term structure of interest rates. Chapter 16 deals with fixed-income investment strategies, including the concepts of duration and immunization.

Part V is devoted to equity securities. Chapter 17 presents the theory of equity valuation, primarily discounted dividend models of progressively greater degrees of complexity and realism. It attempts to reach the level of sophistication at which professional security analysts employ these models. Chapter 18 is devoted to fundamental analysis, including the analysis of financial statements, the preparation of earnings forecasts, and other applied techniques used in trying to identify mispriced common stocks.

Part VI covers derivative assets such as options, futures contracts, and convertible securities. It contains two chapters on options and two on futures. Chapter 19, the first of the two chapters on options, is a general introduction to options markets and option pricing theory. Chapter 20 contains more advanced material on options and discusses warrants and convertible securities as well.

Chapter 21 is a general introduction to futures contracts. It explains the kinds of contracts traded, their uses in hedging and in speculating, and the equilibrium relationships between spot and futures prices. Chapter 22 takes a closer look at several selected futures contracts.

Part VII is devoted to active portfolio management. Chapter 23 develops the theory of active portfolio management. It attempts to integrate the material on security analysis in Parts IV through VI with the material on portfolio selection in Parts II and III by addressing the question of how to combine securities that you believe are mispriced into an overall portfolio that is efficiently diversified. To the best of our knowledge, the material in this chapter has never before appeared in a textbook.

Chapter 24 addresses the evaluation of portfolio performance. It develops the theory behind some of the popularly used risk-adjusted performance measures and explains the methods of determining whether a portfolio manager has superior market timing or security selection ability. Chapter 25 shows how the analysis presented thus far can be extended to a wider context that includes international investments, as well as investments in real estate or precious metals. Chapter 26 discusses some of the key organizational issues in the actual business of money management.

Part VIII is about the process of portfolio management. Chapter 27 lays out the general framework. It contains an extensive explanation of the process of asset allocation based on the theory of efficient diversification. Chapter 28 applies it to the individual investor and to pension funds. This part of the book should be of special interest to students participating in the CFA program, since it covers much of the same ground as the portfolio management parts of the CFA syllabus.

Pedagogical Features and Ancillary Materials

This book contains several features designed to make it easy for the student to understand, absorb, and apply the concepts and techniques presented. Each chapter begins with an **overview**, which states the objectives of the chapter and describes the material to be covered, and ends with a detailed **summary**, which recapitulates the main ideas presented.

Learning investments is in many ways like learning a new language. Before one can communicate, one must learn the basic vocabulary. To facilitate this process, all new terms are presented in **boldface** type the first time we use them, and at the end of each chapter there is a **Key Terms** section listing the most important new terms introduced in that chapter. A **Glossary** of all of the terms used appears at the end of the book.

Boxes containing short articles from business periodicals are included throughout the book. We think they enliven the text discussion with examples from the world of current events. The article in the Prologue from *Business Week* on the invasion of Wall Street by so-called rocket scientists is an example. We chose the boxed material on the basis of relevance, clarity of presentation, and consistency with good sense.

A unique feature of this book is the inclusion of **Concept Checks** in the body of the text. These self-test questions and problems enable the student to determine whether he or she has understood the preceding material and to reinforce that understanding. Detailed solutions to all these questions are provided at the end of the book.

These Concept Checks may be approached in a variety of ways. They may be skipped altogether in a first reading of the chapter with no loss in continuity. They can then be answered with any degree of diligence and application upon the second reading. Finally, they can serve as models for solving the end-of-chapter problems assigned by the instructor.

Each chapter also contains a list of **Selected Readings** that are annotated to guide the student toward useful sources of additional information in specific subject areas.

The **end-of-chapter problems** progress from the simple to the complex. We strongly believe that practice in solving problems is a critical part of learning investments, so we have provided lots of problems. Many are taken from CFA examinations and therefore represent the kinds of questions that professionals in the field believe are relevant to the "real world." The **Student Problems Manual,** which accompanies the text, provides many more practice problems with solutions.

Software is available for use with the text. First, it is designed to enhance the student's understanding of the material presented in the chapter. Second, it shows that the concepts and techniques presented in the chapter can be easily implemented in real-world applications by using the computer.

Many schools now make PC laboratories available for individual or class use. We have found that for some students the integration of the use of the computer into the investments course either as a mandatory or a voluntary component adds a great deal.

The software diskette provides a basic set of programs and data that the student can actually use for analysis or for personal investing.

The **Instructor's Manual** that accompanies this text contains detailed solutions to the end-of-chapter questions and problems, and a **Test Bank** contains multiple-choice problems.

Acknowledgments

This book was developed over a period of 3 years, and it involved the efforts of many dedicated professionals. Our thanks go to Steve Ross, who persuaded us that writing such a text was an endeavor worth undertaking. A distinguished panel of reviewers read the first draft, after which a focus group of selected reviewers met to discuss its content in detail. Their suggestions were incorporated in the second draft, which likewise was reviewed by a highly qualified panel. The text was extensively class tested by experienced instructors, and throughout the production process the material was examined by technical reviewers with specialized expertise in the various subject areas.

These reviewers, each of whom was carefully selected by the Irwin development team, deserve special thanks for their valuable insights and contributions.

John Binder
*University of Illinois
at Chicago*

Richard E. Callaway
*University of Tennessee
at Knoxville*

David C. Distad
*University of California
at Berkeley*

Michael C. Ehrhardt
*University of Tennessee
at Knoxville*

Jeremy Goh
Washington University

Robert G. Hansen
Dartmouth College

Joel Hasbrouck
New York University

Shalom J. Hochman
University of Houston

A. James Ifflander
Arizona State University

Robert Jennings
*Indiana University
at Bloomington*

Susan D. Jordan
*University of Missouri
at Columbia*

Josef Lakonishok
*University of Illinois
at Champaign/Urbana*

Dennis Lasser
*State University of New York
at Binghamton*

Christopher K. Ma
University of Pittsburgh

Anil K. Makhija
University of Pittsburgh

Deryl W. Martin
Emory University

Jean Masson
Washington University

Rick Meyer
University of South Florida

Don B. Panton
University of New Mexico

Leonard Rosenthal
Bentley College

Anthony Sanders
Ohio State University

John Settle
Portland State University

Keith V. Smith
Purdue University

Laura T. Starks
*University of Texas
at Austin*

Jack Treynor
University of Southern California

Hsiu-Kwang Wu
*University of Alabama
at Tuscaloosa*

Thomas J. Zwirlein
*University of Colorado
at Colorado Springs*

For granting us permission to include many of their examination questions in the text, we are grateful to the Institute of Chartered Financial Analysts.

Several colleagues read portions of the manuscript and offered many helpful suggestions. In particular, we would like to acknowledge the contributions of Jeff Daskin, Steve Marks, and Don Smith. We also are indebted to Abraham Abraham for his help with the text.

Much credit is due also to the development and production team: our special thanks go to Glenn Turner, Senior Vice President; Denise Clinton and Mike Junior, Sponsoring Editors; Terry Eynon, Developmental Editor; Carol Wiseman, Project Manager; John A. Rogers, Production Editor; and John Rokusek, Designer.

We also thank Mary Jeanne Curtenaz, Gisele Gauthier, Jeannie O'Brien, and especially Vince Mahler, who typed seemingly endless revisions of the manuscripts with good cheer.

Finally, we thank Judy, Hava, and Sheryl, who contributed to the book with their support and understanding.

Zvi Bodie
Alex Kane
Alan J. Marcus

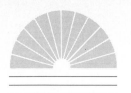

List of Boxes

Contents in Brief

Contents

PART II   *Portfolio Theory*

PART III   *Equilibrium in Capital Markets*

PART IV   *Fixed-Income Securities*

PART V　　*Equities*

PART VI

Derivative Assets: Options and Futures

PART VII   *Active Portfolio Management*

PART VIII   *Players and Strategies*

27   *Principles of Portfolio Management, 808*

28 *Individual Investors and Pension Funds, 837*

Appendix

PART I

Introduction

Prologue

This is a book about investing in securities such as stocks, bonds, options, and futures contracts. It is intended to provide an understanding of how to analyze these securities, how to determine whether they are appropriate for inclusion in your **investment portfolio** (the set of securities you choose to hold), and how to buy and sell them.

We can usefully divide the process of investing, both in theory and in practice, into two parts: security analysis and portfolio management. **Security analysis** is the attempt to determine whether an individual security is correctly valued in the marketplace; that is, it is the search for mispriced securities. **Portfolio management** is the process of combining securities into a portfolio tailored to the investor's preferences and needs, monitoring that portfolio, and evaluating its performance. This book is intended to provide a thorough treatment of both parts of the investment process.

This book is designed first and foremost to impart knowledge of practical value to anyone interested in becoming an investment professional or a sophisticated private investor. It provides a lot of institutional detail, but of necessity it also contains a lot of theory. It is impossible to be a sophisticated investor or investment professional today without a sound basis in valuation theory, modern portfolio theory, and option pricing theory at the level presented in the following chapters.

The Main Themes of Investments

The Risk-Return Trade-off

One simple strategy for an investor to pursue is to keep all of his or her money invested in a bank account. This strategy has a number of advantages. It is safe, and it requires no expertise and little effort on the part of the investor.

However, if an investor is willing to consider the possibility of taking on some risk, there is the potential reward of higher expected returns. A considerable part of this book is devoted to exploring the nature of this **risk-return trade-off** and the principles of rational portfolio choice associated with it. The approach we present is known as **modern portfolio theory** (MPT).

The main organizing principle of MPT is **efficient diversification.** The basic idea is that any investor who is averse to risk, that is, who requires a higher expected return in order to increase exposure to risk, will be made better off by reorganizing the portfolio so as to increase its expected return without taking on additional risk.

In this book we devote considerable space to explaining the principles of efficient diversification and applying them to the issue of **asset allocation.** Asset allocation is the choice of how much to invest in each of the broad asset classes—stocks, bonds, cash, real estate, foreign securities, *derivative securities,*[1] gold, and possibly others to achieve the best portfolio given the investor's objectives and constraints.

Active vs. Passive Management

We define **passive management** as a strategy of holding a well-diversified portfolio of generic security types without attempting to outperform other investors through superior market forecasting or superior ability to find mispriced securities. Depending on the approach used to find the best portfolio mix, passive management can be quite sophisticated. Indeed, as we show in our exposition of the asset allocation decision, efficient diversification can be a rather complex process, requiring many inputs and the aid of a computer.

Active management can take two forms: market timing and security selection. The most popular kind of **market timing** is trying to time the stock market, increasing one's commitment to stocks when one is "bullish" (when one thinks the market will do relatively well), and moving out of stocks when one is "bearish." But market timing is potentially just as profitable in the markets for fixed-income securities, where the name of the game is forecasting interest rates. Successful market timing, whether in the market for stocks or for bonds, requires superior forecasting ability.

Security selection is the attempt to find mispriced securities and to improve one's risk-return trade-off by concentrating on such securities. Security selection can involve both buying those securities believed to be underpriced and selling those believed to be overpriced. Successful security selection requires the sacrifice of some amount of diversification.

There is a large body of empirical evidence to support a theory called the **efficient markets hypothesis** (EMH), which among other things says that active management of both types should not be expected to work for very long. The basic reasoning behind the EMH is that in a competitive financial environment successful trading strategies tend to "self-destruct." Bargains may exist for brief periods, but with so many talented highly paid analysts scouring the markets for them, by the time you or I "discover" them, they are no longer bargains.

To be sure, there are some extremely successful investors, but according to the

---

[1]Derivative securities include options and futures contracts. They are described briefly in Chapter 2 and then discussed in much greater detail in Part VI.

EMH one can account for some or all of them on the basis of luck rather than skill. And even if their success in the past derived from skill at finding some extraordinary bargains, the EMH would say that their chances to continue to find more in the future are slight. Even the legendary Benjamin Graham,[2] the father of modern security analysis and the teacher of some of today's investment giants, has said that the job of finding true bargains has become difficult if not impossible in today's competitive environment. In part, this situation is testimony to the success Graham and his followers have had in teaching the principles of fundamental analysis.

Our view is that markets are nearly efficient. Nevertheless, even in this competitive environment profit opportunities may exist for especially diligent and creative investors. This idea motivates our treatment of active portfolio management in Part VII, which is a section unique to this textbook.

Equilibrium Pricing Relationships

A fascinating feature of financial markets, and one that is not at all apparent to the untrained observer, is that the prices of securities must often have a specific relationship to each other, because if the relationships are violated market forces will come into play to restore them. Financial economists refer to these as *equilibrium pricing relationships,* and in this text we explain them in detail.

Perhaps the best known of these relationships are the following:
1. The security market line (expected return-beta) relationship
2. The put-call parity relationship
3. The Black-Scholes option pricing model
4. The spot-futures parity relationship
5. The international interest rate parity relationship

These relationships are more than just intellectually pleasing theoretical constructs. In most cases if they are violated, the first investors to discover the violation have opportunities for large profits with little or no risk. For example, the recent practice of *program trading* is primarily a systematic method of profiting from violations of equilibrium pricing relationships in the market for the Standard & Poor's 500 stock-index futures contract.

A well-trained investment professional must not only be aware of these equilibrium relationships, but also must understand why they exist and how to profit from any violation of them. We have tried to provide the basis for this knowledge throughout the book, as well as in the specific chapters in which these relationships are presented and explained.

The Use of Options and Futures Contracts in Implementing Investment Strategy

In today's securities markets, there are a variety of ways sophisticated investors can tailor the set of possible investment outcomes to their specific knowledge or pref-

---

[2]We will have much more to say about Graham and his ideas about investing in Chapter 18.

erences regarding security returns. The emergence of markets for so-called derivative securities such as options and futures contracts has made it possible to implement strategies unheard of only a few short years ago. Perhaps in no other area of investments is the recent business school graduate at a greater advantage over the investment veteran who studied investments several years ago.

Probably the most well known of these strategies is *portfolio insurance*. There are a variety of ways an investor can combine stocks and/or bonds with derivative securities to eliminate the possibility of loss of principal while preserving much of the upside potential of an investment in the stock market. These securities and strategies are here to stay. The investment professional must understand and master them if he or she is to avoid technological obsolescence.

In our chapters on derivative securities we explain in some detail and with a minimum of mathematics the use of options and futures in implementing portfolio insurance and other investment strategies.

Text Organization

The text has nine parts, which are fairly independent and may be studied in a variety of sequences. Part I is introductory and contains much institutional material. Part II contains the core of modern portfolio theory as it relates to optimal portfolio selection. Part III contains the core of modern portfolio theory as it relates to the equilibrium structure of expected rates of return on risky assets. It builds on the material in Part II and therefore must be preceded by it.

Part IV, which is on the analysis and valuation of fixed-income securities, is the first of three parts on security valuation. Part V is devoted to equity securities. Part VI covers derivative assets such as options, futures contracts, and convertible securities.

Part VII is devoted to active portfolio management and performance measurement. It has as a prerequisite the material on MPT in Part II. Part VIII is about the process of portfolio management.

Other Features

A unique feature is the inclusion of self-test questions and problems within the following chapters. These Concept Checks are designed to provide the student with a means for determining whether he or she has understood the preceding material and for reinforcing that understanding. Detailed solutions to all Concept Checks are provided at the end of the book.

These in-chapter questions may be used in a variety of ways. They may be skipped altogether in a first reading of the chapter with no loss in continuity. They can then be done with any degree of diligence and intensity upon the second reading. Finally, they can serve as models for solving the end-of-chapter problems.

The end-of-chapter problems progress from the simple to the complex. We strongly believe that practice in solving problems is a critical part of learning investments, so we have provided many opportunities. Many are taken from past Chartered Financial Analyst examinations and therefore represent the kinds of questions that professionals in the field believe are relevant to the "real world." The *Study Guide*, which accompanies the text, provides many more practice problems with solutions.

The Investments Field and Career Opportunities

As with any other field of scientific inquiry, the theory of investments is constantly changing and, we believe, advancing. In that sense we too are always learning something new. What makes it especially exciting is that the lag between discovery and application in investments is extraordinarily short. For example, the Black-Scholes option pricing formula and the dynamic hedging strategy that is its mainspring were developed in 1973.[3] Just a few years later practitioners were busy applying it on the Chicago Board Options Exchange.

Far from being an exception, the example of the Black-Scholes formula has become the paradigm for the relationship between the academic and applied worlds in investments. Indeed, Fischer Black himself is an example of this development, moving from a professorship at MIT's Sloan School of Management to a full partnership in the investment banking firm of Goldman Sachs.

We believe that the field of investments offers great opportunities for careers that are both fascinating and lucrative, but the competition is fierce. A mastery of the material in this text will, we hope, give you a competitive advantage.

Key Terms

Investment portfolio	Asset allocation
Security analysis	Passive management
Portfolio management	Active management
Risk-return trade-off	Market timing
Modern portfolio theory	Security selection
Efficient diversification	Efficient markets hypothesis

---

[3] See Black, Fischer, and Scholes, M., "The Pricing of Options and Corporate Liabilities," *Journal of Political Economy*, May-June 1973.

Rocket Scientists Are Revolutionizing Wall Street

Former Academics Are Pioneering Ways to Make More Money With Less Risk

Before coming to Wall Street in 1980, Henry Nicholas Hanson was a physicist at Brown University, where he researched the properties of helium at low temperatures. Now, Hanson, a Salomon Brothers vice-president, is one of Wall Street's leading authorities on stock-index futures.

Stanley Diller is a former economics professor. In the mid-1970s, at the age of 40, he started a bond research department at Goldman, Sachs & Co. Now at Bear, Stearns & Co., Diller is said to earn at least $500,000 a year and tells his colleagues: "Never call me doctor. It would cut my salary by 75%."

Fischer Black, one of the nation's leading finance academics, left a tenured full professorship at Massa-

Fischer Black

chusetts Institute of Technology in early 1984 to become a vice-president at Goldman Sachs. Black is internationally known for developing an option-pricing model that traders use to value stock options.

The three men represent Wall Street's new breed, known as the "rocket scientists" or "quants." These

former academics, trained in mathematics, and the whiz kids, most from the physical sciences, who have come after them, are revolutionizing the stock and bond markets. They are the brains behind program trading—the controversial use of stock-index futures to lock in high risk-free yields. They have introduced a plethora of new financial products, including interest rate swaps, zero-coupon bonds, and new types of mortgage-backed securities. In the process, they've made hundreds of millions of dollars for the brokerage houses that employ them and for the firms' clients.

Today the top firms employ more than 1,000 rocket scientists and usually pay them well over six figures. Indeed, the Wall Street whiz kids—just like top traders and salesmen—can become millionaires in only a few years. "There is no other way a technical guy is going to make that kind of money," says Diller.

Pigeonholed

The first rocket scientists on Wall Street were cut from a different mold. In the early 1970s they and their computer programs were used for back-office functions such as data processing to handle increased trading volume. Although they vastly increased the efficiency of the brokerage industry, they were pigeonholed by top management.

But by the end of that decade, as interest rates began fluctuating wildly and the deregulation of the financial markets was picking up steam, Wall Street houses turned to the quants in increasing numbers. The firms desperately needed ways to protect against the calamitous movements in bond prices that could wipe out their capital. To their horror, they found that the old way of hedging one bond against another of a different maturity was often producing big losses. Rocket scientists solved the problem using "convexity," a tool from calculus that describes the behavior of bond prices when interest rates move violently. They also designed new hedges using options and futures contracts.

Continued.

Now the quants are in the mainstream of virtually all activity in the markets. They helped develop the hottest game on Wall Street: program trading. To play, a brokerage house or institutional client usually buys stocks that make up an index, such as the Standard & Poor's 500-stock index, and simultaneously sells short a matching futures contract that generally commands a premium over the underlying stocks. Risk-free profits come because on expiration the value of the futures contract must equal the value of the stock index.

The trick is to buy as few stocks as possible, both to mimimize transaction costs and to make sure that both sides of the trade are done at the same time. Yet the basket of securities must still track the entire index. For example, the rocket scientists showed the program traders how they can approximate the S&P 500 with 95% accuracy by buying only about half the stocks in the index.

The quants are also involved in other types of buy programs that have nothing to do with risk-free arbitrage. They are using their computers to decide when to buy as many as 2,000 different stocks at a time worth hundreds of millions of dollars. Doing such trades all at once saves transaction fees and reduces the risk that the market will change before the trade can be accomplished. "Clients call us, and we will commit to buy or sell an entire portfolio at a given price," says Arthur S. Estey, a vice-president at Shearson Lehman Brothers and a former finance professor. Indeed, a good part of the 34-point rise in the Dow industrials on April 8 resulted from a $300 million buy program that was unrelated to arbitrage.

Nervous Clients

The whiz kids have also developed a kind of insurance that is being sold to portfolio managers. As the stock market has soared, nervous clients have sought to guard their gains. By selling short futures, big investors can protect themselves against general market declines and still stay invested in individual stocks. Such "insurance" has helped keep the stock market at high levels while reducing the level of risk to investors. "People don't have to use their capital to make major moves just to play the direction of the market," says Hugh A. Johnson, chief investment strategist with First Albany Corp.

The rocket scientists continue to streamline the bond markets. Even during periods of relative interest rate stability, bond managers incur risks if they don't protect themselves against an uptick in rates. But if they're not careful, the hedge they use can kill them. Since October, interest rates have fallen 3 percentage points. The typical hedge—usually the short sale of futures—created a big loss. The offsetting gain should have been in the bond itself.

But companies have the right to call bonds if interest rates fall steeply. Thus a bondholder who sells futures contracts short could find himself losing a fortune on the short sale without making anything on the bonds themselves. The quants again were summoned, and they devised hedge programs that overcame the call problem. The quants' solution "is the talk of the town right now," says Dexter E. Senft, a managing director of First Boston Corp.

Senft, 33, has become a role model for the new Wall Street whiz kid. In 1983, he invented the collateralized-mortgage obligation, [CMO], a type of mortgage-backed security. Rather than keep him in a corner, First Boston rewarded him with the title and money of managing director. But no one argues that he is overpaid. The CMO market, starting from nothing three years ago, is approaching $35 billion.

Other phenomenally successful products of the quants include zero-coupon bonds, which are issued at a huge discount but pay no interest. Currently, there are over $200 billion worth of outstanding Treasury zeros alone. Interest rate swaps, which permit two companies to exchange fixed-rate debt for the floating-rate variety, is also a $200 billion business. Neither interest rate swaps nor zero-coupon bonds even existed before 1981.

Direct Involvement

The rise of the older rocket scientists on Wall Street has inspired a whole new generation, many of whom have abandoned other careers. James Kennedy, head of Merrill Lynch & Co.'s Debt Strategy Group, went to medical school in New Zealand. A member of his team, John H. Carlson, is a meteorologist who, before coming to Merrill, sold long-range weather forecasts to commodity brokers.

Continued.

James A. Tilley's Ph.D. thesis was titled *The Effects of Spin-Orbit Interactions in Itinerant Ferromagnets*. Now at Morgan Stanley & Co., Tilley helps insurance companies meet their policyholder obligations by matching those cash needs with the flows generated from investments. He exhibits the polish of the typical investment banker—not the dishevelment of the stereotyped technician.

More and more rocket scientists, like Tilley, are getting directly involved with corporate clients. Kennedy of Merrill Lynch recalls a client that had a series of payments totaling $45 million to make over 5 years and owned bonds whose cash flows precisely matched those obligations. Merrill's rocket scientists were asked whether there might be a less expensive way to do it. They constructed a new portfolio that would save the client $1 million. They also developed a solution that could save the company even more money if the client was willing to borrow money for a short period. The company did, and saved $3 million.

The successful Wall Street rocket scientists have learned to operate within time and budget constraints.

Some analytical problems, such as matching the cash flows of assets and liabilities, "if run to completion, would occupy the largest computer mainframes for weeks," says First Boston's Senft. "Rocket scientists get the computer to give answers that are close enough in a short time—like 15 minutes—to reduce the risk of a change in market prices during the analysis."

The message that Wall Street wants rocket scientists is being heard on university campuses. From MIT to the University of California at Berkeley, big firms are actively courting students with advanced degrees in all scientific fields. Meanwhile, investment managers around the country are struggling to keep up with the latest techniques of the quants. "We make sure we make a quarterly pilgrimage to the esoteric pillars of money management," says Bruce P. Bedford, chairman of Flagship Financial Inc. in Dayton, Ohio. "Some of it is above our heads, yeah." But "that's where the action is."

CHAPTER 1

The Investment Environment

Even a cursory glance at *The Wall Street Journal* reveals a bewildering collection of securities, markets, and financial institutions. Although it may appear so, the financial environment is not chaotic: there is rhyme and reason behind the array of instruments and markets. The central message we want to convey in this chapter is that financial markets and institutions evolve in response to the desires, technologies, and regulatory constraints of the investors in the economy. In fact, we could *predict* the general shape of the investment environment (if not the design of particular securities) if we knew nothing more than these desires, technologies, and constraints.

This chapter provides a broad overview of the investment environment. We begin by examining the differences between financial assets and real assets. We proceed to the three broad sectors of the financial environment: households, businesses, and government. We see how many features of the investment environment are natural responses of profit-seeking firms and individuals to opportunities created by the demands of these sectors, and we examine the driving forces behind financial innovation. Next, we discuss recent trends in financial markets. Finally, we conclude with a discussion of the relationship between households and the business sector.

1.1 Real Assets vs. Financial Assets

The material wealth of a society is determined ultimately by the productive capacity of its economy, the goods and services that can be provided to its members. This productive capacity is a function of the **real assets** of the economy: the land, buildings, knowledge, and machines that are used to produce goods and the workers whose skills are necessary to use those resources. Together, physical and "human" assets generate the entire spectrum of output produced and consumed by the society.

In contrast to such real assets are **financial assets** such as stocks or bonds. These assets, per se, do not represent a society's wealth. Shares of stock are no more than sheets of paper; they do not directly contribute to the productive capacity of the economy. Instead, financial assets contribute to the productive capacity of the economy *indirectly,* because they allow for separation of the ownership and management of the firm and facilitate the transfer of funds to enterprises with attractive investment opportunities. Financial assets certainly contribute to the wealth of the individuals or firms holding them. This is because financial assets are *claims* to the income generated by real assets or claims on income from the government.

When the real assets used by a firm ultimately generate income, the income is allocated to investors according to their ownership of financial assets, or securities, issued by the firm. Bondholders, for example, are entitled to a flow of income based on the interest rate and par value of the bond. Equityholders or stockholders are entitled to any residual income after bondholders and other creditors are paid. In this way the values of financial assets are derived from and depend on the values of the underlying real assets of the firm.

Real assets are income-generating assets, whereas financial assets define the allocation of income or wealth among investors. Individuals can choose between consuming their current endowments of wealth today and investing for the future. When they invest for the future, they may choose to hold financial assets. The money a firm receives when it issues securities (sells them to investors) is used to purchase real assets. Ultimately then, the returns on a financial asset come from the income produced by the real assets that are financed by the issuance of the security. In this way, it is useful to view financial assets as the means by which individuals hold their claims on real assets in well-developed economies. Most of us cannot personally own auto plants. But we can hold shares of General Motors or Ford, which provide us with income derived from the production of automobiles.

An operational distinction between real and financial assets involves the balance sheets of individuals and firms in the economy. Real assets appear only on the asset side of the balance sheet. In contrast, financial assets always appear on both sides of balance sheets. Your financial claim on a firm is an asset, but the firm's issuance of that claim is the firm's liability. When we aggregate over all balance sheets, financial assets will cancel out, leaving only the sum of real assets as the net wealth of the aggregate economy.

Another way of distinguishing between financial and real assets is to note that financial assets are created *and destroyed* in the ordinary course of doing business. For example, when a loan is paid off, both the creditor's claim (a financial asset) and the debtor's obligation (a financial liability) cease to exist. In contrast, real assets are destroyed only by accident or by wearing out over time.

The distinction between real and financial assets is apparent when we compare the composition of national wealth in the United States, presented in Table 1.1, with the financial assets and liabilities of U.S. households shown in Table 1.2. National wealth consists of structures, equipment, inventories of goods, and land. (It does not include the value of "human capital," the value of the earnings potential of the work force.) In contrast, Table 1.2 includes financial assets such as bank accounts, corporate equity, bonds, and mortgages.

Persons in the United States tend to hold their financial claims in an indirect form. In fact, only about 20% of the adult U.S. population holds shares directly. The claims of most individuals on firms are mediated through institutions that hold shares

TABLE 1.1   National Net Worth, 1986

Assets	$ Billion
Residential structures	3,748
Plant and equipment	3,922
Inventories	863
Consumer durables	1,525
Land	3,239
Gold and SDRs	19
Net claims on foreigners	−147
TOTAL	**13,170***

Data from *Balance Sheets for the U.S. Economy 1947-86*, Washington, D.C.: Board of Governors of the Federal Reserve System, October 1987.
*Column sum may differ from total because of rounding errors.

on their behalf: institutional investors such as pension funds, insurance companies, mutual funds, and college endowments.

Concept Check

Question 1. Are the following assets real or financial?
a. Patents
b. Lease obligations
c. Customer goodwill
d. A college education
e. A $5-bill

1.2   *Clients of the Financial System*

We start our analysis with a broad view of the major clients that place demands on the financial system. By considering the needs of these clients, we can gain considerable insight into why organizations and institutions have evolved as they have.

We can classify the clientele of the investment environment into three groups: the household sector, the corporate sector, and the government sector. This trichotomy is not perfect. It excludes some organizations such as not-for-profit agencies and has difficulty with some hybrids such as unincorporated or family-run businesses. Nevertheless, from the standpoint of capital markets, the three-group classification is useful.

The Household Sector

Households constantly make economic decisions concerning such activities as work, job training, retirement planning, and savings vs. consumption. We will take

TABLE 1.2   Balance Sheet of U.S. Households, 1986

Assets	$ Billion	% Total	Liabilities and Net Worth	$ Billion	% Total
Tangible Assets					
Houses	2,709	16.2	Mortgages	1,691	10.1
Land	1,081	6.5	Consumer credit	723	4.3
Durables	1,525	9.1	Other loans	220	1.3
Other	366	2.1	Other	104	0.6
Total tangibles	**5,681**	**33.9**	**Total liabilities**	**2,738**	**16.3**
Financial Assets					
Deposits	2,860	17.1			
Life insurance reserves	274	1.6			
Pension reserves	2,055	12.3			
Corporate equity	2,210	13.2			
Equity in noncorporate business	2,384	14.2			
Debt securities	1,087	6.5			
Other	200	1.2			
Total financial assets	**11,070**	**66.1**	Net worth	14,013	83.7
TOTAL	**16,751**	**100.0**		**16,751**	**100.0**

Data from *Balance Sheets for the U.S. Economy 1947-86*, Board of Governors of the Federal Reserve System, October 1987.

most of these decisions as being already made and focus on financial decisions specifically. Essentially, we concern ourselves only with what financial assets households desire to hold.

Even this limited focus, however, leaves a broad range of issues to consider. Most households are potentially interested in a wide array of assets, and the assets that are attractive can vary considerably depending on the household's economic situation. Even a limited consideration of taxes and risk preferences can lead to widely varying asset demands, and this demand for variety is, as we shall see, a driving force behind financial innovation.

Taxes lead to varying asset demands because people in different tax brackets "transform" before-tax income to after-tax income at different rates. For example, high tax–bracket investors naturally will seek tax-free securities, compared with low tax–bracket investors who want primarily higher yielding taxable securities. A desire to minimize taxes also leads to demand for securities that are exempt from state and local taxes. This in turn causes demand for portfolios that specialize in tax-exempt bonds of one particular state.

In other words, differential tax status creates "tax clienteles" that in turn give rise to demand for a range of assets with a variety of tax implications. The demand of investors encourages entrepreneurs to offer such portfolios, for a fee of course!

Risk considerations also create demand for a diverse set of investment alternatives. At an obvious level, differences in risk tolerance create demand for assets with a variety of risk-return combinations. Individuals also have particular hedging requirements that contribute to diverse investment demands.

Consider, for example, a resident of New York City who plans to sell her house and retire to Miami, Florida, in 15 years. Such a plan seems feasible if real estate prices in the two cities do not diverge before her retirement. How can one hedge Miami real estate prices now, short of purchasing a home there immediately rather than at retirement? One way to hedge the risk is to purchase securities that will increase in value if Florida real estate becomes more expensive. This creates a hedging demand for an asset with a particular risk characteristic. Such demands lead profit-seeking financial corporations to supply the desired goods: observe Florida real estate investment trusts (REITs) that allow individuals to invest in securities whose performance is tied to Florida real estate prices. If Florida real estate becomes more expensive, the REIT will increase in value. The individual's loss as a potential purchaser of Florida real estate is offset by her gain as an investor in that real estate. This is only one example of how a myriad of risk-specific assets are demanded *and created* by agents in the financial environment.

Risk motives also lead to demand for ways that investors can easily diversify their portfolios and even out their risk exposure. We will see that these diversification motives inevitably give rise to mutual funds that offer small individual investors the ability to invest in a wide range of stocks, bonds, precious metals, and virtually all other financial instruments.

The Business Sector

Whereas household financial decisions are concerned with how to invest money, businesses typically need to raise money to finance their investments in real assets: plant, equipment, technological know-how, and so forth. Table 1.3 presents balance sheets of U.S. corporations as a whole for 1986. The heavy concentration on tangible assets is obvious. Broadly speaking, there are two ways for businesses to raise money—they can borrow it, either from banks or directly from households by issuing bonds, or they can "take in new partners" by issuing stocks, which are ownership shares in the firm.

Businesses issuing securities to the public have several objectives. First, they want to get the best price possible for their securities. Second, they want to market the issues to the public at the lowest possible cost. This has two implications. First, businesses might want to farm out the marketing of their securities to firms that specialize in such security issuance, because it is unlikely that any single firm is in the market often enough to justify a full-time security issuance division. Issue of securities requires immense effort. The security issue must be brought to the attention of the public. Buyers then must subscribe to the issue, and records of subscriptions and deposits must be kept. The allocation of the security to each buyer must be determined, and subscribers finally must exchange money for securities. These activities clearly call for specialists. The complexities of security issuance have been the catalyst for creation of an investment banking industry to cater to business demands. We will return to this industry shortly.

The second implication of the desire for low-cost security issuance is that most businesses will prefer to issue fairly simple securities that require the least extensive

TABLE 1.3   Balance Sheet of Nonfinancial U.S. Businesses, 1986 (Farm, Corporate, Noncorporate)*

Assets	$ Billion	% Total	Liabilities and Net Worth	$ Billion	% Total
Tangible Assets					
Equipment and structures	4,510	49.4	Money market securities	76	.8
Land	2,045	22.4	Bonds and mortgages	1,535	16.8
Inventories	863	9.5	Bank loans	604	6.6
Total tangibles	**7,418**	**81.3**	Other loans	349	3.8
			Trade debt	519	5.7
			Other	341	3.7
			Total liabilities	**3,424**	**37.5**
Financial Assets					
Deposits and cash	307	3.4			
Marketable securities	244	2.7			
Consumer credit	93	1.0			
Trade credit	636	6.7			
Other	423	4.6			
Total financial assets	**1,703**	**18.7**	Net worth	5,697	62.5
TOTAL	**9,121**	**100.0**		**9,121**	**100.0**

Data from *Balance Sheets for the U.S. Economy 1947-86*, Board of Governors of the Federal Reserve System, October 1987.
*Column sums may differ from total because of rounding error.

incremental analysis and, correspondingly, are the least expensive to arrange. Such a demand for simplicity or uniformity by business-sector security issuers is likely to be at odds with the household sector's demand for a wide variety of risk-specific securities. This mismatch of objectives gives rise to an industry of middlemen who act as intermediaries between the two sectors, specializing in transforming simple securities to complex issues that suit particular market niches.

The Government Sector

Like businesses, governments often need to finance their expenditures by borrowing. Unlike businesses, governments cannot sell equity shares; they are restricted to borrowing to raise funds when tax revenues are not sufficient to cover expenditures. They also can print money, of course, but this source of funds is limited by its inflationary implications, and so most governments usually try to avoid excessive use of the printing press.

Governments have a special advantage in borrowing money because their taxing power makes them very creditworthy and therefore able to borrow at the lowest rates. The financial component of the federal government's balance sheet is presented in Table 1.4. Notice that the major liabilities are government securities.

A second, special role of the government is in regulating the financial environment. Some government regulations are relatively innocuous. For example, the Securities and Exchange Commission is responsible for disclosure laws that are designed

TABLE 1.4   Financial Assets and Liabilities of the U.S. Government, 1986

Assets	$ Billion	% Total	Liabilities	$ Billion	% Total
Deposits, currency, gold	62	17.4	Currency	19	.9
Mortgages	54	15.1	Government securities	1,812	90.1
Loans	200	56.0	Pension fund reserves	170	8.4
Other	41	11.5	Life insurance reserves	11	0.6
TOTAL	357	100.0	TOTAL	2,012	100.0

Data from *Flow of Funds Accounts: Financial Assets and Liabilities, Year-End, 1963-86,* Board of Governors of the Federal Reserve System, September 1987.

to enforce truthfulness in various financial transactions. Other regulations have been much more controversial.

One example is Regulation Q, which for decades put a ceiling on the interest rates that banks were allowed to pay to depositors, until it was repealed by the Depository Institutions Deregulation and Monetary Control Act of 1980. These ceilings were supposedly a response to widespread bank failures during the Great Depression. By curbing interest rates, the government hoped to limit further failures. The idea was that if banks could not pay high interest rates to compete for depositors, their profits and safety margins presumably would improve. The result was predictable: instead of competing through interest rates, banks competed by offering "free" gifts for initiating deposits and by opening more numerous and convenient branch locations. Another result also was predictable: bank competitors stepped in to fill the void created by Regulation Q. The great success of money market funds in the 1970s came in large part from depositors leaving banks that were prohibited from paying competitive rates. Indeed, much financial innovation may be viewed as responses to government tax and regulatory rules.

1.3   *The Environment Responds to Clientele Demands*

When enough clients demand and are willing to pay for a service, it is likely in a capitalistic economy that a profit-seeking supplier will find a way to provide and charge for that service. This is the mechanism that leads to the diversity of financial markets. Let us consider the market responses to the disparate demands of the three sectors.

Financial Intermediation

Recall that the financial problem facing households is how best to invest their funds. The relative smallness of most households makes direct investment intrinsically difficult. A small investor obviously cannot advertise his willingness in the local newspaper to lend money to businesses that need to finance investments. Instead,

TABLE 1.5   Balance Sheet of Financial Institutions, 1986*

Assets	$ Billion	% Total	Liabilities and Net Worth	$ Billion	% Total
Tangible Assets			**Liabilities**		
Equipment and structures	186	2.2	Deposits	3,097	37.4
Land	12	.1	Mutual fund shares	413	5.0
Total tangibles	**198**	**2.4**	Life insurance reserves	264	3.2
			Pension reserves	1,886	22.8
			Money market securities	821	9.9
			Bonds and mortgages	272	3.3
			Other	1,100	13.3
			Total liabilities	**7,853**	**94.9**
Financial Assets					
Deposits and cash	299	3.6			
Government securities	1,676	20.3			
Corporate bonds	776	9.4			
Money market securities	366	4.4			
Mortgages	1,598	19.3			
Consumer credit	630	7.6			
Other loans	972	11.8			
Corporate equity	969	11.7			
Other	788	9.5			
Total financial assets	**8,074**	**97.6**	Net worth	419	5.1
TOTAL	**8,272**	**100.0**		**8,272**	**100.0**

Data from *Balance Sheets for the U.S. Economy 1947-86*, Board of Governors of the Federal Reserve System, October 1987.
*Column sums may differ from total because of rounding error.

financial intermediaries such as banks, investment companies, insurance companies, or credit unions naturally evolve to bring the two sectors together. Financial intermediaries sell their own liabilities to raise funds that are used to purchase liabilities of other corporations.

For example, a bank raises funds by borrowing (taking in deposits) and lending that money to (purchasing the loans of) other borrowers. The spread between the rates paid to depositors and the rates charged to borrowers is the source of the bank's profit. In this way, lenders and borrowers do not need to contact each other directly. Instead, each goes to the bank, which acts as an intermediary between the two. The problem of matching lenders with borrowers is solved when each comes independently to the common intermediary. The convenience and cost savings the bank offers the borrowers and lenders allow it to profit on the spread between the rates on its loans and the rates on its deposits. In other words, the problem of coordination creates a market niche for the bank as intermediary. Profit opportunities alone dictate that banks will emerge in a trading economy.

Financial intermediaries are distinguished from other businesses in that both their assets and their liabilities are overwhelmingly financial. Table 1.5 shows that the balance sheets of financial institutions include very small amounts of tangible assets. Compare Table 1.5 with Table 1.3, the balance sheet of the nonfinancial corporate sector. The contrast arises precisely because intermediaries are middlemen, simply moving funds from one sector to another. In fact, from a bird's-eye view, this is the primary social function of such intermediaries, to channel household savings to the business sector.

Other examples of financial intermediaries are investment companies, insurance companies, and credit unions. All these firms offer similar advantages, in addition to playing a middleman role. First, by pooling the resources of many small investors, they are able to lend considerable sums to large borrowers. Second, by lending to many borrowers, intermediaries achieve significant diversification, meaning they can accept loans that individually might be risky. Third, intermediaries build expertise through the volume of business they do. One individual trying to borrow or lend directly would have much less specialized knowledge of how to structure and execute the transaction with another party.

Investment companies, which pool together and manage the money of many investors, also arise out of the "smallness problem." Here, the problem is that most household portfolios are not large enough to be spread among a wide variety of securities. It is very expensive in terms of brokerage fees to purchase one or two shares of many different firms, and it clearly is more economical for stocks and bonds to be purchased and sold in large blocks. This observation reveals a profit opportunity that has been filled by mutual funds offered by many investment companies. **Mutual funds** pool the limited funds of small investors into large amounts, thereby gaining the advantages of large-scale trading; investors are assigned a prorated share of the total funds according to the size of their investment. This system gives small investors advantages that they are willing to pay for via a management fee to the mutual fund operator. Mutual funds are logical extensions of an investment club or cooperative, in which individuals themselves team up and pool funds. The fund sets up shop as a firm that accepts the assets of many investors, acting as an investment agent on their behalf. Again, the advantages of specialization are sufficiently large that the fund can provide a valuable service and still charge enough for it to clear a handsome profit.

Investment companies also can design portfolios specifically for large investors with particular goals. In contrast, mutual funds are sold in the retail market, and their investment philosophies are differentiated mainly by strategies that are likely to attract a large number of clients. Some investment companies manage "commingled funds," in which the monies of different clients with similar goals are merged into a "mini-mutual fund," which is run according to the common preferences of those clients.

Economies of scale also explain the proliferation of analytic services available to investors. Newsletters, data bases, and brokerage house research services all exploit the fact that the expense of collecting information is best borne by having a few agents engage in research to be sold to a large client base. This setup arises naturally. Investors clearly want information, but, with only small portfolios to manage, they do not find it economical to incur the expense of collecting it. Hence, a profit opportunity emerges: a firm can perform this service for many clients and charge for it.

Investment Banking

Just as economies of scale and specialization create profit opportunities for ...-cial intermediaries, so too do these economies create niches for firms that perform specialized services for businesses. We said before that firms raise much of their capital by selling securities such as stocks and bonds to the public. Because these firms do not do so frequently, however, investment banking firms that specialize in such activities are able to offer their services at a cost below that of running an in-house security issuance division.

Investment bankers such as Goldman Sachs, Merrill Lynch, or Salomon Brothers advise the issuing firm on the prices it can charge for the securities issued, market conditions, appropriate interest rates, and so forth. Ultimately, the investment banking firm handles the marketing of the security issue to the public.

Investment bankers also can help firms design securities with special desirable properties. As an example of this practice, consider a pharmaceutical company undertaking a risky R&D project for a new drug. It needs to raise money for research costs and realizes that if the research is successful it will need to build a new manufacturing plant requiring still more financing. To deal with this contingency, the investment banker might design a bond-with-warrant issue. (A *warrant* is a security giving its holder the option to purchase stock from the firm at a specified price up until the warrant's expiration date.) The bonds and warrants are issued, and the research commences. If the research is eventually successful, the stock price will increase, the warrant holders will find it advantageous to exercise their options to purchase additional shares, and as they purchase those shares, additional funds will flow to the firm precisely as they are needed to finance the new manufacturing plant. The design of the financing scheme lets the firm avoid two separate security offerings and saves the considerable costs of the second offering. The exercise of the warrants provides additional financing at no additional flotation costs.

Financial Innovation

The example of the pharmaceutical company illustrates one source of financial innovation. The company's need for initial and contingent financing led to a creative packaging of securities that met the particular needs of the firm. The investment diversity desired by households, however, is far greater than most businesses have a desire to satisfy. Most firms find it simpler to issue "plain vanilla" securities, leaving exotic variants to others who specialize in financial markets. This, of course, creates a profit opportunity for innovative security design and repackaging that investment bankers are only too happy to fill.

Consider the astonishing changes in the mortgage markets since 1970, when mortgage pass-through securities were first introduced by the Government National Mortgage Association (GNMA, or Ginnie Mae). These pass-throughs aggregate individual home mortgages into relatively homogeneous pools. Each pool acts as backing for a **GNMA pass-through security.** GNMA securityholders receive prorated shares of all the principal and interest payments made on the underlying mortgage pool. For example, the pool might total $100 million of 12%, 30-year conventional mortgages.

The rights to the cash flows could then be sold as 5,000 units, each worth $20,000. Each unit holder would then receive 1/5,000 of all monthly interest and principal payments made on the pool. The banks that originated the mortgages continue to service them, but no longer own the mortgage investments; these have been passed through to the GNMA securityholders.

Pass-through securities were a tremendous innovation in mortgage markets. The *securitization* of mortgages meant that mortgages could be traded just like other securities in national financial markets. Availability of funds no longer depended on local credit conditions; with mortgage pass-throughs trading in national markets, mortgage funds could flow from any region to wherever demand was greatest.

The next round of innovation came when it became apparent that investors might be interested in mortgage-backed securities with different effective times to maturity. Thus was born the *collateralized mortgage obligation,* or CMO. The CMO meets the demand for mortgage-backed securities with a range of maturities by dividing the overall pool into a series of classes called tranches. The so-called fast-pay tranche receives all the principal payments made on the entire mortgage pool until the total investment of the investors in the tranche is repaid. In the meantime investors in the other tranches receive only interest on their investment. In this way the fast-pay tranche is retired first and is the shortest-term mortgage-backed security. The next tranche then receives all of the principal payments until it is retired, and so on, until the slow-pay tranche, the longest-term class, finally receives payback of principal after all other tranches have been retired.

Although these securities are relatively complex, the message here is that security demand elicited a market response. The waves of product development in the last 2 decades are responses to perceived profit opportunities created by as-yet unsatisfied demands for securities with particular risk, return, tax, and timing attributes. As the investment banking industry becomes even more sophisticated, security creation and customization become more routine. Most new securities are created by dismantling and rebundling more basic securities. For example, the CMO is a dismantling of a simpler mortgage-backed security into component tranches. A Wall Street joke asks how many investment bankers it takes to sell a light bulb. The answer is 100—one to break the bulb and 99 to sell off the individual fragments.

This discussion leads to the notion of primitive vs. derivative securities. A **primitive security** offers returns based only on the status of the issuer. For example, bonds make stipulated interest payments depending only on the solvency of the issuing firm. Dividends paid to stockholders depend as well on the board of directors' assessment of the firm's financial position. In contrast, **derivative securities** yield returns that depend on additional factors pertaining to the prices of other assets. For example, the payoff to stock options depends on the price of the underlying stock. In our mortgage examples the derivative mortgage-backed securities offer payouts that depend on the original mortgages, which are the primitive securities. Much of the innovation in security design may be viewed as the continual creation of new types of derivative securities from the available set of primitive securities.

Response to Taxation and Regulation

We have seen that much financial innovation and security creation may be viewed as a natural market response to unfulfilled investor needs. Another driving force behind innovation is the ongoing game played between governments and investors on taxation and regulation. Many financial innovations are direct responses to government attempts either to regulate or to tax investments of various sorts. We can illustrate this with several examples.

We have already noted how Regulation Q, which limited bank deposit interest rates, spurred the growth of the money market industry. It also was one reason for the birth of the Eurodollar market. Because Regulation Q did not apply to dollar-denominated time deposits in foreign accounts, many U.S. banks and foreign competitors established branches in Western Europe, where they could offer competitive rates outside the jurisdiction of U.S. regulators. The growth of the Eurodollar market was also the result of another U.S. regulation: reserve requirements. Foreign branches were exempt from such requirements and were thus better able to compete for deposits. Ironically, despite the fact that Regulation Q no longer exists, the Eurodollar market continues to thrive, thus complicating the lives of U.S. monetary policymakers.

Another innovation attributable largely to tax avoidance motives is the long-term deep discount, or zero-coupon, bond. These bonds, often called "zeros," pay little or no interest, instead providing returns to investors through a redemption price that is higher than the initial sales price. Corporations were allowed for tax purposes to impute an implied interest expense based on this built-in price appreciation. The government's technique for imputing tax-deductible interest expenses, however, proved to be too generous in the early years of the bonds' lives, so corporations issued these bonds widely to exploit the resulting tax benefit. Ultimately, the Treasury caught on, amended its interest imputation procedure, and the flow of new zeros dried up.

Meanwhile, however, the financial markets had discovered that zeros were useful ways to lock in a long-term investment return. When the supply of primitive zero-coupon bonds ended, financial innovators created derivative zeros by purchasing U.S. Treasury bonds, "stripping" off the coupons, and selling them separately as zeros.

Another tax-induced innovation is the **dual fund.** Under old U.S. tax laws, capital gains were taxed at lower rates than were dividends. The differential meant high tax–bracket investors preferred capital gains, whereas tax-exempt investors were happy to receive dividends. Entrepreneurs then created dual funds (the derivative asset) in which *income* and *capital* shares on a portfolio of stocks (the primitive assets) were sold separately. The income shareholders receive the dividends on the portfolio, plus their share of the initial value when the portfolio is cashed in. The capital shareholders receive their share of initial value plus any accumulated capital gains.

There are plenty of other examples. The Eurobond market came into existence as a response to changes in U.S. tax law. Financial futures markets were stimulated by abandonment in the early 1970s of the system of fixed exchange rates and by new federal regulations that overrode state laws treating some financial futures as gambling arrangements.

The general tendency is clear: tax and regulatory pressures on the financial system very often lead to unanticipated financial innovations when profit-seeking investors make an end run around the government's restrictions. The constant game of regulatory catch-up sets off another flow of new innovations.

1.4   *Markets and Market Structure*

Just as securities and financial institutions come into existence as natural responses to investor demands, so too do markets evolve to meet needs. Consider what would happen if organized markets did not exist. Households that wanted to borrow would need to find others that wanted to lend. Inevitably, a meeting place for borrowers and lenders would be settled on, and that meeting place would evolve into a financial market. A pub in old London called Lloyd's launched the maritime insurance industry. A Manhattan curb on Wall Street became synonymous with the financial world.

We can differentiate four types of markets: direct search markets, brokered markets, dealer markets, and auction markets.

A **direct search market** is the least organized market. Here, buyers and sellers must seek each other out directly. One example of a transaction taking place in such a market would be the sale of a used refrigerator in which the seller advertises for buyers in a local newspaper. Such markets are characterized by sporadic participation and low-priced and nonstandard goods. It does not pay most people or firms to seek profits by specializing in such an environment.

The next level of organization is a **brokered market.** In markets where trading in a good is sufficiently active, brokers can find it profitable to offer search services to buyers and sellers. A good example is the real estate market, where economies of scale in searches for available homes and for prospective buyers make it worthwhile for participants to pay brokers to conduct the searches for them. Brokers in given markets develop specialized knowledge on valuing assets traded in that given market.

An important brokered investment market is the so-called **primary market,** where new issues of securities are offered to the public. In the primary market investment bankers act as brokers; they seek out investors to purchase securities directly from the issuing corporation. By contrast, purchase and sale of existing securities among investors take place in the **secondary market,** which means on established security exchanges or in the over-the-counter market.

Another brokered market is that for large **block transactions,** in which very large blocks of stock are bought or sold. These blocks are so large (more than 10,000 shares) that brokers or "block houses" often are engaged to search directly for other large traders, rather than bringing the trade directly to the stock exchange where relatively smaller investors trade.

When trading activity in a particular type of asset increases, **dealer markets** arise. Here, dealers specialize in various commodities, purchase assets for their own inventory, and sell goods for a profit from their inventory. Dealers, unlike brokers, trade assets for their own accounts. The dealer's profit margin is the "bid-asked" spread, the difference between the price at which the dealer buys for and sells from inventory. Dealer markets save traders on search costs because market participants can easily look up the prices at which they can buy from or sell to dealers. Obviously, a fair amount of market activity is required before dealing in a market is an attractive source of income. The over-the-counter securities market is one example of a dealer market.

The most integrated market is an **auction market,** in which all transactors in a good converge at one place to bid on or offer a good. The New York Stock Exchange (NYSE) is an example of an auction market. An advantage of auction markets over dealer markets is that one need not search to find the best price for a good. If all participants converge, they can arrive at mutually agreeable prices and thus save the bid-asked spread. Continuous auction markets (as opposed to periodic auctions such as in the art world) require very heavy and frequent trading to cover the expense of maintaining the market. For this reason, the NYSE and other exchanges set up listing requirements, which limit the shares traded on the exchange to those of firms in which sufficient trading interest is likely to exist.

Concept Check	Question 4. Many assets trade in more than one type of market. What types of markets do the following trade in? a. Used cars b. Paintings c. Rare coins

1.5 *Recent Trends*

We have recently seen four trends in the contemporary investment environment:

1. Globalization   3. Credit enhancement
2. Securitization   4. Bundling and unbundling

Each is a logical consequence of the demand and supply forces that give rise to specialized markets and instruments.

Globalization

If a wider array of investment choices can improve welfare, why should we limit ourselves to purely domestic assets? **Globalization** requires efficient communication technology and the dismantling of regulatory constraints. These tendencies in worldwide investment environments have encouraged international investing in recent years.

U.S. investors commonly can take advantage of foreign investment opportunities in two ways:

1. Purchase of foreign securities using American Depository Receipts (ADRs), which are domestically traded securities representing claims to shares of foreign stocks

2. Purchase of foreign securities that are offered in dollars

Once upon a time a U.S. investor who wished to hold a French stock had to engage in four transactions: (1) purchase French francs, (2) purchase the stock on the French Bourse, (3) sell the stock in France, and (4) sell the French francs for dollars. Today, the same investor can purchase ADRs of this stock. Brokers who act as intermediaries for these transactions hold an inventory of stock from which they sell shares, denominated in U.S. dollars. Now, there is no more technical difference between investing in a French or a U.S. stock than there is in holding a Massachusetts-based stock compared with a California-based stock. Of course, the investment implications may differ: ADRs still expose investors to exchange rate risk.

Many foreign firms are so eager to lure U.S. investors that they will save these investors the expense of paying the higher commissions that are associated with the ADRs. Figure 1.1 shows a case in point. Cadbury Schweppes is a United Kingdom-based corporation that marketed its stock directly to U.S. investors in ADRs. Each ADR represents a claim to 10 shares of Cadbury Schweppes stock.

An example of how far globalization has progressed appears in Figure 1.2. Here, Walt Disney is selling debt claims denominated in European Currency Units (ECUs), an index of a basket of European currency values.

Securitization

Until recently, financial intermediaries served to channel funds from national capital markets to smaller local ones. **Securitization,** however, now allows borrowers to enter capital markets directly. In this procedure pools of loans typically are aggregated into pass-through securities, such as mortgage pass-throughs. Then, investors can invest in securities backed by those pools. The transformation of these pools into standardized securities enables issuers to deal in a volume large enough that they can bypass intermediaries. We have already discussed this phenomenon in the context of the securitization of the mortgage market.

Another example of securitization is the collateralized automobile receivable (CAR), a pass-through arrangement for car loans. Figure 1.3 shows an example of such a note. The loan originator passes the loan payments through to the holder of the CAR.

FIGURE 1.1
Globalization and
American Depository
Receipts.

This announcement is neither an offer to sell nor a solicitation of an offer to buy any of these Securities.
This offer is made only by the Prospectus.

Cadbury Schweppes p.l.c.

6,000,000 American Depositary Shares

Representing

60,000,000 Ordinary Shares

———

Price $17 an American Depositary Share

———

Copies of the Prospectus may be obtained in any State from only such of the
undersigned as may legally offer these Securities in compliance
with the securities laws of such State.

MORGAN STANLEY & CO.
Incorporated

LEHMAN BROTHERS
Shearson Lehman American Express Inc.

KLEINWORT, BENSON
Incorporated

BEAR, STEARNS & CO.	THE FIRST BOSTON CORPORATION	ALEX. BROWN & SONS Incorporated
DILLON, READ & CO. INC.		DONALDSON, LUFKIN & JENRETTE Securities Corporation
DREXEL BURNHAM LAMBERT Incorporated	GOLDMAN, SACHS & CO.	HAMBRECHT & QUIST Incorporated
HOARE GOVETT LTD.	E. F. HUTTON & COMPANY INC.	KIDDER, PEABODY & CO. Incorporated
LAZARD FRERES & CO.	MERRILL LYNCH CAPITAL MARKETS	SAMUEL MONTAGU & CO. Limited
PAINEWEBBER Incorporated	PRUDENTIAL-BACHE Securities	ROBERTSON, COLMAN & STEPHENS
L. F. ROTHSCHILD, UNTERBERG, TOWBIN		SALOMON BROTHERS INC.
SMITH BARNEY, HARRIS UPHAM & CO. Incorporated	WERTHEIM & CO., INC.	DEAN WITTER REYNOLDS INC.

September 12, 1984

FIGURE 1.2
Globalization: a debt
issue denominated in
European Currency
Units.

New Issue December, 1985

ECU 62,500,000

Walt Disney Productions

8¾% Notes Due February 25, 1994

Salomon Brothers International Limited

Crédit Commercial de France	**Kredietbank International Group**
BankAmerica Capital Markets Group	**Banque Bruxelles Lambert S.A.**
Banque Générale du Luxembourg S.A.	**Banque Internationale à Luxembourg S.A.**
Banque Nationale de Paris	**Banque Paribas Capital Markets Limited**
Caisse des Dépôts et Consignations	**Crédit Agricole**
Crédit Lyonnais	**Deutsche Bank Capital Markets Limited**
EBC Amro Bank Limited	**Generale Bank**
Genossenschaftliche Zentralbank AG Vienna	**IBJ International Limited**
Mitsubishi Finance International Limited	**Morgan Guaranty Ltd**
Morgan Stanley International	**Nippon European Bank S.A.**
Nomura International Limited	**Société Génerale**
Swiss Bank Corporation International Limited	**Union Bank of Switzerland (Securities) Limited**
S. G. Warburg & Co. Ltd.	**Westpac Banking Corporation**

FIGURE 1.3
Securitization of
automobile loans.

NEW ISSUE   July 7, 1987

$25,675,000

Asset Backed Securities Corporation

Asset Backed Obligations, Series 3

Collateralized by Automotive Receivables

$15,250,000	$10,425,000
7.40% Class 3-A Notes Due June 15, 1990	7.45% Class 3-B Notes Due June 15, 1992
Price 99.9375%	Price 97.1875%
plus accrued interest at the applicable rate from June 15, 1987	plus accrued interest at the applicable rate from June 15, 1987

---

*The Notes will be secured by a pool of recently originated retail automotive installment sale contracts (the
"Receivables") purchased from General Electric Credit Corporation (the "Company"), all monies
due thereunder net of servicing and other fees, security interests in the vehicles financed
thereby, the Company's limited guaranty of payments under the Receivables, and
certain other collateral. The Receivables will be secured by new, and used
automobiles and light trucks and will be serviced by the Company.*

*Copies of the Prospectus and the related Prospectus Supplement may be obtained
in any State in which this announcement is circulated where the undersigned
may legally offer these securities in such State.*

 # The First Boston Corporation

FIGURE 1.4

Aetna's credit enhancement of the Rockefeller Group's bond.

Offering Circular

$100,000,000

Rockefeller Group International Finance N.V.

13¼% Notes Due 1989

Unconditionally Guaranteed as to Payment of Principal and Interest by

Rockefeller Group, Inc.

and under a Surety Bond Issued by

The Ætna Casualty and Surety Company

Issue Price 99¾%

Principal of, premium, if any, and interest on the Notes will be payable without deduction for, or on account of, United States or Netherlands Antilles withholding taxes, all as set forth herein. Interest will be payable annually on June 21, commencing in 1985.

The Notes will mature on June 21, 1989. The Notes are redeemable (i) as a whole or from time to time in part, on or after June 21, 1987 at a redemption price equal to 101¼% of the principal amount of the Notes if made prior to June 21, 1988 and 100½% of the principal amount of the Notes if made on or after June 21, 1988, plus, in each case, accrued interest to the date fixed for redemption, and (ii) as a whole at any time in the event of certain developments involving United States or Netherlands Antilles withholding taxes, at their principal amount plus accrued interest to the date fixed for redemption. See "Description of the Notes". The Notes may also be redeemed as a whole, at a redemption price equal to their principal amount plus accrued interest to the date fixed for redemption, at the option of The Ætna Casualty and Surety Company ("Ætna") upon the occurrence of certain events. See "Description of the Surety Bond".

The Notes will be unconditionally guaranteed as to the payment of principal, premium, if any, and interest and certain other amounts by Rockefeller Group, Inc. As a private corporation, Rockefeller Group, Inc., does not disclose financial information to the public. Accordingly, arrangements have been made for payments of principal of, premium, if any, and interest on, and certain other amounts with respect to, the Notes to be guaranteed under a Surety Bond issued by Ætna. See "Description of the Notes" and "Description of the Surety Bond".

Application has been made to list the Notes on the Luxembourg Stock Exchange.

The Notes have not been registered under the United States Securities Act of 1933 and may not be offered or sold, directly or indirectly, in the United States of America, or its territories or possessions or to citizens, nationals or residents thereof, except as set forth herein. See "Underwriting".

A temporary global Note without interest coupons in the amount of $100,000,000 will be delivered to a depositary in London for the account of participants in Euro-clear and CEDEL S.A. on or about June 21, 1984 and will be exchangeable for definitive Notes not earlier than 90 days after the completion of the distribution upon certification that such Notes are not beneficially owned by United States citizens, nationals or residents, as set forth herein. Interest on the Notes will not be payable until issuance of the definitive Notes. See "Description of the Notes—Denominaton and Transfer".

MORGAN GUARANTY LTD

AMRO INTERNATIONAL LIMITED	**CHASE MANHATTAN LIMITED**
CREDIT SUISSE FIRST BOSTON LIMITED	**DEUTSCHE BANK AKTIENGESELLSCHAFT**
DRESDNER BANK AKTIENGESELLSCHAFT	**ENSKILDA SECURITIES** SKANDINAVISKA ENSKILDA LIMITED
LEHMAN BROTHERS INTERNATIONAL SHEARSON LEHMAN/AMERICAN EXPRESS INC	**SAMUEL MONTAGU & CO. LIMITED**
ORION ROYAL BANK LIMITED	**SOCIÉTÉ GÉNÉRALE**
SOCIÉTÉ GÉNÉRALE DE BANQUE S.A.	**SWISS BANK CORPORATION INTERNATIONAL LIMITED**
UNION BANK OF SWITZERLAND (SECURITIES) LIMITED	**S. G. WARBURG & CO. LTD.**

May 25, 1984

Securitization also may represent a way for U.S. banks to unload their portfolios of third-world debt. Many observers believe these loans will be joined into pools, with claims to these pools then sold to outside investors.

Credit Enhancement

In the past, a corporation that was not in the best of financial conditions would be able to obtain loans only through commercial banks. The banks' credit departments scrutinized each customer. A business shopping around for a loan might be sized up simultaneously by several different banks.

Today, the credit-hungry corporation can arrange for **credit enhancement.** It engages an insurance company to put its credit behind the corporation's, for a fee. The firm can then float a bond of "enhanced" credit rating directly to the public.

Figure 1.4 shows an example of credit enhancement in a joint financial venture between the Rockefeller Group and Aetna Casualty and Surety. The Rockefeller Group is a privately held corporation and thus exempt from a large part of typical disclosure rules. It cannot issue publicly traded bonds at reasonably low yields without revealing information to the public that it wishes to keep private. Instead, it purchases Aetna's backing. Aetna can perform its own credit analysis, keeping the information revealed confidential.

Bundling and Unbundling

Disparate investor demands elicit a supply of exotic securities. Creative security design often calls for **bundling** primitive and derivative securities into one composite security. One such example appears in Figure 1.5. The Chubb Corporation, with the aid of Goldman Sachs, has combined three primitive securities—stocks, bonds, and preferred stock—into one hybrid security.

Chubb is issuing preferred stock that is convertible into common stock, at the option of the holder, and exchangeable into convertible bonds at the option of the firm. Hence, this security is a bundling of preferred stock with several options.

Quite often, creating a security that appears to be attractive requires **unbundling** of an asset. An example is given in Figure 1.6. There, a mortgage pass-through certificate is unbundled into two classes. Class 1 receives only principal payments from the mortgage pool, whereas class 2 receives only interest payments. Another example of unbundling was given in the discussion on financial innovation and CMOs in Section 1.3.

Concept Check

Question 5. How can tax motives contribute to the desire for unbundling?

FIGURE 1.5
Bundling creates a
complex security.

3,000,000 Shares
The Chubb Corporation
$4.25 Convertible Exchangeable Preferred Stock
(Stated Value $50 Per Share)

The $4.25 Convertible Exchangeable Preferred Stock (the "Preferred Stock"), $1.00 par value, of The Chubb Corporation (the "Corporation") offered hereby is convertible at the option of the holder at any time, unless previously redeemed, into Common Stock, $1.00 par value, of the Corporation (the "Common Stock") at the rate of .722 shares of Common Stock for each share of Preferred Stock (equivalent to a conversion price of $69.25 per share), subject to adjustment under certain conditions. On March 25, 1985, the last reported sale price of the Common Stock on the New York Stock Exchange was $57¼ per share.

The Preferred Stock also is exchangeable in whole at the sole option of the Corporation on any dividend payment date beginning April 15, 1988 for the Corporation's 8½% Convertible Subordinated Debentures due April 15, 2010 (the "Debentures") at the rate of $50 principal amount of Debentures for each share of Preferred Stock. See "Description of Debentures".

The Preferred Stock is redeemable for cash at any time, in whole or in part, at the option of the Corporation at redemption prices declining to $50 on April 15, 1995, plus accrued and unpaid dividends to the redemption date. However, the Preferred Stock is not redeemable prior to April 15, 1988 unless the closing price of the Common Stock on the New York Stock Exchange shall have equaled or exceeded 140% of the then effective conversion price per share for at least 20 consecutive trading days ending within 5 days prior to the notice of redemption. Dividends on the Preferred Stock will be cumulative and are payable quarterly on January 15, April 15, July 15 and October 15. The initial dividend will be payable on July 15, 1985 and will accrue from the date of issuance. See "Description of Preferred Stock".

Application will be made to list the Preferred Stock on the New York Stock Exchange.

THESE SECURITIES HAVE NOT BEEN APPROVED OR DISAPPROVED BY THE SECURITIES AND EXCHANGE COMMISSION NOR HAS THE COMMISSION PASSED UPON THE ACCURACY OR ADEQUACY OF THIS PROSPECTUS. ANY REPRESENTATION TO THE CONTRARY IS A CRIMINAL OFFENSE.

	Initial Public Offering Price	Underwriting Discount	Proceeds to Corporation(1)
Per Share	$50.00	$1.375	$48.625
Total	$150,000,000	$4,125,000	$145,875,000

(1) Before deducting expenses payable by the Corporation estimated at $500,000.

The shares of Preferred Stock are offered severally by the Underwriters, as specified herein, subject to receipt and acceptance by them and subject to their right to reject any order in whole or in part. It is expected that certificates for the shares of Preferred Stock will be ready for delivery at the offices of Goldman, Sachs & Co., New York, New York on or about April 2, 1985.

Goldman, Sachs & Co.

The date of this Prospectus is March 26, 1985.

This announcement appears as a matter of record only.

$200,000,000*

Federal National Mortgage Association

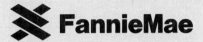 **FannieMae**

Stripped Mortgage-Backed Securities

**Principal and Interest payable on the 25th day of
each month, commencing August 25, 1987**

SMBS Trust 20-CL—Fixed-Rate Residential Mortgage Loans

SMBS Class 1: 100% of Principal Payments on Underlying
9$\frac{1}{2}$% Fannie Mae Guaranteed Mortgage Pass-Through Certificates

SMBS Class 2: 100% of Interest Payments on Underlying
9$\frac{1}{2}$% Fannie Mae Guaranteed Mortgage Pass-Through Certificates

---

The obligations of Fannie Mae under its guaranty of the SMBS Certificates are
obligations of Fannie Mae and are not backed by the full faith and credit of the United
States. The SMBS Certificates are exempt from the registration requirements of the
Securities Act of 1933 and are "Exempted Securities" within the meaning of the
Securities Exchange Act of 1934.

Class 1	$200,000,000 Principal Amount*
Class 2	$200,000,000 Notional Principal Amount*

Goldman, Sachs & Co.

July 9, 1987   *Approximate

1.6   *On the Relationship Between Households and Businesses*

Occasional waves of takeovers, particularly with the development of exotic defenses, have brought to the surface public misgivings about "unproductive speculation" on Wall Street. Many see a need to curb such activities that supposedly divert funds from productive use and cause plant shutdowns and unemployment. An important related issue that may not come up in the public debate is the inherent conflict among households, the direct and indirect shareholders of businesses, and the professional managers who run them. This issue is an important feature of the investment environment.

The control structure of a standard, publicly traded firm is modeled on a democratic arrangement. Its main features are, in theory, as follows:

1. No one has to own shares. Willing investors buy shares, satisfied shareholders can buy more, and unsatisfied shareholders can unload the stock at any time.
2. Management has to disclose to the public a great deal of information, which is audited by independent experts.
3. Important decisions of management must be approved by voting in shareholder meetings.
4. In any election, the rule is one-share one-vote; thus shareholder voting power is proportional to the shareholder's stake in the corporation. Absentee shareholders can vote by proxy.
5. Corporate management, from the president down, is subject to control by the board of directors led by the chairman. Individual directors are elected by shareholders, who can unseat directors in any meeting. Shareholder meetings can be called by shareholders, as well as by management. One annual meeting is mandatory.

Given such a system, what can go wrong? If management is unsatisfactory, the board in principle will oust it. If the board members are not on their toes, shareholders will oust them. In the end, if all works as intended, the corporation will be run by management that executes the (aggregate) will of shareholders.

Management, however, can hurt shareholders in two ways. First, incompetent managers may be very expensive to shareholders (and to corporate employees, who also are stakeholders). Second, management's control of pecuniary rewards and other perquisites comes directly from the pockets of shareholders. This creates a conflict between management and shareholders, which is called the **agency problem.** A great deal of financial theory is dedicated to the analysis of this problem. Corporate executives are probably the best compensated professionals in the nation, which is fine as long as shareholders are happy. After all, competition itself should assure that managerial resource compensation is allocated as efficiently as any production factor in the economy.

This is not a minor issue, because a lot of money is at stake. The mere size of modern corporations and the risk imposed by complex and changing environment and technology mean a large amount of wealth is endangered every day.

When we have large corporations and many diversified investors, however, control is very dispersed. In many cases even the largest shareholder holds less than 2% of the shares. Management, as a whole, through executive stock options and compensation shares, may become important shareholders. By and by, one finds that management controls the board, rather than vice versa.

What about proxy fights to wrest control of the firm from current management? Evidence shows that the cost of an average proxy fight is in the millions of dollars. Shareholders who attempt such a fight have to use their own funds. Management that defends against it uses corporate coffers in addition to already existing communication channels to shareholders at large. Little wonder that few such attempts are made. When they are, 75% fail. Dissidents win some seats on the board of directors in a majority of cases, but seldom enough seats to assume control of the company. Ousting the management of a large corporation is a modern-day version of David's battle with Goliath.

Are shareholders in trouble? Not yet. Their greatest protection is the hunger and might of other businesses. How does this sword of Damocles work? A bad management team, whether incompetent or excessively greedy, presumably causes the firm's shares to sell at a price that reflects its poor performance. Now imagine the management of one business observing another that is underperforming. All it has to do is acquire the underperforming business, fire current management, put in place their own (presumably better) people, and the stock price should reflect their expectations of improved performance. The acquiring firm might therefore be willing to bid up the price of shares of the target firm by as much as 50% to acquire it. In the process, the economy gets rid of one bad management team and becomes more efficient.

Just the threat of this mechanism ought to keep management on its toes. However, give management the ability to engage in expensive takeover defenses (at shareholder expense, of course), and their vulnerability is limited. The danger of antitakeover regulation that allows poor managers to protect their positions is clear.

What about the arguments that takeovers lead to shutdowns and unemployment, and that funds for takeovers are diverted from productive resources? A firm that takes over another one must believe that it can improve operations. If it pays a premium for the acquisition, the acquiring firm must believe it can create additional value to justify the purchase price. Potential efficiency gains might therefore be expected to be an impetus for mergers and acquisitions. Of course, one might argue that some acquisitions are motivated more by tax motives than true economic efficiency, but this seems more a reason to modify tax law than intrude in the market for corporate control.

The argument that takeover funds are diverted from productive uses is without merit. After all, the money that is paid by the acquirer to the target firm's shareholders does not disappear; it is reinvested in financial markets. If shareholders had needed the money for food, they would have sold their shares in the first place. In the end, the displacement of bad management ought to bring in, if anything, more investment funds in this newly created opportunity.

Summary

1. Real assets are used to produce the goods and services created by an economy. Financial assets are claims to the income generated by real assets. Securities are financial assets. Financial assets are part of an investor's wealth, but not part of national wealth. Instead, financial assets determine how the "national pie" is split up among investors.

2. The three sectors of the financial environment are households, businesses, and government. Households decide on investing their funds. Businesses and government, in contrast, typically need to raise funds.

3. The diverse tax and risk preferences of households create a demand for a wide variety of securities. In contrast, businesses typically find it more efficient to offer relatively uniform forms of securities. This conflict gives rise to an industry that creates complex derivative securities from primitive ones.

4. The smallness of households leads to a market niche for financial intermediaries, mutual funds, and investment companies. Economies of scale and specialization are factors supporting the investment banking industry.

5. Four types of markets may be distinguished: direct search, brokered, dealer, and auction markets. Securities are sold in all but direct search markets.

6. Four recent trends in the financial environment are globalization, securitization, credit enhancement, and bundling and unbundling.

7. Stockholders own the corporation and, in principle, can oust an unsatisfactory management team. In practice, ouster may be difficult because of the advantage that management has in proxy fights. The threat of takeover helps keep management doing its best for the firm.

Key Terms

Real assets	Primary market
Financial assets	Secondary market
Financial intermediaries	Block transactions
Mutual funds	Dealer markets
Investment bankers	Auction market
Pass-through security	Globalization
Primitive security	Securitization
Derivative security	Credit enhancement
Dual fund	Bundling
Direct search market	Unbundling
Brokered market	Agency problem

Selected Readings

An excellent discussion of financial innovation may be found in:
   Miller, Merton H., "Financial Innovation: The Last Twenty Years and the Next," *Journal of Financial and Quantitative Analysis, 21,* December 1986, pp. 459-471.
Detailed discussions of a variety of financial markets and market structures are provided in:
   Garbade, Kenneth D., *Securities Markets,* New York: McGraw Hill, 1982.
   Wood, John H., and Wood, Norm L., *Financial Markets,* San Diego: Harcourt Brace Jovanovich, 1985.
Several trends in the capital market are discussed in:
   Recent Trends in International Banking, Bank for International Settlements, 1986.

Problems

1. Suppose you discover a treasure chest of $10 billion in cash.
   a. Is this a real or financial asset?
   b. Is society any richer for the discovery?
   c. Are you wealthier?
   d. Can you reconcile your answers to (b) and (c)? Is anyone worse off as a result of the discovery?

2. Examine the balance sheet of the financial sector. What is the ratio of tangible assets to total assets? What is that ratio for nonfinancial firms? Why should this difference be expected?

3. In the 1960s, the U.S. government instituted a 30% withholding tax on interest payments on bonds sold in the United States to overseas investors. (It has since been repealed.) What connection does this have to the contemporaneous growth of the huge Eurobond market, where U.S. firms issue dollar-denominated bonds overseas?

4. Consider Figure 1.7, on page 36, which describes an issue of American gold certificates.
   a. Is this issue a primary or secondary market transaction?
   b. Are the certificates primitive or derivative assets?
   c. What market niche is filled by this offering?

5. Why would you expect securitization to take place only in highly developed capital markets?

6. Suppose that you are an executive of General Motors, and that a large share of your potential income is derived from year-end bonuses that depend on GM's annual profits.
   a. Would purchase of GM stock be an effective hedging strategy for the executive who is worried about the uncertainty surrounding his bonus?
   b. Would purchase of Toyota stock be an effective hedge strategy?

7. Consider again the GM executive in question 6. In light of the fact that the design of the annual bonus exposes the executive to risk that she would like to shed, why doesn't GM instead pay her a fixed salary that doesn't entail this uncertainty?

8. What is the relationship between securitization and the role of financial intermediaries in the economy? What happens to financial intermediaries as securitization progresses?

9. Although we stated that real assets comprise the true productive capacity of an economy, it is hard to conceive of a modern economy without well-developed financial markets and security types. How would the productive capacity of the U.S. economy be affected if there were no markets in which one could trade financial assets?

10. In Section 1.5 the possibility of the securitization of third-world debt was raised. How might such a third-world pass-through security be designed?

11. Why does it make sense that the first futures markets introduced in nineteenth century America were for trades in agricultural products? For example, why did we not see instead futures markets for goods such as paper or pencils?

FIGURE 1.7
A gold-backed security.

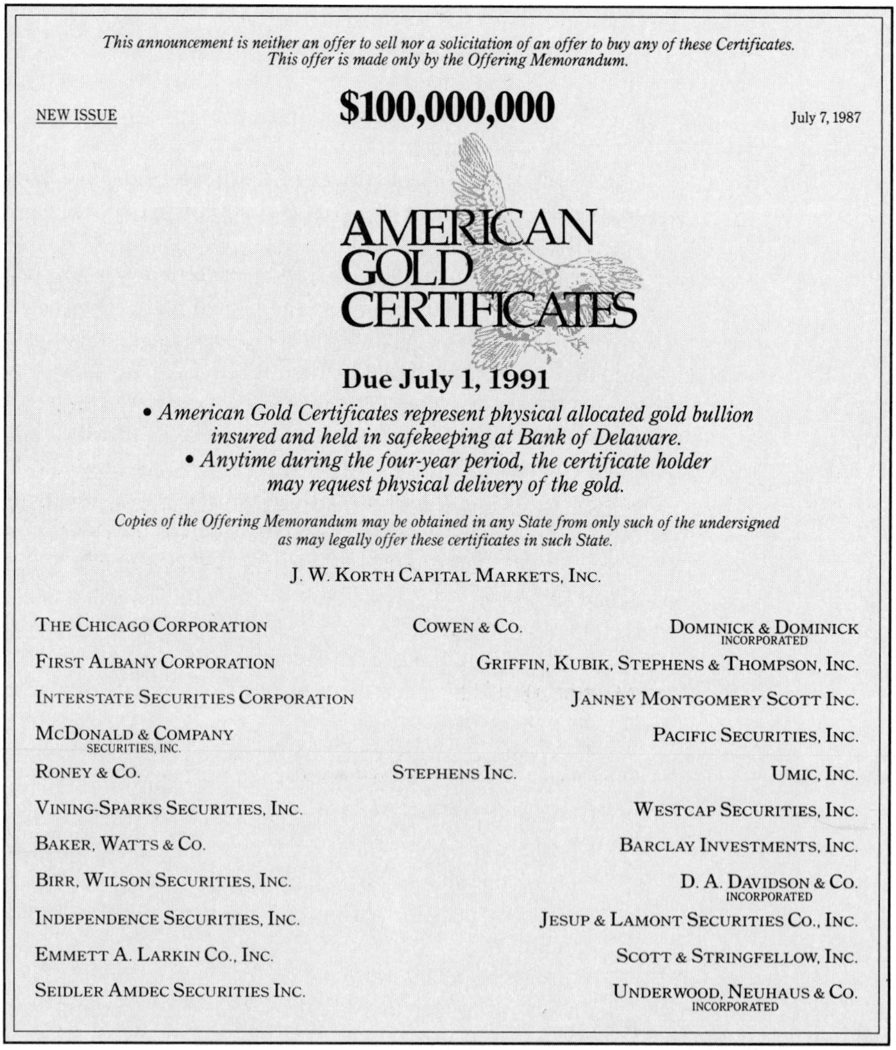

This announcement is neither an offer to sell nor a solicitation of an offer to buy any of these Certificates. This offer is made only by the Offering Memorandum.

NEW ISSUE

$100,000,000

July 7, 1987

AMERICAN GOLD CERTIFICATES

Due July 1, 1991

- *American Gold Certificates represent physical allocated gold bullion insured and held in safekeeping at Bank of Delaware.*
- *Anytime during the four-year period, the certificate holder may request physical delivery of the gold.*

Copies of the Offering Memorandum may be obtained in any State from only such of the undersigned as may legally offer these certificates in such State.

J. W. KORTH CAPITAL MARKETS, INC.

THE CHICAGO CORPORATION	COWEN & CO.	DOMINICK & DOMINICK INCORPORATED
FIRST ALBANY CORPORATION		GRIFFIN, KUBIK, STEPHENS & THOMPSON, INC.
INTERSTATE SECURITIES CORPORATION		JANNEY MONTGOMERY SCOTT INC.
McDONALD & COMPANY SECURITIES, INC.		PACIFIC SECURITIES, INC.
RONEY & CO.	STEPHENS INC.	UMIC, INC.
VINING-SPARKS SECURITIES, INC.		WESTCAP SECURITIES, INC.
BAKER, WATTS & CO.		BARCLAY INVESTMENTS, INC.
BIRR, WILSON SECURITIES, INC.		D. A. DAVIDSON & CO. INCORPORATED
INDEPENDENCE SECURITIES, INC.		JESUP & LAMONT SECURITIES CO., INC.
EMMETT A. LARKIN CO., INC.		SCOTT & STRINGFELLOW, INC.
SEIDLER AMDEC SECURITIES INC.		UNDERWOOD, NEUHAUS & CO. INCORPORATED

CHAPTER 2

Markets and Instruments

This chapter covers a range of financial securities and the markets in which they trade. Our goal is to introduce you to the features of various security types. This foundation will be necessary to understand the more analytic material that follows in later chapters.

We refer to the traditional classification of securities, money market instruments or capital market instruments. The **money market** includes short-term, marketable, liquid, low-risk debt securities. Money market instruments sometimes are called cash equivalents because of their safety and liquidity. **Capital markets,** in contrast, include longer-term and riskier securities. Securities in the capital market are much more diverse than those found within the money market. For this reason, we will subdivide the capital market into four segments. Accordingly, this chapter contains a discussion of five markets overall: the money market, longer-term fixed income capital markets, equity markets, and the two so-called derivative markets, options and futures markets.

2.1 *The Money Market*

The money market is a subsector of the bond market. It consists of very short-term debt securities that usually are highly marketable. Many of these securities trade in large denominations, and so are out of the reach of individual investors. Money market funds, however, are easily accessible to small investors. These mutual funds pool the resources of many investors and purchase a wide variety of money market securities on their behalf.

Figure 2.1 is a reprint of a money rates listing from *The Wall Street Journal*. It includes the various instruments of the money market that we will describe in detail. Table 2.1 lists outstanding volume in 1987 of the major instruments of the money market.

MONEY RATES

Monday, May 23, 1988

The key U.S. and foreign annual interest rates below are a guide to general levels but don't always represent actual transactions.

PRIME RATE: 9%. The base rate on corporate loans at large U.S. money center commercial banks.

FEDERAL FUNDS: 7¼% high, 7 1/16% low, 7% near closing bid, 7⅛% offered. Reserves traded among commercial banks for overnight use in amounts of $1 million or more. Source: Fulton Prebon (U.S.A.) Inc.

DISCOUNT RATE: 6%. The charge on loans to depository institutions by the New York Federal Reserve Bank.

CALL MONEY: 8¼% to 8½%. The charge on loans to brokers on stock exchange collateral.

COMMERCIAL PAPER placed directly by General Motors Acceptance Corp.: 7% 30 to 43 days; 7.15% 44 to 69 days; 7.20% 70 to 100 days; 7.15% 101 to 179 days; 7% 180 to 270 days.

COMMERCIAL PAPER: High-grade unsecured notes sold through dealers by major corporations in multiples of $1,000: 7.15% 30 days; 7.20% 60 days; 7.25% 90 days.

CERTIFICATES OF DEPOSIT: 6.73% one month; 6.84% two months; 6.90% three months; 7.13% six months; 7.45% one year. Average of top rates paid by major New York banks on primary new issues of negotiable C.D.s, usually on amounts of $1 million and more. The minimum unit is $100,-000. Typical rates in the secondary market: 7.05% one month; 7.28% three months; 7.60% six months.

BANKERS ACCEPTANCES: 7.02% 30 days; 7.08% 60 days; 7.13% 90 days; 7.18% 120 days; 7.28% 150 days; 7.28% 180 days. Negotiable, bank-backed business credit instruments typically financing an import order.

LONDON LATE EURODOLLARS: 7 5/16% to 7 3/16% one month; 7½% to 7⅜% two months; 7 9/16% to 7 7/16% three months; 7⅜% to 7½% four months; 7¾% to 7⅝% five months; 7 13/16% to 7 11/16% six months.

LONDON INTERBANK OFFERED RATES (LIBOR): 7⅜% one month; 7 9/16% three months; 7 13/16% six months; 8¼% one year. The average of interbank offered rates for dollar deposits in the London market based on quotations at five major banks.

FOREIGN PRIME RATES: Canada 10.25%; Germany 6%; Japan 3.375%; Switzerland 5%; Britain 7.50%. These rate indications aren't directly comparable; lending practices vary widely by location. Source: Morgan Guaranty Trust Co.

TREASURY BILLS: Results of the Monday, May 23, 1988, auction of short-term U.S. government bills, sold at a discount from face value in units of $10,000 to $1 million: 6.34%, 13 weeks; 6.71%, 26 weeks.

FEDERAL HOME LOAN MORTGAGE CORP. (Freddie Mac): Posted yields on 30-year mortgage commitments for delivery within 30 days. 10.44%, standard conventional fixed-rate mortgages; 7.125%, 2% rate capped one-year adjustable rate mortgages. Source: Telerate Systems Inc.

FEDERAL NATIONAL MORTGAGE ASSOCIATION (Fannie Mae): Posted yields on 30 year mortgage commitments for delivery within 30 days (priced at par). 10.43%, standard conventional fixed rate-mortgages; 8.95%, 6/2 rate capped one-year adjustable rate mortgages. Source: Telerate Systems Inc.

MERRILL LYNCH READY ASSETS TRUST: 5.99%. Annualized average rate of return after expenses for the past 30 days; not a forecast of future returns.

TABLE 2.1   Components of the Money Market (October 1987)

	$ Billion
Overnight repurchase agreements	85.4
Term repurchase agreements*	106.9
Small-denomination time deposits†	882.5
Large-denomination time deposits‡	475.9
Term Eurodollars	93.7
Short-term Treasury securities	272.3
Bankers' acceptances	44.5
Commercial paper	256.4
Money market deposit accounts	532.6

Data from *Economic Report of the President*, U.S. Government Printing Office, 1988.
*Includes overnight Eurodollars.
†Less than $100,000 denomination.
‡More than $100,000 denomination.

U.S. *Treasury bills* are the most marketable of all money market instruments. T-bills represent the simplest form of borrowing: the government raises money by selling bills to the public. Investors buy the bills at a discount from the stated maturity value. At the bill's maturity, the holder receives from the government a payment equal to the face value of the bill. The difference between the purchase price and ultimate maturity value constitutes the investor's earnings.

T-bills with initial maturities of 91 days or 182 days are issued weekly. Offerings of 52-week bills are made monthly. Sales are conducted via auction, at which investors can submit competitive or noncompetitive bids. A competitive bid is an order for a given quantity of bills at a specific offered price. The order is filled only if the bid is high enough relative to other bids to be accepted. A noncompetitive bid is an unconditional offer to purchase bills at the average price of the successful competitive bids.

The Treasury rank-orders bids by offering price and accepts bids in order of descending price until the entire issue is absorbed by competitive and noncompetitive bids. Competitive bidders face two dangers: they may bid too high and overpay for the bills, or they may bid too low and be shut out of the auction. Noncompetitive bidders by contrast pay the average price for the issue, and all noncompetitive bids are accepted up to a maximum of $1 million per bid. In recent years noncompetitive bids have absorbed between 10% and 25% of the total auction.

Individuals can purchase T-bills directly at auction or on the secondary market from a government securities dealer. T-bills are highly liquid; that is, they are easily converted to cash and sold at low transaction cost and with not much price risk. Unlike most other money market instruments, which sell in minimum denominations of $100,000, T-bills sell in minimum denominations of only $10,000. The income earned on T-bills is exempt from all state and local taxes, another characteristic distinguishing them from other money market instruments.

Bank discount yields

T-bill yields are not quoted in the financial pages as effective annual rates of return. Instead, the **bank discount yield** is used. To illustrate this method, consider a $10,000 par value T-bill sold at $9,600 with a maturity of a half year, or 182 days. With the bank discount method, the bill's discount from par value, which here equals $400, is "annualized" based on a 360-day year. The $400 discount is annualized as

$$\$400 \times (360/182) = \$791.21$$

The result is divided by the $10,000 par value to obtain a bank discount yield of 7.912% per year. Rather than report T-bill prices, the financial pages report these discount yields.

The bank discount yield is not an accurate measure of the effective annual rate of return. To see this, note that the half-year holding period return on the bill is 4.17%:

the \$9,600 investment provides \$400 in earnings, and 400/9600 = .0417. The compound interest–annualized rate of return, or **effective annual yield,** is therefore

$$(1.0417)^2 - 1 = .0851$$
$$= 8.51\%$$

We can highlight the source of the discrepancy between the bank discount yield and effective annual yield by examining the bank discount formula:

$$r_{\text{BD}} = \frac{10,000 - P}{10,000} \times \frac{360}{n} \tag{2.1}$$

where P is the bond price, n is the maturity of the bill in days, and r_{BD} is the bank discount yield. (Actually, because of the convention of *skip-day settlement,* n is calculated as though the T-bill sale is not consummated until 2 business days after the date on which the T-bill price is quoted.)

The bank discount formula thus takes the bill's discount from par as a fraction of par value and then annualizes by the factor $360/n$. There are three problems with this technique, and they all combine to reduce the bank discount yield compared with the effective annual yield. First, the bank discount yield is annualized using a 360-day year rather than a 365-day year. Second, the annualization technique uses simple interest rather than compound interest. Multiplication by $360/n$ does not account for the ability to earn interest on interest, which is the essence of compounding. Finally, the denominator in the first term in equation 2.1 is the par value, \$10,000, rather than the purchase price of the bill, P. We really want an interest rate to tell us the rate that we can earn per dollar invested, but dollars invested here are P, not \$10,000. Less than \$10,000 is required to purchase the bill.

Figure 2.2 shows Treasury bill listings from *The Wall Street Journal* for prices on May 12, 1988. The discount yield on the bill maturing on July 14 is 6.08% based on the bid price of the bond and 6.01% based on the asked price. (The bid price is the price at which a customer can sell the bill to a dealer in the security, whereas the asked price is the price at which the customer can buy a security from a dealer. The difference in bid and asked prices is a source of profit to the dealer.)

FIGURE 2.2

Treasury bill listings.

U.S. Treas. Bills Mat. date	Bid	Asked	Yield Discount	Mat. date	Bid	Asked	Yield Discount
-1988-				-1988-			
5-19	5.01	4.89	4.96	9-15	6.31	6.24	6.47
5-26	5.11	4.99	5.07	9-22	6.38	6.31	6.55
6- 2	5.66	5.54	5.63	9-29	6.42	6.35	6.60
6- 9	5.73	5.66	5.76	10- 6	6.44	6.37	6.63
6-16	5.76	5.69	5.80	10-13	6.44	6.37	6.64
6-23	5.82	5.75	5.87	10-20	6.44	6.37	6.65
6-30	5.75	5.68	5.80	10-27	6.50	6.43	6.72
7- 7	5.99	5.92	6.06	11- 3	6.50	6.43	6.73
7-14	6.08	6.01	6.16	11-10	6.44	6.40	6.70
7-21	6.12	6.05	6.21	11-25	6.59	6.52	6.84
7-28	6.13	6.06	6.22	12-22	6.65	6.58	6.91
8- 4	6.19	6.15	6.33	-1989-			
8-11	6.22	6.18	6.36	1-19	6.71	6.65	7.00
8-18	6.24	6.17	6.36	2-16	6.77	6.71	7.09
8-25	6.18	6.11	6.31	3-16	6.81	6.74	7.15
9- 1	6.34	6.27	6.48	4-13	6.86	6.79	7.23
9- 8	6.33	6.26	6.48	5-11	6.84	6.80	7.27

To determine the bill's true market price, we must solve equation 2.1 for P. Rearranging equation 2.1, we obtain

$$P = 10,000 \times [1 - r_{BD} \times (n/360)] \qquad (2.2)$$

Equation 2.2 in effect first "deannualizes" the bank discount yield to obtain the actual proportional discount from par, then finds the fraction of par for which the bond sells (which is the expression in brackets), and finally multiplies the result by par value, or $10,000. In the case at hand, $n = 61$ days for the July 14 maturity bond (63 days minus 2 days for skip-day settlement). The discount yield based on the asked price is 6.01% or .0601, so that the asked price of the bill is

$$\$10,000 \times [1 - .0601 \times (61/360)] = \$9,898.164$$

Concept Check

Question 1. Find the bid price of the preceding bill based on the bank discount yield at bid.

The "yield" column in Figure 2.2 is the **bond equivalent yield** of the T-bill. This is the bill's yield over its life, assuming that it is purchased for the asked price, and annualized using simple interest techniques. The bond equivalent yield (r_{BEY}) is expressed as

$$r_{BEY} = \frac{10,000 - P}{P} \times \frac{365}{n} \qquad (2.3)$$

In equation 2.3 the holding period return of the bill is computed in the first term on the right-hand side as the price increase of the bill if held until maturity per dollar paid for the bill. The second term annualizes that yield. Note that the bond equivalent yield correctly uses the price of the bill in the denominator of the first term and uses a 365-day year in the second term to annualize. It still, however, uses a simple interest procedure to annualize, also known as *annual percentage rate,* or APR, and so problems still remain in comparing yields on bills with different maturities. Nevertheless, yields on most securities with less than a year to maturity are annualized using a simple interest approach.

Thus for our demonstration bill

$$r_{BEY} = \frac{10,000 - 9,898.164}{9,898.164} \times \frac{365}{61} = .06156$$

or 6.16%, as reported in *The Wall Street Journal.*

A convenient formula relating the bond equivalent yield to the bank discount yield is

$$r_{BEY} = \frac{365 \times d}{360 - (d \times n)}$$

where d is the discount yield. Here, $d = .0601$, so that

$$r_{BEY} = \frac{365 \times .0601}{360 - (.0601 \times 61)} = .06156$$

as derived previously.

Finally, the effective annual yield on the bill based on the asked price, \$9,898.164, is 6.32%. The bond's 61-day return equals $(10,000 - 9,898.164)/9,898.164$, or 1.0288%. Annualizing this return, we obtain $(1.010288)^{365/61} = 1.0632$, implying an effective annual interest rate of 6.32%.

This example illustrates the general rule that the bank discount yield is less than the bond equivalent yield, which in turn is less than the compounded, or effective, annual yield.

Certificates of Deposit

A *certificate of deposit,* or CD, is a time deposit with a bank. Time deposits may not be withdrawn on demand. The bank pays interest and principal to the depositor only at the end of the fixed term of the CD. CDs issued in denominations greater than \$100,000 are usually negotiable, however; that is, they can be sold to another investor if the owner needs to cash in the certificate before its maturity date. Short-term CDs are highly marketable, although the market significantly thins out for maturities of 6 months or more. CDs are treated as bank deposits by the Federal Deposit Insurance Corporation, so they are insured for up to \$100,000 in the event of a bank insolvency.

Commercial Paper

Large, well-known companies often issue their own short-term unsecured debt notes rather than borrow directly from banks. These notes are called *commercial paper*. Very often, commercial paper is backed by a bank line of credit, which gives the borrower access to cash that can be used (if needed) to pay off the paper at maturity. Commercial paper maturities range up to 270 days; longer maturities would require registration with the Securities and Exchange Commission and so are almost never issued. Most often, commercial paper is issued with maturities of less than 1 or 2 months. Usually, it is issued in multiples of \$100,000. Therefore small investors can invest in commercial paper only indirectly, via money market mutual funds.

Commercial paper is considered to be a fairly safe asset, because a firm's condition presumably can be monitored and predicted over a term as short as 1 month. Many firms issue commercial paper intending to roll it over at maturity, that is, issue new paper to obtain the funds necessary to retire the old paper. If lenders become complacent about a firm's prospects and grant rollovers heedlessly, they can suffer big losses. When Penn Central defaulted in 1970, it had $82 million of commercial paper outstanding. However, the Penn Central episode was the only major default on commercial paper in the past 40 years.

Bankers' Acceptances

A *bankers' acceptance* starts as an order to a bank by a bank's customer to pay a sum of money at a future date, typically within 6 months. At this stage, it is similar to a postdated check. When the bank endorses the order for payment as "accepted," it assumes responsibility for ultimate payment to the holder of the acceptance. At this point, the acceptance may be traded in secondary markets like any other claim on the bank. Bankers' acceptances are considered very safe assets because traders can substitute the bank's credit standing for their own. They are used widely in foreign trade where the creditworthiness of one trader is unknown to the trading partner. Acceptances sell at a discount from the face value of the payment order, just as T-bills sell at a discount from par value.

Eurodollars

Eurodollars are dollar-denominated deposits at foreign banks or foreign branches of American banks. By locating outside the United States, these banks escape regulation by the Federal Reserve Board. Despite the tag "Euro," these accounts need not be in European banks, although that is where the practice of accepting dollar-denominated deposits outside the United States began.

Most Eurodollar deposits are for large sums, and most are time deposits of less than 6 months' maturity. A variation on the Eurodollar time deposit is the Eurodollar certificate of deposit. A Eurodollar CD resembles a domestic bank CD except that it is the liability of a non-U.S. branch of a bank, typically a London branch. The advantage of Eurodollar CDs over Eurodollar time deposits is that the holder can sell the asset to realize its cash value before maturity. Eurodollar CDs are considered less liquid and riskier than domestic CDs, however, and thus offer higher yields. Firms also issue Eurodollar bonds, which are dollar-denominated bonds in Europe, although bonds are not a money market investment because of their long maturities.

Repos and Reverses

Dealers in government securities use *repurchase agreements,* also called "repos" or "RPs," as a form of short-term, usually overnight, borrowing. The dealer sells government securities to an investor on an overnight basis, with an agreement to buy back those securities the next day at a slightly higher price. The increase in the price is the overnight interest. The dealer thus takes out a 1-day loan from the investor, and the securities serve as collateral.

A *term repo* is essentially an identical transaction, except that the term of the implicit loan can be 30 days or more. Repos are considered very safe in terms of credit risk because the loans are backed by the government securities. A *reverse repo* is the mirror image of a repo. Here, the dealer finds an investor holding government securities and buys them, agreeing to sell them back at a specified higher price on a future date.

The repo market was upset by several failures of government security dealers in 1985. In these cases the dealers had entered into the typical repo arrangements with investors, pledging government securities as collateral. The investors did not take physical possession of the securities as they could have under the purchase and resale arrangement. Some of the dealers, unfortunately, fraudulently pledged the same securities as collateral in different repos; when the dealers went under, the investors found that they could not collect the securities that they had "purchased" in the first phase of the repo transaction. In the wake of the scandal repo rates for nonprimary dealers increased, whereas rates for some well-capitalized firms fell as investors became more sensitive to credit risk.[1] Investors can best protect themselves by taking delivery of the securities, either directly or through an agent such as a bank custodian.

Federal Funds

Just as most of us maintain deposits at banks, banks maintain deposits of their own at a Federal Reserve bank. Each member bank of the Federal Reserve System, or "the Fed," is required to maintain a minimum balance in a reserve account with the Fed. The required balance depends on the total deposits of the bank's customers. Funds in the bank's reserve account are called *federal funds* or *fed funds*. At any time, some banks have more funds than required at the Fed. Other banks, primarily big New York and other financial center banks, tend to have a shortage of federal funds. In the federal funds market, banks with excess funds lend to those with a shortage. These loans, which are usually overnight transactions, are arranged at a rate of interest called the federal funds rate.

Brokers' Calls

Individuals who buy stocks on margin borrow part of the funds to pay for the stocks from their broker. The broker in turn may borrow the funds from a bank, agreeing to repay the bank immediately (on call) if the bank requests it. The rate paid on such loans is usually about 1% greater than the rate on short-term T-bills.

The LIBOR Market

The **London Interbank Offered Rate** (LIBOR) is the rate at which large banks in London are willing to lend money among themselves. This rate has become the pre-

---

[1]Lumpkin, Stephen A., "Repurchase and Reverse Repurchase Agreements," in Cook, T, and Rowe T. (editors), *Instruments of the Money Market*, Richmond, Va.: Federal Reserve Bank of Richmond, 1986.

mier short-term interest rate quoted in the European money market, and it serves reference rate for a wide range of transactions. For example, a corporation might bo. row at a rate equal to LIBOR plus 2%.

Yields on Money Market Instruments

Although most money market securities are of low risk, they are not risk-free. For example, as we noted earlier, the commercial paper market was rocked by the Penn Central bankruptcy, which precipitated a default on $82 million of commercial paper. Money market investors became more sensitive to creditworthiness after this episode, and the yield spread between low- and high-quality paper widened.

The securities of the money market do promise yields greater than those on default-free T-bills, at least in part because of greater relative riskiness. In addition, many investors require more liquidity; thus they will accept lower yields on securities such as T-bills that can be quickly and cheaply sold for cash. Figure 2.3 shows that bank CDs, for example, consistently have paid a risk premium over T-bills. Moreover, that risk premium increased with economic crises such as the energy price shocks associated with the two OPEC disturbances, or the failures of Continental Illinois and Penn Square banks.

FIGURE 2.3

The spread between 3-month certificates of deposit and T-bill rates.
(From Cook, Timothy Q., "Treasury Bills," in Cook, Timothy Q., and Rowe, Timothy D. [editors], *Instruments of the Money Market,* Federal Reserve Bank of Richmond, Richmond, Va., 1986.)

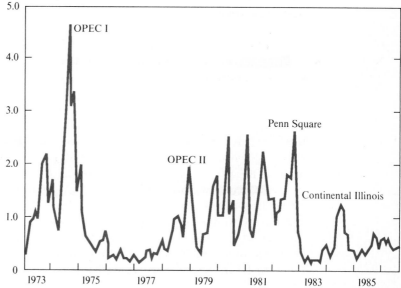

The Fixed-Income Capital Market

The fixed-income capital market is composed of longer term borrowing instruments than those that trade in the money market. This market includes Treasury notes and bonds, corporate bonds, municipal bonds, mortgage securities, and federal agency debt.

Treasury Notes and Bonds

The U.S. government borrows funds in large part by selling *Treasury notes* and *Treasury bonds*. T-note maturities range up to 10 years, whereas bonds are issued with maturities ranging from 10 to 30 years. Both are issued in denominations of $1,000 or more. Both make semiannual coupon payments that are set at an initial level that enables the government to sell the securities at or near par value. Aside from their differing maturities at issuance, the only major distinction between T-notes and T-bonds is that T-bonds may be callable during a given period, usually the last 5 years of the bond's life. The call provision gives the Treasury the right to repurchase the bond at par value.

Figure 2.4 is an excerpt from a listing of Treasury issues in *The Wall Street Journal*. Note the bond *(arrow)* that matures in August 1994. The coupon income, or interest, paid by the bond is 8¾% of par value, meaning that for a $1,000 face value bond $87.50 in annual interest payments will be made in two semiannual installments of $43.75 each. Despite their appearance, the numbers to the right of the decimal point in the bid and asked prices are not part of a decimal. They actually represent units of ⅟₃₂ of a point.

The bid price of the August 1994 bond is 100¹⁰⁄₃₂, or 100.31. The asked price is 100¹⁴⁄₃₂, or 100.44. Although bonds are sold in denominations of $1,000 par value, the prices are quoted as a percentage of par value. Thus the bid price of 100.31 should be interpreted as 100.31% of par or $1,003.10 for the $1,000 par value bond. Similarly, the bond could be bought from a dealer for $1004.40. The −.01 bid change means the closing bid price on this day fell ⅟₃₂ (as a percentage of par value) from the previous day's closing bid price. Finally, the yield to maturity on the bond based on the asked price is 8.65%.

The **yield to maturity** reported in the financial pages is calculated by determining the semiannual yield and then doubling it, rather than compounding it for two half-year periods. This use of a simple interest technique to annualize means that the yield is quoted on an annual percentage rate (APR) basis rather than as an effective annual yield. The APR method in this context is also called the bond equivalent yield.

Figure 2.4 indicates that the yields on most bonds are fairly similar. Some bonds, however, such as the 3 Feb 1995 and the 3½ Nov 1998 bonds, offer seemingly quite low yields. These bonds are known as *flower bonds*. They are special because they may be used to settle federal estate taxes at par value under certain conditions. Because individuals who use these bonds for estate-tax purposes may in effect sell them

FIGURE 2.4

Treasury bonds and notes.

(From *The Wall Street Journal*, May 13, 1988.) Reprinted by permission of *The Wall Street Journal*. © Dow Jones & Company, Inc. 1988. All rights reserved.

TREASURY BONDS, NOTES & BILLS

Thursday, May 12, 1988

Representative Over-the-Counter quotations based on transactions of $1 million or more as of 4 p.m. Eastern time.

Hyphens in bid-and-asked and bid changes represent 32nds; 101-01 means 101 1/32. a-Plus 1/64. b-Yield to call date. d-Minus 1/64. k-Nonresident aliens exempt from withholding taxes. n-Treasury notes. p-Treasury note; nonresident aliens exempt from withholding taxes.

Source: Bloomberg Financial Markets

Treasury Bonds and Notes

Rate	Mat.	Date	Bid	Asked	Bid Chg.	Yld.
8¼	1988	May n	99-31	100-02	....	0.00
7⅛	1988	May p	99-31	100-02	....	5.67
9⅞	1988	May n	99-30	100-01—	01	3.99
10	1988	May n	99-30	100-01	....	4.11
7	1988	Jun p	100	100-03	....	6.13
13⅜	1988	Jun n	100-27	100-30—	01	6.15
6⅜	1988	Jul p	99-29	100 +	01	6.50
14	1988	Jul n	101-06	101-09	....	6.23
6⅛	1988	Aug p	99-23	99-26	....	6.68
9½	1988	Aug n	100-19	100-22	....	6.64
10½	1988	Aug n	100-28	100-31	....	6.52
6⅜	1988	Sep p	99-24	99-27+	01	6.74
11⅜	1988	Sep n	101-19	101-22	....	6.76
15⅜	1988	Oct n	103-21	103-24	....	6.21
6⅜	1988	Oct p	99-21	99-24	....	6.91
6¼	1988	Nov p	99-16	99-19+	01	7.01
8¾	1988	Nov n	100-25	100-28	....	6.96
8⅜	1988	Nov p	100-23	100-26+	01	6.96
11¾	1988	Nov n	102-07	102-10—	01	7.01
10⅝	1988	Dec n	101-29	102-01	....	7.25
6¼	1988	Dec n	99-09	99-13	....	7.21
6⅛	1989	Jan n	99-04	99-08	....	7.20
14⅜	1989	Jan n	104-25	104-29—	02	6.99
8	1989	Feb p	100-12	100-16+	01	7.29
6¼	1989	Feb p	99-02	99-06	....	7.30
11⅜	1989	Feb n	102-25	102-29	....	7.33
11¼	1989	Mar p	103-04	103-08	....	7.36
6⅜	1989	Mar n	99-02	99-06+	01	7.33
7⅛	1989	Apr p	99-19	99-23	....	7.43
14⅜	1989	Apr n	106-02	106-06	....	7.31
6⅞	1989	May n	99-10	99-14	....	7.47
9¼	1989	May n	101-19	101-25+	01	7.38
8	1989	May n	100-12	100-16+	01	7.49
11¾	1989	May n	103-31	104-03	....	7.45
7⅜	1989	Jun p	99-23	99-27+	01	7.51
9⅝	1989	Jun p	102-03	102-07	....	7.53
7⅜	1989	Jul p	99-29	100-01	....	7.58
14½	1989	Jul n	107-15	107-19—	03	7.58
7¾	1989	Aug p	99-31	100-03	....	7.66
6⅜	1989	Aug p	98-21	98-25	....	7.65
13⅞	1989	Aug n	107-07	107-11	....	7.62
8½	1989	Sep k	100-28	101	....	7.71
9⅜	1989	Sep p	102	102-04	....	7.71
11⅞	1989	Oct n	105-11	105-15	....	7.73
7⅞	1989	Oct p	100-03	100-07	....	7.71
6⅜	1989	Nov p	98	98-04+	01	7.72
10¾	1989	Nov n	104-04	104-08	....	7.71
12¾	1989	Nov p	106-29	107-01	....	7.71
7¾	1989	Nov p	99-27	99-31+	01	7.77
7⅞	1989	Dec p	99-30	100-02+	01	7.82
8½	1989	Dec p	100-23	100-27+	01	7.80
7⅜	1990	Jan k	99-05	99-09+	01	7.82
10½	1990	Jan n	103-30	104-02	....	7.85
3½	1990	Feb	93	93-18+	02	7.47
6½	1990	Feb k	97-22	97-26+	01	7.85
7⅛	1990	Feb k	98-22	98-26+	01	7.84
11				105-03+		

Rate	Mat.	Date	Bid	Asked	Bid Chg.	Yld.
7⅜	1993	Apr p	95-08	95-12	....	8.54
7⅝	1993	May	96-08	96-12	....	8.51
10½	1993	May n	106-06	106-10	....	8.55
7¼	1993	Jul p	94-14	94-18+	01	8.57
7½	1988-93	Aug	95-08	95-14—	01	8.59
8⅜	1993	Aug	100-06	100-14+	03	8.51
11⅞	1993	Aug n	113-15	113-19	....	8.60
7⅛	1993	Oct p	93-16	93-20	....	8.62
8⅝	1993	Nov	99-29	100-03—	03	8.60
11¾	1993	Nov	113-07	113-11	....	8.65
7	1994	Jan	92-16	92-20+	01	8.67
9	1994	Feb	101-11	101-15	....	8.67
7	1994	Apr p	92-03	92-07+	02	8.71
4⅛	1989-94	May	92-31	93-17	....	5.40
13⅛	1994	May p	120-05	120-09	....	8.72
8	1994	Jul n	96-11	96-15+	01	8.75
8¾	1994	Aug	100-10	100-14—	01	8.65
12⅜	1994	Aug p	118-08	118-12+	01	8.74
9½	1994	Oct k	103-07	103-11	....	8.80
10⅛	1994	Nov	106-11	106-15	....	8.80
11⅝	1994	Nov	113-21	113-25	....	8.80
8⅝	1995	Jan p	98-23	98-27+	01	8.85
3	1995	Feb	92-31	93-17	....	4.11
10½	1995	Feb	108-06	108-10—	02	8.83
11¼	1995	Feb p	111-27	111-31—	01	8.85
8⅜	1995	Apr p	97-16	97-20	....	8.84
10⅜	1995	May	107-21	107-25—	02	8.86
11¼	1995	May p	112-02	112-06+	01	8.88
12⅜	1995	May	120-07	120-11	....	8.69
10½	1995	Aug p	108-07	108-11—	01	8.91
9½	1995	Nov p	102-31	103-03—	01	8.93
11½	1995	Nov	114-01	114-05	....	8.88
8⅞	1996	Feb p	99-12	99-16	....	8.96
7⅜	1996	May p	90-26	90-30	....	8.99
7¼	1996	Nov p	89-16	89-20—	01	9.02
8⅝	1997	Aug k	97-04	97-08	....	9.07
8½	1997	May k	96-21	96-25+	03	9.03
8⅞	1997	Nov	98-20	98-24+	02	9.07
8⅛	1998	Feb p	93-27	93-31+	01	9.07
7	1993-98	May	87-04	87-08	....	8.96
3½	1998	Nov	92-31	93-17—	01	4.27
8½	1994-99	May	95-15	95-19—	01	9.14
7⅞	1995-00	Feb	90-18	90-22—	01	9.18
8⅜	1995-00	Aug	93-30	94-02+	03	9.19
11¾	2001	Feb	118-27	119-01+	03	9.18
13⅛	2001	May	129-07	129-13+	03	9.20
8	1996-01	Aug	91-11	91-17+	02	9.11
13¾	2001	Aug	131-18	131-24+	03	9.18
15¾	2001	Nov	150-15	150-21+	03	9.14
14¼	2002	Feb	139-03	139-09+	03	9.16
11⅝	2002	Nov	118-11	118-17+	06	9.28
10¾	2003	Feb	111-10	111-16+	03	9.30
10¾	2003	May	111-11	111-17+	01	9.31
11⅛	2003	Aug	114-15	114-21	....	9.30
11⅞	2003	Nov	120-20	120-26+	03	9.31
12⅜	2004	May	124-26	125 +	03	9.34
13¾	2004	Aug	136-21	136-27+	03	9.30
11⅝	2004	Nov k	118-27	119-01+	01	9.34
8¼	2000-05	May	91-12	91-18+	02	9.24
12	2005	May k	122-10	122-16+	04	9.33
10¾	2005	Aug	111-21	111-27—	01	9.35
9⅜	2006	Feb k	101-01	101-07+	03	9.23
7⅞	2002-07	Feb	85-13	85-19+	04	9.25
7⅞	2002-07	Nov	87-11	87-17+	03	9.27
8⅜	2003-08	Aug	91-09	91-15+	03	9.32
8¾	2003-08	Aug	94-11	94-17+	03	9.35
~2004-09		May	97-23	97-?0+	01	9.35
		Nov	107-			9.40

to the U.S. government for their full par value, these bonds sell at close to par value despite their low coupon payments. The Treasury no longer issues flower bonds.

You can pick out the callable bonds in Figure 2.4 because a range of years appears in the maturity-date column. These are the years during which the bond is callable. Yields on premium bonds (bonds selling above par value) are calculated as the yield to the first call date, whereas yields on discount bonds are calculated as the yield to maturity date.

Concept Check

Question 2. Why does it make sense to calculate yields on discount bonds to maturity and yields on premium bonds to the first call date?

Federal Agency Debt

Some government agencies issue their own securities to finance their activities. These agencies usually are formed to channel credit to a particular sector of the economy that Congress believes is not receiving adequate credit through normal private sources. Figure 2.5 reproduces listings of some of these securities from *The Wall Street Journal*. The majority of the debt is issued in support of farm credit and home mortgages.

The major mortgage-related agencies are the Federal Home Loan Bank (FHLB), the Federal National Mortgage Association (FNMA, or Fannie Mae), the Government National Mortgage Association (GNMA, or Ginnie Mae), and the Federal Home Loan Mortgage Corporation (FHLMC, or Freddie Mac). The FHLB borrows money by issuing securities and lends this money to savings and loan institutions to be lent in turn to individuals borrowing for home mortgages.

Freddie Mac and Ginnie Mae were organized to provide liquidity to the mortgage market. Until the pass-through securities sponsored by these agencies were established (see the discussion of mortgages and mortgage-backed securities in this section), the lack of a secondary market in mortgages hampered the flow of investment funds into mortgages and made mortgage markets dependent on local, rather than national, credit availability.

The farm credit agencies consist of

1. The 12 district Banks for Cooperatives, which make seasonal loans to farm cooperatives
2. The 12 Federal Land Banks, which make mortgage loans on farm properties
3. The 12 Federal Intermediate Credit Banks, which provide short-term financing for production and marketing of crops and livestock

Although the debt of federal agencies is not explicitly insured by the federal government, it is widely assumed that the government would step in with assistance if an agency neared default. Thus these securities are considered extremely safe assets, and their yield spread above Treasury securities is quite small.

FIGURE 2.5

Government agency issues.

(From *The Wall Street Journal*, May 25, 1988.) Reprinted by permission of *The Wall Street Journal*. © Dow Jones & Company, Inc. 1988. All rights reserved.

GOVERNMENT AGENCY ISSUES

Tuesday, May 24, 1988

Mid-afternoon Over-the-Counter quotations usually based on large transactions, sometimes $1 million or more.

Hyphens in bid-and-asked represent 32nds; 101-01 means 101 1/32. a-Plus 1/64. b-Yield to call date. d-Minus 1/64.

Source: Bloomberg Financial Markets

FNMA Issues

Rate	Mat	Bid	Asked	Yld
10.50	6-88	100-01	100-05	6.43
9.40	8-88	100-10	100-14	7.08
16.38	8-88	101-21	101-27	7.06
8.55	9-88	100-05	100-11	7.24
13.20	9-88	101-16	101-20	7.41
9.50	10-88	100-22	100-25	7.27
8.38	1-91	99-19	99-29	8.41
6.90	2-91	96-05	96-15	8.38
7.65	2-91	98-03	98-09	8.36
12.00	3-91	108-13	108-23	8.42
12.50	3-91	109-09	109-27	8.47
7.20	4-91	96-21	96-27	8.45
8.00	4-91	98-25	98-29	8.43
7.45	5-91	97-07	97-17	8.41
8.55	6-91	99-21	99-31	8.56
7.65	7-91	97-05	97-15	8.59
8.70	8-91	100-07	100-13	8.54
8.40	8-91	99-07	99-17	8.56
7.00	9-91	95-05	95-15	8.60
7.80	10-91	97-25	98-03	8.46
7.38	10-91	96-03	96-13	8.62
9.55	11-91	102-13	102-19	8.66
11.75	12-91	108-30	109-08	8.66
8.50	1-92	99-11	99-17	8.65
7.00	3-92	94-19	94-29	8.60
12.00	4-92	110-18	110-24	8.67
8.45	5-92	98-24	98-30	8.77
8.50	5-92	98-29	99-03	8.77
7.05	6-92	94-03	94-13	8.72
10.13	6-92	104-09	104-15	8.79
8.45	7-92	98-21	98-31	8.75
10.60	10-92	105-27	106-05	8.87
9.88	12-92	103-21	103-31	8.79
10.90	1-93	107-05	107-15	8.89
7.95	2-93	96-19	96-25	8.80
7.90	3-93	96-13	96-23	8.75
10.95	3-93	107-15	107-25	8.91
7.55	4-93	94-27	95-01	8.82
10.88	4-93	107-09	107-19	8.92
10.75	5-93	106-25	107-03	8.95
7.75	11-93	94-26	95	8.93
7.38	12-93	93-07	93-13	8.91
7.65	4-94	93-15	93-21	9.06
8.90	8-94	98-31	99-05	9.08
10.10	10-94	103-29	104-03	9.23
9.25	11-94	100-05	100-11	9.18
9.00	1-95	98-19	98-23	9.26
11.95	1-95	112-11	112-21	9.34
11.50	2-95	110-10	110-16	9.35
11.70	5-95	111-15	111-25	9.36
11.15	6-95	108-29	109-03	9.36
10.50	9-95	105-07	105-17	9.43
10.60	11-95	106-03	106-09	9.41
9.20	1-96	98-17	98-27	9.41
7.00	2-96	85-31	86-09	9.55
9.35	2-96	99-11	99-21	9.41
8.75	6-96	96-03	96-13	9.40
8.00	7-96	91-13	91-19	9.51
8.15	8-96	92-07	92-11	9.51
7.70	12-96	89-15	89-25	9.47
7.60	1-97	88-25	88-31	9.50
9.20	6-97	97-27	98-01	9.53
8.95	7-97	96-11	96-17	9.52
9.55	9-97	99-21	99-27	9.57
9.55	11-97	99-19	99-25	9.58
7.10	12-97	84-09	84-19	9.60
9.55	12-97	99-19	99-25	9.58
9.80	12-97	100-15	101-01	9.51
8.65	2-98	94-09	94-15	9.53
9.15	4-98	97-05	97-11	9.57
12.35	12-13	112-29	113-07	9.25
12.65	3-14	114-[illegible]		9.25
[illegible]	7-14			

Fed. Home Loan Bank

Rate	Mat	Bid	Asked	Yld
7.38	5-88	99-31	100-02	2.77
10.15	5-88	99-30	100-02	5.38
7.25	6-88	99-31	100-02	6.35
8.80	6-88	100-03	100-06	6.45
10.80	6-88	100-08	100-11	6.62
9.15	7-88	100-06	100-10	7.04
12.50	9-89	105-13	105-23	7.88
14.55	9-89	107-24	108-02	8.03
9.35	10-89	101-19	101-23	8.03
6.60	11-89	98-03	98-09	7.83
11.55	11-89	104-16	104-26	8.09
8.13	11-89	99-30	100-04	8.03
6.55	12-89	97-26	98	7.91
8.25	12-89	100-01	100-05	8.14
11.20	1-90	104-07	104-17	8.22
6.55	1-90	97-17	97-23	8.03
6.70	3-90	97-19	97-25	8.01
7.30	3-90	98-17	98-27	7.98
11.90	3-90	105-25	106-03	8.24
7.05	4-90	98-01	98-07	8.07
7.70	4-90	99-07	99-11	8.07
8.25	5-90	99-27	100-01	8.23
7.75	6-90	98-27	99-05	8.19
9.50	6-90	102-03	102-13	8.21
9.75	7-90	102-11	102-21	8.37
7.80	7-90	98-23	98-29	8.35
8.10	8-90	99-07	99-13	8.38
8.88	9-90	100-23	100-29	8.43
12.50	9-90	108-07	108-17	8.38
10.30	9-90	103-17	103-27	8.44
7.05	10-90	97-09	97-15	8.22
8.40	11-90	99-23	99-29	8.44
13.70	11-90	111-09	111-19	8.46
10.90	12-90	105-05	105-15	8.49
8.70	12-90	100-13	100-23	8.38
8.30	1-91	99-09	99-19	8.47
9.10	1-91	101-11	101-21	8.39
7.10	2-91	96-13	96-23	8.45
7.65	2-91	97-27	98-05	8.41
11.88	2-91	107-31	108-09	8.43
7.75	3-91	97-23	98-01	8.54
7.35	4-91	96-31	97-05	8.47
7.88	5-91	97-27	98-05	8.58
8.50	5-91	99-21	99-25	8.58
7.50	7-91	96-23	97-01	8.58
7.20	8-91	96-01	96-07	8.55
11.10	8-91	106-19	106-29	8.61
7.40	9-91	96-03	96-13	8.66
11.75	9-91	108-09	108-19	8.71
9.95	10-91	103-13	103-19	8.71
7.15	11-91	95-03	95-13	8.70
7.00	12-91	94-17	94-27	8.70
11.40	12-91	107-14	107-24	8.83
7.00	1-92	94-09	94-19	8.75
11.45	2-92	107-27	108-05	8.84
7.10	3-92	94-13	94-23	8.75
8.15	4-92	97-25	98-03	8.73
8.30	4-92	98-23	99-01	8.59
11.70	4-92	108-27	109-05	8.88
8.60	5-92	99-01	99-11	8.80
8.40	6-92	98-09	98-19	8.81
8.38	7-92	98-05	98-15	8.82
8.60	8-92	98-31	99-09	8.80
10.35	8-92	104-19	104-29	8.93
10.85	10-92	106-13	106-23	8.97
11.10	11-92	107-11	107-21	8.99
8.80	11-92	99-13	99-23	8.88
9.05	12-92	100-09	100-19	8.89
10.70	1-93	106-07	106-17	8.95
9.50	1-93	101-27	102-05	8.92
8.05	2-93	96-23	97-01	8.82
8.10	3-93	96-31	97-05	

Rate	Mat	Bid	Asked	Yld
			102-01	
		81-15	81-25	10.1[illegible]
8.95	2-18	88-26	89	10.12
0.00	10-19	5-16	5-26	9.28

Federal Farm Credit

Rate	Mat	Bid	Asked	Yld
6.45	6-88	99-30	100-01	4.51
7.20	6-88	99-30	100-01	5.14
8.00	6-88	99-30	100-01	5.90
6.70	7-88	99-29	100	6.64
7.60	7-88	100	100-03	6.46
11.50	7-88	100-15	100-20	7.08
11.70	7-88	100-17	100-21	7.07
6.90	8-88	99-30	100-01	6.70
7.00	8-88	99-29	100	6.85
6.60	9-88	99-25	99-28	6.97
12.88	9-88	101-07	101-11	7.51
7.00	10-88	99-25	99-29	7.20
11.50	10-88	101-13	101-17	7.50
7.05	11-88	99-30	100-01	6.94
7.50	12-88	99-29	100-01	7.43
8.75	1-89	100-19	100-23	7.59
11.65	1-89	102-14	102-18	7.57
13.05	1-89	103-10	103-14	7.58
6.88	3-89	99-11	99-14	7.62
12.50	4-89	103-29	104-01	7.77
7.35	6-89	99-13	99-19	7.77
13.70	7-89	106-03	106-09	7.87
7.75	9-89	99-21	99-27	7.87
10.60	10-89	103-05	103-11	8.03
15.65	10-89	109-22	109-28	8.09
12.45	10-89	105-14	105-20	8.14
10.95	1-90	103-29	104-07	8.16
11.15	1-90	104-07	104-17	8.16
10.85	2-90	103-23	104-01	8.22
11.35	4-90	105-03	105-13	8.21
14.10	6-90	110-09	110-19	8.29
9.55	7-90	102-11	102-17	8.24
10.40	7-90	103-31	104-05	8.25
12.50	9-90	107-31	108-09	8.41
10.60	10-90	104-15	104-21	8.42
7.65	3-91	97-27	98-01	8.45
7.55	4-91	97-11	97-21	8.47
14.10	4-91	113-19	113-29	8.59
9.10	7-91	101-07	101-17	8.53
14.70	7-91	116-03	116-13	8.64
10.60	10-91	104-29	105-07	8.79
13.65	12-91	113-20	113-30	8.94
11.50	1-92	107-28	108-06	8.82
15.20	1-92	118-26	119-04	8.94
13.75	7-92	115-29	116-07	8.98
10.65	1-93	106-01	106-11	8.95
11.80	10-93	111-15	111-25	8.99
12.35	3-94	113-17	113-23	9.22
14.25	4-94	122-07	122-13	9.24
13.00	9-94	117-23	118-01	9.15
11.45	12-94	110-05	110-15	9.27
11.90	10-97	113-19	113-29	9.62

Student Loan Marketing

Rate	Mat	Bid	Asked	Yld
9.63	5-88	99-29	100-01	3.82
11.70	7-88	100-12	100-16	6.85
7.90	7-89	99-26	100-04	7.77
12,85	9-89	105-06	105-24	7.96
13.15	9-90	105-18	106-04	7.94
10.90	2-90	103-29	104-07	8.26
6.95	8-90	96-31	97-05	8.36
7.90	9-90	98-21	98-31	8.39
8.45	12-90	99-29	100-03	8.41
7.38	2-91	97-21	97-31	8.47
8.55	5-91	99-15	99-25	8.63
7.75	6-91	97-11	97-21	8.63
7.60	6-91	96-27	97-05	8.65
5.60	8-91	91-21	91-31	8.53
8.00	8-91	98-07	98-17	8.53
8.25	6-92	97-11	97-29	8.87
9.25	9-92	100-21	100-31	8.76
8.80	12-92	99-03	99-13	8.96
10.50	4-93	105-25	105-31	8.97
7.35	5-93	93-17	93-27	8.92
8.20	5-93	96-29	97-03	8.92
0.00	9-95	54-13	54-31	9.52
7.75	12-96	89-21	89-27	9.50
7.63	1-97	88-23	88-29	9.53
9.50	9-97	99-05	99-23	9.54
0.00	5-14	7-13	7-23	10.11
[illegible]	10-22			

Rate	Mat	Bid	Asked	Yld
				[illegible].85
	[illegible]			8.86
8.90	5-93	99-21	99-25	8.96
10.75	5-93	106-13	106-23	9.05
7.75	7-93	95-03	95-09	8.90
11.70	7-93	110-29	111-03	8.96
7.45	8-93	93-22	94	8.90
11.95	8-93	111-23	112-01	9.02
7.95	9-93	95-21	95-27	8.94
7.88	10-93	95-17	95-23	8.89
7.38	11-93	93-04	93-14	8.91
7.38	12-93	92-31	93-05	8.96
12.15	12-93	113-20	113-26	8.95
7.30	1-94	92-22	92-28	8.93
7.45	2-94	93-10	93-16	8.91
12.00	2-94	113-05	113-11	8.97
8.50	4-94	98-01	98-07	8.89
10.00	6-95	102-27	103-05	9.38
10.30	7-95	104-11	104-17	9.41
8.10	3-96	91-27	92-01	9.56
7.75	4-96	89-25	89-31	9.58
8.25	5-96	92-17	92-23	9.57
8.25	6-96	92-17	92-23	9.56
8.00	7-96	91-05	91-09	9.56
7.70	8-96	89-11	89-17	9.56
8.25	9-96	92-11	92-17	9.57
7.88	2-97	90-03	90-13	9.51
7.65	3-97	88-27	89-01	9.51
9.20	8-97	98-05	98-15	9.45

World Bank Bonds

Rate	Mat	Bid	Asked	Yld
15.00	12-88	103-22	104-06	7.84
11.00	10-89	103-10	103-26	8.37
4.50	2-90	94-07	94-23	8.27
5.38	7-91	90-20	91-04	8.92
16.63	11-91	121-07	121-23	9.23
15.13	12-91	117-07	117-23	9.30
5.38	4-92	87-27	88-11	9.20
14.75	6-92	118-09	118-25	9.18
13.63	9-92	115-28	116-12	9.03
10.90	3-93	106-30	107-14	9.07
10.38	5-93	105-08	105-24	9.04
5.88	9-93	86-24	87-04	9.10
6.50	3-94	87-15	87-31	9.35
6.38	10-94	85-28	86-12	9.38
11.63	12-94	110-14	110-29	9.45
8.63	8-95	95-24	96-16	9.45
8.13	8-96	92-26	93-18	9.40
9.35	12-00	96-21	97-11	9.82
8.85	7-01	92-30	93-20	9.82
8.38	12-01	89-15	90-06	9.80
8.25	5-02	88-11	88-29	9.80
8.35	8-02	89	89-16	9.80
12.38	10-02	118-21	119-21	9.91

GNMA Issues

Rate	Mat	Bid	Asked	Bond Yld
8.00		86-21	86-25	10.14
8.50		89-20	89-24	10.19
9.00		92-18	92-22	10.25
9.50		95-18	95-22	10.30
10.00		98-18	98-22	10.35
10.50		101-17	101-21	10.41
11.00		104-17	104-21	10.46
11.50		106-23	106-27	10.63
12.00		108-24	108-28	10.82
12.50		109-30	110-04	11.13
13.00		111-10	111-16	11.41
13.50		112-10	112-16	11.74
14.00		113-12	113-18	12.06
14.50		113-30	114-06	12.47
15.00		114-30	115-02	12.78

Inter-Amer. Devel. Bk.

Rate	Mat	Bid	Asked	Yld
14.63	8-92	118-28	119-12	9.10
12.13	10-93	112-16	113	9.15
11.63	12-94	110-04	110-20	9.50
11.38	5-95	109	109-16	9.55
7.50	12-96	87-20	88-04	9.65
9.50	10-97	102-08	102-20	8.85
8.50	3-11	85-24	86-08	10.12

Source – Bear Stearns

Federal Land Bank

Rate	Mat	Bid	Asked	Yld
8.20	1-90	100-03	100-09	8.00
7.95	4-91	98-11	98-21	8.48
7.9[illegible]	[illegible]	90-11	90-21	9.59

Municipal Bonds

Municipal bonds are issued by state and local governments. They are similar to Treasury and corporate bonds except that their interest income is exempt from federal income taxation. The interest income also is exempt from state and local taxation in the issuing state. Capital gains taxes, however, must be paid on "munis," when the bonds mature or if they are sold for more than the investor's purchase price.

Two types of municipal bonds may be distinguished. These are *general obligation* bonds, which are backed by the "full faith and credit" (that is, the taxing power) of the issuer, and *revenue bonds,* which are issued to finance particular projects and are backed either by the revenues from that project or by the particular municipal agency operating the project. Typical issuers of revenue bonds are airports, hospitals, and turnpike or port authorities. Obviously, revenue bonds are riskier in terms of default than are general obligation bonds.

An *industrial developmental bond* is a revenue bond that is issued to finance commercial enterprises, such as the construction of a factory that can be operated by a private firm. In effect, this device gives the firm access to the municipality's ability to borrow at tax-exempt rates. Figure 2.6 shows the volume of new offerings of municipal bonds in recent years. Note the increasing importance of revenue bonds in the last few years.

Like Treasury bonds, municipal bonds vary widely in maturity. A good deal of the debt issued is in the form of short-term *tax anticipation notes,* which raise funds to pay for expenses before actual collection of taxes. Other municipal debt is long term and used to fund large capital investments. Maturities range up to 30 years.

FIGURE 2.6

State and local government security issues.

(Modified from the *1985 Historical Chart Book,* Board of Governors of the Federal Reserve Board.)

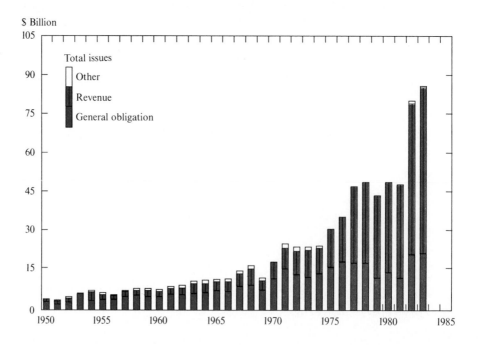

The key feature of municipal bonds is their tax-exempt status. Because in\ need not pay federal (and possibly state) taxes on the interest proceeds, they are will-ing to accept lower yields on these securities. These lower yields represent a huge savings to state and local governments. Correspondingly, they constitute a huge drain of potential tax revenue from the federal government, and the government has shown some dismay over the explosive increase in use of industrial development bonds. These so-called *private purpose bonds* increased from 22% of new municipal offer-ings in 1975 to 62% in 1983.

There is some concern that these bonds are being used to take advantage of the tax-exempt feature of municipal bonds rather than as a source of funds for publicly desirable investments. The Tax Reform Act of 1986 placed new restrictions on the issuance of tax-exempt bonds. As of 1988, each state is allowed to issue mortgage revenue and private purpose tax-exempt bonds only up to a limit of $50 per capita or $150 million, whichever is larger.

An investor choosing between taxable and tax-exempt bonds must compare after-tax returns on each bond. An exact comparison requires a computation of after-tax rates of return that explicitly accounts for taxes on income and realized capital gains. In practice, there is a simpler rule of thumb. If we let t denote the investor's marginal tax bracket and r denote the total before-tax rate of return available on taxable bonds, then $r(1 - t)$ is the after-tax rate available on those securities. If this value exceeds the rate on municipal bonds, r_m, the investor does better holding the taxable bonds. Otherwise, the tax-exempt municipals provide higher after-tax returns.

One way to compare bonds is to determine the interest rate on taxable bonds that would be necessary to provide an after-tax return equal to that of municipals. To de-rive this value, we set after-tax yields equal, and solve for the **equivalent taxable yield** of the tax-exempt bond. This is the rate a taxable bond must offer to match the after-tax yield on the tax-free municipal.

$$r(1 - t) = r_m \qquad (2.4)$$

or

$$r = r_m/(1 - t) \qquad (2.5)$$

Thus the equivalent taxable yield is simply the tax-free rate divided by $1 - t$. Table 2.2 presents equivalent taxable yields for several municipal yields and tax rates.

TABLE 2.2   Equivalent Taxable Yields Corresponding to Various Tax-Exempt Yields

Marginal Tax Rate	Tax-Exempt Yield				
	4%	6%	8%	10%	12%
20%	5.0	7.5	10.0	12.5	15.0
30%	5.7	8.6	11.4	14.3	17.1
40%	6.7	10.0	13.3	16.7	20.0
50%	8.0	12.0	16.0	20.0	24.0

This table frequently appears in the marketing literature for tax-exempt mutual bond funds because it demonstrates to high tax–bracket investors that municipal bonds offer highly attractive equivalent taxable yields. Each entry is calculated from equation 2.5. If the equivalent taxable yield exceeds the actual yields offered on taxable bonds, the investor is better off after taxes holding municipal bonds. Notice that the equivalent taxable interest rate increases with the investor's tax bracket; the higher the bracket, the more valuable the tax-exempt feature of municipals. Thus high tax–bracket investors tend to hold municipals.

We also can use equations 2.4 or 2.5 to find the tax bracket at which investors are indifferent between taxable and tax-exempt bonds. The cutoff tax bracket is given by solving equation 2.4 for the tax bracket at which after-tax yields are equal. Doing so, we find that

$$t = 1 - r_m/r \tag{2.6}$$

Thus the yield ratio r_m/r is a key determinant of the attractiveness of municipal bonds. The higher the yield ratio, the lower the cutoff tax bracket, and the more individuals will prefer to hold municipal debt. Figure 2.7 graphs the yield ratio since 1970. Notice that the ratio seems to have risen over time. This implies that municipals have become desirable to investors in progressively lower tax brackets.

FIGURE 2.7

Ratios of yields on tax-exempt bonds to taxable bonds.

(Data from Federal Reserve Board bulletins.)

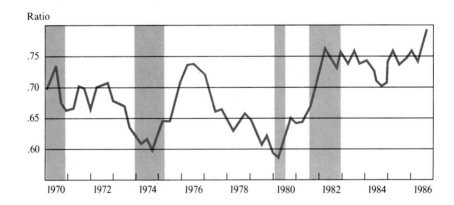

Question 3. What economic policy changes in the 1980s might have contributed to the increase in the yield ratio?

Introduction

Corporate Bonds

Corporate bonds enable private firms to borrow money directly from the public. These bonds are similar in structure to Treasury issues—they typically pay semiannual coupons over their lives and return the face value to the bondholder at maturity. However, they differ most importantly from Treasury bonds in degree of risk. Default risk is a real consideration in the purchase of corporate bonds, and Chapter 14

FIGURE 2.8
Corporate bond listings.

(From *The Wall Street Journal*, May 25, 1988.) Reprinted by permission of *The Wall Street Journal*. © Dow Jones & Company, Inc. 1988. All rights reserved.

NEW YORK EXCHANGE BONDS

Tuesday, May 24, 1988

Total Volume $26,430,000

SALES SINCE JANUARY 1

1988	1987	1986
$3,145,200,000	$4,118,523,000	$4,642,511,000

	Domestic Tue.	Domestic Mon.	All Issues Tue.	All Issues Mon.
Issues traded	657	667	659	668
Advances	234	184	234	184
Declines	262	326	264	326
Unchanged	161	157	161	158
New highs	3	9	3	9
New lows	14	15	14	15

Dow Jones Bond Averages

	−1986− High	Low	−1987− High	Low	−1988− High	Low		−1988−	−−−Tuesday−−− −1987−	−1986−
	93.65	83.73	95.51	81.26	91.25	86.92	20 Bonds	87.42 +0.02	87.64 +0.57	90.59 ....
	95.79	81.85	98.23	79.51	91.88	86.20	10 Utilities	86.20	87.88 +0.84	90.60 −0.03
	91.64	84.82	93.10	83.00	90.64	86.96	10 Industrial	88.64 +0.04	87.40 +0.31	90.58 +0.02

Bonds	Cur Yld	Vol	Close	Net Chg.
ColuG 8¾95	9.1	3	95¾	− ¼
ColuG 9⅝95	9.4	17	97	− 1¼
ColuG 12¾00	12.3	10	104	...
Cmdis 9.65s02	10.7	30	90	− 1½
CmwE 8s03	10.0	13	79⅞	− ⅜
CmwE 9⅞04	10.3	2	91¼	− ¼
CmwE 9⅛08	10.6	9	86¼	...
CmwE 15¾00	13.5	5	114	+ 1
Crane 7s93	7.6	1	92⅜	− ⅜
Crane 7s94	8.2	5	85	...
Crane 10⅛94	10.5	20	100	− ⅞
CrayRs 6⅛11	cv	25	105½	− ½
CrdF zr90s	...	25	80¼	...
CrdF 13⅞92	13.2	3	105¼	− 5⅝
CritAc 12¼14	12.0	1	102⅜	− ⅛
CritAc 13⅛14	12.7	1	103⅝	− ⅛
DaytH 10¾13	11.1	141	97	...
DaytP 8½07	10.0	5	85	...
Deere 9s08	cv	121	120	+ 4½
DetEd 9s99	9.9	5	90¾	+ ¾
DetEd 9.15s00	10.0	10	91⅜	− 1½
DetEd 8.75s00	9.8	2	83⅛	− 1¾
DetEd 8½01	9.8	10	82⅜	− ⅞
DetEd 7¾01	9.6	5	77	− ⅝
DetEd 9⅞04	10.6	1	93	− ½
Dow 8⅞2000	9.2	202	96¼	+ ¾
Dow 8⅜08	9.8	6	88	...
duPnt 8½06	9.6	35	88⅞	...
duPnt 14s91	13.6	8	103²¹⁄₃₂	...
duPnt dc6s01	8.4	5	71¾	+ ½
duPnt 12⅞92	12.1	42	106¼	...
duPnt 8½16	9.4	10	90⅜	...
duPnt 7½93	8.0	45	93⅞	+ ⅜
DukeP 7¾02	9.2	22	84⅛	+ ⅛
DukeP 7¾02	9.1	5	80¼	+ ⅛
DukeP 7¾03	9.1	20	84¾	+ ⅛
DukeP 8½03	9.4			+ ¾

Bonds	Cur Yld	Vol	Close	Net Chg.
Fuqua 9⅞97	10.2	5	97¼	− ¼
GAF 11⅜95	11.4	163	99⅝	− ⅜
GATX 11½96	11.2	63	103	...
GnATr 5¾99	cv	265	95	+ 1
GnDev 12⅞05	13.4	32	94	− ½
GdDyn 5¾11	...	9	88	...
GnEl 8½04	9.3	25	91⅜	+ ¾
GEICr 8¾49f	8.8	16	93¼	+ ½
GTE 6⅞91	7.1	4	93¾	− ¼
Gene dc9¾93	11.2	9	87¼	− ¾
GaPw 8⅞00	10.0	5	89	+ ¼
GaPw 7½02J	9.6	5	78½	− 1½
GaPw 11¾00	11.3	10	103	...
GaPw 9¾08	10.7	25	91½	− 1⅜
GaPw 10½09	10.6	23	98⅜	...
GaPw 11s09	11.1	27	99½	− 2⅜
GaPw 13⅛12	12.3	3	106½	+ 1½
GaPw 16s14	14.8	17	108⅜	...
GaPw 10¾17	10.9	60	99	...
GibFn 9¼08	cv	4	69	− 1
vjGloM dc16s01f	...	10	18⅜	...
vjGloMr 16½02f	...	28	18½	− ½
vjGloM dc13s03f	cv	10	18	− ¼
GdNaFg 13¼95	13.0	120	102⅛	− ⅜
Gdrch 8¼34f	8.8	15	94	...
Grace 4¼90	cv	10	101⅛	...
GreyF zr94	...	34	51¼	+ ⅛
GrowGp 12½94	12.9	62	97	− 1
GrowGp 8½06	cv	46	101	− ⅛
Grumn 9¼09	cv	5	101½	+ ⅛
Gulfrd 6s12	cv	10	79	− 1½
GlfWn 7s03A	9.3	16	75	...
Harns dc12s04	12.1	17	99¼	− ¾
Hawn 8.35s03	9.5	8	87¾	+ ¼
Hellr 7¾92	8.2	12	94	− 1
Hellr 8¾02			91	− 4
Holldy 10⅛??			?7½	+ ⅛
Holld				

Bonds	Cur Yld	Vol	Close	Net Chg.
vjJoneL 6¾94f	...	50	28	− 1¾
KerrMc 8½06	9.7	50	87¼	− 1¾
KerrMc 7¼12	cv	6	102	− 1
Kolmrg 8¾09	cv	10	82	− ½
vjLTV 5s88f	...	45	34⅜	− ⅛
vjLTV 11s07f	...	15	33	...
vjLTV 14s04f	...	6	45⅜	+ ⅝
vjLTV 8¾98f	...	15	31½	...
McDInv 8s11	cv	2	81	...
vjMcLn 12s03f	...	110	7⅛	+ ¼
vjMcLn 14¼94f	...	50	7¼	− ⅜
Mead 6s12	cv	5	92	...
Melln 8.6s09	10.5	6	82	+ 1⅞
Melln 7¼99	8.7	5	83	+ ½
MerLy zr06	...	75	23⅜	...
MesaCap 12s96	12.0	5	99⅞	− ⅛
MichB 7s12	9.7	8	72¼	− 1
MichB 9.6s08	9.9	58	96⅞	...
MichB 8⅛15	10.0	13	81¼	− 1¾
MichB 9⅛18	10.1	15	90	...
MKT 4s90	4.5	13	89	...
MKT 5½33f	...	55	62½	+ ½
MKT 5½33f	...	30	62½	...
MPac 4¾20f	...	144	48⅞	...
MPac 4¼30f	...	17	48	− ¾
MPac 5s45f	...	20	49¾	...
Mobil 8½01	9.4	7	90⅞	+ ⅛
Mobil 14.4s04	13.5	21	106¾	...
Mobil 7¾91	7.8	15	97⅜	...
MobO 7¾01	8.8	10	83⅜	− ⅜
Mobil 13.76s04	13.0	3	106⅛	− ⅜
Mobil 8⅜94	8.8	119	97½	+ ⅛
Mobil 8¾90	8.7	14	100⅜	− ⅜
Monog 10s99	12.5	5	80	+ 2⅞
Monog 11s04	12.9	20	85	− 2½
Moran 8¾08f	cv	2	6?	− 3½
MtSTl 7¾11	9.?			...

discusses this issue in considerable detail. For now, we distinguish only among *secured bonds,* which have specific collateral backing them in the event of firm bankruptcy, unsecured bonds called *debentures,* which have no collateral, and *subordinated debentures,* which have a lower priority claim to the firm's assets in the event of bankruptcy.

Corporate bonds usually come with options attached. *Callable bonds* give the firm the option to repurchase the bond from the holder at a stipulated call price. *Convertible bonds* give the bondholder the option to convert each bond into a stipulated number of shares of stock. These options are treated in more detail in Chapter 14.

Figure 2.8 is a partial listing of corporate bond prices from *The Wall Street Journal.* The listings are similar to those for Treasury bonds. The first du Pont bond listed has a coupon rate of 8½% and a maturity date of 2006. Its **current yield,** defined as annual coupon income divided by price, is 9.6%. (Note that current yield is a different measure from yield to maturity. The differences are explored in Chapter 17.) A total of 35 bonds traded on this particular day. The closing price of the bond was 88⅞% of par, or $888.75, which was unchanged from the previous day's close. Notice that, in contrast to Treasury bonds, price quotes on corporate bonds use explicit fractions instead of decimals that represent 32nds of a point.

Mortgages and Mortgage-Backed Securities

An investments text of 20 years ago probably would not include a section on mortgage loans, since investors could not invest in these loans. Now, because of the explosion in mortgage-backed securities, almost anyone can invest in a portfolio of mortgage loans, and these securities have become a major component of the fixed-income market.

Until the 1970s almost all home mortgages were written for a long term (15- to 30-year maturity), with a fixed interest rate over the life of the loan, and with equal fixed monthly payments. These so-called conventional mortgages are still the most popular, but a diverse set of alternative mortgage designs has developed.

Fixed-rate mortgages have posed difficulties to banks in years of increasing interest rates. Because banks commonly issue short-term liabilities (the deposits of their customers) and hold long-term assets such as fixed-rate mortgages, they suffer losses when interest rates increase: the rates they pay on deposits increase while their mortgage income remains fixed.

A relatively recent introduction is the *adjustable rate mortgage.* These mortgages require the borrower to pay an interest rate that varies with some measure of the current market interest rate. For example, the interest rate might be set at 2 points above the current rate on 1-year Treasury bills and might be adjusted once a year. Often, a contract sets a limit, or cap, on the maximum size of an interest rate change within a year and over the life of the contract. The adjustable rate contract shifts the risk of fluctuations in interest rates from the lender to the borrower.

Because of the shifting of interest rate risk to their customers, banks are willing to offer lower rates on adjustable rate mortgages than on conventional fixed-rate mortgages. This proved to be a great inducement to borrowers during a period of high interest rates in the early 1980s. As interest rates fell, however, conventional mortgages appear to have regained popularity. Although adjustable rate mortgages accounted for about half of all mortgage lending at year-end 1983, that figure fell to about 30% by mid-1986.

A *mortgage-backed security* is either an ownership claim in a pool of mortgages or an obligation that is secured by such a pool. These claims represent securitization of mortgage loans. Mortgage lenders originate loans and then sell packages of these loans in the secondary market. Specifically, they sell their claim to the cash inflows from the mortgages as those loans are paid off. The mortgage originator continues to service the loan, collecting principal and interest payments, and passes these payments along to the purchaser of the mortgage. For this reason, these mortgage-backed securities are called *pass-throughs*.

Mortgage-backed pass-through securities were first introduced by the Government National Mortgage Association (GNMA, or Ginnie Mae) in 1970. GNMA pass-throughs carry a guarantee from the U.S. government that ensures timely payment of principal and interest, even if the borrower defaults on the mortgage. This guarantee increases the marketability of the pass-through. Thus investors can buy or sell GNMA securities like any other bond.

Other mortgage pass-throughs have since become popular. These are sponsored by FNMA (Federal National Mortgage Association, or Fannie Mae) and FHLMC (Federal Home Loan Mortgage Corp, or Freddie Mac). The success of mortgage-backed pass-throughs has encouraged introduction of pass-through securities backed by other assets. For example, the Student Loan Marketing Association (SLMA, or Sallie Mae) sponsors pass-throughs backed by loans originated under the Guaranteed Student Loan Program and by other loans granted under various federal programs for higher education.

Although pass-through securities often guarantee payment of interest and principal, they do not guarantee the rate of return. Holders of mortgage pass-throughs therefore can be severely disappointed in their returns in years when interest rates drop significantly. This is because homeowners usually have an option to prepay, or pay ahead of schedule, the remaining principal outstanding on their mortgages. This right is essentially an option held by the borrower to "call back" the loan for the remaining principal balance, quite analogous to the option held by government or corporate issuers of callable bonds. The prepayment option gives the borrower the right to buy back the loan at the outstanding principal amount rather than at the present discounted value of the *scheduled* remaining payments. When interest rates fall, so that the present value of the scheduled mortgage payments increases, the borrower may choose to take out a new loan at today's lower interest rate and use the proceeds of the loan to prepay or retire the outstanding mortgage. This refinancing may disappoint pass-through investors, who are liable to "receive a call" just when they might have anticipated capital gains from interest rate declines.

2.3 *Equity Securities*

Common Stock as Ownership Shares

Common stocks, also known as equity securities or equities, represent ownership shares in a corporation. Each share of common stock entitles its owner to one vote on any matters of corporate governance that are put to a vote at the corporation's annual meeting and to a share in the financial benefits of ownership.[2]

The corporation is controlled by a board of directors elected by the shareholders. The board, which meets only a few times each year, selects managers who actually run the corporation on a day-to-day basis. Managers have the authority to make most business decisions without the board's specific approval. The board's mandate is to oversee the management to ensure that it acts in the best interests of shareholders. The members of the board are elected at the annual meeting. Shareholders who do not attend the annual meeting can vote by *proxy,* empowering another party to vote in their name. Management usually solicits the proxies of shareholders and normally gets a vast majority of these proxy votes. Occasionally, however, a group of shareholders intent on unseating the current management or altering its policies will wage a proxy fight to gain the voting rights of shareholders not attending the annual meeting. Thus, although management usually has considerable discretion to run the firm as it sees fit—without daily oversight from the equityholders who actually own the firm—both oversight from the board and the possibility of a proxy fight serve as checks on management's jurisdiction.

Another related check on management's discretion is the possibility of a corporate takeover. In these episodes, an outside investor who believes that the firm is mismanaged will attempt to acquire the firm. Usually, this is accomplished with a *tender offer,* which is an offer made to purchase at a stipulated price, usually substantially above the current market price, some or all of the shares held by the current stockholders. If the tender is successful, the acquiring investor purchases enough shares to obtain control of the firm and can replace its management.

The common stock of most large corporations can be bought or sold freely on one or more stock exchanges. A corporation whose stock is not publicly traded is said to be closely held. In most closely held corporations, the owners of the firm also take an active role in its management. Takeovers are therefore generally not an issue.

Thus, although there is substantial separation of the ownership and the control of large corporations, there are at least some implicit controls on management that tend to force it to act in the interests of the shareholders.

---

[2]A corporation sometimes issues two classes of common stock, one bearing the right to vote, the other not. Because of its restricted rights, the nonvoting stock should sell for a lower price.

Characteristics of Common Stock

The two most important characteristics of common stock as an investment are its **residual claim** and **limited liability** features.

Residual claim means that stockholders are the last in line of all those who have a claim on the assets and income of the corporation. In a liquidation of the firm's assets the shareholders have a claim to what is left after all other claimants such as the tax authorities, employees, suppliers, bondholders, and other creditors have been paid. For a firm not in liquidation, shareholders have claim to the part of operating income left over after interest and taxes have been paid. Management can either pay this residual as cash dividends to shareholders or reinvest it in the business to increase the value of the shares.

Limited liability means that the greatest amount shareholders can lose in event of failure of the corporation is their original investment. Unlike owners of unincorporated businesses, whose creditors can lay claim to the personal assets of the owner (house, car, furniture), corporate shareholders may at worst have worthless stock. They are not personally liable for the firm's obligations.

Concept Check

Question 4.
a. If you buy 100 shares of IBM stock, to what are you entitled?
b. What is the most money you can make on this investment over the next year?
c. If you pay $50 per share, what is the most money you could lose over the year?

Stock Market Listings

Figure 2.9 is a partial listing from *The Wall Street Journal* of stocks traded on the New York Stock Exchange. The NYSE is one of several markets in which investors may buy or sell shares of stock. We will examine these markets in detail in Chapter 3.

To interpret the information provided for each traded stock, consider the listing for Baltimore Gas and Electric, BaltGE. The first two columns provide the highest and lowest price at which the stock has traded in the last 52 weeks, 34 and 19 respectively. The 2.00 figure means that dividend payout to its shareholders over the last quarter was $2.00 per share at an annual rate. This value corresponds to a dividend yield of 6.3%, meaning that the dividend paid per dollar value of each share is .063. That is, BaltGE stock is selling at 31⅝ (the last recorded, or "close" price in the next-to-last column), so that the dividend yield is 2.00/31.625 = .0632, or 6.3%. The stock listings show that dividend yields vary widely among firms. It is important to recognize that high dividend–yield stocks are not necessarily better investments than low-yield stocks. Total return to an investor comes from dividends and **capital**

FIGURE 2.9

Stock market listings.

(From *The Wall Street Journal*, May 25, 1988.) Reprinted by permission of *The Wall Street Journal*. © Dow Jones & Company, Inc. 1988. All rights reserved.

NEW YORK STOCK EXCHANGE COMPOSITE TRANSACTIONS

Tuesday, May 24, 1988

Quotations include trades on the Midwest, Pacific, Philadelphia, Boston and Cincinnati stock exchanges and reported by the National Association of Securities Dealers and Instinet

52 Weeks High	Low	Stock	Div.	Yld %	P-E Ratio	Sales 100s	High	Low	Close	Net Chg.
30½	11¾	AnchGl	.08	.5	14	128	17⅛	16⅞	17	...
34⅜	18½	Angelic	.72	2.9	13	36	24¾	24½	24⅝	+ ⅛
14⅝	9⅝	AngelRI	1.52	14.0	44	18	10⅞	10¾	10⅞	...
40⅛	25¾	Anheus	.60	2.0	14	10853	30¼	29¾	30⅛	+ ½
17⅜	6¾	Anthm s	...	...	18	74	11¾	11⅜	11¾	+ ⅛
14⅞	7¾	Anthony	.44b	3.4	8	167	13	12¾	13	...
29⅞	20½	Aon cp	1.28	5.3	10	304	24	23¾	24	+ ¼
12½	6⅝	Apache	.28	3.6	...	101	8	7⅞	7⅞	...
8⅜	2⅝	ApcP un	.35	12.2	...	313	2⅞	2¾	2⅞	+ ⅛
36	17	ApplBk	...	...	7	51	28	27⅝	27⅝	...
20⅞	8½	ApplM s	...	...	14	296	14¾	14½	14⅝	+ ⅛
27¾	17½	ArchDn	.10b	.5	11	3246	21⅜	21	21¼	...
38¼	17	ArcoCh	.60e	1.9	...	492	31	29⅞	31	+ 1⅛
39	16¾	Aristec	.80	2.8	5	2878	29½	28¼	28¾	− ¾
24¾	8⅛	ArkBst	.36	1.5	17	639	24⅞u	24⅜	24¾	...
26½	15⅝	Arkla	1.08	6.0	18	425	18	17¾	18	+ ¾
59	34½	Arkla pf	3.00	7.4	...	20	40½	40	40½	+1
14½	7¾	Armada	...	...	...	7	11¾	11½	11¾	...
14¾	7⅛	Armco	...	...	20	1435	9⅞	9½	9¾	+ ⅛
46	37¾	Armc pf	4.50	11.1	...	180	40½	40½	40½	...
47⅜	22½	ArmWI	1.00	2.7	11	620	36½	36	36½	+ ⅜
31¼	13	Armtek	.48	1.9	11	357	24⅞	24⅜	24⅜	+ ⅛
12⅛	4⅞	ArowE	...	...	...	357	8⅛	8	8	...
21½	12	ArowE pf	1.94	12.3	...	1064	15¾	15½	15¾	...
33	11	Artra	...	...	...	512	28½	27⅞	28¼	− ⅛
37⅜	14¾	Arvin	.68	3.7	19	1770	18½	18¼	18½	+ ⅛
34¼	15	Asarco	.30e	1.3	3	1004	23¾	23½	23¾	+ ¼
72½	46½	AshlOil	2.00	2.9	12	x1050	68½	67¾	68½	+ ¼
12	3⅝	AsiaPc	...	...	...	132	6⅜	6¼	6¼	− ⅛
12¾	5	AtalSos	.40e	5.8	8	12	7	6⅞	6⅞	...
23⅛	9⅞	Athlone	1.60	11.4	...	16	14	13⅞	14	+ ¼
27¼	19⅜	AtlGas	1.76	6.8	10	76	25¾	25¾	25¾	− ⅛
36½	28¾	AtlEnrg	2.68a	8.3	8	121	32⅜	32½	32⅜	+ ⅛
99½	58¾	AtlRich	4.00	4.7	11	1597	84⅞	83¾	84¼	− ½
235¾	155½	AtlRc pr	2.80	1.4	...	3	200¾	200⅝	200¾	− 3¼
53	21¾	AtlasCp	...	...	34	51	31¾	31½	31¾	+ ¾
8	3	AudVd	...	...	19	136	5⅛	5	5	− ¼
28⅝	10⅝	Augat	.40	3.1	22	206	12¾	12	12¾	+ ⅜
32½	10	Ausimt	.60	1.9	16	3003	32¼	31⅜	32⅛	+ ⅜
54½	32¼	AutoDt	.52	1.4	18	1678	37¾	37½	37½	+ ⅛
8	4½	Avalon	.20e	3.8	...	269	5¼	4⅞	5¼	+ ½
25¼	14⅜	AVMCO	.34	1.4	12	6	24⅛	24¼	24⅛	...
29¼	15⅜	Avery	.48	2.3	24	703	21⅛	20⅞	21⅛	+ ⅜
39¼	18½	Avnet	.50	2.1	18	521	23¾	23¼	23⅝	+ ⅛
38⅝	19¼	Avon	2.00	8.6	11	2170	23¼	22¾	23⅛	+ ⅜
35⅝	16	Aydin	...	...	10	37	20	19⅞	19⅞	− ⅛

— B–B–B —

32⅜	23⅛	BCE g	2.44	...	...	303	29⅞	29¾	29⅞	...
20¼	13⅜	BET n	.77e	4.5	13	26	17¼	17	17⅛	+ ½
9⅞	3¼	BMC	...	...	8	815	6¾	6½	6¾	+ ¼
32⅜	23½	BRE	2.40	8.3	13	33	29½	29	29	...
19⅝	14½	BRT	2.48	13.8	7	159	18⅛	18	18	− ⅛
42¼	20	Bairnco	.80	2.5	11	147	31⅞	31½	31¾	...
27⅛	11⅛	BakrHu	.46	2.7	...	1986	16½	16¼	16¾	+ ⅛
67	38⅝	BkrH pf	3.50	7.3	...	4	48½	48¼	48¼	− ½
28	17	Baldor	.52	2.0	23	24	25½	25¼	25⅜	+ ⅛
48½	25⅝	Ball	.96	3.4	10	325	28½	27¾	28⅜	+ ⅝
27¾	10½	BallyMf	.24	1.5	6	2615	16	15½	16	+ ½
21¼	9¾	BaltBcp	.50	3.3	8	229	15	14⅞	15	+ ⅜
34	19	BaltGE	2.00	6.3	9	541	31⅜	31⅛	31⅜	+ ⅜
27⅜	16⅛	BncOne	.92b	3.7	12	756	24¾	24¼	24¾	...
4¼	1⅛	BanTx n	...	...	...	31	1¼	1¼	1¼	...
69	42	Bandag	...	...	15	283	61½	60⅜	61¼	+ ½
3⁰							24⅜	24¼		¾

52 Weeks High	Low	Stock	Div.	Yld %	P-E Ratio	Sales 100s	High	Low	Close	Net Chg.
28	19¾	CinnBel	1.12	3.9	13	289	28½u	27½	28½	+ ¾
27¾	23⅛	CinGE	2.24	8.5	12	359	26⅜	26	26⅜	+ ¼
44	39	CinG pf	4.00	9.5	...	z150	42	42	42	+1
77¼	65½	CinG pf	7.44	10.1	...	z600	73½	73	73½	...
35	14	CinMil	.72	3.2	...	366	22⅞	22¼	22⅜	− ¼
15⅜	8¼	CineOd	...	...	8	223	8⅜	8¼	8⅜	...
18½	7	CircleK	.28	2.0	15	603	13¾	13⅜	13¾	+ ⅜
40	17	CirCty	.08	.3	12	76	26¾	26½	26¾	+ ⅜
33½	17½	Circus s	...	...	16	81	27	26½	27	+ ½
34⅛	15⅞	Citicrp s	1.48	6.6	...	14107	22½	21¾	22½	+ ¾
82⅜	66¼	Citcp pf	6.00e	8.8	...	406	68	68	68	+ ⅜
100¾	73	Citcp pfA	7.00e	8.5	...	1223	83	81¾	82	− 1½
8	1⅞	Clabir	.04l	...	...	243	2	2	2	...
11⅜	2⅜	ClairSt	.10b	3.8	10	685	2⅞	2¾	2⅝	− ⅛
35⅞	17¼	ClarkE	...	...	...	349	31¾	30¾	31¾	+1
13⅜	7	ClayHm	...	...	9	63	9½	9¼	9¾	+ ⅛
9¾	4⅜	ClmGlb n	...	...	...	19	6¼	6⅛	6⅛	...
21⅞	9¼	ClvClf	...	...	14	146	19⅞	19¼	19½	− ½
21½	14⅞	ClvCl pf	2.00	9.8	...	2	20¾	20½	20½	− ⅛
76¾	64	ClvEl pf	7.40	11.0	...	z200	67½	67½	67½	+ 1¼
36	23½	Clorox	1.04	3.6	12	557	28⅞	28¼	28⅞	+ ⅜
27	9	ClubMd	.20	1.5	13	183	13½	13⅜	13½	+ ½
12¾	6⅝	Coachm	.40	4.3	463	415	9⅞	9	9¼	− ⅜
9	3¾	Cstam n	...	...	11	6	6¾	6¼	6⅝	− ⅛
22	12¾	CoastSL	.40	2.6	4	219	15¾	15⅜	15¾	− ½
40⅜	21	Coastal	.40	1.5	13	x372	27½	27¼	27¾	...
38½	24¼	Cstl pf	2.11	7.4	...	250	28⅜	28⅜	28⅜	+ ⅛
53⅞	29	CocaCl	1.20	3.4	14	6621	35¾	35¼	35⅜	+ ⅜
21¼	10½	CocaCE	.05	.3	22	1202	14⅞	14⅜	14¾	+ ⅜
11⅜	1⅞	Coleco	...	...	...	1414	2	d	1¾	1¾ − ¼
43½	26¼	Colemn	1.20	3.0	12	80	40	39¾	40	+ ¼
52⅜	28	ColgPal	1.48	3.5	44	1940	41½	41	41¾	+ ⅜
23½	10⅜	ColFds	.16	1.2	11	152	13½	13⅛	13¼	+ ⅛
9⅜	7¼	ColFd pf	.75e	8.1	...	x412	9¾	9½	9¼	+ ¼
19¾	7½	Colt n	...	...	7	113	17	16¾	17	+ ⅛
56½	26⅝	ColGas	2.00	6.9	12	792	29¼	28⅞	29¼	+ ⅛
58	51	ColGs pf	5.12	9.9	...	40	51¾	51¾	51¾	...
16⅛	6¾	ColPict	...	...	...	3088	8⅜	8⅜	8¼	...
12¾	5½	ColumS	.28	4.1	...	198	6¾	6¾	6¾	+ ¼
12¾	5½	ColSv pf	...	...	...	9	7	7	7	+ ¼
118	111	CSP pr n	15.25	13.4	...	z90	114⅛	114¼	114⅛	...
45⅜	22⅜	CmbEn	1.00	3.3	19	298	30⅛	30	30	+ ¼
36½	12	Comdis	.24	1.2	33	867	20½	19½	19¾	...
34⅜	17	CmcCrd	.28	1.2	32	865	23⅝	22⅞	23¾	+ ⅞
28¼	14½	CmMtl s	.44	1.8	12	23	25	24¾	24⅞	+ ⅜
11⅜	6¼	Comdre	...	...	8	1245	10½	9⅝	10	+ ⅛
36½	22¾	CmwE	3.00	12.8	5	2256	23¾	23½	23½	− ⅛
21⅜	16½	CwE pr	1.90	10.6	...	81	18	17⅞	17⅞	− ⅛
22¾	17¼	CwE pr	2.00	10.7	...	10	19¼	18⅜	18⅜	+ ⅜
85½	75	CwE pf	8.38	10.7	...	z100	78	78	78	+1
28⅛	25½	CwE pf	2.87	10.8	...	52	26½	26⅜	26½	+ ⅜
34⅜	25¼	ComES	2.80	10.5	8	74	26⅞	26½	26⅜	...
9	3¼	CmwMt	1.05	30.0	...	143	3¾	3⅜	3½	− ⅛
33⅞	22	Comsat	1.20	4.3	...	73	28⅜	27¾	28	+ ⅛
32¼	19	CPsyc s	.36	1.7	16	623	21¾	21¾	21½	+ ⅜
78½	34	Compaq	...	...	12	2155	48⅞	48⅛	48⅞	+ ½
27¾	18½	Compgr	.60	2.3	72	1	26⅜	26⅜	26⅜	+ ⅛
37¼	15½	CmpAsc	...	...	19	2884	25½	24¼	25½	+ 1⅛
27½	7½	CmpFct	...	...	12	2501	13½	13	13	− ⅛
73	38	CompSc	...	...	15	604	41	40½	40½	+ ¼
16⅞	9⅛	CmpTsk	.05	.5	15	119	10¾	10⅛	10¼	− ⅛
10⅛	10	Comstk n	...	...	...	1052	10½	10	10	− ⅛
38	20⅞	ConAgr	.67	2.4	15	...	27⅛	27¾	27¾	+ ⅝
25¾	18¾	ConnE	1.76	...	...	...	...	22		− ¼

gains, or appreciation in the value of the stock. Low dividend–yield firms presumably offer greater prospects for capital gains, or investors would not be willing to hold the low-yield firms in their portfolios.

The P-E ratio, or **price-earnings ratio,** is the ratio of the current stock price to last year's earnings. The P-E ratio tells us how much stock purchasers must pay per dollar of earnings that the firm generates for each share. The P-E ratio also varies widely across firms. Where the dividend yield and P-E ratio are not reported in Figure 2.9 the firms have zero dividends, or zero or negative earnings. We shall have much to say about P-E ratios in Chapter 17.

The sales column shows that 541 hundred shares of the stock were traded on May 24. Shares commonly are traded in round lots of 100 shares each. Investors who wish to trade in smaller "odd lots" generally must pay higher commissions to their stock brokers. The highest price and lowest price per share at which the stock traded on that day were 31⅝ and 31⅛, respectively. The last, or closing, price of 31⅝ was up ⅝ from the closing price of the previous day.

Preferred Stock

Preferred stock has features similar to both equity and debt. Like a bond, it promises to pay to its holder fixed dividends each year. In this sense preferred stock is similar to an infinite-maturity bond, that is, a perpetuity. It also resembles a bond in that it does not convey voting power regarding the management of the firm. Preferred stock is an equity investment, however, in the sense that failure to pay the dividend does not precipitate corporate bankruptcy. Instead, preferred dividends are usually *cumulative;* that is, unpaid dividends cumulate and must be paid in full before any dividends may be paid to holders of common stock.

Preferred stock also differs from bonds in terms of its tax treatment for the firm. Because preferred stock payments are treated as dividends rather than interest, they are not tax-deductible expenses for the firm. This disadvantage is somewhat offset by the fact that corporations may exclude 80% of dividends received from domestic corporations in the computation of their taxable income. Preferred stocks therefore make desirable fixed-income investments for some corporations. Even though they rank after bonds in the event of corporate bankruptcy, preferred stock often sells at lower yields than do corporate bonds. Presumably, this reflects the value of the dividend exclusion, because risk considerations alone indicate that preferred stock ought to offer higher yields than bonds. Individual investors, who cannot use the 80% exclusion, generally will find preferred stock yields unattractive relative to those on other available assets.

Preferred stock is issued in variations similar to those of corporate bonds. It can be callable by the issuing firm, in which case it is said to be *redeemable*. It also can be convertible into common stock at some specified conversion ratio. A recent innovation in the market is adjustable rate preferred stock, which, similar to adjustable rate mortgages, ties the dividend rate to current market interest rates.

2.4   Stock and Bond Market Indices

Stock Market Indices

The daily performance of the Dow Jones Industrial Average is a staple portion of the evening news report. Although the Dow is the best-known measure of the performance of the stock market, it is only one of several indicators of stock market performance. Other more broadly based indices are computed and published daily. In addition, several indices of bond market performance are widely available.

Dow Jones Averages

The Dow Jones Industrial Average of 30 large "blue-chip" corporations has been computed since 1896. Its long history probably accounts for its preeminence in the public mind. (The average covered only 20 stocks until 1928.) The Dow is a **price-weighted average,** which means that it is computed by adding the prices of the 30 companies and dividing by a "divisor."

Originally, the divisor was simply 20 when 20 stocks were included in the index; thus the index was no more than the average price of the 20 stocks. This makes the index performance a measure of the performance of a particular portfolio strategy that buys one share of each firm in the index. Therefore the weight of each firm in the index is proportional to the share price rather than the total outstanding market value of the shares. For example, if shares of firm XYZ sell for $100 each and it has 1 million shares outstanding, while shares of firm ABC sell for $25 each but it has 20 million shares outstanding, the "Dow portfolio" would have four times as much invested in XYZ as in ABC ($100 compared with $25) despite the fact that ABC is a more prominent firm in the economy ($500 million market value of equity vs. only $100 million for XYZ).

Table 2.3 illustrates this point. Suppose that ABC increases by 20%, from $25 to $30, while XYZ increases by only 10%, from $100 to $110. The return on a price-weighted average of the two stocks would come to only 12%, whereas the combined market value of the two stocks actually increases by more than 18%. Because of its lower price, the superior performance of ABC relative to XYZ has a smaller effect on the price-weighted average than it does on the actual combined value of the stocks.

TABLE 2.3   Price-Weighted Returns

Stock	Initial Price	Final Price	Shares (Million)	Initial Value of Outstanding Stock ($ Million)	Final Value of Outstanding Stock ($ Million)
ABC	25	30	20	500	600
XYZ	100	110	1	100	110
Average	62.5	70	**Total market value 600**		710

Increase in average price = 12% = 70/62.5 − 1
Increase in market value = 18.3% = 710/600 − 1

Concept Check

Question 5. Suppose that shares of XYZ increase in price to $110 whi[le]
of ABC fall to $20. Find the percentage change in the price-weighted
of these two stocks. Compare that to the percentage return of a portfolio that
holds one share in each company.

As stocks are added to or dropped from the average, or stocks split over time, the
Dow divisor is continually adjusted to leave the average unaffected by the change.
For example, if XYZ were to split two for one, and its share price were therefore to
fall to $50, we would not want the average to fall, because that would incorrectly
indicate a fall in the general level of market prices. Following a split, the divisor
must be reduced to a value that leaves the average unaffected by the split. Table 2.4
illustrates this point. The initial share price of XYZ, which was $100 in Table 2.3,
falls to $50 if the stock splits at the beginning of the period. Notice that the number
of shares outstanding doubles, leaving the market value of total shares unaffected.
The divisor, d, which originally was 2.0 when the two-stock average was initiated,
must be reset to a value that leaves the average unchanged. Because the sum of the
postsplit stock prices is 75 and the presplit average price was 62.5, we calculate the
new value of d by solving $75/d = 62.5$. The value of d therefore falls from its original value of 2.0 to $75/62.5 = 1.20$, and the initial value of the average is indeed
unaffected by the split: $75/1.20 = 62.5$. At period-end, shares of ABC will sell for
$30, while shares of XYZ will sell for $55, representing the same 10% return it was
assumed to earn in Table 2.3. The new value of the price-weighted average is $(30 + 55)/1.20 = 70.83$, and the "rate of return" on the average is $70.83/62.5 - 1 = .133$,
or 13.3%. Notice that this return is greater than that calculated in Table 2.3. The
relative weight of XYZ, which is the poorer-performing stock, is lower after the split
because its price is lower; the performance of the average therefore improves. This
example illustrates again that the implicit weighting scheme of a price-weighted average is somewhat arbitrary, being determined by the prices rather than the outstanding market values of the shares in the average.

TABLE 2.4 Price-Weighted Returns After a Stock Split

Stock	Initial Price	Final Price	Shares (Million)	Initial value of Outstanding Stock ($ Million)	Final Value of Outstanding Stock ($ Million)
ABC	25	30	20	500	600
XYZ	50	55	2	100	110
Index value	$\frac{75}{1.20} = 62.5$	$\frac{85}{1.2} = 70.83$			
Market value				600	710

In the same way that the divisor is updated for stock splits, if one firm is dropped from the average and another firm with a different price is added, the divisor has to be updated to leave the average unchanged by the substitution. By now, the divisor for the Dow Jones Industrial Average has fallen to a value of about .75.

Dow Jones & Company also computes a Transportation Average of 20 airline, trucking, and railroad stocks; a Public Utility Average of 15 electric and natural gas utilities; and a Composite Average combining the 65 firms of the three separate averages. Each is a price-weighted average, and thus overweights the performance of high-priced stocks.

Figure 2.10 reproduces some of the data reported on the Dow Jones Averages from *The Wall Street Journal* (which is owned by Dow Jones). The bars show the range of values assumed by the average on each day. The cross hatch (✝) indicates the closing value of the average.

FIGURE 2.10
Dow Jones Averages.
(From *The Wall Street Journal,* May 17, 1988.) Reprinted by permission of *The Wall Street Journal.* © Dow Jones & Company, Inc. 1988. All rights reserved.

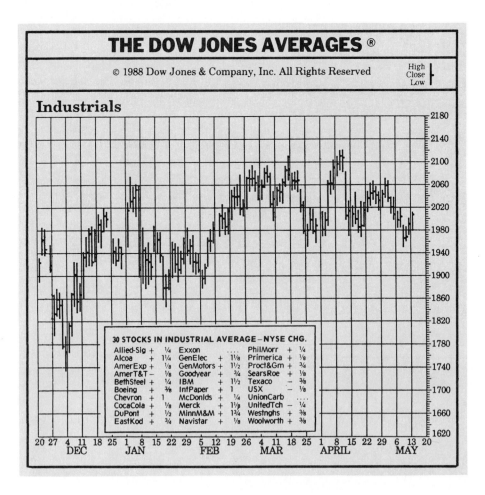

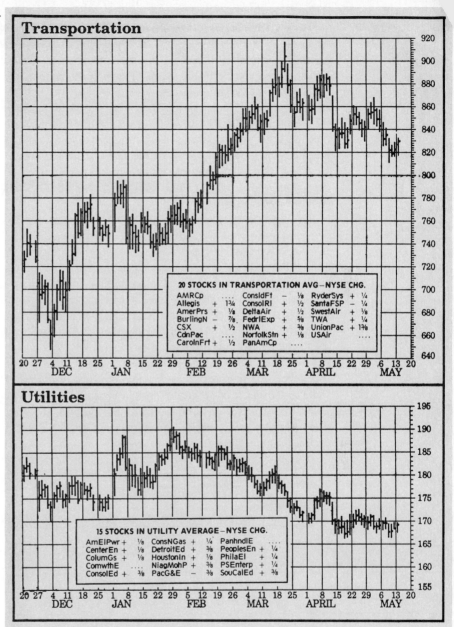

Transportation

20 STOCKS IN TRANSPORTATION AVG—NYSE CHG.

AMRCp	....	ConsldFt	− ⅛	RyderSys	+ ¼
Allegis	+ 1¾	ConsolRl	+ ½	SantaFSP	− ¼
AmerPrs	+ ⅛	DeltaAir	+ ½	SwestAir	+ ⅛
BurlingN	− ⅞	FedrlExp	+ ⅝	TWA	+ ¼
CSX	+ ½	NWA	+ ⅜	UnionPac	+ 1⅜
CdnPac	....	NorfolkStn	+ ⅛	USAir	....
CarolnFrt	+ ½	PanAmCp	....		

Utilities

15 STOCKS IN UTILITY AVERAGE—NYSE CHG.

AmElPwr	+ ⅛	ConsNGas	+ ¼	PanhndlE	....
CenterEn	+ ⅛	DetroitEd	+ ⅜	PeoplesEn	+ ¼
ColumGs	+ ⅛	HoustonIn	+ ⅛	PhilaEl	+ ¼
ComwthE	....	NiagMohP	+ ⅜	PSEnterp	+ ¼
ConsolEd	+ ⅜	PacG&E	− ⅜	SouCalEd	+ ⅜

Standard & Poor's indices

The Standard & Poor's Composite 500-Stock Index improves on the Dow Jones in two ways. First, it is a more broadly based index of 500 firms. Second, it is a **market value–weighted index.** In the case of the firms XYZ and ABC that we mentioned above, the S&P 500 would give ABC five times the weight given to XYZ because the market value of its outstanding equity is five times larger. The S&P 500 is computed by calculating the total market value of the 500 firms in the index and the total market value of those firms on the previous day of trading. The percentage increase in the total market value from one day to the next represents the increase in the index. The rate of return of the index therefore equals the rate of return that would be earned by an investor holding a portfolio of all 500 firms in the index in proportion to their market value, except that the index does not reflect cash dividends paid out by those firms.

To illustrate, look again at Table 2.3. If the initial level of a market value–weighted index of stocks ABC and XYZ were set equal to an arbitrarily chosen starting value such as 100, the index value at year-end would be 100 $\times$ (710/600) = 118.3. The increase in the index reflects the 18.3% return earned on a portfolio consisting of those two stocks held in proportion to outstanding market values.

Note also from Tables 2.3 and 2.4 that market value–weighted indices are unaffected by stock splits. The total market value of outstanding XYZ stock increases from $100 million to $110 million regardless of the stock split, thereby rendering the split irrelevant to the performance of the index.

A nice feature of both market value–weighted and price-weighted indices is that they reflect the returns to buy-and-hold portfolio strategies. If one were to buy each share in the index in proportion to its outstanding market value, the value-weighted index would perfectly track capital gains on the underlying portfolio. Similarly, a price-weighted index tracks the returns on a portfolio composed of equal shares of each firm.

Investors today can purchase shares in mutual funds that hold shares in proportion to their representation in the S&P 500. These **index funds** yield a return equal to that of the S&P 500 index and so provide a low-cost passive investment strategy for equity investors.

Standard & Poor's also publishes a 400-Stock Industrial Index, a 20-Stock Transportation Index, a 40-Stock Utility Index, and a 40-Stock Financial Index.

Concept Check	Question 6. Reconsider the stock of firms XYZ and ABC from question 5. Calculate the percentage change in the market value–weighted index. Compare that to the rate of return of a portfolio that holds $500 of ABC stock for every $100 of XYZ stock, that is, an index portfolio.

FIGURE 2.11

Performance of stock indices.

(From *The Wall Street Journal*, May 25, 1988.) Reprinted by permission of *The Wall Street Journal*. © Dow Jones & Company, Inc. 1988. All rights reserved.

STOCK MARKET DATA BANK   May 24, 1988

Major Indexes

HIGH	LOW	(12 MOS)	CLOSE	NET CH	% CH	12 MO CH	%	FROM 12/31	%
DOW JONES AVERAGES									
2722.42	1738.74	30 Industrials	x1962.53	+ 21.05	+ 1.08	− 335.41	−14.60	+ 23.70	+ 1.22
1101.16	661.00	20 Transportation	794.95	+ 10.90	+ 1.39	− 162.43	−16.97	+ 46.09	+ 6.15
213.79	160.98	15 Utilities	169.16	+ 1.19	+ 0.71	− 29.31	−14.77	− 5.92	− 3.38
992.21	653.76	65 Composite	x727.29	+ 7.99	+ 1.11	− 132.49	−15.41	+ 13.02	+ 1.82
NEW YORK STOCK EXCHANGE									
187.99	125.91	Composite	143.53	+ 1.32	+ 0.93	− 19.19	−11.79	+ 5.30	+ 3.83
231.05	149.43	Industrials	173.71	+ 1.49	+ 0.87	− 24.64	−12.42	+ 6.67	+ 3.99
80.22	61.63	Utilities	68.75	+ 0.67	+ 0.98	− 2.62	− 3.67	+ 1.44	+ 2.14
168.20	104.76	Transportation	123.89	+ 1.62	+ 1.32	− 17.14	−12.15	+ 5.32	+ 4.49
165.36	107.39	Finance	120.29	+ 1.42	+ 1.19	− 26.32	−17.95	+ 5.72	+ 4.99
STANDARD & POOR'S INDEXES									
336.77	223.92	500 Index	253.51	+ 2.68	+ 1.07	− 35.60	−12.31	+ 6.43	+ 2.60
393.17	255.43	Industrials	293.49	+ 2.75	+ 0.95	− 42.41	−12.63	+ 7.63	+ 2.67
274.20	167.59	Transportation	191.05	+ 3.29	+ 1.75	− 40.06	−17.33	+ 0.88	+ 0.46
121.11	91.80	Utilities	103.66	+ 1.44	+ 1.41	− 4.01	− 3.72	+ 1.54	+ 1.51
32.56	20.39	Financials	22.42	+ 0.37	+ 1.68	− 5.78	−20.50	+ 0.79	+ 3.65
NASDAQ									
455.26	291.88	Composite	365.16	+ 1.90	+ 0.52	− 46.28	−11.25	+ 34.69	+10.50
488.92	288.30	Industrials	374.87	+ 2.28	+ 0.61	− 67.05	−15.17	+ 35.93	+10.60
475.78	333.66	Insurance	386.28	+ 1.76	+ 0.46	− 24.16	− 5.89	+ 35.22	+10.03
510.24	365.63	Banks	437.84	+ 2.42	+ 0.56	− 26.49	− 5.70	+ 47.18	+12.08
195.37	124.98	Nat. Mkt. Comp.	157.74	+ 0.86	+ 0.55	− 17.96	−10.22	+ 15.15	+10.62
187.94	110.21	Nat. Mkt. Indus.	144.98	+ 0.93	+ 0.65	− 23.49	−13.94	+ 13.87	+10.58
OTHERS									
365.01	231.90	AMEX	290.52	− 0.16	− 0.06	− 34.82	−10.70	+ 30.17	+11.59
1926.2	1232.0	Fin. Times Indus.	1428.3	+ 20.7	+ 1.47	− 249.5	−14.87	+ 55.0	+ 4.00
27819.98	21036.80	Nikkei Stock Avg.	27312.66	+ 62.90	+ 0.23	+2731.76	+11.11	+5748.66	+26.66
289.02	181.09	Value-Line(geom)	222.09	+ 1.33	+ 0.60	− 35.87	−13.91	+ 20.47	+10.15
3299.44	2188.11	Wilshire 5000	2528.15	+ 21.21	+ 0.85	− 334.96	−11.70	+ 111.02	+ 4.59

Other market value indices

The New York Stock Exchange publishes a market value–weighted composite index of all NYSE-listed stocks, in addition to sub-indices for industrial, utility, transportation, and financial stocks. The American Stock Exchange, or Amex, also computes a market value–weighted index of its stocks. These indices are even more broadly based than the S&P 500. The National Association of Securities Dealers publishes an index of nearly 3,000 OTC firms using the NASDAQ quotation service.

The ultimate equity index so far computed is the Wilshire 5,000 index of the market value of all NYSE and Amex stocks plus actively traded OTC stocks. Figure 2.11 reproduces a *Wall Street Journal* listing of stock index performance.

Equally weighted indices

Market performance is sometimes measured by an equally weighted average of the returns of each stock in an index. Such an averaging technique, by placing equal weight on each return, corresponds to an implicit portfolio strategy that places equal dollar values on each stock. This is in contrast to both price weighting (which requires equal numbers of shares of each stock) and market value weighting (which requires investments in proportion to outstanding value).

Unlike price- or market value–weighted indices, equally weighted indices do not correspond to buy-and-hold portfolio strategies. Suppose that you start with equal dollar investments in the two stocks of Table 2.3, ABC and XYZ. Because ABC increases in value by 20% over the year while XYZ increases by only 10%, your portfolio no longer is equally weighted. It is now more heavily invested in ABC. To reset the portfolio to equal weights, you would need to rebalance: either sell off some ABC stock and/or purchase more XYZ stock. Such rebalancing would be necessary to align the return on your portfolio with that on the equally weighted index.

The Value Line index

The Dow Jones and market value–weighted indices all use arithmetic averaging: they all sum up either prices or market values and divide by a divisor. In contrast, the Value Line index is an equally weighted **geometric average** of the performance of about 1,700 firms. To compare geometric and arithmetic averages, suppose that three firms have returns on a trading day as follows:

Stock	Return
A	10%
B	−5%
C	20%

An equally weighted arithmetic average of these returns would be

$$[.10 + (-.05) + .20]/3 = .0833$$
$$= 8.33\%$$

In contrast, the geometric average, r_G, is computed as

$$1 + r_G = [(1 + .10)(1 - .05)(1 + .20)]^{\frac{1}{3}}$$
$$= 1.0784$$

for a geometric average of 7.84%. The general formula for the geometric average is

$$1 + r_G = [(1+r_1)(1 + r_2) \ldots (1 + r_n)]^{1/n}$$

where r_i is the return on the ith security in the index.

Note that the geometric average is less than the arithmetic average. This is a general property: whenever there is variation in performance among the stocks in an index, the geometric average will be less than the arithmetic average. For this reason the Value Line index provides a downward-biased measure of the rate of return that would be earned by an investor purchasing an equally weighted portfolio of all the stocks in the index. In fact, there is no portfolio strategy that results in a rate of return equal to that of a geometric index.

TABLE 2.5   Shearson Lehman Hutton Bond Market Indices

	Averages					Total Market Value ($ Million)	Total Index (%)	
	Duration*	Coupon	Maturity	Price	Yield		Gov./Corp.	Aggregate
Government/Corporate Bond Index	5.12	8.96	9.48	101.91	8.13	1642854	100.00	71.33
Government bond index	4.63	9.03	8.13	104.30	7.72	1230452	74.90	53.42
Corporate bond index	6.58	8.78	13.49	95.38	9.35	412402	25.10	17.91
Mortgage backed securities index	5.79	9.41	10.40	99.65	9.21	607938	100.00	26.40
Yankee bond index	6.67	9.80	13.40	102.16	9.11	52377	100.00	2.27
Aggregate bond index	5.33	9.10	9.81	101.31	8.44	2303169	0.00	100.00
Government/Corporate Bond Index	5.12	8.96	9.48	101.91	8.13	1642854	100.00	71.33
Intermediate	3.30	8.94	4.13	103.12	7.75	1157988	70.49	50.28
Long term	9.48	9.01	22.25	99.11	9.05	484866	29.51	21.05
Government Bond Index	4.63	9.03	8.13	104.30	7.72	1230452	74.90	53.42
Intermediate	3.10	8.97	3.83	104.03	7.49	952805	58.00	41.37
Long term	9.88	9.22	22.90	105.25	8.55	277647	16.90	12.05
Treasury	4.78	9.26	8.67	107.17	7.70	1053525	64.13	45.74
Intermediate	3.08	8.94	3.79	104.23	7.42	784468	47.75	34.06
Long term	9.74	10.30	22.87	116.76	8.53	269058	16.38	11.68
Agency	3.76	7.86	4.95	89.96	7.85	176927	10.77	7.68
Intermediate	3.23	9.11	4.00	103.07	7.79	168337	10.25	7.31
Long term	14.30	1.76	23.57	25.75	8.96	8589	0.52	0.37
Corporate Bond Index	6.58	8.78	13.49	95.38	9.35	412402	25.10	17.91
Intermediate	4.20	8.80	5.51	99.13	8.97	205183	12.49	8.91
Long term	8.94	8.76	21.39	91.93	9.72	207220	12.61	9.00
Industrial	6.70	9.12	13.66	96.98	9.46	118010	7.18	5.12
Intermediate	4.48	9.17	5.98	100.19	9.09	58597	3.57	2.54
Long term	8.89	9.08	21.23	94.02	9.81	59412	3.62	2.58
Utility	7.97	8.78	18.50	94.53	9.60	153195	9.32	6.65
Intermediate	4.78	8.09	6.35	95.27	9.17	38539	2.35	1.67
Long term	9.04	9.01	22.58	94.29	9.74	114656	6.98	4.98
Finance	4.98	8.50	7.92	94.98	8.98	141198	8.59	6.13
Intermediate	3.85	8.87	4.96	100.00	8.82	108047	6.58	4.69
Long term	8.68	7.50	17.57	81.61	9.48	33151	2.02	1.44

Modified from *The Bond Market Report*, Shearson Lehman Hutton Inc., February 1988.
*Duration is defined and discussed in Chapter 16.

Bond Market Indicators

Just as stock market indices provide guidance concerning the performance of the overall stock market, several bond market indicators measure the performance of various categories of bonds. The two most well-known groups of indices are those of Shearson-Lehman Hutton and Salomon Brothers. Table 2.5 lists some of the indices compiled by Shearson Lehman Hutton, as well as some characteristics of those indices as of February 1988. The Shearson Lehman Hutton Government/Corporate Bond Index is perhaps the premier indicator of bond market performance.

The indices are all computed monthly, and all measure total returns as the sum of capital gains plus interest income derived from the bonds during the month. Any intra-month cash distributions received from the bonds are assumed to be invested during the month at the T-bill rate.

The major problem with these indices is that true rates of return on many bonds are difficult to compute because the infrequency with which the bonds trade make reliable up-to-date prices difficult to obtain. In practice, prices often must be estimated from bond valuation models. These "matrix" prices may differ substantially from true market values.

2.5 *Derivative Markets*

One of the most significant developments in financial markets in recent years has been the growth of futures and options markets. These instruments provide payoffs that depend on the values of other assets such as commodity prices, bond and stock prices, or market index values. For this reason these instruments sometimes are called **derivative assets,** or **contingent claims.** Their values derive from or are contingent on the values of other assets.

Options

A *call option* gives its holder the right to purchase an asset for a specified price, called the *exercise* or *strike price,* on or before a specified expiration date. For example, a July call option on IBM stock with an exercise price of $120 entitles its owner to purchase IBM stock for a price of $120 at any time up to and including the expiration date in July. Each option contract is for the purchase of 100 shares. However, quotations are made on a per-share basis. The holder of the call need not exercise the option; it will be profitable to exercise only if the market value of the asset that may be purchased exceeds the exercise price.

When the market price exceeds the exercise price, the option holder may "call away" the asset for the exercise price and reap a profit equal to the difference between the stock price and the exercise price. Otherwise, the option will be left unexercised. If not exercised before the expiration date of the contract, the option simply expires and no longer has value. Calls therefore provide greater profits when stock prices increase and thus represent bullish investment vehicles.

In contrast, a *put option* gives its holder the right to sell an asset for a specified exercise price on or before a specified expiration date. A July put on IBM with an exercise price of $120 thus entitles its owner to sell IBM stock to the put writer at a price of $120 at any time before expiration in July, even if the market price of IBM is lower than $120. Whereas profits on call options increase when the asset increases in value, profits on put options increase when the asset value falls. The put is exercised only if its holder can deliver an asset worth less than the exercise price in return for the exercise price.

FIGURE 2.12
Options market listings.

(From *The Wall Street Journal*, May 17, 1988.) Reprinted by permission of *The Wall Street Journal*. © Dow Jones & Company, Inc. 1988. All rights reserved.

Figure 2.12 gives listed stock option quotations from *The Wall Street Journal*. The first option listed on the Chicago Board Options Exchange is for shares of Alcoa. The numbers below Alcoa indicate that the last recorded price for Alcoa stock was 45⅜ per share. Options are traded on Alcoa with exercise prices of 40, 45, and 50. These values, the exercise price or strike price, are given in the first column of numbers. Note that the exercise prices bracket the price of Alcoa.

The next three columns of numbers provide the prices of call options on Alcoa shares with expiration dates of May, June, and July. The prices of Alcoa call options decrease as one moves down each column, corresponding to progressively higher exercise prices. This makes sense, because the right to purchase a share of Alcoa at a given exercise price is worth less as the exercise price increases. For example, with an exercise price of 40, the May call lists for 5 per share, whereas the option to purchase the stock for an exercise price of 50 is worth only ¹⁄₁₆. The footnote "r" indicates that the option was not traded on that day, and "s" indicates that the option with that exercise price and expiration date has not been introduced by the exchange.

The last three columns report prices of put options with various strike prices and times to maturity. Put prices, of course, increase with the exercise price. The right to sell a share of Alcoa at a price of 40 is less valuable than the right to sell it at 50.

Concept Check	Question 7. What would be the profit or loss per share of stock to an investor who bought the May maturity Alcoa call option with exercise price 45 on May 16, 1988, if the stock price at the expiration of the option is 48? What about a purchaser of the put option with the same exercise price and maturity?

Futures Contracts

The *futures contract* calls for delivery of an asset or its cash value at a specified delivery or maturity date for an agreed-upon price, called the futures price, to be paid at contract maturity. The *long position* is held by the trader who commits to purchasing the commodity on the delivery date. The trader who takes the short position commits to delivering the commodity at contract maturity.

Figure 2.13 illustrates the listing of several financial futures contracts as they appear in *The Wall Street Journal*. The top line in boldface type gives the contract name, the exchange on which the futures contract is traded in parentheses, and the contract size. Thus the second contract listed on the right is for the S&P 500 index, traded on the Chicago Mercantile Exchange (CME). Each contract calls for delivery of 500 times the value of the S&P 500 stock price index.

The next several rows detail price data for contracts expiring on various dates. The June 1988 maturity contract opened during the day at a futures price of 264 per unit of the index. (The last line of the entry shows that the S&P 500 index was at 266.69 at close of trading on the day of the listing.) The highest futures price during the day was 268.50, the lowest was 263.15, and the settlement price (a representative trading price during the last few minutes of trading) was 266.85. The settlement price increased by 3.90 from the previous trading day. The highest and lowest futures prices over the contract's life to date have been 347.90 and 190.00 respectively. Finally, open interest, or the number of outstanding contracts, was 92,080. Corresponding information is given for each maturity date.

The trader holding the long position profits from price increases. Suppose that at expiration the S&P 500 index is at 270. The long position trader who entered the contract at the futures price of 266.85 on June 1 would pay the previously agreed-upon 266.85 for each unit of the index, which at contract maturity would be worth 270. Because each contract calls for delivery of 500 times the index, ignoring brokerage fees, the profit to the long position would equal $500 \times (270 - 266.85) = \$1,575$. Conversely, the short position must deliver 500 times the value of the index for the previously agreed-upon futures price. The short position's loss equals the long position's profit.

FIGURE 2.13

Financial futures listings.

(From *The Wall Street Journal*, June 22, 1988.) Reprinted by permission of *The Wall Street Journal*. © Dow Jones & Company, Inc. 1988. All rights reserved.

FUTURES PRICES

Wednesday, June 1, 1988

Open Interest Reflects Previous Trading Day.

	Open	High	Low	Settle	Change	Lifetime High	Low	Open Interest
May	....	....	....	60.70	− 1.05	65.15	56.40	426
July	....	....	....	60.80	− 1.05	63.00	56.50	141

Est vol 5,000; vol Tues 5,507; open int 32,811, +745.

ORANGE JUICE (CTN)—15,000 lbs.; cents per lb.

	Open	High	Low	Settle	Change	Lifetime High	Low	Open Interest
July	168.00	168.75	167.25	168.65	+ 1.05	178.25	124.00	5,967
Sept	163.25	164.20	162.85	164.10	+ 1.05	177.00	125.00	2,925
Nov	156.75	157.25	156.50	157.25	+ .80	172.75	132.00	1,583
Ja89	152.25	152.75	152.25	152.75	+ .75	171.25	132.00	781
Mar	151.80	152.00	151.80	152.05	+ .50	167.90	151.80	123

Est vol 700; vol Tues 968; open int 11,396, +98.

SUGAR—WORLD (CSCE)—112,000 lbs.; cents per lb.

	Open	High	Low	Settle	Change	Lifetime High	Low	Open Interest
July	9.68	9.98	9.66	9.96	+ .49	10.38	6.79	38,864
Oct	9.75	9.92	9.65	9.91	+ .46	10.35	7.00	70,131
Mr89	9.64	9.86	9.58	9.80	+ .44	10.32	7.66	46,877
May	9.65	9.80	9.56	9.78	+ .43	10.20	7.87	4,570
July	9.70	9.80	9.65	9.80	+ .42	9.80	8.10	362

Est vol 33,021; vol Tues19,614; open int 150,872, +251.

SUGAR—DOMESTIC (CSCE)—112,000 lbs.; cents per lb.

	Open	High	Low	Settle	Change	Lifetime High	Low	Open Interest
July	22.30	22.35	22.30	22.34	+ .10	22.35	21.55	1,789
Sept	22.20	22.21	22.20	22.21	+ .03	22.21	21.52	2,537
Nov	22.01	22.03	22.01	22.03	+ .03	22.03	21.50	1,937
Ja89	21.93	21.93	21.93	21.93	+ .01	21.93	21.70	320
Mar	21.87	21.87	21.87	21.87		21.88	21.75	130

Est vol 522; vol Tues176; open int 6,748, −28.

—METALS & PETROLEUM—

COPPER (CMX)—25,000 lbs.; cents per lb.

	Open	High	Low	Settle	Change	Lifetime High	Low	Open Interest
June	96.00	98.75	96.00	98.55	+ 4.15	98.75	87.50	180
July	93.00	93.80	92.55	93.55	+ 2.25	102.30	62.30	16,226
Sept	88.20	89.30	88.20	88.80	+ 1.65	97.30	59.45	5,770
Dec	85.80	86.00	85.60	85.60	+ 1.55	96.50	64.70	4,817
Mr89	83.00	83.20	82.35	82.80	+ 1.35	93.00	66.50	1,227
May	82.20	82.20	82.20	81.60	+ 1.35	89.00	73.15	136
July	80.00	80.00	80.00	80.60	+ 1.35	80.00	77.50	197
Sept	....	....	80.00	+ 1.35	80.00	76.00	96
Dec	....	....	80.00	+ 1.35	82.20	77.50	174

Est vol 6,000; vol Tues 5,537; open int 28,841, −265.

GOLD (CMX)—100 troy oz.; $ per troy oz.

	Open	High	Low	Settle	Change	Lifetime High	Low	Open Interest
June	457.50	459.00	455.60	457.60	+ 2.60	523.00	399.00	9,408
July	....	....	459.90	+ 2.60	458.50	458.40	160
Aug	462.00	463.30	460.30	462.40	+ 2.60	537.00	425.00	52,683
Oct	466.80	468.40	465.80	467.30	+ 2.50	533.50	429.00	12,677
Dec	472.00	473.50	470.50	472.30	+ 2.40	546.00	430.00	23,958
Fb89	477.80	479.50	476.00	477.50	+ 2.20	549.50	446.00	9,610
Apr	....	....	482.80	+ 2.00	550.00	451.00	7,128
June	485.80	485.80	485.80	488.30	+ 1.80	570.00	455.50	10,216
Aug	....	....	494.10	+ 1.60	575.00	482.20	5,894
Oct	....	....	500.30	+ 1.40	575.50	466.30	7,249
Dec	....	....	506.60	+ 1.20	510.00	472.50	5,580
Fb90	....	....	512.90	+ 1.00	516.00	502.00	1,898

Est vol 36,000; vol Tues 31,639; open int 146,461, −2,872.

PLATINUM (NYM)—50 troy oz.; $ per troy oz.

	Open	High	Low	Settle	Change	Lifetime High	Low	Open Interest
June	619.00	....	....	....	+ 4.20	619.00	580.00	251
July	417....	....	....	....	....	....	.00	13,448

—INDEXES—

MUNI BOND INDEX(CBT)$1,000; times Bond Buyer MBI

	Open	High	Low	Settle	Chg	High	Low	Open Interest
June	87-19	87-23	87-09	87-22	+ 23	89-26	70-03	10,247
Sept	84-28	85-14	84-21	85-12	+ 37	88-08	81-02	5,086
Dec	82-27	83-13	82-27	83-13	+ 37	86-29	80-16	518
Mr89	80-27	81-19	80-27	81-19	+ 38	85-05	78-25	322
June	79-10	79-28	79-10	79-28	+ 38	80-19	77-06	363

Est vol 7,500; vol Tues 5,925; open int 16,536, +118.
The index: Close 87-29; Yield 8.37.

S&P 500 INDEX (CME) 500 times index

	Open	High	Low	Settle	Change	High	Low	Open Interest
June	264.00	268.50	263.15	266.85	+ 3.90	347.90	190.00	92,080
Sept	265.90	270.30	265.05	268.75	+ 4.05	343.50	193.00	41,106
Dec	267.60	271.90	266.50	270.60	+ 4.20	277.50	252.20	889
Mr89	269.50	273.60	268.50	271.95	+ 4.05	279.10	253.90	100

Est vol 73,974; vol Tues 64,531; open int 134,175, −2,848.
Indx prelim High 267.43; Low 262.10; Close 266.69 +4.55

NYSE COMPOSITE INDEX (NYFE) 500 times index

	Open	High	Low	Settle	Change	High	Low	Open Interest
June	149.20	151.80	148.85	150.75	+ 1.85	194.60	113.00	6,268
Sept	150.10	152.65	149.75	151.65	+ 1.90	155.75	128.50	2,220
Dec	151.00	153.45	151.00	152.55	+ 1.95	156.60	137.95	816

Est vol 10,002; vol Tues 9,861; open int 9,534, −101.
The index: High 150.62; Low 147.96; Close 150.34 +2.31

KC VALUE LINE INDEX (KC) 500 times index

	Open	High	Low	Settle	Change	High	Low	Open Interest
June	228.50	233.10	228.50	232.40	+ 4.10	287.00	177.20	2,602
xSept	235.50	240.20	235.50	239.70	+ 4.40	244.20	225.00	760
xDec	....	....	241.50	+ 4.40	240.00	237.25	5

Est vol 1,200; vol Tues 800; open int 3,367, +70.
X- New index: High 234.80; Low 231.39; Close 234.70 +3.29

MAJOR MKT INDEX (CBT) $250 times index

	Open	High	Low	Settle	Change	High	Low	Open Interest
June	398.00	405.50	396.20	401.80	+ 5.85	478.00	373.90	7,23
July	398.50	406.60	398.00	402.95	+ 5.65	406.60	376.70	187
Sept	400.00	407.30	398.50	403.80	+ 5.90	543.30	249.00	105

Est vol 7,000; vol Tues 4,208; open int 7,433, −206.
The index: High 404.77; Low 394.93; Close 402.27 +6.86

STERLING (LIFFE)—£500,000; pts of 100%

	Open	High	Low	Settle	Change	High	Low	Open Interest
June	91.95	92.01	91.68	91.73	− .30	92.22	89.28	15,514
Sept	91.10	91.10	90.73	90.79	− .38	91.47	89.26	12,230
Dec	90.63	90.63	90.31	90.38	− .31	91.15	89.22	3,395
Mr89	90.40	90.40	90.15	90.28	− .14	90.94	89.25	1,933
June	90.11	90.12	90.05	90.12	− .10	90.66	89.65	809
Sept	....	....	90.09	− .11	90.47	89.65	415
Dec	....	....	89.99	− .11	90.22	89.76	325
Mar	....	....	89.89	− .11	89.98	89.80	190

Est vol 33,925; vol Tues 8,125; open int 34,811, −1,132.

T—BONDS (LIFFE) $1 mil.; pts of 100%

	Open	High	Low	Settle	Change	High	Low	Open Interest
June	86-16	86-31	86-09	86-30	+ 1-11	88-02	85-03	2,700
Sept	85-22	86-02	85-14	86-02	+ 1-11	86-26	84-12	1,578

Est vol 11,487; vol Tues 7,280; open int 4,278, −1,085.

LONG GILT (LIFFE)—£50,000; 32nds of 100%

	Open	High	Low	Settle	Change	High	Low	Open Interest
June	120-04	120-11	119-24	120-07	+ 0-01	123-25	117-05	18,503
Sept	95-21	95-26	95-07	95-26	+ 0-05	98-20	95-07	18,524

Est vol 26,802; vol Tues 15,942; open int 37,061, +1,448.

EURODOLLAR (IMM)—$1 million; pts of 100%

		High	Low	Settle	C...			Open Interest

The right to purchase the asset at an agreed-upon price, as opposed to the obligation, distinguishes call options from long positions in futures contracts. A futures contract *obliges* the long position to purchase the asset at the futures price; the call option, in contrast, *conveys the right* to purchase the asset at the exercise price. The purchase will be made only if it yields a profit.

Clearly, a holder of a call has a better position than does the holder of a long position on a futures contract with a futures price equal to the option's exercise price. This advantage, of course, comes only at a price. Call options must be purchased; futures investments may be entered into without cost. The purchase price of an option

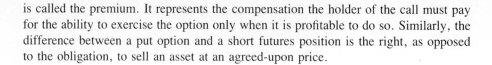

is called the premium. It represents the compensation the holder of the call must pay for the ability to exercise the option only when it is profitable to do so. Similarly, the difference between a put option and a short futures position is the right, as opposed to the obligation, to sell an asset at an agreed-upon price.

Summary

1. Money market securities are very short-term debt obligations. They are usually highly marketable and have relatively low credit risk. Their low maturities and low credit risk ensure minimal capital gains or losses. These securities trade in large denominations, but may be purchased indirectly through money market funds.

2. Much of the U.S. government borrowing is in the form of Treasury bonds and notes. These are coupon-paying bonds usually issued at or near par value. Treasury bonds are similar in design to coupon-paying corporate bonds.

3. Municipal bonds are distinguished largely by their tax-exempt status. Interest payments (but not capital gains) on these securities are exempt from federal income taxes. The taxable equivalent yield offered by a municipal bond equals $r_m/(1 - t)$, where r_m is the municipal yield and t is the investor's tax bracket.

4. Mortgage pass-through securities are pools of mortgages sold in one package. Owners of pass-throughs receive all principal and interest payments made by the borrower. The bank that originally issued the mortgage merely services the mortgage, simply "passing through" the payments to the purchasers of the mortgage. The government may guarantee the timely payment of interest and principal on mortgages pooled into these pass-through securities.

5. Common stock is an ownership share in a corporation. Each share entitles its owner to one vote on matters of corporate governance and to a prorated share of the dividends paid to shareholders. Stock, or equity, owners are the residual claimants on the income earned by the firm.

6. Preferred stock usually pays fixed dividends for the life of the firm; it is a perpetuity. A firm's failure to pay the dividend due on preferred stock, however, does not precipitate corporate bankruptcy. Instead, unpaid dividends simply cumulate. New varieties of preferred stock include convertible and adjustable-rate issues.

7. Many stock market indices measure the performance of the overall market. The Dow Jones Averages, the oldest and best-known indicators, are price-weighted indices. Today, many broad-based, market value–weighted indices are computed daily. These include the Standard & Poor's 500-Stock Index, the NYSE and Amex indices, the NASDAQ index, and the Wilshire 5000 Index. The Value Line index is a geometrically weighted average of about 1,700 firms.

8. A call option is a right to purchase an asset at a stipulated exercise price on or before a maturity date. A put option is the right to sell an asset at some exercise price. Calls increase in value while puts decrease in value as the value of the underlying asset increases.

9. A futures contract is an obligation to buy or sell an asset at a stipulated futures price on a maturity date. The long position, which commits to purchasing, gains if

the asset value increases while the short position, which commits to delivering the asset, loses.

Key Terms

Money market	Limited liability
Capital markets	Capital gains
Bank discount yield	Price-earnings ratio
Effective annual yield	Price-weighted average
Bond equivalent yield	Market value–weighted index
London Interbank Offered Rate	Index funds
Yield to maturity	Geometric average
Equivalent taxable yield	Derivative assets
Current yield	Contingent claims
Residual claim	

Selected Readings

The standard reference to the securities, terminology, and organization of the money market is:
Stigum, Marcia, *The Money Market,* Homewood, Ill.: Dow Jones-Irwin, 1983.
A more detailed treatment of money market securities is contained in the following collection of articles:
Cook, Timothy Q., and Rowe, Timothy D., *Instruments of the Money Market,* Richmond, Va.: Federal Reserve Bank of Richmond, 1986.
A collection of essays on a wide variety of fixed-income securities is:
Fabozzi, Frank J., and Pollack, Irving M. (editors), *The Handbook of Fixed Income Securities,* Homewood, Ill.: Dow Jones-Irwin, 1987.
A discussion of trends in the municipal bond market may be found in:
Rubin, Laura S., "Recent Developments in the State and Local Government Sector," *Federal Reserve Bulletin, 70,* November 1984.
A good treatment of the institutional organization of option markets is contained in:
Reference Manual, Chicago: The Chicago Board Options Exchange, 1982.
A textbook emphasizing institutional features of futures markets is:
Kolb, Robert, *Understanding Futures Markets,* Glenview, Ill.: Scott Foresman & Co., 1985.

Problems

1. The following multiple-choice problems are based on questions that appeared in the 1986 CFA examination.
   a. Preferred stock
      i. Is actually a form of equity
      ii. Pays dividends not fully taxable to U.S. corporations
      iii. Is normally considered a fixed-income security
      iv. All of the above
   b. Straight preferred stock yields usually are lower than yields on straight bonds of the same quality because of:
      i. Marketability

    ii. Risk

    iii. Taxation

    iv. Call protection

2. The investment manager of a corporate pension fund has purchased a U.S. Trea-
sury bill with 180 days to maturity at a price of $9,600 per $10,000 face value.
The manager has computed the bank discount yield at 8%. (CFA examination,
Level II, 1986.)

   a. Calculate the bond equivalent yield for the Treasury bill. Show calculations.
(Ignore skip-day settlement.)

   b. Briefly state two reasons why a Treasury bill's bond equivalent yield is always different from the discount yield.

3. A bill has a bank discount yield of 6.81% based on the asked price, and 6.90%
based on the bid price. The maturity of the bill (already accounting for skip-day
settlement) is 60 days. Find the bid and asked prices of the bill.

4. Reconsider the T-bill of question 3. Calculate its bond equivalent yield and effective annual yield based on the ask price. Confirm that these yields exceed the
discount yield.

5. Which security offers a higher effective annual yield?

   a.   i. A 3-month bill selling at $9,764

      ii. A 6-month bill selling at $9,539

   b. Calculate the bank discount yield on each bill.

6. Find the after-tax return to a corporation that buys a share of preferred stock at
$40, sells it at year-end at $40, and receives a $4 year-end dividend. The firm is
in the 30% tax bracket.

7. Consider the three stocks in the following table. P_t represents price at time t, and
Q_t represents shares outstanding at time t. Stock C splits two for one in the last
period.

	P_0	Q_0	P_1	Q_1	P_2	Q_2
A	90	100	95	100	95	100
B	50	200	45	200	45	200
C	100	200	110	200	55	400

   a. Calculate the rate of return on a price-weighted index of the three stocks for
the first period ($t = 0$ to $t = 1$).

   b. What must happen to the divisor for the price-weighted index in year 2?

   c. Calculate the price-weighted index for the second period ($t = 1$ to $t = 2$).

8. Using the data in problem 7, calculate the first period rates of return on the following indices of the three stocks:

   a. A market value–weighted index

   b. An equally weighted index

   c. A geometric index

9. An investor is in a 28% tax bracket. If corporate bonds offer 9% yields, what
must municipals offer for the investor to prefer them to corporate bonds?

10. Which security should sell at a greater price?
    a. A 10-year Treasury bond with a 9% coupon rate vs. a 10-year T-bond with a 10% coupon
    b. A 3-month maturity call option with an exercise price of $40 vs. a 3-month call on the same stock with an exercise price of $35
    c. A put option on a stock selling at $50, or a put option on another stock selling at $60 (all other relevant features of the stocks and options may be assumed to be identical)
    d. A 3-month T-bill with a discount yield of 6.1% vs. a 3-month bill with a discount yield of 6.2%
11. Why do call options with exercise prices greater than the price of the underlying stock sell for positive prices?
12. Both a call and a put currently are traded on stock XYZ; both have strike prices of $50 and maturities of 6 months. What will be the profit to an investor who buys the call for $4 in the following scenarios for stock prices in 6 months?
    a. $40
    b. $45
    c. $50
    d. $55
    e. $60
    What will be the profit in each scenario to an investor who buys the put for $6?
13. Explain the difference between a put option and a short position in a futures contract.
14. Examine the first 25 stocks listed in Figure 2.9. For how many of these stocks is the 52-week high price at least 50% greater than the 52-week low price? What do you conclude about the volatility of prices on individual stocks?

CHAPTER 3

How Securities Are Traded

We examine in this chapter how securities are bought and sold, how firms issue securities, and how they are traded on various exchanges or in the over-the-counter market. We explain short sales and buying securities on margin. We also examine the roles of insurance and regulatory agencies and explain how an individual can invest in securities either through a broker or through a mutual fund.

3.1 *How Firms Issue Securities*

When firms need to raise capital they may choose to sell (or *float*) new securities. These new issues of stocks, bonds, or other securities typically are marketed to the public by investment bankers in what is called the **primary market.** Purchase and sale of already issued securities among private investors takes place in the **secondary market.**

There are two types of primary market issues of common stock. *Initial public offerings,* or *IPOs,* are stocks issued by a formerly privately owned company selling stock to the public for the first time. *Seasoned new issues* are offered by companies that already have floated equity. A sale by IBM of new shares of stock, for example, would constitute a seasoned new issue.

In the case of bonds we also distinguish between two types of primary market issues, a *public offering,* which is an issue of bonds sold to the general investing public that can then be traded on the secondary market, and a *private placement,* which is an issue that is sold to a few institutional investors at most, and is generally held to maturity.

Investment Bankers

Public offerings of both stocks and bonds typically are marketed via an **underwriting** by investment bankers. In fact, more than one investment banker usually markets the securities. A lead firm forms an *underwriting syndicate* of other investment bankers to share the responsibility for the stock issue.

The bankers advise the firm regarding the terms on which it should attempt to sell the securities. A preliminary registration statement must be filed with the Securities and Exchange Commission (SEC) describing the issue and the prospects of the company. This *preliminary prospectus* is known as a *red herring* because of a statement printed in red that the company is not attempting to sell the security before the registration is approved. When the statement is finalized and approved by the SEC, it is called the **prospectus.** At this time the price at which the securities will be offered to the public is announced.

There are two methods of underwriting a securities issue. In a *firm commitment* underwriting arrangement the investment bankers purchase the securities from the issuing company and then resell them to the public. The issuing firm sells the securities to the underwriting syndicate for the public offering price less a spread that serves as compensation to the underwriters. In such an arrangement the underwriters assume the full risk that the shares cannot in fact be sold to the public at the stipulated offering price.

An alternative to this arrangement is the *best-efforts* agreement. In this case the investment banker agrees to help the firm sell the issue to the public, but does not actually purchase the securities. The banker simply acts as an intermediary between the public and the firm and thus does not bear the risk of being unable to resell purchased securities at the offering price. The best-efforts procedure is more common for initial public offerings of common stock, for which the appropriate share price is less certain.

Corporations engage investment bankers either by negotiation or by competitive bidding. Negotiation is more common. Besides being compensated by the spread between the purchase price and the public offering price, an investment banker may receive shares of common stock or other securities of the firm. In the case of competitive bidding, a firm may announce its intent to issue securities and invite investment bankers to submit bids for the underwriting. Such a bidding process may reduce the cost of the issue; it might also bring fewer services from the investment banker. Many public utilities are required to solicit competitive bids from underwriters.

Shelf Registration

An important innovation in the method of issuing securities was introduced in 1982, when the SEC approved Rule 415, which allows firms to register securities and gradually sell them to the public for 2 years after the initial registration. Because the securities are already registered, they can be sold on short notice with little additional paperwork. In addition, they can be sold in small amounts without incurring substantial flotation costs. The securities are "on the shelf," ready to be issued, which has given rise to the term *shelf registration*.

Underpricing

Underwriters face a peculiar conflict of interest. On the one hand, acting in the best interest of the issuing firm, they should attempt to market securities to the public at the highest possible price, thereby maximizing the revenue realized from the offering. On the other hand, if they set the offering price higher than the public will pay, they will be unable to market the securities to customers. Underwriters left with unmarketable securities will be forced to sell them at a loss on the secondary market. Underwriters therefore must balance their own interests against those of their clients. The lower the public offering price, the less capital the firm raises, but the greater the chance that the securities can be sold at that price. Also, the lower the price, the less effort needed to find investors to purchase the securities. If the offering is made at a low enough price, investors will beat down the doors of the underwriters to purchase the securities.

In fact, there is some evidence that IPOs of common stock often are underpriced compared with the price at which they could be marketed. In a study of the pricing of 112 IPOs, Ibbotson[1] found that an investor who purchased shares of each issue at the initial offering price and then resold the stock 1 month later would have earned an average *abnormal* return of 11.4%.[2] Such an abnormal return would indicate that the stock was offered to the public at a price substantially below that which investors were willing to pay. Such underpricing means that IPOs commonly are oversubscribed; that is, there is demand from the public for more of the shares at the offering price than there are shares being offered.

3.2 Where Securities Are Traded

Once securities are issued to the public, investors may trade them among themselves. Purchase and sale of already issued securities take place in the secondary markets, which consist of (1) national and local securities exchanges, (2) the over-the-counter market, and (3) direct trading between two parties.

The Secondary Markets

There are nine major **stock exchanges** in the United States. Two of these, the New York Stock Exchange (NYSE) and the American Stock Exchange (ASE, or Amex), are national in scope. The others are regional exchanges, which list firms located in a particular geographic area. There also are several exchanges for the trading of options and futures contracts, which we will discuss in the options and futures chapters.

An exchange provides a facility for its members to trade securities, and only members of the exchange may trade there. Therefore memberships, or *seats,* on the exchange are valuable assets. The exchange member charges investors for executing trades on their behalf. This is the means by which brokerage firms operate. They own seats on exchanges and advertise their willingness to execute trades for customers for

---

[1]Ibbotson, Roger G., "Price Performance of Common Stock New Issues," *Journal of Financial Economics, 2,* September 1975.

[2]Abnormal return measures the return on the investment net of the portion that can be attributed to general market movements. See the discussion of this concept in Chapter 13.

a fee. The commissions that can be earned through this activity determine the market value of a seat. A seat on the NYSE sold for more than $1 million in 1987. However, after the market crash in October 1987 stock market prices and trading volume fell, and commissions earned by brokerage firms also decreased. The value of a seat on the NYSE fell almost 50% by January 1988 to $625,000. Although this value later rose to $800,000 in May 1988, it was still more than 30% below its former level.

The NYSE is by far the largest single exchange. The shares of approximately 1,500 firms trade there, and over 2,000 stock issues (common and preferred stock) are listed. Daily trading volume on the NYSE regularly exceeds 100 million shares. Table 3.1 shows the market value of securities listed on the nine stock exchanges as of December 1987, as well as trading volume on each exchange during that year.

From Table 3.1 you can see that the NYSE accounts for about 85% of the market value of shares traded on the exchanges. The Amex also is national in scope, but it focuses on listing smaller and younger firms than does the NYSE. Regional exchanges provide a market for trading shares of local firms that do not meet the listing requirements of the national exchanges. The national exchanges are willing to list a stock (allow trading in that stock on the exchange) only if it meets certain criteria of size and stability.

TABLE 3.1 Stock Exchanges, December 1987

	Market Value of Listed Securities ($ Million)	% of Total	Trading Volume During the Year (Thousands of Shares)	% of Total
New York	124,179	87.10	4,373,747	82.94
Midwest	7,684	5.39	285,541	5.41
Pacific	3,748	2.63	177,661	3.37
American	2,899	2.03	279,960	5.31
Boston	1,867	1.31	72,074	1.37
Philadelphia	1,503	1.05	59,821	1.13
Cincinnati	682	0.48	22,402	0.42
Spokane	2	0.00	2,283	0.04
Intermountain	0	0.00	0	0.00
TOTAL	**142,564**	**100.00**	**5,273,489**	**100.00**

From the Securities and Exchange Commission *Monthly Statistical Review, 47,* February 1988.

Table 3.2 gives the initial listing requirements for the NYSE. These requirements ensure that a firm is of significant trading interest before the NYSE will allocate facilities for it to be traded on the floor of the exchange. If a listed company suffers a decline and fails to meet the criteria in Table 3.2, it may be delisted from the exchange.

Regional exchanges also sponsor trading of some firms that are traded on national exchanges. This dual listing enables local brokerage firms to trade in shares of large firms without needing to purchase a membership on the NYSE.

TABLE 3.2   Initial Listing Requirements for the NYSE

Pretax income in last year	$ 2,500,000
Average annual pretax income in previous 2 years	$ 2,000,000
Net tangible assets	$18,000,000
Market value of publicly held stock	$18,000,000
Shares publicly held	1,100,000
Number of holders of 100 shares or more	2,000

Data from the New York Stock Exchange *Fact Book*, 1988.

Although most common stocks are traded on the exchanges, most bonds and other fixed-income securities are not. Corporate bonds are traded both on the exchanges and over the counter, but all federal and municipal government bonds are traded only over the counter.

The Over-the-Counter Market

There are nearly 7,000 issues traded on the **over-the-counter market** (OTC) and any security may be traded there, but the OTC market is not a formal exchange. There are no membership requirements for trading, nor are there listing requirements for securities. In the OTC market thousands of brokers register with the SEC as dealers in OTC securities. Security dealers quote prices at which they are willing to buy or sell securities. A broker can execute a trade by contacting the dealer listing an attractive quote.

Before 1971, all OTC quotations of stock were recorded manually and published daily. The so-called pink sheets were the means by which dealers communicated their interest in trading at various prices. This was a cumbersome and inefficient technique, and published quotes were a full day out of date. In 1971 the National Association of Securities Dealers Automated Quotation system, or **NASDAQ,** began to offer immediate information on a computer-linked system of bid and asked prices for stocks offered by various dealers. The **bid price** is that at which a dealer is willing to purchase a security; the **asked price** is that at which the dealer will sell a security. The system allows a dealer who receives a buy or a sell order from an investor to examine all current quotes, call the dealer with the best quote, and execute a trade. About 3,500 stocks are quoted on the NASDAQ system.

To be listed on NASDAQ, a firm must satisfy one of two sets of criteria:
1. a. 350,000 publicly held shares
   b. Market value of publicly held shares of $2 million
   c. Minimum bid price of $3
   d. Annual net income of $300,000 in either the last fiscal year or 2 of the last 3 years
2. a. 800,000 publicly held shares
   b. Market value of publicly held shares of $8 million
   c. Net worth of $8 million
   d. Incorporation of at least 4 years

NASDAQ has three levels of subscribers. The highest, Level 3, is for f
ing, or "making markets," in OTC securities. These market makers maintaiï
tories of a security and continually stand ready to buy these shares from or sel
to the public at the quoted bid and asked prices. They earn profits from the sp
between the bid price and the asked price. Level 3 subscribers may enter the bid a
asked prices at which they are willing to buy or sell stocks into the computer network
and update these quotes as desired.

Level 2 subscribers receive all bid and asked quotes but cannot enter their own
quotes. These subscribers tend to be stockbrokers who execute trades for clients but
do not actively deal in the stocks on their own account. Brokers attempting to buy or
sell shares call the market maker who has the best quote to execute a trade.

Level 1 subscribers receive only the median, or "representative," bid and asked
prices on each stock. Level 1 subscribers are investors who are not actively buying
and selling securities, yet the service provides them with general information.

For bonds, the over-the-counter market is a loosely organized network of dealers
linked together by a computer quotation system. In practice, the corporate bond market often is quite "thin," in that there are few investors interested in trading a particular bond at any particular time. The bond market is subject to a type of "liquidity
risk," because it can be difficult to sell holdings quickly if the need arises.

The Third and Fourth Markets

The **third market** refers to trading of exchange-listed securities on the OTC market. Until recently, members of an exchange were required to execute all their trades
of exchange-listed securities on the exchange and to charge commissions according to
a fixed schedule. This schedule was disadvantageous to large traders, who were pre-
vented from realizing economies of scale on large trades. The restriction led brokerage firms that were not members of the NYSE, and so not bound by its rules, to
establish trading in the OTC market on large NYSE-listed firms. These trades took
place at lower commissions than would have been charged on the NYSE, and the
third market grew dramatically until 1972 when the NYSE allowed negotiated commissions on orders exceeding $300,000. On May 1, 1975, frequently referred to as
"May Day," commissions on all orders became negotiable.

The **fourth market** refers to direct trading between investors in exchange-listed
securities without benefit of a broker. Large institutions who wish to avoid brokerage
fees altogether may engage in direct trading.

The National Market System

The Securities Act Amendments of 1975 directed the Securities and Exchange
Commission to implement a national competitive securities market. Such a market
would entail centralized reporting of transactions and a centralized quotation system,
and would result in enhanced competition among market makers. In 1975 a "Consolidated Tape" began reporting trades on the NYSE, the Amex, and the major regional
exchanges, as well as on NASDAQ-listed stocks. In 1977 the Consolidated Quota-

tions Service began providing on-line bid and asked quotes for NYSE securities also ʇraded on various other exchanges. This enhances competition by allowing traders to ɪd the best exchange for a desired trade. In 1978 the Intermarket Trading System ɪ implemented to link seven exchanges by computer (NYSE, Amex, Boston, Cincinnati, Midwest, Pacific, and Philadelphia). Brokers and market makers can thus display quotes on all markets and execute cross-market trades.

A central limit-order book would be the ultimate centralization of the marketplace. In such a system orders from all exchanges would be listed centrally, and all traders could fill all orders.

3.3 Trading on Exchanges

Most of the material in this section applies to all securities traded on exchanges. Some of it, however, applies just to stocks, and in such cases we use the terms "stocks" or "shares."

The Participants

When an investor instructs a broker to buy or sell securities, a number of players must act to consummate the trade. We start our discussion of the mechanics of exchange trading with a brief description of the potential parties to a trade.

The investor places an order with a broker. The brokerage firm owning a seat on the exchange contacts its *commission broker,* who is on the floor of the exchange, to execute the order. *Floor brokers* are independent members of the exchange who own their own seats and handle work for commission brokers when those brokers have too many orders to handle.

Registered traders are frequent traders who use their membership to execute trades for their own accounts. By trading directly, they avoid the commissions that would be incurred if they had to trade through a broker. The **specialist** is central to the trading process. Specialists maintain a market in one or more listed securities. We will examine their role in detail shortly.

Types of Orders

Investors may issue several types of orders to their brokers. *Market orders* are simple buy or sell orders that are to be executed immediately at current market prices. In contrast, investors can issue *limit orders,* whereby they specify prices at which they are willing to buy or sell a security. If the stock falls below the limit on a limit-buy order, then the trade is to be executed. If stock XYZ is selling at $45, for example, a limit-buy order may instruct the broker to buy the stock if and when the share price falls below $43. Correspondingly, a limit-sell order instructs the broker to sell as soon as the stock price goes above the specified limit. Orders also can be limited by a time period. Day orders, for example, expire at the close of the trading day. If it is not executed on that day, the order is canceled. *Open* or *good-till-canceled orders,* in contrast, remain in force for up to 6 months unless canceled by the customer.

Stop-loss orders are similar to limit orders in that the trade is not to be executed unless the stock hits a price limit. In this case, however, the stock is to be sold if its price falls *below* a stipulated level. As the name suggests, the order lets the stock be sold to stop further losses from accumulating. Symmetrically, *stop-buy orders* specify that the stock should be bought when its price rises above a given limit. These trades often accompany short sales, and they are used to limit potential losses from the short position. Short sales are discussed in greater detail in Section 3.6.

Specialists and the Execution of Trades

The specialist, who is the central figure in the execution of trades, makes a market in the shares of one or more firms. Part of this task is simply mechanical. The specialist maintains a "book" listing all outstanding unexecuted limit orders entered by brokers on behalf of clients. Actually, the book is now a computer console. When limit orders can be executed at market prices, the specialist sees to the trade. In this role the specialist merely acts as a facilitator. As buy and sell orders at mutually agreeable prices cross the trading desk, the market maker matches the two parties to the trade.

The specialist is required to use the highest outstanding offered purchase price and lowest outstanding offered selling price when matching trades. Therefore the specialist system results in an auction market—all buy orders and all sell orders come to one location, and the best bids "win" the trades.

The more interesting function of the specialist is to maintain a "fair and orderly market" by dealing personally in the stock. In return for the exclusive right to make the market in a specific stock on the exchange, the specialist is required to maintain an orderly market by buying and selling shares from inventory. Specialists maintain bid and asked prices at which they are obligated to meet at least a limited amount of market orders. If market buy orders come in, specialists must sell shares from their own accounts at the maintained asked price; if sell orders come in, they must stand willing to buy at the listed bid price.

Ordinarily, in an active market specialists can cross buy and sell orders without direct participation on their own accounts. That is, the specialist's own inventory need not be the primary means of order execution. However, sometimes the specialist's bid and asked prices will be better than those offered by any other market participant. Therefore, at any point the effective asked price in the market is the lower of either the specialist's offered asked price or the lowest of the unfilled limit-sell orders. Similarly, the effective bid price is the highest of unfilled limit-buy orders or the specialist's bid. These procedures ensure that the specialist provides liquidity to the market.

By standing ready to trade at quoted bid and asked prices, the specialist is exposed somewhat to exploitation by other traders. Large traders with ready access to late-breaking news will trade with specialists only if the specialists' quoted prices are temporarily out of line with assessments based on the traders' (possibly superior) information. Specialists who cannot match the information resources of large traders will be at a disadvantage when their quoted prices offer profit opportunities to more informed traders.

You might wonder why specialists do not protect their interests by setting a low bid price and a high asked price. A specialist using that strategy would not suffer losses by maintaining a too-low asked price or a too-high bid price in a period of dramatic movements in the stock price. Specialists who offer a narrow spread between the bid and the asked prices have little leeway for error and must constantly monitor market conditions to avoid offering other investors advantageous terms.

There are two reasons why large bid-asked spreads are not viable options for the specialist. First, one source of the specialist's income is derived from frequent trading at the bid and asked prices, with the spread as a trading profit. A too-large spread would tend to discourage investors from trading, and the specialist's business would dry up. Another reason specialists cannot use large bid-ask spreads to protect their interests is that they are obligated to provide price continuity to the market.

To illustrate the principle of price continuity, suppose that the highest limit-buy order for a stock is $30 while the lowest limit-sell order is at $32. When a market buy order comes in, it is matched to the best limit-sell at $32. A market sell order would be matched to the best limit-buy at $30. As market buys and sells come to the floor randomly, the stock price would fluctuate between $30 and $32. The exchange authorities would consider this excessive volatility, and the specialist would be expected to step in with bid and/or asked prices in between these values to reduce the bid-asked spread to an acceptable level, such as $\frac{1}{4}$ or $\frac{1}{2}$ point.

Specialists earn income both from commissions for acting as brokers for orders and from the spread between the bid and asked prices at which they buy and sell securities. It also appears that specialists' access to their "book" of limit orders gives them unique knowledge about the probable direction of price movement over short periods of time. For example, suppose the specialist sees that a stock now selling for $45 has limit-buy orders for over 100,000 shares at prices ranging from $44.50 to $44.75. This latent buying demand provides a cushion of support, because it is unlikely that enough sell pressure could come in during the next few hours to cause the price to drop below $44.50. If there are very few limit-sell orders above $45, some transient buying demand could raise the price substantially. The specialist in such circumstances realizes that a position in the stock offers little downside risk and substantial upside potential. Such unique access to the trading intentions of other market participants seems to allow a specialist to earn substantial profits on personal transactions.

The specialist system was subject to extraordinary pressure during the market crash of October 19, 1987, when stock prices fell about 25% on 1 day. In the face of overwhelming sell pressure, market makers were called upon to purchase huge amounts of stock. Specialists as a whole bought $486 million of stock on this single day.[3] However, as prices continued to fall, these market makers suffered large losses, thereby eliminating much of their net worth. This in turn made banks wary of

---

[3]This discussion is based on the Brady Commission report. See the Selected Readings.

Introduction

lending additional funds to specialist firms and precluded further share purchases by those firms. Only assurances by the Federal Reserve to make ample credit available to the financial system reestablished banks' willingness to lend. Nevertheless, the stock market came close to a halt during the crash. Since the crash, the NYSE has sharply increased the capital requirements for its specialist firms.

Moreover, in the wake of the market collapse many specialists apparently decided not to sacrifice their own capital in a seemingly hopeless effort to shore up prices. Although specialists as a whole were net purchasers of stock, fully 30% of the specialists in a sample of large stocks were net sellers on October 19. These firms came under criticism for failing to live up to their mandate to attempt to support an orderly market.

Block Sales

Institutional investors frequently trade blocks of several thousand shares of stock. Table 3.3 shows that **block transactions** of over 10,000 shares now account for about half of all trading on the NYSE. Such transactions are often too large to be handled comfortably by specialists who do not wish to hold such large blocks of stock in their inventory. Moreover, specialists are prohibited from soliciting interest in shares from other institutional traders, and so cannot easily lay off large positions that they might assume in dealing with institutional traders.

In response to this problem, "block houses" have evolved to aid in the placement of block trades. Block houses are brokerage firms that help to find potential buyers or sellers of large block trades. Once a trader has been located, the block is sent to the exchange floor where the trade is executed by the specialist. If such traders cannot be identified, the block house might purchase all or part of a block sale for its own account. The broker then can resell the shares to the public.

Settlement

An order executed on the exchange must be settled within 5 working days. The purchaser must deliver the cash, and the seller must deliver the stock to the broker,

TABLE 3.3 Block Transactions on the New York Stock Exchange

Year	Shares (Thousands)	Percentage of Reported Volume	Average Number of Block Transactions per Day
1965	48,262	3.1	9
1970	450,908	15.4	68
1975	778,540	16.6	136
1980	3,311,132	29.2	528
1985	14,222,272	51.7	2,139
1986	17,811,335	49.9	2,631
1987	24,497,241	51.2	3,639

Data from the New York Stock Exchange *Fact Book*, 1988.

who in turn delivers it to the buyer's broker. Transfer of the shares is made easier when the firm's clients keep their securities in *street name,* meaning that the broker holds the shares registered in the firm's own name on behalf of the client.

Settlement is simplified further by a clearinghouse. The trades of all exchange members are recorded each day, with members' transactions netted out, so that each member need only transfer or receive the net number of shares sold or bought that day. Each member settles only with the clearinghouse, instead of with each firm with whom trades were executed.

3.4   *Trading on the OTC Market*

On the exchanges all trading takes place through a specialist. Trades on the OTC market, however, are negotiated directly through dealers. Each dealer maintains an inventory of selected securities. Dealers sell from their inventories at asked prices and buy for them at bid prices.

An investor who wishes to purchase or sell shares engages a broker who tries to locate the dealer offering the best deal on the security. This contrasts with exchange trading, where all buy or sell orders are negotiated through the specialist, who arranges for the best bids to get the trade. In the OTC market brokers must search the offers of dealers directly to find the best trading opportunity.

Exchange trading is effectively conducted in an auction market, whereas OTC trading is conducted in a **dealer market.** The NASDAQ system facilitates access for subscribers to the Level 2 or Level 3 service who can obtain a full set of dealer bid and asked quotes. Dealers who make a market in securities will subscribe to the Level 3 service where they can list their offers, as well as view those of other dealers. Brokers need only Level 2 subscriptions to gain access to all offers.

Because this system bypasses the specialist system, OTC trades do not require a centralized trading floor as do exchange-listed stocks. Dealers can be located anywhere, as long as they can communicate effectively with other buyers and sellers.

3.5   *Buying on Margin*

Investors who purchase stocks on **margin** borrow part of the purchase price of the stock from their brokers. The brokers in turn borrow money from banks at the call money rate to finance these purchases, and charge their clients that rate plus a service charge for the loan. All securities purchased on margin must be left with the brokerage firm in street name, because the securities are used as collateral for the loan.

The Board of Governors of the Federal Reserve System sets limits on the extent to which stock purchases can be financed via margin loans. Currently, the maximum margin is 50%, meaning that at most 50% of the purchase price may be borrowed.

The percentage margin is defined as the ratio of the net worth, or "equity value" of the account to the market value of the securities. To demonstrate, suppose that the investor initially pays $6,000 toward the purchase of $10,000 worth of stock (100 shares at $100 per share), borrowing the remaining $4,000 from the broker. The account will have a balance sheet as follows:

Assets		Liabilities and Owner's Equity	
Value of stock	$10,000	Loan from broker	$4,000
		Equity	$6,000

The initial percentage margin is $6,000/$10,000 = 60%. If the stock's price declines to $70 per share, the account balance becomes:

Value of stock	$7,000	Loan from broker	$4,000
		Equity	$3,000

The equity in the account falls by the full decrease in the stock value, and the percentage margin is now $3,000/$7,000 = 43%.

If the stock value were to fall below $4,000, equity would become negative, meaning that the value of the stock is no longer sufficient collateral to cover the loan from the broker. To guard against this possibility, the broker sets a *maintenance margin*. If the percentage margin falls below the maintenance level, the broker will issue a *margin call* requiring the investor to add new cash or securities to the margin account. If the investor does not act, the broker may sell the securities from the account to pay off enough of the loan to restore the percentage margin to an acceptable level.

An example will show how the maintenance margin works. Suppose the maintenance margin is 30%. How far could the stock price fall before the investor would get a margin call? To answer this question requires some algebra.

Let P be the price of the stock. The value of the investor's 100 shares is then $100P$, and the equity in his account is $100P - \$4,000$. The percentage margin is therefore $(100P - \$4,000)/100P$. The price at which the percentage margin equals the maintenance margin of .3 is found by solving the equation:

$$\frac{100P - \$4,000}{100P} = .3$$
$$100P - \$4,000 = 30P$$
$$70P = \$4,000$$
$$P = \$57.14$$

If the price of the stock were to fall below $57.14 per share, the investor would get a margin call.

Concept Check

Question 1. If the maintenance margin in the example we have discussed were 40%, how far could the stock price fall before the investor would get a margin call?

Why do investors buy stock (or bonds) on margin? They do so when they wish to invest an amount greater than their own money alone would allow. Thus they can achieve greater upside potential, but they also expose themselves to greater downside risk.

To see how, let us suppose that an investor is bullish (optimistic) on IBM stock, which is currently selling at $100 per share. The investor has $10,000 to invest and expects IBM stock to go up in price by 30% during the next year. Ignoring any dividends, the expected rate of return would thus be 30% if the investor spent only $10,000 to buy 100 shares.

But now let us assume that the investor also borrows another $10,000 from the broker and invests it in IBM also. The total investment in IBM would thus be $20,000 (for 200 shares). Assuming an interest rate on the margin loan of 9% per year, what will be the investor's rate of return now (again ignoring dividends) if IBM stock does go up 30% by year's end?

The 200 shares will be worth $26,000. Paying off $10,900 of principal and interest on the margin loan leaves $15,100 ($26,000 − $10,900). The rate of return therefore will be

$$\frac{\$15,100 - \$10,000}{\$10,000} = 51\%$$

The investor has parlayed a 30% rise in the stock's price into a 51% rate of return on the $10,000 investment.

Doing so, however magnifies the downside risk. Suppose that instead of going up by 30% the price of IBM stock goes down by 30% to $70 per share. In that case the 200 shares will be worth $14,000, and the investor is left with $3,100 after paying off the $10,900 of principal and interest on the loan. The result is a disastrous rate of return:

$$\frac{\$3,100 - \$10,000}{\$10,000} = -69\%$$

Table 3.4 summarizes the possible results of these hypothetical transactions. Note that, if there is no change in IBM's stock price, the investor loses 9%, the cost of the loan.

TABLE 3.4 Illustration of Buying Stock on Margin

Change in Stock Price	End of Year Value of Shares	Repayment of Principal and Interest	Investor's Rate of Return*
30% increase	$26,000	$10,900	51%
No change	20,000	10,900	−9%
30% decrease	14,000	10,900	−69%

*Assuming the investor buys $20,000 worth of stock by borrowing $10,000 at an interest rate of 9% per year.

Question 2. Suppose that in the previous example the investor borrows only $5,000 at the same interest rate of 9% per year. What will be the rate of return if the price of IBM stock goes up by 30%? If it goes down by 30%? If it remains unchanged?

3.6 *Short Sales*

A **short sale** allows investors to profit from a decline in a security's price. In this procedure an investor borrows shares of stock from another investor through a broker and sells the shares. Later, the investor (the short seller) must repurchase the shares in the market in order to replace the shares that were borrowed. This is called covering the short position. If the stock price has fallen, the shares will be repurchased at a lower price than that at which they were initially sold, and the short seller reaps a profit. Short sellers must not only return the shares but also give the lender any dividends paid on the shares during the period of the short sale, because the lender of the shares would have received the dividends directly from the firm had the shares not been lent.

Exchange rules permit short sales only after an *uptick,* that is, only when the last recorded change in the stock price is positive. This rule apparently is meant to prevent waves of speculation against the stock. In other words, the votes of "no confidence" in the stock that short sales represent may be entered only after a price increase.

Finally, exchange rules require that proceeds from a short sale must be kept on account with the broker. The short seller therefore cannot invest these funds to generate income. In addition, short sellers are required to post margin (which is essentially collateral) with the broker to ensure that the trader can cover any losses sustained should the stock price rise during the period of the short sale.[4]

To illustrate the actual mechanics of short selling, suppose that you are bearish (pessimistic) on IBM stock, and that its current market price is $100 per share. You tell your broker to sell short 1,000 shares. The broker borrows 1,000 shares either from another customer's account or from another broker.

The $100,000 cash proceeds from the short sale are credited to your account. Suppose the broker has a 50% margin requirement on short sales. This means that you must have other cash or securities in your account worth at least $50,000 that can serve as margin (that is, collateral) on the short sale. Let us suppose that you have

---

[4]We should note that although we have been describing a short sale of a stock, bonds also may be sold short.

$50,000 in Treasury bills. Your account with the broker after the short sale will then be:

Assets		Liabilities and Owner's Equity	
Cash	$100,000	Short position in IBM stock	$100,000
T-bills	$ 50,000	(1,000 shares owed)	
		Equity	$ 50,000

Now if you are right, and IBM stock falls to $70 per share, you can cover your short sale for a profit of $30,000. If the price of IBM stock goes up while you are short, however, you may get a margin call from your broker.

Let us suppose that the broker has a maintenance margin of 30% on short sales. This means that the equity in your account must be at least 30% of the value of your short position at all times. How far can the price of IBM stock go up before you get a margin call?

Let P be the price of IBM stock. Then the value of your short position is $1,000P$, and the equity in your account is $150,000 - 1,000P$. Your short position margin ratio is $(\$150,000 - 1,000P)/1,000P$. The critical value of P is thus

$$\frac{\$150,000 - 1,000P}{1,000P} = .3$$
$$\$150,000 - 1,000P = 300P$$
$$1,300P = \$150,000$$
$$P = \$115.38 \text{ per share}$$

If IBM stock should rise above $115.38 per share, you will get a margin call, and you will either have to put up additional cash or cover your short position.

Concept Check

Question 3. If the short position maintenance margin in the preceding example were 40%, how far could the stock price rise before the investor would get a margin call?

3.7 Regulation of Securities Markets

Trading in securities markets in the United States is regulated under a myriad of laws. The two major laws are the Securities Act of 1933 and the Securities Exchange Act of 1934. The 1933 Act requires full disclosure of relevant information relating to the issue of new securities. This is the Act that requires registration of new securities and the issuance of a prospectus that details the financial prospects of the firm. The 1934 Act established the Securities and Exchange Commission to administer the provisions of the 1933 Act. It also extended the disclosure principle of the 1933 Act by requiring firms with issued securities on secondary exchanges to perio.. relevant financial information.

SEC approval of a prospectus or financial report does not mean that it vie.. security as a good investment. The SEC cares only that the relevant facts are di.. closed; investors make their own evaluations of the security's value. The 1934 Act also empowered the SEC to register and regulate securities exchanges, OTC trading, brokers, and dealers. The Act thus established the SEC as the administrative agency responsible for broad oversight of the securities markets. The SEC, however, shares oversight with other regulatory agencies. For example, the Commodity Futures Trading Commission (CFTC) regulates trading in futures markets, whereas the Federal Reserve has broad responsibility for the health of the U.S. financial system. In this role the Fed sets margin requirements on stocks and stock options and regulates bank lending to securities markets participants.

The Securities Investor Protection Act of 1970 established the Securities Investor Protection Corporation (SIPC) to protect investors from losses if their brokerage firms fail. Just as the Federal Deposit Insurance Corporation provides federal protection to depositors against bank failure, the SIPC ensures that investors will receive securities held for their account in street name by the failed brokerage firm up to a limit of $500,000 per customer. The SIPC is financed by levying an "insurance premium" on its participating, or member, brokerage firms. It also may borrow money from the SEC if its own funds are insufficient to meet its obligations.

In addition to federal regulations, security trading is subject to state laws. The laws providing for state regulation of securities are known generally as blue sky laws, because they attempt to prevent the false promotion and sale of securities representing nothing more than blue sky. State laws to outlaw fraud in security sales were instituted before the Securities Act of 1933. Varying state laws were somewhat unified when many states adopted portions of the Uniform Securities Act, which was proposed in 1956.

Much of the securities industry relies on self-regulation. The SEC delegates to secondary exchanges much of the responsibility for day-to-day oversight of trading. Similarly, the National Association of Securities Dealers oversees trading of OTC securities. The Institute of Chartered Financial Analysts' Code of Ethics and Professional Conduct sets out principles that govern the behavior of CFAs.

The market collapse of October 19, 1987 has prompted several suggestions for regulatory change. For example, the Brady Commission has suggested the following:
1. A single agency to coordinate issues that affect several financial markets
2. Unified clearing systems across markets
3. Consistent margin requirement across markets
4. "Circuit breakers" to halt trading when market conditions warrant such action
5. Information gathering and dissemination across markets

One of the important restrictions on trading involves *insider trading*. It is illegal for anyone to transact in securities to profit from **inside information**, that is, private information held by officers, directors, or major stockholders that has not yet been divulged to the public. The difficulty is that the definition of insiders can be ambiguous. Although it is obvious that the chief financial officer of a firm is an insider, it is less clear whether the firm's biggest supplier can be considered an insider. However, the supplier may deduce the firm's near-term prospects from significant changes in orders. This gives the supplier a unique form of private information, yet the supplier does not necessarily qualify as an insider. These ambiguities plague security analysts, whose job is to uncover as much information as possible concerning the firm's expected prospects. The distinction between legal private information and illegal inside information can be fuzzy (see nearby box).

The SEC requires officers, directors, and major stockholders of all publicly held firms to report all of their transactions in their firm's stock. A compendium of insider trades is published monthly in the SEC's *Official Summary of Securities Transactions and Holdings*. The idea is to inform the public of any implicit votes of confidence or no confidence made by insiders.

Do insiders exploit their knowledge? The answer seems to be, to a limited degree, yes. Two forms of evidence support this conclusion. First, there is massive evidence of "leakage" of useful information to some traders before any public announcement of that information. For example, share prices of firms announcing dividend increases (which the market interprets as good news concerning the firm's prospects) commonly increase in value a few days *before* the public announcement of the increase.[5] Clearly, some investors are acting on the good news before it is released to the public. Similarly, share prices tend to increase a few days before the public announcement of above-trend earnings growth.[6] At the same time, share prices still rise substantially on the day of the public release of good news, indicating that insiders, or their associates, have not fully bid up the price of the stock to the level commensurate with that news.

The second sort of evidence on insider trading is based on returns earned on trades by insiders. Researchers have examined the SEC's summary of insider trading to measure the performance of insiders. In one of the best known of these studies, Jaffee[7] examines the abnormal return on stocks over the months following purchases or sales by insiders. For months in which insider purchasers of a stock exceeded insider sellers of the stock by three or more, the stock had an abnormal return in the following 8 months of about 5%. When insider sellers exceeded insider buyers, however, the stock tended to perform poorly.

3.8 *Selecting a Broker*

Basically, individuals may choose from two kinds of brokers: full-service or discount. Full-service brokers, who provide a variety of services, often are referred to as account executives or financial consultants. Besides carrying out the basic services of executing orders, holding securities for safekeeping, extending margin loans, and fa-

[5]See, for example, Aharony, J., and Swary, I., "Quarterly Dividend and Earnings Announcement and Stockholders' Return: An Empirical Analysis," *Journal of Finance, 35,* March 1980.

[6]See, for example, Foster, George, Olsen, Chris, and Shevlin, Terry, "Earnings Releases, Anomalies, and the Behavior of Security Returns," *The Accounting Review,* October 1984.

[7]Jaffee, Jeffrey F., "Special Information and Insider Trading," *Journal of Business, 47,* July 1974.

Cloudy Cases: Insider-Trading Law Leads to an Array of Interpretations

You go to a party and meet a lawyer who advises Rupert Omnivore, a notorious corporate raider. The lawyer gives you a tip: Mr. Omnivore will soon "make a run at" Deadwood Industries Inc. You promptly buy stock in Deadwood. A week later, its share price surges as Mr. Omnivore goes public with his intentions.

Are you guilty of insider trading?

That sort of hypothetical question has legal experts, investment bankers and stock-market investors tied up in knots these days. Nicholas Brady, chairman of Dillon, Read & Co., said in Senate testimony last month that he is confused about what is permissible and what isn't. "There needs to be clarification of exactly what conduct is to be prohibited by the concept of insider trading," said Mr. Brady.

Some practices clearly are illegal, as shown by the recent guilty pleas in Wall Street's widening insider-trading scandal. Just last week, investment banker Martin Siegel pleaded guilty to leaking information about pending takeovers to arbitrager Ivan Boesky. Mr. Siegel's payoff: briefcases filled with cash, which he would pick up in secret meetings with Mr. Boesky's couriers.

But there are plenty of gray areas in insider-trading law. In fact, the Securities and Exchange Commission says it has resisted efforts to spell out precise guidelines, partly because it worries that shrewd market players may find ways to evade the spirit of the law, while just barely complying with the letter. "The current approach gives the SEC a lot more scope," says Irwin Schneiderman, a securities lawyer at the New York firm of Cahill, Gordon & Reindel. Mr. Schneiderman represents the investment banking firm of Drexel Burnham Lambert Inc., which has been a focus of the government's current insider-trading investigations.

Here are some examples of what legal experts say are ambiguous areas that ordinary investors may have to worry about—along with some sense of how the law currently stands.

The Raider's Tip

To some top lawyers, the example at the start of this story looks like a big loophole in current law. Unlike Mr. Siegel's situation, where he breached clients' confidences when he leaked information, raiders may be perfectly willing to have intermediaries tip off other investors about their next move. That's because such leaks can help move shares into "sympathetic hands," aiding raiders in later stages of a battle for corporate control.

"There is a real debate" about whether such practices are illegal, says Dillon Read's Mr. Brady. Lawyers generally say they aren't too comfortable with raiders leaking their intentions, and they certainly aren't about to assure a raider that it's safe to do so. But so far, there hasn't been a test case, says Philip Parker, chief counsel in the SEC's enforcement division.

A critical issue is whether a tender offer is involved, says John Coffee, a securities-law professor at Stanford University. If so, Rule 14e-3 under the Securities Exchange Act strictly limits trading by interested parties. But if a raider hasn't yet decided how to wage a fight, Rule 14e-3 might not apply, lawyers say.

Still, buying on the basis of a tip may have another set of worries for investors, says Geoffrey Hazard, a professor at Yale Law School. If they are acting in concert with the raider, the entire group may be required to disclose its holdings, once these exceed 5% of a company's stock.

"Insider trading isn't the only law pertaining to these situations," says Prof. Hazard. "That's a point worth remembering when people hem and haw about the ambiguities of insider-trading law."

The Chain

You're an officer of Ennui Enterprises, and you're about to report disappointing quarterly earnings. You know not to sell before the news, but you tell your col-

Continued.

lege roommate. He tells his daughter, who's married to a stockbroker. The broker tells his clients. They dump their stock in Ennui—hours before the earnings are reported and the stock falls.

Have the clients done anything wrong? Have you?

Lawyers say the critical question for recipients of such tips is whether they knew, or had reason to know, that any of the sources were breaching a fiduciary duty in leaking information. If so, tip recipients shouldn't trade on the information.

In practical terms, the longer the chain, the less likely regulators are to pursue the case. Bevis Longstreth, a former SEC commissioner, recalls one inquiry that led from former Deputy Defense Secretary Paul Thayer to a series of brokers, to a group of world-class backgammon players. "It was pretty remote," he recalls, "and ultimately we didn't go after the backgammon players." (Officials did, successfully, bring a case against Mr. Thayer.)

Law-enforcement officials do pursue some chains, and the original leaker can face heavy sanctions. Just this week, criminal charges were filed against Israel Grossman, a New York lawyer who allegedly leaked nonpublic information to six friends and relatives about Colt Industries Inc.'s 1986 recapitalization. The recipients of the leak weren't criminally charged, but were charged in a civil case.

Early Word of News Stories

It could involve television, the business press or a medical journal. But you know in advance about a news report that should boost a company's stock. Is it legal to trade on this information?

The law is still in flux here, says Stanford's Prof. Coffee. A former Wall Street Journal reporter, R. Foster Winans, was convicted of securities fraud for leaking information about future Journal articles. His case is due to be reviewed by the Supreme Court.

On the other hand, the SEC chose not to bring a case against an Arizona researcher who traded in G.D. Searle options before appearing on CBS-TV to discuss Searle's Aspartame sweetener. The researcher said of his trading at the time: "I don't feel it's unethical. I feel it's the American way."

An important test here is how such traders learned of the future news reports, says Prof. Coffee. If they misappropriated information from their employer, in violation of company policy, they would seem to be guilty of insider trading under the current Winans ruling. But it's questionable whether any insider-trading offense would occur if the investor didn't have a fiduciary duty to the news organization.

The Overheard Tip

Tired of your duties at Ennui Enterprises, you take off for the golf course instead. You can't help overhearing another group talking about their corporate acquisition plans. You buy the stock they mention. Sure enough, their bid comes a week later, bringing you big profits.

Have the other executives done anything wrong? Have you?

If the leak really was inadvertent, despite sensible precautions to avoid it, the overheard executives face little legal risk, experts say. They add that accidental tip recipients are probably in the clear, too, as long as they haven't taken unusual steps to glean the information.

But enforcement officials may ask a lot of questions before they're convinced that a leak was an accident. And Mr. Longstreth, currently a partner in the New York law firm of Debevoise & Plimpton, says investors should think a little about their conscience, as well as the law.

"For all the talk about gray areas, my clients can sense what's all right and what isn't," he says. "They don't call me and say: 'Where's the line, so I can stay just barely on the safe side of it.' "

cilitating short sales, normally they provide information and advice relating to investment alternatives. Full-service brokers usually are supported by a research staff that issues analyses and forecasts of general economic, industry, and company conditions and often makes specific buy or sell recommendations. Some customers take the ultimate leap of faith and allow a full-service broker to make buy and sell decisions for them by establishing a *discretionary account*. This step requires an unusual degree of trust on the part of the customer, because an unscrupulous broker can "churn" an account, that is, trade securities excessively, in order to generate commissions.

Discount brokers, on the other hand, provide "no-frills" services. They buy and sell securities, hold them for safekeeping, offer margin loans, and facilitate short sales, and that is all. The only information they provide about the securities they handle consists of price quotations.

In recent years discount brokerage services have become increasingly available. Today, many banks, thrift institutions, and mutual fund management companies offer such services to the investing public as part of a general trend toward the creation of one-stop financial "supermarkets."

One important service that most brokers, both full-service and discount, offer their customers is an automatic cash management feature allowing cash generated from the sale of securities or from the receipt of dividends or interest to be almost immediately invested in a money market fund. This ensures that there will never be "idle" cash (uninvested cash) in the investor's account.

3.9   Cost of Trading

We can look at the cost of buying or selling securities as having an explicit part—the broker's commission—and an implicit part—the dealer's **bid-asked spread.** Sometimes the broker is a dealer in the security being traded and will charge no commission, but will collect the fee entirely in the form of the bid-asked spread.

Another implicit cost of trading that some observers would distinguish is the price concession an investor may be forced to make for trading in any quantity that exceeds the quantity the dealer is willing to trade at the posted bid or asked price.

The commission for trading common stocks is generally around 2% of the value of the transaction, but it can vary significantly. Before 1975 the schedule of commissions was fixed, but in today's environment of negotiated commissions there is substantial flexibility. On some trades, full-service brokers will offer even lower commissions than will discount brokers. In general, it pays the investor to shop around.

Total trading costs consisting of the commission, the dealer bid-asked spread, and the price concession can be substantial. According to one study, the round-trip costs (costs of purchase and resale) of trading large blocks of stocks of small companies can be as high as 30%.[8]

However, in most cases costs of trades are far smaller. Table 3.5 compares trad-

---

[8]Loeb, T.F., "Trading Cost: The Critical Link Between Investment Information and Results," *Financial Analysts Journal,* May-June, 1983.

TABLE 3.5   Commission Rates at Several Brokerage Firms*

Number of Shares	Brokerage Firms				
Full Service:	**Merrill Lynch**	**Shearson Lehman**	**Prudential-Bache**	**Kidder Peabody**	**Paine Webber**
Share Price: $5					
25	$31.25	$12.50	$35.00	$9.45	$21.25
	(25.0%)	(10.0%)	(28.0%)	(7.6%)	(17.0%)
100	$50.00	$35.00	$39.25	$35.63	$36.00
	(10.0%)	(7.0%)	(7.9%)	(7.1%)	(7.2%)
1,000	$189.50	$201.25	$205.50	$173.95	$201.00
	(3.8%)	(4.0%)	(4.1%)	(3.5%)	(4.0%)
Share Price: $20					
25	$50.00	$35.00	$39.25	$19.73	$36.00
	(10.0%)	(7.0%)	(7.9%)	(3.9%)	(7.2%)
100	$71.00	$57.25	$63.00	$63.81	$59.00
	(3.6%)	(2.9%)	(3.2%)	(3.2%)	(3.0%)
1,000	$356.00	$415.75	$410.50	$375.15	$397.00
	(1.8%)	(2.1%)	(2.1%)	(1.9%)	(2.0%)
Share Price: $70					
25	$63.00	$52.13	$58.00	$44.86	$54.50
	(3.6%)	(3.0%)	(3.3%)	(2.6%)	(3.1%)
100	$97.00	$98.00	$109.25	$102.89	$102.00
	(1.4%)	(1.4%)	(1.6%)	(1.5%)	(1.5%)
1,000	$680.00	$730.75	$764.50	$690.20	$750.00
	(1.0%)	(1.0%)	(1.1%)	(1.0%)	(1.1%)
Discount:	**Brown & Co.**	**Citicorp Brokerage**	**Fidelity Brokerage**	**Quick & Reilly**	**Charles Schwab**
Share Price: $5					
25	$26.00	$38.00	$33.00	$35.00	$34.00
	(20.80%)	(30.40%)	(26.40%)	(28.00%)	(27.20%)
100	$29.00	$38.00	$33.00	$35.00	$34.00
	(5.70%)	(7.60%)	(6.60%)	(7.00%)	(6.80%)
1,000	$65.00	$100.00	$68.00	$50.00	$76.00
	(1.30%)	(2.00%)	(1.36%)	(1.00%)	(1.52%)
Share Price: $20					
25	$26.25	$38.00	$33.00	$35.00	$34.00
	(5.25%)	(7.60%)	(6.60%)	(7.00%)	(6.80%)
100	$30.00	$38.00	$46.60	$35.00	$51.00
	(1.50%)	(1.90%)	(2.33%)	(1.75%)	(2.55%)
1,000	$75.00	$136.00	$123.00	$97.62	$122.00
	(0.38%)	(0.68%)	(0.62%)	(0.49%)	(0.61%)
Share Price: $70					
25	$27.00	$38.00	$44.03	$35.00	$47.00
	(1.54%)	(2.17%)	(2.52%)	(2.00%)	(2.69%)
100	$33.00	$91.00	$80.40	$48.44	$83.00
	(0.47%)	(1.30%)	(1.15%)	(0.69%)	(1.19%)
1,000	$105.00	$211.00	$182.00	$179.59	$204.00
	(0.15%)	(0.30%)	(0.26%)	(0.26%)	(0.29%)

Modified from *The Wall Street Journal*, July 16, 1987, and August 24, 1987. Reprinted by permission of *The Wall Street Journal*. © Dow Jones & Company, Inc. 1987. All rights reserved.
*Numbers in parentheses are commissions as a percentage of value of traded stock.

for a sample of full-service and discount brokerage firms. The commissions can be as low as .25% of the value of stocks traded for large transactions made through discount houses.

3.10   *Mutual Funds and Other Investment Companies*

As an alternative to investing in securities through a broker (or in addition to it), many individuals invest in mutual funds sponsored by investment companies. This section explains how these institutions work.

Mutual Funds

Mutual funds are firms that manage pools of other people's money. Individuals buy shares of mutual funds, and the funds invest the money in certain specified types of assets, (for example, common stocks, tax-exempt bonds, mortgages). The shares issued to the investors entitle them to a pro rata portion of the income generated by these assets.

Mutual funds perform several important functions for their shareholders:
1. Record keeping and administration. The funds prepare periodic status reports and reinvest dividends and interest.
2. Diversification and divisibility. By pooling their money, investment companies enable shareholders to hold fractional shares of many different securities. Funds can act as large investors even if any individual shareholder cannot.
3. Professional management. Many, but not all, mutual funds have full-time staffs of security analysts and portfolio managers who attempt to achieve superior investment results for their shareholders.
4. Lower transaction costs. By trading large blocks of securities, investment companies can achieve substantial savings on brokerage fees and commissions.

There are two types of mutual funds: **closed-end funds** and **open-end funds.** Open-end funds stand ready to redeem or issue shares at their net asset value (NAV), which is the market value of all securities held divided by the number of shares outstanding. The number of shares outstanding of an open-end fund changes daily as investors buy new shares or redeem old shares. Closed-end funds do not redeem or issue shares at net asset value. Shares of closed-end funds are traded through brokers, as are other common stocks, and their price can therefore differ from NAV.

Figure 3.1 shows a listing of closed-end funds' NAVs and prices from *The Wall Street Journal*. The list of these "Publicly Traded Funds" appears weekly on Mondays. Note that in most cases the stock price is different from the NAV, and many are trading below NAV.[9]

Many investors consider closed-end fund shares selling at a discount to their NAV

---

[9]The divergence of the market price of a closed-end fund's shares from NAV constitutes a major puzzle, yet to be satisfactorily explained by finance theorists.

FIGURE 3.1

Closed-end mutual funds.

(From *The Wall Street Journal*, April 22, 1988.) Reprinted by permission of *The Wall Street Journal*. © Dow Jones & Company, Inc. 1988. All rights reserved.

PUBLICLY TRADED FUNDS

Friday, April 29, 1988

Following is a weekly listing of unaudited net asset values of publicly traded investment fund shares, reported by the companies as of Friday's close. Also shown is the closing listed market price or a dealer-to-dealer asked price of each fund's shares, with the percentage of difference.

	N.A. Value	Stk Price	% Diff
Diversified Common Stock Funds			
AdmExp	16.85	15½	− 8.01
BakerFen	49.94	39½	−20.91
BlueChipVal	7.11	5¾	−19.13
Clmnte-Gbl	8.62	6⅜	−26.04
EqGuard	b9.69	9¼	− 4.58
GemIICap	14.65	10¾	−26.62
GemII Inc	9.58	12⅜	+29.22
GenAmInv	18.25	14⅝	−19.90
GlobGrCap	8.53	8	− 6.21
GlobGrInc	9.38	9⅜	...
GSO Trust	9.62	9¼	− 3.80
Lehman	13.83	12	−13.20
LbtyAll-Star	8.30	6½	−21.70
NiagaraSh	15.74	13⅛	−16.61
NchApGrEq	8.11	6¼	−22.93
QuestFVICp	10.20	8	−21.57
QuestFVIInc	11.77	10	−15.04
RoyceValue	z	z	z
SchaferValu	8.60	7	−18.60
Source	38.36	38⅛	− 0.61
Tri-Contl	24.14	21¼	−12.00
WorldwdVal	19.14	14⅜	−24.90
ZweigFund	10.06	10⅛	− 0.65
Closed End Bond Funds			
CIM High	a9.61	10⅛	+ 5.35
ZenithIF	9.24	10⅛	+ 9.60
Specialized Equity and Convertible Funds			
AmCapCv	23.01	21¼	− 7.65
ASA	bc52.40	45	−14.10
AsiaPacific	8.01	6¼	−21.97
BancrftCv	22.70	20⅞	− 8.02
BGR PM	be14.44	10¾	−25.55
Brazil	11.57	10⅜	−10.33
CNV HdgCap	9.67	5	−48.29
CNV HldgInc	9.44	10¾	+13.88
Castle	22.64	21½	− 6.14
CenFdCan	b6.32	5⅝	−11.00
CentSec	12.39	10⅜	−16.26

	N.A. Value	Stk Price	% Diff
Claremont	50.99	50½	− 1.00
CounsTndC	7.31	5½	−24.76
CypressFd	9.45	7	−25.93
DufPhUtils	7.56	8½	+12.40
EllsworthCv	8.61	7⅜	−14.32
Engex	13.30	9⅝	−27.63
Fin NwCmp	15.59	13	−16.61
1stAustralia	9.61	7¾	−19.35
FstFnFd	8.64	6¾	−21.87
FstIberian	9.16	8¾	− 4.50
FranceFd	b10.19	9	−11.60
GabelliE	10.81	8¾	−19.06
GermanyFd	7.45	6¾	− 9.40
H&Q Health	8.09	6½	−19.65
Ham Cap	b9.07	7⅝	−15.93
Ham UtPf	b48.04	48¾	+ 1.48
Helvetia Fd	11.49	10¾	− 6.44
Italy Fd	b9.29	7⅜	−20.61
Korea fd	39.31	72	+83.16
Malaysia Fd	8.31	7	−15.76
Mexico Fd	b6.28	5	−20.38
MG SLCap	8.95	7⅝	−14.80
Pete&Res	26.93	26⅛	− 2.99
Pil Reg	9.23	7⅛	−22.81
Prg Inc	8.71	8⅛	− 7.20
RegFinI/Shs	7.48	6	−19.79
Scndinvla	8.70	6⅞	−21.00
ScudrNAsia	13.71	10¾	−21.59
Taiwan Fd	b22.84	42⅛	+84.40
TCW Cvt	b8.45	7¼	−14.20
TplEmgMk	b8.74	7	−19.90
Thai Fd	11.38	16	+40.60
U.K. Fd	11.41	8¾	−23.31
Z-Seven	d14.32	14⅝	+ 2.13

a-Ex-dividend. b-As of Thursday's close. c-Translated at Commercial Rand exchange rate. d-NAV reflects $1.60 per share for taxes. e-In Canadian Dollars. z-Not available.

to be a true bargain. Even if the market price never rises to the level of NAV, the dividend yield on an investment in the fund would exceed the dividend yield on the same securities held outside of the fund. To see this, imagine a fund with a NAV of $10 per share and a market price of $9 that pays an annual dividend of $1 per share. Its dividend yield based on NAV is 10% per year, which is the yield obtainable by buying the securities directly. But the dividend yield to someone buying shares in the fund at $9 would be 11.11% per year.

The market price of open-end funds, on the other hand, cannot fall below NAV because these funds redeem shares at NAV. The offer price will exceed NAV, however, if the fund carries a load. Shares of a **load fund** are sold by security brokers, many insurance brokers, and others. A load is in effect a sales commission, usually from 3% to 8.5% of NAV, which is paid to the seller.

MUTUAL FUNDS

Friday, April 29, 1988
Price ranges for investment companies, as quoted by the National Association of Securities Dealers. NAV stands for net asset value per share; the offering includes net asset value plus maximum sales charge, if any.

		Offer NAV				Offer NAV	
	NAV	Price	Chg.		NAV	Price	Chg.
SelReg r	8.94	9.12+	.02	IDS Tax r	p3.92	4.13	...
SelRetl r	11.56	11.80−	.04	IDS Ag r	p9.20	9.20+	.03
SelSL r	8.57	8.74−	.04	IDS Eq r	p7.27	7.27−	.01
SelSoft r	14.35	14.64+	.04	IDS Inc r	p5.67	5.67	...
SelTec r	18.22	18.59+	.02	IDS Pan	p4.20	4.20	...
SelTele r	16.52	16.86−	.01	**IFG Funds:**			
SelUtil r	24.67	25.17−	.01	Divrsf f	10.87	10.87−	.06
Fidelity Plymouth Fds:				Intmn f	10.15	10.15	...
Agg Inc	p9.70	10.10−	.01	Intl Fd f	11.41	11.41+	.11
Glob Nat	p11.10	11.56−	.07	Intl Cash	p14.75	14.95−	.03
Gov Sec	p9.25	9.64−	.01	Inv Resrch	4.89	5.34−	.02
Grw Opp	p13.10	13.65−	.04	IRI Stock	p6.74	7.17−	.13
HI Mun	p10.23	10.66	...	Istel Fund	p12.63	N.L.−	.03
Inc Gwth	p10.59	11.03+	.03	**Ivy Funds:**			
Spec Sit	p14.36	14.96−	.01	Grwth		12.79	N.L.−	.03
ST Bd	p10.04	10.19	...	Inst		99.20	N.L.−	.30
Fidu CapG	15.14	N.L.+	.04	Intl		15.01	N.L.+	.03
Financial Programs:				JP Growth	12.18	13.24−	.05
Dynam	xd6.65	6.65−	.06	JP Income	9.17	9.97	...
Hi Yield	xd7.94	7.94−	.07	**Janus Funds:**			
Industl	3.53	3.53−	.02	Jan Fnd	10.93	N.L.+	.01
Income	7.65	7.65−	.04	Janus Vl	9.69	N.L.+	.01
Select	xd6.42	6.42−	.05	Jans Vn	26.93	N.L.+	.11
Tax Free	13.62	13.62	...	Japan Fd	19.88	N.L.−	.05
Wld Tch	9.81	9.81	...	**John Hancock Funds:**			
FBS Gov	xd6.93	6.93−	.04	Bond Fd	14.68	16.04−	.02
FSP Egy	9.69	9.69	...	Globl Tr	15.09	16.49−	.06
FSP Eur	8.56	8.56−	.01	Growth	13.19	14.42−	.03
FSP Fin	7.10	7.10−	.02	High Inc	p9.30	9.76−	.01
FSP Gld	5.55	5.55+	.02	Fed PI	9.61	10.09	...
FSP HS	12.49	12.49−	.07	Pac Bas	p11.03	11.58−	.02
FSP Ls	10.77	10.77+	.01	Spcl Eqt	4.96	5.42	...
FSP PaB	12.46	12.46+	.06	Tax Ex	p10.25	10.76−	.01
FSP Tc	10.50	10.50−	.07	Gtd Mtg	9.95	10.87	...
FSPUt	xd7.94	7.94−	.07	US Govt	8.86	9.68	...
Fst Eagle	10.96	N.L.+	.03	Kauf Fund	.86	N.L.−	.01
First Investors Fund:				**Kemper Funds:**			
Bond Ap	p10.79	11.63+	.01	Blue Chp	9.12	9.55−	.06
Discovr	p9.05	9.89	...	Cal Tax	7.04	7.37	...
Govt	˄11.01	11.87+		Enh	˄˄	9.32−	.01
		5.8⁵					

Shares of a **no-load fund** are bought directly from the fund at NAV and carry no sales charge.[10] The investment performance of no-load funds does not differ systematically from that of load funds, so it would seem that an investor who buys into a load fund is simply paying the retail price for an equivalent item readily available wholesale.

Figure 3.2 shows part of the listings for mutual funds published every weekday in *The Wall Street Journal*. Load funds are the ones whose offer price exceeds their NAV.

At the end of 1986 there were 1,669 open-end mutual funds with assets of $699.5

---

[10]No-load funds advertise in the financial pages of newspapers and usually have toll-free telephone numbers for prospective investors to call for information and application forms.

TABLE 3.6   Classification of Mutual Funds By Size and Type (as of December 31, 1986)

	Number of Funds	Combined Assets (Thousands)	Total (%)
Size of Fund			
Over $1 billion	167	$ 442,851,500	63.3
$500 million-$1 billion	159	111,655,000	16.0
$300 million-$500 million	123	47,411,400	6.7
$100 million-$300 million	369	68,954,600	9.8
$50 million-$100 million	235	17,195,300	2.5
$10 million-$50 million	380	10,330,700	1.5
$1 million-$10 million	206	1,046,500	0.2
Under $1 million	30	16,000	0.0
	1,669	$ 699,461,000	100.0
Type of Fund			
Common Stock:			
Maximum capital gain	99	$ 31,842,200	4.6
Growth	268	44,826,600	6.4
Growth and income	134	50,970,000	7.3
Specialized:			
Canadian and international	44	9,182,800	1.3
Gold and precious metals	18	1,177,900	0.2
Industry	49	3,803,400	0.5
Government securities	113	118,589,100	16.9
Tax-exempt bond funds	270	80,628,000	11.5
Technology	5	283,100	0.0
Other	13	2,852,900	0.4
Balanced	26	5,290,000	0.8
Income	199	61,053,300	8.7
Bond and preferred stock	45	14,413,700	2.1
Money market	280	217,569,600	31.1
Tax-free money markets	106	56,978,400	8.2
	1,669	$ 699,461,000	100.0

From *Investment Companies 1987*, Wiesenberger Investment Companies Services.

billion. Of these, 386 were money market funds (including tax-free money market funds) with assets of $274.5 billion. Table 3.6 gives a breakdown of the number of mutual funds and their assets by size and type of fund at the end of 1986.

Management Companies and Mutual Fund Investment Policies

Management companies are firms that manage a family of mutual funds. They typically organize the funds and then collect a management fee for operating them. Some of the most well-known management companies are Fidelity, Dreyfus, and Vanguard. Each offers an array of open-end mutual funds with different investment

FIGURE 3.3

The Fidelity Group of mutual funds.

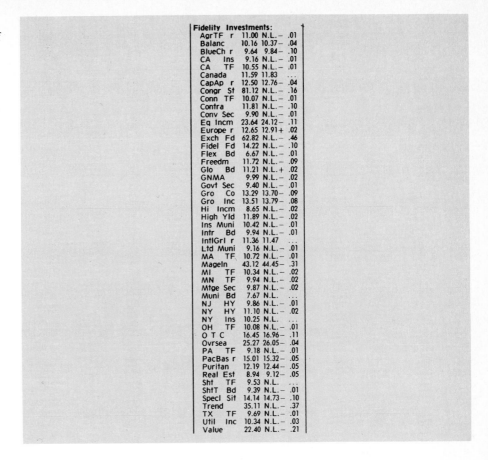

Fidelity Investments:			
AgrTF r	11.00	N.L.−	.01
Balanc	10.16	10.37−	.04
BlueCh r	9.64	9.84−	.10
CA Ins	9.16	N.L.−	.01
CA TF	10.55	N.L.−	.01
Canada	11.59	11.83	
CapAp r	12.50	12.76−	.04
Congr St	81.12	N.L.−	.16
Conn TF	10.07	N.L.−	.01
Contra	11.81	N.L.−	.10
Conv Sec	9.90	N.L.−	.01
Eq Incm	23.64	24.12−	.11
Europe r	12.65	12.91+	.02
Exch Fd	62.82	N.L.−	.46
Fidel Fd	14.22	N.L.−	.10
Flex Bd	6.67	N.L.−	.01
Freedm	11.72	N.L.−	.09
Glo Bd	11.21	N.L.+	.02
GNMA	9.99	N.L.−	.02
Govt Sec	9.40	N.L.−	.01
Gro Co	13.29	13.70−	.09
Gro Inc	13.51	13.79−	.08
Hi Incm	8.65	N.L.−	.02
High Yld	11.89	N.L.−	.02
Ins Muni	10.42	N.L.−	.01
Intr Bd	9.94	N.L.−	.01
IntlGrl r	11.36	11.47	
Ltd Muni	9.16	N.L.−	.01
MA TF	10.72	N.L.−	.01
Mageln	43.12	44.45−	.31
MI TF	10.34	N.L.−	.02
MN TF	9.94	N.L.−	.02
Mtge Sec	9.87	N.L.−	.02
Muni Bd	7.67	N.L.	
NJ HY	9.86	N.L.−	.01
NY HY	11.10	N.L.−	.02
NY Ins	10.25	N.L.	
OH TF	10.08	N.L.−	.01
O T C	16.45	16.96−	.11
Ovrsea	25.27	26.05−	.04
PA TF	9.18	N.L.−	.01
PacBas r	15.01	15.32−	.05
Puritan	12.19	12.44−	.05
Real Est	8.94	9.12−	.05
Sht TF	9.53	N.L.	
ShtT Bd	9.39	N.L.−	.01
Specl Sit	14.14	14.73−	.10
Trend	35.11	N.L.−	.37
TX TF	9.69	N.L.−	.01
Util Inc	10.34	N.L.−	.03
Value	22.40	N.L.−	.21

policies. Table 3.7 lists the 12 largest mutual fund families and discusses some of their features.

Figure 3.3 gives a listing of the funds offered by the Fidelity Group. The name of each fund often describes its investment policy. Fidelity Massachusetts Tax-Free Bond Fund (MA TF), for example, invests exclusively in bonds that are tax-exempt in the Commonwealth of Massachusetts. Some funds have promotional names like the High Income Fund, which invests exclusively in "junk" (speculative grade) bonds.

The names of common stock funds often give little or no clue as to their investment policies. An example is Fidelity's Puritan Fund. Wiesenberger's manual classifies common stock funds as having the following objectives:

1. Maximum capital gain
2. Growth
3. Growth and income

"arranged in descending order of emphasis on capital appreciation and, consequently,

TABLE 3.7   The Major Mutual Fund Families

Family	Total Net Assets ($ Billions)*	Number of Funds*	Range of Up-Front or Deferred Sales Charges (%)	Basic Switching Limits or Charges‡	Comments
American Funds Group	$16.5	19	4.75 to 8.5	None	Vaunted 60-person research staff deserves much of the credit for strong overall family performance.
Dean Witter	20.0	14	4 to 5.5	None	Highly sales-driven group: last year 7,500 brokers hawked $1.2 billion in bond funds in 22 days.
Dreyfus Group	14.0	36	0 to 4.5	None	Chairman Howard Stein's launch of six risky (but top-gaining) strategic funds revitalized group.
Fidelity Investments	35.7	89	0 to 3.0†	4 switches a year	Incentive plan can boost fund managers' pay as much as 50% for market-whipping performance.
Franklin Group	30.0	42	4.0	$5 per switch	Early marketers of triple-tax-free muni funds; beware of 2.5% to 4% load on reinvested dividends.
Kemper	17.4	19	4.5 to 8.5	2 switches a month	High expense ratios (2% on average) cripple returns on popular, broker-sold Investment Portfolio series.

Modified from *Money*, May 1988.
*Excludes money-market, institutional, and closed-end funds. Totals as of 12/31/87.
†Contractual-plan funds carry higher fees.
‡Excludes sector and international funds; rules for some funds may differ.
¶Switch out and return equals one round trip.

in ascending order of the importance placed on current income and relative price stability."[11]

Some funds are designed as candidates for an individual's whole investment portfolio. Wiesenberger's manual classifies such funds, which hold both equities and fixed-income securities, as *income* or *balanced funds*. Income funds "provide as liberal a current income from investments as possible," whereas balanced funds "minimize investment risks so far as this is possible without unduly sacrificing possibilities for long-term growth and current income."

Finally, an **index fund** tries to match the performance of a broad market index. For example, Vanguard Index Trust is a no-load mutual fund that replicates the composition of the Standard & Poor's 500-Stock Index, thus providing a relatively low-cost way for small investors to pursue a passive common stock investment strategy.

---

[11]*Investment Companies 1987*, Wiesenberger Investment Companies Services.

Family	Total Net Assets ($ Billions)*	Number of Funds*	Range of Up-Front or Deferred Sales Charges (%)	Basic Switching Limits or Charges‡	Comments
Merrill Lynch	23.0	27	0 to 6.5	2 switches a month	Standout growth-and-income managers generally follow relatively low-risk, value-oriented approach.
Putnam	29.7	30	4.75 to 8.5	$5 per switch	Excellent research, superior stock and muni bond fund performance, but, oh, those 8.5% loads.
Scudder	11.1	30	None	3 round trips per year¶	First big group to offer international funds (1953); Japan Fund, up 233%, among top 3-year gainers.
T. Rowe Price	8.3	20	None	2 switches per 120 days	First-rate service but middling overall performance; exceptions: international stock and bond funds.
Twentieth Century Investors	4.5	10	0 to 0.5	1 switch a month	Fee on small stock funds compensates existing shareholders with 0.5% of new investments or withdrawals.
Vanguard Group	18.4	38	None	2 switches a year	Lowest expense ratios in the business (average: 0.4%) help bond and money-market fund returns.

(The Fidelity Group does not offer an index fund.)

When choosing a mutual fund, an individual investor should consider not only the fund's stated investment policy, but also its management fees and other expenses. Comparative data on virtually all important aspects of mutual funds are available in the annual volumes prepared by Wiesenberger Investment Companies Services, which can be found in most academic libraries.

Unit Investment Trusts

Unit investment trusts are pools of money invested in a portfolio that, in contrast to mutual funds, is fixed for the life of the fund. To form a unit trust, a sponsor, typically a brokerage firm, buys a set of securities and sells shares called *redeemable trust certificates* to investors at a premium above NAV. All income and repayments of principal are paid out by the fund's trustee (a bank or trust company) to the shareholders. Most unit trusts hold fixed-income securities and expire at their maturity.

There is no active management of a unit trust by definition, because the portfolio composition is fixed.

Commingled Funds

Commingled funds are investment pools managed by banks and insurance companies for trust or retirement accounts that are too small to warrant managing on a separate basis. A commingled fund is similar in form to an open-end mutual fund. Instead of shares, though, the fund offers units that are bought and sold at net asset value. A bank or insurance company may offer an array of different commingled funds for trust or retirement accounts to choose from, for example, a money market fund, a bond fund, and a common stock fund.

Real Estate Investment Trusts (REITs)

A REIT is similar to a closed-end mutual fund. REITs invest in real estate or loans secured by real estate. Besides issuing shares, they raise capital by borrowing from banks and issuing bonds and mortgages. Most of them are highly leveraged (debt-financed) with a typical debt ratio of 70%.

There are two principal kinds of REITs. *Equity trusts* invest in real estate directly, whereas *mortgage trusts* invest primarily in mortgages and construction loans. REITs generally are established by banks, insurance companies, or mortgage companies, which then serve as investment managers to earn a fee.

REITs are exempt from taxes as long as at least 95% of their taxable income is distributed to shareholders. For shareholders, however, the dividends are taxable as personal income.

Summary

1. Firms issue securities to raise the capital necessary to finance their investments. Investment bankers market these securities to the public on the primary market. Investment bankers generally act as underwriters who purchase the securities from the firm and resell them to the public at a markup. Before the securities may be sold to the public, the firm must publish an SEC-approved prospectus that provides information on the firm's prospects.

2. Issued securities are traded on the secondary market, that is, on organized stock exchanges. Securities also trade on the over-the-counter market and, for large traders, through direct negotiation. Only members of exchanges may trade on the exchange. Brokerage firms holding seats on the exchange sell their services to individuals, charging commissions for executing trades on their behalf. The NYSE and, to a lesser extent, the Amex have fairly strict listing requirements. Regional exchanges provide listing opportunities for local firms who do not meet the requirements of the national exchanges.

3. Trading of common stocks in exchanges takes place through specialists. Specialists act to maintain an orderly market in the shares of one or more firms, maintaining "books" of limit-buy and limit-sell orders and matching trades at mutually acceptable prices. Specialists also will accept market orders by selling from or buying for their own inventory of stocks when an imbalance of buy and sell orders exists.

4. The over-the-counter market is not a formal exchange but an informal network of brokers and dealers who negotiate sales of securities. The NASDAQ system provides on-line computer quotes offered by dealers in the stock. When an individual wishes to purchase or sell a share, the broker can search the listing of offered bid and asked prices, call the dealer who has the best quote, and execute the trade.

5. Block transactions are a fairly recent, but fast-growing, segment of the securities market, which currently accounts for about half of trading volume. These trades often are too large to be handled readily by specialists, and thus block houses have developed that specialize in these transactions, identifying potential trading partners for their clients.

6. Buying on margin means borrowing money from a broker in order to buy more securities. By buying securities on margin, an investor magnifies both the upside potential and the downside risk. If the equity in a margin account falls below the required maintenance level, the investor will get a margin call from the broker.

7. Short selling is the practice of selling securities that the seller does not own. The short seller borrows the securities sold through a broker and may be required to cover the short position at any time on demand. The cash proceeds of a short sale are always kept in escrow by the broker, and the broker usually requires that the short seller deposit additional cash or securities to serve as margin (collateral) for the short sale.

8. Securities trading is regulated by the Securities and Exchange Commission, as well as by self-regulation of the exchanges. Many of the important regulations have to do with full disclosure of relevant information concerning the securities in question. Insider trading rules also prohibit traders from attempting to profit from inside information.

9. In addition to providing the basic services of executing buy and sell orders, holding securities for safekeeping, making margin loans, and facilitating short sales, full-service brokers offer investors information, advice, and even investment decisions. Discount brokers offer only the basic brokerage services but usually charge less.

10. Total trading costs consist of commissions, the dealer's bid-asked spread, and price concessions. These costs can represent as much as 30% of the value of the securities traded.

11. As an alternative to investing in securities through a broker, many individuals invest in mutual funds and other investment companies. Mutual funds free the individual from many of the administrative burdens of owning individual securities and offer the prospect of superior investment results. Mutual funds are classified according to whether they are open-end or closed-end, load or no-load, and by the type of securities in which they invest. REITs are specialized investment companies that invest in real estate and loans secured by real estate.

Key Terms

Primary market

Secondary market

Underwriting

Prospectus

Stock exchanges

Over-the-counter market

NASDAQ

Bid price

Asked price

Third market

Fourth market

Specialist

Block transactions

Dealer market

Margin

Short sale

Inside information

Bid-asked spread

Closed-end fund

Open-end fund

Load fund

No-load fund

Index fund

Selected Readings

A good treatment of investment banking is:
Smith, Clifford W., "Investment Banking and the Capital Acquisition Process," *Journal of Financial Economics, 15,* January-February 1986.

An overview of securities markets is provided in:
Garbade, Kenneth D., *Securities Markets,* New York: McGraw-Hill, 1982.

The specialist system is examined in:
Stoll, Hans R., "The Stock Exchange Specialist System: An Economic Analysis," *Monograph Series in Finance and Economics,* Graduate School of Business Administration, New York University, 1985.

An examination of market functioning during the October 1987 crash is:
The Brady Commission Report, or formally, the *Report of the Presidential Task Force on Market Mechanisms,* Washington, D.C.: United States Goverment Printing Office, 1988.

The New York Stock Exchange Fact Book, published annually, contains extensive data on exchange trading and is available from the New York Stock Exchange, Eleven Wall Street, New York, N.Y.

Problems

1. FBN, Inc. has just sold 100,000 shares in an initial public offering. The underwriter's explicit fees were $70,000. The offering price for the shares was $50, but immediately upon issue the share price jumped to $53.
   a. What is your best guess as to the total cost to FBN of the equity issue?
   b. Is the entire cost of the underwriting a source of profit to the underwriters?

2. Suppose that you sell short 100 shares of IBM, now selling at $120 per share.
   a. What is your maximum possible loss?
   b. What happens to the maximum loss if you simultaneously place a stop-buy order at $128?

3. An expiring put will be exercised and the stock will be sold if the stock price is below the exercise price. A stop-loss order causes a stock sale when the stock price falls below some limit. Compare and contrast the two strategies of purchasing put options vs. issuing a stop-loss order.

4. Compare call options and stop-buy orders.

5. Do you think it is possible to replace market-making specialists by a fully automated computerized trade-matching system?

6. Consider the following limit-order book of a specialist. The last trade in the stock took place at a price of $50.

Limit-Buy Orders		Limit-Sell Orders	
Price ($)	**Shares**	**Price ($)**	**Shares**
49.75	500	50.25	100
49.50	800	51.50	100
49.25	500	54.75	300
49.00	200	58.25	100
48.50	600		

   a. If a market-buy order for 100 shares comes in, at what price will it be filled?

   b. At what price would the next market-buy order be filled?

   c. If you were the specialist, would you desire to increase or decrease your inventory of this stock?

7. Consider the following data*:

Year	Market Value of Shares Traded on NYSE (Millions)	Price of an NYSE Seat	
		High	**Low**
1960	$ 37,960	$162,000	$135,000
1965	73,200	250,000	190,000
1970	103,063	320,000	130,000
1975	133,819	138,000	55,000
1980	397,670	275,000	175,000
1985	1,023,202	480,000	310,000

   a. What do you conclude about the relationship between trading volume and the price of a seat?

   b. What happened in 1975 to upset this relationship?

8. You are bullish on AT&T stock. The current market price is $50 per share, and you have $5,000 of your own to invest. You borrow an additional $5,000 from your broker at an interest rate of 8% per year and invest $10,000 in the stock.

   a. What will be your rate of return if the price of AT&T stock goes up by 10% during the next year? (Ignore the expected dividend.)

   b. How far does the price of AT&T stock have to fall for you to get a margin call if the maintenance margin is 30%?

9. You are bearish on AT&T stock and decide to sell short 100 shares at the current market price of $50 per share.

   a. How much in cash or securities must you put into your brokerage account if

---

*Data from the New York Stock Exchange *Fact Book,* 1986.

the broker's initial margin requirement is 50% of the value of the short position?

    b. How high can the price of the stock go before you get a margin call if the maintenance margin is 30% of the value of the short position?

10. Call one full-service broker and one discount broker and find out the transaction costs of implementing the following strategies:

    a. Buying 100 shares of IBM now and selling them 6 months from now

    b. Investing an equivalent amount in 6-month at-the-money call options (calls with strike price equal to the stock price) on IBM stock now and selling them 6 months from now

The following questions are from the 1986 Level I CFA examination:

11. If you place a stop-loss order to sell 100 shares of stock at $55 when the current price is $62, how much will you receive for each share if the price drops to $50?

    a. $50

    b. $55

    c. $54⅞

    d. Cannot tell from the information given

12. You wish to sell short 100 shares of XYZ Corporation stock. If the last two transactions were at 34⅛ followed by 34¼, you only can sell short on the next transaction at a price of

    a. 34⅛ or higher

    b. 34¼ or higher

    c. 34¼ or lower

    d. 34⅛ or lower

13. Specialists on the New York Stock Exchange do all of the following *except:*

    a. Act as dealers for their own accounts

    b. Execute limit orders

    c. Help provide liquidity to the marketplace

    d. Act as odd-lot dealers

CHAPTER 4

Concepts and Issues

This chapter introduces some key concepts and issues that are central to informed investment decision-making. The material presented is basic to the development of the theory in subsequent parts of the book. We start with the determination of real and nominal interest rates and risk premiums on risky securities. Then we review the historical record of rates of return on bills, bonds, and stocks, as well as the relationship between bill rates and inflation. We also distinguish between real and nominal risk. We conclude by introducing the law of one price, which states that securities or combinations of securities will be priced so that no investor can make riskless arbitrage profits by trading them.

4.1 Determinants of the Level of Interest Rates

The Equilibrium Real Rate of Interest

Perhaps the single most important factor in investment decision-making is the level of interest rates. Decisions depend to a great extent on what investors think interest rates will do.

For example, suppose that you have $10,000 in a savings account. The bank pays you a variable interest rate tied to some short-term reference rate such as the 30-day Treasury bill rate. You have the option of moving some or all of your money into a longer-term certificate of deposit that offers a fixed rate over the term of the deposit.

Your decision depends critically on your outlook for interest rates. If you think rates will fall, you will want to lock in the current higher rates by investing in a relatively long-term CD. If, on the other hand, you expect rates to rise, you will want to postpone committing any funds to long-term CDs.

Forecasting interest rates is one of the most notoriously difficult parts of applied macroeconomics. Nonetheless, we do have a good understanding of the following fundamental factors that determine the level of interest rates:

1. The supply of funds from savers, primarily households

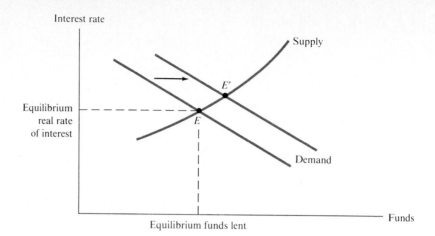

2. The demand from businesses for funds to be used to finance physical investments in plant, equipment, and inventories (real assets or capital formation)
3. The government's net supply and/or demand for funds as modified by actions of the monetary authority

These three basic factors determine the level of the **real interest rate**, that is, the interest rate in a no-inflation world. The level of nominal interest rates, which is the rate we actually observe, is the real rate plus the expected rate of inflation. Thus a fourth factor affecting the interest rate is the expected rate of inflation.

Although there are many different interest rates economy-wide (as many indeed as there are different types of securities), economists frequently talk as if there were a single representative rate. We can use this abstraction to gain some insight into the determination of the real rate of interest if we consider the supply and demand curves for funds.

Figure 4.1 shows a downward sloping demand curve and an upward sloping supply curve. On the horizontal axis we measure the quantity of funds, and on the vertical axis we measure the real rate of interest.

The supply curve slopes up from left to right because the higher the real interest rate, the greater the supply of household savings. The assumption is that at higher real interest rates households will choose to postpone some current consumption and set aside or invest more of their disposable income for future use.[1]

The demand curve slopes down from left to right because the lower the real interest rate, the more businesses will want to invest in physical capital. Assuming that businesses rank projects by the expected real return on invested capital, the lower the real interest rate on the funds needed to finance those projects, the more of them firms will undertake.

---

[1]There is a considerable amount of controversy among experts on the issue of whether household saving does in fact go up in response to an increase in the real interest rate. See, for example, Carlino, Gerald, "Interest Rate Effects and Intertemporal Consumption," *Journal of Monetary Economics*, March 1982.

Equilibrium is at the point of intersection of the supply and demand curves, point *E* in Figure 4.1.

The government can shift these supply and demand curves either to the right or to the left through its fiscal and monetary policies. For example, consider an increase in the government's budget deficit. This increases the government's borrowing demand and shifts the demand curve to the right up to the dashed line, which causes the equilibrium real interest rate to rise to point *E'*. Hence a revised forecast indicating higher than expected government borrowing might increase expected future interest rates. The monetary authority may offset such a rise through an expansionary monetary policy, which will shift the supply to the right.

Thus the fundamental determinants of the real interest rate are the propensity of households to save and the expected productivity (or profitability) of investment in physical capital. However, the real rate can be affected as well by government fiscal and monetary policies.

The Equilibrium Nominal Rate of Interest

Until recently we could not directly observe what the risk-free real rate of interest in the U.S. economy was. However, since January 1988 the Franklin Savings and Loan Association of Ottawa, Kansas has been issuing certificates of deposit insured by the Federal Savings and Loan Insurance Corporation that offer a guaranteed real rate of interest for maturities ranging from 1 to 10 years.[2] The actual nominal rate of interest credited to your account is the promised real rate plus the rate of inflation as measured by the proportional increase in the Consumer Price Index.

Conventional certificates of deposit offer a guaranteed **nominal rate of interest**. Thus you can only infer what the expected real rate is by subtracting your expectation of what the rate of inflation will be. For example, if the interest rate on 1-year conventional CDs is 8%, we can only infer what the expected real rate is by subtracting an estimate of the expected rate of inflation over the next year. Thus, if we estimate expected inflation to be 5%, the expected real rate would be 3%.

Actually, the exact relationship between the real and nominal interest rates on a conventional CD is given by

$$1 + R = (1 + r)/(1 + i)$$

or equivalently,

$$R = (r - i)/(1 + i)$$

where R is the real rate, r is the nominal rate,[3] and i is the rate of inflation. The relationship $R = r - i$ holds exactly only for continuously compounded rates. Otherwise it is only an approximation. See the appendix to this chapter for further details.

---

[2]They are called "Inflation-Plus CDs."
[3]To be more exact, r is the effective annual rate of interest on the CD.

TABLE 4.1   Probability Distribution of HPR on the Stock Market

State of the Economy	Probability	Ending Price	HPR
Boom	.25	$140	44%
Normal growth	.50	110	14%
Recession	.25	80	−16%

4.2   *Risk and Risk Premiums*

Risk means uncertainty about future rates of return. We quantify that uncertainty using probability distributions.

For example, suppose you are considering investing some of your money, which is all currently invested in a bank account, in a stock market index fund. The price of a share in the fund is currently $100, and your *time horizon* is 1 year. You expect the cash dividend during the year to be $4, and therefore your expected *dividend yield* is 4%.

Your total **holding period return** (HPR) will depend on the price you expect to prevail 1 year from now. Suppose your best guess is that it will be $110 per share. Then your *capital gain* will be $10, and your HPR will be 14%. The definition of the holding period return is

$$\text{HPR} = \frac{\text{Ending price of a share} - \text{Beginning price} + \text{Cash dividend}}{\text{Beginning price}}$$

In our case we have

$$\text{HPR} = \frac{\$110 - \$100 + \$4}{\$100}$$
$$= .14$$
$$= 14\%$$

However, there is considerable uncertainty about the price of a share a year from now and therefore about the HPR. Let us assume that we can quantify our beliefs about the state of the economy and the stock market in terms of three possible scenarios with the probabilities presented in Table 4.1.

How can we evaluate this probability distribution? Throughout this book we will characterize probability distributions of rates of return in terms of their expected or mean return, $E(r)$, and their standard deviation, σ. The expected rate of return is a probability-weighted average of the rates of return in all scenarios. Calling $Pr(s)$ the probability of each scenario and $r(s)$ the HPR in each scenario, where scenarios are labeled, or "indexed" by the variable s, we may write the expected return as

$$E(r) = \Sigma Pr(s)r(s) \tag{4.1}$$

Applying this formula to Table 4.1, we find that the expected rate of return on the index fund is

$$E(r) = .25 \times 44\% + .5 \times 14\% + .25 \times -16\%$$
$$= 14\%$$

The standard deviation of the rate of return, σ, is a measure of risk. It is defined as the square root of the variance, which in turn is defined as the expected value of the squared deviations from the expected return. Symbolically,

$$\sigma^2 = \Sigma Pr(s)[r(s) - E(r)]^2 \qquad (4.2)$$

Therefore in our example,

$$\sigma^2 = .25 \times (44 - 14)^2 + .5 \times (14 - 14)^2 + .25 \times (-16 - 14)^2$$
$$= 450$$

and

$$\sigma = 21\%$$

Clearly, what troubles us as potential investors in the index fund is the downside risk of a -16% rate of return, not the upside potential of a 44% rate of return. The standard deviation of the rate of return does not distinguish between these two; it treats both as deviations from the mean. As long as the probability distribution is more or less symmetric about the mean, σ is an adequate measure of risk. In the special case where we can assume that the probability distribution is normal—that is, the well-known bell-shaped curve—$E(r)$ and σ are perfectly adequate to completely characterize the distribution.

Now getting back to our example, how much if anything should we invest in the index fund? First, we must ask how much of a reward there is for our taking on risk by investing some of our money in stocks.

We measure the reward as the difference between the expected HPR on the index fund and the **risk-free rate** we can earn by leaving our money in the bank. We call this difference the **risk premium** on common stocks. If the risk-free rate in our example is 6% per year, then the risk premium on stocks is 8% per year.

The degree to which we are willing to commit funds to stocks depends on our *risk aversion*. Finance theorists generally assume that investors are risk-averse in the sense that, if the risk premium were zero, they would not be willing to invest any money at all in stocks. In theory then, there must always be a positive risk premium on stocks to induce risk-averse investors to hold the existing supply.

Although this simple scenario analysis serves to illustrate the concepts behind the quantification of risk and return, the next question is how can we get a more realistic estimate of $E(r)$ and σ for common stocks and other types of securities?

4.3   *The Historical Record*

Bills, Bonds, and Stocks: 1926 to 1986

The record of past rates of return is one possible source of information about risk premiums and standard deviations. We can estimate the historical risk premium by

TABLE 4.2   Rates of Return, 1926 to 1986

Date	Stocks	Long-Term Government Bonds	Treasury Bills	Inflation (CPI)
1926	0.1162	0.0777	0.0327	−0.0149
1927	0.3749	0.0893	0.0312	−0.0208
1928	0.4361	0.001	0.0324	−0.0097
1929	−0.0842	0.0342	0.0475	0.0019
1930	−0.249	0.0466	0.0241	−0.0603
1931	−0.4334	−0.0531	0.0107	−0.0952
1932	−0.0819	0.1684	0.0096	−0.103
1933	0.5399	−0.0008	0.003	0.0051
1934	−0.0144	0.1002	0.0016	0.0203
1935	0.4767	0.0498	0.0017	0.0299
1936	0.3392	0.0751	0.0018	0.0121
1937	−0.3503	0.0023	0.0031	0.031
1938	0.3112	0.0553	−0.0002	−0.0278
1939	−0.0041	0.0594	0.0002	−0.0048
1940	−0.0978	0.0609	0	0.0096
1941	−0.1159	0.0093	0.0006	0.0972
1942	0.2034	0.0322	0.0027	0.0929
1943	0.259	0.0208	0.0035	0.0316
1944	0.1975	0.0281	0.0033	0.0211
1945	0.3644	0.1073	0.0033	0.0225
1946	−0.0807	−0.001	0.0035	0.1817
1947	0.0571	−0.0263	0.005	0.0901
1948	0.055	0.034	0.0081	0.0271
1949	0.1879	0.0645	0.011	−0.018
1950	0.3171	0.0006	0.012	0.0579
1951	0.2402	−0.0394	0.0149	0.0587
1952	0.1837	0.0116	0.0166	0.0088
1953	−0.0099	0.0363	0.0182	0.0063
1954	0.5262	0.0719	0.0086	−0.005
1955	0.3156	−0.013	0.0157	0.0037
1956	0.0656	−0.0559	0.0246	0.0286
1957	−0.1078	0.0745	0.0314	0.0302
1958	0.4336	−0.061	0.0154	0.0176

Data from the Center for Research of Security Prices, University of Chicago, Chicago, Ill.

taking an average of the past differences between the HPRs on the asset type and the risk-free rate. Table 4.2 presents the annual HPRs on three asset classes for the period 1926 to 1986.

The third column shows the 1-year HPR on a policy of "rolling-over" 30-day Treasury bills as they mature. Because this rate changes from month to month, it is risk-free only for a 30-day holding period. The second column presents the annual HPR an investor would have earned by investing in U.S. Treasury bonds with 20-year maturities. The first column illustrates the HPR on the Standard & Poor's Composite Index of common stocks, which is a value-weighted stock portfolio of 500 of

Date	Stocks	Long-Term Government Bonds	Treasury Bills	Inflation (CPI)
1959	0.1196	−0.0226	0.0295	0.015
1960	−0.0047	0.1378	0.0266	0.0148
1961	0.2689	0.0097	0.0213	0.0067
1962	−0.0873	0.0689	0.0273	0.0122
1963	0.228	0.0121	0.0312	0.0165
1964	0.1648	0.0351	0.0354	0.0119
1965	0.1245	0.0071	0.0393	0.0192
1966	−0.1006	0.0365	0.0476	0.0335
1967	0.2398	−0.0919	0.0421	0.0304
1968	0.1106	−0.0026	0.0521	0.0472
1969	−0.085	−0.0508	0.0658	0.0611
1970	0.0401	0.121	0.0653	0.0549
1971	0.1431	0.1323	0.0439	0.0336
1972	0.1898	0.0568	0.0384	0.0341
1973	−0.1466	−0.0111	0.0693	0.088
1974	−0.2647	0.0435	0.08	0.122
1975	0.372	0.0919	0.058	0.0701
1976	0.2384	0.1675	0.0508	0.0481
1977	−0.0718	−0.0067	0.0512	0.0677
1978	0.0656	−0.0116	0.0718	0.0903
1979	0.1844	−0.0122	0.1038	0.1331
1980	0.3242	−0.0395	0.1124	0.124
1981	−0.0491	0.0185	0.1471	0.0894
1982	0.2141	0.4035	0.1054	0.0387
1983	0.2251	0.0068	0.088	0.038
1984	0.0627	0.1543	0.0985	0.0395
1985	0.3216	0.3097	0.0772	0.0377
1986	0.1847	0.2444	0.0616	0.0113
Average	0.1212	0.0470	0.0351	0.0314
Standard deviation	0.2104	0.0848	0.0334	0.0480
Minimum	−0.4334	−0.0919	−0.0002	−0.1030
Maximum	0.5399	0.4035	0.1471	0.1817

largest corporations in the United States. (We discussed the S&P 500 stock index in Chapter 2.) Finally, the last column gives the annual inflation rate as measured by the rate of change in the consumer price index.

At the bottom of each column are four descriptive statistics. The first is the arithmetic mean or average HPR. For bills it is 3.51%, for bonds it is 4.70%, and for common stock it is 12.12%. These numbers imply an average risk premium of 1.19% per year on bonds and 8.61% on stocks (the average HPR less the risk-free rate of 3.51%).

The second statistic reported at the bottom of Table 4.2 is the standard deviation.

FIGURE 4.2

Rates of return on bills, bonds, and stocks, 1926 to 1986.

(Data from Ibbotson, Roger, and Sinquefield, Rex A., *Stocks, Bonds, Bills and Inflation: The Past and the Future,* Charlottesville, Va.: Financial Analysts Research Foundation, 1987.)

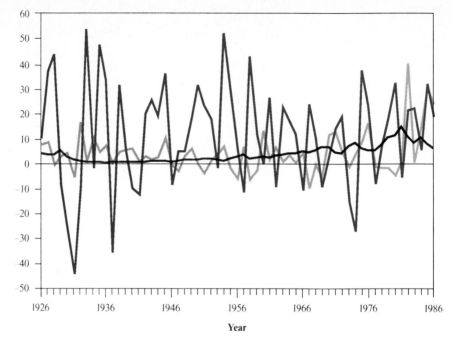

FIGURE 4.3

The normal distribution.

(From Ross, Stephen A., and Westerfield, Randolph W., *Corporate Finance,* St. Louis: The C.V. Mosby Co., 1988.)

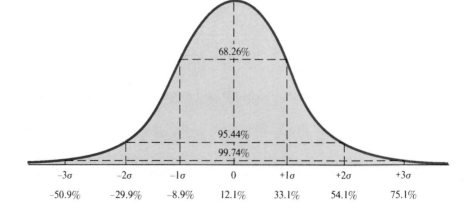

The higher the standard deviation, the higher the variability of the HPR.

This standard deviation is based on historical data rather than forecasts of *future* scenarios as in equation 4.2. The formula for historical variance, however, is similar to equation 4.2. It is as follows:

$$\sigma^2 = \frac{n}{n-1} \sum_{t=1}^{n} \frac{(r_t - \bar{r})^2}{n} \tag{4.3}$$

Here, each year's outcome is taken as a possible scenario.[4] Deviations are simply taken from the historical average, $\bar{r}$, instead of the expected value $E(r)$. Each historical outcome is taken as equally likely, and given a "probability" of $1/n$.

Figure 4.2 gives a graphic representation of the relative variabilities of the annual HPR on the three different asset classes. We have plotted the three time series on the same set of axes, each in a different manner. Clearly, the annual HPR on stocks is the most variable series. The standard deviation of stock returns has been 21%, compared to 8.5% for bonds and 3.3% for bills. Here is evidence of the risk-return trade-off that characterizes security markets: the markets with the highest average returns also are the most volatile.

The other summary measures at the bottom of Table 4.2 show the highest and lowest annual HPR (the range) for each asset over the 60-year period. The size of this range is another possible measure of the relative riskiness of each asset class. It too confirms the ranking of stocks as the riskiest and bills as the least risky of the three asset classes.

An all-stock portfolio with a standard deviation of 21% would constitute a very volatile investment. For example, if stock returns are normally distributed with that standard deviation and an expected rate of return of 12.1% (the historical average), then in roughly 1 year out of 3, returns will be less than −8.9% (12.1% − 21%) or greater than 33.1% (12.1% + 21%).

Figure 4.3 is a graph of the normal curve with a mean of 12.1% and a standard deviation of 21%. The graph shows the theoretical probability of rates of return within various ranges given these parameters.

Figure 4.4 presents another view of the historical data, the actual frequency distribution of returns on various asset classes over the period 1926 to 1986. Notice the greater range of stock returns relative to bill or bond returns.

We should stress that variability of HPR in the past can be an unreliable guide to risk, at least in the case of the risk-free asset. For an investor with a holding period of 1 year, for example, a 1-year T-bill is risk free with a σ of zero, despite the fact that the standard deviation of the 1-year T-bill rate estimated from historical data is not zero.

---

[4]We multiply by $n/(n-1)$ in equation 4.3 to eliminate statistical bias in the estimate of variance.

FIGURE 4.4

Frequency distributions of the annual HPR on five asset classes.

(Modified from Ibbotson, Roger, and Sinquefeld, Rex A., *Stocks, Bonds, Bills and Inflation* [SBBI]. Updated in *SBBI 1987 Yearbook*. Ibbotson Associates, Chicago.)

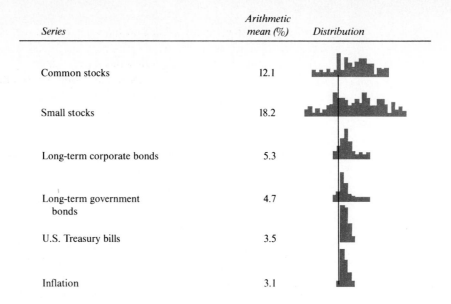

Series	Arithmetic mean (%)	Distribution
Common stocks	12.1	
Small stocks	18.2	
Long-term corporate bonds	5.3	
Long-term government bonds	4.7	
U.S. Treasury bills	3.5	
Inflation	3.1	

FIGURE 4.5

Bills and inflation, 1953 to 1986. Black, T-bills; blue, inflation.

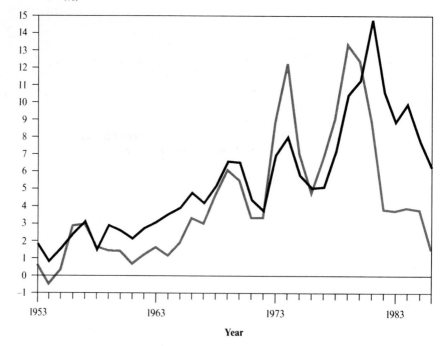

Rate of return (%)

Year

A very important empirical relationship is the connection between inflati[...] rate of return on T-bills. This is apparent in Figure 4.5, which plots both of the time series on the same set of axes. Both series tend to move together, which is consistent with our previous statement that expected inflation is a significant force determining the nominal rate of interest.

In the case of a holding period of 30 days, the difference between actual and expected inflation is not large. The 30-day bill rate will adjust rapidly to changes in expected inflation induced by observed changes in actual inflation. It is not surprising that we see nominal rates on bills move roughly in tandem with inflation over time.

Concept Check

Question 1.

a. Suppose the real interest rate is 3% per year and the expected inflation rate is 8%. What is the nominal interest rate?

b. Suppose the expected inflation rate rises to 10%, but the real rate is unchanged. What happens to the nominal interest rate?

4.4 Real Risk vs. Nominal Risk

The distinction between the real and the nominal rate of interest is crucial in making investment choices, assuming of course that investors have any interest in the future purchasing power of their wealth. Consider the way that a U.S. Treasury bond that offers a "risk-free" nominal rate of return is not truly a risk-free investment—it does not guarantee the future purchasing power of its cash flow.

An example might be a bond that pays $1,000 20 years from now but nothing in the interim. Many people have seen such a zero coupon bond as a convenient way for individuals to lock in attractive, risk-free long-term interest rates (particularly in IRA or Keogh accounts).

However, see Table 4.3 for what the value of the $1,000 will be in 20 years in terms of today's purchasing power.

If we assume that the purchase price of the bond is $103.67, giving a nominal rate of return of 12% per year (since $103.67 \times 1.12^{20} = 1000$), then the real annualized HPR can be computed for each inflation rate.

A simple comparison is at the rate of inflation of 12% per year. At that rate, Table 4.3 shows that the purchasing power of the $1,000 to be received in 20 years would be $103.67, just what was paid initially for the bond. The real HPR in these circumstances is zero: when the rate of inflation equals the nominal rate of interest, the price of goods increases as fast as the money accumulated from the investment, and there is no growth in purchasing power.

At an inflation rate of only 4% per year, however, the purchasing power of $1,000 will be $456.39 in terms of today's prices; that is, the investment of $103.67 grows

TABLE 4.3   Purchasing Power of $1,000 20 Years From Now and 20-Year Real Annualized HPR

Assumed Annual Rate of Inflation	Number of Dollars Required 20 Years From Now to Buy What $1 Buys Today	Purchasing Power of $1,000 to Be Received in 20 Years	Annualized Real HPR
4%	$2.19	$456.39	7.69%
6%	$3.21	$311.80	5.66%
8%	$4.66	$214.55	3.70%
10%	$6.73	$148.64	1.82%
12%	$9.65	$103.67	0

Purchase price of bond is $103.67.
Nominal 20-year annualized HPR is 12% per year.
Purchasing power = $1,000/(1 + inflation rate)^{20}.
Real HPR, R, is computed from the following relationship:

$$R = (1 + r)/(1 + i) - 1$$
$$= 1.12/(1 + i) - 1$$

to a real value of $456.39, for a real 20-year annualized HPR of 7.69% per year.

Even professional economic forecasters admit that their inflation forecasts are hardly certain even for the next year, not to mention the next 20 years. When we look at an asset from the perspective of its future purchasing power, we realize that an asset that is risk free in nominal terms can be very risky in real terms.

Again, looking at Table 4.3, we see that an investor expecting an inflation rate of 8% per year anticipates a real annualized HPR of 3.70%. If the actual rate of inflation turns out to be 10% per year, the resulting real HPR is only 1.82% per year. These differences show the important distinction between expected and actual inflation rates.

Concept Check

Question 2. Suppose the rate of inflation turns out to be 13% per year. What will be the real annualized 20-year HPR on the nominally risk-free bond?

4.5   Risk in a Portfolio Context

The riskiness of a security should never be judged in isolation from an investor's entire portfolio of assets. Sometimes, adding a seemingly risky asset to a portfolio actually reduces the risk of the portfolio as a whole. Investing in an asset that reduces the overall risk of a portfolio is called **hedging.**

The most direct example of hedging is an insurance contract, which is a legal arrangement transferring a specific risk from the insured to the insurer for a specified

Investing: What to Buy When?

In making broad-scale investment decisions, investors may want to know how various types of investments have performed during booms, recessions, high inflation, and low inflation. The table shows how 10 asset categories performed during representative years since World War II. But history rarely repeats itself, so historical performance is only a rough guide to the future.

Investment	Average Annual Return on Investment*			
	Recession	Boom	High Inflation	Low Inflation
Bonds (long-term government)	17%	4%	−1%	8%
Commodity Index	1	−6	15	−5
Diamonds (1-carat investment grade)	−4	8	79	15
Gold† (bullion)	−8	−9	105	19
Private home	4	6	6	5
Real estate‡ (commercial)	9	13	18	6
Silver (bullion)	3	−6	94	4
Stocks (blue chip)	14	7	−3	21
Stocks (small growth-company)	17	14	7	12
Treasury bills (3-month)	6	5	7	3

Modified from *The Wall Street Journal*, November 13, 1987. Reprinted by permission of *The Wall Street Journal*. © Dow Jones & Company, Inc. 1987. All rights reserved.

*In most cases, figures are computed as follows: Recession—average of performance during calendar years 1946, 1975, and 1982; boom—average of 1951, 1965, and 1984; high inflation—average of 1947, 1974, and 1980; low inflation—average of 1955, 1961, and 1986.

†Gold figures are based only on data since 1971 and may be less reliable that others.

‡Commercial real estate figures are based only on data since 1978 and may be less reliable than others.

Sources: Commerce Dept.; Commodity Research Bureau; DeBeers Inc.; Diamond Registry; Dow Jones & Co.; Dun & Bradstreet; Handy & Harman; Ibbotson Associates; Charles Kroll (Diversified Investor's Forecast); Merrill Lynch; National Council of Real Estate Investment Fiduciaries; Frank B. Russell Co.; Shearson Lehman Bros.; T. Rowe Price New Horizons Fund.

cost (the insurance premium). Suppose you own a $100,000 house and have total net worth of $300,000. There is a small distinct possibility that your house will burn to the ground within the coming year. If it does, your net wealth will be reduced by $100,000. If it does not, your wealth remains unchanged (independent of any income from this and other investments, which we shall ignore to simplify the example).

Let us say that your probability assessment of the event "the house will burn to the ground during the coming year" is .002. Your expected loss (.002 × $100,000 = $200) is small in terms of your overall wealth. On the other hand, fire will reduce your wealth by a full one third.

An insurance contract to cover this risk might cost $220, a price that exceeds the expected loss and thereby provides expected profit to the insurer. Consider the payoff to the insurance contract evaluated in isolation as a seemingly risky security.

Not only is the expected profit of the policy negative (−$20), and the expected rate of return negative (−$20/$220 = −9.09%), but the risk also seems to be substantial. The standard deviation of the policy's payoff is identical to that of the uninsured house. You receive either $100,000 (with probability .002) or nothing (with probability .998).

Does this mean that only risk-lovers should purchase insurance? Clearly not. Instead, the example illustrates the fallacy of evaluating the risk of an asset (the insurance contract) in isolation.

Consider the insured house as a portfolio that includes the insurance contract and the house.

Portfolio Component	Value if No Fire	Value if Fire
House	$100,000	0
Insurance contract	0	$100,000

The *portfolio* payoff in the two outcomes is identical, and equal to $100,000, because the house is insured for its precise value, and the insurance pays only when the value of the house goes to zero (in the event of a fire). Thus the portfolio's overall risk has been reduced to zero.

People are concerned about the overall volatility of the value of their portfolios. They do not necessarily dislike volatility in individual components of their portfolios, though. Indeed, most risk-averse persons would invest in the "risky" insurance policy in this example even with its negative expected HPR.

4.6   The Law of One Price and Arbitrage

One of the most fundamental concepts in investments is arbitrage, as you will see again and again throughout this book. **Arbitrage** is the act of buying an asset at one price and simultaneously selling it or its equivalent at a higher price.

If you can buy IBM stock over-the-counter for $128 per share and sell it on the New York Stock Exchange for $128.50, you can make a risk-free arbitrage profit of 50 cents per share. Furthermore, by synchronizing the purchase and sale you might not have to tie up any of your own funds in the transaction. You can use the proceeds from the sale at $128.50 to finance the purchase at $128, and clear the 50 cents without actually investing any of your own money.

Pure arbitrage opportunities of this sort are very rare, because it requires only the participation of a few (maybe only one) arbitrageurs to eliminate the price differential. The increased demand for IBM by arbitrageurs buying on the OTC market would tend to drive the price above $128, and the increased supply of IBM on the NYSE would drive the price down, until the stock would reach a single price in both markets.

This is a somewhat simplified example of arbitrage and the activity of arbitrageurs. In practice there are transaction costs to deal with, and often the arbitrage opportunity involves not one security but combinations of securities. We will see in later chapters that IBM stock can be created synthetically, using IBM options plus T-bills, and arbitrage considerations therefore dictate a pricing relationship that must hold among these securities.

Practitioners and academicians may often disagree about the right way to characterize equilibrium yield and price relationships, but almost everyone would agree that the *law of one price* holds almost all of the time in the securities markets. Stated simply, the law of one price is that equivalent securities or bundles of securities are priced so that risk-free arbitrage is not possible.

Summary

1. The economy's equilibrium level of real interest rates depends on the willingness of households to save, as reflected in the supply curve of funds, and on the expected profitability of business investment in plant, equipment, and inventories, as reflected in the demand curve for funds. It depends also on government fiscal and monetary policy.

2. In the United States investors today can invest in securities offering a risk-free real rate of interest. Their nominal rate of return depends on the actual rate of inflation.

3. The equilibrium expected rate of return on any security is the sum of the risk-free rate and a security-specific risk premium.

4. Investors face a trade-off between risk and expected return. Historical data confirm our intuition that assets with low degrees of risk provide lower returns on average than do those of higher risk.

5. Assets with guaranteed nominal interest rates are risky in real terms because the future inflation rate is uncertain.

6. The riskiness of a security should always be viewed in the context of an investor's total portfolio of assets. Some securities, such as insurance contracts, that would seem quite risky in isolation actually help reduce the risk of an investor's overall portfolio.

7. The law of one price says that two securities or groups of securities with the same payoff structure must sell for the same price. If two identical securities are selling in two markets at different prices it should be profitable to simultaneously buy the security in the low-priced market and sell it in the high-priced market. In the process arbitrageurs, who engage in this activity for a profit, drive up the price in the low-priced market and drive down the price in the high-priced market, eliminating the price differential.

Key Terms

Real interest rate	Risk premium
Nominal rate of interest	Hedging
Holding period return	Arbitrage
Risk-free rate	

Selected Readings

The classic article on the determination of the level of interest rates is:

Fisher, Irving, *The Theory of Interest: As Determined by Impatience to Spend Income and Opportunity to Invest It,* New York: Augustus M. Kelley, Publishers, 1965 (originally published in 1930).

The standard reference for historical returns on a variety of instruments, updated on an ongoing basis, is:

Ibbotson, Roger G., and Sinquefield, Rex A., *Stocks, Bonds, Bills and Inflation: The Past and the Future,* Charlottesville, Va.: Financial Analysts Research Foundation, 1987.

For an in-depth treatment of the distinction between real and nominal risk read:

Bodie, Zvi, "Investment Strategy in an Inflationary Environment," in Friedman, Benjamin M. (editor), *The Changing Roles of Debt and Equity in Financing U.S. Capital Formation,* Chicago: University of Chicago Press, 1982.

Problems

1. You have $5,000 to invest for the next year and are considering the following three alternatives:
   a. A money market fund with an average maturity of 30 days offering a current yield of 6% per year
   b. A 1-year savings deposit at a bank offering an interest rate of 7.5%
   c. A 20-year U.S. Treasury bond offering a yield to maturity of 9% per year
   What role does your forecast of future interest rates play in your decision?

2. Use Figure 4.1 in the text to analyze the effect of the following on the level of real interest rates:
   a. Businesses become more optimistic about future demand for their products and decide to increase their capital spending.
   b. Households are induced to save more because of increased uncertainty about their future Social Security benefits.
   c. The Federal Reserve Board undertakes open-market sales of U.S. Treasury securities to reduce the supply of money.

3. You are considering the choice between investing $50,000 in a conventional 1-year bank CD offering an interest rate of 8% and a 1-year Inflation-Plus CD offering 3% per year plus the rate of inflation.
   a. Which is the safer investment?
   b. Which offers the higher expected return?
   c. If you expect the rate of inflation to be 4% over the next year, which is the better investment? Why?
   d. If we observe a risk-free nominal interest rate of 8% per year and a risk-free real rate of 3%, can we infer that the market's expected rate of inflation is 5% per year?

4. Suppose that you revise your expectations regarding the stock market, which were summarized in Table 4.1 in the text, as follows:

State of the Economy	Probability	Ending Price	HPR
Boom	.3	$140	44%
Normal growth	.4	110	14%
Recession	.3	80	−16%

Use equations 4.1 and 4.2 to compute the mean and standard deviation of the HPR on stocks. Compare your revised parameters with your previous ones.

5. Derive the probability distribution of the 1-year holding period return on a 30-year U.S. Treasury bond with a 9% coupon if it is currently selling at par and the probability distribution of its yield to maturity (YTM) a year from now is as follows:

State of the Economy	Probability	YTM (%)
Boom	.25	12.0
Normal growth	.50	9.0
Recession	.25	7.5

For simplicity assume that the entire 9% coupon is paid at the end of the year rather than every 6 months.

6. Using the historical risk premiums as your guide, if the current risk-free interest rate is 8%, what is your estimate of the expected annual HPR on the S&P 500 stock portfolio?

7. Compute the means and standard deviations of the annual holding period returns listed in Table 4.2 of the text using only the last 30 years, 1957 to 1986. How do they compare with these same statistics computed from data for the period 1926 to 1956? Which do you think are the most relevant statistics to use for projecting into the future?

8. During a period of severe inflation, a bond offered a nominal HPR of 80% per year. The inflation rate was 70% per year.
   a. What was the real HPR on the bond over the year?
   b. Compare this real HPR to the approximation $R = r - i$.

9. You own a house worth $250,000 and intend to insure it fully against fire for the next year. Suppose that the probability of its burning to the ground during the year is .001 and that an insurance policy covering the full value costs $500. Consider the insurance policy as a security.
   a. What is its expected holding period return?
   b. What is the standard deviation of its HPR?
   c. Is the policy a risky asset? Why?

10. You own an export business for which the only source of risk is foreign currency fluctuations. This year your main contract is to ship $1 million worth of goods to West Germany. You have already invested your own money in the goods and signed a contract for the delivery 90 days from now for 2.2 million deutsche-marks (DM). The exchange rate is currently 2 DM to the U.S. dollar.

Suppose the 90 day risk-free interest rate in the United States is now 6% per year and in West Germany it is 8% per year (for loans denominated in DM).

a. If you can borrow and lend at the risk-free interest rates in each country, how could you completely eliminate the risk of fluctuations in the dollar value of your 2.2 million DM to be received 90 days from now?

b. If you can sell the DM in the forward market, what is the minimum price you would require?

c. What general conclusion can you draw from this about the relationship between the interest rates in both countries and the forward price of the currencies?

11. You are faced with the probability distribution of the holding period return on the stock market index fund given in Table 4.1 of the text. Suppose the price of a put option on a share of the index fund with an exercise price of $110 and a maturity of 1 year is $12.

a. What is the probability distribution of the HPR on the put option?

b. What is the probability distribution of the HPR on a portfolio consisting of one share of the index fund and a put option?

c. In what sense does buying the put option constitute a purchase of insurance in this case?

d. Explain why the market price of the put option cannot be less than $10 as long as the market price of the underlying stock is $100.

12. Take as given the conditions described in the previous question, and suppose that the risk-free interest rate is 6% per year. You are contemplating investing $114/1.06 in a 1-year CD and simultaneously buying a call option on the stock market index fund with an exercise price of $110 and a maturity of 1 year.

a. What is the probability distribution of your dollar return at the end of the year?

b. What must be the market price of the call option and why?

Appendix:
Continuous Compounding

Suppose your money earns interest at an annual percentage rate (APR) of 6% compounded semiannually. What is your *effective* annual rate of return, accounting for compound interest?

We find the answer by first computing the per-period rate, 3% per half year, and then computing the future value (FV) at the end of the year per dollar invested at the beginning of the year. In this example we get

$$FV = (1.03)^2$$
$$= 1.0609$$

The effective annual rate (r_{EFF}) is just this number minus 1.0.

TABLE 4A.1   Effective Annual Rates for an APR of 6%

Compounding Frequency	n	r_{EFF} (%)
Annually	1	6.00
Semiannually	2	6.09
Quarterly	4	6.13636
Monthly	12	6.16778
Weekly	52	6.17998
Daily	365	6.18313

$$r_{EFF} = 1.0609 - 1$$
$$= .0609$$
$$= 6.09\% \text{ per year}$$

The general formula for the effective annual rate is

$$r_{EFF} = \left(1 + \frac{r}{n}\right)^n - 1$$

where r is the annual percentage rate, and n is the number of compounding periods per year. Table 4A.1 presents the effective annual rates corresponding to an annual percentage rate of 6% for different compounding frequencies.

As the compounding frequency increases, $(1 + r/n)^n$ gets closer and closer to e^r, where e is the number 2.71828 (rounded off to the fifth decimal place). In our example, $e^{.06} = 1.0618365$. Therefore, if interest is continuously compounded, $r_{EFF} = .0618365$, or 6.18365% per year.

As we noted in Section 4.1 of this chapter, using continuously compounded rates simplifies the algebraic relationship between real and nominal rates of return. To see how, let us compute the real rate of return, first using annual compounding and then using the continuous compounding. Assume the nominal interest rate is 6% compounded annually and the rate of inflation is 4% compounded annually. Using the relationship

$$\text{Real rate} = \frac{1 + \text{Nominal rate}}{1 + \text{Inflation rate}} - 1$$
$$R = \frac{(1 + r)}{(1 + i)} - 1$$
$$= \frac{(r - i)}{(1 + i)}$$

we find that the real rate is

$$R = \frac{1.06}{1.04} - 1$$
$$= .01923$$
$$= 1.923\% \text{ per year}$$

With continuous compounding the relationship becomes

$$e^R = e^r/e^i$$
$$= e^{r-i}$$

Taking the natural logarithm we get

$$R = r - i$$

Real rate = Nominal rate − Inflation rate

all expressed as annual percentage rates, continuously compounded.

Thus, if we assume a nominal interest rate of 6% per year compounded continuously and an inflation rate of 4% per year compounded continuously, the real rate is 2% per year compounded continuously.

PART II

Portfolio Theory

CHAPTER 5

Risk and Risk Aversion

The investment process consists of two broad tasks. One task is security and market analysis, by which we assess the risk and expected-return attributes of the entire set of possible investment vehicles. The second task is the formation of an optimal portfolio of assets. This task involves the determination of the best risk-return opportunities available from feasible investment portfolios and the choice of the best portfolio from that feasible set. We start our formal analysis of investments with this latter task, called portfolio theory. We return to the security analysis task in later chapters.

This chapter introduces three themes in portfolio theory, all centering on risk. The first is the basic tenet that investors avoid risk and demand a reward for engaging in risky investments. The reward is taken as a risk premium, an expected rate of return higher than that available on alternative risk-free investments.

The second theme allows us to summarize and quantify investors' personal trade-offs between portfolio risk and expected return. To do this we introduce the utility function, which assumes that investors can assign a welfare, or "utility," score to any investment portfolio depending on its risk and return.

Finally, the third fundamental principle is that we cannot evaluate the risk of an asset separate from the portfolio of which it is a part; that is, the proper way to measure the risk of an individual asset is to assess its impact on the volatility of the entire portfolio of investments. Taking this approach, we find that seemingly risky securities may be portfolio stabilizers and actually low-risk assets.

Appendix A to this chapter describes the theory and practice of measuring portfolio risk by the variance or standard deviation of returns. We discuss other potentially relevant characteristics of the probability distribution of portfolio returns, as well as the circumstances in which variance is sufficient to measure risk. Appendix B discusses the classical theory of risk aversion.

5.1 *Risk and Risk Aversion*

Risk With Simple Prospects

The presence of risk means that more than one outcome is possible. A *simple prospect* is an investment opportunity in which a certain initial wealth is placed at risk, and there are only two possible outcomes. For the sake of simplicity, it is useful to begin our analysis and elucidate some basic concepts using simple prospects.[1]

Take as an example initial wealth, W, of $100,000, and assume two possible results. With a probability, p, of .6, the favorable outcome will occur, leading to final wealth, W_1, of $150,000. Otherwise, with probability $1 - p = .4$, a less favorable outcome, $W_2 = \$80,000$, will occur. We can represent the simple prospect using an event tree:

$$W = \$100,000 \quad \overset{\textstyle p = .6 \quad W_1 = \$150,000}{\underset{\textstyle 1 - p = .4 \quad W_2 = \$80,000}{\Big\langle}}$$

Suppose that an investor, Susan, is offered an investment portfolio with a payoff in 1 year that is described by such a simple prospect. How can she evaluate this portfolio?

First, she could try to summarize it using descriptive statistics. For instance, her mean or expected end-of-year wealth, denoted $E(W)$, is

$$\begin{aligned} E(W) &= pW_1 + (1 - p)W_2 \\ &= .6 \times 150,000 + .4 \times 80,000 \\ &= \$122,000 \end{aligned}$$

The expected profit on the $100,000 investment portfolio is $22,000: $122,000 - 100,000$. The variance, σ^2, of the portfolio's payoff is calculated as the expected value of the squared deviations of each possible outcome from the mean:

$$\begin{aligned} \sigma^2 &= p[W_1 - E(W)]^2 + (1 - p)[W_2 - E(W)]^2 \\ &= .6(150,000 - 122,000)^2 + .4(80,000 - 122,000)^2 \\ &= 1,176,000,247 \end{aligned}$$

The standard deviation, σ, which is the square root of the variance, is therefore $34,292.86.

Clearly, this is risky business: the standard deviation of the payoff is large, much larger than the expected profit of $22,000. Whether the expected profit is large enough to justify such risk depends on the alternative portfolios.

---

[1]Chapters 5 through 7 rely on some basic results from elementary statistics. For a refresher, see the Quantitative Review in the Appendix at the end of the book.

Let us suppose Treasury bills are one alternative to Susan's risky portfolio. Suppose that at the time of the decision, a 1-year T-bill offers a rate of return of 5%; $100,000 can be invested to yield a sure profit of $5,000. We can now draw Susan's decision tree:

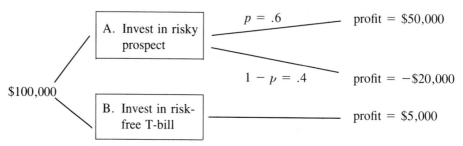

Earlier, we showed the expected profit on the portfolio to be $22,000. Therefore the expected marginal, or incremental, profit of the risky portfolio over investing in safe T-bills is

$$\$22,000 - \$5,000 = \$17,000$$

meaning that one can earn an expected **risk premium** of $17,000 as compensation for the risk of the investment.

The question of whether a given risk premium provides adequate compensation for the investment's risk is age-old. Indeed, one of the central concerns of finance theory (and much of this text) is the measurement of risk and the determination of the risk premiums that investors can expect of risky assets in well-functioning capital markets.

Concept Check

Question 1.
What is the risk premium of Susan's risky portfolio in terms of rate of return rather than dollars?

Risk, Speculation, and Gambling

One definition of *speculation* is "the assumption of considerable business risk in obtaining commensurate gain." Although this definition is fine linguistically, it is useless without first specifying what is meant by "commensurate gain" and "considerable risk."

By "commensurate gain" we mean a positive expected profit beyond the risk-free alternative. This is the risk premium. In our example the dollar risk premium is the profit net of the alternative, which is the sure T-bill profit. The risk premium is the incremental expected gain from taking on the risk. By "considerable risk" we mean that the risk is sufficient to affect the decision. An individual might reject a prospect that has a positive risk premium because the added gain is insufficient to make up for the risk involved.

To gamble is "to bet or wager on an uncertain outcome." If you compare this definition to that of speculation, you will see that the central difference is the lack of "good profit." Economically speaking, a gamble is the assumption of risk for no purpose but enjoyment of the risk itself, whereas speculation is undertaken because one perceives a favorable risk-return trade-off. To turn a gamble into a speculative prospect requires an adequate risk premium for compensation to risk-averse investors for the risks that they bear. Hence *risk aversion and speculation are not inconsistent*.

In some cases a gamble may appear to the participants as speculation. Suppose that two investors disagree sharply about the future exchange rate of the U.S. dollar against the British pound. They may choose to bet on the outcome. Suppose that Paul will pay Mary $100 if the value of 1 pound exceeds $1.30 1 year from now whereas Mary will pay Paul if the pound is worth less than $1.30. There are only two relevant outcomes: (1) the pound will exceed $1.30, or (2) it will fall below $1.30. If both Paul and Mary agree on the probabilities of the two possible outcomes, and if neither party anticipates a loss, it must be that they assign $p = .5$ to each outcome. In that case the expected profit to both is zero and each has entered one side of a gambling prospect.

What is more likely, however, is that the bet results from differences in the probabilities that Paul and Mary assign to the outcome. Mary assigns it $p > .5$ whereas Paul's assessment is $p < .5$. They perceive, subjectively, two different prospects. Economists call this case of differing beliefs "heterogeneous expectations." In such cases investors on each side of a financial position see themselves as speculating rather than gambling.

Both Paul and Mary should be asking, "Why is the other willing to invest in the side of a risky prospect that I believe offers a negative expected profit?" The ideal way to resolve heterogeneous beliefs is for Paul and Mary to "merge their information," that is, for each party to verify that he or she possesses all relevant information and processes the information properly. Of course, the acquisition of information and the extensive communication that is required to eliminate all heterogeneity in expectations is costly, and thus up to a point heterogeneous expectations cannot be taken as irrational. If, however, Paul and Mary enter such contracts frequently, they would recognize the information problem in one of two ways: either they will realize that they are creating gambles when each wins half of the bets, or the consistent loser will admit that he or she has been betting on inferior forecasts.

Question 2. Assume that dollar-denominated T-bills in the United States and pound-denominated bills in the United Kingdom offer equal yields to maturity. Both are short-term assets, and both are free of default risk. Neither offers investors a risk premium. However, a U.S. investor who holds U.K. bills is subject to exchange rate risk since the pounds earned on the U.K. bills eventually will be exchanged for dollars at the future exchange rate. What expectation about future exchange rates would determine whether a U.S. investor who purchases U.K. bills is engaging in speculation or gambling?

Risk Aversion and Utility Values

We have discussed risk with simple prospects and how risk premiums bear on speculation. A prospect that has a zero risk premium is called a *fair game*. Investors who are **risk averse** reject investment portfolios that are fair games or worse. Risk-averse investors are willing to consider only risk-free or speculative prospects. Loosely speaking, a risk-averse investor "penalizes" the expected rate of return of a risky portfolio by a certain percentage (or penalizes the expected profit by a dollar amount) to account for the risk involved. The greater the risk the investor perceives, the larger the penalization. (One might wonder why we assume risk aversion as fundamental. We believe that most investors accept this view from simple introspection, but we discuss the question more fully in Appendix B of this chapter.)

We can formalize this notion of a risk-penalty system. To do so, we will assume that each investor can assign a welfare, or **utility,** score to competing investment portfolios based on the expected return and risk of those portfolios. The utility score may be viewed as a means of ranking portfolios. Higher utility values are assigned to portfolios with more attractive risk-return profiles. Portfolios receive higher utility scores for higher expected returns and lower scores for higher volatility. Many particular "scoring" systems are legitimate. One reasonable function that is commonly employed by financial theorists assigns a portfolio with expected return $E(r)$ and variance of returns σ^2 the following utility score:

$$U = E(r) - \tfrac{1}{2} A\sigma^2 \qquad (5.1)$$

where U is the utility value and A is an index of the investor's aversion to taking on risk. (The factor of $\tfrac{1}{2}$ is a scaling convention that will simplify calculations in later chapters. It has no economic significance, and we could eliminate it simply by defining a "new" A with half the value of the A used here.)

Equation 5.1 is consistent with the notion that utility is enhanced by high expected returns and diminished by high risk. (Whether variance is an adequate measure of portfolio risk is discussed in Appendix A.) The extent to which variance lowers utility depends on A, the investor's degree of risk aversion. More risk-averse investors (who have the larger As) penalize risky investments more severely. Investors choosing among competing investment portfolios will select the one providing the highest utility level.

Notice in equation 5.1 that the utility provided by a risk-free portfolio is simply the rate of return on the portfolio, since there is no penalization for risk. This provides us with a convenient benchmark for evaluating portfolios. For example, recall Susan's investment problem, choosing between a portfolio with expected return .22 (22%) and standard deviation $\sigma = .34$, and T-bills providing a risk-free return of 5%. Although the risk premium on the risky portfolio is large, 17%, the risk of the project is so great that Susan does not need to be very risk averse to choose the safe all-bills strategy. Even for $A = 3$, a moderate risk-aversion parameter, equation 5.1 shows the risky portfolio's utility value as $.22 - \frac{1}{2} \times 3 \times .34^2 = .0466$, or 4.66%, which is slightly lower than the risk-free rate. In this case Susan would reject the portfolio in favor of T-bills.

The downward adjustment of the expected return as a penalty for risk is $\frac{1}{2} \times 3 \times .34^2 = .1734$, or 17.34%. If Susan were less risk averse (more risk tolerant), for example with $A = 2$, she would adjust the expected rate of return downward by only 11.56%. In that case the utility level of the portfolio would be 10.44%, higher than the risk-free rate, leading her to accept the prospect.

Concept Check	Question 3. A portfolio has an expected rate of return of .20, and standard deviation of .20. Bills offer a sure rate of return of .07. Which investment alternative will be chosen by an investor whose $A = 4$? What if $A = 8$? *Note:* treat the interest rates as decimals (for example, $E(r) = .20$, not 20%) to answer this question.

Because we can compare utility values to the rate offered on risk-free investments when choosing between a risky portfolio and a safe one, we may interpret a portfolio's utility value as its "certainty equivalent" rate of return to an investor. That is, the **certainty equivalent rate** of a portfolio is the rate that risk-free investments would need to offer with certainty to be considered equally attractive to the risky portfolio.

Now we can say that a portfolio is desirable only if its certainty equivalent return exceeds that of the risk-free alternative. A sufficiently risk-averse investor may assign any risky portfolio, even one with a positive risk premium, a certainty equivalent rate of return that is below the risk-free rate, which will cause the investor to reject the portfolio. At the same time a less risk-averse (more risk-tolerant) investor will assign the same portfolio a certainty equivalent rate that exceeds the risk-free rate and thus will prefer the portfolio to the risk-free alternative. If the risk premium is zero or negative to begin with, any downward adjustment to utility only makes the portfolio look worse. Its certainty equivalent rate will be below that of the risk-free alternative for all risk-averse investors.

In contrast to risk-averse investors, **risk-neutral** investors judge risky prospects

FIGURE 5.1

The trade-off between
risk and return of a
potential investment
portfolio.

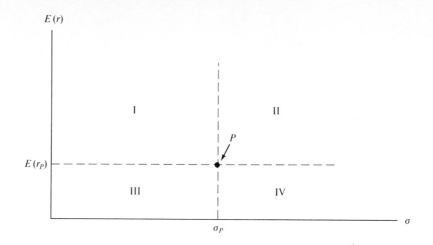

solely by their expected rates of return. The level of risk is irrelevant to the risk-neutral investor, meaning that there is no penalization for risk. For this investor a portfolio's certainty equivalent rate is simply its expected rate of return.

A **risk lover** is willing to engage in fair games and gambles; this investor adjusts the expected return upward to take into account the "fun" of confronting the prospect's risk. Risk lovers will always take a fair game because their upward adjustment of utility for risk gives the fair game a certainty equivalent that exceeds the alternative of the risk-free investment.

We can depict the individual's trade-off between risk and return by plotting the characteristics of potential investment portfolios that the individual would view as equally attractive on a graph with axes measuring the expected value and standard deviation of portfolio returns. Figure 5.1 plots the characteristics of one portfolio.

Portfolio P, which has expected return $E(r_P)$ and standard deviation σ_p, is preferred by risk-averse investors to any portfolio in quadrant IV because it has an expected return equal to or greater than any portfolio in that quadrant and a standard deviation equal to or smaller than any portfolio in that quadrant. Conversely, any portfolio in quadrant I is preferable to portfolio P because its expected return is equal to or greater than P's and its standard deviation is equal to or smaller than P's.

This is the mean-standard deviation, or equivalently, **mean-variance (M-V) criterion.** It can be stated as A dominates B if

$$E(r_A) \geq E(r_B)$$

and

$$\sigma_A \leq \sigma_B$$

and at least one inequality is strict.

In the expected return–standard deviation graph the preferred direction is northwest, because in this direction we simultaneously increase the expected return *and*

FIGURE 5.2
The indifference
curve.

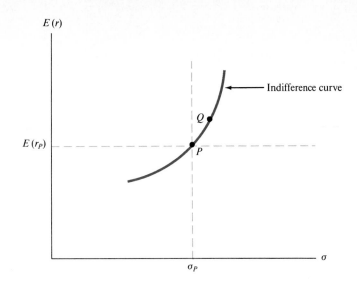

decrease the variance of the rate of return. This means that any portfolio that lies northwest of P is superior to P.

What can be said about portfolios in the quadrants II and III? Their desirability, compared with P, depends on the exact nature of the investor's risk aversion. Suppose an investor identifies all portfolios that are equally attractive as portfolio P. Starting at P, an increase in standard deviation lowers utility; it must be compensated for by an increase in expected return. Thus point Q is equally desirable to this investor as P. Investors will be equally attracted to portfolios with high risk and high expected returns compared with other portfolios with lower risk but lower expected returns.

These equally preferred portfolios will lie on a curve in the mean-standard deviation graph that connects all portfolio points with the same utility value (Figure 5.2). This is called the **indifference curve.**

To determine some of the points that appear on the indifference curve, examine the utility values of several possible portfolios for an investor with $A = 4$, presented in Table 5.1. Note that each portfolio offers identical utility, since the high-return portfolios also have high risk. Although in practice the exact indifference curves of various investors cannot be known, this analysis can take us a long way in determining appropriate principles for portfolio selection strategy.

TABLE 5.1   Utility Values of Possible Portfolios

Expected Return, E(r)	Standard Deviation, σ	Utility = $E(r) - \frac{1}{2}A\sigma^2$
.10	.200	$.10 - .5 \times 4 \times .04 = .02$
.15	.255	$.15 - .5 \times 4 \times .065 = .02$
.20	.300	$.20 - .5 \times 4 \times .09 = .02$
.25	.339	$.25 - .5 \times 4 \times .115 = .02$

5.2 Portfolio Risk

Asset Risk vs. Portfolio Risk

We have focused so far on the return and risk of an individual's overall investment portfolio. Such portfolios are composed of diverse types of assets. In addition to their direct investment in financial markets, investors have stakes in pension funds, life insurance policies with savings components, homes, and, not least, the earning power of their skills (human capital).

We saw in Chapter 4 that, sometimes, adding a seemingly risky asset to a portfolio actually reduces the risk of the overall portfolio. The example we cited was that of a fire insurance policy. Although the policy viewed in isolation had a very uncertain and volatile payoff, it clearly was a portfolio risk reducer because it provided a positive payoff precisely when another major part of the portfolio, the investor's house, fared poorly. Investing in an asset with a payoff pattern that offsets your exposure to a particular source of risk is called **hedging.**

Insurance contracts are obvious hedging vehicles. In many contexts financial markets offer similar, although perhaps less direct, hedging opportunities. For example, consider two firms, one producing suntan lotion, the other producing umbrellas. The shareholders of each firm face weather risk of an opposite nature. A rainy summer lowers the return on the suntan-lotion firm but raises it on the umbrella firm. Shares of the umbrella firm act as "weather insurance" for the suntan-lotion firm shareholders in precisely the same way that fire insurance policies insure houses. When the lotion firm does poorly (bad weather), the "insurance" asset (umbrella shares) provides a high payoff that offsets the loss.

Another means to control portfolio risk is **diversification,** by which we mean that investments are made in a wide variety of assets so that the exposure to the risk of any particular security is limited. By placing one's eggs in many baskets, overall portfolio risk actually may be less than the risk of any component security considered in isolation.

To examine these effects more precisely, and to lay a foundation for the mathematical properties that will be used in coming chapters, we will consider an example with less than perfect hedging opportunities, and in the process review the statistics underlying portfolio risk and return characteristics.

Consider the problem of Humanex, a nonprofit organization deriving most of its income from the return of its endowment. Years ago, the founders of Best Candy willed a large block of Best Candy stock to Humanex with the provision that Humanex may never sell it. This block of shares now comprises 50% of Humanex's endowment. Humanex has free choice as to where to invest the remainder of its portfolio.[2]

The value of Best Candy stock is sensitive to the price of sugar. In years when the Caribbean sugar crop fails, the price of sugar rises significantly and Best Candy suffers considerable losses. We can describe the fortunes of Best Candy stock using the following scenario analysis:

| | Normal Year for Sugar | | Abnormal Year |
	Bullish Stock Market	Bearish Stock Market	Sugar Crisis
Probability	.5	.3	.2
Rate of return	.25	.10	−.25

To summarize these three possible outcomes using conventional statistics, we review some of the key rules governing the properties of risky assets and portfolios.

Rule 1. The mean or **expected return** of an asset is a probability-weighted average of its return in all scenarios. Calling $Pr(s)$ the probability of scenario s and $r(s)$ the return in scenario s, we may write the expected return, $E(r)$, as

$$E(r) = \sum_s Pr(s)r(s) \tag{5.2}$$

Applying this formula to the case at hand, with three possible scenarios, we find that the expected rate of return of Best Candy's stock is

$$E(r_{Best}) = .5 \times .25 + .3 \times .10 + .2(-.25)$$
$$= .105$$
$$= 10.5\%$$

Rule 2. The **variance** of an asset's returns is the expected value of the squared deviations from the expected return. Symbolically,

$$\sigma^2 = \sum_s Pr(s)[r(s) - E(r)]^2 \tag{5.3}$$

Therefore in our example

$$\sigma^2_{Best} = .5(.25 - .105)^2 + .3(.10 - .105)^2 + .2(-.25 - .105)^2$$
$$= .035725$$

---

[2]The portfolio restriction is admittedly unrealistic. We use this example only to illustrate the various strategies that might be used to control risk and to review some useful results from statistics.

The **standard deviation** of Best's return, which is the square root of the variance, is $\sqrt{.035725} = .189$, or 18.9%.

Humanex has 50% of its endowment in Best's stock. To reduce the risk of the overall portfolio, it could invest the remainder in T-bills, which yield a sure rate of return of 5%. To derive the return of the overall portfolio, we apply rule 3:

Rule 3. The rate of return on a portfolio is a weighted average of the rates of return of each asset comprising the portfolio, with portfolio proportions as weights. This implies that the *expected* rate of return on a portfolio is a weighted average of the *expected* rate of return on each component asset.

In this case the portfolio proportions in each asset are .5, and the portfolio's expected rate of return is

$$E(r_{Humanex}) = .5E(r_{Best}) + .5r_{Bills}$$
$$= .5 \times .105 + .5 \times .05$$
$$= .0775$$
$$= 7.75\%$$

The standard deviation of the portfolio may be derived from the following:

Rule 4. When a risky asset is combined with a risk-free asset, the portfolio standard deviation equals the risky asset's standard deviation multiplied by the portfolio proportion invested in the asset.

In this case, the Humanex portfolio is 50% invested in Best stock and 50% invested in risk-free bills. Therefore

$$\sigma_{Humanex} = .5\sigma_{Best}$$
$$= .5 \times .189$$
$$= .0945$$
$$= 9.45\%$$

By reducing its exposure to the risk of Best by half, Humanex reduces its portfolio standard deviation by half. The cost of this risk reduction, however, is a reduction in expected return. The expected rate of return on Best stock is 10.5%. The expected return on the one-half T-bill portfolio is 7.75%. This makes the risk premiums over the 5% rate on risk-free bills 5.5% for Best stock and 2.75% for the half T-bill portfolio. By reducing the share of Best stock in the portfolio by one half, Humanex reduces its portfolio risk premium by one half, from 5.5% to 2.75%.

In an effort to improve the contribution of the endowment to the operating budget, Humanex's trustees hire Sally, a recent MBA, as a consultant. Investigating the sugar and candy industry, Sally discovers, not surprisingly, that during years of sugar crisis in the Caribbean basin, SugarKane, a big Hawaiian sugar company, reaps unusual profits and its stock price soars. A scenario analysis of SugarKane's stock looks like this:

	Normal Year for Sugar		Abnormal Year
	Bullish Stock Market	Bearish Stock Market	Sugar Crisis
Probability	.5	.3	.2
Rate of return	.01	−.05	.35

The expected rate of return on SugarKane's stock is 6%, and its standard deviation is 14.73%. Thus SugarKane is almost as volatile as Best, yet its expected return is only a notch better than the T-bill rate. This cursory analysis makes SugarKane appear to be an unattractive investment. For Humanex, however, the stock holds great promise.

SugarKane offers excellent hedging potential for holders of Best stock because its return is highest precisely when Best's return is lowest—during a Caribbean sugar crisis. Consider Humanex's portfolio when it splits its investment evenly between Best and SugarKane. The rate of return for each scenario is the simple average of the rates on Best and SugarKane because the portfolio is split evenly between the two stocks (see Rule 3).

	Normal Year for Sugar		Abnormal Year
	Bullish Stock Market	Bearish Stock Market	Sugar Crisis
Probability	.5	.3	.2
Rate of return	.13	.025	.05

The expected rate of return on Humanex's hedged portfolio is .0825 with a standard deviation of .0483, or 4.83%.

Sally now summarizes the reward and risk of the three alternatives:

Portfolio	Expected Return	Standard Deviation
All in Best Candy	.105	.1890
Half in T-bills	.07575	.0945
Half in SugarKane	.0825	.0483

The numbers speak for themselves. The hedge portfolio including SugarKane clearly dominates the simple risk-reduction strategy of investing in safe T-bills. It has higher expected return *and* lower standard deviation than the one-half T-bill portfolio. The point is that, despite SugarKane's large standard deviation of return, it is a risk reducer for some investors—in this case those holding Best stock.

The risk of the individual assets in the portfolio must be measured in the context of the effect of their return on overall portfolio variability. This example demonstrates that assets with returns that are inversely associated with the initial risky position are the most powerful risk reducers.

Question 5. Suppose that the stock market offers an expected rate of return of 20%, with a standard deviation of 15%. Gold has an expected rate of return of 18%, with a standard deviation of 17%. In view of the market's higher expected return and lower uncertainty, will anyone choose to hold gold in a portfolio?

To quantify the hedging or diversification potential of an asset, we use the concepts of covariance and correlation. The **covariance** measures how much the returns on two risky assets move in tandem. A positive covariance means that asset returns move together. A negative covariance means that they vary inversely, as in the case of Best and SugarKane.

To measure covariance, we look at return "surprises" or deviations from expected value in each scenario. Consider the product of each stock's deviation from expected return in a particular scenario:

$$[r_{Best} - E(r_{Best})]\,[r_{Kane} - E(r_{Kane})]$$

This product will be positive if the returns of the two stocks move together across scenarios, that is, if both returns exceed their expectations or both fall short of those expectations in the scenario in question. On the other hand, if one stock's return exceeds its expected value when the other's falls short, the product will be negative. Thus a good measure of how much the returns move together is the *expected value* of this product across all scenarios, which is defined as the covariance:

$$\mathrm{Cov}(r_{Best}, r_{Kane}) = \sum_s Pr(s)\,[r_{Best}(s) - E(r_{Best})]\,[r_{Kane}(s) - E(r_{Kane})] \quad (5.4)$$

In this example, with $E(r_{Best}) = .105$ and $E(r_{Kane}) = .06$ and with returns in each scenario summarized as follows, we find the covariance from a simple application of equation 5.4.

	Normal Year for Sugar		Abnormal Year
	Bullish Stock Market	Bearish Stock Market	Sugar Crisis
Probability	.5	.3	.2
Stock			
Best Candy	.25	.10	−.25
SugarKane	.01	−.05	.35

The covariance between the two stocks is

$$\text{Cov}(r_{\text{Best}}, r_{\text{Kane}}) = .5(.25 - .105)(.01 - .06)$$
$$+ .3(.10 - .105)(-.05 - .06) + .2(-.25 - .105)(.35 - .06)$$
$$= -.02405$$

The negative covariance confirms the hedging quality of SugarKane stock relative to Best Candy. SugarKane's returns move inversely with Best's.

An easier statistic to interpret than the covariance is the **correlation coefficient,** which scales the covariance to a value between -1 (perfect negative correlation) and $+1$ (perfect positive correlation). The correlation coefficient between two variables equals their covariance divided by the product of the standard deviations. Denoting the correlation by the Greek letter ρ, we find that

$$\rho(\text{Best, SugarKane}) = \frac{\text{Cov}[r_{\text{Best}}, r_{\text{SugarKane}}]}{\sigma_{\text{Best}} \sigma_{\text{SugarKane}}}$$
$$= \frac{-.0240}{.189 \times .1473}$$
$$= -.86$$

This large negative correlation (close to -1) confirms the strong tendency of Best and SugarKane stocks to move inversely, or "out of phase" with one another.

The impact of the covariance of asset returns on portfolio risk is apparent in the following formula for portfolio variance.

Rule 5. When two risky assets with variances σ_1^2 and σ_2^2, respectively, are combined into a portfolio with portfolio weights w_1 and w_2, respectively, the portfolio variance σ_P^2 is given by

$$\sigma_P^2 = w_1^2 \sigma_1^2 + w_2^2 \sigma_2^2 + 2w_1 w_2 \text{Cov}(r_1, r_2)$$

In this example, with equal weights in Best and SugarKane, $w_1 = w_2 = .5$, and with $\sigma_{\text{Best}} = .189$, $\sigma_{\text{Kane}} = .1473$, and Cov $(r_{\text{Best}}, r_{\text{Kane}}) = -.02405$, we find that

$$\sigma_P^2 = .5^2 \times .189^2 + .5^2 \times .1473^2 + 2 \times .5 \times .5 (-.02405) = .00233$$

or that $\sigma_P = \sqrt{.00233} = .0483$, precisely the same answer for the standard deviation of the returns on the hedged portfolio that we derived directly from the scenario analysis.

Rule 5 for portfolio variance highlights the effect of covariance on portfolio risk. A positive covariance increases portfolio variance, and a negative covariance acts to reduce portfolio variance. This makes sense because returns on negatively correlated assets tend to be offsetting, which stabilizes portfolio returns.

Basically, hedging involves the purchase of a risky asset that is negatively correlated with the existing portfolio. This negative correlation makes the volatility of the hedge asset a risk-reducing feature. A hedge strategy is a powerful alternative to the simple risk-reduction strategy of including a risk-free asset in the portfolio.

In later chapters we will see that, in a rational equilibrium, hedge assets must offer relatively low expected rates of return. The perfect hedge, an insurance contract, is by design perfectly negatively correlated with a specified risk. As one would expect in a "no free lunch" world, the insurance premium reduces the portfolio's expected rate of return.

Concept Check

Question 6. Suppose that the distribution of SugarKane stock is as follows:

Bullish Stock Market	Bearish Stock Market	Sugar Crisis
.07	−.05	.20

a. What would be its correlation with Best?
b. Is SugarKane stock a useful hedge asset now?
c. Calculate the portfolio rate of return in each scenario and the standard deviation of the portfolio from the scenario returns. Then evaluate σ_P using rule 5.
d. Are the two methods of computing portfolio standard deviation consistent?

Summary

1. Speculation is the undertaking of a risky investment for its risk premium. The risk premium has to be large enough to compensate a risk-averse investor for the risk of the investment.

2. A fair game is a risky prospect that has a zero-risk premium. It will not be undertaken by a risk-averse investor.

3. Investor's preferences toward the expected return and volatility of a portfolio may be expressed by a utility function that is higher for higher expected returns and lower for higher portfolio variances. More risk-averse investors will apply greater penalties for risk. We can describe these preferences graphically using indifference curves.

4. The desirability of a risky portfolio to a risk-averse investor may be summarized by the certainty equivalent value of the portfolio. The certainty equivalent rate of return is a value that, if it is received with certainty, would yield the same utility as the risky portfolio.

5. Hedging is the purchase of a risky asset to reduce the risk of a portfolio. The negative correlation between the hedge asset and the initial portfolio turns the volatility of the hedge asset into a risk-*reducing* feature. When a hedge asset is perfectly negatively correlated with the initial portfolio, it serves as a perfect hedge and works like an insurance contract on the portfolio.

Key Terms

Risk premium	Hedging
Risk averse	Diversification
Utility	Expected return
Certainty equivalent rate	Variance
Risk neutral	Standard deviation
Risk lover	Covariance
Mean-variance criterion	Correlation coefficient
Indifference curve	

Selected Readings

A classic work on risk and risk aversion is:
   Arrow, Kenneth, *Essays in the Theory of Risk Bearing,* North Holland, Amsterdam, 1971.
Some good statistics texts with business applications are:
   Levy, Haim, and Ben-Horim, Moshe, *Statistics: Decisions and Applications in Business and Economics,* New York: Random House, 1984.
   Wonnacott, Thomas H., and Wonnacott, Ronald J., *Introductory Statistics for Business and Economics,* New York: John Wiley & Sons, 1984.

Problems

1. Consider a risky portfolio. The end-of-year cash flow derived from the portfolio will be either $50,000 or $150,000 with equal probabilities of .5. The alternative risk-free investment in T-bills pays 5% per year.
    a. If you require a risk premium of 10%, how much will you be willing to pay for the portfolio?
    b. Suppose that the portfolio can be purchased for the amount you found in (a). What will be the expected rate of return on the portfolio?
    c. Now suppose that you require a risk premium of 15%. What is the price that you will be willing to pay?
    d. Comparing your answers to (a) and (c), what do you conclude about the relationship between the required risk premium on a portfolio and the price at which the portfolio will sell?
2. Consider a portfolio that offers an expected rate of return of 10% and a standard deviation of 15%. T-bills offer a risk-free 8% rate of return. What is the maximum level of risk aversion for which the risky portfolio is still preferred to bills?
3. Draw the indifference curve in the expected return-standard deviation plane corresponding to a utility level of .05 for an investor with a risk aversion coefficient of 3. Hint: choose several possible standard deviations, ranging from .05 to .25,

and find the expected rates of return providing a utility level of .05. Then plot the expected return-standard deviation points so derived.

4. Now draw the indifference curve corresponding to a utility level of .04 for an investor with risk aversion coefficient $A = 4$. Comparing your answers to questions 3 and 4, what do you conclude?
5. Draw an indifference curve for a risk-neutral investor providing utility level .05.
6. What must be true about the sign of the risk aversion coefficient, A, for a risk lover? Draw the indifference curve for a utility level of .05 for a risk lover.

Consider historical data showing that the average annual rate of return on the S&P 500 portfolio over the past 60 years has averaged about 8.5% more than the Treasury bill return and that the S&P 500 standard deviation has been about 21% per year. Assume these values are representative of investors' expectations for future performance and that the current T-bill rate is 6%. Use these values to answer questions 7 to 9.

7. Calculate the expected return and variance of portfolios invested in T-bills and the S&P 500 index with weights as follows:

w_{bills}	w_{market}
0	1.0
.2	.8
.4	.6
.6	.4
.8	.2
1.0	0

8. Calculate the utility levels of each portfolio of question 7 for an investor with $A = 3$. What do you conclude?
9. Repeat question 8 for an investor with $A = 5$. What do you conclude?

Reconsider the Best and SugarKane stock market hedging example in the text, but assume for questions 10 to 13 that the probability distribution of the rate of return on SugarKane stock is as follows:

	Bullish Stock Market	Bearish Stock Market	Sugar Crisis
Probability	.5	.3	.2
Rate of return	.10	−.05	.20

10. If Humanex's portfolio is half Best stock and half SugarKane, what are its expected return and standard deviation? Calculate the standard deviation from the portfolio returns in each scenario.
11. What is the covariance between Best and SugarKane?
12. Calculate the portfolio standard deviation using rule 5 and show that the result is consistent with your answer to question 10.

Appendix A:
A Defense of Mean-Variance Analysis

Describing Probability Distributions

The axiom of risk aversion needs little defense. So far, however, our treatment of risk has been limiting in that it took the variance (or equivalently, the standard deviation) of portfolio returns as an adequate risk measure. In situations in which variance alone is not adequate to measure risk this assumption is potentially restrictive. Here, we provide some justification for mean-variance analysis.

The basic question is how one can best describe the uncertainty of portfolio rates of return. In principle, one could list all possible outcomes for the portfolio over a given period. If each outcome results in a payoff such as a dollar profit or rate of return, then this payoff value is the *random variable* in question. A list assigning a probability to all possible values of the random variable is called the probability distribution of the random variable.

The reward for holding a portfolio is typically measured by the expected rate of return across all possible scenarios, which equals

$$E(r) = \sum_{s=1}^{n} Pr(s)r_s$$

where $s = 1, \ldots, n$ are the possible outcomes or scenarios, r_s is the rate of return for outcome s, and $Pr(s)$ is the probability associated with it.

Actually, the expected value or mean is not the only candidate for the central value of a probability distribution. Other candidates are the median and the mode.

The median is defined as the outcome value that exceeds the outcome values for half the population and is exceeded by the other half. Whereas the expected rate of return is a weighted average of the outcomes, the weights being the probabilities, the median is based on the rank order of the outcomes and takes into account only the order of the outcome values rather than the values themselves.

The median differs significantly from the mean in cases where the expected value is dominated by extreme values. One example is the income (or wealth) distribution in a population. A relatively small number of households command a disproportionate share of total income (and wealth). The mean income is "pulled up" by these extreme values, which makes it nonrepresentative. The median is free of this effect, since it equals the income level that is exceeded by half the population, regardless of by how much.

Finally, a third candidate for the measure of central value is the mode, which is the most likely value of the distribution or the outcome with the highest probability. However, the expected value is by far the most widely used measure of central or average tendency.

We now turn to the characterization of the risk implied by the nature of the probability distribution of returns. In general, it is impossible to quantify risk by a single number. We can, however, describe the probabilities and magnitudes of the possible deviations from the mean, or the "surprises," in a concise fashion, to illuminate the risk-return trade-off. The easiest way to accomplish this is to answer a set of questions in order of their informational value and to stop at the point where additional questions would not affect our notion of the risk-return trade-off.

The first question is, "What is a typical deviation from the expected value?" A natural answer would be, "The expected deviation from the expected value is _____." Unfortunately, this answer is meaningless because it is necessarily zero: positive deviations from the mean are offset exactly by negative deviations.

There are two ways of getting around this problem. The first is to use the expected *absolute* value of the deviation. This is known as MAD (mean absolute deviation), which is given by

$$\sum_{s=1}^{n} Pr(s) \times \text{Absolute Value}[r_s - E(r)]$$

The second is to use the expected *squared* deviation from the expected, or mean, value, which is simply the variance of the probability distribution:

$$\sigma^2 = \sum_{s=1}^{n} Pr(s) [r_s - E(r)]^2$$

Note that the unit of measurement of the variance is "percent squared." To return to our original units, we compute the standard deviation as the square root of the variance, which is measured in percentage terms, as is the expected value.

The variance also is called the *second central moment* around the mean, with the expected return itself being the first moment. Although the variance measures the average squared deviation from the expected value, it does not provide a full description of risk. To see why, consider the two probability distributions for rates of return on a portfolio, in Figure 5A.1.

A and *B* are probability distributions with identical expected values and variances. The graphs show that the variances are identical because probability distribution *B* is the mirror image of *A*.

What is the principal difference between *A* and *B*? *A* is characterized by more likely but small losses and less likely but extreme gains. This pattern is reversed in *B*. The difference is important. When we talk about risk, we really mean "*bad* surprises." The "bad surprises" in *A,* although they are more likely, are small (and limited) in magnitude. The "bad surprises" in *B* could be extreme, indeed unbounded. A risk-averse investor will prefer *A* to *B* on these grounds; hence it is worthwhile to quantify this characteristic. The asymmetry of the distribution is called skewness, which we measure by the *third central moment,* given by

$$M_3 = \sum_{s=1}^{n} Pr(s) [r_s - E(r)]^3$$

Skewed probability
distributions for rates
of return on a
portfolio.

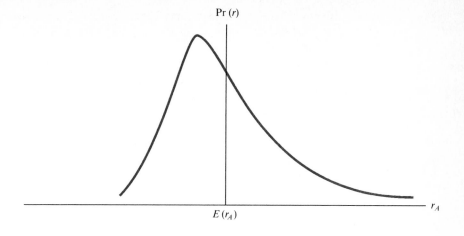

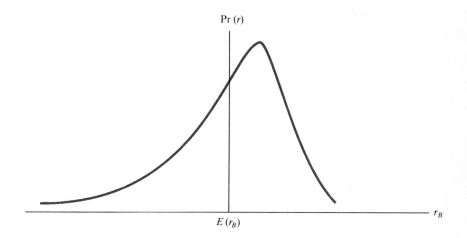

Cubing the deviations from expected value preserves their signs, which allows us
to distinguish good from bad surprises. Because this procedure gives greater weight
to larger deviations, it causes the "long tail" of the distribution to dominate the measure of skewness. Thus the skewness of the distribution will be positive for a right-
skewed distribution such as A and negative for a left-skewed distribution such as B.
The asymmetry is a relevant characteristic, although it is not as important as the magnitude of the standard deviation.

To summarize, the first moment (expected value) represents the expected reward.
The second and higher central moments characterize the uncertainty of the reward.
All the even moments (variance, M_4, and so on) represent the likelihood of extreme
values. Larger values for these moments indicate greater uncertainty. The odd mo-

ments (M_3, M_5, and so on) represent measures of asymmetry. Positive numbers are associated with positive skewness and hence are desirable.

We can characterize the risk aversion of any investor by the preference scheme that the investor assigns to the various moments of the distribution. In other words, we can write the utility value derived from the probability distribution as

$$U = E(r) - b_0\sigma^2 + b_1M_3 - b_2M_4 + b_3M_5 - \ldots$$

where the importance of the terms lessens as we proceed to higher moments. Notice that the "good" (odd) moments have positive coefficients whereas the "bad" (even) moments have minus signs in front of the coefficients.

How many moments are needed to describe the investor's assessment of the probability distribution adequately? Samuelson's "Fundamental Approximation Theorem of Portfolio Analysis in Terms of Means, Variances, and Higher Moments"[a] proves that in many important circumstances:

1. The importance of all moments beyond the variance is much smaller than that of the expected value and variance. In other words, disregarding moments higher than the variance will not affect portfolio choice.
2. The variance is as important as the mean to investor welfare.

Samuelson's proof is the major theoretical justification for mean-variance analysis. Under the conditions of this proof mean and variance are equally important, and we can overlook all other moments without harm.

The major assumption that Samuelson makes to arrive at this conclusion concerns the "compactness" of the distribution of stock returns. The distribution of the rate of return on a portfolio is said to be compact if the risk can be controlled by the investor. Practically speaking, we test for compactness of the distribution by posing a question: Will the risk of my position in the portfolio decline if I hold it for a shorter period, or will the risk approach zero if I hold the risky portfolio for only an instant? If the answer is yes, then the distribution is compact.

In general, compactness may be seen as being equivalent to continuity of stock prices. If stock prices do not take sudden jumps, then the uncertainty of stock returns over smaller and smaller time periods decreases. Under these circumstances investors who can rebalance their portfolios frequently will act so as to make higher moments of the stock return distribution so small as to be unimportant. It is not that skewness, for example, does not matter in principle. It is, instead, that the actions of investors in frequently revising their portfolios will limit higher moments to negligible levels.

Continuity or compactness is not, however, an innocuous assumption. Portfolio revisions entail transaction costs, meaning that rebalancing must of necessity be somewhat limited and that skewness and other higher moments cannot entirely be ignored. Compactness also rules out such phenomena as the major stock price jumps that occur in response to takeover attempts. It also rules out such dramatic events as the 25% 1-day decline of the stock market on October 19, 1987. Except for these relatively unusual events, however, mean-variance analysis is adequate. In most

---

[a]Samuelson, Paul A., "The Fundamental Approximation Theorem of Portfolio Analysis in Terms of Means, Variances, and Higher Moments," *Review of Economic Studies, 37,* 1970.

cases, if the portfolio may be revised frequently, we need to worry about the mean and variance only.

Portfolio theory, for the most part, is built on the assumption that the conditions for mean-variance (or mean-standard deviation) analysis are satisfied. Accordingly, we typically ignore higher moments.

Concept Check

Question 5A.1. How does the simultaneous popularity of both lotteries and insurance policies confirm the notion that individuals prefer positive to negative skewness of portfolio returns?

Normal and Lognormal Distributions

Modern portfolio theory, for the most part, assumes that asset returns are normally distributed. This is a convenient assumption because the normal distribution can be described completely by its mean and variance, which provides another justification for mean-variance analysis. The argument has been that, even if individual asset returns are not exactly normal, the distribution of returns of a large portfolio will resemble a normal distribution quite closely.

The data support this argument. Table 5A.1 shows summaries of the results of 1-year investments in many portfolios selected randomly from NYSE stocks. The portfolios are listed in order of increasing degrees of diversification; that is, the numbers of stocks in each portfolio sample are 1, 8, 32, and 128. The percentiles of the distribution of returns for each portfolio are compared to what one would have ex-

TABLE 5A.1 Frequency Distributions of Rates of Return From a 1-Year Investment in Randomly Selected Portfolios from NYSE-Listed Stocks

Statistic	N = 1 Observed	N = 1 Normal	N = 8 Observed	N = 8 Normal	N = 32 Observed	N = 32 Normal	N = 128 Observed	N = 128 Normal
Minimum	−71.1	NA	−12.4	NA	6.5	NA	16.4	NA
5th centile	−14.4	−39.2	8.1	4.6	17.4	16.7	22.7	22.6
20th centile	−.5	−6.3	16.3	16.1	22.2	22.3	25.3	25.3
50th centile	19.6	28.2	26.4	28.2	27.8	28.2	28.1	28.2
70th centile	38.7	49.7	33.8	35.7	31.6	32.9	30.0	30.0
95th centile	96.3	95.6	54.3	51.8	40.9	39.9	34.1	33.8
Maximum	442.6	NA	136.7	NA	73.7	NA	43.1	NA
Mean	28.2	28.2	28.2	28.2	28.2	28.2	28.2	28.2
Standard deviation	41.0	41.0	14.4	14.4	7.1	7.1	3.4	3.4
Skewness (M_3)	255.4	0.0	88.7	0.0	44.5	0.0	17.7	0.0
Sample size	1,227	—	131,072	—	32,768	—	16,384	—

From Fisher, Lawrence, and Lorie, James H.: "Some Studies of Variability of Returns on Investments in Common Stocks," *Journal of Business, 43,* April 1970; published by the University of Chicago.

pected from portfolios identical in mean and variance but drawn from a normal distribution.

Looking first at the single stock portfolio ($n = 1$), the departure of the return distribution from normality is significant. The mean of the sample is 28.2%, and the standard deviation is 41.0%. In the case of a normal distribution with the same mean and standard deviation, we would expect the fifth percentile stock to lose 39.2%, but the fifth percentile stock actually lost 14.4%. In addition, while the normal distribution's mean coincides with its median, the actual sample median of the single stock was 19.6%, far below the sample mean of 28.2%.

In contrast, the returns of the 128-stock portfolios are virtually identical in distribution to the hypothetical normally distributed portfolio. The normal distribution therefore is a pretty good working assumption for well-diversified portfolios. How large a portfolio must be for this result to take hold depends on how far the distribution of the individual stocks is from normality. It appears that a portfolio typically must include at least 32 stocks for the 1-year return to be close to normally distributed.

There remain theoretical objections to the assumption that individual stock returns are normally distributed. Given that a stock price cannot be negative, the normal distribution cannot be truly representative of the behavior of a holding period rate of return because it allows for any outcome, including the whole range of negative prices. Specifically, rates of return lower than -100% are theoretically impossible because they imply the possibility of negative security prices. The failure of the normal distribution to rule out such outcomes must be viewed as a shortcoming.

An alternative assumption is that the continuously compounded annual rate of return is normally distributed. If we call this rate r and we call the effective annual rate r_e, then $r_e = e^r - 1$, and since e^r can never be negative, the smallest possible value for r_e is -1 or -100%. Thus this assumption nicely rules out the troublesome possibility of negative prices while still conveying the advantages of working with normal distributions.

Under this assumption the distribution of r_e will be *lognormal*. This distribution is depicted in Figure 5A.2.

For *short* holding periods, that is, where t is small, the approximation of $r_e(t) = e^{rt} - 1$ by rt is quite accurate and the normal distribution provides a good approximation to the lognormal. With rt normally distributed, the effective annual return over short time periods may be taken as approximately normally distributed.

For short holding periods, therefore, the mean and standard deviation of the effective holding period returns are proportional to the mean and standard deviation of the annual, continuously compounded rate of return on the stock and to the time interval.

Therefore, if the standard deviation of the annual continuously compounded rate of return on a stock is 40% ($\sigma = .40$), then the variance of the holding period return for 1 month, for example, is for all practical purposes

$$\sigma^2(\text{monthly}) = \frac{\sigma^2}{12} = \frac{.16}{12} = .0133$$

and the standard deviation is $\sqrt{.0133} = .1155$.

FIGURE 5A.2

The lognormal
distribution for three
values of σ^2.

(From Atchison, J., and
Brown, J.A.C., *The
Lognormal Distribution*,
New York: Cambridge
University Press, 1976.)

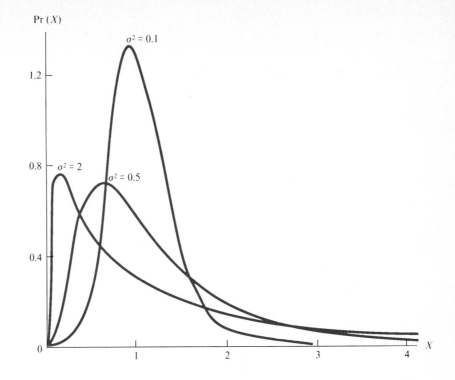

To illustrate this principle, suppose that the Dow Jones Industrials went up 1 day by 30 points from 2,100 to 2,130. Is this a "large" move? Looking at annual, continuously compounded rates on the Dow Jones portfolio, we find that the annual standard deviation historically has been about 27%. Under the assumption that the return on the Dow Jones portfolio is lognormally distributed and that returns between successive subperiods are uncorrelated, the 1-day distribution has a standard deviation (based on 250 trading days per year) of

$$
\begin{aligned}
\sigma(\text{day}) &= \sigma(\text{year}) \sqrt{1/250} \\
&= \frac{.27}{\sqrt{250}} \\
&= .0171 \\
&= 1.71 \ \% \text{ per day}
\end{aligned}
$$

Applying this to the opening level of the Dow Jones on that trading day, 2100, we find that the daily standard deviation of the Dow Jones index is 2100 × .0171 = 35.9 points per day.

Since the daily rate on the Dow Jones portfolio is approximately normal, we know that in 1 day out of 3, the Dow Jones will move (from a starting level of 2100) by more than 36 points either way. Thus a move of 30 points is hardly an unusual event.

Summary: Appendix A

1. The probability distribution of the rate of return can be characterized by its moments. The reward from taking the risk is measured by the first moment, which is the mean of the return distribution. Higher moments characterize the risk. Even moments provide information on the likelihood of extreme values, and odd moments provide information on the asymmetry of the distribution.

2. Investors' risk preferences can be characterized by their preferences for the various moments of the distribution. The fundamental approximation theorem shows that when portfolios are revised often enough, and prices are continuous, the desirability of a portfolio can be measured by its mean and variance alone.

3. The rates of return on well-diversified portfolios for holding periods that are not too long can be approximated by a normal distribution. For short holding periods (up to 1 month), the normal distribution is a good approximation for the lognormal.

Problem: Appendix A

1. The Smartstock investment consulting group prepared the following scenario analysis for the end-of-year dividend and stock price of Klink Inc., which is selling now at $12 per share:

Scenario	Probability	End-of-Year	
		Dividend ($)	Price ($)
1	.10	0	0
2	.20	.25	2.00
3	.40	.40	14.00
4	.25	.60	20.00
5	.05	.85	30.00

Compute the rate of return for each scenario and
a. The mean, median and mode
b. The standard deviation and mean absolute deviation
c. The first moment, and the second and third moments around the mean
Is the probability distribution of Klink stock positively skewed?

Appendix B:
Risk Aversion and Expected Utility

We digress here to examine the rationale behind our contention that investors are risk averse. Recognition of risk aversion as central in investment decisions goes back at least to 1738. Daniel Bernoulli, one of a famous Swiss family of distinguished mathematicians, spent the years 1725 through 1733 in St. Petersburg, where he analyzed the following coin-toss game. To enter the game one pays an entry fee. Thereafter, a coin is tossed until the *first* head appears. The number of tails, denoted by n, that appears until the first head is tossed is used to compute the payoff, R, to the participant, as

$$R(n) = 2^n$$

The probability of no tails before the first head ($n = 0$) is ½ and the corresponding payoff is $2^0 = \$1$. The probability of one tail and then heads ($n = 1$) is ½ × ½ with payoff $2^1 = \$2$, the probability of two tails and then heads ($n = 2$) is ½ × ½ × ½, and so forth.

The following table illustrates the probabilities and payoffs for various outcomes:

Tails	Probability	Payoff = $R(n)$	Probability × Payoff
0	½	$1	$1/2
1	¼	$2	$1/2
2	⅛	$4	$1/2
3	¹⁄₁₆	$8	$1/2
•	•	•	•
•	•	•	•
n	$(1/2)^{n+1}$	2^n	$1/2

The expected payoff is therefore

$$E(R) = \sum_{n=0}^{\infty} Pr(n)R(n)$$
$$= \tfrac{1}{2} + \tfrac{1}{2} + \ldots$$
$$= \infty$$

This game is called the "St. Petersburg Paradox." Although the expected payoff is infinite, participants obviously will be willing to purchase tickets to play the game only at a finite, and possibly quite modest, entry fee.

Bernoulli resolved the paradox by noting that investors do not assign the same value per dollar to all payoffs. Specifically, the greater their wealth, the less their "appreciation" for each extra dollar. We can make this insight mathematically precise by assigning a welfare or utility value to any level of investor wealth. Our utility function should increase as wealth is higher, but each extra dollar of wealth should increase utility by progressively smaller amounts.[b] (Modern economists would say that investors exhibit "decreasing marginal utility" from an additional payoff dollar.) One particular function that assigns a subjective value to the investor from a payoff of $R, which has a smaller value per dollar the greater the payoff, is the function $\log(R)$. If this function measures utility values of wealth, the subjective utility value of the game is indeed finite.[c] The certain wealth level necessary to yield this utility value is $2.38, because $\log (2.38) = .866$. Hence the certainty equivalent value of the risky payoff is $2.38, which is the maximum amount that this investor will pay to play the game.

Von Neumann and Morgenstern adapted this approach to investment theory in a complete axiomatic system in 1946. Avoiding unnecessary technical detail, we restrict ourselves here to an intuitive exposition of the rationale for risk aversion.

Imagine two individuals who are identical twins, except that one of them is less fortunate than the other. Peter has only $1,000 to his name while Paul has a net worth of $200,000. How many hours of work would each twin be willing to offer to earn 1 extra dollar? It is likely that Peter (the poor twin) has more essential uses for the extra money than does Paul. Therefore Peter will offer more hours. In other words, Peter derives a greater personal welfare or assigns a greater "utility" value to the 1,001*st* dollar than Paul does to the 200,001*st*.

Figure 5B.1 depicts graphically the relationship between wealth and the utility value of wealth that is consistent with this notion of decreasing marginal utility.

Individuals have different rates of decrease in their marginal utility of wealth. What is constant is the *principle* that per-dollar utility decreases with wealth. Functions that exhibit the property of decreasing per-unit value as the number of units grows are called concave. A simple example is the log function, familiar from high school mathematics. Of course, a log function will not fit all investors, but it is consistent with the risk aversion that we assume for all investors.

Now consider the following simple prospect:

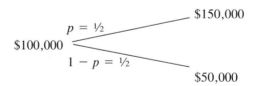

This is a fair game in that the expected profit is zero. Suppose, however, that the curve in Figure 5B.1 represents the investor's utility value of wealth, assuming a log utility function. Figure 5B.2 shows this curve with the numerical values marked.

---

[b]This utility function is similar in spirit to the one that assigns a satisfaction level to portfolios with given risk-and-return attributes. However, the utility function here refers not to investor's satisfaction with alternative portfolio choices but only to the subjective welfare they derive from different levels of wealth.

[c]If we substitute the "utility" value, $\log(R)$, for the dollar payoff, R, to obtain an expected utility value of the game (rather than expected dollar value), we have, calling $V(R)$ the expected utility,

$$V(R) = \sum_{n=0}^{\infty} Pr(n) \log[R(n)] = \sum_{n=0}^{\infty} (1/2)^{n+1} \log(2^n) \approx 0.866$$

$U(W)$

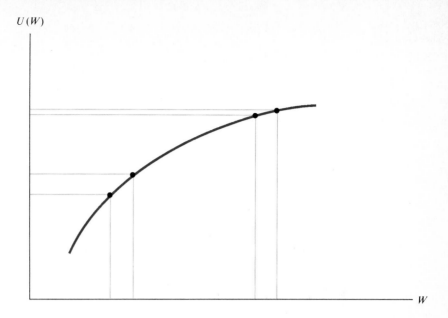

W

Figure 5B.2 shows that the loss in utility from losing $50,000 exceeds the gain from winning $50,000. Consider the gain first. With probability $p = .5$, wealth goes from $100,000 to $150,000. Using the log utility function, utility goes from $\log(100,000) = 11.51$ to $\log(150,000) = 11.92$, the distance G on the graph. This gain is $G = 11.92 - 11.51 = .41$. In expected utility terms, then, the gain is $pG = .5 \times .41 = .21$.

Now consider the possibility of coming up on the short end of the prospect. In that case, wealth goes from $100,000 to $50,000. The loss in utility, the distance L on the graph, is $L = \log(100,000) - \log(50,000) = 11.51 - 10.82 = .69$. Thus the loss in expected utility terms is $(1 - p)L = .5 \times .69 = .35$, which exceeds the gain in expected utility from the possibility of winning the game.

We compute the expected utility from the risky prospect:

$$
\begin{aligned}
E[U(W)] &= pU(W_1) + (1 - p)U(W_2) \\
&= \tfrac{1}{2}\log(50,000) + \tfrac{1}{2}\log(150,000) \\
&= 11.37
\end{aligned}
$$

If the prospect is rejected, the utility value of the (sure) $100,000 is $\log(100,000) = 11.51$, greater than that of the fair game (11.37). Hence the risk-averse investor will reject the fair game.

Using a specific investor utility function (such as the log utility) allows us to compute the certainty equivalent value of the risky prospect to a given investor, Mary Smith. This is the amount that, if received with certainty, the investor would consider equally attractive as the risky prospect.

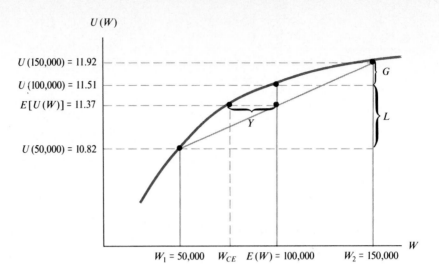

If log utility describes the investor's preferences toward wealth outcomes, then Figure 5B.2 can also tell us what is, for her, the dollar value of the prospect. We ask, "What sure level of wealth has a utility value of 11.37 (which equals the expected utility from the prospect)?" A horizontal line drawn at the level 11.37 intersects the utility curve at the level of wealth W_{CE}. This means that

$$\log(W_{CE}) = 11.37$$

which implies that

$$W_{CE} = e^{11.37}$$
$$= \$86{,}681.86$$

W_{CE} is therefore the certainty equivalent of the prospect. The distance Y in Figure 5B.2 is the penalty, or the downward adjustment, to the expected profit that is attributable to the risk of the prospect.

$$Y = E(W) - W_{CE}$$
$$= \$100{,}000 - \$86{,}681.86$$
$$= \$13{,}318.13$$

Smith views $86,681.56 for certain as being equal in utility value as $100,000 at risk. Therefore she would be indifferent between the two.

Question 5B.1. Suppose the utility function is $U(W) = \sqrt{W}$.
a. What is the utility level at wealth levels $50,000 and $150,000?
b. What is expected utility if p still equals .5?
c. What is the certainty equivalent of the risky prospect?
d. Does this utility function also display risk aversion?
e. Does this utility function display more or less risk aversion than the log utility function?

Does revealed behavior of investors demonstrate risk aversion? Looking at prices and past rates of return in financial markets, we can answer with a resounding "yes." With remarkable consistency, riskier bonds are sold at lower prices than are safer ones with otherwise similar characteristics. Riskier stocks also have provided higher average rates of return over long periods of time than less risky assets such as T-bills. For example, over the 1926 to 1987 period, the average rate of return on the S&P 500 portfolio exceeded the T-bill return by about 8.5% per year.

It is abundantly clear from financial data that the average, or representative, investor exhibits substantial risk aversion. For readers who recognize that financial assets are priced to compensate for risk by providing a risk premium and at the same time feel the urge for some gambling, we have a constructive recommendation: direct your gambling desire to investment in financial markets. As Von Neumann once said, "the stock market is a casino with the odds in your favor." A small risk-seeking investment may provide all the excitement you want with a positive expected return to boot!

Problems: Appendix B

1. Suppose that your wealth is $250,000. You buy a $200,000 house and invest the remainder in a risk-free asset paying an annual interest rate of 6%. There is a probability of .001 that your house will burn to the ground and its value be reduced to zero. With a log utility of end-of-year wealth, how much would you be willing to pay for insurance (at the beginning of the year)? (Assume that, if the house does not burn down, its end of year value still will be $200,000.)
2. If the cost of insuring your house is $1 per $1,000 of value, what will be the certainty equivalent of your end-of-year wealth if you insure your house at:
   a. ½ its value
   b. Its full value
   c. 1½ times its value

CHAPTER 6

Capital Allocation Between the Risky Asset and the Risk-Free Asset

There are two methods to control investment risk. The first is to shift funds out of risky securities into safe Treasury bills. We call this an **asset allocation decision** because it requires choosing among broad asset markets: in this case the choice is between equity securities and money market securities. The following box describes the asset allocation strategies of several well-known brokerage houses.

The second method is to make choices in the actual portfolio of risky assets. Choosing the portfolio of risky assets is called the **security selection decision.** For Humanex (in the Chapter 5 example), security selection included identifying a hedge asset (shares in SugarKane stock) to add to the equity portfolio to improve the risk-return characteristics of that portfolio.

The asset allocation and security selection decisions are in some ways independent. A "bottom-up" treatment of portfolio choice would start with security selection within each asset class. Then, given the investor's choice for the best combination of risky securities, that portfolio would be mixed with risk-free assets to form a complete portfolio. We prefer a "top-down" approach, however, so we start with asset allocation: how to mix the broad asset classes of an investor's portfolio. Only then do we consider how to select the securities within each asset class. This treatment offers a bird's-eye view of portfolio construction that avoids getting lost in the intricacies of the security selection problem. Our assumption is that asset allocation provides a greater perspective as background for the analytically more difficult security selection decision.

Therefore this chapter covers the allocation of an investor's funds between a risky asset and a risk-free asset. Although investors in fact hold many risky assets in their portfolios, for now we will assume that a given optimal combination of those risky assets has been determined and that its risk-and-return characteristics have been determined. We refer to this optimal risky portfolio as "the" **risky asset.** At this stage the investor decides how much to invest in it, placing the remainder of the investment fund in the risk-free asset.

Evaluating Brokers' Advice on Asset Mix

Six of 10 Firms Beat '87 Return of S&P 500

Just as baseball fans claim that pitching is at least 70% of the game, many professional investors say that asset allocation is the most valuable skill in investing.

It's "more important than stock selection," claims Edward Kerschner, chief investment strategist for Paine-Webber Inc., echoing a comment made by top research officials at several other firms.

YOUR
MONEY
MATTERS

Asset allocation is the art of placing an investor's funds into different types of assets to come up with a strategically balanced portfolio. Some financial advisers slice the pie into many pieces and include real estate, gold or esoteric investments like oil-and-gas partnerships. But brokerage houses usually use just three categories: stocks, bonds and cash. ("Cash," in this case, means safe investments like Treasury bills or money market funds, not dollars under the mattress.)

Following last fall's stock market crash, asset allocation became a hot topic on Wall Street—and for good reason. People caught with too much of their money in stocks needed a trip to the financial hospital. Those who had diversified their investment portfolios escaped with cuts and bruises.

How good is the asset-allocation advice doled out by major brokerage houses? To find out, *The Wall Street Journal* surveyed that advice given last year by the 10 largest brokerage houses, based on the number of registered representatives. Wilshire Associates, a securities-research firm in Santa Monica, Calif., then estimated how investors who followed the suggestions would have fared. The accompanying table shows the results and what each house recommends now.

As it turns out, most of the brokerage houses offered useful allocation advice in 1987. Indeed, six of the 10 beat last year's return on stocks, and all of them bested the annual return on bonds. Still, some did

much better than others. Here's a firm-by-firm rundown.

Kidder Peabody & Co.: Cash was king for Kidder in 1987. For most of the year, it suggested that investors keep 35% of their funds in cash, the highest level recommended by any of the firms. That caution paid off: Last year, cash (as measured by Treasury bills) outperformed both stocks and bonds on an annual basis. Bonds, overall, were the worst investment, but at no point did Kidder recommend more than a 20% bond position.

As for stocks, Kidder suggested a 45% weighting, which it lowered to 40% in November. The firm's cautious stance "reflected our assessment that the financial markets were likely to face a protracted period of great uncertainty and volatility," says R. Joseph Fuchs, Kidder's director of research. "We were communicating an overriding concern with capital preservation."

Paine Webber: "We're the only firm that has a totally objective model as opposed to a committee decision," says Mr. Kerschner, the company's investment-strategist. The model turns on historical data about "risk premiums." For the past 20 years, Mr. Kerschner says, investors have generally demanded 2.7 percentage points of extra return for investing in stocks, as opposed to bonds, to compensate for the extra risk. When the spread diminishes to less than that, bonds generally look like the better buy, he says. And that's exactly what happend in 1987: As stock prices rose and interest rates climbed, the gap narrowed. Thus, Paine Webber started the year recommending that investors put 47% of their funds into stocks, then progressively lightened that percentage to 6% just before the crash.

Dean Witter Reynolds Inc.: "What we did right was pay attention to the fundamentals, as opposed to the psychology of the moment," says John Connolly, the firm's chief investment strategist. When 1987 began, Dean Witter recommended a 71% weighting in stocks and, in three cuts, chipped that down to 50%. Still, the final cut came in May, three months before the market peaked. "If there was a fault, it was being a

Continued.

little bit too early," Mr. Connolly says, "but I guess you can't have it both ways."

Merrill Lynch: "If I was right all the time, I'd be (sailing) my yacht," says Charles Clough, chief investment strategist for Merrill Lynch & Co. Before the crash, Merrill stepped down its weighting on stocks to 40% from 50%; at the same time, it increased its weighting on bonds to 40%. "I had the timing of the moves right," says Mr. Clough, "but I should have made" more dramatic changes.

Shearson Lehman Hutton: Investment strategist Michael Sherman says he has two regrets about the advice he gave last year. First, it was "wrong-footed" of him to suggest raising cash levels to 20% as early as he did, in May. Second, he wishes he'd done more to prepare for the crash. Between April and October, Mr. Sherman recommended that investors gradually lower their stock holdings to 50% of their total portfolio, from 65%. Now, of course, he wishes he'd advised them to lower it more. After all, he says, "I was writing articles all summer long about how inflated the (stock) market was."

Shearson was the only firm to recommend that investors buy gold. But the amount was so small—just 5%—that it had a negligible impact on the firm's annual results.

A.G. Edwards: The prize for "most cautious" among the 10 firms probably goes to A.G. Edwards & Sons Inc. At the start of last year, the St. Louis-based firm recommended that investors put only 35% of their money in stocks. Before the crash, it lowered that to 30%; after the crash, it lowered the weighting again, to 25%. "We are basically a conservative company," says chief economist Raymond Worseck. "As the stock market got crazier and crazier, we thought that bonds represented good value."

Smith Barney: At the start of 1987, John Hoffman, chief investment strategist at Smith Barney, Harris Upham & Co., urged a 30% position in bonds and only a 50% position in stocks. "After two good years in 1985 and 1986, I don't think we anticipated how strong the stock market would be in early 1987," he says. "We

were late in a bull market.... We were getting a little nervous at that point."

Smith Barney raised its stock allocation to 60% in the spring, then ducked back to 50% in September. Naturally, Mr. Hoffman now wishes he'd ducked lower, but he figures no one really foresaw the crash.

Thomson McKinnon: The good news is that prior to the crash, Thomson McKinnon Securities Inc. told investors to raise their cash position to 25%. The bad news is it suggested that money come out of bonds, not stocks: Throughout most of the year, Thomson recommended a position in equities that hovered around 50%. Early in 1987, Thomson urged a 48% allocation to bonds. That proved another unwise move: the bond market sputtered for much of the year.

Drexel Burnham: The calculations for Drexel Burnham Lambert Inc. are based on its advice to institutional clients; the firm doesn't have a blend for retail customers. At its most bullish, Drexel will only recommend an allocation of 60% in stocks; similarly, the highest it will go in bonds is 40%. When it foresees trouble for either market, cash can be substituted for some of the stocks or bonds.

During most of 1987, Drexel recommended a 58% position in stocks and a 25% position in bonds. After the crash it held to the 58% stock weighting but raised the bond component to 32%. According to Abby Joseph Cohen, the firm's chief investment strategist, this post-crash advice has paid off handsomely, even if in the 1987 totals it's largely offset by losses elsewhere.

Prudential-Bache: Throughout 1987, Prudential Bache Securities Inc. urged an intense commitment to stocks. As the year started, it suggested that aggressive small investors be 95% invested in stocks. That dipped to 85% by midyear, then rose to 90% before the crash. In October, Pru-Bache ran bullishly right off the cliff.

Alone among the 10 firms, Pru-Bache advised investors to avoid bonds altogether during 1987. Greg Smith, chief investment strategist, says he felt the economy would be stronger than expected and the dollar weak—both bad for bonds. Thus, some Prudential Bache followers probably missed the post-crash bond rally.

Continued.

The asset allocation decision has two components. First, we determine the risk-return trade-off offered by the set of feasible portfolios. Second, we show how the individual's degree of risk aversion dictates the optimal mix of risky assets and risk-free assets. Finally, we look at so-called passive strategies, which call for allocation of the investment budget between a money market (risk-free) fund and an index fund of common stocks.

6.1 Risk Reduction With the Risk-Free Asset

Throughout this chapter we will consider investors holding a risky portfolio, called P, and some risk-free securities such as T-bills. When we shift wealth from the risky portfolio to the risk-free asset, we do not change the relative proportions of the various risky assets within the risky portfolio. Rather, we reduce the relative weight of the risky portfolio as a whole in favor of risk-free assets.

For example, assume that the total market value of an initial portfolio is $300,000, of which $90,000 is invested in the Ready Asset money market fund, a risk-free asset for practical purposes. The remaining $210,000 is invested in risky equity securities—$113,400 in IBM and $96,600 in GM. The IBM and GM holding is "the" risky portfolio, 54% in IBM and 46% in GM:

$$\text{IBM:} \quad w_1 = \frac{113,400}{210,000}$$
$$= .54$$

$$\text{GM:} \quad w_2 = \frac{96,600}{210,000}$$
$$= .46$$

The weight of the risky portfolio, P, in the **complete portfolio,** including risk-free investments, is denoted by y:

$$y = \frac{210,000}{300,000}$$
$$= .7 \text{ (risky assets)}$$

$$1 - y = \frac{90,000}{300,000}$$
$$= .3 \text{ (risk-free assets)}$$

The weights of each stock in the complete portfolio are as follows:

$$\text{IBM:} \quad \frac{\$113,400}{\$300,000} = .378$$

$$\text{GM:} \quad \frac{\$96,600}{\$300,000} = .322$$

$$\text{Risky portfolio} \quad = .700$$

The risky portfolio is 70% of the complete portfolio.

Suppose that the owner of this portfolio wishes to decrease risk by reducing the exposure to the risky portfolio from $y = .7$ to $y = .56$. The risky portfolio would total only $168,000 (.56 × $300,000 = $168,000), requiring the sale of $42,000 of the original $210,000 risky holdings, with the proceeds used to purchase more shares in Ready Asset (the money market fund). Total holdings in the risk-free asset will increase to $300,000(1 - .56) = \$132,000$, or the original holdings plus the new contribution to the money market fund:

$$\$90,000 + \$42,000 = \$132,000$$

The key point, however, is that we leave the proportions of each stock in the risky portfolio unchanged. Because the weights of IBM and GM in the risky portfolio are .54 and .46, respectively, we sell $.54 \times \$42,000 = \$22,680$ of IBM and $.46 \times \$42,000 = \$19,320$ of GM. After the sale the proportions of each share in the risky portfolio are in fact unchanged:

$$\text{IBM:} \quad w_1 = \frac{113,400 - 22,680}{210,000 - 42,000}$$
$$= .54$$

$$\text{GM:} \quad w_2 = \frac{96,600 - 19,320}{210,000 - 42,000}$$
$$= .46$$

Rather than thinking of our risky holdings as IBM and GM stock separately, we may view our holdings as if they were in a single fund that holds IBM and GM in fixed proportions. In this sense we treat the risky fund as a single risky asset, that asset being a particular bundle of securities. As we shift in and out of safe assets, we simply alter our holdings of that bundle of securities commensurately.

Given this assumption, we can now turn to the desirability of reducing risk by changing the risky/risk-free asset mix, that is, reducing risk by decreasing the proportion y. As long as we do not alter the weights of each stock within the risky portfolio, the probability distribution of the rate of return on the risky portfolio remains unchanged by the asset reallocation. What will change is the probability distribution of the rate of return on the complete, or overall, portfolio that consists of the risky asset and the risk-free asset.

Concept Check

Question 1. What will be the dollar value of your position in IBM, and its proportion in your overall portfolio, if you decide to hold 50% of your investment budget in Ready Asset?

6.2 *The Risk-Free Asset*

By virtue of its power to tax and control the money supply, only the government can issue default-free bonds. Actually, the default-free guarantee by itself is not sufficient to make the bonds risk-free in real terms. The only risk-free asset in real terms would be a perfectly price-indexed bond. Moreover, a default-free perfectly indexed bond offers a guaranteed real rate to an investor only if the maturity of the bond is identical to the investor's desired holding period. Even indexed bonds are subject to interest rate risk, because real interest rates change unpredictably through time. When future real rates are uncertain, so is the future price of perfectly indexed bonds.

Nevertheless, it is common practice to view Treasury bills as "the" **risk-free asset.** Their short-term nature makes their values insensitive to interest rate fluctuations. Indeed, an investor can lock in a short-term nominal return by buying a bill and holding it to maturity. The inflation uncertainty over the course of a few weeks, or even months, is negligible compared with the uncertainty of stock market returns.

In practice, most investors use a broader range of money market instruments as a risk-free asset. All the money market instruments are virtually free of interest rate risk because of their short maturities and are fairly safe in terms of default or credit risk.

Most money market funds hold, for the most part, three types of securities: Treasury bills, bank certificates of deposit (CDs), and commercial paper (CP), differing slightly in their default risk. The yields to maturity on CDs and CP for identical maturity, for example, are always slightly higher than those of T-bills. The pattern of this yield spread for 90-day CDs is shown in Figure 6.1.

Money market funds have changed their relative holdings of these securities over time, but by and large, T-bills make up only about 15% of their portfolios. Nevertheless, the risk of such blue-chip short-term investments as CDs and CP is miniscule compared with that of most other assets such as long-term corporate bonds, common stocks, or real estate. Hence, we treat money market funds as the most easily accessible risk-free asset for most investors.

6.3 *Portfolios of One Risky Asset and One Risk-Free Asset*

In this section we examine the risk-return combinations available to investors. This is the "technological" part of asset allocation; it deals with only the opportunities available to investors given the features of the broad asset markets in which they can invest. In the next section we address the "personal" part of the problem, the specific individual's choice of the best risk-return combination from the set of feasible combinations.

Suppose that the investor has already decided on the composition of the optimal risky portfolio. The investment proportions in all the available risky assets are known. Now the final concern is with the proportion of the investment budget, y, to

FIGURE 6.1

The pattern of the yield spread for 90-day certificates of deposit vs. 3-month Treasury bills.

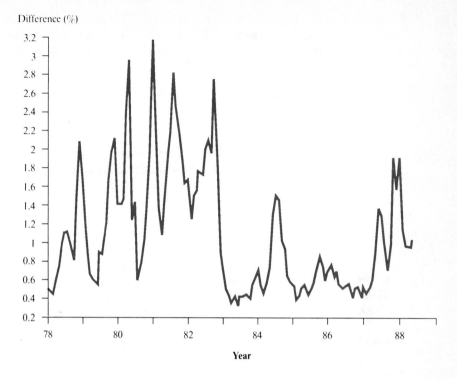

Difference (%)

Year

be allocated to the risky portfolio, P. The remaining proportion, $1 - y$, is to be invested in the risk-free asset, F.

Denote the risky rate of return by r_P and denote the expected rate of return on P by $E(r_P)$ and its standard deviation by σ_P. The rate of return on the risk-free asset is denoted as r_f. In the numerical example we assume that $E(r_p) = 15\%$, $\sigma_P = 22\%$, and that the risk-free rate is $r_f = 7\%$. Thus the risk premium on the risky asset is $E(r_P) - r_f = 8\%$.

With a proportion, y, in the risky portfolio, and $1 - y$ in the risk-free asset, the rate of return on the *complete* portfolio, denoted C, is r_C where

$$r_C = yr_P + (1 - y)r_f$$

Taking the expectation of this portfolio's rate of return,

$$\begin{aligned} E(r_C) &= yE(r_P) + (1 - y)r_f \\ &= r_f + y[E(r_P) - r_f] \\ &= .07 + y(.15 - .07) \end{aligned} \qquad (6.1)$$

This result is easily interpreted. The base rate of return for any portfolio is the risk-free rate. In addition, the portfolio is *expected* to earn a risk premium that depends on the risk premium of the risky portfolio, $E(r_P) - r_f$, and the investor's exposure to the risky asset, denoted by y. Investors are assumed to be risk averse and thus unwilling to take on a risky position without a positive risk premium.

As we noted in Chapter 5, when we combine a risky asset and a risk-free asset in a portfolio, the standard deviation of that portfolio is the standard deviation of the risky asset multiplied by the weight of the risky asset in that portfolio. In our case, the complete portfolio consists of the risky asset and the risk-free asset. Since the standard deviation of the risky portfolio is $\sigma_P = .22$,

$$\sigma_C = y\sigma_P \qquad\qquad (6.2)$$
$$= .22y$$

which makes sense because the standard deviation of the portfolio is proportional to both the standard deviation of the risky asset and the proportion invested in it. In sum, the rate of return of the complete portfolio will have expected return $E(r_C) = r_f + y[E(r_P) - r_f] = .07 + .08y$ and standard deviation $\sigma_C = .22y$.

The next step is to plot the portfolio characteristics (as a function of y) in the expected return-standard deviation plane. This is done in Figure 6.2. The expected return-standard deviation combination for the risk-free asset, F, appears on the vertical axis because the standard deviation is zero. The risky asset, P, is plotted with a standard deviation, $\sigma_P = .22$, and expected return of .15. If an investor chooses to invest solely in the risky asset, then $y = 1.0$, and the resulting portfolio is P. If the chosen position is $y = 0$, then $1 - y = 1.0$, and the resulting portfolio is the risk-free portfolio F.

What about the more interesting midrange portfolios where y lies between zero and 1? These portfolios will graph on the straight line connecting points F and P. The slope of that line is simply $[E(r_P) - r_f]/\sigma_P$ (or rise/run), in this case $.08/.22$.

FIGURE 6.2
Expected return-standard deviation combinations.

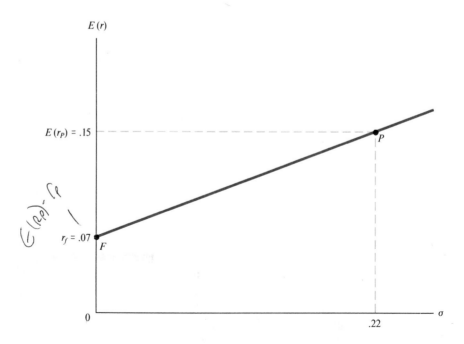

The conclusion is straightforward. Increasing the fraction of the overall portfolio invested in the risky asset increases the expected return by the risk premium of equation 6.1, which is .08. It also increases portfolio standard deviation according to equation 6.2 at the rate .22. The extra return per extra risk is thus .08/.22 = .36.

To derive the exact equation for the straight line between F and P, we rearrange equation 6.2 to find that $y = \sigma_C/\sigma_P$, and substitute for y in equation 6.1 to describe the expected return-standard deviation trade-off:

$$E[r_C(y)] = r_f + y[E(r_P) - r_f]$$

$$= r_f + \frac{\sigma_C}{.22}[E(r_P) - r_f]$$

$$= .07 + \frac{.08}{.22}\sigma_C$$

Thus the expected return of the portfolio as a function of its standard deviation is a straight line, with intercept r_f and slope as follows:

$$S = \frac{E(r_P) - r_f}{\sigma_P}$$

$$= \frac{.08}{.22}$$

Figure 6.3 graphs the *investment opportunity set,* which is the set of feasible expected return and standard deviation pairs of all portfolios resulting from different values of y. The graph is a straight line originating at r_f and going through the point labeled P.

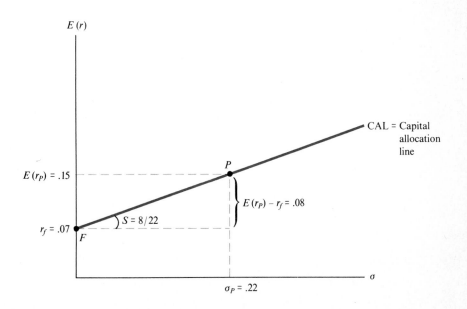

FIGURE 6.3
The investment opportunity set with a risky asset and a risk-free asset.

This straight line is called the **capital allocation line** (CAL). It depicts all the risk-return combinations available to investors. The slope of the CAL, S, equals the increase in the expected return of the chosen portfolio per unit of additional standard deviation—in other words, the measure of extra return per extra risk. For this reason, the slope also is called the **reward-to-variability ratio.**

A portfolio equally divided between the risky asset and the risk-free asset, that is, where $y = .5$, will have an expected rate of return of $E(r_C) = .07 + .5 \times .08 = .11$, implying a risk premium of 4%, and a standard deviation of $\sigma_C = .5 \times .22 = .11$, or 11%. It will plot on the line FP midway between F and P. The reward-to-variability ratio is $S = .08/.22 = .36$.

Concept Check

Question 2. Can the reward-to-variability ratio, $S = [E(r_C) - r_f]/\sigma$, of any combination of the risky asset and the risk-free asset be different from the ratio for the risky asset taken alone, $[E(r_P) - r_f]/\sigma$, which in this case is .36?

What about points on the line to the right of portfolio P in the investment opportunity set? If investors can borrow at the (risk-free) rate of $r_f = 7\%$, they can construct portfolios that may be plotted on the CAL to the right of P.

Suppose the investment budget is $300,000, and our investor borrows an additional $120,000, investing the total available funds in the risky asset. This is a *leveraged* position in the risky asset; it is financed in part by borrowing. In that case

$$y = \frac{420,000}{300,000}$$

$$= 1.4$$

and $1 - y = 1 - 1.4 = -.4$, reflecting a short position in the risk-free asset, which is a borrowing position. Rather than lending at a 7% interest rate, the investor borrows at 7%. The distribution of the portfolio rate of return still exhibits the same reward-to-variability ratio:

$$E(r_C) = .07 + (1.4 \times .08)$$
$$= .182$$
$$\sigma_C = 1.4 \times .22$$
$$= .308$$
$$S = \frac{E(r_C) - r_f}{\sigma_C}$$
$$= \frac{.182 - .07}{.308}$$
$$= .36$$

FIGURE 6.4

The opportunity set
with differential
borrowing and lending
rates.

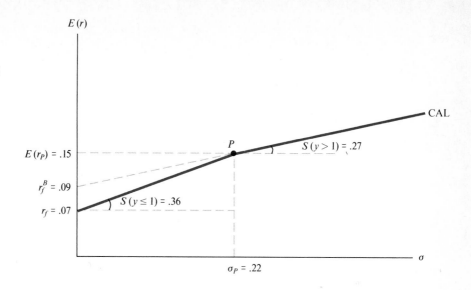

As one might expect, the leveraged portfolio has a higher standard deviation than does an unleveraged position in the risky asset.

Of course, nongovernment investors cannot borrow at the risk-free rate. The risk of a borrower's default causes lenders to demand higher interest rates on loans. Therefore the nongovernment investor's borrowing cost will exceed the lending rate of $r_f = 7\%$. Suppose that the borrowing rate is $r_f^B = 9\%$. Then, in the borrowing range the reward-to-variability ratio, the slope of the CAL, will be $[E(r_P) - r_f^B]/\sigma_P = .06/.22 = .27$. The CAL will therefore be "kinked" at point P as shown in Figure 6.4. To the left of P the investor is lending at 7%, and the slope of the CAL is .36. To the right of P, where $y > 1$, the investor is borrowing to finance extra investments in the risky asset, and the slope is .27.

In practice, borrowing to invest in the risky portfolio is easy and straightforward if you have a margin account with a broker. All you have to do is tell your broker that you want to buy "on margin." Margin purchases may not exceed 50% of the purchase value. Therefore, if your net worth in the account is $300,000, the broker is allowed to lend you up to $300,000 to purchase additional stock.[1] You would then have $600,000 on the asset side of your account and $300,000 on the liability side, resulting in $y = 2.0$.

---

[1]Margin purchases require the investor to maintain the securities in a margin account with the broker. If the value of the securities declines below a "maintenance margin," a "margin call" is sent out, requiring a deposit to bring the net worth of the account up to the appropriate level. If the margin call is not met, regulations mandate that some or all of the securities be sold by the broker and the proceeds used to reestablish the required margin. See Chapter 3, Section 3.5, for a further discussion.

6.4 Risk Tolerance and Asset Allocation

We have shown how to develop the CAL, the graph of all feasible risk-return combinations available from different asset-allocation choices. The investor confronting the CAL now must choose one optimal combination from the set of feasible choices. This choice entails a trade-off between risk and return. Individual investor differences in risk aversion imply that, given an identical opportunity set (as described by a risk-free rate and a reward-to-variability ratio), different investors will choose different positions in the risky asset. In particular, the more risk-averse investors will choose to hold less of the risky asset and more of the risk-free asset.

In Chapter 5 we showed that the utility an investor derives from a portfolio with a given probability distribution of rates of return can be described by the expected return and variance of the portfolio rate of return. Specifically, we developed the following representation:

$$U = E(r) - \tfrac{1}{2}A\sigma^2$$

where A is the coefficient of risk aversion. We interpret this expression to say that the utility from a portfolio increases as the expected rate of return increases, and it decreases when the variance increases. The relative magnitude of these changes is governed by the coefficient of risk aversion A. For risk-neutral investors, $A = 0$. Higher levels of risk aversion are reflected in larger values for A.

An investor who faces a risk-free rate, r_f, and a risky portfolio with expected return $E(r_P)$ and standard deviation σ_P will find that, for any choice of y, the expected return of the complete portfolio is given by equation 6.1, part of which we repeat here:

$$E(r_C) = r_f + y[E(r_P) - r_f]$$

From equation 6.2, the variance of the overall portfolio is

$$\sigma_C^2 = y^2\sigma_P^2$$

The investor attempts to maximize his or her utility level, U, by choosing the best allocation to the risky asset, y. Typically, we write this problem as follows:

$$\operatorname*{Max}_{y} U = E(r_C) - \tfrac{1}{2}A\sigma_C^2 = r_f + y[E(r_P) - r_f] - \tfrac{1}{2}y^2 A\sigma_P^2$$

where A is the coefficient of risk aversion.

Students of calculus will remember that the maximization problem is solved by setting the derivative of this expression to zero. Doing so and solving for y yields the optimal position for risk-averse investors in the risky asset, y^*, as follows[2]:

$$y^* = \frac{E(r_P) - r_f}{A\sigma_P^2}$$

(6.3)

This solution shows that the optimal position in the risky asset is, as one would expect, *inversely* proportional to the level of risk aversion and the level of risk, as measured by the variance, and directly proportional to the risk premium offered by the risky asset.

Going back to our numerical example [$r_f = 7\%$, $E(r_P) = 15\%$, and $\sigma_P = 22\%$], the optimal solution for an investor with a coefficient of risk aversion, $A = 4$, is

$$y^* = \frac{.15 - .07}{4 \times .22^2}$$

$$= .41$$

In other words, this particular investor will invest 41% of the investment budget in the risky asset and 59% in the risk-free asset. (Note that r_f, $E(r_P)$, and σ_P must be expressed as decimals, or else it is necessary to change the scale of A.)

With 41% invested in the risky portfolio, the rate of return of the complete portfolio will have an expected return and standard deviation as follows:

$$E(r_C) = .07 + .41 \times (.15 - .07)$$

$$= .1028$$

$$\sigma_C = .41 \times .22$$

$$= .0902$$

The risk premium of the complete portfolio is $E(r_C) - r_f = 3.28\%$, which is obtained by taking on a portfolio with a standard deviation of 9.02%. Notice that 3.28/9.02 = 36, which is the reward-to-variability ratio assumed for this problem.

A less mathematical way of presenting this decision problem is to use indifference curve analysis. Recall from Chapter 5 that the indifference curve is a graph in the expected return–standard deviation plane of all points that result in a given level of utility. The curve then displays the investor's required trade-off between expected return and standard deviation.

For example, suppose that the initial portfolio under consideration is the risky asset itself, $y = 1$. The dark blue curve in Figure 6.5 represents the indifference curve for an investor with a degree of risk aversion, $A = 4$, that passes through the risky asset with $E(r_P) = 15\%$ and $\sigma_P = 22\%$. The light blue curve, by contrast, shows an indifference curve going through P with a smaller degree of risk aversion, $A = 2$. The dashed indifference curve is flatter, that is, the more risk-tolerant (less risk-

---

[2]The derivative with respect to y equals $E(r_P) - r_f - yA\sigma_P^2$. Setting this expression equal to zero and solving for y yields equation 6.3.

FIGURE 6.5
Two indifference
curves through a risky
asset.

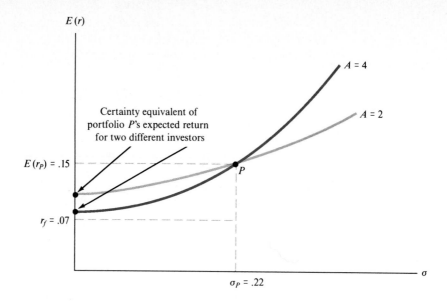

FIGURE 6.6
A set of indifference
curves.

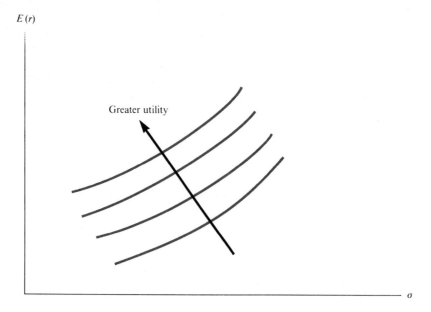

FIGURE 6.7

The graphical solution
to the portfolio
decision.

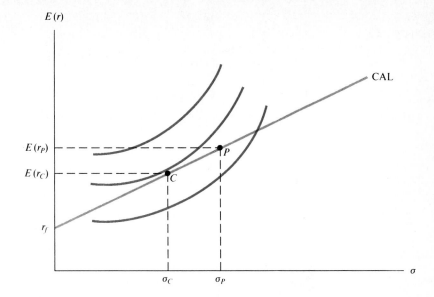

averse) investor requires a smaller increase in expected return to compensate for a
given increase in standard deviation. The intercept of the indifference curve with the
vertical axis is the *certainty equivalent* of the risky portfolio's expected rate of return
because it gives a risk-free return with the same utility as the risky portfolio. Notice
in Figure 6.5 that the less risk-averse investor (with $A = 2$) has a higher certainty
equivalent for a risky portfolio such as P than the more risk-averse investor ($A = 4$).

Indifference curves can be drawn for many benchmark portfolios, representing
various levels of utility. Figure 6.6 shows this set of indifference curves.

To show how to use indifference curve analysis to determine the choice of the
optimal portfolio for a specific CAL, Figure 6.7 superimposes the graphs of the indifference curves on the graph of the investment opportunity set, the CAL.

The investor seeks the position with the highest feasible level of utility, represented by the highest possible indifference curve that touches the investment opportunity set. This is the indifference curve tangent to the CAL.

This optimal overall portfolio is represented by point C, on the investment opportunity set. Such a graphical approach yields the same solution as the algebraic approach:

$$E(r_C) = .1028$$

and

$$\sigma_C = .0902$$

which yields $y^* = .41$.

In summary, the asset allocation process can be broken down into two steps: (1)
determine the CAL, and (2) find the point of highest utility along that line.

Question 4.

a. If an investor's coefficient of risk aversion is $A = 3$, how does the optimal asset mix change? What are the new $E(r_C)$ and σ_C?

b. Suppose that the borrowing rate, $r_f^B = 9\%$, is greater than the lending rate, $r_f = 7\%$. Show, graphically, how the optimal portfolio choice of some investors will be affected by the higher borrowing rate. Which investors will *not* be affected by the borrowing rate?

6.5 Passive Strategies: The Capital Market Line

The CAL is derived with the risk-free asset and "the" risky portfolio P. Determination of the assets to include in risky portfolio P may result from a passive or an active strategy. A **passive strategy** describes a portfolio decision that avoids *any* direct or indirect security analysis.[3] At first blush, a passive strategy would appear to be naive. As will become apparent, however, forces of supply and demand in large capital markets may make such a strategy a reasonable choice for many investors.

Two researchers, Roger Ibbotson and Rex Sinquefield, provide a comprehensive compilation of the history of rates of return on different asset classes in the twentieth century on an ongoing basis.[4] Their data are available on computer tape from the University of Chicago's Center for Research in Security Prices (CRSP). This data base includes rates of return on 30-day T-bills, long-term T-bonds, long-term corporate bonds, and common stocks. The CRSP tapes provide a monthly rate of return series for the period 1926 to the present and, for common stocks, a daily rate of return series from 1964 to the present. We can use these data to develop various passive strategies.

A natural candidate for a passively held risky asset would be a well-diversified portfolio of common stocks. We have already said that a passive strategy requires that we devote no resources to acquiring information on any individual stock or group of stocks, so we must follow a "neutral" diversification strategy. One way is to select a diversified portfolio of stocks that mirrors the value of the corporate sector of the U.S. economy. This results in a value-weighted portfolio in which, for example, the proportion invested in GM stock will be the ratio of GM's total market value to the market value of all listed stocks.

The value-weighted stock portfolio in the Ibbotson-Sinquefield study is the Stan-

---

[3] By "indirect security analysis" we mean the delegation of that responsibility to an intermediary such as a professional money manager.

[4] Ibbotson, R.G., and Sinquefield, R.A., *Stocks, Bond, Bills, and Inflation* (SBBI), Updated in *SBBI 1987 Yearbook*, Chicago: Ibbotson Associates, 1987.

TABLE 6.1   Annual Rates of Return for Common Stocks and 1-Month Bills, and the Risk Premium Over Bills on Common Stock

	Common Stocks		1-Month Bills		Risk Premium Over Bills on Common Stocks	
	Mean	S.D.	Mean	S.D.	Mean	S.D.
1926-1940	8.5	30.1	1.3	1.5	7.2	30.2
1941-1951	15.3	14.8	.6	.4	14.7	14.7
1952-1967	14.8	18.0	2.7	1.0	12.1	18.6
1968-1987	10.6	16.4	7.5	2.7	3.1	16.7
1926-1987	12.0	20.9	3.5	3.3	8.5	21.4

dard & Poor's composite index of the 500 largest capitalization corporations (S&P 500). (Before March 1957 it consisted of 90 of the largest stocks.) Table 6.1 shows the historical record of this portfolio.

The last pair of columns shows the average risk premium over T-bills and the standard deviation of the common stock portfolio. The risk premium of 8.5% and standard deviation of 21.4% over the entire period are similar to the figures we assumed for the risky portfolio we used as an example in Section 6.4.

We call the capital allocation line provided by 1-month T-bills and a broad index of common stocks the **capital market line** (CML). A passive strategy generates an investment opportunity set that is represented by the CML.

How reasonable is it for an investor to pursue a passive strategy? Of course, we cannot answer such a question without comparing the strategy to the costs and benefits accruing to an active portfolio strategy. Some thoughts are relevant at this point, however.

First, the alternative active strategy is not free. Whether you choose to invest the time and cost to acquire the information needed to generate an optimal active portfolio of risky assets, or whether you delegate the task to a professional who will charge a fee, construction of an active portfolio is more expensive than a passive one. The passive portfolio requires only small commissions on purchases of T-bills (or zero commissions if you purchase bills directly from the government) and management fees to a mutual fund company that offers a market index fund to the public. Vanguard, for example, operates the Index Trust Fund that mimics the S&P 500 index. It purchases shares of the firms constituting the S&P 500 in proportion to the market values of the outstanding equity of each firm, and therefore essentially replicates the S&P 500 index. The fund thus duplicates the performance of this market index. It has one of the lowest operating expenses (as a percentage of assets) of all mutual stock funds precisely because it requires minimal managerial effort.

A second reason supporting a passive strategy is the free-rider benefit. If we assume there are many active, knowledgeable investors who quickly bid up prices of undervalued assets and bid down overvalued assets (by selling), we have to conclude that at any time most assets will be fairly priced. Therefore a well-diversified portfolio of common stock will be a reasonably fair buy, and the passive strategy may not be inferior to that of the average active investor. (We will explain this assumption and provide a more comprehensive analysis of the relative success of passive strategies in later chapters.)

To summarize, however, a passive strategy involves investment in two passive portfolios: virtually risk-free short-term T-bills (or, alternatively, a money market fund), and a fund of common stocks that mimics a broad market index. The capital allocation line representing such a strategy is called the capital market line. Historically, based on 1926 to 1987 data, the passive risky portfolio offered an average risk premium of 8.5% and a standard deviation of 21.4%, resulting in a reward-to-variability ratio of .40. Passive investors allocate their investment budgets among instruments according to their degree of risk aversion.

We can use our analysis to deduce a typical investor's risk-aversion parameter. In 1987 the total market value of the S&P 500 stocks was about four times as large as the market value of all outstanding T-bills of less than 6 months' maturity. If we ignore all other assets (long-term bonds and real estate, for example), and pretend that all investors followed a passive strategy, then the average investor's position in the risky asset (the S&P 500) was

$$y = \frac{4}{1 + 4}$$
$$= .8$$

What degree of risk aversion must investors have for this portfolio to be optimal?

Assuming that the average investor uses the historical average risk premium (8.5%) and standard deviation (21.4%) to forecast future return and standard deviation, and noting that the weight in the risky portfolio was .8, we can work out the average investor's risk tolerance as follows:

$$y^* = \frac{E(r_M) - r_f}{A\sigma_M^2}$$
$$= .8$$
$$= \frac{.085}{A \times .214^2}$$

which implies a coefficient of risk aversion of

$$A = \frac{.085}{.8 \times .214^2}$$
$$= 2.32$$

This is, of course, mere speculation. We have assumed without basis that the average 1987 investor held the naive view that historical average rates of return and standard deviations are the best estimates of expected rates of return and risk, looking to the future. To the extent that in 1987 the average investor took advantage of contemporary information in addition to simple historical data, our estimate of $A = 2.32$ would be an unjustified inference. Nevertheless, a broad range of studies, taking into account the full range of available assets, places the degree of risk aversion for the representative investor in the range of 2.0 to 4.0.[5]

Concept Check

Question 5. Suppose that expectations about the S&P 500 index and the T-bill rate are the same as they were in 1987, but you find that today a greater proportion is invested in T-bills than in 1987. What can you conclude about the change in risk tolerance over the years since 1987?

Summary

1. Shifting funds from the risky portfolio to the risk-free asset is the simplest way to reduce risk. Other methods involve diversification of the risky portfolio. We take up these methods in later chapters.

2. T-bills provide a perfectly risk-free asset in nominal terms only. Nevertheless, the standard deviation of real rates on short-term T-bills is small compared to that of other assets such as long-term bonds and common stocks, so for the purpose of our analysis we consider T-bills as the risk-free asset. Money market funds hold, in addition to T-bills, short-term relatively safe obligations such as CP and CDs. These entail some default risk, but again the additional risk is small relative to most other risky assets. For convenience, we often refer to money market funds as risk-free assets.

3. An investor's risky portfolio (the risky asset) can be characterized by its reward-to-variability ratio, $S = [E(r_P) - r_f]/\sigma_P$. This ratio is also the slope of the CAL, the line that, when graphed, goes from the risk-free asset through the risky asset. All combinations of the risky asset and the risk-free asset lie on this line. All things considered, an investor would prefer a steeper-sloping CAL, because that means higher expected return for any level of risk. If the borrowing rate is greater than the lending rate, the CAL will be "kinked" at the point of the risky asset.

4. The investor's degree of risk aversion is characterized by the slope of his or her indifference curve. Indifference curves show, at any level of expected return and risk, the required risk premium for taking on one additional percentage of standard

---

[5]See for example, Friend, I., and Blume, M., "The Demand for Risky Assets," *American Ecnomic Review, 64,* 1974, or Grossman, S.J., and Shiller, R.J., "The Determinants of the Variability of Stock Market Prices," *American Economic Review, 71,* 1981.

deviation. More risk-averse investors have steeper indifference curves; that is, they require a greater risk premium for taking on more risk.

5. The exact optimal position, y^*, in the risky asset, is proportional to the risk premium and inversely proportional to the variance and degree of risk aversion:

$$y^* = \frac{E(r_P) - r_f}{A\sigma_P^2}$$

Graphically, this portfolio represents the point at which the indifference curve is tangent to the CAL.

6. A passive investment strategy disregards security analysis, targeting instead the risk-free asset and a broad portfolio of risky assets such as the S&P 500 stock portfolio. If in 1987 investors took the mean historical return and standard deviation of the S&P 500 as proxies for its expected return and standard deviation, then the market values of outstanding T-bills and the S&P 500 stocks would imply a degree of risk aversion of about $A = 2.3$ for the average investor. This is in line with other studies, which estimate typical risk aversion in the range of 2.0 through 4.0.

Key Terms

Asset allocation decision	Capital allocation line
Security selection decision	Reward-to-variability ratio
Risky asset	Passive strategy
Complete portfolio	Capital market line
Risk-free asset	

Selected Readings

The classic article describing the asset allocation choice, whereby investors choose the optimal fraction of their wealth to place in risk-free assets is:
 Tobin, James, "Liquidity Preference as Behavior Towards Risk," *Review of Economic Studies, 25,* February 1958.
A three-asset class asset allocation problem is considered in:
 Bodie, Zvi, Kane, Alex, and McDonald, Robert, "Inflation and the Role of Bonds in Investor Portfolios," in Friedman, Benjamin (editor), *Corporate Capital Structures in the United States,* Chicago: University of Chicago Press, 1985.
Practitioner-oriented approaches to asset allocation may be found in:
 Maginn, John L., and Tuttle, Donald L., *Managing Investment Portfolios: A Dynamic Process,* New York: Warren, Gorham, & Lamont, Inc., 1983.

Problems

You manage a risky portfolio with an expected rate of return of 17% and a standard deviation of 27%. The T-bill rate is 7%.

1. Your client chooses to invest 70% of a portfolio in your fund and 30% in a T-bill money market fund. What is the expected value and standard deviation of the rate of return on your client's portfolio?

2. Suppose that your risky portfolio includes the following investments in the given proportions:

Stock A:	27%
Stock B:	33%
Stock C:	40%

What are the investment proportions of your client's overall portfolio, including the position in T-bills?

3. What is the reward-to-variability ratio (S) of your risky portfolio?

4. Draw the CAL of your portfolio on an expected return-standard deviation diagram. What is the slope of the CAL? Show the position of your client on your fund's CAL.

5. Suppose that your client decides to invest in your portfolio a proportion y of the total investment budget so that the overall portfolio will have an expected rate of return of 15%.
   a. What is the proportion y?
   b. What are your client's investment proportions in your three stocks and the T-bill fund?
   c. What is the standard deviation of the rate of return on your client's portfolio?

6. Suppose that your client prefers to invest in your fund a proportion y that maximizes the expected return on the overall portfolio subject to the constraint that the overall portfolio's standard deviation will not exceed 20%.
   a. What is the investment proportion, y?
   b. What is the expected rate of return on the overall portfolio?

7. Your client's degree of risk aversions is $A = 3.5$.
   a. What proportion, y, of the total investment should be invested in your fund?
   b. What is the expected value and standard deviation of the rate of return on your client's optimized portfolio?

You estimate that a passive portfolio, that is, one invested in a risky portfolio that mimics the S&P 500 stock index, yields an expected rate of return of 13% with a standard deviation of 25%.

8. Draw the CML and your fund's CAL on an expected return-standard deviation diagram.
   a. What is the slope of the CML?
   b. Characterize in one short paragraph the advantage of your fund over the passive fund.

9. Your client ponders whether to switch the 70% that is invested in your fund to the passive portfolio.
   a. Explain to your client the disadvantage of the switch.
   b. Show your client the maximum fee you could charge (as a percentage of the investment in your fund deducted at the end of the year) that would still leave

the client at least as well off investing in your fund as in the passive one. (Hint: The fee will lower the slope of your client's CAL by reducing the expected return net of the fee.)

10. Consider the client in question 7 with $A = 3.5$.

   a. If the client chose to invest in the passive portfolio, what proportion, y, would be selected?

   b. What fee (percentage of the investment in your fund, deducted at the end of the year) can you charge to make the client indifferent between your fund and the passive strategy?

11. Look at the data in Table 6.1 on the average risk premium of the S&P 500 over T-bills, and the standard deviation of that risk premium. Suppose that the S&P 500 is your risky portfolio.

   a. If your risk-aversion coefficient is 4 and you believe that the entire 1926-1987 period is representative of future expected performance, what fraction of your portfolio should be allocated to T-bills and what fraction to equity?

   b. What if you believe that the 1968-1987 period is representative?

   c. What do you conclude upon comparing your answers to (a) and (b)?

12. What do you think would happen to the expected return on stocks if investors perceived higher volatility in the equity market? Relate your answer to equation 6.3.

CHAPTER 7

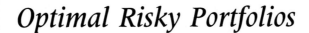

Optimal Risky Portfolios

In Chapter 6 we discussed the capital allocation decision. That decision governs how an investor chooses between risk-free assets and "the" optimal portfolio of risky assets. This chapter explains how to construct that optimal risky portfolio.

We begin at the simplest level, with a discussion of how diversification can reduce the variability of portfolio returns. After establishing this basic point, we examine efficient diversification strategies. We start with a portfolio of two risky securities and use that example to investigate the relationship between investment proportions and the resulting portfolio expected returns and standard deviations. We then add one risk-free asset, a T-bill, to the menu of assets and determine the optimal portfolio. We do this by combining the principles of optimal allocation between risky assets and risk-free assets (from Chapter 6) with the risky-portfolio construction methodology.

Moving beyond two risky assets, we can generalize our analysis to a universe of many risky assets. This generalization relies on some celebrated research, the Markowitz portfolio selection model.[1] We discuss the efficient set of risky portfolios and show how the best attainable capital allocation line emerges from the Markowitz algorithm.

Finally, in the last two appendices, we examine common fallacies regarding the power of diversification in the contexts of the insurance principle and the notion of time diversification.

7.1 *Diversification and Portfolio Risk*

Suppose that your risky portfolio is composed of only one stock, Digital Equipment Corporation. What would be the sources of risk to this "portfolio"? You might

---

[1]Markowitz, Harry M., *Portfolio Selection: Efficient Diversification of Investments*. New York: John Wiley & Sons, Inc., 1959.

think of two broad sources of uncertainty. First, there is the risk that comes from conditions in the general economy, such as the business cycle, the inflation rate, interest rates, and exchange rates. None of these macroeconomic factors can be predicted with certainty, and all affect the rate of return that Digital stock eventually will provide. In addition to these macroeconomic factors there are firm-specific influences, such as Digital's success in research and development, and personnel changes. These factors affect Digital without noticeably affecting other firms in the economy.

Now consider a naive **diversification** strategy, in which you include additional securities in your risky portfolio. For example, suppose that you place half of your risky portfolio in Exxon, leaving the other half in Digital. What should happen to portfolio risk? To the extent that the firm-specific influences on the two stocks differ, we should reduce portfolio risk. For example, when oil prices fall, hurting Exxon, computer prices might rise, helping Digital. The two effects are offsetting, and stabilize portfolio return.

But why end diversification at only two stocks? If we diversify into many more securities, we continue to spread out our exposure to firm-specific factors, and portfolio volatility should continue to fall. Ultimately, however, even if we include a large number of risky securities in our portfolio, we cannot avoid risk altogether. To the extent that virtually all securities are affected by the common macroeconomic factors, we cannot eliminate our exposure to these risk sources. For example, if all stocks are affected by the business cycle, we cannot avoid exposure to business cycle risk no matter how many stocks we hold.

When all risk is firm-specific, as in Figure 7.1, A, diversification can reduce risk to arbitrarily low levels. The reason is that with all risk sources independent, and with the portfolio spread across many securities, the exposure to any particular source of risk is reduced to a negligible level. This is just an application of the well-known law of averages. The reduction of risk to very low levels in the case of independent risk sources is sometimes called the **insurance principle,** because of the conventional belief that an insurance company depends on the risk reduction achieved though diversification when it writes many policies insuring against many indepen-

FIGURE 7.1

Portfolio risk as a function of the number of stocks in the portfolio.

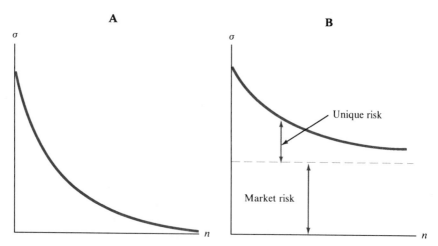

dent sources of risk, each policy being a small part of the company's overall portfolio. (See Appendix B for a discussion of the insurance principle.)

When common sources of risk affect all firms, however, even extensive diversification cannot eliminate risk. In Figure 7.1, *B*, portfolio standard deviation falls as the number of securities increases, but it cannot be reduced to zero.[2] The risk that remains even after extensive diversification is called **market risk,** risk that is attributable to market-wide risk sources. Such risk is also called **systematic risk,** or **nondiversifiable risk.** In contrast, the risk that *can* be eliminated by diversification is called **unique risk, firm-specific risk, nonsystematic risk,** or **diversifiable risk.**

This analysis is borne out by empirical studies. Figure 7.2 shows the effect of portfolio diversification, using data on NYSE stocks.[3] The figure shows the average standard deviation of equally weighted portfolios constructed by selecting stocks at random as a function of the number of stocks in the portfolio. On average, portfolio risk does fall with diversification, but the power of diversification to reduce risk is limited by systematic or common sources of risk.

---

[2]The interested reader can find a more rigorous demonstration of these points in Appendix A. That discussion, however, relies on tools developed later in this chapter.

[3]Fisher, L., and Lorie, J.H., "Some Studies of the Variability of Returns on Investments in Common Stocks," *Journal of Business, 43,* April 1970.

FIGURE   7.2

Portfolio diversification. The average standard deviation of returns of portfolios composed of only one stock was .554. The average portfolio risk fell rapidly as the number of stocks included in the portfolio increased. For 32 stocks the portfolio standard deviation was down to .325. In the limit, portfolio risk could be reduced to only .315, showing that a typical 32-stock portfolio had only a small amount of diversifiable risk.

(From Fisher, Lawrence, and Lorie, James H., "Some Studies of the Variability of Returns on Investments in Common Stocks," *Journal of Business, 43,* April 1970; published by the University of Chicago.)

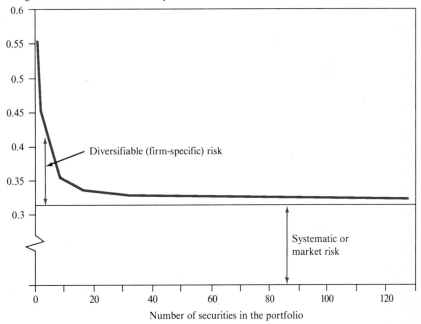

Average annual standard deviation of portfolio

TABLE 7.1 Descriptive Statistics for Two Stocks

	Digital	Exxon
Expected return, $E(r)$	.20	.15
Standard deviation, σ	.45	.32
Covariance, $Cov(r_D, r_E)$	.0475	
Correlation coefficient, ρ_{DE}	.33	

7.2 Portfolios of Two Risky Assets

In the last section we analyzed naive diversification, examining the risk of equally weighted portfolios of several securities. It is time now to study efficient diversification, whereby we construct risky portfolios to provide the lowest possible risk for any given level of expected return.

Constructing the optimal risky portfolio is an immensely difficult statistical task. The *principles* we follow, however, are the same as those used to construct a portfolio from two risky assets only. We will analyze this easier process first and then backtrack a bit to see how we can generalize the technique to apply to more realistic cases.

Assume for this purpose that an investor is limited to two stocks: Digital Equipment Corporation and Exxon, with the parameters of the joint probability distribution as shown in Table 7.1.

A proportion denoted by w_D is invested in Digital stock, and the remainder, $1 - w_D$, denoted w_E, is invested in Exxon stock. The rate of return on this portfolio will be

$$r_p = w_D r_D + w_E r_E$$

where r_p stands for the rate of return on the portfolio, r_D the return on investment in Digital, and r_E the return on investment in Exxon.

As we noted in Chapter 5, the expected rate of return on the portfolio is a weighted average of expected returns on the component securities with portfolio proportions as weights:

$$E(r_p) = w_D E(r_D) + w_E E(r_E) \tag{7.1}$$

The variance of the two-asset portfolio (Rule 5 of Chapter 5) is

$$\sigma_p^2 = w_D^2 \sigma_D^2 + w_E^2 \sigma_E^2 + 2 w_D w_E Cov(r_D, r_E) \tag{7.2}$$

The first observation is that the variance of the portfolio, unlike the expected return, is *not* a weighted average of the security variances. To understand the formula for the portfolio variance more clearly, recall that the covariance of a variable (which in this case is the uncertain rate of return) with itself is the variance of that variable; that is

$$\text{Cov}(r_D, r_D) = \sum_{\text{scenarios}} \text{Pr(scenario)}[r_D - E(r_D)] \, [r_D - E(r_D)]$$

$$= \sum_{\text{scenarios}} \text{Pr(scenario)}[r_D - E(r_D)]^2$$

$$= \sigma_D^2$$

Therefore another way to write the variance of the portfolio is as follows:

$$\sigma_p^2 = w_D w_D \text{Cov}(r_D, r_D) + w_E w_E \text{Cov}(r_E, r_E) + 2 w_D w_E \text{Cov}(r_D, r_E)$$

In words, the variance of the portfolio is a weighted sum of covariances, where each weight is the product of the portfolio proportions of the pair of assets in the covariance term.

Why do we double the covariance between the two *different* assets in the last term of equation 7.2? This should become clear in the covariance matrix, Table 7.2, which is bordered by the portfolio weights.

The diagonal (from top left to bottom right) of the covariance matrix is made up of the asset variances. The off-diagonal elements are the covariances. Note that

$$\text{Cov}(r_D, r_E) = \text{Cov}(r_E, r_D)$$

so that the matrix is symmetric. To compute the portfolio variance, we sum over each term in the matrix, first multiplying it by the product of the portfolio proportions from the corresponding row and column. Thus we have *one* term for each asset variance, but twice the term for each covariance pair because each covariance appears twice.

TABLE 7.2   Bordered Covariance Matrix

Portfolio Weights	Covariances	
	w_D	w_E
w_D	σ_D^2	$\text{Cov}(r_D, r_E)$
w_E	$\text{Cov}(r_E, r_D)$	σ_E^2

Concept Check

Question 1.

a. Confirm that this simple rule for computing portfolio variance from the covariance matrix is consistent with equation 7.2.

b. Consider a portfolio of three stocks, X, Y, Z, with weights w_X, w_Y, and w_Z. Show that the portfolio variance is

$$w_X^2 \sigma_X^2 + w_Y^2 \sigma_Y^2 + w_Z^2 \sigma_Z^2 + 2 w_X w_Y \text{Cov}(r_X, r_Y)$$
$$+ 2 w_X w_Z \text{Cov}(r_X, r_Z) + 2 w_Y w_Z \text{Cov}(r_Y, r_Z)$$

As we discussed in Chapter 5, the portfolio variance is reduced if the covariance term is negative. This is the case in the use of hedge assets. It is important to recognize that even if the covariance term is positive, thereby increasing portfolio volatility, the *portfolio* standard deviation still is less than the weighted average of the individual security standard deviations, unless the two securities are perfectly positively correlated.

To see this, recall from Chapter 5, equation 5.5, that the covariance can be written as

$$\text{Cov}(r_D, r_E) = \rho_{DE}\sigma_D\sigma_E$$

Substituting into equation 7.2, we can rewrite the variance and standard deviation of the portfolio as

$$\sigma_p^2 = w_D^2\sigma_D^2 + w_E^2\sigma_E^2 + 2w_Dw_E\sigma_D\sigma_E\rho_{DE} \tag{7.3}$$

$$\sigma_p = \sqrt{\sigma_p^2} \tag{7.4}$$

You can see from this information that the covariance term adds the most to the portfolio variance when the correlation coefficient, ρ_{DE}, is highest, that is, when it equals 1—as it would in the case of perfect positive correlation. In this case the right-hand side of equation 7.3 is a perfect square, so it may be rewritten as follows:

$$\sigma_p^2 = (w_D\sigma_D + w_E\sigma_E)^2$$

or

$$\sigma_p = w_D\sigma_D + w_E\sigma_E$$

In other words, the standard deviation of the portfolio in the case of perfect positive correlation is just the weighted average of the component standard deviations. In all other cases the correlation coefficient is less than 1, making the portfolio standard deviation *less* than the weighted average of the component standard deviations.

We know already from Chapter 5 that a hedge asset reduces the portfolio variance. This algebraic exercise adds the additional insight that the standard deviation of a portfolio of assets is less than the weighted average of the component security standard deviations, even when the assets are positively correlated. Because the portfolio expected return is always the weighted average of its component expected returns, while its standard deviation is less than the weighted average of the component standard deviations, *portfolios of less than perfectly correlated assets always offer better risk-return opportunities than the individual component securities on their own.* The less correlation between assets, the greater the gain in efficiency.

How low can portfolio standard deviation be? The lowest possible value of the correlation coefficient is −1, representing perfect negative correlation, in which case the portfolio variance is as follows[4]:

---

[4]This expression also can be derived from equation 7.3. When $\rho_{DE} = -1$, equation 7.3 is a perfect square that can be factored as shown.

$$\sigma_p^2 = (w_D\sigma_D - w_E\sigma_E)^2$$

and the portfolio standard deviation is

$$\sigma_p = \text{Absolute value } (w_D\sigma_D - w_E\sigma_E)$$

Where $\rho = -1$, the investor has the opportunity of creating a perfectly hedged position. If the portfolio proportions are chosen as

$$w_D = \frac{\sigma_E}{\sigma_D + \sigma_E}$$

$$w_E = \frac{\sigma_D}{\sigma_D + \sigma_E} = 1 - w_D$$

the standard deviation of the portfolio will equal zero.[5]

Let us apply this analysis to the data of Digital and Exxon as presented in Table 7.1. Using these data, the formulas for the expected return, variance, and standard deviation of the portfolio are

$$E(r_p) = w_D(.20) + w_E(.15) \tag{7.5}$$

$$\sigma_p^2 = w_D^2(.45^2) + w_E^2(.32)^2 + 2w_Dw_E(.0475) \tag{7.6}$$
$$\sigma_p = \sqrt{\sigma_p^2}$$

Now we are ready to experiment with different portfolio proportions to observe the effect on portfolio expected return and variance. Suppose we change the proportion invested in Digital. The effect on the portfolio's expected return is plotted in Figure 7.3. When the proportion invested in Digital varies from zero to 1 (so that the proportion in Exxon varies from 1 to zero), the portfolio expected return goes from 15% (Exxon's expected return) to 20% (Digital's expected return).

What happens to the right of this region, when $w_D > 1$ and $w_E < 0$? In this case portfolio strategy would be to sell Exxon short and invest the proceeds of the short sale in Digital to increase the expected portfolio return. For example, when $w_D = 2$ and $w_E = -1$, expected portfolio return increases to 25% [$2 \times .20 + (-1) \times .15$]. At this point the value of Digital stock in the portfolio is twice the net worth of the account. This extreme position is financed in part by short selling Exxon stock equal in value to the portfolio's net worth.

The reverse happens when $w_D < 0$ and $w_E > 1$. This strategy calls for selling Digital short and using the proceeds to finance additional purchases of Exxon.

Of course, varying investment proportions has an effect on portfolio standard deviation. Table 7.3 presents portfolio standard deviations for different portfolio weights calculated from equations 7.3 and 7.4 for the assumed value of the correlation coefficient, .33, as well as for other values of ρ. Figure 7.4 shows the relationship between standard deviation and portfolio weights. The graphs show that as

---

[5]It is possible to drive portfolio variance to zero with perfectly positively correlated assets as well, but this would require short sales.

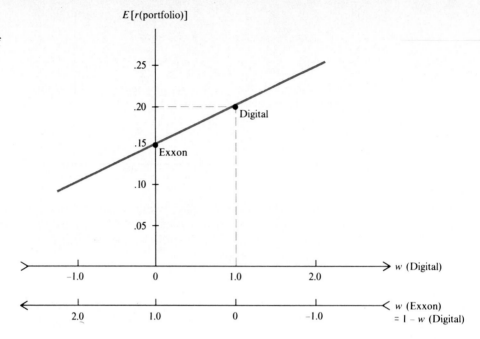

TABLE 7.3 Portfolio Standard Deviation as a Function of Investment Proportions

w_D	$\rho = -1$	$\rho = 0$	$\rho = .33$	$\rho = 1$
0	.3200	.3200	.3200	.3200
.25	.1275	.2651	.2968	.3525
.50	.0650	.2761	.3162	.3850
.75	.2575	.3469	.3717	.4175
1.00	.4500	.4500	.4500	.4500
minimum σ_p	0	.2608	.2960	—
w_D at minimum σ_p	.42	.34	.26	—

the portfolio weight in Exxon increases from zero to 1, portfolio standard deviation first falls with the initial diversification into Exxon, but then rises again as the portfolio becomes heavily concentrated in Exxon stock, and again is undiversified.

What is the minimum level to which portfolio deviation can be held? For the parameter values stipulated in Table 7.1, the portfolio weights that solve this minimization problem turn out to be[6]:

---

[6]This solution uses the minimization techniques of elementary calculus. Write out the expression for portfolio variance from equation 7.2, substitute $1 - w_D$ for w_E, differentiate the result with respect to w_D, set the derivative equal to zero, and solve for w_D.

FIGURE 7.4

Portfolio standard deviation as a function of investment proportions.

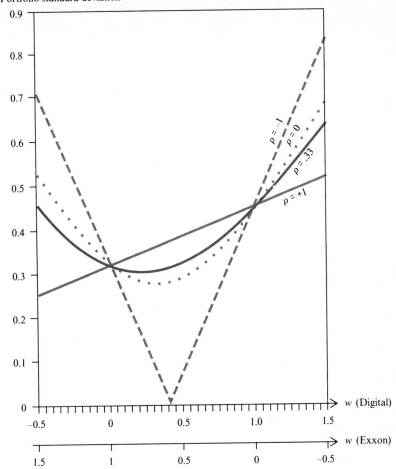

Portfolio standard deviation

$$w_{Min}(D) = \frac{\sigma_E^2 - Cov(r_D, r_E)}{\sigma_D^2 + \sigma_E^2 - 2Cov(r_D, r_E)} \tag{7.7}$$

$$= \frac{.32^2 - .0475}{.45^2 + .32^2 - 2 \times .0475}$$

$$= .26$$

$$w_{Min}(E) = 1 - .26$$

$$= .74$$

This minimum variance portfolio has a standard deviation of

$$\sigma_{Min}(P) = [.26^2 \times .45^2 + .74^2 \times .32^2 + 2 \times .26 \times .74 \times .0475]^{1/2}$$

$$= .296$$

or 29.6%, as indicated in the next-to-last line of Table 7.3 for the column $\rho = .33$.

The dark blue line in Figure 7.4 represents the portfolio standard deviation when $\rho = .33$ as a function of the investment proportions. It passes through the two undiversified portfolios of $w_D = 1$ and $w_E = 1$. Note that the **minimum-variance portfolio** has a standard deviation smaller than that of either of the individual component stocks. This indicates the effect of diversification.

The other three lines in Figure 7.4 show how portfolio risk varies for other values of the correlation coefficient, holding the variances of each stock constant. These lines plot the values in the other three columns of Table 7.3.

The straight line connecting the undiversified portfolios of all-Digital or all-Exxon portfolios, $w_D = 1$ or $w_E = 1$, demonstrates portfolio standard deviation with perfect positive correlation, $\rho = 1$. In this case there is no advantage from diversification, and the portfolio standard deviation is the simple weighted average of the component stock standard deviations.

The dotted curve below the $\rho = .33$ curve depicts portfolio risk for the case of uncorrelated securities, $\rho = 0$. With lower correlation between the two stocks, diversification is more effective and portfolio risk is lower (at least when both stocks are held in positive amounts). The minimum portfolio standard deviation when $\rho = 0$ is .2608 (see Table 7.3), again lower than the standard deviation of either stock.

Finally, the upside-down triangular broken line illustrates the perfect hedge potential when the two stocks are perfectly negatively correlated ($\rho = -1$). In this case the solution for the minimum-variance portfolio is

$$w_{\text{Min}}(D;\rho = -1) = \frac{\sigma_E}{\sigma_D + \sigma_E}$$

$$= \frac{.32}{.45 + .32}$$

$$= .42$$

$$w_{\text{Min}}(E;\rho = -1) = 1 - .42$$

$$= .58$$

and the portfolio variance (and standard deviation) is zero.

We can combine Figures 7.3 and 7.4 to demonstrate the relationship between the portfolio's level of risk (standard deviation) and the expected rate of return on that portfolio—given the parameters of the available stocks. This is done in Figure 7.5. For any pair of investment proportions, w_D, w_E, we read the expected return from Figure 7.3 and the standard deviation from Figure 7.4. The resulting pairs of portfolio expected return and standard deviation are tabulated in Table 7.4 and plotted in Figure 7.5.

The dark blue line in Figure 7.5 shows the **portfolio opportunity set** for $\rho = .33$. We call it the portfolio opportunity set because it shows the combination of expected return and standard deviation of all the portfolios that can be constructed from the two available assets. The broken and dotted lines show the portfolio opportunity set for other values of the correlation coefficient. The line farthest to the right, which is the straight line connecting the undiversified portfolios, shows that there is no ben-

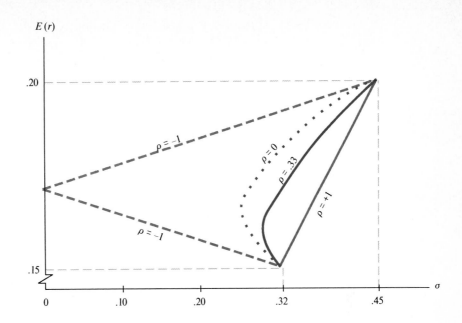

TABLE 7.4   Portfolio Expected Return as a Function of Standard Deviation

W_D	$\rho = -1$		$\rho = 0$		$\rho = .33$		$\rho = +1$	
	$E(r)$	σ	$E(r)$	σ	$E(r)$	σ	$E(r)$	σ
0	.1500	.3200	.1500	.3200	.1500	.3200	.1500	.3200
.25	.1625	.1275	.1625	.2651	.1625	.2968	.1625	.3525
.50	.1750	.065	.1750	.2760	.1750	.3162	.1750	.3850
.75	.1875	.2575	.1875	.3469	.1875	.3717	.1875	.4175
1.00	.2000	.4500	.2000	.4500	.2000	.4500	.2000	.4500
Minimum σ portfolio	.1710	0	.1670	.2608	.1630	.2960	—	—

efit from diversification when the correlation between the two assets is perfectly positive ($\rho = 1$). The dotted line to the left of the dark blue curve shows that there is greater benefit from diversification when the correlation coefficient is zero than when it is positive.

Finally, the $\rho = -1$ lines shows the effect of perfect negative correlation. The portfolio opportunity set is linear, but now it offers a perfect hedging opportunity and the maximum advantage for diversification.

To summarize, although the expected rate of return of any portfolio is simply the weighted average of the asset expected returns, this is not true of the portfolio standard deviation. Potential benefits from diversification arise when correlation is less than perfectly positive. The lower the correlation coefficient, the greater the potential benefit of diversification. In the extreme case of perfect negative correlation, we have a perfect hedging opportunity and can construct a zero-variance portfolio.

7.3 The Optimal Risky Portfolio With a Risk-Free Asset and Two Risky Assets

What if we were still confined to the Digital and Exxon stocks, but now could also invest in risk-free T-bills yielding 8%? We start with a graphical solution. Figure 7.6 shows the opportunity set generated from the joint probability distribution of Digital and Exxon, using the data from Table 7.1.

Two possible capital allocation lines (CALs) are drawn from the risk-free rate $(r_f = 8\%)$ to two feasible portfolios. The first possible CAL is drawn through the minimum-variance portfolio A, which is invested 26% in Digital and 74% in Exxon (equation 7.7). Portfolio A's expected return is $E(r_A) = 16.3\%$, and its standard deviation is $\sigma_A = 29.6\%$. With a T-bill rate of $r_f = 8\%$, the **reward-to-variability ratio,** which is the slope of the CAL combining T-bills and the minimum-variance portfolio, is

$$S_A = \frac{E(r_A) - r_f}{\sigma_A}$$
$$= \frac{.163 - .08}{.296}$$
$$= .28$$

Now consider the CAL that uses portfolio B instead of A. Portfolio B invests 35% in Digital and 65% in Exxon. Its expected return is 16.75% (giving it a risk premium of 8.75%), and its standard deviation is 29.95%. Thus the reward-to-variability ratio on the CAL that is generated using portfolio B is

$$S_B = \frac{.0875}{.2995}$$
$$= .29$$

slightly higher than the reward-to-variability ratio of the CAL that we obtained using the minimum-variance portfolio and T-bills.

If the CAL that uses portfolio B has a better reward-to-variability ratio than the CAL that uses portfolio A, then for any level of risk (standard deviation) that an in-

FIGURE 7.6

The opportunity set of
Digital and Exxon and
two possible CALs.

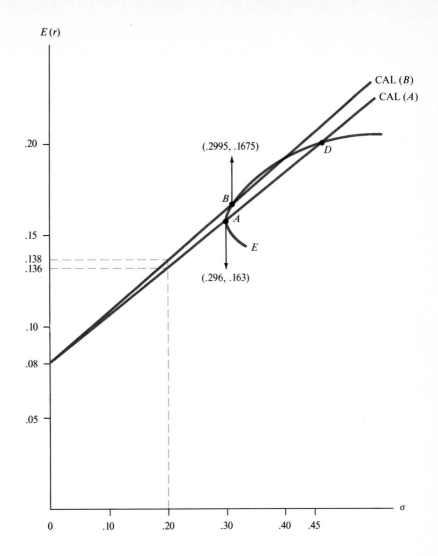

vestor is willing to bear, the expected return is higher with portfolio B. Figure 7.6 reflects this in showing that the CAL for portfolio B is above the CAL for portfolio A. In this sense portfolio B dominates portfolio A.

In fact, the difference between the reward-to-variability ratios is

$$S_B - S_A = .01$$

This means we get one extra basis point expected return with CAL_B for each percentage point increase in standard deviation.

Look at Figure 7.6 again. If we are willing to bear a standard deviation of $\sigma_p = .20$, we can achieve a 13.6% expected return with the CAL of portfolio A:

$$E(r_p)(\text{CAL}_A; \sigma_p = .20) = r_f + .20S_A$$
$$= .08 + .20 \times .28$$
$$= .136$$

With the CAL of portfolio B, we get expected return of 13.8%:

$$E(r_p)(\text{CAL}_B; \sigma_p = .20) = r_f + .20S_B$$
$$= .08 + .20 \times .29$$
$$= .138$$

This is a difference of $.01 \times .20 = .20$, which is .2% or 20 basis points.

But why stop at portfolio B? We can continue to ratchet the CAL upward until it ultimately reaches the point of tangency with the investment opportunity set. This must yield the CAL with the highest feasible reward-to-variability ratio. Therefore the tangency portfolio, P, drawn in Figure 7.7, is the optimal risky portfolio to mix with T-bills. We can read the expected return and standard deviation of portfolio P from the graph in Figure 7.7.

$$E(r_P) = 17.57\%$$
$$\sigma_P = 31.85\%$$

In practice, we obtain an algebraic solution to this problem with a computer program. We can describe the process briefly, however.

The objective is to find the weights w_D, w_E that result in the highest slope of the CAL (that is, the yield of the risky portfolio with the highest reward-to-variability ratio). Therefore the objective is to maximize the slope of the CAL for any possible portfolio, p. Thus our *objective function* is the slope that we have called S_p:

$$S_p = \frac{E(r_p) - r_f}{\sigma_p}$$

For the portfolio with two risky assets, the expected return and standard deviation of portfolio p are

$$E(r_p) = w_D E(r_D) + w_E E(r_E)$$
$$= w_D(.20) + w_E(.15)$$
$$\sigma_p = [w_D^2 \sigma_D^2 + w_E^2 \sigma_E^2 + 2w_D w_E \text{Cov}(r_D, r_E)]^{1/2}$$
$$= [w_D^2(.2025) + w_E^2(.1024) + 2w_D w_E(.0475)]^{1/2}$$

When we maximize the objective function, S_p, we have to satisfy the constraint that the portfolio weights sum to one (100%), that is $w_D + w_E = 1$. Therefore we solve a mathematical problem formally written as

$$\underset{w_i}{\text{Max}} \, S_p = \frac{E(r_p) - r_f}{\sigma_p}$$

subject to $\Sigma w_i = 1$. This is a standard problem in calculus.

FIGURE 7.7

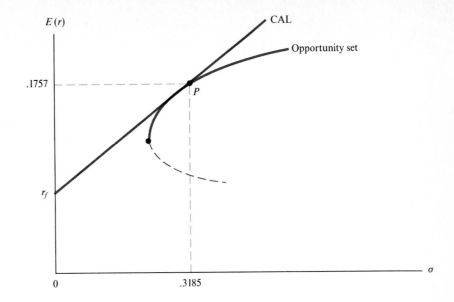

The opportunity set of
Digital and Exxon
with the optimal CAL
and the optimized
portfolio.

In the case of two risky assets, the solution for the weights of the **optimal risky
portfolio,** P, can be shown to be as follows[7]:

$$(7.8)$$

$$w_D = \frac{[E(r_D) - r_f]\sigma_E^2 - [E(r_E) - r_f]\text{Cov}(r_D, r_E)}{[E(r_D) - r_f]\sigma_E^2 + [E(r_E) - r_f]\sigma_D^2 - [E(r_D) - r_f + E(r_E) - r_f]\text{Cov}(r_D, r_E)}$$

$$w_E = 1 - w_D$$

Substituting our data, the solution is

$$w_D = \frac{(.20 - .08).1024 - (.15 - .08).0475}{(.20 - .08).1024 + (.15 - .08).2025 - (.20 - .08 + .15 - .08).0475}$$

$$= .5140$$

$$= 51.40\%$$

$$w_E = 1 - .5140$$

$$= 48.60\%$$

The expected return of this optimal risky portfolio is 17.57% [$E(r_P) = .5140 \times
.20 + .4860 \times .15$]. The standard deviation is 31.85%:

$$\sigma_P = (.5140^2 \times .2025 + .4860^2 \times .1024 + 2 \times .5140 \times .4860 \times .0475)^{1/2}$$

$$= .3185$$

---

[7]The solution procedure is as follows. Substitute for $E(r_p)$ from equation 7.1 and for σ_p from equation 7.2. Substitute $1 -
w_D$ for w_E. Differentiate the resulting expression for S_p with respect to w_D, set the derivative equal to zero, and solve for
w_D.

The CAL with this optimal portfolio has a slope of

$$S_P = (.1757 - .08)/.3185 = .30$$

which is the reward-to-variability ratio of portfolio P. Notice that this slope exceeds the slope of any of the other feasible portfolios that we have considered, as it must if it is to be the slope of the best feasible CAL.

In Chapter 6 we found the optimal *complete* portfolio given an optimal risky portfolio and the CAL generated by a combination of this portfolio and T-bills. Now that we have constructed the optimal risky portfolio, P, we can use the individual investor's degree of risk aversion, A, to calculate the optimal proportion of the complete portfolio to invest in the risky component.

An investor with a coefficient of risk aversion, $A = 4$, would take a position in portfolio P of

$$
\begin{aligned}
y &= \frac{E(r_P) - r_f}{A\sigma_P^2} \\
&= \frac{.1757 - .08}{4 \times .3185^2} \\
&= .2358
\end{aligned}
\tag{7.9}
$$

Thus the investor will invest 23.58% of his or her wealth in portfolio P and 76.42% in T-bills. Portfolio P consists of 51.40% in Digital, so the percentage of wealth in Digital will be $yw_D = .5140 \times .2358 = 12.12\%$. Similarly, the investment in Exxon will be $yw_E = .4860 \times .2358 = 11.46\%$. The graphical solution of this problem is presented in Figures 7.8 and 7.9.

Once we have reached this point, generalizing to the case of many risky assets is straightforward. Before we move on, let us briefly summarize the steps we followed to arrive at the complete portfolio.

1. Specify the return characteristics of all securities (expected returns, variances, covariances).
2. Establish the risky portfolio:
   a. Calculate the optimal risky portfolio, P (equation 7.8).
   b. Calculate the properties of portfolio P using the weights determined in step (a) and equations 7.1 and 7.2.
3. Allocate funds between the risky portfolio and the risk-free asset:
   a. Calculate the fraction of the complete portfolio allocated to portfolio P (the risky portfolio) and to T-bills (the risk-free asset) (equation 7.9).
   b. Calculate the share of the complete portfolio invested in each asset and in T-bills.

FIGURE   7.8
Determination of the
optimal overall
portfolio.

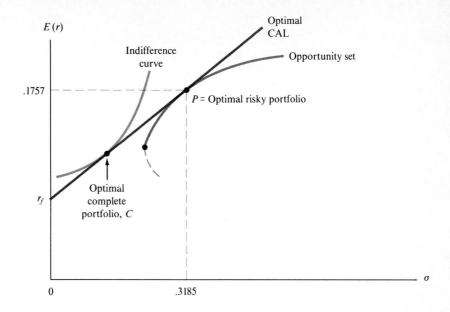

FIGURE   7.9
The proportions of the
optimal overall
portfolio.

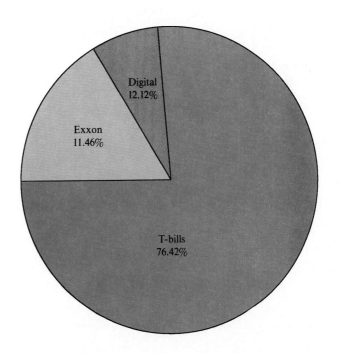

Question 3. The universe of available securities includes two risky stocks, A and B, and T-bills. The data for the universe are as follows:

	Expected Return	Standard Deviation
A	.10	.20
B	.30	.60
T-bills	.05	0

The correlation coefficient between stocks A and B is $-.2$.
a. Draw the opportunity set of stocks A and B.
b. Find the optimal risky portfolio P and its expected return and standard deviation.
c. Find the slope of the CAL supported by T-bills and portfolio P.
d. How much will an investor with $A = 5$ invest in stocks A and B, and in T-bills?

FIGURE 7.10

The minimum-variance frontier of risky assets.

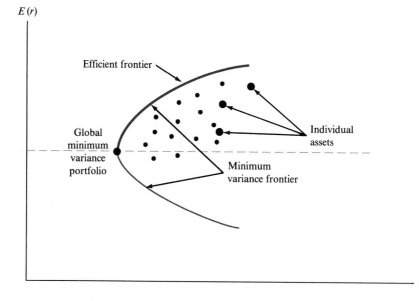

7.4 *The Markowitz Portfolio Selection Model*

Now we can generalize the portfolio construction problem to the case of many risky assets and a risk-free asset. As in the two risky assets example, the problem has three parts. First, we identify the risk-return combinations available from the set of risky assets. Next, we identify the optimal portfolio of risky assets by finding the portfolio that results in the steepest CAL. Finally, we choose an appropriate complete portfolio by mixing the risk-free asset, T-bills, with the optimal risky portfolio. Before describing the process in detail, let us first present an overview.

The first step is to determine the risk-return opportunities available to the investor. These are summarized by the **minimum-variance frontier** of risky assets. This frontier is a graph of the lowest possible portfolio variance that can be attained for a given portfolio expected return. Given the set of data for expected returns, variances, and covariances, we can calculate the minimum-variance portfolio (or equivalently, minimum standard deviation portfolio) for any targeted expected return. Performing such a calculation for many such expected return targets results in a pairing between expected returns and minimum-risk portfolios that offer those expected returns. The plot of these expected return–standard deviation pairs is presented in Figure 7.10.

Notice that all the individual assets lie to the right inside the frontier, at least when we allow short sales in the construction of risky portfolios.[8] This tells us that risky portfolios constituted of only a single asset are inefficient. Diversifying investments allows construction of portfolios with higher expected returns and lower standard deviations.

All the portfolios that lie on the minimum-variance frontier, from the global minimum-variance portfolio and upward, provide the best risk-return combinations and thus are candidates for the optimal portfolio. The part of the frontier that lies above the global minimum-variance portfolio, therefore, is called the **efficient frontier.** For any portfolio on the lower portion of the minimum-variance frontier, there is a portfolio with the same standard deviation and a greater expected return positioned directly above it. Hence, the bottom part of the minimum-variance frontier is inefficient.

The second part of the optimization plan involves the risk-free asset. As before, we search for the capital allocation line with the highest reward-to-variability ratio (that is, the steepest slope) as shown in Figure 7.11.

The CAL that is supported by the optimal portfolio, *P,* is, as before, the one that is tangent to the efficient frontier. This CAL dominates all alternative feasible lines (the broken lines that are drawn through the frontier). Portfolio *P,* therefore, is the optimal risky portfolio.

---

[8]When short sales are prohibited, single securities may lie on the frontier. For example, the security with the highest expected return must lie on the frontier, as that security represents the *only* way that one can obtain a return that high, and so it must also be the minimum-variance way to obtain that return. When short sales are feasible, however, portfolios can be constructed that offer the same expected return and lower variance. These portfolios typically will have short positions in low-expected-return securities.

FIGURE 7.11
The efficient frontier
of risky assets with
the optimal CAL.

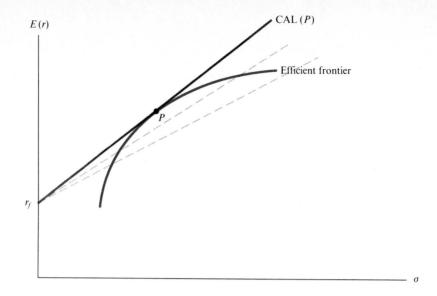

Finally, in the last part of the problem the individual investor chooses the appropriate mix between the optimal risky portfolio P and T-bills, exactly as in Figure 7.8.

Now let us consider each part of the portfolio construction problem in more detail. In the first part of the problem, risk-return analysis, the portfolio manager needs, as inputs, a set of estimates for the expected returns of each security and a set of estimates for the covariance matrix. (In Part V, Equities, we will examine the security valuation techniques and methods of financial analysis that analysts use. For now, we will assume that analysts already have spent the time and resources to prepare the inputs.)

Suppose that the horizon of the portfolio plan is 1 year. Therefore all estimates pertain to a 1-year holding period return. Our security analysts cover n securities. As of now, time zero, we observed these security prices: $P_1^0, \ldots, P_n^0$. The analysts derive estimates for each security's expected rate of return by forecasting end-of-year (time 1) prices: $E(P_1^1), \ldots, E(P_n^1)$, and the expected dividends for the period: $E(D_1), \ldots, E(D_n)$. The set of expected rates of return is then computed from

$$E(r_i) = \frac{E(P_i^1) + E(D_i) - P_i^0}{P_i^0}$$

The covariances among the rates of return on the analyzed securities (the covariance matrix) usually are estimated from historical data. Another method is to use a scenario analysis of possible returns from all securities instead of, or as a supplement to, historical analysis.

The portfolio manager is now armed with the n estimates of $E(r_i)$ and an estimated covariance matrix in which the n diagonal elements are estimates of the variances, σ_i^2, and the $n^2 - n = n(n - 1)$ off-diagonal elements are the estimates of the covariances between each pair of asset returns. We know that each covariance appears twice in this table, so actually we have $n(n - 1)/2$ different covariances estimates. If our portfolio management unit covers 50 securities, our security analysts need to deliver 50 estimates of expected returns, 50 estimates of variances, and $50 \times 49/2 = 1,225$ different estimates of covariances. This is a daunting task! (We show later how the number of required estimates can be reduced substantially.)

Once these estimates are compiled, the expected return and variance of any risky portfolio with weights in each security, w_i, can be calculated from the following formulas[9]:

$$E(r_p) = \sum_{i=1}^{n} w_i E(r_i) \tag{7.10}$$

$$\sigma_p^2 = \sum_{i=1}^{n} w_i^2 \sigma_i^2 + \sum_{\substack{i=1 \\ i \neq j}}^{n} \sum_{j=1}^{n} w_i w_j \text{Cov}(r_i, r_j) \tag{7.11}$$

We mentioned earlier that the idea of diversification is age-old. The phrase "don't put all your eggs in one basket" existed long before modern finance theory. It was not until 1952, however, that Harry Markowitz published a formal model of portfolio selection embodying diversification principles, thereby entering the hall of fame of financial economics. His model is precisely step one of portfolio management: the identification of the efficient set of portfolios, or, as it is often called, the efficient frontier of risky portfolios.

The principal idea behind the frontier set of risky portfolios is that, for any risk level, we are interested only in that portfolio with the highest expected return. An alternative way of describing the frontier set of risky portfolios is as the set of minimum-variance portfolios corresponding to alternative targeted expected returns.

Indeed, the two methods of computing the efficient set of risky portfolios are highly similar. To see this, consider the graphical representation of these procedures. Figure 7.12 shows the minimum-variance frontier.

The points marked by rectangles are the result of a variance-minimization program. We first draw the constraint, that is, a horizontal line at the level of required expected return. We then look for the portfolio with the lowest standard deviation that plots on this horizontal line—we look for the portfolio that will plot farthest to the left (smallest standard deviation) on that line. When we repeat this for various levels of required expected returns, the shape of the minimum-variance frontier emerges. We then discard the bottom (dotted) half of the frontier, because it is inefficient.

In the alternative approach, we draw a vertical line that represents the standard deviation constraint. We then consider all portfolios that plot on this line (have the same standard deviation) and choose the one with the highest expected return, that is,

---

[9]Equation 7.11 follows from our discussion in Section 7.2 on using the bordered covariance matrix to obtain each term in the formula for the variance of a portfolio.

FIGURE 7.12

The efficient portfolio
set.

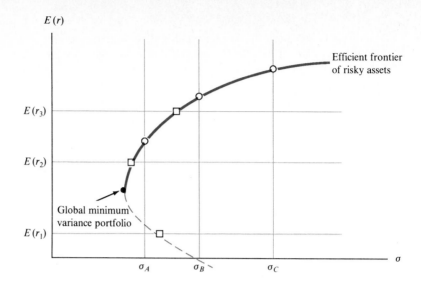

that portfolio falling highest on this vertical line. Repeating this procedure for various vertical lines (levels of standard deviation) gives us the points marked by circles that trace the upper portion of the minimum-variance frontier, the efficient frontier.

When this step is completed, we have a list of efficient portfolios, because the solution to the optimization program includes the portfolio proportions, w_i, and the expected return, $E(r_p)$, and standard deviation, σ_p.

Let us restate what our portfolio manager has done so far. The estimates generated by the analysts were transformed into a set of expected rates of return and a covariance matrix. This group of estimates we shall call the input list. This input list is then fed into the optimization program.

Before we proceed to the second step of choosing the optimal risky portfolio from the frontier set, let us consider a practical point. Some clients may be subject to additional constraints. For example, many institutions are prohibited from taking short positions in any asset. For these clients the portfolio manager will add to the program constraints that rule out negative (short) positions in the search for efficient portfolios. In this special case it is possible that single assets may be, in and of themselves, efficient risky portfolios. For example, the asset with the highest expected return will be a frontier portfolio because, without the opportunity of short sales, the only way to obtain that rate of return is to hold the asset as one's entire risky portfolio.

Short-sale restrictions are by no means the only such constraints. For example, some clients may want to assure a minimal level of expected dividend yield, on the optimal portfolio. In this case the input list will be expanded to include a set of expected dividend yields $d_1, \dots, d_n$ and the optimization program will include an additional constraint that ensures that the expected *portfolio* dividend yield will equal or exceed the desired level, d.

Portfolio managers can tailor the efficient set to conform to any desire of the cli-

FIGURE 7.13
Capital allocation
lines with various
portfolios from the
efficient set.

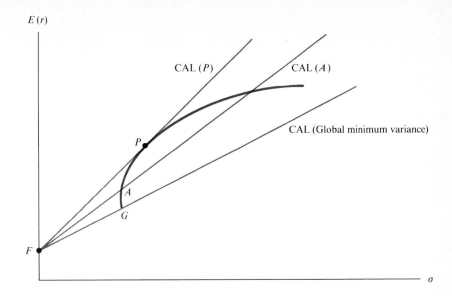

ent. Of course, any constraint carries a price tag in the sense that an efficient frontier constructed subject to extra constraints will offer a reward-to-variability ratio inferior to that of a less constrained one. The client should be made aware of this cost and should reconsider constraints that are not mandated by law.

Another currently prominent constraint is against stocks of companies doing business in South Africa. The nearby box contains an article from *The Wall Street Journal* concerning socially responsible funds that constrain portfolio choice along several criteria. The article points out that one cost of such a policy is a potential increase in volatility.

We are now ready to proceed to step two. This step introduces the risk-free rate. Figure 7.13 shows the efficient frontier plus three CALs representing various portfolios from the efficient set. As before, we ratchet up the CAL by selecting different portfolios until we reach portfolio *P*, which is the tangency point of a line from *F* to the efficient frontier. Portfolio *P* maximizes the reward-to-variability ratio, the slope of the line from *F* to portfolios on the efficient frontier. At this point our portfolio manager is done. Portfolio *P* is the optimal risky portfolio for the manager's clients. This is a good time to ponder our results and their implementation.

The most striking conclusion is that a portfolio manager will offer the same risky portfolio, *P*, to all clients regardless of their degree of risk aversion.[10] The degree of risk aversion of the client comes into play only in the selection of the desired point on the CAL. Thus the only difference between clients' choices is that the more risk-averse client will invest more in the risk-free asset and less in the optimal risky port-

---

[10]Clients who impose special restrictions (constraints) on the manager, such as dividend yield, will obtain another optimal portfolio. Any constraint that is added to an optimization problem leads, in general, to a different and less desirable optimum compared to an unconstrained program.

Doing Good and Doing All Right: Investors Applying Ethical Values

George Pillsbury, a weathy Bostonian who spends a lot of time steering foundation money to liberal causes, decided last summer that his personal portfolio should more closely reflect his social views.

YOUR
MONEY
MATTERS

So he put $400,000 in the hands of Franklin Research & Development Corp., a Boston firm specializing in what it calls "socially responsible investing." A year later, Mr. Pillsbury's account had grown 44%, to $576,000, beating the return of the Standard & Poor's 500-stock index by about eight percentage points.

At a time when many states, cities and universities are selling stock in companies that do business in South Africa, a growing number of individuals are putting their money where their ethical values are. Last year, says the Boston-based Social Investment Forum, individuals invested more than $8 billion with money managers using social and political criteria.

To some critics, avoiding a company to contest apartheid, industrial pollution or a lack of women in positions of authority is like throwing money away. "If you make noneconomic choices, you will get noneconomic results—less profit," says Jack Albertine, vice chairman of Chicago-based Farley Industries Inc.

Being Charitable

Indeed, few investors can expect to match Mr. Pillsbury's good fortune over any extended time. And the performance of some money managers can be charitably described as only mediocre.

But individuals who exclude investments in companies that don't meet certain social or political criteria probably don't do any worse, on average, than the typical investor. While none of the nine "socially responsible" mutual funds tracked by Lipper Analytical Services Inc. outperformed the S&P 500 in the year through June 30, neither did the average mutual fund.

"By restricting your investments in any way, you cannot be better off," says Marshall Blume, a professor of finance at the University of Pennsylvania's Wharton School. In fact, he says, "you are probably worse off—but the amount may be so trivial that you can ignore it," particularly with a small personal portfolio.

Allan Emkin, vice prsident of Wilshire Associates, a Santa Monica, Calif., investment consulting firm, agrees. "When you limit the number of opportunities, you limit some of the potential for return," he says. By restricting investment choices for large institutional portfolios, he says, "you're going to forego something."

PROFITS IN CONSCIENCE
"Socially Responsible" Mutual Funds

Fund	Assets (In millions)*	Total Return (In percent)†
New Alternatives	$ 1.0	35.4%
Calvert Social Investment Managed Growth Portfolio	52.4	32.9
Pioneer Three	520.8	30.4
Parnassus	1.9	28.9
Pioneer II	2,672.5	26.5
Pax World	40.8	25.2
Pioneer	1,526.4	24.3
Dreyfus Third Century	184.3	18.4
Pioneer Bond	26.1	15.3
Mutual Fund Average		27.7
Standard & Poor's 500-Stock Index		35.6

*On 3/31/86
†12 months through 6/30/86
Source: Lipper Analytical Services Inc.

Continued.

The loss isn't necessarily great, however, because the universe of potential investments is huge even if one eliminates some companies. With small personal portfolios, which by their nature are limited in breadth, "it probably doesn't matter," Mr. Emkin says.

Richard Dixon, an associated with Wilshire, says the real problem isn't return, but market risk. Restricted portfolios tend to eliminate large multinational corporations, replacing them with smaller firms whose stock is more volatile, says Mr. Dixon. Investments with low market risk typically fall less rapidly than more volatile investments in a down market and rise less sharply in a bull market.

"The greater risk should actually improve return" over long periods of time because active stocks tend to gain more than they lose, he says. "But for the risk-averse investor, the greater volatility of smaller capitalization companies may be something to avoid."

A recent study by Wilshire compared hypothetical portfolios with and without South Africa-related securities from 1979 to 1984. The 21.1% return of the "South Africa-free" portfolio outperformed the unrestricted portfolio by almost seven points, says Mr. Dixon. But the stock of the generally smaller companies in the restricted portfolio reacted more severely to swings in the market, he adds.

When looking at actual mutual funds, however, the risk factor doesn't loom that large. Spero Kripotos, vice president of CDA Investment Technologies Inc., a Silver Spring, Md., firm that tracks mutual fund performance, says that mutual funds in general are investments with low to average risk. Comparisons by CDA show that funds using social and political investment criteria are no different.

Proponents of social investing, moreover, have little doubt on the wisdom of their approach. Robert J. Schwartz, a New York broker who encourages clients to set their own ethical standards, says he can shape portfolios to avoid investments in South Africa, nuclear utilities or weapons makers without sacrificing return. In 1985, he says, his "socially screened" equity and fixed-income accounts grew an average of 25.2%.

Julie Wendrich, a broker with E.F. Hutton Inc. in Cambridge, Mass., says concern about a company's social responsibility can actually improve return by helping investors avoid potential problems. "A company that will be spending millions to clean up its pollutions or on product liability suits ... could get torn up," she says. By practicing what she preaches with her own money, Ms. Wendrich says she turned $21,000 into $55,000 in the past nine months.

A Sacrifice?

Amy L. Domini, vice president of Franklin Research & Development, says she can't promise profits like Mr. Pillsbury's 44% first-year return. But she says Franklin, which handles $55 million in balanced portfolios for some 90 clients, had a 15.2% average annual return in the five years through 1985, about half a point better than the S&P 500. "Looking at our performance," she adds, "do you think our clients are sacrificing anything?"

At first glance, it might seem that social responsibility had been costly for investors in Dreyfus Third Century Fund. But Jeffrey Friedman, its portfolio manager, says the practice of excluding investments on ethical grounds isn't the reason the fund's total return in the 12 months through June 30 was only 18.4%, far short of the 27.7% mutual-fund average.

"Over the long term, the social criteria don't interfere," Mr. Friedman says. What hurt this past year, he says, was an old-fashioned mistake: being too cautious during a bull market. "I don't think the economy could support this kind of market."

Ultimately, investment performance is in the eye of the beholder. People who put their money in a do-good fund expect psychic returns in addition to profits.

Anne Kessler, a San Francisco banker who says she looks for ways to "put money to use for human value," invested $9,000 last year in the Parnassus Fund "because there wasn't a trade-off" between her social and financial goals. Parnassus, which combines social criteria with the contrarian approach of investing in out-of-favor businesses, has recently been edging out the industry average; it had a 28.9% return for the year ended June 30.

Says Ms. Kessler: "I want to invest in things I believe in long-term, as well as make money now."

folio, *P,* than will a less risk-averse client. However, both will use portfolio *P* as their optimal risky investment vehicle.

This result is called a **separation property;** it tells us that the portfolio choice problem may be separated into two independent tasks. The first task, determination of the optimal risky portfolio, *P,* is purely technical. Given the manager's input list, the best risky portfolio is the same for all clients, regardless of risk aversion. The second task, however, allocation of the complete portfolio to T-bills vs. the risky portfolio, depends on personal preference. Here the client is the decision maker.

The crucial point is that the optimal portfolio *P* that the manager offers is the same for all clients. This result makes professional management more efficient and hence less costly. One management firm can serve any number of clients with relatively small incremental administrative costs.

In actual practice, however, different managers will estimate different input lists, thus deriving different efficient frontiers, and offer different "optimal" portfolios to their clients. The source of the disparity lies in the security analysis. It is worth mentioning here that the rule of GIGO (garbage in-garbage out) applies to security analysis too. If the quality of the security analysis is poor, a passive portfolio such as a market index fund will result in a better CAL than an active portfolio that uses low-quality security analysis to tilt the portfolio weights toward seemingly favorable (mispriced) securities.

As we have seen, the optimal risky portfolios for different clients also may vary because of portfolio constraints such as dividend-yield requirements, tax considerations, or other client preferences. Nevertheless, this analysis suggests that only a very limited number of portfolios may be sufficient to serve the demands of a wide range of investors. This is the theoretical basis of the mutual fund industry.

The (computerized) optimization technique is the easiest part of the portfolio construction problem. The real arena of competition among portfolio managers is in sophisticated security analysis.

Concept Check

Question 4. Suppose that two portfolio managers who work for competing investment management houses each employs a group of security analysts to prepare the input list for the Markowitz algorithm. When all is completed, it turns out that the efficient frontier obtained by portfolio manager *A* dominates that of manager *B.* By domination we mean that *A*'s optimal risky portfolio lies northwest of *B*'s. Hence, given a choice, investors will always prefer the risky portfolio that lies on the CAL of *A.*

a. What should be made of this outcome?

b. Should it be attributed to better security analysis by *A*'s analysts?

c. Could it be that *A*'s computer program is superior?

d. If you were advising clients (and had an advance glimpse at the efficient frontiers of various managers), would you tell them to periodically switch their money around to the manager with the most northwesterly portfolio?

7.5 *Optimal Portfolios With Restrictions on the Risk-Free Investment*

The availability of a risk-free asset greatly simplifies the portfolio decision. When all investors can borrow and lend at that risk-free rate, we are led to a *unique* optimal risky portfolio that is appropriate for all investors. This portfolio maximizes the reward-to-variability ratio. All investors use the same risky portfolio and differ only in the proportion they invest in it and in the risk-free asset.

What if a risk-free asset is not available? Although T-bills are risk-free assets in nominal terms, their real returns are uncertain. Without a risk-free asset, there is no tangency portfolio that is best for all investors. In this case investors have to choose a portfolio from the efficient frontier of risky assets redrawn in Figure 7.14.

Each investor will now choose the optimal risky portfolio by superimposing a particular set of indifference curves on the efficient frontier, as Figure 7.14 shows. The optimal portfolio, *P,* for the investor whose risk aversion is represented by the set of indifference curves in Figure 7.14 is tangent to the highest attainable indifference curve.

Investors who are more risk averse than the one represented in Figure 7.14 would have steeper indifference curves, meaning that the tangency portfolio will be of smaller standard deviation and expected return than portfolio *P,* such as portfolio *Q.* Conversely, investors who are more risk tolerant than the one represented in Figure 7.14 would be characterized by flatter indifference curves, resulting in a tangency portfolio of higher expected return and standard deviation than portfolio *P.* The common feature of all these rational investors is that they choose portfolios on the efficient frontier; that is, they choose mean-variances efficient portfolios.

Even if virtually risk-free lending opportunities are available, many investors do

FIGURE 7.14
Individual portfolio
selection without a
risk-free asset.

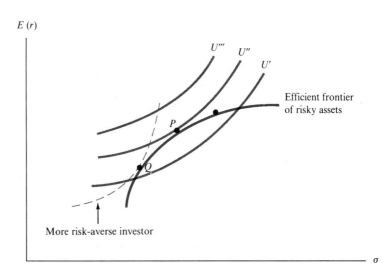

FIGURE 7.15
Individual portfolio
selection with
risk-free lending only.

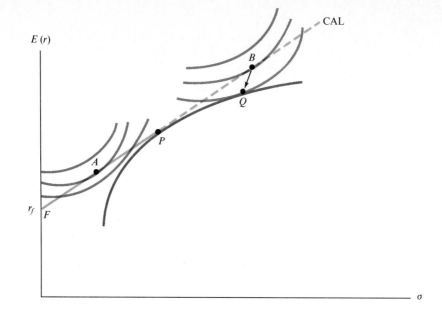

face borrowing restrictions. They may be unable to borrow altogether, or, more real-istically, they may face a borrowing rate that is significantly greater than the lending rate. Let us first consider investors who can lend without risk, but are prohibited from borrowing.

When a risk-free investment is available, but an investor can take only positive positions in it (he or she can lend at r_f, but cannot borrow), a CAL exists but is lim-ited to the line FP as in Figure 7.15.

Any investors whose preferences are represented by indifference curves with tan-gency portfolios on the portion FP of the CAL, such as portfolio A, are unaffected by the borrowing restriction. For such investors the borrowing restriction is a nonbinding constraint, because they are net *lenders*, lending some of their money at rate r_f.

Aggressive or more risk-tolerant investors, who would choose portfolio B in the absence of the borrowing restriction, are affected, however. For them, the borrowing restriction is a binding constraint. Such investors will be driven to portfolios on the efficient frontier, such as portfolio Q, which have higher expected return and stan-dard deviation than does portfolio P. Portfolios such as Q, which are on the efficient frontier of risky assets, represent a zero investment in the risk-free asset.

Finally, we consider a more realistic case, that of feasible borrowing, but at a higher rate than r_f. An individual who borrows to invest in a risky portfolio will have to pay an interest rate higher than the T-bill rate. The lender will require a premium commensurate with the probability of default. For example, the call money rate charged by brokers on margin accounts is higher than the T-bill rate.

Investors who face a borrowing rate greater than the lending rate confront a three-part CAL such as in Figure 7.16. CAL_1, which is relevant in the range FP_1, repre-

FIGURE 7.16
The investment
opportunity set with
differential rates for
borrowing and
lending.

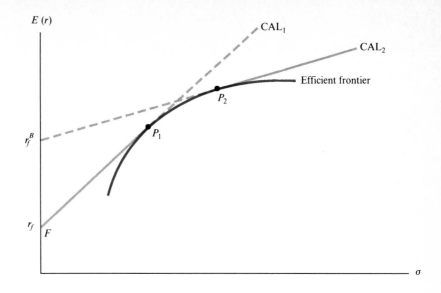

FIGURE 7.17
The optimal portfolio
of defensive investors
with differential
borrowing and lending
rates.

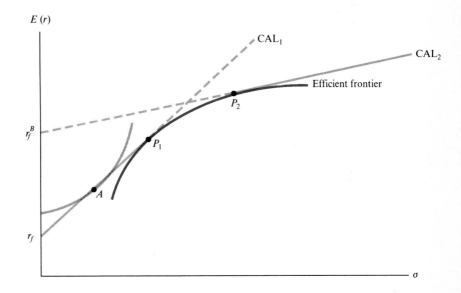

sents the efficient portfolio set for defensive (risk-averse) investors. These investors
invest part of their funds in T-bills at rate r_f. They find that the tangency portfolio is
P_1, and they choose a complete portfolio such as portfolio A in Figure 7.17.

CAL$_2$, which is relevant in a range to the right of portfolio P_2, represents the efficient portfolio set for more aggressive, or risk-tolerant, investors. This line starts at
the borrowing rate, r_f^B, but it is unavailable in the range $r_f^B P_2$, because *lending* (investing in T-bills) is available only at the risk-free rate r_f, less than r_f^B.

FIGURE 7.18
The optimal portfolio of aggressive investors with differential borrowing and lending rates.

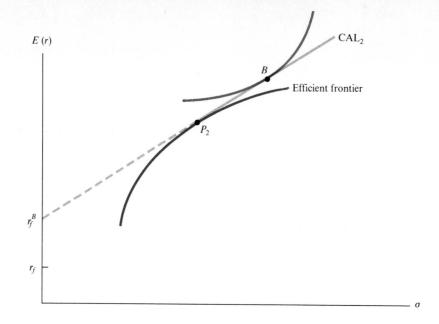

FIGURE 7.19
The optimal portfolio of moderately risk-tolerant investors with differential borrowing and lending rates.

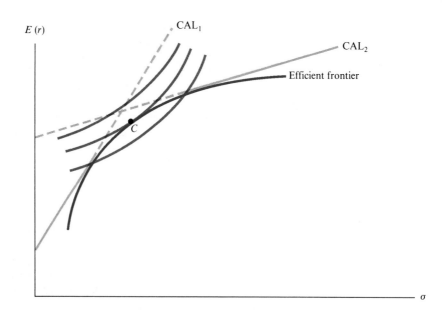

Investors who are willing to *borrow* at the higher rate, r_f^B, to invest in an optimal risky portfolio will choose portfolio P_2 as their risky investment vehicle. Such a case is described in Figure 7.18, which superimposes a relatively risk tolerant investor's indifference curve on CAL_2 of Figure 7.16. The investor with the indifference curve in Figure 7.18 chooses portfolio P_2 as the optimal risky portfolio and borrows to invest in it, arriving at overall portfolio B.

Investors in the middle range, neither defensive enough to invest in T-bills nor aggressive enough to borrow, choose a risky portfolio from the efficient frontier in the range P_1P_2. This case is described in Figure 7.19. The indifference curve representing the investor in Figure 7.19 leads to a tangency portfolio on the efficient frontier, portfolio C.

Concept Check

Question 5. With differential lending and borrowing rates, only investors with about average degrees of risk aversion will choose a portfolio in the range P_1P_2 in Figure 7.17. Other investors will choose a portfolio on CAL_1 if they are more risk averse, or on CAL_2 if they are more risk tolerant.
  a. Does this mean that investors with average risk aversion are more dependent on the quality of the forecasts that generate the efficient frontier?

Summary

1. The expected return of a portfolio is the weighted average of the component asset expected returns with the investment proportions as weights.

2. The variance of a portfolio is the weighted sum of the elements of the covariance matrix with the product of the investment proportions as weights. Thus the variance of each asset is weighted by the square of its investment proportion. Each covariance of any pair of assets appears twice in the covariance matrix, and thus the portfolio variance includes twice each covariance weighted by the product of the investment proportions in each of the two assets.

3. Even if the covariances are positive, the portfolio standard deviation is less than the weighted average of the component standard deviations, as long as the assets are not perfectly positively correlated. Thus portfolio diversification is of value as long as assets are less than perfectly correlated.

4. The greater an asset's *covariance* with the other assets in the portfolio, the more it contributes to portfolio variance. An asset that is perfectly negatively correlated with a portfolio can serve as a perfect hedge. The perfect hedge asset can reduce the portfolio variance to zero.

5. The efficient frontier is the graphical representation of a set of portfolios that maximize expected return for each level of portfolio risk. Rational investors will choose a portfolio on the efficient frontier.

6. A portfolio manager identifies the efficient frontier by first establishing estimates for the asset expected returns and the covariance matrix. This input list is then fed into an optimization program that reports as outputs the investment proportions, expected returns, and standard deviations of the portfolios on the efficient frontier.

7. In general, portfolio managers will arrive at different efficient portfolios because of difference in methods and quality of security analysis. Managers compete on the quality of their security analysis relative to their management fees.

8. If a risk-free asset is available and input lists are identical, all investors will choose the same portfolio on the efficient frontier of risky assets: the portfolio tangent to the CAL. All investors with identical input lists will hold an identical risky portfolio, differing only in how much each allocates to this optimal portfolio and to the risk-free asset. This result is characterized as the separation principle of portfolio construction.

9. When a risk-free asset is not available, each investor chooses a risky portfolio on the efficient frontier. If a risk-free asset is available but borrowing is restricted, only aggressive investors will be affected. They will choose portfolios on the efficient frontier according to their degree of risk tolerance.

Key Terms

Diversification	Diversifiable risk
Insurance principle	Minimum-variance portfolio
Market risk	Portfolio opportunity set
Systematic risk	Reward-to-variability ratio
Nondiversifiable risk	Optimal risky portfolio
Unique risk	Minimum-variance frontier
Firm-specific risk	Efficient frontier
Nonsystematic risk	Separation property

Selected Readings

Two frequently cited papers on the impact of diversification on portfolio risk are:
Evans, John L., and Archer, Stephen H., "Diversification and the Reduction of Dispersion: An Empirical Analysis," *Journal of Finance,* December 1968.
Wagner, W.H., and Lau, S.C., "The Effect of Diversification on Risk," *Financial Analysts Journal,* November-December 1971.

The seminal works on portfolio selection are:
Markowitz, Harry M., "Portfolio Selection," *Journal of Finance,* March 1952.
Markowitz, Harry M., *Portfolio Selection: Efficient Diversification of Investments.* New York: John Wiley & Sons, Inc., 1959.

Also see:
Samuelson, Paul A., "Risk & Uncertainty: A Fallacy of Large Numbers," *Scientia, 98,* 1963.

Problems

The following data apply to Questions 1 through 8:

A pension fund manager is considering three mutual funds. The first is a stock fund, the second is a long-term government and corporate bond fund, and the third is a T-bill money market fund that yields a rate of 9%. The probability distribution of the risky funds is as follows:

	Expected Return	Standard Deviation
Stock fund (S)	.22	.32
Bond fund (B)	.13	.23

The correlation between the fund returns is .15.

1. What are the investment proportions of the minimum-variance portfolio of the two risky funds, and what is the expected value and standard deviation of its rate of return?

2. Tabulate and draw the investment opportunity set of the two risky funds. Use investment proportions for the stock fund of zero to 100% in increments of 20%.

3. Draw a tangent from the risk-free rate to the opportunity set. What does your graph show for the expected return and standard deviation of the optimal portfolio?

4. Solve numerically for the proportions of each asset, and for the expected return and standard deviation of the optimal risky portfolio.

5. What is the reward-to-variability ratio of the best feasible CAL?

6. You require that your portfolio yield an expected return of 15%, and that it be efficient on the best feasible CAL.
   a. What is the standard deviation of your portfolio?
   b. What is the proportion invested in the T-bill fund and each of the two risky funds?

7. If you were to use only the two risky funds, and still require an expected return of 15%, what must be the investment proportions of your portfolio? Compare its standard deviation to that of the optimized portfolio in question 6. What do you conclude?

8. Suppose that you face the same opportunity set, but you cannot borrow. You wish to construct a portfolio with an expected return of 29%. What are the appropriate portfolio proportions and the resulting standard deviation? What reduction in standard deviation could you attain if you were allowed to borrow at the risk-free rate?

9. Stocks offer an expected rate of return of 18%, with a standard deviation of 22%. Gold offers an expected return of 10% with a standard deviation of 30%.
   a. In light of the apparent inferiority of gold with respect to both mean return and volatility, would anyone hold gold? If so, demonstrate graphically why one would do so.
   b. Given the data above, reanswer question (a) with the additional assumption that the correlation coefficient between gold and stocks equals 1. Draw a

graph illustrating why one would or would not hold gold in one's portfolio. Could this set of assumptions for expected returns, standard deviations, and correlation represent an equilibrium for the security market?

10. Suppose that there are many stocks in the market and that the characteristics of stocks *A* and *B* are given as follows:

Stock	Expected Return	Standard Deviation
A	.10	.05
B	.15	.10
	Correlation $= -1$	

Suppose that it is possible to borrow at the risk-free rate, r_f. In equilibrium r_f is greater than .10 (true or false?).

11. Assume that expected returns and standard deviations for all securities (including the risk-free rate for borrowing and lending) are known. In this case all investors will have the same optimal risky portfolio (true or false?).

12. The standard deviation of the portfolio is always equal to the weighted average of the standard deviations of the assets in the portfolio (true or false?).

13. Suppose that you have a project that has a .7 chance of doubling your investment in a year and a .3 chance of halving your investment in a year. What is the standard deviation of the rate of return on this investment?

14. Suppose that you have $1 million and the following two opportunities from which to construct a portfolio:
    a. Risk-free asset earning .12 per year
    b. Risky asset earning .30 per year with a standard deviation of .40
    If you construct a portfolio with a standard deviation of .30, what will be the rate of return?

The following data apply to questions 15 through 17 (CFA Examination, Level III, 1982):

Hennessy & Associates manages a $30 million equity portfolio for the multi-manager Wilstead Pension Fund. Jason Jones, financial vice president of Wilstead, noted that Hennessy had rather consistently achieved the best record among the Wilstead's six equity managers. Performance of the Hennessy portfolio had been clearly superior to that of the S&P 500 in 4 of the past 5 years. In the one less favorable year, the shortfall was trivial.

Hennessy is a "bottom-up" manager. The firm largely avoids any attempt to "time the market." It also focuses on selection of individual stocks, rather than the weighting of favored industries.

There is no apparent conformity of style among the six equity managers. The five managers, other than Hennessy, manage portfolios aggregating $250 million made up of more than 150 individual issues.

Jones is convinced that Hennessy is able to apply superior skill to stock selection, but the favorable results are limited by the high degree of diversification in the portfolio. Over the years, the portfolio generally held 40-50 stocks, with about 2% to 3%

of total funds committed to each issue. The reason Hennessy seemed to do well most years was because the firm was able to identify each year 10 or 12 issues which registered particularly large gains.

Based on this overview, Jones outlined the following plan to the Wilstead pension committee:

"Let's tell Hennessy to limit the portfolio to no more than 20 stocks. Hennessy will double the commitments to the stocks that it really favors, and eliminate the remainder. Except for this one new restriction, Hennessy should be free to manage the portfolio exactly as before."

All the members of the pension committee generally supported Jones' proposal, because all agreed that Hennessy had seemed to demonstrate superior skill in selecting stocks. Yet, the proposal was a considerable departure from previous practice, and several committee members raised questions. Respond to each of these questions:

15. Answer the following:
    a. Will the limitation of 20 stocks likely increase or decrease the risk of the portfolio? Explain.
    b. Is there any way Hennessy could reduce the number of issues from 40 to 20 without significantly affecting risk? Explain.

16. One committee member was particularly enthusiastic concerning Jones' proposal. He suggested that Hennessy's performance might benefit further from reduction in the number of issues to 10. If the reduction to 20 could be expected to be advantageous, explain why reduction to 10 might be less likely to be advantageous. (Assume that Wilstead will evaluate the Hennessy portfolio independently of the other portfolios in the fund.)

17. Another committee member suggested that, rather than evaluate each managed portfolio independently of other portfolios, it might be better to consider the effects of a change in the Hennessy portfolio on the total fund. Explain how this broader point of view could affect the committee decision to limit the holdings in the Hennessy portfolio to either 10 or 20 issues.

Appendix A:
The Power of Diversification

Section 7.1 introduced the concept of diversification and the limits to the benefits of diversification caused by systematic risk. Given the tools we have developed, we can reconsider this intuition more rigorously and at the same time sharpen our insight regarding the power of diversification.

Recall from equation 7.11 that the general formula for the variance of a portfolio is

$$\sigma_p^2 = \sum_{i=1}^{n} w_i^2 \sigma_i^2 + \sum_{\substack{j=1 \\ j \neq i}}^{n} \sum_{i=1}^{n} w_i w_j \text{Cov}(r_i, r_j) \qquad (7A.1)$$

Consider now the naive diversification strategy in which an equally weighted portfolio is constructed, meaning that $w_i = 1/n$ for each security. In this case equation 7A.1 may be rewritten as follows:

$$\sigma_p^2 = \frac{1}{n} \sum_{i=1}^{n} \frac{1}{n} \sigma_i^2 + \sum_{\substack{j=1 \\ j \neq i}}^{n} \sum_{i=1}^{n} \frac{1}{n^2} \text{Cov}(r_i, r_j) \tag{7A.2}$$

Note that there are n variance terms and $n(n-1)$ covariance terms in equation 7A.2.

If we define the average variance and average covariance of the securities as

$$\overline{\sigma}^2 = \frac{1}{n} \sum_{i=1}^{n} \sigma_i^2$$

$$\overline{\text{Cov}} = \frac{1}{n(n-1)} \sum_{\substack{i=1 \\ j \neq i}}^{n} \sum_{j=1}^{n} \text{Cov}(r_i, r_j)$$

we can express portfolio variance as

$$\sigma_p^2 = \frac{1}{n} \overline{\sigma}^2 + \frac{n-1}{n} \overline{\text{Cov}} \tag{7A.3}$$

Now examine the effect of diversification. When the average covariance among security returns is zero, as it is when all risk is firm-specific, portfolio variance can be driven to zero. We see this from equation 7A.3: the second term on the right-hand side will be zero in this scenario while the first term approaches zero as n becomes larger. Hence, when security returns are uncorrelated, the power of diversification to limit portfolio risk is unlimited.

However, the more important case is the one in which economy-wide risk factors impart positive correlation among stock returns. In this case, as the portfolio becomes more highly diversified (n increases) portfolio variance remains positive. While firm-specific risk, represented by the first term in equation 7A.3, is still diversified away, the second term simply approaches $\overline{\text{Cov}}$ as n becomes greater. [Note that $(n-1)/n = 1 - 1/n$, which approaches 1 for large n.] Thus the irreducible risk of a diversified portfolio depends on the covariance of the returns of the component securities, which in turn is a function of the importance of systematic factors in the economy.

To see further the fundamental relationship between systematic risk and security correlations, suppose for simplicity that all securities have a common standard deviation, σ, and all security pairs have a common correlation coefficient ρ. Then the covariance between all pairs of securities is $\rho\sigma^2$, and equation 7A.3 becomes

$$\sigma_p^2 = \frac{1}{n} \sigma^2 + \frac{n-1}{n} \rho\sigma^2 \tag{7A.4}$$

Risk Reduction of Equally Weighted Portfolios in Correlated and Uncorrelated Universes

Universe Size *n*	Optimal Portfolio Proportion *1/n (%)*	$\rho = 0$		$\rho = .4$	
		Standard Deviation (%)	Reduction in σ	Standard Deviation (%)	Reduction in σ
1	100	50.00		50.00	
2	50	35.36	14.64	41.83	8.17
5	20	22.36		36.06	
6	16.67	20.41	1.95	35.36	.70
10	10	15.81		33.91	
11	9.09	15.08	.73	33.71	.20
20	5	11.18		32.79	
21	4.76	10.91	.27	32.73	.06
100	1	5.00		31.86	
101	.99	4.98	.02	31.86	.00

The effect of correlation is now explicit. When $\rho = 0$, we again obtain the insurance principle, where portfolio variance approaches zero as *n* becomes greater. For $\rho > 0$, however, portfolio variance remains positive. In fact, for $\rho = 1$, portfolio variance equals σ^2 regardless of *n*, demonstrating that diversification is of no benefit: in the case of perfect correlation, all risk is systematic. More generally, as *n* becomes greater, equation 7A.4 shows that systematic risk becomes $\rho\sigma^2$.

Table 7A.1 presents portfolio standard deviation as we include ever greater numbers of securities in the portfolio for two cases: $\rho = 0$ and $\rho = .40$. The table takes σ to be 50%. As one would expect, portfolio risk is greater when $\rho = .40$. More surprising, perhaps, is that portfolio risk diminishes far less rapidly as *n* increases in positive correlation case. The correlation among security returns limits the power of diversification.

Note that, for a 100-security portfolio, the standard deviation is 5% in the uncorrelated case—still significant when we consider the potential of zero standard deviation. For $\rho = .40$, the standard deviation is high, 31.86%, yet it is very close to undiversifiable systematic risk in the infinite-sized universe, $\sqrt{\rho\sigma^2} = \sqrt{.4 \times .50^2} = .3162$, or 31.62%. At this point, further diversification is of little value.

Concept Check

Question 7A.1. Suppose that the universe of available risky securities consists of a large number of stocks, identically distributed with $E(r) = 15\%$, $\sigma = 60\%$, and a common correlation coefficient of $\rho = .5$.

a. What is the expected return and standard deviation of an equally weighted risky portfolio of 25 stocks?

b. What is the smallest number of stocks necessary to generate an efficient portfolio with a standard deviation equal to or smaller than 43%?

c. What is the systematic risk in this universe?

d. If T-bills are available and yield 10%, what is the slope of the CAL?

We also can derive an important result from this exercise. When we hold diversified portfolios, the contribution to portfolio risk of a particular security will depend on the *covariance* of that security's return with those of other securities, and *not* on the security's variance. As we shall see in Chapter 8, this implies that fair risk premiums also should depend on covariances rather than total variability of returns.

Appendix B:
The Insurance Principle: Risk-Sharing vs. Risk-Pooling

Mean-variance analysis has taken a strong hold among investment professionals, and insight into the mechanics of efficient diversification has become quite widespread. Common misconceptions or fallacies about diversification still persist, however, and we will try to put some to rest.

It is commonly believed that a large portfolio of independent insurance policies is a necessary and sufficient condition for an insurance company to shed its risk. The fact is that a multitude of independent insurance policies is neither necessary nor sufficient for a sound insurance portfolio. Actually, an individual insurer who would not insure a single policy also would be unwilling to insure a large portfolio of independent policies.

Consider Paul Samuelson's (1963) story. He once offered a colleague 2-to-1 odds on a $1,000 bet on the toss of a coin. His colleague refused, saying, "I won't bet because I would feel the $1,000 loss more than the $2,000 gain. But I'll take you on if you promise to let me make a hundred such bets."

Samuelson's colleague, as many others, might have explained his position, not quite correctly, that "One toss is not enough to make it reasonably sure that the law of averages will turn out in my favor. But in a hundred tosses of a coin, the law of averages will make it a darn good bet."

Another way to rationalize this argument is to think in terms of rates of return. In each bet you put up $1,000 and then get back $3,000 with a probability of one half, or zero with a probability of one half. The probability distribution of the rate of return is 200% with $p = \frac{1}{2}$ and -100% with $p = \frac{1}{2}$.

The bets are all independent and identical and therefore the expected return is $E(r) = \frac{1}{2}(200) + \frac{1}{2}(-100) = 50\%$, regardless of the number of bets. The standard deviation of the rate of return on the portfolio of independent bets is[a]

$$\sigma(n) = \frac{\sigma}{\sqrt{n}}$$

---

[a]This follows from equation 7.11, setting $w_i = 1/n$ and all covariances equal to zero because of the independence of the bets.

where σ is the standard deviation of a single bet:

$$\sigma = [\tfrac{1}{2}(200 - 50)^2 + \tfrac{1}{2}(-100 - 50)^2]^{\frac{1}{2}}$$
$$= 150\%$$

The rate of return on a sequence of bets, in other words, has a smaller standard deviation than that of a single bet. By increasing the number of bets we can reduce the standard deviation of the rate of return to any desired level. It seems at first glance that Samuelson's colleague was correct. But he was not.

The fallacy of the argument lies in the use of a rate of return criterion to choose from portfolios *that are not equal in size.* Although the portfolio is equally weighted across bets, each extra bet increases the scale of the investment by $1,000. Recall from traditional corporate finance that when choosing among mutually exclusive projects you cannot use the internal rate of return (IRR) as your decision criterion when the projects are of different sizes. You have to use the net present value (NPV) rule.

Consider the dollar profit (as opposed to rate of return) distribution of a single bet:

$$E(R) = \tfrac{1}{2} \times 2,000 + \tfrac{1}{2} \times (-1,000)$$
$$= \$500$$
$$\sigma_R = [\tfrac{1}{2}(2,000 - 500)^2 + \tfrac{1}{2}(-1,000 - 500)^2]^{\frac{1}{2}}$$
$$= \$1,500$$

These are independent bets where the total profit from n bets is the sum of the profits from the single bets. Therefore, with n bets

$$E[R(n)] = \$500n$$

$$\text{Variance } \left(\sum_{i=1}^{n} R_i\right) = n\sigma_R^2$$

$$\sigma_R(n) = \sqrt{n\sigma_R^2}$$

$$= \sigma_R\sqrt{n}$$

so that the standard deviation of the dollar return *increases* by a factor equal to the square root of the number of bets, n, in contrast to the standard deviation of the rate of return, which *decreases* by a factor of the square root of n.

As further evidence, consider the standard coin-tossing game. Whether one flips a fair coin 10 times or 1,000 times, the expected percentage of heads flipped is 50%. One expects the actual proportion of heads in a typical running of the 1,000-toss experiment to be closer to 50% than in the 10-toss experiment. This is the law of averages.

But the actual number of heads will typically depart from its expected value by a greater amount in the 1,000-toss experiment. For example, 504 heads is close to 50%

and is 4 more than the expected number. To exceed the expected number of heads by 4 in the 10-toss game would require 9 out of 10 heads, which is a much more extreme departure from the mean. In the many-toss case, there is more volatility of the number of heads and less volatility of the percentage of heads. This is the same when an insurance company takes on more policies: the dollar variance of its portfolio increases while the rate of return variance falls.

The lesson is this: rate-of-return analysis is appropriate when considering mutually exclusive portfolios of equal size, which is what we did in all the examples so far. We applied a fixed investment budget, and we investigated only the consequences of varying investment proportions in various assets. But if an insurance company takes on more and more insurance policies, it is increasing portfolio dollar investments. The analysis that is called for in that case must be cast in terms of dollar profits, in much the same way that NPV is called for instead of IRR when we compare different-sized projects. This is why risk-pooling (that is, accumulating independent risky prospects) does not act to eliminate risk.

Samuelson's colleague should have counteroffered: "Let's make 1,000 bets, each with your $2 against my $1." Then he would be holding a portfolio of fixed size, equal to $1,000, which is diversified into 1,000 identical independent prospects. This would make the insurance principle work.

Another way for Samuelson's colleague to get around the riskiness of this tempting bet is to share the large bets with friends. Consider a firm engaging in 1,000 of Paul Samuelson's bets. In each bet the firm puts up $1,000 and receives $3,000 or nothing as before. Each bet is too large for you. Yet if you hold a 1/1,000 share of the firm, your position is exactly the same as if you were to make 1,000 small bets of $2 against $1. A 1/1,000 share of a $1,000 bet is equivalent to a $1 bet. Holding a small share of many large bets essentially allows you to replace a stake in one large bet with a diversified portfolio of manageable bets.

How does this apply to insurance companies? Investors can purchase insurance company shares in the stock market, so they can choose to hold as small a position in the overall risk as they please. No matter how great the risk of the policies, a large group of individual small investors will agree to bear the risk if the expected rate of return exceeds the risk-free rate. Thus it is the sharing of risk among many shareholders that makes the insurance industry tick.

Appendix C:
The Fallacy of Time Diversification

The insurance story just discussed illustrates a misuse of rate of return analysis, specifically the mistake of comparing portfolios of different sizes. A more insidious version of this error often appears under the guise of "time diversification."

Consider the case of Mr. Frier, who has $100,000. He is trying to figure out the appropriate allocation of this fund between risk-free T-bills that yield 10% and a risky portfolio that yields an annual rate of return with $E(r_p) = 15\%$ and $\sigma_p = 30\%$.

Mr. Frier took a course in finance in his youth. He likes quantitative models, and after careful introspection determines that his degree of risk aversion, A, is 4. Consequently, he calculates that his optimal allocation to the risky portfolio is

$$y = \frac{E(r_p) - r_f}{A\sigma_p^2} = \frac{.15 - .10}{4 \times .3^2}$$
$$= .14$$

that is, a 14% investment ($14,000) in the risky portfolio.

With this strategy, Mr. Frier calculates his complete portfolio expected return and standard deviation by

$$E(r_C) = r_f + y[E(r_p) - r_f]$$
$$= 10.70\%$$
$$\sigma_C = y\sigma_p$$
$$= 4.20\%$$

At this point, Mr. Frier gets cold feet because this fund is intended to provide the mainstay of his retirement wealth. He plans to retire in 5 years, and any mistake will be burdensome.

Mr. Frier calls Ms. Mavin, a highly recommended financial advisor. Ms. Mavin explains that indeed the time factor is all important. She cites academic research showing that asset rates of return over successive holding periods are independent. Therefore she argues that over a 5-year period returns in good years and bad years will cancel out, making the average rate of return on the portfolio over the investment period less risky than would appear from an analysis of single-year volatility. Because returns in each year are independent, Ms. Mavin tells Mr. Frier that a 5-year investment is equivalent to a portfolio of five equally weighted independent assets. With such a portfolio, the (5-year) holding period return has a mean of

$$E[r_p(5)] = 15\% \text{ per year}$$

and standard deviation of[b]

$$\sigma_p(5) = \frac{30}{\sqrt{5}}$$
$$= 13.42\% \text{ per year}$$

Mr. Frier is relieved. He believes that the effective standard deviation has fallen from 30% to 13.42%, and that the reward-to-variability ratio is much better than his first assessment.

---

[b]The calculation for standard deviation is only approximate, because it assumes that the 5-year return is the sum of each of the five 1-year returns, and this formulation ignores compounding. The error is small, however, and does not affect the point we want to make.

Average rates of
return on common
stocks. Simulated total
return distributions for
the period 1977-2000.
Geometric average
annual rates.

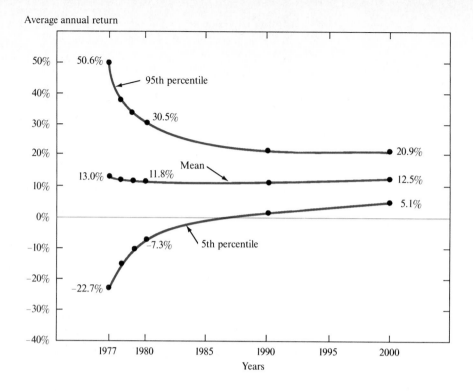

Is Mr. Frier's newfound sense of security warranted? Specifically, is Ms. Mavin's time diversification really a risk-reducer? Is it true that the standard deviation of the annualized *rate* of return over 5 years really is only 13.42% as Mavin claims, compared with the 30% 1-year standard deviation? But what about the volatility of Mr. Frier's total retirement fund? With a standard deviation of the 5-year average return of .1342, a one-standard-deviation disappointment in Mr. Frier's average return over the 5-year period will affect final wealth by a factor of $(1 - .1342)^5 = .487$, meaning that final wealth will be less than one half its expected value. This is a larger impact than the 30% 1-year-swing.

Ms. Mavin is wrong: time diversification does not reduce risk. Although it is true that the per year average rate of return has a smaller standard deviation for a longer time horizon, it also is true that the uncertainty compounds over a greater number of years. Unfortunately, this latter effect dominates in the sense that the *total return* becomes more uncertain the longer the investment horizon.

Figures 7A.1 and 7A.2 from a study by Ibbotson and Sinquefield[c] show the fal-

---

[c]Ibbotson, Roger G., and Sinquefield, Rex A., *Stocks, Bonds, Bills, and Inflation: The Past (1926-76) and the Future (1977-2000),* Chicago: Financial Analysts Research Foundation, 1977.

FIGURE 7A.2

Dollar returns on common stocks. Simulated distributions of nominal wealth index for the period 1977-2000 (year-end 1976 equals 1.00).

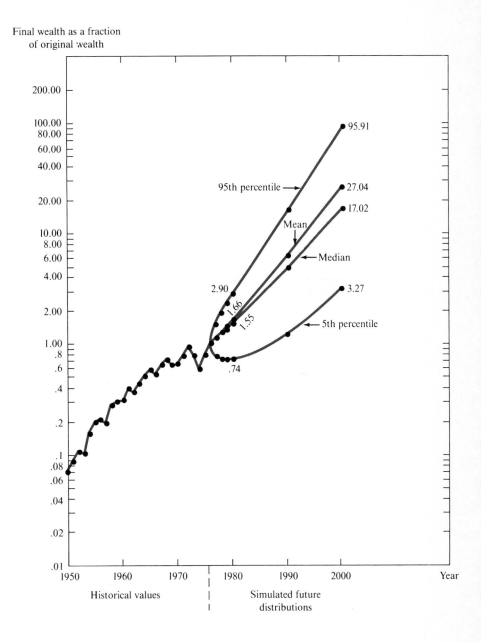

Final wealth as a fraction of original wealth

lacy of time diversification. They represent simulated returns to a stock investment and show the range of possible outcomes. While the confidence band around the expected rate of return on the investment narrows with investment life, the dollar confidence band widens.

Again, the coin-toss analogy is helpful. Think of each year's investment return as one flip of the coin. After many years, the average number of heads approaches 50 percent, but the possible deviation of total heads from one-half the number of flips still will be growing.

The lesson is, once again, that one should not use rate of return analysis to compare portfolios of different size. Investing for more than one holding period means that the amount at risk is growing. This is analogous to an insurer taking on more insurance policies. The fact that these policies are independent does not offset the effect of placing more funds at risk. Focus on the standard deviation of the rate of return should never obscure the more proper emphasis on the possible dollar values of a portfolio strategy.

PART III

Equilibrium in Capital Markets

CHAPTER 8

The Capital Asset Pricing Model

The capital asset pricing model, almost always referred to as the CAPM, is a centerpiece of modern financial economics. The model gives us a precise prediction of the relationship that we should observe between the risk of an asset and its expected return. This relationship serves two vital functions. First, it provides a benchmark rate of return for evaluating possible investments. For example, if we are analyzing securities, we might be interested in whether the expected return we forecast for a stock is more or less than its "fair" return given risk. Second, the model helps us to make an educated guess as to the expected return on assets that have not yet been traded in the marketplace. For example, how do we price an initial public offering of stock? How will a major new investment project affect the return investors require on a company's stock? Although the CAPM does not fully withstand empirical tests, it is widely used because of the insight it offers and because its accuracy suffices for many important applications.

In this chapter we start with the basic version of the CAPM. We also show how the simple version may be extended without losing the insight and applicability of the model.

8.1 The Capital Asset Pricing Model

The capital asset pricing model is a set of predictions concerning equilibrium expected returns on risky assets. We intend to explain it in one short chapter but do not expect this to be easy going. Harry Markowitz laid down the foundation of modern portfolio management in 1952. The CAPM was developed 12 years later in articles by William Sharpe,[1] John Lintner,[2] and Jan Mossin.[3] The time for this gestation indi-

---

[1] Sharpe, William, "Capital Asset Prices: A Theory of Market Equilibrium," *Journal of Finance*, September 1964.
[2] Lintner, John, "The Valuation of Risk Assets and the Selection of Risky Investments in Stock Portfolios and Capital Budgets," *Review of Economics and Statistics*, February 1965.
[3] Mossin, Jan, "Equilibrium in a Capital Asset Market," *Econometrica*, October 1966.

cates that the leap from Markowitz's portfolio selection model to the CAPM is not trivial.

We will approach the CAPM by posing the question "what if" where the "if" part refers to a simplified world. Positing an admittedly unrealistic world allows a relatively easy leap to the "then" part. Once we accomplish this, we can add complexity to the hypothesized environment one step at a time and see how the conclusions must be amended. This process allows us to derive a reasonably realistic and comprehensible model.

We can summarize the simplifying assumptions that lead to the basic version of the CAPM in the following list. The thrust of these assumptions is that we try to ensure that individuals are as alike as possible, with the notable exceptions of initial wealth and risk tolerance. We will see that conformity of investor behavior vastly simplifies our analysis.

1. There are many investors, each with an endowment (wealth) that is small compared to the total endowment of all investors. Investors are price-takers, in that they act as though security prices are unaffected by their own trades. This is the usual perfect competition assumption of microeconomics.

2. All investors plan for one identical holding period. This behavior sometimes is said to be myopic (short-sighted) in that it ignores everything that might happen after the end of the single-period horizon. Myopic behavior is, in general, suboptimal.

3. Investments are limited to a universe of publicly traded financial assets, such as stocks and bonds, and to risk-free borrowing or lending arrangements. This assumption rules out investment in nontraded assets such as in education (human capital), private enterprises, and governmentally funded assets such as town halls and nuclear submarines. It is assumed also that investors may borrow or lend any amount at a fixed, risk-free rate.

4. Investors pay no taxes on returns and no transaction costs (commissions and service charges) on trades in securities. In reality, of course, we know that investors are in different tax brackets and that this may govern the type of assets in which they invest. For example, tax implications may differ depending on whether the income is from interest, dividends, or capital gains. Furthermore, trading is costly, and commissions and fees depend on the size of the trade and the good standing of the individual investor.

5. All investors are rational mean-variance optimizers, meaning that they all use the Markowitz portfolio selection model.

6. All investors analyze securities in the same way and share the same economic view of the world. The result is identical estimates of the probability distribution of future cash flows from investing in the available securities; that is, for any set of security prices, they all derive the same input list to feed into the Markowitz model. Given a set of security prices and the risk-free interest rate, all investors use the same expected returns and covariance matrix of security returns to generate the efficient frontier and the unique optimal risky portfolio. This assumption is often referred to as **homogeneous expectations** or beliefs.

These assumptions represent the "if" of our "what if" analysis. Obviously, they ignore many real-world complexities. With these assumptions, however, we can gain some powerful insights into the nature of equilibrium in security markets.

We can summarize the equilibrium that will prevail in this hypothetical world of securities and investors briefly. The rest of the chapter explains and elaborates on these implications.

1. All investors will choose to hold a portfolio of risky assets in proportions that duplicate representation of the assets in the **market portfolio** *(M)*, which includes all traded assets. For simplicity, we often shall refer to all risky assets as stocks. The proportion of each stock in the market portfolio equals the market value of the stock (price per share multiplied by the number of shares outstanding) divided by the total market value of all stocks.

2. Not only will the market portfolio be on the efficient frontier, but it also will be the tangency portfolio to the optimal capital allocation line (CAL) derived by each and every investor. As a result, the capital market line (CML), the line from the risk-free rate through the market portfolio, *M*, is also the best attainable capital allocation line. All investors hold *M* as their optimal risky portfolio, differing only in the amount invested in it vs. in the risk-free asset.

3. The risk premium on the market portfolio will be proportional to the risk of the market portfolio and the market degree of risk aversion. Mathematically,

$$E(r_M) - r_f = \overline{A}\, \sigma_M^2$$

where σ_M^2 is the variance of the market portfolio and $\overline{A}$ is the average degree of risk aversion across investors. Note that because *M* is the optimal portfolio, which is efficiently diversified across all stocks, σ_M^2 is the systematic risk of this universe.

4. The risk premium on individual assets will be proportional to the risk premium on the market portfolio, *M*, and the *beta coefficient* of the security, relative to the market portfolio. We will see that beta measures the extent to which returns on the stock and the market move together. Formally, beta is defined as

$$\beta_i = \frac{\text{Cov}(r_i, r_M)}{\sigma_M^2}$$

and we can write

$$E(r_i) - r_f = \frac{\text{Cov}(r_i, r_M)}{\sigma_M^2}[E(r_M) - r_f]$$
$$= \beta_i[E(r_M) - r_f]$$

We will elaborate on these results and their implications shortly.

Why Do All Investors Hold the Market Portfolio?

Given the assumptions of the previous section, it is easy to see that all investors will desire to hold identical risky portfolios. If all investors use identical Markowitz analysis (assumption 5) applied to the same universe of securities (assumption 3) for

Equilibrium in Capital Markets

FIGURE 8.1

The efficient frontier
and the capital market
line.

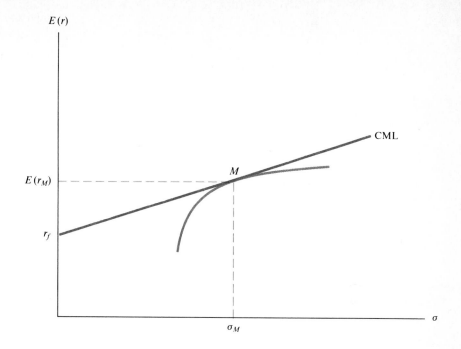

the same time horizon (assumption 2) and use the same input list (assumption 6), they all must arrive at the same determination of the optimal risky portfolio, the portfolio on the efficient frontier identified by the tangency line from T-bills to that frontier, as in Figure 8.1. This implies that if the weight of GM stock, for example, in each common risky portfolio is 1%, then when we sum over all investors' portfolios to obtain the aggregate market portfolio, GM also will comprise 1% of the market portfolio. The same principle applies to the proportion of any stock in each investor's risky portfolio. As a result, the optimal risky portfolio of all investors is simply a share of the market portfolio, which we label M in Figure 8.1.

Now suppose that the optimal portfolio of our investors does not include the stock of some company such as Delta Airlines. When all investors avoid Delta stock, the demand is zero, and Delta's price takes a free fall. As Delta stock gets progressively cheaper, it becomes ever more attractive an investment and all other stocks look (relatively) less attractive. Ultimately, Delta reaches a price where it is profitable enough to include in the optimal stock portfolio.

Such a price adjustment process guarantees that all stocks will be included in the optimal portfolio. It shows that *all* assets have to be included in the market portfolio. The only issue is the price at which investors will be willing to include a stock in their optimal risky portfolio.

This may seem a roundabout way to derive a simple result: if all investors hold an identical risky portfolio, this portfolio has to be M, the market portfolio. Our intention, however, is to demonstrate a connection between this result and its underpinnings, the equilibrating process that is fundamental to security market operation.

The Passive Strategy Is Efficient

In Chapter 6 we defined the CML (capital market line) as the CAL (capital allocation line) that is constructed from either a money market account or T-bills and the market portfolio. Perhaps now you can fully appreciate why the CML is an interesting CAL. In the simple world of the CAPM, M is the optimal tangency portfolio on the efficient frontier. This is shown in Figure 8.1.

In this scenario the market portfolio, M, that all investors hold is based on the common input list, thereby incorporating all relevant information about the universe of securities. This means an investor can skip the trouble of doing specific analysis and obtain an efficient portfolio simply by holding the market portfolio. (Of course, if everyone were to follow this strategy, no one would perform security analysis, and this result would no longer hold. We discuss this issue in depth in Chapter 13 on market efficiency.)

Thus the passive strategy of investing in a market index portfolio is efficient. For this reason, we sometimes call this result a **mutual fund theorem.** The mutual fund theorem is another incarnation of the separation property discussed in Chapter 7. Assuming that all investors choose to hold a market index mutual fund, we can separate portfolio selection into two components—a technological problem, creation of mutual funds by professional managers—and a personal problem that depends on an investor's risk aversion, allocation of the complete portfolio between the mutual fund and risk-free assets.

Concept Check

Question 1. If there are only a few investors who perform security analysis, and all others hold the market portfolio M, would the CML still be the efficient CAL for investors who do not engage in security analysis? Why or why not?

Of course, in reality different investment managers do create risky portfolios that differ from the market index. We attribute this in part to the use of different input lists in the formation of the optimal risky portfolio. Nevertheless, the significance of the mutual fund theorem is that a passive investor may view the market index as a reasonable first approximation of an efficient risky portfolio. Indeed, the nearby box shows that index mutual funds are increasingly popular investment strategies among individual investors.

Investors Latching on to Index Funds

If you can't beat the stock market, why not buy it? Thousands of investors are doing just that—flocking to stock index mutual funds.

Index funds—mutual funds that simply buy and hold stocks in all the companies that make up a certain stock market index—are hot. Index Trust was the Vanguard Group's third best selling of its 19 stock funds this year. "And we haven't spent a penny to advertise it," says Vanguard's Brian Mattes.

It's no wonder index funds are in demand: They consistently show better total returns, on average, than other stock mutual funds. Last year, the average general stock fund was up 13.4% (including dividends and capital gains), well below the 18.7% gain by the Standard & Poor's Corp. 500 stock index. The gap was even worse in the just-ended second quarter: The average fund was up only 1.6%, compared with a 5% gain by the S&P 500.

An index fund's performance will be slightly off the index it uses because a small part of its assets go for management fees and it keeps some cash in money market securities to pay shareholders who redeem their shares.

A plus: An index fund costs less to operate than a regular stock fund: It doesn't have to pay a high-priced Ivy League MBA to choose stocks, and the buy-and-hold strategy keeps transaction costs at a minimum. The savings are passed on to investors.

For example: The $904 million Vanguard Index Trust charges 0.28% of assets each year to operate the fund. That compares with 0.75% as a median fee (in addition to any sales fee) for all funds more than $250 million in assets. For smaller funds, the median fee is as high as 1.49%. "Those fees chip away at your investment, and after several years it really adds up," says Gerald Perritt, editor of *Mutual Fund Letter*.

Index funds long have been available to institutional investors, such as pension funds. But they're relatively new to individual investors. The grand-daddy is Vanguard Index Trust, an 11-year-old fund that invests in the S&P 500. The rest are no more than 2 years old.

The latest twist: Funds that mirror a specific segment of the stock market. Dimensional Fund Advisors Inc. in Santa Monica, Calif., and Colonial Group in Boston have created small-company index funds that buy stocks of the smallest companies on the NYSE.

SOME INDEX MUTUAL FUNDS

Fund	Index followed	Total return* Year to date, 1987	Sales fee
Bench Blue Chip	Dow Jones Ind.	24.4%	2.00%
Colonial Internat'l	EAFA†	25.6%	4.75%
Colonial Small Stock	Small Stock‡	21.6%	4.75%
Colonial U.S. Index	S&P 500	25.7%	4.75%
Continental Heritage	S&P 100	24.4%	3.75%
DFA Small Stock	Small Stock‡	19.9%	1%
Principal Preservation	S&P 100	26.8%	4.5%
Rushmore OTC Indx.	NASDAQ 100	32.6%	none
Stk. MarketAmerica	Large Stock‡	27.2%	4.5%
Vanguard Index Trust	S&P 500	27.3%	none

*Assumes all dividends and capital gains are reinvested.
†Morgan Stanley index of stocks in Europe, Australia and Far East.
‡Index created by fund managers.
Source: Lipper Analytical Services Inc.
From *USA TODAY*, July 13, 1987. Copyright 1987, *USA TODAY*. Reprinted with permission.

In Chapter 6 we discussed how individual investors go about deciding how much to invest in the risky portfolio. Returning now to the decision of how much to invest in portfolio M vs. in the risk-free asset, what can we deduce about the equilibrium risk premium of portfolio M?

We asserted earlier that the equilibrium risk premium on the market portfolio, $E(r_M) - r_f$, will be proportional to the average degree of risk aversion of the investor population and the risk of the market portfolio, σ_M^2. Now we can explain this result.

Recall that each individual investor chooses a proportion, y, allocated to the optimal portfolio M, such that

$$y = \frac{E(r_M) - r_f}{A\sigma_M^2} \qquad (8.1)$$

In the simplified CAPM economy risk-free investments involve borrowing and lending among investors. Any borrowing position must be offset by the lending position of the creditor. This means that net borrowing and lending across all investors must be zero, and in consequence the average position in the risky portfolio is 100% or $\bar{y} = 1$. Setting $y = 1$ in equation 8.1 and rearranging, we find that the risk premium on the market portfolio is related to its variance by the average degree of risk aversion:

$$E(r_M) - r_f = \bar{A}\sigma_M^2 \qquad (8.2)$$

Concept Check

Question 2. Data from the period 1926 to 1987 for the S&P 500 index yield the following statistics: Average excess return, 8.5%; standard deviation, 21%.
a. To the extent that these averages approximated investor expectations for the period, what must have been the average coefficient of risk aversion?
b. If the coefficient of risk aversion were actually 3.5, what risk premium would have been consistent with the market's historical standard deviation?

Expected Returns on Individual Securities

The CAPM is built on the insight that the appropriate risk premium on an asset will be determined by its contribution to the risk of investors' overall portfolios. Portfolio risk is what matters to investors and is what governs the risk premiums they demand.

Suppose, for example, that we want to gauge the portfolio risk of GM stock. We measure the contribution to the risk of the overall portfolio from holding GM stock by its covariance with the market portfolio. To see why this is so, let us look again at the way the variance of the market portfolio is calculated. To calculate the variance of the market portfolio, we use the covariance matrix bordered by market portfolio weights, as discussed in Chapter 7. We highlight GM in this depiction of the n stocks in the market portfolio.

Portfolio Weights:	w_1	w_2	$\cdots$	w_{GM}	$\cdots$	w_n
w_1	$\text{Cov}(r_1,r_1)$	$\text{Cov}(r_1,r_2)$	$\cdots$	$\text{Cov}(r_1,r_{GM})$	$\cdots$	$\text{Cov}(r_1,r_n)$
w_2	$\text{Cov}(r_2,r_1)$	$\text{Cov}(r_2,r_2)$	$\cdots$	$\text{Cov}(r_2,r_{GM})$	$\cdots$	$\text{Cov}(r_2,r_n)$
$\cdot$	$\cdot$	$\cdot$		$\cdot$		$\cdot$
$\cdot$	$\cdot$	$\cdot$		$\cdot$		$\cdot$
$\cdot$	$\cdot$	$\cdot$		$\cdot$		$\cdot$
w_{GM}	$\text{Cov}(r_{GM},r_1)$		$\cdots$	$\text{Cov}(r_{GM},r_{GM})$	$\cdots$	$\text{Cov}(r_{GM},r_n)$
$\cdot$		$\cdot$		$\cdot$		$\cdot$
$\cdot$	$\cdot$	$\cdot$		$\cdot$		$\cdot$
$\cdot$	$\cdot$	$\cdot$		$\cdot$		$\cdot$
w_n	$\text{Cov}(r_n,r_1)$	$\text{Cov}(r_n,r_2)$	$\cdots$	$\text{Cov}(r_n,r_{GM})$	$\cdots$	$\text{Cov}(r_n,r_n)$

Recall that we calculate the variance of the portfolio by summing over all the elements of the covariance matrix and multiplying each element by the portfolio weights from the row and the column. The contribution of one stock to portfolio variance therefore can be expressed as the sum of all the covariance terms in the row corresponding to the stock where each covariance is multiplied by both the portfolio weight from its row and the weight from its column.[4]

For example, the contribution of GM's stock to the variance of the market portfolio is

$$w_{GM}[w_1\text{Cov}(r_1,r_{GM}) + w_2\text{Cov}(r_2,r_{GM}) + \ldots + w_{GM}\text{Cov}(r_{GM},r_{GM}) + \ldots + w_n\text{Cov}(r_n,r_{GM})] \tag{8.3}$$

Equation 8.3 provides a clue about the respective roles of variance and covariance in determining asset risk. It shows us that, when there are many stocks in the economy, there will be many more covariance terms than variance terms. Consequently, the covariance of a particular stock with all other stocks might be expected to have more to do with that stock's contribution to total portfolio risk than does its variance. In fact, since each stock in equation 8.3 is weighted by its share in the market portfolio, we may summarize the term in brackets in the equation simply as the covariance of GM with the market portfolio. In other words, we can best measure the stock's contribution to the risk of the market portfolio by its covariance with that portfolio.

---

[4]An alternative and equally valid approach would be to measure GM's contribution to market variance as the sum of the elements in the row *and* the column corresponding to GM. In this case, GM's contribution would be twice the sum in equation 8.3. The approach that we take in the text allocates contributions to portfolio risk among securities in a convenient manner in that the sum of the contributions of each stock equals the total portfolio variance, whereas the alternative measure of contribution would sum to twice the portfolio variance. This results from a type of double-counting, because adding both the rows and the columns for each stock would result in each entry in the matrix being added twice.

This should not surprise us. For example, if the covariance between GM and the rest of the market is negative, then GM makes a "negative contribution" to portfolio risk: by providing returns that move inversely with the rest of the market, GM stabilizes the return on the overall portfolio. If the covariance is positive, GM makes a positive contribution to overall portfolio risk because its returns amplify swings in the rest of the portfolio.

To prove this more rigorously, note that the rate of return on the market portfolio may be written as

$$r_M = \sum_{k=1}^{n} w_k r_k$$

Therefore the covariance of the return on GM with the market portfolio is

$$\mathrm{Cov}(r_{GM}, r_M) = \mathrm{Cov}\left(r_{GM}, \sum_{k=1}^{n} w_k r_k\right) = \sum_{k=1}^{n} w_k \mathrm{Cov}(r_{GM}, r_k) \tag{8.4}$$

Comparing the last term of equation 8.4 to the term in brackets in equation 8.3, we can see that the covariance of GM with the market portfolio is indeed proportional to the contribution of GM to the variance of the market portfolio.

Having measured the contribution of GM stock to market variance, we may determine the appropriate risk premium for GM. We note first that the market portfolio has a risk premium of $E(r_M) - r_f$ and a variance of σ_M^2, for a reward-to-risk ratio of

$$\frac{E(r_M) - r_f}{\sigma_M^2} \tag{8.5}$$

This ratio often is called the **market price of risk**[5] because it quantifies the extra return that investors demand to bear portfolio risk. The ratio of risk premium to variance tells us how much extra return must be earned per unit of portfolio risk.

Suppose that investors wish to increase their position in the market portfolio by a tiny fraction, δ, financed by borrowing at the risk-free rate. The increment to the portfolio expected excess return will be

$$\Delta E(r) = \delta[E(r_M) - r_f]$$

The portfolio variance will increase by the variance of the incremental position in

---

[5]We open ourselves to ambiguity in using this term, because the market portfolio's reward-to-variability ratio

$$\frac{E(r_M) - r_f}{\sigma_M}$$

sometimes is referred to as the market price of risk. Note that since the appropriate risk measure of GM is its covariance with the market portfolio (its contribution to the variance of the market portfolio), this risk is measured in percent squared. Accordingly, the price of this risk, $[E(r_M) - r_f]/\sigma^2$, is defined as the percentage of expected return per percent square of variance.

the market *plus* twice its covariance with the original position (100% in the market):

$$\Delta\sigma^2 = \delta^2\sigma_M^2 + 2\delta\text{Cov}(r_M, r_M)$$

If δ is infinitesimal, then its square will be negligible,[6] leaving the incremental variance as

$$\Delta\sigma^2 = 2\delta\text{Cov}(r_M, r_M) = 2\delta\sigma_M^2$$

The trade-off between the *incremental risk premium* and *incremental risk,* referred to as the marginal price of risk, is given by the ratio

$$\frac{\Delta E(r)}{\Delta\sigma^2} = \frac{E(r_M - r_f)}{2\sigma_M^2}$$

and equals one half the market price of risk in equation 8.5.

Now suppose that, instead, investors were to invest the increment δ in GM stock, financed by borrowing at the risk-free rate. The increase in mean excess return is

$$\Delta E(r) = \delta[E(r_{\text{GM}}) - r_f]$$

The increase in variance, here too, includes the variance of the incremental position in GM *plus* twice its covariance with the market:

$$\Delta\sigma^2 = \delta^2\sigma_{\text{GM}}^2 + 2\delta\text{Cov}(r_{\text{GM}}, r_M)$$

Dropping the negligible term, the *marginal price of risk* of GM is

$$\frac{\Delta E(r)}{\Delta\sigma^2} = \frac{E(r_{\text{GM}}) - r_f}{2\text{Cov}(r_{\text{GM}}, r_M)}$$

In equilibrium, the marginal price of risk of GM stock has to equal that of the market portfolio. Because, when the marginal price of risk of GM is greater than the market's, investors can increase their portfolio *average* price of risk by increasing the weight of GM in their portfolio. Moreover, as long as the price of GM stock does not rise relative to the market, investors will keep buying GM stock. The process will continue until stock prices adjust so that marginal price of risk of GM equals that of the market. (The same process, in reverse, will equalize marginal prices of risk when GM's initial marginal price of risk is less than that of the market portfolio.) Equating the marginal price of risk of GM's stock to that of the market gets us the relationship between the risk premium of GM and that of the market.

$$\frac{E(r_{\text{GM}}) - r_f}{2\text{Cov}(r_{\text{GM}}, r_M)} = \frac{E(r_M) - r_f}{2\sigma_M^2}$$

To determine the fair risk premium for GM stock, we need only multiply the risk that GM stock contributes to the variance of the market portfolio, which is

---

[6]For example, if δ is 1% (.01 of wealth), then its square is .0001 of wealth, one hundredth of the original value. The term $\delta\sigma_M^2$ will be smaller than $2\delta\text{Cov}(r_M, r_M)$ by an order of magnitude.

Cov(r_{GM},r_M), by the market price of risk. We thus find that $E(r_{GM}) - r_f$, which is GM's risk premium, should be

$$E(r_{GM}) - r_f = \text{Cov}(r_{GM}, r_M) \times \frac{E(r_M) - r_f}{\sigma_M^2}$$

Rearranging slightly, we obtain

$$E(r_{GM}) - r_f = \frac{\text{Cov}(r_{GM}, r_M)}{\sigma_M^2} [E(r_M) - r_f] \tag{8.6}$$

The term $\text{Cov}(r_{GM}, r_M)/\sigma_M^2$ measures the contribution of GM stock to the variance of the market portfolio as a fraction of the total variance of the market portfolio and is referred to by the Greek letter **beta**, β. Using this measure, we can restate equation 8.6 as

$$E(r_{GM}) = r_f + \beta_{GM}[E(r_M) - r_f] \tag{8.7}$$

This **expected return-beta relationship** is the most familiar expression of the CAPM to practitioners. We will have a lot more to say about the expected return-beta relationship shortly.

We see now why the assumptions that made individuals act similarly are so useful. If everyone holds an identical risky portfolio, then everyone will find that the beta of each asset with the market portfolio equals the asset's beta with his or her own risky portfolio. Hence everyone will agree on the appropriate risk premium for each asset.

Does this mean that the fact that few real-life investors actually hold the market portfolio implies that the CAPM is of no practical importance? Not necessarily. Recall from Chapter 7 that reasonably well-diversified portfolios shed firm-specific risk and are left with only systematic or market risk. Even if one does not hold the precise market portfolio, a well-diversified portfolio will be so very highly correlated with the market that a stock's beta relative to the market still will be a useful risk measure.

In fact, several authors have shown that modified versions of the CAPM will hold true even if we consider differences among individuals leading them to hold different portfolios. For example, Brennan[7] examines the impact of differences in investors' personal tax rates on market equilibrium, and Mayers[8] looks at the impact of non-traded assets such as human capital (earning power). Both find that, although the market is no longer each investor's optimal risky portfolio, the expected return-beta relationship still should hold in a somewhat modified form.

If the expected return-beta relationship holds for any individual asset, it must hold for any combination of assets. Suppose that some portfolio P has weight w_k for stock k, where k takes on values 1, . . . , n. Writing out the CAPM equation 8.7 for each

---

[7]Brennan, Michael J., "Taxes, Market Valuation, and Corporate Finance Policy," *National Tax Journal*, December 1973.
[8]Mayers, David, "Nonmarketable Assets and Capital Market Equilibrium Under Uncertainty," in Jensen, M.C. (editor), *Studies in the Theory of Capital Markets*, New York: Praeger, 1972.

stock, and multiplying each equation by the weight of the stock in the portfolio, we obtain these equations, one for each stock:

$$w_1 E(r_1) = w_1 r_f + w_1 \beta_1 [E(r_M) - r_f]$$
$$+ w_2 E(r_2) = w_2 r_f + w_2 \beta_2 [E(r_M) - r_f]$$
$$+ \quad \ldots = \ldots$$
$$+ w_n E(r_n) = w_n r_f + w_n \beta_n [E(r_M) - r_f]$$
$$E(r_P) = r_f + \beta_P [E(r_M) - r_f]$$

Summing each column shows that the CAPM holds for the overall portfolio because $E(r_P) = \sum_k w_k E(r_k)$ is the expected return on the portfolio, and $\beta_P = \sum_k w_k \beta_k$ is the portfolio beta. Incidentally, this result has to be true for the market portfolio itself,

$$E(r_M) = r_f + \beta_M [E(r_M) - r_f]$$

Indeed, this is a tautology because $\beta_M = 1$, as we can verify by demonstrating that

$$\beta_M = \frac{\text{Cov}(r_M, r_M)}{\sigma_M^2} = \frac{\sigma_M^2}{\sigma_M^2}$$

This also establishes 1 as the weighted average value of beta across all assets. If the market beta is 1, and the market is a portfolio of all assets in the economy, the weighted average beta of all assets must be 1. Hence betas greater than 1 are considered aggressive in that investment in high-beta stocks entails above-average sensitivity to market swings. Betas below 1 can be described as defensive.

Concept Check

Question 3. Suppose that the risk premium on the market portfolio is estimated at 8% with a standard deviation of 22%. What is the risk premium on a portfolio invested 25% in GM and 75% in Ford, if both have a beta of 1.15?

A word of caution: we are all accustomed to hearing that well-managed firms will provide high rates of return. We agree this is true if one measures the *firm's* return on investments in plant and equipment. The CAPM, however, predicts returns on investments in the *securities* of the firm.

Let us say that everyone knows a firm is well run. Its stock price will therefore be bid up, and consequently returns to stockholders who buy at those high prices will not be excessive. Security prices, in other words, reflect public information about a firm's prospects, but only the risk of the company (as measured by beta in the context of the CAPM) should affect expected returns. In a rational market investors receive high expected returns only if they are willing to bear risk.

FIGURE 8.2
The security market
line.

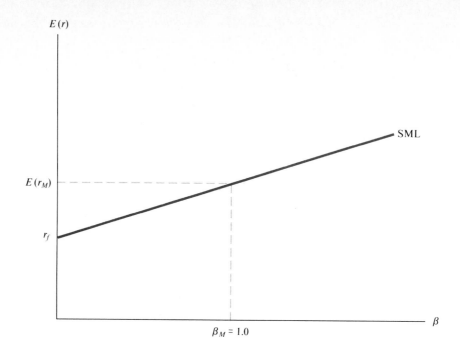

The Security Market Line

We can view the expected return-beta relationship as a reward-risk equation. The beta of a security is the appropriate measure of its risk because beta is proportional to the risk that the security contributes to the optimal risky portfolio.

Risk-averse investors measure the risk of the optimal risky portfolio by its variance. In this world we would expect the reward, or the risk premium on individual assets, to depend on the risk that an individual asset contributes to the portfolio. The beta of a stock measures the stock's contribution to the variance of the market portfolio as a fraction of the total portfolio variance. Hence we expect, for any asset or portfolio, the required risk premium to be a function of beta. The CAPM confirms this intuition, stating further that the security's risk premium is directly proportional to both the beta and the risk-premium of the market portfolio; that is, the risk premium equals $\beta[E(r_M) - r_f]$.

The expected return-beta relationship can be portrayed graphically as the **security market line** (SML) in Figure 8.2. Its slope is the risk premium of the market portfolio. At the point where $\beta = 1$ on the horizontal axis (which is the market portfolio's beta) we can read off the vertical axis the expected return on the market portfolio.

It is useful to compare the security market line to the capital market line. The CML graphs the risk premiums of efficient portfolios (that is, portfolios composed of the market and the risk-free asset) as a function of portfolio standard deviation. This is appropriate because standard deviation is a valid measure of risk for efficiently diversified portfolios that are candidates for an investor's overall portfolio. The SML,

FIGURE 8.3
The SML and a
positive-alpha stock.

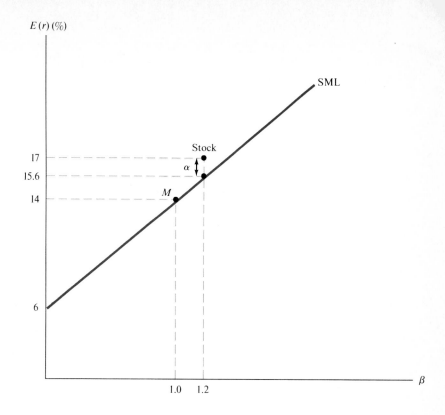

in contrast, graphs *individual asset* risk premiums as a function of asset risk. The relevant measure of risk for individual assets held as parts of well-diversified portfolios is not the asset's standard deviation or variance; it is, instead, the contribution of the asset to the portfolio variance, which we measure by the asset's beta. The SML is valid for both efficient portfolios and individual assets.

The security market line provides a benchmark for the evaluation of investment performance. Given the risk of an investment, as measured by its beta, the SML provides the required rate of return from that investment to compensate investors for risk, as well as the time value of money.

Because the security market line is the graphic representation of the expected return-beta relationship, "fairly priced" assets plot exactly on the SML; that is, their expected returns are commensurate with their risk. Given the assumptions we made in Section 8.2, all securities must lie on the SML in market equilibrium. Nevertheless, we see here how the CAPM may be of use in the money-management industry. Suppose that the SML relation is used as a benchmark to assess the fair expected return on a risky asset. Then security analysis is performed to calculate the return actually expected. (Notice that we depart here from the simple CAPM world in that some investors now apply their own unique analysis to derive an "input list" that may differ from their competitors'.) If a stock is perceived to be a good buy, or underpriced, it will provide an expected return in excess of the fair return stipulated by the SML. Underpriced stocks therefore plot above the SML: given their betas, their expected returns are greater than dictated by the CAPM. Overpriced stocks plot below the SML.

The difference between the fair and actually expected rates of return on a stock is called the stock's **alpha,** denoted α. For example, if the market is expected to be 14%, a stock has a beta of 1.2, and the T-bill rate is 6%, the SML would predict an expected return on the stock of $6 + 1.2(14 - 6) = 15.6\%$. If one believed the stock would provide a return of 17%, the implied alpha would be 1.4% (see Figure 8.3).

Concept Check

Question 4. Stock XYZ has an expected return of 12% and risk of $\beta = 1$. Stock ABC has expected return of 13% and $\beta = 1.5$. The market's expected return is 11%, and $r_f = 5\%$.
a. According to the CAPM, which stock is a better buy?
b. What is the alpha of each stock? Plot the SML and each stock's risk-return point on one graph. Show the alphas graphically.

The CAPM also is useful in capital budgeting decisions. For a firm considering a new project, the CAPM can provide the return that the project needs to yield, based on its beta, to be acceptable to investors. Managers can use the CAPM to obtain this cutoff internal rate of return (IRR) or "hurdle rate" for the project.

Concept Check

Question 5. The risk-free rate is 8% and the expected return on the market portfolio is 16%. A firm considers a project that is expected to have a beta of 1.3.
a. What is the required rate of return on the project?
b. If the expected IRR of the project is 19%, should it be accepted?

Yet another use of the CAPM is in utility rate-making cases. In this case the issue is the rate of return that a regulated utility should be allowed to earn on its investment in plant and equipment. Suppose that the equityholders have invested $100 million in the firm and that the beta of the equity is .6. If the T-bill rate is 6% and the market risk premium is 8%, then the fair profits to the firm would be assessed as $6 + .6(8) = 10.8\%$ of the $100 million investment, or $10.8 million. The firm would be allowed to set prices at a level expected to generate these profits.

8.2 *Extensions of the CAPM*

The assumptions that allowed Sharpe to derive the simple version of the CAPM are admittedly unrealistic. Financial economists have been at work ever since the CAPM was devised to extend the model to more realistic scenarios.

There are two classes of extensions to the simple version of the CAPM. The first attempts to relax the assumptions that we outlined at the outset of the chapter. The second acknowledges the fact that investors worry about sources of risk other than the uncertain value of their securities, such as unexpected changes in relative prices of consumer goods. This idea involves the introduction of additional risk factors besides security returns, and we will discuss it further in Chapter 11.

The CAPM With Restricted Borrowing: The Zero-Beta Model

The CAPM is predicated on the assumption that all investors share an identical input list that they feed into the Markowitz algorithm. Thus all investors agree on the location of the efficient (minimum-variance) frontier, where each portfolio has the lowest variance among all feasible portfolios at a target expected rate of return. When all investors can borrow and lend at the safe rate, r_f, all agree on the optimal tangency portfolio and choose to hold a share of the market portfolio.

When there are constraints on risk-free lending and/or borrowing, we will see that the market portfolio is no longer the common optimal portfolio for all investors. One "restriction" on risk-free borrowing and lending is that in a strict sense, once we account for inflation uncertainty, there is no truly risk-free asset in the U.S. economy. Only Treasury securities are entirely free of default risk, but these are nominal obligations, meaning that their real values are exposed to price level risk. In this sense there is no risk-free asset in the economy. Other restrictions have to do with differences in the rates at which investors can borrow and lend.

When investors no longer can borrow or lend at a common risk-free rate, they may choose risky portfolios from the entire set of efficient frontier portfolios according to how much risk they choose to bear. The market is no longer the common optimal portfolio. In fact, with investors choosing different portfolios, it is no longer obvious whether the market portfolio, which is the aggregate of all investors' portfolios, will even be on the efficient frontier. If the market portfolio is no longer mean-variance efficient, then the expected return-beta relationship of the CAPM will no longer characterize market equilibrium.

An equilibrium expected return-beta relationship in the case of restricted risk-free investments has been developed by Fischer Black.[9] Black's model is fairly difficult and requires a good deal of facility with mathematics. Therefore we will satisfy ourselves with a sketch of Black's argument and spend more time with its implications.

---

[9]Black, Fischer, "Capital Market Equilibrium with Restricted Borrowing," *Journal of Business,* July 1972.

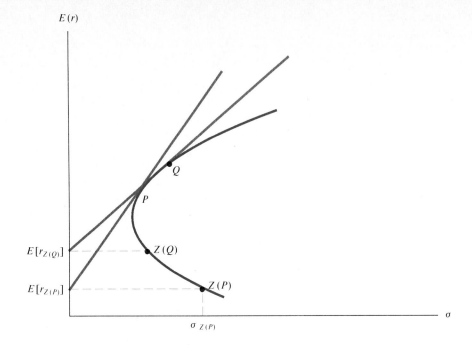

Black's model of the CAPM in the absence of a risk-free asset rests on the three following properties of mean-variance efficient portfolios:

1. Any portfolio constructed by combining efficient portfolios is itself on the efficient frontier.
2. Every portfolio on the efficient frontier has a "companion" portfolio on the bottom half (the inefficient part) of the minimum-variance frontier with which it is uncorrelated. Because the portfolios are uncorrelated, the companion portfolio is referred to as the **zero-beta portfolio** of the efficient portfolio.

   The expected return of an efficient portfolio's zero-beta companion portfolio can be derived by the following graphical procedure. From any efficient portfolio such as P in Figure 8.4 draw a tangency line to the vertical axis. The intercept will be the expected return on portfolio P's zero-beta companion portfolio, denoted $Z(P)$. The horizontal line from the intercept to the minimum-variance frontier identifies the standard deviation of the zero-beta portfolio. Notice in Figure 8.4 that different efficient portfolios such as P and Q have different zero-beta companions.

   These tangency lines are helpful constructs only. They do *not* signify that one can invest in portfolios with expected return-standard deviation pairs along the line. That would be possible only by mixing a risk-free asset with the tangency portfolio. In this case, however, we assume that risk-free assets are not available to investors.

3. The expected return of any asset can be expressed as an exact, linear function of the expected return on any two frontier portfolios. Consider, for example,

FIGURE 8.5

Portfolio selection
with no risk-free
assets.

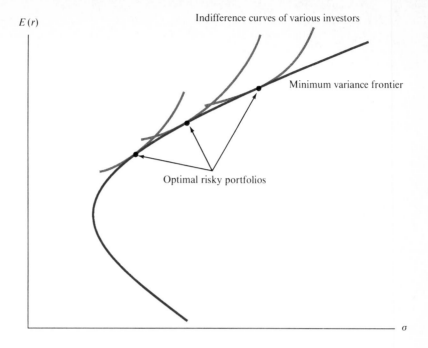

the minimum-variance frontier portfolios P and Q. Black shows that the expected return on any asset i can be expressed as

$$E(r_i) = E(r_Q) + [E(r_P) - E(r_Q)] \frac{\text{Cov}(r_i, r_P) - \text{Cov}(r_P, r_Q)}{\sigma_P^2 - \text{Cov}(r_P, r_Q)} \qquad (8.8)$$

Note that this last property has nothing to do with market equilibrium. It is a purely mathematical property relating frontier portfolios and individual securities.

Given these three properties, it is easy to derive Black's model. The assumption of homogeneous expectations assures us that all investors use the same input list and compute the same minimum-variance frontier. Each investor will invest in an efficient portfolio according to his or her degree of risk aversion, as in Figure 8.5. The market portfolio, which is just the aggregate of all investors' portfolios, therefore is a combination of efficient portfolios, and by property 1, must itself be an efficient portfolio.

Next, recall equation 8.8 from property 3. Instead of using the arbitrarily chosen frontier portfolios P and Q in the equation, let us instead use as our two frontier portfolios the market portfolio, M, and its zero-beta companion, $Z(M)$. This is a convenient pairing of portfolios because their mutual covariance is zero, causing equation 8.8 to simplify. Specifically, because $\text{Cov}[r_M, r_{Z(M)}] = 0$, the expected return of any asset i, using M and $Z(M)$ as the benchmark frontier portfolios, can be expressed as

$$E(r_i) = E[r_{Z(M)}] + E[r_M - r_{Z(M)}] \frac{\text{Cov}(r_i, r_M)}{\sigma_M^2} \qquad (8.9)$$

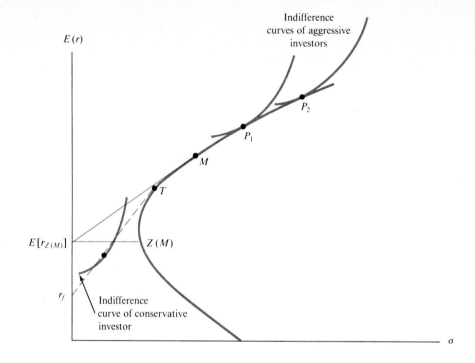

FIGURE 8.6

Capital market equilibrium with risk-free lending but no risk-free borrowing.

where P from equation 8.8 has been replaced by M and Q has been replaced by $Z(M)$. Note that this is a variant of the simple CAPM, in which r_f simply has been replaced with $E[r_{Z(M)}]$.

Although Black derived this variant of the CAPM for the case in which no risk-free asset exists, the approach we have taken can be applied to many related scenarios. For example, consider an economy in which investors can lend at the risk-free rate (can buy T-bills, for example) but cannot borrow funds to invest. We first explored portfolio selection for this situation in Section 7.5. Now we can explore market equilibrium.

Figure 8.6 shows that relatively conservative (risk-averse) investors will select the tangency portfolio, T, as their optimal risky portfolio and mix T with the safe asset. Relatively aggressive investors will choose efficient portfolios like P_1 or P_2. The market portfolio, M, will be a combination of these portfolios, all of which are efficient, meaning that the market also will be an efficient portfolio. Therefore the zero-beta version of the CAPM will apply in this situation also.

A more realistic scenario is one in which the investor can lend at the risk-free rate, r_f, and can borrow at a higher rate, r_f^B. This case also was considered in Chapter 7. The same arguments that we have just employed also can be used to establish the zero-beta CAPM in this situation. Problem 18 at the end of this chapter asks you to fill in the details of the argument for this situation.

Lifetime Consumption: The CAPM With Dynamic Programming

One of the restrictive assumptions of the simple version of the CAPM is that investors are myopic—they plan for one common holding period. Investors actually may be concerned with a lifetime consumption plan and a possible desire to leave a bequest to children. Consumption plans that are feasible for them depend on current wealth and future rates of return on the investment portfolio. These investors will want to rebalance their portfolios as often as required by changes in wealth.

However, Eugene Fama[10] shows that, even if we extend our analysis to a multi-period setting, the single CAPM still may be appropriate. The key assumptions that Fama uses to replace myopic planning horizons are that investor preferences are unchanging over time and that the risk-free interest rate and probability distribution of security returns do not change unpredictably over time. Of course, this latter assumption is itself somewhat unrealistic. However, the extensions to the CAPM engendered by considering random changes to the so-called "investment opportunity set" must wait until Chapter 11.

Summary

1. The CAPM assumes that investors are single-period planners who agree on a common input list from security analysis and seek mean-variance optimal portfolios.

2. The CAPM assumes that security markets are ideal in the sense that:

   a. They are large, and investors are price-takers.

   b. There are no taxes or transaction costs.

   c. All risky assets are publicly traded.

   d. Investors can borrow and lend any amount at a fixed risk-free rate.

3. With these assumptions, all investors hold identical risky portfolios. The CAPM holds that in equilibrium the market portfolio is the unique mean-variance efficient tangency portfolio. Thus a passive strategy is efficient.

4. The CAPM market portfolio is a value-weighted portfolio. Each security is held in a proportion equal to its market value divided by the total market value of all securities.

5. If the market portfolio is efficient and the average investor neither borrows nor lends, then the risk premium on the market portfolio is proportional to its variance, σ_M^2, and to the average coefficient of risk aversion across investors A:

---

[10]Fama, Eugene F., "Multiperiod Consumption-Investment Decisions," *American Economic Review, 60,* 1970.

$$E(r_M) - r_f = \overline{A}\sigma_M^2$$

6. The CAPM implies that the risk premium on any individual asset or portfolio is the product of the risk premium on the market portfolio and the beta coefficient:

$$E(r) - r_f = \beta[E(r_M) - r_f]$$

where the beta coefficient is the covariance of the asset with the market portfolio as a fraction of the variance of the market portfolio

$$\beta = \frac{\text{Cov}(r, r_M)}{\sigma_M^2}$$

7. When risk-free investments are restricted but all other CAPM assumptions hold, then the simple version of the CAPM is replaced by its zero-beta version. Accordingly, the risk-free rate in the expected return-beta relationship is replaced by the zero-beta portfolio's expected return rate of return:

$$E(r_i) = E[r_{Z(M)}] + \beta_i E[r_M - r_{Z(M)}]$$

8. The simple version of the CAPM assumes that investors are myopic. When investors are assumed to be concerned with lifetime consumption and bequest plans, but investors' tastes and security return distributions are stable over time, the market portfolio remains efficient and the simple version of the expected return-beta relationship holds.

Key Terms

Homogeneous expectations	Expected return-beta relationship
Market portfolio	Security market line
Mutual fund theorem	Alpha
Market price of risk	Zero-beta portfolio
Beta	

Selected Readings

A good introduction to the intuition of the CAPM is:
Malkiel, Burton G., *A Random Walk Down Wall Street,* New York: W.W. Norton & Company, Inc., 1985.

The four articles that established the CAPM are:
Sharpe, William, "Capital Asset Prices: A Theory of Market Equilibrium," *Journal of Finance,* September 1964.
Lintner, John, "The Valuation of Risk Assets and the Selection of Risky Investments in Stock Portfolios and Capital Budgets," *Review of Economics and Statistics,* February 1965.
Mossin, Jan, "Equilibrium in a Capital Asset Market," *Econometrica,* October 1966.
Treynor, Jack, "Towards a Theory of Market Value of Risky Assets," unpublished manuscript, 1961.

A review of the simple CAPM and its variants is contained in:
Jensen, Michael C., "The Foundation and Current State of Capital Market Theory," in Jensen, Michael C. (editor), *Studies in the Theory of Capital Markets,* New York: Praeger Publishers, 1972.

Equilibrium in Capital Markets

The zero-beta version of the CAPM appeared in:
  Black, Fischer, "Capital Market Equilibrium with Restricted Borrowing," *Journal of Business,* July 1972.
Excellent practitioner-oriented discussions of the CAPM are:
  Mullins, David, "Does the Capital Asset Pricing Model Work," *Harvard Business Review,* January/February 1982.
  Rosenberg, Barr, and Rudd, Andrew, "The Corporate Uses of Beta," in Stern, J.M., and Chew, D.H., Jr. (editors), *The Revolution in Corporate Finance,* New York: Basil Blackwell, 1986.

Problems

1. What is the beta of a portfolio with $E(r_p) = 20\%$, if $r_f = 5\%$ and $E(r_M) = 15\%$?
2. The market price of a security is $40. Its expected rate of return is 13%. The risk-free rate is 7% and the market risk premium is 8%. What will be the market price of the security if its covariance with the market portfolio doubles (and all other variables remain unchanged)? Assume that the stock is expected to pay a constant dividend in perpetuity.
3. You are a consultant to a large manufacturing corporation that is considering a project with the following net after-tax cash flows (in millions of dollars):

Years From Now	After-Tax Cash Flow
0	−20
1-9	10
10	20

   The project's beta is 1.7. Assuming that $r_f = 9\%$ and $E(r_M) = 19\%$, what is the net present value of the project? What is the highest possible beta estimate for the project before its NPV becomes negative?
4. Are the following true or false?
   a. Stocks with a beta of zero offer an expected rate of return of zero.
   b. The CAPM implies that investors require a higher return to hold highly volatile securities.
   c. You can construct a portfolio with beta of .75 by investing .75 of the budget in bills and the remainder in the market portfolio.
5. Consider the following table, which gives a security analyst's expected return on two stocks for two particular market returns:

Market Return	Aggressive Stock	Defensive Stock
.05	.02	.035
.20	.32	.14

   a. What are the betas of the two stocks?
   b. What is the expected rate of return on each stock if the market return is equally likely to be 5% or 20%?

c. If the T-bill rate is 8% and the market return is equally likely to be 5% or 20%, draw the SML for this economy.

d. Plot the two securities on the SML graph. What are the alphas of each?

e. What hurdle rate should be used by the management of the aggressive firm for a project with the risk characteristics of the defensive firm's stock?

If the simple CAPM is valid, which of the following situations in problems 6 to 12 are possible? Explain. Consider each situation independently.

6.

Portfolio	Expected Return	Beta
A	.20	1.4
B	.25	1.2

7.

Portfolio	Expected Return	Standard Deviation
A	.30	.35
B	.40	.25

8.

Portfolio	Expected Return	Standard Deviation
Risk-free	.10	0
Market	.18	.24
A	.16	.12

9.

Portfolio	Expected Return	Standard Deviation
Risk-free	.10	0
Market	.18	.24
A	.20	.22

10.

Portfolio	Expected Return	Beta
Risk-free	.10	0
Market	.18	1.0
A	.16	1.5

11. Portfolio	Expected Return	Beta
Risk-free	.10	0
Market	.18	1.0
A	.16	.9

12. Portfolio	Expected Return	Standard Deviation
Risk-free	.10	0
Market	.18	.24
A	.16	.22

In problems 13 to 15 assume that the risk-free rate of interest is 8% and the expected rate of return on the market is 18%.

13. A share of stock sells for $100 today. It will pay a dividend of $9 per share at the end of the year. Its beta is 1. What do investors expect the stock to sell for at the end of the year?

14. I am buying a firm with an expected cash flow of $1,000 but am unsure of its risk. If I think the beta of the firm is zero, when in fact the beta is really 1, how much *more* will I offer for the firm than it is truly worth?

15. A stock has an expected rate of return of 6%. What is its beta?

16. Two investment advisors are comparing performance. One averaged a 19% rate of return and the other a 16% rate of return. However, the beta of the first investor was 1.5, whereas that of the second was 1.

    a. Can you tell which investor was a better predictor of individual stocks (aside from the issue of general movements in the market)?

    b. If the T-bill rate were 6% and the market return during the period were 14%, which investor would be the superior stock selector?

    c. What if the T-bill rate were 3% and the market return were 15%?

17. In 1987 the rate of return on short-term government securities (perceived to be risk free) was about 6%. Suppose the expected rate of return required by the market for a portfolio with a beta measure of 1 is 15%. According to the capital asset pricing model (security market line):

    a. What is the expected rate of return on the market portfolio?

    b. What would be the expected rate of return on a stock with $\beta = 0$?

    c. Suppose you consider buying a share of stock at $40. The stock is expected to pay $3 dividends next year and to sell then for $41. The stock risk has been evaluated by $\beta = -.5$. Is the stock overpriced or underpriced?

18. Suppose that you can invest risk free at rate r_f but can borrow only at a higher rate, r_f^B. This case was considered in Section 7.5.

    a. Draw a minimum-variance frontier. Show on the graph the risky portfolio that will be selected by defensive investors. Show the portfolio that will be selected by aggressive investors.

    b. What portfolios will be selected by investors who neither borrow nor lend?

c. Where will the market portfolio lie on the efficient frontier?

d. Will the zero-beta CAPM be valid in this scenario? Explain. Show graphically the expected return on the zero-beta portfolio.

19. Consider an economy with two classes of investors. Tax-exempt investors can borrow or lend at the safe rate, r_f. Taxed investors pay tax rate t on all interest income, so their net-of-tax safe interest rate is $r_f(1 - t)$. Show that the zero-beta CAPM will apply to this economy and that $(1 - t)r_f < E[r_{Z(M)}] < r_f$.

20. Suppose that borrowing is restricted so that the zero-beta version of the CAPM holds. The expected return on the market portfolio is 17%, and on the zero-beta portfolio it is 8%. What is the expected return on a portfolio with a beta of .6?

CHAPTER 9

Index Models

Chapter 7 introduced the Markowitz portfolio selection model, which shows how to obtain the maximum return possible for any level of portfolio risk. Implementation of the Markowitz portfolio selection model, however, requires a huge number of estimates of covariances between all pairs of available securities. Moreover, these estimates have to be fed into a mathematical optimization program that requires vast computer capacity to perform the necessary calculations for large portfolios. Because the data requirements and computer capacity called for in the full-blown Markowitz procedure are overwhelming, we must search for a strategy that reduces the necessary compilation and processing of data. We will introduce in this chapter a simplifying assumption that at once eases our computational burden and offers significant new insights into the nature of systematic risk vs. firm-specific risk. This abstraction is the notion of an "index model," specifying the process by which security returns are generated. Our discussion of the index model also will introduce the concept of factor models of security returns, a concept at the heart of contemporary investment theory and its applications.

9.1 *A Single-Index Security Market*

Systematic Risk vs. Firm-Specific Risk

The success of a portfolio selection rule depends on the quality of the input list, that is, the estimates of expected security returns and the covariance matrix. In the long run efficient portfolios will beat portfolios with less reliable input lists and consequently inferior reward-to-risk trade-offs.

Suppose your security analysts can thoroughly analyze 50 stocks. This means that your input list will include the following:

$$
\begin{aligned}
n &= \quad 50 \text{ estimates of expected returns} \\
n &= \quad 50 \text{ estimates of variances} \\
(n^2 - n)/2 &= \underline{1225} \text{ estimates of covariances} \\
& \qquad 1325 \text{ estimates}
\end{aligned}
$$

This is a formidable task, particularly in light of the fact that a 50-security portfolio is relatively small. Doubling n to 100 will nearly quadruple the number of estimates to 5,150. If $n = 1,600$, roughly the number of NYSE stocks, we need nearly 1.3 *million* estimates.

Covariances between security returns occur because the same economic forces affect the fortunes of many firms. Some examples of common economic factors are business cycles, inflation, money-supply changes, technological changes, and prices of raw materials. All these (interrelated) factors affect almost all firms. Thus unexpected changes in these variables cause, simultaneously, unexpected changes in the rates of return on the entire stock market.

Suppose that we group all these economic factors and any other relevant common factors into one macroeconomic indicator and assume that it moves the security market as a whole. We further assume that, beyond this common effect, all remaining uncertainty in stock returns is firm-specific; that is, there is no other source of correlation between securities. Firm-specific events would include new inventions, deaths of key employees, and other factors that affect the fortune of the individual firm without affecting the broad economy in a measurable way.

We can summarize the distinction between macroeconomic and firm-specific factors by writing the return, r_i, realized on any security during some holding period as

$$r_i = E(r_i) + m_i + e_i \tag{9.1}$$

where $E(r_i)$ is the expected return on the security as of the beginning of the holding period, m_i is the impact of unanticipated macro events on the security's return during the period, and e_i is the impact of unanticipated firm-specific events. Both m_i and e_i have zero expected values because each represents the impact of unanticipated events, which by definition must average out to zero.

We can gain further insight by recognizing that different firms have different sensitivities to macroeconomic events. Thus, if we denote the unanticipated component of the macro factor by F, and denote the responsiveness of security i to macroevents by the Greek letter beta, β_i, then equation 9.1 becomes[1]

$$r_i = E(r_i) + \beta_i F + e_i \tag{9.2}$$

Equation 9.2 is known as a **factor model** for stock returns. It is easy to imagine that a more realistic decomposition of security returns would require more than one factor in equation 9.2. We treat this issue in Chapter 10. For now, let us examine the easy case with only one macro factor.

Of course, a factor model is of little use without specifying a way to measure the factor that is posited to affect security returns. One reasonable approach is to assert that the rate of return on a broad index of securities such as the S&P 500 is a valid proxy for the common macro factor. This approach leads to an equation similar to the factor model, which is called a **single-index model** because it uses the market index to proxy for the common or systematic factor.

---

[1] You may wonder why we choose the notation β for the responsiveness coefficient, since β already has been defined in Chapter 8 in the context of the CAPM. The choice is deliberate, however. Our reason will be obvious shortly.

According to the index model, we can separate the actual or realized rate of return on a security into macro (systematic) and micro (firm-specific) components in a manner similar to that in equation 9.2. We write the rate of return on each security as a sum of three components:

	Symbol
1. The stock's expected return if the market is neutral, that is, if the market's excess return, $r_M - r_f$, is zero	α_i
2. The component of return due to movements in the overall market; β_i is the security's responsiveness to market movements	$\beta_i(r_M - r_f)$
3. The unexpected component due to unexpected events that are relevant only to this security (firm-specific)	e_i

The holding period excess rate of return on the stock, which measures the stock's relative performance, then can be stated as

$$r_i - r_f = \alpha_i + \beta_i(r_M - r_f) + e_i$$

Let us denote security excess returns over the risk-free rate using capital R, and so rewrite this equation as

$$R_i = \alpha_i + \beta_i R_M + e_i \qquad (9.3)$$

You may wonder why we write the index model in terms of excess returns over r_f rather than in terms of total returns. This is because the level of the stock market return represents the state of the macro economy only to the extent that it exceeds or falls short of the rate of return on risk-free T-bills. For example, in the 1950s, when T-bills were yielding only a 1% or 2% rate of return, a return of 8% or 9% on the stock market would be considered good news. In contrast, in the early 1980s, when bills were yielding over 10%, that same 8% or 9% stock market return would signal disappointing macroeconomic news.[2]

Equation 9.3 says that each security therefore has two sources of risk: *market or "systematic" risk,* attributable to its sensitivity to macroeconomic factors as reflected in R_M, and *firm-specific* risk as reflected in e. If we denote the variance of the excess return on the market, R_M, as σ_M^2, then we can break the variance of the rate of return on each stock into two components:

	Symbol
1. The variance attributable to the uncertainty of the common macroeconomic factors	$\beta_i^2 \sigma_M^2$
2. The variance attributable to firm-specific uncertainty	$\sigma^2(e_i)$

---

[2]In practice, however, a "modified" index model is often used that is similar to equation 9.3 except that it uses total rather than excess returns. This practice is most common when daily data are used. In this case the rate of return on bills is on the order of only about .02% per day, so total and excess returns are almost indistinguishable.

The covariance between R_M and e_i is zero because e_i is defined as firm-specific, that is, independent of movements in the market. Hence, calling σ_i^2 the variance of the rate of return on security i, we find that

$$\sigma_i^2 = \beta_i^2 \sigma_M^2 + \sigma^2(e_i)$$

The covariance between the excess rates of return on two stocks, for example, R_i and R_j, derives only from the common factor, R_M, because e_i, and e_j are each firm-specific and therefore presumed to be uncorrelated. Hence the covariance between two stocks is

$$\text{Cov}(R_i, R_j) = \text{Cov}(\beta_i R_M, \beta_j R_M) = \beta_i \beta_j \sigma_M^2 \qquad (9.4)$$

These calculations show that if we have

> n estimates of the expected returns, $E(R_i)$
>
> n estimates of the sensitivity coefficients, β_i
>
> n estimates of the firm-specific variances, $\sigma^2(e_i)$
>
> 1 estimate for the variance of the (common) macroeconomic factor, σ_M^2,

then these $(3n + 1)$ estimates will enable us to prepare the input list for this single-index security universe. Thus for a 50-security portfolio we will need 151 estimates rather than 1,325, and for a 100-security portfolio we will need only 301 estimates rather than 5,150.

It is easy to see why the index model is such a useful abstraction. For large universes of securities the data estimates required for the Markowitz procedure are only a small fraction of what otherwise would be needed (see the nearby box).

Another advantage is less obvious but equally important. The index model abstraction is crucial for specialization of effort in security analysis. If a covariance term had to be calculated directly for each security pair, then security analysts could not specialize by industry. For example, if one group were to specialize in the computer industry and another in the auto industry, who would have the common background to estimate the covariance between IBM and GM? Neither group would have the deep understanding of other industries necessary to make an informed judgment of co-movements among industries. In contrast, the index model suggests a simple way to compute covariances. Covariances among securities are due to the influence of the single common factor, represented by the market index return, and can be easily estimated using equation 9.4.

The simplification derived from the index model assumption is, however, not without cost. The "cost" of the model lies in the restrictions it places on the structure of asset return uncertainty. The classification of uncertainty into a simple dichotomy—macro vs. micro risk—oversimplifies sources of real-world uncertainty and misses some important sources of dependence in stock returns. For example, this dichotomy rules out industry events, events that may affect many firms within an industry without substantially affecting the broad macro economy.

Statistical analysis shows that the firm-specific components of some firms are cor-

Securities Firms Are Cooking Up Potpourri of World Stock Indexes

As investors grow hungrier for worldwide investments, demand for an accurate financial calorie counter increases as well.

As a result, some of the biggest securities firms are introducing world stock market indexes, each firm boasting it provides a comprehensive measure of world investing patterns.

Last week, Salomon Brothers Inc. launched its Salomon-Russell Global Equity Index, tracing $3.565 trillion of equities world-wide. Three similar measures are already available. Laszlo Birinyi Jr., vice president for Salomon's equity market analysis group, says, "We're trying to provide reliable, consistent information on global securities."

The Salomon index has formidable competition. For most of the past 20 years, investors who wanted to compare their success, or that of their investment advisers, to markets around the world turned to the Capital International Indices, a pioneering measure computed by Capital International S.A., starting in 1968. Morgan Stanley Group Inc. acquired the index, the related data base and other publications in early 1986. The indexes, currently known as the Morgan Stanley Capital International Indices, cover equities in 2,000 companies in 21 countries.

First Boston Corp. teamed with London-based Euromoney last year to launch its Global Index. In February, Goldman, Sachs & Co. and Wood MacKenzie & Co. joined the London-based Financial Times to follow suit with the FT-Actuaries World Indices. Shearson Lehman Brothers Inc. has one in the works, too.

Designing a global index is far from easy, starting with the question of which stocks to track. Some analysts fault the Morgan Stanley index for being too inclusive, because many countries have restrictions on foreign ownership. The Morgan Stanley index, for example, counts securities in Swedish banks that can't be purchased outside Sweden. But Morgan Stanley says foreign investors can purchase these stocks by seeking permission from the company.

Some new rival indexes adjust for "cross-holdings"

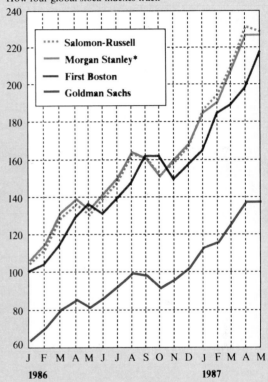

Variations on a Theme

How four global stock indexes track

- Salomon-Russell
- Morgan Stanley*
- First Boston
- Goldman Sachs

1986   1987

*Adjusted for comparison

of one company in another, such as Seagram Co.'s 22.5% stake in Du Pont Co. Morgan Stanley's index, however, generally doesn't do so.

Once the universe of securities has been selected, the figures require constant recalculation and adjustment. Expensive computer resources and highly trained analysts track exchange rates, mergers, stock splits, dividend payments and changes in capitalization. New companies must be added constantly.

All this concern is the result of growing internation-

Continued.

alization of financial markets. U.S. institutions are investing heavily abroad, and stock markets outside the U.S. have surged. First Boston estimates that U.S. institutions will have $45 billion to $50 billion in foreign equities by year's end, up from about $4 billion in 1980.

While the U.S. stock market, as measured by the Dow Jones Industrial Average, rose almost 23% in 1986, Morgan Stanley's European-Australia-Far Eastern Index, which includes the world other than the U.S., rose almost 70%. Salomon's International Equity Index rose 67.5%.

As interest in global investing rises, there is a lot of ego in getting a firm's name on a popular measuring stick. "Competitors of Morgan Stanley find it impalatable to put Morgan Stanley's name on their research," says Mark Sladkus, a vice president at Morgan Stanley.

Still, Mr. Sladkus concedes there aren't great differences in the competing measures. "They all track one another extremely closely. That would discount all claims that one is the best." He adds he is "quite certain that five years from now, there will only be two or three indexes in the market."

In addition, Mr. Sladkus says that because the Morgan Stanley index has been around much longer than competing indexes, it provides a useful historical benchmark for investors.

Tony Regan, head of international investments at Putnam Cos. in Boston, says, "Unless (competitors) can prove superiority, they've all got a problem in dislodging Morgan Stanley. It will be interesting to see if any differences in performance do emerge. Then we owe it to ourselves to see why."

However, Greg Smith, chief investment strategist for Prudential-Bache Securities Inc., says, "There'll never be a time when we have an industry standard. We're probably just splitting hairs to some people, but they're important hairs in the international market."

From *The Wall Street Journal*, June 17, 1987. Reprinted by permission of *The Wall Street Journal*.

related. Examples are the nonmarket components of stocks in a single industry, such as computer stocks or auto stocks. At the same time, statistical significance does not always correspond to economic significance. Economically speaking, the question that is more relevant to the assumption of a single-index model is whether portfolios constructed using covariances that are estimated on the basis of the single-factor or single-index assumption are significantly different from, and less efficient than, portfolios constructed using covariances that are estimated directly for each pair of stocks. In Part VII on active portfolio management, we explore this issue further.

Concept Check

Question 1. Suppose that the index model for stocks A and B is estimated with the following results:

$$R_A = .01 + .9R_M + e_A$$
$$R_B = -.02 + 1.1R_M + e_B$$
$$\sigma_M = .20$$
$$\sigma(e_A) = .3$$
$$\sigma(e_B) = .1$$

Find the standard deviation of each stock and the covariance between them.

FIGURE 9.1

Characteristic line for
GM.

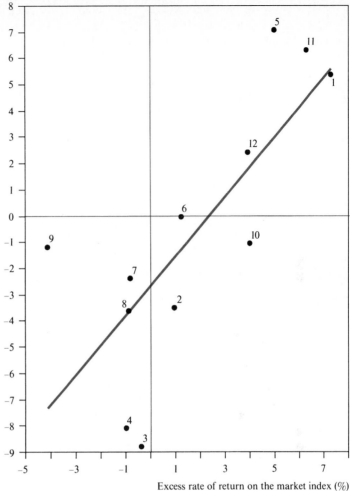

Excess rate of return on GM stock (%)

Excess rate of return on the market index (%)

Estimating the Index Model

Equation 9.3 also suggests how we might go about actually measuring market and firm-specific risk. Suppose that we observe the excess return on the market index and a specific asset over a number of holding periods. We use as an example monthly excess returns on the S&P 500 index and GM stock for 1985. We can summarize the results for a sample period in a **scatter diagram** as illustrated in Figure 9.1.

The horizontal axis in Figure 9.1 measures the excess return (over the risk-free rate) on the market index, whereas the vertical axis measures the excess return on the asset in question (GM stock in our example). A pair of excess returns (one for the market index, one for GM stock) over a holding period constitutes one point on this scatter diagram. The points are numbered 1 through 12, representing excess returns for the S&P 500 and GM for each month from January through December 1985. The single-index model states that the relationship between the excess returns on GM and the S&P 500 is given by

$$R_{GMt} = \alpha_{GM} + \beta_{GM}R_{Mt} + e_{GMt}$$

Note the resemblance of this relationship to a **regression equation.**

In a single-variable linear regression equation the dependent variable plots around a straight line with an intercept α and a slope β. The deviations from the line, e_t, are assumed to be mutually independent and independent of the right-hand variable. Because these assumptions are identical to those of the index model we can look at the index model as a regression model. The sensitivity of GM to the market, measured by β_{GM}, is the slope of the regression line. The intercept of the regression line is α, and deviations of particular observations from the regression line are denoted e. These **residuals** are the parts of stock returns not explained by the independent variable (the market-index return); therefore they measure the impact of firm-specific events during the particular month. The parameters of interest, α, β, and Var(e), can be estimated using standard regression techniques.

Estimating the regression equation of the single-index model gives us the **security characteristic line** (SCL), which is plotted in Figure 9.1. (The regression results and raw data appear in Table 9.1.) The SCL is a plot of the typical excess return on a security over the risk-free rate as a function of the excess return on the market.

This sample of holding period returns is, of course, too small to yield reliable statistics. We use it only for demonstration. For this sample period we find that the beta coefficient of GM stock, as estimated by the slope of the regression line, is 1.1357, and that the intercept for this SCL is -2.59% per month.

For each month, our estimate of the residual, e, which is the deviation of GM's excess return from the prediction of the SCL, equals

$$\text{deviation} = \text{actual} - \text{predicted return}$$
$$e_{GMt} = R_{GMt} - (\beta_{GM}R_{Mt} + \alpha_{GM})$$

These residuals are estimates of the monthly unexpected *firm-specific* component of the rate of return on GM stock. Hence we can estimate the firm-specific variance by[3]

$$\sigma^2(e_{GM}) = \frac{1}{10} \sum_{t=1}^{12} e_t^2 = 12.60$$

Therefore the standard deviation of the firm-specific component of GM's return, $\sigma(e_{GM})$, equals 3.55% per month.

---

[3]Because the mean of e_t is zero, e_t^2 is the squared deviation from its mean. The average value of e_t^2 is therefore the estimate of the variance of the firm-specific component. We divide the sum of squared residuals by the degrees of freedom of the regression, $n - 2 = 12 - 2 = 10$ to obtain an unbiased estimate of $\sigma^2(e)$.

Equilibrium in Capital Markets

TABLE 9.1   Characteristic Line for GM Stock

Month	Market Return	GM Return	Monthly T-Bill Rate	Excess Market Return	Excess GM Return
January	7.89	6.06	0.65	7.24	5.41
February	1.51	−2.86	0.58	0.93	−3.44
March	0.23	−8.18	0.62	−0.38	−8.79
April	−0.29	−7.36	0.72	−1.01	−8.08
May	5.58	7.76	0.66	4.92	7.10
June	1.73	0.52	0.55	1.18	−0.03
July	−0.21	−1.74	0.62	−0.83	−2.36
August	−0.36	−3.00	0.55	−0.91	−3.55
September	−3.58	−0.56	0.60	−4.18	−1.16
October	4.62	−0.37	0.65	3.97	−1.02
November	6.85	6.93	0.61	6.25	6.32
December	4.55	3.08	0.65	3.90	2.43
Mean	2.38	0.02	0.62	1.75	−0.60
Std Dev	3.33	4.97	0.05	3.32	4.97
Regression Results	$r_{GM} - r_f = \alpha + \beta(r_M - r_f)$				

	α	β
Estimated coefficient	−2.590	1.1357
Standard error of estimate	(1.547)	(0.309)

Variance of residuals = 12.601
Standard deviation of residuals = 3.550
R-SQR = 0.575

The Index Model and Diversification

The index model, which was first suggested by Sharpe,[4] also offers insight into portfolio diversification. Suppose that we choose an equally weighted portfolio of n securities. The excess rate of return on each security is given by

$$R_i = \alpha_i + \beta_i R_M + e_i$$

Similarly, we can write the excess return on the portfolio of stocks as

$$R_P = \alpha_P + \beta_P R_M + e_P \tag{9.5}$$

We now show that, as the number of stocks included in this portfolio increases, the part of the portfolio risk attributable to nonmarket factors becomes ever smaller. This part of the risk is diversified away. In contrast, the market risk remains, regardless of the number of firms combined into the portfolio.

---

[4]Sharpe, William F., "A Simplified Model of Portfolio Analysis," *Management Science*, January 1963.

To understand these results, note that the excess rate of return on this equally weighted portfolio, for which $w_i = 1/n$, is

$$R_P = \sum_{i=1}^{n} w_i R_i = \frac{1}{n} \sum_{i=1}^{n} R_i = \frac{1}{n} \sum_{i=1}^{n} (\alpha_i + \beta_i R_M + e_i)$$

$$= \frac{1}{n} \sum_{i=1}^{n} \alpha_i + \left(\frac{1}{n} \sum_{i=1}^{n} \beta_i \right) R_M + \frac{1}{n} \sum_{i=1}^{n} e_i \qquad (9.6)$$

Comparing equations 9.5 and 9.6, we see that the portfolio has a sensitivity to the market given by

$$\beta_P = \frac{1}{n} \sum_{i=1}^{n} \beta_i$$

(which is the average of the individual β_is), and has a nonmarket return component of a constant (intercept)

$$\frac{1}{n} \sum_{i=1}^{n} \alpha_i$$

(which is the average of the individual alphas,) plus the zero mean variable

$$e_P = \frac{1}{n} \sum_{i=1}^{n} e_i$$

which is the average of the firm-specific components. Hence the portfolio's variance is

$$\sigma_P^2 = \beta_P^2 \sigma_M^2 + \sigma^2(e_P) \qquad (9.7)$$

The systematic risk component of the portfolio variance, which we defined as the part that depends on marketwide movements, is $\beta_P^2 \sigma_M^2$ and depends on the average of the sensitivity coefficients of the individual securities. This part of the risk depends on portfolio beta and σ_M^2 and will persist regardless of the extent of portfolio diversification. No matter how many stocks are held, their common exposure to the market will be reflected in portfolio systematic risk.[5]

In contrast, the nonsystematic component of the portfolio variance is $\sigma^2(e_P)$ and is attributable to firm-specific components, e_i. Because these e_is are independent, and all have zero expected value, the law of averages can be applied to conclude that as more and more stocks are added to the portfolio the firm-specific components tend to

---

[5] Of course, one can always construct a portfolio with zero systematic risk by mixing negative β and positive β assets. The point of our discussion is that the vast majority of securities have a positive β, implying that well-diversified portfolios with small holdings in large numbers of assets will indeed have positive systematic risk.

cancel out, resulting in ever-smaller nonmarket risk. Such risk is thus termed *diversifiable*. To see this more rigorously, examine the formula for the variance of the equally weighted "portfolio" of firm-specific components. Because the e_is are all uncorrelated,

$$\sigma^2(e_P) = \sum_{i=1}^{n} \left(\frac{1}{n}\right)^2 \sigma^2(e_i) = \frac{1}{n}\overline{\sigma}^2(e)$$

where $\overline{\sigma}^2(e)$ is the average of the firm-specific variances. Since this average is independent of n, when n gets large, $\sigma^2(e_p)$ becomes negligible.

Concept Check

Question 2. Reconsider the two stocks in Concept Check 1. Suppose we form an equally weighted portfolio of A and B. What will be the nonsystematic standard deviation of that portfolio?

To summarize, as diversification increases, the total variance of a portfolio approaches the systematic variance, defined as the variance of the market factor multiplied by the square of the portfolio sensitivity coefficient, β_P. This is shown in Figure 9.2.

Figure 9.2 shows that, as more and more securities are combined into a portfolio, variance decreases because of the diversification of firm-specific risk. However, the

FIGURE 9.2

The variance of a portfolio with β in the single-factor economy.

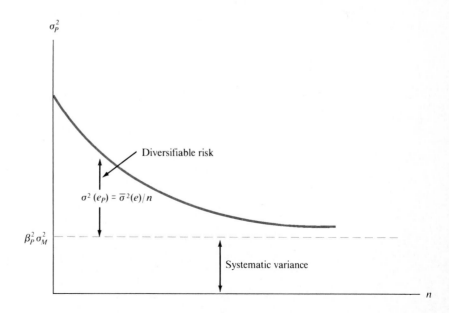

power of diversification is limited. Even for very large *n*, risk remains because of the exposure of virtually all assets to the common, or market, factor. Therefore this systematic risk is said to be nondiversifiable.

This analysis is borne out by empirical analysis. We saw the effect of portfolio diversification on portfolio standard deviations in Figure 7.2. These empirical results are similar to the theoretical graph presented here in Figure 9.2.

9.2   *The CAPM and the Index Model*

Actual Returns vs. Expected Returns

The CAPM is an elegant model. The question is whether it has real-world value, whether its implications are borne out by experience. Chapter 12 provides a range of empirical evidence on this point, but for now we will focus briefly on a more basic issue: is the CAPM testable even in principle?

For starters, one central prediction of the CAPM is that the market portfolio is a mean-variance efficient portfolio. Consider that the CAPM treats all traded risky assets. To test the efficiency of the CAPM market portfolio, we would need to construct a value-weighted portfolio of a huge size and test its efficiency. So far, this task has been infeasible. An even more difficult problem, however, is that the CAPM implies relationships among *expected* returns, whereas all we can observe are actual or realized holding period returns, and these need not equal prior expectations. Even supposing we could construct a portfolio to represent the CAPM market portfolio satisfactorily, how would we test its mean-variance efficiency? We would have to show that the reward-to-variability ratio of the market portfolio is higher than that of any other portfolio. However, this reward-to-variability ratio is set in terms of expectations, and we have no way to observe these expectations directly.

The problem of measuring expectations haunts us as well when we try to establish the validity of the second central set of CAPM predictions, the expected return-beta relationship. Remember that the CAPM equation is defined in terms of expected returns $E(r_i)$ and $E(r_M)$:

$$E(r_i) = r_f + \beta_i[E(r_M) - r_f] \tag{9.8}$$

The upshot is that, as elegant and insightful as the CAPM is, we must make additional assumptions to make it implementable and testable.

The Index Model and Realized Returns

We have said that the CAPM is a statement about ex ante or expected returns, whereas in practice all anyone can observe directly are ex post or realized returns. To make the jump from expected to realized returns, we can employ the index model, which we will use in excess return form as

$$R_i = \alpha_i + \beta_i R_M + e_i \tag{9.9}$$

We saw in Section 9.1 how to apply standard regression analysis to estimate equation 9.9 using observable realized returns over some sample period. Let us now see how this framework for statistically decomposing actual stock returns meshes with the CAPM.

We start by deriving the covariance between the returns on stock i and the market index. By definition, the firm-specific or nonsystematic component is independent of the marketwide or systematic component, that is, $Cov(R_M, e_i) = 0$. From this relationship, it follows that the covariance of the excess rate of return on security i with that of the market index is

$$Cov(R_i, R_M) = Cov(\beta_i R_M + e_i, R_M)$$
$$= \beta_i Cov(R_M, R_M) + Cov(e_i, R_M)$$
$$= \beta_i \sigma_M^2$$

Note that we can drop α_i from the covariance terms because α_i is a constant and thus has zero covariance with all variables.

Because $Cov(R_i, R_M) = \beta_i \sigma_M^2$, the sensitivity coefficient, β_i, in equation 9.9, which is the slope of the regression line representing the index model, equals

$$\beta_i = \frac{Cov(R_i, R_M)}{\sigma_M^2}$$

The index model beta coefficient turns out to be the same beta as that of the CAPM expected return-beta relationship, except that we replace the (theoretical) market portfolio of the CAPM with the well-specified and observable market index.

This should not be a surprising result. Consider what happens when we merge many stocks into a portfolio. Firm-specific risk is diversified away, leaving only systematic, or market, risk. It is only systematic risk that needs to be compensated for through a risk premium, and the natural risk measure of a stock as part of a portfolio is its contribution to the portfolio's exposure to the market factor, which is the stock's beta coefficient in the index model. Beta measures both the contribution of a stock to the variance of the market portfolio *and* the sensitivity of that stock's return to the macro factor. Regardless of which interpretation we choose, we conclude that beta is the risk measure that should determine the stock's fair risk premium.

Question 3. The data below is drawn from a three-stock financial market that satisfies the single index model.

Stock	Capitalization	Beta	Mean Excess Return	Standard Deviation
A	$3,000	1.0	.10	.40
B	$1,940	.2	.02	.30
C	$1,360	1.7	.17	.50

The single factor in this economy is perfectly correlated with the value-weighted index of the stock market. The standard deviation of the market index portfolio is 25%.
a. What is the mean excess return of the index portfolio?
b. What is the covariance between stock A and the index?
c. Break down the variance of stock B into its systematic and firm-specific components.

The Index Model and the Expected Return-Beta Relationship

Recall that the CAPM expected return-beta relationship is, for any asset i and the (theoretical) market portfolio,

$$E(r_i) - r_f = \beta_i[E(r_M) - r_f]$$

where $\beta_i = \text{Cov}(r_i, r_M)/\sigma_M^2$. This is a statement about the mean or expected excess return of assets relative to the mean excess return of the (theoretical) market portfolio.

Taking the expectation of each side of equation 9.9 shows that the index model specification is

$$E(r_i) - r_f = \alpha_i + \beta_i[E(r_M) - r_f]$$

A comparison of the index model relationship to the CAPM expected return-beta relationship shows that the CAPM predicts that α_i must be zero for all assets. The alpha of a stock is its expected return in excess of (or below) the fair expected return as predicted by the CAPM. If the stock is fairly priced, its alpha must be zero.

We emphasize again that this is a statement about expected returns on a security. After the fact, of course, some securities will do better or worse than expected and will have returns higher or lower than predicted by the CAPM relationship; that is, they will exhibit positive or negative alphas over a sample period. But this superior or inferior performance could not have been forecast in advance.

Therefore, if we estimate the index model for several firms, using equation 9.9 as a regression equation, we should find that the ex post or realized alphas (the regres-

FIGURE 9.3

Frequency distribution
of alphas.

(From Jensen, Michael C.,
"The Performance of Mutual
Funds in the Period
1945-1964," *Journal of
Finance, 23,* May 1968.)

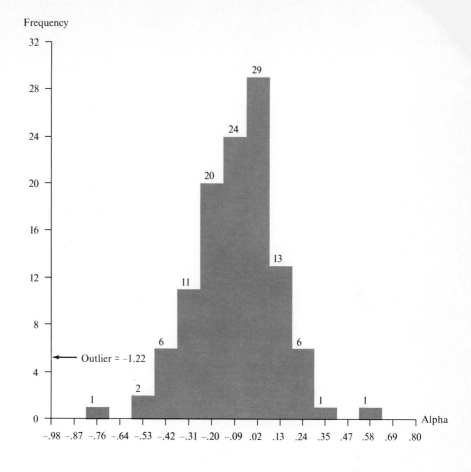

sion intercepts) for the firms in our sample center around zero. If the initial expectation for alpha were zero, as many firms would be expected to have a positive as a negative alpha for some sample period. The CAPM states that the *expected* value of alpha is zero for all securities, whereas the index model representation of the CAPM holds that the *realized* value of alpha should average out to zero for a sample of historical observed returns.

Some interesting evidence on this property was compiled by Michael Jensen,[6] who examined the alphas realized by mutual funds over the 10-year period 1955 to 1964. Figure 9.3 shows the frequency distribution of these alphas, which do indeed seem to be distributed around zero.

There is yet another applicable variation on the intuition of the index model, the **market model.** Formally, the market model states that the return "surprise" of any

---

[6] Jensen, Michael C., "The Performance of Mutual Funds in the Period 1945-1964," *Journal of Finance, 23,* May 1968.

security is proportional to the return surprise of the market, plus a firm-specific surprise:

$$r_i - E(r_i) = \beta_i[r_M - E(r_M)] + e_i$$

This equation divides returns into firm-specific and systematic components somewhat differently from the index model. If the CAPM is valid, however, you can see that, substituting for $E(r_i)$ from equation 9.8, the market model equation becomes identical to the index model we have just presented. The market model also predicts a zero value for the intercept term of the regression equation. For this reason the terms "index model" and "market model" are sometimes used interchangeably.

Concept Check

Question 4. Can you sort out the nuances of the following maze of models?
a. CAPM
b. single factor model
c. single index model
d. market model

9.3 The Industry Version of the Index Model

Not surprisingly, the index model has attracted the attention of practitioners. To the extent that it is approximately correct, it provides a convenient benchmark for security analysis.

A modern practitioner using the CAPM who has no special information about a security, or insight that is unavailable to the general public, will conclude that the security is "properly" priced. By "properly" priced, the analyst means that the expected return on the security is fair, given its risk, and therefore plots on the security market line. For instance, if one has no private information about GM's stock, then one should expect

$$E(r_{GM}) = r_f + \beta_{GM}[E(r_M) - r_f]$$

A portfolio manager who has a forecast for the market index, $E(r_M)$, and observes the risk-free T-bill rate, r_f, can use the model to determine the benchmark expected return for any stock. The beta coefficient, the market risk, σ_M^2, and the firm-specific risk, $\sigma^2(e)$, can be estimated from historical SCLs, that is, from regressions of security excess returns on market index excess returns.

There are many sources for such regression results. One widely used source is the Research Computer Services Department of Merrill Lynch, Pierce, Fenner and Smith, Inc., which publishes a monthly *Security Risk Evaluation* book, commonly called the "beta book."

Security Risk Evaluation uses the S&P 500 index as the proxy for the market portfolio. It relies on the 60 most recent monthly observations to calculate the regression parameters. Merrill Lynch and most services[7] use total returns, rather than excess returns (deviations from T-bill rates), in their regressions. In this way they estimate a variant of our index model, which is

$$r = a + br_M + e*$$ (9.10)

instead of

$$r - r_f = \alpha + \beta(r_M - r_f) + e$$ (9.11)

To see the effect of this departure, we can rewrite equation 9.11 as

$$r = r_f + \alpha + \beta r_M - \beta r_f + e = \alpha + r_f(1 - \beta) + \beta r_M + e$$ (9.12)

Comparing equations 9.10 and 9.12, you can see that if r_f is constant over the sample period both equations have the same independent variable, r_M, and residual, e. Therefore the slope coefficient will be the same in the two regressions.[8]

However, the intercept that Merrill Lynch calls alpha is really, using the parameters of the CAPM, an estimate of $\alpha + r_f(1 - \beta)$. The apparent justification for this procedure is that, on a monthly basis, $r_f(1 - \beta)$ is small and is apt to be swamped by the volatility of actual stock returns. However, it is worth noting that for $\beta \neq 1$, the regression intercept in equation 9.10 will not equal the CAPM alpha as it does when excess returns are used as in equation 9.11.

Another way the Merrill Lynch procedure departs from the index model is in its use of percentage of changes in price instead of total rates of return. This means that the index model variant of Merrill Lynch ignores the dividend component of stock returns.

Table 9.2 illustrates a page from the beta book showing the estimates for GM. The third column, "Close Price," shows the stock price at the end of the sample period. The next two columns show the beta and alpha coefficients. Remember that Merrill Lynch's alpha is actually $\alpha + r_f(1 - \beta)$.

The next column, R-SQR, shows the square of the correlation coefficient between r_i and r_M. The R-square statistic, which is sometimes called the coefficient of determination, gives the fraction of the variance of the dependent variable (the return on the stock) that is explained by movements in the independent variable (the return on the S&P 500 index). Recall from Section 9.1 that the part of the total variance of the rate of return on an asset, σ^2, that is explained by market returns is the systematic variance, $\beta^2\sigma_M^2$. Hence the R-square is systematic variance over total variance, which tells us what fraction of a firm's volatility is attributable to market movements:

$$R\text{-square} = \frac{\beta^2\sigma_M^2}{\sigma^2}$$

---

[7] Value Line is another common source of security betas. Value Line uses weekly rather than monthly data and uses the New York Stock Exchange index instead of the S&P 500 as the market proxy.

[8] Actually, r_f does vary over time and so should not be grouped casually with the constant term in the regression. However, variations in r_f are tiny compared with swings in the market return. The actual volatility in the T-bill rate has only a small impact on the estimated value of β.

TABLE 9.2   Market Sensitivity Statistics

Ticker Symbol	Security Name	February 1986 Close Price	Beta	Alpha	R-SQR	RESID STD DEV—N	Standard Error Beta	Standard Error Alpha	Adjusted Beta	Number of Observations
GHSE	General Housewares Corp	11.250	1.18	.42	.16	10.47	.34	1.39	1.12	60
GRC	General Instr Corp	20.750	1.70	−1.32	.29	10.48	.34	1.39	1.46	60
GMIC	General Microwave Corp	15.000	1.22	1.46	.15	11.36	.37	1.52	1.14	59
GTS	General Mls Inc	69.250	.51	1.11	.11	5.54	.18	.74	.68	60
GM	General Mtrs Corp	77.750	.83	.12	.25	5.66	.18	.75	.89	60 ◀
GME	General Motors Corp CLE	42.000	1.27	2.80	.18	10.55	.34	1.40	1.18	60
GNCI	General Nutrition Inc	5.750	1.18	−.63	.10	13.13	.42	1.75	1.12	60
GPU	General Pub Utils Corp	19.500	.74	2.03	.13	7.27	.24	.97	.83	60
GNR	General RE Corp	118.000	.91	1.73	.24	6.41	.21	.85	.94	60
GRS	General Real Estate Sh Ben I	8.500	.08	−.11	.02	8.84	.29	1.18	.39	60
GRX	General Refractories Co	11.250	1.74	−.42	.19	13.94	.46	1.85	1.49	60
GSE	General Secs Inc	13.610	1.07	−.75	.69	2.87	.09	.38	1.05	60
GSH	General Small Prods Corp	23.250	.71	1.63	.63	12.80	.41	1.70	.81	60
GSX	General Signal Corp	50.250	1.01	−.63	.39	5.00	.16	.67	1.00	60
GCO	Genesco Inc	3.500	1.75	−1.77	.28	11.05	.36	1.47	1.50	60

Modified from *Security Risk Evaluation,* Research Computer Services Department of Merrill Lynch, Pierce, Fenner and Smith, Inc.
Based on S&P 500 index, using straight regression.

The firm-specific variance, $\sigma^2(e)$, is the part of the asset variance that is unexplained by the market index. Therefore, because

$$\sigma^2 = \beta^2 \sigma_M^2 + \sigma^2(e)$$

the coefficient of determination also may be expressed as

$$R\text{-square} = 1 - \frac{\sigma^2(e)}{\sigma^2} \tag{9.13}$$

Accordingly, the column following *R*-SQR reports the standard deviation of the nonsystematic component, $\sigma(e)$, calling it RESID STD DEV-*N,* in reference to the fact that the *es* are estimated by the regression residuals. This variable is an estimate of firm-specific risk.

The following two columns appear under the heading of Standard Error. These are statistics that allow us to test the significance of the regression coefficients. The standard error of an estimate is the standard deviation of the possible estimation error of the coefficient, which is a measure of the precision of the estimate. A rule of thumb is that if an estimated coefficient is less than twice its standard error, we cannot reject

Ticker Symbol	Security Name	February 1986 Close Price	Beta	Alpha	R-SQR	RESID STD DEV—N	Standard Error Beta	Standard Error Alpha	Adjusted Beta	Number of Observations
GENB	Genesee Brewing Inc Cl B	52.750	.16	1.48	.01	8.92	.29	1.19	.44	60
GES	Genesco Technology Corp	5.750	1.66	−1.64	.23	12.07	.39	1.61	1.44	60
GNVA	Genova Inc	4.625	.30	2.94	.01	17.78	.58	2.37	.53	60
GDG	Genovese Drug Stores Inc	13.625	.67	2.75	.03	12.07	.39	1.61	.78	60
GRAD	Genrad Inc	12.375	1.75	−1.10	.27	11.25	.36	1.50	1.49	60
GST	Genstak Corp	28.250	2.41	−1.74	.52	9.23	.30	1.23	1.94	60
GPC	Genuine Parts Co	39.000	1.00	.49	.31	5.88	.19	.78	1.00	60
GWSH	George Washington Corp	4.125	.64	−.07	.04	10.28	.33	1.37	.76	60
GXWI	Geo Intl Corp	2.625	1.28	−4.68	.15	11.50	.37	1.53	1.17	60
GBFB	Georgia Bonded Fibres Inc	6.375	.97	.57	.04	16.40	.53	2.18	.98	60
GP	Georgia Pac Corp	29.625	1.56	−1.13	.48	6.50	.21	.87	1.37	60
GTH	Geothermal Res Intl Inc	14.000	.83	.28	.06	11.65	.38	1.55	.88	60
GEB	Gerber Prods Co	39.625	.74	1.55	.13	7.26	.23	.97	.83	60
GRB	Gerber Scientific Inc	23.000	2.42	.58	.35	13.16	.43	1.75	1.94	60
GEMC	Geriatric & Med Ctrs Inc	6.875	1.28	2.73	.12	13.18	.43	1.75	1.18	60

the hypothesis that the true coefficient is zero. The ratio of the coefficient to its standard error is the *t*-statistic that you may have studied in statistics. A *t*-statistic greater than 2 is the traditional cutoff for statistical significance. The two columns of the standard error of the estimated alpha and beta allow us a quick check on the statistical significance of these estimates.

The next-to-last column is called adjusted beta. The motivation for adjusting beta estimates is the observation that, on average, the beta coefficients of stocks seem to move toward 1 over time. One explanation for this phenomenon is intuitive. A business enterprise usually is established to produce a specific product or service, and a new firm may be more unconventional than an older one in many ways, from technology to management style. As it grows, however, a firm diversifies, first expanding to similar products and later to more diverse operations. As the firm becomes more conventional, it starts to resemble the rest of the economy even more. Thus its beta coefficient will tend to change in the direction of 1.

Another explanation for this phenomenon is statistical. We know that the average beta over all securities is 1. Thus, before estimating the beta of a security our guess would be that it is 1. When we estimate this beta coefficient over a particular sample period, we sustain some unknown sampling error of the estimated beta. The greater the difference between our beta estimate and 1, the greater is the chance that we incurred a large estimation error and that, when we estimate this same beta in a subsequent sample period, the new estimate will be closer to 1.

The sample estimate of the beta coefficient is the best guess for the sample period. Given that beta has a tendency to evolve toward 1, however, a forecast of the future beta coefficient should adjust the sample estimate in that direction.

Merrill Lynch adjusts beta estimates in a simple way. They take the sample estimate of beta and average it with 1, using the weights of two thirds and one third:

$$\text{Adjusted beta} = \tfrac{2}{3} \text{ Sample beta} + \tfrac{1}{3}(1)$$

Finally, the last column shows the number of observations, which is 60 months, unless the stock is newly listed and fewer observations are available.

For the 60 months ending in February 1986, GM's beta was estimated at .83. Note that the adjusted beta for GM is .89, taking it a third of the way toward 1.

The sample period regression alpha is .12. Since GM's beta is less than 1, we know that this means that the index model alpha estimate is somewhat smaller. As we did in equation 9.11, we have to subtract $(1 - \beta)r_f$ from the regression alpha to obtain the index model alpha. Even so, the standard error of the alpha estimate is .75. The estimate of alpha is far less than twice its standard error. Consequently, we cannot reject the hypothesis that the true alpha is zero.

Concept Check

Question 5. What was GM's CAPM alpha per month during the period covered by the Merrill Lynch regression if during this period the average monthly rate of return of T-bills was 0.6%.

More importantly, these alpha estimates are ex post (after the fact) measures. They do not mean that anyone could have forecasted these alpha values ex ante (before the fact). In fact, the name of the game in security analysis is to forecast alpha values ahead of time. A well-constructed portfolio that includes long positions in future positive alpha stocks and short positions in future negative alpha stocks will outperform the market index. The key term here is "well-constructed," meaning that the portfolio has to balance concentration on high alpha stocks with the need for risk-reducing diversification. The beta and residual variance estimates from the index model regression make it possible to achieve this goal. (We examine this technique in more detail in Part VII on active portfolio management.)

Note that GM's RESID STD DEV-N is 5.66% per month and its R-SQR is .25. This tells us that $\sigma_{GM}^2(e) = .0566^2 = .003204$ and, because R-SQR $= 1 - \sigma^2(e)/\sigma^2$, we can solve for the estimate of GM's total standard deviation by rearranging equation 9.12 as follows:

$$\sigma_{GM} = \left[\frac{\sigma_{GM}^2(e)}{1 - R^2} \right]^{1/2} = \left(\frac{.003204}{.75} \right)^{1/2} = .0654 = 6.54\% \text{ per month}$$

This is GM's monthly standard deviation for the sample period. Therefore the annualized standard deviation for that period was $6.54 \sqrt{12} = 22.64\%$.

In the absence of special information concerning GM, if our forecast for the market index is 14% and T-bills pay 6%, we learn from the Merill Lynch beta book that the CAPM forecast for the rate of return on GM stock is

$$E(r_{GM}) = r_f + \text{adjusted beta} \times [E(r_M) - r_f]$$
$$= .06 + .89(.14 - .06)$$
$$= .1312$$
$$= 13.12\%$$

9.4 *Predicting Betas*

We saw in the previous section that betas estimated from past data may not be the best estimates of future betas: betas seem to drift toward 1 over time. This suggests that we might want a forecasting model for beta.

One simple approach would be to collect data on beta in different periods and then estimate a regression equation:

$$\text{Current beta} = a + b \text{ (Past beta)} \qquad (9.14)$$

Given estimates of *a* and *b,* we would then forecast future betas using the rule

$$\text{Forecast beta} = a + b \text{ (Current beta)}$$

There is no reason, however, to limit ourselves to such simple forecasting rules. Why not also investigate the predictive power of other financial variables in forecasting beta? For example, if we believe that firm size and debt ratios are two determinants of beta, we might specify an expanded version of equation 9.13 and estimate

$$\text{Current beta} = \alpha$$
$$+ b_1 \text{ (Past beta)}$$
$$+ b_2 \text{ (Firm size)}$$
$$+ b_3 \text{ (Debt ratio)}$$

Now we would use estimates of α and b_1 through b_3 to forecast future betas.

Such an approach has been followed by Rosenberg and Guy,[9] who found the following variables to help predict betas:

1. Variance of earnings
2. Variance of cash flow
3. Growth in earnings per share
4. Market capitalization (firm size)

---

[9]Rosenberg, Barr, and Guy, J., "Prediction of Beta from Investment Fundamentals, Parts 1 and 2," *Financial Analysts Journal,* May-June and July-August 1976.

5. Dividend yield

6. Debt to asset ratio

Rosenberg and Guy also find that, even after controlling for a firm's financial characteristics, industry group helps to predict beta. For example, they find that the beta values of gold mining companies are on average .827 lower than would be predicted based on financial characteristics alone. This should not be surprising; the −.827 "adjustment factor" for the gold industry reflects the fact that gold values are inversely related to market returns.

Table 9.3 presents beta estimates and adjustment factors for a subset of firms in the Rosenberg and Guy study.

TABLE 9.3   Industry Betas and Adjustment Factors

Industry	Beta	Adjustment Factor
Agriculture	.99	−.140
Drugs and medicine	1.14	−.099
Telephone	.75	−.288
Energy utilities	.60	−.237
Gold	.36	−.827
Construction	1.27	.062
Air transport	1.80	.348
Trucking	1.31	.098
Consumer durables	1.44	.132

Concept Check

Question 6. Compare the first five and last four industries in Table 9.3. What characteristic seems to determine whether the adjustment factor is positive or negative?

Summary

1. A single-factor model of the economy classifies sources of uncertainty as systematic (macroeconomic) factors or firm-specific (microeconomic) factors. The index model assumes that the macro factor can be represented by a broad index of stock returns.

2. The single-index model drastically reduces the necessary inputs into the Markowitz portfolio selection procedure. It also aids in specialization of labor in security analysis.

3. If the index model specification is valid, then the systematic risk of a portfolio or asset equals $\beta^2 \sigma_M^2$, and the covariance between two assets equals $\beta_i \beta_j \sigma_M^2$.

4. The index model is estimated by applying regression analysis to excess rates of return. The slope of the regression curve is the beta of an asset, whereas the intercept

is the asset's alpha during the sample period. The regression line is also called the security characteristic line. The regression beta is equivalent to the CAPM beta, except that the regression uses actual returns and the CAPM is specified in terms of expected returns. The CAPM predicts that the average value of alphas measured by the index model regression will be zero.

5. Practitioners routinely estimate the index model using total rather than excess rates of return. This makes their estimate of alpha equal to $\alpha + r_f(1 - \beta)$.

6. Betas show a tendency to evolve toward 1 over time. Beta forecasting rules attempt to predict this drift. Moreover, other financial variables can be used to help forecast betas.

Key Terms

Factor model	Residuals
Single-index model	Security characteristic line
Scatter diagram	Market model
Regression equation	

Selected Readings

The seminal paper relating the index model to the portfolio selection problem is:
  Sharpe, William F., "A Simplified Model of Portfolio Analysis," *Management Science,* January 1963.
Papers on the tendency of betas to drift over time are:
  Blume, Marshall, "Betas and Their Regression Tendencies," *Journal of Finance, 10,* June 1975.
  Klemkosky, R.C., and Martin, J.D., "The Adjustment of Beta Forecasts," *Journal of Finance, 10,* September 1975.
  Vasicek, O., "A Note on Using Cross-Sectional Information in Bayesian Estimation of Security Betas," *Journal of Finance, 8,* December 1973.
Papers on the relation between beta and firm characteristics are:
  Rosenberg, Barr, and Guy, J., "Predictions of Beta from Investment Fundamentals," *Financial Analyst Journal, 32,* May-June 1976.
  Robichek, A.A., and Cohn, R.A., "The Economic Determinants of Systematic Risk," *Journal of Finance,* May 1974.

Problems

1. A portfolio management organization analyzes 75 stocks and constructs a mean-variance efficient portfolio that is constrained to these 75.
   a. How many estimates of expected returns, variances, and covariances are needed to optimize this portfolio?
   b. If one could safely assume that stock market returns closely resemble a single-index structure, how many estimates would be needed?

2. The following are estimates for two of the stocks in Question 1.

Stock	Expected Return	Beta	Firm-Specific Standard Deviation
A	.14	.6	.32
B	.25	1.3	.37

The market index has a standard deviation of .26.

a. What is the standard deviation of stocks A and B?

b. Suppose that we were to construct a portfolio with proportions:

Stock A:	.33	
Stock B:	.38	
T-bills:	.29	$(r_f = 9\%)$

Compute the expected return, standard deviation, beta, and nonsystematic standard deviation of the portfolio.

3. Consider the following two regression curves for stocks A and B.

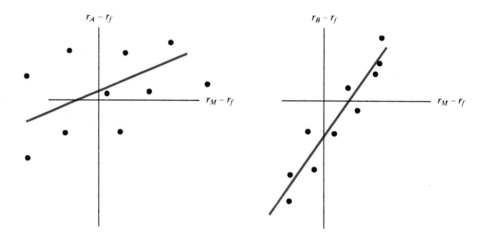

a. What stock has higher firm specific risk?

b. Which stock has greater systematic (market) risk?

c. Which stock has higher R-square?

d. Which stock has higher alpha?

e. Which stock has higher correlation with the market?

4. Consider the two (excess return) index model regression results for stocks A and B:

$R_A = .01 + 1.2R_M$

R-SQR = .576

RESID STD DEV-N = 10.3%

$R_B = -.02 + .8R_M$

R-SQR = .436

RESID STD DEV-N = 9.1%

a. Which stock has more firm-specific risk?
b. Which has greater market risk?
c. For which stock does market movement explain a greater fraction of return variability?
d. Which stock had an average return in excess of that predicted by the CAPM?
e. If r_f were constant at 6% and the regression had been run using total rather than excess returns, what would have been the regression intercept for stock A?

Use the following data for problems 5 through 11. Suppose that the index model for stocks A and B is estimated with the following results:

$$R_A = .02 + .65R_M + e_A$$
$$R_B = .04 + 1.10R_M + e_B$$
$$\sigma_M = .25; \ R\text{-}SQR_A = .15; \ R\text{-}SQR_B = .30$$

5. What is the standard deviation of each stock?
6. Break down the variance of each stock to the systematic and firm-specific components.
7. What is the covariance and correlation coefficient between the two stocks?
8. What is the covariance between each stock and the market index?
9. Are the intercepts of the two regressions consistent with the CAPM? Interpret their values.
10. For portfolio P with investment proportions of .60 in A and .40 in B, rework problems 5, 6, and 8.
11. Rework problem 10 for portfolio Q with investment proportions of .50 in P, .30 in the market index, and .20 in T-bills.
12. In a two stock capital market, the capitalization of stock A is twice that of B. The standard deviation of the excess return on A is .30 and on B is .50. The correlation coefficient between the excess returns is .7.
    a. What is the standard deviation of the market index portfolio?
    b. What is the beta of each stock?
    c. What is the residual variance of each stock?
    d. If the index model holds and stock A is expected to earn 11% in excess of the risk-free rate, what must be the risk premium on the market portfolio?

13. A stock recently has been estimated to have a beta of 1.24:
    a. What will Merrill Lynch compute as the "adjusted beta" of this stock?
    b. Suppose that you estimate the following regression describing the evolution of beta over time:

$$\beta_t = .3 + .7\beta_{t-1}$$

What would be your predicted beta for next year?

14. (Based on CFA Examination, Level I, 1982)

When the annualized quarterly percentage rates of return for a stock market index were regressed against the returns for KM and WMT stocks over the period 1971 to 1980 in an ordinary least squares regression, the following results were obtained:

Statistic	KM	WMT
Alpha	−3.68%	13.96%
Beta	.69	.97
R-square	.25	.22
Residual standard deviation	13.02%	21.45%

Explain what these regression results tell the analyst about risk-and-return relationships for each stock over the 1971 to 1980 period. Comment on their implications for future risk-and-return relationships, assuming both stocks were included in a diversified common stock portfolio, especially in view of the following data obtained from two large brokerage houses in late December 1981:

Brokerage House	Beta of KM	Beta of WMT
A	.80	1.45
B	.75	1.20

where A's betas are calculated on weekly price change data over the preceding 52 weeks and B's betas are calculated on monthly price change data over the preceding 60 months.

CHAPTER 10

Arbitrage Pricing Theory

T the exploitation of security mispricing in such a way that risk-free economic profits may be earned is called **arbitrage.** It typically involves the simultaneous purchase and sale of equivalent securities (usually in different markets) in order to profit from discrepancies in their price relationship. The concept of arbitrage is central to the theory of capital markets. This chapter discusses the nature, and illustrates the use, of arbitrage. We show how to identify arbitrage opportunities and why investors will take as large a position as they can in arbitrage portfolios.

Perhaps the most basic principle of capital market theory is that equilibrium market prices are rational in that they rule out risk-free arbitrage opportunities. Pricing relationships that guarantee the absence of risk-free arbitrage possibilities are extremely powerful. If actual security prices allow for risk-free arbitrage, the result will be strong pressure on security prices to restore equilibrium. Only a few investors need be aware of arbitrage opportunities to bring about a large volume of trades, and these trades will bring prices back into balance.

The CAPM of the last two chapters gave us the security market line, a relationship between expected return and risk as measured by beta. The model discussed in this chapter, called the Arbitrage Pricing Theory, or APT, also stipulates a relationship between expected return and risk, but it uses different assumptions and techniques. We explore this relationship using well-diversified portfolios, showing that these portfolios are priced to satisfy the CAPM expected return-beta relationship. Because all well-diversified portfolios have to satisfy that relationship, we show that all individual securities almost certainly satisfy this same relationship. This reasoning allows the derivation of an SML relationship that avoids reliance on the unobservable, theoretical market portfolio that is central to the CAPM. Next, we show how the simple single-factor APT easily can be generalized to a richer multifactor version. Finally, we discuss the similarities and differences between the APT and the CAPM and the APT and the index model.

10.1   Arbitrage: Profits and Opportunities

A risk-free arbitrage opportunity arises when an investor can construct a **zero investment portfolio** that will yield a sure profit. A zero investment portfolio means that the investor need not use any of his or her own money. Obviously, to be able to construct a zero investment portfolio one has to be able to sell short at least one asset and use the proceeds to purchase (go long on) one or more assets. Even a small investor using borrowed money in this fashion can take a large position in such a portfolio.

An obvious case of an arbitrage opportunity arises when the law of one price is violated, as discussed in Chapter 4. When an asset is trading at different prices in two markets (and the price differential exceeds transaction costs), a simultaneous trade in the two markets can produce a sure profit (the net price differential) without any investment. One simply sells short the asset in the high-priced market and buys it in the low-priced market. The net proceeds are positive, and there is no risk because the long and short positions offset each other.

In modern markets with electronic communications and instantaneous execution, such opportunities have become rare but not extinct. The same technology that enables the market to absorb new information quickly also enables fast operators to make large profits by trading huge volumes at the instant that an arbitrage opportunity appears. This is the essence of program trading, to be discussed in Chapter 22.

From the simple case of a violation of the law of one price, let us proceed to a less obvious (yet just as profitable) arbitrage opportunity. Imagine that four stocks are traded in an economy with only four distinct, possible scenarios. The rates of return on the four stocks for each inflation-interest rate scenario appear in Table 10.1. The current prices of the stocks and rate of return statistics are shown in Table 10.2.

Eyeballing the rate of return data, there seems no clue to any arbitrage opportunity lurking in this set of investments. The expected returns, standard deviations, and correlations do not reveal any particular abnormality.

Consider, however, an equally weighted portfolio of the first three stocks (Apex, Bull, and Crush), and contrast its possible future rates of return with those of the fourth stock, Dreck.

	High Real Interest Rates		Low Real Interest Rates	
	Inflation Rate		Inflation Rate	
	High	**Low**	**High**	**Low**
Equally weighted portfolio (A, B, and C)	23.33	23.33	20.00	36.67
Dreck	15.00	23.00	15.00	36.00

TABLE 10.1   Rate of Return Projections

| | High Real Interest Rates | | Low Real Interest Rates | |
	High Inflation	Low Inflation	High Inflation	Low Inflation
Probability:	.25	.25	.25	.25
Stock				
Apex (A)	−20	20	40	60
Bull (B)	0	70	30	−20
Crush (C)	90	−20	−10	70
Dreck (D)	15	23	15	36

TABLE 10.2   Rate of Return Statistics

| Stock | Current Price | Expected Return | Standard Deviation (%) | Correlation Matrix | | | |
				A	B	C	D
A	$10	25	29.58	1.00	−.15	−.29	.68
B	$10	20	33.91	−.15	1.00	−.87	−.38
C	$10	32.5	48.15	−.29	−.87	1.00	.22
D	$10	22.25	8.58	.68	−.38	.22	1.00

This analysis reveals that in all scenarios the equally weighted portfolio will outperform Dreck. The rate of return statistics of the two alternatives are

	Mean	Standard Deviation	Correlation
Three-stock portfolio	25.83	6.40	.94
Dreck	22.25	8.58	

The two investments are not perfectly correlated; that is, they are not perfect substitutes, meaning there is no violation of the law of one price here. Nevertheless, the equally weighted portfolio will fare better under *any* circumstances; thus any investor, no matter how risk averse, can take advantage of this dominance. All that is required is for the investor to take a short position in Dreck and use the proceeds to purchase the equally weighted portfolio.[1] Let us see how it would work.

Suppose that we sell short 300,000 shares of Dreck and use the $3 million proceeds to buy 100,000 shares each of Apex, Bull, and Crush. The dollar profits in each of the four scenarios will be as follows:

---

[1]Short selling is discussed in Chapter 3.

| Stock | Dollar Investment | High Real Interest Rates | | Low Real Interest Rates | |
| | | Inflation Rate | | Inflation Rate | |
		High	Low	High	Low
Apex	$1,000,000	$-200,000	$200,000	$400,000	$600,000
Bull	1,000,000	0	700,000	300,000	-200,000
Crush	1,000,000	900,000	-200,000	-100,000	700,000
Dreck	-3,000,000	-450,000	-690,000	-450,000	-1,080,000
Portfolio	0	$250,000	$10,000	$150,000	$20,000

The first column verifies that the net investment in our portfolio is zero. Yet this portfolio yields a positive profit according to any scenario. This is a money machine. Investors will want to take an infinite position in such a portfolio because larger positions entail no risk of losses, yet yield ever growing profits. Theoretically, even a single investor would take such large positions that the market would react to the buying and selling pressure: the price of Dreck has to come down and/or the prices of Apex, Bull, and Crush have to go up. The arbitrage opportunity will be eliminated.

Concept Check

Question 1. Suppose that Dreck's price starts falling without any change in its per-share dollar payoffs. How far must the price fall before arbitrage between Dreck and the equally weighted portfolio is no longer possible? (Hint: what happens to the amount of the equally weighted portfolio that can be purchased with the proceeds of the short sale as Dreck's price falls?)

The idea that equilibrium market prices ought to be rational in the sense that prices will move to rule out arbitrage opportunities is perhaps the most fundamental concept in capital market theory. Violation of this restriction would indicate the grossest form of market irrationality.

The critical property of a risk-free arbitrage portfolio is that any investor, regardless of risk aversion or wealth, will want to take an infinite position in it so that profits will be driven to an infinite level. Because those large positions will force prices up or down until the opportunity vanishes, we can derive restrictions on security prices that satisfy the condition that no arbitrage opportunities are left in the marketplace.

There is an important difference between risk-free arbitrage and risk-vs.-return dominance arguments in support of equilibrium price relationships. A dominance argument holds that when an equilibrium price relationship is violated, many investors will make portfolio changes. Each individual investor will make a limited change, though, depending on his or her degree of risk aversion. Aggregation of these limited portfolio changes over many investors is required to create a large volume of buying and selling, which in turn restores equilibrium prices. When risk-free arbitrage opportunities exist, by contrast, each investor wants to take as large a position as possible; hence it will not take many investors to bring about the price pressures necessary to restore equilibrium. For this reason, implications for prices derived from the no-arbitrage argument are stronger than implications derived from a risk-vs.-return dominance argument.

The CAPM is an example of a dominance argument. The CAPM argues that all investors hold mean-variance efficient portfolios. If a security (or a bundle of securities) is mispriced, then investors will tilt their portfolios toward the underpriced and away from the overpriced securities. The resulting pressure on equilibrium prices results from many investors shifting their portfolios, each by a relatively small dollar amount. The assumption that a sufficiently large number of investors are mean-variance sensitive is critical, whereas the essence of the no-arbitrage condition is that even relatively few investors are enough to identify an arbitrage opportunity and then mobilize large dollar amounts to take advantage of it. Pressure on prices can result from only a few arbitrageurs.

Practitioners often use the terms "arbitrage" and "arbitrageurs" in ways other than our strict definition. "Arbitrageur" often is used to refer to a professional searching for mispriced securities in specific areas such as merger-target stocks, rather than to one who seeks strict risk-free arbitrage opportunities in the sense that no loss is possible. The search for mispriced securities rather than the more restrictive search for sure bets sometimes is called **risk arbitrage** to distinguish it from pure arbitrage.

To leap ahead, in Part VI we discuss "derivative" securities such as futures and options, where market values are completely determined by the prices of other securities or portfolios. For example, a call option on a stock has a value at maturity that is fully determined by the price of the stock. For such securities, strict risk-free arbitrage is a practical possibility, and the condition of no-arbitrage leads to exact pricing. In the case of stocks and other "primitive" securities (whose values are not determined strictly by a single asset or bundle of assets), we will have to obtain no-arbitrage conditions by appealing to diversification arguments.

10.2 *Well-Diversified Portfolios and the APT*

Stephen Ross developed the **Arbitrage Pricing Theory** (APT) in 1976.[2] As with our analysis of the CAPM, we begin with the simple version of his model, which assumes that only one systematic factor affects security returns. However, the usual discussion of the APT is concerned with the multifactor case, and we treat this richer model in Section 10.5.

Ross starts by examining a single-factor model similar in spirit to the market model introduced in Chapter 9. As in that model, uncertainty in asset returns has two sources: a common or macroeconomic factor, and a firm-specific or microeconomic

---

[2]Ross, Stephen A., "Return, Risk and Arbitrage," in Friend, I., and Bicksler, J. (editors), *Risk and Return in Finance*, Cambridge, Mass.: Ballinger, 1976.

cause. In the factor model the common factor is assumed to have zero expected value, and it is meant to measure new information concerning the macroeconomy. New information has, by definition, zero expected value. There is no need, however, to assume that the factor can be proxied by the return on a market index portfolio.

If we call F the deviation of the common factor from its expected value, β_i the sensitivity of firm i to that factor, and e_i the firm-specific disturbance, the factor model states that the actual return on firm i will equal its expected return plus a (zero expected value) random amount attributable to unanticipated economy-wide events, plus another (zero expected value) random amount attributable to firm-specific events.

We can formulate that rate of return as

$$r_i = E(r_i) + \beta_i F + e_i$$

where $E(r_i)$ is the expected return on stock i, β_i is the sensitivity of the stock to the common factor, F, and e_i is the firm-specific disturbance. All the nonsystematic returns, the e_is, are uncorrelated among themselves and uncorrelated with the factor, F.

To make the factor model more concrete, consider an example. Suppose that the macro factor, F, is taken to be the unexpected percentage change in GNP, and that the consensus is that GNP will increase by 4% this year. Suppose also that a stock's β value is 1.2. If GNP increases by only 3%, then the value of F would be -1%, representing a 1% disappointment in actual growth vs. expected growth. Given the stock's beta value, this disappointment would translate into a return on the stock that is 1.2% lower than previously expected. This macro surprise together with the firm-specific disturbance, e_i, determine the total departure of the stock's return from its originally expected value.

Well-Diversified Portfolios

Now we look at the risk of a portfolio of stocks. We first show that if a portfolio is well diversified, its firm-specific or nonfactor risk can be diversified away. Only factor (or systematic) risk remains. If we construct an n-stock portfolio with weights, w_i; $\Sigma w_i = 1$, then the rate of return on this portfolio is as follows:

$$r_P = E(r_P) + \beta_P F + e_P \tag{10.1}$$

where

$$\beta_P = \Sigma w_i \beta_i$$

is the weighted average of the β_i of the n securities. The portfolio nonsystematic component (which is uncorrelated with F) is

$$e_P = \Sigma w_i e_i$$

which also is a weighted average, in this case of the e_i of each of the n securities.

We can divide the variance of this portfolio into systematic and nonsystematic sources, as we saw in Chapter 9. The portfolio variance is

$$\sigma_P^2 = \beta_P^2 \sigma_F^2 + \sigma^2(e_P)$$

where σ_F^2 is the variance of the factor F, and $\sigma^2(e_P)$ is the nonsystematic risk of the portfolio, which is given by

$$\sigma^2(e_P) = \text{Variance}(\Sigma w_i e_i) = \Sigma w_i^2 \sigma^2(e_i)$$

Note that, in deriving the nonsystematic variance of the portfolio, we depend on the fact that the firm-specific e_is are uncorrelated and hence that the variance of the "portfolio" of nonsystematic e_is is the weighted sum of the individual nonsystematic variances (with the square of the investment proportions as weights).

If the portfolio were equally weighted, $w_i = 1/n$, then the nonsystematic variance would be

$$\sigma^2\left(e_P; w_i = \frac{1}{n}\right) = \Sigma \left(\frac{1}{n}\right)^2 \sigma^2(e_i) = \frac{1}{n}\Sigma \frac{\sigma^2(e_i)}{n} = \frac{1}{n}\overline{\sigma^2(e_i)}$$

In this case, we divide the average nonsystematic variance, $\overline{\sigma^2(e_i)}$, by n, so that when the portfolio gets large (in the sense that n is large and the portfolio remains equally weighted across all n stocks), the nonsystematic variance approaches zero.

Concept Check

Question 2. What will be the nonsystematic standard deviation of the equally weighted portfolio if the average value of $\sigma^2(e_i)$ equals .30, and (a) $n = 10$, (b) $n = 100$, (c) $n = 1,000$, and (d) $n = 10,000$. What do you conclude about the nonsystematic risk of large, diversified portfolios?

The set of portfolios for which the nonsystematic variance approaches zero as n gets large consists of more portfolios than just the equally weighted portfolio. Any portfolio for which each w_i becomes consistently smaller as n gets large (specifically where each w_i^2 approaches zero as n gets large) will satisfy the condition that the portfolio nonsystematic risk will approach zero as n gets large.

In fact, this property motivates us to define a **well-diversified portfolio** as one that is diversified over a large enough number of securities with proportions, w_i, each small enough that for practical purposes the nonsystematic variance, $\sigma^2(e_P)$, is negligible. Because the expected return of e_P is zero, if its variance also is zero, we can conclude that any realized value of e_P will be virtually zero. Rewriting equation 10.1, we conclude that for a well-diversified portfolio for all practical purposes

$$r_P = E(r_P) + \beta_P F$$

and

$$\sigma_P^2 = \beta_P^2 \sigma_F^2; \quad \sigma_P = \beta_P \sigma_F$$

Large (mostly institutional) investors hold portfolios of hundreds and even thousands of securities; thus the concept of well-diversified portfolios clearly is operational in contemporary financial markets. Well-diversified portfolios, however, are not necessarily equally weighted.

As an illustration, consider a portfolio of 1,000 stocks. Let our position in the first stock be $w\%$. Let the position in the second stock be $2w\%$, the position in the third $3w\%$, and so on. In this way our largest position (in the thousandth stock) is $1,000w\%$. Can this portfolio possibly be well diversified, considering the fact that the largest position is 1,000 times the smallest position? Surprisingly, the answer is yes.

To see this, let us determine the largest weight in any one stock, in this case, the thousandth stock. The sum of the positions in all stocks must be 100%; therefore

$$w + 2w + \ldots + 1,000w = 100$$

Solving for w, we find that

$$w = .0002\%$$
$$1000w = .2\%$$

Our *largest* position amounts to only .2 of 1%. And this is very far from an equally weighted portfolio. Yet, for practical purposes this still is a well-diversified portfolio.

Betas and Expected Returns

Because nonfactor risk can be diversified away, only factor risk commands a risk premium in market equilibrium. Nonsystematic risk across firms cancels out in well-diversified portfolios, so that only the systematic risk of a security can be related to its expected returns.

The solid line in Figure 10.1, *A*, plots the return of a well-diversified portfolio with $\beta = 1$ for various realizations of the systematic factor. The expected return of portfolio *A* is 10%: this is where the solid line crosses the vertical axis. At this point the systematic factor is zero, implying no macro surprises. If the macro factor is positive, the portfolio's return exceeds its expected value; if it is negative, the portfolio's

FIGURE 10.1
Returns as a function of the systematic factor. **A,** Well-diversified portfolio, **B,** Single stock.

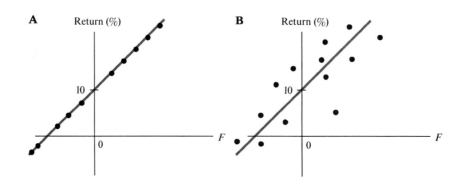

Equilibrium in Capital Markets

return falls short of its mean. The return on the portfolio is therefore

$$E(r_A) + \beta_A F = .10 + 1.0 \times F$$

Compare Figure 10.1, *A*, with Figure 10.1, *B*, which is a similar graph for a single stock with $\beta = 1$. The undiversified stock is subject to nonsystematic risk, which is seen in a scatter of points around the line. The well-diversified portfolio's return, in contrast, is determined completely by the systematic factor.

Now consider Figure 10.2, where the dashed line plots the return on another well-diversified portfolio, Portfolio *B*, with an expected return of 8% and β also equal to 1.0. Could portfolios *A* and *B* coexist with the return pattern depicted? Clearly not: no matter what the systematic factor turns out to be, portfolio *A* outperforms portfolio *B*, leading to an arbitrage opportunity.

If you sell short $1 million of *B* and buy $1 million of *A*, a zero net investment strategy, your return would be $20,000, as follows:

$(.10 + 1.0 \times F) \times$ \$1 million	(from long position in *A*)
$-(.08 + 1.0 \times F) \times$ \$1 million	(from short position in *B*)
$.02 \times$ \$1 million $= \$20,000$	(net proceeds)

You make a risk-free profit because the factor risk cancels out across the long and short positions. Moreover, the strategy requires zero net investment. You should pursue it on an indefinitely large scale until the return discrepancy between the two portfolios disappears. Portfolios with equal betas must have equal expected returns in market equilibrium, or risk-free arbitrage opportunities exist.

What about portfolios with different betas? We show now that their risk premiums must be proportional to beta. To see why, consider Figure 10.3. Suppose that the risk-free rate is 4% and that well-diversified portfolio *C*, with a beta of .5, has an expected return of 6%. Portfolio *C* plots below the line from the risk-free asset to portfolio *A*. Consider therefore a new portfolio, *D*, composed of half of portfolio *A*

FIGURE 10.2

Returns as a function of the systematic factor: an arbitrage opportunity.

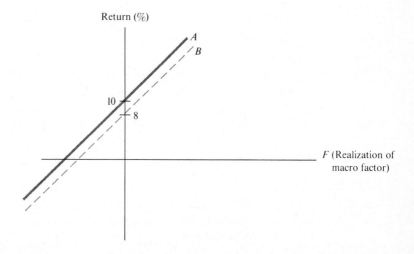

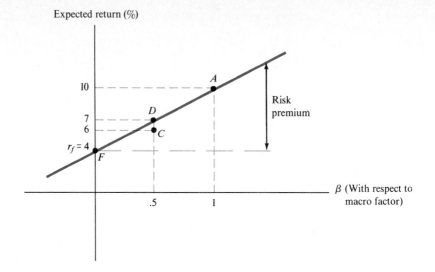

FIGURE 10.3
An arbitrage
opportunity.

Expected return (%)

10

7
6

$r_f = 4$

F

A

D

C

Risk
premium

β (With respect to
macro factor)

.5   1

and half of the risk-free asset. Portfolio D's beta will be $(\frac{1}{2} \times 0 + \frac{1}{2} \times 1.0) = .5$, and its expected return will be $(\frac{1}{2} \times 4 + \frac{1}{2} \times 10) = 7\%$. Now portfolio D has an equal beta but a greater expected return than does portfolio C. From our analysis in the previous paragraph we know that this constitutes an arbitrage opportunity.

We conclude that, to preclude arbitrage opportunities, the expected return on all well-diversified portfolios must lie on the straight line from the risk-free asset in Figure 10.3. The equation of this line will dictate the expected return on all well-diversified portfolios.

Concept Check

Question 3. Suppose that portfolio E is well diversified with a beta of $\frac{2}{3}$ and expected return of 9%. Would an arbitrage opportunity exist? If so, what would be the arbitrage opportunity?

Notice in Figure 10.3 that risk premiums are indeed proportional to portfolio betas. The risk premium is depicted by the vertical arrow, which measures the distance between the risk-free rate and the expected return on the portfolio. The risk premium is zero for $\beta = 0$, and rises in direct proportion to β.

The Security Market Line

Now consider the market portfolio as a well-diversified portfolio, and let us measure the systematic factor as the unexpected return on the market portfolio. The beta of the market portfolio is 1, since that is the beta of the market portfolio with itself.

FIGURE 10.4

The security market
line.

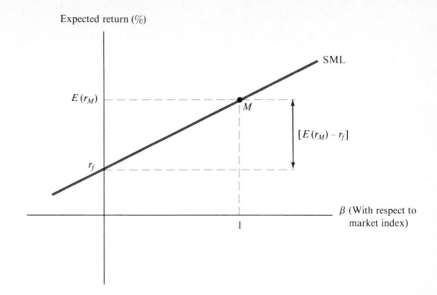

Because the market portfolio is on the line in Figure 10.3, we can use it to determine the equation describing the line. As Figure 10.4 shows, the intercept is r_f, and the slope is $E(r_M) - r_f$ [rise $= E(r_M) - r_f$; run $= 1$], implying that the equation of the line is

$$E(r_P) = r_f + [E(r_M) - r_f]\beta_P \qquad (10.2)$$

Hence, Figures 10.3 and 10.4 are identical to the SML relation of the CAPM.

We have used the no-arbitrage condition to obtain an expected return-beta relationship identical to that of the CAPM, without the restrictive assumptions of the CAPM. This suggests that despite its restrictive assumptions the main conclusion of the CAPM, namely, the SML expected return-beta relationship, is likely to be at least approximately valid.

It is worth noting that in contrast to the CAPM the APT does not require that the benchmark portfolio in the SML relationship be the true market portfolio. Any well-diversified portfolio lying on the SML of Figure 10.3 may serve as the benchmark portfolio. For example, one might define the benchmark portfolio as the well-diversified portfolio most highly correlated with whatever systematic factor is thought to affect stock returns. Accordingly, the APT has more flexibility than does the CAPM because problems associated with an unobservable market portfolio are not a concern.

In addition, the APT provides further justification for use of the index model in the practical implementation of the SML relationship. Even if the index portfolio is not a precise proxy for the true market portfolio, which is a cause of considerable concern in the context of the CAPM, we now know that if the index portfolio is sufficiently well diversified, the SML relationship should still hold true according to the APT.

So far we have demonstrated the APT relationship for well-diversified portfolios only. The CAPM expected return-beta relationship applies to single assets, as well as to portfolios. In the next section we generalize the APT result one step further.

10.3 Individual Assets and the APT

We have demonstrated that, if arbitrage opportunities using well-diversified portfolios are to be ruled out, each portfolio's expected excess return must be proportional to its beta. For any two well-diversified portfolios P and Q, this can be written as

$$\frac{E(r_P) - r_f}{\beta_P} = \frac{E(r_Q) - r_f}{\beta_Q} \tag{10.3}$$

The question is whether this relationship tells us anything about the expected rates of return on the component stocks. The answer is that if this relationship is to be satisfied by all well-diversified portfolios, it almost surely must be satisfied by all individual securities, although the proof of this proposition is somewhat difficult. We note at the outset that, intuitively, we must prove simply that nonsystematic risk does not matter for security returns. The expected return-beta relationship that holds for well-diversified portfolios also must hold for individual securities.

First, we show that if individual securities satisfy equation 10.3, so will all portfolios. If for any two stocks, i and j, the same relationship holds exactly, that is,

$$\frac{E(r_i) - r_f}{\beta_i} = \frac{E(r_j) - r_f}{\beta_j} = K$$

where K is a constant for all securities, then by cross-multiplying, we can write, for any security, i,

$$E(r_i) = r_f + \beta_i K$$

Therefore for any portfolio P with security weights w_i we have

$$E(r_P) = \sum w_i E(r_i) = r_f \sum w_i + K \sum w_i \beta_i$$

Because $\Sigma w_i = 1$ and $\beta_P = \Sigma w_i \beta_i$, we have

$$E(r_P) = r_f + \beta_P K$$

Thus for all portfolios,

$$\frac{E(r_P) - r_f}{\beta_P} = K$$

and since all portfolios have the same K,

$$\frac{E(r_P) - r_f}{\beta_P} = \frac{E(r_Q) - r_f}{\beta_Q}$$

In other words, if the expected return-beta relationship holds for all single assets, then it will hold for all portfolios.

Concept Check

Question 4. Confirm the property expressed in equation 10.3 with a simple numerical example. Suppose that portfolio P has an expected return of 10%, and β of .5, whereas portfolio Q has an expected return of 15% and β of 1. The risk-free rate, r_f, is 5%.
a. Find K for these portfolios, and confirm that they are equal.
b. Find K for an equally weighted portfolio of P and $Q,$ and show that it equals K for each individual security.

Thus, to satisfy the no-arbitrage condition for well-diversified portfolios, equation 10.3, it is sufficient that all securities individually satisfy that condition. Now we show that it also is necessary that all securities satisfy the condition. To avoid extensive mathematics, we will satisfy ourselves with a less rigorous argument.

First, as we have shown, when the expected return-beta relationship holds for all single assets, it also holds for any pair of well-diversified portfolios. Suppose that this relationship is violated for all single assets. Now create a pair of well-diversified portfolios from these assets. What are the chances that, in spite of the fact that for any two single assets this relationship

$$\frac{E(r_i) - r_f}{\beta_i} = \frac{E(r_j) - r_f}{\beta_j}$$

does not hold, the relationship *will* hold for the well-diversified portfolios as follows:

$$\frac{E(r_P) - r_f}{\beta_P} = \frac{E(r_Q) - r_f}{\beta_Q}$$

The chances are small, but it is possible that the relationships among the single securities are violated in offsetting ways so that somehow it holds for the pair of well-diversified portfolios.

Now construct yet another well-diversified portfolio. What are the chances that the violation of the relationships for single securities are such that the third portfolio also will fulfill the no-arbitrage expected return-beta relationship? Obviously, the chances are smaller still. But the relationship is possible. Continue with a fourth well-diversified portfolio, and so on. If the no-arbitrage expected return-beta relationship has to hold for infinitely many different, well-diversified portfolios, it must be virtually certain that the relationship holds for all individual securities.

We use the term "virtually certain" advisedly because we must distinguish this conclusion from the statement that all securities surely fulfill this relationship. The reason we cannot make the latter statement has to do with a property of well-diversified portfolios.

Recall that for a portfolio to qualify as well diversified it has to have very small positions in all securities. If, for example, only one security violates the expected return-beta relationship, then the effect of this violation for a well-diversified portfolio will be too small to be of importance for any practical purpose, and meaningful arbitrage opportunities will not arise. But if many securities violate the expected return-beta relationship, the relationship will no longer hold for well-diversified portfolios, and arbitrage opportunities will be available.

Consequently, we conclude that imposing the no-arbitrage condition on a single-factor security market implies maintenance of the expected return-beta relationship for all well-diversified portfolios and for all but, possibly, a *small* number of individual securities.

The APT serves many of the same functions as the CAPM. It gives us a benchmark for fair rates of return that can be used for capital budgeting, security evaluation, or investment performance evaluation. Moreover, the APT highlights the crucial distinction between nondiversifiable risk (factor risk) that requires a reward in the form of a risk premium and diversifiable risk that does not.

10.4 *The APT and the CAPM*

The APT is an extremely appealing model. It depends on the assumption that a rational equilibrium in capital markets precludes arbitrage opportunities. A violation of the APT's pricing relationships will cause extremely strong pressure to restore them even if only a limited number of investors become aware of the disequilibrium.

Furthermore, the APT yields an expected return-beta relationship using a well-diversified portfolio that practically can be constructed from a large number of securities. In contrast, the CAPM is derived assuming an inherently unobservable "market" portfolio.

In spite of these appealing differences, the APT does not fully dominate the CAPM. The CAPM provides an unequivocal statement on the expected return-beta relationship for all assets, whereas the APT implies that this relationship holds for all but perhaps a small number of securities. This is an important difference, yet it is fruitless to pursue because the CAPM is not a readily testable model in the first place. A more productive comparison is between the APT and the index model.

Recall that the index model relies on the assumptions of the CAPM with additional assumptions that: (1) a specified market index is virtually perfectly correlated with the (unobservable) theoretical market portfolio, and (2) the probability distribution of stock returns is stationary so that sample period returns can provide valid estimates of expected returns and variances.

The implication of the index model is that the market index portfolio is efficient and that the expected return-beta relationship holds for all assets. The assumption that the probability distribution of the security returns is stationary and the observability of the index make it possible to test the efficiency of the index and the expected return-beta relationship. The arguments leading from the assumptions to these implications rely on mean-variance efficiency; that is, if any security violates the expected beta relationship, then all investors (each relatively small) will tilt their portfolios so that their combined overall pressure on prices will restore an equilibrium that satisfies the relationship.

In contrast, the APT uses a single-factor security market assumption and arbitrage arguments to obtain the expected return-beta relationship for well-diversified portfolios. Because it focuses on the no-arbitrage condition, without the further assumptions of the market or index model, the APT cannot rule out a violation of the expected return-beta relationship for any particular asset. For this, we need the CAPM assumptions and its dominance arguments.

10.5   A Multifactor APT

We have assumed all along that there is only one systematic factor affecting stock returns. This simplifying assumption is in fact too simplistic. It is easy to think of several factors that might affect stock returns: business cycles, interest rate fluctuations, inflation rates, oil prices, and so on. Presumably, exposure to any of these factors will affect a stock's perceived riskiness and appropriate expected rate of return. We can use a multifactor version of the APT to accommodate these multiple sources of risk.

Suppose that we generalize the factor model expressed in equation 10.1 to a two-factor model:

$$r_i = E(r_i) + \beta_{i1} F_1 + \beta_{i2} F_2 + e_i \tag{10.4}$$

Factor 1 might be, for example, departures of GNP growth from expectations, and factor 2 might be unanticipated inflation. Each factor has a zero expected value because each measures the surprise in the systematic variable rather than the level of the variable. Similarly, the firm-specific component of unexpected return, e_i, also has zero expected value. Extending such a two-factor model to any number of factors is straightforward.

Establishing a multifactor APT proceeds along lines very similar to those we followed in the simple one-factor case. First, we introduce the concept of a **factor portfolio,** which is a well-diversified portfolio constructed to have a beta of 1 on one of the factors and a beta of 0 on any other factor. This is an easy restriction to satisfy because we have a large number of securities to choose from, and a relatively small number of factors. Factor portfolios will serve as the benchmark portfolios for a multifactor generalization of the security market line relationship.

Suppose that the two factor portfolios, called portfolios 1 and 2, have expected returns $E(r_1) = 10\%$ and $E(r_2) = 12\%$. Suppose further that the risk-free rate is 4%. The risk premium on the first factor portfolio becomes $10\% - 4\% = 6\%$, whereas that on the second factor portfolio is $12\% - 4\% = 8\%$.

Now consider an arbitrary well-diversified portfolio, portfolio A, where beta on the first factor, $\beta_{A1} = .5$, and beta on the second factor, $\beta_{A2} = .75$. The multifactor APT states that the overall risk premium on this portfolio must equal the sum of the risk premiums required as compensation to investors for each source of systematic risk. The risk premium attributable to risk factor 1 should be the portfolio's exposure to factor 1, β_{A1}, multiplied by the risk premium earned on the first factor portfolio, $E(r_1) - r_f$. Therefore the portion of portfolio A's risk premium that is compensation for its exposure to the first risk factor is $\beta_{A1}[E(r_1) - r_f] = .5\,(.10 - .04) = .03$, whereas the risk premium attributable to risk factor 2 is $\beta_{A2}\,[E(r_2) - r_f] = .75\,(.12 - .04) = .06$. The total risk premium on the portfolio should be $.03 + .06 = .09$. Therefore the total return on the portfolio should be .13, or 13%:

.04	Risk-free rate
+.03	Risk premium for exposure to factor 1
+.06	Risk premium for exposure to factor 2
.13	Total expected return

To see why the expected return on the portfolio must be 13%, consider the following argument. Suppose that the expected return on portfolio A were 12% rather than 13%. This return would give rise to an arbitrage opportunity. Form a portfolio from the factor portfolios with the same betas as portfolio A. This requires weights of .5 on the first factor portfolio, .75 on the second factor portfolio, and $-.25$ on the risk-free asset. This portfolio has exactly the same factor betas as portfolio A: it has a beta of .5 on the first factor because of its .5 weight on the first factor portfolio, and a beta of .75 on the second factor.

However, in contrast to portfolio A, which has a 12% expected return, this portfolio's expected return is $(.5 \times 10) + (.75 \times 12) - (.25 \times 4) = 13\%$. A long position in this portfolio and a short position in portfolio A would yield an arbitrage profit. The total return per dollar long or short in each position would be

$.13 + .5\,F_1 + .75\,F_2$	(long position in factor portfolios)
$-(.12 + .5\,F_1 + .75\,F_2)$	(short position in portfolio A)
$.01$	

for a positive and risk-free return on a zero net investment position.

To generalize this argument, note that the factor exposure of any portfolio, P, is given by its betas, β_{P1} and β_{P2}. A competing portfolio formed from factor portfolios with weights β_{P1} in the first factor portfolio, β_{P2} in the second factor portfolio, and $1 - \beta_{P1} - \beta_{P2}$ in T-bills will have betas equal to those of portfolio P, and expected return of

$$E(r_P) = \beta_{P1}\,E(r_1) + \beta_{P2}\,E(r_2) + (1 - \beta_{P1} - \beta_{P2})\,r_f \qquad (10.5)$$
$$= r_f + \beta_{P1}\,[E(r_1) - r_f] + \beta_{P2}\,[E(r_2) - r_f]$$

Hence any well-diversified portfolio with betas β_{P1} and β_{P2} must have the return given in equation 10.5 if arbitrage opportunities are to be precluded. If you compare equations 10.2 and 10.5, you will see that equation 10.5 is simply a generalization of the one-factor SML.

Finally, the extension of the multifactor SML of equation 10.5 to individual assets is precisely the same as for the one-factor APT. Equation 10.5 cannot be satisfied by every well-diversified portfolio unless it is satisfied by virtually every security taken individually. This establishes a multifactor version of the APT. Hence the fair rate of return on any stock with $\beta_1 = .5$ and $\beta_2 = .75$ is 13%. Equation 10.5 thus represents the multifactor SML for an economy with multiple sources of risk.

Concept Check	Question 5. Find the fair rate of return on a security with $\beta_1 = .2$ and $\beta_2 = 1.4$.

One shortcoming of the multifactor APT is that it gives no guidance concerning the determination of the risk premiums on the factor portfolios. In contrast, the CAPM implies that the risk premium on the market is determined by the market's variance and the average degree of risk aversion across investors. As it turns out, the CAPM also has a multifactor generalization, sometimes called the consumer service model, to be discussed in the next chapter. This model provides some guidance concerning the risk premiums on the factor portfolios.

Summary

1. A risk-free arbitrage opportunity arises when two or more security prices enable investors to construct a zero net investment portfolio that will yield a sure profit.

2. Rational investors will want to take infinitely large positions in arbitrage portfolios regardless of their degree of risk aversion.

3. The presence of arbitrage opportunities and the resulting large volume of trades will create pressure on security prices. This pressure will continue until prices reach levels that preclude arbitrage. Only a few investors need to become aware of arbitrage opportunities to trigger this process because of the large volume of trades in which they will engage.

4. When securities are priced so that there are no risk-free arbitrage opportunities, we say that they satisfy the no-arbitrage condition. Price relationships that satisfy the no-arbitrage condition are important because we expect them to hold in real-world markets.

5. Portfolios are called "well-diversified" if they include a large number of securities and the investment proportion in each is sufficiently small. The proportion of a security in a well-diversified portfolio is small enough so that for all practical purposes a reasonable change in that security's rate of return will have a negligible effect on the portfolio rate of return.

6. In a single-factor security market, all well-diversified portfolios have to satisfy the expected return-beta relationship of the security market line to satisfy the no-arbitrage condition.

7. If all well-diversified portfolios satisfy the expected return-beta relationship, then all but a small number of securities also must satisfy this relationship.

8. The assumption of a single-factor security market made possible by the simple version of the APT, together with the no-arbitrage condition, implies the same expected return-beta relationship as does the CAPM, yet it does not require the restrictive assumptions of the CAPM and its (unobservable) market portfolio. The price of this generality is that the APT does not guarantee this relationship for all securities at all times.

9. A multifactor APT generalizes the single-factor model to accommodate several sources of systematic risk.

Key Terms

Arbitrage	Arbitrage Pricing Theory
Zero investment portfolio	Well-diversified portfolio
Risk arbitrage	Factor portfolio

Selected Readings

Stephen Ross developed the arbitrage pricing theory in two articles:

Ross, S.A. "Return, Risk and Arbitrage." In Friend, I., and Bicksler, J. (editors), *Risk and Return in Finance,* Cambridge, Mass.: Ballinger, 1976.

Ross, S.A., "Arbitrage Theory of Capital Asset Pricing," *Journal of Economic Theory,* December 1976.

Articles exploring the factors that influence common stock returns are:

Bower, D.A., Bower, R.S., and Logue, D.E., "Arbitrage Pricing and Utility Stock Returns," *Journal of Finance,* September 1984.

Chen, N.F., Roll, R., and Ross, S., "Economic Forces and the Stock Market: Testing the APT and Alternative Asset Pricing Theories," *Journal of Business,* July 1986.

Sharpe, W., "Factors in New York Stock Exchange Security Returns, 1931-1979," *Journal of Portfolio Management,* summer 1982.

Problems

1. Suppose that two factors have been identified for the U.S. economy: the growth rate of industrial production, IP, and the inflation rate, IR. IP is expected to be 4%, and IR 6%. A stock with a beta of 1 on IP and .4 on IR currently is expected to provide a rate of return of 14%. If industrial production actually grows by 5%, while the inflation rate turns out to be 7%, what is your revised estimate of the expected rate of return on the stock?

2. Suppose that there are two independent economic factors, F_1 and F_2. The risk-free rate is 7%, and all stocks have independent firm-specific components with a standard deviation of 50%. The following are well-diversified portfolios:

Portfolio	Beta on F_1	Beta on F_2	Expected Return
A	1.8	2.1	40
B	2.0	−0.5	10

What is the expected return-beta relationship in this economy?

Equilibrium in Capital Markets

3. Consider the following data for a one-factor economy. All portfolios are well diversified.

Portfolio	E(r)	Beta
A	10%	1
B	4%	0

Suppose that portfolio B is well diversified with a beta of ⅔ and expected return of 9%. Would an arbitrage opportunity exist? If so, what would be the arbitrage strategy?

4. The following is a scenario for three stocks constructed by the security analysts of Pf Inc.

Stock	Price ($)	Scenario Rate of Return (%)		
		Recession	Average	Boom
A	10	−15	20	30
B	15	25	10	−10
C	50	12	15	12

a. Construct an arbitrage portfolio using these stocks.
b. How might these prices change when equilibrium is restored? Give an example where a change in stock C's price is sufficient to restore equilibrium, assuming that the dollar payoffs to stock C remain the same.

5. Assume that both portfolios A and B are well diversified, that $E(r_A) = .10$, and $E(r_B) = .12$. If the economy has only one factor, and $\beta_A = 1$, whereas $\beta_B = 1.1$, what must be the risk-free rate?

6. Assume that stock market returns have the market index as a common factor, and that all stocks in the economy have a beta of 1 on the market index. Firm-specific returns all have a standard deviation of .30.

Suppose that an analyst studies 20 stocks, and finds that one half have an alpha of 3%, and the other half an alpha of −3%. Suppose the analyst buys $1 million of an equally weighted portfolio of the positive alpha stocks, and shorts $1 million of an equally weighted portfolio of the negative alpha stocks.

a. What is the expected profit (in dollars) and standard deviation of the analyst's profit?
b. How does your answer change if the analyst examines 50 stocks instead of 20 stocks? 100 stocks?

7. Assume that security returns are generated by the single index model

$$R_i = \alpha_i + \beta_i R_M + e_i$$

where R_i is the excess return for security i, and R_M is the market's excess return. Suppose also that there are three securities A, B, and C characterized by the following data:

Security	β_i	$E(R_i)$	$\sigma^2(e_i)$
A	.8	.10	.05
B	1.0	.12	.01
C	1.2	.14	.10

a. If $\sigma_M^2 = .04$, calculate the variance of returns of securities A, B, and C.

b. Now assume that there are an infinite number of assets with return characteristics identical to those of A, B, and C respectively. If one forms a well-diversified portfolio of type A securities, what will be the mean and variance of the portfolio's excess returns? What about portfolios composed only of type B or C stocks?

c. Is there an arbitrage opportunity in this market? What is it? Analyze the opportunity graphically.

8. The SML relationship states that the expected risk premium on a security in a one-factor model must be directly proportional to the security's beta. Suppose that this were not the case. For example, suppose that expected return rises more than proportionately with beta as in the figure below.

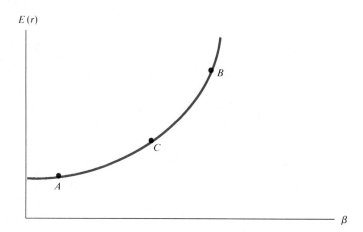

a. How could you construct an arbitrage portfolio? (Hint: Consider combinations of portfolios A and B, and compare the resultant portfolio to C.)

b. We will see in Chapter 12 that some researchers have examined the relationship between average return on diversified portfolios and the β and β^2 of those portfolios. What should they have discovered about the effect of β^2 on portfolio return?

9. If the APT is to be a useful theory, the number of systematic factors in the economy must be small. Why?

10. The APT itself does not provide guidance concerning the factors that one might expect to determine risk premiums. How should researchers decide which factors to investigate? Why, for example, is industrial production a reasonable factor to test for a risk premium?

Equilibrium in Capital Markets

CHAPTER 11

Equilibrium With Multiple Sources of Risk: The Multifactor CAPM

The CAPM and the one-factor APT describe a fundamental expected return-beta relationship. Such a simple relationship implies that investors are concerned with, and hedge, only one source of risk: uncertainty about future security prices. In the real world investors may be concerned with a number of uncertainties that affect their future consumption plans, such as the relative prices of goods and services or future investment opportunities. If it is true that investors are concerned about additional uncertainties, and if security returns are correlated with other sources of uncertainties, we would expect that investors will want to hold hedge portfolios that will reduce these uncertainties in addition to the market portfolio.

The multifactor CAPM, which is concerned with these hedging demands, describes the resulting equilibrium security returns that are consistent with such demands. The model demonstrates that individuals should be concerned with more than just the expected value and uncertainty of their wealth. They also should hedge factors that determine the future purchasing power of their wealth (relative price levels) and factors that determine the future earning power of their portfolios (such as the future level of the interest rate). Each of these additional factors requires a hedging response beyond that predicted by traditional mean-variance analysis. The result is a multifactor expected return-beta relationship that constitutes a generalized version of the CAPM.

11.1 The Multifactor CAPM

The basic form of the CAPM uses a set of simplifying assumptions to establish that the market portfolio is efficient and that the expected excess return on any security is proportional to its covariance with the market portfolio. This is the expected return-beta relationship:

$$E(r_i) - r_f = \beta_i \left[E(r_M) - r_f \right]$$

In Chapter 8 we discussed how relaxing some assumptions (particularly, that risk-free lending and borrowing is feasible, that all assets are publicly traded, and that investors have a one-period investment horizon) may affect the slope of the security market line, but preserve the simple form of the expected return-beta relationship that the expected excess return on a security is proportional to its beta. Such a simple single-variable relationship, however, assumes that investors face only *one* source of risk—namely, uncertainty about future values of securities—and that the dollar value of wealth is the only determinant of economic welfare.

Obviously, there are other sources of uncertainty that real-world investors face. Some important ones are as follows:

1. Uncertainty about future tastes
2. Uncertainty about the variety of consumer goods that will be available in the future
3. Uncertainty about future investment opportunities expressed by the means, variances, and covariances of the rates of return that can be earned on investments
4. Uncertainty about labor income
5. Uncertainty about relative prices of consumption goods
6. Uncertainty about life expectancy

We have noted that the simple version of the CAPM and its various extensions treat only uncertainty about the future value of securities. The extent to which any additional uncertainty will differentially affect security prices or returns depends on whether securities can be used to hedge these uncertainties. Although these risks may be very real to investors, as long as those risks are independent of security returns they will have no bearing on portfolio choice and therefore should leave security prices unaffected.

For example, surely there is no financial security that could reduce the uncertainties associated with future tastes or the future variety of consumer goods. In addition, although uncertain life expectancy is a factor for all investors—life insurance was created in response to it—the event of death is reasonably statistically independent across individuals. It is unlikely that returns on securities (other than life insurance policies) would be statistically dependent on the event of an individual's death. We therefore would not expect life expectancy concerns to have differential effects on security prices.

The following sources of uncertainty, however, might be expected to affect security prices:

1. Uncertainty about the future values of securities
2. Uncertainty about future investment opportunities
3. Uncertainty about future labor income
4. Uncertainty about prices of consumption goods

Robert C. Merton[1] is responsible for the development of an expanded CAPM that accounts for the potential effect of these **extra-market sources of uncertainty** on security prices. The focal point of the model is not dollar returns *per se* but the consumption and investment made possible by the individual's wealth. Investors facing a

---

[1]Merton, Robert C., "An Intertemporal Capital Asset Pricing Model," *Econometrica, 41,* 1973, and "A Reexamination of the CAPM," in Friend, I., and Bicksler, J. (editors), *Risk and Return in Finance,* New York: Ballinger Publishing, 1976.

broad list of risk factors must do more than hedge just the dollar value of their portfolios. Once we accept the existence of extra hedge demands, we must generalize the simple expected return-beta relationship.

Example: Hedging Oil-Price Risk

We can use an extremely simple example to illustrate the logic of the multifactor CAPM.

Imagine a consumer-investor, George Green, who has reached a stage in his life where he consumes each year his labor income of $40,000 plus the return on his investment portfolio of $100,000. George subscribes to the simple version of the CAPM and therefore uses as his risky investment vehicle a mutual fund that mimics the S&P 500. The rate of return on this fund, r_P, has an expected value of 15% and a standard deviation of 25%. The risk-free rate is 8%.

George's degree of risk aversion is such that he invests 50% of his wealth in the risky market-index mutual fund. His annual expenditure budget, B, has a mean and standard deviation of

$$E(B) = 40,000 + 100,000 \left[r_f + y[E(r_P) - r_f] \right]$$
$$= 40,000 + 100,000 (.08 + .5 \times .07) = \$51,500$$
$$\sigma_B = 100,000 \ y\sigma_P = 100,000 \times .5 \times .25 = \$12,500$$

Sarah Kalm (remember her?) points out that at current prices George spends $15,000 annually on energy-related items. Sarah figures that George's use of energy is inflexible; that is, he will consume the same amount of energy regardless of prices. Thus, if we denote the energy expenditure by F (for fuel), the consumption level, C, on "satisfying" goods is actually $C = B - F$.

Suppose that George is using 15,000 energy "units" annually at a current cost of $1 per unit. The percentage increase in the energy price has a zero expected value, but it is uncertain. Sarah estimates that the standard deviation of the rate of increase is 20%. Therefore the standard deviation of the dollar expenditure on energy is $15,000 \times .20 = \$3,000$. She also believes that the correlation between the rate of oil-price increase and the portfolio return is zero. (That is a somewhat unrealistic assumption, but it simplifies calculations and does not alter the principles involved.)

Using these data, George calculates that the expected value of his consumption budget (as opposed to total expenditures including energy) is

$$E(C) = E(B) - E(F) = 51,500 - 15,000$$
$$= \$36,500$$

and that the standard deviation is

$$\sigma_C = (\sigma^2_B + \sigma^2_F)^{\frac{1}{2}} = (12,500^2 + 15,000^2 \times .20^2)^{\frac{1}{2}}$$
$$= \$12,855$$

because the covariance between B and F is zero.

Since the standard deviation of the portfolio proceeds is $12,500, the marginal risk to George's consumption attributable to energy price uncertainty is measured by the increment of $355 over the standard deviation that he would bear if energy prices were certain.

Notice that George's problem is now more complex than the traditional mean-variance framework recognizes. Even if George were to select a risk-free portfolio, he would continue to face uncertainty in his consumption because of energy-price risk. George's risk-management techniques must account for energy-price uncertainty, as well as the usual risk of portfolio returns.

Sarah observes that George could lessen consumption risk to the pre-energy price uncertainty level in two ways. First, he could reduce his exposure to portfolio risk. Instead of investing 50% of his wealth in the risky mutual fund, George could decrease his position to 48.54%. At this position the standard deviation of the overall expenditure budget is $.4854 \times 100,000 \times .25 = \$12,135$, and the standard deviation of satisfying consumption is once again

$$\sigma_C = (12{,}135^2 + 3{,}000^2)^{1/2}$$
$$= \$12{,}500$$

This reduction in consumption risk to its original level comes at the expense of the risk premium on the 1.46% of the portfolio that is shifted from the risky portfolio to the risk-free asset. With a risk premium of 7% on the risky portfolio, this amounts to a loss in expected dollar consumption of $\$100,000 \times .0146 \times .07 = \$102.20$. The expected dollar expenditure on consumption items (excluding energy) becomes

$$\$40{,}000 + \$100{,}000 \, (.08 + .4854 \times .07) - \$15{,}000 = \$36{,}397.80$$

rather than $36,500.

Another way to eliminate the oil-price risk is by hedging. Sarah calls this a better method, maintaining that energy stocks are a natural hedge in this case. (Remember the Humanex Hospital example of Chapter 5.) Let us consider her argument.

Suppose that Oilex is a mutual fund that specializes in maintaining a portfolio of energy stocks that is perfectly positively correlated with oil prices. To simplify calculations, assume also that the Oilex fund has a zero beta so that oil prices are uncorrelated with security prices. Now, *under the simple CAPM hypothesis,* the zero-beta Oilex fund should have a zero risk premium; that is, we expect it to earn the risk-free rate of 8% that we have posited. Therefore, if the simple CAPM is correct and Oilex has the same expected rate of return as the risk-free asset, then investing in Oilex rather than in the risk-free asset will not affect the expected value of the consumption budget. This means that if George maintains his investment in the S&P 500 mutual fund at 50% of his wealth, his expected satisfying consumption level will remain at the original $36,500, regardless of how much he invests in Oilex.

A natural choice for the proportion invested in Oilex would be the amount that minimizes risk. Since Oilex is uncorrelated with the S&P 500 fund and perfectly correlated with oil-price increases, George can use Oilex to hedge the oil-price risk completely while maintaining the (original level of) standard deviation ($12,500) attributable to his speculative portfolio.

The hedge works as follows. On the one hand, an oil-price increase results in a loss in the consumption budget because more dollars must be spent on energy. Balancing this, however, is the fact that the rate of return on the Oilex fund increases with oil prices, thereby increasing the budget available for consumption. The net effects are offsetting, which makes the Oilex fund a perfect hedge for energy risk.

Suppose that the Oilex fund standard deviation is 22%. Recall that energy price uncertainty is only 20%, and that George will purchase 15,000 energy units at an expected price of $1 each. Because Oilex and energy prices are perfectly correlated, George fully eliminates his energy exposure by diverting $15,000 × (.20/.22) = $13,636 from T-bills to the Oilex fund. Since Oilex, by virtue of its zero beta, has the same expected rate of return as T-bills (if the CAPM is correct), George can eliminate energy risk without giving up any expected consumption. With the oil-price risk eliminated, the standard deviation of the satisfying consumption budget reverts to $12,500, as it stood before we introduced this extra source of risk.

The key point is that George has deviated from strict adherence to the tenets of traditional mean-variance analysis. His portfolio is not mean-variance efficient in terms of dollar returns. It is heavily skewed toward Oilex. But in terms of *consumption risk* (as opposed to dollar risk), George is following precisely the correct strategy. Traditional mean-variance analysis ignores this extra source of consumption risk, namely, the risk of relative prices.

The hedging strategy we show in the Oilex example is more sophisticated than the one called for in the Humanex example in Chapter 5. Humanex chose assets to hedge only the dollar rate of return on its portfolio. In this case George looks beyond dollar values to hedge extra sources of risk to his consumption. Thus he must hedge not only the dollar risk on his investment portfolio, but also the price risk of consumer goods.

| **Concept Check** | Question 1. Show that George's portfolio with the hedge position in Oilex is *not* mean-variance efficient in terms of portfolio rate of return. Do so by comparing the expected return and standard deviation of the portfolio rate of return of the hedging strategy with that of George's original unhedged position.

Question 2. What does our analysis so far suggest about the appropriateness of beta as the measure of security risk? Why is beta incomplete in this scenario? |

Hedging Demands and the CAPM

One way to summarize the essentials of George's problem and Sarah's solution is to say that George's optimal risky portfolio is not the market portfolio, contrary to the implications of the CAPM. Rather, it is a combination of two portfolios: the market portfolio and a **hedge portfolio,** in this case the energy hedge (Oilex) fund.

Note that we did not fully optimize George's portfolio because we held the proportion invested in the market index fund arbitrarily constant. Complete optimization would have included a revision of his consumption-investment plan to obtain the best investment position. We also simplified the example by assuming either zero or perfect correlations between various rates. Our point, however, is that no matter how complex the patterns of possible scenarios and how sophisticated the optimization technique, it is clear that the energy hedge portfolio will enter at least some investor portfolios.

Now consider the fact that if a significant number of investors shift their portfolios away from the market portfolio toward a specific direction such as energy stocks, the CAPM expected return-beta relationship will no longer obtain. Relative prices of securities will change to reflect this extra hedging demand for energy stocks.

Suppose, as is in fact the case, that energy is a significant component in many expenditure budgets, and that future energy prices are uncertain. Further, suppose that some combination of securities can be selected for a portfolio so as to maximize the portfolio's correlation with energy-price changes. This is the portfolio that will be the hedge portfolio in which many investors, to varying degrees, will take long positions to hedge energy-price risk. This extra demand (in excess of that predicted by the simple, single source of risk CAPM) will drive up the prices of the securities in the hedge portfolio, thereby driving down their expected rates of return. In the case of Oilex such extra **hedging demand** would force its rate of return below the risk-free rate despite its (assumed) zero beta. The simple CAPM expected return-beta relationship would have to be generalized to account for the effects of this extra source of hedging demand.

We have said that the chosen hedge portfolio will be the portfolio with the maximum correlation with the source of risk it is designed to hedge. The demand for this hedge portfolio will exceed the demand predicted by the CAPM, which ignores risk sources other than the variance of the portfolio itself. The excess demand for a portfolio that hedges an extra source of uncertainty will depend on the aggregate desire of consumer-investors to hedge this source of uncertainty, and the effectiveness of the (most effective) hedge portfolio in hedging this source of uncertainty.

The equilibrium risk premium on this portfolio will be denoted $E(r_H) - r_f$, where $E(r_H)$ is the expected return on the hedge portfolio. Practically speaking, there is no way to predict the magnitude of this risk premium without information regarding the exact preferences of all investors for all consumer goods in all future periods. All we can say is that the risk premium is smaller than the simple CAPM would predict for this portfolio when it implies that all investors ignore the extra source of risk. We are left with the result that hedge portfolios carry risk premiums that we have to assess empirically.

Concept Check

Question 3. Consider a security whose rate of return is negatively correlated with energy prices. How will the demand for this security compare with the single source of risk model? How will its expected rate of return compare to that predicted by the simple CAPM?

Extra hedging demands require generalizing the CAPM into a multifactor model. With K extra sources of risk, let $E(r_{Hk}) - r_f$ denote the risk premium on the kth hedge portfolio, and call β_{ik} the sensitivity of stock i to the kth source of extra risk. Then the risk premium on individual assets and portfolios is determined by a multifactor expected return-beta relationship:

$$E(r_i) - r_f = \beta_{iM}[E(r_M) - r_f] + \beta_{i1}[E(r_{H1}) - r_f] + \ldots + \beta_{ik}[E(r_{Hk}) - r_f] \quad (11.1)$$

$$= \beta_{iM}[E(r_M) - r_f] + \sum_{k=1}^{K} \beta_{ik}[E(r_{Hk}) - r_f]$$

Note that equation 11.1 is no more than a multifactor generalization of the one-factor security market line, which we explore further later in this chapter. Just as we can estimate beta in the traditional index model using a simple regression (the security characteristic line), we can measure the multiple "betas" in this extended model in a multiple regression that allows for several explanatory or systematic factors. Instead of regressing security returns on just market index returns, we also include, as explanatory variables, returns on those portfolios most highly correlated with each extra source of risk. These portfolios serve as indices for the extra-market risk factors.

Suppose that there exists a security, j, that has no hedge value at all, in that it is uncorrelated with all extra-market sources of risk. In that case all the β_{jk} coefficients will be zero, and this security (and only such securities) will have a risk premium that conforms to the simple version of the CAPM.

For any other security, the beta coefficient from a simple regression on the market portfolio will differ from the correct beta coefficient in the appropriate multifactor regression equation that properly identifies all hedge portfolios. Therefore, whenever extra-market risk is empirically significant, most securities will not conform to the simple CAPM expected return-beta relationship.

Note also that the magnitude of the beta coefficient of a specific security on one of the hedge portfolios represents the "importance" of this security in the hedge portfolio. A higher beta of a security means that this security return is more sensitive to the extra source of risk that this portfolio serves to hedge.

Extra Sources of Risk

Now we can again focus our attention on the extra sources of risk and ask how we might expect them to affect security prices. Our list includes (1) uncertainty about the future investment opportunity set, (2) uncertainty about labor income, and (3) uncertainty about relative prices of consumption goods.

One example of uncertainty about the future opportunity set is the future risk-free rate of interest. Although we use the T-bill rate as the risk-free rate, in reality T-bills offer risk-free returns only for short maturities. The relevant maturity depends on personal circumstances.

For example, suppose that an investor, Kay, revises her portfolio once a month. In that case the yield-to-maturity on a 1-month bill (observed at the beginning of the 1-month holding period) is the operational risk-free rate. Because the level of this 1-

month rate will change through time, Kay knows that the investment opportunities available next month are uncertain. How does this uncertainty affect the current composition of her portfolio?

Looking ahead to the next period, Kay may believe that, compared to today, the next period is riskier. As of now, the level of the next month's risk-free rate is unknown, which compounds next-period uncertainty.

If uncertainty about the future risk-free rate increases future-period uncertainty, Kay should be looking for a hedge to offset this risk. Suppose that there exists a security whose rate of return is perfectly correlated with changes in the future T-bill rate. This correlation means that, if the T-bill rate next month increases from its current level, the hedge security will end the month with a higher than currently expected rate of return. If investors increase the proportion they invest in this hedge security, they will enter next month with more wealth than they would otherwise if T-bill rates go up, and less if rates go down.

Should investors take positive or negative positions in the hedge security? We cannot answer this question without knowing the exact nature of their preferences. The correct position in the interest rate hedge security (short or long) depends on whether an unexpected increase in the T-bill rate would be a pleasant or unpleasant surprise. For a net lender of funds, increases in interest rates are beneficial, whereas borrowers presumably do not welcome an increase. Those for whom an increase in interest rates is undesirable will take a long position in the hedge security so that any unpleasant increase in the T-bill rate will be offset by a pleasant increase in the return realized on the hedge asset. If the majority of investors turn out to be long hedgers, the resulting extra demand for the hedge asset will drive up its price, driving its expected return below that predicted by the one-factor CAPM.

The lesson to be learned? In some cases we cannot predict whether a hedge security will have more or less of a risk premium than will a security with no hedge value. This example of uncertainty differs from the energy price case. In that case the oil-price increase was unambiguously unpleasant to energy consumers, resulting in increased demand for hedge assets. In this case an increase in the T-bill rate is not necessarily good news or bad news, so we cannot know how most investors will try to offset this risk.

Another source of risk beyond portfolio return is uncertainty in labor income. The present value of future labor income is sometimes called "human capital." To compute the value of the human capital of a specific investor we would discount his expected labor income in all future periods by an appropriate discount rate. The riskier the labor income, the higher the discount rate and the less the value of this investor's human capital.

The uncertainty surrounding labor income differs across investors. Consequently, the makeup of hedge portfolios for labor income uncertainty also will differ across investors. For example, automakers are subject to different kinds of uncertainties than are physicians. Can we establish a common denominator for these hedge portfolios and thus better predict expected excess returns for securities that hedge labor income uncertainty?

To start with, we can differentiate between corporations (and their outstanding securities) on the basis of the labor intensity vs. capital intensity of their production technology. For many investors, therefore, investing in firms that are relatively labor-intensive will provide a hedge for labor income uncertainty: when wages are low, the profits of these firms will be high. Thus the expected rate of return on the stocks of these firms may be pushed downward (relative to securities of capital-intensive firms) if the majority of investors desire to hedge labor income.

Finally, let us consider price risk. General price-level uncertainty (measured by price indices such as the CPI) may cause differential demand for different-maturity fixed income securities such as bonds and mortgages. Consumers reasonably differentiate among the amount they allot to broad classes of consumption (for example, housing, food, energy, transportation, clothing, and recreation). Differential demands for shares in different industries may be the result.

Concept Check

Question 4. Consider the following regression results for stock X.

$$r_X = .01 + .7 \, (\% \text{ change in oil prices})$$

a. If I live in Louisiana, where the local economy is heavily dependent on oil industry profits, does stock X represent a useful asset to hedge my overall economic well-being? Why or why not?

b. What if I live in Boston, where most individuals and firms are energy *consumers*?

c. If energy consumers are far more numerous than energy producers, will high oil-beta stocks have higher or lower expected rates of return in market equilibrium than low oil-beta stocks?

What Is Gained by the Multifactor CAPM?

Merton's **multifactor CAPM** is a formidable theoretical construct. Consumer-investors are modeled as though they derive optimal lifetime consumption and portfolio rules when they face any number of sources of uncertainty, in addition to the uncertainty surrounding the future value of securities. The portfolio demands of these investors are in the form of desired investment proportions in "mutual funds." One of these funds is the market portfolio that hedges security price risk by diversification. The other "mutual funds" are designed to hedge each extra specific source of risk. Each "mutual fund" is a hedge portfolio designed to maximize correlation with the particular source of risk to be hedged.

We have shown that extra sources of risk do not affect all investors in the same way (and to the same degree). Therefore the positions taken in the hedge portfolios generally will not be the same for all investors. Sources of risk that are common to many investors, however, will be hedged by similar portfolios across investors. This demand will give rise to the emergence of hedge portfolios for sectors such as transportation, energy, and bond funds.

Imposing equilibrium conditions on these demands for the various portfolios gives us equation 11.1, the generalized expected return-beta relationship of the multifactor CAPM. In equation 11.1, β_{iM} and β_{ik} represent the sensitivity of security i to the portfolio best correlated with risk factor k. The "betas" are the measures of systematic risks.

FIGURE 11.1
The multifactor SML.

A   Contribution to risk premium

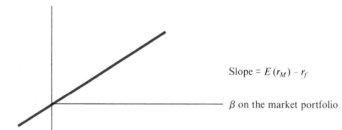

Slope = $E(r_M) - r_f$

β on the market portfolio

B   Contribution to risk premium

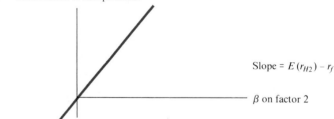

Slope = $E(r_{H2}) - r_f$

β on factor 2

C   Contribution to risk premium

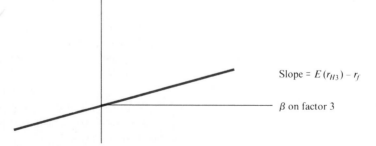

Slope = $E(r_{H3}) - r_f$

β on factor 3

We have noted already that the generalized expected return-beta relationship of the multifactor CAPM is really a multidimensional security market line (SML), as Figure 11.1 shows. The horizontal axis of the market-risk SML is the market beta of the securities, β_{iM}. The vertical axis of the market-risk SML in Figure 11.1, A, gives the part of the expected return of a security attributable to the market-risk exposure of the security as measured by the market beta. The slope of this dimension of the SML is $E(r_M) - r_f$.

The horizontal axes of the other SMLs in Figure 11.1, B and C, are the hedge betas of the securities, β_{ik}. The vertical axes of these SMLs are the increments of the security excess returns attributable to the hedge value of the securities as given by their β_{ik} coefficients. The slopes of these SMLs are $E(r_{Hk}) - r_f$.

By suggesting what types of extra hedge factors are likely to be important to investors, the multifactor CAPM provides us with a guide as to what kind of deviations from the single-source-of-risk CAPM we can expect for various securities. The model does not resolve all issues, however. We must determine which sources of risk are indeed priced in capital markets (that is, which ones command risk premiums), and what portfolios most efficiently hedge those risks. This adds further complexity on top of the CAPM's "old" drawback that we cannot observe the market portfolio.

With the simple version of the CAPM, we were able to finesse the difficulty posed by the unobservable market portfolio by assuming a single-factor security market, where some broad market index was assumed to be perfectly correlated with the factor. Further, the single-factor arbitrage pricing theory (APT) verified that in a single-factor security market the expected return-beta relationship should hold for well-diversified portfolios and should be approximately valid for individual securities. The expanded CAPM, however, directs us to a *multifactor* risk-reward trade-off.

11.2   *The APT and the Multifactor CAPM*

Just as the single-factor CAPM and APT are very similar, so are their multifactor generalizations. Let's explore the similarities.

Start with the APT, and assume that there are K factors. Let the first of our K well-diversified portfolios be a broad value-weighted market index called M, with risk premium $E(r_M) - r_f$. Let the risk premiums on the other factors be denoted $E(r_k) - r_f$ for each factor k. Then the multifactor APT states that for any security i,

$$E(r_i) - r_f = \beta_{iM}[E(r_M) - r_f] + \sum_{k=2}^{K} \beta_{ik}[E(r_k) - r_f] \qquad (11.2)$$

Now recall that the multifactor CAPM predicts that

$$E(r_i) - r_f = \beta_{iM}[E(r_M) - r_f] + \sum_{h=1}^{H} \beta_{ih}[E(r_h) - r_f] \qquad (11.3)$$

where there are H extra sources of risk and a portfolio to hedge each source. The sensitivity of the ith security to the hedge portfolio for a given source of risk is β_{ih}, and the risk premium on the hth hedge portfolio is $E(r_h) - r_f$.

If you look at equations 11.2 and 11.3, the APT and the multifactor CAPM seem identical. Are they? We can summarize the issue of the mutual validity of the APT and the multifactor CAPM as follows:

1. If you believe in the relevance of the multifactor CAPM, you expect a multifactor security market and a multifactor expected return-beta relationship. You cannot be sure which of the risk factors actually will be priced, but the relationship you expect is fully consistent with the one expected from the APT.

2. If you believe in the APT, you also expect a multifactor expected return-beta relationship. However, there is no factor that is assumed ahead of time not to be priced. The multifactor CAPM, in contrast, predicts that factors that are irrelevant to consumption uncertainty *will not* be priced. Thus an expected return-beta relationship can satisfy the APT and still be at odds with the multifactor CAPM if irrelevant factors can be shown to command risk premiums.

3. The APT implication is exact only for well-diversified portfolios. The expected return-beta relationship for less-than-well-diversified portfolios is only approximate. The CAPM and the multifactor CAPM require more restrictive assumptions and therefore make a stronger statement; that is, the expected return-beta relationship is exact for all assets. This difference applies to the single-factor APT and CAPM, as well as the multifactor versions of the theories.

Concept Check

Question 6. An example of a factor that might be identified as explaining stock returns, but not appear in the multifactor CAPM, is the return on a particular industry group such as machine tools.

  a. Why might this industry factor seem to be a useful explanatory variable in describing security returns, yet still not appear in the multifactor CAPM?

  b. Would you expect this factor to command a significant risk premium? More generally, what types of factors will not be priced?

Perhaps the most relevant question is whether the APT and the multifactor CAPM are distinguishable empirically. The answer is "Yes, in theory," but it is very doubtful whether we can prove this in the field. Our analysis suggests that the only way we can make a distinction is by identifying priced factors that should not be priced according to our understanding of the multifactor CAPM.

Empirically, to make the judgment that a priced factor is irrelevant to future consumption uncertainty seems next to impossible. Of course, if we find that one of the priced factors is the number of shooting stars per month, we would tend to reject it as inconsistent with the multifactor CAPM.

On the other hand, consider a factor such as industrial production. On the surface it would appear that uncertainty about future industrial production in and of itself is not an item affecting future consumption risk. It is conceivable, however, that industrial production is a proxy for the business cycle, or for the strength of manufacturing firms relative to service firms, which are more labor intensive. The factor in some way may be related to future labor income uncertainty. More generally, seemingly irrelevant factors may appear to command risk premiums if they indirectly proxy for relevant sources of risk.

The chance that we will get an empirical verdict that the APT is valid, but at the same time that the multifactor CAPM is not, is quite remote.

Summary

1. Investors are concerned with a host of extra-market sources of uncertainty pertaining to future consumption. These concerns give rise to demands for securities that hedge these extra uncertainties.

2. In order to hedge an extra-market source of uncertainty, a portfolio of securities must be correlated with this uncertainty.

3. Extra hedging demand will be reflected in security prices if many investors use similar hedge portfolios. Reasonable sources of hedging demands might revolve around the following extra-market sources of uncertainty:
   a. Uncertainty about future investment opportunities
   b. Uncertainty about future labor income
   c. Uncertainty about future relative prices of consumption goods

4. Investors will hold a number of additional portfolios to hedge extra sources of relevant uncertainty in addition to their position in the market portfolio (to hedge security price uncertainty by diversification). Each hedge portfolio is designed to maximize its correlation with one of the relevant sources of uncertainty.

5. With the extra hedging demands, equilibrium security returns will satisfy the multifactor expected return-beta relationship,

$$E(r_i) - r_f = \beta_{iM} \left[E(r_M) - r_f \right] + \sum_{k=1}^{K} \beta_{ik} \left[E(r_{Hk}) - r_f \right]$$

where the last term is the sum of the incremental risk premiums resulting from the hedge value of the security.

6. The multifactor CAPM does not explicitly predict which hedge portfolios are relevant. Any portfolio that can hedge a source of consumption uncertainty is a candidate. But a nonzero incremental risk premium will arise only if there is an aggregate desire to hedge this uncertainty *and* an effective hedge portfolio can be constructed.

7. The multifactor CAPM and the APT arrive at identical expressions for security returns. The first difference between the two models is the one we know already; that is, the APT need hold only for well-diversified portfolios, whereas the multifactor CAPM holds for all assets. This difference reflects the cost of replacing the set of simplifying assumptions of the CAPM with one no-arbitrage condition.

8. Neither the APT nor the multifactor CAPM predict the magnitude of risk premiums of priced factors. Further, the APT does not preclude the pricing of any factor. Thus the APT is "less discriminating" than the multifactor CAPM, which, at least in theory, does not price factors that are unrelated to future consumption risk.

9. Empirically, we do not expect to be able to distinguish the multifactor versions of the CAPM and the APT. The effect of a priced factor that cannot be directly related to a relevant source of consumption uncertainty may be attributable to correlation with a yet-unidentified source of consumption risk.

Key Terms

Extra-market sources of uncertainty Hedging demand
Hedge portfolio Multifactor CAPM

Selected Readings

This material is intrinsically difficult, and most readings are correspondingly complex. A good introduction is:

Merton, Robert C., "A Reexamination of the CAPM," in Friend, I., and Bicksler, J. (editors), *Risk and Return in Finance,* New York: Ballinger Publishing, 1976.

A related model based explicitly on consumption uncertainty that is a useful counterpoint to Merton's treatment of the subject is:

Breeden, Douglas, "An Intertemporal Asset Pricing Model with Stochastic Consumption and Investment Opportunities," *Journal of Financial Economics, 7,* 1979.

More advanced treatments of multifactor equilibrium models are:

Merton, Robert C., "An Intertemporal Capital Asset Pricing Model," *Econometrica, 41,* 1973.

Cox, John C., Ingersoll, Jonathan E., and Ross, Stephen A., "An Intertemporal Asset Pricing Model with Rational Expectations," *Econometrica, 53,* 1985.

Problems

1. The total annual income of Don and Linda Miller is expected to be $180,000. The market value of their portfolio is $600,000, of which 40% is invested in a money market fund yielding a virtually risk-free rate of 7%. The balance is invested in a market index fund. The market index risk premium is 9% and has a standard deviation of 25%.

   It occurs to Don and Linda (D&L) that their labor income has become significantly risky. They estimate its standard deviation to be 10%.

   Assume that D&L's labor income is uncorrelated with the market portfolio, and that there exists a hedge portfolio with a standard deviation of 20%. The hedge portfolio is perfectly *negatively* correlated with D&L's labor income and is uncorrelated with the market portfolio.

   a. What is D&L's expected labor income (in dollars)? What is the standard deviation of this income?

   b. What would be the standard deviation of total income if their labor income were risk-free?

   c. How much money should be shifted from the market index fund into the money market fund to lower total risk to the level in question b? What would be D&L's expected annual income in this case?

d. If instead the funds were shifted from the money market fund to the hedge portfolio, how much should be shifted to completely eliminate labor income risk? If the (zero-beta) hedge portfolio were expected to earn the risk-free rate of 7%, what would be expected annual income?

e. What risk premium on the hedge portfolio would make D&L indifferent between reducing risk using the hedge portfolio compared with shifting from the market index into the money market fund? (Hint: the risk premium that results in indifference will be negative. Why?)

f. What types of securities might make up the labor income hedge portfolio? What is the likely correlation between such a portfolio and the market index?

g. How might D&L's ages affect their investment strategy?

2. Consider the following regression results for stock X.

$$r_X = .01 + 1.7(\text{inflation})$$

a. If I am retired and live on my pension, which provides a fixed number of dollars each month, does stock X represent a useful asset to hedge my overall economic well-being? Why or why not?

b. What if I am a gold producer, and I am aware that gold prices increase when inflation accelerates?

c. If retirees are far more numerous than gold producers in this economy, will high inflation–beta stocks have higher or lower expected rates of return in market equilibrium than low inflation–beta stocks?

CHAPTER 12

Empirical Evidence on Security Returns

Before we discuss what sort of evidence supports the implications of the CAPM and APT, we must note that these implications already have been accepted in widely varying applications. Consider the following:

1. Many professional portfolio managers use the expected return-beta relationship of security returns. Furthermore, many firms rate the performance of portfolio managers according to the reward-to-variability ratios they maintain and the average rates of return they realize relative to the SML.
2. Regulatory commissions use the expected return-beta relationship along with forecasts of the market index return as one factor in determining the cost of capital for regulated firms.
3. Court rulings on torts cases sometimes use the expected return-beta relationship to determine discount rates to evaluate claims of lost future income.
4. Many firms use the SML to obtain a benchmark hurdle rate for capital budgeting decisions.

These practices show that the financial community has passed a favorable judgment on the CAPM and the APT, if only implicitly.

In this chapter we consider the evidence along more explicit and rigorous lines. The first part of the chapter presents the methodology that has been deployed in testing the single-factor CAPM and APT and assesses the results. The second part of the chapter provides an overview of current efforts to establish the validity of the multifactor versions of the CAPM and APT.

Why lump together empirical works on the CAPM and APT? The CAPM is a theoretical construct that predicts *expected* rates of return on assets, relative to a market portfolio of all risky assets. It is difficult to test these predictions empirically because both expected returns and the exact market portfolio are unobservable (see Chapter 9). To overcome this difficulty, a single-factor or multifactor capital market usually is postulated, where a broad-based market index portfolio (such as the S&P 500) is assumed to represent the factor, or one of the factors. Furthermore, to obtain more reliable statistics, most tests have been conducted on the rates of return on well-diversified portfolios rather than on individual securities. For both of those reasons tests that have been directed at the CAPM actually have been more suitable to establish the validity of the APT. We will see that it is more useful to distinguish the empirical work on the basis of the factor structure that is assumed or estimated, rather than to distinguish between tests of the CAPM and the APT.

12.1 *The Index Model and the Single-Factor APT*

The Expected Return-Beta Relationship

Recall that if the expected return-beta relationship holds with respect to an observable ex ante efficient index, M, the expected rate of return on any security i is

$$E(r_i) = r_f + \beta_i[E(r_M) - r_f] \tag{12.1}$$

where β_i is defined as $Cov(r_i, r_M)/\sigma_M^2$.

This is the most commonly tested implication of the CAPM. Early simple tests followed three basic steps: establishing sample data, estimating the SCL (security characteristic line), and estimating the SML (security market line).

Setting up the sample data

Determine a sample period of, for example, 60 monthly holding periods (5 years). For each of the 60 holding periods collect the rates of return on 100 stocks, a market portfolio proxy (the S&P 500), and 1-month (risk-free) T-bills. Your data thus consist of

r_{it} $i = 1, \ldots, 100$, and $t = 1, \ldots, 60$:
     Returns on the 100 stocks over the 60-month sample period

r_{Mt} Returns on the S&P 500 index over the sample period; and

r_{ft} Risk-free rate each month

This constitutes a table of $102 \times 60 = 6{,}120$ rates of return.

Estimating the SCL

View equation 12.1 as a security characteristic line (SCL) as in Chapter 9. For each stock, i, you estimate the beta coefficient as the slope of a **first-pass regression** equation. (The terminology *first-pass* regression is due to the fact that the estimated coefficients will be used as input into a **second-pass regression.**)

$$r_{it} - r_{ft} = a_i + b_i(r_{Mt} - r_{ft}) + e_{it}$$

You will use the following statistics in later analysis:

$\overline{r_i - r_f}$ = Sample averages (over the 60 observations) of the excess return on each of the 100 stocks

b_i = Sample estimates of the beta coefficients of each of the 100 stocks

$\overline{r_M - r_f}$ = Sample average of the excess return of the market index

$\sigma^2(e_i)$ = Estimates of the variance of the residuals for each of the 100 stocks

The sample average excess returns on each stock and the market porfolio are taken as estimates of expected excess returns, and the values of b_i are estimates of the true beta coefficients for the 100 stocks during the sample period. The $\sigma^2(e_i)$ estimates the nonsystematic risk of each of the 100 stocks.

Estimating the SML

Now view equation 12.1 as a security market line (SML) with 100 observations for the stocks in your sample. You can estimate γ_0 and γ_1 in the following second-pass regression equation with b_i from the first pass as the independent variable:

$$\overline{r_i - r_f} = \gamma_0 + \gamma_1 b_i \qquad i = 1, \ldots , 100 \qquad (12.2)$$

Compare equations 12.1 and 12.2; you should conclude that if the CAPM is valid, then γ_0 and γ_1 must satisfy

$$\gamma_0 = 0 \qquad \gamma_1 = \overline{r_M - r_f}$$

In fact, however, you can go a step further and argue that the key property of the expected return-beta relationship described by the SML is that the expected excess return on securities is determined *only* by the systematic risk (as measured by beta) and should be independent of the nonsystematic risk, as measured by the variance of the residuals, $\sigma^2(e_i)$, which also were estimated from the first-pass regression. These estimates can be added as a variable in equation 12.2 of an expanded SML that now looks like this:

$$\overline{r_i - r_f} = \gamma_0 + \gamma_1 b_i + \gamma_2 \sigma^2(e_i) \qquad (12.3)$$

This *second-pass* regression is estimated with the hypotheses:

$$\gamma_0 = 0 \qquad \gamma_1 = \overline{r_M - r_f} \qquad \gamma_2 = 0$$

To the disappointment of early researchers, tests following this pattern consistently failed to support the index model and the results from such a test (first conducted by John Lintner[1] and later replicated by Merton Miller and Myron Scholes[2])

---

[1]Lintner, John, "Security Prices, Risk and Maximal Gains from Diversification," *Journal of Finance, 20*, December 1965.

[2]Miller, Merton H., and Scholes, Myron, "Rate of Return in Relation to Risk: A Reexamination of Some Recent Findings," in Jensen, Michael C. (editor), *Studies in the Theory of Capital Markets*, New York: Praeger Publishers, 1972.

using annual data on 631 NYSE stocks for 10 years, 1954 to 1963, are

Coefficient:	$\gamma_0 = .127$	$\gamma_1 = .042$	$\gamma_2 = .310$
Standard error:	.006	.006	.026
Sample average:		$\overline{r_M - r_f} = .165$	

Such results are totally inconsistent with the CAPM. First, the estimated SML is "too flat"; that is, the γ_1 coefficient is too small. The slope should be $\overline{r_M - r_f} = .165$ (16.5% per year), but it is estimated at only .042. The difference, .122, is about 20 times the standard error of the estimate, .006, which means that the measured slope of the SML is lower than it should be by a statistically significant margin. At the same time, the intercept of the estimated SML, γ_0, which is hypothesized to be zero, in fact equals .127, which is more than 20 times its standard error of .006.

Concept Check

Question 2.
a. What is the implication of the empirical SML being "too flat"?
b. Do high- or low-beta stocks tend to outperform the predictions of the CAPM?

Second, and more damaging to the CAPM, is that nonsystematic risk seems to predict expected excess returns. The coefficient of the variable that measures nonsystematic risk, $\sigma^2(e_i)$, is .310, more than 10 times its standard error of .026.

There are, however, two principal flaws in these tests. The first is that statistical variation in stock returns introduces **measurement error** into the beta estimates, the b coefficients from the first-pass regressions. Using these estimates in place of the true beta coefficients in the estimation of the second-pass regression for the SML biases the estimates in the direction that we have observed: the measurement errors in the beta coefficients will lead to an estimate of the SML that is too flat and that has a positive (rather than zero) intercept.

The second problem results from the fact that the variance of the residuals is correlated with the beta coefficients of stocks. Stocks that have high betas tend also to have high nonsystematic risk. Add this effect to the measurement problem, and the coefficient of nonsystematic risk, γ_2, in the second-pass regression will be upward biased.

Indeed, a well-controlled simulation test by Miller and Scholes[2] confirms these arguments. In this test a random number generator simulated rates of return with covariances similar to observed ones. The average returns were made to agree exactly with the CAPM expected return-beta relationship. Miller and Scholes then used these randomly generated rates of return in the tests we have described as if they were observed from a sample of stock returns. The results of this "simulated" test were virtually identical to those reached using real data, despite the fact that the simulated returns were *constructed* to obey the SML, that is, the true γ coefficients were $\gamma_0 = 0$, $\gamma_1 = .165 = \overline{r_M - r_f}$, and $\gamma_2 = 0$.

This postmortem of the early test gets us back to square one. We can explain away the disappointing test results, but we have no positive results to support the CAPM-APT implications.

The next wave of tests was designed to overcome the measurement error problems that led to biased estimates of the SML. The innovation in these tests was to investigate the rate of return on portfolios rather than individual securities. Combining securities into portfolios diversifies away most of the firm-specific part of returns, thereby enhancing the precision of the estimates of beta and the expected rate of return of the portfolio of securities. This mitigates the statistical problems that arise from measurement error in the beta estimates.

Obviously, however, combining stocks into portfolios reduces the number of observations left for the second-pass regression. For example, suppose that we wish to group 100 stocks into portfolios of 20 stocks each. If the assumption of a single-factor market is reasonably accurate, then the residuals of the 20 stocks in each portfolio will be practically uncorrelated and hence the variance of the portfolio residual will be about one twentieth the residual variance of the average stock. Thus the portfolio beta in the first-pass regression will be estimated with far better accuracy. However, now consider the second-pass regression. With individual securities we had 100 observations to estimate the second-pass coefficients. With portfolios of 20 stocks each we are left with only five observations for the second-pass regression.

To get the best of this trade-off, we need to construct portfolios with the largest possible dispersion of beta coefficients. Other things being equal, a sample yields more accurate regression estimates the more widely spaced are the observations of the independent variables. Consider the first-pass regressions in the test of the CAPM where we estimate the relationship between the market's excess return and each stock's. If we have a sample with a great dispersion of market returns, we have a better shot at accurately estimating the effect of a change in the market return on the return of the stock. In our case, however, we have no control over the range of the market returns. But we can control the range of the independent variable of the second-pass regression, the portfolio betas. Rather than allocate 20 stocks to each portfolio randomly, we can rank portfolios by betas. Portfolio 1 will include the 20 highest-beta stocks and Portfolio 5 the 20 lowest-beta stocks. In that case a set of portfolios with small nonsystematic components, e_P, and widely spaced betas will yield reasonably powerful tests of the SML.

A study by Black, Jensen, and Scholes[3] (BJS) pioneered this method. The researchers used an elaborate method to design the sample portfolios and estimate their betas. To illustrate, let us assume that the data set consists of 500 stocks over a long sample period. We would split the sample period into three subperiods:

---

[3]Black, Fischer, Jensen, Michael C., and Scholes, Myron, "The Capital Asset Pricing Model: Some Empirical Tests," in Jensen, Michael C. (editor), *Studies in the Theory of Capital Markets,* New York: Praeger Publishers, 1972.

Subperiod I

Estimate *individual* stock betas and order them from highest to lowest beta. Form equally weighted portfolios of 50 stocks each, resulting in 10 portfolios from highest to lowest beta. This is a preparatory step for the first-pass regression.

Subperiod II

Reestimate the betas of the 10 portfolios. These estimates will be used as the true betas for the SML estimates. The errors in measuring these betas are independent of the errors in the betas used to form the portfolios. This is the first-pass regression.

Subperiod III

Use the average excess returns on the 10 portfolios from this period as estimates of the expected excess returns to regress on the betas from the previous subperiod. This is the second-pass regression.

The BJS study uses all available NYSE stock returns over the period 1931 to 1965. The number of available stocks increased from 582 in 1931 to 1,094 in 1965. The available stocks are allocated to 10 portfolios; thus portfolio size varies over the period from 58 to 110 stocks. The size and diversification of these portfolios reduces measurement error considerably.

Summary statistics for the 10 portfolios appear in Table 12.1. The betas of the 10 portfolios for the entire period (420 months) are shown in the first line of the table. They range from .4992 to 1.5614 and are fairly evenly spaced. The next two lines show the intercepts (denoted by α) of the SCL for each portfolio. These values are small, and the ratios of these values to their standard errors [the *t*-statistics, $t(\alpha)$] are less than 2.0 for 9 out of the 10 portfolios. The pattern of these alpha values, however, begins to tell the story of the test results. The alphas are negative for high-beta portfolios ($\beta > 1$) and positive for low-beta portfolios ($\beta < 1$). This is a clue that, contrary to what the SML would imply, lower beta portfolios earned consistently better risk-adjusted returns than higher beta portfolios.

TABLE 12.1 Summary of Statistics for Time Series Tests (January 1931–December 1965)

| Item* | \multicolumn{11}{c}{Portfolio Number} |
	1	2	3	4	5	6	7	8	9	10	$\bar{R}_M$
β	1.5614	1.3838	1.2483	1.1625	1.0572	0.9229	0.8531	0.7534	0.6291	0.4992	1.0000
$\hat{\alpha} \cdot 10^2$	−0.0829	−0.1938	−0.0649	−0.0167	−0.0543	0.0593	0.0462	0.0812	0.1968	0.2012	
$t(\alpha)$	−0.4274	−1.9935	−0.7597	−0.2468	−0.8869	0.7878	0.7050	1.1837	2.3126	1.8684	
$\rho(\bar{R}, \bar{R}_M)$	0.9625	0.9875	0.9882	0.9914	0.9915	0.9833	0.9851	0.9793	0.9560	0.8981	
$\rho(\bar{e}_t, \bar{e}_{t-1})$	0.0549	−0.0638	0.0366	0.0073	−0.0708	−0.1248	0.1294	0.1041	0.0444	0.0992	
$\sigma(\bar{e})$	0.0393	0.0197	0.0173	0.0137	0.0124	0.0152	0.0133	0.0139	0.0172	0.0218	
$\bar{R}$	0.0213	0.0177	0.0171	0.0163	0.0145	0.0137	0.0126	0.0115	0.0109	0.0091	0.0142
σ	0.1445	0.1248	0.1126	0.1045	0.0950	0.0836	0.0772	0.0685	0.0586	0.0495	0.0891

Modified from Fischer Black, Michael C. Jensen, and Myron Scholes, "The Capital Asset Pricing Model: Some Empirical Tests," in *Studies in the Theory of Capital Markets,* Michael C. Jensen, Ed. [Praeger Publishers, New York, 1972]. Copyright © 1972 by Praeger Publishers, Inc. Reprinted with permission.

*$\bar{R}$ = Average monthly excess returns, σ = Standard deviation of the monthly excess returns, r = Correlation coefficient. Sample size for each regression, 420.

The next two lines in Table 12.1 show the correlation coefficients of the portfolio returns with the market index, $\rho(R_P, R_M)$, and the serial correlation of the nonsystematic component, e, of the portfolios between successive periods, $\rho(e_t, e_{t-1})$. The large size and corresponding diversification of the portfolios is such that we expect returns to be highly correlated with the market index. Indeed, the correlation coefficients range from .8981 to .9915. The nonsystematic components are virtually independent from period to period: $\rho(e_t, e_{t-1})$ ranges from $-.1248$ to .1294, as we would expect from random noise.

From the last three lines of the table we note first that most of the risk of the 10 portfolios is systematic. The first of these lines shows the standard deviation of the residuals, our estimate of nonsystematic risk, $\sigma(e)$. The bottom line shows the standard deviation of the excess rate of return, σ. For the highest-beta portfolio the monthly standard deviation was 14.45% per month, of which 3.93% is nonsystematic. For the lowest-beta portfolio the standard deviation of the excess return was 4.95% per month, of which 2.18% is nonsystematic.

The next-to-last line in the table shows the average monthly excess returns for the 10 portfolios and the market (NYSE) index. The market index excess return averages 1.42% per month, and the average excess returns for the 10 portfolios range from .91% to 2.13% per month. As we should expect from the CAPM, the portfolios with betas lower than 1 earned less than the market index, and the portfolios with betas higher than 1 earned more.

Figure 12.1 shows the second-pass regression estimate of the SML for the entire period. The upper left-hand corner of Figure 12.1 reveals the disappointing result for the CAPM hypothesis. The intercept of the estimated SML, the γ_0 coefficient, is .359% per month with a standard error of only .055% (its t-statistic is 6.53), so that the intercept, which is hypothesized by the CAPM to be zero, is positive and statistically significant.

The slope of the SML is 1.08. The CAPM hypothesis is that this slope, γ_1, should equal the expected excess return on the market index. For the sample period the market index averaged 1.42% per month. The difference, $\gamma_1 - \overline{(r_M - r_f)}$, for this sample is thus $-.34\%$ per month. The estimated SML is too flat again. The standard error of the estimate of γ_1 is .052%, so the difference (.34%) is 6.54 times the standard error. Thus the results are inconsistent with the CAPM hypothesis for γ_1.

Breaking the analysis into subperiods, BJS found no better results. Figure 12.2 shows the estimated SMLs for four subperiods. The intercepts are positive and statistically significant in three out of the four subperiods. Worse even, in the 1957 to 1965 subperiod, the slope of the SML has the wrong sign.

At this point, BJS bring up the possibility that perhaps the sample results may verify the zero-beta version of the CAPM. Recall from Chapter 8 that when borrowing is restricted the CAPM expected return-beta relationship must be amended. As it turns out, all that is called for in moving to the zero-beta version of the CAPM is replacing the risk-free rate with the expected excess return on the zero-beta portfolio (that is, the efficient portfolio uncorrelated with the market portfolio).

FIGURE   12.1

The second-pass regression estimate of the security market line.

(From Fischer Black, Michael C. Jensen, and Myron Scholes, "The Capital Asset Pricing Model: Some Empirical Tests," in *Studies in the Theory of Capital Markets,* Michael C. Jensen, Ed. [Praeger Publishers, New York, 1972]. Copyright © 1972 by Praeger Publishers, Inc. Reprinted with permission.)

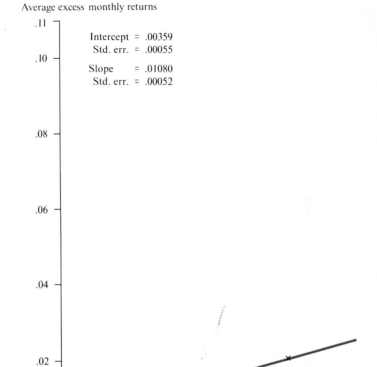

Average excess monthly returns

Intercept = .00359
Std. err. = .00055

Slope   = .01080
Std. err. = .00052

Systematic risk

FIGURE 12.2

The estimated security market lines for four subperiods.

(From Fischer Black, Michael C. Jensen, and Myron Scholes, "The Capital Asset Pricing Model: Some Empirical Tests," in *Studies in the Theory of Capital Markets,* Michael C. Jensen, Ed. [Praeger Publishers, New York, 1972]. Copyright © 1972 by Praeger Publishers, Inc. Reprinted with permission.

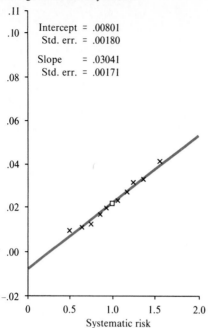

June 1931 - September 1939

Average excess monthly returns

Intercept = .00801
Std. err. = .00180

Slope   = .03041
Std. err. = .00171

Systematic risk

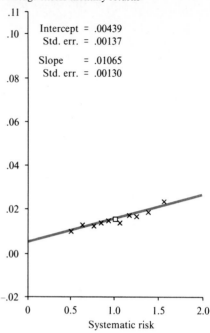

October 1939 - June 1948

Average excess monthly returns

Intercept = .00439
Std. err. = .00137

Slope   = .01065
Std. err. = .00130

Systematic risk

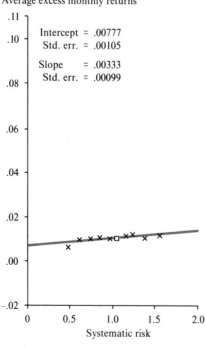

July 1948 - March 1957

Average excess monthly returns

Intercept = .00777
Std. err. = .00105

Slope   = .00333
Std. err. = .00099

Systematic risk

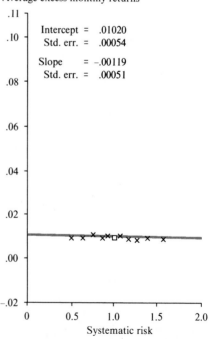

April 1957 - December 1965

Average excess monthly returns

Intercept = .01020
Std. err. = .00054

Slope   = −.00119
Std. err. = .00051

Systematic risk

The two representations of the CAPM expected return-beta relationships are as follows:

1. No restriction on risk-free investment:

$$E(r_i) - r_f = \beta_i[E(r_M) - r_f]$$

2. Restriction on risk-free investment (the zero-beta CAPM):

$$E(r_i) - E(r_{Z(M)}) = \beta_i[E(r_M) - E(r_{Z(M)})] \tag{12.4}$$

where $r_{Z(M)}$ is the rate of return on the zero-beta portfolio.

If we shift $E(r_{Z(M)})$ to the right-hand side and substract the risk-free rate from both sides, equation 12.4 takes this form:

$$E(r_i) - r_f = E(r_{Z(M)}) - r_f + \beta_i[E(r_M) - E(r_{Z(M)})] \tag{12.5}$$

If we were to test this version of the CAPM, we would hypothesize that

$$\gamma_0 = E(r_{Z(M)}) - r_f$$

$$\gamma_1 = E(r_M) - E(r_{Z(M)})$$

To conduct their test, BJS needed to estimate returns on the zero-beta portfolio from the available data. To obtain these rates, they rearranged equation 12.5 and concluded that the actual rate of return on any stock in period t (as opposed to the expected return) would be described by

$$r_{it} = r_{Zt}(1 - \beta_i) + r_{Mt}\beta_i + e_{it} \tag{12.6}$$

Using the previously estimated beta coefficient, the zero-beta rate is *estimated* from the return of each stock by

$$r_Z = (r_{it} - \beta_i r_{Mt})/(1 - \beta_i) \tag{12.7}$$

Note that the rate of return on each stock provides one estimate of the zero-beta rate. BJS use a statistically efficient technique to average these estimates across stocks and thus obtain, for each period, an efficient estimate of the zero-beta rate.

Using the time series of the estimated zero-beta rates for each subperiod, in conjunction with the market and individual stock returns, BJS examined the validity of the zero-beta version of the CAPM. Their major conclusions follow:

1. The average return of the zero-beta portfolio is significantly greater than the risk-free rate.
2. The excess rate of return on the zero-beta portfolio explains some of the deviation of the results from the simple version of the CAPM, yet the regression estimates are not fully consistent with the zero-beta version of the CAPM either.

The fact that the average return on the zero-beta portfolio exceeds the risk-free rate is consistent with the restricted borrowing models of the CAPM presented in Chapter 8. It also is consistent with BJS's finding that the empirical SML is flatter than predicted by the simple CAPM.

> **Question 3.** What should be the average return on the zero-beta portfolio in the BJS test according to the zero-beta version of the CAPM?

BJS tested the SML equation directly with negative results, with and without restrictions on risk-free lending and borrowing. They did not concern themselves with other specific implications of the CAPM, such as that expected returns are independent of nonsystematic risk or that the relationship between expected returns and beta is linear.

Fama and MacBeth[4] use the BJS methodology to verify that the observed relationship between average excess returns and beta is indeed linear and that nonsystematic risk does not explain average excess returns. Using 20 portfolios constructed according to the BJS methodology, Fama and MacBeth expand the estimation of the SML equation to include the square of the beta coefficient (to test for linearity of the relationship between returns and betas) and the estimated standard deviation of the residual (to test for the explanatory power of nonsystematic risk). For a sequence of many subperiods they estimate, for each subperiod, the equation

$$r_i = \gamma_0 + \gamma_1\beta_i + \gamma_2\beta_i^2 + \gamma_3\sigma(e_i)$$

The term γ_2 measures potential nonlinearity of return, and γ_3 measures the explanatory power of nonsystematic risk, $\sigma(e_i)$. The Fama-MacBeth results show that the beta relationship is in fact linear (γ_2 is not significantly different from zero) and that nonsystematic risk does not explain average returns (γ_3 also is insignificant). At the same time, however, the authors report that the SMLs, in general, remain too flat and have a positive significant intercept.

We can summarize these conclusions:

1. The insights that are supported by the single-factor CAPM and APT are as follows:
   a. Expected rates of return are linear and increase with beta, the measure of systematic risk.
   b. Expected rates of return are not affected by nonsystematic risk.
2. The single-variable expected return-beta relationship predicted by either the risk-free rate or the zero-beta version of the CAPM is not fully consistent with empirical observation.

Thus, although the CAPM seems *qualitatively* correct, in that β matters and $\sigma(e_i)$ does not, empirical tests do not validate its *quantitative* predictions.

---

[4]Fama, Eugene, and MacBeth, James, "Test of the Multiperiod Two Parameter Model," *Journal of Financial Economics,* March 1977.

The Efficiency of the Market Index—Roll's Critique

In 1977, while researchers were improving test methodology in an effort to conclusively endorse or reject the validity of the CAPM, Richard Roll[5] threw a monkey wrench into their machinery. In the now classic "Roll's Critique" he argues not only that the tests of the expected return-beta relationship are invalid, but also that it is doubtful that CAPM can ever be tested.

Roll's critique includes the following observations:

1. There is a single testable hypothesis associated with the CAPM: the market portfolio is mean-variance efficient.

2. All the other implications of the model, the best-known being the linear relation between expected return and beta, follow from the market portfolio's efficiency and therefore are not independently testable. There is an "if and only if" relation between the expected return-beta relationship and the efficiency of the market portfolio.

3. In any sample of observations of individual returns there will be an infinite number of ex post mean-variance efficient portfolios using the sample period returns and covariances (as opposed to the ex ante expected returns and covariances). Sample betas calculated between each such portfolio and individual assets will be exactly linearly related to sample mean returns. In other words, if betas are calculated against such portfolios, they will satisfy the SML relation exactly whether or not the true market portfolio is mean-variance efficient in an ex ante sense.

4. The CAPM is not testable unless we know the exact composition of the true market portfolio and use it in the tests. This implies that the theory is not testable unless *all* individual assets are included in the sample.

5. Using a proxy such as the S&P 500 for the market portfolio is subject to two difficulties. First, the proxy itself might be mean-variance efficient even when the true market portfolio is not. Conversely, the proxy may turn out to be inefficient, but obviously this alone implies nothing about the true market portfolio's efficiency. Furthermore, most reasonable market proxies will be very highly correlated with each other and with the true market whether or not they are mean-variance efficient. Such a high degree of correlation will make it seem that the exact composition of the market portfolio is unimportant, whereas the use of different proxies can lead to quite different conclusions. This problem is often referred to as **benchmark error,** since it refers to the use of an incorrect benchmark (market proxy) portfolio in the tests of the theory.

---

[5]Roll, Richard, "A Critique of the Asset Pricing Theory's Tests: Part I: On Past and Potential Testability of the Theory," *Journal of Financial Economics, 4,* 1977.

Roll's criticism requires us to think in terms of two contexts and three portfolios. The contexts are as follows:

1. Ex ante expectations of rates of return and covariances
2. Ex post (sample) averages of rates of return and estimates of covariances

Clearly, the ex post (realized) rates of returns are random, and their measured averages and covariances are not necessarily equal to those that were expected ex ante.

Now Roll argues that we have to worry about three types of portfolios:

1. The true (unobservable) market portfolio
2. The portfolio that happens to be ex post efficient for a given sample of realized returns
3. The portfolio that is chosen as the proxy for the market portfolio and is used to conduct the test

Roll argues that the third portfolio, the market proxy, will be highly correlated with the first two portfolios. Since we do not know the exact composition of the true market portfolio, even if the data seem to support the expected return-beta relationship, we cannot tell whether this is (a) because we have tested the tautology that the ex post efficient portfolio (2) is indeed efficient, and therefore the expected return-beta relationship appears valid, or (b) that our index portfolio is in fact close enough to the unobservable market portfolio (1), and that *this* is the reason for the empirical finding of an expected return-beta relationship. Conversely, if we find that the results indicate that the expected return-beta relationship does not hold, we cannot tell whether the tests do not confirm the theory, or, instead, that the choice of the proxy for the market portfolio is inadequate.

Roll's critique is a serious blow to the CAPM. Indeed, it led to a now famous article in *Institutional Investor* called "Is Beta Dead?" However, the problems in testing the CAPM should not obscure the value of the model. The nearby box presents what we believe is a reasonably balanced view of the controversy.

With Roll's critique of the BJS and Fama-MacBeth methodology in mind, let us reassess the test results so far and consider what alternative tests might make sense. BJS used an equally weighted portfolio of all NYSE stocks as their proxy for the market portfolio. Since this portfolio included between 582 and 1,094 stocks throughout the sample period, there is no question that their market proxy was a well-diversified portfolio. The 10 test portfolios were equally weighted portfolios of between 58 and 110 stocks, also fairly well diversified. Perhaps we can view the BJS test really as a test of the APT, which applies only to well-diversified portfolios. As tests of the CAPM, however, Roll shows that the procedures are objectionable. Roll's critique tells us that all we can say about the BJS and Fama-MacBeth tests is that they, at best, constitute an attempt to verify a zero-beta version of the APT but provide no evidence about the CAPM.

Another inference we can draw from Roll's critique is that one way to test the CAPM is to test the efficiency of a market proxy. If we were to verify empirically that a legitimate market proxy is *the* efficient portfolio, we could endorse the CAPM's validity.

This is an important, albeit confusing, point. To relate it to first principles, we need first to distinguish portfolio mean-variance efficiency from informational effi-

Beta Is Dead! Long Live Beta!

Introduction

The philosophy of natural science as expounded by Karl Popper prescribes a logicoempiricist methodology for invalidating new theoretical models of the observed world, such as those hypothesized in the applied investment field by Harry Markowitz and Bill Sharpe. Their particular paradigm-shift has resulted in a plethora of theoretical investment models, including the Capital Asset Pricing Model (CAPM). Recent papers by Richard Roll, however, have suggested that the CAPM may not be susceptible to invalidation by such methodological tests.

The above paragraph shows quite clearly that it is, in fact, possible to do several things at once. Several imposing names are dropped, lots of long words are used, and a relatively simple statement is made utterly confusing—all in the same paragraph. The next Guiness Book of Records will surely have a new entry in this category, awarded to the author of the 1980 *Institutional Investor (I.I.)* article entitled "Is Beta Dead?," who managed to keep up this kind of thing for seven pages, thereby utterly confusing hundreds of investment managers.

About Theories

Modern Portfolio Theory (MPT) developed from the work done by Harry Markowitz in 1952 on Portfolio Selection. In essence, it is based on the single observation that the proper task of the investment manager is not simply to maximize expected return, but to do so at an acceptable level of risk. If this were not so, portfolios would consist solely of managers' favorite stocks, instead of combining different stocks which, although all not equally attractive when considered individually, together offer the maximum expected return for a given level of risk.

This observation itself was not new. The originality of Markowitz's contribution lay in showing how investment risk could be measured and, hence, how mathematics could be used to select the best possible portfolio from all the different combinations of a chosen list of stocks.

There have been many refinements of the theory since. What is now commonly referred to as MPT is no longer a single theory, but several different theories or models, together with their applications. These models may be grouped into three main categories: versions of the Market Model, versions of the Capital Asset Pricing Model (CAPM), and versions of the Efficient Market Hypothesis (EMH).

The most common misconception about MPT is that these three theoretical constructs are all part of the same one and that, therefore, they stand or fall together. While some of the applications depend on two or more of the models, the individual models themselves do not depend heavily on each other. It is thus quite possible that one could be "wrong" while the others were "right."

It is, in any case, a mistake to think in terms of theories being "right" or "wrong" absolutely. All theories are "wrong" in that sense, including, for example, Einstein's Theory of Relativity.

Karl Popper (see first sentence) is a philosopher of science who has pointed out that, even if a particular theory were "right," you could never actually prove it. All you can ever hope to do is prove that it is wrong. If you have a new theory, you keep testing it in as many different ways as possible to see if it doesn't work. As long as it works fairly well, you can assume that it might be right, but you will never know for sure. A good theory is generally reckoned to be one that works quite well most of the time.

Newton's theory about the way planets and stars move was considered to be a good theory for several hundred years. Then some smart engineer invented an extra-powerful telescope with a very accurate scale, and a bored astronomer who had nothing else to do one evening noticed that the orbit of Mercury, the smallest planet around these parts, wasn't quite where it should be. Suddenly, Newton's theory wasn't so hot any more, and we all had to wait a few more years for Einstein to come along and say, "Well it's nearly right, but if you put in this extra wrinkle here . . .," and so invent Relativity.

Continued.

Unfortunately for Einstein, smart engineers and bored astronomers are two a penny these days, even allowing for inflation, and they've already noticed one or two places where his theory is a tiny bit out.

Newton's theory is still taught in schools, and is widely used in many different applications. To give a somewhat gruesome example, it is used for ranging artillery fire. The theory may not be exactly right, but it is certainly right enough to kill people. On the other hand, Einstein's theory was used to plot the flight of the Apollo spacecraft because Newton's theory wasn't good enough to provide the rigorous degree of accuracy required.

This point about a theory being useful without needing to be right was also made about the CAPM in the *I.I.* article mentioned earlier. In that article, Barr Rosenberg was quoted as saying, "While the model is false, it's not very false." All models are false in this sense; what matters is how false they are, and to what extent this affects their application.

Much Ado About Nothing Very Much

Presumably, you may say, the *Institutional Investor* article on the demise of beta was supposed to be about something—but what exactly? The story the article was based on is actually more than five years old, and is quite simple.

In 1977 Richard Roll, the noted professor at U.C.L.A., published the first of a series of academic papers showing that there is a bit of a problem with the CAPM. The problem has to do with something else Karl Popper said about theories: namely, that any new theory that someone thinks up should not be given the time of day unless it can be tested.

In the Middle Ages any young priest who wanted to get ahead would think up a new theory about how many angels could balance on the head of a pin. Karl Popper would have said that they were all wasting their time, since there was no way of testing their theories.

What Richard Roll did was to point out that the CAPM can't be tested either. His reason was that to test it you first need to get hold of "the market," and that can't be done. A lot of so-called testing had already been done using "market proxies" such as the S&P 500. Roll pointed out, quite correctly, that using different proxies gave you different answers; and that, in any case, a proxy was merely a proxy and not what

we were supposed to be testing.

The problem with using a proxy is that it is not the efficient market portfolio one would like it to be, but is an inefficient portfolio (i.e., one containing diversifiable risk), representing a subset of the market. Roll showed that one of the mathematical consequences of this was likely to be consistent errors in the betas.

It is worth pointing out that nearly everyone now agrees with this just as everyone agrees that the CAPM is clearly not true. These errors are fundamentally different from the random errors that arise from the fact that betas are estimated statistically, rather than measured directly. We might also note, en passant, that the gentlemen with calculators continue to work out Discounted Present Values, and that stocks still tend to go up and down together. The validity of EMH and the Market Model, meanwhile, remains unaffected by this controversy over CAPM.

The crucial point is this: beta is supposed to measure the market-related risk of a stock or portfolio. By using the S&P 500 index as a market proxy, we are going to get betas that actually measure S&P 500-related risk. What we were hoping to do is to separate the total risk of a stock into its diversifiable and non-diversifiable components. By using a proxy that is itself an inefficient portfolio, we run the risk of not separating the total risk into the correct proportions. The S&P 500-related beta could be bigger or smaller than the "real" beta.

The "furious controversy" that the *I.I.* article described is about how important these consistent errors in the betas are. If they are small (and there are good, though complex, reasons why this is likely to be the case), then we do not have much of a problem. If they are large, then we will have to be rather careful in those applications in which it is likely to matter.

No doubt the "furious controversy" will continue to rage in academic circles for some time yet, and when the dust settles it may well turn out that the current version of the CAPM belongs in the same basket as theories about angels and pins. More than likely, though, academics will have thought up a different version of the CAPM that can be tested. And when some subtle variant of the present CAPM is finally vindicated, it is a fairly safe bet that beta will remain (though possibly in a different manifestation) the reigning measure of investment risk.

Continued.

Is beta dead? One way to answer the question is to calculate (or buy) a few, and then watch what happens as the market goes up and down. The question then becomes fairly simply: do portfolios of high (or medium, or low) beta stocks exaggerate (or match, or dampen) market swings? Answer: yes.

The fact of the matter is that betas do work, more or less well depending mostly on how sensible we've been in calculating them. All betas are relative to one or another market proxy. According to Einstein, everything else is relative too, so this should not be too much of a problem. Naturally something's beta will change if it is measured against different market indices. It will also change if it measured against hemlines, which many experienced market men believe to be a very reliable market proxy. The point is that it has to be measured against something, and it is therefore up to the user to decide which market proxy is most appropriate.

We know that these theories are not perfectly "right," but we also know that they are not too "wrong." Using MPT can provide valuable information on the risks incurred in different investment strategies. In short, while the model is false, it's not very false, and even a model that is a bit false is a great deal better than no model at all.

From MacQueen, Jason, in Stern, Joel M., and Chew, Donald H. (editors), *The Revolution in Corporate Finance*, Oxford, England: Basil Blackwell, 1986. Originally published in *Chase Financial Quarterly*, Chase Manhattan Bank, New York. Reprinted with permission.

ciency. The concept of informational efficiency relates to the question of whether an asset or portfolio is "fairly priced." By "fairly" we mean that the price reflects all available information. For example, does the price of Digital Equipment stock reflect all available information about the earning potential of the corporation that arises from its current and expected future business plans? Chapter 13 is devoted to this concept and to the empirical issue of whether capital markets are informationally efficient.

The question of the informational efficiency of capital markets cannot be divorced from the question of mean-variance efficiency of asset portfolios, however. A central assumption of the simple CAPM is that all investors deduce the same input list from security analysis and hence construct identical efficient frontiers. Under these circumstances trade leads to the mean-variance efficiency of the market portfolio. However, this means that all investors use the same information when analyzing each asset. Therefore, according to CAPM hypothesis, all assets are informationally efficiently priced.

It is possible that capital markets are *informationally* efficient, but at the same time the CAPM is not valid and the market is not a *mean-variance* efficient portfolio. Roll, in addition to providing us with his now classic critique, realized this point and came up with a positive conclusion: studies of the performance of professionally managed portfolios that were intended to test informational efficiency also may serve as indirect tests of the CAPM. If these tests lead to the conclusion that a market proxy portfolio consistently beats all professionally managed portfolios (on a risk-adjusted basis), then we may conclude that the market proxy is mean-variance efficient and the CAPM is valid. Conversely, if a professionally managed portfolio consistently outperforms the market proxy, then either the proxy is inadequate or the CAPM is invalid.

The motivation for comparing the performance of professional portfolio managers against the market proxy portfolio is simple. Professional managers are the best qualified to choose efficient portfolios, since they spend considerable resources on selecting and revising portfolios. Yet the CAPM predicts that all their efforts will fail, that one portfolio (the market portfolio) will outperform them all. If we find that, indeed, professional managers fail to beat the market proxy, the CAPM prediction is upheld. On the other hand, if professional managers can beat the proxy, we would have to conclude that the market proxy is inadequate and/or that the CAPM must be rejected.

The evidence on the performance of professional managers relative to a market proxy is strong. Sharpe[6] pioneered this line of investigation by studying the reward-to-variability ratio of 34 mutual funds. He concludes:

> We have shown that performance can be evaluated with a simple yet theoretically meaningful measure that considers both average return and risk. This measure precludes the 'discovery' of differences in performance due solely to differences in objectives (e.g., the high average returns typically obtained by funds that consciously hold risky portfolios). However, even when performance is measured in this manner there are differences among funds; and such differences do not appear to be entirely transitory. To a major extent they can be explained by differences in expense ratios, lending support to the view that the capital market is highly efficient and that good managers concentrate on evaluating risk and providing diversification, spending little effort (and money) on the search for incorrectly priced securities. However, past performance per se also explains some of the differences. Further work is required before the significance of this result can be properly evaluated. But the burden of the proof may reasonably be placed on those who argue the traditional view—that the search for securities whose prices diverge from their intrinsic value is worth the expense required.

Sharpe records the annual rate of return that investors realized from 34 mutual funds over the 10-year period 1954 to 1963. He then measures the reward-to-variability ratio for each fund, dividing the average rate of return by the standard deviation of returns, and compares these reward-to-variability ratios to that of the Dow Jones Industrials portfolio. The results are graphed in Figure 12.3. The figure shows that only 11 out of the 34 funds outperformed the Dow Jones Industrial portfolio, which is itself far from a satisfactory proxy for the theoretically efficient market portfolio.

Today, the picture is similar. Studies following Sharpe investigated more funds, used shorter intervals (months instead of years) to estimate variables, and, most important, included a more reasonable proxy for the market portfolio, such as the S&P 500 or the NYSE index.

One example is a study by McDonald[7] that uses 123 mutual fund monthly returns over the 10-year period 1960 to 1969. The proxy for the market portfolio is the equally weighted portfolio of all NYSE stocks. Results of this study appear in Table 12.2, which shows the average reward-to-variability measure and other performance

---

[6]Sharpe, William, "Mutual Fund Performance," *Journal of Business, Supplement on Security Prices, 39,* January 1966.
[7]McDonald, John G., "Objectives and Performance of Mutual Funds, 1960-1969," *Journal of Financial and Quantitative Analysis, 9,* June 1974.

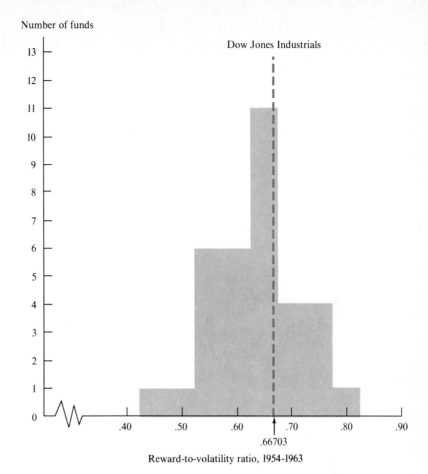

FIGURE 12.3

Mutual fund performance compared with the Dow Jones Industrials, 1954 to 1963.

(From Sharpe, William, "Mutual Fund Performance," *Journal of Business Supplement on Security Prices, 39,* January 1966; published by the University of Chicago.)

Number of funds

Dow Jones Industrials

.66703

Reward-to-volatility ratio, 1954-1963

measures for each decile of the sample of funds ranked by systematic risk (beta). The bottom line in the table shows the reward-to-variability ratio for the market proxy. None of the deciles (with 12 to 13 funds in each decile) had a better reward-to-variability ratio than the proxy. The 123-fund average ratio for the period was .112, the proxy's was .133.

Table 12.3 shows a breakdown by fund objective, from "maximum capital gains" to "income." Again, no category, on average, outperformed the proxy. In all, 84 funds out of 123 were outperformed by the NYSE equally weighted portfolio. These are typical results from studies of this nature and so is McDonald's conclusion: "For the mutual funds as a whole, the data clearly show neither significantly 'superior' nor 'inferior' performance over the decade 1960-1969."

TABLE 12.2 Systematic Risk and Performance

	Systematic Risk			Performance Measures		
Risk Decile	Beta Range	Mean Beta	Monthly Excess Return (%)	Sharpe* Measure	Treynor† Measure	Jensen‡ Measure
10	1.22-1.46	1.34	.755	.122	.563	.128
9	1.09-1.21	1.14	.672	.130	.590	.144
8	1.02-1.07	1.04	.476	.107	.458	−.003
7	.97-1.02	.99	.454	.110	.458	−.003
6	.92-.96	.94	.458	.112	.487	.023
5	.88-.92	.90	.520	.120	.578	.103
4	.82-.87	.84	.442	.118	.526	.055
3	.73-.81	.77	.461	.128	.599	.105
2	.65-.72	.69	.291	.091	.420	−.028
1	.00-.64	.49	.213	.078	.435	−.014
Sample means		.92	.477	.112	.518	.051
Market-based portfolios	—	—		.133	.510	0

Modified from McDonald, John G., "Objectives and Performance of Mutual Funds, 1960-1969," *Journal of Financial and Quantitative Analysis, 9,* June 1974.
*Reward-to-variability ratio: mean excess return divided by the standard deviation of fund return.
†Reward-to-systematic risk ratio: mean excess return divided by beta.
‡Alpha: estimated constant from least-squares regression of fund excess returns on market excess returns.

TABLE 12.3 Objectives and Performance

	Risk		Performance Measures			
Objective of Fund	Systematic Risk (Beta)	Total Variability (S.D.)	Mean Monthly Excess Return (%)	Sharpe* Measure	Treynor† Measure	Jensen‡ Measure
Maximum capital gain	1.22	5.90	.693	.117	.568	.122
Growth	1.01	4.57	.565	.124	.560	.099
Growth-income	.90	3.93	.476	.121	.529	.058
Income-growth	.86	3.80	.398	.105	.463	.004
Balanced	.68	3.05	.214	.070	.314	−.099
Income	.55	2.67	.252	.094	.458	−.002
Sample means	.92	4.17	.477	.112	.518	.051
Market-based portfolios	—	—	—	.133	.510	0
Stock market index	1.00	3.83	.510	.133	.510	0
Bond market index¶	.18	1.42	.093	.065	.516	Not available

Modified from McDonald, John G., "Objectives and Performance of Mutual Funds, 1960-1969," *Journal of Financial and Quantitative Analysis, 9,* June 1974.
*Reward-to-variability ratio: mean excess return divided by the standard deviation of fund return.
†Reward-to-volatility ratio: mean excess return divided by beta.
‡Alpha: estimated constant from least-squares regression of fund excess returns on market excess returns (Jensen's delta).
¶Proxy measure based on arithmetic means of results for Keystone B-1 and B-4 funds, with returns adjusted for .042% per month average management fee.

12.2 *Multiple Factors in Security Returns*

Research into the multifactor nature of security returns is still in its infancy. Identifying the factors and investigating the risk premiums of securities as a function of their factor loadings (betas) present greater statistical difficulties.

Two lines of inquiry are being pursued. In the first, researchers analyze security returns statistically to discern the significant factors and to construct portfolios that are highly correlated with those factors. They then estimate the average returns on these portfolios to determine whether these factors command risk premiums.

The second approach is to prespecify likely economic factors and identify portfolios that are highly correlated with these factors. The risk premiums on these portfolios are then estimated from sample average returns.

Identifying Factors From Security Returns

In exploratory factor analysis the exact number of factors is not known. Typically, a model with no factors is first fit to the data. This model assumes that asset returns are mutually uncorrelated. The goodness-of-fit measure from the model serves as a base value to express the total variability in returns. The researcher then fits a succession of factor models with increasing numbers of factors, comparing the goodness-of-fit measures of the various models. As each additional factor is added, a large improvement in the goodness-of-fit measures suggests the existence of an important underlying factor that should be included. A small improvement in the fit suggests that the additional factor may have no real significance.

Factor analysis involving a large number of securities is a difficult task. In one of the most comprehensive studies to date, Lehman and Modest[8] used 750 NYSE and Amex stocks to identify the factors. They concluded that, although the test results "may be interpreted as very weak evidence in favor of a ten factor model," the tests actually "provide very little information regarding the number of factors which underlie the APT. As the analysis suggests, the tests have little power to discriminate among models with different numbers of factors."

Paralleling the difficulty in identifying the factor structure from security returns, it has been difficult to demonstrate significant risk premiums on the **factor portfolios** that are constructed from this analysis. Although results may not be strong enough to disprove the hypothesis that the factor portfolios have insignificant risk premiums, the tests have little power to reject the hypothesis even when it is false. Reinganum and Conway[9] have developed evidence that the large number of factors identified by factor analysis techniques may be a statistical fluke. Their work uses a cross-valida-

---

[8]Lehman, Bruce, and Modest, David, "The Empirical Foundation of the Arbitrage Pricing Theory I: The Empirical Tests," New York: Graduate School of Business, Columbia University, 1985.
[9]Reinganum, Marc, and Conway, Dolores, "Cross Validation Tests of the APT," working paper, 1987.

tion technique to confirm the explanatory power of factor portfolios that are generated by factor analysis.

The cross-validation method splits the sample period rates of return into two sub-samples of odd- and even-date rates of return. Factor analysis is used to identify factor portfolios from the odd-date subsample security returns. The rates of return from the even-date subsample are then used to test the explanatory power of these factor portfolios.

Suppose that the odd-date subsample produces 10 factor portfolios. We now compute the rates of return on the 10 portfolios for all the even dates. Let us assume that the first of the portfolios is the market index portfolio, r_M. Denote the other nine factor portfolio returns by $r_{P2}, \ldots, r_{P10}$. Next, we estimate 10 regression equations for all the stocks ($i = 1, \ldots, n$) using all the even-date returns ($t = 2, 4, 6, \ldots$) in the sample.

$$(1) \qquad r_{it} = r_{ft} + \beta_{iM}(r_{Mt} - r_{ft}) + e_{i1t}$$
$$(2) \qquad r_{it} = r_{ft} + \beta_{iM}(r_{Mt} - r_{ft}) + \beta_{iP2}(r_{P2} - r_{ft}) + e_{i2t}$$

.

.

.

$$(10) \qquad r_{it} = r_{ft} + \beta_{iM}(r_{Mt} - r_{ft}) + \beta_{iP2}(r_{P2} - r_{ft}) + \beta_{iP3}(r_{P3} - r_{ft}) + \ldots$$
$$+ \beta_{iP10}(r_{P10} - r_{ft}) + e_{i10t}$$

For each of the 10 regressions we estimate the variance of the residual $\sigma^2(e_{ikt})$, $k = 1, \ldots, 10$. The cross-validation test requires each additional factor portfolio to reduce the residual variance significantly.

The 10 first-pass factor portfolios appear in an order determined by their significance in the factor analysis of the odd-date subsample. In the second-pass (even-date) cross-validation test, Reinganum and Conway found that, of the 10, only one factor portfolio (the market index) remained significant, whereas just one other was border-line significant in explaining the variability of the residuals. The results demonstrate the statistical difficulties in identifying the factors that drive stock returns.

By design, these factor analysis tests are in the spirit of the APT rather than the consumer service model. The portfolios that researchers identify statistically as factor portfolios are not constructed with regard to any economic meaning, and the chance that any of them can be identified as an obvious hedge for some prespecified risk to future consumption is small.

Tests of Multifactor Equilibrium Models With Prespecified Hedge Portfolios

The other avenue to test the multifactor equilibrium CAPM or APT is to choose portfolios that are predesigned to hedge specific risks and to test the multifactor model with these portfolios.

A full-blown test of the multifactor equilibrium model, with prespecified factors and hedge portfolios, is as yet unavailable. A test of this hypothesis requires three stages:

1. Specification of risk factors

2. Identification of hedge portfolios
3. Test of the explanatory power and risk premiums of the hedge portfolios

A major step in this direction was made by Chen, Roll, and Ross,[10] who hypothesized several possible variables that might proxy for systematic factors:

1. MP = Monthly growth rate in industrial production
2. DEI = Changes in expected inflation measured by changes in short-term (T-bill) interest rates
3. UI = Unexpected inflation defined as the difference between actual and expected inflation
4. UPR = Unexpected changes in borne risk premiums measured by the difference between the returns on corporate Baa bonds and long-term government bonds
5. UTS = Unexpected changes in the term premium measured by the difference between the returns on long- and short-term government bonds

With the identification of these potential economic factors, Chen, Roll, and Ross skip the procedure of identifying factor portfolios (the portfolios that have the highest correlation with the factors). Instead, by using the factors themselves, they implicitly assume that factor portfolios exist that are perfectly correlated with the factors. The factors are now used in a test similar to that of Fama-MacBeth.

A critical part of the methodology is the grouping of stocks into portfolios. Recall that in the single-factor tests portfolios were constructed to span a wide range of betas to enhance the power of the test. In a multifactor framework the efficient criterion for grouping is less obvious. Chen, Roll, and Ross chose to group the sample stocks into 20 portfolios by market value of outstanding equity, a variable that is known to be associated with stock returns.

They first use 5 years of monthly data to estimate the factor betas of the 20 portfolios in a first-pass regression. This is accomplished by estimating the following regressions for each portfolio:

$$r = a + \beta_M r_M + \beta_{MP} MP + \beta_{DEI} DEI + \beta_{UI} UI + \beta_{URS} URS + \beta_{UTS} UTS + e$$

where M stands for the stock market index. Chen, Roll, and Ross use as the market index both the value-weighted NYSE index (VWNY) and the equally weighted NYSE index (EWNY).

Using the 20 sets of first-pass estimates of factor betas as the independent variables, they now estimate the second-pass regression (with 20 observations, one for each portfolio):

$$r = \gamma_0 + \gamma_M \beta_M + \gamma_{MP} \beta_{MP} + \gamma_{DEI} \beta_{DEI} + \gamma_{UI} \beta_{UI} + \gamma_{URS} \beta_{URS} + \gamma_{UTS} \beta_{UTS} + e$$

where the gammas become estimates of the risk premiums on the factors.

Chen, Roll, and Ross ran this second-pass regression for every month of their

---

[10]Chen, Nai-Fu, Roll, Richard, and Ross, Stephen, "Economic Forces and the Stock Market," *Journal of Business, 59,* 1986.

TABLE 12.4 Economic Variables and Pricing (Percent per Month × 10), Multivariate Approach

A	Years	YP	MP	DEI	UI	UPR	UTS	Constant
	1958-84	4.341	13.984	−.111	−.672	7.941	−5.87	4.112
		(.538)	(3.727)	(−1.499)	(−2.052)	(2.807)	(−1.844)	(1.334)
	1958-67	.417	15.760	.014	−.133	5.584	.535	4.868
		(.032)	(2.270)	(.191)	(−.259)	(1.923)	(.240)	(1.156)
	1968-77	1.819	15.645	−.264	−1.420	14.352	−14.329	−2.544
		(.145)	(2.504)	(−3.397)	(−3.470)	(3.161)	(−2.672)	(−.464)
	1978-84	13.549	8.937	−.070	−.373	2.150	−2.941	12.541
		(.774)	(1.602)	(−.289)	(−.442)	(.279)	(−.327)	(1.911)

B	Years	MP	DEI	UI	UPR	UTS	Constant
	1958-84	13.589	−.125	−6.29	7.205	−5.211	4.124
		(3.561)	(−1.640)	(−1.979)	(2.590)	(−1.690)	(1.361)
	1958-67	13.155	.006	−.191	5.560	−.008	4.989
		(1.897)	(.092)	(−.382)	(1.935)	(−.004)	(1.271)
	1968-77	16.966	−.245	−1.353	12.717	−13.142	−1.889
		(2.638)	(−3.215)	(−3.320)	(2.852)	(−2.554)	(−.334)
	1978-84	9.383	−.140	−.221	1.679	−1.312	11.477
		(1.588)	(−.552)	(−.274)	(.221)	(−.149)	(1.747)

C	Years	EWNY	MP	DEI	UI	UPR	UTS	Constant
	1958-84	5.021	14.009	−.128	.848	.130	−5.017	6.409
		(1.218)	(3.774)	(−1.666)	(−2.541)	(2.855)	(−1.576)	(1.848)
	1958-67	6.575	14.936	−.005	−.279	5.747	−.146	7.349
		(1.199)	(2.336)	(−.060)	(−.558)	(2.070)	(−.067)	(1.591)
	1968-77	2.334	17.593	−.248	−1.501	12.512	−9.904	3.542
		(.283)	(2.715)	(−3.039)	(−3.366)	(2.758)	(−2.015)	(.558)
	1978-84	6.638	7.563	−.132	−.729	5.273	−4.993	9.164
		(.906)	(1.253)	(−.529)	(−.847)	(.663)	(−.520)	(1.245)

D	Years	VWNY	MP	DEI	UI	UPR	UTS	Constant
	1958-84	−2.403	11.756	−.123	.795	8.274	−5.905	10.713
		(−.633)	(3.054)	(−1.600)	(−2.376)	(2.972)	(−1.879)	(2.755)
	1958-67	1.359	12.394	.005	−.209	5.204	−.086	9.527
		(.277)	(1.789)	(.064)	(−.415)	(1.815)	(−.040)	(1.984)
	1968-77	−5.269	13.466	−.255	−1.421	12.897	−11.708	8.582
		(−.717)	(2.038)	(−3.237)	(−3.106)	(2.955)	(−2.299)	(1.167)
	1978-84	−3.683	8.402	−.116	.739	6.056	−5.928	15.452
		(−.491)	(1.432)	(−.458)	(−.869)	(.782)	(−.644)	(1.867)

Modified from Chen, Nai-Fu, Roll, Richard, and Ross, Stephen, "Economic Forces and the Stock Market," *Journal of Business, 59*, 1986; published by the University of Chicago.
VWNY = Return on the value-weighted NYSE index; EWNY = Return on the equally weighted NYSE index; MP = Monthly growth rate in industrial production; DEI = Change in expected inflation; UI = Unanticipated inflation; UPR = Unanticipated change in the risk premium (Baa and under return—long-term government bond return); UTS = Unanticipated change in the term structure (long-term government bond return—Treasury-bill rate); and YP = Yearly growth rate in industrial production. *t*-statistics are in parentheses.

sample period, reestimating the first-pass factor betas once every 12 months. They ran the second-pass tests in four variations. First (Table 12.4, parts *A* and *B*), they excluded the market index altogether and used two alternative measures of industrial production (*YP* based on annual growth of industrial production and *MP* based on monthly growth). Finding that *MP* is a more effective measure, they next included the two versions of the market index, *ENYSE* and *VNYSE,* one at a time (Table 12.4, parts *C* and *D*). The estimated risk premiums (the values for the parameters, γ) were averaged over all the second-pass regressions corresponding to each subperiod listed in Table 12.4.

Note in Table 12.4, parts *C* and *D,* that the two market indices *EWNY* (equally weighted index of NYSE) and *VWNY* (the value-weighted NYSE index) are not significant (their *t*-statistics of 1.218 and −.633 are less than 2 for the overall sample period and for each subperiod). Note also that the *VWNY* factor has the wrong sign in that it seems to imply a negative market-risk premium. Industrial production *(MP),* the risk premium on bonds *(UPR),* and unanticipated inflation *(UI)* are the factors that appear to have significant explanatory power.

These results are only preliminary, but they indicate that it may be possible to hedge some economic factors that affect future consumption risk with appropriate portfolios. A CAPM or APT multifactor equilibrium expected return-beta relationship may one day supersede the now widely used single-factor model.

It is very difficult to identify the portfolios that serve to hedge common sources of risk to future consumption opportunities. The two lines of research explore the data in search of such portfolios. Factor analysis techniques indicate the portfolios that may be providing hedge services. Researchers can then try to figure out what the source of risk is and how important it is. The second line of research attempts to guess the identity of economic variables that are correlated with consumption risk and determine whether they indeed explain rates of return.

Concept Check

Question 5. Compare the strategy of prespecifying the risk factor (as in Chen, Roll, and Ross's work) with that of exploratory factor analysis.

Summary

1. Although the single-factor expected return-beta relationship has not yet been confirmed by scientific standards, its use is already commonplace in economic life.

2. Early tests of the single-factor CAPM rejected the SML, finding that nonsystematic risk did explain average security returns.

3. Later tests controlling for the measurement error in beta found that nonsystematic risk does not explain portfolio returns but also that the estimated SML is too flat compared with what the CAPM would predict.

4. Roll's critique implies that the usual CAPM test is a test only of the mean-variance efficiency of a prespecified market proxy and therefore that tests of the linearity of the expected return-beta relationship do not bear on the validity of the model.

5. Tests of the mean-variance efficiency of professionally managed portfolios against the benchmark of a prespecified market index conform with Roll's critique in that they provide evidence of the efficiency of the prespecific market index.

6. Empirical evidence suggests that most professionally managed portfolios are outperformed by market indices, which lends weight to acceptance of the efficiency of those indices and hence the CAPM.

7. Factor analysis of security returns suggests that more than one factor may be necessary for a valid expected return-beta relationship. This technique, however, does not identify the economic factors behind the factor portfolios.

8. Work on prespecified economic factors is ongoing. Preliminary results suggest that factors such as unanticipated inflation do play a role in the expected return-beta relationship of security returns.

Key Terms

Single-factor models	Measurement error
First-pass regression	Benchmark error
Second-pass regression	Factor portfolios

Selected Readings

The key readings concerning tests of the CAPM are still:
Black, Fischer, Jensen, Michael C., and Scholes, Myron, "The Capital Asset Pricing Model: Some Empirical Tests," in Jensen, Michael C. (editor), *Studies in the Theory of Capital Markets,* New York: Praeger Publishers, 1972.
Fama, Eugene, and MacBeth, James, "Test of the Multiperiod Two Parameter Model," *Journal of Financial Economics,* March 1977.
Roll, Richard, "A Critique of the Asset Pricing Theory's Tests," *Journal of Financial Economics, 4,* 1977.

A test of the model using more recent econometric tools is:
Gibbons, Michael, "Multivariate Tests of Financial Models," *Journal of Financial Economics, 10,* 1982.

The factor analysis approach to testing multivariate models is treated in:
Roll, Richard, and Ross, Stephen, "An Empirical Investigation of the Arbitrage Pricing Theory," *Journal of Finance, 20,* 1980.
Lehman, Bruce, and Modest, David, "The Empirical Foundation of the Arbitrage Pricing Theory, I: The Empirical Tests," New York: Graduate School of Business, Columbia University, 1985.

A good paper that tests the APT with prespecified factors is:
Chen, Nai-Fu, Roll, Richard, and Ross, Stephen A., "Economic Forces and the Stock Market," *Journal of Business, 59,* 1986.

Problems

The following annual excess rates of return were obtained for six portfolios and a market index portfolio:

	Portfolios						
Year	Market Index	*A*	*B*	*C*	*D*	*E*	*F*
1	26.4	38.1	32.6	23.6	15.2	11.9	38.0
2	17.9	21.9	20.2	17.6	14.6	11.8	19.8
3	13.4	13.4	15.1	13.0	13.2	9.0	14.4
4	10.6	9.8	10.4	11.4	12.1	11.0	9.7

1. Perform the first-pass regressions as did Black, Jensen, and Scholes and tabulate the summary statistics as in Table 12.1.
2. Specify the hypotheses for a test of a second-pass regression for the SML.
3. Perform the second-pass SML regression by regressing the average excess return on each portfolio on its beta.
4. Summarize your test results and compare them to the reported results in the text.
5. Group the six portfolios into three, maximizing the dispersion of the betas of the three resultant portfolios. Repeat the test and explain any changes in the results.
6. Explain Roll's critique as it applies to the tests performed in problems 1 to 5.
7. Compare the mean variance efficiency of the six portfolios and the market index. Does the comparison support the CAPM?

Suppose that, in addition to the market factor that has been considered in problems 1 to 7, a second factor is considered. The values of this factor for years 1 to 4 were as follows:

Year	Factor Value (%)
1	13
2	17
3	−21
4	27

8. Perform the first-pass regressions as did Chen, Roll, and Ross and tabulate the relevant summary statistics. (Hint: use a multivariable regession as in the Lotus spreadsheet package. Estimate the betas of the six portfolios on the two factors.)
9. Specify the hypothesis for a test of a second-pass regression for the multidimensional SML.
10. Do the data suggest a two-factor economy?
11. Can you identify a factor portfolio for the second factor?

12. (CFA Examination, Level III, 1981)

Richard Roll, in an article on using the capital asset pricing model (CAPM) to evaluate portfolio performance, indicated that it may not be possible to evaluate portfolio management ability if there is an error in the benchmark used.

a. In evaluating portfolio performance, describe the general procedure, with emphasis on the benchmark employed.

b. Explain what Roll meant by the benckmark error and identify the specific problem with this benchmark.

c. Draw a graph that shows how a portfolio that has been judged as superior relative to a "measured" security market line (SML) can be inferior relative to the "true" SML.

d. Assume that you are informed that a given portfolio manager has been evaluated as superior when compared to the Dow Jones Industrial Average, the S&P 500, and the NYSE Composite Index. Explain whether this consensus would make you feel more comfortable regarding the portfolio manager's true ability.

e. While conceding the possible problem with benchmark errors as set forth by Roll, some contend this does not mean the CAPM is incorrect, but only that there is a measurement problem when implementing the theory. Others contend that because of benchmark errors the whole technique should be scrapped. Take and defend one of these positions.

CHAPTER 13

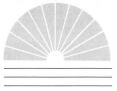

Market Efficiency

In the 1950s an early application of computers in economics was for analysis of economic time series. Business cycle theorists felt that tracing the evolution of several economic variables over time would clarify and predict the progress of the economy through boom and bust periods. A natural candidate for analysis was the behavior of stock market prices over time. Assuming that stock prices reflect the prospects of the firm, recurrent patterns of peaks and troughs in economic performance ought to show up in those prices.

Maurice Kendall examined this proposition in 1953.[1] He found to his great surprise that he could identify *no* predictable patterns in stock prices. Prices seemed to evolve randomly. They were as likely to go up as they were to go down on any particular day, regardless of past performance. The data provided no way to predict price movements.

At first blush, Kendall's results were disturbing to some financial economists. They seemed to imply that the stock market is dominated by erratic market psychology, or "animal spirits," that it follows no logical rules. In short, the results appeared to confirm the irrationality of the market. On further reflection, however, economists came to reverse their interpretation of Kendall's study.

It soon became apparent that random price movements indicated a well-functioning or efficient market, not an irrational one. In this chapter we will explore the reasoning behind what may seem a surprising conclusion. We show how competition among analysts leads naturally to market efficiency, and we examine the implications of the efficient market hypothesis for investment policy. We also consider empirical evidence that supports and contradicts the notion of market efficiency.

---

[1] Kendall, Maurice, "The Analysis of Economic Time Series, Part I: Prices," *Journal of the Royal Statistical Society, 96,* 1953.

13.1 Random Walks and the Efficient Market Hypothesis

Suppose Kendall had discovered that stock prices are predictable. What a gold mine this would have been for investors! If they could use Kendall's equations to predict stock prices, investors would reap unending profits simply by purchasing stocks that the computer model implied were about to increase in price and by selling those stocks about to fall in price.

A moment's reflection should be enough to convince yourself that this situation could not persist for long. For example, suppose that the model predicts with great confidence that XYZ stock price, currently at $100 per share, will rise dramatically in 3 days to $110. What would all investors with access to the model's prediction do today? Obviously, they would place a great wave of immediate buy orders to cash in on the prospective increase in stock price. No one holding XYZ, however, would be willing to sell. The net effect would be an *immediate* jump in the stock price to $110. The forecast of a future price increase will lead instead to an immediate price increase. In other words, the stock price will immediately reflect the "good news" implicit in the model's forecast.

This simple example illustrates why Kendall's attempt to find recurrent patterns in stock price movements was doomed to failure. A forecast about favorable *future* performance leads instead to favorable *current* performance, as market participants all try to get in on the action before the price jump.

More generally, one might say that any information that could be used to predict stock performance must already be reflected in stock prices. As soon as there is any information indicating that a stock is underpriced and therefore offers a profit opportunity, investors flock to buy the stock and immediately bid up its price to a fair level, where only ordinary rates of return can be expected. These "ordinary rates" are simply rates of return commensurate with the risk of the stock.

However, if prices are bid immediately to fair levels, given all available information, it must be that they increase or decrease only in response to new information. New information, by definition, must be unpredictable; if it could be predicted, then the prediction would be part of today's information. Thus stock prices that change in response to new (unpredictable) information also must move unpredictably.

This is the essence of the argument that stock prices should follow a **random walk,** that is, that price changes should be random and unpredictable.[2] Far from a proof of market irrationality, randomly evolving stock prices are the necessary consequence of intelligent investors competing to discover relevant information on which to buy or sell stocks before the rest of the market becomes aware of that information.

---

[2]Actually, we are being a little loose with terminology here. Strictly speaking, we should characterize stock prices as following a submartingale, meaning that the expected change in the price can be positive, presumably as compensation for the time value of money and systematic risk. Moreover, the expected return may change over time as risk factors change. A random walk is more restrictive in that it constrains successive stock returns to be independent *and* identically distributed. Nevertheless, the term "random walk" is commonly used in the looser sense that price changes are essentially unpredictable. We will follow this convention.

Indeed, if stock price movements were predictable, that would be damning evidence of stock market inefficiency, because the ability to predict prices would indicate that all available information was not already reflected in stock prices. Therefore the notion that stocks already reflect all available information is referred to as the **efficient market hypothesis** (EMH).[3]

Competition as the Source of Efficiency

Why should we expect stock prices to reflect "all available information"? After all, if you are willing to spend time and money on gathering information, it might seem reasonable that you could turn up something that has been overlooked by the rest of the investment community. When information is costly to uncover and analyze, one would expect investment analysis calling for such expenditures to result in an increased expected return. This point has been stressed by Grossman and Stiglitz.[4] They argue that investors will have an incentive to spend time and resources to analyze and uncover new information only if such activity is likely to generate higher investment returns. Therefore in market equilibrium it makes sense that efficient information gathering activity should be fruitful. Although we would not, therefore, go so far as to say that you absolutely cannot come up with new information, it still makes sense to consider the competition.

Consider an investment management fund currently managing a $5 billion portfolio. Suppose that the fund manager can devise a research program that could increase the portfolio rate of return by one tenth of one percent per year, a seemingly modest amount. This program would increase the dollar return to the portfolio by $5 billion × .001, or $5 million. Therefore the fund would be willing to spend up to $5 million per year on research to increase stock returns by a mere one tenth of one percent per year. With such large rewards for such small increases in investment performance, it should not be surprising that professional portfolio managers are willing to spend large sums on industry analysts, computer support, and research effort, and therefore that price changes are, generally speaking, difficult to predict.

With so many well-backed analysts willing to spend considerable resources on research, there will not be many easy pickings in the market. Moreover, the incremental rates of return on research activity are likely to be so small that only managers of the largest portfolios will find them worth pursuing.

Although it may not literally be true that "all" relevant information will be uncovered, it is virtually certain that there are many investigators hot on the trail of any leads that may improve investment performance. Competition among these many well-backed, highly paid, aggressive analysts ensures that, as a general rule, stock prices ought to reflect available information regarding their proper levels.

---

[3] Market efficiency should not be confused with the idea of efficient portfolios introduced in Chapter 7. An informationally efficient *market* is one in which information is rapidly disseminated and reflected in prices. An efficient *portfolio* is one with the highest expected return for a given level of risk.

[4] Grossman, Sanford J., and Stiglitz, Joseph E., "On the Impossibility of Informationally Efficient Markets," *American Economic Review, 70,* June 1980.

It is common to distinguish among three versions of the EMH: the weak, semi-strong, and strong forms of the hypothesis. These versions differ by their notions of what is meant by the term "all available information."

The **weak-form** hypothesis asserts that stock prices already reflect all information that can be derived by examining market trading data such as the history of past prices, trading volume, or short interest. This version of the hypothesis implies that trend analysis is fruitless. Past stock price data are publicly available and virtually costless to obtain. The weak-form hypothesis holds that if such data ever conveyed reliable signals about future performance, all investors would have learned already to exploit the signals. Ultimately, the signals lose their value as they become widely known because a buy signal, for instance, would result in an immediate price increase.

The **semistrong-form** hypothesis states that all publicly available information regarding the prospects of a firm must be reflected already in the stock price. Such information includes, in addition to past prices, fundamental data on the firm's product line, quality of management, balance sheet composition, patents held, earning forecasts, and accounting practices. Again, if any investor has access to such information from publicly available sources, one would expect it to be reflected in stock prices.

Finally, the **strong-form** version of the efficient market hypothesis states that stock prices reflect all information relevant to the firm, even including information available only to company insiders. This version of the hypothesis is quite extreme. Few would argue with the proposition that corporate officers have access to pertinent information long enough before public release to enable them to profit from trading on that information. Indeed, much of the activity of the Securities and Exchange Commission is directed toward preventing insiders from profiting by exploiting their privileged situation. Rule 10b-5 of the Security Exchange Act of 1934 sets limits on trading by corporate officers, directors, and substantial owners, requiring them to report trades to the SEC. These insiders, their relatives, and any associates who trade on information supplied by insiders are considered in violation of the law.

Defining insider trading is not always easy, however. After all, stock analysts are in the business of uncovering information not already widely known to market participants. As we saw in Chapter 3, the distinction between private and inside information is sometimes murky.

Concept Check | Question 1. If the weak form of the efficient market hypothesis is valid, must the strong form also hold? Conversely, does strong-form efficiency imply weak-form efficiency?

13.2 *Implications of the EMH for Investment Policy*

Technical Analysis

Technical analysis is essentially the search for recurrent and predictable patterns in stock prices. Although technicians recognize the value of information regarding future economic prospects of the firm, they believe that such information is not necessary for a successful trading strategy. This is because whatever the fundamental reason for a change in stock price, if the stock price responds slowly enough, the analyst will be able to identify a trend that can be exploited during the adjustment period. The key to successful technical analysis is a sluggish response of stock prices to fundamental supply-and-demand factors. This prerequisite, of course, is diametrically opposed to the notion of an efficient market.

Technical analysts are sometimes called "chartists" because they study records or charts of past stock prices, hoping to find patterns they can exploit to make a profit. Figure 13.1 shows some of the types of patterns a chartist might hope to identify. The chartist may draw lines connecting the high and low prices for the day to examine any trends in the prices (Figure 13.1, *A*). The cross-bars indicate closing prices. This is called a search for "momentum." More complex patterns, such as the "breakaway" (Figure 13.1, *B*) or "head and shoulders" (Figure 13.1, *C*), are also believed to convey clear buy or sell signals. The head and shoulders is named for its rough resemblance to a portrait of a head with surrounding shoulders. Once the right shoulder is penetrated (known as piercing the neckline) chartists believe the stock is on the verge of a major decline in price.

Other chartist techniques involve moving averages. In one version of this approach average prices over the past several months are taken as indicators of the "true value" of the stock. If the stock price is above this value, it may be expected to fall. In another version the moving average is taken as indicative of long-run trends. If the trend has been downward and if the current stock price is below the moving average, then a subsequent increase in the stock price above the moving average line (a "breakthrough") might signal a reversal of the downward trend.

Another technique is called the *relative strength* approach. The chartist compares stock performance over a recent period to performance of the market or other stocks in the same industry. A simple version of relative strength takes the ratio of the stock price to a market indicator such as the S&P 500 index. If the ratio increases over time, the stock is said to exhibit relative strength because its price performance is better than that of the broad market. Such strength presumably may continue for a long enough period of time to offer profit opportunities.

One of the most commonly heard components of technical analysis is the notion of **resistance levels** or **support levels.** These values are said to be price levels above which it is difficult for stock prices to rise, or below which it is unlikely for them to fall, and they are believed to be levels determined by market psychology.

FIGURE   13.1

Technical analysis. **A,**
Momentum (upward).
B, Breakaway. **C,**
Head and shoulders.

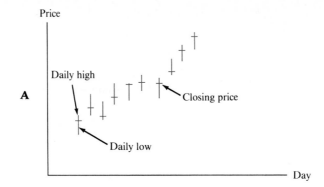

A

Price

Daily high

Closing price

Daily low

Day

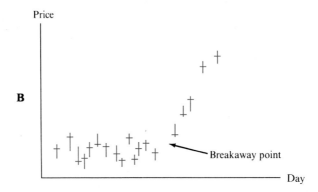

B

Price

Breakaway point

Day

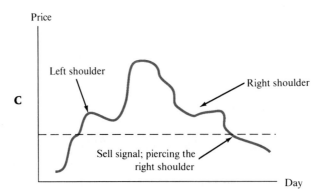

C

Price

Left shoulder

Right shoulder

Sell signal; piercing the
right shoulder

Day

Consider, for example, stock XYZ, which traded for several months at a price of $72, and then declined to $65. If the stock eventually begins to increase in price, $72 is considered a resistance level (according to this theory) because investors who bought originally at $72 will be anxious to sell their shares as soon as they can break even on their investment. Therefore at prices near $72 a wave of selling pressure would exist. Such activity imparts a type of "memory" to the market that allows past price history to influence current stock prospects.

Technical analysts also focus on the volume of trading. The idea is that a price fall accompanied by heavy trading volume signals a more bearish market than if volume were smaller, because the price decline is taken as representing broader-based selling pressure.

The efficient market hypothesis implies that technical analysis is without merit. The past history of prices and trading volume is publicly available at minimal cost. Therefore any information that was ever available from analyzing past prices has already been reflected in stock prices. As investors compete to exploit their common knowledge of a stock's price history, they necessarily drive stock prices to levels where expected rates of return are exactly commensurate with risk. At those levels one cannot expect abnormal returns.

As an example of how this process works, consider what would happen if the market believed that a level of $72 truly were a resistance level for stock XYZ. No one would be willing to purchase the stock at a price of $71.50, because it would have almost no room to increase in price, but ample room to fall. However, if no one would buy it at $71.50, then $71.50 would become a resistance level. But then, using a similar analysis, no one would buy it at $71, or $70, and so on. The notion of a resistance level is a logical conundrum. Its simple resolution is the recognition that if the stock is ever to sell at $71.50, investors *must* believe that the price can as easily increase as fall. The fact that investors are willing to purchase the stock at $71.50 is evidence of their belief that they can earn a fair expected rate of return at that price.

Concept Check

Question 2. If everyone in the market believes in resistance levels, why do these beliefs not become self-fulfilling prophecies?

Fundamental Analysis

Fundamental analysis uses earnings and dividend prospects of the firm, expectations of future interest rates, and risk evaluation of the firm to determine proper stock prices. Ultimately, it represents an attempt to determine the present discounted value of all the payments a stockholder will receive from each share of stock. If that value exceeds the stock price, the fundamental analyst would recommend purchasing the stock.

Fundamental analysts usually start with a study of past earnings and an examination of company balance sheets. They supplement this analysis with further detailed economic analysis, ordinarily including an evaluation of the quality of the firm's management, the firm's standing within its industry, and the prospects for the industry as a whole. The hope is to attain insight into future performance of the firm that is not yet recognized by the rest of the market. Chapters 17 and 18 provide a detailed discussion of the types of analyses that underlie fundamental analysis.

Once again, the efficient market hypothesis predicts that *most* fundamental analysis also is doomed to failure. If the analyst relies on publicly available earnings and industry information, his or her evaluation of the firm's prospects is not likely to be significantly more accurate than those of rival analysts. There are many well-informed, well-financed firms conducting such market research, and in the face of such competition it will be difficult to uncover data not also available to other analysts. Only analysts with a unique insight will be rewarded.

Fundamental analysis is much more difficult than merely identifying well-run firms with good prospects. Discovery of good firms does an investor no good in and of itself if the rest of the market also knows those firms are good. If the knowledge is already public, the investor will be forced to pay a high price for those firms and will not realize a superior rate of return. The trick is not to identify firms that are good, but to find firms that are *better* than everyone else's estimate. Similarly, poorly run firms can be great bargains if they are not quite as bad as their stock prices suggest. This is why fundamental analysis is difficult. It is not enough to do a good analysis of a firm; you can make money only if your analysis is better than that of your competitors because the market price is expected already to reflect all commonly available information.

Active vs. Passive Portfolio Management

By now it is apparent that casual efforts to pick stocks are not likely to pay off. Competition among investors ensures that any easily implemented stock evaluation technique will be used widely enough so that any insights derived will be reflected in stock prices. Only serious, time-consuming, and expensive techniques are likely to generate the *differential* insight necessary to generate trading profits.

Moreover, these techniques are economically feasible only for managers of large portfolios. If you have only $100,000 to invest, even a 1% per year improvement in performance generates only $1,000 per year, hardly enough to justify herculean efforts. The billion-dollar manager, however, reaps extra income of $10 million annually from the same 1% increment.

If small investors are not in a favored position to conduct active portfolio management, what are their choices? The small investor probably is better off placing funds in a mutual fund. By pooling resources in this way, small investors can gain from economies of size.

More difficult decisions remain, though. Can investors be sure that even large mutual funds have the ability or resources to uncover mispriced stocks? Further, will any mispricing be sufficiently large to repay the costs entailed in active portfolio management?

Proponents of the efficient market hypothesis believe that active management is largely wasted effort and unlikely to justify the expenses incurred. Therefore they advocate a **passive investment strategy** that makes no attempt to outsmart the market. A passive strategy aims only at establishing a well-diversified portfolio of securities without attempting to find under- or overvalued stocks. Passive management is usually characterized by a buy-and-hold strategy. Because the efficient market theory indicates that stock prices are at fair levels, given all available information, it makes no sense to buy and sell securities frequently, which generates large brokerage fees without increasing expected performance.

One common strategy for passive management is to create an *index fund*. Such a fund aims to mirror the performance of a broad-based index of stocks. For example, the Vanguard Group of mutual funds sponsors a mutual fund called the Index Trust that holds stocks in direct proportion to their weight in the Standard & Poor's 500 stock price index. The performance of the Index Trust fund therefore replicates the performance of the S&P 500. Investors in this fund obtain broad diversification with relatively low management fees. The fees can be kept to a minimum because Vanguard does not need to pay analysts to assess stock prospects and does not incur transaction costs from high portfolio turnover.

Indexing has grown in appeal considerably since 1970. Many institutional investors now hold indexed bond portfolios, as well as indexed stock portfolios. These portfolios aim to replicate the features of well-known bond indices such as the Shearson Lehman or Salomon Brothers indices. In 1987 fully one third of all fixed-income investments of tax exempt institutional investors went into index bond funds.[5]

Managers of large portfolios, such as those of pension funds, often create their own indexed funds rather than paying a mutual fund manager such as Vanguard to do so for them. A hybrid strategy also is fairly common, where the fund maintains a *passive core,* which is an indexed position, and augments that position with one or more actively managed portfolios.

Concept Check

Question 3. What would happen to market efficiency if *all* investors attempted to follow a passive strategy?

The Role of Portfolio Management in an Efficient Market

If the market is efficient, why not throw darts at *The Wall Street Journal* instead of trying rationally to choose a stock portfolio? This is a tempting conclusion to draw from the notion that security prices are fairly set, but it is far too facile. There is a role for rational portfolio management, even in perfectly efficient markets.

You have learned that a basic principle in portfolio selection is diversification. Even if all stocks are priced fairly, each still poses firm-specific risk that can be eliminated through diversification. Therefore rational security selection, even in an effi-

---

[5]*Pensions and Investment Age,* February 8, 1988.

cient market, calls for the selection of a well-diversified portfolio providing the systematic risk level that the investor wants.

Rational investment policy also requires that tax considerations be reflected in security choice. High tax–bracket investors generally will not want the same securities that low-bracket investors find favorable. At an obvious level high-bracket investors find it advantageous to buy tax-exempt municipal bonds despite their relatively low pretax yields, while those same bonds are unattractive to low tax–bracket investors. At a more subtle level high-bracket investors might want to tilt their portfolios in the direction of capital gains as opposed to dividend or interest income, because the option to defer the realization of capital gain income is more valuable the higher the current tax bracket. Hence these investors may prefer stocks that yield lower dividends yet offer greater expected capital gain income. They also will be more attracted to investment opportunities for which returns are sensitive to tax benefits, such as real estate ventures.

A third argument for rational portfolio management relates to the particular risk profile of the investor. For example, a General Motors executive whose annual bonus depends on GM's profits generally should not invest additional amounts in auto stocks. To the extent that his or her compensation already depends on GM's well-being, the executive is already overinvested in GM and should not exacerbate the lack of diversification.

Investors of varying ages also might warrant different portfolio policies with regard to risk bearing. For example, older investors who are essentially living off savings might choose to avoid long-term bonds whose market values fluctuate dramatically with changes in interest rates (discussed in Part IV). Because these investors are living off accumulated savings, they require conservation of principal. In contrast, younger investors might be more inclined toward long-term bonds. The steady flow of income over long periods of time that is locked in with long-term bonds can be more important than preservation of principal to those with long life expectancies.

In conclusion, there is a role for portfolio management even in an efficient market. Investors' optimal positions will vary according to factors such as age, tax bracket, risk aversion, and employment. The role of the portfolio manager in an efficient market is to tailor the portfolio to these needs, rather than to beat the market.

Book Values vs. Market Values

A somewhat common belief is the notion that book values are intrinsically more trustworthy than market values. Many firms, for example, are reluctant to issue additional stock when the market price of outstanding equity is lower than the book value of those shares. Issue under these circumstances is said to cause dilution of the original stockholder's ownership claim.

Perhaps this faith in book values derives from their stability. Although market values fluctuate daily, book values remain the same day in and day out. The stability of book values actually is a misleading virtue. Market prices fluctuate for a good reason: they move in response to new information about the economic prospects of the firm.

The stability of book values in the face of new information is testament to their essential unreliability.

As an example of how book values can go wrong, imagine what would happen to the price of Exxon stock if the price of oil were to double overnight. The stock price would increase for the very good reason that Exxon's assets are now far more valuable. Yet the book value of Exxon's assets would remain unchanged. Its stability in the face of changing conditions clearly shows it is not a guide to true value.

13.3   Event Studies

The notion of informationally efficient markets leads to a powerful research methodology. If security prices reflect all currently available information, then price changes must reflect new information. Therefore it seems that one should be able to measure the importance of an event of interest by examining price changes during the period in which the event occurs.

An **event study** describes a technique of empirical financial research that enables an observer to assess the impact of a particular event on a firm's stock price. A stock market analyst might want to study the impact of dividend changes on stock prices, for example. An event study would quantify the relationship between dividend changes and stock returns. Using the results of such a study together with a superior means of predicting dividend changes, the analyst could in principle earn superior trading profits.

Analyzing the impact of an announced change in dividends is more difficult than it might at first appear. On any particular day stock prices respond to a wide range of economic news such as updated forecasts for GNP, inflation rates, interest rates, or corporate profitability. Isolating the part of a stock price movement that is attributable to a dividend announcement is not a trivial exercise.

The statistical approach that researchers commonly use to measure the impact of a particular information release, such as the announcement of a dividend change, is a marriage of efficient market theory with the index model discussed in Chapter 9. We want to measure the unexpected return that results from an event. This is the difference between the actual stock return and the return that might have been expected given the performance of the market. This expected return can be calculated using the index model.

Recall that the index model holds that stock returns are determined by a market factor and a firm-specific factor. The stock return (in excess of the risk-free rate), R_t, during a given period, t, would be expressed mathematically as

$$R_t = a + bR_{Mt} + e_t \qquad (13.1)$$

Where R_{Mt} is the market's excess rate of return during the period and e_t is the part of a security's return resulting from firm-specific events. The parameter b measures sensitivity to the market return, and a is the average excess rate of return the stock would realize in a period with a zero market excess return. Equation 13.1 therefore provides a decomposition of R_t into market and firm-specific factors. The firm-specific return may be interpreted as the unexpected return that results from the event.

Determination of the firm-specific return in a given period requires that we obtain an estimate of the term e_t. Therefore we rewrite equation 13.1:

$$e_t = R_t - (a + bR_{Mt}) \qquad (13.2)$$

Equation 13.2 has a simple interpretation: to determine the firm-specific component of a stock's return, subtract the return that the stock ordinarily would earn for a given level of market performance from the actual rate of return on the stock. The residual, e_t, is the stock's return over and above what one would predict based on broad market movements in that period, given the stock's sensitivity to the market.

For example, suppose that the analyst has estimated that $a = .5\%$ and $b = .8$. On a day that the market goes up by 1%, you would predict from equation 13.1 that the stock should rise by an expected value of $.5\% + .8 \times 1\% = 1.3\%$.[6] If the stock actually rises by 2%, the analyst would infer that firm-specific news that day caused an additional stock return of $2\% - 1.3\% = .7\%$. We sometimes refer to the term e_t in equation 13.2 as the **abnormal return**—the return beyond what would be predicted from market movements alone.

The general strategy in event studies is to estimate the abnormal return around the date that new information about a stock is released to the market and attribute the abnormal stock performance to the new information. The first step in the study is to estimate parameters a and b for each security in the study. These typically are calculated using index model regressions as described in Chapter 9 in a period before that in which the event occurs. The prior period is used for estimation so that the impact of the event will not affect the estimates of the parameters. Next, the information release dates for each firm are recorded. For example, in a study of the impact of merger attempts on the stock prices of target firms, the announcement date is the date on which the public is informed that a merger is to be attempted. Finally, the abnormal returns of each firm surrounding the announcement date are computed, and the statistical significance and magnitude of the typical abnormal return is assessed to determine the impact of the newly released information.

One concern that complicates event studies arises from *leakage* of information. Leakage occurs when information regarding a relevant event is released to a small group of investors before official public release. In this case the stock price might start to increase (in the case of a "good news" announcement) days or weeks before the official announcement date. Any abnormal return on the announcement date is then a poor indicator of the total impact of the information release. A better indicator would be the **cumulative abnormal return,** which is simply the sum of all abnormal returns over the time period of interest. The cumulative abnormal return thus captures the total firm-specific stock movement for an entire period when the market might be responding to new information.

---

[6]Actually, we should subtract the risk-free rate here to obtain excess returns, but the risk-free rate of return over 1 day is negligible.

FIGURE 13.2

Cumulative abnormal returns before takeover attempts: target companies.

(From Keown, Arthur, and Pinkerton, John, "Merger Announcements and Insider Trading Activity," *Journal of Finance, 36,* September 1981.)

Cumulative abnormal return

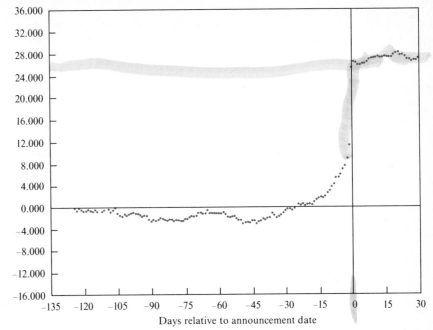

Days relative to announcement date

Figure 13.2 presents the results from a fairly typical event study. The authors of this study were interested in leakage of information before merger announcements and constructed a sample of 194 firms that were targets of a takeover attempt. In most takeovers, stockholders of the acquired firms sell their shares to the acquirer at substantial premiums over market value. Announcement of a takeover attempt is good news for shareholders of the target firm and therefore should cause stock prices to jump.

Figure 13.2 confirms the good-news nature of the announcements. On the announcement day, called day 0, the average cumulative abnormal return (CAR) for the sample of takeover candidates increases substantially, indicating a large and positive abnormal return on the announcement date. Notice that immediately after the announcement date the CAR no longer increases or decreases significantly. This is in accord with the efficient market hypothesis. Once the new information became public, the stock prices jumped almost immediately in response to the good news. With prices once again fairly set, reflecting the effect of the new information, further abnormal returns on any particular day are equally likely to be positive or negative. In fact, for a sample of many firms, the average abnormal return will be extremely close to zero, and thus the CAR will show neither upward nor downward drift. This is precisely the pattern shown in Figure 13.2.

The pattern of returns for the days preceding the public announcement date yields some interesting evidence about efficient markets and information leakage. If insider trading rules were perfectly obeyed and perfectly enforced, stock prices should show no abnormal returns on days before the public release of relevant news, because no special firm-specific information would be available to the market before public announcement. Instead, we should observe a clean jump in the stock price only on the announcement day. In fact, the prices of these takeover targets clearly start an upward drift 30 days before the public announcement. There are two possible interpretations of this pattern. One is that information is leaking to some market participants who then purchase the stocks before the public announcement. At least some abuse of insider trading rules is occurring.

Another interpretation is that in the days before a takeover attempt the public becomes suspicious of the attempt as it observes someone buying large blocks of stock. As acquisition intentions become more evident, the probability of an attempted merger is gradually revised upward so that we see a gradual increase in CARs. Although this interpretation is certainly a valid possibility, evidence of leakage appears almost universally in event studies, even in cases where the public's access to information is not gradual. It appears as if insider trading violations do occur.

Actually, the SEC itself can take some comfort from patterns such as that in Figure 13.2. If insider trading rules were widely and flagrantly violated, we would expect to see abnormal returns earlier than they appear in these results. The CAR would turn positive as soon as acquiring firms decided on their takeover targets, because insiders would start trading immediately. By the time of the public announcement, the insiders would have bid up the stock prices of target firms to levels reflecting the merger attempt, and the abnormal returns on the actual public announcement date would be close to zero. The dramatic increase in the CAR that we see on the announcement date indicates that a good deal of these announcements are indeed news to the market and that stock prices did not already reflect complete knowledge about the takeovers. It would appear, therefore, that SEC enforcement does have a substantial effect on restricting insider trading, even if some amount of it still persists.

Concept Check

Question 4. Suppose that we see negative abnormal returns (declining CARs) after an announcement date. Is this a violation of efficient markets?

13.4 Are Markets Efficient?

The Issues

Not surprisingly, the efficient market hypothesis does not exactly arouse enthusiasm in the community of professional portfolio managers. It implies that a great deal of the activity of portfolio managers—the search for undervalued securities—is at best wasted effort, and quite probably harmful to clients because it costs money and leads to imperfectly diversified portfolios. Consequently, the EMH has never been widely accepted on Wall Street, and debate continues today on the degree to which security analysis can improve investment performance. Before discussing empirical tests of the hypothesis, we want to note three factors that together imply that the debate probably never will be settled: the *magnitude issue,* the *selection bias issue,* and the *lucky event issue*.

The magnitude issue

Consider an investment manager overseeing a $2 billion portfolio. If she can improve performance by only one tenth of one percent per year, that effort will be worth .001 × $2 billion = $2 million annually. This manager clearly would be worth her salary! Yet can we, as observers, statistically measure her contribution? Probably not: a one-tenth of one percent contribution would be swamped by the yearly volatility of the market. Remember, the annual standard deviation of the well-diversified S&P 500 index has been more than 20% per year. Against these fluctuations a small increase in performance would be hard to detect. Nevertheless, $2 million remains an extremely valuable improvement in performance.

All might agree that stock prices are very close to fair values, and that only managers of large portfolios can earn enough trading profits to make the exploitation of minor mispricing worth the effort. According to this view, the actions of intelligent investment managers are the driving force behind the constant evolution of market prices to fair levels. Rather than ask the qualitative question "are markets efficient?" we ought instead to ask a more quantitative question: "how efficient are markets?"

The selection bias issue

Suppose that you discover an investment scheme that could really make money. You have two choices: either publish your technique in *The Wall Street Journal* to win fleeting fame, or keep your technique secret and use it to earn millions of dollars. Most investors would choose the latter option, which presents us with a conundrum. Only investors who find that an investment scheme cannot generate abnormal returns will be willing to report their findings to the whole world. Hence opponents of the efficient markets view of the world always can use evidence that various techniques do not provide investment rewards as proof that the techniques that do work simply are not being reported to the public. This is a problem in *selection bias;* the outcomes we are able to observe have been preselected in favor of failed attempts. Therefore we cannot fairly evaluate the true ability of portfolio managers to generate winning stock market strategies.

The lucky event issue

In virtually any month it seems we read an article about some investor or investment company with a fantastic investment performance over the recent past. Surely the superior records of such investors disprove the efficient market hypothesis.

Yet this conclusion is far from obvious. As an analogy to the investment game, consider a contest to flip the most number of heads out of 50 trials using a fair coin. The expected outcome for any person is, of course, 50% heads and 50% tails. If

HOW TO GUARANTEE A SUCCESSFUL MARKET NEWSLETTER

Suppose you want to make your fortune publishing a market newsletter. You need first to convince potential subscribers that you have talent worth paying for. Ah, but what if you have no talent? The solution is simple: start eight newsletters.

In year 1, let four of your newsletters predict an up-market and four a down-market. In year 2, let half of the originally optimistic group of newsletters continue

newsletters, and market the eighth newsletter based on its perfect track record. If we want to establish a newsletter with a perfect track record over a 4-year period, we need $2^4 = 16$ newsletters. A 5-year period requires 32 newsletters, and so on.

After the fact, the one newsletter that was always right will attract attention for your uncanny foresight and investors will rush to pay large fees for its advice.

Newsletter Predictions

Year	1	2	3	4	5	6	7	8
1	U	U	U	U	D	D	D	D
2	U	U	D	D	U	U	D	D
3	U	D	U	D	U	D	U	D

to predict an up-market and the other half a down-market. Do the same for the originally pessimistic group. Continue in this manner to obtain the above pattern of predictions (U = prediction of an up-market, D = prediction of a down-market).

After 3 years, no matter what has happened to the market, one of the newsletters would have had a perfect prediction record. This is because after 3 years there are $2^3 = 8$ outcomes for the market, and we have covered all eight possibilities with the eight newsletters. Now, we simply slough off the seven unsuccessful

Your fortune is made, and you never even researched the market!

WARNING: This scheme is illegal! The point, however, is that with hundreds of market newsletters, you can find one that has stumbled onto an apparently remarkable string of successful predictions without any real degree of skill. After the fact, *someone's* prediction history can seem to imply great forecasting skill. This person is the one we will read about in *The Wall Street Journal;* the others will be forgotten.

10,000 people, however, compete in this contest, it would not be surprising if at least one or two contestants flipped more than 75% heads. In fact, elementary statistics tells us that the expected number of contestants flipping 75% or more heads would be two. It would be silly, though, to crown these people the "head-flipping champions of the world." Obviously, they are simply the contestants who happened to get lucky on the day of the event. (See box above.)

The analogy to efficient markets is clear. Under the hypothesis that any stock is fairly priced given all available information, any bet on a stock is simply a coin toss. There is equal likelihood of winning or losing the bet. However, if many investors using a variety of schemes make fair bets, statistically speaking, *some* of those investors will be lucky and win a great majority of the bets. For every big winner, there may be many big losers, but we never hear of these managers. The winners, though, turn up in *The Wall Street Journal* as the latest stock market gurus; then they can make a fortune publishing market newsletters.

Our point is that after the fact there will have been at least one successful investment scheme. A doubter will call the results luck, the successful investor will call it skill. The proper test would be to see whether the successful investors can repeat their performance in another period, yet this approach is rarely taken.

With these caveats in mind, we turn now to some of the empirical tests of the efficient markets hypothesis.

Concept Check	Question 5. The Magellan Fund managed by Fidelity was one of the top five funds for 8 of the 10 years of the decade ending 1986. Is this performance sufficient to dissuade you from a belief in efficient markets? If not, would *any* performance record be sufficient to dissuade you?

Tests of Technical Analysis

Early tests of efficient markets were tests of the weak form. Could speculators find trends in past prices that would enable them to earn abnormal profits? This is essentially a test of the efficacy of technical analysis.

The already-cited work of Kendall and of Roberts,[7] both of whom analyzed the possible existence of patterns in stock prices, suggest that such patterns are not to be found. Fama[8] later analyzed "runs" of stock prices to see whether the stock market exhibits "momentum" that can be exploited. (A run is a sequence of consecutive price increases or decreases.) For example, if the last three changes in daily stock prices were positive, could we be more confident that the next move also would be up?

Fama classified daily stock price movements of each of the 30 Dow Jones industrial stocks as positive, zero, or negative in order to test persistence of runs. He found that neither positive nor negative returns persisted to an extent that could contradict the efficient market hypothesis. Although there was some evidence of runs over very short time intervals (less than 1 day), the tendency for runs to persist was so slight that any attempt to exploit them would generate trading costs in excess of the expected abnormal returns.

A more sophisticated version of trend analysis is a **filter rule.** A filter technique gives a rule for buying or selling a stock depending on past price movements. One rule, for example, might be: "buy if the last two trades each resulted in a stock price increase." A more conventional one might be: "buy a security if its price increased by 1%, and hold it until its price falls by more than 1% from the subsequent high."

---

[7]Roberts, Harry, "Stock Market 'Patterns' and Financial Analysis: Methodological Suggestions," *Journal of Finance, 14,* March 1959.
[8]Fama, Eugene, "The Behavior of Stock Market Prices," *Journal of Business, 38,* January 1965.

Alexander[9] and Fama and Blume[10] found that such filter rules generally could not generate trading profits.

One exception to this conclusion relates to very short-term filters. If you could actually sit on the floor of the stock exchange and observe each trade, or at least observe prices every hour or so and then act on what you see, the empirical results of these studies show that filter rules with extremely low filters could generate slight abnormal profits. Even then, these profits would be exceeded by the costs of so frequently buying and selling the securities, and thus would not offer a money-making opportunity. Floor traders themselves could not gain from the profits thus generated, for even the small clearinghouse fees on a trader's activity would be enough to wipe out the abnormal returns. Thus, although the potential gross profit from such filters might be statistically significant, such profits are not significant net of transactions costs.

Similar results were obtained by Levy,[11] who identified 32 standard patterns used by chartists and tested their predictive power. He concluded that none of the patterns produced better-than-average trading results for anyone who cannot buy and sell securities free of commissions. Moreover, the most bullish results tended to be generated by patterns that technical analysts typically described as bearish.

The conclusion of the vast majority of weak-form tests is that the efficient market hypothesis is validated by stock market data. To be fair, however, one should note the criticism of efficient market skeptics, who argue that any filter rule or trend analysis that can be tested statistically is overly mechanical and cannot capture the finesse with which human investors can detect subtle but exploitable patterns in past prices.

Moreover, more sophisticated recent tests of the random walk hypothesis have found some interesting violations of the model. Lo and MacKinlay[12] find evidence of serial correlation[13] in stock returns, while Keim and Stambaugh[14] find variables that can be used to predict changes in expected returns. These studies do not necessarily imply stock market inefficiency. They may indicate only that fair risk premiums vary systematically over time. In addition, it is not clear that these empirical results could be used to formulate trading strategies to yield abnormal profits after transaction costs. Nevertheless, they provide food for thought.

---

[9]Alexander, Sidney, "Price Movements in Speculative Markets: Trends or Random Walks. No. 2," in Cootner, Paul (editor), *The Random Character of Stock Market Prices*, Cambridge, Mass.: MIT Press, 1964.

[10]Fama, Eugene, and Blume, Marshall, "Filter Rules and Stock Market Trading Profits," *Journal of Business, 39,* (Supplement) January 1966.

[11]Levy, Robert A., "The Predictive Significance of Five-Point Chart Patterns," *Journal of Business, 44,* July 1971.

[12]Lo, Andrew W., and MacKinlay, A. Craig, "Stock Market Prices Do Not Follow Random Walks: Evidence From a Simple Specification Test," NBER Working Paper No. 2168, February 1987.

[13]Serial correlation measures the tendency for above-average returns to be followed by more above-average returns, and below-average returns to be followed by below-average returns.

[14]Keim, Donald B. and Stambaugh, Robert F., "Predicting Returns in the Stock and Bond Markets," *Journal of Financial Economics 17,* December 1986.

Fundamental analysis calls on a much wider range of information to create portfolios than does technical analysis, and tests of the value of fundamental analysis are thus correspondingly more difficult to evaluate. They have, however, revealed a number of so-called anomalies, that is, evidence that seems inconsistent with the efficient market hypothesis. We will review several such anomalies in the following pages.

We must note before starting that one major problem with these tests is that most require risk adjustments to portfolio performance and most tests use the CAPM to make the risk adjustments. We know that, although beta seems to be a relevant descriptor of stock risk, the empirically measured quantitative trade-off between risk as measured by beta and expected return differs from the predictions of the CAPM. If we use the CAPM to adjust portfolio returns for risk, we run the risk that inappropriate adjustments will lead to the conclusion that various portfolio strategies can generate superior returns, when in fact it simply is the risk adjustment procedure that has failed.

Another way to put this is to note that tests of risk-adjusted returns are *joint tests* of the efficient market hypothesis *and* the risk adjustment procedure. If it appears that a portfolio strategy can generate superior returns, we must then choose between rejecting the EMH or rejecting the risk adjustment technique. Usually, the risk adjustment technique is based on more questionable assumptions than is the EMH; by opting to reject the procedure, we are left with no conclusion about market efficiency.

An example of this issue is the discovery by Basu[15] that portfolios of low price-earnings ratio stocks have higher average returns than do high P/E portfolios. The **P/E effect** holds up even if returns are adjusted for portfolio beta. Is this a confirmation that the market systematically misprices stocks according to P/E ratio? This would be an extremely surprising and, to us, disturbing conclusion, because analysis of P/E ratios is such a simple procedure. Although it may be possible to earn superior returns using hard work and much insight, it hardly seems possible that such a basic technique is enough to generate abnormal returns. One possible interpretation of these results is that the model of capital market equilibrium is at fault in that the returns are not properly adjusted for risk. This in fact is the conclusion that Basu reached in 1983.

The small-firm effect

One of the most important anomalies with respect to the efficient market hypothesis is the so-called size, or **small-firm effect,** originally documented by Banz.[16] Banz found that both total and risk-adjusted rates of return tend to fall with increases in the relative size of the firm, as measured by the market value of the firm's out-

---

[15]Basu, Sanjoy, "The Investment Performance of Common Stocks in Relation to their Price-Earnings Ratios: A Test of the Efficient Market Hypothesis," *Journal of Finance, 32,* June 1977, pp. 663-682; and "The Relationship between Earnings Yield, Market Value, and Return for NYSE Commnon Stocks: Further Evidence," *Journal of Financial Economics, 12,* June 1983.

[16]Banz, Rolf, "The Relationship between Return and Market Value of Common Stocks," *Journal of Financial Economics, 9,* March 1981.

standing equity. Dividing all NYSE stocks into five quintiles according to firm size, Banz found that the average annual return of firms in the smallest-size quintile was 19.8% greater than the average return of firms in the largest-size quintile.

This is a huge premium; imagine earning a premium of this size on a billion-dollar portfolio. Yet it is remarkable that following a simple (even simplistic) rule such as "invest in low capitalization stocks" should enable an investor to earn excess returns. After all, any investor can measure firm size at little cost. One would not expect such minimal effort to yield such large rewards.

Later studies (Keim,[17] Reinganum,[18] and Blume and Stambaugh[19]) showed that the small-firm effect occurs virtually entirely in January, in fact, in the first 2 weeks of January. The size effect is in fact a "small-firm-in-January" effect.

Figure 13.3 illustrates the January effect. Keim ranked firms in order of increasing size as measured by market value of equity and then divided them into 10 portfolios grouped by the size of each firm. In each month of the year, he calculated the difference in the average excess return of firms in the smallest-firm portfolio and largest-firm portfolio. The average monthly differences over the years 1963 to 1979 appear in Figure 13.3. January clearly stands out as an exceptional month for small firms, with an average small-firm premium of .714% per day.

The results for the first 5 trading days in January are even more compelling. The difference in excess returns between the smallest-firm and largest-firm portfolios for the first 5 trading days of the year are as follows:

Trading Day	Differential Excess Return (Average for 1963-1979)
1	3.20
2	1.68
3	1.25
4	1.14
5	0.89
TOTAL	**8.16**

The total differential return is an amazing 8.16% over only 5 trading days.

Some researchers believe that the January effect is tied to tax-loss selling at the end of the year. The hypothesis is that many people sell stocks that have declined in price during the previous months to realize their capital losses before the end of the tax year. Such investors do not put the proceeds from these sales back into the stock market until after the turn of the year. At that point the rush of demand for stock places an upward pressure on prices that results in the January effect. Finally, the January effect is said to show up most dramatically for the smallest firms because the

[17]Keim, Donald B., "Size Related Anomalies and Stock Return Seasonality: Further Empirical Evidence," *Journal of Financial Economics, 12,* June 1983.

[18]Reinganum, Marc R., "The Anomalous Stock Market Behavior of Small Firms in January: Empirical Tests for Tax-Loss Effects," *Journal of Financial Economics, 12,* June 1983.

[19]Blume, Marshall E., and Stambaugh, Robert F., "Biases in Computed Returns: An Application to the Size Effect," *Journal of Finance Economics,* 1983.

FIGURE 13.3

Average difference
between daily excess
returns (in
percentages) of
lowest-firm-size and
highest-firm-size
deciles for each month
between 1963 and
1979.

(Data from Keim, Donald
B., "Size Related Anomalies
and Stock Return
Seasonality: Further
Empirical Evidence,"
*Journal of Financial
Economics, 12,* June 1983.)

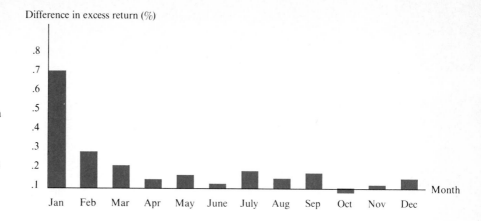

small-firm group includes, as an empirical matter, stocks with the greatest variability of prices during the year. The group therefore includes a relatively large number of firms that have declined sufficiently to induce tax-loss selling.

From a theoretical standpoint, this theory has substantial flaws. First, if the positive January effect is a manifestation of buying pressure, it should be matched by a symmetric negative December effect when the tax-loss incentives induce selling pressure. Second, the predictable January effect flies in the face of efficient market theory. If investors who do not already hold these firms know that January will bring abnormal returns to the small-firm group, they should rush to purchase stock in December to capture those returns. This would push buying pressure from January to December. Rational investors should not "allow" such predictable abnormal January returns to persist. However, small firms outperform large ones in January in every year of Keim's study, 1963 to 1979.

Despite these theoretical objections, much empirical evidence supports the belief that the January effect is connected to tax-loss selling. For example, Reinganum found that, within size class, firms that had declined more severely in price had larger January returns. This pattern is illustrated in Figure 13.4. Reinganum divided firms into quartiles based on the extent to which stock prices had declined during the year. Big price declines would be expected to generate big January returns if these firms tend to be unloaded in December and enjoy demand pressure in January. The figure shows that the lowest quartile (biggest tax loss) portfolios within each size group show the greatest January effect.

A size effect continues to persist, however, even after adjusting for taxes. Small firms that rose in price continue to show abnormal January returns (Figure 13.4, *B*), while large firms that declined in price show no special January effect. Hence, although taxes appear to be associated with the abnormal January returns (Figure 13.4,

FIGURE 13.4

Average daily returns in January for securities in the upper quartile and bottom quartile of the tax-loss selling distribution by market-value portfolio.

(From Reinganum, Marc R., "The Anomalous Stock Market Behavior of Small Firms in January: Empirical Tests for Tax-Loss Effects," *Journal of Financial Economics, 12,* June 1983.)

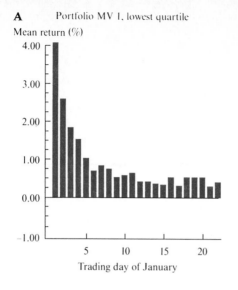

A Portfolio MV 1, lowest quartile

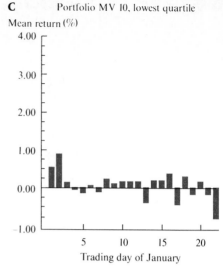

C Portfolio MV 10, lowest quartile

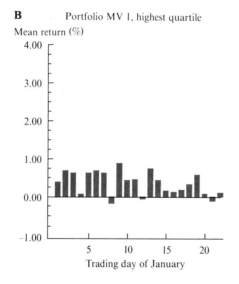

B Portfolio MV 1, highest quartile

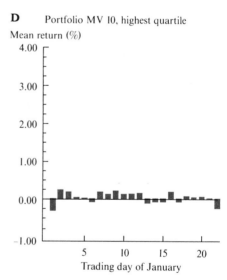

D Portfolio MV 10, highest quartile

A compared with *B, C* compared with *D*), size per se remains a factor in January (Figure 13.4, *A* compared with *C, B* compared with *D*).

The fundamental question is why market participants do not exploit the January effect and thereby ultimately eliminate it by bidding stock prices to appropriate levels. One possible explanation lies in segmentation of the market into two groups: institutional investors who invest primarily in large firms, and individual investors who invest disproportionately in smaller-sized firms. According to this view, managers of large institutional portfolios are the moving force behind efficient markets. It is professionals who seek out profit opportunities and bid prices to their appropriate levels. Institutional investors do not seem to buy at the small-size end of the market, perhaps because of limits on allowed portfolio positions, so the small-firm anomaly persists without the force of their participation.

Concept Check

Question 6. Does this market segmentation theory get the efficient market hypothesis off the hook, or are there still market mechanisms that in theory ought to act to eliminate the small firm anomaly?

The neglected-firm effect

Arbel and Strebel[20] give another interpretation of the small-firm effect. Because small firms tend to be neglected by large institutional traders, information about such firms is less available. This information deficiency makes smaller firms riskier investments that command higher returns. "Brand-name" firms, after all, are subject to considerable monitoring from institutional investors that assures high-quality information, and presumably investors do not purchase "generic" stocks without the prospect of greater returns.

As evidence for the **neglected-firm effect,** Arbel[21] measures the information deficiency of firms using the coefficient of variation of analysts' forecasts of earnings. (The coefficient of variation is the ratio of standard deviation to mean and measures the dispersion of forecasts. It is a "noise-to-signal" ratio.) The correlation coefficient between the coefficient of variation and total return was .676, quite high, and statistically significant. In a related test Arbel divided firms into highly researched, moderately researched, and neglected groups based on the number of institutions holding the stock. Table 13.1 shows that the January effect was largest for the neglected firms.

The day-of-the-week effect

The small-firm-in-January effect is one example of seasonality in stock market returns, a recurrent pattern of turn-of-the-year abnormal returns. Another recurrent pattern, and in several ways an even odder one, is the **weekend effect,** documented by French[22] and Gibbons and Hess.[23] These researchers studied the pattern of stock returns from close of trading on Friday afternoon to close on Monday, to determine

---

[20]Arbel, Avner, and Strebel, Paul J., "Pay Attention to Neglected Firms," *Journal of Portfolio Management*, winter 1983.

[21]Arbel, Avner, "Generic Stocks: An Old Product in a New Package." *Journal of Portfolio Management*, summer 1985.

[22]French, Kenneth, "Stock Returns and the Weekend Effect," *Journal of Financial Economics, 8,* March 1980.

[23]Gibbons, Michael, and Hess, Patrick, "Day of the Week Effects and Asset Returns," *Journal of Business, 54,* October 1981.

TABLE 13.1   January Effect by Degree of Neglect (1971-1980)

	Average January Return (%)	Average January Return Minus Average Return During Rest of Year (%)	Average January Return After Adjusting for Systematic Risk (%)
S&P 500 Companies			
Highly researched	2.48	1.63	-1.44
Moderately researched	4.95	4.19	1.69
Neglected	7.62	6.87	5.03
Non-S&P 500 Companies			
Neglected	11.32	10.72	7.71

From Arbel, Avner, "Generic Stocks: An Old Product in a New Package," *Journal of Portfolio Management,* summer 1985.

whether the 3-day return spanning the weekend would be three times the typical return on a weekday. This was to be a test of whether the market operates on calendar time or trading time.

Much to their surprise, the typical Friday-to-Monday return was not larger than that of other weekdays—in fact, it was negative! Following is the mean return of the S&P 500 portfolio for each day of the week over the period July 1962 through December 1978. The Monday return is based on closing price Friday to closing price Monday, the Tuesday return is based on Monday closing to Tuesday closing, and so on:

	Monday	Tuesday	Wednesday	Thursday	Friday
Mean Return:	−.134%	.002%	.096%	.028%	.084%

The negative Monday effect is extremely large. On an annualized basis, assuming 250 trading days a year, the return is −33.5% (−.134% × 250). Gibbons and Hess report that for the overall period all 30 Dow Jones Industrial stocks had negative mean Monday returns. Thus it is quite unlikely that the weekend effect can be attributed to statistical fluke.

The weekend effect poses a problem for efficient market theorists. In frictionless markets one would expect this recurrent pattern to be "arbitraged away." Specifically, investors would sell stocks short late Friday afternoon, and repurchase them on Monday afternoon at an expected lower price, thereby capturing an abnormal return. The selling on Friday would drive prices down on Friday to a fair level in the sense that the Friday-Monday return would be expected to be positive and commensurate with the risk of the stock market.

In practice of course, such arbitrage activity would not pay. The magnitude of the weekend effect is not nearly large enough to offset the transaction costs involved in short selling and repurchasing the stocks. Hence market frictions prevent the direct elimination of the weekend effect. Nevertheless, the effect should not be observed in efficient markets, even in the absence of direct arbitrage. If there is a predictable weekend effect, one would expect investors to shy away from purchases on Fridays, delaying them until Monday instead. Conversely, sales of stock originally scheduled for Monday optimally would be pushed up to the preceding Friday. This reshuffling of buying and selling would be enough to increase buy relative to sell pressure on Mondays to the point where the weekend effect would be dissipated. The persistence of the effect seems to indicate that investors have not paid attention to the predictable price pattern.

One explanation of this anomaly is that firms may tend to release bad news to the public over the weekend while the financial markets are closed. This is an appealing but problematic interpretation. If investors come to expect weekends to bring bad news, they will treat any weekend that passes without such news as a relief, and prices will, in response, increase on Monday morning. Averaging over the "bad-news" and "relief" weekends, one should expect mean Friday-Monday returns to be fair, and certainly not negative.

Inside information

It would not be surprising if insiders were able to make superior profits trading in their firm's stock. The ability of insiders to trade profitably in their own stock has been documented in studies by Jaffee,[24] Seyhun,[25] Givoly and Palmon,[26] and others. Jaffee's was one of the earlier studies that documented the tendency for stock prices to rise after insiders intensively bought shares and to fall after intensive insider sales.

To enhance fairness, the Securities and Exchange Commission requires all insiders to register their trading activity. The SEC publishes these trades in an *Official Summary of Insider Trading*. Once the *Official Summary* is published, the knowledge of the trades becomes public information. At that point, if markets are efficient, fully and immediately processing the information released in the *Official Summary* of trading, an investor should no longer be able to profit from following the pattern of those trades.

Surprisingly, early studies like Jaffee's seemed to indicate that following insider transactions, buying after insider purchases were reported in the *Official Summary* and selling after insider sales, could offer substantial abnormal returns to an outside investor. This would be a clear violation of market efficiency, as the data in the *Official Summary* are publicly available. However, a more recent and extensive study by Seyhun, which carefully tracked the public release dates of the *Official Summary,* found that following insider transactions would be to no avail. Although there is some tendency for stock prices to increase even after the *Official Summary* reports insider buying, the abnormal returns are not of sufficient magnitude to overcome transaction costs.

---

[24]Jaffee, Jeffrey F., "Special Information and Insider Trading," *Journal of Business, 47,* July 1974.

[25]Seyhun, H. Nejat, "Insiders' Profits, Costs of Trading and Market Efficiency," *Journal of Financial Economics, 16,* 1986.

[26]Givoly, Dan, and Palmon, Dan, "Insider Trading and Exploitation of Inside Information: Some Empirical Evidence," *Journal of Business, 58,* 1985.

The Value Line enigma

The Value Line Investor Survey is an investment advisory service that ranks securities on a timeliness scale of one (best buy) to five (sell). Ranks are based on relative earnings and price performance across securities, price momentum, quarterly earnings momentum, and a measure of unexpected earnings in the most recent quarter.

Several studies have examined the predictive value of the Value Line recommendations. Black[27] found that Portfolio 1 (the "buy" portfolio) had a risk-adjusted excess rate of return of 10%, while Portfolio 5 (the "sell" portfolio) had an abnormal return of −10%. These results imply a fantastic potential value to the Value Line forecasts. Copeland and Mayers[28] performed a similar study using a more sophisticated risk-adjustment technique, and found that the difference in the risk-adjusted performance of Portfolios 1 and 5 was much smaller; Portfolio 1 earned an abnormal 6-month rate of return of 1.52%, while Portfolio 5 earned an abnormal return of −2.97%. Even this smaller difference, however, seems to be a substantial deviation from the prediction of the efficient market hypothesis.

Given Value Line's apparent success in predicting stock performance, we would expect that changes in Value Line's timeliness rankings would result in abnormal returns for affected stocks. This seems to be the case. Stickel[29] shows that Value Line rerankings generally are followed by abnormal stock returns in the expected direction. Interestingly enough, smaller firms tend to respond with greater sensitivity to rerankings. This pattern is consistent with the neglected-firm effect in that the information contained in a reranking carries greater weight for firms that are less intensively monitored.

The market crash of October 1987

The market crash of October 1987 seems to be a glaring counterexample to the efficient market hypothesis. If prices reflect market fundamentals, then defenders of the EMH must look for news on the nineteenth of October consistent with the 23% 1-day decline in stock prices. Yet no events of such importance seem to have transpired on that date. The fantastic price swing is hard to reconcile with market fundamentals. The nearby box presents a discussion of the crash in the context of efficient market theory.

Concept Check

Question 7. Some say that continued worry concerning the U.S. trade deficit brought down the market on October 19. Is this explanation consistent with the EMH?

---

[27]Black, Fischer, "Yes, Virginia, There is Hope: Tests of the Value Line Ranking System," Graduate School of Business, University of Chicago, 1971.

[28]Copeland, Thomas E., and Mayers, David, "The Value Line Enigma (1965-1978): A Case Study of Performance Evaluation Issues," *Journal of Financial Economics, 11,* November 1982.

[29]Stickel, Scott E., "The Effect of Value Line Investment Survey Rank Changes on Common Stock Prices," *Journal of Financial Economics, 14,* 1985.

The 'Efficient Market' Was a Good Idea
—and Then Came the Crash

It Launched a Revolution, but the Theory Can't Explain Why Investors Panicked on Oct. 19

The Oct. 19 stock market collapse crushed more than $500 billion in investor wealth. It also struck a blow against one of the most powerful ideas in finance—the efficient market theory (EMT). "It was the nail in the coffin of the theory," says economist Bruce Greenwald, a staff member on the Brady commission, which studied the crash.

That theory bucked the popular view that stocks move on the latest fad or the speculative fever of the crowd. Well-informed investors could make a bundle, went the conventional wisdom. Not so, says the EMT. The stock market is an efficient information processing machine. Investors act rationally, and stock prices reflect whatever information people have about the fundamentals, such as present and future earnings. Stock prices change only on fresh news—and that doesn't include crowd psychology.

Herd Instinct

The theory had few believers back in the early 1960s. But the EMT ended up launching a market revolution. Finance professors and math whizzes built careers on Wall Street exploiting its insights. For instance, the theory says that you can't consistently outperform the market averages, since only unexpected news moves prices. Did the EMT catch on with big money? You bet. Many pension-fund sponsors turned their backs on money managers who claimed that they could beat the market and bought some $175 billion in index funds that track the market.

Then came Bloody Monday. Efficient market theory is useless in explaining the biggest stock market calamity in 58 years. What new information jarred investors into slashing their estimate of the value of Corporate America's assets by some 23% in the 6½ hours the New York Stock Exchange was open? Hardly enough news came out that day, or over the weekend, to account for the plunge.

Indeed, a survey by Yale University's Robert Shiller of nearly 1,000 big and small investors showed that the reason for selling was not a change in the fundamentals. Rather, it was the declines that took place in the market itself the Thursday and Friday before, as well as the sharp sell-off on the morning of Oct. 19. "Lots of nervous people came to believe the price drops themselves signaled a crash, and everyone tried to be the first out the door," says Shiller. Investors panicked because the market was falling like a stone. There was no rationality, only herd instinct.

The rout of the efficient markets theory holds important implications not only for investors but also for the idea that the market is the best possible way to channel capital to its most productive uses. According to this belief, investors allowed to choose in a competitive market will funnel money to those companies with the best prospects. It's no coincidence that the EMT was mainly developed at the University of Chicago, a laissez-faire bastion. Moreover, the so-called derivative securities—stock index futures and options—were conceived in the Windy City and traded on the Chicago exchanges largely because of the impetus from the university's free market theorists, who argued that the new instruments would make the stock market even more efficient.

Reason to Believe

But if crowd psychology, not rationality, rules stock prices, investors and policymakers might be getting the wrong signals from the market. Money might flow to unproductive businesses, such as junk-bond-financed leveraged buyouts. Meanwhile, companies spending a lot on future products and cultivating markets could starve for cheap capital. Even Chicago's pioneering efficient-market theorist Eugene Fama admits the EMT is "a matter of belief" to him. If prices are not being set the way the theory assumes, then the free market system is not allocating resources efficiently, says Fama.

Continued.

Signs that the EMT doesn't work began to show up in the stock market well before Bloody Monday. The crash is only the latest, most dramatic, instance of the theory's failure. A cottage industry has sprung up in academe documenting market "anomalies" inconsistent with the EMT. Take the "January effect." Small-capitalization stocks repeatedly show large returns during the first five trading days of the year. According to the EMT, the January effect shouldn't persist. Sophisticated investors, anticipating the easy gains, should have bid up prices well before the beginning of the year.

Other economists believe they have found further instances of investor irrationality. A study by economists Richard Thaler and Werner De Bondt shows that a stock portfolio made up of the 35 worst-performing NYSE issues consistently outperformed the market by an average of 19.6% over a period of three years. The reason, explains Thaler, is that investors overreacted to the bad news and drove the dogs way down—far below what they were truly worth. Stocks again and again overshoot the fundamentals, a finding that doesn't square with the EMT.

Never Say Die

The EMT is far from dead, however. Yale University's Stephen Ross challenges the view that there was little news to account for the crash. He says volatility rose as investors became nervous about the market weeks before Oct. 19. Under the circumstances, "only a small change in news can start an avalanche," says Ross.

The market should have been able to hold back the avalanche, says the EMT theorist, but the exchanges simply broke down. The Brady report pointed out that many NYSE specialists buckled under pressure on Oct. 19 and 20 and were selling, not buying. At the same time, the Big Board computers could not handle the volume. The institutions that make up the market failed, not the EMT.

Still, there is evidence that the stock market is not as competitive as the efficient-market theorists believe. The Brady report said that a handful of mutual and pension funds unleashed enormous selling pressure at the opening of the market on Bloody Monday, swamping the system. For the EMT to work, no one seller should be able to influence the market very much. More telling, four months after the crash, the Dow Jones industrial average is still some 800 points below its peak in August. What changes in U.S. business prospects can account for such a downgrading?

The arguments over the EMT are likely to continue. But the theory's apparent failure to explain the greatest stock market crash in history may suggest to policymakers and to the exchanges that the "market" is not all that it was cracked up to be.

Stock market fads

Recent studies have found stock returns to follow patterns that might be consistent with "fads" in stock prices. For example, Poterba and Summers[30] find evidence that the stock market as a whole has a tendency to perform relatively poorly following periods in which it performed well, and vice versa. The results of this study indicate either that the required risk premium on the market portfolio varies over time or that the market exhibits irrationality: the tendency for stocks to do well following periods of poor performance suggests that the market may systematically be overreacting to relevant news. This overshooting phenomenon is not corrected for a period of some years, implying that stock prices can deviate from fundamental values for extended

[30]Poterba, James M., and Summers, Lawrence H., "Mean Reversion in Stock Prices: Evidence and Implications," National Bureau of Economic Research Working Paper 2343, August 1987.

periods. However, the tendency for the market as a whole to exhibit this behavior is fairly weak; it does not suggest a powerful trading strategy.

A similar overshooting phenomenon at the level of individual firms has been documented by Lehman.[31] He finds a strong tendency for very poorly performing firms in a given week to experience sizable reversals over the subsequent week, while the best performing group of stocks in a given week fares poorly in the following week. Lehman's study indicates that this tendency is strong enough to be exploited profitably and so presents a strong challenge to market efficiency. However, many investors are now attempting to exploit this phenomenon. The true test of market efficiency will be to see whether the "reversal effect" persists now that participants are aware of it.

Mutual fund performance

We have documented some of the apparent chinks in the armor of efficient market proponents. Ultimately, however, the issue of market efficiency boils down to whether skilled investors can make consistent abnormal trading profits. The best test is simply to look at the performance of market professionals to see if that performance is superior to that of a passive index fund that buys and holds the market.

Casual evidence does not support claims that professionally managed portfolios can beat the market. In most of the past 15 years the S&P 500 has outperformed the median professionally managed fund. SEI Funds Evaluation Services evaluates equity manager performance each year and compares those funds to the S&P 500. In the decade ending in 1982 the S&P 500 beat two thirds of managed funds in the SEI sample. In the 5-year period ending 1986 the S&P 500 beat 75% of managed funds.

Of course, one might argue that there are good managers and bad managers, and that the good managers can, in fact, consistently outperform the index. The real test of this notion is to see whether managers with good performance in a given year can repeat that performance in a following year. In other words, is the abnormal performance due to luck or skill? Jensen[32] performed such a test using 10 years of data on 115 mutual funds, a total of 1,150 annual observations.

Jensen first risk-adjusted all returns using the CAPM to obtain portfolio alphas, or returns in excess of required return given risk. Then he tested to see whether managers with positive alphas tended to repeat their performance in later years. If markets are efficient, and abnormal performance is due solely to the luck of the draw, the probability of following superior performance in a given year with superior performance the next year should be 50%: each year's abnormal return is essentially like the toss of a fair coin. This is precisely the pattern that Jensen found. Table 13.2 is reproduced from Jensen's study.

In row 1, we see that 574 positive alphas were observed out of the 1,150 observations, virtually 50% on the nose. Of these 574 positive alphas, 50.4% were followed

---

[31]Lehman, Bruce N., "Fads, Martingales, and Market Efficiency," National Bureau of Economic Research Working Paper 2533, March 1988.
[32]Jensen, Michael C., "Risk, the Pricing of Capital Assets, and the Evaluation of Investment Portfolios," *Journal of Business, 42,* April 1969.

TABLE 13.2   Mutual Fund Performance

Number of Consecutive Positive Alphas So Far	Number of Observations	Cases in Which the Next Alpha Is Positive (%)
1	574	50.4
2	312	52.0
3	161	53.4
4	79	55.8
5	41	46.4
6	17	35.3

From Jensen, Michael C.,"Risk, the Pricing of Capital Assets, and the Evaluation of Investment Portfolios," *Journal of Business, 42,* April 1969; published by The University of Chicago.

by positive alphas. So far, it appears that obtaining a positive alpha is pure luck, like a coin toss. Row 2 shows that 312 cases of two consecutive positive alphas were observed. Of these observations, 52% were followed by yet another positive alpha. Continuing, we see that 53.4% of three-in-a-row were followed by a fourth, and 55.8% of four-in-a-row were followed by a fifth.

The results so far are intriguing. They seem to suggest that most positive alphas are indeed obtained through luck. However, as more and more stringent filters are applied, the remaining managers show greater tendency to follow good performance with more good performance. This might suggest that there are a few, rare, superior managers who can consistently beat the market. However, at this point, the pattern collapses. Only 46.4% of the five-in-a-row group repeats the superior performance. Yet the sample size is too small to make statistically precise inferences about the population of managers. The ultimate interpretation of these results is thus to some extent a matter of faith. However, it seems clear that it is not wise to invest with an actively managed fund chosen at random. The average alpha of all funds was slightly negative even *before* subtracting all the costs of management.

In a more recent study Dunn and Theisen[33] examined the performance of several institutional portfolios over the 1973 to 1982 period. Dividing the funds into four quarters, based on total investment return for different subperiods, they posed the following question: "Do funds that performed well in one period tend to perform well in subsequent periods?"

The answer seems to be no, suggesting that superior performance in any period is more a matter of luck than underlying consistent ability. For example, Table 13.3 shows investment results for a base period 1973 to 1977 and subsequent period 1978 to 1982. The first row shows the relative performance of the first-quartile managers from the 1973 to 1977 base period in the subsequent 1978 to 1982 period. Only 26% of those managers repeated their first-quartile performance; another 26% dropped to the *bottom* quartile in the latter period. Second quartile performers in the base period also fared poorly in the subsequent period; only 10% ended up in the top quartile,

---

[33]Dunn, Patricia, and Theisen, Rolf D., "How Consistently Do Active Managers Win?" *Journal of Portfolio Management, 9,* summer 1983.

TABLE 13.3   Quartile Comparison of Investment Results

Base Period Quartile	Subsequent Period Quartile			
	Q1	Q2	Q3	Q4
Q1	26%	37%	11%	26%
Q2	10	25	25	40
Q3	25	30	40	10
Q4	30	15	35	20

From Dunn, Patricia, and Theisen, Rolf, D., "How Consistently Do Active Managers Win?" *Journal of Portfolio Management, 9,* summer 1983.

and 25% continued in the second quartile. Thus we cannot reject the hypothesis that relative rank is independent from one period to the next.

So, Are Markets Efficient?

There is a telling joke about two economists walking down the street. They spot a $20 bill on the sidewalk. One starts to pick it up, but the other one says, "Don't bother; if the bill were real someone would have picked it up already."

The lesson is clear. An overly doctrinaire belief in efficient markets can paralyze the investor and make it appear that no research effort can be justified. This extreme view is probably unwarranted. There are enough anomalies in the empirical evidence to justify the search for underpriced securities that clearly goes on.

The bulk of the evidence, however, suggests that any supposedly superior investment strategy should be taken with many grains of salt. The market is competitive *enough* that only differentially superior information or insight will earn money; the easy pickings have been picked. In the end it is likely that the margin of superiority that any professional manager can add is so slight that the statistician will not be able to detect it.

We conclude that markets are very efficient, but that rewards to the especially diligent, intelligent, or creative may in fact be waiting.

Summary

1. Statistical research has shown that stock prices seem to follow a random walk with no discernible predictable patterns that investors can exploit. Such findings are now taken to be evidence of market efficiency, that is, of evidence that market prices reflect all currently available information. Only new information will move stock prices, and this information is equally likely to be good news or bad news.

2. Market participants distinguish among three forms of the efficient market hypothesis. The weak form asserts that all information to be derived from past stock prices already is reflected in stock prices. The semistrong form claims that all publicly available information is already reflected. The strong form, usually taken only

as a straw man, asserts that all information, including insider information, is reflected in prices.

3. Technical analysis focuses on stock price patterns and on proxies for buy or sell pressure in the market. Fundamental analysis focuses on the determinants of the underlying value of the firm, such as current profitability and growth prospects. Since both types of analysis are based on public information, neither should generate excess profits if markets are operating efficiently.

4. Proponents of the efficient market hypothesis often advocate passive as opposed to active investment strategies. The policy of passive investors is to buy and hold a broad-based market index. They expend resources neither on market research nor on frequent purchase and sale of stocks. Passive strategies may be tailored to meet individual investor requirements.

5. Event studies are used to evaluate the economic impact of events of interest, using abnormal stock returns. Such studies usually show that there is some leakage of inside information to some market participants before the public announcement date. Therefore insiders do seem to be able to exploit their access to information to at least a limited extent.

6. Empirical studies of technical analysis do not support the hypothesis that such analysis can generate superior trading profits. Only very short-term filters seem to offer any hope for profits, yet these are extremely expensive in terms of trading costs. These costs exceed potential profits even for floor traders.

7. Several anomalies regarding fundamental analysis have been uncovered. These include the P/E effect, the small-firm effect, the neglected-firm effect, the weekend effect, and the Value Line Ranking System.

8. By and large, the performance record of professionally managed funds lends little credence to claims that professionals can consistently beat the market.

Key Terms

Random walk	Event study
Efficient market hypothesis	Abnormal return
Weak-form EMH	Announcement date
Semistrong-form EMH	Cumulative abnormal return
Strong-form EMH	Filter rule
Technical analysis	P/E effect
Resistance levels	Small-firm effect
Support levels	Neglected-firm effect
Fundamental analysis	Weekend effect
Passive investment strategy	

Selected Readings

One of the best treatments of the efficient market hypothesis is:
   Malkiel, Burton G., *A Random Walk Down Wall Street,* New York: W.W. Norton & Co., Inc. 1985. This paperback book provides an entertaining and insightful treatment of the ideas presented in this chapter as well as fascinating historical examples of securities markets in action.

A more rigorous introduction to the theoretical underpinnings of the EMH, as well as a review of early empirical work, may be found in:

Fama, Eugene F., "Efficient Capital Markets: A Review of Theory and Empirical Work," *Journal of Finance, 25,* May 1970.

The June 1983 edition of the *Journal of Financial Economics* is devoted to a symposium on the small-firm effect and other empirical anomalies.

Problems

1. If markets are efficient, what should be the correlation coefficient between stock returns for two nonoverlapping time periods?

2. Which of the following most appears to contradict the proposition that the stock market is *weakly* efficient? Explain.
   a. Over 25% of mutual funds outperform the market on average.
   b. Insiders earn abnormal trading profits.
   c. Every January, the stock market earns above-normal returns.

3. Suppose that, after conducting an analysis of past stock prices, you come up with the following observations. Which would appear to *contradict* the *weak* form of the efficient market hypothesis? Explain.
   a. The average rate of return is significantly greater than zero.
   b. The correlation between the return during a given week and the return during the following week is zero.
   c. One could have made superior returns by buying stock after a 10% rise in price and selling after a 10% fall.
   d. One could have made higher than average capital gains by holding stock with low dividend yields.

4. Which of the following statements are true if the efficient market hypothesis holds?
   a. It implies that future events can be forecast with perfect accuracy.
   b. It implies that prices reflect all available information.
   c. It implies that security prices change for no discernible reason.
   d. It implies that prices do not fluctuate.

5. Which of the following observations would provide evidence *against* the *semi-strong-form* of the efficient market theory? Explain.
   a. Mutual fund managers do not on average make superior returns.
   b. You cannot make superior profits by buying (or selling) stocks after the announcement of an abnormal rise in dividends.
   c. Low P/E stocks tend to have positive abnormal returns.
   d. In any year approximately 50% of pension funds outperform the market.

6. A successful firm like IBM has consistently generated large profits for years. Is this a violation of the EMH?

7. Suppose you find that prices of stocks before large dividend increases show on average consistently positive abnormal returns. Is this a violation of the EMH?

8. "If the business cycle is predictable, and a stock has a positive beta, the stock's returns also must be predictable." Respond.

9. "If all securities are fairly priced, all must offer equal market rates of return." Comment.

10. An index model regression applied to past monthly excess returns in General Motors' stock price produces the following estimates, which are believed to be stable over time:

$$R_{GM} = .10\% + 1.1 R_M$$

If the market index subsequently rises by 8% and General Motors' stock price rises by 7%, what is the abnormal change in General Motors' stock price? The T-bill return during the month is 1%.

11. The monthly rate of return on T-bills is 1%. The market went up this month by 1.5%. In addition, AmbChaser, Inc., which has an equity beta of 2, surprisingly just won a lawsuit that awards them $1 million immediately.
    a. If the original value of AmbChaser equity were $100 million, what would you guess was the rate of return of its stock this month?
    b. What is your answer to (a) if the market had expected AmbChaser to win $2 million?

12. We know that the market should respond positively to good news, and that good-news events such as the coming end of a recession can be predicted with at least some accuracy. Why then can we not predict that the market will go up as the economy recovers?

13. If prices are as likely to increase as decrease, why do investors earn positive returns from the market on average?

14. You know that firm XYZ is very poorly run. On a scale of 1 (worst) to 10 (best), you would give it a score of 3. The market consensus evaluation is that the management score is only 2. Should you buy or sell the stock?

15. Examine the figure[34] on p. 375, which presents cumulative abnormal returns both before and after dates on which insiders buy or sell shares in their firms. How do you interpret this figure? What are we to make of the pattern of CARs before and after the event date?

16. Suppose that during a certain week the Fed annnounces a new monetary growth policy, Congress surprisingly passes legislation restricting imports of foreign automobiles, and Ford comes out with a new car model that it believes will increase profits substantially. How might you go about measuring the market's assessment of Ford's new model?

---

[34]From Seyhun, Nejat, H., "Insiders, Profits, Costs of Trading and Market Efficiency," *Journal of Financial Economics, 16,* 1986.

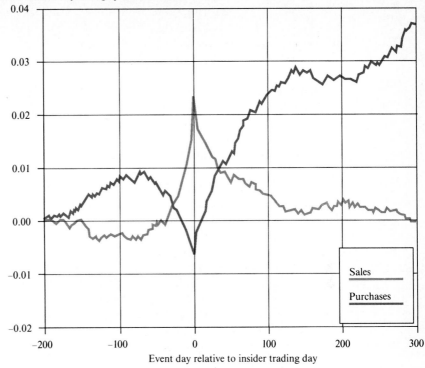

Cumulative daily average prediction errors

Event day relative to insider trading day

Sales

Purchases

17. (Adapted from CFA Examination, Level I, 1981)

Some authors contend that professional managers are incapable of outperforming the market. Others come to an opposite conclusion. Compare and contrast the assumptions about the stock market that support (1) passive portfolio management, and (2) active portfolio management.

(CFA Examination, Level III, 1985)

The following information should be used in solving problems 18 and 19:

As director of research for a medium-sized investment firm, Jeff Cheney was concerned about the mediocre investment results experienced by the firm in recent years. He met with his two senior equity analysts to consider alternatives to the stock selection techniques employed in the past.

One of the analysts suggested that the current literature has examined the relationship between price earnings ratios (P/E) and securities returns. A number of studies had concluded that high P/E stocks tended to have higher betas and lower risk-adjusted returns than stocks with low P/E ratios.

The analyst also referred to recent studies analyzing the relationship between security returns and company size as measured by equity capitalization. The studies concluded that when compared to the S&P 500 Index, small capitalization stocks tended to provide above-average risk-adjusted returns while large capitalization stocks tended to provide below-average risk-adjusted returns. It was further noted that little correlation was found to exist between a company's P/E ratio and the size of its equity capitalization.

Jeff's firm has employed a strategy of complete diversification and the use of beta as a measure of portfolio risk. He and his analysts were intrigued as to how these recent studies might be applied to their stock selection techniques and thereby improve their performance. Given the results of the studies indicated above:

18. Explain how the results of these studies might be used in the stock selection and portfolio management process. Briefly discuss the effects on the objectives of diversification and on the measurement of portfolio risk.
19. List the reasons and briefly discuss why this firm might *not* want to adopt a new strategy based on these studies in place of their current strategy of complete diversification and the use of beta as a measure of portfolio risk.

PART IV

Fixed-Income Securities

CHAPTER 14

Bond Prices and Yields

In the previous chapters on risk-and-return relationships, we have treated securities at a high level of abstraction. We have assumed implicitly that a prior, detailed analysis of each security already has been performed, and that its risk-and-return features have been assessed.

We turn now to specific analyses of particular security markets. We examine valuation principles, determinants of risk and return, and portfolio strategies commonly used within and across the various markets.

We begin by analyzing **fixed-income securities.** A fixed-income security is a claim on a specified periodic stream of income. Fixed-income securities have the advantage of being relatively easy to understand because much of the element of risk is absent. The level of payments is fixed in advance, so risk considerations are minimal as long as the issuer of the security is sufficiently creditworthy. Hence these securities are a convenient starting point for our analysis of the universe of potential investment vehicles.

This chapter reviews the principles of bond pricing. It shows how bond prices are set in accordance with market interest rates, and why bond prices change with those rates. After examining the Treasury bond market, where default risk may be ignored, we move to the corporate bond sector. Here, we look at the determinants of credit risk and the default premium built into bond yields. Finally, we examine the impact of call and convertibility provisions on prices and yields.

14.1 Bond Prices and Yields

The basic fixed-income security is the bond. A **bond** is a simple borrowing arrangement in which the borrower issues (sells) an IOU to the investor. The arrangement obligates the issuer to make specified payments to the bondholder on specified dates. A typical *coupon bond* obligates the issuer to make semiannual payments of interest, called coupon payments, to the bondholder for the life of the bond, and then to repay the original **principal,** or borrowed money, at the maturity of the bond. The **coupon rate** of the bond is the coupon payment divided by the bond's **par value.** To illustrate, a bond with par value of $1,000 and coupon rate of 8% is sold to a buyer for a $1,000 payment. The bondholder is then entitled to a payment of 8% of $1,000, or $80 per year, for the stated life of the bond, for example 30 years. That $80 payment typically comes in two semiannual installments of $40 each. After the 30-year life of the bond, the borrower (issuer) repays the original $1,000 principal to the lender (the bondholder).

Review of the Present Value Relationship

Because a bond's coupon payments and principal repayment all occur months or years into the future, the price that an investor would be willing to pay for the claim to those payments depends on the value of dollars to be received in the future compared with dollars in hand today. The *present value* of a claim to a dollar to be paid in the future is the market price at which that claim would sell if it were traded in the securities market.

We know that the present value of a dollar to be received in the future is less than $1. This is because the time spent waiting to receive the dollar imposes an opportunity cost on the investor—if the money is not in hand today, it cannot be invested to start generating income immediately. Denoting the current market interest rate by r, the present value of a dollar to be received n years from now is $1/(1 + r)^n$.

To see why this must be, consider an example in which the interest rate is 5%, $r = .05$. According to the present value rule, the value of $1 to be received in 10 years would be $1/(1.05)^{10} = \$.614$. This is precisely the amount that would be paid in the marketplace for a claim to a payment of $1 in 10 years. This is because an investor currently investing at the going 5% rate of interest realizes that only $.614 needs to be set aside now in order to provide a final value of $1 in 10 years, since $.614 \times 1.05^{10} = \$1$. The present value formula tells us exactly how much an investor should be willing to pay for a claim to a future cash flow. This value will be the current price of the claim.

We simplify for now by assuming that there is one interest rate that is appropriate for discounting cash flows of any maturity, but we can relax this assumption easily. In practice, there may be different discount rates for cash flows accruing in different periods. For the time being, however, we ignore this refinement until the next chapter.

Bond Pricing

In the previous example we asserted that the 8% coupon bond could be sold to the public at an issue price of $1,000; that is, we assumed that the bond could be sold at its par value. This is a bit of a leap, because we do not yet know whether investors would be willing to pay $1,000 for the 60 semiannual payments of $40 and the ultimate repayment of the $1,000 in year 30. To arrive at the price they would be willing to pay for the bond, investors need to compute the present value of the cash flows they stand to receive from purchasing the bond.

In our case, the bond would indeed sell at $1,000 if the market interest rate were exactly equal to the 8% coupon rate, or more precisely, if the market interest rate were 4% per 6-month period. In this event it is easy to confirm that the present value of the bond's 60 semiannual coupon payments of $40 each would equal $904.94, while the $1,000 principal repayment would have a present value of $1,000/(1.04)^{60} = $95.06, for a total bond value of $1,000. You can perform these calculations easily on any financial calculator or use a set of present value tables from any introductory finance textbook.

Symbolically, we write

$$\$1,000 = \sum_{t=1}^{60} \frac{\$40}{(1.04)^t} + \frac{\$1,000}{(1.04)^{60}} \tag{14.1}$$

The summation sign in equation 14.1 directs us to add 60 terms, each of which is $40 divided by 1.04 to a power that ranges from 1 to 60. This first expression thus gives us the present value of a $40 annuity. For expositional simplicity we can write equation 14.1 as

$$1,000 = 40 \times PA(4\%, 60) + 1,000 \times PF(4\%, 60)$$

where PA(4%, 60) represents the present value of an annuity of $1 when the interest rate is 4% and the annuity is to last for 60 periods, and PF (4%, 60) similarly represents the present value of a single payment of $1 to be received in 60 periods. In our example each "period" is 6 months.

Of course, if the interest rate were not equal to the bond's coupon rate, the bond would not sell at par value. For example, if the interest rate were to rise to 10% (5% per 6 months), the bond's price would fall by $189.29 to $810.71, as follows:

$$\$40 \times PA(5\%, 60) + \$1,000 \times PF(5\%, 60)$$
$$= \$757.17 \qquad\qquad + \$53.54$$
$$= \$810.71$$

At the higher current interest rate, the present value of the payments to be received by the bondholder is lower. This illustrates the general property that bond prices and market interest rates are inversely related.

TABLE 14.1   Bond Prices at Different Interest Rates (8% Coupon Bond)

Time to Maturity	Bond Price at Given Market Interest Rate				
	4%	6%	8%	10%	12%
1 year	1,038.83	1,019.13	1,000.00	981.41	963.33
10 years	1,327.03	1,148.77	1,000.00	875.38	770.60
20 years	1,547.11	1,231.15	1,000.00	828.41	699.07
30 years	1,695.22	1,276.76	1,000.00	810.71	676.77

FIGURE 14.1
The inverse
relationship between
bond prices and
yields.

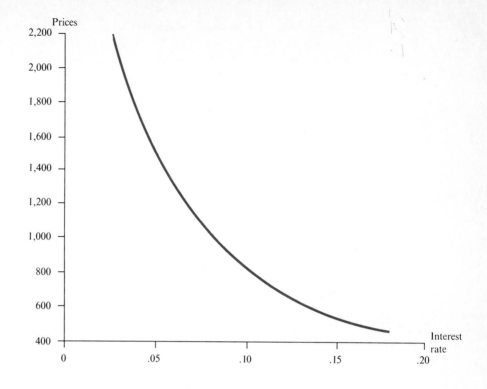

Figure 14.1 shows the price of the 30-year, 8% coupon bond for a range of interest rates. The negative slope illustrates the inverse relationship between prices and yields. Note also from the figure (and from Table 14.1) that the shape of the curve implies that an increase in the interest rate results in a price decline that is smaller than the price gain resulting from a decrease of equal magnitude in the interest rate.

Concept Check

Question 1. Calculate the price of the bond for a market interest rate of 3% per half year. Compare the capital gains for the interest rate decline to the losses incurred when the rate increases to 5%.

Corporate bonds at issue typically sell at par value. Thus the underwriters of the bond issue (the firms that market the bonds to the public for the issuing corporation) must choose a coupon rate that very closely approximates market yields. In such a primary issue the underwriters attempt to sell the newly issued bonds directly to their customers. If the coupon rate is inadequate, the bonds will not be salable at par value.

After the bonds are issued, bondholders may buy or sell bonds in secondary markets such as the New York Bond Exchange, or the over-the-counter market, where most bonds trade. In these secondary markets bond prices move in accordance with market forces. The bond prices fluctuate inversely with the market interest rate.

The inverse relationship between prices and yields is a central feature of fixed-income securities. Interest rate fluctuations represent the main source of risk for this market, and we devote considerable attention in Chapter 16 to assessing the sensitivity of bond prices to market yields. For now, however, it is sufficient to highlight one key factor that determines that sensitivity, namely, the maturity of the bond.

A general rule in evaluating bond price risk is that the greater the maturity of the bond, the greater the sensitivity of price to fluctuations in the interest rate. For example, consider Table 14.1, which presents the price of an 8% coupon bond at different market yields and times to maturity. For any departure of the interest rate from 8% (the rate at which the bond sells at par value), the change in the bond price is smaller for shorter times to maturity.

This makes sense. If you buy the bond at par with an 8% coupon rate, and market rates subsequently rise, then you suffer a loss: you have tied up your money earning 8% when alternative investments offer higher returns. This is reflected in the capital loss on the bond. The longer the period for which your money is tied up, the greater the loss, and correspondingly the greater the drop in the bond price. In Table 14.1 the row for 1-year maturity bonds shows little price sensitivity—with only 1 year's earning at stake, changes in interest rates are not too threatening. However, for 30-year maturity bonds, interest rate swings have a large impact on bond prices.

This is why short-term Treasury securities such as T-bills are considered to be the safest. They are free not only of default risk, but also largely of price risk attributable to interest-rate volatility.

Yield to Maturity

In practice, an investor considering the purchase of a bond is not quoted a promised rate of return. Instead, the investor must use the bond price, maturity date, and coupon payments to infer the return offered by the bond over its life. The **yield to maturity** is a measure of the average rate of return that will be earned on a bond if it is bought now and held until maturity. To calculate the yield to maturity, we solve the bond price equation for the interest rate, given the bond's price.

For example, suppose that the 8% 30-year coupon bond were selling at $1,276.76. What rate of return would be earned by an investor purchasing the bond at market price? To answer this question, we solve for r in the equation following:

$$1,276.76 = \sum_{t=1}^{60} \frac{40}{(1 + r)^t} + \frac{1,000}{(1 + r)^{60}}$$

or equivalently,

$$1,276.76 = 40 \times PA(r, 60) + 1,000 \times PF(r, 60)$$

These equations have only one unknown variable, the interest rate, r. Y financial calculator to confirm that the solution to the equation is $r = .03$, half year.[1] This is considered the bond's yield to maturity, since the bond would be fairly priced at $1,276.76 if the fair market rate of return on the bond over its entire life were 3% per half year. The bond's yield to maturity would be quoted in the financial press at an annual percentage rate (APR) of 6%, despite the fact that its effective annual yield is 6.09% ($1.03^2 - 1 = .0609$).

Notice that the bond's yield to maturity is the internal rate of return on an investment in the bond. The yield to maturity can be interpreted as the compound rate of return over the life of the bond under the assumption that all bond coupons can be reinvested at an interest rate equal to the bond's yield to maturity. If this is not the case, the yield to maturity will not be the same as the return over the bond's life. Yield to maturity is widely accepted as a proxy for average return, however, because alternative measures require forecasts of future reinvestment rates. We discuss some of the alternative measures in Chapter 15.

You should be aware that yield to maturity differs from the *current yield* of a bond. The current yield is the bond's annual coupon payment divided by the bond price. For example, for the 8% 30-year bond currently selling at $1,276.76, the current yield would be $80/$1,276.76 = .0627$, or 6.27% per year. In contrast, recall that the effective annual yield to maturity is 6.09%. For this bond, which is selling at a premium over par value ($1,276 rather than $1,000), the coupon rate exceeds the current yield, which exceeds the yield to maturity. The coupon rate exceeds current yield because the coupon rate divides the coupon payments by par value ($1,000) rather than by the bond price ($1,276). Similarly, the current yield exceeds yield to maturity because the yield to maturity accounts for the built-in capital loss on the bond: the bond bought today for $1,276 will eventually fall in value to $1,000 at maturity.

| Concept Check | Question 2. What will be the relationship between coupon rate, current yield, and yield to maturity for bonds selling at discounts from par? |

14.2 Bond Prices Over Time

Although bonds generally promise a fixed flow of income to their owners, that income stream is not in fact risk free unless the investor can be sure that the issuer will not default on the obligation. All corporate bonds, for example, entail some risk of default. Even though the promised cash flows are specified when the bond is purchased, the actual bond payments are uncertain, because they depend to some extent on the ultimate financial status of the firm. In contrast, U.S. government fixed-

---

[1] Without a financial calculator we still could solve the equation, but we would need to use a trial-and-error approach.

income securities may be treated as virtually free of default risk.

Because these securities are free of default risk they present fewer complicating issues for analysis. Hence we will illustrate the properties of bond prices using Treasury securities as our example, deferring until later in the chapter the discussion of riskier nongovernment securities.

Zero Coupon Bonds

Borrowers also, but less commonly, issue *original issue discount bonds* in addition to coupon bonds issued at par. These are bonds that are issued intentionally with low coupon rates that cause the bond to sell at a discount from par value. An extreme example of this type of bond is the **zero coupon bond,** which carries no coupons and must provide all its return in the form of price appreciation. "Zeros" provide only one cash flow to their owners, and that is on the maturity date of the bond.

U.S. Treasury bills are examples of short-term zero coupon instruments. The Treasury issues, or sells, a bill for some amount less than $10,000, agreeing to repay $10,000 at the bill's maturity. All of the investor's return comes in the form of price appreciation over time.

In addition, longer-term zero coupon bonds can be created synthetically. Several investment banking firms buy coupon-paying Treasury bonds and sell rights to single payments backed by the bonds. These bonds are said to be *stripped* of coupons. They often have colorful names such as CATS (certificates of accrual on Treasury securities, issued by Salomon Brothers) or TIGRs (Treasury investment growth receipts, issued by Merrill Lynch). The single payments are, in essence, zero coupon bonds collateralized by the original Treasury securities and thus are virtually free of default risk. (See the nearby box.)

Treasury bills are issued with initial maturities of less than 1 year. Thus, if a bill with a 6-month maturity is issued at a price of $9,600, we would determine the half-year yield to maturity over the bill's life by solving

$$\$9,600 = \$10,000/(1 + r)$$

to find that $r = .0417$, or 4.17% per half year. The effective annual rate would be 8.51% ($1.0417^2 = 1.0851$).

Recall from Chapter 2, however, that bill yields are quoted using the bank discount method, which is not easily comparable either to the APR or to the effective yield. Thus, to keep our eyes on principles rather than institutional details, we will confine our discussion to effective interest rates.

What should happen to T-bill prices as time passes? On their maturity dates bills must sell for $10,000 because the payment of par value is imminent. Before maturity, however, bills should sell at discounts from par, as the present value of the future $10,000 payment is less than $10,000. As time passes, then, the bill's price will increase at exactly the rate of interest.

To see this, consider a Treasury bill with 8 months until maturity, and suppose that the market interest rate is 1% per month. The price of the bill today will be

Lyons And Tigrs, No Bears, Oh, My! Lyons And Tigrs, No . . .

Blame it all on Merrill Lynch & Co.

The firm's TIGRs—Treasury investment growth receipts—were successful enough to spawn a slew of imitators. Salomon Brothers Inc. soon followed with CATS, or certificates of accrual on Treasury securities. Now, more than animals are running amok on Wall Street.

How About a Test Drive?

Salomon is selling securities backed by auto loans called CARs, or certificates of automobile receivables. Drexel Burnham Lambert Inc. calls its version of the same thing FASTBACs, or first automotive short-term bonds and certificates.

One type of securities can be bought, depending on the firm, as STARS, or short-term auction-rate stock; DARTS, or Dutch-auction-rate transferable securities; MAPS, market-auction preferred stock; AMPS, auction-market preferred stock; and CAMPS, cumulative auction-market preferred stock.

Shearson Lehman Brothers Inc. recently tagged a floating-rate mortgage-backed security with one of Wall Street's most popular words: FIRSTS, or floating-interest-rate short-term securities.

Merrill Lynch, knowing no boundaries, added COLTS, or continuously offered long-term securities, and OPOSSMS, options to purchase or sell specific mortgage-backed securities. Salomon bolstered its lineup with HOMES, or homeowner-mortgage Euro securities, and CARDs, certificates for amortizing revolving debts, backed by credit-card receivables.

A Salomon spokeswoman gives one explanation for the practice: "Names without acronyms can be tongue-twisting and hard to remember." A Merrill official offers another: "It's one-upmanship."

Some officials say the trend has gotten out of hand. Wesley Jones, head of product development at First Boston Corp., says if an acronym "sounds like an animal, it won't describe what you've got."

ZCCBs and SLOBs

Likewise, by the time a name has been massaged to produce an acronym, it may tell little of the product. For example, Merrill Lynch offers LYONs, or liquid-yield option notes; these are really zero-coupon convertible bonds, but calling them ZCCBs wouldn't sound nearly as good for these companions of TIGRs.

Of course, the uncontrived names of some securities actually form acronyms, but these rarely make useful marketing tools. First Boston, for instance, once underwrote an offering of secured-lease obligation bonds. It used the full name.

FIGURE 14.2
The price of a 10-year
zero coupon bond
over time. Price
equals $1{,}000/(1.10)^t$,
where t is time until
maturity.

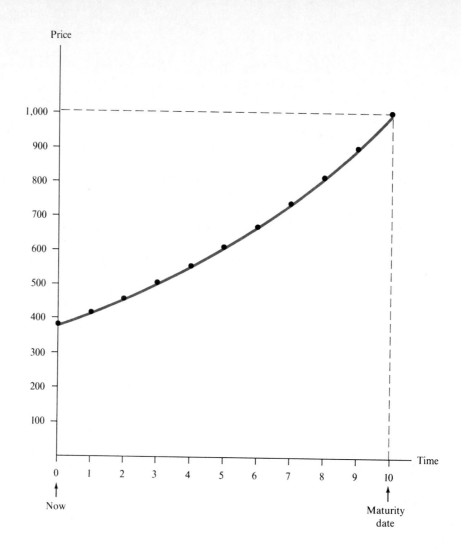

$10,000/1.01^8$, or $9,234.83. Next month, with only 7 months until maturity, the bill price will be $10,000/1.01^7$, or $9,327.18, a 1% increase over its value the previous month. Because the present value of the bill is now discounted for 1 fewer month, its price has increased by the 1-month discount factor.

Figure 14.2 presents the price path of a 10-year zero coupon bond until its maturity date for an annual market interest rate of 10%. Notice that the bond price rises exponentially, not linearly, until its maturity.

The Internal Revenue Service recognizes that the "built-in" price appreciation on orginal issue discount (OID) bonds such as T-bills or other zero coupon bonds in fact represents an implicit interest payment to the holder of the security. The IRS calculates a price appreciation schedule to impute interest income for any portion of the built-in appreciation that accrues to the investor during the tax year even if the asset is not sold or does not mature until future years. Any additional gains or losses that arise from changes in market interest rates are treated as capital gains or losses if the OID bond is sold during the tax year. We work through an example of this procedure later in this section.

Coupon Bonds

We will use U.S. Treasury bonds and notes as our prototype default-free coupon bond. Like bills, T-notes and T-bonds pose no default risk. T-note maturities range up to 10 years, whereas bonds are issued with maturities ranging from 10 to 30 years. Both are issued in denominations of $1,000 or more. Both make semiannual coupon payments that are set at an initial level that enables the government to sell the securities at or near par value. Aside from their differing maturities at issuance, the only major distinction between T-notes and T-bonds is that T-bonds may be *callable* for a given period, usually during the last 5 years of the bond's life. The call provision gives the Treasury the right to repurchase the bond at par value.

Figure 14.3 is an excerpt from the listing of Treasury issues in *The Wall Street Journal*. Note the bond (*arrow*) that matures in December 1990. Its coupon rate is 6⅝%. Recall from the discussion in Chapter 2 that even though they look like decimals, the bid and asked prices are quoted in points plus fractions of ⅟₃₂ of a point, and that although bonds are sold in denominations of $1,000 par value, the prices are quoted as a percentage of par value. Therefore the bid price of the bond is 96²³⁄₃₂ = 96.71875% of par value, or $967.1875, while the asked price is 96²⁷⁄₃₂, or $968.4375.

As we have noted, the reported yield to maturity, 8.05%, is calculated by determining the 6-month yield and then doubling it, rather than compounding it for two half-year periods. Using a simple-interest technique to annualize means that the yield is quoted on an APR basis rather than as an effective annual yield. The APR method in this context is also called the **bond equivalent yield.**

As you look at Figure 14.3, you will see that the yields on most bonds are fairly similar. Some bonds, however, such as the 3 Feb 1995 and the 3½ Nov 1998 bonds offer seemingly quite low yields. These bonds, known as *flower bonds*, are special because they may be used to settle federal estate taxes at par value under certain conditions. Because individuals using these bonds for estate tax purposes may in effect sell them to the U.S. government for their full par value, these bonds sell at close to par value despite their low coupon payments. Flower bonds are no longer issued by the Treasury.

The callable bonds are easily identified in Figure 14.3 because a range of the years in which the bond is callable appears in the maturity date column. Recall from Chapter 2 that yields on premium bonds (bonds selling above par value) are calculated as the yield to the first call date, whereas yields on discount bonds are calculated as the yield to maturity date.

In practice, a bond buyer must pay the asked price for the bond plus any accrued interest. Recall that interest payments are made every 6 months. If a bond is pur-

TREASURY BONDS, NOTES & BILLS

Tuesday, July 5, 1988

Representative Over-the-Counter quotations based on transactions of $1 million or more as of 4 p.m. Eastern time.

Hyphens in bid-and-asked and bid changes represent 32nds; 101-01 means 101 1/32. a-Plus 1/64. b-Yield to call date. d-Minus 1/64. k-Nonresident aliens exempt from withholding taxes. n-Treasury notes. p-Treasury note; nonresident aliens exempt from withholding taxes.

Source: Bloomberg Financial Markets

Treasury Bonds and Notes

Rate	Mat. Date	Bid	Asked	Chg.	Yld.
6⅜	1988 Jul p	99-29	100	....	6.44
14	1988 Jul n	100-04	100-07	....	4.82
6⅛	1988 Aug p	99-26	99-29	....	6.61
9½	1988 Aug p	100-07	100-10	....	6.40
10½	1988 Aug n	100-10	100-13	− 01	6.51
6⅜	1988 Sep p	99-25	99-28	....	6.80
11¾	1988 Sep p	100-30	101-01	....	6.71
15⅝	1988 Oct n	102-13	102-16	....	5.96
6⅜	1988 Oct p	99-23	99-26	....	6.90
6¼	1988 Nov p	99-18	99-21	− 01	7.09
8¾	1988 Nov n	100-17	100-20	....	6.88
8⅝	1988 Nov p	100-14	100-17	....	7.02
11¾	1988 Nov n	101-17	101-20	− 01	6.99
10⅜	1988 Dec p	101-14	101-18	− 01	7.27
6¼	1988 Dec n	99-13	99-17	....	7.25
6⅛	1989 Jan n	99-08	99-12	....	7.25
14⅝	1989 Jan p	103-29	104-01	− 02	6.67
8	1989 Feb p	100-08	100-12	− 01	7.34
6¼	1989 Feb n	99-05	99-09	− 01	7.38
11¾	1989 Feb n	102-07	102-11	− 01	7.35
11¼	1989 Mar p	102-17	102-21	− 01	7.43
6¾	1989 Mar p	99-04	99-08	− 01	7.42
7⅛	1989 Apr p	99-18	99-22	− 01	7.51
14⅜	1989 Apr n	105-11	105-15	− 02	6.97
6⅞	1989 May p	99-10	99-14	− 01	7.55
9¼	1989 May n	101-10	101-16	....	7.39
8	1989 May n	100-07	100-11	− 03	7.58
11¾	1989 May n	103-10	103-14	− 01	7.51
7⅜	1989 Jun p	99-22	99-26	− 01	7.57
9⅜	1989 Jun p	101-25	101-29	....	7.57
7⅜	1989 Jul p	99-27	99-31	− 02	7.65
14½	1989 Jul n	106-23	106-27	− 01	7.43
7¾	1989 Aug p	99-30	100-02	− 01	7.68
6⅜	1989 Aug p	98-25	98-29	....	7.66
13⅜	1989 Aug p	106-13	106-17	− 02	7.61
8½	1989 Sep k	100-23	100-27	− 02	7.75
9⅜	1989 Sep p	101-23	101-27	− 02	7.76
11⅞	1989 Oct n	104-26	104-30	....	7.71
7⅞	1989 Oct p	100	100-04	....	7.76
6¾	1989 Nov p	98-03	98-07	− 01	7.77
10¾	1989 Nov n	103-20	103-24	− 01	7.77
12¾	1989 Nov p	106-09	106-13	....	7.68
7¾	1989 Nov p	99-25	99-29	− 01	7.81
7⅞	1989 Dec p	99-28	100	− 02	7.87
8⅜	1989 Dec p	100-19	100-23	− 03	7.85
7⅜	1990 Jan k	99-05	99-09	− 01	7.87
10½	1990 Jan p	103-18	103-22	− 01	7.88
3½	1990 Feb	94	94-18	+ 02	7.13
6½	1990 Feb p	97-27	97-31	− 01	7.86
7⅛	1990 Feb k	98-22	98-26	− 02	7.90
11	1990 Feb	104-14	104-18	− 03	7.91
7⅛	1990 Mar p	98-26	98-30	− 02	7.91
7¾	1990 Mar p	99-01	99-05	− 02	7.89
8	1990 Jun p	99-29	100-01	− 02	7.98
10¾	1990 Jul n	104-29	105-01	− 02	8.01
7⅞	1990 Aug k	99-20	99-24	− 03	8.00
9⅞	1990 Aug p	103-11	103-15	− 05	8.05
10¾	1990 Aug n	105-03	105-07	− 01	8.00
6¾	1990 Sep p	97-08	97-12	− 04	8.05
11½	1990 Oct n	106-27	106-31	− 03	8.07
8	1990 Nov p	99-24	99-28	− 03	8.05
9⅜	1990 Nov p	103-05	103-09	− 02	8.06
13	1990 Nov n	110-10	110-14	− 02	8.04
6⅝	1990 Dec p	96-23	96-27	− 01	8.05
11¾	1991 Jan n	108-02	108-06	− 04	8.10
7¾	1991 Feb p	98-06	98-10	− 04	8.10
9½	1991 Feb k	102-06	102-10	− 04	8.12
3	1995 Feb	94-02	94-20	+ 06	3.93
10½	1995 Feb	108-31	109-03	− 10	8.66
11¼	1995 Feb p	112-21	112-25	− 09	8.67
8⅜	1995 Apr p	98-12			7
10⅜		May			
11½		v p			

Rate	Mat. Date	Bid	Asked	Bid Chg.	Yld.
12⅜	1995 May	120-10	120-14	− 11	8.61
10½	1995 Aug p	109-05	109-09	− 11	8.72
9½	1995 Nov p	104	104-04	− 09	8.72
11½	1995 Nov	115-01	115-05	− 08	8.67
8⅞	1996 Feb p	100-20	100-24	− 09	8.74
7¾	1996 May p	92	92-04	− 09	8.78
7¼	1996 Nov p	90-25	90-29	− 10	8.81
8⅝	1997 Aug k	98-18	98-22	− 09	8.84
8½	1997 May k	97-28	98	− 09	8.83
8⅞	1997 Nov p	100	100-04	− 11	8.85
8⅛	1998 Feb p	95-09	95-13	− 07	8.84
9	1998 May	101-03	101-07	− 10	8.81
7	1993-98 May	89-05	89-09	− 09	8.63
3½	1998 Nov	94-03	94-21	+ 04	4.14
8½	1994-99 May	97-10	97-14	− 08	8.87
7⅞	1995-00 Feb	92-14	92-18	− 08	8.91
8¾	1995-00 Aug	95-29	96-01	− 06	8.92
11¾	2001 Feb	120-22	120-28	− 15	8.95
13⅛	2001 May	131-07	131-13	− 17	8.96
8	1996-01 Aug	93-26	94	− 23	8.78
13⅜	2001 Aug	133-15	133-21	− 10	8.96
15¾	2001 Nov	152-05	152-11	− 10	8.95
14¼	2002 Feb	140-24	140-30	− 10	8.98
11⅝	2002 Nov	120-05	120-11	− 10	9.06
10¾	2003 Feb	113-08	113-14	− 11	9.07
10¾	2003 Feb	113-09	113-15	− 10	9.08
11⅛	2003 Aug	116-12	116-18	− 06	9.09
11⅛	2003 Nov	122-18	122-24	− 10	9.09
12⅜	2004 May	126-30	127-04	− 10	9.11
13¾	2004 Aug	139	139-06	− 10	9.07
11⅝	2004 Nov k	121-02	121-08	− 09	9.10
8¼	2000-05 May	93-08	93-14	− 10	9.01
12	2005 May k	124-17	124-23	− 10	9.10
10¾	2005 Aug k	113-26	114	− 08	9.12
9⅜	2006 Feb k	103-01	103-07	− 10	9.01
7⅝	2002-07 May	87-10	87-16	− 08	9.02
7⅞	2002-07 Nov	89-09	89-15	− 08	9.03
8⅜	2003-08 Aug	92-27	93-01	− 12	9.14
8¾	2003-08 Nov	96-02	96-08	− 12	9.16
9⅛	2004-09 May	99-13	99-19	− 11	9.17
10⅜	2004-09 Nov	109-23	109-29	− 12	9.19
11¾	2005-10 Feb	121-13	121-19	− 11	9.19
10	2005-10 May	106-16	106-22	− 11	9.21
12¾	2005-10 Nov	130-17	130-23	− 11	9.18
13⅞	2006-11 May	140-29	141-03	− 11	9.16
14	2006-11 Nov	142-15	142-21	− 11	9.16
10⅜	2007-12 Nov	110-11	110-17	− 11	9.20
12	2008-13 Aug	125-14	125-20	− 11	9.18
13¼	2009-14 May	137-14	137-20	− 11	9.17
12½	2009-14 Aug k	130-18	130-24	− 11	9.18
11¾	2009-14 Nov	124-15	124-21	− 10	9.11
11¼	2015 Feb k	121-26	122	− 11	9.05
10⅜	2015 Aug k	115-15	115-21	− 24	9.06
9⅞	2015 Nov	107-27	108-01	− 19	9.07
9¼	2016 Feb k	101-26	102	− 13	9.05
7¼	2016 May k	81-27	82-01	− 09	9.02
7½	2016 Nov k	84-09	84-15	− 10	9.02
8¾	2017 May k	96-30	97-04	− 16	9.03
8⅞	2017 Aug k	98-15	98-21	− 12	9.00
9⅛	2018 May k	102-14	102-20	− 15	8.87

U.S. Treas. Bills Mat. date	Bid	Asked	Yield Discount
-1988-			
7- 7	6.51	5.49	5.57
7-14	4.96	3.94	4.00
7-21	5.41	5.29	5.38
7-28	6.04	5.92	6.02
8- 4	6.33	6.21	6.33
8-11	6.30	6.23	6.36
8-18	6.30	6.23	6.36
8-25	6.30	6.23	6.37
9- 1	6.43	6.39	6.54
9- 8	6.43	6.39	6.55
9-15	6.47	6.43	6.60
9-22	6.51	6.47	6.65
9-29	6.56	6.52	6.71
10- 6	6.55	6.48	6.68
10-13	6.51	6.44	6.65
10-20	6.55	6.48	6.70
10-27	6.59	6.53	6.7

Mat. date	Bid	Asked	Yield Discount
-1988-			
11- 3	6.62	6.56	6.80
11-10	6.63	6.57	6.82
11-17	6.64	6.58	6.84
11-25	6.70	6.64	6.91
12- 1	6.67	6.61	6.89
12- 8	6.67	6.61	6.90
12-15	6.73	6.67	6.97
12-22	6.76	6.70	7.01
12-29	6.71	6.67	6.99
-1989-			
1-19	6.78	6.74	7.08
2-16	6.84	6.78	7.13
3-16	6.86	6.80	7.17
4-13		6.87	7.27
		6.94	7.37

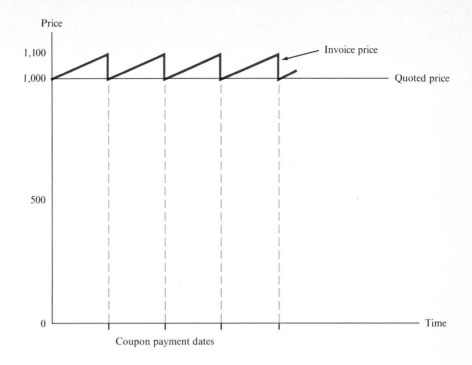

FIGURE 14.4
Invoice price of a coupon bond over time.

chased between coupon payments, the buyer must pay the seller for the prorated share of the upcoming coupon. For example, if 40 days have passed since the last coupon payment, and there are 182 days in the semiannual coupon period, the seller is entitled to a payment of accrued interest of 40/182 of the semiannual coupon. The sale, or invoice price, of the bond would equal the stated price plus the accrued interest.

Figure 14.4 illustrates the pattern of bond prices over time. Assume that a bond paying annual coupons is issued at par at a coupon rate of 10%, and that market rates remain at 10%. The quoted price of the bond remains at $1,000, whereas the invoice price follows a ratchet pattern, gradually reaching $1,100 just before a coupon payment and falling back to $1,000 just after the coupon is paid.

This explains why the price of a maturing bond is listed at $1,000 rather than $1,000 plus one coupon payment. A purchaser of an 8% coupon bond 1 day before the bond's maturity would in fact receive $1,040 on the following day and therefore should be willing to pay a total price of $1,040 for the bond. However, $40 of that total payment would constitute the accrued interest for the preceding half-year period that is owed to the bond seller. The bond price is quoted net of accrued interest in the financial pages and thus appears as $1,000.

As we noted earlier, a T-bond will sell at par value when its coupon rate equals the market interest rate. In these circumstances the investor receives fair compensation for the time value of money in the form of the recurrent interest payments. No further capital gain is necessary to provide fair compensation. If the coupon rate were lower than the market interest rate, the coupon payments alone would not provide investors as high a return as they could earn elsewhere in the market. To receive a fair return on such an investment, investors also would need to earn capital gains on their bonds to augment the insufficient interest income. The bonds therefore would have to sell below par value to provide a "built-in" capital gain on the investment.

To illustrate this point, suppose a bond was issued several years ago when the interest rate was 7%. The bond's annual coupon rate was thus set at 7%. Now, with 3 years left in the bond's life, the interest rate is 4% per half year, slightly more than 8% per year compounded. The bond's fair market price is therefore the present value of the remaining semiannual coupons plus principal repayment. If the next coupon is to be paid in 6 months, that present value is

$$\$35 \times PA(4\%, 6) + \$1,000 \times PF(4\%, 6) = \$973.79$$

which is less than par value.

In 6 months, after the next coupon is paid, the bond would sell at

$$\$35 \times PA(4\%, 5) + \$1,000 \times PF(4\%, 5) = \$977.74$$

thereby yielding a capital gain over the 6-month period of $3.95. If an investor had purchased the bond at $973.79, the total return over the 6-month period would equal the coupon payment plus capital gain, or $35 + $3.95 = $38.95. This represents a 6-month rate of return of 38.95/973.79, or 4%, exactly the current 6-month rate of return available elsewhere in the market.

Concept Check

Question 3. What will the bond price be in another 6 months, when four half-year periods remain until maturity? What is the rate of return to an investor who purchases the bond at $977.74 and sells it in 6 months?

When bond prices are set according to the present value formula, any discount from par value provides an anticipated capital gain that will augment a below-market coupon rate just sufficiently to provide a fair total rate of return. Conversely, if the coupon rate exceeds the market interest rate, then the interest income by itself is greater than that available elsewhere in the market. Investors will bid up the price of these bonds above their par values. As the bonds approach maturity, they will fall in value because fewer of these above-market coupon payments remain. The resulting capital losses offset the large coupon payments so that the bondholder again receives only a fair rate of return.

Problem 5 at the end of this chapter asks you to work through the case of the high-coupon bond. Figure 14.5 traces the price paths of high- and low-coupon bonds (net of accrued interest) as time to maturity approaches. The low-coupon bond enjoys capital gains, whereas the high-coupon bond suffers capital losses.

We use these examples to make the important point that each bond offers investors the same total rate of return. Although the capital gain and income components dif-

FIGURE   14.5

Price paths of coupon
bonds.

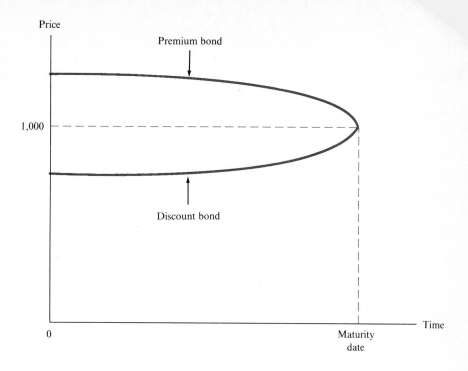

fer, the price of each bond is set to provide competitive rates, as we should expect in
well-functioning capital markets. Security returns all should be comparable on an after-tax risk-adjusted basis. If not, investors will try to sell low-return securities,
thereby driving down their prices until their total return at the now-lower price is
competitive with other securities. Price should continue to adjust until all securities
are fairly priced in that expected returns are appropriate (given necessary risk and tax
adjustments).

After-Tax Returns

We have noted that coupon payments are taxable as interest income, and that discounts from par value on original issue discount bonds are amortized and also treated
as interest income. Capital gains or losses also result in tax obligations or benefits in
the year they are realized. Because investors should focus on after-tax income, we
will examine the after-tax rate of return on two types of bonds: a zero-coupon bond
and a par bond.

Suppose that you have a 1-year investment horizon and are trying to decide between these two bonds. Both mature in 20 years. The zero-coupon bond pays $1,000
at maturity. For simplicity, assume the par bond, which has a 10% coupon rate, pays
the $100 coupon once each year. Both bonds now offer yields to maturity of 10%.
The 10% coupon bond sells at par, whereas the zero sells at $1,000/(1.10)^{20} =
$148.64.

First, let us calculate after-tax returns over the coming year assuming that yields to maturity remain at 10% and assuming a personal tax bracket of 30%. At the end of the year the time to maturity of each bond will be 19 years. The coupon bond still will sell at par value (why?), and will have provided a $100 coupon payment. Total income is $100, and the before-tax yield is therefore 10%. However, the $100 coupon payment generates $30 in tax obligations and thus results in only $70 net income, providing an after-tax rate of return of 7%.

The zero-coupon bond will have increased in price to $1,000/(1.10)^{19} = \$163.51$, a pretax gain of 10%. However, that gain of $14.87 ($163.51 − $148.64) is treated by the IRS as imputed interest, with 30% of it taxed away. Therefore the net-of-tax increase in value for the zero is $10.41, for an after-tax rate of return of 10.41/148.64 = .07, or 7%. Thus for both bonds the after-tax yield equals $10\% \times (1 - .30)$, or 7%.

Now let us see what happens if the interest rate changes. Suppose the yields on each bond fall to 9% by next year. The price of the coupon bond will rise to $1,089.50, at which point it is sold. The pretax return on the bond will be the $100 coupon plus the capital gain of $89.50, a total return of 18.95%. The tax due on the bond is 30% of the $100 coupon plus 30% of $89.50, because under U.S. tax law realized capital gains are taxed at the same rate as ordinary income. Thus taxes will be $30 + $26.85, leaving net-of-tax income of $132.65, which figures as an after-tax rate of return of 13.265%. Note that, although realized capital gains and interest income are taxed equally, it still is important to distinguish between capital gains and other income because capital gains are taxed only when realized.

The zero-coupon bond will sell at $1,000/(1.09)^{19} = \$194.49$ by year-end, for a pretax gain of $45.85 and a pretax rate of return of 30.85%. Of this total return, $14.87 will be taxed as ordinary income as the imputed or "built-in" interest at the original 10% yield. The remaining $30.98 income is treated as a capital gain that will be taxed if the bond is sold. Therefore total taxes owed if the bond is sold are $(.30 \times \$14.87) + (.30 \times \$30.98) = \$13.76$, leaving net-of-tax income of $32.09, and an after-tax rate of return of $32.09/\$148.64 = 21.59\%$.

14.3   Corporate Bonds

Like the government, corporations borrow money by issuing bonds. Figure 14.6 is an excerpt of the corporate bond listings from *The Wall Street Journal*. The data presented differ only slightly from U.S. Treasury bond listings. For example, the IBM 9⅜ bond pays a coupon rate of 9.375% and matures in 2004. Unlike Treasury bonds, corporate bonds trade in increments of ⅛ point. IBM's *current yield* is 9.4%, which is simply the annual coupon payment divided by the bond price ($93.75/$997.50). Recall that current yield, unlike yield to maturity, ignores any prospective capital gains or losses based on the bond's price relative to par value. The trading volume column shows that 69 bonds traded on that day. The high, low, and closing prices for the day are given, as well as the change from yesterday's closing price. Like govern-

FIGURE 14.6

Corporate bond listing.

(From *The Wall Street Journal*, July 6, 1988.) Reprinted by permission of *The Wall Street Journal*. © Dow Jones & Company, Inc. 1988. All rights reserved.

NEW YORK EXCHANGE BONDS

Tuesday, July 5, 1988

Total Volume $23,150,000

	Domestic Tue.	Fri.	All Issues Tue.	Fri.
Issues traded	598	532	599	533
Advances	274	268	275	269
Declines	206	150	206	150
Unchanged	118	114	118	114
New highs	10	10	11	10
New lows	3	4	3	4

SALES SINCE JANUARY 1

1988	1987	1986
$3,971,428,000	$5,954,103,000	$5,619,926,000

Dow Jones Bond Averages

-1986- High Low	-1987- High Low	-1988- High Low		---Tuesday--- -1988-	-1987-	-1986-
93.65 83.73	95.51 81.26	91.25 86.92	20 Bonds	89.19 +0.19	89.11 +0.04	91.09 -0.38
95.79 81.85	98.23 79.51	91.88 86.05	10 Utilities	88.80 -0.01	90.06 +0.07	91.43 -0.72
91.64 84.82	93.10 83.00	90.64 86.96	10 Industrial	89.58 +0.40	88.15 +0.01	90.74 -0.05

Bonds	Cur Yld	Vol	Close	Net Chg.	Bonds	Cur Yld	Vol	Close	Net Chg.	Bonds	Cur Yld	Vol	Close	Net Chg.
Beverly zr03	...	46	28½	...	duPnt 8.45s04	9.2	25	91⅞	+ ½	Holidy 11s99	11.6	43	95⅛	+ ⅝
BoisC 7s16	cv	25	118	+ ¾	duPnt 8½06	9.3	10	91½		HollyFar 6s17	cv	51	81½	+ ½
BoltBer 6s12	cv	11	79		duPnt 14s91	13.6	15	102²³⁄₃₂	- ⁹⁄₃₂	HoCp 8½08	cv	21	101	+ ¼
Bordn 8⅜16	10.0	15	84⅛	- ⅞	duPnt dc6s01	8.1	21	74¼	- ¼	HoCp 9s98	cv	25	100	+ ½
BrkUn 8¾99	9.1	15	96⅜	+ 3⅝	duPnt 12⅞92	12.1	20	106½		Humn 8½09	cv	29	101	+ ⅛
BwnSh 9¼05	cv	13	98	- 2	duPnt 8½16	9.4	10	90⅛	- 1¼	vjHuntIR 9⅞e04f	...	30	9½	+ 4
BwnFer 6¼12	cv	61	90⅜	+ 1⅛	DukeP 9¾04	9.7	20	100½	+ ½	IBM Cr 7⅛89	7.2	25	99¼	+ ⅛
BurNo 9⅝96	9.6	10	100⅜	+ 1	DukeP 9⅜08	9.7	104	96¾	- 1⅛	IBM Cr 8¾90	8.3	8	101¼	+ ⅞
BusInd 8s06	cv	15	116½	- 2	EKod 8⅜16	10.0	98	86⅜	- ⅛	ICN 12⅞98	14.5	16	89	- ½
BusInd 5½07	cv	1	79½		Enron 10¾98	10.5	5	102	+ ½	IFRB 9¾99f	...	5	27½	- 1¾
CBS 10⅞95	10.3	12	105⅛	- ⅜	Equitc 10s04	cv	6	72		IllBel 7⅜06	9.1	14	84	- ¼
CIT 9½95	9.5	52	99½	- ⅞	Exxon 6s97	7.4	33	80¾		IllBel 8s04	9.2	13	87	- ¼
CIT 8⅜s01	9.9	15	84¾		Exxon 6½98	7.7	35	84	+ 1	IllPw 8⅜06	10.0	3	86½	+ ⅛
CaroFrt 6¼11	cv	10	77	- ¾	FedSt 10¼10	11.7	64	87½	+ ½	InldStl 9½00	10.0	20	95	+ 4
CartHaw 12½02	13.8	31	90⅞	- ⅛	Fldcst 6s12	cv	25	65¾	+ ¾	InldStl 7.9s07	10.1	10	78½	...
Champ 6½11	cv	16	118	+ 1	FinCpA 6s88	7.8	2	76½	- 3½	InspRs 8½12	cv	7	109	
ChartC 12s99	12.8	24	93⅞	- ⅛	FinCpA 11⅞98	28.4	6	41⅞	+ 1⅞	ItgRs 10⅞96	11.2	1	96¼	...
vjChmtrn 9s94f	...	20	83¾	+ ⅛	FinCp dc11½02	cv	42	29½	- ¾	ItgRs 10s90	9.9	15	101	+ ⅞
CPoV 7¼12	9.5	5	76¼	- ⅜	FtRepub 8¼99f	cv	28	22½	- 1½	Intlgc 11.99s96	15.9	25	75½	+ 1
CPoV 8⅝09	9.5	22	90⅜	+ 1⅝	FtRep flt04f	...	10	28¾	- ¼	IBM 9¾04	9.4	69	99¾	- ⅛
ChvrnC 11¾88	11.6	5	101	...	FUnRE 10¼09	cv	21	107	+ ¼	IBM 7⅞04	cv	335	104⅞	+ ¼
ChvrnC 11s90	10.8	60	101⅝	- ⅛	FisbM 4¾97	cv	9	35	- 1	IBM 10¼95	9.7	155	105⅜	+ ⅛
ChvrnC 7⅞97	8.5	10	92¼	+ 1	FisbCp 8½05	cv	5	52	+ 1	IBM 9s98	9.0	45	100	- ⅛
Chvrn 8¾05	9.4	19	93¼	+ ¼	FlowGn 14.30s04	14.2	8	100½	+ ¼	IPap 8.85s00	9.1	5	96¾	
Chvrn 8¾96	9.0	60	97⅞	- ⅛	Ford 8⅛90	8.2	17	99½	+ 1⅝	IPap dc5⅞12	...	44	56½	- ⅞
Chvrn 9⅜16	9.9	30	94½	- ⅛	FrdC 8.7s99	9.0	5	97	+ 2	IntRec 9s10	cv	20	72½	+ 1¼
ChiPac 6½12	cv	32	90½	+ 1½	FrdC 8¾01	9.2	10	91	+ ¼	IntTT 10s00	10.0	2	99¾	- ⅞
ChckFul 7s12	cv	107	101	+ 2½	FreptM 8¾13	cv	46	107	+ ½	InTT 14¾91	14.3	10	103½	- 1
ChCft 13s99	12.7	4	102	- ½	Fruf 13½96	16.8	127	80¼	+ ¾	vjJnM 9.7s85mf	...	7	132⅛	- 1¾
Chryslr 13s97	11.2	29	116		Fuqua 9½98	10.0	6	93⅜		vjJonsLI 6¾94f	...	38	32¼	...
Chryslr 10.95s17	10.6	10	102⅞	+ 1⅞	Fuqua 9⅞97	10.1	4	97½	+ ⅜	K mart 8⅛97	8.7	15	93½	- ½
ChryF 8.35s91	8.4	10	99⅛		GAF 11⅜95	11.5	156	99	+ ¼	Kenn 7⅞01	8.8	6	89⅜	+ ⅛
ChryF 12⅛90	11.5	4	105	+ ⅞	GATX 11½96	11.2	1	103	- ¾	KerrGl 13s96	12.7	5	102	+ ½
ChryF 9¾91	9.3	25	100⅞	- ¾	GnDev 12⅜05	15.6	138	81	- 7	KerrMc 7¼12	cv	21	103¼	...
ChryF 7...	8.2	25					20	92½	+	...⅞90				

ment bonds, corporate bonds sell in units of $1,000 par value but are quoted as a percentage of par value.

Although the bonds listed in Figure 14.6 trade on a formal exchange, the New York Bond Exchange, we should note that most bonds are traded over-the-counter, meaning that the market for the bonds is a loosely organized network of bond dealers linked together by a computer quotation system. (See Chapter 3 for a comparison of exchange and OTC trading.) In practice, the bond market can be quite "thin," in that there are few investors interested in trading a particular bond at any particular time. Figure 14.6 shows that trading volume of many bonds on the New York Bond Exchange is quite low. On any day it might be difficult to find a buyer or seller for a particular issue, which introduces some "liquidity risk" into the bond market. It may be difficult to sell one's holdings quickly if the need arises.

Bonds issued in the United States today generally are *registered* bonds, meaning that the issuing firm keeps records of the owner of the bond and can mail interest checks to the owner. Registration of bonds is clearly helpful to tax authorities in the enforcement of tax collection. In contrast, *bearer bonds* are traded without any record of ownership. The investor's physical possession of the bond certificate is the only evidence of ownership.

Promised Yields vs. Expected Yields

Corporate bonds always are subject to potential default of the bond issuer. If the issuer declares bankruptcy, the bondholders will not receive all the payments that were promised to them when the bonds were issued. Because of this, we must distinguish between the bond's promised yield to maturity and its expected yield. The promised or stated yield will be realized only if the firm ultimately meets the obligations of the bond issue. Therefore the stated yield is the maximum possible yield to maturity of the bond.[2] In contrast, the expected yield to maturity must take into account the possibility of a default.

To compensate investors for the possibility of bankruptcy, a corporate bond must offer a **default premium.** The premium is a differential in promised yield between the corporate bond and an otherwise identical government bond that is risk free in terms of default. If the corporation remains solvent, and the investor actually receives the promised yield, the investor will realize a higher total yield to maturity than can be realized from the government bond. If, however, the firm goes bankrupt, the corporate bond is likely to provide a return lower than the government bond. The corporate bond thus holds the possibility of both better and worse performance than the default-free Treasury bond. It is important to keep in mind, therefore, that the stated yield to maturity on risky bonds is not the expected yield—it is the yield to maturity that will be realized if the corporation survives over the life of the bond.

The pattern of default premiums offered on risky bonds is sometimes called the risk structure of interest rates. The greater the default risk, the higher the default premium. Such default risk is measured by both Moody's and Standard & Poor's, both of which assign letter grades to the bonds of corporations and municipalities to reflect their assessment of the safety of the bond issue. The top rating is AAA (Standard & Poor's) or Aaa (Moody's). Moody's modifies each rating class with a 1, 2, or 3 suf-

---

[2]The realized compound yield to maturity (see Chapter 15) can exceed the promised yield of maturity if the reinvestment rate turns out to be high. The conventional yield to maturity, however, is independent of reinvestment rates and cannot exceed the promised yield upon purchase of the bond.

FIGURE 14.7

Definitions of each
bond rating class.

(From Ross, Stephen A.,
and Westerfield, Randolph
W., *Corporate Finance*, St.
Louis: Times Mirror/Mosby
College Publishing, 1988.)

Bond Ratings

	Very high quality	High quality	Speculative	Very poor
Standard & Poor's	AAA AA	A BBB	BB B	CCC D
Moody's	Aaa Aa	A Baa	Ba B	Caa C

At times both Moody's and Standard & Poor's have used adjustments to these ratings.
S&P uses plus and minus signs: A+ is the strongest A rating and A− the weakest.
Moody's uses a 1, 2, or 3 designation—with 1 indicating the strongest.

Moody's	S&P	
Aaa	AAA	Debt rated Aaa and AAA has the highest rating. Capacity to pay interest and principal is extremely strong.
Aa	AA	Debt rated Aa and AA has a very strong capacity to pay interest and repay principal. Together with the highest rating, this group comprises the high grade bond class.
A	A	Debt rated A has a strong capacity to pay interest and repay principal, although it is somewhat more susceptible to the adverse effects of changes in circumstances and economic conditions than debt in higher rated categories.
Baa	BBB	Debt rated Baa and BBB is regarded as having an adequate capacity to pay interest and repay principal. Whereas it normally exhibits adequate protection parameters, adverse economic conditions or changing circumstances are more likely to lead to a weakened capacity to pay interest and repay principal for debt in this category than in higher rated categories. These bonds are medium grade obligations.
Ba B Caa Ca	BB B CCC CC	Debt rated in these categories is regarded, on balance, as predominantly speculative with respect to capacity to pay interest and repay principal in accordance with the terms of the obligation. BB and Ba indicate the lowest degree of speculation, and CC and Ca the highest degree of speculation. Although such debt will likely have some quality and protective characteristics, these are outweighed by large uncertainties or major risk exposures to adverse conditions. Some issues may be in default.
C	C	This rating is reserved for income bonds on which no interest is being paid.
D	D	Debt rated D is in default, and payment of interest and/or repayment of principal is in arrears.

Data from various editions of *Standard & Poor's Bond Guide* and *Moody's Bond Guide*.

fix (for example, Aaa1, Aaa2, Aaa3) to provide a finer gradation of ratings. S&P uses a + or − modification.

Bonds rated BBB or above (S&P) or Baa or above (Moody's) are considered **investment grade bonds,** whereas lower-rated bonds are classified as **speculative grade** or **junk bonds.** Certain regulated institutional investors such as insurance companies have not always been allowed to invest in speculative grade bonds. (Some observers have expressed doubt over the value of the bond rating system; see the discussion in the nearby box.)

Figure 14.7 contains data from the *Standard & Poor's Credit Overview* and from *Moody's Industrial Manual* that provide the definitions of each bond rating classification. Figure 14.8 shows yields to maturity of bonds of different risk classes since 1930. The figure shows clear evidence of the presence of default-risk premiums on promised yields. Although yield spreads vary over time, higher promised yields clearly are associated with lower ratings.

One particular manner in which yield spreads seem to vary over time is related to the business cycle. Yield spreads tend to be wider when the economy is in a recession. Apparently, investors perceive a higher probability of bankruptcy when the economy is faltering, even holding bond ratings constant. They require a commensurately higher default premium. This is sometimes termed a *flight to quality,* meaning that investors move their funds into safer bonds unless they can obtain larger premiums on lower-rated securities.

FIGURE 14.8

Long-term bond yields.

(From the *1984* Historical *Chart Book,* Board of Governors of the Federal Reserve System, Washington, D.C.: United States Government Printing Office.)

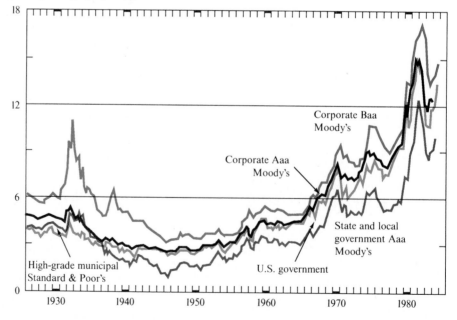

Quarterly averages per year (%)

Value of Bond Ratings Questioned by a Growing Number of Studies

Investors put a lot of faith in bond ratings. But a growing body of research indicates that ratings provide an incomplete and often outdated guide to credit quality.

The studies note that ratings do provide one valuable service: distinguishing between investment-grade bonds and low-rated "junk" bonds. Beyond that, however, the research:

- Questions the significance of the assorted letter grades or notches separating one investment-grade bond from another.
- Finds that there is less correlation than might be expected between ratings and the likelihood of default.
- Indicates that ratings don't tell investors much about other measures of risk like volatility and market performance.
- "Ratings provide information, albeit with a lag, to investors who don't have the resources to investigate a firm," says Jerome Fons, an economist at the Federal Reserve Bank of Cleveland. "But there are questions about (their) usefulness."

Paying for Safety

For investors, the implications are significant. With yield differences between ratings grades amounting to as much as half a percentage point, the perception of greater safety can be expensive. The investor who opts for a triple-A bond rather than a single-A may earn a return of 7.35% rather than 8.35%.

Deciding whether to sacrifice yield for safety has become increasingly important this year as bond prices—including those of top-rated bonds—have slumped. Meanwhile a federal investigation into possible violations involving some 100 municipal bond issues has also focused investor attention on bond rat-ings; several of the issues under scrutiny received the top rating of triple-A.

The two companies with the lion's share of the ratings business are Standard & Poor's Corp. and Moody's Investors Service Inc. Together, they have evaluated more than 92% of the $260 billion of corporate and municipal bonds issued so far this year, according to Securities Data Co., a New York research firm. Both companies bill issuers from $1,000 to $50,000, depending upon the size and complexity of the issues.

Ratings are based on the financial strength and flexibility of the issuer, on its management's expertise and on either the economic outlook for the municipality or the industrial outlook for the company, says Leo O'Neill, head of S&P's debt-rating division. Investment-grade ratings range from triple-A down to triple-B minus (at S&P) or Baa3 (at Moody's). Junk bonds—typically issued by troubled municipalities or heavily indebted companies to repay bank loans, buy out shareholders or finance takeovers—are rated double-B-plus (at S&P) or Ba1 (at Moody's) and below. In general, the higher the rating, the cheaper it is for the issuer to sell bonds.

The two companies defend the usefulness of their services, arguing that they don't pretend to answer all questions about a bond—only the likelihood of default. Edward Kerman, a managing director at Moody's, says the ratings offer "an independent arbiter's assessment of relative risk." S&P's Mr. O'Neill acknowledges that there isn't a "huge, wide differential" between top-rated, triple-A bonds and debt that is rated single-A. But he adds that triple-A bonds are "the creme de la creme," which investors will be happy they have "in periods of economic stress."

Much of the research on bond ratings has been spurred by the growth of the $146 billion junk-bond market, which itself challenged the ratings system. The studies do show that junk bonds are riskier.

According to Edward Altman, a professor of finance at New York University and a consultant to Merrill

Continued.

Lynch & Co., corporate bonds had an average annual default rate of 0.14% through 1986 compared with 1.67% for junk bonds. Moreover, he adds, of the $14.2 billion of rated corporate bonds that have gone into default since 1970, about 70% were rated as junk debt at the time of sale.

But studies also indicate that a well-diversified portfolio of junk debt or a mutual fund that includes junk bonds isn't significantly riskier—and may actually be

ASSIGNING GRADES

Total Value of Corporate and Municipal Bonds Sold Between Jan. 1 and Sept. 15, in Billions of Dollars:

	S & P	Moody's
Investment Grade		
AAA	$80.81	$49.78
AA/Aa	50.39	32.29
A	44.76	53.09
BBB/Baa	19.69	22.53
"Junk" Ratings		
BB/Ba	$ 5.41	$ 4.29
B	17.77	22.12
CCC/Caa	.68	.24

Source: Securities Data Co.

less risky—than an investment-grade bonds portfolio, says Marshall Blume, a professor of Finance at the University of Pennsylvania's Wharton School. The reason: Lower-rated debt tends to move up or down in price in line with the issuer's fortunes, avoiding the larger day-to-day swings in the bond market.

Studies also indicate that investors are well compensated for the added risk of junk bonds. Given past default rates, the yield premium on corporate junk debt should be about one percentage point, says Jonathan Kolatch, director of corporate bond research for Goldman, Sachs & Co. Instead, the premium is hovering at about 2.25 percentage points, he says.

In one study that compared the Salomon Brothers Inc. "high-yield" bond index with a universe of triple-

A-rated debt, Mr. Fons of the Cleveland Federal Reserve Bank found that default rates implied by the yields on the junk bonds exceeded actual default rates. The promised return "appears to sufficiently compensate—almost overcompensate—holders for the loss they can experience," he says.

Most research into bond credit ratings has been done with corporate debt. But institutional investors in municipals think the same criticisms of ratings apply to their market.

"There's been numerous examples of the rating agencies' failure to warn investors of potential problems," says Roger Dennis, president of Massachusetts Financial Services Inc.'s managed municipal bond trust. "During all the major crises in the market, the rating agencies caught on after the fact."

A Record Default

Perhaps the best-known incident involved the record $2.25 billion of bonds sold in the late 1970s and early 1980s for two nuclear power plants built by the Washington Public Power Supply System. The ratings firms assigned the debt single-A-plus and single-A1 ratings, including a strong capacity to pay interest and principal.

In May of 1981, analysts at Merrill Lynch Capital Markets Inc. and Drexel Burnham Lambert Inc. predicted the power plants would never be built. The ratings agencies downgraded the debt soon after, but it remained investment-grade. It wasn't until seven months later, when the power plants were canceled, that Moody's and S&P assigned the debt junk status. The bonds went into default in June 1982, the biggest default in the history of the municipal market.

Discussing the rating agencies' timeliness, Mr. Kerman of Moody's says only that his agency "reviews and updates ratings periodically" to insure their "accuracy and currency."

The risk that a bond might be downgraded is also an important consideration for investors. And a top rating doesn't guarantee that a bond won't be affected. Indeed, most triple-A debt has two chances of being downgraded. That's because such bonds usually have a "security blanket" of insurance or a letter of credit from

Continued.

Junk Bonds

Junk bonds are nothing more than speculative grade (low-rated or unrated) bonds. Before 1977 almost all junk bonds were "fallen angels," that is, bonds originally issued by firms with investment-grade ratings but since downgraded. In 1977, however, firms began to issue "original-issue junk." Much of the credit for this innovation is given to Drexel Burnham Lambert, and especially its trader, Michael Milken. Drexel had long enjoyed a niche as a junk-bond trader and had thereby established a network of potential investors in junk bonds. They began to market original-issue junk, so-called emerging credits, in the belief that default rates on these bonds did not justify the large yield spreads commonly exhibited in the marketplace. Firms not able to muster an investment-grade rating were happy to have Drexel (and other investment bankers) market their bonds directly to the public because this opened up a new source of financing. Previously, these firms were forced to borrow from banks, and junk issues were a lower-cost financing alternative.

Junk bonds gained some notoriety in the 1980s when they were used commonly as financing vehicles in leveraged buyouts and hostile takeover attempts. Since then, Drexel has estimated that only about 15% of junk bonds are connected with merger and acquisition activity.

Milken's belief that the yield premium on junk bonds has been excessive compared with the actual default risk seems to be borne out by historical experience. In a study of data on default experience of low-rated debt and all-rated debt for the 1970 to 1985 period, Altman and Nammacher[3] found that the default rate on junk was 2.15% over that period. This compares to yield spreads of junk bonds relative to Treasury bonds of 3% to more than 5% in the 1980s.

---

[3]Altman, Edward I., and Nammacher, Scott, "The Default Experience on High-Yield Corporate Debt," *Financial Analysts Journal, 41*, July-August 1985.

Indeed, junk bonds have been popular with investors. In 1977 they comprised 3.7% of the market in straight debt; by 1987, they accounted for 23%.[4]

Determinants of Bond Safety

Bond rating agencies base their quality ratings largely on an analysis of the level and trend of some of the issuer's financial ratios. The key ratios used to evaluate safety follow:

1. *Coverage ratios* (ratios of company earnings to fixed costs). For example, the *times-interest-earned ratio* is the ratio of earnings before interest payments and taxes to interest obligations. The *fixed-charge coverage ratio* adds lease payments and sinking fund payments to interest obligations to arrive at the ratio of earnings to all fixed cash obligations. Low or falling coverage ratios signal possible cash flow difficulties.

2. *Leverage ratios* (debt-to-equity ratio). A too-high leverage ratio indicates excessive indebtedness, signaling the possibility that the firm will be unable to earn enough to satisfy the obligations on its bonds.

3. *Liquidity ratios*. The two common liquidity ratios are the *current ratio* (current assets/current liabilities) and the *quick ratio* (current assets excluding inventories/current liabilities). These ratios measure the firm's ability to pay bills coming due with cash currently being collected.

4. *Profitability ratios* (measures of rates of return on assets or equity). Profitability ratios are indicators of a firm's overall financial health. The *return on assets* (earnings before interest and taxes divided by total assets) is the most popular of these measures. Firms with higher return on assets should be better able to raise money in security markets because they offer prospects for better returns on the firm's investments.

5. *Cash flow to debt ratio*. This is the ratio of total cash flow to outstanding debt.

Standard & Poor's has computed 3-year median values of selected ratios for firms in each of their rating classes, which we present in Table 14.2. Of course, ratios must be evaluated in the context of industry standards, and analysts differ in the weights they place on particular ratios. Nevertheless, Table 14.2 demonstrates the tendency of ratios to improve along with the firm's rating class. In fact, the heavy dependence of bond ratings on publicly available financial data is evidence of an interesting phenomenon. You might think that an increase or decrease in bond rating would cause substantial bond price gains or losses, but this is not the case. Weinstein[5] finds that bond prices move in *anticipation* of rating changes, which is evidence that investors themselves track the financial status of bond issuers. This is consistent with an efficient market. Rating changes actually largely confirm a change

---

[4]Perry, Kevin, and Taggart, Robert A., "The Growing Role of Junk Bonds in Corporate Finance," *Continental Bank Journal of Applied Corporate Finance, 1,* spring 1988.

[5]Weinstein, Mark I., "The Effect of a Rating Change Announcement on Bond Price," *Journal of Financial Economics,* December 1977.

TABLE 14.2   Rating Classes and Median Financial Ratios, 1983-1985

Rating Category	Fixed-Charge Coverage Ratio	Cash Flow to Long-Term Debt	Return on Capital (%)	Long-Term Debt to Capital (%)
AAA	7.48	3.09	25.60	8.85
AA	4.43	1.18	22.05	18.88
A	2.93	.75	18.03	24.46
BBB	2.30	.46	12.10	31.54
BB	2.04	.27	13.80	42.52
B	1.51	.19	12.01	52.04
CCC	0.75	.15	2.70	69.28

Data from Standard & Poor's *Debt Rating Criteria*, 1986.

in status that has been reflected in security prices already. Holthausen and Leftwich,[6] however, find that bond rating downgrades (but not upgrades) are associated with abnormal returns in the stock of the affected company.

Many studies have tested whether financial ratios can in fact be used to predict default risk. One of the best-known series of tests has been conducted by Edward Altman, who has used discriminant analysis to predict bankruptcy. With this technique a firm is assigned a score based on its financial characteristics. If its score exceeds a cutoff value, the firm is deemed creditworthy. A score below the cutoff value indicates significant bankruptcy risk in the near future.

To illustrate the technique, suppose that we were to collect data on the return on equity (ROE) and coverage ratios of a sample of firms, and then keep records of any corporate bankruptcies. In Figure 14.9 we plot the ROE and coverage ratios for each firm using X for firms that eventually went bankrupt and O for those that remained solvent. Clearly, the X and O firms show different patterns of data, with the solvent firms typically showing higher values for the two ratios.

The discriminant analysis determines the equation of the line that best separates the X and O observations. Suppose that the equation of the line is $.75 = .9$ ROE $+ .4$ Coverage. Each firm is assigned a "Z-score" equal to $.9$ ROE $+ .4$ Coverage using the firm's ROE and coverage ratios. If the Z-score exceeds $.75$, the firm plots above the line and is considered a safe bet; Z-scores below $.75$ foretell financial difficulty.

Altman[7] found the following equation to best separate failing and nonfailing firms:

$$Z = 3.3 \frac{\text{EBIT}}{\text{Total assets}} + 99.9 \frac{\text{Sales}}{\text{Assets}} + .6 \frac{\text{Market value of equity}}{\text{Book value of debt}}$$
$$+ 1.4 \frac{\text{Retained earnings}}{\text{Total assets}} + 1.2 \frac{\text{Working capital}}{\text{Total assets}}$$

[6]Holthausen, Robert W., and Leftwich, Richard W., "The Effect of Bond Rating Changes on Common Stock Prices," *Journal of Financial Economics, 17,* September 1986.
[7]Altman, Edward I., "Financial Ratios, Discriminant Analysis, and the Prediction of Corporate Bankruptcy," *Journal of Finance, 23,* September 1968.

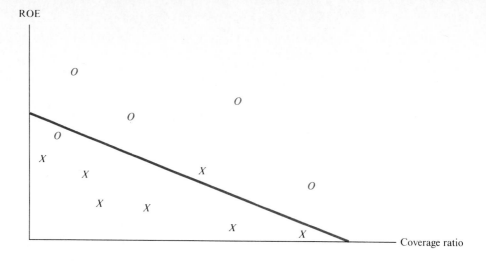

FIGURE 14.9
Discriminant analysis.

Firms with Z-scores above 2.7 were deemed safe: 97% of these were still in business in the next year. In contrast, 94% of bankrupt firms had Z-scores below 2.7 the year before they failed.

Concept Check

Question 4. Suppose we add a new variable equal to current liabilities/current assets to Altman's equation. Would you expect this variable to receive a positive or negative coefficient?

Bond Indentures

A bond is issued with an **indenture,** which is the contract between the issuer and the bondholder. Part of the indenture is a set of restrictions on the firm issuing the bond to protect the rights of the bondholders. Such restrictions include provisions relating to collateral, sinking funds, dividend policy, and allowed further borrowing. The issuing firm agrees to these so-called *protective covenants* in order to market their bonds to investors concerned about the safety of the bond issue.

Sinking funds

Bonds call for the repayment of principal at the end of the bond's life. This repayment constitutes a large cash commitment. To help ensure that the committment does not create a cash flow crisis, the firm agrees to establish a **sinking fund** to spread the principal repayment burden over several years. The fund may operate in one of two ways:

1. The firm may repurchase a fraction of the outstanding bonds in the open market each year.
2. The firm can purchase a fraction of outstanding bonds at a special call price associated with the sinking fund provision. The firm has an option to purchase the bonds at either the market price or the sinking fund call price, whichever is lower. To fairly allocate the burden of the sinking fund call among bondholders, the bonds chosen for the call are selected at random based on serial number.[8]

The sinking fund call differs from a conventional bond call in two important ways. First, the firm can repurchase only a limited fraction of the bond issue at the sinking fund call price. At best, some indentures allow firms to use a *doubling option*, which allows repurchase of double the required number of bonds at the sinking fund call price. Second, the sinking fund call price generally is lower than the call price established by other call provisions in the indenture. The sinking fund call price often is set at the bond's par value.

Although sinking funds ostensibly protect bondholders by making principal repayment more likely, they can in fact act to hurt the investor. If interest rates fall and bond prices rise, firms will benefit from the sinking fund provision that enables them to repurchase their bonds at below-market prices. In these circumstances, the firm's gain is the bondholder's loss.

One bond issue that does not require a sinking fund is a *serial bond* issue. In a serial bond issue, the firm sells bonds with staggered maturity dates. As bonds mature sequentially, the principal repayment burden for the firm is spread out over time just as it is with a sinking fund. Serial bonds do not include call provisions.

Subordination of further debt

One of the factors determining bond safety is total outstanding debt of the issuer. An investor purchasing a bond would be understandably distressed to see the firm soon tripling its outstanding debt. The bondholder would have a bond of lower quality than it appeared when issued. To prevent firms from harming bondholders in this manner, **subordination clauses** restrict the amount of additional borrowing. Additional debt might be required to be subordinated in priority to existing debt; that is, in the event of bankruptcy, *subordinated* or *junior* debtholders will not be paid unless and until the prior senior debt is fully paid. For this reason, subordination is sometimes called a "me-first rule," meaning that the senior bondholders are to be paid first in the event of bankruptcy.

---

[8]Although it is uncommon, the sinking fund provision also may call for periodic payments to a trustee with the payments invested so that the accumulated sum can be used for retirement of the entire issue at maturity.

Dividend restrictions

Firms are limited in the amount of dividends that they are allowed to pay. The limitation on dividend payouts protects the bondholders because it forces the firm to retain assets rather than paying them to stockholders. A typical restriction disallows payment of dividends if cumulative dividends paid since the firm's inception exceed cumulative net income plus proceeds from sales of stock.

Collateral

Some bonds are issued with specific collateral behind them. **Collateral** can take several forms, but it is a particular asset of the firm that the bondholders receive if the firm defaults on the bond. If the collateral is property, the bond is called a *mortgage bond*. If the collateral takes the form of other securities held by the firm, the bond is a *collateral trust bond*. If equipment is used, the bond is known as an *equipment obligation bond*. This last form of collateral is most commonly used by firms such as railroads, where the equipment is fairly standard and can be easily sold to another firm should the firm default and the bondholders acquire the collateral.

Because of the specific collateral that backs them, collateralized bonds generally are considered the safest variety of corporate bonds. In contrast, general **debenture bonds** do not provide for specific collateral; they are *unsecured* bonds. They rely solely on the general earning power of the firm for their safety. If the firm defaults, debenture owners become general creditors of the firm. Because of their greater safety, collateralized bonds generally offer lower yields than do general debentures.

Callable Bonds and Convertible Bonds

Callable bonds allow the issuer to repurchase the bond at a specified price. For example, if a bond is issued with a high coupon rate when market interest rates are high, and interest rates subsequently fall, the firm might like to retire the high-priced debt and issue new bonds at a lower coupon rate, thereby reducing its interest payments. This is called "refunding." In the absence of a call provision the firm would have to pay fair market prices to buy back the original issue. But to the investor those market prices reflect the increased present value of the bond's scheduled payments. The call provision, which allows the firm to repurchase the bond at the call price, lets the issuer avoid paying the full present value to the bondholders. The firm, rather than the bondholder, benefits from falls in interest rates.

Of course, the firm's benefit is the bondholder's burden. Holders of callable bonds will not reap capital gains from falls in the interest rate if the bonds are called away from them. The firm's option to call the bond at a specified price takes away from the bondholder any upside capital gains potential beyond the call price. To compensate investors, callable bonds are issued with higher coupons and promised yields to maturity than are noncallable bonds.

Figure 14.10 illustrates the risk of call to the bondholder. The blue line is the value at various market interest rates of a "straight" (noncallable) bond with par value $100, 8% coupon, and 30-year time to maturity. The black line is the value of the same bond if it is callable at $110. At high interest rates the risk of call is negligible,

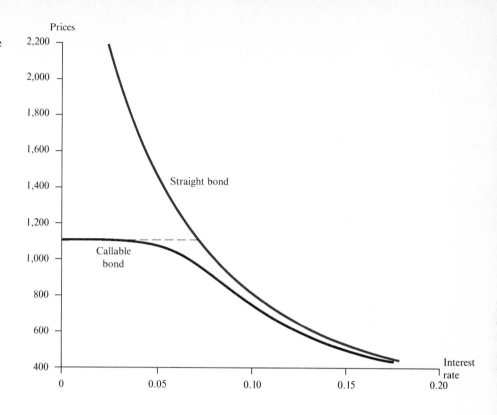

FIGURE 14.10
Bond prices, callable
and straight debt.

and the values of the bonds coincide. At lower rates, however, the values of the
bonds begin to diverge, the difference reflecting the value of the firm's option to reclaim the callable bond at $110. Finally, at very low interest rates, the bond is called,
and its value simply equals $110.

The call price of a bond is commonly set at an initial level about par value plus
one annual coupon payment. As time passes, the call price falls, gradually approaching par value.

Callable bonds typically come with a period of *call protection,* an initial period
during which the bonds are not callable. Such bonds are referred to as *deferred* callable bonds. An implicit form of call protection operates for bonds selling at deep discounts from their call prices. Even if interest rates fall a bit, deep-discount bonds still
will sell below the call price and thus will not be subject to a call. Premium bonds
that might be selling near their call prices, however, are especially apt to be called if
rates fall further. If interest rates fall, a callable premium bond is likely to provide a
lower return than could be earned on a discount bond whose potential price appreciation is not limited by the likelihood of a call. Investors in premium bonds often are
more interested in the bond's yield to call rather than yield to maturity as a consequence, because it may appear to them that the bond will be retired at the call date.

Question 5. The yield to maturity on two 10-year maturity bonds currently is 7%. Each bond has a call price of $1,100. One bond has a coupon rate of 6%, the other 8%. Assume for simplicity that bonds are called as soon as the present value of their remaining payments exceeds their call price. What will be the capital gain on each bond if the market interest rate suddenly falls to 6%?

Question 6. Would you expect a premium bond with the same call price as a discount bond to offer a lower, equal, or higher promised yield to maturity compared with the discount bond?

Figure 14.11 shows the terms of a callable bond issued by IBM as described in *Moody's Industrial Manual*. The bond was issued in 1979 but was not callable until 1983. After 1983 the call price falls until it eventually reaches par value in 1998. In addition, the bond is not callable until 1989 if the purpose of the call is to refinance the firm's debt at a lower interest rate. Therefore bondholders have complete call protection until 1983 and partial protection through 1989. However, *limited* amounts of the bonds may be called at par value starting in 1985 as part of the provisions of the sinking fund.

A relatively new development is the **put bond,** or extendible bond. Whereas the callable bond gives the issuer the option to extend or retire the bond at the call date, the put bond gives the option to the bondholder. Thus, if the bond's coupon rate exceeds current market yields, the bondholder will choose to extend the bond's life. If the bond's coupon rate is too low, it will be optimal not to extend; the bondholder instead reclaims principal that can be invested at current yields.

Convertible bonds convey an option to bondholders to exchange each bond for a specified number of shares of common stock of the firm. The *conversion ratio* gives the number of shares for which each bond may be exchanged. Suppose that a convertible bond that is issued at par value of $1,000 is convertible into 40 shares of a firm's stock. The current stock price is $20 per share, so the option to convert is not currently profitable. However, should the stock price later rise to $30, each bond may be profitably converted into $1,200 worth of stock. The *market conversion value* is the current value of the shares for which the bonds may be exchanged. At the $20 stock price the bond's conversion value is $800. The *conversion premium* is the excess of the bond value over the conversion value of the bond. If the bond currently were selling for $950, its premium would be $150.

Thus convertible bonds give their holders the ability to share in price appreciation of the company's stock. Of course, this benefit comes at a price; convertible bonds offer lower coupon rates and promised yields to maturity than do nonconvertible bonds. At the same time, the actual return on the convertible bond may exceed the stated yield to maturity if the option to convert becomes profitable.

We discuss convertible and callable bonds further in Chapter 20.

FIGURE 14.11

Callable bond issued by IBM.

(From Moody's Investors Services, New York. Reprinted by permission.)

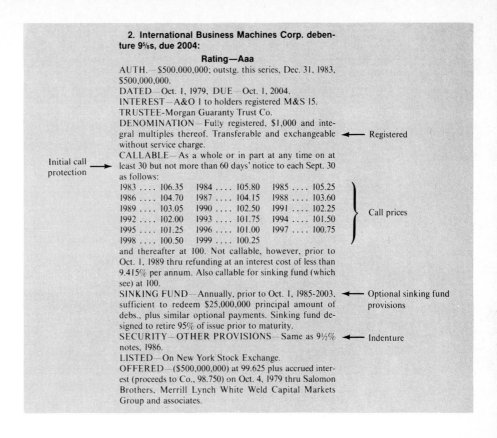

2. International Business Machines Corp. debenture 9⅝s, due 2004:

Rating—Aaa

AUTH.—$500,000,000; outstg. this series, Dec. 31, 1983, $500,000,000.

DATED—Oct. 1, 1979, DUE—Oct. 1, 2004.

INTEREST—A&O 1 to holders registered M&S 15.

TRUSTEE-Morgan Guaranty Trust Co.

DENOMINATION—Fully registered, $1,000 and integral multiples thereof. Transferable and exchangeable without service charge. ← Registered

CALLABLE—As a whole or in part at any time on at least 30 but not more than 60 days' notice to each Sept. 30 as follows:

1983 .... 106.35	1984 .... 105.80	1985 .... 105.25
1986 .... 104.70	1987 .... 104.15	1988 .... 103.60
1989 .... 103.05	1990 .... 102.50	1991 .... 102.25
1992 .... 102.00	1993 .... 101.75	1994 .... 101.50
1995 .... 101.25	1996 .... 101.00	1997 .... 100.75
1998 .... 100.50	1999 .... 100.25	

} Call prices

and thereafter at 100. Not callable, however, prior to Oct. 1, 1989 thru refunding at an interest cost of less than 9.415% per annum. Also callable for sinking fund (which see) at 100.

SINKING FUND—Annually, prior to Oct. 1, 1985-2003, ← Optional sinking fund provisions
sufficient to redeem $25,000,000 principal amount of debs., plus similar optional payments. Sinking fund designed to retire 95% of issue prior to maturity.

SECURITY—OTHER PROVISIONS—Same as 9½% ← Indenture
notes, 1986.

LISTED—On New York Stock Exchange.

OFFERED—($500,000,000) at 99.625 plus accrued interest (proceeds to Co., 98.750) on Oct. 4, 1979 thru Salomon Brothers, Merrill Lynch White Weld Capital Markets Group and associates.

Initial call protection →

Floating-Rate Bonds

Floating-rate bonds mimic short-term bonds in the sense that they are designed to minimize the holder's interest rate risk. As with variable-rate mortgages, the interest rate that the borrower pays is reset periodically depending on market conditions. For example, the rate paid might be adjusted annually to the current T-bill rate plus 2%. At each reset, the bond price should revert to par value, since the bond is now offering the current market yield. Because the bond always pays close to current market rates, its price risk is minimized. The interest rate risk of floaters is more a function of the length of the reset period than of the bond's maturity.

The yield spread on floaters is fixed over the life of the security, which may be many years, in contrast to short-term bonds or money-market instruments. Therefore, if the appropriate yield premium changes, the bond price will not revert to par value. The major risk involved in floaters has to do with changing credit conditions. The financial health of the firm may deteriorate, for example, meaning a greater yield premium is required than is offered by the security. In addition, the risk premium that the market demands for a particular risk category also may change, as in the flight-to-quality phenomenon.

Summary

1. Fixed-income securities are distinguished by their promise to pay a fixed or specified stream of income to their holders. The coupon bond is a typical fixed-income security.

2. The yield to maturity is the single interest rate that equates the present value of a security's cash flows to its price. Bond prices and yields are inversely related.

3. For premium bonds, the coupon rate is greater than the current yield, which is greater than the yield to maturity. The order of these inequalities is reversed for discount bonds.

4. Treasury bills are U.S. government-issued zero coupon bonds with original maturities of up to 1 year. Prices of zero coupon bonds rise exponentially over time, providing a rate of appreciation equal to the interest rate. The IRS treats price appreciation as an imputed interest payment to the investor.

5. Treasury notes and bonds have original maturities greater than 1 year. They are issued at or near par value, with their prices quoted net of accrued interest. T-bonds may be callable during their last 5 years of life.

6. When bonds are subject to potential default, the stated yield to maturity is the maximum possible yield to maturity that can be realized by the bondholder. In the event of default, however, that promised yield will not be realized. To compensate bond investors for default risk, bonds must offer default premiums, that is, promised yields in excess of those offered by default-free government securities. If the firm remains healthy, its bonds will provide higher returns than will government bonds. Otherwise, the returns may be lower.

7. Bond safety is often measured with financial ratio analysis. Bond indentures are another safeguard to protect the claims of bondholders. Common indentures specify sinking fund requirements, collateralization of the loan, dividend restrictions, and subordination of future bond issues.

8. Callable bonds should offer higher promised yields to maturity to compensate investors for the fact that they will not realize full capital gains if the interest rate falls and the bonds are called away from them at the stipulated call price. Bonds often are issued with a period of call protection. In addition, discount bonds selling significantly below their call price offer implicit call protection.

9. Put bonds give the option to terminate or extend the life of the bond to the bondholder rather than to the issuer.

10. Convertible bonds may be exchanged at the bondholder's discretion for a specified number of shares of stock. Convertible bondholders "pay" for this option by accepting a lower coupon rate on the security.

11. Floating-rate bonds pay a fixed premium over a reference short-term interest rate. They limit risk because the rate paid is tied to current market conditions.

Key Terms

Fixed-income securities	Bond equivalent yield	Subordination clauses
Bond	Default premium	Collateral
Principal	Investment grade bond	Debenture bonds
Coupon rate	Speculative grade or	Callable bond
Par value	junk bond	Put bond
Yield to maturity	Indenture	Convertible bonds
Zero-coupon bond	Sinking fund	Floating-rate bonds

Selected Readings

A comprehensive treatment of pricing issues related to fixed-income securities is given in:
Van Horne, James C., *Financial Market Rates and Flows,* Englewood Cliffs, N.J.: Prentice-Hall, 1984.
Surveys of fixed-income instruments and investment characteristics are contained in:
Stigum, Marcia, and Fabozzi, Frank J., *Bond and Money Market Instruments,* Homewood, Ill.: Dow Jones-Irwin, 1987.
Fabozzi, Frank J., and Pollack, Irving M., *The Handbook of Fixed Income Securities,* Homewood, Ill.: Dow Jones-Irwin, 1987.

Problems

1. Treasury bonds paying an 8% coupon rate with *semiannual* payments currently sell at par value. What coupon rate would they have to pay to sell at par if they paid their coupons *annually?*

2. A newly issued 10-year maturity, 7% coupon bond making *annual* coupon payments is sold to the public at a price of $850. What will be an investor's taxable income from the bond over the coming year? The bond will *not* be sold at the end of the year.

3. What is the price of a $1,000 face value bond with a coupon rate of 14% if the bond has an *effective* annual yield to maturity of 21% and 15 years until maturity? Assume that the bond pays semiannual coupons and that the next coupon payment arrives 6 months from now.

4. Which security has a higher *effective* annual interest rate?
   a. A 3-month T-bill selling at $97,645 and par value $100,000
   b. A coupon bond selling at par and paying a 10% coupon semiannually

5. Consider a bond paying a coupon rate of 10% per year semiannually when the market interest rate is only 4% per half year. The bond matures in 3 years.
   a. Find the bond's price today and 6 months from now after the next coupon is paid.
   b. What is the total rate of return on the bond?

6. Assume you have a 1-year investment horizon and are trying to choose among three bonds. All have the same degree of default risk and mature in 10 years. The first is a zero-coupon bond that pays $1,000 at maturity. The second has an 8% coupon rate and pays the $80 coupon once per year. The third has a 10% coupon rate and pays the $100 coupon once per year.
   a. If all three bonds are now priced to yield 8% to maturity, what are their prices?

b. If you expect their yields to maturity to be 8% at the beginning of next year, what will their prices be then? What is your before-tax holding period return on each bond? If you are in the 30% marginal tax bracket, what will your after-tax rate of return be on each?

c. Recalculate your answer to (b) under the assumption that you expect the yields to maturity on each bond to be 7% at the beginning of next year.

7. (Adapted from CFA Examination, Level I, 1983)

Assume that two firms, PG and CLX, were concurrently to undertake private debt placements in 1987 with the following contractual details:

	PG	CLX
Issue size	$1 billion	$100 million
Issue price	100	100
Maturity	1988*	1998
Coupon	11%	12%
Collateral	First mortgage	Unsecured
First call date	1993	1990
Call price	111	106
Sinking fund, beginning	nil	1988
Sinking fund, amount	nil	$5 million/year

*Extendible at the option of the holder for an additional 10 years (to 1998) with no change in coupon rate.

Ignoring credit quality, identify four features of these issues that might account for the lower coupon on the PG debt. Explain.

8. (CFA Examination, Level I, 1982)

Georgia-Pacific Corporation, a large forest products manufacturer, has outstanding two Aa-rated, $150 million par amount, intermediate-term debt issues:

	10.10% Notes	Floating-Rate Notes
Maturity	1990	1987
Issued	6-12-80	9-27-79
At par to yield	10.10%	12.00%
Callable (beginning on)	6-15-86	10-01-84
Callable at	100	100
Sinking fund	None	None
Current coupon	10.10%	16.90%
Changes	Fixed	Every 6 months
Rate adjusts to	—	0.75% above 6 months Treasury bill rate
Range since issued	—	16.90%-12.00%
Current price	73⅜	97
Current yield	13.77%	17.42%
Yield to maturity	15.87%	—
Price range since issue	100-72	102-93

Based on these data:

a. State the minimum coupon rate of interest at which Georgia-Pacific could sell a fixed rate issue at par due in 1990. Assume the same indenture provisions as the 10.10% notes and disregard any tax considerations.

b. Give two reasons why the floating-rate notes are not selling at par (offering price).

c. State and justify whether the risk of call is high, moderate, or low for the fixed rate issue.

d. Assuming a decline in interest rates is anticipated, identify and justify which issue would be most appropriate for an actively managed bond portfolio where total return is the primary objective.

e. Explain why yield to maturity is not valid for the floating-rate note.

9. (CFA Examination, Level I, 1986)

You are given the following information about a convertible bond issue:

Burroughs Corp.
7¼% Due 8/1/2010

Agency rating (Moody's/S&P)	A3/A−
Conversion ratio	12.882
Market price of convertible	$102.00
Market price of common stock	$ 66.00
Dividend per share—common	$ 2.60
Call price (first call—8/1/1990)	$106.00
Estimated floor price	$ 66.50

Using this information, calculate the following data and show calculations:

a. Market conversion value

b. Conversion premium per common share

c. Current yield—convertible

d. Dividend yield—common

10. (Adapted from CFA Examination, Level III, 1982)

As the portfolio manager for a large pension fund, you are offered the following bonds:

	Coupon	Maturity	Price	Call Price	Yield to Maturity
Edgar Corp. (new issue)	14.00%	2002	$101¾	$114	13.75%
Edgar Corp. (new issue)	6.00%	2002	$ 48⅛	$103	13.60%

Assuming that you expect a decline in interest rates over the next three years, identify and justify which of the bonds you would select.

The following multiple-choice problems are based on questions that appeared in the 1986 CFA examination:

11. Which bond probably has the highest credit quality?
    a. Sumter, South Carolina Water and Sewer Revenue Bond
    b. Riley County, Kansas, General Obligations Bond
    c. University of Kansas Medical Center Refunding Revenue Bonds (insured by American Municipal Bond Assurance Corporation)
    d. Euless, Texas, General Obligation Bond (refunded and secured by U.S. governments in escrow to maturity)

12. The spread between Treasury and BAA corporate bond yields widens when:
    a. Interest rates are low
    b. There is economic uncertainty
    c. There is a "flight from quality"
    d. All of the above

13. The market risk of an AAA-rated preferred stock relative to an AAA-rated bond is:
    a. Lower
    b. Higher
    c. Equal
    d. Unknown

14. A bond with a call feature:
    a. Is attractive because the immediate receipt of principal plus premium produces a high return
    b. Is more apt to be called when interest rates are high, because the interest saving will be greater
    c. Will usually have a higher yield than a similar noncallable bond
    d. None of the above

15. The yield-to-maturity on a bond is:
    a. Below the coupon rate when the bond sells at a discount, and above the coupon rate when the bond sells at a premium
    b. The discount rate that will set the present value of the payments equal to the bond price
    c. The current yield plus the average annual capital gain rate
    d. Based on the assumption that any payments received are reinvested at the coupon rate

16. A particular bond has a yield to maturity on an APR basis of 12% but makes equal quarterly payments. What is the effective annual yield to maturity?
    a. 11.45%
    b. 12.00%
    c. 12.55%
    d. 37.35%

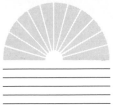

15

The Term Structure of Interest Rates

In Chapter 14 we assumed for the sake of simplicity that the same constant interest rate is used to discount cash flows of any maturity. In the real world this is rarely the case. We have seen, for example, that in 1987 short-term bonds and notes carried yields to maturity only slightly higher than 6% while the longest-term bonds had yields above 8%. At the time when these bond prices were quoted, anyway, the longer-term securities had higher yields. This, in fact, is a common empirical pattern.

In this chapter we explore the pattern of interest rates for different-term assets. We attempt to identify the factors that account for that pattern and determine what information may be derived from an analysis of the so-called **term structure of interest rates,** the structure of interest rates appropriate for discounting cash flows of different maturities.

15.1 *The Term Structure Under Certainty*

What do you conclude from the observation that longer-term bonds offer higher yields to maturity? One possibility is that longer-term bonds are riskier and that the higher yields are evidence of a risk premium that compensates for interest rate risk. Another possibility is that investors expect interest rates to rise and that the higher average yields on long-term bonds reflect the anticipation of high interest rates in the latter years of the bond's life. We will start our analysis of these possibilities with the easiest case: a world with no uncertainty where investors already know the path of future interest rates.

Bond Pricing

The interest rate for a given year is called the **short interest rate** for that period. Suppose that all participants in the bond market are convinced that the short rates for the next 4 years will follow the pattern in Table 15.1.

TABLE 15.1   Interest Rates on 1-Year Bonds in Coming Years

Year	Interest Rate
0 (Today)	8%
1	10%
2	11%
3	11%

TABLE 15.2   Prices and Yields of Zero Coupon Bonds

Time to Maturity	Price	Yield to Maturity
1	$925.93	8.000%
2	$841.75	8.995%
3	$758.33	9.660%
4	$683.18	9.993%

Of course, market participants cannot look up such a sequence of short rates in *The Wall Street Journal*. All they observe there are prices and yields of bonds of various maturities. Nevertheless, we can think of the short-rate sequence of Table 15.1 as the series of interest rates that investors keep in the back of their minds when they evaluate the prices of different bonds. Given this pattern of rates, what prices might we observe on various maturity bonds? To keep the algebra simple, for now we will treat only a zero-coupon bond.

A bond paying $1,000 in 1 year would sell today for $1,000/1.08 = $925.93. Similarly, a 2-year maturity bond would sell today at price

$$P = \frac{\$1,000}{(1.08)\,(1.10)} \tag{15.1}$$
$$= \$841.75$$

This is the present value of the future $1,000 cash flow because $841.75 would need to be set aside now to provide a $1,000 payment in 2 years. After 1 year, the $841.75 set aside would grow to $841.75(1.08) = $909.09 and after the second year to $909.09(1.10) = $1,000.

In general we may write the present value of $1 to be received after n periods as

$$\text{PV of \$1 in } n \text{ periods} = \frac{1}{(1 + r_1)\,(1 + r_2)\,.\,.\,.\,(1 + r_n)}$$

where r_i is the interest rate that will prevail in year i. Continuing in this manner, we find the values of the 3- and 4-year bonds as shown in the first column of Table 15.2.

FIGURE 15.1
Yield curve.

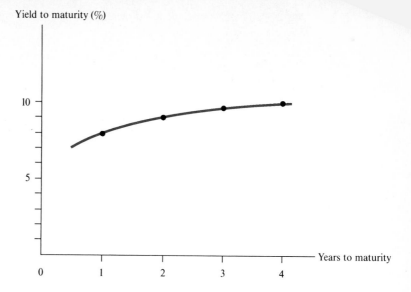

Yield to maturity (%)

From the bond prices we can calculate the yield to maturity on each bond. Recall that the yield is the *single* interest rate that equates the present value of the bond's payments to the bond's price. Although interest rates may vary over time, the yield to maturity is calculated as one "average" rate that is applied to discount all of the bond's payments. For example, the yield on the 2-year zero-coupon bond, which we will call y_2, is the interest rate that satisfies

$$841.75 = 1,000/(1 + y_2)^2 \qquad (15.2)$$

which we solve for $y_2 = .08995$. We repeat the process for the two other bonds, with results as reported in the table. For example, we find y_3 by solving

$$758.33 = 1,000/(1 + y_3)^3$$

Now we can make a graph of the yield to maturity on the four bonds as a function of time to maturity. This graph, which is called the **yield curve,** appears in Figure 15.1.

The yield to maturity on zero-coupon bonds is sometimes called the **spot rate** that prevails today for a period corresponding to the maturity of the zero. The yield curve, or equivalently, the last column of Table 15.2, thus presents the spot rates for four maturities. Note that the spot rates or yields do *not* equal the 1-year interest rates for each year. Instead, the yield on the 2-year bond is close to the average of the short rates for years 1 and 2. This makes sense because, if the yield is a measure of the average return over the life of the bond, it should be determined by the market interest rates available in both years 1 and 2.

In fact, we can say more than this. Notice that equations 15.1 and 15.2 each relate the 2-year bond's price to appropriate interest rates. Combining equations 15.1 and 15.2, we find

$$841.75 = \frac{1,000}{(1.08)(1.10)} = \frac{1,000}{(1 + y_2)^2}$$

so that

$$(1 + y_2)^2 = (1.08)(1.10)$$

and

$$1 + y_2 = [(1.08)(1.10)]^{1/2} = 1.08995$$

Similarly,

$$1 + y_3 = [(1 + r_1)(1 + r_2)(1 + r_3)]^{1/3}$$

and

$$1 + y_4 = [(1 + r_1)(1 + r_2)(1 + r_3)(1 + r_4)]^{1/4} \tag{15.3}$$

and so on. Thus the yields are in fact related to the interest rate in each period. However, the relationship is not an arithmetic average but a geometric one.

Holding Period Returns

What is the rate of return on each of the four bonds in Table 15.2 over a 1-year holding period? You might think at first that higher-yielding bonds would provide higher 1-year rates of return, but this is not the case. In our simple world with no uncertainty all bonds must offer identical rates of return over any holding period. Otherwise, at least one bond would be dominated by the others in the sense that it would offer a lower rate of return than would combinations of other bonds; consequently, the price of that bond would fall. This is no more than an application of the law of one price introduced in Chapter 4. In fact, despite their different yields to maturity, each bond will provide a rate of return over the coming year equal to this year's short interest rate.

To confirm this point, we can compute the rates of return on each bond. The 1-year bond is bought today for $925.93 and matures in 1 year for a return of $1 + r = \$1,000/\$925.93 = 1.08$, or $r = 8\%$. The 2-year bond is bought today for $841.75. Next year the interest rate will be 10%, and the bond will have 1 year left until maturity. It will sell for $\$1,000/1.10 = \$909.09$. Thus the *holding period return* is defined by $1 + r = \$909.09/\$841.75 = 1.08$ for an 8% rate of return. Similarly, the 3-year bond will be purchased for $758.33 and will be sold at year-end for $\$1,000/(1.10)(1.11) = \$819.00$, for a rate of return satisfying $1 + r = \$819.00/\$758.33 = 1.08$, again, an 8% return.

Concept Check

Question 1. Confirm that the return on the 4-year bond also will be 8%.

Therefore we conclude that, when interest rate movements are known with certainty, if all bonds are fairly priced, all will provide equal 1-year rates of return. The higher yields on the longer-term bonds are no more than a reflection of the fact that future interest rates are higher than are current rates, and that the longer bonds are still alive during the higher-rate period. Owners of the short-term bonds receive lower yields to maturity, but they can reinvest or "roll over" their proceeds for higher yields in later years when rates are higher. In the end, both long-term bonds and short-term rollover strategies provide equal returns over the holding period, at least in a world of interest rate certainty.

Forward Rates

Unfortunately, investors do not have access to short-term interest rate quotations for coming years. What they do have are newspaper quotations of bond prices and yields to maturity. Can they infer future short rates from the available data?

Suppose we are interested in the interest rate that will prevail during year 3, and we have access only to the data reported in Table 15.2. We start by comparing two alternatives:

1. Invest in a 3-year zero coupon bond.
2. Invest in a 2-year zero coupon bond. After 2 years reinvest the proceeds in a 1-year bond.

Assuming an investment of $100, under strategy 1, with a yield to maturity of 9.660% on 3-year zero coupon bonds, our investment would grow to $100(1.0966)^3 = \$131.87$. Under strategy 2, the $100 investment in the 2-year bond would grow after 2 years to $100(1.08995)^2 = \$118.80$. Then in the third year it would grow by an additional factor of $1 + r_3$.

In a world of certainty both of these strategies must yield exactly the same final payoff. If strategy 1 were to dominate strategy 2, no one would hold 2-year bonds; their prices would fall and their yields rise. Likewise if strategy 2 dominated strategy 1, no one would hold 3-year bonds. Therefore we can conclude that $131.87 = \$118.80 (1 + r_3)$, which implies that $(1 + r_3) = 1.11$, or $r_3 = 11\%$. This is in fact the rate that will prevail in year 3, as Table 15.1 indicates. Thus our method of obtaining the third-period interest rate does provide the correct solution in the certainty case.

More generally, the comparison of the two strategies establishes that the return on a 3-year bond equals that on a 2-year bond and rollover strategy:

$$100(1 + y_3)^3 = 100(1 + y_2)^2(1 + r_3)$$

so that $1 + r_3 = (1 + y_3)^3/(1 + y_2)^2$. Generalizing, for the certainty case, a simple rule for inferring a future short interest rate from the yield curve of zero-coupon bonds is to use the following formula:

$$(1 + r_n) = (1 + y_n)^n/(1 + y_{n-1})^{n-1} \qquad (15.4)$$

where n denotes the period in question and y_n is the yield to maturity of a zero-coupon bond with an n-period maturity.

Of course, when future interest rates are uncertain, as they are in reality, there is no meaning to inferring "the" future short rate. No one knows today what the future interest rate will be. At best, we can speculate as to its expected value and associated uncertainty. Nevertheless, it still is common to use equation 15.4 to investigate the implications of the yield curve for future interest rates. In recognition of the fact that future interest rates are uncertain, we call the interest rate that we infer in this manner the **forward interest rate** rather than the future short rate, because it need not be the interest rate that actually will prevail at the future date.

If the forward rate for period n is f_n, we then define f_n by the equation

$$1 + f_n = (1 + y_n)^n/(1 + y_{n-1})^{n-1}$$

Equivalently, we may rewrite the equation as

$$(1 + y_n)^n = (1 + y_{n-1})^{n-1}(1 + f_n) \qquad (15.5)$$

In this formulation, the forward rate is *defined* as a "break-even" interest rate that equates the return on an n-period zero-coupon bond to that of a $(n - 1)$-period zero-coupon bond rolled over into a 1-year bond in year n. The total returns on the two n-year strategies will be equal if the spot interest rate in year n turns out to equal f_n.

We emphasize that the interest rate that actually will prevail in the future need not equal the forward rate, which is calculated from today's data. Indeed, it is not even necessarily the case that the forward rate equals the expected value of the future short interest rate. This is an issue that we address in much detail shortly. For now, note that forward rates equal future short rates in the special case of interest rate certainty.

15.2   *Measuring the Term Structure*

Thus far we have focused on default-free zero coupon bonds. These bonds are easiest to analyze because their maturity is given by their single payment. In practice, however, the great majority of bonds pay coupons, and most available data pertain to coupon bonds, so we must develop a general approach to calculate spot and forward rates from prices of coupon bonds.

Equations 15.4 and 15.5 for the determination of the forward rate from available yields apply only to zero coupon bonds. They were derived by equating the returns to competing investment strategies that both used zeros. If coupon bonds had been used in those strategies, we would have had to deal with the issue of coupons paid during the investment period, which complicates the analysis.

A further complication arises from the fact that bonds with different coupon rates can have different yields even if their maturities are equal. For example, consider two bonds, each with a 2-year time to maturity and annual coupon payments. Bond A has a 3% coupon; bond B a 12% coupon. Using the interest rates of Table 15.1, we see that bond A will sell for

$$\frac{\$30}{1.08} + \frac{\$1,030}{(1.08)(1.10)} = \$894.78$$

At this price its yield to maturity is 8.98%. Bond B will sell for

$$\frac{\$120}{1.08} + \frac{\$1,120}{(1.08)(1.10)} = \$1,053.87$$

at which price its yield to maturity is 8.94%. Because bond B makes a greater share of its payments in the first year when the interest rate is lower, its yield to maturity is slightly lower. Because bonds with the same maturity can have different yields, we conclude that a single yield curve relating yields and times to maturity cannot be appropriate for all bonds.

The solution to this ambiguity is to perform all of our analysis using the yield curve for zero coupon bonds, sometimes called the *pure yield curve*. Our goal therefore is to calculate the pure yield curve even if we have to use data on more common coupon-paying bonds.

The trick we use to infer the yield curve from data on coupon bonds is to treat each coupon payment as a separate "mini" zero coupon bond. A coupon bond becomes then just a "portfolio" of many zeros. By determining the price of each of these "zeros" we can calculate the yield to that maturity date for a single-payment security and thereby construct the pure yield curve.

As a simple example of this technique, suppose that we observe an 8% coupon bond with 1 year until maturity selling at \$986.10, and a 10% coupon bond, also with a year until maturity, selling at \$1004.78. To infer the short rates for the next two 6-month periods, we first attempt to find the present value of each coupon payment taken individually, that is, treated as a mini zero coupon bond. Call d_1 the present value of \$1 to be received in half a year, and d_2 the present value of a dollar to be received in 1 year. (The d stands for discounted values.) Then our two bonds must satisfy the simultaneous equations

$$986.10 = d_1 \times 40 + d_2 \times 1,040$$
$$1004.78 = d_1 \times 50 + d_2 \times 1,050$$

In each equation the bond's price is set equal to the discounted value of all of its remaining cash flows. Solving these equations we find that $d_1 = .95694$ and $d_2 = .91137$. Thus, if r_1 is the short rate for the first 6-month period, then $d_1 = 1/(1 + r_1) = .95694$, so that $r_1 = .045$, and $d_2 = 1/[(1 + r_1)(1 + f_2)] = 1/[(1.045)(1 + f_2)] = .91137$, so that $f_2 = .05$. Thus the two short rates are shown to be 4.5% for the first half-year period and 5% for the second.

Question 2. A T-bill with 6-month maturity and $10,000 face value sells for $9,700. A 1-year maturity T-bond paying semiannual coupons of $40 sells for $1,000. Find the current 6-month short rate, and the forward rate for the following 6-month period.

When we analyze many bonds, such an inference procedure is more difficult, in part because of the greater number of bonds and time periods, but also because not all bonds give rise to identical estimates for the discounted value of a future $1 payment. In other words, there seem to be apparent error terms in the pricing relationship.[1] Nevertheless, treating these errors as random aberrations, we can use a statistical approach to infer the pattern of forward rates embedded in the yield curve.

To see how the statistical procedure would operate, suppose that we observe many coupon bonds, indexed by i, selling at prices P_i. The coupon and/or principal payment (the cash flow) of bond i at time t is denoted CF_{it}, and the present value of a $1 payment at time t, which is the implied price of a zero-coupon bond that we are trying to determine, is denoted d_t. Then for each bond we may write the following:

$$P_1 = d_1 CF_{11} + d_2 CF_{12} + d_3 CF_{13} + \ldots + e_1$$
$$P_2 = d_1 CF_{21} + d_2 CF_{22} + d_3 CF_{23} + \ldots + e_2$$
$$P_3 = d_1 CF_{31} + d_2 CF_{32} + d_3 CF_{33} + \ldots + e_3$$

$$\vdots \qquad\qquad\qquad\qquad \vdots \qquad\qquad\qquad\qquad \tag{15.6}$$

$$P_n = d_1 CF_{n1} + d_2 CF_{n2} + d_3 CF_{n3} + \ldots + e_n$$

Each line of equation system 15.6 equates the price of the bond to the sum of its cash flows, discounted according to time until payment. The last term in each equation, e_i, represents the error term that accounts for the deviations of a bond's price from the prediction of the equation.

Students of statistics will recognize that equation 15.6 is a simple system of equations that can be estimated by regression analysis. The dependent variables are the bond prices, the independent variables are the cash flows, and the coefficients d_t are to be estimated from the observed data.[2] The estimates of d_t are our inferences of the present value of $1 to be paid at time t. The pattern of d_t for various times to payment is called the *discount function*, since it gives the discounted value of $1 as a function of time until payment. From the discount function, which is equivalent to a list of zero-coupon bond prices for various maturity dates, we can calculate the yields

---

[1] We will consider later some of the reasons for the appearance of these error terms.

[2] In practice, variations of regression analysis called "splining techniques" are usually used to estimate the coefficients. This method was first suggested by McCulloch in the following two articles: McCulloch, J. Huston, "Measuring the Term Structure of Interest Rates," *Journal of Business, 44,* January 1971; and "The Tax Adjusted Yield Curve," *Journal of Finance, 30,* June 1975.

FIGURE 15.2

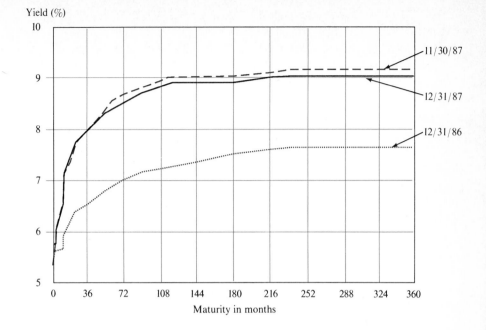

The Treasury yield
curve in 1986 and
1987.

(Redrawn from *The Bond
Market Report,* Shearson,
Lehman, Hutton, December
1987.)

on pure zero-coupon bonds. We would use Treasury securities in this procedure to avoid complications arising from default risk. Figure 15.2 is a plot of the yield curve for Treasury securities as it appeared at year-end 1987 and 1986.[3]

Before leaving the issue of the measurement of the yield curve, it is worth pausing briefly to discuss the error terms. Why is it that all bond prices do not conform exactly to a common discount function that sets price equal to present value? The reason is that two major factors are not accounted for in the regression analysis of equation 15.6: taxes and options associated with the bond.

Taxes affect bond prices because investors care about their after-tax return on investment. Therefore the coupon payments should be treated as net of taxes. Similarly, if a bond is not selling at par value, the IRS imputes a "built-in" interest payment by amortizing the difference between the price and the par value of the bond. These considerations are difficult to capture in a mathematical formulation because different individuals are in different tax brackets, meaning that the net-of-tax cash flows from a given bond depend on the identity of the owner. Moreover, the specification of equation 15.6 implicitly assumes that the bond is held until maturity: it discounts *all* the bond's coupon and principal payments. This of course ignores the investor's option to sell the bond before maturity and so to realize a different stream of income from that described by equation 15.6. Moreover, it ignores the investor's ability to engage in *tax-timing options*. For example, an investor whose tax bracket is

---

[3]Note, however, that this figure is not a graph of the true term structure on zero-coupon bonds. It is simply a curve fit to yields on coupon-paying Treasury bonds of various maturities.

expected to change over time may benefit by realizing capital gains during the period when the tax rate is the lowest.

Another feature affecting bond pricing is the call provision. First, if the bond is callable, how do we know whether to include in equation 15.6 coupon payments in years following the first call date? Similarly, the date of the principal repayment becomes uncertain. More important, one must realize that the issuer of the callable bond will exercise the option to call only when it is profitable to do so. Conversely, the call provision is a transfer of value away from the bondholder who has "sold" the option to call to the bond issuer. The call feature therefore will affect the bond's price, and introduce further error terms in the simple specification of equation 15.6.

15.3   *Interest Rate Uncertainty and Forward Rates*

Let us turn now to the more difficult analysis of the term structure when future interest rates are uncertain. We have argued so far that, in a certain world, different investment strategies with common terminal dates must provide equal rates of return. For example, two consecutive 1-year investments in zeros would need to offer the same total return as an equal-sized investment in a 2-year zero. Therefore under certainty,

$$(1 + r_1)(1 + r_2) = (1 + y_2)^2$$

What can we say when r_2 is not known today?

To be concrete, we will use an example in which the yield on 1-year zero-coupon bonds is 8%, while that on 2-year zeros is 9%. The implied forward rate for year 2 is given by $1 + f_2 = (1.09)^2/(1.08)$, so that $1 + f_2 = 1.10$, or $f_2 = 10\%$.

Consider first a "short-term" investor who wishes to invest only for 1 year. The investor can purchase 1-year maturity zero-coupon bonds with face value $100 for $100/1.08 = \$92.59$. The rate of return on these bonds over the year will be precisely 8%. Alternatively, the investor may purchase longer-term 2-year zero-coupon bonds and resell them at the end of the 1-year holding period.

The 2-year bonds originally will cost $100/(1 + y_2)^2 = \$100/(1.09)^2 = \$84.17$. What will they sell for next year? At that time, the year 2 interest rate will be known, and the bond will have 1 year until maturity. Therefore it will sell for $100/(1 + r_2)$. If the year 2 interest rate *turns out* to equal 10% (which is the forward rate, f_2) then the bond will sell at $100/1.10 = \$90.91$ and provide a 1-year rate of return of 8% ($\$90.91/\$84.17 = 1.08$). This makes sense, since the forward rate was defined as the break-even future short rate that would equate the rates of return on different maturity bonds.

Is it reasonable to assume that the expected value of r_2, which we will denote $E(r_2)$, should be equal to f_2? It is a reasonable presumption if investors do not care about the uncertainty surrounding the resale value of their 2-year bonds. If $E(r_2) = f_2$, then the long-term bond and short-term bond strategies provide equal expected rates of return,[4] and risk-indifferent investors will be equally happy with either bond.

However, if short-term investors wish to avoid unnecessary risk, they will shy away from the long-term bond. They would not be willing to hold it unless they could anticipate an expected return greater than that offered by the 1-year bond. Another way of putting this is to say that investors will require a risk premium to hold the longer-term bond. The more risk-averse investor would be willing to hold the long-term bond only if $E(r_2)$ is less than the break-even value, f_2, because the lower the expectation of r_2 the greater the anticipated return on the long-term bond.

Therefore, if most individuals are short-term investors, bonds must have prices that make f_2 greater than $E(r_2)$. The forward rate will embody a premium compared with the expected future short interest rate. This **liquidity premium** compensates short-term investors for the uncertainty about the price at which they will be able to sell their long-term bonds at the end of the year.[5]

Concept Check

Question 3. Suppose that the required liquidity premium for the short-term investor is 1%. What must $E(r_2)$ be if f_2 is 10%?

Perhaps surprisingly, we also can imagine scenarios in which long-term bonds can be perceived by investors to be *safer* than short-term bonds. To see how, we now consider a "long-term" investor, who wishes to invest for a full 2-year period. The investor can purchase the 2-year $100 par value zero-coupon bond for $84.17 and lock in a guaranteed yield to maturity of $y_2 = 9\%$. Alternatively, the investor can roll over two 1-year investments. In this case an investment of $84.17 would grow in 2 years to $84.17 multiplied by $(1.08)(1 + r_2)$, which is an uncertain amount today because r_2 is not yet known. The break-even year-2 interest rate is, once again, the forward rate, 10%, because the forward rate is defined as the rate that equates the terminal value of the two investment strategies

The expected value of the payoff of the rollover strategy is $84.17(1.08)[1 + E(r_2)]$. If $E(r_2)$ equals the forward rate, f_2, then the expected value of the payoff from the rollover strategy will equal the known payoff from the 2-year maturity bond strategy.

Is this a reasonable presumption? Once again, it is only if the investor does not care about the uncertainty surrounding the final value of the rollover strategy. Whenever that risk is important, the long-term investor will not be willing to engage in the

---

[4]This condition is only approximate. The strategies would provide equal expected payoffs if $1/(1 + f_2)$ equals $E[1/(1 + r_2)]$. When interest rates are uncertain, this condition is not equivalent to $f_2 = E(r_2)$. However, for small variance of r_2 the two conditions are approximately equivalent.

[5]Liquidity refers to the ability to sell an asset easily at a predictable price. Because long-term bonds have greater price risk, they are considered less liquid in this context and thus must offer a premium.

rollover strategy unless its expected return exceeds that of the 2-year bond. In this case the investor would require that

$$(1.08)\left[1 + E(r_2)\right] > (1.09)^2 = (1.08)(1 + f_2)$$

which implies that $E(r_2)$ exceeds f_2. The investor would require that the expected period 2 interest rate exceed the break-even value of 10%, which is the forward rate.

Therefore, if all investors were long-term investors, no one would be willing to hold short-term bonds unless those bonds offered a reward for bearing interest rate risk. In this situation bond prices would be set at levels such that rolling over short bonds resulted in greater expected return than holding long bonds. This would cause the forward rate to be less than the expected future spot rate.

For example, suppose that in fact $E(r_2) = 11\%$. The liquidity premium therefore is negative: $f_2 - E(r_2) = 10\% - 11\% = -1\%$. This is exactly opposite from the conclusion that we drew in the first case of the short-term investor. Clearly, whether forward rates will equal expected future short rates depends on investors' readiness to bear interest rate risk, as well as on their willingness to hold bonds that do not correspond to their investment horizons.

15.4   Theories of the Term Structure

The Expectations Hypothesis

The simplest theory of the term structure is the **expectations hypothesis.** A common version of this hypothesis states that the forward rate equals the market consensus expectation of the future short interest rate; in other words, that $f_2 = E(r_2)$, and that liquidity premiums are zero. Because $f_2 = E(r_2)$, we may relate yields on long-term bonds to expectations of future interest rates. For example, with $(1 + y_2)^2 = (1 + r_1)(1 + f_2)$ from equation 15.5, we may also write that $(1 + y_2)^2 = (1 + r_1)[1 + E(r_2)]$ if the expectations hypothesis is correct. The yield to maturity would thus be determined solely by current and expected future one-period interest rates. An upward-sloping yield curve would be clear evidence that investors anticipate increases in interest rates.

Concept Check

Question 4. If the expectations hypothesis is valid, what can we conclude about the premiums necessary to induce investors to hold bonds of different maturities from their investment horizons?

Liquidity Preference

We noted in our discussion of the long- and short-term investors that short-term investors will be unwilling to hold long-term bonds unless the forward rate exceeds the expected short interest rate, $f_2 > E(r_2)$, whereas long-term investors will be unwilling to hold short bonds unless $E(r_2)$ exceeds f_2. In other words, both groups of investors require a premium to induce them to hold bonds with maturities different from their investment horizons. Advocates of the **liquidity preference theory** of the term structure believe that short-term investors dominate the market so that, generally speaking, the forward rate exceeds the expected short rate. The excess of f_2 over $E(r_2)$, the liquidity premium, is predicted to be positive.

Concept Check	Question 5. The liquidity premium hypothesis also holds that *issuers* of bonds prefer to issue long-term bonds. How would this preference contribute to a positive liquidity premium?

To illustrate the differing implications of these theories for the term structure of interest rates, consider a situation in which the short interest rate is expected to be constant indefinitely. Suppose that $r_1 = 10\%$ and that $E(r_2) = 10\%$, $E(r_3) = 10\%$, and so on. Under the expectations hypothesis the 2-year yield to maturity could be derived from the following:

$$(1 + y_2)^2 = (1 + r_1)[1 + E(r_2)]$$
$$= (1.10)(1.10)$$

so that y_2 equals 10%. Similarly, yields on all-maturity bonds would equal 10%.

In contrast, under the liquidity preference theory f_2 would exceed $E(r_2)$. For sake of illustration, suppose that f_2 is 11%, implying a 1% liquidity premium. Then, for 2-year bonds:

$$(1 + y_2)^2 = (1 + r_1)(1 + f_2)$$
$$= (1.10)(1.11)$$
$$= 1.221$$

implying that $1 + y_2 = 1.105$. Similarly, if f_3 also equals 11%, then the yield on 3-year bonds would be determined by

$$(1 + y_3)^3 = (1 + r_1)(1 + f_2)(1 + f_3)$$
$$= (1.10)(1.11)(1.11)$$
$$= 1.35531$$

implying that $1 + y_3 = 1.1067$. The plot of the yield curve in this situation would be given as in Figure 15.3, *A*. Such an upward-sloping yield curve is commonly observed in practice.

If interest rates are expected to change over time, then the liquidity premium may be overlaid on the path of expected spot rates to determine the forward interest rate. Then the yield to maturity for each date will be an average of the single-period forward rates. Several such possibilities for increasing and declining interest rates appear in Figure 15.3, *B* to *D*.

FIGURE 15.3

Yield curves. **A,** Constant expected short rate. Liquidity premium of 1%. Result is a rising yield curve. **B,** Declining expected short rates. Increasing liquidity premiums. Result is a rising yield curve despite falling expected interest rates.

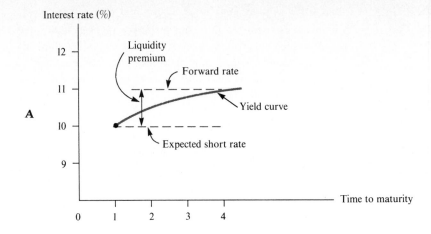

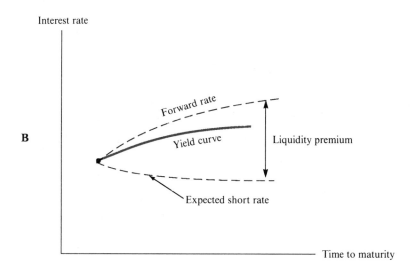

Market Segmentation and Preferred Habitat Theories

Both the liquidity premium and expectations hypothesis theories of the term structure implicitly view bonds of different maturities as some sort of substitutes for each other. An investor considering holding bonds of one maturity possibly can be lured instead into holding bonds of another maturity by the prospect of earning a risk premium. In this sense markets for bonds of all maturities are inextricably linked, and yields on short and long bonds are determined jointly in market equilibrium. Forward rates cannot differ from expected short rates by more than a fair liquidity premium, or else investors will reallocate their fixed-income portfolios to exploit what they per-

FIGURE 15.3

FIGURE 15.3
Continued. C,
Declining expected
short rates. Constant
liquidity premiums.
Result is a
hump-shaped yield
curve. **D,** Increasing
expected short rates.
Increasing liquidity
premiums. Result is a
sharply increasing
yield curve.

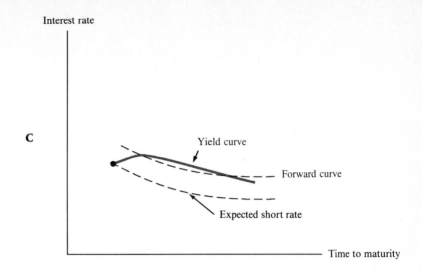

C

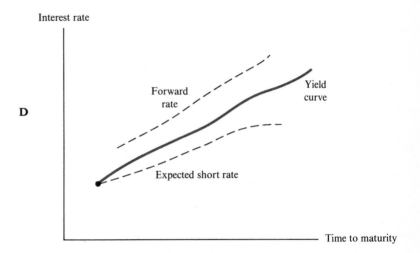

D

ceive as abnormal profit opportunities elsewhere.

In contrast, the **market segmentation theory** holds that long- and short-maturity bonds are traded in essentially distinct or segmented markets, each of which finds its own equilibrium independently. The activities of long-term borrowers and lenders determine rates on long-term bonds. Similarly, short-term traders set short rates independently of long-term expectations. The term structure of interest rates, in this view, is determined by the equilibrium rates set in the various maturity markets.

This view of the market is not common today. Both borrowers and lenders seem to compare long and short rates, as well as expectations of future rates, before deciding whether to borrow or lend long- or short-term. That they make these comparisons, and are willing to move into a particular maturity if it seems sufficiently profitable to do so, means that all-maturity bonds compete with each other for investors' attention, which implies that the rate on a bond of any given maturity is determined with an eye toward rates on competing bonds. This view of the market is called the **preferred habitat theory:** investors prefer specific maturity ranges but can be induced to switch if premiums are sufficient. Markets are not so segmented that an appropriate premium cannot attract an investor who prefers one investment horizon to consider a different one.

15.5 *Interpreting the Term Structure*

We have seen that under certainty, 1 plus the yield to maturity on a zero coupon bond is simply the geometric average of 1 plus the future short rates that will prevail over the life of the bond. This is the meaning of equation 15.3, which we repeat here:

$$1 + y_n = [(1 + r_1)(1 + r_2) \ldots (1 + r_n)]^{1/n}$$

When future rates are uncertain, we modify equation 15.3 by replacing future short rates with forward rates:

$$1 + y_n = [(1 + r_1)(1 + f_2)(1 + f_3) \ldots (1 + f_n)]^{1/n} \tag{15.7}$$

Thus there is a direct relationship between yields on various maturity bonds and forward interest rates. This relationship is the source of the information that can be gleaned from an analysis of the yield curve.

First, we ask what factors can account for a rising yield curve. Mathematically, if the yield curve is rising, f_n must exceed y_{n-1}. In words, the yield curve is upward sloping at any point where the forward rate for the period is greater than the yield to maturity on bonds of a one-period-shorter maturity. This rule follows from the notion of the yield to maturity as an average (albeit a geometric average) of forward rates.

If the yield curve is to rise as one moves to longer maturities, it must be the case that extension to a longer maturity results in the inclusion of a "new" forward rate that is higher than the average of the previously observed rates. This is analogous to the observation that if a new student's test score is to increase the class average, that student's score must exceed the class's average without her score. To raise the yield to maturity, an above-average forward rate must be added to the other rates in the averaging computation.

For example, if the yield to maturity on 3-year bonds is 9%, then the yield on 4-year bonds will satisfy the following equations:

$$(1 + y_4)^4 = (1.09)^3(1 + f_4)$$

If $f_4 = .09$, then y_4 also will equal .09. (Confirm this!) If f_4 is greater than 9%, y_4 will exceed 9%, and the yield curve will slope upward.

Given that an upward-sloping yield curve is always associated with a forward rate higher than the spot, or current, yield, we need to ask next what can account for that higher forward rate. Unfortunately, there always are two possible answers to this question. Recall that the forward rate can be related to the expected future short rate according to this equation:

$$f_n = E(r_n) + \text{Liquidity premium}$$

where the liquidity premium might be necessary to induce investors to hold bonds of maturities that do not correspond to their preferred investment horizons.

By the way, the liquidity premium need not be positive, although that is the position generally taken by advocates of the liquidity premium hypothesis. We showed previously that if most investors have long-term horizons, the liquidity premium could be negative.

In any case, the equation shows that there are two reasons that the forward rate could be high. Either investors expect rising interest rates, meaning that $E(r_n)$ is high, or they require a large premium for holding longer-term bonds. Although often it is tempting to infer from a rising yield curve that investors believe that interest rates will eventually increase, this is not a valid inference. Indeed, Figure 15.3, *A*, provides a simple counterexample to this line of reasoning. There, the spot rate is expected to stay at 10% forever. Yet there is a constant 1% liquidity premium so that all forward rates are 11%. The result is that the yield curve continually rises, starting at a level of 10% for 1-year bonds, but eventually approaching 11% for long-term bonds as more and more forward rates at 11% are averaged into the yields to maturity.

Therefore, although it is true that expectations of increase in future interest rates can result in a rising yield curve, the converse is not true: a rising yield curve does not in and of itself imply expectations of higher future interest rates. This is the heart of the difficulty in drawing conclusions from the yield curve. The effects of possible liquidity premiums confound any simple attempt to extract expectations from the term structure. But estimating the market's expectations is a crucial task, because only by comparing your own expectations to those reflected in market prices can you determine whether you are relatively bullish or bearish on interest rates.

One very rough approach to deriving expected future spot rates is to assume that liquidity premiums are constant. An estimate of that premium can be subtracted from the forward rate to obtain the market's expected interest rate. For example, again making use of the example plotted in Figure 15.3, *A*, the researcher would estimate from historical data that a typical liquidity premium in this economy is 1%. After

FIGURE 15.4

Price volatility of a
30-year Treasury
bond, January 1977 to
December 1987.
(Courtesy Fidelity
Management Trust
Company, Boston.)

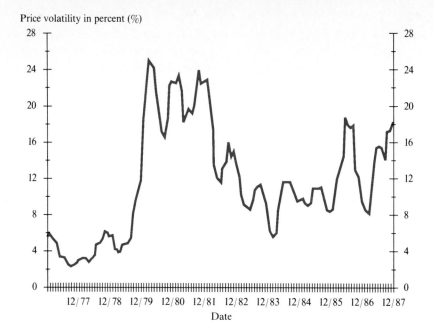

calculating the forward rate from the yield curve to be 11%, the expectation of the future spot rate would be determined to be 10%.

This approach has little to recommend it for two reasons. First, it is next to impossible to obtain precise estimates of a liquidity premium. The general approach to doing so would be to compare forward rates and eventually realized future short rates and to calculate the average difference between the two. However, the deviations between the two values can be quite large and unpredictable because of unanticipated economic events that affect the realized short rate. The data do not contain enough information to calculate a reliable estimate of the expected premium. Second, there is no reason to believe that the liquidity premium should be constant. Figure 15.4 shows the variability of prices of long-term Treasury bonds over a 10-year period. Interest rate risk fluctuated dramatically during the period. So might we expect risk premiums on various duration bonds to fluctuate. Empirical evidence suggests that term premiums do in fact fluctuate over time.[6]

Figure 15.5 presents interest rate spreads between bonds of various maturities for the decade ending in 1987. The figure shows that the yield curve is usually upward sloping at short maturities: 5-year T-notes have consistently higher yields than do 3-month T-bills. At the longer maturities the yield curve flattens. Yield spreads between 10- and 20-year T-bonds fluctuate around zero and are generally quite small.

The usually observed initial upward slope for the yield curve is the empirical basis for the liquidity premium doctrine that long-term bonds offer a positive liquidity pre-

---

[6]See, for example, Startz, Richard, "Do Forecast Errors or Term Premia Really Make the Difference Between Long and Short Rates?" *Journal of Financial Economics, 10,* 1982.

FIGURE 15.5

Selected rate spreads.

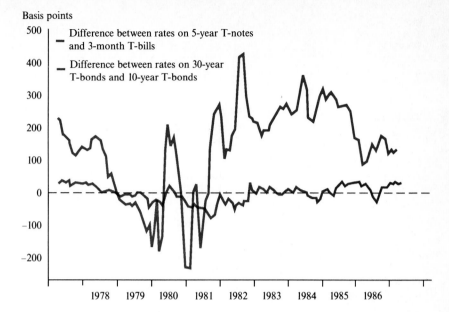

Therefore an expected change in interest rates can be due to changes in either expected real rates or expected inflation rates. Usually, it is important to distinguish between these two possibilities because the economic environments associated with them may vary substantially. High real rates may indicate a rapidly expanding economy, high budget deficits, and tight monetary policy. Although high inflation rates also can arise out of a rapidly expanding economy, inflation also may be caused by rapid expansion of the money supply or supply-side shocks to the economy such as interruptions in oil supplies. These factors have very different implications for investments. Even if we conclude from an analysis of the yield curve that rates will fall, we need to analyze the macroeconomic factors that might cause such a decline.

mium. In the face of this empirical regularity, perhaps it is valid to interpret a downward-sloping yield curve as evidence that interest rates are expected to decline. If **term premiums,** the spread between yields on long- and short-term bonds, generally are positive, then anticipated declines in rates could account for a downward-sloping curve.

Why might interest rates fall? There are two factors to consider: the real rate and the inflation premium. Recall that the nominal interest rate is composed of the real rate plus a factor to compensate for the effect of inflation:

$$1 + \text{Nominal rate} = (1 + \text{Real rate})(1 + \text{Inflation rate})$$

or, approximately,

$$\text{Nominal rate} \approx \text{Real rate} + \text{Inflation rate}$$

Therefore an expected change in interest rates can be due to changes in either expected real rates or expected inflation rates. Usually, it is important to distinguish between these two possibilities because the economic environments associated with them may vary substantially. High real rates may indicate a rapidly expanding economy, high budget deficits, and tight monetary policy. Although high inflation rates also can arise out of a rapidly expanding economy, inflation also may be caused by rapid expansion of the money supply or supply-side shocks to the economy such as interruptions in oil supplies. These factors have very different implications for investments. Even if we conclude from an analysis of the yield curve that rates will fall, we need to analyze the macroeconomic factors that might cause such a decline.

15.6 Realized Compound Yield to Maturity

We have noted that the yield to maturity is calculated by finding the single interest rate that makes the present value of the payments provided by a security equal to its price. This procedure is correct only if interest rates are unchanging over time so that any intermediate cash flows from the bond can be reinvested at the bond's yield to maturity. The yield then would be the appropriate measure of the time value of money for all cash flows from the bond. When rates are not constant, however, the yield to maturity is not the appropriate discount rate for all cash flows.

Let us first examine this problem under certainty using the data shown in Table 15.1. For illustration, consider a 4-year 10% coupon bond making annual coupon payments.

First, we compute the conventionally measured yield to maturity on the bond. The bond will sell at a price equal to the present value of all cash flows; using discount factors derived from Table 15.1 we find:

Time	Cash Flow	Discount Factor	Present Value
1	100	1.08	92.59
2	100	(1.08)(1.10)	84.18
3	100	(1.08)(1.10)(1.11)	75.83
4	1,100	(1.08)(1.10)(1.11)(1.11)	751.50
			1,004.10

The bond will sell at $1,004.10. At this price its yield to maturity works out to 9.871%. This interest rate solves the following equation for y:

$$1,004.10 = 100 \times PA(y,4) + 1,000 \times PF(y,4)$$

The equation applies a single yield, y, to all cash flows.[7]

Instead of calculating yield in this manner, however, we could ask the following question: What would be the realized yield if all coupon payments from the bond are reinvested at the going market interest rate at the time of payment? Suppose that all coupons are invested short-term and rolled over until the bond matures. Then the first coupon payment would grow by a factor of 1.10 in year 2, 1.11 in year 3, and 1.11 in year 4. Figure 15.6 demonstrates the total growth in invested funds over the life of the bond. By the end of year 4, the investor would have accumulated a total of $1,469.74 from the initial investment of $1,004.10. The **realized compound yield** would be computed as $1,004.10(1 + y)^4 = 1,469.74$, which implies that $y = 9.993\%$. Thus the realized yield differs from the conventional yield to maturity, except for zero-coupon bonds, for which there is no issue of reinvesting coupons.

[7]Recall from Chapter 14 that PA is the present value factor for annuities and PF is the present value factor for a one-time payment.

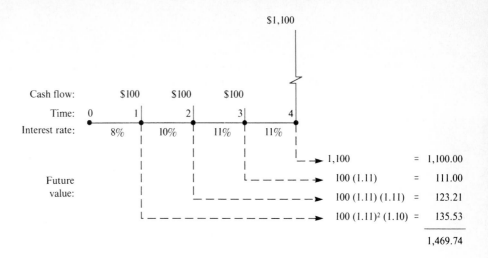

FIGURE 15.6
Growth of invested funds.

Cash flow: $100 $100 $100

Time: 0   1   2   3   4

Interest rate: 8%   10%   11%   11%

Future value:

$1,100

1,100   = 1,100.00

100 (1.11)   =   111.00

100 (1.11) (1.11)   =   123.21

100 (1.11)² (1.10)   =   135.53

                            ─────────
                            1,469.74

Concept Check

Question 7. Compute the conventional and realized compound yield to maturity for a 3-year 12% annual coupon bond using the data from Table 15.1.

This example highlights the problem associated with using conventional yields to maturity when the term structure is not flat. The yield to maturity is computed by mistakenly applying an "average" rate over the bond's life to all of its payments, regardless of their timing. However, the realized yield to maturity method—as an alternative to the conventional yield—is not a cure-all.

In an economy with future interest rate uncertainty, the rates at which interim coupons can be reinvested are not yet known. This fact reduces much of the attraction of the realized yield measure. In practice, we would need either to assume a set of future interest rates at which coupons could be invested, or to use the set of forward rates implied by the yield curve as the assumed path of rates. The appeal of either procedure is dubious, however, because neither the assumed nor the forward rate can confidently be assumed an accurate estimate of future short rates.

Unfortunately, although conventional yields to maturity on coupon bonds pose problems of interpretation, realized yields to maturity raise equally difficult problems of implementation. Probably the best approach to the yield curve is to estimate as well as possible the series of forward rates implied by the pure yield curve, that is, the yield curve that we can plot from a series of zero-coupon bonds. If a series of zeros is not observable, the pure yield curve may be estimated along the lines suggested in Section 15.2. Given the series of forward rates, the analyst must make an educated guess about their implications for future short rates and the resulting implications for portfolio composition. This is part of the art, as opposed to the science, of portfolio management.

Summary

1. The term structure of interest rates refers to the interest rates for various terms to maturity embodied in the prices of default-free zero-coupon bonds.

2. In a world of certainty all investments must provide equal total returns for any investment period. Short-term holding period returns on all bonds would be equal in a risk-free economy, and all equal to the rate available on short-term bonds. Similarly, total returns from rolling over short-term bonds over longer periods would equal the total return available from long-maturity bonds.

3. A pure yield curve could be plotted easily from a complete set of zero-coupon bonds. In practice, however, most bonds carry coupons, payable at different future times, so that yield curve estimates usually must be inferred from prices of coupon bonds. Measurement of the term structure is complicated by tax issues such as tax timing options and the different tax brackets of different investors.

4. The forward rate of interest is the break-even future interest rate that would equate the total return from a rollover strategy to that of a longer-term zero-coupon bond. It is defined by the equation

$$(1 + y_n)^n(1 + f_{n+1}) = (1 + y_{n+1})^{n+1}$$

where n is a given number of periods from today. This equation can be used to show that yields to maturity and forward rates are related by the equation

$$(1 + y_n)^n = (1 + r_1)(1 + f_2)(1 + f_3) \ldots (1 + f_n)$$

5. A common version of the expectations hypothesis holds that forward interest rates are unbiased estimates of expected future interest rates. However, there are good reasons to believe that forward rates differ from expected short rates by a risk premium, also known as a liquidity premium. A liquidity premium can cause the yield curve to slope upward even if no increase in short rates is anticipated.

6. The existence of liquidity premiums makes it extremely difficult to infer expected future interest rates from the yield curve. Such an inference would be made easier if we could assume the liquidity premium remained reasonably stable over time. However, both empirical and theoretical insights cast doubt on the constancy of that premium.

7. An alternative measure to the conventional yield to maturity is the realized compound yield to maturity, computed from the total funds that would accrue if all cash flows from a fixed-income security were reinvested at going market rates. Although such a measure can be superior to conventional yield to maturity when the future path of spot rates is known, realized compound yield has no clear advantage over yield to maturity in the real world of interest rate uncertainty.

Key Terms

Term structure of interest rates	Spot rate
Short interest rate	Forward interest rate
Yield curve	Liquidity premium

Expectations hypothesis	Preferred habitat theory
Liquidity preference theory	Term premiums
Market segmentation theory	Realized compound yield

Selected Readings

A detailed presentation of yield curve analytics and relationships among spot rates, yields to maturity, and realized compound yields is contained in:
Homer, Sidney, and Liebowitz, Martin, *Inside the Yield Book: New Tools for Bond Market Strategy*, Englewood Cliffs, N.J.: Prentice-Hall, 1972.

A discussion of the various versions of the expectations hypothesis is:
Cox, John, Ingersoll, Jonathan, and Ross, Stephen, "A Reexamination of Traditional Hypotheses About the Term Structure of Interest Rates," *Journal of Finance, 36,* September 1981.

A test of the expectations hypothesis using survey data is:
Friedman, Benjamin, "Interest Rate Expectations versus Forward Rates: Evidence from an Expectations Survey," *Journal of Finance, 34,* September 1979.

Evidence on liquidity premiums may be found in:
Nelson, Charles, "Estimation of Term Premiums from Average Yield Differentials in the Term Structure of Interest Rates," *Econometrica,* March 1972.
Fama, Eugene, "The Information in the Term Structure," *Journal of Financial Economics, 13,* 1984.
Fama, Eugene, "Forward Rates as Predictors of Future Spot Rates," *Journal of Financial Economics, 3,* 1976.
Startz, Richard, "Do Forecast Errors or Term Premia Really Make the Difference Between Long and Short Rates?" *Journal of Financial Economics, 10,* 1982.

Problems in the measurement of the yield curve are treated in:
McCulloch, J. Houston, "Measuring the Term Structure of Interest Rates," *Journal of Business, 44,* January 1971.
McCulloch, J. Houston, "The Tax Adjusted Yield Curve," *Journal of Finance, 30,* June 1975.

Problems

1. (CFA Examination, Level I, 1986)
   a. Briefly explain why bonds of different maturities have different yields in terms of the (1) expectations, (2) liquidity, and (3) segmentation hypotheses.
   b. Briefly describe the implications of each of the three hypotheses when the yield curve is (1) upward sloping, and (2) downward sloping.
2. (CFA Examination, Level I, 1986)
   Which one of the following is false?
   a. The liquidity hypothesis indicates that, all other things being equal, longer maturities will have a higher yield.
   b. The basic conclusion of the expectations hypothesis is that the long-term rate is equal to the anticipated short-term rate.
   c. The expectations hypothesis indicates a flat yield curve if anticipated future short-term rates are equal to current short-term rates.
   d. The segmentation hypothesis contends that borrowers and lenders are constrained to particular segments of the yield curve.

3. The following is a list of prices for zero coupon bonds of various maturities. Calculate the yields to maturity of each bond and the implied sequence of forward rates.

Maturity (Years)	Price of Bond ($)
1	943.40
2	898.47
3	847.62
4	792.16

4. Assuming that the expectations hypothesis is valid, compute the expected price path of the 4-year bond in problem 3 as time passes. What is the rate of return of the bond in each year? Show that the expected return equals the forward rate for each year.

5. Consider an 8% coupon bond with 3 years until maturity making *annual* coupon payments. The interest rates in the next 3 years will be, with certainty, $r_1 = 8\%$, $r_2 = 10\%$, $r_3 = 12\%$. Calculate the price, yield to maturity, and realized compound yield of the bond.

6. Would you expect the yield on a callable bond to lie above or below a yield curve fitted from noncallable bonds?

7. The current yield curve for default-free pure discount (zero-coupon) bonds is as follows:

Maturity (Years)	YTM
1	10%
2	11%
3	12%

a. What are the implied 1-year forward rates?

b. Assume that the pure expectations hypothesis of the term structure is correct. If market expectations are accurate, what will the pure yield curve, that is, the yields to maturity on 1- and 2-year pure discount bonds, be next year?

c. If you purchased a 2-year pure discount bond now, what is the expected total rate of return over the next year? If it were a 3-year pure discount bond? (Hint: compute the current and expected future prices.) Ignore taxes.

d. What should be the current price of the 3-year maturity bond with a 12% coupon rate paid annually? If you purchased it at that price, what would your total expected rate of return be over the next year (coupon plus price change)? Ignore taxes.

8. Below is a list of prices for zero coupon bonds of various maturities.

Maturity (Years)	Price of $1,000 Par Bond (Zero Coupon)
1	943.40
2	873.52
3	816.37

a. An 8.5% $1,000 par bond pays an annual coupon and will mature in 3 years. What should the yield to maturity on the bond be?

b. If at the end of the first year the yield curve flattens out at 8%, what will be the 1-year holding period return on the coupon bond?

9. Prices of zero coupon bonds reveal the following pattern of forward rates:

Year	Forward Rate
1	5%
2	7%
3	8%

In addition to the zero coupon bond, investors also may purchase a 3-year bond making annual payments of $60 with par value $1,000.

a. What is the price of the coupon bond?

b. What is the yield to maturity of the coupon bond?

c. Under the expectations hypothesis, what is the expected realized compound yield of the coupon bond?

d. If you forecast that the yield curve in 1 year will be flat at 7%, what is your forecast for the expected rate of return on the coupon bond for the 1-year holding period?

10. You observe the following term structure:

	Effective Annual YTM
6-month bill	6.1%
1-year zero coupon bond	6.2%
1.5-year zero coupon bond	6.3%
2-year zero coupon bond	6.4%

a. If you believe that the term structure in 6 months will be the same as today's, will bills or the 2-year zeros provide a greater expected 6-month return?

b. What if you believe in the expectations hypothesis?

11. (CFA Examination, Level II, 1983)

In June 1982, when the yield to maturity (YTM) on long-term bonds was about 14%, many observers were projecting an eventual decline in these rates. It was not unusual to hear of customers urging portfolio managers to "lock-in" these high rates by buying some new issues with these high coupons. You recognize that it is not possible to really lock-in such returns for coupon bonds because of the potential reinvestment rate problem if rates decline. Assuming the following expectations for a 5-year bond bought at par, compute the total realized compound yield (without taxes) for the bond below.

Coupon: 14% (assume annual interest payments at end of each year)

Maturity: 5 years

1-year reinvestment rates during:

  Year 2, 3; 10%

  Year 4, 5; 8%

CHAPTER 16

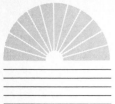

Fixed-Income Portfolio Management

In this chapter we turn to various strategies that fixed-income portfolio managers can pursue, making a distinction between passive and active strategies. A *passive investment strategy* takes market prices of securities as fairly set. Rather than attempting to beat the market by exploiting superior information or insight, passive managers act to maintain an appropriate risk/return balance given market opportunities. One special case of passive management is an immunization strategy that attempts to insulate or immunize the portfolio from interest rate risk.

An *active investment strategy* attempts to achieve returns more than commensurate with risk borne. In the context of fixed-income management this style of management can take two forms. Active managers either use interest rate forecasts to predict movements in the entire fixed-income market, or they employ some form of intramarket analysis to identify particular sectors of the fixed-income market or particular bonds that are relatively mispriced.

We start our discussion with an analysis of the sensitivity of bond prices to interest rate fluctuations. The concept of duration, which measures interest rate sensitivity, is basic to formulating both active and passive fixed-income strategies. We turn next to passive strategies and show how duration-matching strategies can be used to immunize the holding period return of a fixed-income portfolio from interest rate risk. Finally, we explore a variety of active strategies, including intramarket analysis, interest rate forecasting, and interest rate swaps.

16.1   Interest Rate Risk

We have seen already that an inverse relationship exists between bond prices and yields, and we know that interest rates can fluctuate substantially. Indeed, as the nearby box illustrates, bond volatility has exceeded stock volatility for most of the 1980s. As interest rates rise and fall, bondholders experience capital losses and gains. These gains or losses make fixed-income investments risky, even if the coupon and principal payments are guaranteed as in the case of Treasury obligations.

'Boring' Bonds?
They've Been More Volatile Than Stocks

During the 1980s, the corporate bond market has been more volatile than the stock market. The fluctuation in bonds increased sharply after October 1979, when the Federal Reserve adopted a policy allowing wider moves in short-term interest rates. Since then, returns in the bond market generally have varied more than in the stock market, according to the volatility indexes compiled by Shearson Lehman Economics. The highest peak shows a period when bonds were seven times as volatile as stocks. Bonds settled down considerably in late 1986, and stocks have fluctuated more since last October. But, as fears about the dollar's decline and accelerating inflation permeate the fixed-income markets, the volatility of bonds is picking up again.

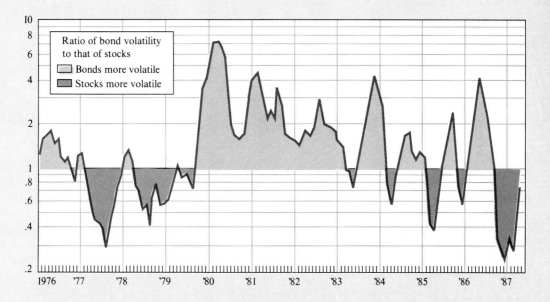

Note: Bond volatility index based on daily yields of triple-A, 20-year corporate bonds and stock volatility index based on daily changes in total return (the change in price and reinvestment of dividends) of the S&P 500-stock index; both are averaged monthly.
Source: Shearson Lehman Brothers Inc.

Why do bond prices respond to interest rate fluctuations? Remember that in a competitive market all securities must offer investors fair expected rates of return. If a bond is issued with an 8% coupon when competitive yields are 8%, then it will sell at par value. If the market rate rises to 9%, however, who would purchase an 8% coupon bond at par value? The bond price must fall until its expected return increases to the competitive level of 9%. Conversely, if the market rate falls to 7%, the 8%

TABLE 16.1   Prices of 8% Coupon Bond

Yield to Maturity (APR)	T = 1 Year	T = 10 Years	T = 20 Years
8%	1,000	1,000	1,000
9%	990.64	934.96	907.99
Change in Price (%)*	0.94%	6.50%	9.20%

*Equals value of bond at a 9% yield to maturity divided by value of bond at (the original) 8% yield, minus 1.

coupon on the bond is attractive compared to yields on alternative investments. In response, investors eager for that return would bid the bond price above its par value until the total rate of return falls to the market rate.

Interest Rate Sensitivity

It is easy to confirm with numerical examples that prices of long-term bonds generally are more sensitive to interest rate movements than are those of short-term bonds. Consider Table 16.1, which gives bond prices for 8% semiannual coupon bonds at different yields to maturity and times to maturity, *T*. (The interest rates are expressed as annual percentage rates (APRs), meaning that the true 6-month yield is doubled to obtain the stated annual yield.)

The shortest-term bond falls in value by less than 1% when the interest rate increases from 8% to 9%. The 10-year bond falls by 6.5%, and the 20-year bond by over 9%. Longer-term bonds are more sensitive to interest rate increases because higher interest rates have a greater impact on more distant future payments. The 1-year bond, for example, is so close to maturity that the present value of the remaining payments is hardly affected at all by the increase in the interest rate. As payments become progressively more distant, however, the effect of discounting at a higher rate becomes progressively more telling, and prices are affected much more by the increase in the interest rate.

Let us now recompute Table 16.1 using a zero-coupon bond rather than the 8% coupon bond. The results are shown in Table 16.2. Notice that for each maturity, there is a higher percentage decrease in the price of the zero-coupon bond attributable to the increase in the interest rate than for the 8% coupon bond. Since we know that long-term bonds are more sensitive to interest rate movements than are short-term bonds, this observation suggests that in some sense a zero-coupon bond represents a longer-term bond than an equal-time-to-maturity coupon bond. In fact, this insight about effective maturity is a useful one that we can make mathematically precise.

For now, we can note that the times to maturity of the two bonds in this example are not perfect measures of the long- or short-term nature of the bonds. The 8% bond makes many coupon payments, most of which come years before the bond's maturity date. Each of these payments may be considered to have its own "maturity date," and the effective maturity of the bond is therefore some sort of average of the maturities of all the cash flows paid out by the bond. The zero-coupon bond, by contrast, makes

TABLE 16.2   Prices of Zero Coupon Bond

Yield to Maturity (APR)	T = 1 Year	T = 10 Years	T = 20 Years
8%	924.56	456.39	208.29
9%	915.73	414.64	171.93
Change in price (%)*	0.96%	9.15%	17.46%

*Equals value of bond at a 9% yield to maturity divided by value of bond at (the original) 8% yield, minus 1.

only one payment at maturity. Its time to maturity is therefore a well-defined concept.

Duration

To deal with the ambiguity of the "maturity" of a bond making many payments, we need a measure of the average maturity of the bond's promised cash flows to serve as a useful summary statistic of the effective maturity of the bond. We would like also to use the measure as a guide to the sensitivity of a bond to interest rate changes, because we have noted that price sensitivity tends to increase with time to maturity.

Frederick Macaulay[1] termed the effective maturity concept the **duration** of the bond, and suggested that duration be computed as the weighted average of the times to each coupon or principal payment made by the bond. He recommended that the weight of each payment be related to the "importance" of each payment to the value of the bond; specifically, that the weight for each payment be the proportion of the total value of the bond accounted for by that payment. This proportion is just the present value of the payment divided by the bond price. Macaulay's duration formula is given by

$$D = \sum_{t=1}^{T} t \times \frac{CF_t/(1+y)^t}{\text{Price}} \qquad (16.1)$$

where
  D is the bond's duration
  t is the time until each payment
  y is the bond's yield to maturity
  CF_t is the cash flow (coupon or principal payment) received by the bond owner at time t
  Price is the bond price

The duration measure is a weighted average of all of the times to payment, t, with weights equal to $[CF_t/(1+y)^t]/$price. These weights sum to exactly 1.0 because the

---

[1]Macaulay, Frederick, *Some Theoretical Problems Suggested by the Movements of Interest Rates, Bond Yields, and Stock Prices in the United States Since 1856,* New York: National Bureau of Economic Research, 1938.

16.3   Calculating the Duration of Two Bonds

	(1) Time Until Payment (in Years)	(2) Payment	(3) Payment Discounted at 5% Semiannually	(4) Weight*	(5) Column 1 Multiplied by Column 4
Bond A					
8% bond	.5	$ 40	$ 38.095	.0395	.0198
	1.0	40	36.281	.0376	.0376
	1.5	40	34.553	.0358	.0537
	2.0	1,040	855.611	.8871	1.7742
Sum:			$964.540	1.0000	1.8853
Bond B					
Zero-coupon	.5-1.5	$ 0	$ 0	0	0
bond	2.0	1,000	822.70	1.0	2
Sum:			$822.70	1.0	2

*Weight = Present value of each payment (column 3) divided by the bond price, $964.54 for bond A and $822.70 for bond B.

sum of the cash flows discounted at the yield to maturity equals the bond price.

As an example of the application of equation 16.1, we derive in Table 16.3 the durations of an 8% coupon and zero-coupon bond, each with 2 years to maturity. We assume that the yield to maturity on each bond is 10%, or 5% per half year.

We calculate the duration of the bonds by adding the numbers in column 5. The duration of the zero-coupon bond is exactly equal to its time to maturity, 2 years. This makes sense, because with only one payment, the average time until payment must be the bond's maturity. The 2-year coupon bond in contrast has a shorter duration of 1.8853 years.

Duration is a key concept in fixed-income portfolio management for at least three reasons. First, it is a simple summary statistic of the effective average maturity of the portfolio. Second, it turns out to be an essential tool in immunizing portfolios from interest rate risk. We will explore this application in Section 16.2. Third, duration is a measure of the interest rate sensitivity of a portfolio, which we will explore here.

We have already noted that long-term bonds are more sensitive to interest rate movements than are short-term bonds. The duration measure enables us to quantify this relationship. Specifically, it can be shown that when interest rates change, the proportional change in a bond's price can be related to the change in its yield to maturity, y, according to the rule:

$$\frac{\Delta P}{P} = -D \times \left[\frac{\Delta(1 + y)}{1 + y} \right] \tag{16.2}$$

The proportional price change equals the proportional change in 1 plus the bond's yield times the bond's duration. Therefore bond price volatility is proportional to the bond's duration, and duration becomes a natural measure of interest rate exposure.[2]

To confirm this point, let's compare the interest rate sensitivity of the price of the 2-year coupon bond in Table 16.3, which has a duration of 1.8853 years, to the sensitivity of a zero-coupon bond with maturity and duration of 1.8853 years. Both should have equal interest rate exposure if duration is a useful measure of price sensitivity.

The 2-year bond sells for $964.5405 at the initial semiannual interest rate of 5%. If the bond's semiannual yield increases by 1 basis point (1/100 of a percent) to 5.01%, its price will fall to $964.1942, a percentage decline of .0359%. The zero-coupon bond has a maturity of $1.8853 \times 2 = 3.7706$ half-year periods. (Because we use a half-year interest rate of 5%, we also need to define duration in terms of a number of half-year periods to maintain consistency of units.) At the initial half-year interest rate of 5%, it sells at a price of $831.9623 ($1,000/1.05^{3.7706}$). Its price falls to $831.6636 ($1,000/1.0501^{3.7706}$) when the interest rate increases, for an identical .0359% capital loss. We conclude therefore that equal-duration assets are in fact equally sensitive to interest rate movements.

Incidentally, this example confirms the validity of equation 16.2. Note that the equation predicts that the proportional price change of the two bonds should have been $3.7706 \times .0001/1.05 = .000359$, or .0359%, exactly as we found from direct computation.

Because duration is so important to fixed-income portfolio management, it is worth exploring some of its properties. We have already established the following:

Rule 1 for duration

The duration of a zero-coupon bond equals its time to maturity.

We have also seen that the 2-year coupon bond has a lower duration than the 2-year zero because coupons early in the bond's life lower the bond's weighted average time until payments. This illustrates another general property:

Rule 2 for duration

Holding maturity constant, a bond's duration is higher when the coupon rate is lower.

This rule is attributable to the impact of early coupon payments on the average maturity of a bond's payments. The lower these coupons, the less they reduce the weighted average maturity of the payments.

---

[2]Actually, equation 16.2 is only approximately valid for large changes in the bond's yield. The approximation becomes exact as one considers smaller, or localized, changes in yields. Students of calculus will recognize that duration is proportional to the derivative of the bond's price with respect to changes in the bond's yield:

$$D = (dP/dy)/[P/(1 + y)]$$

As such, it gives a measure of the slope of the bond price curve only in the neighborhood of the current price.

Rule 3 for duration

Holding the coupon rate constant, a bond's duration generally increases with its time to maturity. Duration always increases with maturity for bonds selling at par or at a premium to par.

This property of duration is fairly intuitive. What is surprising is that duration need not always increase with time to maturity. It turns out that for some deep discount bonds, duration may fall with increases in maturity. However, for virtually all traded bonds it is safe to assume that duration increases with maturity.

Figure 16.1 is a graph of duration as a function of time to maturity for bonds of various coupon rates. Notice that for the zero-coupon bond, maturity and duration are equal. However, for coupon bonds duration increases by less than a year with a year's increase in maturity. The slope of the duration graph is less than one.

Although long-maturity bonds generally will be high-duration bonds, duration is a better measure of the long-term nature of the bond because it also accounts for coupon payments. Only when the bond pays no coupons is time to maturity an adequate statistic; then maturity and duration are equal.

Notice also in Figure 16.1 that the two 15% coupon bonds have different durations when they sell at different yields to maturity. The lower-yield bond has greater duration. This makes sense, because at lower yields the more distant payments made by the bond have relatively greater present values and account for a greater share of the

FIGURE 16.1

Duration vs. maturity.
(From Nemerever, William
L., "Managing Bond
Portfolios Throu^h
Immunization S. .egies,"
*The Revolution in
Techniques for Managing
Bond Portfolios,*
Charlottesville, Va.: The
Institute of Chartered
Financial Analysts.)

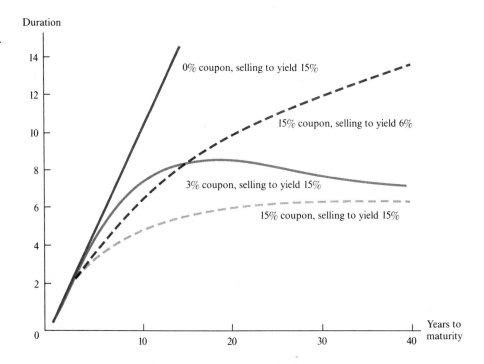

bond's total value. Thus in the weighted-average calculation of duration the distant payments receive greater weights, which results in a higher duration measure. This establishes rule 4:

Rule 4 for duration

Holding other factors constant, the duration of a coupon bond is higher when the bond's yield to maturity is lower.

Rule 4 applies to coupon bonds. For zeros, of course, duration equals time to maturity, regardless of the yield to maturity.

Finally, we develop some algebraic rules for the duration of securities of special interest. These rules are derived from and consistent with the formula for duration given in equation 16.1 but may be easier to use for long-term bonds.

Rule 5 for duration

The duration of a level perpetuity is $(1 + y)/y$. For example, at a 10% yield, the duration of a perpetuity that pays $100 once a year forever will equal $1.10/.10 = 11$ years, but at an 8% yield it will equal $1.08/.08 = 13.5$ years.

Rule 5 makes it obvious that maturity and duration can differ substantially. The maturity of the perpetuity is infinite, whereas the duration of the instrument at a 10% yield is only 11 years. The present-value-weighted cash flows early on in the life of the perpetuity dominate the computation of duration.

Concept Check

Question 1. Show that the duration of the perpetuity increases as the interest rate decreases in accordance with Rule 4.

Rule 6 for duration

The duration of a level annuity is equal to the following:

$$\frac{1 + y}{y} - \frac{T}{(1 + y)^T - 1}$$

where T is the number of payments and y is the annuity's yield per payment period. For example, a 10-year annual annuity with a yield of 8% will have duration

$$\frac{1.08}{.08} - \frac{10}{1.08^{10} - 1} = 4.87 \text{ years}$$

Rule 7 for duration

The duration of a coupon bond equals the following:

$$\frac{1 + y}{y} - \frac{(1 + y) + T(c - y)}{c[(1 + y)^T - 1] + y}$$

where c is the coupon rate per payment period, T is the number of payment periods, and y is the bond's yield per payment period. For example, a 10% coupon bond with 20 years until maturity, paying coupons semiannually, would have a 5% semiannual coupon and 40 payment periods. If the yield to maturity were 4% per half-year period, the bond's duration would be

$$\frac{1.04}{.04} - \frac{1.04 + 40(.05 - .04)}{.05[1.04^{40} - 1] + .04} = 19.74 \text{ half-years}$$

$$= 9.87 \text{ years}$$

This calculation reminds us again of the importance of maintaining consistency between the time units of the payment period and interest rate. When the bond pays a coupon semiannually, we must use the effective semiannual interest rate and semiannual coupon rate in all calculations. This unit of time (1 half-year) is then carried into the duration measure, when we calculate duration to be 19.74 half-year periods.

Rule 8 for duration

For coupon bonds selling at par value, rule 7 simplifies to the following formula for duration:

$$\frac{1 + y}{y} \left[1 - \frac{1}{(1 + y)^T} \right]$$

Durations can vary widely among traded bonds. Table 16.4 presents durations computed from rule 7 for several bonds all assumed to pay semiannual coupons and to yield 4% per half year. Notice that duration decreases as coupon rates increase, and generally increases with time to maturity. According to Table 16.4 and equation 16.2, if the interest rate were to increase from 8% to 8.1%, the 6% coupon 20-year bond would fall in value by about 1.01% (10.922 × .1%/1.08), while the 10% cou-

TABLE 16.4 Bond Durations (in Years) (Initial Bond Yield = 8% APR)

Years to Maturity	Coupon Rates (per year)			
	6%	8%	10%	12%
1	.985	.980	.976	.972
5	4.361	4.218	4.095	3.990
10	7.454	7.067	6.772	6.541
20	10.922	10.292	9.870	9.568
Infinite (perpetuity)	13.000	13.000	13.000	13.000

pon 1-year bond would fall by only 0.090%. Notice also from Table 16.4 that only for the perpetual bond is duration independent of coupon rate.

16.2 *Passive Bond Management*

Passive managers take bond prices as fairly set and seek to control only the risk of their fixed-income portfolio. Generally, there are two ways of viewing this risk, depending on the circumstances of the particular investor. Some institutions such as banks are concerned with protecting the current net worth or net market value of the firm against interest rate fluctuations. Other investors such as pension funds may have an investment goal to be reached after a given number of years. These investors are more concerned with protecting the future values of their portfolios.

What is common to the bank and the pension fund, however, is interest rate risk. The net worth of the firm or the ability to meet future obligations fluctuate with interest rates. These institutions presumably might be interested in methods to control that risk. We will see that, by properly adjusting the maturity structure of their portfolios, these institutions can shed their interest rate risk. **Immunization** techniques refer to strategies used by such investors to shield their overall financial status from exposure to interest rate fluctuations. Let us therefore turn to a discussion of how interest rate risk arises and how it can be controlled using immunization strategies. We will use the bank and pension fund as two examples of firms that might be interested in such strategies.

Net Worth Immunization

Many banks have a natural mismatch between asset and liability maturity structures. Bank liabilities are primarily the deposits owed to customers, most of which are very short-term in nature, and consequently of low duration. Bank assets by contrast are composed largely of outstanding commercial and consumer loans or mortgages. These assets are of longer duration than are deposits, and their values are correspondingly more sensitive to interest rate fluctuations. In periods when interest rates increase unexpectedly, banks can suffer serious decreases in net worth—their assets fall in value by more than their liabilities.

Flannery and James[3] have shown that prices of bank stock do in fact tend to fall when interest rates rise. In another study, Kopcke and Woglom[4] found that when measured by market values total liabilities exceeded total assets for some savings banks in Connecticut in several years during the 1970s, a period following significant increases in interest rates. Had these banks been required to carry their assets at mar-

---

[3]Flannery, Mark J., and James, Christopher M., "The Effect of Interest Rate Changes on the Common Stock Returns of Financial Institutions," *Journal of Finance, 39,* September 1984.

[4]Kopcke, Richard W., and Woglom, Geoffrey R.H., "Regulation Q and Savings Bank Solvency—The Connecticut Experience," *The Regulation of Financial Institutions,* Federal Reserve Bank of Boston Conference Series, No. 21, 1979.

ket value on their balance sheets, they would have been declared insolvent. Clearly, banks are subject to interest rate risk.

The watchword in bank portfolio strategy in the 1970s and early 1980s was asset and liability management. Techniques called gap management were developed to limit the "gap" between asset and liability durations. Adjustable rate mortgages were one way to reduce the duration of bank asset portfolios. Unlike conventional mortgages, adjustable rate mortgages do not fall in value when market interest rates rise, because the rates they pay are tied to an index of the current market rate. Even if the indexing is imperfect or entails lags, indexing greatly diminishes sensitivity to interest rate fluctuations. On the other side of the balance sheet, the introduction of bank certificates of deposit with fixed terms to maturity served to lengthen the duration of bank liabilities, also reducing the duration gap.

One way to view gap management is that the bank is attempting to equate the durations of assets and liabilities to effectively immunize its overall position from interest rate movements. Because bank assets and liabilities are roughly equal in size, if their durations also are equal, any change in interest rates will affect the values of assets and liabilities equally. Interest rates would have no effect on net worth, in other words. Therefore net worth immunization requires a portfolio duration of zero. This will result if assets and liabilities are equal in both magnitude and duration.

Concept Check

Question 2. If assets and liabilities are not equal, then immunization requires that $D_A A = D_L L$ where D denotes duration and A and L denote assets and liabilities, respectively. Explain why the simpler condition $D_A = D_L$ is no longer valid in this case.

Target Date Immunization

Pension funds are different from banks. They think more in terms of future commitments than current net worth. Pension funds have an obligation to provide workers with a flow of income upon their retirement, and they must have sufficient funds available to meet these commitments. As interest rates fluctuate, both the value of the assets held by the fund and the rate at which those assets generate income fluctuate. The pension fund manager therefore may want to protect or "immunize" the future accumulated value of the fund at some target date against interest rate movements.

Pension funds are not alone in this concern. Any institution with a future fixed obligation might consider immunization a reasonable risk management policy. Insurance companies, for example, also pursue immunization strategies. Indeed, the notion of immunization was introduced by F.M. Redington,[5] an actuary for a life insurance company.

---

[5]Redington, F.M., "Review of the Principle of Life-Office Valuations," *Journal of the Institute of Actuaries*, 78, 1952.

The idea behind immunization is that with duration-matched assets and liabilities the ability of the asset portfolio to meet the firm's obligations should be unaffected by interest rate movements. As a concrete example, consider a pension fund that has purchased $10,000 in 20-year coupon bonds to fund an obligation of $29,859.84 in 6 years. At a market interest rate of 20%, the pension plan has fully funded the obligation, since the present value of the obligation is exactly $10,000.

As interest rates change, however, two offsetting influences will affect the ability of the fund to grow to the targeted value of $29,859.84. On the one hand, if interest rates rise, the fund will suffer a capital loss, impairing its ability to satisfy the obligation. The value of the bonds in 6 years will be lower than it would have been had interest rates remained at 20%. On the other hand, at the now-higher interest rate, reinvested coupons will grow at a faster rate, offsetting the capital loss. This demonstrates that there are two offsetting types of interest rate risk that face fixed-income investors: price risk and reinvestment rate risk. Increases in interest rates cause capital losses but increase the rate at which reinvested income will grow. If the portfolio duration is chosen appropriately, these two effects will cancel out exactly. It turns out that if the portfolio duration is set equal to the investor's horizon date the accumulated value of the investment fund at the horizon date will be unaffected by interest rate fluctuations. For a horizon equal to the portfolio's duration, price risk and reinvestment risk exactly cancel out, as illustrated in Figure 16.2.

As an example of immunization, suppose that a pension fund is obligated to pay out $14,693.28 in 5 years. If the current market interest rate is 8%, the present value of that obligation is $10,000. The plan chooses to fund the obligation with $10,000 of 8% *annual* coupon bonds, selling at par value, with 6 years to maturity. As the duration of the bond is (from rule 8) 5 years, the single-payment obligation should be immunized by the bond.

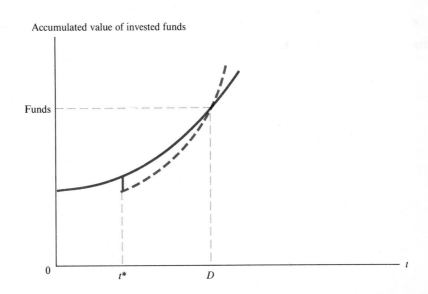

FIGURE 16.2

Growth of invested funds. The solid blue curve represents the growth of portfolio value at the original interest rate. If interest rates increase at time t^* the portfolio value falls but increases thereafter at the faster rate represented by the broken gray curve. At time D (duration) the curves cross.

Accumulated value of invested funds

TABLE 16.5   Terminal Value of a Bond Portfolio After 5 Years (All Proceeds Reinvested)

Payment Number	Time Remaining Until Obligation	Accumulated Value of Invested Payment		
Rates Remain at 8%				
1	4	$800 \times (1.08)^4$	=	$ 1,088.39
2	3	$800 \times (1.08)^3$	=	1,007.77
3	2	$800 \times (1.08)^2$	=	933.12
4	1	$800 \times (1.08)^1$	=	864.00
5	0	$800 \times (1.08)^0$	=	800.00
Sale of bond	0	$10,800/1.08$	=	10,000.00
				$ 14,693.28
Rates Fall to 7%				
1	4	$800 \times (1.07)^4$	=	$ 1,048.64
2	3	$800 \times (1.07)^3$	=	980.03
3	2	$800 \times (1.07)^2$	=	915.92
4	1	$800 \times (1.07)^1$	=	856.00
5	0	$800 \times (1.07)^0$	=	800.00
Sale of bond	0	$10,800/1.07$	=	10,093.46
				$ 14,694.05
Rates Increase to 9%				
1	4	$800 \times (1.09)^4$	=	$ 1,129.27
2	3	$800 \times (1.09)^3$	=	1,036.02
3	2	$800 \times (1.09)^2$	=	950.48
4	1	$800 \times (1.09)^1$	=	872.00
5	0	$800 \times (1.09)^0$	=	800.00
Sale of bond	0	$10,800/1.09$	=	9,908.26
				$ 14,696.02

The sale price of the bond portfolio equals the portfolio's final payment ($10,800) divided by $1 + r$, because the time to maturity of the bonds will be 1 year at the time of sale.

Let us now investigate whether the bond can generate enough income to pay off the obligation 5 years from now regardless of interest rate movements. Table 16.5 shows that if interest rates remain at 8%, then the accumulated funds from the bond will grow to exactly the $14,693.28 obligation. Over the 5-year period the year-end coupon income of $800 is reinvested at the prevailing 8% market interest rate. At the end of the period the bonds can be sold for $10,000; they still will sell at par value because the coupon rate still equals the market interest rate. Total income after 5 years from reinvested coupons and the sale of the bond is precisely $14,693.28.

However, Table 16.5 shows that if interest rates fall to 7%, the total funds will accumulate to $14,694.05, providing a small surplus of 77 cents. If rates increase to 9% as at the bottom of Table 16.5, the fund accumulates to $14,696.02, providing a small surplus of $2.74.

Several points are worth highlighting. First, notice that duration-matching balances the trade-off between the accumulated value of the coupon payments (reinvest-

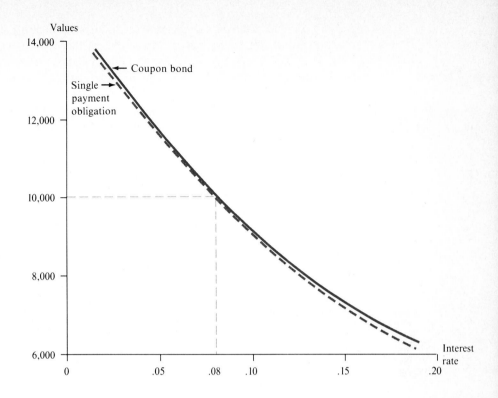

FIGURE 16.3
Immunization.

ment rate risk) and the sale value of the bond (price risk). For example, when interest rates fall, the coupons grow less than in the base case, but the gain on the sale of the bond slightly more than offsets the coupon shortfall. When interest rates rise, the re-sale value of the bond falls, but the coupons more than make up for this loss with their higher accumulated interest. The net surplus in the fund is trivial, especially compared to the change in the value of the accumulated coupons or resale value taken alone.

As we noted, immunization also can be analyzed in terms of present values as opposed to future values. Figure 16.3 presents a graph of the present values of the bond and the single-payment obligation as a function of the interest rate. Notice that at the current rate of 8% the values are equal and the obligation is fully funded by the bond. Moreover, the two present value curves are tangent at $y = 8\%$. As market yields change, the change in value of both the asset and the obligation is equal, so the obligation remains fully funded. For greater changes in the interest rate, however, the present value curves diverge. This is related to the fact that the fund actually shows some surplus in year 5 at market interest rates other than 8%.

Why is there any surplus in the fund? After all, we claimed that a duration-matched asset and liability mix would result in indifference to interest rate shifts. Actually, such a claim is valid only for *small* changes in the interest rate, because as bond yields change, so too does duration. (Recall rule 4 for duration and footnote 2.)

In our example, although the duration of the bond is indeed equal to 5 years at a yield to maturity of 8%; it rises to 5.02 years when its yield falls to 7% and drops to 4.97 years at $y = 9\%$; that is, the bond and the obligation were not duration-matched *across* the interest rate shift, so that the position was not fully immunized.

This example highlights the importance of **rebalancing** immunized portfolios. As interest rates and asset durations change, a manager must rebalance the portfolio of fixed-income assets continually to realign its duration with the duration of the obligation. Moreover, even if interest rates do not change, asset durations *will* change solely because of the passage of time. Recall from Figure 16.2 that duration generally decreases less rapidly than does maturity. Thus, even if an obligation is immunized at the outset, as time passes the durations of the asset and liability will fall at different rates. Without portfolio rebalancing, durations will become unmatched and the goals of immunization will not be realized. Obviously, immunization is a passive strategy only in the sense that it does not involve attempts to identify undervalued securities. Immunization managers still actively update and monitor their positions.

As an example of the need for rebalancing, consider a portfolio manager facing an obligation of $19,487 in 7 years, which, at a current market interest rate of 10%, has a present value of $10,000. Right now, suppose that the manager wishes to immunize the obligation by holding only 3-year zero coupon bonds and perpetuities paying annual coupons. (Our focus on zeros and perpetuities will serve to keep the algebra simple.) At current interest rates, the perpetuities have a duration of $1.10/.10 = 11$ years. The duration of the zero is simply 3 years.

For assets with equal yields, the duration of a portfolio is the weighted average of the durations of the assets comprising the portfolio. To achieve the desired portfolio duration of 7 years, the manager would have to choose appropriate values for the weights of the zero and the perpetuity in the overall portfolio. Call w the zero's weight and $(1 - w)$ the perpetuity's weight. Then w must be chosen to satisfy the equation

$$w \times 3 \text{ years} + (1 - w) \times 11 \text{ years} = 7 \text{ years}$$

which implies that $w = \frac{1}{2}$. The manager invests $5,000 in the zero coupon bond and $5,000 in the perpetuity, providing annual coupon payments of $500 per year indefinitely. The portfolio duration is then 7 years, and the position is immunized.

Next year, even if interest rates do not change, rebalancing will be necessary. The present value of the obligation has grown to $11,000, because it is 1 year closer to maturity. The manager's funds also have grown to $11,000: the zero-coupon bonds have increased in value from $5,000 to $5,500 with the passage of time, while the perpetuity has paid its annual $500 coupon and still is worth $5,000. However, the portfolio weights must be changed. The zero-coupon bond now will have duration of 2 years, while the perpetuity remains at 11 years. The obligation is now due in 6 years. The weights must now satisfy the equation

$$w \times 2 + (1 - w) \times 11 = 6$$

which implies that $w = \frac{5}{9}$. Now, the manager must invest a total of $11,000 \times \frac{5}{9} = \$6,111.11$ in the zero. This requires that the entire $500 coupon payment be invested in the zero and that an additional $111.11 of the perpetuity be sold and invested in the zero in order to maintain an immunized position.

Concept Check

Question 3. What would be the immunizing weights in the second year if the interest rate had fallen to 8%?

Of course, rebalancing of the portfolio entails transaction costs as assets are bought or sold, so one cannot rebalance continuously. In practice an appropriate compromise must be established between the desire for perfect immunization, which requires continual rebalancing, and the need to control trading costs, which dictates less frequent rebalancing.

Cash Flow Matching and Dedication

The problems associated with immunization seem to have a simple solution. Why not simply buy a zero-coupon bond that provides a payment in an amount exactly sufficient to cover the projected cash outlay? If we follow the principle of **cash flow matching** we automatically immunize the portfolio from interest rate movements because the cash flow from the bond and the obligation exactly offset each other.

Cash flow matching can be accomplished on a multiperiod basis. In this case the manager selects either zero-coupon or coupon bonds that provide total cash flows in each period that match a series of obligations. Such a matching principle is referred to as a **dedication strategy.** In 1985, for example, General Electric purchased $824 million of zero-coupon bonds to finance part of its pension plan. Other major pension plan dedications have been as follows: American Information Technologies Corp, for $2.4 billion, Chrysler Corp for $1.1 billion, and Bethlehem Steel for $700 million. Unlike GE, these firms used conventional bonds rather than zeros in their dedications.

Cash flow matching is not more widely pursued probably because of the constraints that it imposes on bond selection. Immunization-dedication strategies are appealing to firms that do not wish to bet on general movements in interest rates, but these firms may want to immunize using bonds that they perceive are undervalued. Cash flow matching, however, places so many more constraints on the bond selection process that it can be impossible to pursue a dedication strategy using only "underpriced" bonds. Firms looking for underpriced bonds give up exact and easy dedication for the possibility of achieving superior returns from the bond portfolio.

Concept Check

Question 4. How would an increase in trading costs affect the attractiveness of dedication vs. immunization?

If you look back at the definition of duration in equation 16.1, you note that it uses the bond's yield to maturity to calculate the weight applied to each coupon payment. Given this definition and limitations on the proper use of yield to maturity, it is perhaps not surprising that this notion of duration is strictly valid only for a flat yield curve for which all payments are discounted at a common interest rate.

If the yield curve is not flat, then the definition of duration must be modified and $CF_t/(1 + y)^t$ replaced with the present value of CF_t, where the present value of each cash flow is calculated by discounting with the appropriate interest rate from the yield curve corresponding to the date of the *particular* cash flow, instead of by discounting with the *bond's* yield to maturity. Moreover, even with this modification, duration matching will immunize portfolios only for parallel shifts in the yield curve. Clearly, this sort of restriction is unrealistic. As a result, much work has been devoted to generalizing the notion of duration. Multifactor duration models have been developed to allow for tilts and other distortions in the shape of the yield curve, in addition to shifts in its level. (We refer to some of this work in the bibliography to this chapter.) However, it does not appear that the added complexity of such models pays off in terms of substantially greater effectiveness.[6]

Finally, immunization can be an inappropriate goal in an inflationary environment. Immunization is essentially a nominal notion and makes sense only for nominal liabilities. It makes no sense to immunize a projected obligation that will grow with the price level using nominal assets such as bonds. For example, if your child will attend college in 15 years and if the annual cost of tuition is expected to be $15,000 at that time, immunizing your portfolio at a locked-in terminal value of $15,000 is not necessarily a risk-reducing strategy. The tuition obligation will vary with the realized inflation rate, whereas the asset portfolio's final value will not. In the end, the tuition obligation will not necessarily be matched by the value of the portfolio.

On this note, it is worth pointing out that immunization is a goal that may well be inappropriate for many investors who would find a zero-risk portfolio strategy unduly conservative. Full immunization is a fairly extreme position for a portfolio manager to pursue.

16.3 *Active Bond Management*

Sources of Potential Profit

Broadly speaking, there are two sources of potential value in active bond management. The first is interest rate forecasting, which tries to anticipate movements across the entire spectrum of the fixed-income market. If interest rate declines are anticipated, managers will increase portfolio duration (and vice versa). The second source of potential profit is identification of relative mispricing within the fixed-income mar-

---

[6]Bierwag, G.O., Kaufman, G.C., and Toevs, A. (editors), *Innovations in Bond Portfolio Management: Duration Analysis and Immunization,* Greenwich, Conn.: JAI Press, 1983.

ket. An analyst for example, might believe that the default premium on one particular bond is unnecessarily large and therefore that the bond is underpriced.

It is worth emphasizing that these techniques will generate abnormal returns only if the analyst's information or insight is superior to that of the market. It is pretty hard to profit from knowledge that rates are about to fall if everyone else in the market is aware of this. In that case the anticipated lower future rates are already built into bond prices in the sense that long-duration bonds are already selling at higher prices that reflect the anticipated fall in future short rates. If the analyst does not have information before the market does, it will be too late to act on that information— prices will have responded already to the news. We discussed this topic in great detail in Chapter 13.

For now we simply repeat that valuable information is differential information. In this context it is worth noting that interest rate forecasters have a notoriously poor track record. If you consider this record, you will approach attempts to time the bond market with caution.

Homer and Liebowitz[7] have coined a popular taxonomy of active bond portfolio strategies. They characterize portfolio rebalancing activities as one of four types of *bond swaps* as follows:

1. The **substitution swap** is an exchange of one bond for a nearly identical substitute. The substituted bonds should be of essentially equal coupon, maturity, quality, call features, sinking fund provisions, and so on. This swap would be motivated by a belief that the market has temporarily mispriced the two bonds, and that the discrepancy between the prices of the bonds represents a profit opportunity.

2. The **intermarket spread swap** is pursued when an investor believes that the yield spread between two sectors of the bond market is temporarily out of line. For example, if the current spread between corporate and government bonds is considered too wide and is expected to narrow, the investor will shift from government bonds into corporate bonds. If the yield spread does in fact narrow, corporates will outperform governments.

   In these two swaps the investor typically believes that the yield relationship between bonds or sectors is only temporarily out of alignment. When the aberration is eliminated, gains can be realized on the underpriced bond. The period of realignment is called the *workout period*.

3. The **rate anticipation swap** is pegged to interest rate forecasting. In this case if investors believe that rates will fall, they will swap into bonds of greater duration. Conversely, when rates are expected to rise, they will swap into low duration bonds.

4. The **pure yield pickup swap** is pursued not in response to perceived mispricing, but as a means of increasing return by holding higher yield bonds. This must be viewed as an attempt to earn an expected term premium in higher yield bonds.

---

[7]Homer, Sidney, and Liebowitz, Martin L., *Inside the Yield Book: New Tools for Bond Market Strategy,* Englewood Cliffs, N.J.: Prentice-Hall, 1972.

The investor is willing to bear the interest rate risk that this strategy entails.

We can add a fifth swap, called a **tax swap** to this list. This simply refers to a swap to exploit some tax advantage. For example, an investor may swap from one bond that has decreased in price to another if realization of capital losses is advantageous for tax purposes.

Investors and analysts commonly use this classification of strategies, at least implicitly. For example, consider these quotations from the Merrill Lynch Fixed-Income Strategy booklet of April 1986.[8]

Projected returns at alternative settings of the funds rate strongly favors ownership of short-term notes. At almost every [projected] setting of the [federal] funds rate, returns from both ten-year notes and thirty-year bonds would be negative . . . In a rising interest rate environment, where yields rise by 35 basis points for two-year notes and 25 basis points for three-year notes, the two-year is projected to outperform by approximately 50 basis points [page 10].

This analysis is motivated by rate anticipation, which follows from Merrill's overall macroeconomic analysis. Given Merrill's belief in rising rates, it recommends short asset durations.

Following this general analysis comes a sector-oriented intermarket spread analysis that expresses Merrill's view that yield relationships across two fixed-income submarkets are temporarily out of line. The history of 1982 to 1984 leads Merrill to believe that corporate yields will fall relative to Treasury yields, making corporates attractive relative to Treasuries:

Corporate/Treasury yield ratios are unusually high for both intermediate- and long-term securities. These ratios are now [April 1986] almost as high as those that emerged late in 1982, following a sharp drop in bond yields. The respective yield ratios for new-issue long-term AA utilities and AA industrials were 1.17 and 1.13 at the end of this past quarter, compared with 1.22 and 1.15 in December 1982. By mid-1983, these ratios had declined to 1.10 and 1.08, respectively. By July 1984, they had declined further, to 1.08 and 1.05. Yield ratios for intermediate corporates display a similar pattern. This record suggests that corporate/Treasury yield ratios are likely to fall in the months ahead if, as we expect, the Treasury yield curve steepens [page 16].

Finally, we see an example of a yield pickup recommendation:

Although the slope of the corporate yield curve is 30 to 50 basis points steeper than that of the Treasury curve, it has flattened by approximately the same degree. Thus any steepening in the Treasury curve would probably spark a similar response in corporates, hurting the long corporate market much more than the short and intermediate coupons. Consequently, the two- to ten-year maturity sector performs far better in the total return simulations [than longer-term issues]. Moreover, since this is the steepest area of the yield curve, it offers investors the opportunity to capture more than 90% of the yield on long bonds while owning ten-year rather than thirty-year maturities [page 17].

The Merrill Lynch strategy book is devoted to broad sectors of the fixed-income market, and so does not include any examples of substitution swaps.

---

[8]Reprinted from *Fixed Income Strategy* by permission of Merrill Lynch, Pierce, Fenner & Smith Incorporated © Copyright 1986.

Horizon Analysis

One form of interest rate forecasting is called **horizon analysis.** The analyst using this approach selects a particular holding period and predicts the yield curve at the end of that period. Given a bond's time to maturity at the end of the holding period, its yield can be read from the predicted yield curve and its end-of-period price calculated. Then the analyst adds the coupon income and prospective capital gain of the bond to obtain the total return on the bond over the holding period.

For example, suppose that a 20-year maturity 10% coupon bond currently yields 9% and sells at $1,092.01. An analyst with a 5-year time horizon would be concerned about the bond's price and the value of reinvested coupons 5 years hence. At that time the bond will have a 15-year maturity, so the analyst will predict the yield on 15-year maturity bonds at the end of the 5-year period to determine the bond's expected price. Suppose that the yield is expected to be 8%. Then the bond's end-of-period price will be (assuming 30 semiannual coupon payments):

$$50 \times PA(4\%,30) + 1,000 \times PF(4\%,30) = \$1,172.92$$

The capital gain on the bond therefore will be $80.91.

Meanwhile, the coupons paid by the bond will be reinvested over the 5-year period. The analyst must predict a reinvestment rate at which the invested coupons can earn interest. Suppose that the assumed rate is 4% per 6-month period. If all coupon payments are reinvested at this rate, the value of the 10 semiannual coupon payments with accumulated interest at the end of the 5 years will be $600.31. (This amount can be solved for as the future value of a $50 annuity after 10 periods with per period interest of 4%.) The total return provided by the bond over the 5-year period will be $80.91 + $600.31 = $681.22 for a total 5-year holding period return of $681.22/ $1,092.01 = .624, or 62.4%.

The analyst repeats this procedure for many bonds and selects the ones promising superior holding period returns for the portfolio.

Concept Check

Question 5. Consider a 30-year 8% coupon bond currently selling at $896.81. The analyst believes that in 5 years the yield on 25-year bonds will be 8.5%. Should she purchase the 20-year bond just discussed or the 30-year bond today?

A particular version of horizon analysis is called **riding the yield curve.** If the yield curve is upward sloping *and* if it is projected that the curve will not shift during the investment horizon, then as bond maturities fall with the passage of time, their yields also will fall as they "ride" the yield curve toward the lower yields of shorter-term bonds. The decrease in yields will contribute to capital gains on the bonds.

To illustrate, suppose that the yield to maturity on 10-year bonds currently is 9%, while that on 9-year bonds is 8.8%. A $1,000 par value 10-year zero-coupon bond can be bought today for $\$1,000/1.09^{10} = \$422.41$. In 1 year, if yields on 9-year bonds are still 8.8%, the bond will sell for $\$1,000/1.088^9 = \$468.10$, for a 1-year return of 10.82%. In contrast, if the bond's yield remained at 9%, it would sell after 1 year for $\$1,000/1.09^9 = \$460.43$, offering a 9% rate of return.

The danger of riding the yield curve is that the yield curve will in fact rise over time. Indeed, according to the expectations hypothesis, an upward sloping curve is evidence that market participants expect interest rates to be rising over time.

Contingent Immunization

Contingent immunization is a mixed passive-active strategy suggested by Liebowitz and Weinberger.[9] To illustrate, suppose that interest rates currently are 10% and that a manager's portfolio is worth $10 million right now. At current rates the manager could lock in, via conventional immunization techniques, a future portfolio value of $12.1 million after 2 years. Now suppose that the manager wishes to pursue active management but is willing to risk losses only to the extent that the terminal value of the portfolio would not drop lower than $11 million. Since only $9.09 million ($11 million/1.1^2) is required to achieve this minimum acceptable terminal value, and the portfolio currently is worth $10 million, the manager can afford to risk some losses at the outset and might start off with an active strategy rather than immediately immunizing.

The key is to calculate the funds required to lock in via immunization a future value of $11 million at current rates. If T denotes the time left until the horizon date, and r is the market interest rate at any particular time, then the value of the fund necessary to guarantee an ability to reach the minimum acceptable terminal value is $11 million/$(1 + r)^T$, because this size of portfolio, if immunized, will grow risk-free to $11 million by the horizon date. This value becomes the trigger point: if and when actual portfolio value dips to the trigger point, active management will cease. *Contingent* upon reaching the trigger, an immunization strategy is initiated instead, guaranteeing that the minimal acceptable performance can be realized.

Figure 16.4 illustrates two possible outcomes in a contingent immunization strategy. In Figure 16.4, *A*, the portfolio falls in value and hits the trigger at time t^*. At that point, immunization is pursued and the portfolio rises smoothly to the $11 million terminal value. In Figure 16.4, *B*, the portfolio does well, never reaches the trigger point, and is worth more than $11 million at the horizon date.

Concept Check

Question 6. What would be the trigger point with a 3-year horizon, an interest rate of 12%, and a minimum acceptable terminal value of $10 million?

---

[9]Liebowitz, Martin L., and Weinberger, Alfred, "Contingent Immunization—Part I: Risk Control Procedures," *Financial Analysts Journal, 38,* November-December 1982.

FIGURE 16.4

Contingent
immunization.

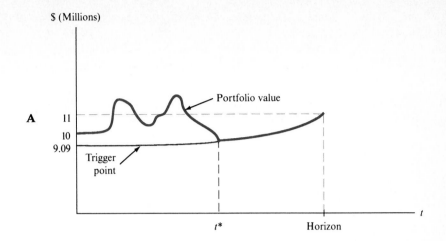

$ (Millions)

Portfolio value

A 11

10
9.09

Trigger
point

t^*

Horizon

t

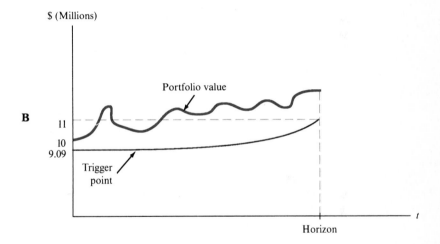

$ (Millions)

Portfolio value

B 11

10
9.09

Trigger
point

Horizon

t

An Example of a Fixed-Income Investment Strategy

As an example of a reasonable active fixed-income portfolio strategy, we might
consider the policies of Sanford Bernstein & Co., as presented in a 1985 speech by
its manager of fixed-income investments, Francis Trainer. The company believes that
big bets on general market-wide interest movements are unwise. Instead, it concen-
trates on exploiting numerous instances of perceived *relative* minor pricing misalign-
ments *within* the fixed-income sector. The firm takes as a risk benchmark the Shearson Lehman Hutton Government/Corporate Bond Index, which contains a vast majority of publicly traded bonds with maturity greater than 1 year. The index is seen as a
passive or neutral position from which any deviation for the portfolio must be justified by active analysis. Bernstein considers a neutral porfolio duration to be equal to

that of the index, which was 4½ years in September 1985, the date of Trainer's speech.

The firm is willing to make some bets on interest rate movements, but only to a limited degree. As Francis Trainer puts it in his speech:

If we set duration of our portfolios at a level equal to the Index and never allow them to vary, this would imply that we are perpetually neutral on the direction of interest rates. However, as those of you who have followed our economic forecasts are aware, this is rarely the case. We believe the utilization of these forecasts will add value and, therefore, we incorporate our economic forecast into the bond management process by altering the durations of our portfolios.

However, in order to prevent fixed-income performance from being dominated by the accuracy of just a single aspect of our research effort, we limit the degree to which we are willing to alter our interest rate exposure. Under the vast majority of circumstances, we will not permit the duration of our portfolios to differ from that of the Shearson Lehman Index by more than one year [page 4].

The company expends most of its effort in exploiting perceived numerous but minor inefficiencies in bond prices that result from lack of attention from its competitors. Its analysts follow about 1,000 securities, attempting to "identify specific securities that are attractive or unattractive as well as identify trends in the richness or cheapness of industries and sectors [p. 6]." These two activities would be characterized as substitution swaps and intermarket spread swaps in the Homer/Liebowitz scheme.

Sanford Bernstein & Co. realizes that market opportunities will arise, if at all, only in sectors of the bond market that present the least competition from other analysts. For this reason it tends to avoid recently issued bonds because "most of the attention that is focused on the bond market is concentrated on those securities that have been recently issued [p. 7]." Similarly, it tends to focus on relatively more complicated bond issues in the belief that extensive research efforts give the firm a comparative advantage in that sector. Finally, the company does not take unnecessary risks. If there do not appear to be enough seemingly attractive bonds, remaining funds are placed in Treasury securities as a "neutral" parking space until new opportunities are identified.

To summarize the key features of Bernstein & Co.'s strategy, we can make the following observations:

1. The firm has a respect for market prices. It believes that usually only minor mispricing can be detected. It works to gain meaningful abnormal returns by combining numerous *small* profit opportunities, not by hoping for success of one big bet.
2. The firm recognizes that to have value its information cannot already be reflected in market prices. It maintains a large research staff and focuses on market niches that appear to be neglected by others.
3. It avoids dependence on forecasting interest rate movements, recognizing that such movements are extremely hard to predict, and that attempts to time the market easily can wipe out all its profits from intramarket analysis.

How well has Sanford Bernstein & Co. done? Figure 16.5 charts its performance over 2¾ years of activity. The horizontal lines in each rectangle are drawn at the rate

FIGURE 16.5

Bond funds background: total funds rate of return for periods ending September 30, 1985.
(Courtesy Sanford C. Bernstein & Co. Inc.)

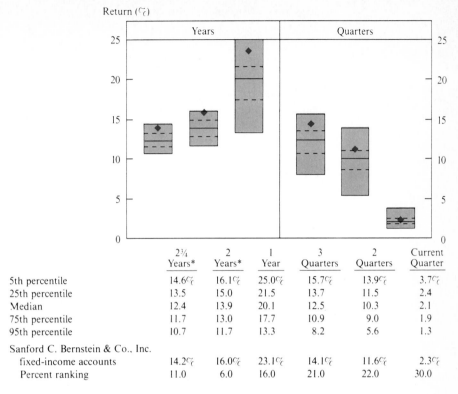

	2¾ Years*	2 Years*	1 Year	3 Quarters	2 Quarters	Current Quarter
5th percentile	14.6%	16.1%	25.0%	15.7%	13.9%	3.7%
25th percentile	13.5	15.0	21.5	13.7	11.5	2.4
Median	12.4	13.9	20.1	12.5	10.3	2.1
75th percentile	11.7	13.0	17.7	10.9	9.0	1.9
95th percentile	10.7	11.7	13.3	8.2	5.6	1.3
Sanford C. Bernstein & Co., Inc. fixed-income accounts	14.2%	16.0%	23.1%	14.1%	11.6%	2.3%
Percent ranking	11.0	6.0	16.0	21.0	22.0	30.0

*Annualized returns.

of return realized by the 5th, 25th, 50th, 75th and 95th percentile manager in a sample of fixed-income managers. The diamond is Sanford Bernstein & Co.'s performance, which has been above average over the period. Of course, 2 or 3 years is too short a time to reach a conclusion about whether we can expect this above average performance to continue. We cannot know whether over the long run the company will be successful in its analysis of security and sector underpricing that its strategy statement calls for. However, the strategy is reasonable for those who wish to pursue active bond management.

16.4 Interest Rate Swaps

Interest rate swaps recently have emerged as a major fixed-income tool. They arose originally as a means of managing interest rate risk. Since 1980 the volume of swaps has increased from virtually zero to about $300 billion in 1986.[10] (Interest rate

---

[10]Levich, Richard, "Financial Innovation in International Financial Markets," Working Paper No. 2277, National Bureau of Economic Research, 1987.

swaps do not have anything to do with the Homer/Liebowitz bond swap taxonomy set out earlier.)

A typical risk management swap is between two parties exposed to opposite types of interest rate risk. For example, on one side may be a savings and loan institution with short-term variable-rate liabilities (deposits) and long-term fixed-rate assets such as conventional mortgages. The S&L will suffer losses if interest rates rise. On the other side of the swap might be a corporation that has issued long-term noncallable fixed rate bonds and has invested in short-term or variable-rate assets. The corporation will lose if interest rates fall.

A swap would work as follows. The S&L would agree to make fixed-rate payments to the corporation based on some *notional* principal amount and fixed interest rate. For example, with a fixed rate of 10%, and notional principal of $10 million, the S&L would pay $1 million per year for the period of the swap. On the other side, the corporation pays an agreed-upon short-term interest rate multiplied by the notional principal to the S&L. Typically, that short rate is tied to the London Interbank Offered Rate (LIBOR), which is an interest rate at which banks borrow from each other in the Eurodollar market. For example, the corporation may pay LIBOR plus 50 basis points. (A basis point is 1/100 of 1%, so that 50 points is a half-percentage point premium.) If LIBOR currently is 8%, the corporation initially will pay 8.5% of the notional principal, or $850,000 per year to the S&L. As LIBOR changes, so too will the corporation's payments.

How does a swap affect the net interest rate exposure of each party? The S&L started with long-term fixed-rate assets and variable-rate liabilities. The swap imposes a long-term fixed-rate liability on the bank, but brings variable-rate inflows from the corporation. The S&L's net interest rate exposure has thus been reduced or eliminated. The corporation has done the reverse. It can fund its variable-rate obligation under the swap arrangement with its short-term assets, and can use the fixed-rate payments received from the swap to make the coupon payments on its long-term debt.

Table 16.6 depicts the balance sheets of the two parties before and after the swap.

TABLE 16.6   Interest Rate Swap

Bank		Corporation	
Assets	*Liabilities*	*Assets*	*Liabilities*
Before the Swap			
Long-term loans	Short-term deposits	Variable-rate or short-term assets	Long-term bonds
	Net worth		Net worth
After the Swap			
Long-term loans Claim to variable-rate cash flows	Short-term deposits Obligation to make fixed cash payments	Short-term assets Claim to fixed cash flows	Long-term bonds Obligation to make variable-rate payments
	Net worth		Net worth

Note that, although each party is maturity-mismatched before the swap, each has both short- and long-term assets and liabilities after the swap, which eliminates the original mismatch.

Interestingly, the swap arrangement does not mean that a new loan has been made. The participants have agreed only to exchange a fixed cash flow for variable cash flow stream. In practice, participants to a swap do not deal with each other directly. Instead, each usually trades with a dealer who acts as an intermediary. The dealer makes a market in swaps, entering one side of a swap with one party and the other side with another party. In some cases swaps are brokered, meaning that the two parties are matched up directly instead of each trading with a dealer.

Concept Check

Question 7. A pension fund holds a portfolio of money market securities that the analyst believes are providing excellent interest rates. What type of swap will mitigate the fund's interest rate risk?

One might ask why firms go to the trouble of arranging these swaps. Why the corporation, for example, did not originally borrow short-term instead of borrowing long and entering a swap? In the early years of the swap market the answer seemed to lie in systematic differences in the perceived credit ratings in different markets. Participants in these markets claimed that European banks placed more weight than U.S. banks on a firm's size, name recognition, and product line compared with its credit rating. Thus it could have paid for a firm that wanted to borrow long-term to instead borrow short-term in the United States and swap into long-term obligations with a European trading partner. The practice exploited a type of market inefficiency—specifically, differences in credit assessments across national markets. Now, however, these inefficiencies seem to have been arbitraged away. Swaps simply provide a means to restructure balance sheets and manage risk very quickly with small transaction costs.

Swaps create an interesting problem for financial statement analysis. Firms are not required to disclose interest rate swaps in corporate financial statements unless they have a "material impact" on the firm, and even then they appear only in the footnotes. Therefore the firm's true net obligations may be quite different from its apparent or presented debt structure.

Summary

1. Even default-free bonds such as Treasury issues are subject to interest rate risk. Longer-term bonds generally are more sensitive to interest rate shifts than are short-term bonds. A measure of the average life of a bond is Macaulay's duration, defined as the weighted average of the times until each payment made by the security, with weights proportional to the present value of the payment.

2. Duration is a direct measure of the sensitivity of a bond's price to a change in its yield. The proportional change in a bond's price equals the negative of duration multiplied by the proportional change in $1 + y$.

3. Immunization strategies are characteristic of passive fixed-income portfolio management. Such strategies attempt to render the individual or firm immune from movements in interest rates. This may take the form of immunizing net worth or, instead, immunizing the future accumulated value of a fixed-income portfolio.

4. Immunization of a fully funded plan is accomplished by matching the durations of assets and liabilities. To maintain an immunized position as time passes and interest rates change, the portfolio must be periodically rebalanced. Classic immunization also depends on parallel shifts in a flat yield curve. Given that this assumption is unrealistic, immunization generally will be less than complete. To mitigate this problem, multifactor duration models can be used to allow for variation in the shape of the yield curve.

5. A more direct form of immunization is dedication, or cash flow matching. If a portfolio is perfectly matched in cash flow with projected liabilities, rebalancing will be unnecessary.

6. Active bond management consists of interest rate forecasting techniques and intermarket spread analysis. One popular taxonomy classifies active strategies as substitution swaps, intermarket spread swaps, rate anticipation swaps, or pure yield pickup swaps.

7. Horizon analysis is a type of interest rate forecasting. In this procedure the analyst forecasts the position of the yield curve at the end of some holding period, and from that yield curve predicts corresponding bond prices. Bonds then can be ranked according to expected total returns (coupon plus capital gain) over the holding period.

8. Interest rate swaps are major recent developments in the fixed-income market. In these arrangements parties trade the cash flows of different securities without actually exchanging any securities directly. This is a useful tool to manage the duration of a portfolio. It also has been used by corporations to borrow at advantageous interest rates in foreign credit markets that are viewed as more hospitable than domestic credit markets.

Key Terms

Duration	Rate anticipation swap
Immunization	Pure yield pickup swap
Rebalancing	Tax swap
Cash flow matching	Horizon analysis
Dedication strategy	Riding the yield curve
Substitution swap	Contingent immunization
Intermarket spread swap	Interest rate swaps

Selected Readings

Duration and immunization are analyzed in a very extensive literature. Good treatments are:

Bierwag, G.O., *Duration Analysis,* Cambridge, Mass.: Ballinger Publishing Company, 1987.

Weil, Roman, "Macaulay's Duration: An Appreciation," *Journal of Business, 46,* October 1973.

Useful general references to techniques of fixed-income portfolio management may be found in two books of readings used by the Institute of Chartered Financial Analysts:

Tuttle, Donald L., "Fixed Income Portfolio Strategies," in Maginn, John L., and Tuttle, Donald L. (editors), *Managing Investment Portfolios: A Dynamic Process, 1985-1986 Update,* Boston: Warren, Gorham & Lamont, 1985.

Tuttle, Donald L., (editor), *The Revolution in Techniques for Managing Bond Portfolios,* Charlottesville, Va.: Institute of Chartered Financial Analysts, 1983.

Active bond management strategies are discussed in:

Homer, Sidney, and Liebowitz, Martin L., *Inside the Yield Book: New Tools for Bond Market Strategy,* Englewood Cliffs, N.J.: Prentice-Hall, 1972.

Liebowitz, Martin L., "Horizon Analysis: A New Analytic Framework for Managed Bond Portfolios," *Journal of Portfolio Management,* spring 1975.

Our discussion of interest rate swaps follows an article in Barron's:

Forsyth, Randall W., "The $150 Billion Baby," *Barron's,* August 19, 1985.

For a detailed analysis of swaps with an emphasis on foreign currency swaps, see the following:

Smith, Clifford W., Smithson, Charles W., and Wakeman, L. Macdonald, "The Evolving Market for Swaps," *Midland Corporate Finance Journal, 3,* winter 1986.

Problems

1. A 9-year bond has a yield of 10% and a duration of 7.194 years. If the market yield changes by 50 basis points, what is the change in the bond's price?

2. Find the duration of a 6% coupon bond making *annual* coupon payments if it has 3 years until maturity and has a yield to maturity of 6%. What is the duration if the yield to maturity is 10%?

3. Find the duration of the bond in problem 2 if the coupons are paid semiannually.

4. Rank the durations of the following pairs of bonds:
   a. Bond *A* is an 8% coupon bond, with a 20-year time to maturity selling at par value. Bond *B* is an 8% coupon bond, with a 20-year maturity time selling below par value.
   b. Bond *A* is a 20-year noncallable coupon bond with a coupon rate of 8%, selling at par. Bond *B* is a 20-year callable bond with a coupon rate of 9%, also selling at par.

5. (CFA Examination Level I, 1985)
   Rank the following bonds in order of descending duration:

Bond	Coupon (%)	Time to Maturity (Years)	Yield to Maturity (%)
A	15	20	10%
B	15	15	10
C	0	20	10
D	8	20	10
E	15	15	15

6. Currently, the term structure is as follows: 1-year bonds yield 7%, 2-year bonds yield 8%, 3-year bonds and greater maturity bonds all yield 9%. An investor is choosing between 1-, 2-, and 3-year maturity bonds all paying *annual* coupons of 8%, once a year. Which bond should you buy if you strongly believe that at year-end the yield curve would be flat at 9%?

7. You will be paying $10,000 a year in tuition expenses at the end of the next 2 years. Bonds currently yield 8%.
   a. What is the present value and duration of your obligation?
   b. What maturity zero-coupon bond would immunize your obligation?
   c. Suppose you buy a zero-coupon bond with value and duration equal to your obligation. Now suppose that rates immediately increase to 9%. What happens to your net position, that is, to the difference between the value of the bond and that of your tuition obligation? What if rates fall to 7%?

8. What types of interest rate swap would be appropriate for a corporation holding long-term assets that it funded with floating-rate bonds?

9. You are managing a portfolio of $1 million. Your target duration is 10 years, and you can choose from two bonds: a zero-coupon bond with maturity of 5 years, and a perpetuity, each currently yielding 5%.
   a. How much of each bond will you hold in your portfolio?
   b. How will these fractions change *next year* if target duration is now 9 years?

10. My pension plan will pay me $10,000 once a year for a 10-year period. The first payment will come in exactly 5 years. The pension fund wants to immunize its position.
    a. What is the duration of its obligation to me? The current interest rate is 10% per year.
    b. If the plan uses 5-year and 20-year zero-coupon bonds to construct the immunized position, how much money ought to be placed in each bond? What will be the *face value* of the holdings in each zero?

11. (CFA Examination, Level III, 1983)
    The ability to *immunize* a bond portfolio is very desirable for bond portfolio managers in some instances.
    a. Discuss the components of interest rate risk—that is, assuming a change in interest rates over time, explain the two risks faced by the holder of a bond.
    b. Define immunization and discuss why a bond manager would immunize his portfolio.
    c. Explain why a duration-matching strategy is a superior technique to a maturity-matching strategy for the minimization of interest rate risk.
    d. Explain in specific terms how you would use a zero-coupon bond to immunize a bond portfolio. Discuss why a zero-coupon bond is an ideal instrument in this regard.
    e. Explain how contingent immunization, another bond portfolio management technique, differs from *classical immunization*. Discuss why a bond portfolio manager would engage in *contingent immunization*.

12. (CFA Examination, Level I, 1981)

You are the manager for the bond portfolio of a pension fund. The policies of the fund allow for the use of active strategies in managing the bond portfolio.

It appears that the economic cycle is beginning to mature, inflation is expected to accelerate, and in an effort to contain the economic expansion central bank policy is moving toward constraint. For each of the situations below, *state* which one of the two bonds you would prefer. *Briefly justify* your answer in each case.

a. Government of Canada (Canadian pay) 10% due in 1984 and priced at 98.75 to yield 10.50% to maturity.

or

Government of Canada (Canadian pay) 10% due in 1995 and priced at 91.75 to yield 11.19% to maturity.

b. Texas Power and Light Co., 7½ due in 2002, rated AAA, and priced at 62 to yield 12.78% to maturity.

or

Arizona Public Service Co. 7.45 due in 2002, rates A−, and priced at 56 to yield 14.05% to maturity.

c. Commonwealth Edison 2¾ due in 1999, rated Baa, and priced at 25 to yield 14.9% to maturity.

or

Commonwealth Edison 15⅜ due in 2000, rated Baa, and priced at 102.75 to yield 14.9% to maturity.

d. Shell Oil Co. 8½ sinking fund debentures due in 2000, rated AAA (sinking fund begins 9/80 at par), and priced at 69 to yield 12.91% to maturity.

or

Warner-Lambert 8⅞ sinking fund debentures due in 2000, rated AAA (sinking fund begins 4/86 at par), and priced at 75 to yield 12.31% to maturity.

e. Bank of Montreal (Canadian pay) 12% Certificates of Deposit due in 1985, rated AAA, and priced at 100 to yield 12% to maturity.

or

Bank of Montreal (Canadian pay) Floating Rate Notes due in 1991, rated AAA. Coupon currently set at 10.65% and priced at 100 (coupon adjusted semiannually to .5% above the 3-month Government of Canada Treasury bill rate).

13. (CFA Examination, Level I, 1983)

Active bond management as contrasted with a passive buy and hold strategy, has gained increased acceptance as investors have attempted to maximize the total return on bond portfolios under their management.

The following bond swaps could have been made in recent years as investors attempted to increase the total return on their portfolio.

From the information presented below, identify the reason(s) investors may have made each swap.

Action			Call	Price	YTM (%)
a.	Sell	Baa1 Georgia Pwr. 1st mtg. 11⅝% due 2000	108.24	75⅝	15.71
	Buy	Baa1 Georgia Pwr. 1st mtg. 7⅜% due 2001	105.20	51⅛	15.39
b.	Sell	Aaa Amer. Tel & Tel notes 13¼% due 1991	101.50	96⅛	14.02
	Buy	U.S. Treasury notes 14¼% due 1991	NC	102.15	13.83
c.	Sell	Aa1 Chase Manhattan zero coupon due 1992	NC	25¼	14.37
	Buy	Aa1 Chase Manhattan float rate notes due 2009	103.90	90¼	—
d.	Sell	A1 Texas Oil & Gas 1st mtg. 8¼% due 1997	105.75	60	15.09
	Buy	U.S. Treasury bond 8¼% due 2005	NC	65.60	12.98
e.	Sell	A1 K mart convertible deb. 6% due 1999	103.90	62¾	10.83
	Buy	A2 Lucky Stores S.F. deb. 11¾% due 2005	109.86	73	16.26

PART V

Equities

CHAPTER 17

Equity Valuation

$\mathbf{W}$e said in Chapter 7 that investors who believe in stock market efficiency would do best by pursuing a passive investment strategy of indexing. But what if you are interested in trying to beat the market? It is easier said than done.

We are reminded of Will Rogers' explanation of how to make money in the stock market. He once gave a lecture in which he advised his listeners, "Why, making money in the stock market is the easiest thing in the world. You find an attractive stock, buy it, and watch its price go up for a while. Then when it reaches its peak, you sell it, and make a handsome profit."

One rather skeptical listener interrupted the speaker: "But Mr. Rogers, what if the price doesn't go up?" "Then don't buy it," came the reply.

To help you in that first step of identifying the right stocks to buy (or those that you should sell short), we devote this chapter to an examination of the methods and models that professional stock analysts use. All of the models presented in this chapter are employed by **fundamental analysts.** They are to be distinguished from the models used by **technical analysts.** (Technical analysis was discussed in Chapter 13.)

Remember that the purpose of all of these models is to identify stocks that are mispriced. The question of how much of your portfolio to invest in such mispriced stocks was discussed briefly in Chapter 7 and will be addressed again in detail in Chapter 25.

17.1 Balance Sheet Valuation Methods

A common valuation measure is **book value,** which is the net worth of a company as shown on the balance sheet. Table 17.1, gives the balance sheet totals for IBM to illustrate how to calculate book value per share.

Book value of IBM stock on December 31, 1987 was $64.06 per share ($38,263 million divided by 597,326,059 shares). On that same date IBM stock had a market price of $115.50. Would it be fair then to say that IBM stock was overpriced?

TABLE 17.1   IBM Balance Sheet, December 31, 1987 ($ Million)

Assets	Liabilities and Owners' Equity	
$63,668	Liabilities	$25,425
	Common equity	$38,263
	597,326,059 shares outstanding	

If you think further, you will recognize that the book value is the result of applying a set of arbitrary accounting rules to spread the acquisition cost of assets over a specified number of years, whereas the market price of a stock takes account of the firm's value as a going concern. In other words, the market price reflects the present value of its expected future cash flows. It would therefore be unusual if the market price of IBM stock were exactly equal to its book value.

Can book value represent a "floor" for the stock's price, below which level the market price can never fall? Although IBM's book value per share on December 31, 1987 was less than its market price, other evidence from the same date disproves this notion. On December 31, 1987, ITT stock had a book value of $53.83 per share and a market price of $41.75. Clearly, book value cannot always be a floor for the stock's price.

A better measure of a floor for the stock price is the **liquidation value** per share of the firm. This represents the amount of money that could be realized by breaking up the firm, selling its assets, repaying its debt, and distributing the remainder to the shareholders. The reasoning behind this concept is that if the market price of equity drops below liquidation value of the firm, the firm becomes attractive as a takeover target. A corporate raider such as Carl Icahn or T. Boone Pickens would find it profitable to buy enough shares to gain control and then actually to liquidate because the liquidation value exceeds the value of the business as a going concern.

Another balance sheet concept that is of interest in valuing a firm is the **replacement cost** of its assets less its liabilities. Some analysts believe that the market value of the firm cannot get too far above its replacement cost because, if it did, then competitors would try to replicate the firm. The competitive pressure of other similar firms entering the same industry would drive down the market value of all firms until they came into equality with replacement cost.

This idea is popular among economists, and the ratio of market price to replacement cost of a firm's common stock is known as **Tobin's q.**[1] In the long run, according to this view, the ratio of market price to replacement cost will tend toward 1, but the evidence is that this ratio can differ significantly from 1 for very long periods of time.[2]

---

[1]The ratio is named after the Nobel prize–winning economist James Tobin. For a discussion of Tobin's q and its role in monetary theory, see Tobin, James, "A General Equilibrium Approach to Monetary Theory," *Journal of Money, Credit, and Banking,* February 1969.

[2]See, for example, Summers, Lawrence H., "Taxation and Corporate Investment: A q-Theory Approach," *Brookings Papers on Economic Activity,* 1981.

Although focusing on the balance sheet can give some useful information about a firm's liquidation value or its replacement cost, the analyst must usually turn to the expected future cash flows for a better estimate of the firm's value as a going concern. We now examine the quantitative models that analysts use to value common stock in terms of the future earnings and dividends the firm will yield.

17.2   *Intrinsic Value vs. Market Price*

The most popular model for assessing the value of a firm as a going concern takes off from the observation that an investor in stock expects a return consisting of cash dividends and capital gains or losses. We begin by assuming a 1-year holding period and supposing that ABC stock has an expected dividend per share, $E(D_1)$, of $4, the current price of a share (P_0) is $48, and the expected price at the end of a year, $E(P_1)$, is $52.

The holding period return that the investor expects is $E(D_1)$ plus the expected price appreciation, $E(P_1) - P_0$, all divided by the current price P_0:

$$
\begin{aligned}
\text{Expected HPR} &= E(r) \\
&= \frac{E(D_1) + [E(P_1) - P_0]}{P_0} \\
&= \frac{4 + (52 - 48)}{48} \\
&= 0.167 \\
&= 16.7\%
\end{aligned}
$$

Note that $E(\ )$ denotes an expected future value. Thus $E(P_1)$ represents the stock price 1 year from now. $E(r)$ is referred to as the stock's expected holding period return. It is the sum of the expected dividend yield, $E(D_1)/P_0$, and the expected rate of price appreciation, the capital gains yield, $[E(P_1) - P_0]/P_0$.

But what is the investor's required rate of return on the stock? From the CAPM we know that the required rate, k, is equal to $r_f + \beta [E(r_M) - r_f]$. Suppose $r_f = 6\%$, $\beta = 1.2$, and $E(r_M) - r_f = 5\%$. Then the value of k is

$$
\begin{aligned}
k &= 6\% + 1.2 \times 5\% \\
&= 12\%
\end{aligned}
$$

For ABC the rate of return that the investor expects exceeds the required rate based on ABC's risk by a margin of 4.7%. Naturally, the investor will want to include more of ABC stock in the portfolio than a passive strategy would dictate.

Another way to see this is to compare the **intrinsic value, V_0,** of a share of stock to its current market price:

$$
V_0 = \frac{E(D_1 + P_1)}{1 + k}
$$

In the case of ABC the intrinsic value based on present value of expected cash flows to the stockholder is

$$V_0 = \frac{\$4 + \$52}{1.12}$$
$$= \$50$$

In other words, the intrinsic value is the present value of the expected future cash inflow (that is, the dividend plus the terminal price at which the stock can be sold) discounted by the required rate of return. Whenever the intrinsic value, or the investor's estimate of what the stock is really worth, exceeds the market price, the stock is undervalued. In the ABC case, $V_0 > P_0$ ($50 > $48), so the stock is undervalued by the market. Investors will want to buy more ABC than they would following a passive strategy.

If the intrinsic value turns out to be lower than the current market price, investors should buy less of it than under the passive strategy. It might even pay to *go short* ABC stock, as we discussed in Chapter 3. It is useful to think of shorting a stock as a way to hold a negative number of shares of a firm.

In market equilibrium the current market price will reflect an average of the intrinsic value estimates of all market participants. This means that the individual investor whose intrinsic V_0 estimate differs from the market price, P_0, in effect must disagree with some or all of the market consensus estimates of D_1, P_1, or k. Another way to refer to the market consensus value of k is by the term **market capitalization rate,** which we use often throughout this chapter.

Concept Check

Question 1. You expect the price of IBX stock to be $59.77 per share a year from now. Its current market price is $50, and you expect it to pay a dividend 1 year from now of $2.15 per share.
a. What is the stock's expected dividend yield, rate of price appreciation, and HPR?
b. If the stock has a beta of 1.15, the risk-free rate is 6% per year, and the expected rate of return on the market portfolio is 14% per year, what is the required rate of return on IBX stock?
c. What is the intrinsic value of IBX stock, and how does it compare to the current market price?

17.3 *Discounted Dividend Models*

The model we have used so far relies on an estimate of the end-of-year price, P_1. However, you may want to know how investors can forecast this price. Using the same logic employed to derive V_0, the intrinsic value of ABC stock at the beginning of the second year is

$$E(P_1) = E(V_1)$$
$$= \frac{E(D_2) + E(P_2)}{1 + k}$$

where we assume that future price will equal future intrinsic value.

By substitution, we can express V_0 in terms of $E(D_1)$, $E(D_2)$, and $E(P_2)$:

$$V_0 = \frac{1}{1 + k} E(D_1 + P_1)$$
$$= \frac{1}{1 + k} E\left(D_1 + \frac{D_2 + P_2}{1 + k}\right)$$
$$= \frac{E(D_1)}{1 + k} + \frac{E(D_2 + P_2)}{(1 + k)^2}$$

By continually repeating this chain of substitutions, we get the basic formula of the **discounted dividend model** (DDM):

$$V_0 = \frac{E(D_1)}{1 + k} + \frac{E(D_2)}{(1 + k)^2} + \frac{E(D_3)}{(1 + k)^3} + \cdot \cdot \cdot$$
$$= \sum_{t = 1}^{n} \frac{E(D_t)}{(1 + k)^t}$$

In other words, the intrinsic value of a share of stock is the present value of all expected future dividends.

Note that, despite what seems like its exclusive focus on dividends, the discounted dividend model is not in conflict with the notion that investors look at both dividends and expected capital gains when they evaluate a stock. On the contrary, we have just seen that the DDM can be derived from that assumption.[3]

The Constant Growth Rate Model

To apply the DDM, an investor must specify a procedure for estimating the series of expected future dividends. The simplest assumption is that dividends will grow at a constant rate, g, the **constant growth model.** We can return to the ABC example to see how the DDM works under the assumption that $g = 4\%$ per year. The expected stream of future dividends would be

$E(D_1)$	$E(D_2)$	$E(D_3)$	. . .
$4	$4.16	$4.3264	. . .

---

[3]If investors never expected a dividend to be paid, then this model implies that the stock would have no value. To reconcile the fact that non-dividend-paying stocks do have a market value with this model, one must assume that investors expect that some day it may pay out some cash, even if only a liquidating dividend.

The present value of a perpetual stream of dividends growing at a constant rate, g, is[4]

$$V_0 = \frac{E(D_1)}{k - g} \qquad (17.1)$$

With the ABC data this implies that the intrinsic value of ABC stock is:

$$V_0 = \frac{\$4}{.12 - .04}$$
$$= \frac{\$4}{.08}$$
$$= \$50$$

Because the constant growth DDM is so widely used by stock market analysts, it is worth exploring some of its implications and limitations. The constant growth rate DDM implies that a stock's value will be greater:

1. The larger its expected dividend per share, $E(D_1)$
2. The lower the market capitalization rate, k
3. The higher the expected growth rate of dividends, g

Another implication of the constant growth model is that the stock price is expected to grow at the same rate as dividends. To see this, suppose that ABC stock is selling at its intrinsic value of $50 (that is, $P_0 = V_0$).

Therefore,

$$P_0 = \frac{E(D_1)}{k - g}$$
$$= \$50$$

---

[4]Proof that the intrinsic value, V_0, of a stream of cash dividends growing at a constant rate, g, is equal to $\frac{E(D_1)}{k - g}$:

By definition,

$$V_0 = \frac{E(D_1)}{1 + k} + \frac{E(D_1)\,(1 + g)}{(1 + k)^2} + \frac{E(D_1)\,(1 + g)^2}{(1 + k)^3} + \ \cdots \qquad (a)$$

Multiplying through by $(1 + k)/(1 + g)$, we obtain

$$\frac{(1 + k)}{(1 + g)}\,V_0 = \frac{E(D_1)}{(1 + g)} + \frac{E(D_1)}{(1 + k)} + \frac{E(D_1)\,(1 + g)}{(1 + k)^2} + \ \cdots \qquad (b)$$

Subtracting equation a from equation b, we find that

$$\frac{(1 + k)}{(1 + g)}\,V_0 - V_0 = \frac{E(D_1)}{(1 + g)}$$

which implies

$$\frac{(k - g)V_0}{(1 + g)} = \frac{E(D_1)}{(1 + g)}$$
$$V_0 = \frac{E(D_1)}{k - g}$$

Next year's price is expected to be

$$E(P_1) = \frac{E(D_2)}{k - g}$$

However, because

$$E(D_2) = E(D_1)(1 + g)$$

we get by substitution:

$$E(P_1) = \frac{E(D_1)(1 + g)}{k - g}$$
$$= P_0(1 + g)$$

and the expected capital gains yield is

$$\frac{E(P_1) - P_0}{P_0} = \frac{P_0(1 + g) - P_0}{P_0}$$
$$= g$$

For the case of ABC stock, where g is 4% per year:

$$E(P_1) = \$50(1.04)$$
$$= \$52$$

and

$$\frac{E(P_1) - P_0}{P_0} = \frac{\$2}{\$50}$$

$$= .04 \text{ per year}$$

Therefore the DDM implies that in the case of constant growth of dividends the rate of price appreciation in any year will equal that constant growth rate, g.

Note that for a stock whose market price equals its intrinsic value ($P_0 = V_0$) the expected HPR will be

$$E(r) = \frac{E(D_1)}{P_0} + \frac{E(P_1) - P_0}{P_0} = \frac{E(D_1)}{P_0} + g$$

The first component, $E(D_1)/P_0$, is the expected dividend yield, and the second is the rate of capital appreciation, which in the constant growth case equals the rate of growth of dividends. In our example,

$$E(r) = (\$4/\$50) + .04 = .08 + .04 = .12 = 12\%$$

Note that, in order for the constant growth rate DDM to be applicable, the expected growth rate, g, must be less than the market capitalization rate, k. If this condition is violated, then the estimated intrinsic value will either be negative (if $k < g$) or undefined (if $k = g$, since one cannot divide by zero).

If an analyst ends up with an estimate of g that is greater than k, probably it is unsustainable in the long run. The appropriate valuation model to use in this case is one of the multistage DDMs that we discuss later rather than the constant growth rate model.

Question 2. a. IBX's stock dividend at the end of this year is expected to be $2.15, and it is expected to grow at 11.2% per year forever. If the required rate of return on IBX stock is 15.2% per year, what is its intrinsic value?
   b. If IBX's current market price is equal to this intrinsic value, what is next year's expected price?
   c. If an investor were to buy IBX stock now and sell it after receiving the $2.15 dividend a year from now, what is the expected capital gain (that is, the price appreciation) in percentage terms? What is the dividend yield, and what would the HPR be?

Convergence of Price to Intrinsic Value

Now suppose that the current market price of ABC stock is only $48 per share and therefore that the stock now is undervalued by $2 per share. In this case the expected rate of price appreciation depends on an additional assumption about whether the discrepancy between the intrinsic value and the market price will disappear, and if so, when.

One fairly common assumption is that the discrepancy will never disappear and that the market price will continue to grow at rate g forever. This implies that the discrepancy between intrinsic value and market price also will grow at that same rate. In our example:

Now	Next Year
$V_0 = \$50$	$E(V_1) = \$50 \times 1.04 = \$52$
$P_0 = \$48$	$E(P_1) = \$48 \times 1.04 = \$49.92$
$V_0 - P_0 = \$2$	$E(V_1 - P_1) = \$2 \times 1.04 = \$2.08$

Under this assumption the expected HPR will exceed the required rate, because the dividend yield is higher than it would be if P_0 were equal to V_0. In our example the dividend yield would be 8.33% instead of 8%, so that the expected HPR would be $12\frac{1}{3}\%$ rather than 12%.

$$E(r) = \frac{E(D_1)}{P_0} + g$$
$$= \frac{\$4}{\$48} + .04$$
$$= .0833 + .04$$
$$= 12\frac{1}{3}\% \text{ per year}$$

An investor who identifies this undervalued stock can get an expected dividend yield that exceeds the required yield by 33 basis points. This excess return is earned each year, and the market price never catches up to intrinsic value.[5]

A second possible assumption is that the gap between market price and intrinsic value will disappear by the end of the year. In that case we would have $E(P_1) = E(V_1) = \$52$, and

$$
\begin{aligned}
E(r) &= \frac{E(D_1)}{P_0} + \frac{E(P_1) - P_0}{P_0} \\
&= \frac{4}{48} + \frac{52 - 48}{48} \\
&= .0833 + .0833 \\
&= .1667 = 16\tfrac{2}{3}\% \text{ per year}
\end{aligned}
$$

The assumption of complete catch-up to intrinsic value produces a much larger 1-year HPR. In future years the stock is expected to generate only fair rates of return.

Many stock analysts assume that a stock's price will approach its intrinsic value gradually over time—for example, over a 5-year period. This puts their expected 1-year HPR somewhere between the bounds of $12\tfrac{1}{3}\%$ and $16\tfrac{2}{3}\%$.

Relating Value to Investment Opportunities

How do stock analysts derive forecasts of g, the expected growth rate of dividends? Usually, they first assume a constant dividend payout ratio (that is, ratio of dividends to earnings), which implies that dividends will grow at the same rate as earnings. Then they try to relate the expected growth rate of earnings to the expected profitability of the firm's *future* investment opportunities.

The exact relationship is

$$ g = b \times \text{ROE} \tag{17.2} $$

where b is the proportion of the firm's earnings that is reinvested in the business, called the **plowback ratio** or the **earnings retention ratio,** and ROE is the rate of return (return on equity) on new investments.[6] If all of the variables are specified correctly, equation 17.2 is true by definition, which we will now see. The relevant variables are E_0, the firm's current earnings, I, the amount of earnings to be reinvested this period by the firm, and ΔE, the increase in earnings resulting from future new investment.

The earnings variable must be interpreted as earnings net of the funds necessary to maintain the productivity of the firm's capital, that is, earnings net of "economic depreciation." In other words, the earnings figure should be interpreted as the maximum amount of money that the firm could pay out each year in perpetuity without deplet-

---

[5]Closed-end investment companies selling at a discount to their net asset value (discussed in Chapter 3) are an example.
[6]The appropriate measure of ROE in equation 17.2 is really the internal rate of return (IRR) on the firm's future investments of equity capital.

ing its productive capacity. For this reason the earnings number may be quite different from the accounting earnings figure that the firm reports in its financial statements. (This is explored further in Chapter 18.)

Now let us return to the case of ABC. Suppose that the firm's current earnings are $10 million, and earnings retained and reinvested in the firm are $4 million, so that b is .4. By definition, the expected growth rate of earnings is equal to the change in earnings divided by current earnings:

$$g = \frac{\Delta E}{E_0}$$

By multiplying both numerator and denominator by I, reinvested earnings, we find

$$g = \frac{I}{E_0} \times \frac{\Delta E}{I}$$

Now note that the first term on the right-hand side, I/E_0, is the plowback or retention ratio, b; it is the ratio of reinvested earnings to total earnings. Next, note that $\Delta E/I$ is the incremental earnings per unit of new investment and therefore the return on equity for the new investment. Let us assume that ROE is 10% per year in this example.

Substituting b for I/E_0 and ROE for $\Delta E/I$, we are able to verify equation 17.2:

$$g = b \times \text{ROE}$$
$$= .4 \times 10\%$$
$$= 4\% \text{ per year}$$

Equation 17.2 highlights the two factors that determine growth in earnings: the profitability of future investments (ROE) and the proportion of earnings reinvested in the business (b).

You might jump from this observation to the conclusion that higher growth necessarily leads to higher market value of the stock, but that is only half true. If higher expected growth is due to higher expected profitability of future investments, it indeed should cause the market price to rise. However, if higher growth is attributable to a higher plowback ratio, which under our assumptions means a lower **dividend payout ratio,** its effect on market price can go either way, depending on whether the expected return on investment is higher or lower than the required rate of return on investment.

To clarify these points, consider a numerical example. Suppose XYZ has just paid a dividend and expects this coming year's earnings per share to be $1 ($E(E_1) = \$1$ per share). Its market capitalization rate is 12% per year.

Table 17.2, A and B, shows the values of g and P_0 that correspond to various assumptions about ROE and b. The entries in the table are derived by substituting into the two formulas:

1. $g = b \times \text{ROE}$

2. $P_0 = \dfrac{E(D_1)}{k - g} = \dfrac{(1 - b)E(E_1)}{k - g}$

TABLE 17.2   Effect of ROE and Plowback

Expected ROE	Plowback Ratio (b)			
	0	.25	.50	.75
A. On Growth Rate (g):				
10%	0	2.5%	5.0%	7.5%
12%	0	3.0%	6.0%	9.0%
14%	0	3.5%	7.0%	10.5%
B. On Price (P_0):				
10%	$8.33	$7.89	$ 7.14	$ 5.56
12%	$8.33	$8.33	$ 8.33	$ 8.33
14%	$8.33	$8.82	$10.00	$16.67

Assumptions: $E(E_1) = \$1$ per share, and $k = 12\%$ per year.

where $E(E_1) = \$1$ per share and $k = 12\%$ per year.

Table 17.2, A, shows that g increases with both the plowback ratio and expected ROE. You can see the impact of the plowback ratio by going across the rows. For example, let us follow the row corresponding to an expected ROE of 10%. As the plowback ratio rises from zero to .75, the growth rate of earnings increases from zero to 7.5% per year.

You can see the impact of ROE on g by going down columns two and three. At a plowback ratio of .5, the growth rate increases from a low of 5% per year (when ROE is 10%) to a high of 7% (when ROE is 14%). For any plowback ratio, with the exception of zero, g rises as ROE rises.

The impact of ROE and b on P_0 can be seen by looking at Table 17.2, B.

ROE has an unambiguous effect. For any plowback ratio other than zero, price rises with ROE. On the other hand, the impact of changes in the plowback ratio on price depends on whether expected ROE is above or below 12%, the market capitalization rate.

Looking across the middle row in Table 17.2, B, an ROE of 12%, we see that the price of $8.33 is unaffected by the plowback ratio. The top row at an ROE of 10% shows that price decreases to $5.56 as the plowback ratio increases to .75, whereas the bottom row corresponding to an ROE of 14% shows that price increases to $16.67 as the plowback ratio rises to .75.

This pattern has a simple interpretation. When the expected ROE is less than the required return, k, investors prefer that the firm pay out earnings as dividends, rather than reinvest earnings in the firm at an inadequate rate of return. That is, for ROE lower than k, the value of the firm falls as plowback increases. Conversely, when ROE exceeds k, the firm offers superior investment opportunities, so the value of the firm is enhanced as those opportunities are more fully exploited by raising the plowback ratio.

Finally, for ROE = k, the firm offers "break-even" investment opportunities with just fair rates of return. In this case investors are indifferent between reinvestment of earnings in the firm or elsewhere at the market capitalization rate, because the rate of return in either case is 12%. In this case the stock price is unaffected by the plowback ratio.

One way to summarize these relationships is to say that a higher plowback ratio will bring a higher growth rate but not necessarily a higher stock price. A higher plowback rate increases price only if investments undertaken by the firm offer an expected rate of return higher than the market capitalization rate. Otherwise, higher plowback hurts investors because it means that more money is sunk into projects with inadequate rates of return.

Concept Check

Question 3. Your analysis of IBX stock suggests that the expected ROE on future investments is 16% per year. The dividend payout ratio is .3, and the required market capitalization rate is 15.2% per year. Next year's earnings are expected to be $7.17 per share.
a. What is the plowback ratio and the expected growth rate?
b. What is the intrinsic value of a share?
c. If the current market price is $50 per share, what is the expected 1-year HPR if:
   i. the market price grows at the same rate as dividends?
   ii. the market price converges to the intrinsic value by the end of the year?

Price-Earnings Ratios and Future Investment Opportunities

Much of the real-world discussion of stock market valuation focuses on the ratio of a stock's price to its earnings per share, known as the **price-earnings multiple.** This makes sense because absolute levels of stock values across companies cannot be compared. The price-earnings multiple is also called the P/E ratio.

How does the DDM we have discussed relate to a stock's price-earnings multiple? We can use Table 17.2, B, to demonstrate. Note that the price P_0 is always equal to $8.33 per share when the plowback ratio, and therefore g, equals zero. For this no-growth case, $P_0 = E(E_1)/k$, the price is simply the present value of a perpetual expected stream of earnings, all paid out as dividends. In this case the price-earnings multiple, defined as P_0 divided by $E(E_1)$, equals 1 divided by k, or the inverse of the market capitalization rate.

When ROE exceeds k, that is, when the expected rate of return on future investment opportunities exceeds the required rate of return, the price-earnings multiple will exceed $1/k$. Assuming rational firm management, the firm will undertake only future investments yielding an expected ROE greater than k. The net present value of those projects therefore will be positive. If such is the case, $1/k$ is the lowest value that the $P_0/E(E_1)$ ratio can take.

In the numerical example in Table 17.2 the firm's management will select a plowback ratio greater than zero only if it thinks future ROE will exceed 12%. In such a case the P/E ratio would exceed the 8.33 value for the no-growth case.

If management thinks ROE is going to be less than 12%, it will set the plowback ratio equal to zero. In that case the P/E ratio would equal 8.33. In the case where the future ROE is expected to equal the 12% market capitalization rate, the P/E ratio is 8.33 regardless of the plowback ratio.

It is common to think of a stock with a high growth rate of earnings as having a relatively high P/E ratio. Our analysis, however, should suggest to you that it is not growth *per se* that produces a high P/E multiple, but rather the presence of future investment opportunities that may yield an ROE greater than k.

To see these relationships more clearly, substitute $b \times$ ROE for g in equation 17.1 to get:

$$\frac{P_0}{E(E_1)} = \frac{(1 - b)}{k - (b \times \text{ROE})} \tag{17.3}$$

Equation 17.3 shows that an increase in b may either increase or decrease the P/E ratio, depending on whether ROE is greater or less than k. If ROE $= k$ then equation 17.3 reduces to

$$P_0 = \frac{(1 - b)E(E_1)}{k - bk}$$
$$= \frac{(1 - b)E(E_1)}{(1 - b)k}$$
$$= \frac{E(E_1)}{k}$$

So that

$$\frac{P_0}{E(E_1)} = \frac{1}{k}$$

Concept Check

Question 4. ABC stock has an expected ROE of 12% per year, expected earnings per share of $2, and expected dividends of $1.50 per share. Its market capitalization rate is 10% per year.
a. What are its expected growth rate, its price, and its P/E ratio?
b. If the plowback ratio were .4, what would be the expected dividend per share, the growth rate, price, and P/E ratio?

Multistage Discounted Dividend Models

A major limitation of the constant growth model is that it fails to capture the real-world pattern of dividends of many firms. Some firms go through periods in which they pay no dividends at all. Others see periods of very rapid growth in dividends, which cannot be sustained forever. To allow for this variation, stock analysts use multistage dividend discount models.

The simplest of the multistage DDMs is the two-stage model, where an initial stage of dividend growth at rate g_1 lasts for a limited number of years and is followed thereafter by constant growth at a lower rate, g_2. We can illustrate the two-stage model with an example for which there are no dividends at all in the first stage.

Consider what we will call Growth Dynamics (GD), a young firm experiencing rapid growth, reinvesting all its earnings, and paying no dividends. Its most recent earnings per share were $1, and its ROE is 25% per year.

Analysts assume that GD's high ROE will fall to 15% per year 3 years from now, and that at that point GD's management will start paying out all earnings as dividends. If the required rate of return, k, on GD stock is 12% per year, what can we say about GD's current and future intrinsic values?

Since its ROE in the first 3 years is expected to be 25% per year and the plowback ratio is 1.0, the growth rate of earnings, g, is 25% per year. Earnings per share will grow from the current value of $1 to $1.953125 in year 3. Starting in year 3, GD will pay annual dividends of $1.953125 per share forever, at which point further growth is zero, since plowback into the firm is zero.

The pattern of expected future earnings and dividends is as follows:

$t:$	0	1	2	3	4	5
E_t	$1	$1.25	$1.5625	$1.953125	$1.953125	→
D_t	0	0	0	$1.953125	$1.953125	→

The firm is expected to reach a constant growth phase 2 years from now (with $g = 0$). At this point we can obtain its price from the discounted dividend model. The expected price of a share 2 years from now, P_2, is therefore simply D_3/k, or $1.953125/.12 = 16.2760. Therefore its value today is the present value of that expected future price, discounted at 12% per year, which is $16.2760/(1.12)^2 = 12.9752.

Between now and 3 years from now, the investor's return will be entirely in the form of price appreciation at a rate of 12% per year. Starting in year 3 the return will come entirely in the form of a 12% per year dividend yield.

The $12.9752 present value of expected future dividends represents our DDM intrinsic value estimate for GD stock, assuming a 12% per year market capitalization rate. But how do we estimate the *expected* rate of return on the stock, given its current market price?

Suppose the current market price is $10 per share. According to the DDM, the stock is worth $12.9752, or $2.9752 more than this. As in the earlier constant growth rate DDM, the expected rate of return to stockholders depends on how rapidly the market price will converge to its intrinsic value.

One measure of expected return we can derive from analogy with bond returns is a yield to maturity measure, which is the discount rate that would make the present value of all expected future dividends equal to the current market price.

In the case of GD, the expected future flow of dividends is $1.953125 per year starting 3 years from now and lasting forever. The yield to maturity analog y can be found by solving for y:

$$P_0 = \$10 = \frac{1}{(1+y)^2} \frac{D_3}{y}$$

$$= \frac{1.953125}{(1+y)^2 y} \tag{17.4}$$

This equation sets the current price equal to the present value of the expected perpetual stream of dividends. The present value of the perpetuity equals D_3/y discounted for an extra 2 years, because the dividend stream starts in 3 years rather than in 1 year as is usually the case. Solving this equation by a trial-and-error procedure, we find that $y = 14.81\%$ per year.[7]

Note that y is the expected rate of return for someone who will hold the stock in perpetuity. It is not, in general, the same as the expected HPR for shorter time horizons, because y is analogous to the yield to maturity on a bond.

Alternatively, we can assume, as we did in the case of the constant growth rate DDM, that the market price will converge to its intrinsic value by the end of the first year.

The intrinsic value 1 year from now is

$$\frac{P_2}{1+k} = \frac{16.2760}{1.12}$$
$$= \$14.5321$$

as the expected price at time 2 is now 1 year closer.

The expected HPR is thus

$$E(r) = \frac{P_1 - P_0}{P_0}$$
$$= \frac{\$14.5321 - \$10}{\$10}$$
$$= .45321 = 45.32\% \text{ per year}$$

This high 1-year HPR is generated by the immediate "catch-up" of market price to intrinsic value.

Two points are worth noting about this example of a multistage DDM. The first is that, even when the market price equals the intrinsic value, the expected rate of price appreciation is not equal to the growth rate of earnings until the final stage, where g once again is constant. This feature differentiates the multistage from the constant growth DDM. The second point, which is true of any DDM, is that when market

---

[7]The value of y that satisfies this equation is found by an iterative search procedure. The general procedure is to start with an initial guess, and then through a systematic trial-and-error process make progressively better approximations.

price equals intrinsic value the expected HPR, the sum of the expected dividend yield plus the expected rate of price appreciation, equals the market capitalization rate.

If the GD stock is priced at its intrinsic value, we have $P_0 = \$12.9752$, and the expected rate of capital appreciation in the first stage is 12% ([$\$14.53 - 12.98$]/$\$12.98$), which is the market capitalization rate. In the second stage the growth rate is expected to fall to zero, and all earnings are paid out as dividends. Price is expected to remain constant at $16.276 per year.

Note that in both stages of GD's growth the sum of expected dividend yield and price appreciation is 12% per year. In stage one it is all price appreciation; in stage two it is all dividend yield.

You might well ask how realistic this example is. Market history shows many cases of firms that proceeded through an early growth stage when they paid no dividends and then subsequently started to pay cash dividends that have grown at a roughly constant rate. Perhaps the best-known case is IBM. Still other companies are in the first stage, yet to pay a cash dividend. Digital Equipment Corporation is one example.

More generally, however, we can allow for dividends to be paid in both stages of growth. To see how an analyst would actually apply the two-stage DDM to a stock that is currently paying a cash dividend, let us now use it to value the stock of the IBM Corporation.

Our assumptions are:

1. Next year's earnings per share: $11.25
2. Earnings per share 3 years from now: $19.93
3. The dividend payout ratio: .4
4. Return on equity 3 years from now: 19%
5. β: .95

Let us assume that the risk-free rate is 6% per year and the risk premium on the market portfolio 8% per year. We will assume that earnings and dividends grow smoothly at a rate of 21% per year between now and 3 years from now, since that is the growth rate implied by assumptions 1 and 2.

Under these assumptions the ultimate growth rate beyond year 4 is 11.4% per year ($b \times \text{ROE} = .6 \times 19\%$), and the market capitalization rate 13.6% ($r_f + \beta[E(r_M) - r_f] = 6\% + .95 \times 8\%$). The cash flow diagram is therefore

t:	0	1	2	3	4	. . .
E_t		$11.25	$13.61	$16.47	$19.93	. . .
D_t		$4.50	$5.45	$6.59	$7.97	. . .

The estimated price at $t = 3$ is:

$$P_3 = \frac{D_4}{k - g}$$
$$= \frac{\$7.97}{.136 - .114}$$
$$= \$362.27$$

The intrinsic value is the present value (PV) of dividends in years 1 through 3 plus the PV of P_3.

$$V_0 = \frac{\$4.50}{1.136} + \frac{\$5.45}{1.136^2} + \frac{\$6.59 + 362.27}{1.136^3}$$
$$= \$259.79$$

Concept Check

Question 5. The Two-Stage Corporation just paid a dividend of $2 per share, and it is expected to grow by 10% per year for the next 3 years. Starting at the end of year 3, the dividend growth rate is expected to fall to 4% per year and to stay there forever. The appropriate market capitalization rate for Two-Stage stock is 12% per year.
a. What should be the price of the stock?
b. What is its expected price 1 year from now?
c. What is the expected dividend yield and rate of capital appreciation?

In practice, the multistage DDMs that security analysts use often are more complex than our two-stage model. Usually, they allow for a more gradual transition from the initial high-growth stage to the ultimate steady state. In addition, computers make it relatively easy to generate patterns of expected future dividends that conform to any plausible scenario, and to estimate the corresponding intrinsic value and expected rate of return.

There is, however, one multistage DDM that does not require computer aid and still allows the assumed growth rate of dividends to start high and to fall gradually over time to a long-run steady state level. The so-called H-model is gaining in popularity because of its relative simplicity.[8]

The H model assumes that the dividend growth rate starts at a level g_a and declines linearly over $2H$ years to a long-run constant growth rate of g_n. Therefore at H years the growth rate is halfway between g_a and g_n.

Under these assumptions the equation for the stock's price is:

$$P_0 = \frac{D_0(1 + g_n)}{k - g_n} + \frac{D_0 H(g_a - g_n)}{k - g_n} \tag{17.5}$$

The first term on the right-hand side of equation 17.5 represents the value of a share if dividends were expected to grow at the long-run growth rate, g_n, starting with the very first period. The second term is the premium because of higher than g_n growth rates expected during the first $2H$ years. The longer the half-life of the period of higher growth (H) and the higher the initial growth rate (g_a), the more the premium is.

---

[8]For a detailed exposition of this model see Fuller, R.J., and Hsia, C.C., "A Simplified Model for Estimating Stock Prices for Growth Firms," *Financial Analysts Journal*, September-October 1984.

To demonstrate how the *H*-model works, suppose the stream of future dividends per share of the HIJ Corporation is expected to start at $1 per share, with an initial growth rate of 25% per year that falls to a long-run rate of 5% per year after 10 years. In this case

$$D_0 = \$1$$
$$g_a = .25$$
$$g_n = .05$$
$$H = 5 \text{ years}$$

Assume further that its market capitalization rate is 10% per year.

$$P_0 = \frac{1.05}{.1 - .05} + \frac{1.0 \times 5(.25 - .05)}{.1 - .05}$$
$$= 21 + 20$$
$$= \$41.00 \text{ per share}$$

The *H* model also has a simple expression for the expected yield to maturity *(y)* on the expected dividend stream, given its market price. Recall that *y* is the discount rate that makes the present value of all expected future dividends equal to the current market price. For the *H* model it is given by

$$y = \frac{D_0}{P_0}[1 + g_n + H(g_a - g_n)] + g_n$$

If the market price of a share of HIJ is $20, the expected yield to maturity is

$$y = \frac{1}{20}[(1.05) + 5(.25 - .05)] + .05$$
$$= \frac{2.05}{20} + .05$$
$$= .1525$$
$$= 15.25\% \text{ per year}$$

If the market price were $41 rather than $20 per share, *y* would be 10% per year, which is the market capitalization rate.

Concept Check

Question 6. The Unlimited Corporation is a rapidly growing retailer of women's clothing. Its most recent dividend per share was $2, and its market capitalization rate is 12% per year. You are an analyst who believes that Unlimited's dividend growth rate will be 35% this year and will decline gradually to 6% per year 20 years from now. Thereafter, growth will level off at 6% per year forever.

a. What is your estimate of the intrinsic value of a share of Unlimited's stock?

b. If the market price of a share is currently $100, what is the expected yield to maturity on an investment in the stock?

17.4 Capitalized Earnings Models

Equity valuation often focuses on earnings rather than dividends. As you know from earlier discussion, the relationship between earnings and dividends in any period t, assuming no external equity financing, is

$$\text{Dividends}_t = \text{Earnings}_t - \text{Reinvested earnings}_t$$

It follows that the present value of all expected dividends must equal the present value of expected earnings minus the present value of expected reinvested earnings. Therefore

$$V_0 = \sum_{t=1}^{\infty} \frac{D_t}{(1+k)^t} = \sum_{t=1}^{\infty} \frac{E_t}{(1+k)^t} - \sum_{t=1}^{\infty} \frac{I_t}{(1+k)^t} \qquad (17.6)$$

Recognize that equation 17.6 does *not* imply that the value of a firm is equal to the PV of expected future earnings. It says that the firm's value equals the PV of expected future earnings *less* the PV of the earnings reinvested in the firm.

If the expected ROE on reinvested earnings is equal to k, then even the most complicated multistage DDM reduces to the simplest capitalized earnings model:

$$V_0 = E(E_1)/k$$

The reason is that in this special case the net present value of all new investment is zero, so the firm is worth the same as if it paid all earnings out as dividends and was not expected to grow at all.

For example, let us return to our two-stage growth model of IBM stock. We assumed that the ROE in years 4 and beyond was going to be 19% per year, while the market capitalization rate was 13.6%. Had we assumed that the ROE in years 4 and beyond was going to be 13.6% rather than 19% per year, then our estimate of P_3 would be $E(E_4)/k = \$19.93/.136 = \$146.54$, rather than \$362.27. The resulting intrinsic value would therefore be \$163.08, rather than \$259.79.

Note that, if IBM continues to plow back 60% of its earnings in years 4 and beyond, the growth rate of earnings and dividends will be 8.16% per year ($.6 \times 13.6\%$). The expected price of a share at $T = 3$, however, will be the same as if it paid out all earnings as dividends.

$$P_3 = E(D_4)/(k - g) = \$7.97/(.136 - .0816) = \$146.51$$

Many analysts employ a simple two-step earnings-based approach to equity valuation. First, they forecast earnings per share, and then they multiply this forecast by an "appropriate" earnings multiplier. Usually, this multiplier is chosen according to some ad hoc empirical rule. The simplest such rule would be to apply the P/E multiple for the S&P 500.

For example, if our estimate of IBM's next earnings per share is \$11.25, and the P/E multiple for the S&P 500 is 12, then our estimate of the intrinsic value of a share of IBM stock would be $135. A more sophisticated version of this approach is to compute P/E multiples by industry group. Thus we might find that for companies in the electrical equipment industry the average P/E multiple is 14. When we apply this multiplier to IBM's estimated EPS of $11.25, we get an intrinsic value of $157.50 per share.

An even more sophisticated approach would be to base the multiplier on factors such as the firm's beta, its expected growth rate of earnings, and its dividend payout ratio. If done in the way described in earlier sections of this chapter, the resultant estimate of intrinsic value will be the same as that produced by the DDM. Usually, however, analysts who employ the earnings multiplier approach do not worry about whether their results are consistent with the DDM.

17.5 *Corporate Finance and the Free Cash Flow Approach*

In both the discounted dividend and capitalized earnings approaches to equity valuation we made the assumption that the only source of financing of new equity investment in the firm was retained earnings. How would our results be affected if we allowed external equity financing of new investments? How would they be affected if we assumed debt financing of new investments? In other words, how do dividend policy and capital structure affect the value of a firm's shares?

The classic answer to these questions was provided by Modigliani and Miller (MM) in a series of articles that have become the foundation for the modern theory of corporate finance,[9] and we will briefly explain the main points of their theory.[10]

MM claim that if we take as given a firm's future investments, then the value of its existing common stock is not affected by how those investments are financed. Therefore neither the firm's dividend policy nor its capital structure should affect the value of a share of its equity.

The basic reasoning underlying the MM theory is that the intrinsic value of the equity in a firm is the present value of the net cash flows to shareholders that can be produced by the firm's existing assets plus the net present value of any investments to be made in the future. Given those existing and expected future investments, the firm's dividend and financing decisions will affect only the form in which existing shareholders will receive their future returns, that is, as dividends or capital gains, but not their present value.

As a by-product of their proof of these propositions, MM show the equivalence of three seemingly different approaches to valuing the equity in a firm. The first two are the discounted dividend and capitalized earnings approaches presented in the earlier

---

[9]The original two papers are Miller, M., and Modigliani, F., "Dividend Policy, Growth and the Valuation of Shares," *Journal of Business,* October 1961; and Modigliani, F., and Miller, M., "The Cost of Capital, Corporation Finance, and the Theory of Investment," *American Economic Review,* June 1958. Miller has revised his views in "Debt and Taxes," *Journal of Finance,* May 1976, and Modigliani his in "Debt, Dividend Policy, Taxes, Inflation and Market Valuation," *Journal of Finance,* May 1982.

[10]For a more complete treatment see Ross, Stephen A., and Westerfield, Randolph W., *Corporate Finance,* Times Mirror/Mosby, 1988, Chapters 14 and 15.

parts of this chapter. The third is the free cash flow approach.

This third approach starts with an estimate of the value of the firm as a whole and derives the value of the equity by subtracting the market value of all nonequity claims. The estimate of the value of the firm is found as the present value of cash flows, assuming all-equity financing plus the net present value of tax shields created by using debt. This approach is similar to that used by the firm's own management in capital budgeting, or the valuation approach that another firm would use in assessing the firm as a possible acquisition target.

For example, consider the MiMo Corporation. Its cash flow from operations before interest and taxes was $1 million in the year just ended, and it expects that this will grow by 6% per year forever. To make this happen, the firm will have to invest an amount equal to 15% of pretax cash flow each year. The tax rate is 30%. Depreciation was $100,000 in the year just ended and is expected to grow at the same rate as the operating cash flow. The appropriate market capitalization rate for the unleveraged cash flow is 10% per year, and the firm currently has debt of $2 million outstanding.

MiMo's projected free cash flow for the coming year is

Before-tax cash flow from operations	$1,060,000
Depreciation	106,000
Taxable income	954,000
Taxes (at 30%)	286,200
After-tax unleveraged income	667,800
After-tax cash flow from operations (After-tax unlevered income plus depreciation)	773,800
New investment (15% of cash flow from operations)	159,000
Free cash flow (after-tax cash flow from operations minus new investment)	614,800

It is important to realize that this projected free cash flow is what the firm's cash flow would be under all-equity financing. It ignores the interest expense on the debt, as well as any tax savings resulting from the deductibility of the interest expense.

The present value of all future free cash flows is

$$V_0 = \frac{C_1}{k - g}$$
$$= \frac{\$614,800}{.1 - .06} = \$15,370,000$$

Thus the value of the whole firm, debt plus equity, is $15,370,000. Since the value of the debt is $2 million, the value of the equity is $13,370,000.

If we believe that the use of financial leverage enhances the total value of the firm, then we should add to the $15,370,000 estimate of the firm's unleveraged value the gain from leverage. Thus, if in our example we believe that the tax shield provided by the deductibility of interest payments on the debt increases the firm's total value by $.5 million, the value of the firm would be $15,870,000 and the value of the equity $13,870,000.

In reconciling this free cash flow approach with either the discounted dividend or the capitalized earnings approaches, it is important to realize that the capitalization rate to be used in the present value calculation is different. In the free cash flow approach it is the rate appropriate for unleveraged equity, whereas in the other two approaches it is the rate appropriate for leveraged equity. Since leverage affects the stock's beta, these two capitalization rates will be different.

17.6   *Inflation and Equity Valuation*

What about the effects of inflation on stock prices? We can study that by starting with the sample case where the current price is unaffected by inflation, then explore the ways in which reality might differ.

Consider the case of Inflatotrend, a firm that in the absence of inflation pays out all earnings as dividends. Earnings and dividends per share are $1, and there is no growth. We will use asterisked (*) letters to denote variables in the no-inflation case, or what represents the real value of variables. We again consider an equilibrium capitalization rate, k^*, of 10% per year. The price per share of this stock should be $10:

$$P_0 = \frac{\$1}{.1} = \$10$$

Now imagine that inflation *(i)* is 6% per year, but that the values of the other economic variables adjust so as to leave their real values unchanged. Specifically, the *nominal* interest or capitalization rate, k, becomes $(1 + k^*)(1 + i) - 1 = 1.10 \times 1.06 - 1 = .166$ or 16.6%, and the expected nominal growth rate of dividends, g, is now 6%, which is necessary to maintain a constant level of real dividends. The *nominal* dividend expected at the end of this year is therefore $1.06 per share.

If we apply the constant growth DDM to these nominal variables we get the same price as in the no-inflation case:

$$\begin{aligned}
P_0 &= \frac{E(D_1)}{k - g} \\
&= \frac{\$1.06}{.166 - .060} \\
&= \frac{\$1.06}{.106} \\
&= \$10
\end{aligned}$$

Thus, as long as real values are unaffected, the stock's current price is unaffected by inflation.

Note that the expected nominal dividend yield, $E(D_1)/P_0$, is 10.6% and the expected nominal capital gains rate, $[E(P_1) - P_0]/P_0$ is 6%. Almost the entire 6.6% increase in nominal HPR comes in the form of expected capital gains. A capital gain is necessary if the real value of the stock is to remain unaffected by inflation.

Let us see how these assumptions affect the other variables: earning and the plowback ratio. To illuminate what otherwise may be confusing implications, we can explore a simplified story behind the examples above.

Inflatotrend produces a product that requires purchase of inventory at the beginning of each year, processing, and sale of the finished product at the end of the year. Last year there was no inflation. The inventory cost $10 million. Labor, rent, and other processing costs (paid at year-end) were $1 million, and revenue was $12 million. Assuming no taxes, earnings were $1 million.

Revenue	$12 million
−Labor and rent	1 million
−Cost of goods sold	10 million
Earnings	$1 million

All earnings are distributed as dividends to the 1 million shareholders. Because the only invested capital is the $10 million in inventory, the ROE is 10%.

This year inflation of 6% is expected, and all prices are expected to rise at that rate. As inventory is paid for at the beginning of the year it will still cost $10 million. However, revenue will be $12.72 million instead of $12 million, and other costs will be $1.06 million.

Nominal Earnings

Revenue	$12.72 million
−Labor and rent	1.06 million
−Cost of goods sold	10.00 million
Earnings	$1.66 million
ROE	16.6%

Note that the amount required to replace inventory at year's end is $10.6 million, rather than the beginning cost of $10 million, so the amount of cash available to distribute as dividends is $1.06 million, not the reported earnings of $1.66 million.

A dividend of $1.06 million would be just enough to keep the real value of dividends unchanged and at the same time allow for maintenance of the same real value of inventory. The reported earnings of $1.66 million overstate true economic earnings, in other words.

We thus have the following set of relationships:

	No Inflation	6% Inflation
Dividends	$1 million	$1.06 million
Reported earnings	$1 million	$1.66 million
ROE	10%	16.6%
Plowback ratio	0	.36145
Price of a share	$10	$10
P/E ratio	10	6.0241

There are some surprising findings in this case of "neutral" inflation, that is, inflation that leaves the real interest rate and real earnings unaffected. While nominal dividends rise at the rate of inflation, 6%, reported earnings increase initially by 66%. In subsequent years, as long as inflation remains at a constant rate of 6%, earnings will grow at 6%.

Note also that the plowback ratio rises from 0 to .36145. Although plowback in the no-inflation case was zero, positive plowback of reported earnings now becomes necessary to maintain a constant value real inventory level. Inventory must rise from a nominal level of $10 million to a level of $10.6 million to maintain its real value. This inventory investment requires reinvested earnings of $.6 million.

Thus the proportion of reported income that must be retained and reinvested to keep the real growth rate of earnings at zero is .36145 if inflation is 6% per year. Multiplying this plowback ratio by the nominal ROE of 16.6% produces a nominal growth rate of dividends of 6%, which is equal to the inflation rate:

$$g = b \times \text{ROE}$$
$$= .36145 \times 16.6\%$$
$$= 6\% \text{ per year}$$

More generally, the relationship between nominal and real variables is:

Variable	Real	Nominal
Growth rate	g^*	$g = (1 + g^*)(1 + i) - 1$
Capitalization rate	k^*	$k = (1 + k^*)(1 + i) - 1$
Return on equity	ROE^*	$\text{ROE} = (1 + \text{ROE}^*)(1 + i) - 1$
Expected dividend	$E(D_1^*)$	$E(D_1) = (1 + i)E(D_1^*)$
Plowback ratio	b^*	$b = \dfrac{(1 + b^* \times \text{ROE}^*)(1 + i) - 1}{(1 + \text{ROE}^*)(1 + i) - 1}$

Note that it is not true that $E(E_1) = (1 + i)E(E^*_1)$. That is, expected reported earnings do not, in general, equal expected real earnings times one plus the inflation rate. The reason, as you have seen, is that stated earnings do not accurately measure the cost of replenishing assets.

For example, cost of goods sold is treated as if it were $10 million, even though it now costs $10.6 million to replace the inventory. Original cost accounting in this case distorts the measured cost of goods sold, which in turn distorts the reported earnings figures. We will return to this point in Chapter 18.

Note also the effect of inflation on the P/E ratio. In our example the P/E ratio drops from 10 in the no-inflation scenario to 6.0241 in the 6% inflation scenario. This is entirely a result of the fact that the reported earnings figure gets distorted by inflation and overstates true economic earnings.

This is true in the real world too, not just in our simplified example. Many companies show gains in reported earnings during inflationary periods, even though real earnings may be unaffected. This is one reason analysts must interpret data on the past behavior of P/E ratios over time with great care.

Concept Check

Question 7. Assume that Inflatotrend has a 4% annual expected constant growth rate of earnings if there is no inflation. $E(E^*_1) = \$1$ per share; ROE* = 10% per year; $b^* = .4$; and $k^* = 10\%$ per year.
a. What is the current price of a share ex-dividend?
b. What are the expected real dividend yield and rate of capital appreciation?
c. If the firm's real revenues and dividends are unaffected by inflation, and expected inflation is 6% per year, what should be the nominal growth rate of dividends, the expected nominal dividend yield, the expected ROE, and the nominal plowback ratio?

For many years financial economists considered stocks to be an inflation-neutral investment in the sense that we have described. They believed, and many of them still believe, that changes in the rate of inflation, whether expected or unexpected, have no effect on the expected real rate of return on common stocks.

Recent empirical research, however, seems to indicate that real rates of return are negatively correlated with inflation. In terms of the simple constant growth rate DDM, this would mean that an increase in inflation is associated with (but is not necessarily caused by) either a decrease in $E(D_1)$, an increase in k, a decrease in g, or some combination of all three.

One school of thought[11] believes that economic "shocks" such as the OPEC oil price hikes have caused a simultaneous increase in the inflation rate and decline of expected real earnings (and dividends). This would demonstrate a negative correlation between inflation and real stock returns.

A second view[12] is that the higher the rate of inflation, the riskier real stock returns are perceived to be. The reasoning here is that higher inflation is associated with greater uncertainty about the economy, which tends to induce a higher required rate of return on equity. In addition, a higher k implies a lower level of stock prices.

A third perspective[13] is that higher inflation results in lower real dividends because our tax system causes lower after-tax real earnings as the inflation rate rises.

Finally, there is the view[14] that most investors in the stock market suffer from a form of "money illusion." Investors mistake the rise in the nominal rate of interest for a rise in the real rate. As a result, they undervalue stocks in a period of higher inflation.

We will have more to say about the behavior of the aggregate stock market in the face of inflation and the hypotheses advanced to account for it in Section 17.7.

[11] See Fama, Eugene, F., "Stock Returns, Real Activity, Inflation, and Money," *American Economic Review*, September 1981.

[12] See Malkiel, Burton, *A Random Walk Down Wall Street*, ed. 4, New York: W.W. Norton & Co., Inc., 1985.

[13] See Feldstein, Martin, "Inflation and the Stock Market," *American Economic Review*, December 1980.

[14] See Modigliani, Franco, and Cohn, Richard, "Inflation, Rational Valuation, and the Market," *Financial Analysts Journal*, March-April 1979.

FIGURE 17.1

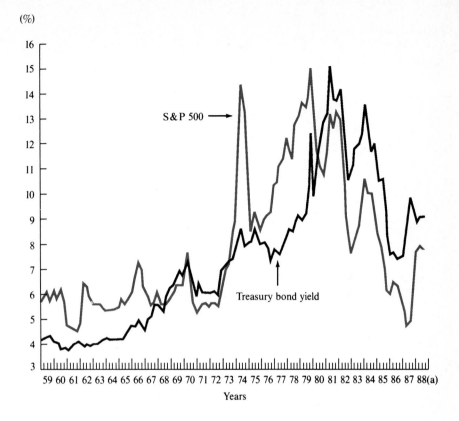

Earnings yield of
S&P 500 compared
with Treasury bond
yield. (*88a*, as of June
10, 1988)
(From Kidder, Peabody
Investment Policy Group).

17.7 *Behavior of the Aggregate Stock Market*

Explaining Past Behavior

It has been well documented that the stock market is a leading economic indicator.[15] This means that it tends to fall before a recession and to rise before an economic recovery. As the nearby box shows, however, the relationship is far from perfectly reliable.

Most scholars and serious analysts would agree that, although the stock market appears to have a substantial life of its own, responding perhaps to bouts of mass euphoria and then panic, economic events and the anticipation of such events do have a substantial effect on stock prices.[16] Perhaps the two factors with the greatest impact are interest rates and corporate profits.

Figure 17.1 shows the behavior of the earnings-to-price ratio (that is, the earnings

---

[15]See, for example, Fischer, Stanley, and Merton, Robert C., "Macroeconomics and Finance: The Role of the Stock Market," *Carnegie-Rochester Conference Series on Public Policy, 21,* 1984.

[16]For a discussion of the current debate on the rationality of the stock market, see the Suggested Readings at the end of this chapter.

The Stock Market Is a Lousy Economic Forecaster

People wait anxiously for the other shoe to drop: The stock market has crashed—508 points in one day, 983 points over two months. Now, what happens to the economy? Will it, too, crash or at least take a nasty spill?

If the history of the past six decades is a guide, the answer is probably not. Barrie A. Wigmore of Goldman, Sachs & Co. is author of *The Crash and Its Aftermath,* a definitive economic history of the early 1930s. Here's what he says: "This year's boom has had little to do with the underlying strength of the U.S. economy. So why should the recent crash?" FORBES has dusted off the history books and picked the nine great

market breaks beginning with 1929. What we found confirms Wigmore's view of this tenuous relationship. Our conclusion: no depression, probably no recession. At least not now.

FORBES researchers identified the nine occasions when the stock market crashed by 25% or more as measured by the Dow Jones industrials. Four of these "crashes" were followed by strong economic advances. Three were followed by short economic downturns. One was followed by a big, fat depression—1929.

That's not much of a forecasting record.

Sept. 3, 1929 to July 8, 1932. A market collapse that altogether wiped out 89% of the Dow industrials' value, the greatest peacetime economic loss in modern history. As we know now, that crash ushered in the Great Depression. But people didn't know that then. In two months the Dow industrials lost 48% of their value, but the economy kept on growing and ended the year with GNP substantially above year-earlier levels. Even business writer Alexander Dana Noyes, who had been predicting the bust for months, believed the selling was overdone.

Unfortunately, the first wave of selling was followed by another collapse in

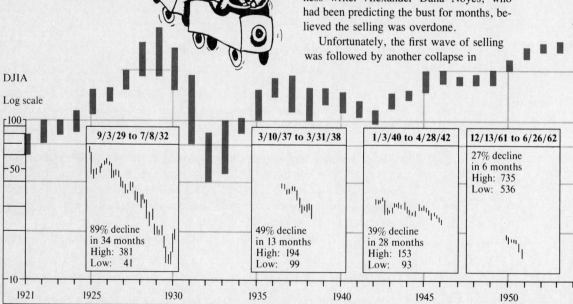

DJIA

Log scale

9/3/29 to 7/8/32

89% decline
in 34 months
High: 381
Low: 41

3/10/37 to 3/31/38

49% decline
in 13 months
High: 194
Low: 99

1/3/40 to 4/28/42

39% decline
in 28 months
High: 153
Low: 93

12/13/61 to 6/26/62

27% decline
in 6 months
High: 735
Low: 536

1930 (April to December), when the stock market lost 47% of its value. In the third selloff (February 1931 to December 1931) the Dow lost 62% in value. By now the economy, too, was on the ropes. By year's end, the GNP had dropped 7.7% below 1930 levels in constant dollars, and unemployment stood at 25% of the labor force.

The fourth slide (March to July 1932) wiped out 54% of what little value the Dow averages still retained. But any brave soul who bought stocks at this point would have come out a rich man. This fourth collapse was followed by a sustained five-year bull market, in which the Dow averages rose 372%.

Mar. 10, 1937 to Mar. 31, 1938, the so-called Roosevelt recession. Here the stock market did accurately predict a slowdown. Ironically, that slowdown came when Roosevelt yielded to pressures similar to those now weighing on Washington and cut spending to balance the budget. Waves of strikes ensued as the economy began slowly to reverse course and slide back into recession. The downturn lasted for about a year, ending when the Administration began some Keynesian pump-priming.

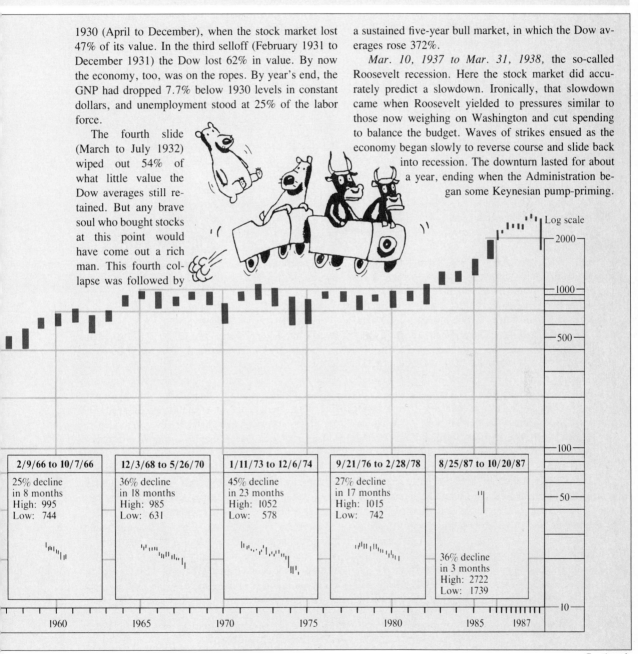

2/9/66 to 10/7/66	12/3/68 to 5/26/70	1/11/73 to 12/6/74	9/21/76 to 2/28/78	8/25/87 to 10/20/87
25% decline in 8 months High: 995 Low: 744	36% decline in 18 months High: 985 Low: 631	45% decline in 23 months High: 1052 Low: 578	27% decline in 17 months High: 1015 Low: 742	

36% decline in 3 months
High: 2722
Low: 1739

1960   1965   1970   1975   1980   1985   1987

Continued.

Jan. 3, 1940 to Apr. 28, 1942. During this 28-month period, Dow stocks lost an average of 39% in value, as investors blamed everything from Roosevelt's health to the danger that Germany and Japan might win the war. Through it all, the economy kept on growing, with the GNP nearly doubling from 1940 to 1943, while war mobilization cut unemployment from 8.1% to 1.1% over the same period.

Dec. 13, 1961 to June 26, 1962. The so-called Kennedy correction. During the six-month period, Dow stocks lost 27% in value. Many investors at the time blamed the Administration's confrontation with the steel industry, leaving fears of an antibusiness era. There was growing international tension with the Bay of Pigs and the Berlin Wall. But whatever the cause, the economy remained strong. Already in the second year of an advance, it continued right on growing, racking up gains of 4% or more in GNP annually through the rest of the decade. This was the longest period of sustained economic growth since the end of World War II.

Feb. 9, 1966 to Oct. 7, 1966. During this eight-month period, Dow stocks dropped 25% in value as investors grew wary of Lyndon Johnson's guns-and-butter economic strategy. But even rising interest rates and tight money from William McChesney Martin Jr. at the Federal Reserve failed to halt growth, and by early 1967, stocks were once again rising smartly.

Dec. 3, 1968 to May 26, 1970. The Nixon slide, 36%. During this 18-month period, Wall Street's speculative excesses of the Johnson era were wiped out, creating a long list of famous casualties, from James Ling of LTV to Bernie Cornfeld of IOS. Corporate casualties included Penn Central Corp., F.I. du Pont & Co. and a host of lesser names on Wall Street.

Then, as now, prophets of doom were not lacking. In May of 1970, at the very trough of the decline, liberal economist John Kenneth Galbraith reportedly likened the year to 1929, suggesting that even more wrenching declines lay ahead. Anyone who listened to Harvard's sage soon regretted doing so. Though the economy declined throughout the remainder of 1970, the stock market took off on a two-year advance.

Jan. 11, 1973, to Dec. 6, 1974. This 23-month bear market, which knocked 45% off the Dow industrials, did precede a recession. But the steepest drop (March to December 1974) came as a consequence of a recession. The economy was already reeling from rising petroleum prices when investors began pulling their money out of Wall Street. Hardest hit: the so-called Nifty Fifty blue-chip stocks like Polaroid and Avon, which had gotten wildly overpriced in the previous bull market and now lost, in some cases, 90% of their value.

The recession—which started before the steepest market collapse—lasted 16 months, until spring 1975. But anyone watching economic indicators for when to return to the market would have missed out. The Dow industrials had begun to improve three months earlier, indicating what wise investors have known all along: The market is a much better predictor of recoveries than of recessions.

Sept. 21, 1976 to Feb. 28, 1978. The economy had been relentlessly advancing since the spring of 1975 when Wall Street grew wary that Jimmy Carter might defeat Gerald Ford and unleash a round of Democratically inspired runaway spending in Washington. Carter did defeat Ford, spending did balloon, inflation did explode, and the stock market did plunge 27% in the following 17 months. Yet through it all, the economy continued to advance for another five years.

The fact is that the stock market often responds to its own internal momentum and, at other times, to a misapprehension of what lies ahead. Take the "Dow theory collapse" that lasted from May to October of 1946. This was not quite rough enough to make our list of crashes, but it was a nasty one all the same. During this five-month period, the Dow industrials dropped 23%, and jittery investors fretted that a new depression was just over the horizon. In fact, as a subsequent study by the Securities & Exchange Commission showed, much of the selling was caused by large numbers of investors reacting to the Dow theory "sell signal" and dumping stocks when the Dow industrial average dropped down through 186.02, a presumed support level.

Does the October crash foreshadow an economic collapse? Only one in nine major crashes has done so in 60 years. The odds are slightly better that it may foreshadow a recession of some kind. But the odds are highest that it presages nothing more severe than correction of the market's own previous excesses on the upside.

Reprinted by permission of *Forbes* magazine, November 30, 1987. © Forbes Inc., 1987. Illustration, Patrick McDonnell and Shelly Dell. © 1987.

yield) of the S&P 500 stock index vs. the yield to maturity on long-term Treasury bonds over the last 30 years. Our discussion of valuation models earlier in this chapter gives us some insights into the relationship between these two yields.

In the absence of inflation and assuming that the expected ROE on future real investments in the corporate sector is equal to the equity capitalization rate and that current earnings per share equal expected future earnings per share, the earnings yield on the S&P 500 represents the expected real rate of return on the stock market. This should be equal to the yield to maturity on Treasury bonds plus a risk premium, which may change slowly over time.

Inflation will alter this relationship for several reasons. First, as shown earlier in this chapter, even in the case of neutral inflation reported earnings tend to rise in a period of high inflation. Thus at least part of the sharp rise in the S&P earnings yield in Figure 17.1 in the 1970s can be attributed to the sharp rise in the rate of inflation during that period.[17]

However, a more important fact is that the yield to maturity on Treasury bonds is a nominal rate that embodies the inflation expectations of market participants. The earnings yield on common stocks, on the other hand, is a real yield. Thus, if stocks are inflation neutral, the difference between the earnings yield on stocks and the yield to maturity on Treasury bonds will reflect both the risk premium on stocks and the expected long-run inflation rate. This implies that when the expected rate of inflation is low the earnings yield on stocks should exceed the yield to maturity on bonds, and when the expected rate of inflation is high the reverse should be true.

For example, suppose that in the absence of inflation the earnings yield on stocks is 9% per year and the yield to maturity on bonds 3% per year, implying an equity risk premium of 6% per year. As you can see in Figure 17.1, this appeared to be the case in the 1960s. Now suppose the expected rate of inflation is 8% per year. If stocks are inflation neutral, the earnings yield will still be 9%. (If, as some have suggested, stocks are perceived to be riskier when the inflation rate rises, then the earnings yield will be higher.) But the yield to maturity on bonds, since it is a nominal rate, will jump to 11% per year. Thus the yield to maturity on bonds will exceed the earnings yield on stocks by 2% per year, the difference between the expected rate of inflation (8% per year) and the equity risk premium (6% per year). These hypothetical relationships are summarized in Table 17.3.

Something like this appears to be what actually happened in the late 1970s and 1980s. Of course, other things that might have affected stock and bond yields were happening during this period as well. Perhaps the most important were changes in the relative risk of stocks and bonds. Long-term bonds, in particular, became much riskier during this period as a result of changes in Federal Reserve monetary policy and the variability in the inflation rate.

---

[17]Franco Modigliani, Richard Cohn, claim that for the S&P 500 stocks as a whole the reported earnings may not be all that distorted during this period because the upward bias induced by historic cost depreciation and FIFO inventory accounting was offset by the downward bias caused by understatement of the real interest expense on the debt. This is discussed further in Chapter 18. See Modigliani, Franco, and Cohn, Richard, "Inflation, Rational Valuation, and the Market," *Financial Analysts Journal*, March-April 1979.

FIGURE 17.2
Risk premiums, 1974
to 1987.

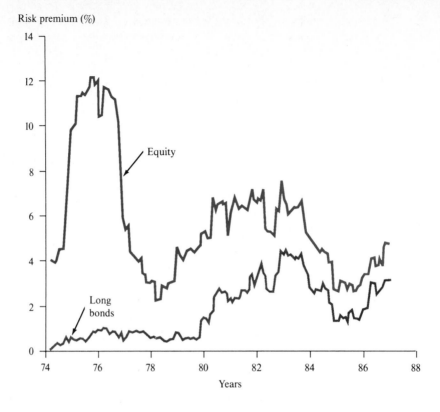

TABLE 17.3   Effect of Inflation on Stock and Bond Yields

Rate of Inflation	Earnings Yield on Stocks	Yield to Maturity on Bonds
0	9% per year	3% per year
8% per year	9% per year	11% per year

Figure 17.2 shows what the capital asset pricing model would have predicted the risk premiums on stocks and bonds to be during the period 1974 to 1987. These risk premiums were generated by asking what set of expected returns were necessary to make the demand for each asset class equal to the supply, given the observed set of variances and covariances during the previous 24 months. Although these are expected 1-month holding period returns and not yields to maturity, they do indicate the direction of change.[18]

---

[18]For a more complete explanation of the methodology used in deriving Figure 17.2, see Bodie, Zvi, Kane, Alex, and McDonald, Robert, "Why Haven't Nominal Rates Declined?" *Financial Analysts Journal,* March/April 1984. Updating of the figure was provided by Michael Rouse.

TABLE 17.4   S&P 500 Price Targets Under Various Scenarios

	9-12 Month Target	Other Interest Rate Possibilities		"The Bull Scenario"
U.S. T-bond interest rate*	9¾%	9¼%	8¾%	8%
P/E ratio	11.5×†	12.1×	12.9×	14.3×
EPS (midpiont of 1988 and 1989 est.)	$21.50	$21.50	$21.50	$24.00
S&P price target 1 year out	247	260	277	343

Modified from Gillard, William J., "The Investment Environment and Portfolio Strategy," June 1988, Kidder, Peabody Investment Policy Group.
*Forecast year-end 30-year Treasury bond.
†Assumes an S&P 500 earnings yield 100 basis points below the bond yield. Our reasoning is that, even though the earnings yield exceeded the bond yield for most of the post-World War II era, the earnings yield has been below the bond yield for most of the recent period, beginning with the high-inflation era and extending into the current time. We believe one of the explanations for this current relationship is the abundant liquidity that is buoying the market. In recognition of the market's willingness to accept a lower earnings yield, we assume an 8.7% earnings yield, which implies a P/E of 11.5×. Other tests validate this type of number.

Forecasting the Stock Market

What can we learn from all of this about the future rate of return on stocks? First, a note of optimism. Although timing the stock market is a very difficult and risky game, it is not impossible.

In the early 1980s several serious scholars of the stock market were predicting that as the rate of inflation came down the stock market would do extraordinarily well. For example, in the fourth edition of his classic book, *A Random Walk Down Wall Street,* Malkiel[19] predicted a compound rate of return of 17% per year during the decade of the 1980s. In fact, the average compound rate of return on the S&P 500 during the 5-year period 1982 to 1987 was 17% per year.

In addition, by the summer of 1987, on the eve of the October 1987 stock market crash, many market analysts were warning that the market was seriously overvalued. The ensuing debacle is now history.

However, if market history teaches us anything at all, it is that the market has great variability. In the language of statistics, the standard deviation is quite large. Thus, although we can use a variety of methods to derive a best point forecast of the expected holding period return on the market, the standard error of that forecast will always be high.

The most popular approach to forecasting the stock market is the earnings multiplier approach applied at the aggregate level. The first step is to forecast corporate profits for the coming period (either a quarter or a full year). Then an estimate of the earnings multiplier is derived based on a forecast of long-term interest rates. The product of the two forecasts is the point forecast of the end-of-period level of the market. Table 17.4 illustrates how the securities firm of Kidder Peabody does it.

Other analysts use an aggregate version of the discounted dividend model. All of

---

[19]Malkiel, Burton, *A Random Walk Down Wall Street,* ed. 4, New York: W.W. Norton Co., 1985.

these models rely heavily on forecasts of such macroeconomic variables as GNP, interest rates, and the rate of inflation, which are themselves very difficult to predict accurately.

An alternative approach is to extrapolate past rates of return on the stock market. The simplest version of this approach is to take as the forecast value of the expected HPR on the stock market the current Treasury bill rate plus the historical average risk premium on equity. This is the approach adopted by Ibbotson and Sinquefield.[20]

There are many variants of this approach. Perhaps the most innovative is a Bayesian approach proposed by Merton. Merton uses past data to estimate the expected HPR return on the stock market, but imposes the reasonable Bayesian "prior" that the risk premium can never be negative.[21]

17.8 *Contingent Claims Approach to Equity Valuation*

In recent years the theory of contingent claims pricing has been applied to common stocks.[22] This approach can be a useful adjunct to the valuation models presented earlier—especially the free cash flow model—if a firm has substantial debt in its capital structure. In this approach common stock is viewed as a call option on the assets of the firm, with an exercise price equal to the face value of the debt.

For example, suppose the Hidett Corporation has assets worth $100 million and debt with a face value of $100 million. Although the book value of the equity may be zero, the common stock may still have a substantial market value. The equity is a call option in the sense that if the shareholders pay off the debt at its face value at maturity, then they can keep the firm's assets; otherwise the assets will belong to the creditors.

Viewing the equity of Hidett Corporation as a call option on the assets of the firm gives considerable insight into the determinants of its value, as well as a well-known methodology for estimating it. A detailed exposition of the techniques used is contained in Part VI, but one insight is worth mentioning now.

How will the value of Hidett's common stock be affected if the riskiness of the firm's assets (as measured by the standard deviation of their market value) increases? The answer is that the value of the common stock will increase, just as the price of an option increases when the standard deviation of the underlying security increases.

Summary

1. This chapter has explored the basic models of common stock valuation. We have distinguished the intrinsic value of a stock, which is the analyst's best guess of

[20]See Ibbotson, R.G., and Sinquefield, R.A., *Stocks, Bonds, Bills and Inflation: The Past and the Future*, Financial Analysts Research Foundation, 1977.

[21]See Merton, Robert C., "On Estimating the Expected Return on the Market," *Journal of Financial Economics*, 8, 1980.

[22]See Mason, Scott, and Merton, Robert C., "The Role of Contingent Claims Analysis in Corporate Finance," in Altman and Subramanyam (editors), *Recent Advances in Corporate Finance*, Homewood, Ill.: Richard D. Irwin, Inc., 1985.

what the stock's price should be, from its actual market price, and we have explored the investment implications of a discrepancy between the two.

2. One approach to estimating intrinsic value is to focus on the firm's book value, either as it appears on the balance sheet or as adjusted to reflect current replacement cost of assets or liquidation value. Another approach is to focus on the present value of expected future dividends, earnings, or free cash flow.

3. We explained the assumptions behind discounted dividend models (DDM) in general and the constant growth rate model in particular. In the constant growth rate DDM, the intrinsic value of a share is equal to

$$V_0 = \frac{\text{Expected future dividends per share}}{\text{Market capitalization rate } - \text{Expected growth rate}}$$

and the growth rate of dividends is equal to the expected rate of price appreciation.

4. The expected growth rate of earnings is related both to the firm's expected profitability and to its dividend policy. The relationship can be expressed as

$$g = (\text{ROE on new investment}) \times (1 - \text{Dividend payout ratio})$$

5. The more realistic DDMs allow for several stages of earnings growth. Usually there is an initial stage of rapid growth, followed by a final stage of constant growth at a lower sustainable rate.

6. You can relate any DDM to a simple capitalized earnings model by comparing the expected ROE on future investments to the market capitalization rate, k. If the two rates are equal, then the stock's intrinsic value reduces to expected earnings per share (EPS) divided by k.

7. Many analysts form their estimate of a stock's value by multiplying their forecast of next year's EPS by a P/E multiple derived from some empirical rule. This rule can be consistent with some version of the DDM, although often it is not.

8. The free cash flow approach is the one used most often in corporate finance. The analyst first estimates the value of the entire firm as the present value of expected future free cash flows, assuming all-equity financing, then adds the value of tax shields arising from debt financing, and finally subtracts the value of all claims other than equity. This approach will be consistent with the DDM and capitalized earnings approaches as long as the capitalization rate is adjusted to reflect financial leverage.

9. We explored the effects of inflation on stock prices in the context of the constant growth DDM. Although traditional theory has been that inflation has a neutral effect on real stock returns, recent historical evidence shows a striking negative correlation between inflation and real stock market returns. There are four different explanations that may account for this negative correlation:
   a. Economic "shocks" that simultaneously produce higher inflation and lower real earnings
   b. Increased riskiness of stocks in a more inflationary environment
   c. Lower real after-tax earnings and dividends attributable to inflation-induced distortions in the tax system
   d. Money "illusion"

10. The models presented in this chapter can be used to explain and to forecast

the behavior of the aggregate stock market. The key macroeconomic variables that determine the level of stock prices in the aggregate are interest rates and corporate profits.

11. The modern theory of contingent claims pricing has been used to value common stocks by viewing them as a call option on the assets of the firm. This approach is especially useful for valuing the equity of highly leveraged firms, where the probability of default is significant.

Key Terms

Book value
Liquidation value
Replacement cost
Tobin's q
Intrinsic value
Market capitalization rate

Discounted dividend model
Constant growth model
Plowback ratio
Earnings retention ratio
Dividend payout ratio
Price/earnings multiple

Selected Readings

For the key issues in the recent debate about the rationality of the stock market see:
Merton, Robert C., "On the Current State of the Stock Market Rationality Hypothesis," in Dornbusch, Rudiger, Fischer, Stanley, and Bossons, John, (editors), *Macroeconomics and Finance, Essays in Honor of Franco Modigliani,* Cambridge, Mass.: MIT press, 1986.
Cutler, David M., Poterba, James M., and Summers, Lawrence H., "What Moves Stock Prices?" Cambridge, Mass.: National Bureau of Economic Research Working Paper No. 2538, March 1988.
West, Kenneth D., "Bubbles, Fads, and Stock Price Volatility Tests: A Partial Evaluation," Cambridge, Mass.: National Bureau of Economic Research Working Paper No. 2574, May 1988.

Problems

1. The P/E ratio of ITT Corporation is currently 6, while the P/E ratio of the S&P 500 is 10. How might you account for the difference?
2. According to the discounted dividend approach, the value of a firm's equity is the present value of expected future dividends. But according to many analysts, a firm's dividend policy does not affect the value of its equity. How can you reconcile these seemingly contradictory points of view?
3. Since the value of the firm increases with the growth rate of dividends, firms should increase the plowback ratio to a value of 1.0 in order to maximize g. Under what circumstances, if any, is this statement true?
4. The FI Corporation's dividends per share are expected to grow indefinitely by 5% per year.
   a. If this year's year-end dividend is $8 and the market capitalization rate is 10% per year, what must the current stock price be according to the DDM?
   b. If the expected earnings per share are $12, what is the implied value of the ROE on future investment opportunities?
   c. How much is the market paying per share for growth opportunities (that is,

for an ROE on future investments that exceeds the market capitalization rate)?

5. (This question is based on the 1987 CFA Examination, Level I). Using the data provided, discuss whether the common stock of United States Tobacco Company is attractively priced based on at least three different valuation approaches. (Hint: use the asset value, DDM, and earnings multiplier approaches.)

	U.S. Tobacco	S&P 500
Recent price	$27.00	290
Book value per share	$6.42	
Liquidation value per share	$4.90	
Replacement costs of assets per share	$9.15	
Anticipated next year's dividend	$1.20	$8.75
Estimated annual growth in dividends and earnings	10.%	7.0%
Required return	13.0%	
Estimated next year's EPS	$2.40	$16.50
P/E ratio based on next year's earnings	11.3	17.6
Dividend yield	4.4%	3.0%

6. The risk-free rate of return is 10%, the required rate of return on the market is 15%, and High-Flyer stock has a beta coefficient of 1.5.
   a. If the dividend per share expected during the coming year, D_1, is $2.50 and $g = 5\%$, at what price shoud a share sell?
   b. If it is selling at $18 per share, what is the expected HPR to a potential investor? (Assume first that the price converges to intrinsic value by the end of the holding period, and then assume that price never converges to intrinsic value.)

7. Your preliminary analysis of two stocks has yielded the information set forth below. The market capitalization rate for both stock A and stock B is 10% per year.

	Stock A	Stock B
Expected return on equity, (ROE)	14%	12%
Estimated earnings per share, $E(E_1)$	$2.00	$1.65
Estimated dividends per share, $E(D_1)$	$1.00	$1.00
Current market price per share, P_0	$27.00	$25.00

   a. What are the expected dividend payout ratios for the two stocks?
   b. What are the expected dividend growth rates for each?
   c. What is the intrinsic value of each stock?
   d. In which, if either, of the two stocks would you choose to invest?
   e. What is the expected 1-year HPR on each of the stocks if:
      i. The market prices grow at the same rate as dividends?
      ii. The market prices converge to their intrinsic values by the end of the year?

8. (This question is based on the 1988 CFA Examination, Level I.) The Tennant

Company, founded in 1870, has evolved into the leading producer of large-sized floor sweepers and scrubbers, which are ridden by their operators. Its latest dividend per share was $.96, its earnings per share were $1.85, and its ROE was 16.9%.

a. Based on these data, calculate a value for Tennant common stock by applying the constant growth dividend discount model. Assume that an investor's required rate of return is a five percentage point premium over the current risk-free rate of return of 7%.

b. To your disappointment, the calculation that you completed in part *a* results in a value below the stock's current market price. Consequently, you apply the constant growth DDM using the same required rate of return as in your calculation for part *a,* but using the company's stated goal of earning 20% per year on stockholders' equity and maintaining a 35% dividend payout ratio. However, you find that you are unable to calculate a meaningful answer. Explain why you cannot calculate a meaningful answer, and identify an alternative DDM that may provide a meaningful answer.

9. (This question is based on the 1986 CFA Examination, Level I.) You are a portfolio manager considering the purchase of Nucor common stock. Nucor is the preeminent "mini-mill" steel producer in the United States. Mini-mills use scrap steel as their raw material and product a limited number of products, primarily for the construction market. You are provided the following information:

Nucor Corporation

Stock price (Dec. 30, 1985)	$ 53.00
1985 Estimated earnings	$ 4.25
1985 Estimated book value	$ 25.00
Indicated dividend	$ 0.40
Beta	1.10
Risk-free return	7.0%
High grade corporate bond yield	9.0%
Risk premium—stocks over bonds	5.0%

a. Calculate the expected stock market return. Show your calculations.

b. Calculate the implied total return of Nucor stock.

c. Calculate the required return of Nucor stock using the security market line model.

d. Briefly discuss the attractiveness of Nucor based on these data.

10. The stock of Nogro Corporation is currently selling for $10 per share. Earnings per share in the coming year are expected to be $2. The company has a policy of paying out 50% of its earnings each year in dividends. The rest is retained and invested in projects that earn a 20% rate of return per year. This situation is expected to continue indefinitely.

a. Assuming the current market price of the stock reflects its intrinsic value as computed using the constant growth rate DDM, what rate of return do Nogro's investors require?

b. By how much does its value exceed what it would be if all earnings were paid as dividends and nothing were reinvested?

c. If Nogro were to cut its dividend payout ratio to 25%, what would happen to its stock price? What if Nogro eliminated the dividend altogether?

d. Suppose that Nogro wishes to maintain its current 50% dividend payout policy but that it also wishes to invest an amount each year equal to that year's total earnings. All the money would be invested in projects earning 20% per year. One way that Nogro could do so would be to issue an amount of new stock each year equal to one half that year's earnings. What do you think would be the effect of this policy on the current stock price?

11. The Digital Electronic Quotation System (DEQS) Corporation pays no cash dividends currently and is not expected to for the next 5 years. Its latest EPS was $10, all of which was reinvested in the company. The firm's expected ROE for the next 5 years is 20% per year, and during this time it is expected to continue to reinvest all of its earnings. Starting 6 years from now the firm's ROE on new investments is expected to fall to 15%, and the company is expected to start paying out 40% of its earnings in cash dividends, which it will continue to do forever after. DEQS' market capitalization rate is 15% per year.

a. What is your estimate of DEQS' intrinsic value per share?

b. Assuming its current market price is equal to its intrinsic value, what do you expect to happen to its price over the next year? The year after?

c. What effect would it have on your estimate of DEQS' intrinsic value if you expected DEQS to pay out only 20% of earnings starting in year 6?

12. Microhard, Inc., is a computer hardware company that has been growing rapidly in recent years. You are an analyst who thinks that over the next 10 years its dividend growth rate will go from 20% per year to a long-run constant rate of 4% per year. The latest dividend per share was $3, and you think the appropriate capitalization rate is 15% per year.

a. What is your estimate of Microhard's intrinsic value per share?

b. If its current market price is $40 per share, what is the expected yield to maturity?

c. If all expectations are realized, and Microhard's stock price moves to its new intrinsic value, what should its price be 1 year from now?

13. The Duo Growth Company just paid a dividend of $1 per share. The dividend is expected to grow at a rate of 25% per year for the next 3 years and then to level off to 5% per year forever. You think the appropriate market capitalization rate is 20% per year.

a. What is your estimate of the intrinsic value of a share of the stock?

b. If the market price of a share is equal to this intrinsic value, what is the expected dividend yield?

c. What do you expect its price to be 1 year from now? Is the implied capital gain consistent with your estimate of the dividend yield and the market capitalization rate?

14. The risk-free rate of return is 8%, the expected rate of return on the market portfolio is 15%, and the stock of Xyrong Corporation has a beta coefficient of 1.2.

Xyrong pays out 40% of its earnings in dividends, and the latest earnings announced were $10 per share. Dividends were just paid and are expected to be paid annually. You expect that Xyrong will earn an ROE of 20% per year on all reinvested earnings forever.

    a. What is the intrinsic value of a share of Xyrong stock?

    b. If the market price of a share is currently $100, and you expect the market price to be equal to the intrinsic value 1 year from now, what is your expected 1-year holding period return on Xyrong stock?

15. You are a different analyst trying to evaluate Xyrong stock. You agree with the previous analyst's assessments of everything except Xyrong's future earnings and dividends. You decide to apply the H model, and you assume that the growth rate of dividends will start at 12% per year and decline linearly to a long-run rate of 4% per year over the next 20 years.

    a. What is your assessment of the intrinsic value of a share of Xyrong stock?

    b. If the current market price of Xyrong stock is $100 per share, what is your estimate of the yield to maturity?

    c. If you expect the market price to be equal to the intrinsic value 1 year from now what is your expected 1-year holding period return on Xyrong stock?

16. The Generic Genetic (GG) Corporation pays no cash dividends currently and is not expected to for the next 4 years. Its latest EPS was $5, all of which was reinvested in the company. The firm's expected ROE for the next 4 years is 20% per year, during which time it is expected to continue to reinvest all of its earnings. Starting 5 years from now, the firm's ROE on new investments is expected to fall to 15% per year. GG's market capitalization rate is 15% per year.

    a. What is your estimate of GG's intrinsic value per share?

    b. Assuming its current market price is equal to its intrinsic value, what do you expect to happen to its price over the next year?

17. The MoMi Corporation's cash flow from operations before interest and taxes was $2 million in the year just ended, and it expects that this will grow by 5% per year forever. To make this happen, the firm will have to invest an amount equal to 20% of pretax cash flow each year. The tax rate is 34%. Depreciation was $200,000 in the year just ended and is expected to grow at the same rate as the operating cash flow. The appropriate market capitalization rate for the unleveraged cash flow is 12% per year, and the firm currently has debt of $4 million outstanding. Use the free cash flow approach to value the firm's equity.

18. The CPI Corporation is expected to pay a real dividend of $1 per share this year. Its expected growth rate of real dividends is 4% per year, and its current market price per share is $20.

    a. Assuming the constant growth DDM is applicable, what must be the real market capitalization rate for CPI?

    b. If the expected rate of inflation is 6% per year, what must be the nominal capitalization rate, the nominal dividend yield, and the growth rate of nominal dividends?

    c. If the expected real earnings per share are $1.80, what would be your estimate of intrinsic value if you used a simple capitalized earnings model?

d. If you inflated the above estimate of EPS using the 6% per year inflation rate and discounted it using the nominal capitalization rate, what estimate of intrinsic value would you get? What conclusion can you draw about adjusting the simple capitalized earnings model for inflation?

19. (This question is based on the 1986 CFA examination, Level II.) You are Paul R. Overlook, CFA, and investment advisor for a large endowment fund. You have recently read about a basic valuation model that values an asset according to the present value of the asset's expected cash flows. You now are using this valuation framework to explain to the fund's trustees how inflation affects the rates of return on stocks. After your presentation, the trustees ask the following:

a. "If common stocks are attractive for hedging inflation, why did stocks perform so poorly in the 1970s when the inflation rate was increasing?"

b. "If stocks are attractive inflation hedges, it seems that stock prices should rise the most when inflation increases. Why then did stock prices appreciate so much from 1982 to 1986 when the inflation rate was declining?"

Explain your response to each of these questions in the context of the valuation model you have just read about.

20. You are trying to forecast the expected return on the aggregate stock market for the next year. Suppose the current 1-year Treasury bill rate is 8%, the yield to maturity on 20-year Treasury bonds is 9% per year, the expected rate of inflation is 5% per year, and the expected EPS for the S&P 500 is $30. What is your forecast and why?

CHAPTER 18

Fundamental Analysis

In this chapter we show how analysts use financial data as inputs into equity valuation models. The basic question is, what can we learn from a company's accounting data that can help us to estimate the intrinsic value of its common stock?

We start by examining how the "bottom line" earnings figure, as reported by accountants following generally accepted accounting principles (GAAP), relates to the theoretical concept of earnings that security analysts use in their valuation models. After pointing out some of the problems associated with relying on accounting earnings, we show how analysts use financial ratios to explore the sources of a firm's profitability and evaluate the "quality" of its earnings in a systematic fashion. Finally, we conclude with a discussion of the limitations of financial statement analysis as a tool in uncovering mispriced securities.

18.1 *What Are Earnings?*

Accounting Earnings vs. Economic Earnings

Let us start by defining earnings in a manner that is consistent with security valuation models used in the financial community. As is usual in the language of finance, we will use the terms "income" and "profit" synonymously with earnings. Recall the simple constant growth rate DDM:

$$V_0 = E(D_1)/(k - g) = E(E_1) \times (1 - b)/(k - g)$$

and

$$g = b \times \text{ROE}$$

In this model, earnings must be interpreted as the expected sustainable cash flow from the firm's existing assets, assuming no new *net* investment. Zero net investment implies that the firm's total, or gross, investment is enough to maintain only a constant real cash flow with zero growth.

We will continue to use asterisks to denote real value of variables, and we find that for the zero net plowback case, the value of the firm's equity is the present value of $E(E_1^*)$ per year in perpetuity, or

$$V_0 = \frac{E(E_1^*)}{k^*}$$

In other words $E(E_1^*)$ is the *real* flow of cash that the firm could pay forever to current shareholders as dividends without any change—either expansion or contraction—in the productive capacity of the firm. We will refer to this definition of earnings as **economic earnings.**

Accounting earnings are what we see on a firm's income statement. How closely do accounting earnings as reported in financial statements approximate economic earnings? The answer depends on how closely generally accepted accounting principles approximate the judgments that security analysts would make regarding the past and future productivity and profitability of the firm's assets.[1]

Depreciation

A key factor in computing true earnings is the measurement of depreciation. The accounting and economic measures of depreciation can differ markedly. According to the *economic* definition, depreciation is the amount of a firm's operating cash flow that must be reinvested in the firm to sustain its real cash flow at the current level.

The *accounting* measurement is quite different. Accounting depreciation is the amount of the original acquisition cost of an asset that is allocated to each accounting period over an arbitrarily specified life of the asset.

Assume, for example, that a firm buys machines with a useful economic life of 20 years at $100,000 apiece. In its financial statements, however, the firm can depreciate the machines over 10 years using the straight-line method, for $10,000 per year in depreciation. Thus after 10 years a machine will be fully depreciated on the books, even though it remains a productive asset that will not need replacement for another 10 years.

In computing accounting earnings this firm will overestimate depreciation in the first 10 years of the machine's economic life and underestimate it in the last 10 years. This will cause reported earnings to be understated compared with economic earnings in the first 10 years and overstated in the last 10 years.[2]

If the management of the firm had a zero plowback policy and distributed as cash dividends only its accounting earnings, it would pay out too little in the first 10 years relative to the sustainable cash flow. Similarly, a security analyst who relied on the (unadjusted) reported earnings figure during the first few years would see understated economic earnings and therefore would underestimate the firm's intrinsic value.

---

[1] In "The Trouble with Earnings," *Financial Analysts Journal,* September-October 1972, Jack Treynor points out some important difficulties with the accounting concept of earnings. In particular he argues that the trouble stems from accountants' attempt to measure the value of assets.

[2] Inflation usually makes the discrepancy between accounting and economic earnings even greater, an issue we treat later in this chapter.

18.2 Earnings and Stock Prices

Earnings Announcements and Stock Price Behavior

Despite some drawbacks in accounting conventions, accountants' net income figures do in fact convey considerable information concerning a firm's prospects. Evidence lies in the fact that stock prices tend to increase when firms announce earnings greater than market analysts or investors had anticipated. We can cite several studies to this effect.

In one study, Niederhoffer and Regan formed three groups of stock: the 50 stocks with the greatest price increases in 1970, the 50 with the greatest price decreases, and 50 randomly selected stocks.[3] In the worst-performing group earnings declined by 83% (compared with analysts' forecasts of a 15.3% *increase*), whereas in the best-performing group, earnings increased 21.4% (the analysts forecast a 7.7% increase). The implication is that deviation of actual earnings from projected earnings is the driving force behind abnormal stock returns.

In a more recent study Foster, Olsen, and Shevlin used time series of earnings for many firms to forecast the coming quarter's earnings announcement.[4] They estimated the following equation for more than 2,000 firms between 1974 and 1981:

$$E_{i,t} = E_{i,t-4} + a_i(E_{i,t-1} - E_{i,t-5}) + g_i$$

where

$E_{i,t}$ = Earnings of firm i in quarter t

a_i = Adjustment factor for firm i

g_i = Growth factor for firm i

The rationale is that this quarter's earnings, $E_{i,t}$, will equal last year's earnings for the same quarter, $E_{i,t-4}$, plus a factor representing recent above-trend earnings performance as measured by the difference between last quarter's earnings and the corresponding quarter's earnings a year earlier, plus another factor that represents steady earnings growth over time. Regression techniques are used to estimate a_i and g_i. Given these estimates, the equation is used together with past earnings to forecast future earnings.

Now it is easy to determine earnings surprises. Simply take the difference between actual earnings and forecasted or expected earnings, and see whether earnings surprises correlate with subsequent stock price movements.

Before doing so, however, these researchers introduced an extra refinement (first suggested by Latane and Jones) to their procedure.[5] Instead of using the earnings forecast error itself as the variable of interest, they first divided the forecast errors for

[3]Niederhoffer, Victor, and Regan, Patrick, "Earnings Changes, Analysts' Forecasts, and Stock Prices," *Financial Analysts' Journal,* May/June 1972.

[4]Foster, George, Olsen, Chris, and Shevlin, Terry, "Earnings Releases, Anomalies, and the Behavior of Security Returns," *The Accounting Review,* 59:4, October 1984.

[5]Latane, H.A., and Jones, C.P., "Standardized Unexpected Earnings—1971-1977," *Journal of Finance,* June 1979.

FIGURE 18.1

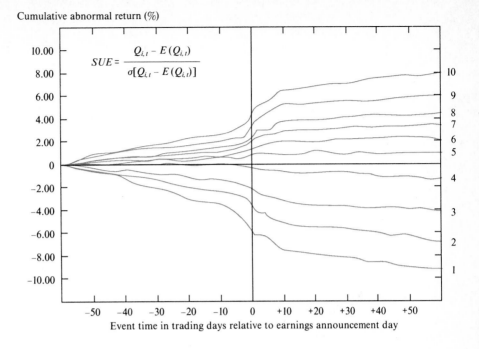

Cumulative abnormal return (%)

$$SUE = \frac{Q_{i,t} - E(Q_{i,t})}{\sigma[Q_{i,t} - E(Q_{i,t})]}$$

Event time in trading days relative to earnings announcement day

each period by the standard deviation of forecast errors calculated from earlier periods; they effectively deflated the error in a particular quarter by a measure of the typical error in an average quarter. This has the effect of discounting forecast errors for firms with historically very unpredictable earnings. For such firms a large error might not be as significant as for a firm with typically very predictable earnings. The resulting "normalized" forecast error commonly is called the "standardized unexpected earnings" (SUE) measure. SUE is the variable that was correlated with stock price movements.

Each earnings announcement was placed in one of 10 deciles ranked by the magnitude of SUE, and the abnormal returns of the stock in each decile were calculated. Figure 18.1 is a graph of the cumulative abnormal returns.

The results of this study are dramatic. The correlation between SUE ranking and abnormal returns across deciles is perfect. There is a large abnormal return (a large increase in cumulative abnormal return) on the earnings announcement day (time 0). The abnormal return is positive for high-SUE and negative for low-SUE (actually negative-SUE) firms.

The more remarkable, and disturbing, result of the study concerns stock price movements *after* the announcement date. The cumulative abnormal returns of high-SUE stocks continue to grow even after the earnings information becomes public, whereas the low-SUE firms continue to suffer negative abnormal returns. The market would appear to adjust to the earnings information only gradually, resulting in a sustained period of abnormal returns.

It appears that one could earn abnormal profits simply by waiting for earnings announcements and purchasing a stock portfolio of high-SUE companies. These are precisely the types of predictable continuing trends that ought to be impossible in an efficient market.

This finding is not unique. Many earnings announcement studies have found similar results. This phenomenon remains a puzzle for future research.

You might wonder whether security analysts can predict earnings more accurately than mechanical time series equations. After all, analysts have access to these statistical equations and to other qualitative and quantitative data. The evidence seems to be that analysts in fact do outperform such mechanical forecasts.

Brown and Rozeff[6] compared earnings forecasts from the *Value Line Investment Survey* with those made using a sophisticated statistical technique called a Box-Jenkins model. The Value Line forecasts generally were more accurate. Whereas 54% of the Box-Jenkins forecasts were within 25% of the realized values, and 26.5% were within 10%, 63.5% of the Value Line forecasts were within 25% and 23% were within 10%. Apparently, the qualitative data and firm-specific fundamental analysis that analysts bring to bear are of value.

The Value Line Ranking System

The Value Line ranking system may be the most celebrated and well-documented example of successful fundamental analysis. Value Line is the largest investment advisory service in the world. Besides publishing the *Value Line Investment Survey,* which provides information on investment fundamentals for approximately 1,700 publicly traded companies, Value Line also ranks each of these stocks according to their anticipated price appreciation over the next 12 months. Stocks ranked in group I are expected to perform the best, whereas those in group V are expected to perform the worst. Value Line calls this "ranking for timeliness."

Figure 18.2 shows the performance of the Value Line ranking system over the 20-year period from 1965 to 1985. Over the total time period the different groups performed just as the rankings would predict, and the differences were quite large. The total 20-year price appreciation for the group I stocks was 1,386% (or 14.4% per year) vs. 28% (or 1.2% per year) for group V.

How does the Value Line ranking system work? As Bernhard[7] explains it, the ranking procedure has three components: (1) relative earnings momentum, (2) earnings surprise, and (3) a value index. Points assigned for each factor determine the stock's overall ranking.

The relative earnings momentum factor comes from each company's year-to-year change in quarterly earnings divided by the average change for all stocks. Stocks

[6]Brown, Lawrence D., and Rozeff, Michael, " The Superiority of Analysts' Forecasts as Measures of Expectations: Evidence from Earnings," *Journal of Finance,* March 1978.
[7]See Bernhard, Arnold, *Value Line Methods of Evaluating Common Stocks,* New York: Arnold Bernhard and Co., 1979.

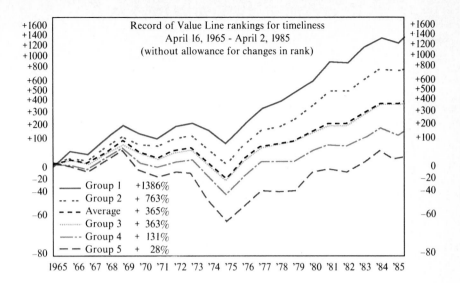

Record of Value Line rankings for timeliness
April 16, 1965 - April 2, 1985
(without allowance for changes in rank)

Group 1	+1386%
Group 2	+ 763%
Average	+ 365%
Group 3	+ 363%
Group 4	+ 131%
Group 5	+ 28%

1965 '66 '67 '68 '69 '70 '71 '72 '73 '74 '75 '76 '77 '78 '79 '80 '81 '82 '83 '84 '85

ranking in the top third of all companies score 1,200 points, the middle third 800 points, and the bottom third 400 points.

The earnings surprise factor has to do with the difference between actual reported quarterly earnings and Value Line's estimate. The points assigned to each stock increase with the percentage difference between reported and estimated earnings.

The value index is calculated from the following regression equation:

$$V = a + b_1 x_1 + b_2 x_2 + b_3 x_3$$

where

x_1 = A score from 1 to 10 depending on the relative earnings momentum ranking, compared with the company's rank for the last 10 years

x_2 = A score from 1 to 10 based on the stock's relative price, with ratios calculated in a similar way to the earnings ratio

x_3 = The ratio of the stock's latest 10-week average relative price (stock price divided by the average price for all stocks) to its 52-week average relative price

and a, b_1, b_2, and b_3 are the coefficients from the regression estimated on 12 years of data.

Each company scores a number of points from 1 to 1,700 for the V value. The last step is to add the points for each of the three factors, and the stocks are classified into five groups according to the total score.

Investing in stocks according to this system does seem to produce superior results on paper, but as the accompanying box points out, in practice Value Line's own mutual funds have not even kept up with the market averages.

Paying the Piper

**On Paper, Value Line's Performance in Picking Stocks Is Nothing Short of Dazzling
. . . for an Investor to Capitalize on That Performance Is a Different Matter**

Value Line, Inc., publishes the *Value Line Investment Survey,* that handy review of 1,652 companies. Each week the survey rates stocks from I (best buys) to V (worst). Can you beat the market following these rankings? Value Line tracks the performance of Group I from April 1965, when a new ranking formula went into effect. If you bought Group I then and updated your list every week, you would have a gain of 15,391% by June 30. That means $10,000 would have grown to about $1.5 million, dividends excluded. The market is up only 245% since 1965, dividends excluded.

Quite an impressive record. There is only one flaw: It ignores transaction costs. Do transaction costs much matter against a performance like that? What does the investor lose in transaction costs? A percentage point a year? Two percent?

None other than Value Line provides an answer to this question, and the answer is almost as startling as the paper performance. Since late 1983 Value Line has run a mutual fund that attempts to track Group I precisely. Its return has averaged a dismal 11 percentage points a year worse than the hypothetical results in Group I. The fund hasn't even kept up with the market *(see chart).*

What went wrong? "Inefficiencies and costs of implementation," says Mark Tavel, manager of the fund, Value Line Centurion.

This is not to denigrate Value Line's undeniably impressive stock-picking record. Far from it: One of the funds run for Value Line by Tavel, Leveraged Growth Investors, shines on Forbes' mutual fund honor roll. (Leveraged Growth and the flagship Value Line Fund use the ranking system, but not as closely as Centurion.)

The point here is to illustrate the folly of constant trading. It's a familiar story, but one that investors are prone to forget in the middle of a bull market. It costs money to run the racetrack, and the fellow who steps up to the betting window pays. Wall Street's revenues top $50 billion a year. People who trade pay the bill, and people who try to beat the market with a lot of trading pay dearly.

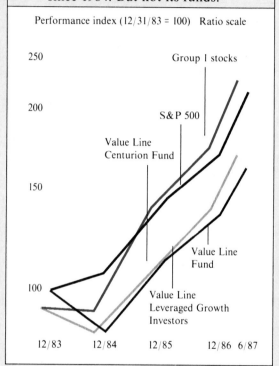

Paper profits

Value Line's hypothetical Group 1 has beaten the market since 1984. But not its funds.

Performance index (12/31/83 = 100) Ratio scale

Group I stocks
S&P 500
Value Line Centurion Fund
Value Line Fund
Value Line Leveraged Growth Investors

250
200
150
100

12/83   12/84   12/85   12/86 6/87

The Value Line Centurion Fund's turnover is 200% a year. That's quite a bit of turnover—although by no means the highest in the business. The turnover is high because in a typical week, 4 of the 100 Group I stocks drop down in rank and have to be replaced with new Group I stocks. It's not impossible for traders like Centurion to beat the market, but they start out with a handicap.

All of which means that paper performance can be pretty fanciful. "Anytime hypothetical returns are offered as proof of a particular investing style, one should also swallow a large grain of salt," says Cam Schmidt of Potomac Investment Management, a money manager in Bethesda, Md. that brought the Value Line discrepancy to *Forbes'* attention.

What are these inefficiencies and costs? And what do they tell investors about the perils of in-and-out trading?

Fund overhead is not a big item. At the $244 million Centurion, which is available only through variable life and annuity policies sold by Guardian Life, the annual expense ratio averages 0.6%. Nor are brokerage commissions large. Funneled at about 5 cents a share mostly to a captive Value Line broker, commissions eat up 0.4% of Centurion's assets per year.

So far we have 1%. Where's the other 10% of the shortfall? Bid-ask spreads, for one. A stock quoted at 39 to sellers might cost a buyer 39½—or even 41 or 42 if the buyer wants a lot of it. With about 95 of the 100 Group I stocks at any given time in the Centurion portfolio, Tavel needs to amass an average $2.5 million position in each. Some of these companies have $150 million or less in outstanding shares. The very smallest Tavel doesn't even try to buy.

Timing explains some of the gulf between hypothetical and actual results. The hypothetical performance assumes a purchase at the Wednesday close before publication of the new rankings. Most subscribers get their surveys on Friday morning, however, and buy at the Friday opening—if they are lucky. An internal Value Line rule forbids the funds to act on rank changes before Friday morning.

Why, then, are Wednesday prices used in the performance claims? Because, says Samuel Eisenstadt, Value Line's chief of statistics, until recently that was all Value Line had in its database. Wednesday prices were gathered because it takes nine days to compute, print and mail the results. The hypothetical buy, then, would come a week after the closing prices used to calculate the rankings, and a day and a half before a real buyer could act on the advice. Eisenstadt says a conversion to Friday night scoring is under way, and will no doubt depress reported performance.

A day makes all the difference. A 1985 study by Scott Stickel, now an assistant professor at Wharton, showed that almost all of the excess return on a Group I stock is concentrated on three days, almost evenly divided: the Friday when subscribers read about the

stock's being promoted into Group I, the Thursday before and the Monday following. Wait until Tuesday to buy and you might as well not subscribe.

Why are prices moving up on Thursday, the day before publication? Eisenstadt suspects the Postal Service of acting with uncharacteristic efficiency in some parts of the country, giving a few subscribers an early start. Another reason for an uptick: Enough is known about the Value Line formula for smart investors to anticipate a rank change by a few days. The trick is to watch Group II (near-top) stocks closely. If a quarterly earnings report comes in far better than the forecast published in *Value Line,* grab the stock. "What happens if you're wrong? You're stuck with a Group II stock with terrific earnings," says Eisenstadt.

Come Friday at 9:30 a.m., the throng is at the starting gate. Tavel says he often gets only a small portion of his position established before the price starts to run away from him. How are the individual investors faring? Probably no better. True, a 200-share order is not by itself going to move the market the way Tavel's 20,000-share order will. But if both orders arrive at the opening bell, the small investor is in no position to get a good price. Individuals aren't paying the fund overhead, but then they pay higher commissions than Tavel.

What of the future? Value Line's magic was built on its computer-quick response to favorable earnings reports. Now computers are nothing special. Significantly, they're becoming a lot more common among individual investors, the people who buy the small-cap stocks where the ranking system has shown its strength. Eisenstadt concedes: "Everyone's playing this earnings surprise game now." But he insists that there's no firm evidence yet that the ranking system is falling apart.

Even if the ranking system loses some of its effectiveness, however, it would be premature to write off Value Line, which trades over-the-counter near 27. Many of the survey's 120,000 subscribers pay $495 a year just to get the detailed financial histories of the companies in it. Indeed, considering that subscriptions are on the upswing and that it costs maybe $50 to print and mail one, favorable earnings surprises may be in store. If you don't like the horses, buy stock in the track.

TABLE 18.1   Nodett's Profitability Over the Business Cycle

Scenario	Sales ($ Millions)	EBIT ($ Millions)	ROA (% per Year)	Net Profit ($ Millions)	ROE (% per Year)
Bad year	80	5	5	3	3
Normal year	100	10	10	6	6
Good year	120	15	15	9	9

18.3   *Return on Equity*

Past vs. Future ROE

We noted in Chapter 17 that **return on equity** (ROE) is one of the two basic factors in determining a firm's growth rate of earnings. There are two sides to using ROE. Sometimes it is reasonable to assume that future ROE will approximate its past value, but a high ROE in the past does not necessarily imply that a firm's future ROE will be high.

A declining ROE, on the other hand, is evidence that the firm's new investments have offered a lower ROE than its past investments. The best forecast of future ROE in this case may be lower than the most recent ROE. The vital point is not to blindly accept historical values as indicators of future values. Data from the recent past may in fact provide information regarding future performance, but the analyst should always keep an eye on the future. It is expectations of future dividends and earnings that determine the intrinsic value of the company's stock.

Financial Leverage and ROE

An analyst interpreting the past behavior of a firm's ROE or forecasting its future value must pay careful attention to the firm's debt-equity mix and to the interest rate on its debt. An example will show why. Suppose that Nodett is a firm that is all-equity financed and has total assets of $100 million. Assume it pays corporate taxes at the rate of 40% of taxable earnings.

Table 18.1 shows the behavior of sales, earnings before interest and taxes, and net profits under three scenarios representing phases of the business cycle. It also shows the behavior of two of the most commonly used profitability measures: **return on assets** (ROA), which equals EBIT/assets, and ROE, which equals net profits/equity.

Somdett is an otherwise identical firm to Nodett, but $40 million of its $100 million of assets are financed with debt bearing an interest rate of 8%. It pays annual interest expense of $3.2 million. Table 18.2 shows how Somdett's ROE differs from Nodett's.

Note that annual sales, EBIT, and ROE for both firms will be the same in each of the three scenarios. Note also that, although Nodett and Somdett have the same ROA in each scenario, Somdett's ROE exceeds that of Nodett in normal and good years and is lower in bad years.

TABLE 18.2 Impact of Financial Leverage on ROE

		Nodett		Somdett	
Scenario	EBIT ($ Millions)	Net Profits ($ Millions)	ROE (%)	Net Profits* ($ Millions)	ROE† (%)
Bad year	5	3	3	1.08	1.8
Normal year	10	6	6	4.08	6.8
Good year	15	9	9	7.08	11.8

*Somdett's after-tax profits are given by .6(EBIT − $3.2 million)
†Somdett's equity is only $60 million.

We can summarize the exact relationship between ROE, ROA and leverage in the following equation[8]:

$$ROE = (1 - \text{Tax rate})\left[ROA + (ROA - \text{Interest rate})\frac{\text{Debt}}{\text{Equity}}\right] \quad (18.1)$$

The relationship has the following implications. If there is no debt or if the firm's ROA equals the interest rate on its debt, its ROE will simply equal (1 minus the tax rate) times ROA. If its ROA exceeds the interest rate, then its ROE will exceed (1 minus the tax rate) times ROA by an amount that will be greater the higher the debt-to-equity ratio.

This result makes intuitive sense: if ROA exceeds the borrowing rate, the firm earns more on its money than it pays out to creditors. The surplus earnings are therefore available to the firm's owners, the equityholders, which raises ROE. If, on the other hand, ROA is less than the interest rate, then ROE will decline by an amount that depends on the debt-to-equity ratio.

To illustrate the application of equation 18.1, we can use the numerical example in Table 18.2. In a normal year Nodett has an ROE of 6%, which is .6 (1 minus the tax rate) times its ROA of 10%. However, Somdett, which borrows at an interest rate

---

[8]The derivation of equation 18.1 is as follows:

$$ROE = \frac{\text{Net profit}}{\text{Equity}}$$

$$= \frac{EBIT - \text{Interest} - \text{Taxes}}{\text{Equity}}$$

$$= \frac{(1 - \text{Tax rate})(EBIT - \text{Interest})}{\text{Equity}}$$

$$= (1 - \text{Tax rate})\frac{(ROA \times \text{Assets} - \text{Interest rate} \times \text{Debt})}{\text{Equity}}$$

$$= (1 - \text{Tax rate})\left[ROA \times \frac{(\text{Equity} + \text{Debt})}{\text{Equity}} - \text{Interest Rate} \times \frac{\text{Debt}}{\text{Equity}}\right]$$

$$= (1 - \text{Tax rate})\left[ROA + (ROA - \text{Interest rate})\frac{\text{Debt}}{\text{Equity}}\right]$$

of 8% and maintains a debt/equity ratio of ⅔, has an ROE of 6.8%. The calculation using equation 18.1 is

$$ROE = .6[10\% + (10\% - 8\%)⅔]$$
$$= .6[10\% + ⅓\%]$$
$$= 6.8\%$$

The important point to remember is that increased debt will make a positive contribution to a firm's ROE only if the firm's ROA exceeds the interest rate on the debt.

Note also that financial leverage increases the risk of the equityholder returns. Table 18.2 shows that ROE on Somdett is worse than that of Nodett in bad years. Conversely, in good years Somdett outperforms Nodett because the excess of ROA over ROE provides additional funds for equityholders. The presence of debt makes Somdett more sensitive to the business cycle than Nodett.

Even if financial leverage increases the expected ROE of Somdett relative to Nodett (as it seems to in Table 18.2), this does not imply that the market value of Somdett's equity will be higher.[9] Financial leverage increases the risk of the firm's equity as surely as it raises the expected ROE.

In the context of the constant growth rate discounted dividend model, $V_0 = (1 - b)E(E_1)/(k - g)$, high leverage might increase $E(E_1)$ and g, which tends to increase value per share, but it also increases k, which reduces value per share. The net effect of leverage thus can be either positive or negative.

Concept Check

Question 1. Mordett is a company with the same assets as Nodett and Somdett, but a debt-to-equity ratio of 1.0 and an interest rate of 9%. What would its net profit and ROE be in a bad year, a normal year, and a good year?

18.4 Ratio Analysis

Decomposition of ROE

In order to understand the factors affecting a firm's ROE, including its trend over time and its performance relative to competitors, analysts often "decompose" ROE into the product of a series of ratios.[10] Each component ratio is in itself meaningful, and the process serves to focus the analyst's attention on the separate factors influencing performance.

---

[9]This is the essence of the debate on the Modigliani-Miller theorems regarding the effect of financial leverage on the value of the firm. For a discussion of the issues and evidence, see footnotes 9 and 10 in Chapter 17.
[10]This kind of decomposition of ROE is often called the Dupont system.

TABLE 18.3 Ratio Decomposition Analysis for Nodett and Somdett

	ROE	(1) Net Profit / Pretax Profit	(2) Pretax Profit / EBIT	(3) EBIT / Sales (ROS)	(4) Sales / Assets (ATO)	(5) Assets / Equity	(6) Compound Leverage Factor (2) × (5)
Bad year							
Nodett	.030	.6	1.000	.0625	.800	1.000	1.000
Somdett	.018	.6	.360	.0625	.800	1.667	.600
Normal year							
Nodett	.060	.6	1.000	.100	1.000	1.000	1.000
Somdett	.068	.6	.680	.100	1.000	1.667	1.134
Good year							
Nodett	.090	.6	1.000	.125	1.200	1.000	1.000
Somdett	.118	.6	.787	.125	1.200	1.667	1.311

One useful decomposition of ROE is

$$\text{ROE} = \underset{(1)}{\frac{\text{Net profits}}{\text{Pretax profits}}} \times \underset{(2)}{\frac{\text{Pretax profits}}{\text{EBIT}}} \times \underset{(3)}{\frac{\text{EBIT}}{\text{Sales}}} \times \underset{(4)}{\frac{\text{Sales}}{\text{Assets}}} \times \underset{(5)}{\frac{\text{Assets}}{\text{Equity}}}$$

Table 18.3 shows all these ratios for Nodett and Somdett Corporations under the three different economic scenarios.

Let us first focus on factors 3 and 4. Notice that their product, EBIT/Assets, gives us the firm's ROA.

Factor 3 is known as the firm's **profit margin** or **return on sales** (ROS). ROS shows operating profits per dollar of sales. In an average year Nodett's ROS is .10 or 10%; in a bad year it is .0625 or 6.25%, and in a good year .125 or 12.5%.

Factor 4, the ratio of sales to assets, is known as **asset turnover** (ATO). It indicates the efficiency of the firm's use of assets in the sense that it measures the annual sales generated by each dollar of assets. In a normal year Nodett's ATO is 1.0 per year, meaning that sales of $1 per year were generated per dollar of assets. In a bad year this ratio declines to .8 per year, and in a good year it rises to 1.2 per year.

For Nodett and Somdett we see that factors 3 and 4 do not depend on a firm's financial leverage. The firms' ratios are equal to each other in all three scenarios.

Similarly, factor 1, the ratio of net income after taxes to pretax profit, is the same for both firms. We call this the tax-burden ratio. Its value reflects both the government's tax code and the policies pursued by the firm in trying to minimize its tax burden. In our example it does not change over the business cycle, remaining a constant .6.

Whereas factors 1, 3, and 4 are not affected by a firm's capital structure, factors 2 and 5 are. Factor 2 is the ratio of pretax profits to EBIT. The firm's pretax profits will be greatest when there are no interest payments to be made to debtholders. In fact, another way to express this ratio is

$$\frac{\text{Pretax profits}}{\text{EBIT}} = \frac{\text{EBIT} - \text{Interest expense}}{\text{EBIT}}$$

We will call this factor the interest-burden (IB) ratio. It takes on its highest possible value, 1, for Nodett, which has no financial leverage. In general, the higher the degree of financial leverage the lower the IB ratio. Nodett's IB ratio does not vary over the business cycle, but because interest expense is fixed in dollar amount, Somdett's IB ratio varies from a low of .36 in a bad year to a high of .787 in a good year.

Factor 5, the ratio of assets to equity, is a measure of the firm's degree of financial leverage. It is called the **leverage ratio** and is equal to 1 plus the debt-to-equity ratio.[11] In our numerical example in Table 18.3, Nodett has a leverage ratio of 1 while Somdett's is 1.667.

From our discussion in Section 18.2 we know that financial leverage helps boost ROE only if ROA is greater than the interest rate on the firm's debt. How is this fact reflected in the ratios of Table 18.3?

The answer is that to measure the full impact of leverage in this framework the analyst must take the product of the IB and leverage ratios (that is, factors 2 and 5, shown in Table 18.3 as column 6). For Nodett, factor 6, which we call the compound leverage factor, remains a constant 1.0 under all three scenarios. But for Somdett we see that the compound leverage factor is greater than 1 in normal years (1.134) and in good years (1.311), indicating the positive contribution of financial leverage to ROE. It is less than 1 in bad years, reflecting the fact that when ROA falls below the interest rate, ROE falls with increased use of debt.

We can summarize all of these relationships as follows: ROE = Tax burden × Interest burden × Margin × Turnover × Leverage. Since

$$\text{ROA} = \text{Margin} \times \text{Turnover}$$

and

$$\text{Compound leverage factor} = \text{Interest burden} \times \text{Leverage}$$

we can decompose ROE equivalently as follows:

$$\text{ROE} = \text{Tax burden} \times \text{ROA} \times \text{Compound leverage factor}$$

Table 18.3 compares firms with the same ROS and ATO but different degrees of financial leverage. Comparison of ROS and ATO usually is meaningful only in evaluating firms in the same industry. Cross-industry comparisons of these two ratios are often meaningless and even can be misleading.

For example, let us take two firms with the same ROA of 10% per year. The first is a supermarket chain, the second is a gas and electric utility.

---

[11] $\dfrac{\text{Assets}}{\text{Equity}} = \dfrac{\text{Equity} + \text{Debt}}{\text{Equity}} = 1 + \dfrac{\text{Debt}}{\text{Equity}}$

TABLE 18.4 Differences Between ROS and ATO Across Industries

	ROS	×	ATO	=	ROA
Supermarket chain	.02		5.0		.10
Utility	.20		0.5		.10

As Table 18.4 shows, the supermarket chain has a "low" ROS of 2% and achieves a 10% ROA by "turning over" its assets five times per year. The capital-intensive utility, on the other hand, has a "low" ATO of only .5 times per year and achieves its 10% ROA by having an ROS of 20%. The point here is that a "low" ROS or ATO ratio need not indicate a troubled firm. Each ratio must be interpreted in light of industry norms.

Even within an industry ROS and ATO sometimes can differ markedly among firms pursuing different marketing strategies. In the retailing industry, for example, Niemann-Marcus pursues a high-margin, low-ATO policy compared to K-mart, which pursues a low-margin, high-ATO policy.

Concept Check

Question 2. Do a ratio decomposition analysis for the Mordett corporation of question 1, preparing a table similar to Table 18.3.

Turnover and Other Asset Utilization Ratios

It is often helpful in understanding a firm's ratio of sales to assets to compute comparable efficiency-of-utilization, or turnover, ratios for subcategories of assets. For example, fixed-asset turnover would be

$$\frac{\text{Sales}}{\text{Fixed assets}}$$

This ratio measures sales per dollar of the firm's money tied up in fixed assets.

To illustrate how you can compute this and other ratios from a firm's financial statements, consider Growth Industries, Inc. (GI). GI's income statement and opening and closing balance sheets for the years 19X1, 19X2, and 19X3 appear in Table 18.5.

GI's total asset turnover in 19X3 was .303, which was below the industry average of .4. To understand better why GI underperformed, we decide to compute asset utilization ratios separately for fixed assets, inventories, and accounts receivable.

GI's sales in 19X3 were $144 million. Its only fixed assets were plant and equipment, which were $216 million at the beginning of the year and $259.2 million at year's end. Average fixed assets for the year were therefore $237.6 million [($216 million + $259.2 million)/2]. GI's fixed asset turnover for 19X3 was therefore $144 million per year/$237.6 million = .606 per year. In other words, for every dollar of

TABLE 18.5   Growth Industries Financial Statements, 19X1–19X3 ($ Thousands)

	19X0	19X1	19X2	19X3
Income Statements				
Sales revenue		100,000	120,000	144,000
Cost of goods sold (including depreciation)		55,000	66,000	79,200
Depreciation		15,000	18,000	21,600
Selling and administrative expenses		15,000	18,000	21,600
Operating income		30,000	36,000	43,200
Interest expense		10,500	19,095	34,391
Taxable income		19,500	16,905	8,809
Income tax (40% rate)		7,800	6,762	3,524
Net income		11,700	10,143	5,285
Balance Sheets (End of Year)				
Cash and marketable securities	50,000	60,000	72,000	86,400
Accounts receivable	25,000	30,000	36,000	43,200
Inventories	75,000	90,000	108,000	129,600
Net plant and equipment	150,000	180,000	216,000	259,200
Total assets	**300,000**	**360,000**	**432,000**	**518,400**
Accounts payable	30,000	36,000	43,200	51,840
Short-term debt	45,000	87,300	141,957	214,432
Long-term debt (8% bonds maturing in 19X7)	75,000	75,000	75,000	75,000
Total liabilities	**150,000**	**198,300**	**260,157**	**341,272**
Shareholders' equity	150,000	161,700	171,843	177,128
(1 million shares outstanding)				
Other Data				
Market price per common share at year end		$93.60	$61.00	$21.00

fixed assets there were $.606 in sales during the year 19X3.

Comparable figures for the fixed asset turnover ratio for 19X1 and 19X2 and the 19X3 industry average are

19X1	19X2	19X3	19X3 Industry Average
.606	.606	.606	.700

GI's fixed asset turnover has been stable over time and below the industry average.

Note that, whenever a financial ratio contains one item from the income statement, which covers a period of time, and another from the balance sheet, which is a "snapshot" at a point in time, the practice is to take the average of the beginning and end-of-year balance sheet figures. Thus in computing the fixed asset turnover ratio we divide sales (from the income statement) by average fixed assets (from the balance sheet).

Another widely followed turnover ratio is the inventory turnover ratio, which is the ratio of cost of goods sold per dollar of inventory. It is usually expressed as cost of goods sold (instead of sales revenue) divided by average inventory. It measures the speed with which inventory is turned over.

In 19X1 GI's cost of goods sold (less depreciation) was $40 million, and its average inventory was $82.5 million [($75 million + $90 million)/2]. Its inventory turnover was therefore .485 per year ($40 million/$82.5 million). In 19X2 and 19X3 inventory turnover remained the same and continued below the industry average of .5 per year.

Another measure of efficiency is the ratio of accounts receivable to sales. The accounts receivable ratio usually is computed as average accounts receivable/sales × 365. The result is a number called the **average collection period,** or *days receivables,* which equals the total credit extended to customers per dollar of daily sales. It is thus the number of days' worth of sales that is tied up in accounts receivable. You can also think of it as the average lag between the date of sale and the date payment is received.

For GI in 19X3 this number was 100.4 days:

$$\frac{(\$36 \text{ million} + \$43.2 \text{ million})/2}{\$144 \text{ million}} \times 365 = 100.4 \text{ days}$$

The industry average was 60 days.

Thus in summary we see that GI's poor total asset turnover relative to the industry is in part caused by lower than average fixed asset turnover and inventory turnover and higher than average days receivables. This suggests that GI may be having problems with excess plant capacity and poor inventory and receivables management procedures.

Liquidity and Coverage Ratios

Liquidity and interest coverage ratios are of great importance in evaluating the riskiness of a firm's securities. They aid in assessing the likelihood of the firm's going bankrupt.

Liquidity ratios include the following:

1. **Current ratio:** current assets/current liabilities. This ratio measures the ability of the firm to pay off its current liabilities by liquidating its current assets (that is, turning them into cash). It thereby measures the firm's ability to avoid insolvency in the short run. GI's current ratio was

19X1	19X2	19X3	19X3 Industry Average
1.46	1.17	.97	2.0

This represents an unfavorable time trend and poor standing relative to the industry.

2. **Quick ratio:** (cash + receivables)/current liabilities. This ratio is also called the **acid test ratio.** It has the same denominator as the current ratio but its numerator

includes only cash, cash equivalents, and receivables. The quick ratio is a better measure of liquidity than the current ratio for firms whose inventory is not readily convertible into cash. GI's quick ratio shows the same trends as its current ratio:

19X1	19X2	19X3	19X3 Industry Average
.73	.58	.49	1.0

3. **Interest coverage ratio:** EBIT/interest expense. This ratio is often called **times interest earned** and is closely related to the interest-burden ratio discussed in the previous section. A high coverage ratio tells the firm's shareholders and lenders that the likelihood of bankruptcy is low since annual earnings are significantly greater than annual interest obligations. It is widely used by both lenders and borrowers in determining the firm's debt capacity and is a major determinant of the firm's bond rating.

GI's interest coverage ratio was

19X1	19X2	19X3	19X3 Industry Average
2.86	1.89	1.26	5

GI's interest coverage ratio has fallen dramatically over this 3-year period, and by 19X3 it is far below the industry average. Probably its credit rating has been declining as well, and no doubt GI is considered a relatively poor credit risk in 19X3.

Market Price Ratios

There are two ratios in this category: the **market-to-book-value ratio** and the **price-earnings ratio.**

The market-to-book-value ratio (P/B) equals the market price of a share of the firm's common stock divided by its *book value,* that is, shareholders' equity per share. Analysts sometimes consider the stock of a firm with a low market-to-book value to be a "safer" investment, thinking that the book value represents a "floor" supporting the market price.

Analysts seemingly view book value as the level below which market price will not fall because the firm always has the option to liquidate, or sell off, its assets for their book values. A low market-to-book-value ratio is seen as providing a "margin of safety," and some analysts will screen out or reject high P/B firms in their stock selection process.

Proponents of the P/B screen would argue that, if all other relevant attributes are the same for two stocks, the one with the lower P/B ratio is safer. Although there may be firms for which this approach has some validity, book value may in fact not represent liquidation value, which renders the margin of safety notion unreliable.

The theory of equity valuation offers some insight into the significance of the P/B ratio. A high P/B ratio is an indication that investors think a firm has opportunities of

TABLE 18.6   Effect of ROE and Plowback Ratio on P/B

ROE	Plowback Ratio (b)			
	0	25%	50%	75%
10%	1.00	.95	.86	.67
12%	1.00	1.00	1.00	1.00
14%	1.00	1.06	1.20	2.00

The assumptions and formulas underlying this table are: $E_1 = \$1$; book value per share $= \$8.33$; $k = 12\%$ per year.

$$g = b \times \text{ROE}$$

$$P_0 = \frac{(1 - b)E(E_1)}{k - g}$$

$$P/B = P_0/\$8.33$$

earning a rate of return on their investment in excess of the fair market rate, k.

To illustrate this point, we can return to the numerical example in Chapter 17, Section 17.3, and its accompanying table. That example assumes that the coming year's expected EPS is $1 and the market capitalization rate is 12% per year. Now add the assumption that the book value per share is $8.33, so that in the case for which the expected ROE on future investments also is 12%, the stock will sell at $1/.12 = $8.33, and the P/B ratio will be 1.

Table 18.6 shows the P/B ratio for alternative assumptions about future ROE and plowback ratio.

Reading down any column, you can see how the P/B ratio changes with ROE. The numbers reveal that, for a given plowback ratio, the P/B ratio is higher, the higher the expected ROE. This makes sense, because the greater the expected profitability of the firm's future investment opportunities, the greater is its market value as an ongoing enterprise compared with the cost of acquiring its assets.

The **price-earnings ratio** that is based on the firm's financial statements and reported in newspaper stock listings is not the same as the price-earnings multiple that we discussed in Chapter 17. The numerator is the same (the market price of the stock), but the denominator is different: the most recent past accounting earnings. The P/E multiple used in valuation models is the ratio of price to expected future economic earnings.

Many security analysts pay careful attention to the accounting P/E ratio in the belief that among low P/E stocks they are somehow more likely to find bargains than with high P/E stocks. The idea is that you can acquire a claim on a dollar of earnings more cheaply if the P/E ratio is low. For example, if the P/E ratio is 8, you pay $8 per share per $1 of *current* earnings, whereas, if P/E is 12, you must pay $12 for a claim on $1 of current earnings.

Note, however, that current earnings may differ substantially from future earnings. The higher P/E stock still may be a bargain relative to the low P/E stock if its earnings and dividends are expected to grow at a faster rate. Our point is that ownership of the stock conveys the right to future earnings, as well as to current earnings. An exclusive focus on the commonly reported accounting P/E ratio can be short-sighted, since it ignores future growth in earnings.

An efficient markets adherent will be skeptical of the notion that a strategy of investing in low P/E stocks would result in an expected rate of return greater than that of investing in high or medium P/E stocks *having the same risk*. The empirical evidence on this question is mixed, but if the strategy had worked in the past, it almost surely would not work in the future because too many investors would be following it.[12]

Before leaving the P/B and P/E ratios, it is worth pointing out the relationship among these ratios and ROE:

$$\text{ROE} = \frac{\text{Earnings}}{\text{Book value}}$$

$$= \frac{\text{Market price}}{\text{Book value}} \div \frac{\text{Market price}}{\text{Earnings}}$$

$$= \text{P/B ratio} \div \text{P/E ratio}$$

By rearranging the terms, we find that a firm's **earnings yield,** the ratio of earnings to price, is equal to its ROE divided by the market-book value ratio:

$$\frac{E}{P} = \frac{\text{ROE}}{\text{P/B}}$$

Thus a company with a high ROE, such as IBM, can have a relatively low earnings yield because its P/B ratio is high. Thus from the point of view of an investor a high ROE does not in and of itself imply that the stock is a good buy: the price of the stock already may be bid up to reflect an attractive ROE. If so, the P/B ratio will be above 1.0, and the earnings yield to stockholders will be below the ROE, as the equation demonstrates. One result of this relationship is that a strategy of investing in the stock of high ROE firms may produce a lower holding period return than investing in those with a low ROE.

Clayman[13] has found that investing in the stocks of 29 "excellent" companies, with mean reported ROE of 19.05% during the period 1976 to 1980, produced results much inferior to investing in 39 "unexcellent" companies, those with a mean ROE of 7.09% during the period. An investor putting equal dollar amounts in the stocks of the unexcellent companies would have earned a portfolio rate of return over the 1981 to 1985 period that was 11.3% higher per year than the rate of return on a comparable portfolio of excellent company stocks.

---

[12]See the discussion of this point in Chapter 13, on market efficiency.
[13]Clayman, Michelle, "In Search of Excellence: The Investor's Viewpoint," *Financial Analysts Journal,* May/June 1987.

Concept Check

Question 3. What were GI's ROE, P/E, and P/B ratios in the year 19X3? How do they compare to the industry average ratios which were:

$$ROE = 8.64\%$$
$$P/E = 8$$
$$P/B = .69$$

How does GI's earnings yield in 19X3 compare to the industry average?

18.5   An Illustration of Ratio Analysis

We can tie together our evaluation ammunition by conducting a full-scale ratio analysis of Growth Industries. Our purpose is to assess GI's performance in the recent past, to evaluate its future prospects, and to determine whether its market price reflects its intrinsic value.

In her 19X3 annual report to the shareholders of Growth Industries, Inc., the president wrote: "19X3 was another successful year for Growth Industries. As in 19X2, sales, assets, and operating income all continued to grow at a rate of 20%."

Is she right?

Table 18.7 shows the full set of key financial ratios that we can compute from GI's financial statements. The president is certainly right about the growth in sales, assets, and operating income. However, upon inspection of GI's key financial ratios, it appears that she is wrong in the first part of her statement: 19X3 was not another successful year for GI—it appears to have been another miserable one.

ROE has been declining steadily from 7.51% in 19X1 to 3.03% in 19X3. Comparing GI's 19X3 ROE to the 19X3 industry average of 8.64% makes the deteriorating time trend appear especially alarming. The low and falling market-to-book-value ratio and the falling price-earnings ratio indicate that investors have been reassessing downward the firm's future profitability.

The fact that ROA has not been declining tells us that the source of the declining

TABLE 18.7   Key Financial Ratios of Growth Industries, Inc.

Year	ROE	(1) Net Profit / Pretax Profit	(2) Pretax Profit / EBIT	(3) EBIT / Sales (ROS)	(4) Sales / Assets (ATO)	(5) Assets / Equity	(6) Compound Leverage Factor (2) × (5)	(7) ROA (3) × (4)	P/E	P/B
19X1	7.51%	.6	.650	30%	.303	2.117	1.376	9.09%	8	.58
19X2	6.08	.6	.470	30	.303	2.375	1.116	9.09	6	.35
19X3	3.03	.6	.204	30	.303	2.723	.556	9.09	4	.12
Industry average	8.64%	.6	.800	30%	.400	1.500	1.200	12.00%	8	.69

time trend in GI's ROE must be inappropriate use of financial leverage. And indeed we see that, while GI's leverage ratio climbed from 2.117 in 19X1 to 2.723 in 19X3, its interest-burden ratio fell from .650 to .204—with the net result that the compound leverage factor fell from 1.376 to .556.

The rapid increase in short-term debt from year to year and the concurrent increase in interest expense make it clear that, to finance its 20% growth rate in sales, GI has incurred sizable amounts of short-term debt at high interest rates. The firm is paying rates of interest greater than the ROA it is earning on the investment financed with the new borrowing. As the firm has expanded, its situation therefore has become ever more precarious.

In 19X3, for example, the average interest rate on short-term debt was 20% vs. an ROA of 9.09%. (We compute the average interest rate on short-term debt by taking the total interest expense of $34,391,000, subtracting $6 million in interest on the bonds, and dividing by the beginning-of-year short-term debt of $141,957,000.)

At this point GI stock might be an attractive investment. Its market price is only 12% of its book value, and with a P/E ratio of 4 its earnings yield is 25% per year. GI is a likely candidate for a takeover by another firm that might replace GI's existing management and build shareholder value through a radical change in policy.

Concept Check

Question 4. You have the following information for IBX Corporation for the years 1987 and 1984 (all figures are in $ millions):

	1987	1984
Net income	253.7	239.0
Pretax income	411.9	375.6
EBIT	517.6	403.1
Average assets	4,857.9	3,459.7
Sales	6,679.3	4,537.0
Shareholders' equity	2,233.3	2,347.3

What is the trend in IBX's ROE, and how can you account for it in terms of tax burden, margin, turnover, and financial leverage?

18.6 *Comparability*

The Problem

When you are comparing the financial results of different companies, it is important to recognize that there is more than one acceptable way to represent various items of revenue and expense according to generally accepted accounting principles (GAAP). This means that two firms may have exactly the same economic income yet very different accounting incomes.

The Many Ways of Figuring
Financial Results

An investor in First Boston Corp. might have had a pleasant surprise while reading the investment-banking company's 1987 financial statement. Despite taking heavy hits in the volatile bond markets and October's stock crash, First Boston reported earnings of $3.12 per share—down 40% from the heights of 1986, but about the same as profits in 1984.

But hold on. Looking through Value Line's *Investment Survey,* the same investor would be dismayed to find that First Boston's earnings for last year were only 59¢ a share. What gives? In this case the explanation is fairly simple. Value Line doesn't take into account the profits First Boston made in selling its Park Avenue headquarters, while the company and other reporting services such as Standard & Poor's do.

This type of discrepancy in reported financial figures is very common (table) and points to a general rule: Where the bottom line falls depends on who's drawing it. S&P's *Stock Report* generally follows the company's accounting in regard to nonrecurring items, but Value Line doesn't. For example, Union Carbide's reserve for Bhopal litigation amounted to 40¢ per share. S&P and Carbide subtracted it from earnings, but Value Line left it in.

THE BOTTOM LINE: TAKE YOUR CHOICE

	1987 Earnings per Share	
	S&P	Value Line
Alcoa	$2.52	$4.14
Affiliated Publ.	4.08	0.61
First Boston	3.12	0.59
Merrill Lynch	3.58	1.52
Union Carbide	1.76	2.17

Data from Standard & Poor's Corp., Value Line Inc.

Forecast Tool

With the rash of mergers, acquisitions, and divestitures in recent years, the varying approaches of reporting services can result in enormous differences. In 1985, for example, when Warner-Lambert cut its losses by selling three hospital-supply units, S&P showed the company losing $4.05 per share for the year, while Value Line reported a gain of $3.05 per share.

To try to get a "clear-cut number," Value Line will remove from earnings such items as gains or losses from discontinued operations and other special items, says a senior analyst at the firm. He says such a number is more useful to investors looking at the future earning power of a company. Similarly, *Business Week's* Corporate Scoreboard shows earnings from continuing operations, excluding special, nonrecurring, or extraordinary items. Dan Mayper at S&P says that S&P's philosophy is to reflect all the special items in the figures and explain their significance in the narrative of the report.

There are also wide variations when it comes to computing a company's book value. That's basically what's left over when you subtract liabilities from assets. Unlike Value Line, S&P gives no credit to such intangible assets as customer lists, patents, trademarks, or franchises. Companies with many intangibles on their books, such as broadcasters and publishers, are bound to look a lot worse in S&P's calculations. For example, Capital Cities/ABC had a 1986 per-share book value of $120.82, said Value Line, while S&P showed a negative net worth of $24.26 per share.

Value Line analyst Marc Gerstein believes that including the intangibles on the balance sheet gives the best idea of a company's value as an ongoing concern. S&P regards its approach as more conservative, designed to approximate the company's liquidation value.

Furthermore, interpreting a single firm's performance over time is complicated when inflation distorts the dollar measuring rod. Comparability problems are especially acute in this case because the impact of inflation on reported results often depends on the particular method the firm adopts to account for inventories and depreciation. The security analyst must adjust the earnings and the financial ratio figures to a uniform standard before attempting to compare financial results across firms and over time.

This section addresses the comparability problems arising out of the flexibility of GAAP guidelines in accounting for inventories and depreciation and in adjusting for the effects of inflation. Other important potential sources of noncomparability include the capitalization of leases and other expenses and the treatment of pension costs, but they are beyond the scope of this book. The nearby box further discusses the types of problems an analyst must be aware of in using financial statements to identify bargain stocks.

Inventory Valuation

There are two commonly used ways to value inventories: **LIFO** (last-in first-out) and **FIFO** (first-in first-out). The difference is best explained using a numerical example.

Suppose Generic Products, Inc., (GPI) has a constant inventory of 1 million units of generic goods. The inventory turns over once per year, meaning that the ratio of cost of goods sold to inventory is 1.

The LIFO system calls for valuing the million units used up during the year at the current cost of production, so that the last goods produced are considered the first ones to be sold.

The FIFO system assumes that the units used up or sold are the ones that were added to inventory first, and therefore that goods sold should be valued at original cost.

If the price of generic goods were constant, for example, at the level of $1, the book value of inventory and the cost of goods sold would be the same $1 million under both systems. But suppose the price of generic goods rises by 10 cents per unit during the year as a result of general inflation.

LIFO accounting would result in a cost of goods sold of $1.1 million, while the end-of-year balance sheet value of the 1 million units in inventory remains $1 million. The balance sheet value of inventories is measured as the cost of the goods still in inventory. Under LIFO the last goods produced are assumed to be sold at the current cost of $1.10; the goods remaining are thus the previously produced goods, at a cost of only $1. You can see that, although LIFO accounting accurately measures the cost of goods sold, it understates the current value of the remaining inventory in an inflationary environment.

In contrast, under FIFO accounting the cost of goods sold would be $1 million, and the end-of-year balance sheet value of the inventory would be $1.1 million. The result is that the LIFO firm has both a lower reported profit and a lower balance sheet value of inventories than the FIFO firm.

LIFO is to be preferred to FIFO in computing economic earnings (that is, real sustainable cash flow), because it uses up-to-date prices to evaluate the cost of goods sold. However, LIFO accounting induces balance sheet distortions when it values investment in inventories at original cost. This practice results in an upward bias in ROE, since the investment base on which return is earned is undervalued.

In computing the gross national product, the U.S. Department of Commerce has to make an inventory valuation adjustment (IVA) to eliminate the effects of FIFO accounting on the cost of goods sold. In effect, it puts all firms in the aggregate onto a LIFO basis.

Depreciation

Depreciation comparability problems include one more wrinkle. A firm can use different depreciation methods for tax purposes than for other reporting purposes. Most firms use accelerated depreciation methods for tax purposes and straight-line depreciation in published financial statements. There also are differences across firms in their estimates of the depreciable life of plant, equipment, and other depreciable assets.

The major problem related to depreciation, however, is caused by inflation. Because conventional depreciation is based on historical costs rather than on the current replacement cost of assets, measured depreciation in periods of inflation is understated relative to replacement cost, and *real* economic income (sustainable cash flow) is correspondingly overstated.

The situation is similar to what happens in FIFO inventory accounting. Conventional depreciation and FIFO both result in an inflation-induced overstatement of real income because both use original cost instead of current cost to calculate income.

For example, suppose Generic Products, Inc., has a machine with a 3-year useful life that originally cost $3 million. Annual straight-line depreciation is $1 million, regardless of what happens to the replacement cost of the machine. Suppose inflation in the first year turns out to be 10%. Then the true annual depreciation expense is $1.1 million in current terms, while conventionally measured depreciation remains fixed at $1 million per year. Accounting income therefore overstates *real* economic income by the inflation factor, $.1 million.

As it does in the case of inventory valuation, the Commerce Department in its computation of GNP tries to adjust aggregate depreciation, which it calls "capital consumption allowances" (CCA), for the distorting effects of conventional depreciation techniques.

Inflation and Interest Expense

If inflation can cause distortions in the measurement of a firm's inventory and depreciation costs, it has perhaps an even greater effect on calculation of *real* interest expense. Nominal interest rates include an inflation premium that compensates the lender for inflation-induced erosion in the *real* value of principal. From the perspective of both lender and borrower, part of what is conventionally measured as interest expense should be treated more properly as repayment of principal.

For example, suppose Generic Products has debt outstanding with a face value of $10 million at an interest rate of 10% per year. Interest expense as conventionally measured is therefore $1 million per year. However, suppose inflation during the year is 6%, so that the real interest rate is 4%. Then $.6 million of what appears as interest expense on the income statement is really an inflation premium, or compensation for the anticipated reduction in the real value of the $10 million principal; only $.4 million is *real* interest expense. The $.6 million reduction in the purchasing power of the outstanding principal may be thought of as repayment of principal, rather than as an interest expense. Real income of the firm is therefore understated by $.6 million.

Mismeasurement of real interest means that inflation deflates the statement of real income. The effects of inflation on the reported values of inventories and depreciation that we have discussed work in the opposite direction.

These distortions might by chance cancel each other out, so that the reported income figure is an unbiased estimate of real economic income. Although this seems extremely improbable for any individual firm, there is some evidence that these distortions have approximately offset one another for the aggregate corporate sector of the U.S. economy during the past 20 years.[14]

Concept Check

Question 5. In a period of rapid inflation companies ABC and XYZ have the same *reported* earnings. ABC uses LIFO inventory accounting, has relatively fewer depreciable assets, and has more debt than XYZ. XYZ uses FIFO inventory accounting. Which company has the higher *real* income and why?

Inflation Accounting

In recognition of the need to adjust for the effects of inflation, the Financial Accounting Standards Board in 1980 issued FASB Rule No. 33 (FASB 33). It required large public corporations to supplement their customary financial statements with data pertaining to the effect of inflation.

A survey conducted in 1983, however, indicated that security analysts, by and large, were ignoring the inflation-adjusted data.[15] One possible reason is that analysts believed that FASB 33 just added another element of noncomparability. In other words, analysts may have judged the inflation-adjusted earnings to be poorer estimates of real economic earnings than the original unadjusted figures.

In 1987, after a lengthy evaluation of the effects of FASB 33, the FASB decided to discontinue it. Today, analysts interested in adjusting reported financial statements for inflation are completely on their own.

---

[14]See Modigliani, F. and Cohn, R., "Inflation, Rational Valuation and the Market," *Financial Analysts Journal,* March/April, 1979.

[15]See Norby, W.C., "Applications of Inflation-Adjusted Accounting Data," *Financial Analysts Journal,* March/April 1983.

18.7 Value Investing: The Graham Technique

No presentation of fundamental security analysis would be complete without a discussion of the ideas of Benjamin Graham, the greatest of the investment "gurus." Until the evolution of modern portfolio theory in the latter half of this century, Graham was the single most important thinker, writer, and teacher in the field of investment analysis. His influence on investment professionals remains very strong.

Graham's magnum opus is *Security Analysis,* written with Columbia Professor David Dodd in 1934. Its message is similar to the ideas presented in this chapter. By analyzing a firm's financial statements carefully, Graham felt one could identify bargain stocks. Over the years he developed many different rules for determining the most important financial ratios and the critical values for judging a stock to be undervalued. Through many editions his book has had a profound influence on investment professionals. It has been so influential and successful, in fact, that widespread adoption of Graham's techniques has led to the elimination of the very bargains they are designed to identify.

In a 1976 seminar Graham said[16]:

I am no longer an advocate of elaborate techniques of security analysis in order to find superior value opportunities. This was a rewarding activity, say, forty years ago, when our textbook 'Graham and Dodd' was first published; but the situation has changed a good deal since then. In the old days any well-trained security analyst could do a good professional job of selecting undervalued issues through detailed studies; but in the light of the enormous amount of research now being carried on, I doubt whether in most cases such extensive efforts will generate sufficiently superior selections to justify their cost. To that very limited extent I'm on the side of the 'efficient market' school of thought now generally accepted by the professors.

Nonetheless, in that same seminar Graham suggested a simplified approach to identify bargain stocks:

My first, more limited, technique confines itself to the purchase of common stocks at less than their working-capital value, or net current-asset value, giving no weight to the plant and other fixed assets, and deducting all liabilities in full from the current assets. We used this approach extensively in managing investment funds, and over a thirty-odd-year period we must have earned an average of some 20% per year from this source. For a while, however, after the mid-1950s, this brand of buying opportunity became very scarce because of the pervasive bull market. But it has returned in quantity since the 1973-1974 decline. In January 1976 we counted over 100 such issues in the Standard & Poor's *Stock Guide*—about 10% of the total. I consider it a foolproof method of systematic investment—once again, not on the basis of individual results but in terms of the expectable group outcome.

There are two convenient sources of information for those interested in trying out the Graham technique. Both Standard & Poor's *Outlook* and *The Value Line Investment Survey* carry lists of stocks selling below net working capital value.

---

[16]As cited by John Train in *Money Masters,* New York: Harper & Row, Publishers, Inc. © 1987.

Summary

1. The primary focus of the security analyst should be the firm's real economic earnings rather than its reported earnings. Accounting earnings as reported in financial statements can be a biased estimate of real economic earnings, although empirical studies reveal that reported earnings convey considerable information concerning a firm's prospects.

2. A firm's ROE is a key determinant of the growth rate of its earnings. ROE is affected profoundly by the firm's degree of financial leverage. An increase in a firm's debt-to-equity ratio will raise its ROE and hence its growth rate only if the interest rate on the debt is less than the firm's return on assets.

3. It is often helpful to the analyst to decompose a firm's ROE ratio into the product of several accounting ratios and to analyze their separate behavior over time and across companies within an industry. A useful breakdown is

$$\text{ROE} = \frac{\text{Net profits}}{\text{Pretax profits}} \times \frac{\text{Pretax profits}}{\text{EBIT}} \times \frac{\text{EBIT}}{\text{Sales}} \times \frac{\text{Sales}}{\text{Assets}} \times \frac{\text{Assets}}{\text{Equity}}$$

4. Other accounting ratios that have a bearing on a firm's profitability and/or risk are fixed asset turnover, inventory turnover, days receivables, and current, quick, and interest coverage ratios.

5. Two ratios that make use of the market price of the firm's common stock in addition to its financial statements are the ratio of market-to-book value and the price-earnings ratio. Analysts sometimes take low values for these ratios as a margin of safety or a sign that the stock is a bargain.

6. A strategy of investing in stocks with high reported ROE seems to produce a lower rate of return to the investor than investing in low ROE stocks. This implies that high reported ROE stocks are overpriced compared with low ROE stocks.

7. A major problem in the use of data obtained from a firm's financial statements is comparability. Firms have a great deal of latitude in how they choose to compute various items of revenue and expense. It is therefore necessary for the security analyst to adjust accounting earnings and financial ratios to a uniform standard before attempting to compare financial results across firms.

8. Comparability problems can be acute in a period of inflation. Inflation can create distortions in accounting for inventories, depreciation, and interest expense.

Key Terms

Economic earnings	Leverage ratio	Times interest earned
Accounting earnings	Average collection period	Market-to-book-value ratio
Return on equity	Days receivables	Price-earnings ratio
Return on assets	Current ratio	Earnings yield
Profit margin	Quick ratio	LIFO
Return on sales	Acid test ratio	FIFO
Asset turnover	Interest coverage ratio	

Selected Readings

The classic book on the use of financial statements in equity valuation, now in its fifth edition, is:
Graham and Dodd's Security Analysis, *by Cottle, S., Murray, R., and Block, F., New York: McGraw-Hill, Inc., 1988.*

Problems

1. The Crusty Pie Co., which specializes in the production of apple turnovers, has a return on sales higher than the industry average, yet its ROA is the same as the industry average. How can you explain this?

2. The ABC Corporation has a profit margin on sales below the industry average, yet its ROA is above the industry average. What does this imply about its asset turnover?

3. Firm *A* and firm *B* have the same ROA, yet firm *A*'s ROE is higher. How can you explain this?

4. (1988 CFA Examination, Level I)
   Which of the following *best* explains a ratio of "net sales to average net fixed assets" that *exceeds* the industry average?
   a. The firm expanded its plant and equipment in the past few years.
   b. The firm makes less efficient use of its assets than other firms.
   c. The firm has a lot of old plant and equipment.
   d. The firm uses straight line depreciation.

5. (1988 CFA Examination, Level I)
   The rate of return on assets is equivalent to:
   a. Profit margin × Total asset turnover
   b. Profit margin × Total asset turnover × Leverage ratio/Interest expense
   c. $\dfrac{\text{Net income} + \text{Interest expense net of income tax} + \text{Minority interest in earnings}}{\text{Average total assets}}$
   d. $\dfrac{\text{Net income} + \text{Minority interest in earnings}}{\text{Average total assets}}$
      i. a only
      ii. a and c
      iii. b only
      iv. b and d

6. (1988 CFA Examination, Level I)
   Which one of the following is *true?*
   a. During inflation, LIFO makes the income statement less representative than if FIFO were used.
   b. During inflation, FIFO makes the balance sheet less representative than if LIFO were used.
   c. After inflation ends, distortion due to LIFO will disappear as inventory is sold.
   d. None of the above.

7. (1987 CFA Examination, Level I)
   The financial statements for Seattle Manufacturing Corporation are to be used to

compute the following ratios for 1986 (Tables 18A and 18B).

a. Return on total assets
b. Earnings per share of common stock
c. Acid test ratio
d. Interest coverage ratio
e. Receivables collection period
f. Leverage ratio

8. (1986 CFA Examination, Level I)

The financial statements for Chicago Refrigerator Inc. are to be used to compute the following ratios for 1985 (Tables 18C and 18D).

a. Quick ratio
b. Return on assets
c. Return on common shareholders' equity
d. Earnings per share of common stock
e. Profit margin
f. Times interest earned
g. Inventory turnover
h. Leverage ratio

9. (1985 CFA Examination, Level I)

The financial statements for Atlas Corporation are to be used to compute the following ratios for 1984 (Tables 18E and 18F).

a. Acid-test ratio
b. Inventory turnover
c. Earnings per share
d. Interest coverage
e. Leverage

10. (This question is based on the 1987 CFA Examination, Level I.) The profit growth of United States Tobacco Company has been excellent over the past 10 years. Identify the five sources of corporate internal earnings growth, and from the data appearing in Tables 18G, 18H, and 18I state whether each has or has not contributed to the profit progress of United States Tobacco Co. over the past 10 years.

11. (This question is based on the 1984 CFA Examination, Level I.) The Coca-Cola Company (KO) and PepsiCo, Inc. (PEP) are the leading companies in the world-wide market for soft drinks and snack foods. Return on shareholders' equity is a prime measure of management's performance and can be analyzed using turnover, leverage, profit margin, and income tax rate. Use the ratios and company data provided in Tables 18J-18M below to:

a. Calculate the return on average common equity for KO and PEP for the 2 years 1977 and 1983.
b. Identify the ratios that account for the level and trend of ROE for each company in these 2 years.

TABLE 18A   Seattle Manufacturing Corp. Consolidated Balance Sheet, as of December 31 ($ Millions)

	1985	1986
Assets		
Current assets		
Cash	$ 6.2	$ 6.6
Short-term investment in commercial paper	20.8	15.0
Accounts receivable	77.0	93.2
Inventory	251.2	286.0
Prepaid manufacturing expense	1.4	1.8
Total current assets	**$ 356.6**	**$ 402.6**
Leased property under capital leases net of accumulated amortization	181.4	215.6
Other	6.2	9.8
Total assets	**$ 544.2**	**$ 628.0**
Liabilities		
Current liabilities		
Accounts payable	$ 143.2	$ 161.0
Dividends payable	13.0	14.4
Current portion of long-term debt	12.0	16.6
Current portion of obligations under capital leases	18.8	22.6
Estimated taxes on income	10.8	9.8
Total current liabilities	**$ 197.8**	**$ 224.4**
Long-term debt	86.4	107.0
Obligations under capital leases	140.8	165.8
Total liabilities	**$ 425.0**	**$ 497.2**
Shareholders' Equity		
Common stock, $10 per value		
4,000,000 shares authorized, 3,000,000 and 2,680,000 outstanding, respectively	$ 26.8	$ 30.0
Cumulative preferred stock, Series A 8%; $25 par value;		
1,000,000 authorized; 600,000 outstanding	15.0	15.0
Additional paid-in capital	26.4	27.0
Retained earnings	51.0	58.8
Total shareholders' equity	**$ 119.2**	**$ 130.8**
Total liabilities and shareholders' equity	**$ 544.2**	**$ 628.0**

TABLE 18B   Seattle Manufacturing Corp. Income Statement, Years Ending December 31 ($ Millions)

	1985	1986
Sales	$ 1,166.6	$ 1,207.6
Other income, net	12.8	15.6
Total revenues	**$ 1,179.4**	**$ 1,223.2**
Cost of sales	$ 912.0	$ 961.2
Amortization of leased property	43.6	48.6
Selling and administrative expense	118.4	128.8
Interest expense	16.2	19.8
Total costs and expenses	**$ 1,090.2**	**$ 1,158.4**
Income before income tax	$ 89.2	$ 64.8
Income tax	19.2	10.4
Net income	$ 70.0	$ 54.4

TABLE 18C   Chicago Refrigerator Inc. Balance Sheet, as of December 31 ($ Thousands)

	1984	1985
Assets		
Current assets		
Cash	$ 683	$ 325
Accounts receivable	1,490	3,599
Inventories	1,415	2,423
Prepaid expenses	15	13
Total current assets	**$ 3,603**	**$ 6,360**
Property, plant, equipment, net	1,066	1,541
Other	123	157
Total assets	**$ 4,792**	**$ 8,058**
Liabilities		
Current liabilities		
Notes payable to bank	$ —	$ 875
Current portion of long-term debt	38	116
Accounts payable	485	933
Estimated income tax	588	472
Accrued expenses	576	586
Customer advance payment	34	963
Total current liabilities	**$ 1,721**	**$ 3,945**
Long-term debt	122	179
Other liabilities	81	131
Total liabilities	**$ 1,924**	**$ 4,255**
Shareholders' Equity		
Common stock, $1 par value		
1,000,000 shares authorized; 550,000 and 829,000 outstanding, respectively	$ 550	$ 829
Preferred stock, Series A 10%; $25.00 par value; 25,000 authorized; 20,000 and 18,000 outstanding, respectively	500	450
Additional paid-in capital	450	575
Retained earnings	1,368	1,949
Total shareholders' equity	**$ 2,868**	**$ 3,803**
Total liabilities and shareholders' equity	**$ 4,792**	**$ 8,058**

TABLE 18D   Chicago Refrigerator Inc. Income Statement, Years Ending December 31 ($ Thousands)

	1984	1985
Net sales	$ 7,570	$ 12,065
Other income, net	261	345
Total revenues	**$ 7,831**	**$ 12,410**
Cost of goods sold	$ 4,850	$ 8,048
General administrative and marketing expense	1,531	2,025
Interest expense	22	78
Total costs and expenses	**$ 6,403**	**$ 10,151**
Net income before tax	$ 1,428	$ 2,259
Income tax	628	994
Net Income	$ 800	$ 1,265

TABLE 18E   Atlas Corporation Consolidated Balance Sheet, as of December 31 ($ Millions)

	1983	1984
Assets		
Current Assets		
Cash	$ 3.1	$ 3.3
Short-term investment in commercial paper	2.9	—
Accounts receivable	38.5	46.6
Inventory	125.6	143.0
Prepaid manufacturing expense	.7	.9
Total current assets	**$ 170.8**	**$ 193.8**
Leased property under capital leases net of accumulated amortization	$ 90.7	$ 107.8
Other	3.1	4.9
Total assets	**$ 264.6**	**$ 306.5**
Liabilities		
Current Liabilities		
Accounts payable	$ 71.6	$ 81.7
Dividends payable	6.5	6.0
Current portion of long-term debt	6.0	8.3
Current portion of obligation under capital leases	9.4	11.3
Estimated taxes on income	5.4	4.9
Total current liabilities	**$ 98.9**	**$ 112.2**
Long-term debt	$ 43.2	$ 53.5
Obligations under capital leases	70.4	82.9
Total liabilities	**$ 212.5**	**$ 248.6**
Shareholders' Equity		
Common stock, $10 par value		
2,000,000 shares authorized;		
1,340,000 and 1,500,000 oustanding, respectively	$ 13.4	$ 15.0
Additional paid-in capital	13.2	13.5
Retained earnings	25.5	29.4
Total shareholders' equity	**$ 52.1**	**$ 57.9**
Total liabilities and shareholders' equity	**$ 264.6**	**$ 306.5**

TABLE 18F   Atlas Corporation Income Statement, Years Ending December 31, ($ Millions)

	1983	1984
Sales	$ 583.3	$ 603.8
Other income, net	6.4	2.8
Main revenues	**$ 589.7**	**$ 606.6**
Cost of sales	$ 456.0	$ 475.6
Amortization of leased property	21.8	24.3
Selling and administrative expense	59.2	64.4
Interest expense	8.1	9.9
Total costs and expenses	**$ 545.1**	**$ 574.2**
Income before income tax	$ 44.6	$ 32.4
Income tax	9.6	5.2
Net income	$ 35.0	$ 27.2

TABLE 18G   The United States Tobacco Company, Historic Income Statement Data ($ Thousands)

| | Revenues | Income Before Interest and Taxes | | Interest Expense | Income Before Taxes | | Taxes | | Net Income | | Earnings per Share | |
		Amount	% of Revs.		Amount	% of Revs.	Amount	Tax Rate	Amount	% Increase	Amount	% Increase
1986	$517,996	$200,274	38.7%	$5,534	$194,740	37.6%	$90,802	46.6%	$103,938	11.1%	$1.79	9.1%
1985	480,021	177,122	36.9	5,898	171,224	35.7	77,695	45.4	93,529	11.7	1.64	14.7
1984	443,792	165,053	37.2	5,147	159,906	36.0	76,179	47.6	83,727	18.5	1.43	19.2
1983	382,783	141,228	36.9	4,688	136,540	35.7	65,892	48.3	70,648	27.7	1.21	19.8
1982	320,448	110,266	34.4	6,575	103,691	32.4	48,356	46.6	55,335	21.2	1.01	20.2
1981	280,229	92,277	32.9	3,622	88,655	31.6	42,993	48.5	45,662	21.2	0.84	20.0
1980	265,762	80,677	30.4	5,149	75,528	28.4	37,842	50.1	37,686	17.6	0.70	16.7
1979	233,262	67,662	29.0	6,943	60,719	26.0	28,685	47.2	32,034	15.1	0.60	3.2
1978	205,861	59,006	28.7	4,766	54,240	26.4	26,412	48.7	27,828	14.3	0.53	12.8
1977	181,033	49,508	27.4	3,807	45,701	25.2	21,354	46.7	24,347	25.6	0.47	23.7
1976	166,405	42,159	25.3	3,403	38,726	23.3	19,342	50.0	19,384	21.0	0.38	11.1

Compound Annual Growth Rates

| 1976-86 | 12% | 17% | | 5% | 18% | | 17% | | 18% | | 17% | |

TABLE 18H   The United States Tobacco Company, Historic Asset and Equity Analysis ($ Thousands)

	Average Total Assets	Revenues/ Average Total Assets	Average Total Equity	Net Income as % of Average Total Equity	Average Total Equity as % of Total Average Capitalization
1986	$496,026	1.04	$347,468	30%	75%
1985	438,295	1.10	302,233	31	73
1984	390,654	1.14	270,563	31	79
1983	352,800	1.08	239,405	30	75
1982	306,810	1.04	202,154	27	74
1981	271,959	1.03	173,821	26	75
1980	252,491	1.05	151,871	25	73
1979	230,072	1.01	133,274	24	71
1978	197,658	1.04	117,316	24	69
1977	166,729	1.09	102,788	24	69
1976	145,820	1.14	89,643	22	66

TABLE 18I   The United States Tobacco Company, Historic Dividend and Retained Earnings Analysis ($ Thousands)

| | Dividends | | Retained Earnings | |
	Amount	% of Net Income	Amount	% of Net Income
1986	$54,744	53%	$49,194	47%
1985	47,835	51	45,694	49
1984	40,494	48	43,233	52
1983	32,493	46	38,155	54
1982	25,722	46	29,613	54
1981	21,892	48	23,770	52
1980	18,863	50	18,823	50
1979	16,395	51	15,639	49
1978	14,144	51	13,684	49
1977	12,257	50	12,090	50
1976	9,492	49	9,892	51

TABLE 18J   Selected Financial Ratios

Fiscal Year	EBIT ÷ Assets		Total Assets ÷ Common Equity		Net Earnings ÷ Pretax Earnings		Net Sales ÷ Total Assets	
	KO	PEP	KO	PEP	KO	PEP	KO	PEP
1983 (est.)	21.1%	14.7%	1.78x	2.56x	56.0%	58.0%	1.33x	1.82
1982	23.7	16.9	1.68	2.57	55.0	57.2	1.47	1.82
1981	24.3	17.7	1.60	2.53	55.4	58.5	1.69	1.89
1980	24.3	18.3	1.59	2.39	55.1	56.5	1.77	1.90
1979	26.2	18.5	1.51	2.20	55.4	59.8	1.70	1.92
1978	27.8	19.8	1.46	2.13	54.4	56.1	1.69	1.89
1977	27.9	20.1	1.41	2.31	54.0	55.4	1.59	1.83
1976	28.3	16.9	1.39	2.55	53.4	54.4	1.57	1.77
Averages								
1980-83	23.3%	16.9%	1.66x	2.51x	55.4%	57.5%	1.57x	1.84x
1976-79	27.6	18.8	1.44	2.30	54.3	56.4	1.64	1.85
1976-83	25.4	17.9	1.55	2.41	54.8	57.0	1.60	1.86

Average of beginning and end of year assets and equity used where applicable in computing ratios.

TABLE 18K   Selected Financial Ratios

Fiscal Year	Pretax Earnings ÷ Net Sales		Net Earnings ÷ Total Assets		Net Earnings ÷ Common Equity		Dividends ÷ Net Earnings	
	KO	PEP	DO	PEP	KO	PEP	KO	PEP
1983 (est.)	14.8%	6.4%	11.0%	6.5%	19.6%	16.6%	64.6%	53.1%
1982	14.9	7.1	12.1	7.4	20.3	18.9	62.8	48.9
1981	13.7	7.2	12.8	8.0	20.6	20.3	59.5	44.1
1980	13.1	7.7	12.8	8.3	20.3	19.8	63.2	44.1
1979	15.2	8.2	14.3	9.4	21.6	20.8	57.6	40.9
1978	16.2	9.2	14.9	9.8	21.8	20.9	57.4	40.6
1977	17.5	9.7	15.1	9.9	21.3	22.8	57.5	38.6
1976	18.0	9.6	15.1	9.2	21.1	23.4	55.7	35.4
Averages								
1980-83	14.1%	7.1%	12.2%	7.6%	20.2%	18.9%	62.5%	47.6%
1976-79	16.7	9.2	14.9	9.6	21.4	22.0	57.1	38.9
1976-83	15.4	8.1	13.5	8.6	20.8	20.4	59.8	43.2

Average of beginning and end-of-year assets and equity used where applicable in computing ratios.

TABLE 18L   Selected Financial Statistics, The Coca-Cola Company ($ Millions)

	Fiscal Year							
	1983 (Est.)	1982	1981	1980	1979	1978	1977	1976
Operations								
Sales	6,820.0	6,249.0	5,889.0	5,621.0	4,689.0	4,095.0	3,394.0	2,989.0
Depreciation	180.0	148.9	136.9	131.0	110.0	91.0	80.0	70.0
Interest	73.0	74.6	38.3	35.1	10.7	7.8	NA	NA
Income taxes	444.0	419.8	360.2	330.4	318.0	303.0	273.0	251.0
Net earnings	565.0	512.2	447.0	406.0	395.0	361.0	321.0	288.0
Financial Position								
Cash	616.4	311.0	393.0	289.0	209.0	369.0	418.0	403.0
Receivables	831.3	751.8	483.5	523.1	435.1	338.3	279.9	237.3
Current assets	2,444.2	2,076.6	1,636.2	1,622.3	1,305.6	1,236.6	1,103.5	1,027.3
Total assets	5,331.0	4,923.3	3,564.8	3,406.0	2,938.0	2,582.8	2,254.5	2,007.0
Current liabilities	1,702.7	1,326.8	1,006.3	1,061.6	884.2	744.0	596.3	506.4
Long-term debt	475.0	462.3	137.3	133.2	31.0	15.2	15.3	11.0
Common equity	2,990.0	2,778.7	2,270.8	2,074.7	1,918.7	1,739.6	1,578.0	1,434.0

TABLE 18M   Selected Financial Statistics, PepsiCo, Inc.* ($ Millions)

	Fiscal Year							
	1983 (Est.)	1982	1981	1980	1979	1978	1977	1976
Operations								
Sales	7,700.0	7,499.0	7,027.0	5975.0	5,089.0	4,300.0	3,649.0	3,109.0
Depreciation	260.0	230.4	205.5	172.9	142.1	117.0	93.7	79.1
Interest	156.0	166.2	149.7	114.7	73.1	52.0	46.0	45.0
Income taxes	206.0	226.8	210.8	200.8	168.2	174.3	158.3	135.3
Net earnings	285.0	303.7†	297.5	260.7	250.4	223.0	196.7	161.7
Financial Position								
Cash and equivalents	397.3	280.3	239.0	232.0	205.0	167.0	256.0	231.0
Receivables	785.7	746.1	741.4	596.7	557.2	433.6	374.4	324.5
Current assets	1,739.4	1,590.6	1,762.5	1,326.5	1,201.4	1,010.5	997.0	903.7
Total assets	4,588.9	4,197.5	4,040.0	3,399.9	2,888.9	2,416.8	2,130.3	1,853.6
Current liabilities	1,440.0	1,345.6	1,430.7	1,005.3	843.6	650.7	574.5	478.9
Long-term debt	786.7	864.2	816.1	781.7	619.0	479.1	427.9	278.6
Common equity	1,786.3	1,650.5	1,556.3	1,381.0	1,247.0	1,165.0	971.9	753.0

*Amounts for 1978-1981 restated to reflect overstatement of net income aggregating $92.1 million.
†Before unusual charge of $79.4 million.

PART VI

Derivative Assets:
Options and Futures

CHAPTER 19

An Introduction to Options Markets

Trading of standardized options contracts on a national exchange started in 1973 when the Chicago Board Options Exchange began listing call options. These contracts were almost immediately a great success, crowding out the over-the-counter trading in stock options that had preceded the inception of the formal exchange. Today, the CBOE is the second-largest securities market in the United States in terms of the value of traded securities; only the New York Stock Exchange is larger.

Options contracts are traded now on several exchanges. They are written on common stock, stock indices, foreign exchange, agricultural commodities, precious metals, and interest rate futures. Popular and potent tools in modifying portfolio characteristics, options have become essential tools that a portfolio manager must understand.

This chapter is an introduction to options markets. It explains how puts and calls work and examines their investment characteristics. Popular option strategies are considered next. Finally, the chapter provides a brief overview of option valuation issues.

19.1 The Option Contract

A **call option** gives its holder the right to purchase an asset for a specified price, called the **exercise price** or **strike price,** on or before a specified expiration date. For example, a July call option on IBM stock with exercise price $120 entitles its owner to purchase IBM stock for a price of $120 at any time up to and including the expiration date in July. The holder of the call is not required to exercise the option. Only if the market value of the asset to be purchased exceeds the exercise price will it be profitable for the holder to exercise it. When the market price does exceed the exercise price, the option holder may either sell the option, or "call away" the asset for the exercise price and reap a profit. Otherwise, the option may be left unexercised. If it is not exercised before the expiration date of the contract, a call option simply expires and no longer has value.

The purchase price of the option is called the *premium*. It represents the compensation the purchaser of the call must pay for the ability to exercise the option if it becomes profitable. Sellers of call options, who are said to *write* calls, receive premium income now as payment against the possibility that they will be forced at some later date to deliver the asset in return for an exercise price lower than the market value of the asset. If the option is left to expire because the exercise price remains above the market price of the asset, then—aside from transaction costs—the writer of the call clears a profit equal to the premium income derived from the initial sale of the option.

A **put option** gives its holder the right to *sell* an asset for a specified exercise or strike price on or before a given expiration date. A July put on IBM with exercise price $120 thus entitles its owner to sell IBM stock to the put writer at a price of $120 at any time before expiration in July even if the market price of IBM is less than $120. Whereas profits on call options increase when the asset increases in value, profits on put options increase when the asset value falls. The put is exercised only if its holder can deliver an asset with market value less than the exercise price in return for the exercise price.

Options and futures contracts are sometimes called *derivative securities*. Their values derive from the values of the underlying primary security. For example, the value of an IBM option depends on the price of IBM stock. For this reason options and futures contracts also are called *contingent claims:* payoff is contingent on prices of other securities.

An option is said to be **in the money** when its exercise would produce profits for its holder. An option is **out of the money** when exercise would be unprofitable. A call option is in the money when the exercise price is below the asset's value because purchase at the exercise price would be profitable. It is out of the money when the exercise price exceeds the asset value; no one would exercise the right to purchase for the exercise price an asset worth less than that price. Conversely, put options are in the money when the exercise price exceeds the asset's value because delivery of the lower-valued asset in exchange for the exercise price would be profitable.

Some options trade on over-the-counter markets. The OTC market offers the advantage that the terms of the option contract—the exercise price, maturity date, and number of shares committed—can be tailored to the needs of the traders. The costs of establishing an OTC option contract, however, are quite high.

Today virtually all option trading takes place on organized exchanges. Options on stocks are traded on five exchanges: the CBOE, and the American, New York, Philadelphia, and Pacific stock exchanges. Options on other assets are traded on several other exchanges.

Options contracts traded on exchanges are standardized by allowable maturity dates and exercise prices for each listed option. Each stock option contract provides for the right to buy or sell 100 shares of stock. (If stock splits occur after the contract is listed, adjustments are required. We discuss adjustments in option contract terms later in this section.)

FIGURE 19.1

Listed stock options quotations.

(From *The Wall Street Journal*, May 10, 1988.) Reprinted by permission of *The Wall Street Journal*. © Dow Jones & Company, Inc. 1988. All rights reserved.

LISTED OPTIONS QUOTATIONS

Monday, May 9, 1988

Options closing prices. Sales unit usually is 100 shares.
Stock close is New York or American exchange final price.

[Figure 19.1: a reproduction of the "Listed Options Quotations" table from The Wall Street Journal showing option & strike price, NY close, and Calls—Last and Puts—Last columns for May, Jun, Jul for numerous companies including AmBrnd, Asarco, BwnFer, Chase, ChemBk, ChemW, Chevrn, Circus, ConAg, Deere, Donely, EmrsEl, GTE, GenRe, Gillet, Hecla, IBM, BkBost, CinMil, Colt, Cmdrln, FarmGp, FedDS, GoldWF, HomeD, Lehman, LinB, La Lnd, Lubriz, MCA, McDin, McGHll, NwmtG, PPG, ParkHa, Pttstn, Sun Co, Tesoro, Trnsam, Un Pac, CalFed, CircK, CirCty, Comdis, Compac, Convrg, Daisy, DayHud, DeluxC, EchoB, Ethyl, FUnion, FostWh, Gannett, Gentch, GMills, HBO, Hasbro, Hilton, Hosp, Jerico, JiffyL, and others.]

Standardization of the terms of listed option contracts means that all market participants trade in a limited and uniform set of securities. This increases the depth of trading in any particular option, which lowers trading costs and results in a more competitive market. Therefore exchanges offer two important benefits: ease of trading, which flows from a central marketplace where buyers and sellers or their representatives congregate, and a liquid secondary market where buyers and sellers of options can establish and trade their positions quickly and cheaply.

Figure 19.1 is a reproduction of listed stock option quotations from *The Wall Street Journal*. Note the option listed (arrowhead) that is for shares of IBM. The column below the company name indicates that the last recorded price on the New York

Stock Exchange for IBM stock was \$110⅜ per share.[1] Options are traded on IBM at exercise prices of \$100 through \$125 in \$5 increments. These values are also called strike prices and are given in the first column of numbers.

The exchanges offer options on stocks with exercise prices that bracket the stock price; exercise prices generally are set at five-point intervals for stocks selling below \$100. Larger intervals may be set for stocks selling above \$100. If the stock price moves outside the range of exercise prices of the existing set of options, new options with appropriate exercise prices may be offered. Therefore at any time both in-the-money and out-of-the-money options will be listed, as in the IBM example.

The next three columns of numbers provide the closing prices of call options on IBM shares with expiration dates of May, June, and July. The contracts expire on the Saturday following the third Friday of the month. Notice that the prices of IBM call options decrease as one moves down each column toward progressively higher exercise prices. This makes sense, because the right to purchase a share at a given exercise price is worth less as that exercise price increases. At an exercise price of \$105, the June IBM call sells for \$7½, whereas the option to purchase for an exercise price of \$120 sells for only \$11⁄16. The note "r" means that the option was not traded on that day, whereas "s" indicates that the option with that exercise price and expiration date has not been opened for trading by the exchange.

Many options may go an entire day without trading. Because trading is infrequent, it is not unusual to find option prices that appear out of line with other prices. You might find, for example, two calls with different exercise prices that seem to sell for equal prices. This discrepancy arises because the last trades for these options may have occurred at different times during the day. At any moment the call with the lower exercise price must be worth more than an otherwise-identical call with a higher exercise price.

The last three columns report prices of put options with various strike prices and times to maturity. Notice that, in contrast to call options, put prices increase with the exercise price. The right to sell a share of IBM at a price of \$100 obviously is less valuable than the right to sell it at \$125.

American and European Options

An **American option** allows its holder to exercise the right to purchase (call) or sell (put) the underlying asset on *or before* the expiration date. A **European option** allows for exercise of the option only on the expiration date. American options, because they allow more leeway than do their European counterparts, generally will be more valuable. Virtually all traded options in this country are American. Foreign currency options and stock index options traded on the Chicago Board Options Exchange are notable exceptions to this rule, however.

---

[1]This price sometimes may not match the closing price listed for the stock on the stock market page. This is because some NYSE stocks also trade on the Pacific Stock Exchange, which closes after the NYSE, and the stock pages may reflect the more recent Pacific Exchange closing price. The options exchanges, however, close with the NYSE, so the closing NYSE stock price is appropriate for comparison with the closing option price.

Adjustments in Option Contract Terms

Because options convey the right to buy or sell shares at a stated price, stock splits would radically alter their value if the terms of the option contract were not adjusted to account for the stock split. For example, reconsider the IBM call options in Figure 19.1. If IBM were to announce a 10-for-1 split, its share price would fall from $110⅜ to about $11. A call option with exercise price $110 would be just about worthless, with virtually no possibility that the stock would sell at more than $110 before the option expired.

To account for a stock split, the exercise price is reduced by the factor of the split, and the number of options held is increased by that factor. For example, the original IBM call option with exercise price of $110 would be altered after a 10-for-1 split to 10 new options, with each option carrying an exercise price of $11. A similar adjustment is made for stock dividends of more than 10%; the number of shares covered by each option is increased in proportion to the stock dividend, and the exercise price is reduced by that proportion.

Concept Check

Question 1. Suppose that IBM's stock price at the exercise date is $120, and the exercise price of the call $110. What is the profit on one option contract? After a 10-for-1 split, the stock price is $12, the exercise price is $11, and the option holder now can purchase 1,000 shares. Show that the split leaves option profits unaffected.

In contrast to stock dividends, cash dividends do not affect the terms of an option contract. Because payment of a cash dividend reduces the selling price of the stock without inducing offsetting adjustments in the option contract, the value of the option is affected by dividend policy. Other things being equal, call option values are lower for high dividend-payout policies, because such policies slow the rate of increase of stock prices; conversely, put values are higher for high dividend payouts. (Of course, the option values do not rise or fall on the dividend payment or ex-dividend dates. Dividend payments are anticipated, so the effect of the payment already is built into the original option price.)

The Option Clearing Corporation

The Option Clearing Corporation (OCC) is jointly owned by the exchanges on which stock options are traded. It is the clearinghouse for options trading. Buyers and sellers of options who agree on a price will consummate the sale of the option. At this point the OCC steps in. The OCC places itself between the two traders, becoming the effective buyer of the option from the writer and the effective writer of the option to the buyer. All individuals therefore deal only with the OCC, which effectively guarantees contract performance.

When an option holder exercises an option, the OCC arranges for a member firm with clients who have written that option to make good on the option obligation. The member firm in turn selects from its clients who have written that option to fulfill the contract. The selected client either must deliver 100 shares of stock at a price equal to the exercise price for each call option contract written, or must purchase 100 shares at the exercise price for each put option contract written.

Because the OCC guarantees contract performances, option writers are required to post margin amounts to guarantee that they can fulfill their obligations under the option contract. The margin required is determined in part by the amount by which the option is in the money, because that value is an indicator of the potential obligation of the option writer upon exercise of the option. When the required margin exceeds the posted margin, the writer will receive a margin call. The holder of the option need not post margin, because the holder will exercise the option only if it is profitable to do so. After purchasing the option, no further money is at risk.

Margin requirements are determined in part by the other securities held in the investor's portfolio. For example, a call option writer owning the stock against which the option is written can satisfy the margin requirement simply by allowing a broker to hold that stock in the brokerage account. The stock is then guaranteed to be available for delivery should the call option be exercised. If the underlying security is not owned, however, the margin requirement is determined by the value of the underlying security, as well as by the amount by which the option is in or out of the money. Out-of-the-money options require less margin from the writer, because expected payouts are lower.

Other Listed Options

Options on assets other than stocks are also widely traded. These include options on market indices and industry indices, on foreign currency, and even on the futures prices of agricultural products, gold, silver, fixed-income securities, and stock indices. We will discuss these in turn.

Index options

An index option is a call or put based on a stock market index such as the S&P 500 or the New York Stock Exchange Index. Index options are traded on several broad-based indices, as well as on a few industry-specific indices. We discussed many of these indices in Chapter 2.

The construction of the indices can vary across contracts or exchanges. For example, the S&P 100 index is a value-weighted average of the 100 stocks in the Standard & Poor's 100 stock group. The weights are proportional to the market value of outstanding equity for each stock. The Major Market Index, by contrast, is a price-weighted average of 20 stocks, most of which are in the Dow Jones Industrial Average group, whereas the Value Line Index is an equally weighted arithmetic average of roughly 1,700 stocks.

In contrast to stock options, index options do not require that the call writer actually "deliver the index" upon exercise or that the put writer "purchase the index."

FIGURE 19.2

Listing of various index options.

(From *The Wall Street Journal*, May 30, 1988.) Reprinted by permission of *The Wall Street Journal*. © Dow Jones & Company, Inc. 1988. All rights reserved.

INDEX OPTIONS

Friday, May 27, 1988

Chicago Board

S&P 100 INDEX

Strike Price	Calls—Last Jun	Jul	Aug	Puts—Last Jun	Jul	Aug
220	....	22	....	1/2	1 3/4	3 1/8
225	....	....	....	7/8	2 1/2	4 3/8
230	12 1/4	15 3/4	....	1 9/16	3 3/8	5 5/8
235	8 3/4	12	....	2 9/16	5 1/8	7 1/4
240	5 3/8	8 3/8	10 1/2	4 1/2	7 1/2	9 1/4
245	2 15/16	5 3/4	8	7 1/2	9 1/4	11 3/4
250	1 7/16	3 5/8	6	11	12 1/4	....
255	5/8	2 1/16	3 3/4	15 1/4	16	....
260	1/4	1 1/8	2 3/8	20 1/4	21 1/2	....
265	1/8	5/8	1 7/16	....	....	....
270	1/16	5/16	7/8	....	....	....
275	....	3/16	....	....	....	....

Total call volume 39,754   Total call open int. 278,352
Total put volume 41,239   Total put open int. 227,762
The index: High 241.96; Low 240.02; Close 240.72, −1.24

S&P 500 INDEX

Strike Price	Calls—Last Jun	Jul	Sep	Puts—Last Jun	Jul	Sep
195	....	....	60	....	....	7/8
200	....	....	54 1/2	1/16	....	1 1/16
205	....	....	49 1/2	....	....	1 1/16
210	....	....	44 3/4	1/16	....	1 1/2
215	....	....	....	1/16	....	1 3/4
220	33 1/2	....	....	....	....	....
225	....	....	....	5/16	....	....
230	....	25 1/2	....	7/16	1 3/4	4 3/4
235	....	....	....	3/4	....	....
240	14 3/4	....	....	1	3 1/2	....
245	....	13	....	2 1/2	4 1/2	....
250	6 5/8	9 3/4	....	3 1/2	6 1/4	10
255	3 3/8	6 3/4	....	5 3/8	7 7/8	....
260	2 1/4	4 3/4	....	9 1/4	....	....
265	1 1/16	3	....	12 3/8	....	....
270	7/16	1 13/16	5 1/4	....	....	....
275	....	....	3 1/2	....	....	....
280	1/16	....	....	....	....	....
295	....	....	....	41 7/8	....	....
315	....	....	....	61 1/2	....	....

Total call volume 29,729   Total call open int. 165,580
Total put volume 6,694   Total put open int. 217,332
The index: High 254.63; Low 252.74; Close 253.42, −1.21.

Philadelphia Exchange

GOLD/SILVER INDEX

Strike Price	Calls—Last Jun	Jul	Aug	Puts—Last Jun	Jul	Aug
95	5 3/8	....	....	1 1/8	2 1/8	....
100	2 9/16	....	....	2 7/8	....	....
110	3/16	....	....	....	....	....

Total call volume 21   Total call open int. 583
Total put volume 29   Total put open int. 493
The index: High 99.84; Low 98.88; Close 99.02, −0.78

VALUE LINE INDEX OPTIONS

Strike Price	Calls—Last Jun	Jul	Aug	Puts—Last Jun	Jul	Aug
205	....	....	....	....	....	2 3/8
210	....	....	....	....	....	2 5/8
215	....	....	....	....	....	3 3/4
220	....	....	....	....	....	5 1/8
235	....	3 1/4	....	....	....	....

Total call volume 50   Total call open int. 667
Total put volume 40   Total put open int. 180
The index: High 227.80; Low 227.03; Close 227.36, −0.36
Based on Value Line arithmetic average.

NATIONAL O-T-C INDEX

Total call volume 0   Total call open int. 9
Total put volume 0   Total put open int. 92
The index: High 237.86; Low 236.68; Close 237.37, −0.49

UTILITIES INDEX

Strike Price	Calls—Last Jun	Jul	Aug	Puts—Last Jun	Jul	Aug
170	7	....	....	....	....	....
175	2 1/2	....	....	....	....	....
180	....	1 1/2	....	....	....	....

Total call volume 58   Total call open int. 2,583
Total put volume   Total put open int. 1,424

N.Y. Stock Exchange

NYSE INDEX OPTIONS

Strike Price	Calls—Last Jun	Jul	Aug	Puts—Last Jun	Jul	Aug
130	....	....	....	1/4	7/8	....
135	....	....	....	9/16	1 9/16	....
137 1/2	7	....	....	15/16	....	....
140	5 1/2	7	....	1 11/16	3 1/8	....
145	1 13/16	3 9/16	....	3 1/2	....	6 1/2
150	1/2	1 11/16	....	7 1/4	8 1/4	....
155	1/16	9/16	....	....	....	....

Total call volume 1,178.   Total call open int. 7,910.
Total put volume 463.   Total put open int. 7,491.
The index: High 144.17; Low 143.35; Close 143.66, −0.57.

Pacific Exchange

FINANCIAL NEWS COMPOSITE INDEX

Strike Price	Calls—Last Jun	Jul	Sep	Puts—Last Jun	Jul	Sep
155	17 3/4	....	....	....	....	....
160	13 1/2	....	....	....	....	....
165	8 7/8	....	....	....	....	2 7/16
170	5	7 3/8	....	2 3/16	4	....
175	2 3/8	....	....	4 3/8	....	....
180	....	....	....	7 3/4	....	....
185	....	....	....	12 3/8	....	....
190	....	....	....	17 1/4	....	....
205	....	....	....	32 3/8	....	....

Total call volume 186   Total call open int. 3,835
Total put volume 589   Total put open int. 3,216
The index: High 173.82; Low 172.34; Close 172.89, −0.92

American Exchange

MAJOR MARKET INDEX

Strike Price	Calls—Last Jun	Jul	Aug	Puts—Last Jun	Jul	Aug
350	....	....	....	11/16	2 7/8	....
355	....	....	....	1 1/16	3 3/8	....
360	22	....	....	1 9/16	4 3/4	....
365	18	....	....	2 7/16	....	....
370	14 1/2	....	....	3 1/2	7 1/4	11 1/8
375	10 1/4	....	19	5 1/8	8 7/8	13 3/4
380	7 1/4	12 1/4	....	7 3/8	11 3/8	....
385	5	....	13 1/2	11 1/8	....	17 1/2
390	3 1/4	7 3/8	....	13 1/8	19 3/8	....
395	2	5 3/8	8 1/4	16 1/2	19 3/8	....
400	1 1/8	4	7 1/8	20 1/2	....	....
405	9/16	2 15/16	5 1/2	....	....	....
410	3/8	1 15/16	4	....	....	....
415	....	1 1/8	....	....	....	....
420	1/8	13/16	....	....	....	....
425	1/16	1/2	....	....	....	....
430	....	1/4	....	....	....	....

Total call volume 6,328   Total call open int. 21,125
Total put volume 3,402   Total put open int. 17,812
The index: High 382.15; Low 378.79; Close 379.92, −2.19.

COMPUTER TECHNOLOGY INDEX

Strike Price	Calls—Last Jun	Jul	Aug	Puts—Last Jun	Jul	Aug
120	....	3/8	....	....	....	....

Total call volume 30   Total call open int. 386
Total put volume 0   Total put open int. 245
The index: High 104.39; Low 103.99; Close 103.99, −0.40.

OIL INDEX

Strike Price	Calls—Last Jun	Jul	Aug	Puts—Last Jun	Jul	Aug
175	....	....	....	....	4 5/8	....
180	1 1/2	....	....	....	....	....
185	1/2	2 1/4	....	....	....	....

Total call volume 9   Total call open int. 150
Total put volume 20   Total put open int. 713
The index: High 177.69; Low 175.43; Close 175.82, −1.87.

INSTITUTIONAL INDEX

Strike Price	Calls—Last Jun	Jul	Aug	Puts—Last Jun	Jul	Aug
	....	....	....	....	3/8	....

Instead, a cash settlement procedure is used. The profits that would accrue upon exercise of the option are calculated, and the option writer simply pays that amount to the option holder. The profits are equal to the difference between the exercise price of the option and the value of the index. For example, if the S&P 100 index is at $220 when a call option on the index with exercise price $210 is exercised, the holder of the call receives a cash payment of $10 multiplied by the contract multiplier of 100, or $1,000 per contract. Figure 19.2 is a sample listing of various index options from *The Wall Street Journal*.

Foreign currency options

A currency option offers the right to buy or sell a quantity of foreign currency for a specified amount of domestic currency. Foreign currency options have traded on the Philadelphia Stock Exchange since December of 1982. Since then, the Chicago Board Options Exchange and Chicago Mercantile Exchange have listed foreign currency options. Currency option contracts call for purchase or sale of the currency in exchange for a specified number of U.S. dollars. Contracts are quoted in cents or fractions of a cent per unit of foreign currency. Figure 19.3 shows a *Wall Street Journal* listing of the contracts traded on the Philadelphia Exchange. The size of each option contract is specified for each listing. The call option on the British pound, for example, entitles its holder to purchase 12,500 pounds for a specified number of cents per pound on or before the expiration date. The June call option with strike price of 185 cents sells for 2.15 cents, which means that each contract costs $.0215 × 12,500 = $268.75. The current exchange rate is 186.02 cents per pound. Therefore the option is in the money by 1.02 cents, the difference between the current exchange rate (186.02 cents) and the exercise price of 185 cents per pound.

Futures options

Futures options give their holders the right to buy or sell a specified futures contract, using as a futures price the exercise price of the option. Although the delivery process is slightly complicated, the terms of futures options contracts are designed in effect to allow the option to be written on the futures price itself. The option holder receives upon exercise a profit equal to the difference between the current futures price on the specified asset and the exercise price of the option. Thus, if the futures price is, for example, $37, and the call has an exercise price of $35, the holder who exercises the call option on the futures gets a payoff of $2.

Interest rate options

Options on particular U.S. Treasury notes and bonds are listed on the American Exchange and the CBOE. Options also are traded on Treasury bills, certificates of deposit, and GNMA pass-through certificates. Options on Treasury bond and Treasury note futures also trade on the Chicago Board of Trade.

FIGURE 19.3

Foreign currency option contracts traded on the Philadelphia exchange.

(From *The Wall Street Journal*, May 18, 1988.) Reprinted by permission of *The Wall Street Journal*. © Dow Jones & Company, Inc. 1988. All rights reserved.

FOREIGN CURRENCY OPTIONS

Tuesday, May 17, 1988

Philadelphia Exchange

Option & Underlying	Strike Price	Calls—Last May	Jun	Sep	Puts—Last May	Jun	Sep
50,000 Australian Dollars-cents per unit.							
ADollr	...75	r	1.74	2.53	r	0.32	1.76
76.53	...76	r	1.03	1.62	r	0.68	r
76.53	...77	r	0.50	1.21	r	1.08	r
76.53	...78	r	0.30	0.98	r	r	r
76.53	...79	r	0.11	0.80	r	r	r
50,000 Australian Dollars-European Style.							
76.53	...79	r	0.14	r	r	r	r
12,500 British Pounds-cents per unit.							
BPound	182½	r	r	5.90	r	0.30	r
186.02	.185	r	2.15	r	r	1.05	r
186.02	187½	r	0.75	3.15	r	2.15	r
186.02	.190	r	0.20	2.35	r	4.20	r
186.02	192½	r	0.15	1.85	r	r	r
186.02	195	r	r	r	r	9.40	r
12,500 British Pounds-European Style.							
186.02	182½	r	4.20	r	r	r	r
50,000 Canadian Dollars-cents per unit.							
CDollr	...79	r	1.84	r	s	r	r
80.84	...81	r	r	r	r	0.60	r
80.84	.81½	r	0.16	r	r	r	r
62,500 West German Marks-cents per unit.							
DMark	..56	r	2.75	r	r	0.01	r
58.58	...57	r	r	r	r	0.05	0.40
58.58	...58	r	0.98	r	r	0.14	0.66
58.58	...59	r	0.28	1.42	r	0.56	1.03
58.58	...60	r	0.04	0.90	r	1.40	r
58.58	...61	r	0.05	0.60	r	2.40	2.40
58.58	...62	r	r	0.42	r	r	r
58.58	...63	r	0.03	0.25	r	r	r
58.58	...64	r	r	0.26	r	r	r
6,250,000 Japanese Yen-100ths of a cent per unit.							
JYen	..73	r	r	r	r	r	0.12
79.49	...75	r	r	r	r	0.01	r
79.49	...76	r	3.50	r	r	0.02	r
79.49	...77	r	r	r	r	0.06	0.51
79.49	...78	r	2.32	r	r	0.09	r
79.49	...79	r	0.92	r	r	0.27	r
79.49	...80	r	0.36	1.80	r	0.66	r
79.49	...81	r	0.13	1.28	r	1.56	2.05
79.49	...82	r	0.05	0.94	r	r	r
79.49	...83	r	0.01	r	r	r	r
79.49	...85	r	r	0.31	r	r	r
62,500 Swiss Francs-cents per unit.							
SFranc	..69	r	r	r	r	0.09	r
70.28	...70	r	r	r	r	0.26	1.02
70.28	...71	r	0.32	r	r	0.71	r
70.28	...72	r	0.10	r	r	1.65	1.94
70.28	...73	r	0.07	r	r	2.32	s
70.28	...74	r	r	r	r	3.32	r
62,500 Swiss Francs-European Style.							
70.28	...73	r	r	r	r	2.14	r

Total call vol.   37,694   Call open int.   529,299
Total put vol.   32,914   Put open int.   506,575
r—Not traded. s—No option offered.
Last is premium (purchase price).

Derivative Assets: Options and Futures

19.2 *Values of Options at Expiration*

Call Options

Recall that a call option gives the right to purchase a security at the exercise price. If you hold a call option on IBM stock with an exercise price of $130 and IBM currently sells at $140, you can exercise your option to purchase the stock at $130 and simultaneously sell the shares at the market price of $140, clearing $10 per share. On the other hand, if the shares sell below $130, you can sit on the option and do nothing, realizing no further gain or loss. The value of the call option at expiration equals:

$$\text{Payoff to call holder} = \begin{matrix} S_T - X & \text{if } S_T > X \\ 0 & \text{if } S_T \leqslant X \end{matrix}$$

where S_T is the value of the stock at expiration and X is the exercise price. This formula emphasizes the option property because the payoff cannot be negative. That is, the option is exercised only if S_T exceeds X. If S_T is less than X, exercise does not occur and the option expires with zero value. The loss to the option holder in this case equals the price originally paid for the right to buy at the exercise price.

The value at expiration of the call on IBM with exercise price $130 is given by the following schedule:

IBM value:	$120	$130	$140	$150	$160
Option value:	0	0	$ 10	$ 20	$ 30

For IBM prices at or below $130, the option is worthless. Above $130, the option is worth the excess of IBM's price over $130. The option's value increases by $1 for each dollar increase in the IBM stock price. This relationship can be depicted graphically, as in the solid (top) line of Figure 19.4.

The solid line of Figure 19.4 depicts the value of the call at maturity. The net *profit* to the holder of the call equals the gross payoff less the initial investment in the call. Suppose the call cost $14. Then the profit to the call holder would be as given in the broken (bottom) line of Figure 19.4. At option expiration, the investor has suffered a loss of $14 if the stock price is less than $130. Profits do not become positive unless the stock price at expiration exceeds $144. The break-even point is $144, because at that point the payoff to the call, $S_T - X = \$144 - \$130 = \$14$, equals the cost paid to acquire the call. Hence the call holder profits only if the stock price is higher.

Conversely, the writer of the call incurs losses if the stock price is high. In that scenario, the writer will receive a call and will be obligated to deliver a stock worth S_T for only X dollars:

$$\text{Payoff to call writer} = \begin{matrix} -(S_T - X) & \text{if } S_T \geqslant X \\ 0 & \text{if } S_T < X \end{matrix}$$

FIGURE 19.4
Payoff and profit to call option at expiration.

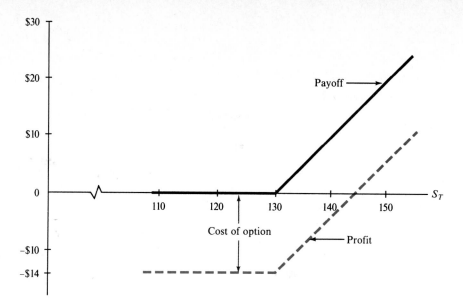

FIGURE 19.5
Payoff and profit to call writers at expiration.

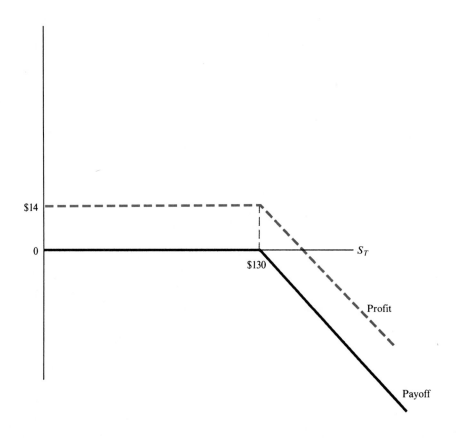

The call writer, who is exposed to losses if IBM stock increases in price, is willing to bear this risk in return for the option premium. Figure 19.5 depicts the payoff and profit diagrams for the call writer. Notice that these are just the mirror images of the corresponding diagrams for call holders. The break-even point for the option writer also is $144. The (negative) payoff at that point just offsets the premium originally received when the option was written.

Put Options

A put option conveys the right to sell an asset at the exercise price. In this case, the holder will not exercise the option unless the asset sells for *less* than the exercise price. For example, if IBM shares were to fall to $110, a put option with exercise price $120 could be exercised to give a $10 profit to its holder. The holder would purchase a share of IBM for $110, and simultaneously deliver it to the put option writer for the exercise price of $120.

The value of a put option at expiration is

$$\text{Payoff to put holder} = \begin{array}{ll} X - S_T & \text{if } S_T \leq X \\ 0 & \text{if } S_T > X \end{array}$$

The solid (top) line in Figure 19.6 illustrates the payoff at maturity to the holder of a put option on IBM stock with an exercise price of $130. If the stock price at option maturity is above $130, the put has no value, because the right to sell the shares at $130 would not be exercised. Below a price of $130 the put value at expiration in-

FIGURE 19.6
Payoff and profit to put option at expiration.

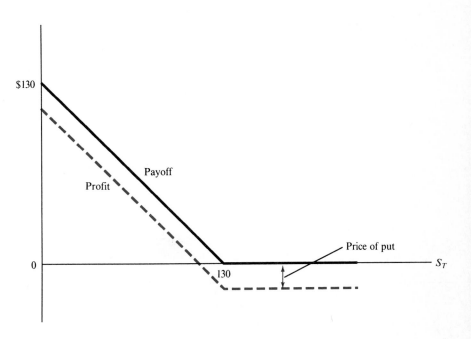

creases by $1 for each dollar that the stock price falls. The broken (bottom) line in Figure 19.6 is a graph of the put option owner's profit at expiration, net of the initial cost of the put.

Concept Check

Question 2. Analyze the strategy of put writing.
a. What is the payoff to a put writer as a function of the stock price?
b. What is the profit?
c. Draw the payoff and profit graphs.
d. When do put writers do well? When do they do poorly?

Writing puts *naked* (that is, writing a put without an offsetting position in the stock for hedging purposes) exposes the writer to losses if the market falls. Writing naked out-of-the-money puts was once considered an attractive way to generate income, since it was believed that as long as the market did not fall sharply before the option expiration the option premium could be collected without the put holder ever exercising the option against the writer. Because only sharp drops in the market could result in losses to the writer of the put, the strategy was not viewed as overly riskly. However, as the nearby box makes clear, in the wake of the market crash of October 1987 such put writers suffered huge losses. Participants now perceive much greater risk to this strategy.

Options vs. Stock Investments

Call options are bullish investments; that is, they provide profits when stock prices increase. Puts, in contrast, are bearish investments. Symmetrically, writing calls is bearish and writing puts is bullish. Because option values depend on market movements, purchase of options may be viewed as a substitute for direct purchase or sale of a stock. Why might an option strategy be preferable to direct stock transactions?

For example, why would you purchase a call option rather than buy IBM stock directly? Maybe you have some information that leads you to believe IBM stock will increase in value from its current level, which in our examples we will take to be $140. You know your analysis could be incorrect, and that IBM also could fall in price. Suppose that a 6-month maturity call option with exercise price $135 currently sells for $14, and that the 6-month interest rate is 5%. Consider these three strategies for investing a sum of money, for example, $14,000. For simplicity, suppose that IBM will not pay any dividends until after the 6-month period.

Strategy A: Purchase 100 shares of IBM stock.
Strategy B: Purchase 1,000 call options on IBM with exercise price $135. (This would require 10 contracts, each for 100 shares.)
Strategy C: Purchase 100 call options for $1,400. Invest the remaining $12,600 in 6-month T-bills, to earn 5% interest.

The Black Hole: How Some Investors Lost All Their Money in the Market Crash

Their Sales of 'Naked Puts' Quickly Come to Grief, Damage Suits Are Filed

When Robert O'Connor got involved in stock-index options, he hoped his trading profits would help put his children through college. His broker, Mr. O'Connor explains, "said we would make about $1,000 a month, and if our losses got to $2,000 to $3,000, he would close out the account."

Instead, Mr. O'Connor, the 46-year-old owner of a small medical X-ray printing concern in Grand Rapids, Mich., got caught in one of the worst investor blowouts in history. In a few minutes on Oct. 19, he lost everything in his account plus an *additional* $91,000—a total loss of 175% of his original investment.

"If I had been told what the real risks were, I would never have done this. We're not big rollers," Mr. O'Connor says. "That's my life savings. That's not money to play with."

Scene of Disaster

For Mr. O'Connor and hundreds of other investors, a little-known corner of the Chicago Board Options Exchange was the "black hole" of Black Monday's market crash. In a strategy marketed by brokers nationwide as a sure thing, these customers had sunk hundreds of millions of dollars into "naked puts"—unhedged, highly leveraged bets that the stock market was in no danger of plunging. Most of these naked puts seem to have been options on the Standard & Poor's 100 stock index, which are traded on the CBOE.

Lulled into complacency by the market's long surge, hundreds of brokers marketed naked puts to ill-informed investors ranging from a retired civil servant in Virginia to a quadriplegic woman in Texas. When stocks crashed, many traders with unhedged positions got margin calls for several times their original investment.

Risky options trades are emerging as the leading single source of investor complaints following the crash, regulators say. Unlike the huge stock-market losses, which remain mostly on paper, individuals' losses on stock-index options were suddenly forced on them at the time of the crash and involved immediate losses of real money. The losses are estimated at several hundred million dollars, and a rash of lawsuits and countersuits between brokers and investors seem certain.

Suitability Questioned

"There are some very serious suitability questions about which investors were put into options," says Scott Staph, the communications director for the North American Securities Administrators Association in Washington. "It's much more dramatic than anything in stocks."

The carnage has sparked investigations by the Chicago Board Options Exchange and the American Stock Exchange, which also has trading in stock-index options. Also scheduled are hearings by several congressional committees. They may press for tighter regulation and stiffer margin requirements, which are regulated by the Securities and Exchange Commission, to curb speculative activity.

The blowout underscores one of the biggest regulatory breakdowns exposed by the market crash: brokers' failure to recognize the riskiness of certain options positions and to require adequate margins, or security deposits. Traders say as much as 25% of the CBOE's stock-index option trades were unhedged—that is, not backed by holdings of the underlying stocks or offsetting trades.

The 'Put' Strategy

The losses were especially sharp in "naked, out-of-the-money puts." A seller of puts agrees to buy stock or stock-index contracts at a set price before the put expires. These contracts are usually sold "out of the money"—priced at a level below current market prices that makes it unprofitable to exercise the option so long as the market rises or stays flat. The seller pockets a small amount per contract.

But if the market plunges, as it did Oct. 19, the op-

Continued.

tion swings into the money. The seller, in effect, has to pay pre-plunge stock prices to make good on his contract—and he takes a big loss.

Moreover, many investors were required to post margin money equal to only 5% to 10% of the face value of the options contracts—a minuscule amount compared with their exposure to loss. That kind of leverage more resembles Russian roulette than the "risk-free" trading that many customers thought they were doing in naked options, says Robert Gordon, the president of Twenty-First Securities Corp., a New York investment firm.

Brokers across the nation are still smarting as well. In San Francisco, Charles Schwab Corp. said a single trader's activity in stock-index options accounted for $15 million of its $22 million in losses in October. Bear, Stearns & Co. and other big Wall Street houses took heavy hits. Options-related losses sank H.B. Shaine & Co., the Grand Rapids brokerage firm where Mr. O'Connor did business. Some $90 million of losses at First Options of Chicago Inc. may drag its parent company, Continental Illinois Corp., into the red in the fourth quarter. And in London, too, a 23-year-old trainee accountant lost nearly one million pounds (about $1.75 million) trading options, according to British press reports.

"You have to recognize that there is unlimited potential for disaster" in selling naked options, says Peter Thayer, executive vice president of Gateway Investment Advisors Inc., a Cincinnati-based investment firm that trades options to hedge its stock portfolios. Last September, Gateway bought out-of-the-money put options on the S&P 100 stock index on the CBOE at $2 to $3 a contract as "insurance" against a plunging market. By Oct. 20, the day after the crash, the value of those contracts had soared to $130. Although Gateway profited handsomely, the parties on the other side of the trade were clobbered.

In many cases, brokers played down the risks to attract more customers to a big-commission business. "Brokers were selling these things like annuities," says Elisabeth Richards, a broker and strategic analyst with Heritage Financial Investments Corp. of Falls Church Va.

In Texas, the 56-year-old quadriplegic, who asked not to be named, says she lost her entire $35,000 nest egg trading naked stock-index options. "It was far too risky for me," she says. She adds that now she is left with only Social Security.

Flying Blind

The North American Securities Administrators Association, which has been fielding investors' post-crash complaints on a new telephone hot line, heard from a Mendocino, Calif., investor who lost $1.3 million in naked puts without even knowing what his position was in the market. The man told association officials that he had switched recently to an aggressive broker who assured him that he would "fill him in as they went along." In a phone call to the association, Mr. Staph says, the man "was asking me what puts and calls are." (A call is an option to buy at a specified price within a specified period.)

Neither the CBOE nor the Amex passes judgment on the riskiness of particular trading strategies. But to help traders caught in sharp moves, the CBOE recently adopted an accelerated opening procedure aimed at starting trading more quickly during heavy volume; it wants to avoid a replay of the morning of Oct. 20, when a huge influx of orders kept some options from trading for an hour and a half.

Firm Sued

Brokers who were pushing naked options assumed that the stock market wouldn't plunge into uncharted territory. Frank VanderHoff, one of the two main brokers who put 50 to 70 H.B. Shaine clients into stock-index options, says he told clients that the strategy's risk was "moderate barring a nuclear attack or a crash like 1929. It wasn't speculative. The market could go up or down, but not *substantially* up or down. If the crash had only been as bad as '29," he adds, "we would have made it." Mr. VanderHoff says that all his customers read and signed option-trading risk-disclosure documents and that he never promised that accounts would have strictly limited losses.

Nevertheless, Mr. O'Connor and other customers are suing the firm in state court in Grand Rapids. They allege that they weren't fully informed of the risks and that Shaine acted negligently by selling out their options accounts without authority from them. The complaint says that the defendants lost about $100,000 each and that they should be reimbursed that amount, plus $500,000 each in damages.

The public's enthusiasm for options trading seems sure to wane. Harry Fluke of Alexandria, Va., was trading naked puts and calls in an arcane strategy known as a "strangle" when the market wiped out the $54,000 in his account. He still owes his brokerage firm $318,500. "It just killed me," he says.

Mr. Fluke's broker, Thomson-McKinnon Securities Inc., contends in a suit filed in federal court in Alexandria to collect money from him that he was well aware of the risks. Mr. Fluke concedes that he had been trading naked puts and calls for several years, but he says nothing had prepared him for the impact of the stock market's unprecedented volatility.

Similarly, a retired engineer in Niagara Falls, N.Y., who asked that his name be withheld, set up a trust for his daughter and grandson 10 years ago, with himself as trustee. The 76-year-old retiree says he lost nearly $360,000 on Black Monday when he was forced to buy back the stock-index options and the trust account was left about $140,000 in debt to Bear Stearns.

His experience is typical: On Oct. 16, he sold 40 S&P 100 stock-index put options for $1,550 each, or a total of $62,000. In essence, he was betting that after the 108.35 point drop in the Dow Jones Industrial Average that Friday, the market wasn't likely to drop much further and probably would soon rally.

But Black Monday's plunge forced him to buy back the puts to cover his margin calls. Meanwhile, the price of the options had jumped 600% to $10,500 a contract—costing him $420,000 for the 40 contracts that he had sold for $62,000 just three days earlier.

Professional Battered

Some professional traders didn't fare much better. On Black Monday, Hwalin Lee took his accustomed place in the CBOE's stock-index-options pit, but unbeknown to other traders, the Taiwan native was already $5 million to $7 million in debt from the Friday plunge. He was under orders from his clearing firm and lender, First Options of Chicago, to close out his big positions in naked puts—to buy back options that he had previously sold. First Options even sent an official variously described in market parlance as a "leg breaker" or "sheriff" onto the CBOE floor with him to make sure he did so. But it was too late. The trader single-handedly lost $52 million.

Mr Lee, 55, had consistently taken huge positions and a dozen times since 1978 had been sanctioned by the CBOE for violating trading limits. First Options didn't shun risk, either. Just a month before, its computers had simulated a 450-point drop in the industrial average. But the computer model assumed that the options market would keep functioning, allowing traders to close out losing positions.

On Black Monday, it didn't. Few were willing to step in front of an oncoming train, and none took the opposite side of Mr. Lee's trades. As the market hit bottom, his losses ballooned.

Mr. Lee couldn't be reached to comment, and officials at Continental Illinois and its options-clearing unit recently declined to be interviewed. However, Jim R. Porter, First Options' chairman, does say another 500-point drop in the industrial average wouldn't cost his firm money because its traders are operating under stricter trading standards and are putting up more margin cash.

Nevertheless, First Options still lets customers, such as James F. Hart, trade in naked, out-of-the-money puts and calls. Mr. Hart says First Options hasn't sought to rein him in. Other brokerage firms, however, have curbed or halted unhedged options trading since the crash.

For small investors such as Mr. Fluke, it's too late. Though not disputing the facts laid out in his broker's suit against him, he is still reeling. He won't comment on his plans, but a lawyer familiar with his case says the former federal employee may file for personal bankruptcy. Mr. Fluke says, "I wish someone had sat down with me and said the risk is greater than you—a retired civil servant—can risk."

FIGURE 19.7
Rates of return to
three strategies.

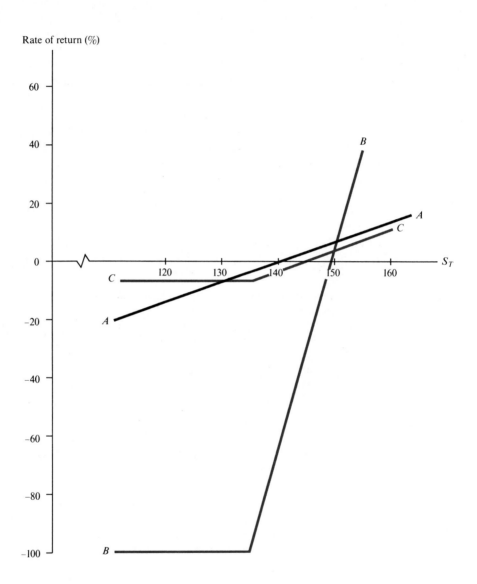

Derivative Assets: Options and Futures

Let us trace the possible values of these three portfolios when the options expire in 6 months as a function of IBM stock price at that time.

IBM Price	$120	$130	$140	$150	$160
Value of portfolio A:	$12,000	$13,000	$14,000	$15,000	$16,000
Value of portfolio B:	0	0	5,000	15,000	25,000
Value of portfolio C:	13,230	13,230	13,730	14,730	15,730

Portfolio A will be worth 100 times the share value of IBM. Portfolio B is worthless unless IBM sells for more than the exercise price of the call. Once that point is reached, the portfolio is worth 1,000 times the excess of the stock price over the exercise price. Finally, portfolio C is worth $13,230 from the investment in T-bills ($12,600 $\times$ 1.05 = $13,230) plus any profits from the 100 call options. Remember that each of these portfolios involves the same $14,000 initial investment. The rates of return on these three portfolios are as follows:

IBM Price	$120	$130	$140	$150	$160
A (all stock)	−14.3%	−7.1%	0.0%	7.1%	14.3%
B (all options)	−100.0%	−100.0%	−64.3%	7.1%	78.6%
C (options plus bills)	−5.5%	−5.5%	−1.9%	5.2%	12.4%

These rates of return are illustrated in Figure 19.7.

Comparing the returns to portfolios B and C to those of the simple investment in IBM stock represented by portfolio A, we see that options offer two interesting features. First, an option offers leverage. Compare the returns of portfolios B and A. When IBM stock falls in price even moderately to $130, the value of portfolio B falls precipitously to zero, a rate of return of −100%. Conversely, if the stock price increases by 14.3%, from $140 to $160, the all-option portfolio jumps in value by a disproportionate 78.6%. In this sense calls are a leveraged investment on the stock. Their values respond more than proportionately to changes in the stock value. Figure 19.7 vividly illustrates this point. The slope of the all-option portfolio is far steeper than the all-stock portfolio, reflecting its greater proportional sensitivity to the value of the underlying security. The leverage factor is the reason that investors (illegally) exploiting inside information commonly choose options as their investment vehicle.

The potential insurance value of options is the second interesting feature, as portfolio C shows. The T-bill plus option portfolio cannot be worth less than $13,230 after 6 months, since the option can always be left to expire worthless. The worst possible rate of return on portfolio C is −5.5%, compared to a (theoretically) worst possible rate of return on IBM stock of −100% if the company were to go bankrupt. Of course, this insurance comes at a price: when IBM does well, portfolio C does not perform quite as well as portfolio A.

The Put-Call Parity Relationship

Suppose that you buy a call option and write a put option, each with the same exercise price, X, and the same expiration date, T. At expiration the payoff on your investment will equal the payoff to the call, minus the payoff that must be made on the put. The payoff for each option will depend on whether the ultimate stock price, S_T, exceeds the exercise price at contract expiration.

	$S_T \leq X$	$S_T > X$
Payoff of call held	0	$S_T - X$
Payoff of put written	$-(X - S_T)$	0
TOTAL	$S_T - X$	$S_T - X$

Figure 19.8 illustrates this payoff pattern. Compare the payoff to that of a portfolio made up of the stock plus a borrowing position, where the money to be paid back will grow, with interest, to X dollars at the maturity of the loan. Such a position, in fact, is a *leveraged* equity position in which $X/(1 + r_f)^T$ dollars is borrowed today (so that X will be repaid at maturity) and S_0 dollars is invested in the stock. The total payoff of the leveraged equity position is $S_T - X$, the same as that of the option strategy. Thus the long call–short put position replicates the leveraged equity position. Again, we see that option trading allows us to construct artificial leverage.

Because the option portfolio has a payoff identical to that of the leveraged equity position, the costs of establishing them must be equal. The net cost of establishing the option position is $C - P$; the call is purchased for C, while the written put generates premium income of P. Likewise, the leveraged equity position requires a net cash outlay of $S_0 - X/(1 + r_f)^T$, the cost of the stock less the proceeds from borrowing. Equating these costs, we conclude that

$$C - P = S_0 - X/(1 + r_f)^T \tag{19.1}$$

Equation 19.1 is called the **put-call parity theorem** because it represents the proper relationship between put and call prices. If the parity relation is ever violated, an arbitrage opportunity arises. For example, suppose that you confront these data for a certain stock:

Stock price	$110
Call price (6-month maturity, $X = \$105$)	$ 17
Put price (6-month maturity, $X = \$105$)	$ 5
Risk-free interest rate:	10.25% annual yield, or 5% per 6 months

We use these data in the put-call parity theorem to see if parity is violated:

$$C - P \stackrel{?}{=} S_0 - X/(1 + r_f)^T \tag{19.2}$$
$$17 - 5 \stackrel{?}{=} 110 - 105/1.05$$
$$12 \stackrel{?}{=} 10$$

FIGURE 19.8

The payoff pattern of
a long call–short put
position.

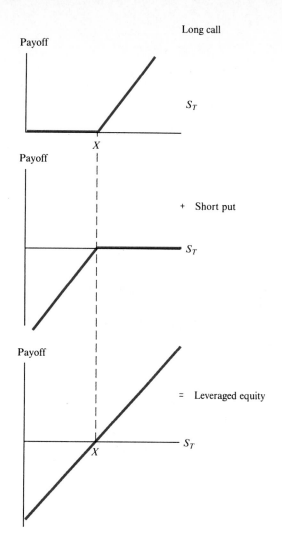

Payoff   Long call

S_T

X

Payoff

+   Short put

S_T

Payoff

=   Leveraged equity

S_T

X

Parity is violated. To exploit the mispricing, you can buy the relatively cheap portfolio (the stock plus borrowing position represented on the right-hand side of equation
19.2) and sell the relatively expensive portfolio (the long call–short put position corresponding to the left-hand side—that is, write a call and buy a put).

Let us examine the payoff to this strategy. In 6 months, the stock will be worth
S_T. The $100 borrowed will be paid back with interest, resulting in a cash outflow of
$105. The written call will result in a cash outflow of $S_T - \$105$ if S_T exceeds $105.

TABLE 19.1   Arbitrage Strategy

| | | Cash Flow in 6 Months | |
Position	Immediate Cash Flow	$S_T \leq 105$	$S_T > 105$
Buy stock	−110	S_T	S_T
Borrow $X/(1 + r_f)^T = \$100$	+100	−105	−105
Sell call	+ 17	0	$-(S_T - 105)$
Buy put	− 5	$105 - S_T$	0
TOTAL	2	0	0

The purchased put pays off $105 − S_T$ if the stock price is below $105.

Table 19.1 summarizes the outcome. The immediate cash inflow is $2. In 6 months the various positions provide exactly offsetting cash flows: the $2 inflow is thus realized without any offsetting outflows. This is an arbitrage opportunity that will be pursued on a large scale until buying and selling pressure restores the parity condition expressed in equation 19.1.

The parity condition actually applies only to options on stocks that pay no dividends before the maturity date of the options. It also applies only to European options, because the cash flow streams from the two portfolios represented by the two sides of equation 19.1 will match only if each position is held until maturity. If a call and a put may be optimally exercised at different times before their common expiration date, then the equality of payoffs cannot be assured, or even expected, and the portfolios will have different values. We will return to these issues in Chapter 20.

For now, however, let's see how well parity works using real data from Figure 19.1. The June call on IBM with exercise price $110 and time to expiration of 39 days cost $4.125, while the put cost $2.875. IBM was selling for $110.375, and the annualized interest rate on this date for 39-day T-bills was 6.5%. According to parity, we should find that

$$\$4.125 - \$2.875 = \$110.375 - \$110/(1.065)^{39/365}$$
$$\$1.25 = \$1.11$$

In this case parity is violated by only 14 cents per share, far too small an amount to outweigh the brokerage fees involved in attempting to exploit the minor mispricing. Moreover, given the infrequent trading of options that we have noted, this small discrepancy from parity could be due to "stale prices."

Combination of Options

An unlimited variety of payoff patterns can be achieved by combining puts and calls with various exercise prices. The following explains the motivation and structure of some of the more popular methods.

Protective put

Imagine that you would like to invest in a stock, for example, IBM, but that you

TABLE 19.2   Payoff to Protective Put Strategy

	$S_T \leq X$	$S_T > X$
Stock	S_T	S_T
Put	$X - S_T$	0
TOTAL	X	S_T

FIGURE 19.9
Value of a protective put position at expiration.

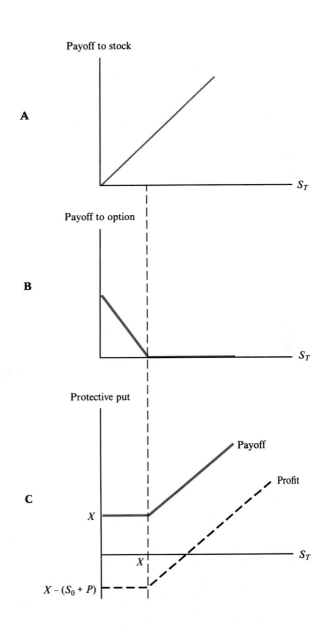

An Introduction to Options Markets

are unwilling to bear potential losses beyond some given level. Investing in the stock alone is quite risky, because in principle you could lose all the money you invest. You might consider instead investing in stock together with a put option on the stock. Table 19.2 illustrates the total value of your portfolio at option expiration.

Whatever happens to the stock price, you are guaranteed a payoff equal to the put option's exercise price because the put gives you the right to sell IBM for the exercise price even if the stock price is below that value.

Figure 19.9 illustrates the payoff and profit to this **protective put** strategy. The solid line in Figure 19.9, C, is the total payoff. The dashed line is displaced downward by the cost of establishing the position, $S_0 + P$. Notice that potential losses are indeed limited.

It is instructive to compare the profit to the protective put strategy with that of the stock investment. For simplicity, consider an at-the-money protective put, so that $X = S_0$. Figure 19.10 compares the profits for the two strategies. The profit on the stock is zero if the stock price remains unchanged, and $S_T = S_0$. It rises or falls by $1 for every $1 swing in the ultimate stock price. The profit on the stock plus put portfolio

FIGURE 19.10
Protective put vs. stock investment.

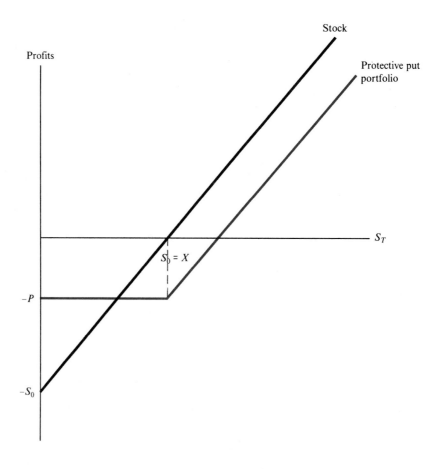

is negative and equal to the cost of the put if S_T is below S_0. The profit on the overall protective put position increases one for one with increases in the stock price, once S_T exceeds S_0.

Figure 19.10 makes it clear that the protective put offers some insurance against stock price declines in that it limits losses. Indeed, as we shall see in Chapter 20, protective put strategies are the conceptual basis for the portfolio insurance industry. The cost of the protection is that, in the case of stock price increases, your profit is reduced by the cost of the put, which turned out to be unneeded.

PROTECTIVE PUTS VS. STOP-LOSS ORDERS

We have seen that protective puts guarantee that the end-of-period value of a portfolio will equal or exceed the put's exercise price. As a specific example, consider a share of stock protected by a European put option with 1-year maturity and an exercise price of $40. Even if the stock at year-end is selling below $40, the put can be exercised and the stock can be sold for the exercise price. The stock-plus-put position will be worth $40, regardless of how far the stock price falls.

Another common tool to protect a portfolio position is the stop-loss order. This is an order to your broker to sell your stock when and if its price falls to some lower boundary such as $40 per share. Thus, should the stock price fall substantially, your shares will be sold before losses mount, so that your proceeds will not fall below $40 per share.

It would seem from this analysis that the stop-loss order provides the same stock price insurance offered by the protective put. The protective put, however, must be obtained by paying for the option, whereas the stop-loss order can be executed by your broker for no extra cost. Does this mean that the stop-loss order is effectively a free put option? What does the put option offer that the stop-loss order does not?

To resolve this seeming paradox, look at Figure 19.11, which graphs one possible path for the stock price over the course of the year. Notice that, although the stock price falls below $40 at time t, it ultimately recovers and ends the year selling at $60. The protective put combination in this circumstance will end the year worth $60—the put will expire worthless, but the stock will be worth $60. The stop-loss order, however, has required that the stock be sold at time t as soon as its price falls below $40. This strategy will yield by year-end only $40 plus any interest accumulated between time t and the end of the year, far less than the payoff on the protective put strategy.

The protective put strategy does offer an advantage over the stop-loss strategy. With a stop-loss order in force, the investor realizes the $40 lower bound if the stock price *ever* reaches that boundary because the stock is sold as soon as the boundary is reached. Whenever the stock price rebounds from the $40 limit, the investor using the stop-loss order will not share in the gain. The holder of the put option, on the other hand, does not have to exercise when the stock hits $40. Instead, the option holder may wait until the end of the year to exercise the option, knowing that the $40 exercise price is guaranteed regardless of how far the stock falls, but that, should the stock price recover, the stock still will be held and any gain will be captured. This is the advantage that justifies the cost required to purchase the protective put option.*

*Another disadvantage of the stop-loss order, which is of a more practical nature, is that the selling price is not guaranteed. Problems in executing trades could lead to a transaction at a price lower than $40.

FIGURE 19.11
Stop-loss vs.
protective put.

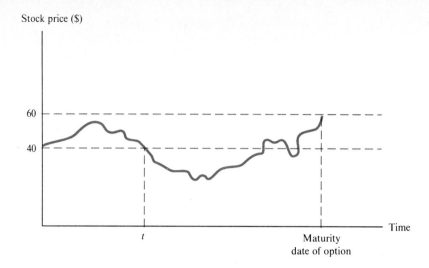

Covered calls

A **covered call** position is the purchase of a share of stock with a simultaneous sale of a call on that stock. The position is "covered" because the obligation to deliver the stock is covered by the stock held in the portfolio. Writing an option without an offsetting stock position is called, by contrast, *naked option writing*. The payoff to a covered call, presented in Table 19.3, equals the stock value minus the payoff of the call. The call payoff is subtracted because the covered call position involves issuing a call to another investor who can choose to exercise it to profit at your expense.

The solid line in Figure 19.12, C, illustrates the payoff pattern. We see that the total position is worth S_T when the stock price at time T is below X, and rises to a maximum of X when S_T exceeds X. In essence the sale of the call option means that the call writer has sold the claim to any stock value above X in return for the initial premium (the call price). Therefore at expiration the position is worth at most X. The broken line of Figure 19.12, C, is the net profit to the covered call.

Writing covered call options has been a popular investment strategy among institutional investors. Consider the managers of a fund invested largely in stocks. They might find it appealing to write calls on some or all of the stock in order to boost income by the premiums collected. Although they thereby forfeit potential capital gains should the stock price rise above the exercise price, if they view X as the price at which they plan to sell the stock anyway, then the call may be viewed as enforcing a kind of "sell discipline." The written call guarantees that the stock sale will take place as planned.

For example, assume a pension fund is holding 1,000 shares of IBM stock, with a current price of $130 per share. Suppose that management intends to sell all 1,000 shares if the share price hits $140 and that a call expiring in 90 days with an exercise price of $140 is currently selling for $5. By writing 10 IBM call contracts (100

TABLE 19.3   Payoff to a Covered Call

	$S \leq X$	$S > X$
Payoff of stock	S_T	S_T
$-$Payoff of call	$\underline{0}$	$\underline{-(S_T - X)}$
TOTAL	S_T	X

FIGURE 19.12

Value of a covered call position at expiration.

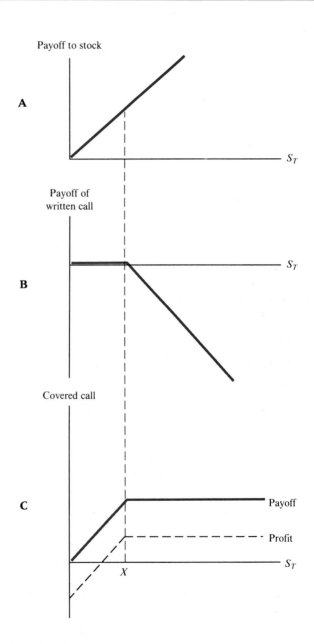

shares each) the fund can pick up $5,000 in extra income. The fund would lose its share of profits from any movement of IBM stock above $140 per share, but given that it would have sold its shares at $140, it would not have realized those profits anyway.

Straddle

A **straddle** is established by buying both a call and a put on a stock, each with the same exercise price, X, and the same expiration date, T. Straddles are useful strategies for investors who believe that a stock will move a lot in price, but are uncertain about the direction of the move. For example, suppose you believe that an important court case that will make or break a company is about to be settled, and the market is not yet aware of the situation. The stock will either double in value if the case is settled favorably, or will drop by half if the settlement goes against the company. The straddle position will do well regardless of the outcome, because its value is highest when the stock price makes extreme upward or downward moves from X.

The kiss of death for a straddle is no movement in the stock price. If S_T equals X, both the call and the put expire worthless, and the investor's outlay for the purchase of the two options is lost. Straddle positions, in other words, are bets on volatility. An investor who establishes a straddle must view the stock as more volatile than the market does. The payoff to a straddle is presented in Table 19.4.

The solid line in Figure 19.13, C, illustrates this payoff. Notice that the portfolio payoff is always positive, except at the one point where the portfolio has zero value, $S_T = X$. You might wonder why all investors do not pursue such a no-lose strategy. Remember, however, that the straddle requires that both the put and call be purchased. The value of the portfolio at expiration, although never negative, still must exceed the initial cash outlay for the investor to clear a profit.

The broken line in Figure 19.13 is the profit to the straddle. The profit line lies below the payoff line by the cost of purchasing the straddle, $P + C$. It is clear from the diagram that the straddle position generates a loss unless the stock price deviates substantially from X. The stock price must depart from X by the total amount expended to purchase the call and the put for the purchaser of the straddle to clear a profit.

Strips and *straps* are variations of straddles. A strip is two puts and one call on a security with the same exercise price and maturity date. A strap is two calls and one put.

TABLE 19.4 Payoff to a Straddle

	$S_T \leq X$	$S_T > X$
Payoff of call	0	$S_T - X$
+ Payoff of put	$+ (X - S_T)$	$+ 0$
TOTAL	$X - S_T$	$S_T - X$

FIGURE 19.13

Payoff and profit to a
straddle at expiration.

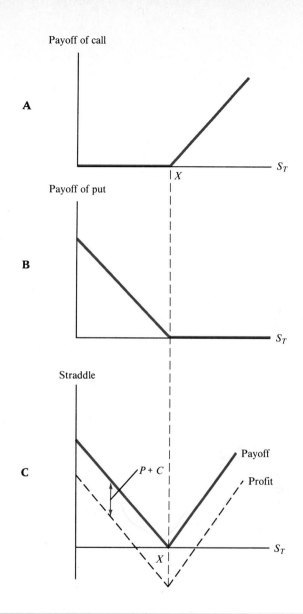

Concept Check

Question 3. Graph the profit and payoff diagrams for strips and straps.

Spreads

A **spread** is a combination of two or more call options (or two or more puts) on the same stock with differing exercise prices or times to maturity. Some options will

TABLE 19.5   Payoff to a Bullish Vertical Spread

	$S_T \leq X_1$	$X_1 < S_T \leq X_2$	$S_T > X_2$
Payoff of call, exercise price = X_1	0	$S_T - X_1$	$S_T - X_1$
$-$ Payoff of call, exercise price = X_2	0	0	$-(S_T - X_2)$
TOTAL	0	$S_T - X_1$	$X_2 - X_1$

FIGURE 19.14
Value of a bullish
spread position at
expiration.

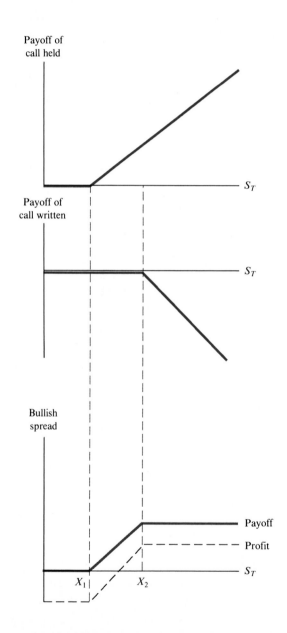

be held long, while others are written. A *vertical* or *money spread* involves the purchase of one option and the simultaneous sale of another with a different exercise price. A *horizontal* or *time* spread refers to the sale and purchase of options with differing expiration dates.

The vertical and horizontal spreads take their names from the way options are listed in the newspaper. Going vertically down a column of option listings such as in Figure 19.1, we find options with identical maturities but different exercise prices. Moving horizontally across the row are options with identical exercise prices but different maturities.

Consider a vertical spread in which one call option is bought with an exercise price X_1, while another call with an identical expiration date but higher exercise price, X_2, is written. The payoff to this position will be the difference in the value of the call held and the value of the call written, as shown in Table 19.5.

Notice that we now have three instead of two outcomes to distinguish: the lowest-price region where S_T is below both exercise prices, a middle region where S_T is between the two exercise prices, and a high-price region where S_T exceeds both exercise prices. Figure 19.14 illustrates the payoff and profit to this strategy, which is called a *bullish spread* because the payoff either increases or is unaffected by stock price increases. Holders of bullish spreads benefit from stock price increases.

A bullish spread would be appropriate for an investor who has a target-wealth goal in mind, but is unwilling to risk losses beyond a certain level. If you are contemplating buying a house for $150,000, for example, you might set this figure as your goal. Your current wealth may be only $145,000, and you are unwilling to risk losing more than $10,000. A bullish spread on 1,000 shares (10 option contracts) with $X_1 = $135 and $X_2 = $150 would give you a good chance to realize the $5,000 capital gain without risking a loss of more than $10,000.

Another motivation for a bullish spread might be that the investor believes that one option is overpriced relative to another. For example, if the investor believes that the $X = $135 call is cheap compared to the $X = $150 call, she might establish the spread, even without a strong desire to take a bullish position in the stock.

19.3 *Option Valuation*

Consider a call option that is out of the money currently, with the stock price below the exercise price. Does this mean that the option is altogether valueless? Clearly not. Even though immediate exercise would be unprofitable, the call retains positive value because there is always a chance that the stock price will increase sufficiently by the expiration date to allow for profitable exercise. If not, the worst that can happen is that the option will expire with zero value.

The value $S_0 - X$ is sometimes called the **intrinsic value** of in-the-money options, because it gives the profit that could be obtained by immediate exercise. Intrinsic value is set equal to zero for out-of-the-money options. The difference between the actual call price and the intrinsic value is commonly called the **time value** of the option. "Time value" is an unfortunate choice of terminology because it may confuse the option's time value with the time value of money. Time value in the options context simply refers to the difference between the option's price and the value the option would have if it were expiring immediately. It is the part of the option's value that may be attributable to the fact that it still has positive time to expiration.

Most of an option's time value is in fact a type of "volatility value." As long as the option holder can choose not to exercise, the payoff cannot be worse than zero. Even if a call option is out of the money now, it still will sell for a positive price because it offers the potential for a profit if the stock price increases while imposing no risk of additional loss should the stock price fall. The volatility value lies in the value of the right not to exercise the option if that action would be unprofitable. The option to exercise, as opposed to the obligation to exercise, provides insurance against poor stock-price performance.

As the stock price increases substantially, it becomes more likely that the option will be exercised by expiration. In this case, with exercise all but assured, the volatility value becomes minimal. As the stock price gets ever greater, the option value approaches the "adjusted" intrinsic value, the stock price minus the present value of the exercise price, $S_0 - PV(X)$.

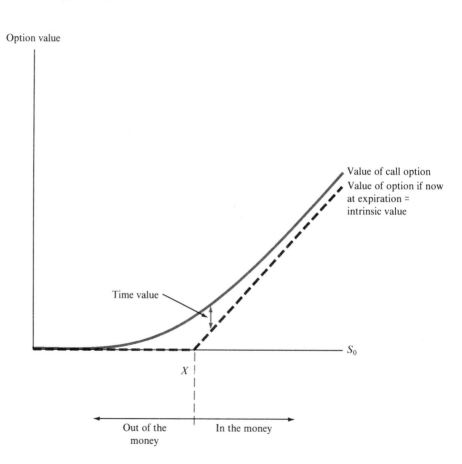

FIGURE 19.15

Call option value before expiration.

Option value

Value of call option
Value of option if now at expiration = intrinsic value

Time value

S_0

X

Out of the money | In the money

Why should this be? If you *know* that the option will be exercised and the stock purchased for X dollars, it is as though you own the stock already. The stock certificate might as well be sitting in your safe deposit box now, because it will be there in only a few months. You just have not paid for it yet. The present value of your obligation is the present value of X, so your net position is $S_0 - PV(X)$.

Figure 19.15 illustrates the call option valuation function. Notice that the option always increases in value with the stock price. The slope is greatest, however, when the option is deep in the money. In this case exercise is all but assured, and the option increases in value one for one with the stock price.

Determinants of the Value of a Call Option

We can identify at least six factors that should affect the value of a call option: the stock price, the exercise price, the volatility of the stock price, the time to expiration, the interest rate, and the dividend rate of the stock. The call option should increase in value with the stock price and decrease in value with the exercise price because the payoff to a call, if exercised, equals $S_T - X$. The magnitude of the expected payoff from the call increases with the difference of $S_0 - X$.

Call option value also increases with the volatility of the underlying stock price. To see why, consider circumstances where possible stock prices at expiration may range from $10 to $50 compared with a situation where stock prices may range only from $20 to $40. In both cases the expected stock price will be $30. Suppose that the exercise price on a call option is also $30. What are the option payoffs?

High-Volatility Scenario

Stock price	$10	$20	$30	$40	$50
Option payoff	0	0	0	$10	$20

If each outcome is equally likely, with probability .2, the expected payoff to the option under high-volatility conditions will be $6.

Low-Volatility Scenario

Stock price	$20	$25	$30	$35	$40
Option payoff	0	0	0	$ 5	$10

Again, with equally likely outcomes, the expected payoff to the option is half as much, only $3.

Despite the fact that the average stock price in each scenario is $30, the average option payoff is greater in the high-volatility scenario. The source of this extra value is the limited loss that an option holder can suffer, or the volatility value of the call. No matter how far below $30 the stock price drops, the option holder will get zero. Obviously, extremely poor stock price performance is no worse for the call option holder than is moderately poor performance. In the case of good stock performance, however, the option will expire in the money, and it will be more profitable the

TABLE 19.6 Determinants of Call Option Values

Variable Increases	Value of Call Option
Stock price, S	Increases
Exercise price, X	Decreases
Volatility, σ	Increases
Time to expiration, T	Increases
Interest rate, r_f	Increases
Cash dividend payouts	Decreases

higher the stock price. Thus extremely good stock outcomes can improve the option payoff without limit, but extremely poor outcomes cannot worsen the payoff below zero. This asymmetry means that volatility in the underlying stock price increases the expected payoff to the option, thereby enhancing its value.[2]

Concept Check

Question 4. Should a put option also increase in value with the volatility of the stock?

Similarly, longer time to expiration increases the value of a call option. For more distant expiration dates, the range of likely stock prices expands, which has an effect similar to that of increased volatility. Moreover, as time to expiration increases, the present value of the exercise price falls, thereby benefiting the call option holder and increasing the option value. As a corollary to this issue, call option values are higher when interest rates rise (holding the stock price constant), because higher interest rates also reduce the present value of the exercise price.

Finally, the dividend payout policy of the firm affects option values. A high-dividend payout policy puts a drag on the rate of growth of the stock price. For any expected total rate of return on the stock, a higher dividend yield must imply a lower expected rate of capital gain. This drag on stock price appreciation decreases the potential payoff from the call option, thereby lowering the call value. Table 19.6 summarizes these relationships.

Concept Check

Question 5. How should the value of a put option respond to the firm's dividend payout policy?

---

[2]Strictly speaking, our demonstration shows only that the expected payoff from the call increases with stock volatility. It does not *necessarily* follow that the price of the call will be greater. This issue is treated in Jagannathan, Ravi, "Call Options and the Risk of Underlying Securities," *Journal of Financial Economics, 13,* September 1984.

Financial economists searched for years for a workable option-pricing model before Black and Scholes[3] and Merton[4] derived a formula for the value of a call option. Now widely used by option-market participants, the **Black-Scholes formula** is

$$C_0 = S_0 N(d_1) - Xe^{-rT}N(d_2) \tag{19.3}$$

where

$$d_1 = \frac{\ln(S_0/X) + (r + \sigma^2/2)T}{\sigma\sqrt{T}}$$

$$d_2 = d_1 - \sigma\sqrt{T}$$

and where

C_0 = Current option value
S_0 = Current stock price
X = Exercise price
r = Risk-free interest rate (the annualized continuously compounded rate on a safe asset with the same maturity as the expiration of the option, which is to be distinguished from r_f, the discrete period interest rate)
T = Time to maturity of option in years
σ = Standard deviation of the annualized continuously compounded rate of return of the stock
ln = Natural logarithm function
e = 2.71828, the base of the natural log function
$N(d)$ = The probability that a random draw from a standard normal distribution will be less than d. This equals the percentage of the area under the normal curve up to d, as shown in Figure 19.16.

Notice one thing that the option value does not depend on: the expected rate of return on the stock. In a sense this information is already built into the formula with inclusion of the stock price, which itself depends on the stock's risk-and-return characteristics. This version of the Black-Scholes formula is predicated on the assumption that the stock pays no dividends. (We address this issue in Chapter 20.)

Although you may find the Black-Scholes formula intimidating, we can explain it first at a somewhat intuitive level. The trick is to view the $N(d)$ terms (loosely!) as risk-adjusted probabilities that the call option will expire in the money. First, look at equation 19.3 when both $N(d)$ terms are close to 1, indicating a very high probability that the option will be exercised. Then the call option value is equal to $S_0 - Xe^{-rT}$, which is what we called earlier the adjusted intrinsic value, $S_0 - PV(X)$. This makes sense: if exercise is certain, we have a claim on a stock with current value S_0 and an

---

[3]Black, Fischer, and Scholes, Myron, "The Pricing of Options and Corporate Liabilities," *Journal of Political Economy, 81* May/June 1973.
[4]Merton, Robert C., "Theory of Rational Option Pricing," *Bell Journal of Economics and Management Science, 4,* spring 1973.

FIGURE   19.16
A standard normal
curve.

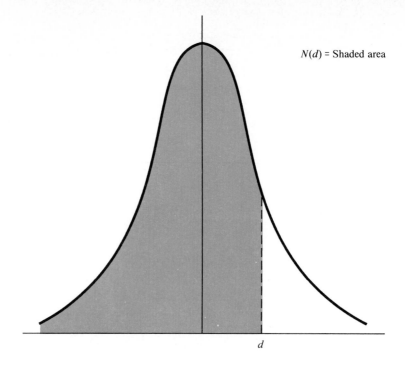

$N(d)$ = Shaded area

d

obligation with present value $PV(X)$, or, with continuous compounding, Xe^{-rT}.

Now look at equation 19.3 when the $N(d)$ terms are close to zero, meaning that the option almost certainly will not be exercised. Then the equation confirms that the call is worth nothing. For middle-range values of $N(d)$ between 0 and 1, equation 19.3 tells us that the call value can be viewed as the present value of the call's potential payoff adjusting for the probability of in-the-money expiration.

How do the $N(d)$ terms serve as risk-adjusted probabilities? This question quickly leads us into advanced statistics. Notice, however, that d_1 and d_2 both increase as the stock price increases. Therefore, $N(d_1)$ and $N(d_2)$ also increase with higher stock prices. This is the property we would desire of our "probabilities." For higher stock prices relative to exercise prices, future exercise is more likely.

In fact, you can use the Black-Scholes formula fairly easily. Suppose that you want to value a call option under the following circumstances:

Stock price	S_0	= 100
Exercise price	X	= 95
Interest rate	r	= .10
Time to expiration	T	= .25 (one fourth year)
Standard deviation	σ	= .5

First calculate

$$d_1 = \frac{\ln(100/95) + (.10 + .5^2/2) \times .25}{.5 \sqrt{.25}} = .43$$
$$d_2 = .43 - .5 \sqrt{.25} = .18$$

Next find $N(d_1)$ and $N(d_2)$. The values of the normal distribution are tabulated and may be found in many statistics textbooks. A table of $N(d)$ is provided here as Table 19.7. The table reveals (using interpolation) that

$$N(.43) = .6664$$
$$N(.18) = .5714$$

Thus the value of the call option is

$$C = 100 \times .6664 - (95e^{-.10 \times .25}) \times .5714$$
$$= 66.64 - 52.94 = \$13.70$$

What if the option price were in fact $15? Is the option mispriced? Maybe, but before betting your fortune on that, you may want to reconsider the valuation analysis. First, like all models, the Black-Scholes formula is based on some simplifying abstractions that make the formula only approximately valid. We consider some of these shortcomings in Chapter 20.

Second, even within the context of the model, you must be sure of the accuracy of the parameters used in the formula. Four of these—S_0, X, T, and r—are straightforward. The stock price, exercise price, and time to maturity may be read directly from the option pages. The interest rate used is the money market rate for a maturity equal to that of the option. The last input, however, the standard deviation of the stock return, is not directly observable. It must be estimated from historical data, from scenario analysis, or from the prices of other options, as we will describe momentarily. Because the standard deviation must be estimated, it is always possible that discrepancies between an option price and its Black-Scholes value are simply artifacts of error in the estimation of the stock's volatility.

In fact, market participants often give the option valuation problem a different twist. Rather than calculating a Black-Scholes option value for a given stock standard deviation, they ask instead, "What standard deviation would be necessary for the option price that I can see to be consistent with the Black-Scholes formula?" This is called the **implied volatility** of the option, the volatility level for the stock that the option price implies. From the implied standard deviation investors judge whether they think the actual stock standard deviation exceeds the implied volatility. If it does, the option is considered a good buy; if actual volatility seems greater than the implied volatility, its fair price would exceed the observed price.

Concept Check

Question 6. Consider the option in the example selling for $15 with Black-Scholes value of $13.70. Is its implied volatility more or less than .5?

TABLE 19.7   Cumulative Normal Distribution

d	$N(d)$	d	$N(d)$	d	$N(d)$
-3.00	.0013	-1.58	.0571	-0.76	.2236
-2.95	.0016	-1.56	.0594	-0.74	.2297
-2.90	.0019	-1.54	.0618	-0.72	.2358
-2.85	.0022	-1.52	.0643	-0.70	.2420
-2.80	.0026	-1.50	.0668	-0.68	.2483
-2.75	.0030	-1.48	.0694	-0.66	.2546
-2.70	.0035	-1.46	.0721	-0.64	.2611
-2.65	.0040	-1.44	.0749	-0.62	.2676
-2.60	.0047	-1.42	.0778	-0.60	.2743
-2.55	.0054	-1.40	.0808	-0.58	.2810
-2.50	.0062	-1.38	.0838	-0.56	.2877
-2.45	.0071	-1.36	.0869	-0.54	.2946
-2.40	.0082	-1.34	.0901	-0.52	.3015
-2.35	.0094	-1.32	.0934	-0.50	.3085
-2.30	.0107	-1.30	.0968	-0.48	.3156
-2.25	.0122	-1.28	.1003	-0.46	.3228
-2.20	.0139	-1.26	.1038	-0.44	.3300
-2.15	.0158	-1.24	.1075	-0.42	.3373
-2.10	.0179	-1.22	.1112	-0.40	.3446
-2.05	.0202	-1.20	.1151	-0.38	.3520
-2.00	.0228	-1.18	.1190	-0.36	.3594
-1.98	.0239	-1.16	.1230	-0.34	.3669
-1.96	.0250	-1.14	.1271	-0.32	.3745
-1.94	.0262	-1.12	.1314	-0.30	.3821
-1.92	.0274	-1.10	.1357	-0.28	.3897
-1.90	.0287	-1.08	.1401	-0.26	.3974
-1.88	.0301	-1.06	.1446	-0.24	.4052
-1.86	.0314	-1.04	.1492	-0.22	.4129
-1.84	.0329	-1.02	.1539	-0.20	.4207
-1.82	.0344	-1.00	.1587	-0.18	.4286
-1.80	.0359	-0.98	.1635	-0.16	.4365
-1.78	.0375	-0.96	.1685	-0.14	.4443
-1.76	.0392	-0.94	.1736	-0.12	.4523
-1.74	.0409	-0.92	.1788	-0.10	.4602
-1.72	.0427	-0.90	.1841	-0.08	.4681
-1.70	.0446	-0.88	.1894	-0.06	.4761
-1.68	.0465	-0.86	.1949	-0.04	.4841
-1.66	.0485	-0.84	.2005	-0.02	.4920
-1.64	.0505	-0.82	.2061	0.00	.5000
-1.62	.0526	-0.80	.2119	0.02	.5080
-1.60	.0548	-0.78	.2177	0.04	.5160

d	N(d)	d	N(d)	d	N(d)
0.06	.5239	0.86	.8051	1.66	.9515
0.08	.5319	0.88	.8106	1.68	.9535
0.10	.5398	0.90	.8159	1.70	.9554
0.12	.5478	0.92	.8212	1.72	.9573
0.14	.5557	0.94	.8264	1.74	.9591
0.16	.5636	0.96	.8315	1.76	.9608
0.18	.5714	0.98	.8365	1.78	.9625
0.20	.5793	1.00	.8414	1.80	.9641
0.22	.5871	1.02	.8461	1.82	.9656
0.24	.5948	1.04	.8508	1.84	.9671
0.26	.6026	1.06	.8554	1.86	.9686
0.28	.6103	1.08	.8599	1.88	.9699
0.30	.6179	1.10	.8643	1.90	.9713
0.32	.6255	1.12	.8686	1.92	.9726
0.34	.6331	1.14	.8729	1.94	.9738
0.36	.6406	1.16	.8770	1.96	.9750
0.38	.6480	1.18	.8810	1.98	.9761
0.40	.6554	1.20	.8849	2.00	.9772
0.42	.6628	1.22	.8888	2.05	.9798
0.44	.6700	1.24	.8925	2.10	.9821
0.46	.6773	1.26	.8962	2.15	.9842
0.48	.6844	1.28	.8997	2.20	.9861
0.50	.6915	1.30	.9032	2.25	.9878
0.52	.6985	1.32	.9066	2.30	.9893
0.54	.7054	1.34	.9099	2.35	.9906
0.56	.7123	1.36	.9131	2.40	.9918
0.58	.7191	1.38	.9162	2.45	.9929
0.60	.7258	1.40	.9192	2.50	.9938
0.62	.7324	1.42	.9222	2.55	.9946
0.64	.7389	1.44	.9251	2.60	.9953
0.66	.7454	1.46	.9279	2.65	.9960
0.68	.7518	1.48	.9306	2.70	.9965
0.70	.7580	1.50	.9332	2.75	.9970
0.72	.7642	1.52	.9357	2.80	.9974
0.74	.7704	1.54	.9382	2.85	.9978
0.76	.7764	1.56	.9406	2.90	.9981
0.78	.7823	1.58	.9429	2.95	.9984
0.80	.7882	1.60	.9452	3.00	.9986
0.82	.7939	1.62	.9474	3.05	.9989
0.84	.7996	1.64	.9495		

Another variation is to compare two options on the same stock with equal expiration dates but different exercise prices. The option with the higher implied volatility would be considered relatively expensive, because a higher standard deviation is required to justify its price. The analyst might consider buying the option with the lower implied volatility and writing the option with the higher implied volatility.

Put Option Valuation

We have concentrated so far on call option valuation. We can derive Black-Scholes European put option values from call option values using the put-call parity theorem. To value the put option, we simply calculate the value of the corresponding call option in equation 19.3 from the Black-Scholes formula, and solve for the put option value:

$$P = C + PV(X) - S_0 \tag{19.4}$$

The data from our Black-Scholes call option example are $C = \$13.70$, $X = \$95$, $S = \$100$, $r = .10$, and $T = .25$. Using these data, we find a European put option on that stock with identical exercise price and time to maturity is worth[5]

$$P = \$13.70 + (\$95e^{-.10 \times .25}) - \$100 = \$6.35$$

As noted, we might then compare this formula value to the actual put price as one step in formulating a trading strategy.

Equation 19.4 is valid for European puts on non-dividend-paying stocks. Listed put options are American options that offer the opportunity of early exercise, however. Because an American option allows its owner to exercise at any time before the expiration date, it must be worth at least as much as the corresponding European option. Therefore equation 19.4 describes only the lower bound on the true value of the American put. We will consider American options further in Chapter 20.

19.4 *Bull and Bear CDs: A Recent Innovation*

A recent innovation is the bull certificate of deposit. Unlike conventional CDs, which pay a fixed rate of interest, *bull CDs* pay depositors a specified fraction of the increase in the rate of return on a market index such as the S&P 500, while guaranteeing a minimum rate of return should the market fall. A bull CD may offer 70% of any market increase, but protect its holder from any market decrease by guaranteeing at least no loss.

This arrangement is clearly a type of call option. If the market rises, the depositor profits according to the *participation rate* or *multiplier,* in this case 70%; if the market falls, the investor is insured against loss. Just as clearly, the bank offering these

---

[5]Notice that we discount the exercise price using continuous compounding rules in accord with the Black-Scholes formula. See the Appendix to Chapter 4 for a review of continuous compounding.

FIGURE 19.17
Bull CD.

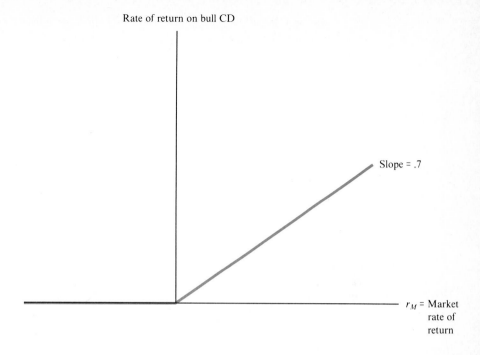

Rate of return on bull CD

Slope = .7

r_M = Market
rate of
return

CDs is in effect writing call options and can hedge its position by buying index calls in the options market. Figure 19.17 shows the nature of the bank's obligation to its depositors.

How might the bank set the appropriate multiplier? To answer this, note various features of the option:

1. The price the depositor is paying for the option is the forgone interest on the conventional CD that could be purchased. The depositor trades in a claim on a risk-free return of r_f for a return that depends on the market's performance. Conversely, the bank can fund its obligation using the interest that it would have paid on a conventional CD.

2. The option we have described is an at-the-money option, meaning that the exercise price equals the current value of the stock index. The option goes into the money as soon as the market index increases from its level at the inception of the contract.

3. We can analyze the option on a per-dollar-invested basis. For example, the option costs the depositor r_f dollars per dollar placed in the bull CD. The market price of the option per dollar invested is C/S_0: the at-the-money option costs C dollars and is written on one unit of the market index, currently at S_0.

Now it is easy to determine the multiplier that the bank can offer on its bull CDs. It receives from its depositors a "payment" of r_f per dollar invested. It costs the bank C/S_0 to purchase the call option on a $1 investment in the market index. Therefore, if r_f is, for example, 70% of C/S_0, the bank can purchase at most .7 call options on the

$1 investment and the multiplier will be .7. More generally, the multiplier on a bull CD is r_f divided by C/S_0.

As an example, suppose that $r_f = 6\%$ per year, and that 6-month maturity at-the-money calls on the market index currently cost $10. The index is at $250. Then the option costs $10/$250 = $.04 per dollar of market value. The CD rate is 3% per 6 months, or $.03 per dollar invested. Therefore the multiplier would be .03/.04 = .75.

This version of the bull CD has several variants. Investors can purchase bull CDs that guarantee a positive minimum return if they are willing to settle for a smaller multiplier. In this case, the option is "purchased" by the depositor for $(r_f - r_{min})$ dollars per dollar invested, where r_{min} is the guaranteed minimum return. Because the purchase price is lower, fewer options can be purchased, which results in a lower multiplier. Another variant is the *bear CD,* which pays depositors a fraction of any *fall* in the market index. For example, a bear CD might offer a rate of return of .6 times any percentage decline in the S&P 500.

Concept Check

Question 7. Continue to assume that $r_f = 6\%$, that at the money calls sell for $10, and that the market index is at 250. What would be the multiplier for bull CDs offering a guaranteed minimum return of 1% on a 6-month deposit?

Summary

1. A call option is the right to buy an asset at an agreed-upon exercise price. A put option is the right to sell an asset at a given exercise price.

2. American options allow exercise on or before the exercise date. European options allow exercise only on the expiration date. Most traded options are American in nature.

3. Options are traded on stocks, stock indices, foreign currencies, fixed-income securities, and several futures contracts.

4. Options can be used either to increase an investor's exposure to an asset price, or to provide insurance against volatility of asset prices. Popular option strategies include covered calls, protective puts, straddles, and spreads.

5. The put-call parity theorem relates the prices of put and call options. If the relationship is violated, arbitrage opportunities will result. Specifically, the relationship that must be satisfied is that

$$C + PV(X) = S_0 + P$$

where X is the exercise price of both the call and the put options, and $PV(X)$ is the present value of a claim to X dollars to be paid at the expiration date of the options.

7. Option values may be viewed as the sum of intrinsic value plus time or "volatility" value. The volatility value is the right to choose not to exercise if the stock

price moves against you. Thus option holders cannot lose more than the cost of the option, regardless of stock price performance.

8. Call options are more valuable when the exercise price is lower, when the stock price is higher, when the interest rate is higher, when the time to maturity is greater, when the stock's volatility is greater, and when dividends are lower.

9. Put option values can be derived using call option values and the put-call parity theorem. For American-style options, such values are only approximate.

10. Bull and bear CDs are in fact options and may be valued by comparing them to the prices of market-traded options.

Key Terms

Call option	Protective put
Exercise price	Covered call
Strike price	Straddle
Put option	Spread
In the money	Intrinsic value
Out of the money	Time value
American option	Black-Scholes formula
European option	Implied volatility
Put-call parity theorem	

Selected Readings

An upper-level textbook that gives a comprehensive treatment of option markets, institutions, and valuation is:
Cox, John, and Rubinstein, Mark, *Options Markets,* Prentice Hall, 1985.
A good treatment of the institutional organization of option markets is:
Chicago Board Options Exchange *Reference Manual.* The CBOE also publishes a *Margin Manual* that provides an overview of margin requirements on many option positions.
An excellent discussion of option trading strategies is:
Black, Fischer, "Fact and Fantasy in the Use of Options," *Financial Analysts Journal,* July/August 1975.
The results of several simulations of various trading strategies are reported in:
Merton, Robert C., Scholes, Myron, and Gladstein, Matthew, "The Returns and Risk of Alternative Call Option Portfolio Strategies," *Journal of Business, 51,* April 1978, and Merton, Robert C., Scholes, Myron, and Gladstein, Matthew, "The Returns and Risks of Alternative Put-Option Portfolio Investment Strategies," *Journal of Business, 55,* January 1982.

Problems

1. Suppose you think Wal-Mart stock is going to appreciate substantially in value in the next 6 months. Suppose that the stock's current price, S_0, is $100, and that the call option expiring in 6 months has an exercise price, X, of $100 and is selling at a price, C, of $10. With $10,000 to invest, you are considering three alternatives.
   a. Invest all $10,000 in the stock, buying 100 shares
   b. Invest all $10,000 in 1,000 options (10 contracts)

c. Buy 100 options (one contract) for $1,000, and invest the remaining $9,000 in a money market fund paying 4% in interest over 6 months (8% per year)

What is your rate of return for each alternative for four stock prices 6 months from now? Summarize your results in the following table and diagram.

Rate of Return on Investment

Stock price:	Price of stock 6 months from now			
	80	100	110	120
a. All stocks (100 shares)				
b. All options (1,000 shares)				
c. Bills + 100 options				

Rate of return

2. The common stock of the PUTT Corporation has been trading in a narrow price range for the past month, and you are convinced that it is going to break far out of that range in the next 3 months. You do not know whether it will go up or down, however. The current price of the stock is $100 per share, and the price of a 3-month call option at an exercise price of $100 is $10.
   a. If the risk-free interest rate is 10% per year, what must be the price of a 3-month put option on PUTT stock at an exercise price of $100?
   b. What would be a simple options strategy to exploit your conviction about the stock price's future movement? How far would it have to move in either direction for you to make a profit on your initial investment?

3. The common stock of the C.A.L.L. Corporation has been trading in a narrow range around $50 per share for months, and you are convinced that it is going to stay in that range for the next 3 months. The price of a 3-month put option with an exercise price of $50 is $4.

a. If the risk-free interest rate is 10% per year, what must be the price of a 3-month call option on C.A.L.L. stock at an exercise price of $50 if it is at the money?

b. What would be a simple options strategy using a put and a call to exploit your conviction about the stock price's future movement? What is the most money you can make on this position? How far can the stock price move in either direction before you lose money?

c. How can you create a position involving a put, a call, and risk-free lending that would have the same payoff structure as the stock at expiration? What is the net cost of establishing that position now?

4. (Based on CFA Examination, Level III, 1984)

Upon the death of his grandmother several years ago, Bill Melody received as a bequest from her estate 2,000 shares of General Motors common stock. The price of the stock at time of distribution from the estate was $75 a share, and this became the cost basis of Melody's holding. Late in 1983, Melody agreed to purchase a new condominium for his parents at a total cost of $160,000, payable in full upon its completion in March 1984. Melody planned to sell the General Motors stock to raise funds to purchase the condominium.

At year-end 1983, GM's market price was around $75 a share, but it appeared to be weakening. This concerned Melody, because if the price of the stock were to drop by a significant amount before he sold, the proceeds would not be sufficient to cover the purchase of the condominium in March 1984.

Melody visited with three different investment counseling firms to seek advice in developing a strategy that, at a minimum, would protect the value of his principal at or near $150,000 ($75 a share). Ideally, the strategy would enhance the value to $160,000 so Melody would have the total cost of the condominium. Four alternatives were discussed:

a. Melody's own opinion was to sell the General Motors stock at $75 a share and invest the proceeds in a 10% certificate of deposit maturing in 3 months.

b. Anderson Investment Advisors suggested that Melody write a March 1984 call option on his General Motors holding at a strike price of $80. The March 1984 calls were quoted at $2.

c. Cole Capital Management suggested that Melody purchase March 1984 at-the-money put contracts on General Motors, now quoted at $2.

d. MBA Associates suggested that Melody keep the stock, purchase March 1984 at-the-money put contracts on GM, and finance the purchase by selling March calls with a strike price of $80.

Disregarding transaction costs, dividend income, and margin requirements, rank the four alternatives in terms of their fulfilling the strategy of at least preserving the value of Melody's principal at $150,000 and preferably increasing the value to $160,000 by March 1984. Support your conclusions by showing the payoff structure of each alternative.

5. a. A butterfly spread is the purchase of one call at exercise price X_1, the sale of two calls at exercise price X_2, and the purchase of one call at exercise price X_3. X_1 is less than X_2, and X_2 is less than X_3 by equal amounts, and all calls

have the same expiration date. Graph the payoff diagram to this strategy.

    b. A vertical combination is the purchase of a call with exercise price X_2, and a put with exercise price X_1, with X_2 greater than X_1. Graph the payoff to this strategy.

6. A bearish spread is the purchase of a call with exercise price X_2 and the sale of a call with exercise price X_1, with X_2 greater than X_1. Graph the payoff to this strategy and compare it to Figure 19.14.

7. We showed in the text that the value of a call option increases with the volatility of the stock. Is this also true of put option values? Use the put-call parity theorem, as well as a numerical example, to confirm your answer.

8. Use the Black-Scholes formula to find the value of a call option on the following stock:

$$
\begin{array}{ll}
\text{Time to maturity} & = 6 \text{ months} \\
\text{Standard deviation} & = 50\% \text{ per year} \\
\text{Exercise price} & = \$50 \\
\text{Stock price} & = \$50 \\
\text{Interest rate} & = 10\% \text{ per year}
\end{array}
$$

9. Recalculate the value of the option in problem 8, successively substituting one of the following changes while keeping the other parameters as in problem 8:

$$
\begin{array}{ll}
\text{Time to maturity} & = 3 \text{ months} \\
\text{Standard deviation} & = 25\% \text{ per year} \\
\text{Exercise price} & = \$55 \\
\text{Stock price} & = \$55 \\
\text{Interest rate} & = 15\%
\end{array}
$$

Consider each scenario independently. Confirm that the option value changes in accordance with the prediction of Table 19.6.

10. If a call option on a non-dividend-paying stock selling at $25 with exercise price $25 and time to maturity of 6 months sells for $2.13, while the corresponding put option sells for $1.39, find the present value of $25 to be paid in 6 months.

11. In each of the following questions you are asked to compare two options with parameters as given. The risk-free interest rate for *all* cases should be assumed to be 6%. Assume that the stocks on which these options are written pay no dividends.

    a.

Put	T	X	σ	Price of Option
A	.5	50	.20	$10
B	.5	50	.25	$10

Which *put* option is written on the stock with the *lower* price?

    i. A

  ii. B

  iii. Not enough information

b.

Put	T	S	σ	Price of Option
A	.5	50	.20	$10
B	.5	50	.20	$12

Which *put* option must be written on the stock with the *lower* price?
  i. *A*
 ii. *B*
iii. Not enough information

c.

Call	S	X	σ	Price of Option
A	50	50	.20	$12
B	55	50	.20	$10

Which *call* option must have the *lower* time to maturity?
  i. *A*
 ii. *B*
iii. Not enough information

d.

Call	T	X	S	Price of Option
A	.5	50	55	$10
B	.5	50	55	$12

Which *call* option is written on the stock with *higher* volatility?
  i. *A*
 ii. *B*
iii. Not enough information

e.

Call	T	X	S	Price of Option
A	.5	50	55	$10
B	.5	55	55	$7

Which *call* option is written on the stock with *higher* volatility?
  i. *A*
 ii. *B*
iii. Not enough information

12. I am attempting to formulate an investment strategy. On the one hand, I think that there is great upward potential in the stock market and would like to participate in the upward move if it in fact materializes. However, I am not able to afford substantial stock market losses and so cannot run the risk of a stock market collapse, which I also think is a possibility. My investment advisor suggests a protective put position: buy both shares in a market-index stock fund and put options on those shares with 3-month maturity and exercise price of $260. The stock index is currently selling for $300. However, my uncle suggests that I instead buy a 3-month call option on the index fund with exercise price $280, and buy 3-month T-bills with face value $280.

a. On the same graph, draw the *payoffs* to each of these strategies as a function of the stock-fund value in three months. (Hint: think of the options as being on one "share" of the stock-index fund, with the current price of each share of the index equal to $300.)

b. Which portfolio must require a greater initial outlay to establish? (Hint: does either portfolio provide a final payoff that is always at least as great as the payoff of the other portfolio?)

c. Suppose that the market prices of the securities are as follows:

Stock fund	$300
T-bill (face value $280)	$270
Call (exercise price $280)	$ 40
Put (exercise price $260)	$ 2

    i. Make a table of the profits realized for each portfolio for the following values of the stock price in 3 months: $S_T = 0$, $260, $280, $300, and $320.

    ii. Graph the profits to each portfolio as a function of S_T on a single graph.

d. Which strategy is riskier? Which should have a higher beta?

e. Explain why the prices for the securities given in part c do *not* violate the put-call parity relationship.

13. Consider a bear CD with a minimum return of zero, and a promise to pay a specified fraction of any percentage fall in the S&P 500 index after a 6-month period. If 6-month maturity at-the-money puts on the index cost $15, the conventional CD rate is 8% per year, and the index is at 250, what multiplier can the bear CD offer?

CHAPTER 20

Options Markets: A Closer Look

This chapter presents more advanced material on option strategies and valuation. We start with a closer look at option pricing. In Chapter 19 we showed some qualitative properties of option pricing and demonstrated one particular valuation formula, the famous Black-Scholes model. Arguably the most significant breakthrough in finance theory in the last three decades, the model still suffers from some unrealistic simplifying assumptions. Two in particular are that the option is exercised only at the exercise date and that the underlying stock pays no dividends. In this chapter we will examine the impact of relaxing these assumptions. Then we will look at some of the more important applications of option pricing theory. We will see how an option hedge ratio can be used in portfolio management and control. One of the most controversial applications of this analysis has been the use of the option hedge ratio in the provision of portfolio insurance.

Option pricing theory also has implications for the valuation of several option-like securities such as callable bonds, convertible bonds, and warrants. Finally, we examine an alternative approach to exact option valuation called "two-state" or "binomial" option pricing.

20.1 More on Option Valuation

The Black-Scholes formula is extremely useful, but like many theoretical constructs, it relies on several simplifying assumptions. You might wonder which properties of option values are truly general and which depend on the particular simplifications. To start with, we will consider some of the more important general properties of option prices. Some of these properties have important implications for the effect of stock dividends on option values and the possible profitability of early exercise of an American option.

Restrictions on the Value of a Call Option

The most obvious restriction on the value of a call option is that its value must be zero or positive. Because the option need not be exercised, it cannot impose any liability on its holder; moreover, as long as there is any possibility that at some point the option can be exercised profitably, the option will command a positive price. Its payoff must be zero at worst, and possibly positive, so that investors are willing to pay a positive amount to purchase it.

We can place another lower bound on the value of a call option. Suppose that the stock will pay a dividend of D dollars just before the expiration date of the option, denoted by T (where today is time zero). Now compare two portfolios, one consisting of a call option on one share of stock and the other a leveraged equity position consisting of that share and borrowing of $(X + D)/(1 + r_f)^T$ dollars. The loan repayment is $X + D$ dollars, due on the expiration date of the option. For example, for a half-year maturity option with exercise price $70, dividends to be paid of $5, and effective annual interest of 10%, you would purchase one share of stock and borrow $75/$(1.10)^{1/2} = \$71.51$. In 6 months, when the loan matures, the payment due is $75.

At that time, the payoff to the leveraged equity position would be

	In General	Our Numbers
Stock value	$S_T + D$	$S_T + 5$
−Payback of loan	$-(X + D)$	-75
TOTAL	$S_T - X$	$S_T - 70$

where S_T denotes the stock price at the option expiration date. Notice that the payoff to the stock is the ex-dividend stock value plus dividends received. Whether the total payoff to the stock-plus-borrowing position is positive or negative depends on whether S_T exceeds X. The net cash outlay required to establish this leveraged equity position is $S_0 - \$71.51$, or, more generally, $S_0 - (X + D)/(1 + r_f)^T$, that is, the current price of the purchased stock, S_0, less the initial cash inflow from the borrowing position.

The payoff to the call option will be $S_T - X$ if the option expires in the money and zero otherwise. Thus the option payoff is equal to the leveraged equity payoff when that payoff is positive and is greater when the leveraged equity position has a negative payoff. Because the option payoff always is greater than or equal to that of the leveraged equity position, the option price must exceed the cost of establishing that position.

In our case the value of the call must be greater than $S_0 - (X + D)/(1 + r_f)^T$, or, more generally,

$$C \geq S_0 - PV(X) - PV(D)$$

where PV(X) denotes the present value of the exercise price and PV(D) is the present value of the dividends the stock will pay at the option's expiration. More generally, we can interpret PV(D) as the present value of any and all dividends to be paid prior to the option expiration date. Because we know already that the value of a call option must be nonnegative, we may conclude that C is greater than the *maximum* of either 0 or $S_0 - PV(X) - PV(D)$.

We also can place an upper bound on the possible value of the call: simply the stock price. No one would pay more than S_0 dollars for the right to purchase a stock currently worth S_0 dollars. Thus $C \leq S_0$.

Figure 20.1 demonstrates graphically the range of prices that is ruled out by these upper and lower bounds for the value of a call option. Any option value outside the shaded area is not possible according to the restrictions we have derived. Before expiration, the call option value normally will be *within* the allowable range, touching neither the upper nor lower bounds, as in Figure 20.2.

Early Exercise and Dividends

A call option holder who wants to close out that position has two choices: exercise the call or sell it. If the holder exercises at time t, the call will provide a profit of $S_t - X$, assuming, of course, that the option is in the money. We have just seen that the option can be sold for at least $S_t - PV(X) - PV(D)$. Therefore, for an option on a nondividend paying stock, C is greater than $S_t - PV(X)$. Because the present value of X is less than X itself, it follows that

$$C \geq S_t - PV(X) \geq S_t - X$$

The implication here is that the proceeds from a sale of the option (at price C) must exceed the proceeds from an exercise ($S_t - X$). It is economically more effective to keep the call option "alive" rather than "killing" it through early exercise. In other words calls on nondividend-paying stocks are worth more alive than dead.

If it never pays to exercise a call option before maturity, the right to exercise early actually must be valueless. The right of the American call holder to exercise early is irrelevant because it will never pay to exercise early. We have to conclude that the values of otherwise-identical American and European call options on stocks paying no dividends are equal. If we can find the value for the European call, we also will have found the value of the American call. Therefore the Black-Scholes formula for European call options will apply as well to American calls on nondividend-paying stocks.

As most stocks do pay dividends, you may wonder whether this result is just a theoretical curiosity. It is not: reconsider our argument and you will see that all that we really require is that the stock pay no dividends *until the option expires*. This condition will be true for many real-world options.

For American *put options*, however, the optimality of early exercise is most definitely a possibility. To see why, consider a simple example. Suppose that you purchase a put option on a stock. Soon the firm goes bankrupt, and the stock price falls to zero. Of course you want to exercise now, because the stock price can fall no lower. Immediate exercise gives you immediate receipt of the exercise price, which can be invested to start generating income. Delay in exercise means a time-value-of-money cost. The right to early exercise of a put option must have value.

Now suppose instead that the firm is only nearly bankrupt, with the stock selling at just a few cents. Immediate exercise may still be optimal. After all, the stock price can fall by only a very small amount, meaning that the proceeds from future exercise cannot be more than a few cents greater than the proceeds from immediate exercise. Against this possibility of a tiny increase in proceeds must be weighed the time-value-of-money cost of deferring exercise. Clearly, there is some stock price below which early exercise is optimal.

Concept Check

Question 1. In light of this discussion, explain why the put-call parity relationship is valid only for European options on nondividend-paying stocks. If the stock pays no dividends, what *inequality* for American options would correspond to the parity theorem?

Dividends and Call Option Valuation

We noted in Chapter 19 that the Black-Scholes call option formula applies to stocks that do not pay dividends. When dividends are to be paid before the option expires, we need to adjust the formula. The payment of dividends raises the possibility of early exercise, and for most realistic dividend payout schemes the valuation formula becomes significantly more complex than the already-intimidating Black-Scholes equation.

We can apply some simple rules of thumb to approximate the option value, however. One popular approach, originally suggested by Black,[1] calls for adjusting the stock price downward by the present value of any dividends that are to be paid before option expiration. Such an adjustment will take dividends into account by reflecting their eventual impact on the stock price. The option value then may be computed as before, assuming that the option will be held to expiration.

This procedure would yield a very good approximation of option value for European call options that must be held until maturity, but it does not allow for the fact that the holder of an American call option might choose to exercise the option just before a dividend. The current value of a call option, assuming that the option will be exercised just before the ex-dividend date, might be greater than the value of the option—assuming it will be held until maturity. Although holding the option until maturity allows greater effective time to expiration, which increases the option value, it also entails more dividend payments, lowering the expected stock price at maturity and thereby lowering the current option value.

For example, suppose that a stock selling at $20 will pay a $1 dividend in 4 months, whereas the call option on the stock does not expire for 6 months. The effective annual interest rate is 10%, so that the present value of the dividend is $1/(1.10)^{1/3} = $0.97. Black suggests that we can compute the option value in one of two ways:

---

[1]Black, Fischer, "Fact and Fantasy in the Use of Options," *Financial Analysts Journal, 31,* July-August 1975.

FIGURE 20.1

Range of possible call
option values.

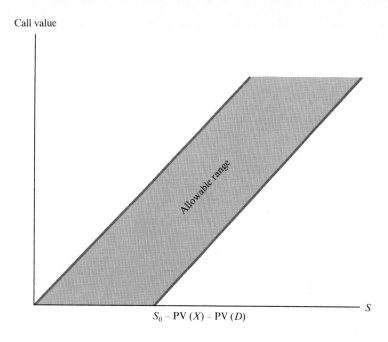

Call value

Allowable range

$S_0 - \text{PV}(X) - \text{PV}(D)$

S

FIGURE 20.2

Call option value as a
function of the stock
price.

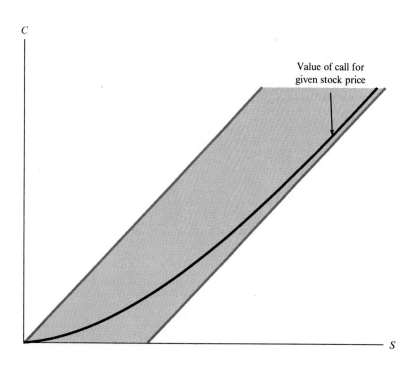

C

Value of call for
given stock price

S

1. Apply the Black-Scholes formula assuming early exercise, thus using the actual stock price of $20 and a time to expiration of four months (the time until the dividend payment)
2. Apply the Black-Scholes formula assuming no early exercise, using the dividend-adjusted stock price of $20 − $0.97 = $19.03 and a time to expiration of 6 months

The greater of the two values is the estimate of the option value, recognizing that early exercise might be optimal. In other words, the so-called *pseudo-American* call option value is the maximum of the value derived by assuming that the option will be held until expiration and the value derived by assuming that the option will be exercised just before an ex-dividend date. Even this technique is not exact, however, for it assumes that the option holder makes an irrevocable decision now on when to exercise, when in fact the decision is not binding until exercise notice is given.[2]

American Put Option Valuation

We saw from the put-call parity theorem for European options with identical maturities and exercise prices written on nondividend-paying stocks, that the put value can be related to the call value as follows:

$$P = C - S_0 + \text{PV}(X) \tag{20.1}$$

We have demonstrated that if the stock pays no dividends the American call has the same value as its European counterpart, whereas the American put is worth more than its European counterpart. Therefore American puts on nondividend-paying stocks must be worth more than the expression on the right-hand side of equation 20.1. Exact put option valuation, however, is difficult because of the complexities associated with the possibility of early exercise. When the stock pays dividends, valuation is even more complicated. In this case both American put options and call options are worth more than their European counterparts.

20.2   Using the Black-Scholes Formula

Hedge Ratios and the Black-Scholes Formula

In Chapter 19 we considered two investments in IBM: 1,000 shares of IBM stock or 10,000 call options on IBM. We saw that the call option position was more sensitive to swings in IBM's stock price than the all-stock position. To analyze the overall exposure to a stock price more precisely, however, it is necessary to quantify these

---

[2]An exact formula for American call valuation on dividend-paying stocks has been developed in Roll, Richard, "An Analytic Valuation Formula for Unprotected American Call Options on Stocks with Known Dividends," *Journal of Financial Economics, 5,* November 1977. The technique has been discussed and revised in Geske, Robert, "A Note on an Analytical Formula for Unprotected American Call Options on Stocks with Known Dividends," *Journal of Financial Economics, 7,* December 1979, and Whaley, Robert E., "On the Valuation of American Call Options on Stocks with Known Dividends," *Journal of Financial Economics, 9,* June 1981. These are difficult papers, however.

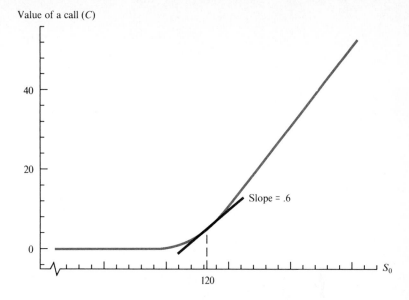

FIGURE 20.3
Call option value and hedge ratio.

Value of a call (C)

40

20

Slope = .6

0

120

S_0

relative sensitivities. A tool that enables us to summarize the overall exposure of portfolios of options with various exercise prices and times to maturity is the **hedge ratio.** An option's hedge ratio is the change in the price of an option for a $1 increase in the stock price. Therefore a call option has a positive hedge ratio and a put option has a negative hedge ratio. The hedge ratio is commonly called the option's **delta.**

If you were to graph the option value as a function of the stock value as we have done for a call option in Figure 20.3, the hedge ratio is simply the slope of the value function evaluated at the current stock price.[3] For example, suppose that the slope of the curve at S_0 = $120 equals .60. As the stock increases in value by $1, the option increases by approximately $.60, as the figure shows.

For every call option written, .60 shares of stock would be needed to hedge the investor's portfolio. For example, if one writes 10 options and holds six shares of stock, according to the hedge ratio of .6, a $1 increase in stock price will result in a gain of $6 on the stock holdings, whereas the loss on the 10 options written will be 10 × $0.60, an equivalent $6. The stock price movement leaves total wealth unaltered, which is what is required of a hedged position. The investor holding the stock and option in proportions dictated by their relative price movements hedges the portfolio.

Black-Scholes hedge ratios are particularly easy to compute. It turns out that the hedge ratio for a call is $N(d_1)$, and the hedge ratio for a put is $N(d_1) - 1$. We defined $N(d_1)$ as part of the Black-Scholes formula (equation 19.3). Recall that $N(d)$ stands

---

[3]Students of calculus will recognize that the hedge ratio also may be viewed as the partial derivative of the formula for the value of the call with respect to the stock price.

for the area under the standard normal curve up to d. Therefore the call option hedge ratio must be positive and less than 1, whereas the put option hedge ratio is negative and of smaller absolute value than 1.

Figure 20.3 verifies the insight that the slope of the call option valuation function is indeed less than 1, approaching 1 only as the stock price becomes extremely large. This tells us that option values change less than one-for-one with changes in stock prices. Why should this be? Suppose that an option is so far in the money that you are absolutely certain it will be exercised. In that case every dollar increase in the stock price would indeed increase the option value by $1. However, if there is a reasonable chance that the call option will expire out of the money, even after a moderate stock price gain, a $1 increase in the stock price will not necessarily increase the ultimate payoff to the call; therefore the call price will not respond by a full dollar.

The fact that hedge ratios are less than 1 does not conflict with our earlier observation that options offer leverage and are quite sensitive to stock price movements. Although *dollar* movements in option prices are slighter than dollar movements in the stock price, the *rate of return* volatility of options remains greater than stock return volatility because options sell at smaller prices. In our example, with the stock selling at $120, and a hedge ratio of 0.6, an option with exercise price $120 may sell for $5. If the stock price increases to $121, the call price would be expected to increase by only $.60 to $5.60. The percentage increase in the option value is $.60/$5.00 = 12%, however, whereas the stock price increase is only $1/$120 = .83%. In this case we would say that the **elasticity** of the option is 12%/.83% = 14.4. For every 1% increase in the stock price, the option price increases by 14.4%.

Concept Check

Question 2. What is the elasticity of a put option currently selling for $4 with exercise price $120, and hedge ratio −.4 if the stock price is currently $122?

The hedge ratio is an essential tool in portfolio management and control. An example will illustrate.

Consider two portfolios, one holding 750 IBM calls and 200 shares of IBM, and the other holding 800 shares of IBM. Which portfolio has greater dollar exposure to IBM price movements? You can answer this question easily using the hedge ratio.

Each option changes in value by H dollars for each dollar change in stock price, where H stands for the hedge ratio. Thus, if H equals 0.6, the 750 options are equivalent to 450 (.6 × 750) shares in terms of the response of their market value to IBM stock price movements. The first portfolio has less dollar sensitivity to IBM, because the 450 share-equivalents of the options plus the 200 shares actually held are less than the 800 shares held in the second portfolio.

This is not to say, however, that the first portfolio is less sensitive to IBM in terms of its rate of return. As we noted in discussing option elasticities, the first portfolio may be of lower total value than the second, so despite its lower sensitivity in terms

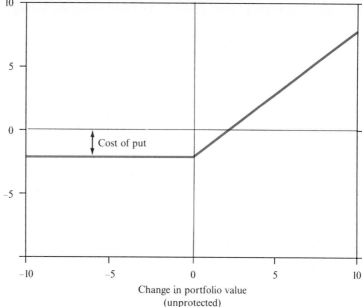

of total market value, it might have greater rate of return sensitivity. Because a call option has a lower market value than the stock, its price changes more than proportionally with stock price changes, even though its hedge ratio is less than 1.

Portfolio Insurance

In Chapter 19 we showed that protective put strategies offer a sort of insurance policy on an asset. The protective put has proved to be extremely popular with investors. Even if the asset price falls, the put conveys the right to sell the asset for the exercise price, which is a way to lock in a minimum portfolio value. With an at-the-money put ($X = S_0$), the maximum loss that can be realized is the cost of the put. The asset can be sold for X, which equals its original value, so even if the asset price falls, the investor's net loss over the period is just the cost of the put. If the asset value increases, however, upside potential is unlimited. Figure 20.4 graphs the profit or loss on a protective put position as a function of the change in the value of the underlying asset.

Although the protective put is a simple and convenient way to achieve **portfolio insurance,** there are practical difficulties in trying to insure a portfolio of stocks. First, unless the investor's portfolio corresponds to a standard market index for which puts are traded, a put option on the portfolio will not be available for purchase. In addition, if index puts are used to protect a nonindexed portfolio, tracking error can result. For example, if the portfolio falls in value while the market index rises, the put will fail to provide the intended protection. Tracking error limits the investor's freedom to pursue active stock selection, because such error will be greater as the managed portfolio departs more substantially from the market index.

Moreover, the desired horizon of the insurance program must match the maturity of a traded put option in order to establish the appropriate protective put position. Whereas most insurance programs have horizons of several years, traded puts until recently have been limited to maturities of less than 1 year, although the CBOE recently initiated trading in European index options with longer maturities. Rolling over a sequence of short-term puts, which might be viewed as a response to this problem, introduces new risks because the prices at which successive puts will be available in the future are not known today.

Providers of portfolio insurance with horizons of several years, therefore, cannot rely on the simple expedient of purchasing protective puts for their clients' portfolios. Instead, they follow trading strategies that replicate the payoffs to the protective put position.

Here is the general idea: Even if a put option on the desired portfolio with the desired expiration date does not exist, a theoretical option pricing model (such as the Black-Scholes model) can be used to determine how that option's price would respond to the portfolio's value if the option did in fact trade. For example, if stock prices were to fall, the put option would increase in value. The option model could quantify this relationship. The net exposure of the (hypothetical) protective put portfolio to swings in stock prices is the sum of the exposures of the two components of the portfolio, the stock and the put. The net exposure of the portfolio equals the equity exposure less the (offsetting) put option exposure. We can create "synthetic" protective put positions by holding a quantity of stocks with the same net exposure to market swings as the hypothetical protective put position. The key to this strategy is the option's delta, or hedge ratio, that is, the change in the price of the protective put option per change in the value of the underlying stock portfolio.

An example will clarify the procedure. Suppose that a portfolio is currently valued at $100 million. An at-the-money put option on the portfolio might have a hedge ratio or delta of $-.6$, meaning that the option's value swings $.60 for every dollar change in portfolio value, but in an opposite direction. Suppose the stock portfolio falls in value by 2%. The profit on a hypothetical protective put position (if the put existed) would be as follows (in millions of dollars):

$$
\begin{array}{lll}
\text{Loss on stocks:} & 2\% \text{ of } \$100 & = \$2.00 \\
\text{Gain on put:} & .6 \times \$2 & = \$1.20 \\
\text{Net loss:} & & \overline{\$.80} \\
\end{array}
$$

We create the synthetic option position by selling a proportion of shares equal to the put option's delta (that is, selling 60% of the shares), and placing the proceeds in risk-free T-bills. The rationale is that the hypothetical put option would have offset 60% of any change in the stock portfolio's value, so one must reduce portfolio risk directly by selling off 60% of the equity and putting the proceeds into a risk-free as-

FIGURE 20.5
Hedge ratios change
as the stock price
fluctuates.

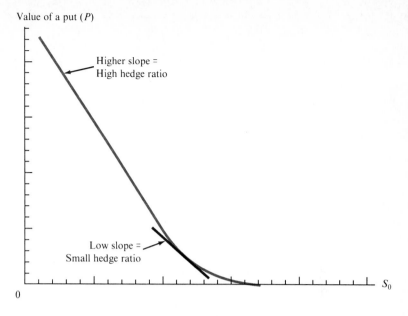

Value of a put (P)

Higher slope =
High hedge ratio

Low slope =
Small hedge ratio

S_0

0

set. Total return on a synthetic protective put position with $60 million in risk-free investments such as T-bills and $40 million in equity is

$$
\begin{array}{lll}
\text{Loss on stocks:} & 2\% \text{ of } \$40 & = \$.80 \\
\text{Loss on bills:} & & = \quad 0 \\
\text{Net loss:} & & \overline{\quad \$.80}
\end{array}
$$

The synthetic and actual protective put positions have equal returns. We conclude that if you sell a proportion of shares equal to the put option's delta and place the proceeds in cash equivalents, your exposure to the stock market will equal that of the desired protective put position.

The difficulty with this procedure is that deltas constantly change. Figure 20.5 shows that, as the stock price falls, the magnitude of the appropriate hedge ratio increases. Therefore market declines require extra hedging, that is, additional conversions of equity into cash. This constant updating of the hedge ratio is called **dynamic hedging.**

Dynamic hedging is one reason portfolio insurance has been said to contribute to market volatility. Market declines trigger additional sales of stock as portfolio insurers strive to increase their hedging. These additional sales are seen as reinforcing or exaggerating market downturns.

In practice, portfolio insurers do not actually buy or sell stocks directly when they update their hedge positions. Instead, they minimize trading costs by buying or selling stock index futures as a substitute for sale of the stocks themselves. As you will see in the following chapters, stock prices and index futures prices usually are very

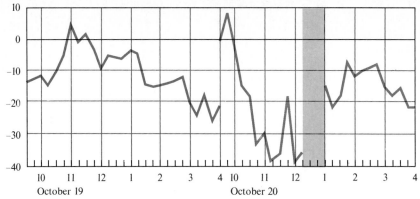

NOTE: Trading in futures contracts halted between 12:15 and 1:05

tightly linked by cross-market arbitrageurs so that futures transactions can be used as reliable proxies for stock transactions. Instead of selling equities based on the put option's delta, insurers will sell an equivalent number of futures contracts.[4]

Several portfolio insurers suffered great setbacks on October 19, 1987, when the Dow Jones Industrial Average fell by more than 500 points. We can describe what happened then so you can appreciate the complexities of applying a seemingly straightforward hedging concept:

1. Market volatility was much greater than ever encountered before. Put option deltas based on historical experience were too low, insurers underhedged, held too much equity, and suffered excessive losses.
2. Prices moved so fast that insurers could not keep up with the necessary rebalancing. They were chasing deltas that kept getting away from them. In addition, the futures market saw a "gap" opening, where the opening price was nearly 10% below the previous day's close. The price dropped before insurers could update their hedge ratios.
3. Execution problems were severe. First, current market prices were unavailable, with the trade execution and price quotation system hours behind, which made computation of correct hedge ratios impossible. Moreover, trading in stocks and stock futures ceased altogether during some periods. The continuous rebalancing capability that is essential for a viable insurance program simply vanished during the precipitous market collapse.
4. Futures prices traded at steep discounts to their proper levels compared to reported stock prices, thereby making the sale of futures (as a proxy for equity sales) to increase hedging seem expensive. Although we will see in the next chapter that stock index futures prices normally exceed the value of the stock index, Figure 20.6 shows that, on October 19, futures sold far below the stock index level. The

---

[4]Notice, however, that the use of index futures reintroduces the problem of tracking error between the portfolio and the market index.

so-called cash-to-futures spread was negative most of the day. When some insurers gambled that the futures price would recover to its usual premium over the stock index, and chose to defer sales, they remained underhedged. As the market fell further, their portfolios experienced substantial losses.

The extent to which the portfolio insurance industry will recover from the market crash is still unclear. Participants are now far more sensitive to the practical difficulties of successfully implementing an insurance program. Direct, rather than synthetic, option strategies now appear more attractive. In this regard, it is noteworthy that the CBOE has introduced longer-term index options. The following box examines the status of portfolio insurance after the crash.

Crash Prompts New Look for Portfolio Insurance

One of the leading proponents of portfolio insurance has an important message: Portfolio insurance is not dead; it's just going to be different in the future.

John O'Brien, chairman of Leland O'Brien Rubinstein Associates Inc. (LOR), a leading portfolio insurance firm and one of the originators of the strategy, believes the death knell that was sounded for dynamic hedging strategy was premature. Granted, portfolio insurance users did incur much higher costs than ever anticipated in the volatile October market. But O'Brien says his clients still had an aggregate return of 5.66% from Jan. 1 to the end of Oct. 19.

"They would have been up several percentage points more than that if they had been able to implement strategies as called for," he adds.

With an estimated $60-$80 billion in assets covered by portfolio insurance, the implementation of this strategy during the stock market crash was like billions of people trying to fit through the same doorway at the same time. While some made it through, the majority got stuck.

Portfolio insurance is supposed to manage exposure to limit downside risk while allowing high levels of average commitment to stock investing. This usually is accomplished by buying stock index futures when stock prices are rising and selling futures when stock prices

fall. The trigger point for buying or selling depends on factors set for the portfolio.

When all the triggers were pulled on Oct. 19, portfolio insurance created wave after wave of sellers who were used to executing their strategies within a normal market environment, using the same market mechanisms and continuous trading to get their orders filled.

Price reporting delays at the New York Stock Exchange, congested SuperDOT terminals used for simultaneous portfolio trading and the ultimate lack of arbitrageurs to narrow the index futures-stocks spreads led to costly delays.

"Because futures contracts were trading at approximately a 10% discount to cash, any additional transactons had the potential to drive (the spread wider) than that," explains O'Brien on why his firm felt further selling of futures contracts on Oct. 19 would have been counterproductive.

Many agree the waves of selling from portfolio insurance contributed to the market's downward spiral. Yet, implementing this strategy in the futures market, mainly in Standard & Poor's (S&P) 500 Index futures at the Chicago Mercantile Exchange (CME), absorbed selling pressure that otherwise would have been directed at the already burdened stock market.

A preliminary study on the crash, commissioned by

Continued.

the CME, concluded portfolio insurers "learned that continuous and smooth exit prices are not obtainable when a collective mass move to an exit occurs. Now that this flaw has been widely exposed, we expect excessive use of this strategy will no longer be a problem."

This "excessive use" also can withhold information needed by the marketplace, according to Gary Ginter, executive vice president of Chicago Research & Trading Group Ltd. Ginter says that replicating a put option with futures rather than buying one allows markets to trade at a much lower implied volatility than it should realistically.

"When show-and-tell time came, their strategy, which reacts to market movements after they have occurred, exacerbated the sell-off," he explains. "Portfolio insurance allows bears to hide in the woods, so to speak, and thereby deprives the market of crucial pricing information it needs to properly perform its function of price discovery. Without a truer measure of just how nervous holders of stock are, without a good reading on the relative balance between bullishness and bearishness among institutional investors, the market will underprice the true cost of insurance."

Jeff Miller, managing partner of Miller Tabak, suggests some kind of size disclosure should be made by users of this strategy to ensure that adequate capital is in the pits in case of another big sell-off.

Many pension funds that had been using this strategy during the crash have since abandoned it. San Diego Gas & Electric had $240 million in equities covered through LOR and has since discontinued the strategy's use, according to Jim Meehan, manager of financial services.

"The thing we are concerned with in portfolio insurance is getting a good handle on the cost of it," he says. "No one could have ever anticipated what the market did and the costs people experienced during that time."

O'Brien estimates the use of portfolio insurance was down 50% in December as institutions waited to see what investigations into the crash would reveal. He says his firm is examining changes in the strategy including longer-run programs with less adjustment in the

hedging rate for any specific change in the index.

What is certain is that institutions want safer ways to insure portfolios.

"Those we deal with are not adverse to getting into the derivative markets," explains J.B. Grossman, managing director of Geldermann's equity index futures and options division. "They're convinced the markets provide more protection than they provide risk. One conclusion I hear our clients reaching is that you should apply the various instruments available on a selective basis. The cunning of a manager is still required as opposed to blind faith in the application of a program."

Brian Johnson, a manager at McKinsey & Co., a management consulting firm, says futures and particularly options have a role in protecting against downside risk as long as they are bought before the fact.

"Those strategies will probably end up using index options and linking returns promised to investors to current conditions in the options markets much as the bank stock market-linked certificates of deposit do currently," he says. "In addition, there seems to be a need for long-term options, one to two years, that can offer a longer-term period of protection in return for an upfront premium."

For the longer-term options, O'Brien expects an over-the-counter (OTC) market will develop, even though the Chicago Board Options Exchange (CBOE) introduced two-year puts on its S&P 500 Index options in October. CBOE Chairman Alger "Duke" Chapman concedes those puts "are not trading at all."

"We need to build institutions on both sides," he says. "It's not a position a market maker wants to take."

Some firms already offer OTC longer-term options. However, they still must manage risk they take through dynamic hedging in the markets.

"This just moves the burden to somebody else's shoulders," one source says. "If you have $100 billion worth of equities to be insured, you need that much more liquidity and capital in the market to do it. A lot of capital in the system is very free to walk away. You need to find a reasonable way to make sure that capital stays in the system at crunch time."

From *Futures* magazine, February 1988. Reprinted by permission.

20.3 *Option-Like Securities*

Even if you never trade an option directly, you still need to appreciate the properties of options in formulating any investment plan. Why? Many other financial instruments and agreements have features that convey implicit or explicit options to one or more parties. If you are to value and use these securities correctly, you must understand these option attributes.

Callable Bonds

You know from Chapter 14 that most corporate bonds are issued with call provisions entitling the issuer to buy bonds back from bondholders at some time in the future at a specified call price. This provision conveys a call option to the issuer, where the exercise price is equal to the price at which the bond can be repurchased. A callable bond arrangement is essentially a sale of a *straight bond* (a bond with no option features such as callability or convertibility) to the investor and the concurrent sale of a call option by the investor to the bond-issuing firm.

There must be some compensation for offering this implicit call option to the firm. If the callable bond were issued with the same coupon rate as a straight bond, we would expect it to sell at a discount to the straight bond equal to the value of the call.

FIGURE   20.7
Values of callable bonds compared with straight bonds.

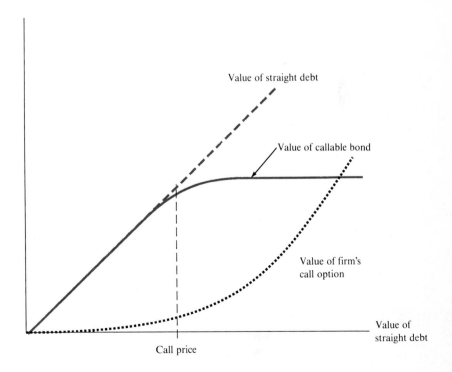

To sell callable bonds at par, firms must issue them with coupon rates higher than the coupons on straight debt. The higher coupons are the investor's compensation for the call option retained by the issuer. Coupon rates usually are selected so that the newly issued bond will sell at par value.

Figure 20.7 illustrates the option-like property of a callable bond. The horizontal axis is the value of a straight bond with terms otherwise identical to the callable bond. The 45-degree broken line represents the value of straight debt. The solid line is the value of the callable bond, and the dotted line is the value of the call option retained by the firm. A callable bond's potential for capital gains is limited by the firm's option to repurchase at the call price.

Concept Check

Question 3. How is a callable bond similar to a covered call strategy on a straight bond?

The option inherent in callable bonds is actually more complex than an ordinary call option because usually it may be exercised only after some initial period of call protection. The price at which the bond is callable may change over time also. Unlike exchange-listed options, these features are defined in the initial bond offering and will depend on the needs of the issuing firm and its perception of the market's tastes.

Concept Check

Question 4. Suppose that the period of call protection is extended. How will the coupon rate that is required for the bond to sell at par value change?

Convertible Securities

Convertible bonds and convertible preferred stock convey options to the holder of the security rather than to the issuing firm. The convertible security typically gives its holder the right to exchange each bond or share of preferred stock for a fixed number of shares of common stock, regardless of the market prices of the securities at the time.

Concept Check

Question 5. Should a convertible bond issued at par value have a higher or lower coupon rate than a nonconvertible bond issued at par?

For example, a bond with a conversion ratio of 10 allows its holder to convert one bond of par value $1,000 into 10 shares of common stock. Alternatively, the conversion price in this case is $100: to receive 10 shares of stock, the investor sacrifices bonds with face value $1,000, or $100 of face value per share. If the present value of the bond's scheduled payments is less than 10 times the value of one share of stock, it may pay to convert; that is, the conversion option is in the money. A bond worth $950 with a conversion ratio of 10 could be converted profitably if the stock were selling above $95, since the value of the 10 shares received for each bond surrendered would exceed $950. Most convertible bonds are issued "deep out of the money"; that is, the issuer sets the conversion ratio so that conversion will not be profitable unless there is a substantial increase in stock prices and/or decrease in bond prices from the time of issue.

A bond's conversion value equals the value it would have if you converted it into stock immediately. Clearly, a bond must sell for at least its conversion value. If it did not, you could purchase the bond, convert it immediately, and clear a risk-free profit. This condition could never persist, because all investors would pursue such a strategy, which ultimately would bid up the price of the bond.

The straight bond value or "bond floor" is the value the bond would have if it were not convertible into stock. The bond must sell for more than its straight bond value because a convertible bond is in fact a straight bond plus a valuable call option. Therefore the convertible bond has two lower bounds on its market price: the conversion value and the straight bond value.

Figure 20.8, A, illustrates the value of the straight debt as a function of the stock price of the issuing firm. For healthy firms the straight debt value is almost independent of the value of the stock because default risk is small. However, if the firm is close to bankruptcy (stock prices are low), default risk increases, and the straight bond value falls. Figure 20.8, B, shows the conversion value of the bond, and C compares the value of the convertible bond to these two lower bounds.

When stock prices are low, the straight bond value is the effective lower bound, and the conversion option is nearly irrelevant. The convertible will trade like straight debt. When stock prices are high, the bond's price is determined by its conversion value. With conversion all but guaranteed, the bond is essentially equity in disguise.

We can illustrate with two examples:

	Bond A	Bond B
Annual coupon	$80	$80
Maturity date	10 years	10 years
Quality rating	Baa	Baa
Conversion ratio	20	25
Stock price	$30	$50
Conversion value	$600	$1,250
Market yield on 10-year Baa-rated bonds	8.5%	8.5%
Value as straight debt	$967	$967
Actual bond price	$972	$1,255
Reported yield to maturity	8.42%	4.76%

FIGURE 20.8

Value of a convertible bond as a function of stock price. **A,** Straight debt value, or bond floor. **B,** Conversion value of the bond. **C,** Total value of convertible bond.

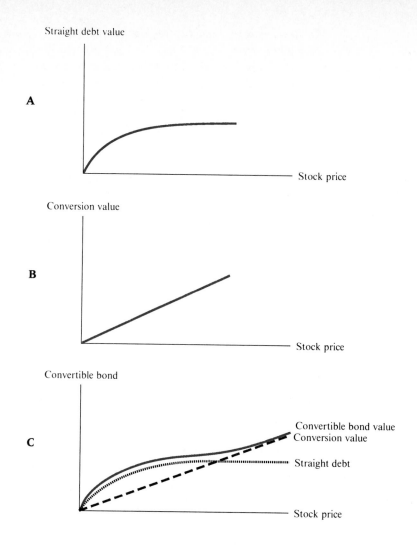

Bond *A* has a conversion value of only $600. Its value as straight debt, in contrast, is $967. This is the present value of the coupon and principal payments at a market rate for straight debt of 8.5%. The bond's price is $972, so the premium over straight bond value is only $5, reflecting the low probability of conversion. Its reported yield to maturity based on scheduled coupon payments and the market price of $972 is 8.42%, close to that of straight debt.

The conversion option on bond *B* is in the money. Conversion value is $1,250, and the bond's price, $1,255, reflects its value as equity (plus $5 for the protection the bond offers against stock price declines). The bond's reported yield is 4.76%, far below the comparable yield on straight debt. The big yield sacrifice is attributable to the far greater value of the conversion option.

In theory, we could value convertible bonds by treating them as straight debt plus call options. In practice, however, this approach is often impractical for several reasons:

1. The conversion price frequently increases over time, which means the exercise price for the option changes.
2. Stocks may pay several dividends over the life of the bond, further complicating the option valuation analysis.
3. Most convertibles also are callable at the discretion of the firm. In essence, the investor and the firm hold options on each other. If the firm exercises its call option to repurchase the bond, the bondholders typically have a month during which they still can convert. When firms use a call option, while knowing that bondholders will choose to convert, the firm is said to have *forced a conversion*. These conditions together mean that the actual maturity of the bond is indeterminate.

Warrants

Warrants are essentially call options issued by the firm. One important difference between calls and warrants is that exercise of a warrant requires the firm to issue a new share of stock to satisfy its obligation—the total number of shares outstanding increases. Exercise of a call option requires only that the writer of the call deliver an already-issued share of stock to discharge the obligation. In this case the number of shares outstanding remains fixed. Also unlike call options, warrants result in a cash flow to the firm when the exercise price is paid by the warrant holder. These differences mean that warrant values will differ somewhat from the values of call options with identical terms.

Like convertible debt, warrant terms may be tailored to meet the needs of the firm. Also like convertible debt, warrants generally are protected against stock splits and dividends in that the exercise price and the number of warrants held are adjusted to offset the effects of the split.

Warrants are often issued in conjunction with another security. Bonds, for example, may be packaged together with a warrant "sweetener," frequently a warrant that may be sold separately. This is called a *detachable warrant*.

Issue of warrants and convertible securities creates the potential for an increase in outstanding shares of stock if exercise occurs. Exercise obviously would affect financial statistics that are computed on a per share basis, so annual reports must provide earnings-per-share (EPS) figures under the assumption that all convertible securities and warrants are exercised. These figures are called fully diluted earnings per share.[5]

---

[5] We should note that the exercise of a convertible bond need not reduce EPS. Diluted EPS will be less than undiluted EPS only if interest saved (per share) on the converted bonds is less than the prior EPS.

Most loan arrangements require that the borrower put up collateral to guarantee that the loan will be paid back. In the event of default, the lender takes possession of the collateral. A nonrecourse loan gives the lender no recourse beyond the right to the collateral; that is, the lender may not sue the borrower for further payment if the collateral turns out not to be valuable enough to repay the loan.

This arrangement, it turns out, gives an implicit call option to the borrower. The borrower, for example, is obligated to pay back L dollars at the maturity of the loan. The collateral will be worth S_T dollars at maturity. (Its value today is S_0.) The borrower has the option to wait until loan maturity and repay the loan only if the collateral is worth more than the L dollars he borrowed. If the collateral is worth less than L, the borrower can default on the loan, discharging the obligation by forfeiting the collateral, which is worth only S_T.

Another way of describing such a loan is to view the borrower as, in effect, turning over collateral to the lender but retaining the right to reclaim it by paying off the loan. The transfer of the collateral with the right to claim it is equivalent to a payment of S_0 dollars, less a future recovery of a sum that resembles a call option with exercise price L. Basically, the borrower turns over collateral and keeps an option to "repurchase" it for L dollars at the maturity of the loan if L turns out to be less than S_T. This is, of course, a call option.

A third way to look at a collateralized loan is to assume the borrower will repay the L dollars with certainty, but also retain the option to sell the collateral to the lender for L dollars, even if S_T is less than L. In this case the sale of the collateral would generate the cash necessary to satisfy the loan. The ability to "sell" the collateral for a price of L dollars represents a put option, which guarantees that the borrower can raise enough money to satisfy the loan by turning over the collateral.

It is strange to think that we can describe the same loan as involving either a put option or a call option, since the payoffs to calls and puts are so different. Yet the equivalence of the two approaches is nothing more than a reflection of the put-call parity relationship. In our call option description of the loan, the value of the borrower's liability is $S_0 - C$: the borrower turns over the asset, which is a transfer of S_0 dollars, but retains a call which is worth C dollars. In the put option description the borrower is obligated to pay L dollars but retains the put, which is worth P: the present value of this net obligation is $L/(1 + r_f)^T - P$. Because these alternative descriptions are equivalent ways of viewing the same loan, the value of the obligations must be equal:

$$S_0 - C = L/(1 + r_f)^T - P \qquad (20.2)$$

Treating L as the exercise price of the option, equation 20.2 is simply the put-call parity relationship.

Figure 20.9, *A*, illustrates the value of the payment to be received by the lender, which equals the minimum of S_T or L. Figure 20.9, *B*, shows that this amount can be expressed as S_T minus the payoff of the call implicitly written by the lender and held by the borrower. Figure 20.9, *C*, shows that it also can be viewed as a receipt of L dollars minus the proceeds of the put option.

FIGURE 20.9

Collateralized loan.

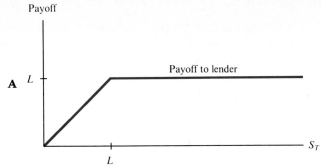

When S_T exceeds L, the loan is repaid and the collateral is reclaimed. Otherwise, the collateral is forfeited and the total loan repayment is worth only S_T.

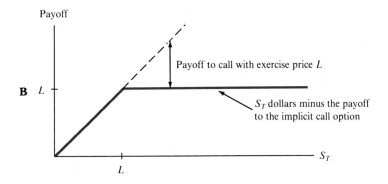

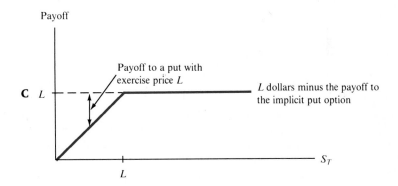

Investors holding stock in incorporated firms are protected by limited liability, which means that if the firm cannot pay its debts, the firm's creditors may attach only the firm's assets, not sue the corporation's equityholders for further payment. In effect, anytime the corporation borrows money, the maximum possible collateral for the loan is the total of the firm's assets. If the firm declares bankruptcy, we can interpret this as an admission that the assets of the firm are insufficient to satisfy the claims against it. The corporation may discharge its obligations by transferring ownership of the firm's assets to the creditors.

Just as with nonrecourse collateralized loans, the required payment to the creditors represents the exercise price of the implicit option, while the value of the firm is the underlying asset. The equityholders have a put option to transfer their ownership claims on the firm to the creditors in return for the face value of the firm's debt.

Alternatively, we may view the equityholders as retaining a call option. They have, in effect, already transferred their ownership claim on the firm to the creditors but have retained the right to reacquire the ownership claims on the firm by paying off the loan. Hence the equityholders have the option to "buy back" the firm for a specified price—they have a call option.

The significance of this observation is that the values of corporate bonds can be estimated using option pricing techniques. The default premium required of risky debt in principle can be estimated using Black-Scholes or more sophisticated option valuation models.

20.4 *Binomial Option Pricing*

Two-State Option Pricing

A complete understanding of the Black-Scholes formula is difficult without a substantial mathematics background. Nevertheless, we can develop valuable insight into option valuation by considering a particularly simple special case. Assume that a stock price can take only two possible values at option expiration: the stock will either increase to a given higher price or decrease to a given lower price. Although this may seem extreme simplification, it allows us to come closer to understanding more complicated and seemingly more realistic models. Moreover, we can extend this approach to accept far more reasonable specifications of stock price behavior. In fact, several major financial firms employ variants of this simple model to value options and securities with option-like features.

Suppose that the stock currently sells at $100 and that by year-end the price will either double to $200 or be cut in half to $50. A call option on the stock might specify an exercise price of $125 and a time to expiration of 1 year. Suppose the interest rate is 8%. At year-end, the payoff to the holder of the call option will be either zero if the stock falls or $75 if the stock price goes to $200.

Compare this payoff to that of a portfolio consisting of one share of the stock and borrowing of $46.30 at the interest rate of 8%. The payoff to this portfolio also depends on the stock price at year-end:

Value of stock	$50	$200
−Repayment of loan with interest	−$50	−$ 50
TOTAL	$0	$150

The payoff of this portfolio is exactly twice the option value regardless of the stock price. In other words two call options will exactly replicate the payoff to the portfolio; two call options should have the same price as the cost of establishing the portfolio, therefore. We know the cost of establishing the portfolio is $100 for the stock, less the $46.30 proceeds from borrowing. Hence the two calls should sell at

$$2C = \$100 - \$46.30$$

or each call should sell at $C = \$26.85$. Thus, given the stock price, exercise price, interest rate, and volatility of the stock price (as represented by the magnitude of the up or down movements), we can derive the fair value for the call option.

This valuation approach relies heavily on the notion of replication. With only two possible end-of-year values of the stock, the returns to the leveraged stock portfolio replicate the returns to the call option, and so need to command the same market price. This notion of replication is behind most option pricing formulas. For more complex price distributions for stocks, the replication technique is correspondingly more complex, but the principles remain the same.

One way to view the role of replication is to note that, using the numbers assumed for this example, a portfolio made up of one share of stock and two call options written is perfectly hedged. Its year-end value is independent of the ultimate stock price:

Stock value	$50	$200
−Obligations from two calls written	− 0	−$150
Net payoff	$50	$ 50

The investor has formed a risk-free portfolio, with a payout of $50. Its value must be the present value of $50, or $50/1.08 = $46.30. The value of the portfolio, which equals $100 from the stock held long, minus $2C$ from the two calls written, should equal $46.30. Hence $100 − 2C = \$46.30$, or $C = \$26.85$.

The ability to create a perfect hedge is the key to this argument. The hedge guarantees the end-of-year payout, which can be discounted using the risk-free interest rate. To find the value of the option in terms of the value of the stock, we do not need to know the option's or the stock's beta or expected rate of return. (Recall that this also was true of Black-Scholes option valuation.) The perfect hedging, or replication, approach enables us to express the value of the option in terms of the current value of the stock without this information. With a hedged position the final stock price does not affect the investor's payoff, so the stock's risk-and-return parameters have no bearing.

The hedge ratio of this example is one share of stock to two calls, or one half. For every option written, one half share of stock must be held in the portfolio to hedge away risk. This ratio has an easy interpretation in this context: it is the ratio of the range of the values of the option to those of the stock across the two possible outcomes. The option is worth either zero or $75, for a range of $75. The stock is worth either $50 or $200, for a range of $150. The ratio of ranges, 75/150, is one half, which is the hedge ratio we have established.

The hedge ratio equals the ratio of ranges because the option and stock are perfectly correlated in this two-state example. When the returns of the option and stock are perfectly correlated, a perfect hedge requires that option and stock be held in a fraction determined only by relative volatility.

The generalization of the hedge ratio for other two-state option problems is

$$H = \frac{C^+ - C^-}{S^+ - S^-}$$

where C^+ and C^- refer to the call option's value when the stock goes up or down, respectively, and S^+ and S^- are the stock prices in the two states. The hedge ratio, H, is thus the ratio of the swings in the possible end-of-period values of the option and the stock. If the investor writes one option and holds H shares of stock, the value of the portfolio will be unaffected by the stock price. In this case option pricing is easy: simply set the value of the hedged portfolio equal to the present value of the known payoff.

Concept Check

Question 6. Intuitively, would you expect the hedge ratio to be higher or lower when the call option is more in the money? You can confirm your intuition in problem 2 at the end of the chapter.

Using our example, the option pricing technique would proceed as follows:
1. Given the possible end-of-year stock prices, $S^+ = 200$ and $S^- = 50$, and the exercise price of 125, calculate that $C^+ = 75$ and $C^- = 0$. The stock price range is thus 150, while the option price range is 75.
2. Find that the hedge ratio is $75/150 = .5$.
3. Find that a portfolio made up of .5 shares with one written option would have an end-of-year value of $25 with certainty.
4. Show that the present value of $25 with a 1-year interest rate of 8% is $23.15.
5. Set the value of the hedged position to the present value of the certain payoff:

$$.5S_0 - C_0 = 23.15$$
$$\$50 - C_0 = \$23.15$$

6. Solve for the call's value, $C_0 = \$26.85$.

What if the option were overpriced, perhaps selling for $30? Then you can make arbitrage profits. Here is how:

	Initial Cash Flow	CF in 1 Year for each Possible Stock Price	
		$S = 50$	$S = 200$
1. Write two options	60	0	−150
2. Purchase one share	−100	50	200
3. Borrow $40 at 8% interest, and repay in 1 year	40	−43.20	−43.20
TOTAL	0	6.80	6.80

Although the net initial investment is zero, the payoff in 1 year is positive and riskless. If the option were underpriced, one would simply reverse this arbitrage strategy: buy the option, and shortsell the stock to eliminate price risk. Note, by the way, that the present value of the profit to the arbitrage strategy above exactly equals twice the amount by which the option is overpriced. The present value of the risk-free profit of $6.80 at an 8% interest rate is $6.30. With two options written in this strategy, this translates to a profit of $3.15 per option, exactly the amount by which the option was overpriced: $30 vs. the "fair value" of $26.85.

Generalizing the Two-State Approach

Although the two-state stock price model seems simplistic, we can generalize it to incorporate more realistic assumptions. To start, suppose that we were to break up the year into two 6-month segments, and then assert that over each half-year segment the stock price could take on two values. In this case we will say it can increase 10% or decrease 5%. A stock initially selling at 100 could follow these possible paths over the course of the year:

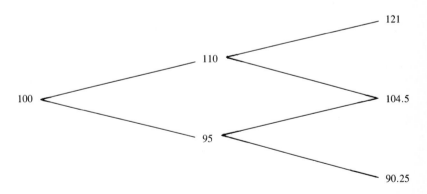

The midrange value of 104.5 can be attained by two paths: an increase of 10% followed by a decrease of 5%, or a decrease of 5% followed by a 10% increase.

There are now three possible end-of-year values for the stock, and three for the option.

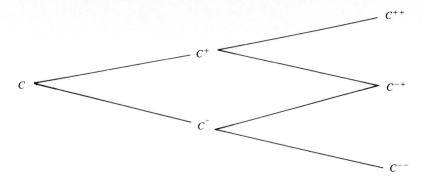

Using methods similar to those we followed above, we could value C^+ from knowledge of C^{++} and C^{+-}, then value C^- from knowledge of C^{-+} and C^{--}, and finally value C from knowledge of C^+ and C^-. There is no reason to stop at 6-month intervals. We could next break up the year into 4 3-month units, or 12 1-month units, or 365 1-day units, each of which would be posited to have a two-state process. Although the calculations become quite numerous and correspondingly tedious, they are easy to program into a computer, and such computer programs are used widely by participants in the securities market.

As we break the year into progressively finer subintervals, the range of possible year-end stock prices expands and, in fact, will ultimately take on a lognormal distribution.[6] This can be seen from an analysis of the event tree for the stock for a period with three subintervals:

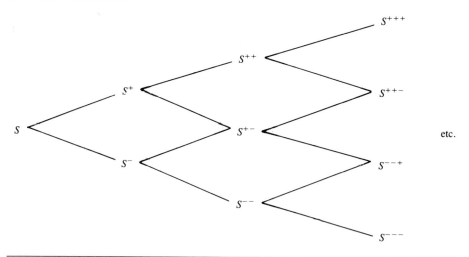

etc.

---

[6]Actually, more complex considerations enter here. The limit of this process is lognormal only if we assume also that stock prices move continuously, by which we mean that over small time intervals only small price movements can occur. This rules out rare events such as sudden, extreme price moves in response to dramatic information (like a takeover attempt). For a treatment of this type of "jump process," see Cox, John C., and Ross, Stephen A., "The Valuation of Options for Alternative Stochastic Processes," *Journal of Financial Economics, 3,* January-March 1976, or Merton, Robert C., "Option Pricing When Underlying Stock Returns Are Discontinuous," *Journal of Financial Economics, 3,* January-March 1976.

First, notice that as the number of subintervals increases the number of possible stock prices also increases. Second, notice that extreme events such as S^{+++} or S^{---} are relatively rare, since they require either three consecutive increases or decreases in the three subintervals. More moderate, or midrange, results such as S^{++-} can be arrived at by more than one path—any combination of two price increases and one decrease will result in stock price S^{++-}. Thus the midrange values will be more likely, and the stock price distribution will acquire the familiar bell-shaped pattern discussed in Chapter 5. The probability of each outcome is described by the binomial distribution, and this multiperiod approach to option pricing is therefore called the **binomial model.**

For example, using our initial stock price of $100, equal probability of stock price increases or decreases, and three intervals for which the possible price increase is 5% and decrease is 3%, we would obtain the probability distribution of stock prices from the following calculations. There are eight possible combinations for the stock price movements in the three periods: $+++$, $++-$, $+-+$, $-++$, $+--$, $-+-$, $--+$, $---$. Each has probability of $\frac{1}{8}$. Therefore the probability distribution of stock prices at the end of the last interval would be as follows:

Event	Probability		Stock Price
3 up movements	$\frac{1}{8}$	100×1.05^3	$= 115.76$
2 up and 1 down	$\frac{3}{8}$	$100 \times 1.05^2 \times .97$	$= 106.94$
1 up and 2 down	$\frac{3}{8}$	$100 \times 1.05 \times .97^2$	$= 98.79$
3 down movements	$\frac{1}{8}$	$100 \times .97^3$	$= 91.27$

The midrange values are three times as likely to occur as the extreme values. Figure 20.10, *A,* is a graph of the frequency distribution for this example. Notice that the graph is beginning to take on the familiar appearance of the bell-shaped curve. In fact, as the number of intervals increases, as in Figure 20.10, *B,* the frequency distribution progressively approaches the lognormal distribution rather than the normal distribution. (Recall our discussion in the appendix to Chapter 5 on why the lognormal distribution is superior to the normal as a means of modeling stock prices.)

Suppose that we were to continue subdividing the interval in which stock prices are posited to move up or down. Eventually, each node of the event tree would correspond to an infinitesimally small time interval. The possible stock price movement within that time interval would be correspondingly small. As those many intervals passed, the end-of-period stock price would more and more closely resemble a lognormal distribution. Thus the apparent oversimplication of the two-state model can be overcome by progressively subdividing any period into many subperiods.

At any node, one still could set up a portfolio that would be perfectly hedged over the next tiny time interval. Then, at the end of that interval, upon reaching the next node, a new hedge ratio could be computed and the portfolio composition could be revised to remain hedged over the coming small interval. By continuously revising the hedge position, the portfolio would remain hedged and would earn a risk-free rate of return over each interval. This is dynamic hedging, which calls for continued updating of the hedge ratio as time passes.

FIGURE 20.10
Probability
distributions.
A, Possible outcomes
and associated
probabilities for stock
prices after three
periods. The stock
price starts at $100,
and in each period it
can increase by 5% or
decrease by 3%.
B, Each period is
subdivided into two
smaller subperiods.
Now there are six
periods, and in each
of these the stock
price can increase by
2.5% or fall by 1.5%.
Notice that as the
number of periods
increases the stock
price distribution
approaches the
familiar bell-shaped
curve.

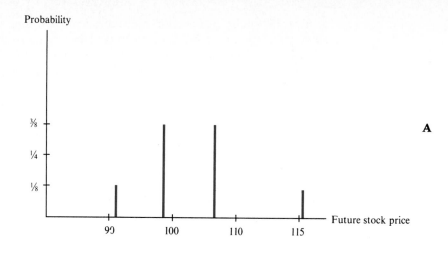

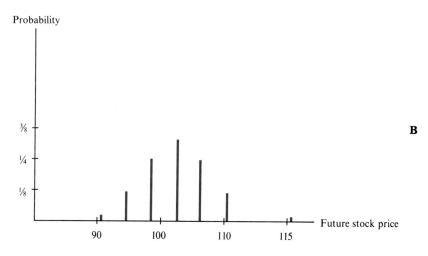

In fact, Black and Scholes used a dynamic hedge approach to derive their option valuation formula, and you saw in our discussion of portfolio insurance that a dynamic hedge strategy is required for the stock plus bills portfolio to replicate the payoff to a protective put.

20.5 *Empirical Evidence*

There have been an enormous number of empirical tests of the option pricing model. For the most part the results of the studies have been positive in that the Black-Scholes model generates option values fairly close to the actual prices at which options trade. At the same time some regular empirical failures of the model have been noted. Geske and Roll[7] have argued that these empirical results can be attributed to the failure of the Black-Scholes model to account for the possible early exercise of American calls on stocks that pay dividends. Indeed, they show that the theoretical bias induced by this failure exactly corresponds to the actual "mispricing" observed empirically.

Whaley[8] examines the performance of the Black-Scholes formula relative to that of the pseudo-American formula and the true American option formula. His findings also indicate that formulas that allow for the possibility of early exercise do better at pricing than the Black-Scholes formula. Whaley's results indicate that the Black-Scholes formula performs worst for options on stocks with high dividend payouts. The true American call option formula, on the other hand, seemed to fare equally well in the prediction of option prices on stocks with high or low dividend payouts.

Summary

1. Call options must sell for at least the stock price less the present value of the exercise price and dividends to be paid before maturity. This implies that a call option on a nondividend-paying stock may be sold for more than the proceeds from immediate exercise. Thus European calls are worth as much as American calls on stocks that pay no dividends because the right to exercise the American call early has no value.

2. The Black-Scholes formula is valid for options on stocks that pay no dividends. Dividend adjustments may be adequate to price European calls on dividend-paying stocks, but the proper treatment of American calls on dividend-paying stocks requires more complex formulas.

3. Put options may be exercised early whether the stock pays dividends or not. Therefore American puts generally are worth more than are European puts.

4. European put values can be derived from the call value and the put-call parity relationship. This technique cannot be applied to American puts for which early exercise is a possibility.

5. The hedge ratio is the number of shares of stock that is required to hedge the price risk involved in writing one option. Hedge ratios are near zero for deep out-of-the-money call options, and approach 1 for deep in-the-money calls.

6. Although hedge ratios are less than 1, call options have elasticities greater than 1. The rate of return on a call (as opposed to the dollar return) responds more than one-for-one with stock price movements.

7. Portfolio insurance can be obtained by purchasing a protective put option on an equity position. When the appropriate put is not traded, portfolio insurance entails a

---

[7]Geske, Robert, and Roll, Richard, "On Valuing American Call Options with the Black-Scholes European Formula," *Journal of Finance, 39,* June 1984.

[8]Whaley, Robert E., "Valuation of American Call Options on Dividend-Paying Stocks: Empirical Tests," *Journal of Financial Economics, 10,* 1982.

dynamic hedge strategy in which a fraction of the equity portfolio equal to the desired put option's delta is sold and placed in risk-free securities.

8. Many commonly traded securities embody option characteristics. Examples of these securities are callable bonds, convertible bonds, and warrants. Other arrangements such as collateralized loans and limited-liability borrowing can be analyzed as conveying implicit options to one or more parties.

9. Options may be priced relative to the underlying stock price using a simple two-period, two-state pricing model. As the number of periods increases, we may approximate more realistic stock price distributions. The Black-Scholes formula may be seen as a limiting case of the binomial option model as the holding period is divided into progressively smaller subperiods.

Key Terms

Hedge ratio	Dynamic hedging
Delta	Warrants
Elasticity	Binomial model
Portfolio insurance	

Selected Readings

The breakthrough articles in option pricing are:
 Black, Fischer, and Scholes, Myron, "The Pricing of Options and Corporate Liabilities," *Journal of Political Economy, 81,* May-June 1973.
 Merton, Robert C., "Theory of Rational Option Pricing," *Bell Journal of Economics and Management Science, 4,* Spring 1973.
A good review of these, as well as an interesting treatment of earlier attempts to value options, appears in:
 Smith, Clifford W., Jr., "Option Pricing: A Review," *Journal of Financial Economics, 3,* January-March 1976.
Good articles on portfolio insurance and replication strategies are:
 Perold, Andre F., and Sharpe, William F., "Dynamic Strategies for Asset Allocation," *Financial Analysts Journal,* January-February 1988.
 Rubinstein, Mark, and Leland, Hayne, "Replicating Options with Positions in Stock and Cash," *Financial Analysts Journal,* July/August 1981.
 The January-February 1988 edition of *Financial Analysts Journal* is devoted to issues surrounding portfolio insurance.
Several applications of option-type analysis to various financial instruments are surveyed in:
 Smith, Clifford, "Applications of Option-Pricing Analysis," in Bicksler, James L. (editor), *Handbook of Financial Economics,* New York: North-Holland Publishing Co., 1979.
The two-state approach was first suggested in:
 Sharpe, William F., *Investments,* Englewood Cliffs, NJ: Prentice-Hall, 1978.
The approach was developed more fully in:
 Rendleman, Richard J. Jr., and Bartter, Brit J., "Two-State Option Pricing," *Journal of Finance, 34,* December 1979.
 Cox, John C., Ross, Stephen A., and Rubinstein, Mark, "Option Pricing: A Simplified Approach," *Journal of Financial Economics, 7,* September 1979.

A summary of the empirical evidence on the accuracy of the option pricing formula may be found in:

Galai, Dan, "A Survey of Empirical Tests of Option Pricing Models," in Brenner, Menachem (editor), *Option Pricing,* Lexington, Mass.: Heath, 1983.

Interesting later work is:

Geske, Robert, and Roll, Richard, "On Valuing American Call Options with the Black-Scholes European Formula," *Journal of Finance, 39,* June 1984.

Whaley, Robert E., "Valuation of American Call Options on Dividend-Paying Stocks: Empirical Tests," *Journal of Financial Economics, 10,* 1982.

Problems

1. Let $p(S,T,X)$ denote the value of a European put on a stock selling at S dollars, with time to maturity T, and with exercise price X, and let $P(S,T,X)$ be the value of an American put.
   a. Evaluate $p(0,T,X)$
   b. Evaluate $P(0,T,X)$
   c. Evaluate $p(S,T,0)$
   d. Evaluate $P(S,T,0)$
   e. What does your answer to (b) tell you about the possibility that American puts may be exercised early?

2. Reconsider the determination of the hedge ratio in the two-state model in Section 20.4 where we showed that one half share of stock would hedge one option. What is the hedge ratio at the following exercise prices: 115, 100, 75, 50, 25, 10? What do you conclude about the hedge ratio as the call option becomes progressively more in the money?

3. Show that Black-Scholes call option hedge ratios also increase as the stock price increases. Consider a 1-year option with exercise price $50 on a stock with annual standard deviation 20%. The T-bill rate is 8% per year. Find $N(d_1)$ for stock prices $45, $50, and $55.

4. Imagine that you are a provider of portfolio insurance. You are establishing a 4-year program. The portfolio you manage is currently worth $100 million, and you hope to provide a minimum return of 0%. The equity portfolio has a standard deviation of 25% per year, and T-bills pay 5% per year risk-free. Assume for simplicity that the portfolio pays no dividends (or that all dividends are reinvested).
   a. What fraction of the portfolio should be placed in bills? What fraction in equity?
   b. What should the manager do if the stock portfolio falls by 3% on the first day of trading?

5. In-The-Money Financial Services Corporation (ITM) is a small firm whose securities are not publicly traded. You are an analyst trying to estimate the value of ITM's common stock and bonds. You have estimated the market value of the firm's assets to be $2 million. The face value of its debt, all of which is going to mature 1 year from now, is $2 million. You estimate the standard deviation of the proportional change in the value of the assets to be .3 per year, and the riskless rate of interest is 10% per year.

a. Write out the payoff to the equityholders at the maturity of the debt. In what way is the equity value like a call option?

b. Use the Black-Scholes option pricing methodology and formula to price ITM's debt and equity, assuming that the total market value of the firm is currently $2 million.

c. What would be the effect of an increase in the standard deviation of the change in asset value on the values of the debt and equity, holding constant the value of the assets and the risk-free interest rate? A numerical answer is not required; just give the direction of change and your explanation.

6. Would you expect a $1 increase in a call option's exercise price to lead to a decrease in the option's value of more or less than $1?

7. The agricultural price support system guarantees farmers a minimum price for their output. Describe the program provisions as an option. What is the asset? The exercise price?

8. In what way is owning a corporate bond similar to writing a put option? A call option?

9. An executive compensation scheme might provide a bonus to a manager of $1,000 for every dollar by which the company's stock price exceeds some cutoff level. In what way is this arrangement equivalent to issuing the manager call options on the firm's stock?

10. We will derive a two-state *put* option value in this problem. Data: $S_0 = 100$; $X = 120$; $1 + r = 1.1$. The two possibilities for S_T are 140 and 80.

a. Show that the range of S is 60 while that of P is 40 across the two states. What is the hedge ratio of the put?

b. Form a portfolio of two shares of stock and three puts. What is the (nonrandom) payoff to this portfolio? What is the present value of the portfolio?

c. Given that the stock currently is selling at 100, solve for the value of the put.

d. Would you exercise this put early?

e. Given your answers to (c) and (d), what is the true value of the put?

f. What do you conclude about the possibility of early exercise?

11. (CFA Examination, Level III, 1987)

You are considering the sale of a call option with an exercise price of $100 and one year to expiration. The underlying stock pays no dividends, its current price is $100, and you believe it has a 50% chance of increasing to $120 and a 50% chance of decreasing to $80. The risk-free rate of interest is 10%.

a. Describe the specific steps involved in applying the binomial option pricing model to calculate the call option's value.

b. Compare the binomial option pricing model to the Black-Scholes option pricing model.

12. XYZ Corp. will pay a $2 per share dividend in 2 months. Its stock price currently is $60 per share. A call option on XYZ has an exercise price of $55 and 3-month time to maturity. The risk-free interest rate is .5% per month, and the stock's volatility (standard deviation) = 7% per month. Find the pseudo-American option value. Hint: try defining one "period" as a month, rather than as a year.

13. Suppose that the risk-free interest rate is zero. Would an American put option ever be exercised early? Explain.

14. You would like to be holding a protective put position on the stock of XYZ Co. to lock in a guaranteed minimum value of $100 at year-end. XYZ currently sells for $100. Over the next year the stock price will increase by 10% or decrease by 10%. The T-bill rate is 5%. Unfortunately, no put options are traded on XYZ Co.

   a. Suppose that the desired put option is traded. How much would it cost to purchase?

   b. What would have been the cost of the protective put portfolio?

   c. What portfolio position in stock and T-bills will ensure you a payoff equal to the payoff that would be provided by a protective put with $X = 100$? Show that the payoff to this portfolio and the cost of establishing the portfolio matches those of the desired protective put portfolio.

15. These three *put* options all are written on the same stock. One has a delta of $-.9$, one a delta of $-.5$, and one a delta of $-.1$. Assign deltas to the three puts by filling in this table.

Put	X	Delta
A	10	
B	20	
C	30	

16. You are *very* bullish (optimistic) on stock EFG, much more so than the rest of the market. In each question choose the portfolio strategy that will give you the greatest dollar profit if your bullish forecast turns out to be correct. Explain your answer.

   a. Choice A: $10,000 invested in calls with $X = 50$
      Choice B: $10,000 invested in EFG stock

   b. Choice A: 10 call options contracts (for 100 shares each), with $X = 50$
      Choice B: 1,000 shares of EFG stock

CHAPTER 21

Futures and Forward Markets: General Principles

Futures and forward contracts are similar to options in that they specify purchase or sale of some underlying security at some future date. The key difference is that the holder of an option to buy is not compelled to buy and will not do so if it is to his or her disadvantage. A futures or forward contract, on the other hand, carries the obligation to go through with the agreed-on transaction. To see how futures and forwards work and how they might be useful, consider the portfolio diversification problem facing a farmer of a single crop, for example, wheat. The entire planting season's revenue depends critically upon the highly volatile crop price. The farmer cannot easily diversify his position because virtually his entire wealth is tied up in the crop.

The miller who must purchase wheat for processing faces a portfolio problem that is the mirror image of the farmer's. He is subject to profit uncertainty because of the unpredictable future cost of the wheat.

Both parties can reduce this source of risk if they enter into a **forward contract** requiring the farmer to deliver the wheat when harvested at a price agreed on now, regardless of the market price at harvest time. No money need change hands at this time. A forward contract is simply a deferred delivery sale of some asset with the sales price agreed on now. All that is required is that each party be willing to lock in the ultimate price to be paid or received for delivery of the commodity. A forward contract protects each party from future price fluctuations.

A forward contract is not an investment in the strict sense that funds are paid for an asset. It is only a commitment today to transact in the future. Forward arrangements are part of our study of investments, however, because they offer powerful means to hedge other investments and generally modify portfolio characteristics, as this farming example illustrates.

Forward markets for future delivery of various commodities go back at least to ancient Greece. Organized *futures markets,* though, are a relatively modern development, dating only to the nineteenth century. Futures markets replace informal forward contracts with highly standardized, exchange-traded securities.

This chapter describes the workings of futures markets, and the mechanics of trading in these markets. We show how futures contracts are useful investment vehicles for both hedgers and speculators and how the futures price relates to the spot price of an asset. Chapter 21 deals with general principles of futures markets. Chapter 22 describes specific futures markets in greater detail.

21.1 *The Futures Contract*

Futures markets formalize and standardize forward contracting. Buyers and sellers do not have to rely on fortuitous matching of their interests; they can trade in a centralized futures market. The futures exchange standardizes the types of **futures contract** that may be traded: it establishes contract size, the acceptable grade of commodity, contract delivery dates, and so forth. Although standardization eliminates much of the flexibility available in informal forward contracting, it has the offsetting advantage of liquidity. Futures contracts also differ from forward contracts in that they call for a daily settling of any gains or losses on the contract. In contrast, in forward contracts no money is exchanged until the delivery date.

In a centralized market buyers and sellers can trade through brokers without personally searching for trading partners. The standardization of contracts and the depth of trading in each contract allow futures positions to be liquidated easily through a broker, rather than personally renegotiated with the other party to the contract. Because the exchange guarantees the performance of each party to the contract, costly credit checks on other traders are not necessary. Instead, each trader simply posts a good faith deposit, called the margin, to guarantee contract performance.

The Basics of Futures Contracts

The futures contract calls for delivery of a commodity at a specified delivery or maturity date, for an agreed-on price, called the futures price, to be paid at contract maturity. The contract specifies precise requirements for the commodity. For agricultural commodities, allowable grades (for example, No. 2 hard winter wheat, or No. 1 soft red wheat) are set by the exchange. The place or means of delivery of the commodity is specified as well. For agricultural commodities, delivery is made by transfer of warehouse receipts issued by approved warehouses. For financial futures, delivery may be made by wire transfer; in the case of index futures delivery may be accomplished by a cash settlement procedure similar to those for index options. (Although the futures contract technically calls for delivery of an asset, delivery in fact rarely occurs. Instead, traders much more commonly close out their positions before contract maturity, taking gains or losses in cash. We will examine how this is done very shortly.)

Because the futures exchange specifies completely the terms of the contract, the traders need bargain only over the futures price. The trader taking the **long position** commits to purchasing the commodity on the delivery date. The trader who takes the **short position** commits to delivering the commodity at contract maturity. The trader in the long position is said to "buy" a contract; the short-side trader "sells" a contract. We are using the words "buy" and "sell" loosely because a contract is not really bought or sold like a stock or bond, but is entered into by mutual agreement. At the

FIGURE 21.1
Prices for agricultural and metals futures.
(From *The Wall Street Journal*, June 6, 1988.) Reprinted by permission of *The Wall Street Journal*.
© Dow Jones & Company, Inc. 1988. All rights reserved.

FUTURES PRICES

Friday, June 3, 1988

Open Interest Reflects Previous Trading Day.

	Open	High	Low	Settle	Change	Lifetime High	Lifetime Low	Open Interest
–GRAINS AND OILSEEDS–								
CORN (CBT) 5,000 bu.; cents per bu.								
July	229	234¾	228½	234½	+ 9¾	234¾	174	66,098
Sept	238	243¾	237	243¾	+10	243¾	180¾	24,029
Dec	252	256¼	251	256¼	+10	256¼	184	82,883
Mr89	260¼	264¼	259½	264¼	+10	264¼	193½	11,257
May	264	269	264	269	+10	269	207½	3,883
July	264½	269¾	264½	269¾	+10	269¾	233	1,975
Est vol 55,000; vol Thur 58,510; open int 190,143, +6,242.								
OATS (CBT) 5,000 bu.; cents per bu.								
July	192	196½	192	196½	+10	196½	144	3,263
Sept	198	200¾	198	200¾	+10	200¾	143	2,956
Dec	209	209¾	207½	209¾	+10	209¾	162	2,073
Mr89	209	212	208	212	+10	212	171	408
Est vol 3,000; vol Thur 2,195; open int 8,720, +176.								
SOYBEANS (CBT) 5,000 bu.; cents per bu.								
July	833	849	831	849	+30	849	488½	57,233
Aug	845	854½	842	854½	+30	854½	512	14,303
Sept	855½	855½	845	855½	+30	855½	503	7,819
Nov	853	864	848	864	+30	864	499¼	75,553
Ja89	856½	871	855	871	+30	871	553	8,360
Mar	866	875	864	875	+30	875	579	3,969
May	869¾	869¾	859	868½	+28⅝	869	647	1,582
July	833	859	847	856	+24½	859	684	1,691
Nov	700½	708	700	704¼	+ 8¾	730	677	657
Est vol 80,000; vol Thur 85,144; open int 171,167, +6,429.								
SOYBEAN MEAL (CBT) 100 tons; $ per ton.								
July	262.70	262.70	259.50	262.70	+10.00	262.70	148.00	29,122
Aug	260.40	260.40	257.00	260.40	+10.00	260.40	148.00	12,509
Sept	259.70	259.70	256.00	259.70	+10.00	259.70	153.00	7,220
Oct	258.00	259.00	256.00	259.00	+10.00	259.00	159.00	6,046
Dec	258.00	258.70	254.00	258.70	+10.00	258.70	159.00	15,022
Ja89	258.00	258.00	254.00	257.70	+ 9.30	258.00	177.00	2,629
Mar	256.00	256.00	252.00	254.70	+ 7.70	256.00	193.50	1,846
May	255.00	256.00	254.00	254.00	+ 6.80	256.00	200.50	787
Est vol 30,000; vol Thur 28,135; open int 75,267, +2,381.								
SOYBEAN OIL (CBT) 60,000 lbs.; cents per lb.								
July	25.35	26.04	25.27	25.77	+ .73	26.04	16.65	35,664
Aug	25.60	26.26	25.55	26.00	+ .74	26.26	16.71	14,130
Sept	25.77	26.50	25.77	26.22	+ .69	26.50	16.55	9,597
Oct	26.00	26.65	25.95	26.47	+ .80	26.65	17.25	7,128
Dec	26.35	27.02	26.30	26.85	+ .78	27.02	18.30	18,223
Ja89	26.55	27.15	26.55	26.95	+ .80	27.15	20.75	1,645
Mar	26.70	27.37	26.70	27.20	+ .83	27.37	21.35	1,479
May	27.40	27.70	27.40	27.65	+ .80	27.70	22.95	596
July	27.60	27.65	27.50	27.50	+ .70	27.65	23.00	145
Est vol 25,000; vol Thur 18,359; open int 88,658, +377.								
WHEAT (CBT) 5,000 bu.; cents per bu.								
July	354	366	355	362¾	+12¼	366	253½	22,618
Sept	363	375	363	372¾	+13¾	375	272	10,029
Dec	373	384	373	383½	+14½	384	289	13,419
Mr89	377½	387½	377½	387	+14	387½	323	1,313
July	346½	346½	342	342	– 2	355	335	104
Est vol 16,500; vol Thur 15,685; open int 47,550, +1,912.								
WHEAT (KC) 5,000 bu.; cents per bu.								
July	351	362½	350	361	+15½	362½	272	11,923
Sept	356	370	356	368	+15½	370	304½	7,333
Dec	365	377½	365	375½	+15¼	377½	301½	3,493
Mr89	377	383	372½	379½	+14½	383	322¾	232
Est vol 4,299; vol Thur 4,919; open int 22,986, +445.								
WHEAT (MPLS) 5,000 bu.; cents per bu.								
July	354½	363¼	350	362½	+18¾	363¼	292½	6,213
Sept	364½	373¼	360½	372¾	+19¼	373¼	296	4,345
Dec	375	382¼	366½	381½	+18¾	382¼	308¾	1,000
Mr89	378	378	377½	378	+20	378	347	108
Est vol n.a.; vol Thur 2,969; open int 11,667, +355.								
BARLEY (WPG) 20 metric tons; Can. $ per ton								
July	104.00	105.00	104.00	105.00	+ 5.00	108.50	71.00	7,662
Oct	108.00	110.00	108.00	110.00	+ 5.00	112.20	75.00	13,080
Nov	109.50	111.00	109.50	111.00	+ 5.00	113.00	78.50	1,139
Dec	110.50	110.50	109.50	110.50	+ 5.00	114.50	78.90	4,391
Mar	....	....	....	114.70	+ 5.00	116.50	105.00	208
Est vol 2,800; vol Thur 3,859; open int 26,480, +512.								
FLAXSEED (WPG) 20 metric tons; Can. $ per ton								
July	284.00	292.50	284.00	292.50	+10.00	292.50	229.70	3,344
Oct	302.00	302.80	297.50	302.80	+10.00	302.80	237.20	1,918
Dec	303.90	308.50	303.90	308.50	+10.00	308.50	242.10	812
Est vol 1,980; vol Thurs 1,472; open int 6,140, –137.								
RAPESEED (WPG) 20 metric tons; Can. $ per ton								
June	392.00	394.70	391.70	394.70	+10.00	394.70	252.90	1,297
Sept	399.00	404.00	399.00	404.00	+10.00	404.00	259.80	11,310
Nov	405.00	405.90	403.50	405.90	+10.00	405.90	261.80	11,018
Ja89	408.00	408.00	406.80	408.00	+10.00	408.00	291.80	4,283

	Open	High	Low	Settle	Change	Lifetime High	Lifetime Low	Open Interest
ORANGE JUICE (CTN)–15,000 lbs.; cents per lb.								
July	169.25	171.00	168.70	171.00	+ 2.10	178.25	124.00	5,991
Sept	164.60	166.00	164.25	165.75	+ 1.35	177.00	125.00	2,964
Nov	157.75	158.40	157.50	158.40	+ .90	172.75	132.00	1,717
Ja89	153.25	153.90	153.25	153.50	+ .50	171.25	132.00	799
Mar	152.90	153.15	152.90	153.05	+ .50	167.90	152.90	129
Est vol 2,000; vol Thurs 977; open int 11,617, +97.								
SUGAR–WORLD (CSCE)–112,000 lbs.; cents per lb.								
July	9.75	10.05	9.72	10.00	+ .22	10.38	6.79	29,426
Oct	9.69	10.01	9.67	9.97	+ .25	10.35	7.00	77,047
Mr89	9.59	9.88	9.56	9.86	+ .24	10.32	7.66	48,492
May	9.62	9.86	9.60	9.86	+ .22	10.20	7.87	4,785
July	9.68	9.90	9.68	9.85	+ .15	9.90	8.10	405
Oct	9.73	9.95	9.73	9.93	+ .23	9.95	8.98	570
Est vol 30,202; vol Thur 23,586; open int 160,734, +3,550.								
SUGAR–DOMESTIC (CSCE)–112,000 lbs.; cents per lb.								
July	22.38	22.40	22.32	22.35	– .03	22.40	21.55	1,711
Sept	22.25	22.25	22.21	22.22	– .02	22.25	21.52	2,591
Nov	22.05	22.06	22.05	22.07	+ .02	22.06	21.50	2,028
Ja89	....	....	....	21.93	....	21.93	21.70	321
Mar	21.88	21.88	21.88	21.88	....	21.88	21.75	140
Est vol 245; vol Thur 334; open int 6,826, –9.								
–METALS & PETROLEUM–								
COPPER (CMX)–25,000 lbs.; cents per lb.								
June	108.00	110.00	108.00	109.45	+ 1.20	110.00	87.50	296
July	102.00	104.90	102.00	103.70	+ 1.95	104.90	62.30	17,175
Sept	95.50	97.70	95.30	95.50	– .35	97.70	59.45	7,145
Dec	93.00	93.00	90.00	90.25	– 1.85	96.50	64.70	5,038
Mr89	86.60	86.90	84.00	84.50	– 2.00	93.00	66.50	1,287
May	84.00	84.00	84.00	82.00	– 2.00	89.00	73.15	138
July	....	....	....	80.80	– 2.00	80.00	77.50	198
Sept	....	....	....	79.80	– 2.00	82.00	76.00	93
Dec	....	....	....	79.80	– 2.00	82.20	77.50	174
Est vol 13,500; vol Thur 18,854; open int 31,562, +1,996.								
GOLD (CMX)–100 troy oz.; $ per troy oz.								
June	467.00	469.50	464.00	464.80	– 2.20	523.00	399.00	4,762
July	466.00	467.50	466.00	466.80	– 2.20	467.50	458.40	305
Aug	470.00	473.80	468.50	469.30	– 2.20	527.00	425.00	56,355
Oct	476.00	479.50	474.30	474.50	– 2.00	533.50	429.00	11,571
Dec	480.50	485.00	479.00	479.80	– 1.80	546.00	430.00	24,339
Fb89	486.50	486.50	484.50	485.10	– 1.80	549.50	446.00	9,586
Apr	490.00	490.00	490.00	490.50	– 1.80	550.00	451.00	7,124
June	496.00	498.00	496.00	496.10	– 1.80	570.00	455.50	10,231
Aug	503.80	503.80	503.80	502.00	– 1.80	575.00	482.20	5,900
Oct	....	....	....	508.30	– 1.80	575.50	466.30	7,240
Dec	....	....	....	514.70	– 1.80	510.00	472.50	5,566
Fb90	....	....	....	521.10	– 1.80	516.00	502.00	2,143
Apr	....	....	....	527.60	– 1.80	....	....	310
Est vol 75,000; vol Thur 58,148; open int 145,422, +4,011.								
PLATINUM (NYM)–50 troy oz.; $ per troy oz.								
June	....	....	....	608.10	–16.90	619.00	580.00	37
July	617.00	622.50	609.10	610.60	–17.40	667.50	443.00	13,219
Oct	623.00	628.00	615.00	616.60	–17.60	667.50	452.00	6,484
Ja89	625.00	632.50	623.00	624.10	–17.60	646.00	459.00	2,998
Apr	640.00	640.00	640.00	631.10	–17.60	643.50	482.00	333
Est vol 10,234; vol Thur 10,269; open int 23,076, +28.								
PALLADIUM (NYM) 100 troy oz.; $ per troy oz.								
June	130.00	132.50	128.50	132.70	+ 1.75	160.50	103.65	996
Sept	129.50	133.00	128.25	132.20	+ 2.15	142.25	103.65	3,959
Dec	130.00	132.00	128.00	131.70	+ 2.15	139.50	104.50	1,949
Mr89	129.00	129.00	128.50	131.20	+ 2.15	129.00	115.50	252
Est vol 1,823; vol Thur 998; open int 7,158, +379.								
SILVER (CMX)–5,000 troy oz.; cents per troy oz.								
June	727.0	727.0	727.0	722.5	– 3.5	727.0	635.0	24
July	723.0	747.0	723.0	727.0	– 3.5	1053.0	580.0	46,201
Sept	735.0	757.0	733.0	736.9	– 3.3	1064.0	588.0	12,253
Dec	750.0	774.0	745.0	752.6	– 3.0	1082.0	606.0	10,691
Mr89	765.0	790.0	765.0	768.6	– 2.7	1073.0	660.0	4,693
May	782.0	787.0	780.0	779.8	– 2.5	948.0	675.0	1,603
July	803.0	803.0	792.0	791.4	– 2.3	985.0	688.0	1,151
Sept	....	....	....	803.1	– 2.1	820.0	698.0	913
Dec	820.0	830.0	818.0	820.5	– 1.8	830.0	722.0	541
Mr90	....	....	....	838.3	– 1.5	777.0	770.0	481
Est vol 50,000; vol Thur 42,073; open int 78,587, +5,552.								
SILVER (CBT)–1,000 troy oz.; cents per troy oz.								
June	721.0	740.0	720.0	724.0	– 1.0	1030.0	600.0	302
Aug	730.0	753.0	729.0	733.0	– 2.5	1004.0	632.0	6,006
Oct	738.0	764.0	738.0	743.0	– 3.0	937.0	637.0	223
Dec	750.0	774.0	748.0	753.0	– 3.0	946.0	648.0	5,991

time the contract is entered into, no money changes hands.

Figure 21.1 shows prices for several agricultural and metals futures contracts as they appear in *The Wall Street Journal*. The boldface line lists the commodity, the exchange where the futures contract is traded in parentheses, the contract size, and the pricing unit. The first contract listed is for corn, traded on the Chicago Board of Trade (CBT). Each contract calls for delivery of 5,000 bushels, and prices are quoted in cents per bushel. The next several rows detail price data for contracts expiring on various dates. The July 1988 maturity corn contract, for example, opened during the day at a futures price of 229 cents per bushel. The highest futures price during the day was $234\frac{3}{4}$, the lowest was $228\frac{1}{2}$, and the settlement price (a representative trading price during the last few minutes of trading) was $234\frac{1}{2}$. The settlement price increased by $9\frac{3}{4}$ cents from the previous trading day. The highest futures price over the contract's life to date was $234\frac{3}{4}$, and the lowest was 174 cents. Finally, open interest, or the number of outstanding contracts, was 66,098. Similar information is given for each maturity date.

The trader holding the long position, who will purchase the good, profits from price increases. Suppose that in July the price of corn turns out to be 239 cents per bushel. The long position trader who entered into the contract at the futures price of $234\frac{1}{2}$ cents on June 3 would pay the agreed-on \$2.345 per bushel to receive corn that at contract maturity is worth \$2.39 per bushel in the market. Since each contract calls for delivery of 5,000 bushels, ignoring brokerage fees, the profit to the long position equals $5,000(\$2.39 - \$2.345) = \$225.00$. Conversely, the short position must deliver 5,000 bushels of corn, each with value \$2.39, for the previously agreed-on futures price of only \$2.345. The short position's loss equals the long position's gain.

To summarize, at maturity:

Profit to long = Spot price at maturity − Original futures price
Profit to short = Original futures price − Spot price at maturity

where the spot price is the actual market price of the commodity at the time of delivery.

Concept Check

Question 1. Graph the profit realized by an investor who enters the long side of a futures contract as a function of the price of the asset on the maturity date. Compare this graph to a graph of the profits realized by the purchaser of the asset itself. Next, try the same exercise for a short futures position and a short sale of the asset.

The futures contract is therefore a zero-sum game, with losses and gains to all positions netting out to zero. Every long position is offset by a short position. The aggregate profits to futures trading, summing over all investors, also must be zero, as is the net exposure to changes in the commodity price. For this reason the establishment of a futures market in a commodity should not have a major impact on the spot market for that commodity. That is, a futures market in IBM stock, were it to be established, should not affect IBM's ability to raise money in the equity market.

Concept Check

Question 2. What is the difference between the futures price and the value of the futures contract?

Question 3. Evaluate the criticism that futures markets siphon off capital from more productive uses.

Existing Contracts

Futures and forward contracts are traded on a wide variety of goods in four broad categories: agricultural commodities, metals and minerals (including energy commodities), foreign currencies, and financial futures (fixed-income securities and stock market indices). The financial futures contracts are recent innovations, for which trading was introduced in 1975. Innovation in financial futures has been quite rapid and is ongoing. (See box.) Table 21.1 enumerates the various contracts trading in the United States in 1987.

TABLE 21.1   Traded Futures Contracts, 1987

Foreign Currencies	Agricultural	Metals and Energy	Financial Futures
British pound	Corn	Copper	Eurodollars
Canadian dollar	Oats	Aluminum	GNMA
Japanese yen	Soybeans	Gold	Treasury bonds
Swiss franc	Soybean meal	Platinum	Treasury bills
French franc	Soybean oil	Palladium	Treasury notes
West German mark	Wheat	Silver	Bank CDs
Short gilt	Barley	Crude oil	Municipal bond index
Long gilt	Flaxseed	Heating oil	Corporate bond index
U.S. dollar index	Rapeseed	Gas oil	S&P 100 index
European Currency Unit	Rye	Gasoline (leaded)	S&P 500 index
Australian dollar	Cattle (feeder)	Gasoline (unleaded)	NYSE index
	Cattle (live)	Propane	Value Line Index
	Hogs		Major Market Index
	Pork bellies		OTC 250 index
	Cocoa		NASDAQ 100 index
	Coffee		Consumer Price Index
	Cotton		Institutional index
	Orange juice		Inflation rate
	Sugar		Russell 2000 Index
	Lumber		Russell 3000 Index
	Potatoes		CRB Index
	Rice		
	Corn syrup		

Modified from *Futures* magazine, 1988 Reference Guide. Reprinted by permission.

Fast Times in the Chicago Pits

Global Trading Hits the Financial-Futures Market

The traders still favor loud-colored polyester jackets. They still bellow and gesture furiously in the "open outcry" system that predates the Civil War. But Chicago's Board of Trade and Mercantile Exchange, those old fogies that dominate the arcane financial-futures business, are positioning themselves to enter the 21st century. As global expansion pushes financial markets toward round-the-clock trading, the Chicago giants are enticing customers with new vehicles and the latest in shopkeeping methods. This week the Board of Trade (BOT) inaugurated a three-hour Sunday-night session to coincide with the opening of business in Tokyo. Within 18 months the Merc plans to introduce global automation—computers that will handle the execution of orders while exhausted traders are at home asleep.

As the prospects for stock and bond prices have turned cloudy—and as the Japanese and other foreigners have piled up American holdings—futures have taken off. Investors use these contracts, which give them the right to buy or sell financial products at fixed times and prices in the future, to hedge against potential losses on securities and currencies. (Speculators use them to bet on future gains.) The expansion has bred new competition for the Chicago exchanges. Security Pacific Corp. plans to trade options on United States government bonds. Jefferies & Co. expects to swap financial futures for its customers without funneling orders through the pits. The Tokyo Stock Exchange trades futures in yen-denominated bonds.

To keep pace with its new rivals, the Chicago traders have had to come up with financial products more complex than their predecessors could have imagined. The Merc plans one futures contract tied to an index of Japanese stocks and another based on stocks in 16 different countries; both should debut in 1988. The BOT is preparing to offer a contract tied to the "Footsie 100"—the Financial Times-London Stock Exchange index of 100 stocks. The costs of marketing a new contract are enormous and the failure rate is high, but the exchanges hope to repeat the success the Merc has had trading in futures linked to the S&P 500 stock index and the BOT's Treasury-bond contract.

Unexpected volume

No contract is of use to foreign investors if the markets aren't open to take their orders. Last April the BOT began trading on four weekday nights, and next month it will extend its evening sessions by 30 minutes to three and a half hours. So far it has done an average nightly volume of 13,000 contracts, almost three times its original estimate of 5,000. The Merc's plan for computerized trading has sparked equal interest: the day after it was announced, 30 bidders lined up to buy exchange memberships.

Some veteran traders fear the advent of the computer will make them obsolete. But market experts say that's unlikely. The pit system makes for liquid markets, letting investors get in and out with ease; jostling on the exchange floor gives traders a "feel" for the market they couldn't get sitting at a desk and increases their propensity to trade. The system has another plus: compared with computers, says University of Chicago professor Merton Miller, "it's so damn cheap." The Chicago traders may hang on to their ancient methods for some time to come—but the rapid changes in today's financial markets are sure to keep them moving with the times.

Outside the futures markets a fairly developed network of banks and brokers has established a forward market in foreign exchange. This forward market is not a formal exchange in the sense that the exchange specifies the terms of the traded contract. Instead, participants in a forward contract may negotiate for delivery of any quantity of goods, as distinguished from futures markets where contract size is set by the exchange. In forward arrangements, banks and brokers simply negotiate contracts for clients (or themselves) as needed.

21.2   Mechanics of Trading in Futures Markets

The Clearinghouse and Open Interest

Trading in futures contracts is more complex than making ordinary stock transactions. If you want to make a stock purchase, your broker simply acts as an intermediary to enable you to buy shares from or sell to another individual through the stock exchange. In futures trading, however, the exchange plays a more active role.

When an investor contacts a broker to establish a futures position, the brokerage firm wires the order to the firm's trader on the floor of the futures exchange. In contrast to stock trading, which involves specialists or market makers in each security, futures trades take place among floor traders in the "trading pit" for each contract. Traders use voice or hand signals to signify their desire to buy or sell. Once a trader willing to accept the opposite side of a trade is located, the trade is recorded and the customer is notified.

At this point, just as is true for options contracts, the **clearinghouse** enters the picture. Rather than having the long and short traders hold contracts with each other, the clearinghouse becomes the seller of the contract for the long position and the buyer of the contract for the short position. The clearinghouse is obligated to deliver the commodity to the long position, and to pay for delivery from the short; consequently, the clearinghouse's position nets to zero. This arrangement makes the clearinghouse the trading partner of each trader, both long and short. The clearinghouse, bound to perform on its side of each contract, is the only party that can be hurt by the failure of any trader to fulfill the obligations of the futures contract. This arrangement is necessary, because a futures contract calls for future performance, which cannot be guaranteed as easily as an immediate stock transaction.

Figure 21.2 A, illustrates what would happen in the absence of the clearinghouse. The trader in the long position would be obligated to pay the futures price to the short position trader; the trader in the short position would be obligated to deliver the commodity. Figure 21.2, B, shows how the clearinghouse becomes an intermediary, acting as the trading partner for each side of the contract. The clearinghouse's position is neutral, since it takes a long and a short position for each transaction.

The existence of the clearinghouse enables traders to liquidate positions easily. If you are currently long in a contract and want to undo your position, you simply instruct your broker to enter the short side of a contract to close out your position. This is called a **reversing trade.** The exchange nets out your long and short positions,

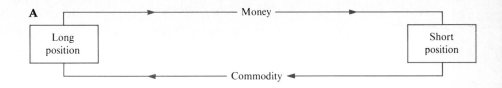

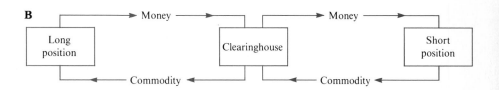

reducing your net position to zero. Your zero net position with the clearinghouse eliminates the need to fulfill at maturity either the original long or the reversing short position.

The **open interest** on the contract is the number of contracts outstanding. (Long and short positions are not counted separately, meaning that open interest can be defined as either the number of long or short contracts outstanding.) The clearinghouse's position nets out to zero, of course, and so is not counted in the computation of open interest. When contracts begin trading, open interest is zero. As time passes, open interest increases as progressively more contracts are entered. Almost all traders, however, liquidate their positions before the contract maturity date. Instead of actually taking or making delivery of the commodity, virtually all traders enter reversing trades to cancel their original positions, thereby realizing the profits or losses on the contract. Actual deliveries and purchases of commodities are then made via regular channels of supply. The percentage of contracts that result in actual delivery is estimated to range from less than 1% to 3%, depending on the commodity and the activity in the contract. The image of a trader awakening one delivery date with a hog in the front yard is amusing, but unlikely.

You can see the typical pattern of open interest in Figure 21.1. In the silver or platinum contracts, for example, the June delivery contracts are close to maturity and open interest is relatively small; most contracts have been reversed already. The next few maturities have significant open interest. Finally, the most distant maturity contract has little open interest, because the contract has only recently been available for trading.

Marking to Market and the Margin Account

Anyone who saw the film *Trading Places* knows that Eddie Murphy as a trader in orange juice futures had no intention of purchasing or delivering orange juice. Traders simply bet on the future price of juice. The total profit or loss realized by the long trader who buys a contract at time zero and closes, or reverses, it at time t is just the change in the futures price over the period, $F_t - F_0$. Symmetrically, the short trader earns $F_0 - F_t$.

The process by which profits or losses accrue to traders is called **marking to market.** At initial execution of a trade, each trader establishes a margin account. The margin is a security account consisting of cash and/or near-cash securities, such as Treasury bills, that ensure the trader is able to satisfy the obligations of the futures contract. Because both parties to a futures contract are exposed to losses, both must post margin. This is in contrast to options, where only the option writer has an obligation and needs to post margin. Because the margin may be satisfied with interest-earning securities, posting the margin does not impose a significant opportunity cost of funds on the trader. The initial margin is usually set between 5% and 10% of the total value of the contract. Contracts written on assets with more volatile prices require higher margins.

On any day that futures markets trade, futures prices may rise or fall. An increase in price benefits long positions that agreed to purchase the good at the lower price that was established when the contract was initiated; conversely, the price increase harms short positions that still must deliver the good at the originally agreed-on futures price. Instead of waiting until the maturity date for traders to realize all gains and losses, the clearinghouse requires all positions to recognize profits as they accrue daily. If the futures price of corn rises from 234 to 236 cents per bushel, the clearinghouse credits the margin account of the long position for 5,000 bushels (which is the standard size of the corn-futures contract) multiplied by 2 cents per bushel, or $100 per contract. Conversely, for the short position the clearinghouse takes this amount from the margin account for each contract held. This daily settling is marking to market.

Therefore the maturity date of the contract does not govern realization of profit or loss. Marking to market ensures that, as futures prices change, the proceeds accrue to the trader's margin account immediately.

Concept Check	Question 4. What must be the net inflow or outlay from marking to the market for the clearinghouse? Hint: what is the net position of the clearinghouse?

If a trader accrues sustained losses from marking to market, the margin account may fall below a critical value called the **maintenance margin** or **variation margin.** Once the value of the account falls below this value, the trader receives a margin call. Either new funds must be transferred into the margin account, or the broker will close out enough of the trader's position to reduce the required margin for that position to a level at or below the trader's remaining margin. This procedure safeguards the position of the clearinghouse. Positions are closed out before the margin account is exhausted—any losses suffered by the trader are thereby covered.

Marking to market is the major way in which futures and forward contracts differ, besides contract standardization. Futures follow a pay- (or receive-) as-you-go-method. Forward contracts are simply held until maturity, and no funds are transferred until that date, although the contracts may be traded.

It is important to note that the futures price on the delivery date will equal the spot price of the commodity on that date. Since a maturing contract calls for immediate delivery, the futures price on that day must equal the spot price—the cost of the commodity from the two competing sources is equalized in a competitive market.[1] You may obtain delivery of the commodity either by purchasing it directly in the spot market or by entering the long side of a futures contract.

A commodity available from two sources (spot or futures market) must be priced identically, or else investors will rush to purchase it from the cheap source in order to sell it in the higher-priced market. Such arbitrage activity could not persist without prices adjusting to eliminate the arbitrage opportunity. Therefore the futures price and spot price must converge at maturity. This is called the **convergence property.**

Because of convergence, the profits realized over the life of futures and forward contracts are quite similar. Call f_0 the forward price at contract inception and P_T the spot price of the commodity on the maturity date, T. The profit to the long position of the forward contract is $P_T - f_0$, that is, the difference between the value of the good received and the price that was contracted to be paid for it. The futures contract, by contrast, uses daily marking to market. The sum of all daily settlements will equal $F_T - F_0$, where F_T stands for the futures price at contract maturity. We have noted, however, that the futures price at maturity equals the spot price, so total futures profits also may be expressed as $P_T - F_0$. Summing the daily mark-to-market settlements results in a profit formula identical to that of the forward contract.

Because these payments accrue continually, we should not, strictly speaking, simply add them up to obtain total profits without first adjusting for interest on interim payments. Some empirical evidence, however, suggests that interest earnings on daily settlements have only a small effect on the determination of futures and forward prices. For this reason, we often ignore this fine point and simply take the profits or losses on a futures contract held to maturity to be $P_T - F_0$ for the long position and $F_0 - P_T$ for the short. Section 4 explores this issue in greater detail.

Concept Check

Question 5. If futures prices are equally likely to go up as to go down by each trading day, what are the expected proceeds from marking to market? The expected interest earnings on those proceeds?

---

[1] Small differences between the spot and futures price at maturity may persist because of transportation costs, but this is a minor factor.

To illustrate the time profile of returns to a futures contract, consider an example for which the current futures price for silver for delivery 5 days from today is $7.60 per ounce. Suppose that over the next 5 days the futures price evolves as follows:

Day	Futures Price
0 (today)	$7.60
1	$7.70
2	$7.75
3	$7.68
4	$7.68
5 (delivery)	$7.71

The spot price of silver on the delivery day is $7.71: the convergence property implies that the price of silver in the spot market must equal the futures price on delivery day.

The daily mark-to-market settlements for each contract held by the long position will be as follows:

Day	Profit (Loss) per Ounce	$\times$ 1,000 Ounces/Contract = Daily Proceeds
1	7.70 − 7.60 = .10	$100
2	7.75 − 7.70 = .05	$ 50
3	7.68 − 7.75 = −.07	−$ 70
4	7.68 − 7.68 = 0	0
5	7.71 − 7.68 = .03	$ 30
		$110

The profit on day 1 is the increase in the futures price from the previous day, or ($7.70−$7.60) per ounce. Because each silver contract on the Chicago Board of Trade calls for purchase and delivery of 1,000 ounces, the total profit per contract is 1,000 multiplied by $.10, or $100. On day 3, when the futures price falls, the long position's margin account will be debited by $70. By day 5, the sum of all daily proceeds is $110. This is exactly equal to 1,000 times the difference between the final futures price of $7.71 and original futures price of $7.60. Thus the sum of all the daily proceeds (per ounce of silver held long) equals $P_T - F_0$.

Cash vs. Actual Delivery

Most futures markets call for delivery of an actual commodity such as a particular grade of wheat or a specified amount of foreign currency if the contract is not reversed before maturity. For agricultural commodities where quality of the delivered good may vary, the exchange sets quality standards as part of the futures contract. In some cases contracts may be settled with higher- or lower-grade commodities. In these cases a premium or discount is applied to the delivered commodity to adjust for the quality difference.

The availability of different grade commodities for delivery reduces the possibility of a *squeeze*. A squeeze occurs when enough long positions hold their contracts to maturity and demand actual delivery that supplies of the commodity are insufficient to cover all contracts. The longs in that case "corner the market." Squeezes have been quite rare in practice, and their legal implications for traders and the exchange are not yet settled. A short squeeze occurs when shorts accumulate a position and threaten to deliver some commodity that is costly to store.

Some futures contracts call for **cash delivery.** An example is a stock index futures contract where the underlying asset is an index such as the Standard & Poor's 500 or the New York Stock Exchange index. Delivery of every stock in the index clearly would be impractical. Hence the contract calls for "delivery" of a cash amount equal to the value that the index attains on the maturity date of the contract. The sum of all the daily settlements from marking to market results in the long position realizing total profits or losses of $S_T - F_0$, where S_T is the value of the stock index on the maturity date T, and F_0 is the original futures price. Cash settlement closely mimics actual delivery, the only difference being that the cash value of the asset rather than the asset itself is delivered by the short position in exchange for the futures price.

More concretely, the S&P 500 index contract calls for delivery of $500 multiplied by the value of the index. At maturity, the index might list at 250, a market value–weighted index of the prices of all 500 stocks in the index. The cash settlement contract calls for delivery of $500 × 250, or $125,000, in return for 500 times the futures price. This yields exactly the same profit as would result from directly purchasing 500 units of the index for $125,000 and then delivering it for 500 times the original futures price.

Regulations

Futures markets are regulated by the Commodities Futures Trading Commission, a federal agency. The CFTC sets capital requirements for member firms of the futures exchanges, authorizes trading in new contracts, and oversees maintenance of daily trading records.

The futures exchange sets limits on the amount by which futures prices may change from one day to the next. For example, the price limit on silver contracts traded on the Chicago Board of Trade is 20 cents, which means that if silver futures close today at $7.40 per ounce, trades in silver tomorrow may vary only between $7.20 and $7.60 per ounce. The exchanges may increase or reduce price limits in response to perceived increases or decreases in price volatility of the contract. Price limits are often eliminated as contracts approach maturity, usually in the last month of trading.

Price limits traditionally are viewed as a means to limit violent price fluctuations. This reasoning seems dubious. Suppose that an international monetary crisis overnight drives up the spot price of silver to $8.50. No one would sell silver futures at prices for future delivery as low as $7.40. Instead, the futures price would rise each day by the 20-cent limit, although the quoted price would represent only an unfilled bid order—no contracts would trade at the low quoted price. After several days of limit moves of 20 cents per day, the futures price would finally reach its equilibrium level, and trading would occur again. This process means no one could unload a position until the price reached its equilibrium level. This example shows that price limits offer no real protection against price fluctuation.

Taxation

Because of the mark-to-market procedure, investors do not have control over the tax year in which they realize gains or losses. Instead, price changes are realized gradually, with each daily settlement. Therefore taxes are paid at year-end on cumulated profits or losses regardless of whether the position has been closed out.

21.3 Futures Markets Strategies

Hedging and Speculating

Hedging and speculating are two polar uses of futures markets. A speculator uses a futures contract to profit from movements in futures prices, a hedger to protect against price movement.

If speculators believe that prices will increase, they will take a long position for expected profits. Conversely, they exploit expected price declines by taking a short position. As an example of a speculative strategy, suppose someone thinks that silver futures prices, currently at $7.20 per ounce, will rise to $7.50 by month's end. Each silver contract on the Chicago Board of Trade (CBT) calls for delivery of 1,000 ounces. If the silver futures price does in fact increase to $7.50, the speculator profits by 1,000 multiplied by $.30, or $300 per contract. If the forecast is incorrect and silver prices decline, the investor loses 1,000 times the decrease in the futures price for each contract purchased. Speculators bet on the direction of futures price movements.

Why does a speculator buy a silver futures contract? Why not buy silver directly? One reason lies in transaction costs, which are far smaller in futures markets. Another reason is storage costs. Holding silver in inventory directly and insuring it is needlessly expensive when futures contracts may be used instead.

A third reason is the leverage that futures trading provides. Each silver contract calls for delivery of 1,000 ounces of silver, worth about $7,200 in our example. The initial margin required for this account might be only $1,000. The $300 per contract gain on the silver translates into a 30% ($300/$1,000) return, despite the fact that the silver futures price increases only 4.2% ($.30/$7.20). Futures margins therefore allow speculators to achieve much greater leverage than is available from direct trading in the commodity.

Hedgers, by contrast, use futures markets to immunize themselves from price movements. Holders of silver, jewelers for example, might want to protect the value of their inventory against price fluctuations. In this case they have no desire to bet on price movements in either direction. To achieve such protection, a hedger takes a short position in silver futures, which obligates the hedger to deliver silver at the contract maturity date for the current futures price. This locks in the sales price for the silver and guarantees that the total value (per ounce) of the silver-plus-futures position at the maturity date is the current futures price.

For illustration, suppose that the futures price for delivery next year is $7.80, and that the only three possible year-end prices per ounce are $7.40, $7.80, and $8.20. If investors currently hold 10,000 ounces of silver, they would take short positions in 10 contracts, each for 1,000 ounces. Protecting the value of an asset with short futures positions is called *short hedging*. Note that the futures position requires no current investment. (We can ignore the margin requirement in the initial investment because it is small relative to the size of the contract, and because it may be posted in interest-bearing securities and so does not present a time-value or opportunity cost.)

Next year, the profits from the short futures position will be 10,000 times any decrease in the futures price, or the sum of the mark-to-market settlements. At maturity the final futures price will equal the spot price of silver because of convergence. Hence the futures profit will be 10,000 times $(F_0 - P_T)$, where P_T is the price of silver on the delivery date and F_0 is the original futures price, $7.80. For the three possible price outcomes, the total portfolio value equals:

	Silver Price at Year-End		
	$7.40	**$7.80**	**$8.20**
Silver holdings	$74,000	$78,000	$82,000
(value = 1,000 P_T)			
Futures profits or losses	$ 4,000	0	−$ 4,000
TOTAL	$78,000	$78,000	$78,000

Note that the total portfolio value is unaffected by the year-end silver price. The gains or losses on the silver holdings are exactly offset by those on the two contracts held short. For example, if silver prices fall to $7.40 per ounce, the losses on the silver inventory are offset by the $4,000 gain on the futures contracts. That profit equals the difference between the futures price on the maturity date (which is the spot price of $7.40) and the originally contracted futures price of $7.80. For short contracts a profit of $.40 per ounce is realized from the fall in the spot price. Because each contract calls for delivery of 10,000 ounces, this results in a $4,000 gain that offsets the decline in the value of silver held. A hedger, in contrast to a speculator, is indifferent to the ultimate price of the spot commodity. The short-hedger who has arranged to sell the commodity for an agreed-on price need not be concerned about further developments in the market price.

To generalize this numerical example, you can note that the silver will be worth P_T at maturity, while the profit on the futures contract is $F_0 - P_T$. The sum of the two positions is therefore F_0 dollars, which is independent of the eventual silver price.

A *long hedge* is the analogue to a short hedge for a purchaser of a commodity. A company that will purchase silver at year-end can lock in the total cost of the purchase by entering the long side of a contract, which commits it to purchasing at the currently determined futures price.

Exact futures hedging may be impossible for some goods because the necessary futures contract is not traded. For example, producers of bauxite, the ore from which aluminum is made, might like to trade in bauxite futures but cannot. Because bauxite and aluminum prices are highly correlated, however, a close hedge may be established by shorting aluminum futures. Hedging a position using futures on another commodity is called *cross hedging*.

Concept Check

Question 6. What are the sources of risk to an investor who uses aluminum futures to hedge an inventory of bauxite?

Futures contracts may be used also as general portfolio hedges. Bodie and Rosansky[2] show that commodity futures returns have had a negative correlation with the stock market. Investors may add a diversified portfolio of futures contracts to a diversified stock portfolio to lower the standard deviation of the overall rate of return. Moreover, the average rate of increase in commodity futures prices has been roughly the same as for common stocks as these figures show:

	1950 to 1976	
	Average Annual Return	**Annual Standard Deviation**
Portfolio of T-bills and 23 commodity futures	13.85%	22.43%
S&P 500 index	13.05%	18.95%

The correlation coefficient between the two portfolios during the estimation period was −.24. This implies that long positions in commodity futures would add substantial diversification benefits to a stock portfolio.

To illustrate, suppose that you invest a fraction of your total wealth in stocks and use the remainder to invest in commodity futures contracts, posting 100% margin with T-bills. The stock-futures-bills portfolio presents you with substantial reduction in risk and no sacrifice in expected return. Bodie and Rosansky found that a portfolio composed of 60% stock and 40% T-bills with futures would have had a return of 13.36% and standard deviation of only 12.68%: virtually an unchanged average return from either portfolio taken alone, but with roughly a one-third reduction in standard deviation.

Commodity futures are also inflation hedges. When commodity prices increase because of unanticipated inflation, returns from long futures positions will increase be-

---

[2]Bodie, Zvi, and Rosansky, Victor, "Risk and Return in Commodity Futures," *Financial Analysts Journal,* May/June 1980.

Derivative Assets: Options and Futures

cause the contracts call for delivery of goods for the price agreed on before the high inflation rate became a reality. A more direct means of hedging inflation is offered by a new contract on the Consumer Price Index, to be discussed at length in Chapter 22.

Basis Risk and Hedging

The **basis** is the difference between the futures price and the spot price. As we have noted, on the maturity date of a contract the basis must be zero: the convergence property implies that $F_T - P_T = 0$. Before maturity, however, the futures price for later delivery may differ substantially from the current spot price.

We discussed the case of a short-hedger who holds an asset and a short position to deliver that asset in the future. If the asset and futures contract are held until maturity, the hedger bears no risk, because the ultimate value of the portfolio on the delivery date is determined completely by the current futures price. Risk is eliminated because the futures price and spot price at contract maturity must be equal: gains and losses on the futures and the commodity position will exactly cancel. If the contract and asset are to be liquidated early, however, the hedger bears **basis risk,** because the futures price and spot price need not move in perfect lockstep at all times before the delivery date. In this case gains and losses on the contract and the asset need not exactly offset each other.

Some speculators try to profit from movements in the basis. Rather than betting on the direction of the futures or spot prices *per se,* they bet on the changes in the difference between the two. A long spot–short futures position will profit when the basis narrows. For example, consider an investor holding 1,000 ounces of silver, who is short one silver futures contract. Silver might sell for $7.20 per ounce, while the futures price for next-year delivery is $7.80. The basis is therefore 60 cents. Tomorrow, the silver spot price might increase to $7.24, while the futures price might increase to $7.81. The basis has narrowed from 60 cents to 57 cents. The investor realizes a capital gain of 4 cents per ounce on her silver holdings, and a loss of 1 cent per ounce from the increase in the futures price. The net gain is the decrease in basis, or 3 cents per ounce.

A related strategy is a **spread** position where the investor takes a long position in a futures contract of one maturity and a short position in a contract on the same commodity, but with a different maturity. Profits accrue if the difference in futures prices between the two contracts changes in the hoped-for direction; that is, if the futures price on the contract held long increases by more (or decreases by less) than the futures price on the contract held short.

Consider an investor who holds a June 1989 maturity contract long with a current futures price of $7.83 an ounce, and an April 1989 contract short with a futures price of $7.73 an ounce. If the June futures price increases by 5 cents to $7.88 while the April futures price increases by 4 cents to $7.77, the net gain will be 5 cents − 4 cents, or 1 cent per ounce. Like basis strategies, spreading aims to exploit movements in relative price structures rather than to profit from movements in the general level of prices.

21.4   *The Determination of Futures Prices*

The Spot-Futures Parity Theorem

There are at least two ways to obtain an asset at some date in the future. One way is to purchase the asset now and store it until the targeted future date. The other way is to take a long futures position that calls for purchase of the asset on the date in question. Since each strategy leads to an equivalent result, namely, the ultimate acquisition of the asset, you would expect the market-determined cost of pursuing these strategies to be equal. There must be a predictable relationship between the current price of the asset, including the costs of holding and storing it, and the futures price.

To make this point more obvious, consider a hypothetical futures contract on a stock that pays no dividends. This is a particularly simple example, because explicit storage costs for stocks are negligible, and because stocks are not subject to seasonal price patterns as most agricultural commodities are. Instead, prices on nondividend-paying stocks are set in market equilibrium at a level such that expected capital gains equal the fair expected rate of return appropriate to the stock's risk level.

Two strategies that will assure possession of the stock at some future date T are:

1. *Strategy A.* Buy the stock at price S_0 now and hold it until time T, when its price will be S_T.
2. *Strategy B.* Initiate a long futures position, and invest enough money now to pay the futures price when the contract matures.

Strategy B will require an immediate investment of the *present value* of the futures price in a risk-free security such as Treasury bills, that is, an investment of $F_0/(1 + r_f)^T$ dollars, where r_f is the rate paid on T-bills. Examine the cash flow streams of these two strategies:

Strategy	Action	Initial Cash Flow	CF at Time T
A	Buy stock	$-S_0$	S_T
B	Enter long position	0	$S_T - F_0$
	Invest $F_0/(1 + r_f)^T$ in bills	$-F_0/(1 + r_f)^T$	F_0
	Total for strategy B	$-F_0/(1 + r_f)^T$	S_T

The initial cash flow of strategy A is negative, reflecting the cash outflow necessary to purchase the stock at the current price S_0. At time T, the stock will be worth S_T.

Strategy B involves an initial investment equal to the present value of the futures price that will be paid at the maturity of the futures contract. By time T, the investment will grow to F_0. In addition, if we simplify by assuming that the entire profit from the futures contract accrues at date T rather than from daily mark-to-market settlements, the profits to the long position at time T will be $S_T - F_0$. The sum of the two components of strategy B will be S_T dollars, exactly enough to purchase the stock at time T regardless of its price at that time.

Note that each strategy results in an identical value at T: a portfolio value of S_T

dollars. Therefore the cost, or initial cash outflow, required by these strategies also must be equal. It follows that

$$F_0/(1 + r_f)^T = S_0$$

or

$$F_0 = S_0(1 + r_f)^T \qquad (21.1)$$

We have derived a relationship between the current price and the futures price of the stock. The interest rate in this case may be viewed as the "cost of carrying" the stock from the present to time T. The cost in this case represents the time-value-of-money opportunity cost—instead of investing in the stock, you could have invested without risk in Treasury bills to earn interest income. To be concrete, suppose the stock currently sells for $40, and the risk-free interest rate is 1% per month. The formula indicates the predicted futures price for 6-month delivery would be $40 × $(1.01)^6$ = $42.46.

Why should the futures price exceed the current stock price by a factor of exactly $(1 + r_f)^T$? The futures contract enables the investor to purchase the stock without tying up funds until the maturity date and without any uncertainty regarding the ultimate purchase price. This advantage must be offset by an equivalent disadvantage, or no one would invest directly in stocks. The offsetting disadvantage is that the futures price must exceed the current stock price by the amount of interest that can be earned on the freed-up funds between now and the delivery date. Equivalently, the futures price must exceed the stock price by the cost of carrying the stock (interest costs in this case) from today until time T. Moreover, because the futures strategy locks in a known purchase price, the appropriate interest rate is the risk-free rate.

If the futures price were not greater than the current spot price, no investor would choose to hold the stock. Instead, each investor could establish a long position in the futures contract, setting aside enough money to cover the futures price. This strategy would enable a cheaper acquisition of the stock. Such a situation could not persist because, if no one is willing to hold the stock at its current price, the stock price would inevitably fall. At the same time the futures price would rise as investors rushed to establish long positions. Ultimately, the stock price relative to the futures price would fall until strategies A and B became equally attractive, and the relationship in equation 21.1 held.

Indeed, if equation 21.1 did not hold, investors could earn arbitrage profits. For example, suppose that the futures price were $43 rather than the "appropriate" value of $42.46 that we just derived. An investor could realize arbitrage profits by pursuing a strategy involving a long position in strategy A and short position in strategy B:

Action	Initial Cash Flow	CF at Time T (6 Months)
Borrow $40, repay with interest at time T	+40	$-40(1.01)^6 = -42.46$
Buy stock for $40	−40	S_T
Enter short futures position (F = $43)	0	$43 - S_T$
TOTAL	0	$0.54

The net initial investment of this strategy is zero. Moreover, its cash flow at time T is positive and risk-free: the total payoff at time T will be \$0.54 regardless of the stock price. (The profit is equal to the mispricing of the futures contract.) Risk has been eliminated because profits and losses on the futures and the stock positions exactly offset each other. The portfolio is perfectly hedged.

Such a strategy produces an arbitrage profit—a risk-free profit requiring no initial net investment. If such an opportunity existed, all market participants would rush to take advantage of it. The results? The stock price would bid up, and/or the future price would bid down until equation 21.1 was satisfied. A similar analysis applies for the possibility that F_0 is less than \$42.46. In this case you simply reverse this strategy to earn riskless profits. We conclude therefore that in a well-functioning market in which arbitrage opportunities are competed away, $F_0 = S_0(1 + r_f)^T$. The arbitrage strategy can be represented more generally as follows:

Action	Initial Cash Flow	CF at Time T
1. Borrow S_0	S_0	$-S_0(1 + r_f)^T$
2. Buy stock for S_0	$-S_0$	S_T
3. Enter short futures position	0	$F_0 - S_T$
TOTAL	0	$F_0 - S_0(1 + r_f)^T$

The initial cash flow is zero by construction: the money necessary to purchase the stock in step 1 is borrowed in step 2, and the futures position in step 3, which is used to hedge the value of the stock position, does not require an initial outlay. Moreover, the total cash flow to the strategy at time T is risk-free because it involves only terms that are already known when the contract is entered. If this risk-free cash flow were positive, then an investor would be able to make risk-free profits without any net investment. This situation could not persist because investors would try to cash in on the arbitrage opportunity. Ultimately, prices would change until the time T cash flow is reduced to zero, at which point F_0 would once again equal $S_0(1 + r_f)^T$.

If F_0 is less than $S_0(1 + r_f)^T$, the cash flow at time T would be risk-free and negative. In this case we would simply reverse the general arbitrage strategy. We would short sell the stock, lend dollars, and enter a long futures position. The long futures–short stock position is again perfectly hedged. The time T cash flow to this reverse strategy would equal $S_0(1 + r_f)^T - F_0$, which again constitutes a risk-free arbitrage profit. Note, however, that this strategy requires the ability to short sell the stock at no cost. When short sales are costly, the opportunity to perform this reverse arbitrage would be limited.

Concept Check

Question 7. What are the three steps of the arbitrage strategy if F_0 is less than $S_0(1 + r_f)^T$? Work out the cash flows of the strategy now and at time T in a table like the one in the text.

Derivative Assets: Options and Futures

Even if short selling is costly, however, one would expect equation 21.1 to hold. Recall that strategies A and B provide identical cash flows at time T. If the initial cost of establishing strategies A and B were to differ, then investors would pursue only the cheaper of the two. If F_0 were less than $S_0(1 + r_f)^T$, no one would be willing to hold the stock directly—it would be cheaper to follow strategy B, which has a payoff identical to that of the stock. With no demand for direct holdings of the stock, the stock price would fall and continue to fall until the costs of establishing strategies A and B are equalized. Hence we arrive once again at the conclusion that the equilibrium relationship between F_0 and S_0 is given by equation 21.1. This result is called the **spot-futures parity theorem,** or **cost-of-carry relationship;** it gives the normal or theoretically correct relationship between spot and futures prices.

We can easily extend the parity theorem to the case where the stock pays dividends. When the stock provides a dividend yield of d, the net cost of carry is only $r_f - d$; the time value cost of the wealth that is tied up in the stock is offset by the flow of dividends from the stock. The net opportunity cost of holding the stock is the foregone interest less the dividends received. Therefore in the dividend-paying case the spot-futures parity relationship[3] is

$$F_0 = S_0(1 + r_f - d)^T \tag{21.2}$$

where d is the dividend yield on the stock. Problem 5 at the end of the chapter leads you through a more formal demonstration of this result.

Spreads

Just as we can predict the relationship between spot and futures prices, there are similar methods to determine the proper relationships among futures prices for contracts of different maturity dates. These relationships are simple generalizations of the spot-futures parity relationship. We will restrict ourselves to stock futures in this discussion and thus avoid the additional complications that arise from noninterest carrying costs.

Call $F(T_1)$ the current futures price for delivery at date T_1, and $F(T_2)$ the futures price for delivery at T_2. Let d be the dividend yield of the stock between T_1 and T_2. We know from the parity equation 21.2 that

$$F(T_1) = S_0(1 + r_f - d)^{T_1}$$
$$F(T_2) = S_0(1 + r_f - d)^{T_2}$$

As a result,

$$F(T_2)/F(T_1) = (1 + r_f - d)^{(T_2 - T_1)}$$

Therefore the basic parity relationship for spreads is

$$F(T_2) = F(T_1)(1 + r_f - d)^{(T_2 - T_1)} \tag{21.3}$$

---

[3]This relationship is only approximate in that it assumes that the dividend is paid just before the maturity of the contract.

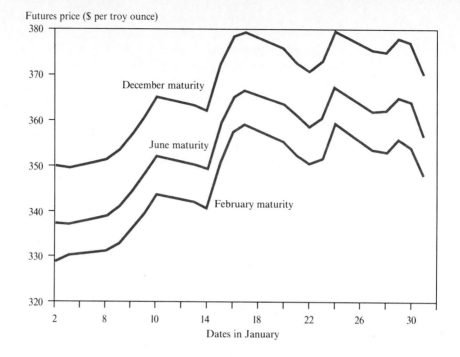

FIGURE 21.3

Futures prices in January 1986 for kilo gold contracts maturing in February, June, and December 1986.

Note that equation 21.3 is quite similar to the spot-futures parity relationship. The major difference is in the substitution of $F(T_1)$ for the current spot price. The intuition is also similar. Delaying delivery from T_1 to T_2 provides the long position the knowledge that the stock will be purchased for $F(T_2)$ dollars at T_2 but does not require that money be tied up in the stock until T_2. The savings realized are the cost of carry between T_1 and T_2 of the money that would have been paid at T_1. Delaying delivery from T_1 until T_2 frees up $F(T_1)$ dollars, which earn risk-free interest at rate r_f. The delayed delivery of the stock also results in the lost dividend yield between T_1 and T_2. The net cost of carry saved by delaying the delivery is thus $r_f - d$. This gives the proportional increase in the futures price that is required to compensate market participants for the delayed delivery of the stock and postponement of the payment of the futures price. If the parity condition for spreads is violated, arbitrage opportunities will arise. (Problem 6 at the end of the chapter explores this phenomenon.)

To see how to use equation 21.3, consider the following data for a hypothetical contract:

Contract Maturity Date	Futures Price
January	105
March	106

Suppose that the effective annual T-bill rate is expected to persist at 10% and that the dividend yield is 4% per year. The "correct" March futures price relative to the January price is, according to equation 21.3,

$$105(1 + .1 - .04)^{\frac{1}{6}} = 106.025$$

The actual March futures price is 106, meaning that the March futures is slightly underpriced compared to the January futures, and that, aside from transaction costs, an arbitrage opportunity seems to be present.

Equation 21.3 shows that futures prices should all move together. Actually, it is not surprising that futures prices for different maturity dates move in unison, because all are linked to the same spot price through the parity relationship. Figure 21.3 plots futures prices on gold for three maturity dates. It is apparent that the prices move in virtual lockstep and that the more distant delivery dates require higher futures prices, as equation 21.3 predicts.

Forward vs. Futures Pricing

Until now we have paid little attention to the differing time profile of returns of futures and forward contracts. Instead, we have taken the sum of daily mark-to-market proceeds to the long position as $P_T - F_0$ and assumed for convenience that the entire profit to the futures contract accrues on the delivery date. The parity theorems we have derived apply strictly to forward pricing because they are predicated on the assumption that contract proceeds are realized only on delivery. Although this treatment is appropriate for a forward contract, the actual timing of cash flows influences the determination of the futures price.

Futures prices will deviate from parity values when marking to market gives a systematic advantage to either the long or short position. If marking to market tends to favor the long position, for example, the futures price should exceed the forward price, since the long position will be willing to pay a premium for the advantage of marking to market.

When will marking to market favor either the long or short trader? A trader will benefit if daily settlements are received when the interest rate is high and are paid when the interest rate is low. Receiving payments when the interest rate is high allows investment of proceeds at a high rate; traders therefore prefer a high correlation between the level of the interest rate and the payments received from marking to market. The long position will benefit if futures prices tend to rise when interest rates are high. In such circumstances the long trader will be willing to accept a higher futures price. Whenever there is a positive correlation between interest rates and changes in futures prices, the "fair" futures price will exceed the forward price. Conversely, a negative correlation means that marking to market favors the short position and implies that the equilibrium futures price should be below the forward price.

In practice, however, it appears that the covariance between futures prices and interest rates is low enough so that futures prices and forward prices differ by negligi-

FIGURE 21.4
Futures price for
delivery at the end of
the harvest, in the
special case that the
expected spot price
remains unchanged.

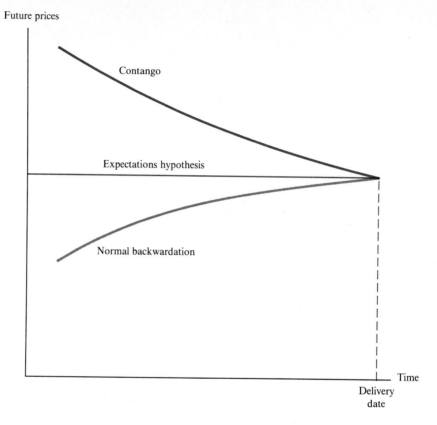

ble amounts. In estimating the theoretically appropriate difference in futures and forward prices on foreign exchange contracts, Cornell and Reinganum[4] found that the
mark-to-market premium is so small that contracts as quoted do not carry enough
decimal points to reflect the predicted difference in the two prices.

21.5 *Futures Prices vs. Expected Spot Prices*

So far we have considered the relationship between futures prices and the current
spot price. One of the oldest controversies in the theory of futures pricing concerns
the relationship between futures price and the expected value of the spot price of the
commodity at some *future* date. Three traditional theories have been put forth: the
expectations hypothesis, normal backwardation, and contango. Today's consensus is
that all of these traditional hypotheses are subsumed by the insights provided by modern portfolio theory. Figure 21.4 shows the expected path of futures prices under the
three traditional hypotheses.

[4]Cornell, Bradford, and Reinganum, Marc R., "Forward and Futures Prices: Evidence from the Foreign Exchange Markets," *Journal of Finance, 36,* December 1981.

Expectations Hypothesis

The *expectations hypothesis* is the simplest theory of futures pricing. It states that the futures price equals the expected value of the future spot price of the asset: $F_0 = E(P_T)$. Under this theory the expected profit to either position of a futures contract would equal zero: the short position's expected profit is $F_0 - E(P_T)$, while the long's is $E(P_T) - F_0$. With $F_0 = E(P_T)$, the expected profit to either side is zero. This hypothesis relies on a notion of risk neutrality. If all market participants are risk neutral, they should agree on a futures price that provides an expected profit of zero to all parties.

The expectations hypothesis bears a resemblance to market equilibrium in a world with no uncertainty; that is, if prices of goods at all future dates are currently known, then the futures price for delivery at any particular date would simply equal the currently known future spot price for that date. It is a tempting but incorrect leap to assert next that under uncertainty the futures price should equal the currently expected spot price. This view ignores the risk premiums that must be built into futures prices when ultimate spot prices are uncertain.

Normal Backwardation

This theory is associated with the famous British economists, John Maynard Keynes and John Hicks. They argued that for most commodities there are natural hedgers who desire to shed risk. For example, wheat farmers will desire to shed the risk of uncertain wheat prices. These farmers will take short positions to deliver wheat in the future at a guaranteed price; they will short hedge. In order to induce speculators to take the corresponding long positions, the farmers need to offer speculators an expectation of profit. Speculators will enter the long side of the contract only if the futures price is below the expected spot price of wheat, for an expected profit of $E(P_T) - F_0$. The speculator's expected profit is the farmer's expected loss, but farmers are willing to bear the expected loss on the contract in order to shed the risk of uncertain wheat prices. The theory of *normal backwardation* thus suggests that the futures price will be bid down to a level below the expected spot price, and will rise over the life of the contract until the maturity date, at which point $F_T = P_T$.

Although this theory recognizes the important role of risk premiums in futures markets, it is based on total variability rather than on systematic risk. (This is not surprising, as Keynes wrote almost 40 years before the development of modern portfolio theory.) The modern view refines the measure of risk used to determine appropriate risk premiums.

Contango

The polar hypothesis to backwardation holds that the natural hedgers are the purchasers of a commodity, rather than the suppliers. In the case of wheat, for example, we would view grain processors as willing to pay a premium to lock in the price that they must pay for wheat. These processors hedge by taking a long position in the futures market; they are long hedgers, as opposed to farmers who are short hedgers.

Because long hedgers will agree to pay high futures prices to shed risk, and because speculators must be paid a premium to enter into the short position, the *contango* theory holds that F_0 must exceed $E(P_T)$.

It is clear that any commodity will have both natural long hedgers and short hedgers. The compromise traditional view, called the "net hedging hypothesis," is that F_0 will be less than $E(P_T)$ when short hedgers outnumber long hedgers and vice versa. The strong side of the market will be the side (short or long) that has more natural hedgers. The strong side must pay a premium to induce speculators to enter into enough contracts to balance the "natural" supply of long and short hedgers.

Modern Portfolio Theory

The three traditional hypotheses all envision a mass of speculators willing to enter either side of the futures market if they are sufficiently compensated for the risk they incur. Modern portfolio theory fine-tunes this approach by refining the notion of risk used in the determination of risk premiums. Simply put, if commodity prices pose positive systematic risk, futures prices must be lower than expected spot prices.

As an example of the use of modern portfolio theory to determine the equilibrium futures price, consider once again a stock paying no dividends. If $E(P_T)$ denotes today's expectation of the time T price of the stock, and k denotes the required rate of return on the stock, then the price of the stock today must equal the present value of its expected future payoff as follows:

$$P_0 = \frac{E(P_T)}{(1 + k)^T} \tag{21.4}$$

We also know from the spot-futures parity relationship that

$$P_0 = \frac{F_0}{(1 + r_f)^T} \tag{21.5}$$

Therefore the right-hand sides of equations 21.4 and 21.5 must be equal. Equating these terms allows us to solve for F_0:

$$F_0 = E(P_T)\left(\frac{1 + r_f}{1 + k}\right)^T \tag{21.6}$$

You can see immediately from equation 21.6 that F_0 will be less than the expectation of P_T whenever k is greater than r_f, which will be the case for any positive-beta asset. This means that the long side of the contract will make an expected profit [F_0 will be lower than $E(P_T)$] when the commodity exhibits positive systematic risk (k is greater than r_f).

Why should this be? A long futures position will provide a profit (or loss) of $P_T - F_0$. If the ultimate realization of P_T involves positive systematic or nondiversifiable risk, the profit to the long position also involves such risk. Speculators with well-diversified portfolios will be willing to enter long futures positions only if they receive compensation for bearing that risk in the form of positive expected profits.

Their expected profits will be positive only if $E(P_T)$ is greater than F_0. The converse is that the short position's profit is the negative of the long's and will have negative systematic risk. Diversified investors in the short position will be willing to suffer an expected loss in order to lower portfolio risk and will be willing to enter the contract even when F_0 is less than $E(P_T)$. Therefore, if P_T has positive beta, F_0 must be less than the expectation of P_T. The analysis is reversed for negative-beta commodities.

Concept Check	Question 8. What must be true of the risk of the spot price of an asset if the futures price is an unbiased estimate of the ultimate spot price?

Summary

1. Forward contracts are arrangements that call for future delivery of an asset at a currently agreed-on price. The long trader is obligated to purchase the good, and the short trader is obligated to deliver it. If the price of the asset at the maturity of the contract exceeds the forward price, the long side benefits by virtue of acquiring the good at the contract price.

2. A futures contract is similar to a forward contract, differing most importantly in the aspects of standardization and marking to market, which is the process by which gains and losses on futures contract positions are settled daily. In contrast, forward contracts call for no cash transfers until contract maturity.

3. Futures contracts are traded on organized exchanges that standardize the size of the contract, the grade of the deliverable asset, the delivery date, and the delivery location. Traders negotiate only over the contract price. This standardization creates increased liquidity in the marketplace and means buyers and sellers can easily find many traders for a desired purchase or sale.

4. The clearinghouse acts as an intermediary between each pair of traders, acting as the short position for each long, and as the long position for each short. In this way traders need not be concerned about the performance of the trader on the opposite side of the contract. In turn, traders post margins to guarantee their own performance on the contracts.

5. The gain or loss to the long side for a futures contract held between time 0 and t is $F_t - F_0$. Because $F_T = P_T$, the long's profit if the contract is held until maturity is $P_T - F_0$, where P_T is the spot price at time T and F_0 is the original futures price. The gain or loss to the short position is $F_0 - P_T$.

6. Futures contracts may be used for hedging or speculating. Speculators use the contracts to take a stand on the ultimate price of an asset. Short hedgers take short positions in contracts to offset any gains or losses on the value of an asset already held in inventory. Long hedgers take long positions to offset gains or losses in the purchase price of a good.

7. The spot-futures parity relationship states that the equilibrium futures price on

an asset providing no services or payments (such as dividends) is $F_0 = P_0(1 + r_f)^T$. If the futures price deviates from this value, then market participants can earn arbitrage profits.

7. If the asset provides services or payments with yield d, the parity relationship becomes $F_0 = P_0(1 + r_f - d)^T$. This model is also called the cost-of-carry model, because it states that the futures price must exceed the spot price by the net cost of carrying the asset until maturity date T.

8. The equilibrium futures price will be less than the currently expected time T spot price if the spot price exhibits systematic risk. This provides an expected profit for the long position that bears the risk and imposes an expected loss on the short position that is willing to accept that expected loss as a means to shed risk.

Key Terms

Forward contract	Open interest	Basis
Futures contract	Marking to market	Basis risk
Long position	Maintenance margin	Spread
Short position	Variation margin	Spot-futures parity theorem
Clearinghouse	Convergence property	Cost-of-carry relationship
Reversing trade	Cash delivery	

Selected Readings

An extensive treatment of the institutional background of several futures markets is provided in:

Kolb, Robert W., *Understanding Futures Markets*, Scott, Foresman, and Co., Glenview, Ill., 1985.

Excellent, although challenging, treatments of the differences between futures and forward markets and the pricing of each type of contract are in:

Jarrow, Robert, and Oldfield, George, "Forward Contracts and Futures Contracts," *Journal of Financial Economics, 9*, December 1981.

Cox, John, Ingersoll, Jonathan, and Ross, Stephen A., "The Relation Between Forward Prices and Futures Prices," *Journal of Financial Economics, 9*, December 1981.

Black, Fischer, "The Pricing of Commodity Contracts," *Journal of Financial Economics, 3*, January-March 1976.

A survey of the issues involved in the regulation of futures markets is provided in:

Edwards, Franklin, "Futures Markets in Transition: The Uneasy Balance between Government and Self-Regulation," *Journal of Futures Markets, 3*, summer 1983.

A discussion of competition between the two regulators of these markets, the SEC and CFTC, is provided in:

Kane, Edward, "Regulatory Structure in Futures Markets: Jurisdictional Competition Between the SEC, CFTC, and Other Agencies," *Journal of Futures Markets, 4*, fall 1984.

For a treatment of the backwardation/contango debate, see:

Cootner, Paul H., "Speculation and Hedging," Food Research Institute Studies, Supplement, Stanford, Calif., 1967.

Keynes, John Maynard, *Treatise on Money*, ed. 2, London: Macmillan, 1930.

Working, Holbrook, "The Theory of Price of Storage," *American Economic Review, 39*, December 1949.

Hicks, J.R., *Value and Capital*, ed. 2, London: Oxford University Press, 1946.

The economics of hedging and spreading is discussed in:

Scholes, Myron, "The Economics of Hedging and Spreading in Futures Markets," *Journal of Futures Markets, 1,* summer 1981.

Problems

1. a. Using the figure below, compute the dollar value of the stocks traded on one contract on the Standard & Poor's 500 index. The closing spot price of the

```
S&P 500 INDEX (CME) 500 times index
Mar   252.20 254.90 251.00 254.30 + 4.40 344.90 181.00 113,445
June  252.80 256.40 252.50 255.75 + 4.40 347.90 190.00   3,255
Est vol 46,886; vol Wed 53,605; open int 116,736, +1,089.
Indx prelim High 253.66; Low 249.39; Close 253.29 +3.91
```

   S&P 500 index is given in the last line of the figure. If the margin requirement is 10% of the futures price times the multiplier of 500, how much must you deposit with your broker to trade the June contract?

   b. If the June futures price were to increase to $260, what rate of return would you earn on your net investment if you entered the long side of the contract at the price shown in the figure?

   c. If the June futures price falls by 1%, what is your rate of return?

2. Why is there no futures market in cement?

3. Why might persons purchase futures contracts rather than the underlying asset?

4. What is the difference in cash flow between short selling an asset and entering a short futures position?

5. Consider a stock that will pay a dividend of D dollars in 1 year, which is when a futures contract matures. Consider the following strategy: buy the stock, short a futures contract on the stock, and borrow S_0 dollars, where S_0 is the current price of the stock.

   a. What are the cash flows now and in 1 year?

   b. Show that the equilibrium futures price must be $F_0 = S_0(1 + r) - D$ to avoid arbitrage.

   c. Call the dividend yield $d = D/S_0$, and conclude that $F_0 = S_0(1 + r - d)$.

6. Consider this arbitrage strategy to derive the parity relationship for spreads: (1) enter a long futures position with maturity date T_1 and futures price $F(T_1)$; (2) enter a short position with maturity T_2 and futures price $F(T_2)$; (3) at T_1, when the first contract expires, buy the asset and borrow $F(T_1)$ dollars at rate r_f; pay back the loan with interest at time T_2.

   a. What are the total cash flows to this strategy at times 0, T_1, and T_2?

   b. Why must profits at time T_2 be zero if no arbitrage opportunities are present?

   c. What must the relationship between $F(T_1)$ and $F(T_2)$ be for the profits at T_2 to be equal to zero? This relationship is the parity relationship for spreads.

7. Suppose that an investor in a 30% tax bracket purchases three soybean futures contracts at a price of $5.40 a bushel and closes them out at price $5.80. What are the after-tax profits to the position?

8. a. A hypothetical futures contract on a nondividend-paying stock with current

price $150 has a maturity of 1 year. If the T-bill rate is 8%, what is the futures price?

    b. What should the futures price be if the maturity of the contract is 3 years?

    c. What if the interest rate is 12% and the maturity of the contract is 3 years?

9. You suddenly receive information that indicates to you that the stock market is about to rise substantially. The market is unaware of this information. What should you do?

10. (CFA Examination, Level III, 1982)

In each of the following cases discuss how you, as a portfolio manager, would use financial futures to protect the portfolio.

    a. You own a large position in a relatively illiquid bond that you want to sell.

    b. You have a large gain on one of your long Treasuries and want to sell it, but would like to defer the gain until the next accounting period, which begins in 4 weeks.

    c. You will receive a large contribution next month that you hope to invest in long-term corporate bonds on a yield basis as favorable as is now available.

11. Suppose the value of the S&P 500 stock index is currently 250. If the 1-year T-bill rate is 8% and the expected dividend yield on the S&P 500 is 5%, what should the 1-year maturity futures price be?

12. It is now January. The interest rate is currently 8% annually. The June futures price for gold is $346.30, while the December futures price is $360. Is there an arbitrage opportunity here? If so, how would you exploit it?

13. The Chicago Board of Trade has just introduced a new futures contract on Brandex stock, a company that currently pays no dividends. Each contract calls for delivery of 1,000 shares of stock in 1 year. The T-bill rate is 6% per year.

    a. If Brandex stock now sells at $120 per share, what should be the futures price?

    b. If Brandex stock immediately decreases by 3%, what will be the change in the futures price and the change in the investor's margin account?

    c. If the margin on the contract is $12,000, what is the percentage return on the investor's position?

14. (Based on CFA Examination, Level III, 1986)

Your client, for whom you are underwriting a $400 million bond issue, is concerned that market conditions will change before the issue is brought to market. He has heard that it may be possible to reduce the risk exposure by hedging in the Government National Mortgage Association (GNMA) futures market. Specifically, he asks you to:

    a. Briefly explain how the hedge works.

    b. Describe *four* practical problems that would limit the effectiveness of the hedge.

15. (CFA Examination, Level III, 1986)

Futures contracts and options on a futures contract can be used to modify risk. Identify the fundamental distinction between a futures contract and an option on a futures contract, and briefly explain the difference in the manner that futures and options modify *portfolio* risk.

CHAPTER 22

Futures Markets: A Closer Look

The previous chapter provided a basic introduction to the operation of futures markets and the principles of futures pricing. This chapter explores selected futures markets in more depth. Figure 22.1 shows the growth that has characterized these markets in the last few years. Most of the growth has been in financial futures, which now dominate trading, so we emphasize these new contracts.

We begin by discussing stock index futures, where we examine the use of program trading. That is followed by a treatment of foreign exchange futures. Next, we move on to the most actively traded markets, those for interest rate futures. Finally, after a look at the oldest markets, those for commodity futures, we discuss some recent developments such as the introduction of inflation futures.

22.1 *Stock Index Futures*

The Contracts

We discussed at length in Chapter 21 a hypothetical futures contract on a share of stock. In practice, stock futures do not trade on individual shares; they trade instead on stock market indices such as the Standard & Poor's 500. In contrast to most futures contracts, which call for delivery of a specified commodity, these contracts are settled by a cash amount equal to the value of the stock index in question on the contract maturity date times a multiplier that scales the size of the contract. The total profit to the long position is $S_T - F_0$, where S_T is the value of the stock index on the maturity date. Cash settlement avoids the costs that would be incurred if the short trader had to purchase the stocks in the index and deliver them to the long position, and if the long position then had to sell the stocks for cash. Instead, the long trader's profit is $S_T - F_0$ dollars, and the short trader's is $F_0 - S_T$ dollars. These profits duplicate those that would arise with actual delivery.

There are several stock index futures contracts currently traded. Table 22.1 lists the major ones, showing under contract size the multiplier used to calculate contract

FIGURE 22.1

Futures and
futures-options trading
volume.

(From The Chicago Board of
Trade *Annual Report*, 1987.)

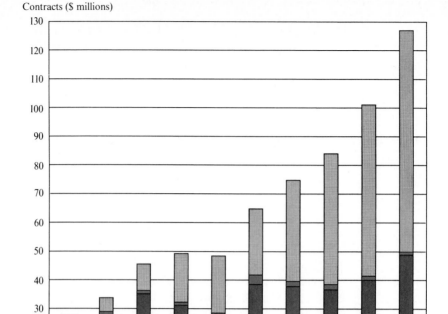

Contracts ($ millions)

Options on futures

Financial instruments

Metals and others

Agricultural futures

settlements. An S&P 500 contract, for example, with a futures price of 250 and a final index value of 255 would result in a profit for the long side of $500 \times (255 - 250) = \$2,500$.

The broad-based stock market indices are all highly correlated. Table 22.2 presents a correlation matrix for four indices calculated over the 20-year period ending in 1981. The only index whose correlation with the others is below .90 is the Value Line index. This index uses an equally weighted average of 1,700 firms, as opposed to the NYSE or S&P indices, which use market value weights. This means that the Value Line contract overweights small firms compared to the other indices, which may explain the lower observed correlation.

TABLE 22.1   Stock Index Futures

Contract	Underlying Market Index	Contract Size	Exchange
S&P 500	Standard & Poor's 500 Index, a value-weighted arithmetic average of 500 stocks	$500 times the S&P 500 index	Chicago Mercantile Exchange
Value Line	Value Line Composite Average; an equally weighted average of about 1,700 firms	$500 times the Value Line index	Kansas City Board of Trade
NYSE	NYSE Composite index; value-weighted arithmetic average of all stocks listed on the NYSE	$500 times the NYSE index	New York Futures Exchange
Major Market	Price-weighted arithmetic average of 20 blue-chip stocks; index is designed to track the Dow Jones Industrial Average	$250 times the Major Market index	Chicago Board of Trade
S&P OTC	Price-weighted arithmetic average of 250 of the largest over-the-counter stocks	$500 times the S&P OTC index	Chicago Mercantile Exchange
Institutional Index	Value-weighted arithmetic average of the 75 most widely held stocks traded by institutional investors	$500 times the Institutional Index	Chicago Board of Trade

TABLE 22.2   Correlation of Stock Market Indices

	Dow Jones	Value Line	S&P 500	NYSE
Dow Jones	1.00	.86	.94	.94
Value Line	.86	1.00	.86	.90
S&P 500	.94	.86	1.00	.98
NYSE	.94	.90	.98	1.00

Modified from Modest, David, and Sundaresan, Mahadevan, "The Relationship Between Spot and Futures Prices in Stock Index Futures Markets: Some Preliminary Evidence," *Journal of Futures Markets, 3,* spring 1983. © John Wiley & Sons, Inc., 1983.

Creating Synthetic Stock Positions

One reason stock index futures are so popular is that they substitute for holdings in the underlying stocks themselves. Index futures let investors participate in broad market movements without actually buying or selling large numbers of stocks.

Because of this, we say futures represent "synthetic" holdings of the market portfolio. Instead of holding the market directly, the investor takes a long futures position in the index. Such a strategy is attractive because the transaction costs involved in establishing and liquidating futures positions are much lower than taking actual spot positions. Investors who wish to frequently buy and sell market positions find it much less costly and easier to play the futures market rather than the underlying spot market. "Market timers," who speculate on broad market moves rather than on individual securities, are large players in stock index futures for this reason.

One means to market time, for example, is to shift between Treasury bills and broad-based stock market holdings. Timers attempt to shift from bills into the market before market upturns, and to shift back into bills to avoid market downturns, thereby profiting from broad market movements. Market timing of this sort, however, can result in huge brokerage fees with the frequent purchase and sale of many stocks. An attractive alternative is to invest in Treasury bills and hold varying amounts of market index futures contracts.

The strategy works like this: When timers are bullish, they will establish many long futures positions that they can liquidate quickly and cheaply when expectations turn bearish. Rather than shifting back and forth between T-bills and stocks, they buy and hold T-bills, and adjust only the futures position. This minimizes transaction costs. An advantage of this technique for timing is that investors can implicitly buy or sell the market index in its entirety, whereas market timing in the spot market would require the simultaneous purchase or sale of all the stocks in the index. This is technically difficult to coordinate and can lead to slippage in execution of a timing strategy.

You can construct a T-bill plus index futures position that duplicates the payoff to holding the stock index itself. Here is how:

1. Hold as many market index futures contracts long as you need to purchase your desired stock position. A desired holding of $1,000 multiplied by the S&P 500 index, for example, would require the purchase of two contracts because each contract calls for delivery of $500 multiplied by the index.

2. Invest enough money in T-bills to cover the payment of the futures price at the contract's maturity date. The necessary investment will equal the present value of the futures price that will be paid to satisfy the contracts. The T-bill holdings will grow by the maturity date to a level equal to the futures price.

For example, suppose that an institutional investor wants to invest $25 million in the market for 1 month and, to minimize trading costs, chooses to buy the S&P 500 futures contract as a substitute for actual stock holdings. If the index is now at 250, the 1-month delivery futures price is 252.50, and the T-bill rate is 1% per month, it would buy 200 contracts. (Each contract controls $500 × 250 = $125,000 worth of stock, and $25 million/$125,000 = 200.) The institution thus has a long position on 100,000 times the S&P 500 index (200 contracts times the contract multiplier of 500). To cover payment of the futures price, it must invest 100,000 times the present value of the futures price in T-bills. This equals 100,000 × (252.50/1.01) = $25 million market value of bills. Notice that the $25 million outlay in bills is precisely equal to the amount that would have been needed to buy the stock directly. The bills will increase in value in 1 month to $25.25 million.

This is an artificial, or synthetic, stock position. What is the value of this portfolio at the maturity date? Call S_T the value of the stock index on the maturity date T, and as usual, let F_0 be the original futures price:

	In General (Per Unit of the Index)	Our Numbers
1. Profits from contract	$S_T - F_0$	$100,000(S_T - 252.50)$
2. Value of T-bills	F_0	$252,500,000$
TOTAL	S_T	$100,000S_T$

The total payoff on the contract maturity date is exactly proportional to the value of the stock index. In other words, adopting this portfolio strategy is equivalent to holding the stock index itself, aside from the issue of interim dividend distributions and tax treatment.

Concept Check

Question 1. This result implies something about the relative cost of pursuing this strategy compared to that of purchasing the index directly. As the payoffs are identical, so should be the costs. What does this say about the spot-futures parity relationship?

The bills-plus-futures strategy may be viewed as a 100% stock strategy. At the other extreme investing in zero futures results in a 100% bills position. Moreover, a short futures position will result in a portfolio equivalent to that obtained by short selling the stock market index, because in both cases the investor gains from decreases in the stock price. Bills-plus-futures mixtures clearly allow for a flexible and low transaction–cost approach to market timing. The futures positions may be established or reversed quickly and cheaply. Also, since the short futures position allows the investor to earn interest on T-bills, it is superior to a conventional short sale of the stock, where the investor typically earns no interest on the proceeds of the short sale.

Empirical Evidence on Pricing of Stock Index Futures

Recall the spot-futures parity relationship between the futures and spot stock price:

$$F_0 = S_0(1 + r_f - d)^T \tag{22.1}$$

Several investigators have tested this relationship empirically. The general procedure has been to calculate the theoretically appropriate futures price using the current value of the stock index and equation 22.1. The dividend yield of the index in question is approximated using historical data. Although dividends of individual securities may fluctuate unpredictably, the annualized dividend yield of a broad-based index such as the S&P 500 is fairly stable, usually in the neighborhood of 3% to 4% per

FIGURE   22.2

Dividend distribution,
Dow Jones 30
Industrials.

(From Kipnis, Gregory M.,
and Tsang, Steve, "Classical
Theory, Dividend Dynamics
and Stock Index Futures
Pricing," in Fabozzi, Frank
J., and Kipnis, Gregory M.
[editors], *Stock Index
Futures,* Homewood, Ill.:
Dow Jones-Irwin, 1982.)

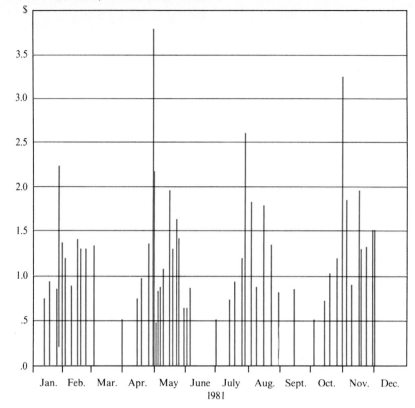

Dividend distribution, Dow Jones 30 Industrials

year. The yield is seasonal with regular and predictable peaks and troughs however, so the dividend yield for the relevant months must be the one used. Figure 22.2 illustrates the dividend distributions of the Dow Jones Industrial stocks during 1981.

If the actual futures price deviates from the value dictated by the parity relationship, then (forgetting transaction costs), an arbitrage opportunity arises. Given an estimate of transaction costs, we can bracket the theoretically correct futures price within a band. If the actual futures price lies within that band, the discrepancy between the actual and the proper futures price is too small to exploit because of the transaction costs; if the actual price lies outside the no-arbitrage band, profit opportunities are worth exploiting.

Modest and Sundaresan[1] constructed such a test using the June and December 1982 S&P 500 contracts. Figure 22.3 replicates an example of their results. The figure shows that the futures prices generally did lie in the theoretically determined no-

[1]Modest, David, and Sundaresan, Mahadevan, "The Relationship Between Spot and Futures Prices in Stock Index Futures Markets: Some Preliminary Evidence," *Journal of Futures Markets, 3,* spring 1983.

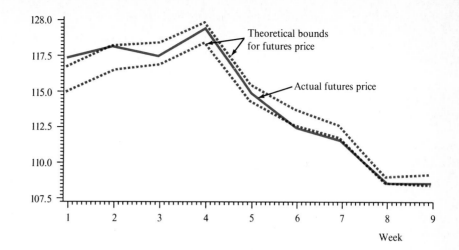

FIGURE 22.3
Prices of S&P 500 contract maturing June 1982. Data plotted for April 21-June 16, 1982.

(From Modest, David, and Sundaresan, Mahadevan, "The Relationship Between Spot and Futures Prices in Stock Index Futures Markets: Some Preliminary Evidence," *Journal of Futures Markets, 3,* spring 1983.) © John Wiley & Sons, Inc., 1983.

arbitrage band, but that profit opportunities occasionally were possible for low-cost transactors.

Such opportunities presented themselves more often in the early years of trading in the contract. Recently, sustained deviations from parity have been far less frequent. This has led some observers[2] to suggest that early deviations from parity are symptomatic of a learning process for market participants; as learning progresses, deviations become rarer. Indeed, the rapid growth of index arbitrage, which attempts to exploit temporary deviations from the parity relationship, is evidence of a dramatic increase in the sophistication of market participants.

Modest and Sundaresan point out that much of the cost of short selling shares is attributable to the investor's inability to invest the entire proceeds from the short sale. Proceeds must be left on margin account, where they do not earn interest. Arbitrage opportunities, or the width of the no-arbitrage band, therefore depend on assumptions regarding the use of short sale proceeds. Figure 22.3 assumes that one half of the proceeds are available to the short seller.

Concept Check

Question 2. What (if anything) would happen to the top of the no-arbitrage band if short sellers could obtain full use of the proceeds from the short sale? What would happen to the low end of the band? Hint: when do violations of parity call for a long futures–short stock position, vs. short futures–long stock?

[2]Figlewski, Stephen, "Explaining the Early Discounts on Stock Index Futures: The Case for Disequilbrium," *Financial Analysts Journal,* July/August 1984.

Whenever the actual futures price falls outside the no-arbitrage band, there is an opportunity for profit. This is why the parity relationships are so important. Far from being theoretical academic constructs, they are in fact a guide to trading rules that can generate large profits. One of the most notable developments in trading activity has been the advent of **index arbitrage,** an investment strategy that exploits divergences between the actual futures price and its theoretically correct parity value.

In theory, index arbitrage is simple. If the futures price is too high, short the futures contract and buy the stocks in the index. If it is too low, go long in futures and short the stocks. You can perfectly hedge your position and should earn arbitrage profits equal to the mispricing of the contract.

In practice, however, index arbitrage can be difficult to implement. The problem lies in buying "the stocks in the index." Selling or purchasing shares in all 500 stocks in the S&P 500 is impractical for two reasons. The first is transaction costs, which may outweigh any profits to be made from the arbitrage. Second, it is extremely difficult to buy or sell stock of 500 different firms simultaneously, and any lags in the execution of such a strategy can destroy the effectiveness of a plan to exploit temporary price discrepancies.

In the real world most arbitrageurs devise portfolios with a small number of stocks that closely mimic the broader market index. These subportfolios are called "baskets," and the traders who develop them are called "basket weavers." Their trades on the spot market are made in this proxy portfolio only, which reduces the execution problems in getting trades off quickly. The substitution, however, creates tracking or basis risk because the futures price on a broad stock index will not correlate as closely with the value of the proxy portfolio as it will with the index itself.

Arbitrageurs need to trade an entire portfolio of stocks quickly and simultaneously if they hope to exploit disparities between the futures price and its corresponding stock index. For this they need a coordinated trading program; hence the term **program trading,** which refers to coordinated purchases or sales of entire portfolios of stocks. The response has been the designated order turnaround (DOT) system, which enables traders to send coordinated buy or sell programs to the floor of the stock exchange via computer.

Index arbitrage seems to have had its own effect on market movements. Four times a year, for example, the S&P 500 futures contract expires at the same time as the S&P 100 index option contract and option contracts on individual stocks. The great volatility of the market at these periods has led people to call the simultaneous expirations the **triple witching hour.**

Expiration-day volatility can be explained by program trading to exploit arbitrage opportunities. Suppose that before a stock index future contract matures, the futures price is a little above its parity value. Arbitrageurs will attempt to lock in superior profits by buying the stocks in the index (the program trading buy order) and taking an offsetting short futures position. If and when the pricing disparity reverses, the position can be unwound at a profit. Alternatively, arbitrageurs can wait until contract maturity day and realize a profit by closing out the offsetting stock and futures positions with "market-on-close" orders, that is, closing out both positions at prices

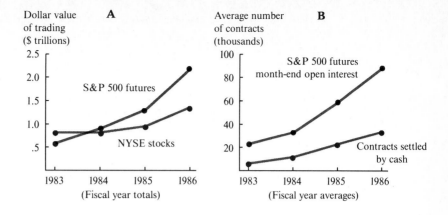

FIGURE 22.4
A, Futures contracts.
B, Arbitrage activity.
(From Merrick, John J.,
"Fact and Fantasy About
Stock-Index Futures Program
Trading," *Business Review,*
Federal Reserve Bank of
Philadelphia,
September/October 1987.)

in the closing range of the day. By waiting until the close of the maturity day, arbitrageurs can be assured that the futures price and stock index price will be aligned—they rely on the convergence property. The nearby box from *The Wall Street Journal* examines both of these versions of index arbitrage.

Obviously, when many program traders follow such a strategy at market close, a wave of program selling passes over the market. The result? Prices go down. This is the expiration-day effect. If execution of the arbitrage strategy calls for a sale (or short sale) of stocks, unwinding on expiration day requires repurchase of the stocks, with the opposite effect: prices will increase.

The success of these arbitrage positions and associated program trades depends on only two things: the relative levels of spot and futures prices and synchronized trading in the two markets. Because arbitrageurs exploit disparities in futures and spot prices, absolute price levels are unimportant. This means that large buy or sell programs can hit the floor even if stock prices are at "fair" levels, that is, at levels consistent with fundamental information. The markets in individual stocks may not be sufficiently deep to absorb the arbitrage-based program trades without significant price movements despite the fact that those trades are not informationally motivated.

Futures trading and index arbitrage have increased dramatically since 1983. Figure 22.4, *A,* shows that the dollar value of stock controlled through futures contracts now exceeds stock value traded on the NYSE. What may be of greater import, contracts held until maturity (settled by cash) also have increased rapidly. Contracts held until maturity are a good proxy for the amount of index arbitrage, because arbitrageurs may hold contracts to maturity to lock in riskless profits from coordinated stock and/ or futures trades. As we know, only at maturity is convergence between futures and stock prices assured.

In an investigation of expiration day effects Stoll and Whaley[3] found that the mar-

---

[3]Stoll, Hans R., and Whaley, Robert E., "Program Trading and Expiration Day Effects," *Financial Analysts Journal* March-April 1987.

ket is in fact more volatile at contract expirations. Table 22.3, for example, shows that the standard deviation of the last-hour return on the S&P 500 index is .641 on expirations of the S&P 500 futures contract, whereas it is only .211 on nonexpiration days. Interestingly, the last-hour volatility of non-S&P 500 stocks appears unaffected by expiration days, consistent with the hypothesis that the effect is related to program trading of the stocks in the index.

If these price swings are based only on temporary market pressure coming from simultaneous program trades, we should expect price declines or advances to reverse after the trades are executed, when profit seekers attempt to buy or sell stocks that are subsequently mispriced according to fundamental information. In fact, Stoll and Whaley found there is a tendency for large price swings to be reversed on the day following the expiration activity.

Although index arbitrage continues to persist, and arguably does affect stock prices occasionally, expiration-day effects seem to have been successfully overcome by a change in the contract settlement procedure. As of June 1987 expiring S&P 500 futures contracts now cease trading on Thursday afternoon rather than Friday. The contract is marked to market for the last time on Friday using the S&P 500 index at market *opening*. Because the final futures price is based on market opening prices, arbitrageurs must use market-on-open orders (instead of market-on-close orders) to assure convergence and lock in a profit from earlier futures mispricing.

The advantage of this procedure is that supply-demand imbalances can be more easily rectified when they occur before market opening. Arbitrageurs must submit

How Index Arbitrage Is Triggered

ROBERT Gordon, president of Twenty-First Securities Corp., New York, uses charts like the one on the right to guide index arbitrage. The chart line, for Feb. 4 and 5, shows the price difference between the March S&P futures (which expire March 18) and the S&P 500 stock index. Mr. Gordon calculates that with 43 days until expiration, the futures index should have a "fair value" of 0.6 points above the stock index. That's the market's way of acknowledging that futures owners are also earning interest on collateral, which stock market investors aren't.

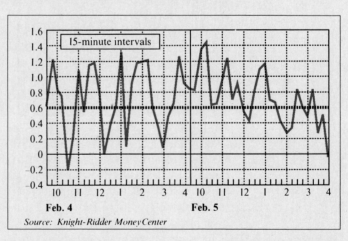

Source: *Knight-Ridder MoneyCenter*

When futures prices fall to parity or to a discount versus stock prices, shown on the chart when the line moves to 0 or below, index arbitragers pounce. They sell the stocks and buy "cheap" futures.

Continued.

THE PROGRAM (Feb. 4)

SELL: 537,877 shares of stock, including 16,191 Exxon shares, 6,854 IBM shares, etc. The proceeds are invested in Treasury bills, paying 5.61% interest. The S&P 500 stock index stands at 252.21; the sale amounts to $20,050,000.

BUY: 159 March futures contracts on the S&P 500 index, which are trading at 252.20. Each contract has 500 times the value of the index, so the purchase amounts to $20,050,000. The T-bills from the stock sale are used as collateral.

ANALYSIS

This type of index arbitrage is done most frequently by index funds, which need to hold at least $20 million of stocks in the same weight as the S&P 500. The goal of this type of fund is to make small profits by shuffling money between stocks and futures, buying whichever is more attractive.

Futures prices can decline for a number of reasons, including when negative sentiment is more prevalent in futures markets than in stock markets.

CASHING OUT

Once index arbitragers have made a trade, they look for a favorable chance to "unwind" it. In this case, the index fund wants to sell futures and buy back stocks. It can do so when the futures expire March 18, or if a good opportunity arises earlier. Each option is shown, as follows:

OPTION 1 (Feb. 5)

SELL: 159 March S&P futures at 251.55. Receive $19,998,225 in proceeds.

BUY: 537,877 shares of stocks in S&P 500 index. Index is at 250.96. Cost: $19,950,628.

ANALYSIS: Futures prices have returned to their "fair value" premium over stocks, justifying the trade. The index arbitrager switches out of futures, back into stocks.

Gain on stock position	$99,372
Loss on futures position	51,775
Interest income/ forgone dividends	negligible
Profit (before commissions)	$47,597
Return above S&P (annualized)	87%

OPTION 2 (March 18)

Let all 159 March S&P futures expire, get margin back.

BUY: An equivalent amount of stocks, simultaneous to futures expiration.

ANALYSIS: In addition to whatever gain or loss the index fund had on the stock market's basic move, it has profited by earning T-bill interest for the 43 days in which it owned futures. That's only partly reduced by forgoing dividend income on stocks.

T-bill interest income	$132,180
Forgone dividend income	84,586
Profit (before commissions)	$ 47,594
Return above S&P (annualized)	2.02%

TABLE 22.3 Mean and Standard Deviation of the Percentage Rates of Return in the Last Hour of Expiration Day by Index Type and Expiration Type (July 1, 1983, through December 27, 1985)*

Index Type	Expiration Type		
	Futures and Options Expiration	Options-Only Expiration	Nonexpiration
S&P 500 Index			
Mean	−0.352†	0.026	0.061
Standard deviation	0.641†	0.261	0.211
Number of observations	10	16	97
S&P 100 Index			
Mean	−0.452†	−0.007	0.033
Standard deviation	0.699†	0.401†	0.252
Number of observations	10	16	97
Non-S&P 500 Stocks‡			
Mean	0.064	0.079	0.077
Standard deviation	0.230	0.211	0.264
Number of observations	10	16	97
Non-S&P 100 Stocks‡			
Mean	−0.168	0.059	0.079
Standard deviation	0.423†	0.202	0.160
Number of observations	10	16	97

Modified from Stoll, Hans R., and Whaley, Robert E., "Program Trading and Expiration Day Effects," *Financial Analysts Journal,* March-April 1987.

*The database contains hourly price observations from closing the day before expiration to 10:30 AM on the first day after expiration.

†The null hypothesis of equal means (*t*-test) or equal standard deviation (*F*-test) is rejected at the 5% probability level.

‡The rate of return for the value-weighted index of non-S&P 500 stocks, R_x, is computed from the following equation:

$$R_{NYSE} = kR_i + (1 - k)R_x$$

where R_{NYSE} is the rate of return on the NYSE composite index, R_i is the rate of return on the S&P 500 or S&P 100 index, and k is the fraction of the NYSE index in the S&P 500 or S&P 100. For the S&P 500, k is .79; for the S&P 100, k is .34.

their market-on-open unwinding orders before 9 AM on expiration day, while the market is closed. If buy-sell imbalances emerge, other participants will be made aware of them. If traders are convinced an imbalance is attributable only to unwinding and is not informationally based, they will be willing to take the opposite side of the trade for only slight price concessions.

During the crash of October 1987 there was a considerable amount of program trading and index arbitrage. (Program trading refers generally to coordinated sales or purchases of entire portfolios, whereas index arbitrage refers specifically to exploitation of violations of spot-futures parity.) Although it is not at all clear that index arbitrage exacerbated the market crash, several firms have since announced that they will forgo such activities—at least for their own accounts—as the nearby box illustrates.

5 Wall St. Firms Move to Restrict Program Trades

In a move intended to restore investor confidence in the stock market, five large Wall Street firms announced yesterday that they had suspended program trading for their own accounts.

The action came in the wake of intense pressure from customers and other member firms who blamed the controversial practice for many of the recent sharp swings in prices since the stock market collapse last October.

Four of the firms will continue to execute such trades for their customers, however. These "program trades" are based on complicated maneuvers to take advantage of the price differences between stocks and stock index futures contracts.

"It's a Small Community"

"The clients and everybody else felt so strongly about it," said Alan C. Greenberg, chairman of Bear, Stearns & Company. Even though he disagreed that the strategy added to market volatility, his firm stopped executing such trades for itself and its customers last Thursday. "We have to live and it's a small community."

In addition to Bear, Stearns, the other firms that suspended their proprietary program trading were Morgan Stanley & Company, Salomon Brothers, Paine Webber Inc. and Kidder, Peabody & Company.

Legislators in Washington as well as professionals in the investment community welcomed the news. "Today's announcement may be some of the best news the markets have had since the October crash," said Representative Edward J. Markey, a Massachusetts Democrat who is the chairman of a House subcommittee that has been conducting hearings on the impact of such trading.

Individual and institutional customers had complained to their Wall Street brokers that program trading was driving them out of the market. "We had heard from a number of clients that it was a destabilizing force," said Donald Marron, chairman of Paine Webber, in an interview. "It is certainly destabilizing in that it is harmful to public confidence."

Morgan Stanley officials apparently set off yesterday's announcements by making a series of phone calls in recent days alerting executives at other firms to its plans.

Even so, executives of the firms maintained that they did not coordinate their decisions to suspend their program trading. "If there was a meeting, I wasn't there," said Paine Webber's Mr. Marron. He and executives of several of the other firms, however, said members of their staffs had telephone conversations over recent weeks discussing with each other the controversy surrounding program trading.

Cooling-Off Period Sought

One executive said that his firm had suspended the practice in hopes of warding off excessive regulation by Washington. In fact, many of the announcements stressed that the firms were acting to provide a cooling-off period so that Wall Street, regulatory authorities and Congress could undertake, as Kidder put it, "a rational review of this activity." Kidder and the other firms dispute the contention that stock index arbitrage increases price volatility.

One official said privately that his firm would resume the practice if legislators sanctioned the strategy.

"The current emotional and often self-serving arguments advanced by various market participants regarding program trading have not produced a constructive dialogue on the structural reforms necessary for these markets," said Max Chapman, chairman of Kidder.

Since the market crash, stock index arbitrage has been blamed as one of the chief contributors to the sharp and sudden intra-day stock price swings. The tactic involves the simultaneous purchase of stock index futures contracts and the sale of the underlying stocks in an index such as the Standard & Poor's 500, or vice versa. In the classic arbitrage, traders are able to capture the "spread," or difference in prices, between the securities in two different markets.

Continued.

Link Seen as Necessary

It is generally agreed by investors, academics and the Presidential commission that investigated the October market crash that this form of arbitrage provides a useful and necessary link between the stock market in New York and the futures markets in Chicago.

But since the crash, however, there have been charges that some on Wall Street have been trading their capital more aggressively by betting on the direction of the stock and futures markets and creating a lopsided arbitrage. The combination of such tactics with a nervous, thinly traded market has made stock prices more volatile, many investors argue.

While index arbitrage trades represent only 10 percent to 12 percent of the daily volume on the New York Stock Exchange, the trades typically are crowded together at short intervals. At times they can account for as much as 35 percent of the volume in a 30-minute period and thus cause even more pressure on prices, said Richard Torrenzano, an executive vice president of the exchange.

Executed for Own Accounts

And on some days, the majority of those trades have been executed by the firms for their own capital accounts. On Jan. 8, for instance, when the Dow Jones industrial average fell more than 140 points, almost 70 percent of the 26.1 million program trade transactions were executed for member firms' own accounts, according to documents prepared for Congress. Only eight million program trades were executed for customers.

Wall Street professionals welcomed yesterday's news. "I think this represents a very positive move toward restoring the confidence in the infrastructure of our capital markets," said Frederic J. Graber, senior partner of Frederic J. Graber & Company, a New York Stock Exchange member and trading firm. "Although obviously much more is yet to be done, this is certainly a step in the right direction."

Jeffrey S. Tabak, partner of Miller Tabak Hirsch & Company, a brokerage firm specializing in stock index futures and options, said, "It should bring back the individual investor."

Volume Extremely Light

Indeed, a number of Wall Street executives said they felt they had to take such action in order to restore confidence to the badly shaken stock market. Trading volume has been extraordinarily light in recent weeks with many individuals and institutional investors sitting on the sidelines.

For months, some institutional money managers have been putting pressure on the Wall Street firms that use the strategy. In fact, Robert G. Kirby, the chairman of the Capital Guardian Trust Company in Los Angeles, and a member of the Presidential commission, had suggested that large investors boycott firms that engage in the strategy for their own accounts.

Additionally, some large corporations had told Wall Street investment bankers that they would take their investment banking business to firms that did not use the strategy, according to an executive of one of the firms suspending the practice yesterday. Earlier this year, Shearson Lehman Brothers Inc., Merrill Lynch & Company and Goldman, Sachs & Company stopped using the strategy.

Denial on Profits

In their announcements, Salomon Brothers and Morgan Stanley both denied recent reports that their profits from program trading were a substantial part of their overall equity trading profits. Morgan Stanley, which has a secondary stock offering scheduled for next week, said that stock index arbitrage resulted in only one-half of 1 percent of its first-quarter revenues. And Salomon said proprietary stock index arbitrage trading on capital of $75 million created gross revenues of only $2.5 million in the first quarter.

Executives at Salomon blamed other factors for the market's volatility. The reduced commissions that institutions pay their brokers have caused some Wall Street firms to risk less capital on their "block trading" for large customers. That in turn has meant that there are fewer buyers and sellers of large blocks of stocks and thus price moves are sharper with less liquidity.

22.2 Foreign Exchange Futures

The Markets

Exchange rates between currencies vary continually and often quite substantially. This variability can be a source of concern for anyone involved in international business. A U.S. exporter who sells goods in England, for example, will be paid in British pounds, and the dollar value of those pounds depends on the exchange rate at the time payment is made. Until that date, the U.S. exporter is exposed to foreign exchange rate risk. This risk, however, is easily hedged through currency futures or forward markets.

The forward market in foreign exchange is fairly informal. It is simply a network of banks and brokers that allows customers to enter forward contracts to purchase or sell currency in the future at a currently agreed-on rate of exchange. Unlike those in futures markets, these contracts are not standardized in a formal market setting. Instead, each is negotiated separately. Moreover, there is no marking to market as would occur in futures markets. The contracts call only for execution at the maturity date.

FIGURE 22.5

Foreign exchange listing.

(From *The Wall Street Journal,* March 16, 1988.) Reprinted by permission of *The Wall Street Journal.* © Dow Jones & Company, Inc. 1988. All rights reserved.

FOREIGN EXCHANGE

Tuesday, March 15, 1988

The New York foreign exchange selling rates below apply to trading among banks in amounts of $1 million and more, as quoted at 3 p.m. Eastern time by Bankers Trust Co. Retail transactions provide fewer units of foreign currency per dollar.

Country	U.S. $ equiv. Tues.	U.S. $ equiv. Mon.	Currency per U.S. $ Tues.	Currency per U.S. $ Mon.
Argentina (Austral) ...	.2107	.2176	4.745	4.595
Australia (Dollar)	.7320	.7300	1.3661	1.3699
Austria (Schilling)	.08547	.08547	11.70	11.70
Belgium (Franc)				
Commercial rate	.02875	.02874	34.78	34.80
Financial rate	.02868	.02868	34.86	34.87
Brazil (Cruzado)	.009363	.009424	106.80	106.11
Britain (Pound)	1.8485	1.8550	.5410	.5391
30-Day Forward	1.8458	1.8521	.5418	.5399
90-Day Forward	1.8399	1.8462	.5435	.5417
180-Day Forward	1.8397	1.8374	.5436	.5442
Canada (Dollar)	.7976	.7956	1.2537	1.2569
30-Day Forward	.7964	.7945	1.2556	1.2587
90-Day Forward	.7943	.7924	1.2590	1.2620
180-Day Forward	.7910	.7892	1.2642	1.2671
Chile (Official rate) ...	.004087	.004090	244.66	244.51
China (Yuan)	.2685	.2687	3.7250	3.7220
Colombia (Peso)	.003632	.003655	275.35	273.60
Denmark (Krone)	.1567	.1573	6.3800	6.3570
Ecuador (Sucre)				
Official rate	.004008	.004090	249.50	244.50
Floating rate	.002522	.002594	396.50	385.50
Finland (Markka)	.2484	.2487	4.0250	4.0205
France (Franc)	.1765	.1771	5.6660	5.6470
30-Day Forward	.1763	.1769	5.6710	5.6520
90-Day Forward	.1759	.1765	5.6860	5.6680
180-Day Forward	.1753	.1759	5.7050	5.6865
Greece (Drachma)	.007502	.007499	133.30	133.35
Hong Kong (Dollar) ...	.1282	.1282	7.7995	7.7980
India (Rupee)	.07722	.07746	12.95	12.91
Indonesia (Rupiah)	.0006024	.0006024	1660.00	1660.00
Ireland (Punt)	1.6080	1.6080	.6219	.6219
Israel (Shekel)	.6359	.6329	1.5725	1.5800
Italy (Lira)	.0008097	.0008130	1235.00	1230.00
Japan (Yen)	.007859	.007888	127.25	126.78
30-Day Forward	.007875	.007905	126.99	126.50
90-Day Forward	.007910	.007940	126.43	125.95
180-Day Forward	.007966	.007996	125.53	125.06
Jordan (Dinar)	2.9027	2.9027	.3445	.3445
Kuwait (Dinar)	3.6376	3.5971	.2749	.278
Lebanon (Pound)	.002710	.002703	369.00	370.00
Malaysia (Ringgit)	.3905	.3923	2.5610	2.5490
Malta (Lira)	3.1104	3.0544	.3215	.3274
Mexico (Peso)				
Floating rate	.0004405	.0004405	2270.00	2270.00
Netherland(Guilder) .	.5338	.5353	1.8735	1.8680
New Zealand (Dollar)	.6705	.6705	1.4914	1.4914
Norway (Krone)	.1582	.1583	6.3225	6.3165
Pakistan (Rupee)	.05685	.05685	17.59	17.59
Peru (Inti)	.03030	.03030	33.00	33.00
Philippines (Peso)	.04746	.04759	21.07	21.01
Portugal (Escudo)	.007348	.007331	136.10	136.40
Saudi Arabia (Riyal) ..	.2666	.2666	3.7505	3.7505
Singapore (Dollar) ...	.4971	.4973	2.0115	2.0110
South Africa (Rand)				
Commercial rate	.4695	.4724	2.1299	2.1169
Financial rate	.3676	.3690	2.7200	2.7100
South Korea (Won) ...	.001321	.001314	757.20	760.90
Spain (Peseta)	.008961	.008953	111.60	111.70
Sweden (Krona)	.1689	.1690	5.9220	5.9160
Switzerland (Franc) ..	.7254	.7294	1.3785	1.3710
30-Day Forward	.7287	.7328	1.3723	1.3646
90-Day Forward	.7344	.7385	1.3616	1.3541
180-Day Forward	.7429	.7469	1.3460	1.3388
Taiwan (Dollar)	.03498	.03498	28.59	28.59
Thailand (Baht)	.03967	.03959	25.21	25.26
Turkey (Lira)	.0008349	.0008449	1190.50	1183.60
United Arab(Dirham) .	.2722	.2722	3.673	3.673
Uruguay (New Peso)				
Financial	.003257	.003289	307.00	304.00
Venezuela (Bolivar)				
Official rate	.1333	.1333	7.50	7.50
Floating rate	.03350	.03401	29.85	29.40
W. Germany (Mark) ..	.5997	.6014	1.6675	1.6628
30-Day Forward	.6015	.6033	1.6624	1.6575
90-Day Forward	.6051	.6067	1.6525	1.6482
180-Day Forward	.6104	.6120	1.6384	1.6340
SDR	1.37719	1.37986	0.726115	0.724713
ECU	1.24393	1.24943	....	....

Special Drawing Rights are based on exchange rates for the U.S., West German, British, French and Japanese currencies. Source: International Monetary Fund.

ECU is based on a basket of community currencies. Source: European Community Commission.

FIGURE 22.6

Foreign exchange futures listing.

(From *The Wall Street Journal*, March 16, 1988.) Reprinted by permission of *The Wall Street Journal*.

FUTURES PRICES

—FINANCIAL—

BRITISH POUND (IMM)—25,000 pounds; $ per pound

	Open	High	Low	Settle	Chg		Lifetime High	Lifetime Low	Open Interest
June	1.8430	1.8520	1.8355	1.8405	−	.0055	1.8780	1.5280	28,409
Sept	1.8350	1.8420	1.8250	1.8320	−	.0060	1.8702	1.6992	783
Dec	1.8250	1.8350	1.8150	1.8236	−	.0074	1.8652	1.6980	177

Est vol 12,645; vol Mon 16,190; open int 53,310, +494.

CANADIAN DOLLAR (IMM)—100,000 dlrs.; $ per Can $

June	.7927	.7950	.7922	.7941	+	.0019	.7985	.7325	15,228
Sept	.7897	.7916	.7896	.7907	+	.0017	.7923	.7307	1,964
Dec	.7861	.7880	.7861	.7873	+	.0015	.7897	.7390	425

Est vol 3,089; vol Mon 4,196; open int 22,086, −936.

JAPANESE YEN (IMM)—12.5 million yen; $ per yen (.00)

June	.7918	.7923	.7900	.7909	−	.0032	.8390	.6735	40,677
Sept	.7973	.7979	.7963	.7968	−	.0031	.8485	.7075	1,005

Est vol 12,734; vol Mon 25,791; open int 70,121, +1,965.

SWISS FRANC (IMM)—125,000 francs-$ per franc

June	.7355	.7365	.7335	.7339	−	.0033	.8040	.6580	19,067
Sept	.7447	.7454	.7425	.7427	−	.0035	.8120	.6950	222

Est vol 14,262; vol Mon 22,400; open int 32,880, +86.

W. GERMAN MARK (IMM)—125,000 marks; $ per mark

June	.6059	.6065	.6041	.6047	−	.0014	.6494	.5410	27,071
Sept	.6115	.6120	.6099	.6105	−	.0014	.6555	.5609	943
Dec	.6158	.6170	.6155	.6164	−	.0014	.6610	.5705	168

Est vol 11,704; vol Mon 16,671; open int 50,014, −874.

EURODOLLAR (LIFFE)—$1 million; pts of 100%

June	92.84	92.87	92.84	92.87	+	.01	93.39	89.89	14,868
Sept	92.58	92.58	92.57	92.58	−	.01	93.13	89.74	6,548
Dec	92.31	92.32	92.29	92.30	−	.01	92.93	89.80	2,416
Mr89	92.05	92.07	92.05	92.05	−	.02	92.33	90.86	726
June	....	....	91.84	−	.02	92.10	91.94	114

Est vol 2,185; vol Mon 4,846; open int 24,696, +1,076.

STERLING (LIFFE)—£500,000; pts of 100%

Mar	91.20	91.28	91.20	91.23	+	.12	91.70	88.60	5,434
June	91.08	91.24	91.08	91.16	+	.14	91.54	89.28	18,402
Sept	90.92	91.00	90.92	90.96	+	.13	91.27	89.26	4,828
Dec	90.75	90.80	90.73	90.77	+	.13	91.12	89.22	2,101
Mr89	90.55	90.59	90.50	90.58	+	.12	90.83	89.25	2,102
June	90.34	90.38	90.33	90.38	+	.08	90.38	89.65	1,057
Sept	90.20	90.20	90.20	90.19	+	.05	90.22	89.65	305
Dec	90.00	90.00	90.00	89.99	+	.01	90.07	89.76	163

Est vol 12,848; vol Mon 8,589; open int 34,392, −416.

LONG GILT (LIFFE)—£50,000; 32nds of 100%

Mar	123-27	123-28	123-19	123-16	+	0-07	125-00	110-26	4,161
June	123-12	123-25	123-05	123-06	+	0-06	123-25	117-05	23,787

Est vol 14,461; vol Mon 17,622; open int 27,963, +555.

EURODOLLAR (IMM)—$1 million; pts of 100%

	Open	High	Low	Settle	Chg	Yield Settle	Yield Chg	Open Interest
June	92.86	92.87	9.285	92.85	+ .01	7.15	− .01	134,946
Sept	92.57	92.58	92.55	92.56	+ .01	7.44	− .01	51,162
Dec	92.30	92.30	92.28	92.28	....	7.72	....	25,568
Mr89	92.06	92.06	92.02	92.03	....	7.97	....	17,936
June	91.85	91.85	91.80	91.81	− .02	8.19	+ .02	12,790
Sept	91.65	91.66	91.63	91.63	− .02	8.37	+ .02	11,047
Dec	91.49	91.50	91.45	91.47	− .02	8.53	+ .02	7,529
Mr90	91.36	91.36	91.33	91.33	− .02	8.67	+ .02	11,121
June	91.23	91.26	91.20	91.21	− .02	8.74	+ .02	10,374
Sept	91.12	91.15	91.10	91.11	− .02	8.89	+ .02	6,938
Dec	91.05	91.06	91.02	91.02	− .02	8.98	+ .02	5,634

Est vol 27,001; vol Mon 56,215; open int 363,248, +5,114.

U.S. DOLLAR INDEX (CTN) 500 times USDX

Mar	89.20	89.36	89.15	89.26	+	.11	102.05	86.07	1,074
June	89.53	89.66	89.37	89.61	+	.26	101.20	86.60	2,000
Sept	90.00	90.00	90.00	90.00	+	.25	92.96	87.42	1,515

Est vol 800; vol Mon 1,122; open int 4,591, −245.
The index: High 89.42; Low 89.10; Close 89.34 +.26

CRB INDEX (NYFE) 500 times index

Mar	226.05	226.70	225.40	225.80	−	.25	242.25	210.00	938
May	225.25	225.40	224.50	225.05	−	.25	237.50	217.10	784
July	225.10	225.10	224.40	225.00	−	.20	235.90	218.50	840
Sept	225.20	225.20	224.75	225.05	−	.15	236.70	221.50	449

Est vol 491; vol Mon 899; open int 3,011, −139.
The index: H... C... 30

For currency futures, however, there are formal markets established by the Chicago Mercantile Exchange (International Monetary Market), the London International Financial Futures Exchange, and the MidAmerican Commodity Exchange. In these-exchanges contracts are standardized by size, and daily marking to market is observed. Moreover, there are standard clearing arrangements that allow traders to enter or reverse positions easily. The resulting liquidity of these contracts is a major advantage of trading in these markets rather than in forward markets. Of course, the standardization that allows for liquidity correspondingly does not permit the flexibility of contract design that is available in the forward market.

Figure 22.5 reproduces a *Wall Street Journal* listing of foreign exchange spot and forward rates. The listing gives the number of U.S. dollars required to purchase some unit of foreign currency and then the amount of foreign currency needed to purchase $1. Figure 22.6 reproduces futures listings, which show the number of dollars needed to purchase a given unit of foreign currency. In Figure 22.5 both spot and forward exchange rates are listed for various delivery dates. The forward quotations always apply to delivery in 30, 90, or 180 days. Thus tomorrow's forward listings will apply to a maturity date 1 day later than today's listing. In contrast, the futures contracts mature in March, June, September, and December, and these four maturity days are the only dates each year when futures contracts settle.

Interest Rate Parity

As is true of stocks and stock futures, there is a spot-futures exchange rate relationship that will prevail in well-functioning markets. Should this so-called interest rate parity relationship be violated, arbitrageurs will be able to make risk-free profits in foreign exchange markets with zero net investment. Their actions will force futures and spot exchange rates back into alignment.

We can illustrate the **interest rate parity theorem** by using two currencies, the U.S. dollar and the British (U.K.) pound. Call E_0 the current exchange rate between the two currencies, that is, E_0 dollars are required to purchase 1 pound. F_0, the forward price, is the number of dollars that is agreed to today for purchase of 1 pound at time T in the future. Call the risk-free interest rates in the United States and United Kingdom r_{US} and r_{UK}, respectively.

The interest rate parity theorem then states that the proper relationship between E_0 and F_0 is given as

$$F_0 = E_0 \left(\frac{1 + r_{US}}{1 + r_{UK}} \right)^T \tag{22.2}$$

For example, if $r_{US} = .06$ and $r_{UK} = .05$ annually, while $E_0 = \$1.80$ per pound, then the proper futures price for a 1-year contract would be

$$\$1.80 \left(\frac{1.06}{1.05} \right) = \$1.817 \text{ per pound}$$

Consider the intuition behind this result. If r_{US} is greater than r_{UK}, money invested in the United States will grow at a faster rate than money invested in the United Kingdom. If this is so, why wouldn't all investors decide to invest their money in the United States? One important reason why not is that the dollar may be depreciating relative to the pound. Although dollar investments in the United States grow faster than pound investments in the United Kingdom, each dollar is worth progressively fewer pounds as time passes. Such an effect will exactly offset the advantage of the higher U.S. interest rate.

To complete the argument, we need only determine how a depreciating dollar will show up in equation 22.2. If the dollar is depreciating, meaning that progressively more dollars are required to purchase each pound, then the forward exchange rate F_0 (which equals the dollars required to purchase 1 pound for delivery in 1 year) must exceed E_0, the current exchange rate. This is exactly what equation 22.2 tells us: when r_{US} exceeds r_{UK}, F_0 must exceed E_0. The depreciation of the dollar embodied in the ratio of F_0 to E_0 exactly compensates for the difference in interest rates available in the two countries. Of course, the argument also works in reverse; if r_{US} is less than r_{UK}, then F_0 is less than E_0.

What if the interest rate parity relationship is violated? For example, suppose the futures price is $1.81 instead of $1.817. You could adopt the following strategy to reap arbitrage profits. In this example let E_1 denote the exchange rate that will prevail in 1 year. E_1 is, of course, a random variable from the perspective of today's investors.

Action	Initial Cash Flow ($)	CF in 1 Year ($)
1. Borrow 1 U.K. pound in London. Convert to dollars.	1.80	$-E_1(1.05)$
2. Lend $1.80 in the United States.	-1.80	$1.80(1.06)$
3. Enter a contract to purchase 1.05 pounds at a (futures) price of $F_0 = \$1.81$.	0	$1.05(E_1 - 1.81)$
TOTAL	0	$.0075

In stage 1, you exchange the 1 pound borrowed in the United Kingdom for $1.80 at the current exchange rate. After 1 year you must repay the pound borrowed with interest. Since the loan is made in the United Kingdom at the U.K. interest rate, you would repay 1.05 pounds, which would be worth $E_1(1.05)$ dollars. The U.S. loan in step 2 is made at the U.S. interest rate of 6%. The futures position in step 3 results in receipt of 1.05 pounds, for which you would first pay F_0 dollars each, and then trade into dollars at rate E_1.

Note that the exchange rate risk here is exactly offset between the pound obligation in step 1 and the futures position in step 3. The profit from the strategy is therefore risk-free and requires no net investment.

To generalize this strategy:

Action	Initial CF ($)	CF in 1 year ($)
1. Borrow 1 U.K. pound in London. Convert to $.	E_0	$-\$E_1(1 + r_{UK})$
2. Use proceeds of borrowing in London to lend in the U.S.	$-\$E_0$	$\$E_0(1 + r_{US})$
3. Enter $(1 + r_{UK})$ futures positions to purchase 1 pound for F_0 dollars	0	$(1 + r_{UK})(E_1 - F_0)$
TOTAL	0	$E_0(1 + r_{US}) - F_0(1 + r_{UK})$

Let us again review the stages of the arbitrage operation. The first step requires borrowing 1 pound in the United Kingdom. With a current exchange rate of E_0, the 1 pound is converted into E_0 dollars, which is a cash inflow. In 1 year the British loan must be paid off with interest, requiring a payment in pounds of $(1 + r_{UK})$, or in dollars of $E_1(1 + r_{UK})$. In the second step the proceeds of the British loan are invested in the United States. This involves an initial cash outflow of $\$E_0$, and a cash inflow of $\$E_0(1 + r_{US})$ in 1 year. Finally, the exchange risk involved in the British borrowing is hedged in step 3. Here, the $(1 + r_{UK})$ pounds that will need to be delivered to satisfy the British loan are purchased ahead in the futures contract.

The net proceeds to the arbitrage portfolio are risk-free and given by $E_0(1 + r_{US}) - F_0(1 + r_{UK})$. If this value is positive, borrow in the United Kingdom, lend in the United States, and enter a long futures position to eliminate foreign exchange risk. If the value is negative, borrow in the United States, lend in the United Kingdom, and take a short position in pound futures. When prices are aligned properly to preclude arbitrage opportunities, the expression must equal zero. If it were positive, investors would pursue the arbitrage portfolio. If it were negative, they would pursue the reverse positions.

Rearranging this expression gives us the relationship

$$F_0 = \frac{1 + r_{US}}{1 + r_{UK}} E_0 \tag{22.3}$$

which is the interest rate parity theorem for a 1-year horizon, known also as the **covered interest arbitrage relationship.**

Concept Check

Question 3. What are the arbitrage strategy and associated profits if the initial futures price is $F_0 = \$1.83/\text{pound}$?

Ample empirical evidence bears out this theoretical relationship. For two other currencies, for example, on December 3, 1987, the *Financial Times* listed the 3-month U.S. interest rate at 1.953% and the 3-month West German rate at .891%.

FIGURE 22.7
U.S. Treasury bond
futures contract
trading volume.
(From the Chicago Board of
Trade, *Financial Futures
Professional, 11,* August
1987.)

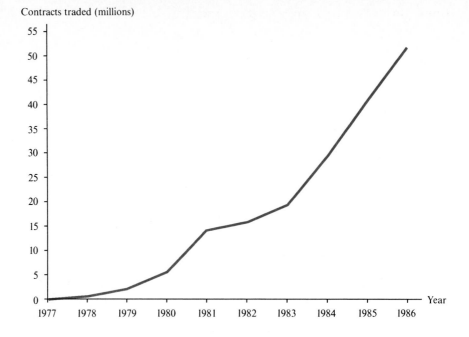

Contracts traded (millions)

The dollar was then worth .6051 West German marks. Substituting these values into equation 22.3 gives $F_0 = .6051(1.01953/1.00891) = .6115$. The actual forward price at that time for 3-month delivery was $.61142 per mark, so close to the parity value that transaction costs would prevent arbitrageurs from profiting from the discrepancy.[4]

22.3 *Interest Rate Futures*

The Markets

The late 1970s and 1980s saw a dramatic increase in the volatility of interest rates, leading to investor desire to hedge returns on fixed-income securities against changes in interest rates. As one example, thrift institutions that had loaned money on home mortgages before 1975 suffered substantial capital losses on those loans when interest rates later increased. An interest rate futures contract could have protected banks against such large swings in yields. Demonstration of these losses has spurred trading in interest rate futures. In fact, the single most actively traded contract today is the Treasury bond futures contract (see Figure 22.7).

The eight major interest rate contracts currently traded are on Eurodollars, Government National Mortgage Association (GNMA) mortgage pass-through securities, Treasury bills, Treasury notes, Treasury bonds, bank certificates of deposit, a munic-

---

[4] The numbers used here are midpoints of the bid-asked spread for all variables.

FIGURE 22.8

Interest rate futures.

(From *The Wall Street Journal,* June 7, 1988.) Reprinted by permission of *The Wall Street Journal.* © Dow Jones & Company, Inc. 1988. All rights reserved.

— FINANCIAL —

EURODOLLAR (IMM) –$1 million; pts of 100%

	Open	High	Low	Settle	Chg	Yield Settle	Chg	Open Interest
June	92.36	92.36	92.31	92.35	−.01	7.65	+ .01	96,714
Sept	91.95	91.97	91.89	91.96	+ .01	8.04	− .01	159,855
Dec	91.64	91.66	91.57	91.63	....	8.37	....	64,412
Mr89	91.46	91.46	91.37	91.43	−.01	8.57	+ .01	44,083
June	91.30	91.30	91.20	91.26	−.02	8.74	+ .02	18,562
Sept	91.14	91.16	91.05	91.12	−.02	8.88	+ .02	16,448
Dec	91.04	91.04	90.94	91.00	−.02	9.00	+ .02	12,587
Mr90	90.94	90.94	90.84	90.90	−.02	9.10	+ .02	14,870
June	90.84	90.84	90.76	90.80	−.03	9.20	+ .03	12,394
Sept	90.75	90.75	90.65	90.71	−.03	9.29	+ .03	10,072
Dec	90.67	90.67	90.59	90.62	−.04	9.38	+ .04	9,227
Mr91	90.59	90.59	90.50	90.53	−.05	9.47	+ .05	5,732

Est vol 106,307; vol Fri 161,939; open int 464,956, +6,463.

U.S. DOLLAR INDEX (FINEX) 500 times USDX

	Open	High	Low	Settle	Chg	Yield Settle	Chg	Open Interest
June	91.07	91.07	90.75	90.81	−.49	101.20	86.60	2,487
Sept	91.08	91.09	90.81	90.86	−.44	92.96	87.42	3,567
Dec	91.10	91.20	91.10	91.15	−.40	92.25	88.40	1,541

Est vol 1,000; vol Fr 712; open int 7,598, +156.
The index: High 91.18; Low 90.86; Close 90.93 −.37

CRB INDEX (NYFE) 500 times Index

	Open	High	Low	Settle	Chg	High	Low	Open Interest
July	256.00	262.00	256.00	261.70	+ 7.70	262.00	218.50	1,471
Sept	256.50	262.00	256.00	261.70	+ 7.50	262.00	221.50	2,225
Dec	255.75	261.30	255.75	261.70	+ 7.10	261.30	231.50	804

Est vol 2,002; vol Fri 1,468; open int 4,500, +635.
The index: High 259.92; Low 255.24; Close 259.52 +4.42

TREASURY BONDS (CBT) –$100,000; pts. 32nds of 100%

	Open	High	Low	Settle	Chg	Yield	Chg	Open Interest
June	88-12	88-12	87-22	88-06	+ 3	9.313	−.011	66,220
Sept	87-15	87-15	86-23	87-08	+ 3	9.428	−.012	252,415
Dec	86-16	86-19	85-29	86-13	+ 3	9.534	−.012	32,318
Mr89	85-22	85-22	85-05	85-19	+ 3	9.638	−.012	18,726
June	85-00	85-00	84-15	84-27	+ 3	9.735	−.012	10,126
Sept	84-04	84-04	84-04	84-04	+ 3	9.829	−.012	405
Dec	83-11	83-15	83-11	83-15	+ 3	9.916	−.012	794
Mr90	82-27	82-29	82-27	82-28	+ 1	9.995	−.005	167

Est vol 300,000; vol Fri 393,941; op int 381,316, +10,732.

TREASURY NOTES (CBT) –$100,000; pts. 32nds of 100%

	Open	High	Low	Settle	Chg	Yield	Chg	Open Interest
June	93-17	93-20	93-08	93-20	+ 3	8.979	−.015	31,815
Sept	93-01	93-01	92-17	92-29	+ 2	9.095	−.010	50,815
Dec	92-02	92-08	91-30	92-08	+ 2	9.202	−.010	1,019

Est vol 16,000; vol Fri 22,986; open int 83,758, +1,971.

5 YR TREAS NOTES (FINEX) $100,000; pts. 32 of 100%

	Open	High	Low	Settle	Chg	Yield	Chg	Open Interest
June	97-20	97-17	97-15	97-20	+ .03	8.59	-- .03	2,982
Sept	97-03	97-035	96-27	97-015	+ .05	8.74	− .01	3,417
Dec	96-19	96-19	96-11	96-175	+ .05	8.87	....	2,498

Est vol 4,500; vol Fri 4,735; open int 8,907, +853.

TREASURY BONDS (MCE) –$50,000; pts. 32nds of 100%

	Open	High	Low	Settle	Chg	Yield	Chg	Open Interest
June	88-09	88-10	87-26	88-08	− 8	9.305	+.031	1,406
Sept	87-09	87-12	86-24	87-10	− 6	9.421	+.024	4,902

Est vol 6,500; vol Fri 11,834; open int 6,373, +1,115.

TREASURY BILLS (IMM) –$1 mil.; pts. of 100%

	Open	High	Low	Settle	Chg	Discount Settle	Chg	Open Interest
Sept	93.32	93.35	93.27	93.33	....	6.67	....	15,806
Dec	93.13	93.13	93.08	93.10	.01	6.90	+ .01	3,079
Mr89	92.96	92.96	92.93	92.94	−.01	7.06	+ .01	390
June	....	....	....	92.75	−.02	7.25	+ .02	163
Sept	....	....	....	92.64	−.02	7.36	+ .02	89

Est vol 4,622; vol Fri 4,167; open int 19,615, +506.

— INDEXES —

MUNI BOND INDEX(CBT)$1,000; times Bond Buyer MBI

	Open	High	Low	Settle	Chg	High	Low	Open Interest
June	87-18	87-20	87-11	87-20	− 2	89-26	70-03	7,848
Sept	85-08	85-09	84-29	85-08	− 4	88-08	81-02	6,486
Dec	83-06	83-11	82-31	83-11	− 4	86-29	80-16	514
Mr89	81-12	81-12	81-08	81-11	− 11	85-05	78-25	421
June	79-22	79-25	79-17	79-25	− 6	80-19	77-06	424

Est vol 5,000; vol Fri 4,905; open int 15,693, −798.
The index: Close 88-02; Yield 8.35.

ipal bond index, and a corporate bond index. These securities thus provide an opportunity to hedge against a wide spectrum of maturities from very short (T-bills) to long term (T-bonds). Figure 22.8 shows listings of some of these contracts in *The Wall Street Journal.*

The Treasury contracts call for delivery of a Treasury bond, bill, or note. Should interest rates rise, the market value of the security at delivery will be less than the original futures price, and the deliverer will profit. Hence the short position in the interest rate futures contract gains when interest rates rise.

GNMA futures have potential for lenders in the mortgage market. Mortgage lenders can pool home mortgages into groups of $1 million minimum size, creating a unit that can be sold by the mortgage originator. The instrument is called a GNMA pass-through certificate, and there is a substantial secondary market for pass-throughs. GNMA futures call for delivery of a GNMA certificate. Because the underlying security here is a pool of mortgages, mortgage lenders can use GNMA futures to hedge the market value of their loans. Similarly, Treasury bond futures can be useful hedging vehicles for bond dealers or underwriters. The newer contracts on municipal and corporate bond indices allow for more direct hedging of long-term bonds other than Treasury issues.

An Application

An episode that occurred in October 1979 is a good illustration of the potential hedging value offered by T-bond contracts. Salomon Brothers, Merrill Lynch, and other underwriters brought out a $1 billion issue of IBM bonds. As is typical, the underwriting syndicate quoted an interest rate at which it guarantees that the bonds can be sold. In essence, the syndicate buys the company's bonds at an agreed-on price and then takes the responsibility of reselling them in the open market. If interest rates increase before the bonds can be sold to the public, the syndicate, not the issuer, bears the capital loss from the fall in the value of the bonds.

In this case the syndicate led by Salomon Brothers and Merrill Lynch brought out the IBM debt to sell at yields of 9.62% for $500 million of 7-year notes and 9.41% for $500 million of 25-year bonds. These yields were only about 4 basis points above comparable-maturity U.S. government bond yields, reflecting IBM's excellent credit rating. The debt issue was brought to market on Thursday, October 4, when the underwriters began placing the bonds with customers. Interest rates, however, rose slightly that Thursday, making the IBM yields less attractive, and not more than 70% of the issue had been placed by Friday afternoon, leaving the syndicate still holding between $250 million to $300 million of bonds.

Then on Saturday, October 6, the Federal Reserve Board announced a major credit-tightening policy. Interest rates jumped by almost a full percentage point. The underwriting syndicate realized that the balance of the IBM bonds could not be placed to its regular customers at the original offering price and decided to sell them in the open bond market. By that time the bonds had fallen nearly 5% in value, so that the underwriter's loss was about $12 million on the unsold bonds. The net loss on the underwriting operation came to about $7 million, because a profit of $5 million had been realized on the bonds that were placed.

As the major underwriter with the lion's share of the bonds, Salomon lost about $3.5 million on the bond issue. Yet, although most of the other underwriters were largely vulnerable to the interest rate movement, Salomon had hedged its bond holdings by shorting about $100 million in GNMA and Treasury bond futures. Holding a short position, Salomon Brothers realized profits on the contract when the interest rate increased. The profits on the short futures position resulted because the value of the bonds required to be delivered to satisfy the contract decreased when interest rates rose. Altogether, Salomon Brothers probably just about broke even on the entire transaction, making estimated gains on the futures position of about $3.5 million, which largely offset the capital loss on the bonds it was holding.

How could Salomon Brothers have constructed the proper hedge ratio, that is, the proper number of futures contracts per bond held in its inventory? The T-bond futures contract nominally calls for delivery of an 8% coupon 20-year maturity government bond in return for the futures price. (In practice, other bonds may be substituted for this standard bond to settle the contract, but we will use the 8% bond for illustration.) Suppose that the market interest rate is 10% and that Salomon is holding $100 million dollars worth of bonds, with a coupon rate of 10%, and 20-year time to maturity. The bonds currently sell at par value of $1,000. If the interest rate were to jump to 11%, the bonds would fall to a market value of $919.77, a loss of $8.02 million. (We use semiannual compounding in this calculation.)

To hedge this risk, Salomon would need to short enough futures so that the profits on the futures position would offset the loss on the bonds. The 8% 20-year bond of the futures contract would sell for $828.41 if the interest rate were 10%. If the interest rate were to jump to 11%, the bond price would fall to $759.31, and the fall in the price of the 8% bond, $69.10, would approximately equal the profit on the short futures position per bond to be delivered.[5] Because each contract calls for delivery of $100,000 par value of bonds (100 bonds at par value of $1,000), the gain on each short position would equal $6,910. Thus, to offset the $8.02 million loss on the value of the bonds, Salomon would need to hold $8.02 million/$6910 = 1,161 contracts short. The total gain on the contracts would offset the loss on the bonds and leave Salomon unaffected by interest rate swings.

The actual hedging problem is more difficult for several reasons: (1) Salomon probably would hold more than one issue of bonds in its inventory, and (2) interest rates on government and corporate bonds will not be equal and need not move in lockstep (and at the time, a corporate bond contract did not exist); (3) the T-bond contract may be settled with any of several bonds instead of the 8% benchmark bond; and (4) taxes could complicate the picture. Nevertheless, the principles illustrated here underlie all hedging activity.

22.4 *Commodity Futures Pricing*

Commodity futures prices are governed by the same general considerations as stock futures. One difference, however, is that the cost of carrying commodities, especially those subject to spoilage, is greater than the cost of carrying financial assets.

---

[5] We say "approximately" because the exact figure depends on the time to maturity of the contract. We assume here that the maturity date is less than a month away so that the futures price and bond price move in virtual lockstep.

Moreover, spot prices for some commodities demonstrate marked seasonal patterns that can affect futures pricing.

Pricing With Storage Costs

The cost of carrying commodities includes, in addition to interest costs, storage costs, insurance costs, and an allowance for spoilage of goods in storage. To price commodity futures, let us reconsider the earlier arbitrage strategy that calls for holding both the asset and a short position in the futures contract on the asset. In this case we will denote the price of the commodity at time T as P_T, and assume for simplicity that all noninterest carrying costs (C) are paid in one lump sum at time T, the contract maturity. Carrying costs appear in the final cash flow.

Action	Initial Cash Flow	CF at Time T
Buy asset; pay carrying costs at T	$-P_0$	$P_T - C$
Borrow P_0; repay with interest at time T	P_0	$-P_0(1 + r_f)$
Short futures position	0	$F_0 - P_T$
TOTAL	0	$F_0 - P_0(1 + r_f) - C$

Because market prices should not allow for arbitrage opportunities, the terminal cash flow of this zero net investment, risk-free strategy should be zero.

If the cash flow were positive, this strategy would yield guaranteed profits for no investment. If the cash flow were negative, the reverse of this strategy also would yield profits. In practice, the reverse strategy would involve a short sale of the commodity. This is unusual but may be done as long as the short sale contract appropriately accounts for storage costs.[6] Thus we conclude that

$$F_0 = P_0(1 + r_f) + C$$

Finally, if we call $c = C/P_0$, and interpret c as the percentage "rate" of carrying costs, we may write

$$F_0 = P_0(1 + r_f + c) \tag{22.4}$$

which is a (1-year) parity relationship for futures involving storage costs. Compare equation 22.4 to the first parity relation for stocks, equation 22.1, and you will see that they are extremely similar. In fact, if we think of carrying costs as a "negative dividend," the equations are identical. This treatment makes intuitive sense because, instead of receiving a dividend yield of d, the storer of the commodity must pay a

---

[6] Jarrow, Robert A., and Oldfield, George S., "Forward Contracts and Futures Contracts," *Journal of Financial Economics, 9,* 1981.

storage cost of c. Obviously, this parity relationship is simply an extension of those we have seen already.

It is vital to note that we derive equation 22.4 assuming that the asset will be bought and stored; it therefore applies only to goods that currently *are* being stored. Two kinds of commodities cannot be expected to be stored. The first is highly perishable goods, such as strawberries, for which storage is technologically not feasible. The second includes goods that are not stored for economic reasons. For example, it would be foolish to buy wheat now, planning to store it for ultimate use in 3 years. Instead, it is clearly preferable to delay the purchase of the wheat until after the harvest of the third year. The wheat is then obtained without incurring the storage costs. Moreover, if the wheat harvest in the third year is comparable to this year's, you could obtain it at roughly the same price as you would pay this year. By waiting to purchase, you avoid both interest and storage costs.

In fact, it is generally not reasonable to hold large quantities of agricultural goods across a harvesting period. Why pay to store this year's wheat, when you can purchase next year's wheat when it is harvested? Maintaining large wheat inventories across harvests make sense only if such a small wheat crop is forecast that wheat prices will not fall when the new supply is harvested.

Concept Check

Question 4. People are willing to buy and "store" shares of stock despite the fact that their purchase ties up capital. Most people, however, are not willing to buy and store wheat. What is the difference in the properties of the expected evolution of stock prices vs. wheat prices that accounts for this result?

Because storage across harvests is costly, equation 22.4 should not be expected to apply for holding periods that span harvest times, nor should it apply to perishable goods that are available only "in season." You can see that this is so if you look at the futures markets page of the newspaper. Figure 22.9, for example, gives futures prices for several times to maturity for soybeans and for gold. Whereas the futures price for gold, which is a stored commodity, increases steadily with the maturity of the contract, the futures price for soybeans is seasonal; it rises within a harvest period as equation 22.4 would predict, but the price then falls across harvests as new supplies become available.

Futures pricing across seasons requires a different approach that is not based on storage across harvest periods. In place of general no-arbitrage restrictions we rely instead on risk premium theory and discounted cash flow (DCF) analysis.

Discounted Cash Flow Analysis for Commodity Futures

We have said that most agricultural commodities follow seasonal price patterns; prices rise before a harvest and then fall at the harvest when the new crop becomes

FIGURE 22.9

Futures prices for soybeans and gold.

(From *The Wall Street Journal*, June 8, 1988.) Reprinted by permission of *The Wall Street Journal*.

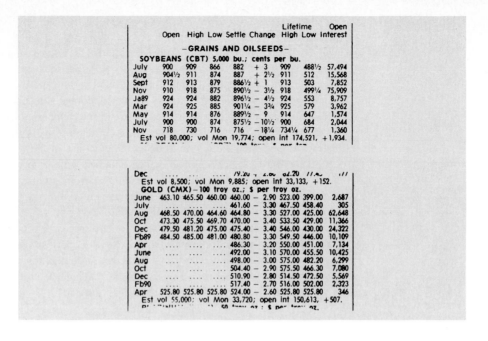

	Open	High	Low	Settle	Change	Lifetime High	Lifetime Low	Open Interest
–GRAINS AND OILSEEDS–								
SOYBEANS (CBT) 5,000 bu.; cents per bu.								
July	900	909	866	882	+ 3	909	488½	57,494
Aug	904½	911	874	887	+ 2½	911	512	15,568
Sept	912	913	879	886½	+ 1	913	503	7,852
Nov	910	918	875	890½	– 3½	918	499¼	75,909
Ja89	924	924	882	896½	– 4½	924	553	8,757
Mar	924	925	885	901¼	– 3¾	925	579	3,962
May	914	914	876	889½	– 9	914	647	1,574
July	900	900	874	875½	– 10½	900	684	2,044
Nov	718	730	716	716	– 18¼	734¼	677	1,360
Est vol 80,000; vol Mon 19,774; open int 174,521, +1,934.								
Dec	....	...	....	[illegible]	[illegible]	[illegible]	[illegible]	[illegible]
Est vol 8,500; vol Mon 9,885; open int 33,133, +152.								
GOLD (CMX) – 100 troy oz.; $ per troy oz.								
June	463.10	465.50	460.00	460.00	– 2.90	523.00	399.00	2,687
July	....	....	....	461.60	– 3.30	467.50	458.40	305
Aug	468.50	470.00	464.60	464.80	– 3.30	527.00	425.00	62,648
Oct	473.30	475.50	469.70	470.00	– 3.40	533.50	429.00	11,366
Dec	479.50	481.20	475.00	475.40	– 3.40	546.00	430.00	24,322
Fb89	484.50	485.00	481.00	480.80	– 3.30	549.50	446.00	10,109
Apr	....	....	....	486.30	– 3.20	550.00	451.00	7,134
June	....	....	....	492.00	– 3.10	570.00	455.50	10,425
Aug	....	....	....	498.00	– 3.00	575.00	482.20	6,299
Oct	....	....	....	504.40	– 2.90	575.50	466.30	7,080
Dec	....	....	....	510.90	– 2.80	514.50	472.50	5,569
Fb90	....	....	....	517.40	– 2.70	516.00	502.00	2,323
Apr	525.80	525.80	525.80	524.00	– 2.60	525.80	525.80	346
Est vol 55,000; vol Mon 33,720; open int 150,613, +507.								

FIGURE 22.10

Typical commodity price pattern over the season. Prices adjusted for inflation.

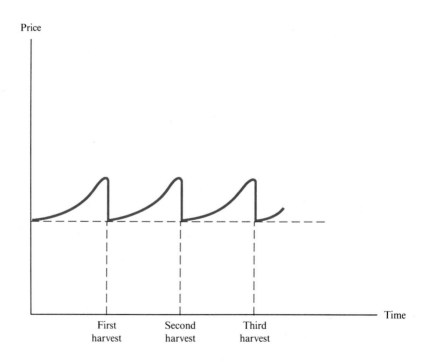

available for consumption. Figure 22.10 graphs this pattern. The price of the commodity following the harvest must rise at the rate of the total cost of carry (interest plus noninterest carrying costs) to induce holders of the commodity to store it willingly for future sale instead of sell it immediately. Inventories will be run down to near zero just before the next harvest.

Clearly, this pattern differs sharply from financial assets such as stocks or gold, for which there is no seasonal price movement. For financial assets, the current price is set in market equilibrium at a level that promises an expected rate of capital gains plus dividends equal to the required rate of return on the asset. Financial assets are stored only if their economic rate of return compensates for the cost of carry. In other words, financial assets are priced so that storing them produces a fair return. Agricultural prices, by contrast, are subject to steep periodic drops as each crop is harvested, which makes storage across harvests consequently unprofitable.

Of course, neither the exact size of the harvest nor the demand for the good is known in advance, so the spot price of the commodity cannot be perfectly predicted. As weather forecasts change, for example, the expected size of the crop and the expected future spot price of the commodity are updated continually.

Given the current expectation of the spot price of the commodity at some future date and a measure of the risk characteristics of that price, we can measure the present value of a claim to receive the commodity at that future date. We simply calculate the appropriate risk premium from a model such as the CAPM or APT and discount the expected spot price at the appropriate risk-adjusted interest rate.

Table 22.4, which presents betas on a variety of commodities, shows that the beta of orange juice, for example, was estimated to be .117 over the period. If the T-bill rate is currently 7%, and the historical market risk premium has been about 8.5%, the appropriate discount rate for orange juice would be given by the CAPM as

$$7\% + .117(8.5\%) = 7.99\%$$

If the expected spot price for orange juice 6 months from now is $1.75 per pound, the present value of a 6-month deferred claim to a pound of orange juice is simply

$$\$1.75/(1.0799)^{1/2} = \$1.68$$

What would the proper futures price for orange juice be? The contract calls for the ultimate exchange of orange juice for the futures price. We have just shown that the present value of the juice is $1.68. This should equal the present value of the futures price that will be paid for the juice. A commitment to a payment of F_0 dollars in 6 months has a present value of $F_0/(1.07)^{1/2} = .967 \times F_0$. (Note that the discount rate is the risk-free rate of 7%, because the promised payment is fixed and therefore independent of market conditions.)

To equate the present values of the promised payment of F_0 and the promised receipt of orange juice, we would set

$$.967F_0 = \$1.68$$

or $F_0 = \$1.74$.

TABLE 22.4 Commodity Betas

Commodity	Beta
Wheat	−0.370
Corn	−0.429
Oats	0.000
Soybeans	−0.266
Soybean oil	−0.650
Soybean meal	0.239
Broilers	−1.692
Plywood	0.660
Potatoes	−0.610
Platinum	0.221
Wool	0.307
Cotton	−0.015
Orange juice	0.117
Propane	−3.851
Cocoa	−0.291
Silver	−0.272
Copper	0.005
Cattle	0.365
Hogs	−0.148
Pork bellies	−0.062
Egg	−0.293
Lumber	−0.131
Sugar	−2.403

From Bodie, Zvi, and Rosansky, Victor, "Risk and Return in Commodity Futures," *Financial Analysts Journal, 36,* May-June 1980.

The general rule, then, to determine the appropriate futures price is to equate the present value of the future payment of F_0 and the present value of the commodity to be received. This gives us

$$\frac{F_0}{(1 + r_f)^T} = \frac{E(P_T)}{(1 + k)^T}$$

or (22.5)

$$F_0 = E(P_T)\left(\frac{1 + r_f}{1 + k}\right)^T$$

where k is the required rate of return on the commodity, which may be obtained from a model of asset market equilibrium such as the CAPM.

Note that equation 22.5 is perfectly consistent with the spot-futures parity relationship. For example, apply equation 22.5 to the futures price for a stock paying no dividends. Because the entire return on the stock is in the form of capital gains, the expected rate of capital gains must equal k, the required rate of return on the stock. Consequently, the expected price of the stock will be its current price times $(1 + k)^T$, or $E(P_T) = P_0(1 + k)^T$. Substituting this expression into equation 22.5 results in F_0

$= P_0(1 + r_f)^T$, which is exactly the parity relationship. This equilibrium derivation of the parity relationship simply reinforces the no-arbitrage restrictions we derived earlier. The spot-futures parity relationship may be obtained from the equilibrium condition that all portfolios earn fair expected rates of return.

Concept Check

Question 5. Suppose that the systematic risk of orange juice were to increase, holding the expected time T price of juice constant. If the expected spot price is unchanged, would the futures price change? In what direction? What is the intuition behind your answer?

The advantage of the arbitrage proofs that we have explored is that they do not rely on the validity of any particular model of security market equilibrium. The absence of arbitrage opportunities is a much more robust basis for argument than the CAPM, for example. Moreover, arbitrage proofs clearly demonstrate how an investor can exploit any misalignment in the spot-futures relationship. To their disadvantage, arbitrage restrictions may be less precise than desirable in the face of storage costs or costs of short selling.

We can summarize by saying that the actions of arbitrageurs force the futures prices of financial assets to maintain a precise relationship with the price of the underlying financial asset. This relationship is described by the spot-futures parity formula. Opportunities for arbitrage are more limited in the case of commodity futures because such commodities often are not stored. Hence, to make a precise prediction for the correct relationship between futures and spot prices, we must rely on a model of security market equilibrium such as the CAPM or APT and estimate the unobservables, the expected spot price, and the appropriate interest rate. Such models will be perfectly consistent with the parity relationships in the benchmark case where investors willingly store the commodity.

22.5 *New Developments in Futures Markets*

The CPI Contract

As potential new demand for hedging or speculating is identified, futures exchanges introduce contracts on new commodities or indices. One example is the inflation futures contract introduced by the Economic Index Market of the Coffee, Sugar, and Cocoa Exchange in 1985. As it turns out, the Coffee Exchange has had a difficult struggle, so far unsuccessful, to make the contract succeed. It is instructive, therefore, to examine the motive behind the new contract and the reasons for its failure to catch on.

The inflation measure originally was based on the Consumer Price Index for Urban Wage Earners and Clerical Workers (CPI-W), which is the index used for wage, lease, and Social Security cost-of-living adjustments. (The government also publishes a CPI-U index for all urban consumers.) The CPI-W contract sets the 1967 price level equal to 100. A price level of 110 means that the average cost of goods is 10% higher than it was in 1967. The level of the CPI-W in September 1987 was 339, which means that goods then cost on average 3.39 times what they did in 1967.

The CPI contract calls for *cash delivery* from the long to the short position of the difference between the original futures price and the value of the CPI-W index at contract maturity. A scaling index of $1,000 is used so that a futures price of 350 and a CPI-W index of 348 at maturity will result in payment of $1,000 × (350 − 348) = $2,000 from the long to the short position.

An inflation futures contract has obvious appeal in a period of uncertain inflation. It can be used to lock in a real rate of return on nominal contracts. Notably, the longest contract maturity will be roughly 3 years, which is just the length of most collective bargaining wage agreements.

To show how such a contract locks in real values, consider this example. Suppose that the nominal interest rate is 9%, and the current level of the CPI is 380. You lend $366,972 today and will be repaid $400,000 in 1 year. This gives you a 9% nominal rate of return. The purchasing power of that payment and the real rate of return on the loan, however, is uncertain, because prices next year depend on inflation experience during the coming year.

The $366,972 that you lend today has a "real value" of $96,572 ($366,972/3.80), meaning that the purchasing power of $366,972 today, when the price level is 380, is equivalent to the purchasing power that $96,572 had in 1967. Real value may be thought of as the price-level adjusted value of your dollar investment. The real value of the $400,000 that you will be repaid will equal $400,000 adjusted for the price level in 1 year.

Consider now the establishment of a long position in the CPI-W contract. If the futures price is 400, the payoff to the long position will be (CPI − 400) × 1,000. Your total portfolio (loan plus futures position) will be:

Loan repayment	400,000
Futures profit	(CPI × 1,000) − 400,000
TOTAL	CPI × 1,000

Note that the portfolio's value is exactly proportional to the price level. In essence, you have sold your original claim to a $400,000 nominal payment for a claim to a payment of 1,000 times the CPI. Your final payment is exactly proportional to the general level of prices, which gives you known purchasing power.

The payment is constant in real terms. Because the CPI is set equal to 100 in 1967, a payment of 1,000 times the CPI has a purchasing power of 1,000 times the purchasing power of $100 in 1967. This is 100,000 real dollars. Thus your original loan of $96,572 in "constant dollars" of 1967 will grow with certainty to a real value of 100,000 constant dollars, thereby yielding a guaranteed real rate of return of 3.55%. The CPI futures contract provides the ability to eliminate completely the effect of inflation on the real rate of return.

To see this point more concretely, suppose that the CPI-W in 1 year will grow from its current level of 380 to either 385, 400, or 415. Hence the price level will be either 3.85, 4.0 or 4.15 times its level in 1967. The futures price on the contract is 400. Your portfolio thus can take on the following values for each price-level scenario:

Price Level CPI	3.85 385	4.00 400	4.15 415
Loan repayment	$400,000	$400,000	$400,000
Futures profit	$1,000(385-400)	0	$1,000(415-400)
Total portfolio value	$385,000	$400,000	$415,000
Portfolio value ÷ Price level	$100,000	$100,000	$100,000

Regardless of the price level, the real value of your position equals $100,000. When the inflation rate is unexpectedly high, so that the nominal loan payment of $400,000 is of less real value than anticipated, the profits from the futures position offset the loss.

The real interest rate that can be locked in using CPI futures is essentially the nominal interest rate paid on bonds adjusted for the implicit inflation forecast built into the CPI futures price. We can use these data to construct a yield curve of real interest rates to compare to the yield curve of nominal interest rates. Figure 22.11 presents such an analysis. Whereas the nominal yield curve at the time of the analysis was upward-sloping, as is common, the inflation rates embedded in the CPI futures were increasing with the maturity date at an even faster pace, so that the real-yield curve actually was downward-sloping.

When it was introduced, economists such as Nobel laureate Milton Friedman hailed the inflation contract. They felt the ability to hedge price risk was of great value and would attract much trading interest. The interest, however, never materialized. We speculate that some reasons for the failure of the contract to date are as follows:

1. Inflation has been low and fairly stable since the contract was introduced, reducing the need for hedging.
2. The contract may have been too difficult for many traders to understand.
3. The value of the "spot commodity," the CPI, is released only monthly. Because the daily value is not known and cannot be traded directly, the spot-futures trading strategies that contribute to volume in other contracts never developed.
4. Many firms already may be inflation hedged, since the prices they pay and charge for goods and services already increase with the general level of prices.
5. Demand for true inflation hedging is more likely to arise to protect long-term interests such as nominal pension benefits. The CPI contract's 3-year maximum maturity is insufficient to hedge these values.

We conclude that ingredients that contribute to successful futures contracts are the presence of natural hedging demands by investors, a closely related spot market for

FIGURE 22.11

Real and nominal
yield curves.

(From *Economic Index
Market newsletter,* Coffee,
Sugar & Cocoa Exchange,
Inc., November 1985.)

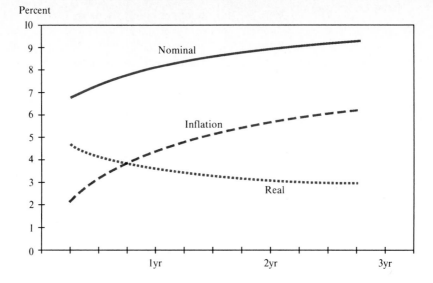

Period ending	Nominal yield	Inflation forecast	Real yield
Dec 85	6.80%	2.11%	4.69%
Mar 86	7.42%	3.23%	4.19%
Jun 86	7.78%	3.91%	3.87%
Dec 86	8.36%	4.85%	3.51%
Jun 87	8.72%	5.40%	3.32%
Dec 87	8.96%	5.83%	3.13%
Jun 88	9.30%	6.21%	3.09%

the commodity and the ability to engage in spot-futures arbitrage strategies, and an easily understood contract design.

Other New Contracts

As it becomes apparent that investors want to speculate on or hedge against a source of uncertainty, the futures exchanges respond by introducing new contracts to satisfy investor demands. The exchanges profit in proportion to the volume of trading on the contract, so it pays them to seek out new contracts with wide appeal to investors. The introduction of the CPI contract is one example of this kind of response. Another is the recent establishment of futures contracts on the U.S. dollar. The dollar index contracts allow investors to bet on (or hedge against) changes in the value of the dollar relative to a bundle of foreign currencies rather than bet on the value of the dollar relative to a particular foreign currency. These contracts are the U.S. Dollar Index Futures and the European Currency Unit Futures traded on the Finex division of the New York Cotton Exchange. Various energy futures similarly arose when oil prices became volatile in the 1970s.

Summary

1. Futures contracts calling for cash settlement are traded on various stock market indices. The contracts may be mixed with Treasury bills to construct artificial equity positions, which makes them potentially valuable tools for market timers. Market index contracts are used also by arbitrageurs who attempt to profit from violations of the parity relationship.

2. Foreign exchange futures trade on several foreign currencies, as well as on a European currency index. The interest rate parity relationship for foreign exchange futures is

$$F_0 = E_0 \left(\frac{1 + r_{US}}{1 + r_{foreign}} \right)^T$$

Deviations of the futures price from this value imply arbitrage opportunity. Empirical evidence, however, suggests that generally the parity relationship is satisfied.

3. Interest rate futures allow for hedging against interest rate fluctuations in several different markets. The most actively traded contract is for Treasury bonds.

4. Commodity futures pricing is complicated by costs for storage of the underlying commodity. When the asset is willingly stored by investors, then the storage costs enter the futures pricing equation as follows:

$$F_0 = P_0(1 + r_f + c)^T$$

The noninterest carrying costs, c, play the role of a "negative dividend" in this context.

5. When commodities are not stored for investment purposes, the correct futures price must be determined using general risk-return principles. In this event

$$F_0 = E(P_T) \left(\frac{1 + r_f}{1 + k} \right)^T$$

The equilibrium (risk-return) and the no-arbitrage predictions of the proper futures price are consistent with one another.

6. As new hedging demands arise among consumers, futures exchanges respond by introducing new contracts. Recent examples are the CPI contract, dollar index contracts, and various energy future contracts.

Key Terms
Index arbitrage
Program trading
Triple witching hour
Interest rate parity theorem
Covered interest arbitrage relationship

Selected Readings

An excellent treatment of stock index futures is:

Modest, David, and Sundaresan, Mahadevan, "The Relationship Between Spot and Futures Prices in Stock Index Futures Markets: Some Preliminary Evidence," *Journal of Futures Markets, 3,* spring 1983.

A good set of readings on index futures is:

Fabozzi, Frank J., and Kipnis, Gregory M. (editors), *Stock Index Futures,* Homewood, Ill.: Dow Jones-Irwin, 1984.

A useful introduction to foreign exchange markets may be found in:

Chrystal, K. Alex, "A Guide to Foreign Exchange Markets," *Federal Reserve Bank of St. Louis,* March 1984.

Two analyses of the use of financial futures to hedge interest rate risk are:

Kolb, Robert, and Gay, Gerald, "Immunizing Bond Portfolios with Interest Rate Futures," *Financial Management, 11,* summer 1982.

Kolb, Robert, and Gay, Gerald, "Interest Rate Futures as a Tool for Immunizing," *Journal of Portfolio Management, 10,* fall 1983.

A survey of the financial futures market with much institutional detail is:

Powers, Mark J., *Inside the Financial Futures Markets,* New York: John Wiley & Sons, 1984.

Analyses of risk and return in commodity futures are in:

Bodie, Zvi, and Rosansky, Victor, "Risk and Return in Commodity Futures," *Financial Analysts Journal, 36,* May-June 1980.

Dusak, Katherine, "Futures Trading and Investor Returns: An Investigation of Commodity Market Risk Premiums," *Journal of Political Economy, 81,* December 1973.

The issue of the storage of commodities is treated in:

Brennan, Michael, "The Supply of Storage," *American Economic Review, 47,* March 1958.

Problems

1. Consider the futures contract written on the S&P 500 index, and maturing in 6 months. The interest rate is 5% per 6-month period, and the future value of dividends expected to be paid over the next 6 months is $8. The current index level is 127.5. Assume that you can short sell the S&P index.
   a. Suppose the expected rate of return on the market is 10% per 6-month period. What is the expected level of the index in 6 months?
   b. What is the theoretical no-arbitrage price for a 6-month futures contract on the S&P 500 stock index?
   c. Suppose the futures price is 124. Is there an arbitrage opportunity here? If so, how would you exploit it?
2. Suppose that the value of the S&P 500 stock index is 250.
   a. If each futures contract costs $25 to trade with a discount broker, how much is the transaction cost per dollar of stock controlled by the futures contract?
   b. If the average price of a share on the NYSE is about $40, how much is the transaction cost per "typical share" controlled by one futures contract?
   c. For small investors, the typical transaction cost per share in trading stocks directly is about 30 cents per share. How many times the transaction costs in futures markets is this?

3. Consider these futures market data for the June delivery S&P 500 contract, exactly 6 months hence. The S&P 500 index is at $249.32, and the June maturity contract is at $F_0 = \$250.70$.

   a. If the current interest rate is 3.25% semiannually, and the average dividend rate of the stocks in the index is 1.5% semiannually, what fraction of the proceeds of stock short sales would need to be available to you to earn arbitrage profits?

   b. Suppose that you in fact have access to 90% of the proceeds from a short sale. What is the lower bound on the futures price that rules out arbitrage opportunities? By how much does the actual futures price fall below the no-arbitrage bound? Formulate the appropriate arbitrage strategy, and calculate the profits to that strategy.

4. You manage a $3 million portfolio, currently all invested in equities, and believe that you have extraordinary market timing skills. You believe that the market is on the verge of a big but short-lived downturn; you would move your portfolio temporarily into T-bills, but you do not want to incur the transaction costs of liquidating and reestablishing your equity position. Instead, you decide to temporarily hedge your equity holdings with S&P 500 index futures contracts.

   a. Should you be long or short on the contracts? Why?

   b. If your equity holdings are invested in a market-index fund, into how many contracts should you enter? The S&P 500 index is now at 300 and the contract multiplier is 500.

   c. How does your answer to (b) change if the beta of your portfolio is .6?

5. Suppose that the spot price of the Swiss franc is currently 40 cents. The 1-year futures price is 44 cents. Is the interest rate higher in the United States or Switzerland?

6. a. The spot price of the British pound is currently $1.50. If the risk-free interest rate on 1-year government bonds is 10% in the United States and 15% in the United Kingdom, what must the forward price of the pound be for delivery 1 year from now?

   b. How could an investor make risk-free arbitrage profits if the forward price were higher than the price you gave in answer to (a)? Give a numerical example.

7. Consider the following information:

$$r_{US} = 15\%$$
$$r_{UK} = 17\%$$
$$E_0 = 2.0 \text{ dollars per pound}$$
$$F_0 = 1.97 \text{ (1-year delivery)}$$

where the interest rates are annual yields on U.S. or U.K. bills. Given this information:

a. Where would you lend?

b. Where would you borrow?

c. How could you arbitrage?

8. (Based on CFA Examination, Level III, 1983)

   In February 1983 the United American Co. is considering the sale of $100 million in 10-year debentures that probably will be rated AAA like the firm's other bond issues. The firm is eager to proceed at today's rate of 10.5%.

   As Treasurer, you know that it will take about 12 weeks (May 1983) to get the issue registered and sold. Therefore you suggest that the firm hedge the pending bond issue using Treasury bond futures contracts. (Each Treasury bond contract is for $100,000.)

   Explain how you would go about hedging the bond issue, and describe the results, assuming that the following two sets of future conditions actually occur. (Ignore commissions and margin costs, and assume a one-to-one hedge ratio.) Show all calculations.

	Case 1	Case 2
Current Values—February 1983		
Bond rate	10.5%	10.5%
June '83 Treasury bond futures	78.875	78.875
Estimated Values—May 1983		
Bond rate	11.0%	10.0%
June '83 Treasury bond futures	75.93	81.84

9. You believe that the spread between municipal bond yields and U.S. Treasury bond yields is going to narrow in the coming month. How can you profit from such a change using the municipal bond and T-bond futures contracts.

10. Salomon Brothers is underwriting an issue of 30-year zero-coupon corporate bonds with a face value of $100 million and a current market value of $5.354 million (a yield of 5% per 6-month period). The firm must hold the bonds for a few days before issuing them to the public, which exposes it to interest rate risk. Salomon wishes to hedge its position by using T-bond futures contracts. The current T-bond futures price is $90.80 per $100 par value, and the T-bond contract will be settled using a 20-year 8% coupon bond paying interest semiannually. The contract is due to expire in a few days, so the T-bond price and the T-bond futures price are virtually identical. The yield implied on the bond is therefore 4.5% per 6-month period. (Confirm this as a first step.) Assume that the yield curve is flat and that the corporate bond will continue to yield 0.5% more than T-bonds per 6-month period, even if the general level of interest rates should change. What hedge ratio should Salomon Brothers use to hedge its bond holdings against possible interest rate fluctuations over the next few days?

11. If the spot price of gold is $350 per troy ounce, the risk-free interest rate is 10%, and storage and insurance costs are zero, what should the forward price of gold be for delivery in 1 year? Use an arbitrage argument to prove your answer. Include a numerical example showing how you could make risk-free arbitrage profits if the forward price exceeded its upper bound value.

12. Assume that the CPI is currently 320 and that the futures price for a CPI contract maturing in 1 year is 340. The 1-year T-bill rate is 8%. What is the risk-free real

rate you could lock in by buying T-bills and going long on CPI futures? What is the amount of money you would have to invest in T-bills today to be perfectly hedged with a single contract? (The contract size is $1,000 times the futures price of the index.)

13. If the corn harvest today is poor, would you expect this fact to have any effect on today's futures prices for corn to be delivered (postharvest) 2 years from today? Under what circumstances will there be no effect?

14. Suppose that the price of corn is risky, with a beta of .5. The monthly storage cost is $.03, and the current spot price is $2.75, with an expected spot price in 3 months of $2.94. If the expected rate of return on the market is 1.8% per month, with a risk-free rate of 1% per month, would you store corn for 3 months?

15. (CFA Examination, Level III, 1985)

You are provided the information outlined as follows to be used in answering this question.

Issue	Price	Yield to Maturity	Modified Duration*
U.S. Treasury bond 11¾% maturing Nov. 15, 2014	100	11.75%	7.6 years
U.S. Treasury long bond futures contract (contract expiration date December 1986)	63.33	11.85%	8.0 years
XYZ Corporation bond 12½% maturing June 1, 2005 (sinking fund debenture, rated AAA)	93	13.50%	7.2 years
Volatility of AAA corporate bond yields relative to U.S. Treasury bond yields = 1.25 to 1.0 (1.25 times)			

Assume no commissions and no margin requirements on U.S. Treasury long bond futures contracts. Assume no taxes.

One U.S. Treasury long bond futures contract is a claim on $100,000 par value long-term U.S. Treasury bonds.

*Modified duration = Duration/$(1 + r)$

Situation A. A fixed-income manager holding a $20 million market value position of U.S. Treasury 11¾% bonds maturing November 15, 2014 expects the economic growth rate and the inflation rate to be above market expectations in the near future. Institutional rigidities prevent any existing bonds in the portfolio from being sold in the cash market.

Situation B. The treasurer of XYZ Corporation has recently become convinced that interest rates will decline in the near future. He believes it is an opportune time to purchase his company's sinking fund bonds in advance of requirements since these bonds are trading at a discount from par value. He is preparing to purchase in the open market $20 million par value XYZ Corporation 12½% bonds maturing June 1, 2005. A $20 million par value position of these bonds is currently offered in the open market at 93. Unfortunately, the treasurer must obtain approval from the Board of Directors for such a purchase, and this approval process can take up to 2 months. The Board of Directors' approval in this instance is only a formality.

For each of these two situations, outline and calculate how the interest rate risk can be hedged using the Treasury long bond futures. Show all calculations, including the total number of futures contracts used.

PART VII

Active Portfolio Management

CHAPTER 23

The Theory of Active Portfolio Management

Thus far we have alluded to active portfolio management in only three instances: the Markowitz methodology of generating the optimal risky portfolio (Chapter 7); security analysis that generates forecasts to use as inputs with the Markowitz procedure (Chapters 17 and 18); and fixed-income portfolio management (Chapter 16). These brief analyses are not adequate to guide investment managers in a comprehensive enterprise of active portfolio management. Probably, you wonder about the seeming contradiction between our equilibrium analysis in Part III—in particular, the theory of efficient markets—and the real-world environment where profit-seeking investment managers use active management to exploit perceived market inefficiencies.

Despite the efficient market hypothesis, there are reasons to believe that active management can have effective results, and we discuss these at the outset. Next we consider the objectives of active portfolio management. We analyze two forms of active management: market timing, which is based solely on macroeconomic factors, and security selection, which includes microeconomic forecasting. At the end of the chapter we show the use of multifactor models in active portfolio management.

23.1   The Lure of Active Management

How can a theory of active portfolio management be reconciled with the notion that markets are in equilibrium? You may want to look back at the analysis in Chapter 13, but we can interpret our conclusions as follows.

Market efficiency prevails when many investors are willing to depart from maximum diversification, or a passive strategy, by adding mispriced securities to their portfolios in the hope of realizing abnormal returns. The competition for such returns ensures that prices will be near their "fair" values. Most managers will not beat the passive strategy on a risk-adjusted basis. However, in the competition for rewards to investing, exceptional managers might beat the average forecasts built into market prices.

There is both economic logic and some empirical evidence to indicate that exceptional portfolio managers can beat the average forecast. Let us discuss economic logic first. We must assume that, if no analyst can beat the passive strategy, investors will be smart enough to divert their funds from strategies entailing expensive analysis to less expensive passive strategies. In that case funds under active management will dry up, and prices will no longer reflect sophisticated forecasts. The consequent profit opportunities will lure back active managers who once again will become successful.[1] Of course, the critical assumption is that investors allocate management funds wisely. Direct evidence on that has yet to be produced.

As for empirical evidence, consider the following: (1) some portfolio managers have produced streaks of abnormal returns that are hard to label as lucky outcomes, (2) the "noise" in realized rates is enough to prevent us from rejecting outright the hypothesis that some money managers have beaten the passive strategy by a statistically small, yet economically significant, margin, and (3) some anomalies in realized returns have been sufficiently persistent to suggest that portfolio managers who identified them in a timely fashion could have beaten the passive strategy over prolonged periods.

These conclusions persuade us that there is a role for a theory of active portfolio management. Active management has an inevitable lure even if investors agree that security markets are nearly efficient.

Suppose that capital markets are perfectly efficient, that an easily accessible market index portfolio is available, and that this portfolio is for all practical purposes the efficient risky portfolio. Clearly, in this case security selection would be a futile endeavor. You would be better off with a passive strategy of allocating funds to a money market fund (the safe asset) and the market index portfolio. Under these simplifying assumptions the optimal investment strategy seems to require no effort or know-how.

Such a conclusion, however, is too hasty. Recall that the proper allocation of investment funds to the risk-free and risky portfolios requires some analysis because the fraction, y, to be invested in the risky market portfolio, M, is given by

$$y = \frac{E(r_M) - r_f}{A\sigma_M^2}$$

where $E(r_M) - r_f$ is the risk premium on M, σ_M^2 its variance, and A is the investor's coefficient of risk aversion. Any rational allocation therefore requires an estimate of σ_M and $E(r_M)$. Even a passive investor needs to do some forecasting, in other words.

Forecasting $E(r_M)$ and σ_M is further complicated by the existence of security classes that are affected by different environmental factors. Long-term bond returns, for example, are driven largely by changes in the term structure of interest rates, whereas equity returns depend on changes in the broader economic environment, including macroeconomic factors beyond interest rates. Once our investor determines relevant forecasts for separate sorts of investments, she might as well use an optimization program to determine the proper mix for the portfolio. It is easy to see how the

[1]This point is worked out fully in Grossman, Sanford J., and Stiglitz, Joseph E., "On the Impossibility of Informationally Efficient Markets," *Amerian Economic Review, 70,* June 1980.

investor may be lured away from a purely passive strategy, and we have not even considered temptations such as international stock and bond portfolios or sector portfolios.

In fact, even the definition of a "purely passive strategy" is problematic, since simple strategies involving only the market index portfolio and risk-free assets now seem to call for market analysis. For our purposes we define purely passive strategies as those that use only index funds *and* weight those funds by fixed proportions that do not vary in response to perceived market conditions. For example, a portfolio strategy that always places 60% in a stock market index fund, 30% in a bond index fund, and 10% in a money market fund is a purely passive strategy.

More important, the lure into active management may be extremely strong because the potential profit from active strategies is enormous. At the same time, competition among the multitude of active managers creates the force driving market prices to near efficiency levels. Although enormous profits may be increasingly difficult to earn, decent profits to diligent analysts must always be the rule rather than the exception. For prices to remain efficient to some degree, some analysts must be able to eke out a reasonable profit. Absence of profits would decimate the active investment management industry, eventually allowing prices to stray from informationally efficient levels. The theory of managing active portfolios is the concern of this chapter.

23.2   *Objectives of Active Portfolios*

What does an investor expect from a professional portfolio manager, and how does this expectation affect the operation of the manager? If the client were risk neutral, that is, indifferent to risk, the answer would be straightforward. The investor would expect the portfolio manager to construct a portfolio with the highest possible expected rate of return. The portfolio manager follows this dictum and is judged by the realized average rate of return.

When the client is risk averse, the answer is more difficult. Without a normative theory of portfolio management, the manager would have to consult each client before making any portfolio decision in order to ascertain that reward (average return) is commensurate with risk. Massive and constant input would be needed from the client-investors, and the economic value of professional management would be questionable.

Fortunately, the theory of mean-variance efficient portfolio management allows us to separate the "product decision," which is how to construct a mean-variance efficient risky portfolio, and the "consumption decision," or the investor's allocation of funds between the efficient risky portfolio and the safe asset. We have seen that construction of the optimal risky portfolio is purely a technical problem, resulting in a single optimal risky portfolio appropriate for all investors. Investors will differ only in how they apportion investment to that risky portfolio and the safe asset. For evidence that the theory of efficient frontiers is seeping through to the practitioner community, see the nearby box, which presents an advertisement by J.P. Morgan.

Another feature of the mean-variance theory that affects portfolio management decisions is the criterion for choosing the optimal risky portfolio. In Chapter 7 we established that the optimal risky portfolio for any investor is the one that maximizes the reward-to-variability ratio, or the expected excess rate of return (over the risk-free rate) divided by the standard deviation. A manager who uses this Markowitz methodology to construct the optimal risky portfolio will satisfy all clients regardless of risk aversion. Clients, for their part, can evaluate managers using statistical methods to draw inferences from realized rates of return to prospective, or ex ante, reward-to-variability ratios.

William Sharpe's assessment of mutual fund performance[2] is the seminal work in the area of portfolio performance evaluation (see Chapter 12). The reward-to-variability ratio has come to be known as **Sharpe's measure:**

$$S = \frac{E(r_P) - r_f}{\sigma_P}$$

It is now a common criterion for tracking performance of professionally managed portfolios.

Briefly, mean-variance portfolio theory implies that the objective of professional portfolio managers is to maximize the (ex ante) Sharpe measure, which entails maximizing the slope of the CAL (capital allocation line). A "good" manager is one whose CAL is steeper than the CAL representing the passive strategy of holding a market index portfolio. Clients can observe rates of return and compute the realized Sharpe measure (the ex post CAL) to evaluate the relative performance of their manager.

Ideally, clients would like to invest their funds with the most able manager, one who consistently obtains the highest Sharpe measure and presumably has real forecasting ability. This is true for all clients regardless of their degree of risk aversion. At the same time, each client must decide what fraction of investment funds to allocate to this manager, placing the remainder in a safe fund. If the manager's Sharpe measure is constant over time (and can be estimated by clients), the investor can compute the optimal fraction (y) to be invested with the manager as

$$y = \frac{E(r_P) - r_f}{A\sigma_P^2}$$

based on the portfolio long-term average return and variance. The remainder will be invested in a money market fund.

The manager's ex ante Sharpe measure from updated forecasts will be constantly varying. Clients would have liked to increase their allocation to the risky portfolio when the forecasts are optimistic, and vice versa. However, it would be impractical to constantly communicate updated forecasts to clients and for them to constantly revise their allocation between the risky portfolios and risk-free asset.

---

[2]Sharpe, William F., "Mutual Fund Performance," *Journal of Business, Supplement on Security Prices, 39,* January 1966.

How J. P. Morgan Investment
sponsors in international

International fixed income securities account for nearly half the world's $5.4 trillion bond market—and offer plan sponsors increasingly attractive opportunities. J.P. Morgan Investment, the leader in this field, manages more than $3 billion of international fixed income securities. We believe you should consider including international bonds in your pension portfolio.

Estimated market value $5.4 trillion
(publicly issued securities)

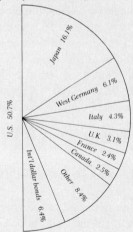

U.S. 50.7%

Japan 16.1%

West Germany 6.1%

Italy 4.3%

U.K. 3.1%

France 2.4%

Canada 2.5%

Other 8.4%

Int'l dollar bonds 6.4%

Shown at J.P. Morgan Investment's London headquarters are international fixed income team members (left to right) Anthony G. Bird, Hans K.-E. Danielsson, Bernard A. Wagenmann, and Adrian F. Lee.

finds opportunities for plan
fixed income markets

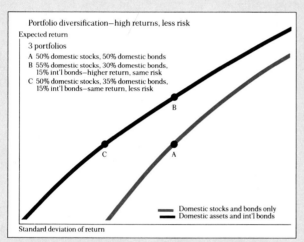

Portfolio diversification—high returns, less risk

Expected return

3 portfolios
A 50% domestic stocks, 50% domestic bonds
B 55% domestic stocks, 30% domestic bonds,
   15% int'l bonds—higher return, same risk
C 50% domestic stocks, 35% domestic bonds,
   15% int'l bonds—same return, less risk

        Domestic stocks and bonds only
        Domestic assets and int'l bonds

Standard deviation of return

The graph above shows that international fixed income investments can reduce your portfolio's risk and improve its return. Even if your pension plan already includes international equities, bonds will provide an effective way to further diversify your portfolio at lower levels of risk. In addition, the immediate outlook for international bonds is particularly favorable due to government fiscal and monetary policies now taking effect in many non-U.S. economies.

Managing markets and currencies

At J.P. Morgan Investment we seek to maximize long-term benefits for our clients, as well as to capitalize on short-term market movements. We select the markets most likely to offer the best return. At the same time we ensure maximum control of currency risk through active hedging.

Using this approach, J.P. Morgan Investment has outperformed return indexes in both rising and falling markets.

Active management, global strength

Our strength in international fixed income management is our global network of portfolio managers, analysts, and traders, and the worldwide resources of The Morgan Bank. Professionals in New York, London, Singapore, and Tokyo continuously monitor and assess market developments to find the opportunities that will produce the best returns for our clients.

To learn more about our ideas and strengths in international fixed income management, write or call: Adrian F. Lee, Vice President, J.P. Morgan Investment Management Inc., 83 Pall Mall, London sw1y 5es; telephone 01-930 9444. Or Anthony P. Wilson, Vice President, 522 Fifth Avenue, New York, NY 10036; telephone (212) 837-2300.

J.P. Morgan Investment—An active investor in world capital markets. J.P. Morgan Investment has managed international bonds since 1977. We participate actively in both U.S. and international fixed income markets. Our International Investment Group, headquartered in London since 1974, serves clients all over the world, and specializes in managing single and multicurrency portfolios for corporations and governments diversifying into other markets.

J.P. Morgan
Investment

Allowing managers to shift funds between their optimal risky portfolio and a safe asset according to their forecasts alleviates the problem. Indeed, many stock funds allow the managers reasonable flexibility to do just that.

23.3 Market Timing

Consider the results of the following two different investment strategies:

1. An investor who put $1,000 in 30-day commercial paper on January 1, 1927, and rolled over all proceeds into 30-day paper (or into 30-day T-bills after they were introduced) would have ended on December 31, 1978, 52 years later, with $3,600.
2. An investor who put $1,000 in the NYSE index on January 1, 1927, and reinvested all dividends in that portfolio would have ended on December 31, 1978, with $67,500.

Suppose we define perfect **market timing** as the ability to tell (with certainty) at the beginning of each month whether the NYSE portfolio will outperform the 30-day paper portfolio. Accordingly, at the beginning of each month, the market timer shifts all funds into either cash equivalents (30-day paper) or equities (the NYSE portfolio), whichever is predicted to do better. Beginning with $1,000 on the same date, how would the perfect timer have ended up 52 years later?

This is how Professor Robert Merton began a seminar with finance professors several years ago. As he collected responses, the boldest guess was a few million dollars. The correct answer: $5.36 *billion*.

Concept Check	Question 1. What was the monthly and annual compounded rate of return for the three strategies over the period 1926 to 1978?

These numbers have some lessons for us. The first has to do with the power of compounding. Its effect is particularly important because more and more of the funds under management represent pension savings. The horizons of such investments may not be as long as 52 years, but by and large they are measured in decades at least, making compounding a significant factor.

Another result that may seem surprising at first is the huge difference between the end-of-period value of the all-safe asset strategy ($3,600) and that of the all-equity strategy ($67,500). Why would anyone invest in safe assets given this historical record? If you have internalized the lessons of previous chapters, you know the reason: risk. The average rates of return and the standard deviations on the all-bills and all-equity strategies are:

	Arithmetic Mean	Standard Deviation
Bills	2.55	2.10
Equities	10.70	22.14

The significantly higher standard deviation of the rate of return on the equity portfolio is commensurate with its significantly higher average return.

Can we also view the rate of return premium on the perfect-timing fund as a risk premium? The answer must be "no," because the perfect timer never does worse than either bills or the market. The extra return is not compensation for the possibility of poor returns but is attributable to superior analysis. It is the value of superior information that is reflected in the tremendous end-of-period value of the portfolio.

The monthly rate-of-return statistics for the all-equity portfolio and the timing portfolio are

Per Month	All Equities (%)	Perfect Timer No Charge (%)	Perfect Timer Fair Charge (%)
Average rate of return	.85	2.58	.55
Average excess return over return on safe asset	.64	2.37	.34
Standard deviation	5.89	3.82	3.55
Highest return	38.55	38.55	30.14
Lowest return	−29.12	.06	−7.06
Coefficient of skewness	.42	4.28	2.84

Ignore for the moment the third column ("Perfect Timer—Fair Charge"). The first two rows of results are self-explanatory. The third item, standard deviation, requires some discussion. The standard deviation of the rate of return earned by the perfect market timer was 3.82%, far greater than the volatility of T-bill returns over the same period. Does this imply that (perfect) timing is a riskier strategy than investing in bills? No. For this analysis standard deviation is a misleading measure of risk.

To see why, consider how you might choose between two hypothetical strategies: the first offers a sure rate of return of 5%; the second strategy offers an uncertain return that is given by 5% *plus* a random number that is zero with probability .5 and 5% with probability .5. The characteristics of each strategy are

	Strategy 1 (%)	Strategy 2 (%)
Expected return	5	7.5
Standard deviation	0	2.5
Highest return	5	10.0
Lowest return	5	5.0

Clearly, strategy 2 dominates strategy 1 since its rate of return is *at least* equal to that of strategy 1 and sometimes greater. No matter how risk averse you are, you will always prefer strategy 2 to strategy 1, despite the significant standard deviation of strategy 2. Compared to strategy 1, strategy 2 provides only "good surprises," so the standard deviation in this case cannot be a measure of risk.

These results are analogous to the case of the perfect timer compared with an all-equity or all-bills strategy. In every period the perfect timer obtains at least as good a return, in some cases a better one. Therefore the timer's standard deviation is a misleading measure of risk compared to an all-equity or all-bills strategy.

Returning to the empirical results, you can see that the highest rate of return is identical for the all-equity and the timing strategies, whereas the lowest rate of return is positive for the perfect timer and disastrous for the all-equity portfolio. Another reflection of this is seen in the coefficient of skewness, which measures the asymmetry of the distribution of returns. Because the equity portfolio is almost (but not exactly) normally distributed, its coefficient of skewness is very low at .42. In contrast, the perfect timing strategy effectively eliminates the negative tail of the distribution of portfolio returns (the part below the risk-free rate). Its returns are "skewed to the right," and its coefficient of skewness is therefore quite large, 4.28.

Now for the third column, "Perfect Timer—Fair Charge," which is perhaps the most interesting of the three. Most assuredly, the perfect timer will charge clients for such a valuable service. (The perfect timer may have other-worldly predictive powers, but saintly benevolence is unlikely.)

Subtracting a fair fee (discussed later) from the monthly rate of return of the timer's portfolio gives us an average rate of return lower than that of the passive, all-equity strategy. However, because the fee is *assumed* to be fair, the two portfolios (the all-equity strategy and the market timing with fee strategy) must be equally attractive after risk adjustment. In this case, again, the standard deviation of the market timing strategy (with fee) is of no help in adjusting for risk because the coefficient of skewness remains high, 2.84. In other words, standard mean-variance analysis is quite complicated for valuing market timing. We need an alternative approach.

Valuing Market Timing as an Option

The key to analyzing the pattern of returns to the perfect market timer is to recognize that perfect foresight is equivalent to holding a call option on the equity portfolio. The perfect timer invests 100% in either the safe asset or the equity portfolio, whichever will yield the higher return. This is shown in Figure 23.1. The rate of return is bounded from below by r_f.

To see the value of information as an option, suppose that the market index currently is at S_0, and that a call option on the index has an exercise price of $X = S_0(1 + r_f)$. If the market outperforms bills over the coming period, S_T will exceed X, whereas it will be less than X otherwise. Now look at the payoff to a portfolio consisting of this option and S_0 dollars invested in bills.

FIGURE 23.1

Rate of return of a
perfect market timer.

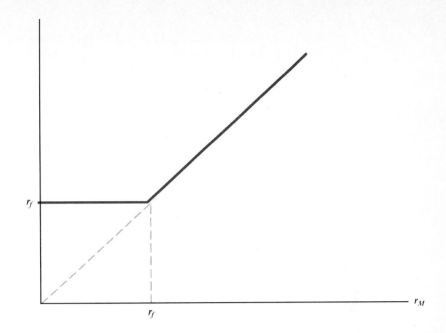

	Payoff to Portfolio	
	$S_T < X$	$S_T \geq X$
Bills:	$S_0(1 + r_f)$	$S_0(1 + r_f)$
Option:	0	$S_T - X$
TOTAL	$S_0(1 + r_f)$	S_T

The portfolio pays the risk-free return when the market is bearish (that is, the market return is less than the risk-free rate), and pays the market return when the market is bullish and beats bills. Such a portfolio is a perfect market timer. Consequently, we can measure the value of perfect ability as the value of the call option, because a call enables the investor to earn the market return only when it exceeds r_f.

This insight lets Merton[3] value timing ability using the theory of option valuation, and from this we calculate our fair charge for timing.

The Value of Imperfect Forecasting

Unfortunately, managers are not perfect forecasters, as you and Merton know. It seems pretty obvious that if managers are right most of the time they are doing very well. However, when we say right "most of the time," we cannot mean merely the

---

[3]Merton, Robert C., "On Market Timing and Investment Performance: An Equilibrium Theory of Value for Market Forecasts," *Journal of Business,* July 1981.

percentage of the time a manager is right. The weather forecaster in Tucson, Arizona, who *always* predicts no rain, may be right 90% of the time. But a high success rate for a "stopped-clock" strategy clearly is not evidence of forecasting ability.

Similarly, the appropriate measure of market forecasting ability is not the overall proportion of correct forecasts. If the market is up 2 days out of 3 and a forecaster always predicts a market advance, the two thirds success rate is not a measure of forecasting ability. We need to examine the proportion of bull markets ($r_M > r_f$) correctly forecast *and* the proportion of bear markets ($r_M < r_f$) correctly forecast.

If we call P_1 the proportion of the correct forecasts of bull markets and P_2 the proportion for bear markets, then $P_1 + P_2 - 1$ is the correct measure of timing ability. For example, a forecaster who always guesses correctly will have $P_1 = P_2 = 1$, and will show ability of 1 (100%). An analyst who always bets on a bear market will mispredict all bull markets ($P_1 = 0$), will correctly "predict" all bear markets ($P_2 = 1$), and will end up with timing ability of $P_1 + P_2 - 1 = 0$. If C denotes the (call option) value of a perfect market timer, then ($P_1 + P_2 - 1$)C measures the value of imperfect forecasting ability.

Concept Check

Question 2. What is the market timing score of someone who flips a fair coin to predict the market?

23.4 Security Selection: The Treynor-Black Model

Overview of the Treynor-Black Model

Security analysis is the other form of active portfolio management besides timing the overall market. Suppose that you are an analyst studying individual securities. It is quite likely that you will turn up several securities that appear to be mispriced. They offer positive anticipated alphas to the investor. But how do you exploit your analysis? Concentrating a portfolio on these securities entails a cost, namely, the firm-specific risk that you could shed by more fully diversifying. As an active manager you must strike a balance between aggressive exploitation of perceived security mispricing and diversification motives that dictate that a few stocks should not dominate the portfolio.

Treynor and Black[4] developed an optimizing model for portfolio managers who use security analysis. It represents a portfolio management theory that assumes security markets are *nearly* efficient. The essence of the model is this:

1. Security analysts in an active investment management organization can analyze in

---

[4]Treynor, Jack, and Black, Fischer, "How to Use Security Analysis to Improve Portfolio Selection," *Journal of Business*, January 1973.

depth only a relatively small number of stocks out of the entire universe of securities. The securities not analyzed are assumed to be fairly priced.

2. For the purpose of efficient diversification, the market index portfolio is the baseline portfolio, which the model treats as the passive portfolio.

3. The macro forecasting unit of the investment management firm provides forecasts of the expected rate of return and variance of the passive (market index) portfolio.

4. The objective of security analysis is to form an active portfolio of a necessarily limited number of securities. Perceived mispricing of the analyzed securities is what guides the composition of this active portfolio.

5. Analysts follow several steps to make up the active portfolio and evaluate its expected performance:

    a. Estimate the beta of each analyzed security and its residual risk. From the beta and the macro forecast, $E(r_M) - r_f$, determine the *required* rate of return of the security.

    b. Given the degree of mispricing of each security, determine its expected return and expected *abnormal* return (alpha).

    c. Calculate the cost of less than full diversification. The nonsystematic risk of the mispriced stock, the variance of the stock's residual, offsets the benefit (alpha) of specializing in an underpriced security.

    d. Use the estimates for the values of alpha, beta, and residual risk to determine the optimal weight of each security in the active portfolio.

    e. Estimate the alpha, beta, and residual risk for the active portfolio according to the weights of the securities in the portfolio.

6. The macroeconomic forecasts for the passive index portfolio and the composite forecasts for the active portfolio are used to determine the optimal risky portfolio, which will be a combination of the passive and active portfolios.

Treynor and Black's model did not take the industry by storm. This is unfortunate for several reasons:

1. Just as even imperfect market timing ability has enormous value, security analysis of the sort Treynor and Black propose has similar potential value. Even with far from perfect security analysis, proper active management can add value.

2. The Treynor-Black model is conceptually easy to implement. Moreover, it is useful even when some of its simplifying assumptions are relaxed.

3. The model lends itself to use in decentralized organizations. This property is essential to efficiency in complex organizations.

Portfolio Construction

Assuming that all securities are fairly priced, and using the index model as a guideline for the rate of return on fairly priced securities, the rate of return on the ith security is given by

$$r_i = r_f + \beta_i(r_M - r_f) + e_i \qquad (23.1)$$

where e_i is the zero mean, firm-specific disturbance.

Absent security analysis, Treynor and Black (TB) take equation 23.1 to represent the rate of return on all securities and assume that the market portfolio, M, is the efficient portfolio. For simplicity, they also assume that the nonsystematic components of returns, e_i, are independent across securities. As for market timing, TB assume that the relevant passive portfolio forecast already has been made, so that the expected return on the market index, r_M, as well as its variance, σ_M^2, has been assessed.

Now a portfolio manager unleashes a team of security analysts to investigate a subset of the universe of available securities. The objective is to form an active portfolio of positions in the analyzed securities to be mixed with the index portfolio. For each security, k, that is researched, we write the rate of return as

$$r_k = r_f + \beta_k(r_M - r_f) + e_k + \alpha_k \tag{23.2}$$

where α_k represents the extra expected return (called the abnormal return) attributable to any perceived mispricing of the security. Thus for each security analyzed the research team estimates the parameters

$$\alpha_k, \ \beta_k, \ \sigma^2(e_k)$$

If all the α_k turn out to be zero, there would be no reason to depart from the passive strategy and the index portfolio M would remain the manager's choice. However, this is a remote possibility. In general, there will be a significant number of nonzero alpha values, some positive and some negative.

One way to get an overview of the TB methodology is to examine what we should do with the active portfolio once we get it. Suppose that the **active portfolio** *(A)* has been constructed somehow and has the parameters

$$\alpha_A, \ \beta_A, \ \sigma^2(e_A)$$

Its total variance is the sum of its systematic variance, $\beta_A^2\sigma_M^2$, plus the nonsystematic variance $\sigma^2(e_A)$. Its covariance with the market index portfolio, M, is

$$\text{Cov}(r_A, r_M) = \beta_A\sigma_M^2$$

Figure 23.2 shows the optimization process with active and passive portfolios. The dashed efficient frontier represents the universe of all securities assuming that they are all fairly priced, that is, that all alphas are zero. By definition, the market index, M, is on this efficient frontier and is tangent to the (broken) capital market line (CML). In practice the analysts do not need to know this frontier. They need only to observe the market index portfolio and construct a portfolio resulting in a capital allocation line that lies above the CML. Given their perceived superior analysis, they will view the market index portfolio as inefficient: the active portfolio, A, constructed from mispriced securities must lie, by design, above the CML.

To locate the active portfolio A in Figure 23.2, we need its expected return and standard deviation. The standard deviation is

$$\sigma_A = [\beta_A^2\sigma_M^2 + \sigma^2(e_A)]^{1/2}$$

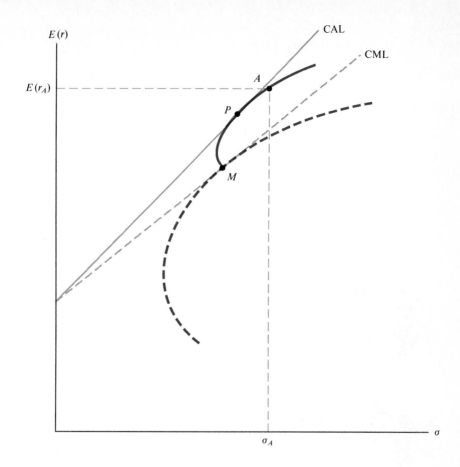

FIGURE 23.2

The optimization
process with active
and passive portfolios.

Because of the positive alpha value that is forecast for *A*, it plots above the (broken) CML with expected return

$$E(r_A) = \alpha_A + r_f + \beta_A[E(r_M) - r_f]$$

The optimal combination of the active portfolio, *A*, with the **passive portfolio,** *M*, is a simple application of the construction of optimal risky portfolios from two component assets that we first encountered in Chapter 7. Because the active portfolio is not perfectly correlated with the market index portfolio, we need to account for their mutual correlation in the determination of the optimal allocation between the two portfolios. This is evident from the solid blue efficient frontier that passes through *M* and *A*. It supports the optimal capital allocation line (CAL) and identifies the optimal risky portfolio, *P*, which combines portfolios *A* and *M*, and is the tangency point of the CAL to the efficient frontier. The active portfolio *A* in this example is not the ultimately efficient portfolio, because we need to mix *A* with the passive market portfolio to achieve greater diversification.

Let us now outline the algebraic approach to this optimization problem. If we invest a proportion, w, in the active portfolio and $1 - w$ in the market index, the portfolio return will be

$$r_p(w) = w\, r_A + (1 - w)r_M$$

We can use this equation to calculate Sharpe's measure (dividing the mean excess return by the standard deviation of the return) as a function of the weight, w, then find the optimal weight, w^*, that maximizes the measure. This is the value of w that makes P the optimal tangency portfolio in Figure 23.2. This maximization ultimately leads to the solution

$$w^* = \frac{w_0}{1 + (1 - \beta_A)w_0} \tag{23.3}$$

where

$$w_0 = \frac{\alpha_A/\sigma^2(e_A)}{[E(r_M) - r_f]/\sigma_M^2}$$

Equation 23.3 actually is a restatement of the formula for determining the optimal weights to invest in two risky assets that you first encountered in Chapter 7. Here we state the equation in terms of portfolio alphas relative to the CAPM, but the approach is identical.

First look at w_0. This would be the optimal weight in the active portfolio *if* its beta (β_A) were 1.0. This weight is a ratio of two measures. In the numerator is the reward from the active portfolio, α_A, reflecting its mispricing, against the nonsystematic risk, $\sigma^2(e_A)$, incurred in holding it. This ratio is divided by an analogous measure for the index portfolio

$$\frac{E(r_M) - r_f}{\sigma_M^2}$$

which is the ratio of the reward from holding the index $E(r_M) - r_f$ to its risk, σ_M^2.

The intuition here is straightforward. We mix the active portfolio with the index for the benefit of diversification. The position to take in the active portfolio relative to the market portfolio depends on the ratio of the active portfolio's abnormal return, α_A, to its potentially diversifiable risk, $\sigma^2(e_A)$. The optimal weights also will depend on the opportunities for diversification, which in turn depend on the correlation between the two portfolios and can be measured by β_A. To adjust the optimal weight for the fact that the beta of the active portfolio may not be 1.0, we compute w^* in equation 23.3.

What is the reward-to-variability ratio of the optimal risky portfolio once we find the best mix, w^*, of the active and passive index portfolio? It turns out that if we compute the square of Sharpe's measure of the risky portfolio, we can separate the contributions of the index and active portfolios as follows:

$$S_P^2 = S_M^2 + \frac{\alpha_A^2}{\sigma^2(e_A)} \tag{23.4}$$

$$= \left[\frac{E(r_M) - r_f}{\sigma_M}\right]^2 + \left[\frac{\alpha_A}{\sigma(e_A)}\right]^2$$

This decomposition of the Sharpe measure of the optimal risky portfolio, which by the way is valid *only* for the optimal portfolio, tells us how to construct the active portfolio. Look at the last equality in equation 23.4. It shows that the highest Sharpe measure for the risky portfolio will be attained when we construct an active portfolio that maximizes the value of $\alpha_A/\sigma(e_A)$. The ratio of alpha to residual standard deviation of the active portfolio will be maximized when we choose a weight for the kth analyzed security as follows:

$$w_k = \frac{\alpha_k/\sigma^2(e_k)}{\displaystyle\sum_{i=1}^{n} \alpha_i/\sigma^2(e_i)} \tag{23.5}$$

This makes sense: the weight of a security in the active portfolio depends on the ratio of the degree of mispricing, α_k, to the nonsystematic risk, $\sigma^2(e_k)$, of the security. The denominator, the sum of the ratio across securities, is a scale factor to guarantee that the weights sum to one.

Note from equation 23.4 that the square of Sharpe's measure of the optimal risky portfolio is increased over the square of the Sharpe measure of the passive (market-index) portfolio by the amount

$$\left[\frac{\alpha_A}{\sigma(e_A)}\right]^2$$

The ratio of the degree of mispricing, α_A, to the nonsystematic standard deviation, $\sigma(e_A)$, becomes a natural performance measure of the active component of the risky portfolio. Sometimes this is called the **appraisal ratio.**

We can also calculate the contribution of a single security in the active portfolio to the portfolio's overall performance. When the active portfolio contains n analyzed securities, the total improvement in the squared Sharpe measure equals the sum of the squared appraisal ratios of the analyzed securities,

$$\left[\frac{\alpha_A}{\sigma(e_A)}\right]^2 = \sum_{i=1}^{n} \left[\frac{\alpha_i}{\sigma(e_i)}\right]^2$$

The appraisal ratio for each security, $\alpha_i/\sigma(e_i)$, is a measure of the contribution of that security to the performance of the active portfolio.

The best way to illustrate the Treynor-Black process is through an example. Suppose that the macroforecasting unit of Drex Portfolio Inc. (DPF) issues a forecast for a 15% market return. The forecast's standard error is 20%. The risk-free rate is 7%. The macro data can be summarized as follows:

$$E(r_M) - r_f = .08 \; ; \; \sigma_M = .20$$

At the same time the security analysis division submits to the portfolio manager the following forecast of annual returns for the three securities that it covers:

Stock	α	β	$\sigma(e)$
1	.07	1.6	.45
2	−.05	1.0	.32
3	.03	.5	.26

Note that the alpha estimates appear reasonably moderate. These estimates of the residual standard deviations are correlated with the betas, just as they are in reality. The magnitudes also reflect typical values for NYSE stocks.

First, let us construct the optimal active portfolio implied by the security analyst input list. To do so we compute the appraisal ratios as follows:

Stock	$\alpha/\sigma^2(e)$		$\dfrac{\alpha_i}{\sigma^2(e_i)} \bigg/ \displaystyle\sum_{i=1}^{3} \dfrac{\alpha_i}{\sigma^2(e_i)}$
1	$.07/.45^2 =$	.3457	$.3457/.3012 = 1.1477$
2	$-.05/.32^2 =$	−.4883	$-.4883/.3012 = -1.6212$
3	$.03/.26^2 =$	.4438	$.4438/.3012 = 1.4735$
TOTAL		.3012	1.0000

The last column presents the optimal positions of each of the three securities in the active portfolio. Obviously, stock 2 has a negative weight. The magnitudes of the individual positions in the active portfolio (114.77% in stock 1, for example) seem quite extreme. However, this should not concern us because the active portfolio will later be mixed with the well-diversified market index portfolio, resulting in much more moderate positions, as we shall see shortly.

The forecasts for the stocks, together with the proposed composition of the active portfolio, lead to the following parameter estimates for the active portfolio:

$$\alpha_A = 1.1477 \times .07 + (-1.6212) \times (-.05) + 1.4735 \times .03 = .2056$$
$$\beta_A = 1.1477 \times 1.6 + (-1.6212) \times 1.0 + 1.4735 \times .5 = .9519$$

$$\sigma(e_A) = [1.1477^2 \times .45^2 + (-1.6212)^2 \times .32^2 + 1.4735^2 \times .26^2]^{1/2} = .8262$$

Note that the negative weight (short position) on the negative alpha stock results in a positive contribution to the alpha of the active portfolio. Note also that because of the assumption that the stock residuals are uncorrelated, the active portfolio's residual variance is simply the weighted sum of the individual stock residual variances, with the squared portfolio proportions as weights.

The parameters of the active portfolio are now used to determine its proportion in the overall risky portfolio.

$$w_0 = \frac{\alpha_A/\sigma^2(e_A)}{[E(r_M) - r_f]/\sigma_M^2}$$

$$= \frac{.2056/.6826}{.08/.04}$$

$$= .1506$$

$$w^* = \frac{w_0}{1 + (1 - \beta_A)w_0}$$

$$= \frac{.1506}{1 + (1 - .9519) \times .1506}$$

$$= .1495$$

Although the active portfolio's alpha is impressive (20.56%), its proportion in the overall risky portfolio, before adjustment for beta, is only 15.06%, because of its large nonsystematic risk (82.62%). Such is the importance of diversification. As it happens, the beta of the active portfolio is almost 1.0, and hence the correction for beta (from w_0 to w^*) is small, from 15.06% to 14.95%. The direction of the change makes sense. If the beta of the active portfolio is low (less than 1.0) there are more potential gains from diversification. Hence a smaller position in the active portfolio is called for. If the beta of the active portfolio were significantly greater than 1.0, a larger correction in the opposite direction would be called for.

The proportions of the individual stocks in the active portfolio, together with the proportion of the active portfolio in the overall risky portfolio, determine the proportions of each individual stock in the overall risky portfolio.

Stock	Final Position		
1	.1495	× 1.1477	= .1716
2	.1495	× (−1.6212)	= −.2424
3	.1495	× 1.4735	= .2202
Active portfolio			.1495
Market portfolio			.8505
			1.0000

The parameters of the active portfolio and market-index portfolio are now used to forecast the performance of the optimal, overall risky portfolio. When optimized, a property of the risky portfolio is that its squared Sharpe measure increases by the square of the active portfolio's appraisal ratio:

$$S_P^2 = \left[\frac{E(r_M) - r_f}{\sigma_M}\right]^2 + \left[\frac{\alpha_A}{\sigma(e_A)}\right]^2$$

$$= .16 + .0619 = .2219$$

and hence the Sharpe measure of the active portfolio is $\sqrt{.2219} = .47$, compared with .40 for the passive portfolio.

23.5 Multifactor Models and Active Portfolio Management

Perhaps in the foreseeable future a multifactor structure of security returns will be developed and accepted as conventional wisdom. So far our analytical framework for active portfolio management seems to rest on the validity of the index model, that is, on a single-factor security model. Despite this appearance, a multifactor structure will not affect the construction of the active portfolio because the entire TB analysis focuses on the residuals of the index model. If we were to replace the one-factor model with a multifactor model, we would continue to form the active portfolio by calculating each security's alpha relative to its fair return (given its betas on *all* factors), and again would combine the active portfolio with the portfolio that would be formed in the absence of security analysis. The multifactor framework, however, does raise several new issues in portfolio management.

You saw in Chapter 7 how the index model simplifies the construction of the input list necessary for portfolio optimization programs. If

$$r_i - r_f = \alpha_i + \beta_i(r_M - r_f) + e_i$$

adequately describes the security market, then the variance of any asset is the sum of systematic and nonsystematic risk: $\sigma^2(r_i) = \beta_i^2\sigma_M^2 + \sigma^2(e_i)$, and the covariance between any two assets is $\beta_i\beta_j\sigma_M^2$.

How do we generalize this rule to use in a multifactor model? To simplify, let us consider a two-factor world, and let us call the two-factor portfolios M and H. Then we generalize the index model to

$$\begin{aligned} r_i - r_f &= \beta_{iM}(r_M - r_f) + \beta_{iH}(r_H - r_f) + \alpha_i + e_i \qquad (23.6) \\ &= r_\beta + e_i \end{aligned}$$

β_M and β_H are the betas of the security relative to portfolios M and H. Given the rates of return on the factor portfolios, r_M and r_H, the fair excess rate of return over r_f on a security is denoted r_β and its expected abnormal return is α_i.

How can we use equation 23.6 to form optimal portfolios? Suppose that investors simply wish to maximize the Sharpe measures of their portfolios. The factor structure of equation 23.6 can be used to generate the inputs for the Markowitz portfolio selection algorithm. The variance and covariance estimates are now more complex, however:

$$\sigma^2(r_i) = \beta_{iM}^2 \sigma_M^2 + \beta_{iH}^2 \sigma_H^2 + 2\beta_{iM}\beta_{iH}\text{Cov}(r_M, r_H) + \sigma^2(e_i)$$

$$\text{Cov}(r_i, r_j) = \beta_{iM}\beta_{jM}\sigma_M^2 + \beta_{iH}\beta_{jH}\sigma_H^2 + (\beta_{iM}\beta_{jH} + \beta_{jM}\beta_{iH})\text{Cov}(r_M, r_H)$$

Nevertheless, the informational economy of the factor model still is valuable, because we can estimate a covariance matrix for an n-security portfolio from:

$$n \text{ estimates of } \beta_{iM}$$
$$n \text{ estimates of } \beta_{iH}$$
$$n \text{ estimates of } \sigma^2(e_i)$$
$$1 \text{ estimate of } \sigma_M^2$$
$$1 \text{ estimate of } \sigma_H^2$$

rather than $n(n + 1)/2$ separate variance and covariance estimates. Thus the factor structure continues to simplify portfolio construction issues.

The factor structure also suggests an efficient method to allocate research effort. Analysts can specialize in forecasting means and variances of different factor portfolios. Having established factor betas, they can form a covariance matrix to be used together with expected security returns generated by the CAPM or APT to construct an optimal passive risky portfolio. If active analysis of individual stocks also is attempted, the procedure of constructing the optimal active portfolio and its optimal combination with the passive portfolio is identical to that followed in the single-factor case.

It is likely, however, that the factor structure of the market has hedging implications. As we saw in Chapter 11, this means that clients will be willing to accept an inferior Sharpe measure (in terms of dollar returns) to maintain a risky portfolio that has the desired hedge qualities. Portfolio optimization for these investors obviously is more complicated, requiring specific information on client preferences. The portfolio manager will not be able to satisfy diverse clients with one portfolio.

In the case of the multifactor market even passive investors (meaning those who accept market prices as "fair") need to do a considerable amount of work. They need forecasts of the expected return and volatility of each factor return, *and* need to determine the appropriate weights on each factor portfolio to maximize their expected utility. Such a process is straightforward in principle, but quickly becomes analytically demanding.

Summary

1. A truly passive portfolio strategy entails holding the market index portfolio and a money market fund. Determining the optimal allocation to the market portfolio requires an estimate of its expected return and variance, which in turn suggests delegating some analysis to professionals.

2. Active portfolio managers attempt to construct a risky portfolio that maximizes the reward-to-variability (Sharpe) ratio.

3. The value of perfect market timing ability is considerable. The rate of return to a perfect market timer will be uncertain. However, its risk characteristics are not measurable by standard measures of portfolio risk, because perfect timing dominates a passive strategy, providing "good" surprises only.

4. Perfect timing ability is equivalent to the possession of a call option on the market portfolio, whose value can be determined using option valuation techniques such as the Black-Scholes formula.

5. With imperfect timing, the value of a timer who attempts to forecast whether stocks will outperform bills is given by the conditional probabilities of the true outcome given the forecasts: $P_1 + P_2 - 1$. Thus, if the value of perfect timing is given by the option value, C, then imperfect timing has the value $(P_1 + P_2 - 1)C$.

6. The Treynor-Black security selection model envisions that a macroeconomic forecast for market performance is available and that security analysts estimate abnormal expected rates of return, α, for various securities. Alpha is the expected rate of return on a security beyond that explained by its beta and the security market line.

7. In the Treynor-Black model the weight of each analyzed security is proportional to the ratio of its alpha to its nonsystematic risk, $\sigma^2(e)$.

8. Once the active portfolio is constructed, its alpha value, nonsystematic risk, and beta can be determined from the properties of the component securities. The optimal risky portfolio, P, is then constructed by holding a position in the active portfolio according to the ratio of α_P to $\sigma^2(e_P)$, divided by the analogous ratio for the market index portfolio. Finally, this position is adjusted by the beta of the active portfolio.

9. When the overall risky portfolio is constructed using the optimal proportions of the active portfolio and passive portfolio, its performance, as measured by the square of Sharpe's measure, is improved (over that of the passive, market index portfolio) by the amount $[\alpha_A/\sigma(e_A)]^2$.

10. The contribution of each security to the overall improvement in the performance of the active portfolio is determined by its degree of mispricing and nonsystematic risk. The contribution of each security to portfolio performance equals $[\alpha_i/\sigma(e_i)]^2$, so that for the optimal risky portfolio,

$$S_P^2 = \left[\frac{E(r_M) - r_f}{\sigma_M^2}\right]^2 + \sum_{i=1}^{n}\left[\frac{\alpha_i}{\sigma(e_i)}\right]^2$$

Key Terms

Sharpe's measure

Market timing

Active portfolio

Passive portfolio

Appraisal ratio

Selected Readings

The valuation of market timing ability using the option pricing framework was developed in:
   Merton, Robert C., "On Market Timing and Investment Performance: An Equilibrium Theory of Value for Market Forecasts," *Journal of Business,* July 1981.
The Treynor-Black model was laid out in:
   Treynor, Jack, and Black, Fischer, "How to Use Security Analysis to Improve Portfolio Selection," *Journal of Business,* January 1973.

Problems

1. The 5-year history of annual rates of return in excess of the T-bill rate for two competing stock funds is

The Bull Fund	The Unicorn Fund
−21.7	−1.3
28.7	15.5
17.0	14.4
2.9	−11.9
28.9	25.4

   a. How would these funds compare in the eye of the risk-neutral potential client?
   b. How would these funds compare by Sharpe's measure?
   c. If a risk-averse investor (with a coefficient of risk aversion $A = 3$) had to choose one of these funds to mix with T-bills, which fund would be better to choose, and how much should be invested in that fund on the basis of the available data?

2. Historical data suggest that the standard deviation of an all-equity strategy is about 5.5% per month. Suppose that the risk-free rate is now 1% per month and that market volatility is at its historical level. What would be a fair monthly fee to a perfect market timer, based on the Black-Scholes formula?

3. In scrutinizing the record of two market timers a fund manager comes up with the following table:

Number of months that $r_M > r_f$	135
Correctly predicted by timer A	78
Correctly predicted by timer B	86
Number of months that $r_M < r_f$	92
Correctly predicted by timer A	57
Correctly predicted by timer B	50

   a. What are the conditional probabilities, P_1 and P_2, and the total ability parameters for timers A and B?

b. Using the historical data of question 2, what is a fair monthly fee for the two timers?

4. A portfolio manager summarizes the input from the macro and micro forecasters in the following table:

Micro Forecasts

Asset	Expected Return (%)	Beta	Residual Standard Deviation
Stock A	20	1.3	58
Stock B	18	1.8	71
Stock C	17	.7	60
Stock D	12	1.0	55

Macro Forecasts

Asset	Expected Return (%)	Standard Deviation
T-bills	8	0
Passive equity Portfolio	16	23

a. Calculate expected excess returns, alpha values, and residual variances for these stocks.
b. Construct the optimal risky portfolio.
c. What is Sharpe's measure for the optimal portfolio and how much of it is contributed by the active portfolio?
d. What should be the exact makeup of the complete portfolio for an investor with a coefficient of risk aversion of 2.8?

5. Recalculate problem 4 for a portfolio manager who is not allowed to short-sell securities.
a. What is the cost in terms of Sharpe's measure of the restriction?
b. What is the utility loss to the investor ($A = 2.8$) given his new complete portfolio?

6. A portfolio management house approximates the return-generating process by a two-factor model and uses two-factor portfolios to construct its passive portfolio. The input table that is constructed by the house analysts looks as follows:

Micro Forecasts

Asset	Expected Return	Beta on M	Beta on H	Residual Standard Deviation
Stock A	20	1.2	1.8	58
Stock B	18	1.4	1.1	71
Stock C	17	.5	1.5	60
Stock D	12	1.0	.2	55

Asset	Expected Return (%)	Standard Deviation
T-bills	8	0
Factor M portfolio	16	23
Factor H portfolio	10	18

The correlation coefficient between the two-factor portfolios is .6.

    a. What is the optimal passive portfolio?

    b. By how much is the optimal passive portfolio superior to the single-factor passive portfolio, M, in terms of Sharpe's measure?

    c. Analyze the utility improvement to the $A = 2.8$ investor relative to holding portfolio M as the sole risky asset that arises from the expanded macro model of the portfolio manager.

7. Construct the optimal active and overall risky portfolio with the data of problem 6 with no restrictions on short sales.

    a. What is the Sharpe measure of the optimal risky portfolio and what is the contribution of the active portfolio to that measure?

    b. Compare the risky portfolio to that from problem 4.

    c. Analyze the utility value of the optimal risky portfolio for the $A = 2.8$ investor. Compare to that of problem 4.

8. Recalculate problem 7 with a short-sale restriction. Compare the results to those from problems 5 and 7.

CHAPTER 24

Portfolio Performance Evaluation

In Chapter 23 we surveyed investment strategies that active managers might pursue. In this chapter we ask how we can evaluate the performance of a portfolio manager. It turns out that even measuring average portfolio returns is not as straightforward as it might seem. In addition, difficulties lie in adjusting average returns for risk, which presents a host of other problems.

We begin with issues on measurement of portfolio returns. From there, we move on to conventional approaches to risk adjustment. We show the problems with these approaches when they are applied in a real and complex world. Finally, we discuss some promising developments in the theory of performance evaluation and examine evaluation procedures used in the field.

24.1 Measuring Investment Returns

The rate of return on an investment is a simple concept in the case of a one-period investment. It is simply the total proceeds derived from the investment per dollar initially invested. Proceeds must be defined broadly to include both cash distributions and capital gains. For stocks, total returns are dividends plus capital gains. For bonds, total returns are coupon or interest paid plus capital gains.

To set the stage for discussing the more subtle issues that follow, let us start with a trivial example. Consider a stock paying a dividend of $2 annually that currently sells for $50. You purchase the stock today and collect the $2 dividend, and then you sell the stock for $53 at year-end. Your rate of return is

$$\frac{\text{Total proceeds}}{\text{Initial investment}} = \frac{\text{Income} + \text{capital gain}}{50}$$

$$= \frac{2 + 3}{50}$$

$$= .10$$

$$= 10\%$$

Another way to derive the rate of return that is useful in the more difficult multiperiod case is to set up the investment as a discounted cash flow problem. Call r the rate of return that equates the present value of all cash flows from the investment with the initial outlay. In our example the stock is purchased for $50 and generates cash flows at year-end of $2 (dividend) plus $53 (sale of stock). Therefore we solve $50 = (2 + 53) / (1 + r)$ to find again that $r = .10$, or 10%.

Time-Weighted Returns vs. Dollar-Weighted Returns

When we consider investments over a period during which cash was added to or withdrawn from the portfolio, measuring the rate of return becomes more difficult. To continue our example, suppose that you were to purchase a second share of the same stock at the end of the first year, and hold both shares until the end of year 2, at which point you sell each share for $54.

Total cash outlays are

Time	Outlay
0	$50 to purchase first share
1	$53 to purchase second share a year later

Proceeds are

Time	Proceeds
1	$2 dividend from initially purchased share
2	$4 dividend from the 2 shares held in the second year, plus $108 received from selling both shares at $54 each

Using the discounted cash flow (DCF) approach, we can solve for the average return over the 2 years by equating the present values of the cash inflows and outflows:

$$50 + \frac{53}{1 + r} = \frac{2}{1 + r} + \frac{112}{(1 + r)^2}$$

resulting in $r = 7.117\%$.

This value is called the internal rate of return or the **dollar-weighted rate of return** on the investment. It is "dollar weighted" because the stock's performance in the second year, when two shares of stock are held, has a greater influence on the average overall return than the first-year return, when only one share is held.

An alternative to the internal or dollar-weighted return is the **time-weighted return.** This method ignores the number of shares of stock held in each period. The stock return in the first year was 10%. (A $50 purchase provided $2 in dividends and $3 in capital gains.) In the second year the stock had a starting value of $53 and sold at year-end for $54, for a total one-period rate of return of $3 ($2 dividend plus $1 capital gain) divided by $53 (the stock price at the start of the second year), or

5.66%. The time-weighted return is the average of 10% and 5.66%, which is 7.83%. This average return considers only the period-by-period returns without regard to the amounts invested in the stock in each period.

Note that the dollar-weighted return is less than the time-weighted return in this example. The reason is that the stock fared relatively poorly in the second year, when the investor was holding more shares. The greater weight that the dollar-weighted average places on the second-year return results in a lower measure of investment performance. In general, dollar- and time-weighted returns will differ, and the difference can be positive or negative depending on the configuration of period returns and portfolio composition.

Which measure of performance is superior? At first, it appears that the dollar-weighted return must be more relevant. After all, the more money you invest in a stock when its performance is superior, the more money you end up with. Certainly your performance measure should reflect this fact.

Time-weighted returns have their own use, however, especially in the money management industry. This is so because in some important applications a portfolio manager may not directly control the timing or the amount of money invested in securities. Pension fund management is a good example. A pension fund manager faces cash inflows into the fund when pension contributions are made, and cash outflows when pension benefits are paid. Obviously, the amount of money invested at any time can vary for reasons beyond the manager's control. Because dollars invested do not depend on the manager's choice, it is inappropriate to weight returns by dollars invested when measuring the investment ability of the manager. Consequently, the money management industry normally uses time-weighted returns for performance evaluation.

Concept Check

> Question 1. Shares of XYZ Corp. pay a $2 dividend at the end of every year on December 31. An investor buys two shares of the stock on January 1 at a price of $20 each, sells one of those shares for $22 a year later on the next January 1, and sells the second share an additional year later for $19. Find the time- and dollar-weighted rates of return on the 2-year investment.

Arithmetic Averages vs. Geometric Averages

Our example takes the arithmetic average of the two annual returns, 10% and 5.66%, as the time-weighted average, 7.83%. Another approach is to take a geometric average, denoted r_G. This approach would entail computing

$$1 + r_G = [(1.10)(1.0566)]^{1/2} \qquad (24.1)$$
$$= 1.0781$$

or

Active Portfolio Management

TABLE 24.1   Average Annual Returns by Investment Class, 1926-1986

	Arithmetic Average	Geometric Average	Difference	Standard Deviation
Common stock of small firms	18.2	12.5	5.7	36.0
Common stock of large firms	12.1	10.0	2.1	21.2
Long-term corporate bonds	5.3	5.0	0.3	8.5
Long-term Treasury bonds	4.7	4.4	0.3	8.6
U.S. Treasury bills	3.5	3.5	<0.1	3.4

From Ibbotson, Roger G., and Rex A. Sinquefield, *Stocks, Bonds, Bills, and Inflation* (SBBI), updated in *SBBI 1987 Yearbook*, Ibbotson Associates, Chicago.

$$r_G = 7.81\%$$

The motivation for this calculation comes from the principle of compounding. If dividend proceeds are reinvested, the accumulated value of an investment in the stock will grow by a factor of 1.10 in the first year and by an additional factor of 1.0566 in the second year. The compound average growth rate is then calculated:

$$(1 + r_G)^2 = (1.10)(1.0566)$$

Taking the square root of each side results in equation 24.1. In general terms, for an *n*-period investment, the geometric average rate of return is given by

$$1 + r_G = [(1 + r_1)(1 + r_2) \ldots (1 + r_n)]^{1/n}$$

where r_t is the return in each time period.

Note that the geometric average return in this example, 7.81%, is slightly less than the arithmetic average return, 7.83%. This is a general property: geometric averages never exceed arithmetic averages, and the difference between the two becomes greater as the variability of period-by-period returns becomes greater.

For example, consider Table 24.1, which presents arithmetic and geometric returns over the 1926 to 1986 period for a variety of investments. The arithmetic averages all exceed the geometric averages, and the difference is greatest for stocks of small firms, where annual returns exhibit the greatest standard deviation. Indeed, the difference between the two averages falls to zero only when there is no variation in yearly returns, although the table indicates that, by the time the standard deviation falls to a level characteristic of T-bills, the difference is quite small.

Here is another return question. Which is the superior measure of investment performance, the arithmetic average or the geometric average? The geometric average has considerable appeal because it represents exactly the constant rate of return we would have needed to earn in each year to match actual performance over some past investment period. It is an excellent measure of *past* performance. However, if our focus is on future performance, then the arithmetic average is the statistic of interest because it is an unbiased estimate of the portfolio's expected future return (assuming of course, that the expected return does not change over time). In contrast, because the geometric return over a sample period is always less than the arithmetic mean, it constitutes a downward-biased estimator of the stock's expected return in any future year.

To illustrate this concept, suppose that in any period a stock will either double in value ($r = 100\%$) with probability of .5, or halve in value ($r = -50\%$) with probability .5. The table following illustrates these outcomes:

Investment Outcome	Final Value of Each Dollar Invested	1-Year Rate of Return
Double	$2	100%
Halve	$0.50	−50%

Suppose that the stock's performance over a 2-year period is characteristic of the probability distribution, doubling in 1 year, and halving in the other. The stock's price ends up exactly where it started, and the geometric average annual return is zero:

$$1 + r_G = [(1 + r_1)(1 + r_2)]^{1/2}$$
$$= [(1 + 1)(1 - .50)]^{1/2}$$
$$= 1$$

so that

$$r_G = 0$$

which confirms that a zero year-by-year return would have replicated the total return earned on the stock.

The expected annual future rate of return on the stock, however, is *not* zero: it is the arithmetic average of 100% and −50%: $(100 - 50)/2 = 25\%$. To confirm this, note that there are two equally likely outcomes for each dollar invested: either a gain of $1 (when $r = 100\%$) or a loss of $.50 (when $r = -50\%$). The expected profit is ($1 − $.50)/2 = $.25, for a 25% expected rate of return. The profit in the good year more than offsets the loss in the bad year, despite the fact that the geometric return is zero. The arithmetic average return thus provides the best guide to expected future returns from an investment.

This argument carries forward into multiperiod investments. Consider, for example, all the possible outcomes over a 2-year period:

Investment Outcome	Final Value of Each Dollar Invested	Total Return Over 2 Years
Double, double	$4	300%
Double, halve	$1	0
Halve, double	$1	0
Halve, halve	$.25	−75%

The expected final value of each dollar invested is $(4 + 1 + 1 + .25)/4 = \$1.5625$ for 2 years, again indicating an average rate of return of 25% per year, equal to the arithmetic average. Note than an investment yielding 25% per year with certainty will yield the same final compounded value as the expected final value of this investment, as $1.25^2 = 1.5625$. The arithmetic average return on the stock is $[300 + 0 + 0 + (-75)]/4 = 56.25\%$ per 2 years, for an effective annual return of 25%, that is, $1.5625^{1/2} - 1$. In contrast, the geometric mean return is zero:

$$[(1 + 3)(1 + 0)(1 + 0)(1 - .75)]^{1/4} = 1.0$$

Again, the arithmetic average is the better guide to *future* performance.

Concept Check

Question 2. Suppose that a stock now selling for $100 will either increase in value by 15% by year-end with probability .5, or fall in value by 5% with probability .5. The stock pays no dividends.
a. What are the geometric and arithmetic mean returns on the stock?
b. What is the expected end-of-year value of the share?
c. Which measure of expected return is superior?

24.2 The Conventional Theory of Performance Evaluation

Calculating average portfolio returns does not mean the task is done. Returns must be adjusted for risk before they can be compared meaningfully. The simplest and most popular way to adjust returns for portfolio risk is to compare rates of return with those of other investment funds with similar risk characteristics. For example, high-yield bond portfolios are grouped into one "universe," growth stock equity funds are grouped into another universe, and so on. Then the (usually time-weighted) average returns of each fund within the universe are ordered, and each portfolio manager receives a percentile ranking depending on relative performance within the **comparison universe.** For example, the manager with the ninth-best performance in a universe of 100 funds would be the 90th percentile manager: her performance was better than 90% of all competing funds over the evaluation period.

These relative rankings are usually displayed in a chart such as that in Figure 24.1. The chart summarizes performance rankings over four periods: 1 quarter, 1 year, 3 years, and 5 years. The top and bottom lines of each box are drawn at the rate of return of the 95th and 5th percentile managers. The three dotted lines correspond to the rates of return of the 75th, 50th (median), and 25th percentile managers. The diamond is drawn at the average return of a particular fund and the square is drawn at the return of a benchmark index such as the S&P 500. The placement of the diamond

FIGURE 24.1
Universe comparison.
Periods ending
December 31, 1988.

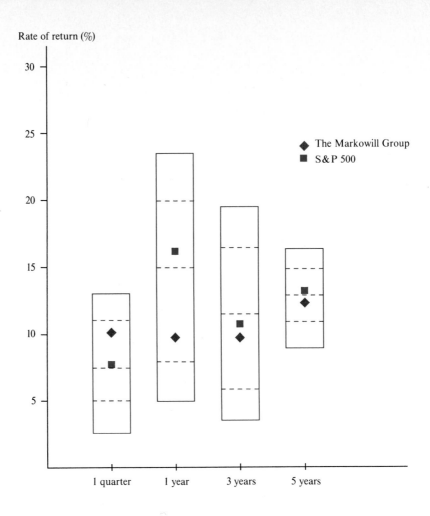

within the box is an easy to read representation of the performance of the fund relative to the comparison universe.

This comparison of performance with other managers of similar investment style is a useful first step in evaluating performance. However, such rankings can be misleading. For example, within a particular universe, some managers may concentrate on particular subgroups, so that portfolio characteristics are not truly comparable. For example, within the equity universe, one manager may concentrate on high-beta stocks. Similarly, within fixed income universes, durations can vary across managers. These considerations suggest that a more precise means for risk adjustment is desirable.

Methods of risk-adjusted performance evaluation using mean-variance criteria came on stage simultaneously with the capital asset pricing model. Jack Treynor,[1] William Sharpe,[2] and Michael Jensen[3] recognized immediately the implications of the CAPM for rating the performance of managers. Within a short time, academicians were in command of a battery of performance measures, and a bounty of scholarly investigation of mutual fund performance was pouring from ivory towers. Shortly thereafter, agents emerged (A.G. Becker is one example) who were willing to supply rating services to portfolio managers eager for regular feedback. This trend has since lost some of its steam.

One explanation for the lagging popularity of risk-adjusted performance measures is the generally negative cast to the performance statistics. In nearly efficient markets it is extremely difficult for analysts to perform well enough to overcome costs of research and transaction costs. Indeed, we have seen that the most professionally managed equity funds generally underperform the S&P 500 index on both risk-adjusted and raw return measures.

Another reason mean-variance criteria may have suffered relates to intrinsic problems in these measures. We will explore these problems, as well as some innovations suggested to overcome them.

For now, however, we can catalog some possible risk-adjusted performance measures and examine the circumstances in which each measure might be most relevant.

1. *Sharpe's measure:* $(\bar{r}_P - \bar{r}_f)/\sigma_P$

   Sharpe's measure divides average portfolio excess return over the sample period by the standard deviation of returns over that period. It measures the reward to (total) volatility trade-off.[4]

2. *Treynor's measure:* $(\bar{r}_P - \bar{r}_f)/\beta_P$

   Like Sharpe's, **Treynor's measure** gives excess return per unit of risk, but uses systematic risk instead of total risk.

3. *Jensen's measure:* $\alpha_P = \bar{r}_P - [\bar{r}_f + \beta_P(\bar{r}_M - \bar{r}_f)]$

   Jensen's measure is the average return on the portfolio over and above that predicted by the CAPM, given the portfolio's beta and the average market return. Jensen's measure is the portfolio's alpha value.

4. *Appraisal ratio:* $\alpha_P/\sigma(e_P)$

   The **appraisal ratio** divides the alpha of the portfolio by the nonsystematic risk of the portfolio. It measures abnormal return per unit of risk that in principle could be diversified away by holding a market index portfolio.

Each measure has some appeal. But each does not necessarily provide consistent assessments of performance, since the risk measures used to adjust returns differ substantially.

---

[1]Treynor, Jack L., "How to Rate Management Investment Funds," *Harvard Business Review, 43*, January-February 1966.
[2]Sharpe, William F., "Mutual Fund Performance," *Journal of Business, 39*, January 1966.
[3]Jensen, Michael C., "The Performance of Mutual Funds in the Period 1945-1964," *Journal of Finance*, May 1968; and "Risk, the Pricing of Capital Assets, and the Evaluation of Investment Portfolios," *Journal of Business*, April 1969.
[4]We place bars over r_f as well as r_P to denote the fact that since the risk-free rate may not be constant over the measurement period, we are taking a sample average, just as we do for r_P.

Question 3. Consider the following data for a particular sample period:

	Portfolio P	Market M
Average return	.35	.28
Beta	1.2	1.0
Standard deviation	.42	.30
Nonsystematic risk, $\sigma(e)$	.18	0

Calculate the following performance measures for portfolio P and the market: Sharpe, Jensen (alpha), Treynor, appraisal ratio. The T-bill rate during the period was .06. By which measures did portfolio P outperform the market?

Sharpe's Measure as the Criterion for Overall Portfolios

Suppose that Jane Close constructs a portfolio and holds it for a considerable period of time. She makes no changes in portfolio composition during the period. In addition, suppose that the daily rates of return on all securities have constant means, variances, and covariances. This assures that the portfolio rate of return also has a constant mean and variance. These assumptions are unrealistic, but they make the problem easy to analyze. They are also crucial to understanding the shortcoming of conventional applications of performance measurement.

Now we want to evaluate the performance of Jane's portfolio. Has she made a good choice of securities? This is really a three-pronged question. First, good choice compared with what alternatives? Second, in choosing between two distinct alternatives, what are the appropriate criteria to use to evaluate performance? Finally, having identified the alternatives and the performance criteria, is there a rule that will separate basic ability from the random luck of the draw?

Fortunately, our earlier chapters of this text help to determine portfolio choice criteria. If investor preferences can be summarized by a mean-variance utility function such as that introduced in Chapter 5, we can arrive at a relatively simple criterion. The particular utility function that we have used in this text is

$$U = E(r_P) - \tfrac{1}{2}A\sigma_P^2$$

where A is the coefficient of risk aversion. With mean-variance preferences, we have seen that Jane will want to maximize her Sharpe measure (that is, the ratio $[E(r_P) - r_f]/\sigma_P$) of her *complete* portfolio of assets. Recall that this is the criterion that led to the selection of the tangency portfolio in Chapter 7. Jane's problem reduces to that of whether her overall portfolio is the one with the highest possible Sharpe ratio.

ı̇o evaluate Jane's portfolio choice, we first ask whether she intends this portfolio to be her exclusive investment vehicle. If the answer is no, we need to know what her "complementary" portfolio is, the portfolio to which she is adding the one in question. The appropriate measure of portfolio performance depends critically on whether the portfolio is the entire investment fund or only a portion of the investor's overall wealth.

Jane's choice portfolio represents her entire risky investment fund

In this simplest case we need to ascertain only whether Jane's portfolio has the highest possible (ex ante) Sharpe measure. But how can this be done? In principle we can follow these four steps:

1. Assume that past security performance is representative of expected future performance, meaning that security returns over Jane's holding period exhibit averages and sample covariances that Jane might have anticipated.
2. Estimate the entire efficient frontier of risk assets from return data over Jane's holding period.
3. Using the risk-free rate at the time of decision, find the portfolio with the highest Sharpe measure.
4. Compare Jane's Sharpe measure to that of the best alternative.

This comprehensive approach, however, is problematic. It requires not only an extensive data base and optimization techniques, but also exacerbates the problem of inference from sample data. We have to rely on a limited sample to estimate the means and covariances of a very large set of securities. The verdict on Jane's choice will be subject to estimation errors. The very complexity of the procedure makes it hard to assess the reliability and significance of the verdict. Is there a second-best alternative?

In fact, it makes sense to compare Jane's choice to a restricted set of alternative portfolios that were easy for her to assess and invest in at the time of her decision. An obvious first candidate for this restricted set is the passive strategy, the market index portfolio. Other candidates are professionally managed active funds. The method to use to compare Jane's portfolio to any specific alternative is the same: compare their Sharpe measures.

In essence, when Jane's portfolio represents her entire investment fund for the holding period in question, the benchmark alternative is the market index or another specific portfolio. The performance criterion is the Sharpe measure of the actual portfolio vs. the benchmark portfolios.

Jane's portfolio is an active portfolio and is mixed with the passive market index portfolio

How do we evaluate the optimal mix in this case? Call Jane's portfolio P, and denote the market portfolio by M. When the two portfolios are mixed optimally, we have seen (in Chapter 23) that the square of the Sharpe measure of the composite portfolio, C, is given by

$$S_C^2 = S_M^2 + \left[\frac{\alpha_P}{\sigma(e_P)}\right]^2$$

where α_P is the abnormal return of the active portfolio, relative to the passive market portfolio, and $\sigma(e_P)$ is the diversifiable risk. The ratio $\alpha_P/\sigma(e_P)$ is thus the correct performance measure for P for this case, since it gives the improvement in the Sharpe measure of the overall portfolio attributable to the inclusion of P.

To see the intuition of this result, recall the single-index model:

$$r_P - r_f = \alpha_P + \beta_P(r_M - r_f) + e_P$$

If P is fairly priced, then $\alpha_P = 0$, and e_P is just diversifiable risk that can be avoided. If P is mispriced, however, α_P no longer equals zero. Instead, it represents the expected abnormal return. Holding P in addition to the market portfolio thus brings a reward of α_P against the nonsystematic risk voluntarily incurred, $\sigma(e_P)$. Therefore the ratio of $\alpha_P/\sigma(e_P)$ is the natural benefit-to-cost ratio for portfolio P. This performance measurement is sometimes called the appraisal ratio:

$$AR_P = \frac{\alpha_P}{\sigma(e_P)}$$

Jane's choice portfolio is one of many portfolios combined into a large investment fund

This third case might describe the situation where Jane, as a corporate financial officer, manages the corporate pension fund. She parcels out the entire fund to a number of portfolio managers. Then she evaluates the performance of individual managers to reallocate parts of the fund to improve future performance. What is the correct performance measure?

We could continue to use the appraisal ratio if it were reasonable to assume that the complementary portfolio to P is approximately equal to the market index portfolio by virtue of its being spread among many managers and thus well-diversified. The appraisal ratio is adequate in these circumstances. But you can imagine that the portfolio managers would take offense at this assumption. Jane, too, is likely to respond, "Do you think I am exerting all this effort just to end up with a passive portfolio?"

If we cannot treat this form of management as the same as investing in the index portfolio, we could make the following approximation. The benefit of portfolio P to the entire diversified fund is measured by P's alpha value. Although α_P is not a full measure of portfolio P's performance value, it will give Jane some indication of P's potential contribution to the overall portfolio. An even better solution, however, is to use Treynor's measure.

Suppose you determine that portfolio P exhibits an alpha value of 2%. "Not bad," you tell Jane. But she pulls out of her desk a report and informs you that another portfolio, Q, has an alpha of 3%. "One hundred basis points is significant," says Jane. "Should I transfer some of my funds from P's manager to Q's?"

You tabulate the relevant data, as in Table 24.2, and graph the results as in Figure 24.2. Note that we plot P and Q in the mean return-beta (rather than the mean-stan-

TABLE 24.2 Portfolio Performance

	Portfolio P	Portfolio Q	Market
Beta	.90	1.60	1.0
Excess return $(\bar{r} - \bar{r}_f)$	.11	.19	.10
Alpha*	.02	.03	0

*Alpha = Excess return − (Beta × Market excess return)
$$= (\bar{r} - \bar{r}_f) - \beta(\bar{r}_M - \bar{r}_f)$$
$$= \bar{r} - [\bar{r}_f + \beta(\bar{r}_M - \bar{r}_f)]$$

FIGURE 24.2
Treynor measure.

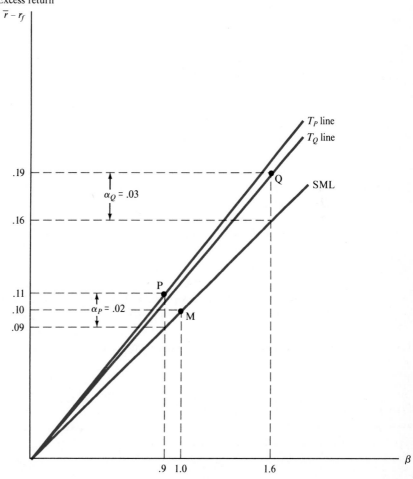

dard deviation) plane, because we assume that P and Q are two of many subportfolios in the fund, and thus that nonsystematic risk will be largely diversified away, leaving beta as the appropriate risk measure. The security market line (SML) shows the value of α_P and α_Q as the distance of P and Q above this line.

Suppose that portfolio Q can be mixed with T-bills. Specifically, if we invest w_Q in Q and $w_F = 1 - w_Q$ in T-bills, the resulting portfolio, Q^*, will have alpha and beta values proportional to Q's alpha and beta and to w_Q:

$$\alpha_{Q^*} = w_Q \alpha_Q$$
$$\beta_{Q^*} = w_Q \beta_Q$$

Thus all portfolios Q^* generated from mixes of Q and T-bills plot on a straight line from the origin through Q. We call it the T-line for the Treynor measure, which is the slope of this line.

Figure 24.2 shows the T-line for portfolio P as well. You can see immediately that P has a steeper T-line; despite its lower alpha, P is a better portfolio in this case after all. For any *given* beta, a mixture of P with T-bills will give a better alpha than a mixture of Q with T-bills.

To see this, suppose that we choose to mix Q with T-bills to create a portfolio Q^* with a beta equal to that of P. We find the necessary proportion by solving for w_Q:

$$w_Q \beta_Q = 1.6 w_Q = \beta_P = .9$$
$$w_Q = \tfrac{9}{16}$$

Portfolio Q^* therefore has an alpha of

$$\alpha_{Q^*} = \tfrac{9}{16} \times 3$$
$$= 1.69\%$$

which in fact is less than that of P.

In other words, the slope of the T-line is the appropriate performance criterion for the third case. The slope of the T-line for P, denoted by T_P, is given by

$$T_P = \frac{\bar{r}_P - \bar{r}_f}{\beta_P}$$

Treynor's performance measure is appealing in the sense that it shows that when an asset is part of a large investment portfolio, you should weight its mean excess return, $\bar{r}_P - \bar{r}_f$ against its *systematic* risk (as measured by beta) rather than against total or diversifiable risk (as measured by its standard deviation) to evaluate its contribution to performance.

Relationships Among the Various Performance Measures

We have shown that under various scenarios one of four different performance measures is appropriate:

$$\text{Sharpe:} \qquad \frac{E(r_P) - r_f}{\sigma_P}$$

$$\text{Treynor:} \qquad \frac{E(r_P) - r_f}{\beta_P}$$

Jensen, or Alpha: α_P

$$\text{Appraisal ratio:} \qquad \frac{\alpha_P}{\sigma(e_P)}$$

It is interesting to see how these measures are related to one another. Beginning with Treynor's measure, note that as the market index beta is 1.0 Treynor's measure for the market index is

$$T_M = \bar{r}_M - \bar{r}_f$$

The mean excess return of portfolio P is

$$\bar{r}_P - \bar{r}_f = \alpha_P + \beta_P(\bar{r}_M - \bar{r}_f)$$

and thus its Treynor measure is

$$
\begin{aligned}
T_P &= \frac{\alpha_P + \beta_P(\bar{r}_M - \bar{r}_f)}{\beta_P} \\
&= \frac{\alpha_P}{\beta_P} + \bar{r}_M - \bar{r}_f \\
&= \frac{\alpha_P}{\beta_P} + T_M
\end{aligned}
\qquad (24.3)
$$

Treynor's measure compares portfolios on the basis of the alpha-to-beta ratio.[5] Note that this is very different in numerical value *and spirit* from the appraisal ratio, which is the ratio of alpha to residual risk.

The Sharpe measure for the market index portfolio is

$$S_M = \frac{\bar{r}_M - \bar{r}_f}{\sigma_M}$$

For portfolio P we have

$$S_P = \frac{\bar{r}_P - \bar{r}_f}{\sigma_P} = \frac{\alpha_P + \beta_P(\bar{r}_M - \bar{r}_f)}{\sigma_P}$$

---

[5]Interestingly, although our definition of the Treynor measure is conventional, Treynor himself initially worked with the alpha-to-beta ratio. In this form the measure is independent of the market. Either measure will rank-order portfolio performance identically, because they differ by a constant (the market's Treynor value). Some call the ratio of alpha to beta "modified alpha" or "modified Jensen's measure," not realizing that this is really Treynor's measure.

With some algebra that relies on the fact that ρ^2 between P and M is

$$\rho^2 = \frac{\beta^2\sigma_M^2}{\beta^2\sigma_M^2 + \sigma^2(e)} = \frac{\beta^2\sigma_M^2}{\sigma_P^2}$$

we find that

$$S_P = \frac{\alpha_P}{\sigma_P} + \frac{\beta_P(\bar{r}_M - \bar{r}_f)}{\sigma_P}$$

$$= \frac{\alpha_P}{\sigma_P} + \rho S_M$$

This expression yields some insight into the process of generating valuable performance with active management. It is obvious that one needs to find significant-alpha stocks to establish potential value. A higher portfolio alpha, however, has to be tempered by the increase in standard deviation that arises when one departs from full diversification. The more we tilt toward high alpha stocks, the lower the correlation with the market index, ρ, and the greater the potential loss of performance value.

We conclude that it is important to use the performance measure that fits the relevant scenario. Evaluating portfolios by different performance measures may yield quite different results.

Actual Performance Measurement: An Example

Now that we have examined possible criteria for performance evaluation, we need to deal with a statistical issue: how can we derive an appropriate performance measure for ex ante decisions using ex post data? Before we plunge into a discussion of this problem, let us look at the rate of return on Jane's portfolio over the last 12 months. Table 24.3 shows the excess return recorded each month for Jane's portfolio P, one of her alternative portfolios Q, and the benchmark market index portfolio M. The last rows in Table 24.3 give sample averages and standard deviations. From these, and regressions of P and Q on M, we obtain the necessary performance statistics.

The performance statistics in Table 24.4 show that portfolio Q is more aggressive than P, in the sense that its beta is significantly higher (1.40 vs. .69). On the other hand, P appears better diversified from its residual standard deviation (1.95% vs. 8.98%). Both portfolios have outperformed the benchmark market index portfolio, as is evident from their larger Sharpe measures and positive alphas.

Which portfolio is more attractive, based on reported performance? If P or Q represents the entire investment fund, Q would be preferable on the basis of its higher Sharpe measure (.51 vs. .45). On the other hand, as an active portfolio to be mixed with the market index, P is preferable to Q, as is evident from its appraisal ratio (.84 vs. .59). For the third scenario, where P and Q are competing for a role as one of a number of subportfolios, the inadequacy of alpha as a performance measure is evident. Whereas Q's alpha is larger (5.28% vs. 1.63%), P's beta is low enough to give

TABLE 24.3 Excess Returns for Portfolios *P* and *Q* and the Benchmark *M* Over 12 Months

Month	Jane's Portfolio P	Alternative Q	Benchmark M
1	3.58	2.81	2.20
2	−4.91	−1.15	−8.41
3	6.51	2.53	3.27
4	11.13	37.09	14.41
5	8.78	12.88	7.71
6	9.38	39.08	14.36
7	−3.66	−8.84	−6.15
8	5.56	.83	2.74
9	−7.72	.85	−15.27
10	7.76	12.09	6.49
11	−4.01	−5.68	−3.13
12	.78	−1.77	1.41
Year's average	2.76	7.56	1.63
Standard deviation	6.17	14.89	8.48

TABLE 24.4 Performance Statistics

	Portfolio P	Portfolio Q	Portfolio M
Sharpe's measure	.45	.51	.19
SCL regression statistics			
Alpha	1.63	5.28	.00
Beta	.69	1.40	1.00
Treynor	4.00	3.77	1.63
$\sigma(e)$	1.95	8.98	.00
Appraisal ratio	.84	.59	.00
R-SQR	.91	.64	1.00

it a better Treynor measure (4.00 vs. 3.77), suggesting that it is superior to *Q* as one portfolio to be mixed with many others.

This analysis is based on 12 months of data only, a period too short to lend statistical significance to the conclusions. Even longer observation intervals may not be enough to make the decision clear-cut, which represents a further problem.

When evaluating a portfolio, the evaluator knows neither the portfolio manager's original expectations nor whether those expectations made sense. One can only observe performance after the fact and hope that random results are not taken for, or do not hide, true underlying ability. But risky asset returns are "noisy," which complicates the inference problem. To avoid making mistakes, we have to determine the "significance level" of a statistic to know whether a portfolio performance measure reliably indicates ability. Quite frequently, however, we can make no significant distinction about performance.

Consider Joe Dart, a portfolio manager. Suppose that his ability is such that his portfolio has an alpha value of 20 basis points per month. (This makes for a hefty 2.4% per year before compounding.) Let us assume that the return distribution of Joe's portfolio has a constant mean, beta, and alpha, a heroic assumption, but one that is in line with the usual treatment of performance measurement. Suppose that for the measurement period Joe's portfolio beta is 1.2 and the monthly standard deviation of the residual (nonsystematic risk) is .02 (2%). With the market portfolio standard deviation of 6.5% per month (22.5% per year), Joe's portfolio systematic variance is

$$\beta^2\sigma_M^2 = 1.2^2 \times .065^2 = .006084$$

and hence the correlation coefficient between his portfolio and the market index is

$$\rho = \left[\frac{\beta^2\sigma_M^2}{\beta^2\sigma_M^2 + \sigma^2(e)}\right]^{1/2}$$

$$= \left[\frac{.006084}{.006084 + .0004}\right]^{1/2}$$

$$= .97$$

which shows that his portfolio appears to be quite well diversified. We calculate these statistics only to show that there is nothing unusual about Joe's portfolio.

To estimate Joe's portfolio alpha, we would estimate the portfolio security characteristic line (SCL), regressing the portfolio excess returns against those of the market index. Suppose that we are in luck in the sense that over the measurement period, the regression estimates yield the true parameters. That means that our SCL estimates for the N months are:

$$\alpha = .2\%, \quad \beta = 1.2, \quad \sigma(e) = 2\%$$

The evaluators who run such a regression, however, do not know the true values, and hence they must compute the t-statistic of the estimated alpha value to determine whether they can reject the hypothesis that Joe's alpha is zero, that is, that he has no ability.

The standard error of the alpha estimate in the SCL regression is approximately

$$\sigma(\alpha) = \frac{\sigma(e)}{\sqrt{N}}$$

where N is the number of observations and $\sigma(e)$ is the sample estimate of nonsystematic risk. The t-statistic for the alpha estimate is then

$$
\begin{aligned}
t(\alpha) &= \frac{\alpha}{\sigma(\alpha)} \\
&= \frac{\alpha\sqrt{N}}{\sigma(e)}
\end{aligned}
\tag{24.2}
$$

Suppose that we require a significance level of 5%. This requires a $t(\alpha)$ value of 1.96 if N is large. With $\alpha = .2$ and $\sigma(e) = 2$ we solve equation 24.2 for N and find that

$$
1.96 = \frac{.2\sqrt{N}}{2}
$$

$$
N = 384 \text{ months}
$$

or 32 years!

What have we shown? Here is an analyst who has very substantial ability. The example is biased in his favor in the sense that we have assumed away statistical problems. Nothing changes in the parameters over a long period of time. Furthermore, the sample period "behaves" perfectly. Regression estimates are all perfect. Still, it will take Joe's entire working career to get to the point where statistics will confirm his true ability. We have to conclude that the problem of statistical inference makes performance evaluation extremely difficult in practice.

Concept Check

Question 4. Suppose an analyst has a measured alpha of .2% with a standard error of 2%, as in our example. What is the probability that the positive alpha is due to luck of the draw and that true ability is zero?

24.3 *Performance Measurement With Changing Portfolio Composition*

We have seen already that the high variance of stock returns requires a very long observation period to determine performance levels with any statistical significance, even if portfolio returns are distributed with constant mean and variance. Imagine how this problem is compounded when portfolio return distributions are constantly changing.

It is acceptable to assume that the return distributions of passive strategies have constant mean and variance when the measurement interval is not too long. However, under an active strategy return distributions change by design, as the portfolio manager updates the portfolio in accordance with the dictates of financial analysis. In such a case estimating various statistics from a sample period assuming a constant mean and variance may lead to substantial errors. Let us look at an example.

Suppose that the Sharpe measure of the passive strategy is .4. A portfolio manager is in search of a better, active strategy. Over an initial period of 52 weeks he executes a low-risk strategy with an annualized mean excess return of 1% and standard deviation of 2%. This makes for a Sharpe measure of .5, which beats the passive strategy. Over the next period of another 52 weeks this manager finds that a *high*-risk strategy is optimal, with an annual mean excess return of 9% and standard deviation of 18%. Here, again, the Sharpe measure is .5. Over the 2-year period our manager maintains a better-than-passive Sharpe measure.

FIGURE 24.3
Portfolio returns.

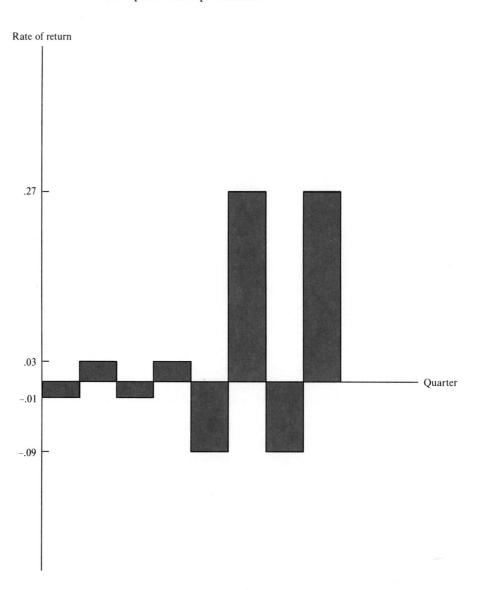

Figure 24.3 shows a pattern of (annualized) quarterly returns that are consistent with our description of the manager's strategy over 2 years. In the first four quarters the excess returns are -1%, 3%, -1%, and 3%, making for an average of 1% and standard deviation of 2%. In the next 4 quarters the returns are: -9%, 27%, -9%, 27%, making for an average of 9% and a standard deviation of 18%. Thus *both* years exhibit a Sharpe measure of .5. However, if we take the 8-quarter sequence as a single measurement period, and measure the portfolio's mean and standard deviation over that full period, we will obtain an average excess return of 5% and standard deviation of 13.42%, making for a Sharpe measure of only .37, apparently inferior to the passive strategy!

What happened? The shift in the mean from the first 4 quarters to the next was not recognized as a shift in strategy. Instead, the difference in mean returns in the 2 years added to the *appearance* of volatility in portfolio returns. The active strategy with shifting means appears riskier than it really is and biases the estimate of the Sharpe measure downward. We conclude that for actively managed portfolios it is crucial to keep track of portfolio composition and changes in portfolio mean and risk. We will see another example of this problem in the next section, which deals with market timing.

24.4 *Market Timing*

In its pure form, market timing involves shifting funds between a market index portfolio and a safe asset, such as T-bills or a money market fund, depending on whether the market as a whole is expected to outperform the safe asset. In practice, of course, most managers do not shift fully between T-bills and the market. How might we measure partial shifts into the market when it is expected to perform well?

To simplify, suppose that the investor holds only the market index portfolio and T-bills. If the weight on the market were constant, for example, .6, then the portfolio beta also would be constant, and the portfolio characteristic line would plot as a straight line with slope .6, as in Figure 24.4, *A*. If, however, the investor could correctly time the market, and shift funds into it in periods when the market does well, the characteristic line would plot as in Figure 24.4, *B*. The idea is that if the timer can predict bull and bear markets the investor will shift more into the market when the market is about to go up. The portfolio beta and the slope of the characteristic line will be higher when r_M is higher, resulting in the curved line that appears in Figure 24.4, *B*.

Treynor and Mazuy[6] propose that such a line can be estimated by adding a squared term to the usual linear index model:

$$r_P - r_f = a + b(r_M - r_f) + c(r_M - r_f)^2 + e_P$$

---

[6]Treynor, Jack L., and Mazuy, Kay, "Can Mutual Funds Outguess the Market," *Harvard Business Review, 43,* July-August 1966.

FIGURE 24.4
Characteristic lines.
A, No market timing,
beta is constant. **B,**
Market timing, beta
increases with
expected market
excess return. **C,**
Market timing with
only two values of
beta.

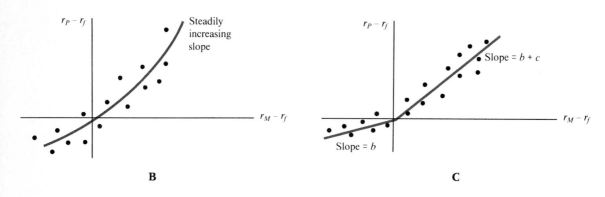

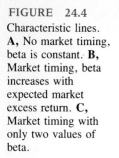

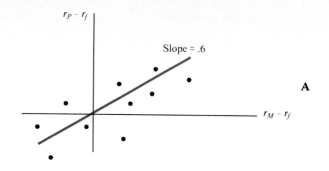

where r_P is the portfolio return, and a, b, and c are estimated by regression analysis. If c turns out to be positive, we have evidence of timing ability, because this last term will make the characteristic line steeper as $r_M - r_f$ is larger. Treynor and Mazuy estimated this equation for a number of mutual funds, but found little evidence of timing ability.

A similar and simpler methodology is proposed by Henriksson and Merton.[7] These authors suggest that the beta of the portfolio take only two values: a large value if the market is expected to do well and a small value otherwise. Under this scheme the portfolio characteristic line appears as Figure 24.4, *C.* Such a line appears in regression form as

$$r_P - r_f = a + b(r_M - r_f) + c(r_M - r_f)D + e_P$$

where D is a dummy variable that equals 1 for $r_M > r_f$ and zero otherwise. Hence the beta of the portfolio is b in bear markets and $b + c$ in bull markets. Again, a positive value of c implies market timing ability.

---

[7]Henriksson, Roy D., and Merton, R.C., "On Market Timing and Investment Performance. II. Statistical Procedures for Evaluating Forecast Skills," *Journal of Business, 54,* October 1981.

Henriksson[8] estimates this equation for 116 mutual funds over the period 1968 to 1980. He finds that the average value of c for the funds was *negative,* and equal to $-.07$, although the value was not statistically significant at the conventional 5% level. Eleven funds had significantly positive values of c, while eight had significantly negative values. Overall, 62% of the funds had negative point estimates of timing ability. In sum, the results showed little evidence of market timing ability. Perhaps this should be expected; given the tremendous values to be reaped by a successful market timer, it would be surprising in nearly efficient markets to uncover clear-cut evidence of such skills.

To illustrate a test for market timing, return to Table 24.3. Regressing the excess returns of portfolios P and Q on the excess returns on M and the square of these returns,

$$r_P - r_f = a_P + b_P(r_M - r_f) + c_P(r_M - r_f)^2 + e_P$$
$$r_Q - r_f = a_Q + b_Q(r_M - r_f) + c_Q(r_M - r_f)^2 + e_Q$$

we derive the following statistics:

Estimate	Portfolio	
	P	**Q**
Alpha (a)	1.77 (1.77)	-2.29 (5.28)
Beta (b)	.70 (.70)	1.10 (1.40)
Timing (c)	.00	.10
R-SQR	.91 (.91)	.98 (.64)

The numbers in parentheses are the regression estimates from the single variable regression reported in Table 24.4. The results reveal that portfolio P shows no timing. It is not clear whether this is a result of Jane's making no attempt at timing or that the effort to time was in vain and served only to increase portfolio variance unnecessarily.

The results for portfolio Q, however, reveal that timing has, in all likelihood, successfully been attempted. The timing coefficient, c, is estimated at .10. This describes a successful timing effort that was offset by unsuccessful stock selection. Note that the alpha estimate, a, is now -2.29% as opposed to the 5.28% estimate derived from the regression equation that did not allow for the possibility of timing activity.

Indeed, this is an example of the inadequacy of conventional performance evaluation techniques that assume constant mean returns and constant risk. The market timer constantly shifts beta and mean return, moving into and out of the market. Whereas the expanded regression captures this phenomenon, the simple SCL does not. The relative desirability of portfolios P and Q remains unclear in the sense that the value of the timing success and selectivity failure of Q compared with P has yet

---

[8]Henriksson, Roy D., "Market Timing and Mutual Fund Performance: An Empirical Investigation," *Journal of Business, 57,* January 1984.

to be evaluated. The important point for performance evaluation, however, is that expanded regressions can capture many of the effects of portfolio composition change that would confound the more conventional mean-variance measures.

24.5 Performance Attribution Procedures

Rather than focus on risk-adjusted returns, practitioners often want simply to ascertain which decisions resulted in superior or inferior performance. Superior investment performance depends on an ability to be in the "right" securities at the right time. Such timing and selection ability may be considered broadly, such as being in equities as opposed to fixed-income securities when the stock market is performing well. Or it may be defined at a more detailed level, such as choosing the relatively better-performing stocks within a particular industry. Portfolio managers constantly make both broad-brush asset-market allocation decisions, as well as more detailed sector and security allocation decisions within markets. Performance attribution studies attempt to decompose overall performance into discrete components that may be identified with a particular level of the portfolio selection process.

Attribution studies start from the broadest asset allocation choices and progressively focus on ever-finer details of portfolio choice. The difference between a managed portfolio's performance and that of a benchmark, or "bogey," portfolio then may be expressed as the sum of the contributions to performance of a series of decisions made at the various levels of the portfolio construction process. For example, one common attribution system decomposes performance into three components: (1) broad asset market allocation choices across equity, fixed-income, and money markets; (2) industry (sector) choice within each market; and (3) security choice within each sector.

To illustrate the allocation of investment results to various decisions at different levels of portfolio construction, consider the attribution results for a hypothetical portfolio. The portfolio invests in stocks, bonds, and money market securities. The attribution analysis is presented in Tables 24.5 through 24.8. The portfolio return

TABLE 24.5   Performance of the Managed Portfolio

Component	Benchmark Weight	Return of Index During Month (%)
Bogey Performance and Excess Return		
Equity (S&P 500)	.60	5.81
Bonds (Shearson Lehman)	.30	1.45
Cash (money market)	.10	0.48
Bogey = (.60 × 5.81) + (.30 × 1.45) + (.10 × 0.48) = 3.97%		
Return of managed portfolio		5.34%
Return of bogey portfolio		3.97
Excess return of managed portfolio		1.37%

over the month was 5.34%. A **bogey,** or benchmark performance level, is calculated based on the performances of an equity index (the S&P 500), a fixed-income index (Shearson Lehman), and a money market index, each weighted using a notion of "usual" or neutral allocation across sectors, or alternatively, using client-specified weights. Here, the standard weights are 60% equity, 30% fixed-income, and 10% cash (money market securities). The bogey portfolio, composed of "investments" in each index with the 60/30/10 weights, returned 3.97%.

The managed portfolio's measure of extra-market performance is positive, and equal to its actual return less the return of the bogey: 5.34 − 3.97 = 1.37%. The next step is to allocate the 1.37% excess return to the separate decisions that contributed to it.

Asset Allocation Decisions

Our hypothetical managed portfolio was invested in the equity, fixed-income, and money markets with weights 70%, 7%, and 23%, respectively. The portfolio's performance can derive from the departure of this weighting scheme from the benchmark 60/30/10 weights, as well as from superior or inferior results *within* each of the three broad markets. To measure only the effect of the manager's asset allocation choice, we measure the performance of a hypothetical portfolio that would have invested in the *indices* for each market with weights 70/7/23. This return measures the individual effect of the shift away from the benchmark 60/30/10 weights, without allowing for any effects attributable to active management of the securities selected within each market. Superior performance relative to the bogey is achieved by over-weighting investments in markets that turn out to perform relatively well, and by un-

TABLE 24.6   Performance Attribution

Market	(1) Actual Weight in Market	(2) Benchmark Weight in Market	(3) Excess Weight	(4) Market Return (%)	(5) = (3) × (4) Contribution to Performance (%)
A. Contribution of Asset Allocation to Performance					
Equity	.70	.60	.10	5.81	.5810
Fixed income	.07	.30	−.23	1.45	−.3335
Cash	.23	.10	.13	0.48	.0624
Contribution of asset allocation					.3099

Market	(1) Portfolio Performance (%)	(2) Index Performance (%)	(3) Excess Performance (%)	(4) Portfolio Weight	(5) = (3) × (4) Contribution (%)
B. Contribution of Selection to Total Performance					
Equity	7.28	5.81	1.47	.70	1.03
Fixed income	1.89	1.45	0.44	.07	.03
Contribution of selection within markets					1.06

TABLE 24.7   Sector Selection Within the Equity Market

Sector	(1) Beginning of Month Weights (%) Portfolio	(2) Beginning of Month Weights (%) S&P 500	(3) Difference in Weights	(4) Sector Return	(5) Sector Over/Under Performance*	(6) = (3) × (5) Sector Allocation Contribution
Basic materials	1.96	8.3	−6.34	6.4	0.9	− 5.7 bp
Business services	7.84	4.1	3.74	6.5	1.0	3.7
Capital goods	1.87	7.8	−5.93	3.7	−1.8	10.7
Consumer cyclical	8.47	12.5	−4.03	8.4	2.9	−11.7
Consumer noncyclical	40.37	20.4	19.97	9.4	3.9	77.9
Credit sensitive	24.01	21.8	2.21	4.6	0.9	2.0
Energy	13.53	14.2	−0.67	2.1	−3.4	2.3
Technology	1.95	10.9	−8.95	−0.1	−5.6	50.1
TOTAL						**129.3 basis points**

*S&P 500 performance, excluding dividends, was 5.5%. Returns compared net of dividends.

derweighting poorly performing markets. The contribution of asset allocation to superior performance equals the sum over all markets of the excess weight in each market multiplied by the return of the market index.

Part *A* of Table 24.6 demonstrates that asset allocation contributed 31 basis points to the portfolio's overall excess return of 137 basis points. The major factor contributing to superior performance in this month was the heavy weighting of the equity market in a month when the equity market had an excellent return of 5.81%.

Sector and Security Allocation Decisions

If .31% of the excess performance can be attributed to advantageous asset allocation across markets, the remaining 1.06% must be attributable to sector selection and security selection within each market. Part *B* of Table 24.6 details the contribution of the managed portfolio's sector and security selection to total performance.

Part *B* shows that the equity component of the managed portfolio had a return of 7.28% vs. a return of 5.81% for the S&P 500. The fixed-income return was 1.89% vs. 1.45% for the Shearson-Lehman index. The superior performance in equity and fixed-income markets weighted by the portfolio proportions invested in each market sums to the 1.06% contribution to performance attributable to sector and security selection.

Table 24.7 documents the sources of the equity market performance by each sector within the market. The first 3 columns detail the allocation of funds within the equity market compared with their representation in the S&P 500. Column 4 shows the rate of return of each sector, and column 5 documents the performance of each sector relative to the return of the S&P 500. The contribution of each sector's allocation presented in column 6 equals the product of the difference in the sector weight and the sector's relative performance.

Note that good performance (a positive contribution) derives from overweighting

TABLE 24.8   Portfolio Attribution: Summary

		Contribution (Basis Points)
1. Asset allocation		31.0
2. Selection	129	
a. Equity excess return	18	
i. Sector allocation		
ii. Security allocation		
	$147 \times .70$ (portfolio weight) =	102.9
b. Fixed income excess return	$44 \times .07$ (portfolio weight) =	3.1
Total excess return of portfolio		**137.0 basis points**

well-performing sectors such as consumer nondurables or underweighting poorly performing sectors such as capital goods. The excess return of the equity component of the portfolio attributable to sector allocation alone is 1.29%. Since the equity component of the portfolio outperformed the S&P 500 by 1.47%, we conclude that the effect of security selection within sectors must have contributed an additional $1.47 - 1.29 = .18\%$ to the performance of the equity component of the portfolio.

A similar sector analysis can be applied to the fixed-income portion of the portfolio, but we do not show those results here.

Summing Up Component Contributions

In this particular month all facets of the portfolio selection process were successful. Table 24.8 details the contribution of each aspect of performance. Asset allocation across the major security markets contributes 31 basis points. Sector and security allocation within those markets contributes 106 basis points, for total excess portfolio performance of 137 basis points. The sector and security allocation of 106 basis points can be partitioned further. Sector allocation within the equity market results in excess performance of 129.3 basis points, and security selection with sectors contributes 18 basis points. (The total equity excess performance of 147 basis points is multiplied by the 70% weight in equity to obtain contribution to portfolio performance.) Similar partitioning could be done for the fixed-income sector.

24.6   *Evaluating Performance Evaluation*

Performance evaluation has two very basic problems:
1. Many observations are needed for significant results even when portfolio mean and variance are constant.
2. Shifting parameters when portfolios are actively managed make accurate performance evaluation all the more elusive.

SEC Requires Clearer Picture of Fund Fees

WASHINGTON—Investors baffled by the complexities of mutual-fund fees soon will get some long-awaited help from regulators.

The Securities and Exchange Commission, after debating the issue for three years, voted 5-0 yesterday to require mutual funds to identify all charges in a standardized fee table prominently located in prospectuses. The table will capsulize how much of a bite fees, sales charges and expenses will take out of a $1,000 investment over various periods of time.

YOUR
MONEY
MATTERS

"Many of these fees are tricky, and they had been under a rock," says Kurt Brouwer, a San Francisco investment adviser specializing in no-load mutual funds. "Now they'll be staring you right in the face."

In a separate rule, the SEC also set stricter guidelines for how mutual funds advertise their performance.

Fees Add Up

Until a few years ago, mutual fund fees were simple. They all charged annual management fees, and some also levied an up-front sales fee, or load. But in recent years, up-front charges have shrunk in favor of new—and usually less obvious—fees.

These include redemption charges and so-called 12b-1 expenses, which allow a fund to deduct an amount from assets to pay for marketing and distribution costs. About 40% of the nearly 1,850 funds tracked by Lipper Analytical Services Inc. can levy the hard-to-spot 12b-1 charges, for instance, and most of them do so. Typically, 12b-1 charges range from 0.25% of annual assets to more than 1%. Although disclosure of these charges already is required, they often are scattered throughout the prospectus. Under the new fee plan, the SEC also will require mutual funds to give a brief description of how they use 12b-1 fees.

The fee issue has become increasingly important to investors. Fund holders these days are likely to be less tolerant of hidden fees, now that they're facing narrower gains after several years of double-digit returns, specialists say. "That's why some (fees) are so insidious," says Sheldon Jacobs, publisher of the No-Load Fund Investor, an industry newsletter.

Take the Kemper Government Plus Portfolio and some of the Keystone Custodian funds, for example, which have no up-front sales charges but are chock-full of other charges. The Kemper fund levies as much as a 5% back-end load, a 1.25% 12b-1 annual charge, and a 0.6% management fee. Several of the Keystone funds charge as much as a 4% back-end load, a 1.25% 12b-1 annual charge, and 0.6% for management costs.

Many industry executives back some aspects of the new rule, such as the standardized fee table. "Investors shouldn't have to beaver through 400 pages of meaningless information to find out what it's going to cost them," says John Butler, president of Financial Programs Inc., a Denver-based mutual-fund group.

But other parts of the regulation—especially determining the fees' impact on a hypothetical investment—have come under fire. Starting May 1, mutual funds will have to report how fees would affect a $1,000 investment assuming a 5% growth rate over one, three, five and 10-year periods.

"Not everything is very easily standardized into a table," says a Keystone spokesman. He says, for instance, that the Keystone fund group's fee structure can vary widely each year and would be difficult to reflect adequately in a table of hypothetical returns. Also, Keystone says that since its fees are lower in the beginning for some funds and then spread out over time, a holder has more money to invest in the beginning.

Wrong Emphasis?

Others in the industry argue that the changes place too much emphasis on fees, which they say are just a small part of the information investors need to pick the right mutual fund. Examining the fees' effect on a hypothetical investment "highlights expense without any reference to any other fund feature, primarily performance," says Charles Kierscht, president of Kemper

Financial Services Inc., Chicago, which charges up-front loads of as much as 8.5% on some funds.

The Investment Company Institute, a trade group, says information on fund performance is more important to investors. Michael Lipper, president of Lipper Analytical, agrees: "Yes, I'd prefer funds with low expenses, but every day I'd take a better performing fund with high expenses."

Many mutual fund investors, however, say the changes will be helpful because they will make fund charges easier to decipher. "Trying to glean through the prospectus is difficult. The fees are hard to figure with all the columns," says Richard Lake, a doctor in Fort Wayne, Ind. "It should be obvious what you're paying for mutual funds."

The SEC yesterday also voted 3-2 to adopt stricter guidelines for mutual-fund advertising. Currently, income funds other than money market funds are free to compute and advertise their yield performance any way they wish, as long as it doesn't violate federal securities laws. As a result, funds use different types of performance figures and disclosure styles, making it more difficult for investors to make meaningful comparisons.

"If interest rates are declining, funds use a one-year average; if rates rise, they give one week—whatever suits the case," says Paul Yurachek, a partner at Dennis Gurtz & Associates, a Washington, D.C., financial planning firm.

Under the new SEC rule, an income fund will have to advertise a uniform, 30-day yield figure. In addition, if any income or equity fund wants to tout performance, it also must include the fund's average annual total return for the past one, five and ten-year periods. The ads also have to disclose whether a sales load is charged and the amount of the load, among other things. After some arm-twisting by SEC Chairman David Ruder, the commissioners voted to require that the procedures on total returns apply to equity funds.

Industry officials who would be reined in by the new advertising guidelines say the rule requires that too much information be crammed into the ads, which would confuse investors. Several fund groups say it will require them to spend more on advertising to buy more space, which will increase costs to investors. "It has to be paid for somehow," says Kemper's Mr. Kierscht.

Some industry officials say the rule shouldn't apply to equity funds since the SEC never identified any abuses in advertising for such funds. Proponents of the rule have said they want to establish standardized comparisons for equity funds.

Meanwhile, on another fee front, the National Association of Securities Dealers this spring is expected to adopt changes to make mutual fund listings in daily newspapers more informative. The NASD plans to add a new footnote to the listings to indicate whether a fund levies a 12b-1 fee.

The footnotes won't indicate the amount of the 12b-1 expense. As a result, more funds with minimal distribution charges likely will eliminate them, says Mr. Jacobs, the newsletter publisher. In recent months, several fund groups, including Neuberger & Berman Management Inc. and Columbia Funds Management Co., have dropped their small 12b-1 charges because of the negative reaction among investors.

The footnotes "will allow investors to be more selective about what they look for" in a mutual fund, says John Taylor, a NASD vice president.

Although these objective difficulties cannot be overcome completely, it is clear that to obtain reasonably reliable performance measures we need to do the following:

1. Maximize the number of observations by taking more frequent return readings.
2. Specify the exact makeup of the portfolio to obtain better estimates of the risk parameters at each observation period.

Suppose an evaluator knows the exact portfolio composition at the opening of each day. Because the daily return on each security is available, the total daily return on the portfolio can be calculated. Furthermore, the exact portfolio composition allows the evaluator to estimate the risk characteristics (variance, beta, residual variance) for each day. Thus daily risk-adjusted rates of return can be obtained. Although a performance measure for 1 day is statistically unreliable, the number of days with such rich data accumulates quickly. Performance evaluation that accounts for frequent revision in portfolio composition is superior by far to evaluation that assumes constant risk characteristics over the entire measurement period.

What sort of evaluation takes place in practice? Performance reports for portfolio managers traditionally have been based on quarterly data over 5 to 10 years. Currently, managers of mutual funds are required to disclose the exact composition of their portfolios only semiannually. Trading activity that immediately precedes the reporting date is known as "window dressing." Rumor has it that window dressing involves changes in portfolio composition to make it look as if the manager chose successful stocks. If IBM performed well over the quarter, for example, a portfolio manager will make sure that his or her portfolio includes a lot of IBM on the reporting date whether or not it did during the quarter and whether or not IBM is expected to perform as well over the next quarter. Of course, portfolio managers deny such activity, and we know of no published evidence to substantiate the allegation. However, if window dressing is quantitatively significant, even the reported quarterly composition data can be misleading. Mutual funds publish portfolio values on a daily basis, which means the rate of return for each day is publicly available, but portfolio composition is not.

Moreover, mutual fund managers have had considerable leeway in the presentation of both past investment performance and fees charged for management services. The resultant noncomparability of net-of-expense performance numbers has made it difficult to meaningfully compare funds. This may be changing, however. As the nearby box describes, the SEC is now moving toward greater disclosure and standardization requirements in the reporting of both fees and performance.

Traditional academic research uses monthly, weekly, and more recently even daily data. But such research makes no use of changes in portfolio composition because the data usually are unavailable. Therefore performance evaluation is unsatisfactory in both the academic and practitioner communities.

Portfolio managers reveal their portfolio composition only when they have to, which so far is quarterly. This is not nearly sufficient for adequate evaluation. However, current computer and communication technology makes it easy to use daily composition data for evaluation purposes. If the technology required for meaningful evaluation is in place, implementation of more accurate performance measurement techniques could improve welfare by enabling the public to identify the truly talented investment managers.

Summary

1. The appropriate performance measure depends on the role of the portfolio to be evaluated. Appropriate performance measures are as follows:
   a. Sharpe: when the portfolio represents the entire investment fund.
   b. Appraisal ratio: when the portfolio represents the active portfolio to be optimally mixed with the passive portfolio.
   c. Treynor: when the portfolio represents one subportfolio of many.

2. Many observations are required to eliminate the effect of the "luck of the draw" from the evaluation process because portfolio returns commonly are very "noisy."

3. The shifting mean and variance of actively managed portfolios make it even harder to assess performance. A typical example is the attempt of portfolio managers to time the market, resulting in ever-changing portfolio betas.

4. A simple way to measure timing and selection success simultaneously is to estimate an expanded SCL, with a quadratic term added to the usual index model.

5. Common attribution procedures partition performance improvements to asset allocation, sector selection, and security selection. Performance is assessed by calculating departures of portfolio composition from a benchmark or neutral portfolio.

Key Terms

Dollar-weighted rate of return	Treynor's measure
Time-weighted return	Jensen's measure
Comparison universe	Appraisal ratio
Sharpe's measure	Bogey

Selected Readings

The mean-variance based performance evaluation literature is based on early papers by:
   Sharpe, William F., "Mutual Fund Performance," *Journal of Business, 39,* January 1966.
   Treynor, Jack L., "How to Rate Management Investment Funds," *Harvard Business Review, 43,* January-February 1966.
   Jensen, Michael C., "The Performance of Mutual Funds in the Period 1945-1964," *Journal of Finance,* May 1968.
   Jensen, Michael C., "Risk, the Pricing of Capital Assets, and the Evaluation of Investment Portfolios," *Journal of Business,* April 1969.
The problems that arise when conventional mean-variance measures are calculated in the presence of a shifting-return distribution are treated in:
   Dybvig, Philip H., and Ross, Stephen A., "Differential Information and Performance Measurement Using a Security Market Line, *Journal of Finance, 40,* June 1985.
The separation of investment ability into timing vs. selection activity derives from:
   Fama, Eugene F., "Components of Investment Performance, *Journal of Finance, 25,* June 1970.

Key empirical papers on timing vs. selection are:

Treynor, Jack, L., and Mazuy, Kay, "Can Mutual Funds Outguess the Market," *Harvard Business Review, 43,* July-August 1966.

Kon, S.J., and Jen, F.D., "The Investment Performance of Mutual Funds: An Empirical Investigation of Timing, Selectivity, and Market Efficiency," *Journal of Business, 52,* April 1979.

Henriksson, Roy D., and Merton, R.C., "On Market Timing and Investment Performance II. Statistical Procedures for Evaluating Forecast Skills," *Journal of Business, 54,* October 1981.

Henriksson, Roy D., "Market Timing and Mutual Fund Performance: An Empirical Investigation," *Journal of Business, 57,* January 1984.

Problems

1. Consider the rate of return of stocks ABC and XYZ.

Year	r_{ABC}	r_{XYZ}
1	.20	.30
2	.10	.10
3	.14	.18
4	.05	.00
5	.01	−.08

   a. Calculate the arithmetic average return on these stocks over the sample period.

   b. Which stock has greater dispersion around the mean?

   c. Calculate the geometric average returns of each stock. What do you conclude?

   d. If you were equally likely to earn a return of 20%, 10%, 14%, 5%, or 1%, in each of the five annual returns for stock ABC, what would be your expected rate of return? What if the five outcomes were those of stock XYZ?

2. XYZ stock price and dividend history are as follows:

Year	Beginning of Year Price	Dividend Paid at Year-end
1991	$100	$4
1992	$110	$4
1993	$ 90	$4
1994	$ 95	$4

   An investor buys three shares of XYZ at the beginning of 1991, buys another two shares at the beginning of 1992, sells one share at the beginning of 1993, and sells all four remaining shares at the beginning of 1994.

   a. What are the arithmetic and geometric average time-weighted rates of return for the investor?

   b. What is the dollar-weighted rate of return? Hint: carefully prepare a chart of cash flows for the *four* dates corresponding to the turns of the year for January 1, 1991, to December 31, 1994. If your calculator cannot calculate internal rate of return you will have to use trial and error.

3. Based on current dividend yields and expected capital gains, the expected rates of return on portfolios A and B are .11 and .14 respectively. The beta of A is 0.8, while that of B is 1.5. The T-bill rate is currently .06, while the expected rate of return of the S&P 500 index is .12. The standard deviation of portfolio A is .10 annually, that of B is .31, and that of the S&P 500 index is .20.

   a. If you currently hold a market-index portfolio, would you choose to add either of these portfolios to your holdings? Explain.

   b. If instead you could invest *only* in T-bills and *one* of these portfolios, which would you choose?

4. Consider the two (excess return) index-model regression results for stocks A and B. The risk-free rate over the period was .06, and the market's average return was .14.

(i) $r_A - r_f = .01 + 1.2(r_M - r_f)$
     R-SQR $= .576$
     Residual standard deviation, $\sigma(e_A) = 10.3\%$
     Standard deviation of $r_A - r_f = .261$

(ii) $r_B - r_f = .02 + .8(r_M - r_f)$
     R-SQR $= .436$
     Residual standard deviation, $\sigma(e_B) = 19.1\%$
     Standard deviation of $r_B - r_f = .249$

   a. Calculate the following statistics for each stock:
     i. Alpha
     ii. Appraisal ratio
     iii. Sharpe measure
     iv. Treynor measure

   b. Which stock is the best choice under the following circumstances?
     i. This is the only risky asset to be held by the investor.
     ii. This stock will be mixed with the rest of the investor's portfolio, currently composed solely of holdings in the market index fund.
     iii. This is one of many stocks that the investor is analyzing to form an actively managed stock portfolio.

5. Evaluate the timing and selection abilities of four managers whose performances are plotted in the following four scatter diagrams.

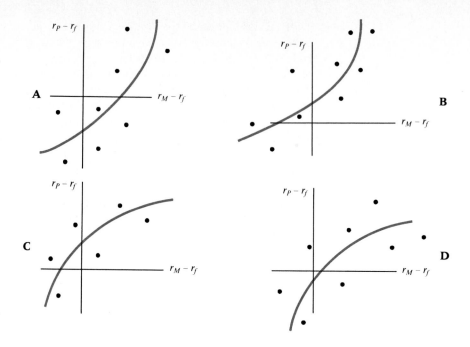

6. Consider the following information regarding the performance of a money manager in a recent month. The table presents the actual return of each sector of the manager's portfolio in column 1, the fraction of the portfolio allocated to each sector in column 2, the benchmark or neutral sector allocations in column 3, and the returns of sector indices in column 4.

	Actual Return	Actual Weight	Benchmark Weight	Index Return
Equity	.02	.70	.60	.025 (S&P 500)
Bonds	.01	.20	.30	.012 (Salomon Brothers index)
Cash	.005	.10	.10	.005

a. What was the manager's return in the month? What was her overperformance or underperformance?
b. What was the contribution of security selection to relative performance?
c. What was the contribution of asset allocation to relative performance? Confirm that the sum of selection and allocation contributions equals her total "excess" return relative to the bogey.

7. Conventional wisdom says that one should measure a manager's investment performance over an entire market cycle. What arguments support this contention? What arguments contradict it?

8. Does the use of universes of managers with similar investment styles to evaluate relative investment performance overcome the statistical problems associated with instability of beta or total variability?

9. During a particular year, the T-bill rate was 6%, the market return was 14%, and a portfolio manager with beta of .5 realized a return of 10%.

a. Evaluate the manager based on the portfolio alpha.

b. Reconsider your answer to part (a) in view of the Black-Jensen-Scholes finding that the security market line is too flat. Now how do you assess the manager's performance?

10. (Based on CFA Examination, Level III, 1983)

The chairman provides you with the following data, covering one year, concerning the portfolios of two of the fund's equity managers (Firm *A* and Firm *B*). Although the portfolios consist primarily of common stocks, cash reserves are included in the calculation of both portfolio betas and performance. By way of perspective, selected data for the financial markets are included in the following table:

	Total Return	Beta
Firm *A*	24.0%	1.0
Firm *B*	30.0	1.5
S&P 500	21.0	
Lehman, Kuhn Loeb Total Bond Index	31.0	
91-day Treasury bills	12.0	

a. Calculate and compare the risk adjusted performance of the two firms relative to each other and to the S&P 500.

b. Explain *two* reasons the conclusions drawn from this calculation may be misleading.

11. (CFA Examination, Level I, 1981)

Carl Karl, a portfolio manager for the Alpine Trust Company, has been responsible since 1975 for the City of Alpine's Employee Retirement Plan, a municipal pension fund. Alpine is a growing community, and city services and employee payrolls have expanded in each of the past 10 years. Contributions to the Plan in fiscal 1980 exceeded benefit payments by a three-to-one ratio.

The Plan's Board of Trustees directed Karl 5 years ago to invest for total return over the long term. However, as Trustees of this highly visible public fund, they cautioned him that volatile or erratic results could cause them embarrassment. They also noted a state statute that mandated that not more than 25% of the Plan's assets (at cost) be invested in common stocks.

At the annual meeting of the Trustees in November 1980, Karl presented the following portfolio and performance report to the Board:

Alpine Employee Retirement Plan

Asset Mix as of 9/30/80	At Cost (Millions)		At Market (Millions)	
Fixed income assets:				
Short-term securities	$ 4.5	11.0%	$ 4.5	11.4%
Long-term bonds and mortgages	26.5	64.7	23.5	59.5
Common stocks	10.0	24.3	11.5	29.1
	$41.0	100.0%	$39.5	100.0%

Investment Performance

	Annual Rates of Return For Periods Ending 9/30/80	
	5 Years	1 Year
Total Alpine Fund:		
Time-weighted	8.2%	5.2%
Dollar-weighted (Internal)	7.7%	4.8%
Assumed actuarial return	6.0%	6.0%
U.S. Treasury bills	7.5%	11.3%
Large sample of pension funds (average 60% equities, 40% fixed income)	10.1%	14.3%
Common stocks—Alpine Fund	13.3%	14.3%
Average portfolio beta coefficient	0.90	0.89
Standard & Poor's 500 Stock Index	13.8%	21.1%
Fixed income securities—Alpine Fund	6.7%	1.0%
Salomon Brothers' Bond Index	4.0%	−11.4%

Karl was proud of his performance and was chagrined when a Trustee made the following critical observations:

a. "Our 1-year results were terrible, and it's what you've done for us lately that counts most."

b. "Our total fund performance was clearly inferior compared to the large sample of other pension funds for the last 5 years. What else could this reflect except poor management judgment?"

c. "Our common stock performance was especially poor for the 5-year period."

d. "Why bother to compare your returns to the return from Treasury bills and the actuarial assumption rate? What your competition could have earned for us or how we would have fared if invested in a passive index (which doesn't charge a fee) are the only relevant measures of performance."

e. "Who cares about time-weighted return? If it can't pay pensions, what good is it!"

Appraise the merits of each of these statements and give counter arguments that Mr. Karl can use.

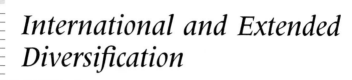

CHAPTER 25

International and Extended Diversification

Although it is common in the United States to use the S&P 500 as the market index portfolio, such practice is in some ways inappropriate. Equities actually comprise less than 25% of total U.S. wealth and a far smaller percentage of world wealth. In this chapter we survey issues of extended diversification. We show how international diversification can improve portfolio performance, examine exchange rate risk, and take a look at investment strategies in an international context. Then we turn to other "nontraditional" asset groups such as real estate and precious metals. These assets, too, may play important roles in investor portfolios.

25.1 *International Investments*

The World Market Portfolio

To appreciate the folly of an exclusive investment focus on U.S. stocks and bonds, examine the components of **world investable wealth** constructed originally by Roger Ibbotson and Laurence Siegel,[1] and updated with Kathryn Love in 1985,[2] presented in Figure 25.1.

The figure gives assessments of both total world wealth and the investable part of world wealth, that is, the part of world wealth that is traded and is therefore accessible to investors. Specifically, in moving from total world wealth to world investable wealth, the authors decided not to include direct investment in durables and foreign real estate. An operational world market index portfolio for 1984 is shown in Table 25.1. According to the authors' estimates, U.S. equities make up only 13.3% of the world index portfolio, whereas world equities comprise about 23%. ("Crossborder assets" in Table 25.1 are those that trade outside the confines of any single country's capital markets.)

---

[1] Ibbotson, R.C., and Siegel, L.B., "The World Market Wealth Portfolio," *Journal of Portfolio Management,* winter 1983.

[2] Ibbotson, R.C., Siegel, L.B., and Love, K.S., "World Wealth: Market Values and Returns," *Journal of Portfolio Management,* fall 1985.

FIGURE 25.1

Total world wealth
and world investable
wealth.

(Redrawn from Ibbotson,
R.C., Siegel, L.B., and
Love, K., "World Wealth:
Market Values and Returns,"
*Journal of Portfolio
Management,* fall 1985.)

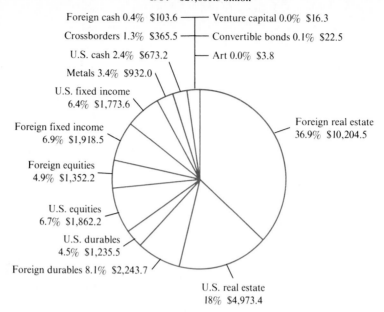

**Total world wealth
1984 = $27,681.5 billion**

Foreign cash 0.4% $103.6 — Venture capital 0.0% $16.3
Crossborders 1.3% $365.5 — Convertible bonds 0.1% $22.5
U.S. cash 2.4% $673.2 — Art 0.0% $3.8
Metals 3.4% $932.0
U.S. fixed income 6.4% $1,773.6
Foreign fixed income 6.9% $1,918.5
Foreign equities 4.9% $1,352.2
U.S. equities 6.7% $1,862.2
U.S. durables 4.5% $1,235.5
Foreign durables 8.1% $2,243.7
Foreign real estate 36.9% $10,204.5
U.S. real estate 18% $4,973.4

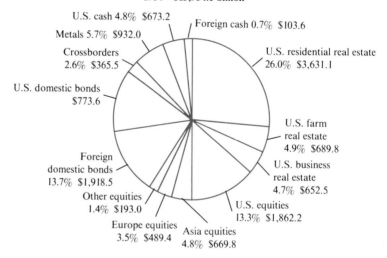

**World investable wealth
1984 = $13,954.1 billion**

U.S. cash 4.8% $673.2
Metals 5.7% $932.0
Crossborders 2.6% $365.5
U.S. domestic bonds $773.6
Foreign domestic bonds 13.7% $1,918.5
Other equities 1.4% $193.0
Europe equities 3.5% $489.4
Asia equities 4.8% $669.8
Foreign cash 0.7% $103.6
U.S. residential real estate 26.0% $3,631.1
U.S. farm real estate 4.9% $689.8
U.S. business real estate 4.7% $652.5
U.S. equities 13.3% $1,862.2

TABLE 25.1 Asset Proportions in Total World Investable Wealth ($13,954.1 Billion in 1984)

Asset Class	Proportion (%)		
	U.S.	Foreign	Crossborder
Cash and equivalents	4.8	.7	—
Bonds	12.7	13.7	2.6
Equities	13.3	9.7	—
Metals	—	—	6.7
U.S. real estate			
Business and farm	9.6	—	—
Residental	26.0	—	—
TOTAL	66.4	24.1	9.3

From Ibbotson, R.C., Siegel, L.B., and Love, K.S., "World Wealth: Market Values and Returns," *Journal of Portfolio Management,* fall 1985.

TABLE 25.2 Comparative Sizes of World Equity Markets, 1986*

Area or Country	$ Billion	% of Total
Europe	**1,338**	**23.7**
United Kingdom	440	7.8
West Germany	246	4.4
Switzerland	132	2.3
France	150	2.7
Netherlands	73	1.3
Sweden	49	0.9
Italy	141	2.5
Spain	42	0.7
Belgium	36	0.6
Pacific Area	**1,910**	**33.9**
Japan	1,746	30.9
Australia	78	1.4
Singapore	33	0.6
Hong Kong	53	0.9
North America	**2,369**	**42.0**
United States	2,203	39.0
Canada	166	2.9
World	**5,642**	**100.0**

From Solnik, Bruno, *International Investments,* © 1988, Addison-Wesley Publishing Co., Inc., Reading, Massachusetts. Tables 2 and 7. Reprinted with permission.
*Column sums may not equal totals because of rounding error.

TABLE 25.3   Size of Major Bond Markets at Year-End, 1985*

Bond Market	Total Publicly Issued	Public Issues in All Markets (%)
U.S. dollar	3,119.0	52.6
Japanese yen	1,082.9	18.2
Deutsche mark	427.2	7.2
Italian lira	276.4	4.7
U.K. sterling	210.8	3.6
French franc	174.4	2.9
Canadian dollar	131.0	2.2
Belgian franc	112.0	1.9
Danish krone	102.0	1.7
Swedish krona	101.7	1.7
Swiss franc	76.6	1.3
Dutch guilder	69.0	1.2
Australian dollar	50.2	0.8
TOTAL	**5,933.2**	**100.0**

Modified from Solnik, Bruno, *International Investments*, Reading, Mass.: Addison-Wesley Publishing Co., Inc., 1988.
*Nominal value outstanding, billions of U.S. dollars equivalent.

Table 25.1 and Figure 25.1 show clearly that "traditional" U.S. assets—stocks, bonds, and bills—are only a small fraction of the potential universe of investments. Tables 25.2 and 25.3 provide insight on the potential importance of international diversification per se, even ignoring diversification into real assets such as metals or real estate. Table 25.2 shows that U.S. equities in 1986 were only 39% of world equity, whereas Table 25.3 shows that U.S. bonds were slightly more than half of world bonds in 1985. Portfolios that exclude non-U.S. assets clearly will pass up important opportunities for diversification.

International Diversification

From our discussion of the power of diversification in Chapter 7 we know that adding to a portfolio assets that are not perfectly correlated will improve the best attainable reward-to-volatility ratio. Given increasing globalization, might not foreign securities provide a feasible way to extend diversification?

Figure 25.2 demonstrates the marked reduction in risk that can be achieved by including foreign, as well as U.S., stocks in a portfolio. The graph presents the standard deviation of equally weighted portfolios of various sizes as a percentage of the average standard deviation of a one-stock portfolio. For example, a value of 20 means that the diversified portfolio has only 20% of the standard deviation of a typical stock. The graphs in Figure 25.2 are presented in terms of the standard deviation of the dollar-denominated returns to make them relevant to U.S. investors.

Figure 25.2 demonstrates that rational investors should invest across borders. Adding international investments to national investments enhances the power of port-

Joys of Diversification:
A Broad Portfolio Pays Off

Over the past two decades, a diversified investment index has outpaced the U.S. stock market and the typical portfolio manager. The index consists of five equally weighted parts: U.S. stocks, foreign stocks, U.S. corporate and government bonds, real estate and Treasury bills. This index has grown at a 10.2% compound rate since 1965, compared with 9.4% for the S&P 500-stock index and 7.9% for the median U.S. money manager invested in both stocks and bonds.

Most of the extra gains came from foreign equities and real estate, which raced ahead of U.S. stocks for much of the 1970s and early 1980s. Analysts differ on whether this performance will continue. But they say diversified portfolios can be less volatile than all-equity accounts, because swings in different parts of a broad portfolio often offset one another somewhat.

Individual investors could approximately duplicate the diversification index with a combination of Treasury bills, stocks of real estate investment trusts or limited partnerships in income-producing real estate, and mutual funds specializing in blue chip and overseas stocks and in fixed-income securities.

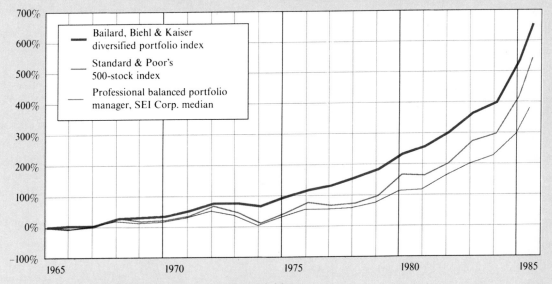

Source: Bailard, Biehl & Kaiser Inc., San Mateo, Calif.

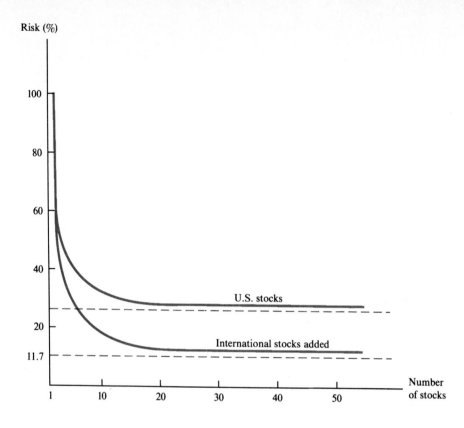

FIGURE 25.2

International diversification.

(Modified from Solnik, B., "Why Not Diversify Internationally Rather Than Domestically," *Financial Analysts Journal*, July/August 1974.)

folio diversification. Table 25.4 presents results from a study of equity returns showing that, although the correlation coefficients between the U.S. stock index and stock index portfolios of other large industrialized economies are positive, they are much smaller than 1. Most correlations are below .5. In contrast, correlation coefficients between diversified U.S. portfolios—with 40 to 50 securities, for example—typically exceed .9. The imperfect correlation across national boundaries allows for the improvement in diversification potential that shows up in Figure 25.2.

Concept Check

Question 1. What would Figure 25.2 look like if we next introduced the possibility of diversifying into real estate investments in addition to foreign equity?

A different perspective on opportunities for international diversification appears in Figure 25.3. Here we examine risk-return opportunities offered by several asset classes, alone and combined into portfolios. For example, we see that world stocks plotted to the northwest of U.S. stocks for this 10-year period, offering higher average return and lower risk than U.S. stocks alone. World stocks and bonds together

TABLE 25.4 Correlation Coefficients of Monthly Percentage Changes in Major Stock Market Indices (Local Currencies, June 1981 to September 1987)

	Australia	Austria	Belgium	Canada	Denmark	France	Germany	Hong Kong	Ireland	Italy	Japan	Malaysia	Mexico	Netherlands	New Zealand	Norway	Singapore	South Africa	Spain	Sweden	Switzerland	U.K.
Austria	.219																					
Belgium	.190	.222																				
Canada	.568	.250	.215																			
Denmark	.217	−.062	.219	.301																		
France	.180	.263	.355	.351	.241																	
Germany	.145	.406	.315	.194	.215	.327																
Hong Kong	.321	.174	.129	.236	.120	.201	.304															
Ireland	.349	.202	.361	.490	.387	.374	.067	.320														
Italy	.209	.224	.307	.321	.150	.459	.257	.216	.275													
Japan	.182	−.025	.223	.294	.186	.361	.147	.137	.183	.241												
Malaysia	.329	−.013	.096	.274	.151	−.134	−.020	.159	.082	−.119	.109											
Mexico	.220	.018	.104	.114	−.174	−.009	.002	.149	.113	.114	−.021	.231										
Netherlands	.294	.232	.344	.545	.341	.344	.511	.395	.373	.344	.333	.151	.038									
New Zealand	.389	.290	.275	.230	.148	.247	.318	.352	.314	.142	−.111	.136	.231	.239								
Norway	.355	.009	.233	.381	.324	.231	.173	.356	.306	.156	.156	.262	.050	.405	.201							
Singapore	.374	.030	.133	.320	.133	−.085	.037	.219	.102	−.038	.066	.891	.202	.196	.212	.280						
South Africa	.279	.159	.143	.385	−.113	.267	.007	−.095	.024	.093	.225	−.013	.260	.058	.038	.156	−.056					
Spain	.147	.018	.050	.190	.019	.255	.147	.193	.175	.290	.248	−.071	.059	.170	.095	.075	.056	−.088				
Sweden	.327	.161	.158	.376	.131	.159	.227	.196	.122	.330	.115	.103	.000	.324	.136	.237	.180	.070	.181			
Switzerland	.334	.401	.276	.551	.283	.307	.675	.379	.290	.287	.130	.099	.026	.570	.397	.331	.157	.112	.192	.334		
U.K.	.377	.073	.381	.590	.218	.332	.263	.431	.467	.328	.354	.193	.068	.534	.014	.313	.250	.168	.209	.339	.435	
United States	.328	.138	.250	.720	.351	.390	.209	.114	.380	.224	.326	.347	.063	.473	.083	.356	.377	.218	.214	.279	.500	.513

Modified from Roll, Richard, "The International Crash of October 1987," Working Paper, University of California, Los Angeles, April 1988.

International and Extended Diversification

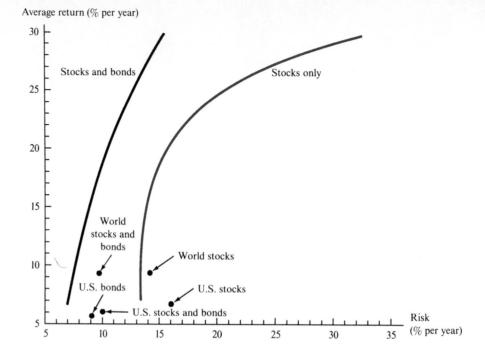

FIGURE 25.3

Efficient frontiers, December 1970 to December 1980.

(From Solnik, B., and Noetzlin, B., "Optimal International Asset Allocation," *Journal of Portfolio Management,* fall 1982.)

offered an even better risk-return combination. (All returns are calculated in terms of U.S. dollars.) Of course, the efficient frontiers generated from these assets offer the best possible risk-return pairs; these are vastly superior to the risk-return profile of U.S. stocks alone.

Evidence that U.S. investors are increasingly aware of the importance of the international sector shows up in the international investments of U.S. pension plans, according to figures compiled by Greenwich Associates and summarized in Table 25.5.

Exchange Rate Risk

International investing poses unique challenges for U.S. investors. Information in foreign markets may be less timely and more difficult to come by. In smaller economies with correspondingly smaller securities markets, one can encounter higher transaction costs and liquidity problems. There also is a need for special expertise concerning political risk. **Political risk** arises from the possibility of the expropriation of assets, changes in tax policy, the possibility of restrictions on the exchange of foreign currency for domestic currency, or other changes in the business climate of a country.

In addition to these risks, international investing entails exchange rate risk. The dollar return from a foreign investment depends not only on the returns in the foreign currency, but also on the exchange rate between the dollar and that currency.

For example, consider an investment in England in risk-free British government

TABLE 25.5 How Projected Dollars Invested Abroad Have Been Changing Millions)

Pension Plan Assets	1982	1983	1986
Over $1 billion	$2,420	$7,118	$17,346
251-1,000 million	1,067	1,285	4,462
100-250 million	313	288	775
Under 100 million	157	71	224
TOTAL	**$3,957**	**$8,762**	**$22,807**

Data from Greenwich Research Associates.

bills paying 10% annual interest in British pounds. These U.K. bills would be the risk-free asset to a British investor—but not for a U.S. investor. Suppose, for example, that the initial **exchange rate** is $2 per pound, and that the U.S. investor starts with $20,000. Those funds can be exchanged for £10,000 and invested at a risk-free 10% rate providing £11,000 in 1 year. However, what if the dollar-pound exchange rate varies over the course of the year? Suppose that the pound depreciates during the year, so that by year-end only $1.80 is required to purchase £1. Despite the positive 10% pound-denominated return, the dollar-denominated return will be negative. The £11,000 can be exchanged at the year-end exchange rate for only $19,800 (11,000 × 1.80), resulting in a loss of $200 relative to the initial $20,000 investment, for a dollar-denominated return of −1%.

Let us generalize. The $20,000 is exchanged for $20,000/$E_0$ pounds, where E_0 denotes the original exchange rate ($2/£). The U.K. investment grows to $(20,000/E_0)[1 + r_f(UK)]$ British pounds, where r_f (UK) is the risk-free rate in the U.K. The pound proceeds ultimately are converted back to dollars at the subsequent exchange rate E_1, for total dollar proceeds of $20,000(E_1/E_0) [1 + r_f(UK)]$. Therefore the dollar-denominated return on the investment in British bills is

$$1 + r(US) = [1 + r_f(UK)] E_1/E_0 \qquad (25.1)$$

We see in equation 25.1 that the dollar-denominated return for a U.S. investor equals the pound-denominated return multiplied by the exchange rate "return." For a U.S. investor, the investment in the British bill in fact is a combination of a safe investment in the U.K. and a risky investment in the performance of the pound relative to the dollar. In this case the pound fared poorly, falling from a value of $2 to only $1.80. The loss on the pound more than offset the earnings on the British bill.

Concept Check

Question 2. Calculate the rate of return in dollars to a U.S. investor holding the British bill if the year-end exchange rate is:
a. E_1 = $2.00/£
b. E_1 = $2.20/£

In this example the exchange rate risk could have been hedged using a forward contract in foreign exchange. If the forward exchange rate had been $F = \$1.93/\pounds$ when the investment was made, the U.S. investor could have locked in a risk-free dollar-denominated return by locking in the year-end exchange rate at $1.93/£. In this case the risk-free U.S. return would have been 6.15%:

$$[1 + r_f(UK)](F/E_0) = (1.10)(1.93/2.00)$$
$$= 1.0615$$

Let us investigate the steps that would be taken to lock in the dollar-denominated returns.

Initial Transaction	End-of-Year Proceeds in Dollars
1. Exchange $20,000 for £10,000 and invest at 10% in U.K.	£11,000 × E_1
2. Enter a contract to deliver £11,000 for dollars at the (forward) exchange rate, $1.93/£.	£11,000(1.93 − E_1)
TOTAL	£11,000 × $1.93/£ = $21,230

The forward contract entered in step 2 exactly offsets the exchange rate risk incurred in step 1.

In fact, you might recall that this is precisely the hedging strategy at the heart of the interest rate parity relationship of Chapter 22. The U.S. investor can lock in a risk-free dollar-denominated return either by investing in the U.K. and hedging exchange rate risk, or by investing in risk-free U.S. assets. Because the returns on two risk-free strategies must be equal, we conclude that

$$[1 + r_f(UK)]\frac{F}{E_0} = 1 + r_f(US)$$

$$\frac{F}{E_0} = \frac{1 + r_f(US)}{1 + r_f(UK)}$$

which is the interest rate parity relationship for a single period.

Unfortunately, such perfect exchange rate hedging is usually not so easy. In our example we knew exactly how many pounds to sell in the forward market because the pound-denominated proceeds in the U.K. were risk-free. If the U.K. investment had not been in bills but instead were in risky U.K. equity, we would not know the ultimate value in pounds of our U.K. investment or therefore how many pounds to sell forward. Thus the hedging opportunity offered by foreign exchange forward contracts would be imperfect. To summarize, the generalization of equation 25.1 is that

$$1 + r(US) = [1 + r(foreign)](E_1/E_0) \tag{25.2}$$

where r(foreign) is the possibly risky return earned in the currency of the foreign investment. The only opportunity for perfect hedging is in the special case that r(foreign) is itself a known number.

Concept Check

Question 3. How many pounds would need to be sold forward to hedge exchange rate risk in the above example if
a. r(UK) = 20%
b. r(UK) = 30%

Passive and Active International Investing

When we discussed investment strategies in the purely domestic context, we used a market index portfolio such as the S&P 500 as a benchmark passive equity investment. This suggests that a world market index might be a useful starting point for a passive international strategy.

One widely used index of non-U.S. stocks is the Europe, Australia, Far East, or **EAFE index** computed by Morgan Stanley. However, there are now several additional indices of world equity performance. Capital International Indices has published several indicators of international equity performance since 1968. Now Salomon Brothers, First Boston, and Goldman Sachs also publish world equity indices. Portfolios designed to mirror or even replicate the country, currency, and company representation of these indices would be the obvious generalization of the purely domestic passive equity strategy.

Active portfolio management in an international context also may be viewed as an extension of active domestic management. In principle, one would form an efficient frontier from the full menu of world securities, and determine the optimal risky portfolio. However, to focus on the special aspects of international investing, we more often view active management from a broader asset-allocation framework. In this case we focus on the following potential sources of abnormal returns: currency selection, country selection, stock selection within countries, and cash/bond selection within countries.

We may measure the contribution of each of these factors in a manner similar to the performance attribution techniques introduced in Chapter 24.

1. **Currency selection** measures the contribution to total portfolio performance attributable to exchange rate fluctuations relative to the investor's benchmark currency, which we will take to be the U.S. dollar. We can measure currency selection as the weighted average of the appreciation, E_1/E_0, of each currency represented in the portfolio, using as weights the fraction of the portfolio invested in each currency. We might use a benchmark such as the EAFE index to compare a portfolio's currency selection for a particular period to a passive benchmark. EAFE currency selection would thus be computed as the weighted average of

---

TABLE 25.6   Example of Performance Attribution: International

	EAFE* Weight	Return on Equity Index	E_1/E_0	Manager's Weight	Manager's Return
Europe	.30	.10	1.10	.35	.08
Australia	.10	.05	.90	.10	.07
Far East	.60	.15	1.30	.55	.18

With the above data we can make the following calculations:

Currency selection:	EAFE: $.30 \times 1.10 + .10 \times .90 + .60 \times 1.30 = 1.20$ (20% appreciation) Manager: $.35 \times 1.10 + .10 \times .90 + .55 \times 1.30 = 1.19$ Loss of 1% relative to EAFE.
Country selection:	EAFE: $.30 \times .10 + .10 \times .05 + .60 \times .15 = .125$ Manager: $.35 \times .10 + .10 \times .05 + .55 \times .15 = .1225$ Loss of .25% relative to EAFE.
Stock selection:	$(.08 - .10).35 + (.07 - .05).10 + (.18 - .15).55 = .0115$ Contribution of 1.15% relative to EAFE.

*E, Europe; A, Australia; FE, Far East.

E_1/E_0 of the currencies represented in the EAFE portfolio, using as weights the fraction of the EAFE portfolio invested in each currency.

2. **Country selection** measures the contribution to performance attributable to investing in the better-performing stock markets of the world. It can be measured as the weighted average of the *equity-index* returns of each country, using as weights the share of the manager's portfolio in each country. We use index returns to abstract from the effect of security selection within countries. To measure a manager's contribution relative to a passive strategy, we might compare country selection to the weighted average across countries of equity index returns, using as weights the share of the EAFE portfolio in each country.

3. **Stock selection** ability may, as in Chapter 24, be measured as the weighted average of equity returns *in excess of the equity index* in each country. In this instance we would use local currency returns and use as weights the investments in each country.

4. **Cash/bond selection** may be measured as the excess return derived from weighting bonds and bills differently from some benchmark weights.

An example of international performance attribution is presented in Table 25.6.

Concept Check

Question 4. What would the manager's country and currency selection have been if his portfolio weights were 40% in Europe, 20% in Australia, and 40% in the Far East?

TABLE 25.7 Relative Importance of World, Industrial, Currency, and Domestic Factors in Explaining Return of a Stock

	Average R-SQR of Regression on Factors				
	Single-Factor Tests				Joint Test
Locality	World	Industrial	Currency	Domestic	All Four Factors
Switzerland	0.18	0.17	0.00	0.38	0.39
West Germany	0.08	0.10	0.00	0.41	0.42
Australia	0.24	0.26	0.01	0.72	0.72
Belgium	0.07	0.08	0.00	0.42	0.43
Canada	0.27	0.24	0.07	0.45	0.48
Spain	0.22	0.03	0.00	0.45	0.45
United States	0.26	0.47	0.01	0.35	0.55
France	0.13	0.08	0.01	0.45	0.60
United Kingdom	0.20	0.17	0.01	0.53	0.55
Hong Kong	0.06	0.25	0.17	0.79	0.81
Italy	0.05	0.03	0.00	0.35	0.35
Japan	0.09	0.16	0.01	0.26	0.33
Norway	0.17	0.28	0.00	0.84	0.85
Netherlands	0.12	0.07	0.01	0.34	0.31
Singapore	0.16	0.15	0.02	0.32	0.33
Sweden	0.19	0.06	0.01	0.42	0.43
All countries	0.18	0.23	0.01	0.42	0.46

Modified from Solnik, Bruno, *International Investments*, © 1988, Addison-Wesley Publishing Co., Inc., Reading, Massachusetts. Tables 2 and 7. Reprinted with permission.

Factor Models and International Investing

International investing presents a good opportunity for an application of multifactor models of security returns. Natural factors might include the following:

1. A world stock index
2. A national (domestic) stock index
3. Industrial sector indices
4. Currency movements

Solnik and de Freitas[3] use such a framework. Table 25.7 presents some of their results for several countries. The first four columns of numbers present the R^2 of various one-factor regressions. Recall that the R^2 measures the percentage of return volatility of a company's stock that can be explained by the factor treated as the independent or explanatory variable. Solnik and de Freitas estimate the factor regressions for many firms in a given country and report the average R^2 across the firms in that country. The table reveals that the domestic factor seems to be the dominant influence on stock returns. Whereas the domestic index alone generates an average R^2 of .42 across all countries, adding the three additional factors (in the last column of the table) increases average R^2 to only .46.

---

[3]Solnik, Bruno, and de Freitas, A., "International Factors of Stock Price Behavior," CESA working paper, February 1986, cited in Solnik, Bruno, *International Investments*, Addison-Wesley Publishing Co., Reading, Mass. 1988.

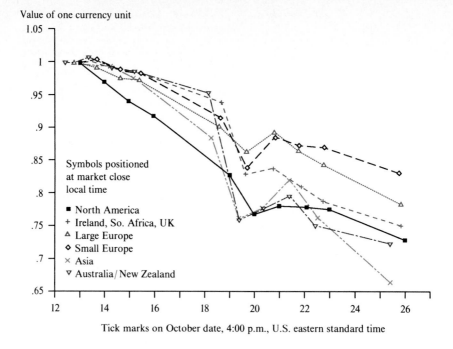

FIGURE 25.4

Regional indices around the crash, October 14–October 26, 1987.

(From Roll, Richard, "The International Crash of October 1987," Working Paper, University of California, Los Angeles, April 1988.)

Value of one currency unit

Symbols positioned at market close local time

■ North America
+ Ireland, So. Africa, UK
△ Large Europe
◇ Small Europe
× Asia
▽ Australia/New Zealand

Tick marks on October date, 4:00 p.m., U.S. eastern standard time

On the other hand, evidence of a world market factor clearly emerges from the market crash of October 1987. Despite the fact that equity returns across borders show only moderate correlation (Table 25.4), equity index returns in October in all 23 countries considered in a study by Richard Roll[4] were negative. Figure 25.4, reproduced from Roll's study, shows the value of regional equity indices (starting from a value of 1.0) during October. The correlation among returns is obvious and suggests some underlying world factor common to all economies. Roll also found that the beta of a country's equity index on a world index (estimated through September 1987) was the best predictor of that index's response to the crash, lending further support to the importance of a world factor.

Equilibrium in International Capital Markets

As for domestic assets, we can look to the CAPM or APT to predict expected rates of return in an international capital market equilibrium. However, these models must be adapted somewhat for the international context.

For example, one might expect that a world CAPM would result simply by replacing a narrow domestic market portfolio with a broad world market portfolio, and measuring betas relative to the world portfolio. Indeed, this approach was pursued in

---

[4]Roll, Richard, "The International Crash of October 1987," Working Paper, University of California, Los Angeles, April 1988.

TABLE 25.8 Equity Returns, 1960-1980

	Average Return	Standard Deviation of Return	Beta	Alpha
Australia	12.20	22.80	1.02	1.52
Austria	10.30	16.90	.01	4.86
Belgium	10.10	13.80	.45	2.44
Canada	12.10	17.50	.77	2.75
Denmark	11.40	24.20	.60	2.91
France	8.10	21.40	.50	.17
Germany	10.10	19.90	.45	2.41
Italy	5.60	27.20	.41	−1.92
Japan	19.00	31.40	.81	9.49
Netherlands	10.70	17.80	.90	.65
Norway	17.40	49.00	−.27	13.39
Spain	10.40	19.80	.04	4.73
Sweden	9.70	16.70	.51	1.69
Switzerland	12.50	22.90	.87	2.66
United Kingdom	14.70	33.60	1.47	1.76
United States	10.20	17.70	1.08	−.69

From Ibbotson, Roger G., Carr, Richard C., and Robinson, Anthony W., "International Equity and Bond Returns," *Financial Analysts Journal,* July/August 1982.

part of a paper by Ibbotson, Carr, and Robinson,[5] who calculated betas of equity indices of several countries against a world equity index. Their results appear in Table 25.8. The betas for different countries show surprising variability.

Whereas such a straightforward generalization of the simple CAPM is a reasonable first step, it is subject to some problems:

1. Taxes, transaction costs, and capital barriers across countries make it difficult and less attractive for investors to hold a world index portfolio. Some assets are simply unavailable to foreign investors.
2. Investors in different countries view exchange rate risk from the perspective of different domestic currencies. Thus they will not agree on the risk characteristics of various securities and therefore will not derive identical efficient frontiers.
3. Investors in different countries tend to consume different baskets of goods, either because of differing tastes, or because of tariffs, transportation costs, or taxes. Therefore, if relative prices of goods vary over time, the inflation risk perceived by investors in different countries also will differ.

These problems suggest that the simple CAPM will not work as well in an international context as it would if all markets were fully integrated. Indeed, some evi-

---

[5]Ibbotson, Roger G., Carr, Richard C., and Robinson, Anthony W., "International Equity and Bond Returns," *Financial Analysts Journal,* July/August 1982.

TABLE 25.9 Investment Characteristics, 1971 to 1983

	90-Day Bills	Salomon Brothers Bond Index	S&P 500	Property Index*
A. Real Annual Rates of Return (%)				
Mean	.3	.2	3.4	3.8
Standard deviation	3.0	14.8	18.7	3.9
B. Correlation Matrix of Real Returns				
Bills	1.0	.7	.4	0
Bonds	.7	1.0	.5	−.4
Stocks	.4	.5	1.0	.3
Property	.0	−.4	.3	1.0

Modified from "Property Revisited: The Role of Property in Pension Fund Investments," Goldman Sachs & Co., Portfolio Strategy publication, October 1984.
*PRISA Index (Prudential Property Investment Separate Account).

dence suggests that assets that are less accessible to foreign investors carry higher risk premiums.[6]

The APT seems better designed for the international context, since the special risk factors that arise in this setting can be treated like any other risk factor. For example, world economic activity and currency movements might simply be added to a list of factors already used in a domestic APT model.

25.2 Real Estate

Like international investments, real estate can play an important role in diversified portfolios. Over the period 1971 to 1983, real estate investments exhibited a risk-return profile far superior to that of the traditional stocks/bonds/bills asset classes. Part *A* of Table 25.9 shows real estate with a mean real return greater than that of stocks, yet a standard deviation of real returns almost as low as bills. These standard deviations probably understate the true volatility of real estate investing. This is because we must use appraisal data when studying real estate returns rather than true transaction prices because most real estate trades only infrequently. Nevertheless, these numbers still suggest outstanding recent performance.

Moreover, real estate exhibits outstanding diversification attributes. Part *B* of Table 25.9 reveals that the correlation of real returns on real estate investments with those of stocks, bonds, and bills has been low or negative, enhancing the opportunity for portfolio risk reduction. Figure 25.5 confirms this point. The efficient frontier

---

[6]Errunza, Vihang, and Losq, Etienne, "International Asset Pricing Under Mild Segmentation: Theory and Test," *Journal of Finance, 40,* March 1985.

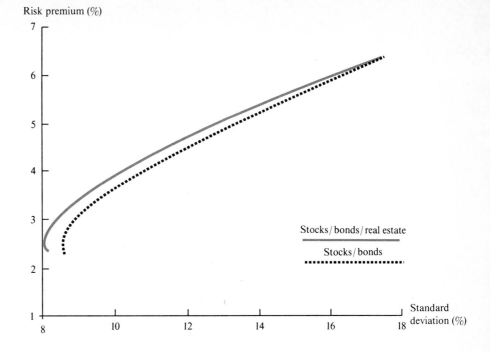

FIGURE 25.5

Attainable efficient frontiers.

(Redrawn from Diermeir, Jeffrey J., Freundlich, Kurt J., and Schlarbaum, Gary G., "The Role of Real Estate in a Multi-Asset Portfolio," in Sale, Tom S. [editor], *Real Estate Investing*, Homewood, Ill.: Dow Jones-Irwin, 1985.)

from stock and bond investments alone is substantially improved when real estate is added to the list of feasible investments.

Another view of the attractive characteristics of real estate investments emerges from the Ibbotson, Siegel, and Love study cited earlier. They performed excess-return index model regressions for several asset classes over the 1959 to 1984 period. U.S. real estate had a beta of only .31 when regressed on the world market portfolio and an annual alpha (abnormal return) of 2.52%. Here again is evidence of low risk and high return, at least for this historical period. Ibbotson and Siegel also found that, when U.S. real estate returns are regressed on the U.S. inflation rate, the slope coefficient was .80, confirming that real estate is an effective inflation hedge. When inflation was higher than expected, so was the nominal return on real estate investments.

25.3 Precious Metals

Precious metals also have been excellent investments in the past. Table 25.10 documents the performance of gold and silver relative to U.S. equities in the 1960 to 1984 period. Although metals have been volatile, their average returns also have been greater than those of equity.

However, the oustanding feature of metals investments has been their ability to serve as an inflation hedge. Ibbotson and Siegel found that a regression of metals

TABLE 25.10   Returns, 1960 to 1984

	Average Return (Arithmetic Mean)	Standard Deviation of Annual Return
Gold	12.62	29.87
Silver	20.51	75.34
Equity (U.S.)	10.20	16.89

From Ibbotson, R.C., Siegel, L.B., and Love, K.S., "World Wealth: Market Values and Returns," *Journal of Portfolio Management,* fall 1985.

returns on U.S. inflation produced a slope coefficient of 5.39, indicating that a 1% increase in inflation was associated with an increased nominal return to metals of more than 5%.

The hedge quality of metals should not be too surprising. We have seen already (Chapter 21) that commodity futures contracts can serve as useful hedge vehicles, and metals are just particular commodities. A related issue concerns the best way to invest in metals. For example, should one buy metals, futures contracts on metals, or companies that mine and refine metals?

Although there is no single correct anwer to this question, some observations are in order. Buying metals (via gold or silver coins, for example) offers the advantage of small-scale transactions. However, it might also entail relatively large storage or insurance costs. Futures contracts offer a low-cost way to bet on prices of traded metals, but require a large minimum investment. Futures contracts also preclude the opportunity for tax timing because of the mark-to-market provision. They also require frequent monitoring as contracts mature and must be rolled over. Finally, investments in stocks of particular companies that mine or refine metals involve issues of firm-specific risk, quality of management, and particular dividend policies that might have beneficial or deleterious tax or cash flow implications for the investor.

Summary

1. U.S. assets comprise only a small fraction of the world wealth portfolio. International capital markets offer important opportunities for portfolio diversification with enhanced risk-return characteristics.

2. Exchange rate risk imparts an extra source of uncertainty to investments denominated in foreign currencies. Much of that risk can be hedged in foreign exchange futures or forward markets, but unless the foreign currency rate of return is known, a perfect hedge is not feasible.

3. Several world market indices can form a basis for passive international investing. Active international management can be partitioned into currency selection, country selection, stock selection, and cash/bond selection.

4. A factor model applied to international investing would include a world factor, as well as the usual domestic factors. Although some evidence suggests that domestic

factors dominate stock returns, the October 1987 crash provides evidence of an important international factor.

5. Real estate and precious metals also offer attractive diversification attributes. Moreover, both of these asset classes have been outstanding inflation hedges.

Key Terms

World investable wealth
Political risk
Exchange rate
EAFE index

Currency selection
Country selection
Stock selection
Cash/bond selection

Selected Readings

Comprehensive textbooks on international facets of investing are:
  Solnik, Bruno, *International Investing*. Reading, Mass.: Addison-Wesley Publishing, Co., Inc., 1988.
  Grabbe, J. Orlin, *International Financial Markets,* New York: Elsevier Science Publishers, 1986.
A text with a greater emphasis on corporate applications and foreign exchange risk management is:
  Shapiro, Alan C., *Multinational Financial Management,* Boston: Allyn & Bacon, Inc., 1986.
A good book of readings is:
  Lessard, Donald R. (editor), *International Financial Management: Theory and Application*, New York: John Wiley & Sons, 1985.

Problems

1. Suppose that a U.S. investor wishes to invest in a British firm currently selling for £40 per share. The investor has $10,000 to invest, and the current exchange rate is $2/£.
   a. How many shares can the investor purchase?
   b. Fill in the table below for rates of return after 1 year in each of the nine scenarios.

Price per Share (£)	Pound-Denominated Return (%)	Dollar-Dominated Return for Year-End Exchange Rate		
		$1.80/£	$2/£	$2.20/£
£35				
£40				
£45				

   c. When is the dollar-denominated return equal to the pound-denominated return?
2. If each of the nine outcomes in question 1 is equally likely, find the standard deviation of both the pound- and dollar-denominated rates of return.
3. Now suppose that the investor in question 1 also sells forward £5,000 at a forward exchange rate of $2.10/£.

a. Recalculate the dollar-denominated returns for each scenario.

b. What happens to the standard deviation of the dollar-denominated return?

4. Calculate the contribution of total performance from currency, country, and stock selection for the following manager:

	EAFE Weight	Return on Equity Index	E_1/E_0	Manager's Weight	Manager's Return
Europe	.30	.20	.9	.35	.18
Australia	.10	.15	1.0	.15	.20
Far East	.60	.25	1.1	.50	.20

5. If the current exchange rate is $1.75/£, the 1-year forward exchange rate is $1.85/£, and the interest rate on British government bills is 8% per year, what risk-free dollar-denominated return can be locked in by investing in the British bills?

6. If you were to invest $10,000 in the British bills of question 5, how would you lock in the dollar-denominated return?

7. Use the data in Table 25.9 to fill in the following table. What do you conclude?

Portfolio	Average Return	Standard Deviation
All stocks		
All bonds		
50% stocks/50% bonds		
One third each in stocks, bonds, and property		

8. (CFA Examination, Level III, 1985)

A U.S. pension plan hired two off-shore firms to manage the non-U.S. equity portion of its total portfolio. Each firm was free to own stocks in any country market included in Capital International's Europe, Australia, and Far East Index (EAFE) and free to use any form of dollar and/or nondollar cash or bonds as an equity substitute or reserve. After 3 years had elapsed, the records of the managers and the EAFE Index were as shown below:

Summary: Contributions to Return

	Currency Selection	Country Selection	Stock Selection	Cash/Bond Allocation	Total Return Recorded
Manager A	9.0%	19.7%	3.1%	0.6%	14.4%
Manager B	7.4	14.2	6.0	2.8	15.6
Composite of A & B	8.2	16.9	4.5	1.7	15.0
EAFE Index	12.9	19.9	—	—	7.0

You are a member of the plan sponsor's Pension Committee, which will soon meet with the plan's consultant to review manager performance. In preparation for this meeting, you go through the following analysis:

a. Briefly describe the strengths and weaknesses of each manager, relative to the EAFE Index data.

b. Briefly explain the meaning of the data in the "Currency" column.

9. (Based on CFA Examination, Level III, 1986)

John Irish, CFA, is an independent investment advisor who is assisting Alfred Darwin, the head of the Investment Committee of General Technology Corporation, to establish a new pension fund. Darwin asks Irish about international equities and whether the Investment Committee should consider them as an additional asset for the pension fund.

a. Explain the rationale for including international equities in General's equity portfolio. Identify and describe *three* relevant considerations in formulating your answer.

b. List *three* possible arguments against international equity investment and briefly discuss the significance of each.

c. To illustrate several aspects of the performance of international securities over time, Irish shows Darwin the accompanying graph of investment results experienced by a U.S. pension fund in the 1970-83 period. Compare the performance of the U.S. dollar and non-U.S. dollar equity and fixed-income asset categories, and explain the significance of the result of the Account Performance Index relative to the results of the four individual asset class indices.

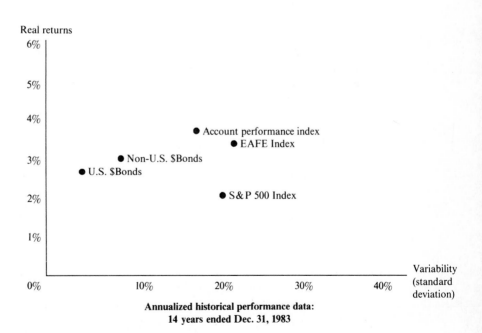

**Annualized historical performance data:
14 years ended Dec. 31, 1983**

CHAPTER 26

Organizational Structure and Management Issues

It is fair to say that there is a certain tension between the investment management community and the academic financial theorist community. The source of this tension is twofold; the first lies in the theory of market efficiency, introduced in the mid-1960s by Eugene Fama. To the professional community the message was that security analysis and macro forecasting—in sum, active portfolio management—are futile because securities are efficiently priced; that is, the passive strategy should be unbeatable. The extreme of this message is epitomized by the joke about the $20 bill (Chapter 13) attributed by professionals to the Chicago School, of which Fama is a prominent professor.

The second source of tension, and perhaps more insidious, is practitioner conviction that financial theory has little to offer in operational guidance for those in the trenches.

As anyone familiar with organizational behavior will see, this tension is more a perception or communication problem than inherent in the nature of financial theory or practical portfolio management. No serious academic would suggest that any effort at active management is futile. (And you can bet that no one would walk by a $20 bill free for the taking.) A fairer characterization of the implication of the theory of market efficiency is that the passive strategy is a good benchmark, that it would take an excellent professional manager to beat it. (And what portfolio manager will suggest that he or she is anything but excellent?)

The question of what financial theory has to offer active portfolio managers is less trivial and is the topic of this chapter. We demonstrate that financial theory provides the following guidelines:

1. How to transform security analysis into operational forecasts
2. How to organize the various functions of portfolio management into decentralized units
3. How to combine the output of the independent units of the portfolio management operation to produce the complete portfolio

4. How to monitor the performance of the various units, evaluate the quality, and compensate the analysts appropriately

Our aim is to establish the complementarity of financial theory and practice. Students of management will recognize that the application of portfolio optimization methods to organization issues accords with general management principles. As more portfolio managers adopt the normative implications of financial theory, portfolio management organizations will more closely resemble the features described in this chapter.

26.1 *The Basic Organization Chart*

The heart of an efficient investment management organization is determination of the macro forecast, construction of the active portfolio, and combining the active portfolio with a passive or market index portfolio to arrive at the optimal risky portfolio. The line units of the organization can be seen as the following:

1. Macro analysis and index portfolio management
2. Micro analysis and active portfolio management
3. Optimization and complete portfolio management

Management is the key word everywhere. So-called passive managers must use sophisticated portfolio techniques to lower the cost of effectively holding the market index portfolio. Many investment management organizations engage in some active management of the safe asset portfolio, instead of "parking cash" in maximum-safety short-term T-bills.

The line units of the operation require two staff units to facilitate, monitor, and evaluate the work of the line units. Successful forecasting requires resources such as data, data processing, and computer assistance. These are provided by a data, resources, and estimation unit. A second staff unit, independent of the forecasters, provides the performance evaluation and attribution function.

As in any organization, logistics are provided by staff units that include accounting and financial control, marketing and sales, personnel and physical plant management, and a clearinghouse unit to take care of market transactions and the relationship with brokers and other intermediaries.

The various units are displayed in the basic organization chart in Figure 26.1.

26.2 *The Index Portfolio Group*

The Index Portfolio Group would be referred to as the Passive Portfolio Group in the Treynor-Black model. However, it is passive only in that it takes security prices as being fairly set. It serves two critical functions: (1) it provides macro forecasts, and (2) it manages the organization's market index portfolio.

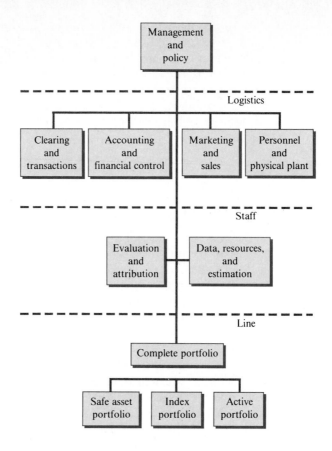

FIGURE 26.1
Basic organization
chart for investment
management.

Management
and
policy

- -

Logistics

| Clearing and transactions | Accounting and financial control | Marketing and sales | Personnel and physical plant |

- -

Staff

| Evaluation and attribution | Data, resources, and estimation |

- -

Line

Complete portfolio

| Safe asset portfolio | Index portfolio | Active portfolio |

Macro Forecasting

Anyone who takes on the responsibility of providing macro forecasts of the rate of return on the market index portfolio needs a lion's heart. Consider first that the stock market index is one of the *leading* indicators in the arsenal of economic forecasters. This means that economists take stock-market prices as *input* into forecasts of future economic activity, which implies that it is difficult to use current economic data to forecast future stock-market prices (returns). Those who can do that well, however, stand to gain enormous profits, as described in Chapter 23.

A corollary to the fact that the stock market is a leading indicator is that forecasting the excess rate of return on the market portfolio by extrapolation from past data will do no good. If you are still undeterred, consider the following[1]:

---

[1]From Maginn, John L., and Tuttle, Donald L., *Managing Investment Portfolios,* sponsored by the Institute of Chartered Financial Analysts, Boston: Warren, Gorham and Lamont, 1983.

Despite the enticing appeal of reducing market exposure through astute sales when securities appear to be overpriced, and bold commitments when prices appear to have declined to attractively low levels, the overwhelming evidence shows that market timing is *not* an effective way to reduce market risk, for the dour but compelling reasons that, *on average* [italics added] and over time, it does not work.

There, you heard it from the horse's mouth—the ICFA. We emphasize the words "on average," because the enormous payoffs to those who can beat the odds make the undertaking irresistible (and there are bound to be those who are above average). The bottom line is that the authors of this text cannot teach anyone how to produce good market forecasts. If we could, we would be out there breaking the bank.

We have talked so far about forecasting the expected excess return (the risk premium) on the market portfolio. We need an estimate of its risk as well, that is, a number for the standard error of the forecast. This estimate is easier to come by, for a reason that constitutes an interesting caveat in estimation theory. The quality of an estimate of the *mean* of a random variable from time-series data depends only on the length of the sample period. Suppose that we are willing to assume that the mean of the rate of return on a stock has been constant over the past 5 years and wish to estimate it. It would make no difference how many observations we may use from the past 5-year period.

Let us assume that the standard deviation of the annual rate of return is 20%. If we take the average of the five annual rates, then the standard error of the estimate will be $20/\sqrt{5}$. Can we improve accuracy by using the 60 monthly observations? Assuming that rates are serially uncorrelated, the monthly standard deviation is $20/\sqrt{12}$. The standard error of the estimate of the *monthly* mean is therefore $20/\sqrt{12 \times 60}$. To obtain the estimate of the *annual* mean and its standard error from the monthly mean, we multiply by 12. The result is that the standard error of the estimate of the annual mean from monthly data is still $20/\sqrt{5}$, because we have only 5 years of data. No improvement in accuracy has been achieved by using 12 times as many observations *within* the sample period. If we had 20 years of data, however, the standard error would be cut in half.

Estimating the variance of the rate of return (as well as covariances with other rates), however, does not require a long measurement interval. The standard error of the estimate of the *standard deviation* of the rate of return over a sample period is approximately inversely proportional to the number of observations within the sample period. Hence, if we were to estimate the standard deviation over the past 5 years to go along with the estimate of the mean, we could improve the estimate from the five annual returns by using monthly observations, cutting the standard error of the estimate to about one fourth of its original value. If we went further, obtaining daily returns and assuming 22 business days per month, the standard error could approach $1/16$ of the original value. Thus, whenever we can assume that the variances and covariances change relatively slowly, we can obtain accurate forecasts for variances and covariances from past data. Most of the actual forecasting of risk involves estimation of variances and covariances from past data.

Picture yourself as manager of the Index Portfolio Group. Your macro forecasting unit constantly feeds you updated forecasts of the excess return on the market index portfolio (risk premium) and its variance (risk). Should you forward these forecasts to the manager of the complete portfolio, to be used in the construction of the optimal risky portfolio? The missing link here involves accounting for the quality of these forecasts. Although the technical aspect of this process is relegated to the Appendix of this chapter, it is important to expound on the principle.

Suppose that the long-run mean excess return on the market portfolio is 8%. Your analyst submits to you a forecast of 15%. The use of a forecast that deviates by 7% from one's uninformed prior (guess) would clearly cause a major shift toward the index portfolio. Do you feel some pressure to shave it a little? The decision should depend on how reliable the *forecaster* is. The 7% deviation should be multiplied first by a discount factor and then added back to the long-run mean. This "shaved" forecast is the one to use at the complete portfolio level.

The discount factor to use is the squared correlation coefficient between the forecasts of market returns and their subsequent realizations. This squared correlation coefficient is a number between zero and one. A perfect forecaster would achieve a correlation of one. There will be no discounting of her forecasts! Forecasts by a forecaster with a correlation of zero would be completely discounted. Furthermore, this ability parameter, the squared correlation coefficient, is used to temper the risk parameter. The difference between the squared correlation coefficient and one (the proportion of the market deviations that is not explained by the forecasts) is used as a discount factor to the *variance* of market return. Thus, with a perfect forecaster, the discount factor is zero and, indeed there is no risk left with her forecasts. With an ability parameter of one half, the risk parameter (the market variance in this case) ought to be discounted to one half its original value.

The process of **adjusting forecasts** requires, as input, the ability parameters of the forecasters. These can be obtained from the record of the forecasters with the organization. The fact that we only estimate, rather than know, these parameters complicates the task. This type of work is the major responsibility of the Evaluation and Attribution Group, to be discussed later.

Concept Check

Question 1. The macro forecasting unit has submitted its 1-year forecast for the market excess return at 15%. The long-run average excess return of the market has been 9%, and the track record of the forecasting unit has been:

Forecast:	20.0	35.0	33.0	−30.0	−50.0	30.0	20.0
Actual:	−17.3	24.1	10.4	−0.6	−11.8	21.9	36.8

Assuming that the sample is representative, what should be the adjusted macro forecast of the organization?

On the face of it, running an index portfolio appears to be a trivial assignment. Nothing is further from the truth. Let us first determine the role of the index portfolio. In a single-factor domestic stock market the foremost goal of the index portfolio is to replicate the market. Ideally, such a portfolio will include all risky assets in the economy. By contemporary standards, the Wilshire 5,000 may be the best alternative. It includes the stocks that are listed on the NYSE and the AMEX and about 3,000 of the more actively traded OTC stocks. Whatever the ideal index portfolio is (call it M^*), it is unlikely that it would serve as the index portfolio, M, for your organization, for two reasons:

1. Some of the stocks in M^* cannot be held by restrictions of the prospectus or client-stated policy.
2. The cost of holding this large portfolio is simply too high.

The objective becomes to create an index portfolio, M, that has the highest possible correlation with M^* and a beta coefficient on M^* as close to one as possible. Operationally, this boils down to a mathematical programming problem. A simple exposition is provided in the Appendix to this chapter.

Construction of the index portfolio requires extensive estimation (of the beta coefficients and residual variance of most stocks in M^*), as well as statistical procedures of selecting random samples leading to the optimization exercise. Execution of these tasks will be shared with the Data, Resources, and Estimation Group.

Once the size and composition of the index portfolio are determined, the index portfolio manager forwards it to the Complete Portfolio Group, where the complete portfolio will be constructed. The index portfolio manager repeats this procedure periodically to ensure that the index portfolio remains reasonably efficient as circumstances change. For ongoing independent assessment of the efforts of the Index Portfolio Group, the Evaluation and Attribution Group will continuously monitor the performance of the index portfolio, M.[2]

If, in addition to equity investments, the organization portfolio is made to include international diversification, or bond portfolio management, or real estate investments, then index portfolio management requires still more work. These additional tasks can be summarized as follows:

1. Identify the relevant factor portfolios.
2. Set up macro forecasting facilities and estimation procedures to supply input for optimal construction of the composite index portfolio.
3. Repeat procedure for generating an efficient down-sized index portfolio for each factor portfolio.
4. Optimize the composite index portfolio, period by period, compute its performance forecast, and communicate this output to the Complete Portfolio Group.

---

[2]The index portfolio can be replaced by futures contracts on a broad market index, thus avoiding the need to go through the procedure of designing an efficient substitute. The procedure will be necessary whenever the passive strategy includes economic factors beyond the stock market index. To construct efficient factor portfolios, the procedure described here is necessary.

FIGURE 26.2

Organization chart of
the Index Portfolio
Group.

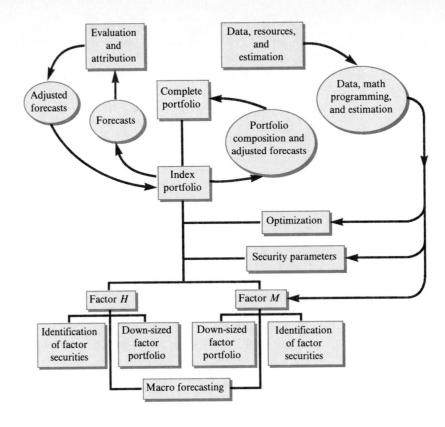

5. Communicate the composition of the composite index portfolio to the Data, Resources, and Estimation Group. Aid in setting up the data base of stock parameters (beta, residual risk) relative to the updated composite portfolio.

The Organization Chart of the Index Portfolio Group

The organization chart of the unit is designed by function. The cooperation and shared facilities that are required within the group are obvious. Figure 26.2 illustrates the communication between the Index Portfolio Group and outside units and also shows output responsibilities.

26.3 The Active Portfolio Group

The consistent quality of the active portfolio will make or break the investment management organization. It is fair to say that the role of all the other units in the organization is to enhance the success of the Active Portfolio Group. As much as the failure of other units may tarnish its performance, if the active portfolio lacks sterling quality, no effort by any other unit will matter. The role of the active portfolio staff is analogous to that of doctors in a hospital. The analysts of the Active Portfolio Group are the "stars" of the operation.

The function of the Active Portfolio Group can be divided into two parts:

1. Micro forecasting: analyze securities and determine the future abnormal return, α, for each security.
2. Optimizing the portfolio: determine the weights of individual securities in the active portfolio, A, so as to maximize the ratio of the reward, α_A, to nonsystematic standard deviation, $\sigma(e_A)$.

Micro Forecasting

Few analysts think in terms of an abnormal return, α, on the security that they analyze, yet this α value is the output that is required to optimize the active portfolio. Let us review two crucial principles of equity valuation:

1. A stock is perceived as mispriced only if your analysis differs from market consensus.
2. An abnormal return can be earned on a mispriced security only if and when the consensus will change so as to agree with your analysis.

Consider the following hypothetical analyst's report:

My prediction is that oil prices are on the rise. History shows that when oil prices rise, profits of oil companies rise while those of manufacturing firms decline. Therefore I'm bullish on oil stocks and bearish on manufacturing stocks.

The value of this analysis is *conditional* on the central issue: whether the analyst's prediction of an imminent oil price increase is more extreme than the consensus among investors. If the prediction is no different from the prevailing forecast, both oil and manufacturing stocks are already priced to reflect that forecast. Furthermore, even if the analyst's forecast is correct, but his prediction is for a *smaller* price increase than that of the consensus forecast, the conclusion ought to be reversed: bearish on oil stocks and bullish on manufacturing stocks.

The conventional benchmark is the readily available report on distribution of earning forecasts by analysts (IBES). We can compare one analyst's bottom-line earnings forecast with the mean of the listed analyst's forecasts, appraise the difference between the two values relative to the dispersion of the forecasts, and judge where the analyst stands in valuation of stocks relative to the consensus.

In a complete security analysis, analysts come up with a fair price that reflects their assessment of the value of the stock, given their forecast of the future of the corporation. When this price is different from the actual market price, the stock is mispriced by the difference between the two. To convert this dollar figure of mispricing to a rate of return, the analyst needs to forecast the rate of amortization of the difference.

Analysts will apply these two principles to supply the Active Portfolio Group manager with constantly updated alpha values for the stocks they are assigned to analyze.

Question 2. Suppose an analyst is using the constant dividend growth model for stock XYZ. There are three inputs:
a. A forecast of the next quarterly dividend, for example, D_1 = 60 cents per share and the permanent (quarterly) dividend growth rate, g = 1.5%
b. The required (quarterly) rate of return on XYZ stock, r_β = 4.5%, given the beta of the XYZ stock and the macro forecast
c. The stock market price of XYZ stock, P_0 = $18.50
What would be the abnormal rate of return on the stock under various amortization rates of the analyst's mispricing estimate? Use 2 and 12 quarters as examples.

Adjusting the Micro Forecasts

The alpha values are subjective values that are only as reliable as the ability of the analyst. Just as we adjust a raw macro forecast, we discount the raw micro forecast by the analyst's ability parameter, which is the square of the correlation coefficient between the analyst's alpha prediction and the subsequent realized values. The adjustment of each analyst's raw alpha forecast is obtained by the Active Portfolio Group with the cooperation of the Evaluation and Attribution Group, which updates the ability parameter from recent forecasts and subsequent realizations. When an analyst submits a forecast of alpha for a stock in the universe of analyzed stocks, it is multiplied by the ability parameter. In addition, the variance of the residual (which ordinarily would be the nonsystematic risk parameter) is multiplied by one minus the ability parameter. Thus the (nonsystematic) risk is also discounted to account for the quality of the forecast.

Question 3. A share of stock of Z, Inc. is currently selling for $12.50. David, the analyst who covers the stock, suggests a fair end-of-quarter price (cum dividend) of $15. Your data files indicate that Z, Inc. has a beta of 1.65. The 90-day T-bill rate stands at 1.5% (per quarter), and the adjusted macro forecast is for a market rate of return of 5% over the next quarter. David's record of similar predictions for Z is summarized below.

Start of Period Price	David's Forecast*	Actual End of Period Price*	Market Forecast†	Actual Rate	T-Bill Rate
5.375	7	6.50	−7.5	−.15	1.75
6.50	9	7.625	−12.5	−2.95	1.40
7.625	7	6.75	7.5	5.48	1.95
6.75	8.625	12.50	5.0	9.20	2.05

*Includes dividends.
†Adjusted.

What is David's forecast, s, for the alpha value of Z and your adjusted forecast, s^*? If the residual standard deviation of Z, Inc. is estimated at 35%, what is the ability adjusted residual variance?

Managing Security Analysis

How do you, a manager of the Active Portfolio Group, allocate your firepower? You have a limited but potentially powerful team of security analysts. There are many stocks out there, a large number of which may be mispriced to varying degrees. Once your team is established, each analyst will have developed expertise on one or more companies and things roll along by routine. However, assuming that you are starting a new unit, are there any rules that provide a short cut to success?

Before analysis, the alpha value of a stock is a zero-mean random variable. Hence all stocks are equally attractive ex ante. On the one hand, there is an advantage to specialization. To produce micro forecasts, sector and industry variables need to be forecast for use in preparing forecasts for individual firms in that sector or industry. Thus it makes sense to allocate your limited group of analysts to a small number of industries, and cover a large number of firms in this small set of industries.

But this approach has a price. Recall that an important assumption in the Treynor-Black security analysis model is that the nonsystematic component of the rate of return on each stock is independent of all other nonsystematic components. All that counts in deciding how much to hold of any stock is the size of alpha relative to the residual variance. You have already developed the intuition that two stocks with residuals that are correlated will make a less desirable active portfolio than two stocks with uncorrelated residuals, because the nonsystematic risk will be less effectively diversified. But correlated residuals are exactly what you can expect when you assign a security analyst to cover, for instance, two automotive stocks. Some of the advantage of the analyst's specialization in the automotive industry will be lost because the nonsystematic components will be correlated to some degree, thereby reducing the effectiveness of the active portfolio.

Optimizing the Active Portfolio

The manager of the Active Portfolio Group needs to obtain estimates for the beta coefficients and the nonsystematic risk values of the actively covered stocks from the Data, Resources, and Estimation Group. With the adjusted forecasts of alpha values, and the paired estimates of nonsystematic risk, $\sigma^2(e)$, the manager determines the optimal positions in the active portfolio from the Treynor-Black model (see Chapter 23). With this portfolio the manager has to communicate to the Complete Portfolio Group the overall performance parameters of the active portfolio, that is, its alpha, beta, and residual variance.

The Organization Chart of the Active Portfolio Group

The chart in Figure 26.3 summarizes the discussion of the operation of this critical group. Note that there is a two-way communication channel between the Evaluation and Attribution Group and the Active Portfolio Group for the adjustment of raw forecasts. The communication channel with the Data, Resources, and Estimation group is

FIGURE 26.3
Organization chart of the Active Portfolio Group.

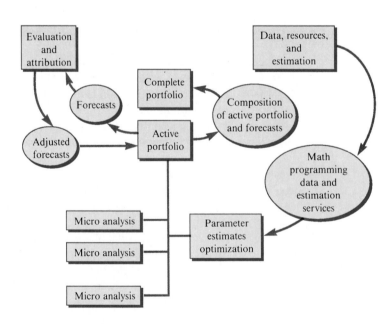

for estimation and optimization needs. Finally, the responsibility line between the manager of the Active Portfolio Group and the Complete Portfolio Group involves the transmission of the micro forecasts and the composition of the optimal portfolio.

26.4 The Safe Asset Group

Managing the Safe Asset Group would appear to be a cinch. After all, all you have to do is park the portfolio's cash in a safe asset such as T-bills. However, the war for an extra basis point rages 24 hours a day. Nothing is simple in this competitive world.

The benchmark decision is to hold the cash in short-term, possibly 30-day, T-bills, as close as possible to a safe asset. Against this benchmark the manager can pit possible deviations along two lines:

1. Hold longer maturity safe (in terms of default) T-bills, thus obtaining some risk premium, known as the **term premium**
2. Obtain some risk premium by holding reasonably safe (in terms of default) assets such as commercial paper (CP), certificates of deposit (CD), or bankers' acceptances (BA)

Going for the Term Premium

Yield curves suggest that in most cases the largest part of the term premium accrues to 1-year maturities. This is sufficient temptation for a money market fund manager (which is really what the Safe Asset Group manager is) to stretch maturity to about 1 year. Of course, theory tells us that this is risky business, and history will usually support a good theory.

In the late 1970s interest rates took off sharply, and many money market funds took a beating. One of them actually went out of business as a result of this exposure. Since then, the typical maturity of money market funds has been shortened to about 30 to 50 days, although funds go different ways. The decision whether to take a fixed, short-maturity position depends not only on the *potential* payoffs and risks, but also on the ability of the Safe Asset Group to produce relatively reliable yield curve forecasts and manage a successful active strategy of shifting between "short" (15- to 30-day) and "long" (up to 1 year) maturity paper.

If the Safe Asset Group intends to engage in active yield–maturity management, then a natural model to apply is Merton's market-timing model. To illustrate, suppose that we decide to shift between 30- and 270-day bills. The 30-day bills can be taken as the truly safe asset, whereas the 270-day bill is analogous to the risky portfolio in Merton's market timing model. The yield-curve forecaster is required to provide the manager with a forecast that is either

1. 270-day bills will outperform 30-day bills

or

2. 30-day bills will outperform 270-day bills

According to the forecast, the Safe Asset Group manager will shift a fixed fraction of funds between the two types of bills. The forecasts will be fed to the Evaluation and Attribution Group to estimate the probability of the two types of errors (P_1 and P_2 in Chapter 23) and to assess the value of this operation.

If it turns out that the unit's efforts are unproductive, it will cease this form of active management. If the quality of the forecasts is significant, the manager should increase the fraction of funds shifted between the different-maturity bills to take better advantage of the group's ability. At least one study shows that the implied option value of this type of market timing is economically significant.[3]

Going for the Risk Premium

A glance at any day's *Wall Street Journal* will show that, for a given maturity, various money market instruments (for example, CP, CD, BA) have slightly higher yields than T-bills. Furthermore, different issuers of each of these instruments carry their unique default risk and thus varying risk premiums.

A decision to play the risk-return trade-off in money market instruments requires quality analysis to beat the market consensus on the appropriate risk premium for each issue of each type of instrument. This type of operation is really active short-term bond-portfolio management.

The Organization Chart of the Safe Asset Group

Figure 26.4 shows the organization chart of the Safe Asset Group, under the assumption that it engages in active management for both the term and risk premiums. When the Safe Asset Group manager submits the composition of the safe portfolio to the Complete Portfolio Group, she also encloses the expected excess rate of return on this portfolio over the 30-day T-bill rate. The latter remains the benchmark risk-free rate for the active and index portfolio. The mean and variance of the excess return on the Safe Asset Group portfolio make for an extra gain (or loss) to be incorporated with the active portfolio contribution.

---

[3]Kane, Alex, and Marks, Stephen G., "The Rocking Horse Analyst," *The Journal of Portfolio Management,* spring 1987.

FIGURE 26.4

Organization chart of
the Safe Asset Group.

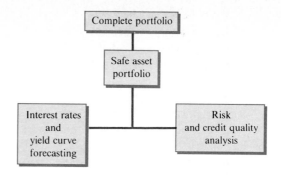

26.5 *The Complete Portfolio Group*

The Complete Portfolio Group serves two functions: (1) to optimize the risky and the complete portfolios, and (2) to manage the entire operation of constructing the active, index, and safe asset portfolios.

Optimizing the Complete Portfolio

The first function is straightforward. We know already how the optimal risky portfolio is constructed from the active and index portfolios. Given the forecasts for the mean and variance of the optimized risky portfolio, and using a managerial "risk aversion" coefficient, the complete portfolio is constructed. A summary of the process is provided in the Appendix to this chapter.

The Complete Portfolio Group manager now submits to the Clearing and Transaction Group the desired position in the specific securities that will make up the organization's complete portfolio, C. These are computed from the following:

1. The composition of the active portfolio, A
2. The composition of the index portfolio, M
3. The proportions of the active and index portfolios in the optimal risky portfolio, P
4. The proportion of the optimized risky portfolio in the complete portfolio
5. The composition of the safe asset portfolio

Concept Check

Question 5. With a management response ("risk aversion") coefficient of 2.0, and the data from questions 1 and 4, what is the optimal complete portfolio and its projected performance?

Management of the Complete Portfolio Group is complicated. In addition to managing three important groups (the active, index, and safe asset portfolios), the manager must handle the complex network of communications with the Data, Resources, and Estimation Group and the Evaluation and Attribution Group. In particular, communication with the latter involves the delicate task of assigning ability parameters to all the operators in the group.

Experience shows that managing professionals who routinely make decisions under uncertainty requires all available "people skills." One example of the dynamics of "forecaster image" is apparent in the behavior of television weather forecasters. When the broadcast desk people banter with the weather person on the air they never mention forecasting record. Instead they seem to hold the weather person responsible for good and bad *weather* (rather than for good or bad forecasts). They applaud forecasts of change for the better and blame the forecaster for a "bad" reversal forecast. Soon enough, the weather person begins to speak as if this were the case, apologizing for bad news and appearing to take credit for improvements.

Things are much the same (if not more so) with financial forecasters. Yet their economic well-being actually is on the line with every forecast. Even if we were to apply the most sophisticated statistics to maximize the chance of fair assessment, we cannot reduce to zero the probability of judging forecasters unfairly.

26.6 *The Data, Resources, and Estimation Group*

Sophisticated investment management requires a fair bit of estimation and maintenance of fairly extensive data bases. The benefits of specialization dictate that this function should be centered in one organizational unit that serves the entire organization. The Data, Resources, and Estimation (DRE) Group includes computer and quantitative experts.

Data Bases

The principal data bases that the DRE group has to maintain are the following:
1. Daily rates of return on the relevant universe of stocks
2. Parameter estimates of the relevant universe of securities
3. In-house expert forecasts and realizations
4. Portfolio composition with parameter forecasts and realizations
5. Evaluation and attribution files (ability parameters and performance statistics)

This list suggests extensive communications between the DRE group and the other organization units. Let us examine these data bases in turn.

Daily returns

At any time, any of the stocks in the relevant universe may be candidates for inclusion in the index or active portfolios. The decision to include a stock in one of the organization portfolios hinges on the stock parameters: its beta, residual variance, and covariance with other stocks. To estimate these measures, the DRE needs a sample of rates of return. Daily returns are required because of the perennial trade-off between the virtues of a large sample and the constancy of parameters within the sample.

Today's technology makes obtaining this data base only a minor problem. A number of services provide daily prices and dividends that can be entered directly into the client's computer over the telephone lines. Converting the daily prices, dividends, and stock split data into daily returns is a simple matter.

Parameter estimates

The organization needs easy, immediate access to the parameters of various stocks. The DRE group routinely updates estimation of these parameters and maintains them in an accessible data base.

TABLE 26.1   Data Base of Expert Forecasts and Realizations

Forecast	*Heading and Time Series*				
Expectations (means) micro	Forecaster: John Doe Parameter: Abnormal returns Security: ABC XYZ				
	Date	Forecast	Realization	Forecast	Realization
	. . .	. . .	. . .	. . .	. . .
	. . .	. . .	. . .	. . .	. . .
Expectations (means) macro	Forecaster: Jane Close Parameter: Deviations from long-run mean Security: Index portfolio				
	Date	Forecast	Realization		
	. . .	. . .	. . .		
	. . .	. . .	. . .		
Risk micro	Forecaster: John Doe Parameter: Residual variance Security: ABC XYZ				
	Date	Forecast	Realization	Forecast	Realization
	. . .	. . .	. . .	. . .	. . .
	. . .	. . .	. . .	. . .	. . .
Risk macro	Forecaster: Jane Close Parameter: Index portfolio variance Security: Index portfolio				
	Date	Forecast	Realization		
	. . .	. . .	. . .		
	. . .	. . .	. . .		

Expert forecasts and realizations

Whenever macro and micro forecasters complete a forecast, they communicate it to the Evaluation and Attribution Group, which then uses it to update ability parameters. Updates require analysis of the time series of past forecasts against subsequent realizations. The data base must allow easy access to paired forecasts and realizations.

The expert forecast data base actually is a collection of data bases that cut across the identities of securities, parameters, and forecasters. Table 26.1 gives an example.

Portfolio composition

This data base serves a number of purposes:

1. The changes in portfolio composition are used by the Clearing and Transactions Group to determine the necessary transactions that have to be executed to maintain the desired complete portfolio.
2. The updated portfolio composition is used to compile its realized rates of return for both accounting and evaluation purposes.
3. The updated portfolio composition is necessary to compile portfolio forecasts for optimization, evaluation, and attribution purposes.

The data base itself is a collection of the individual unit portfolios plus the aggregate of these portfolios, as shown in Table 26.2, of two securities on two different dates.

TABLE 26.2 Data Base of Portfolio Composition, Parameter Forecasts, and Realizations (a Two-Security Portfolio)

Weight and Parameters		Residual		Beta		Residual Risk		Mean	
Date	Weight	F	R	F	R	F	R	F	R
Security 1: active portfolio									
. . .	. . .	. . .	. . .	. . .	. . .	. . .	. . .	. . .	. . .
. . .	. . .	. . .	. . .	. . .	. . .	. . .	. . .	. . .	. . .
Security 2: active portfolio									
. . .	. . .	. . .	. . .	. . .	. . .	. . .	. . .	. . .	. . .
. . .	. . .	. . .	. . .	. . .	. . .	. . .	. . .	. . .	. . .
Index portfolio									
. . .	. . .	. . .	. . .	. . .	. . .	. . .	. . .	. . .	. . .
. . .	. . .	. . .	. . .	. . .	. . .	. . .	. . .	. . .	. . .
Complete portfolio									
. . .	. . .	. . .	. . .	. . .	. . .	. . .	. . .	. . .	. . .
. . .	. . .	. . .	. . .	. . .	. . .	. . .	. . .	. . .	. . .

F = forecast, R = realization.

Evaluation and attribution files

These files are of three types:
1. Bias and efficiency (ability) of individual forecasters
2. Forecast value and performance statistics at the portfolio level
3. Record of overall performance attribution to individual units
We discuss the nature of the data in these files in Section 26.7.

Estimation, Optimization, and Computing Resources

The DRE unit serves as the scientific resource for statistics (estimation), mathematics (optimization), and computer science (data base management).

Organization chart of the Data, Resources, and Estimation Group

Figure 26.5 shows the internal organization of the DRE group. To keep it simple, we show only responsibility lines. The necessary communication channels are clear from the titles of the various units in the group.

FIGURE 26.5

Organization chart of the Data, Resources, and Estimation Group.

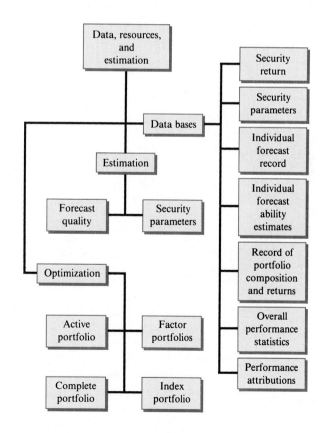

26.7 *The Evaluation and Attribution Group*

The economic value of the entire investment management organization depends on the value of its forecasts and estimates. Forecasters and estimators should be retained and compensated or fired on the basis of their true value. Evaluation and Attribution (EA) is an independent, separate organizational group.

In Chapter 24 we discussed how investors can evaluate performance, looking at an organization from the outside. In this section we seek to evaluate the organization's performance from the inside. These two activities are very different. Clients and outside investors observe only the realized rates of return of the complete portfolio of the organization. The EA group, however, has access to all intermediate forecasts, resulting decisions, and portfolio composition. The problems and alternative solutions for the two types of evaluation are miles apart.

We can follow the process of internal evaluation and attribution from ground level to top, that is, from individual forecasts to performance at the complete portfolio level. However, we first need to establish the principles underlying in-house performance measurement and attribution.

Principles and Hierarchy of In-House Performance Evaluation and Attribution

To understand the principle that drives in-house performance evaluation requires two steps:

1. Take a bird's-eye view of the overall activity in the organization.
2. Comprehend the implications of using forecast-adjustment techniques.

For the first step, we start with the flowchart that leads from analysts' forecasts to portfolio decisions, portfolio forecasts, and subsequent deviations from these forecasts (Figure 26.6). The critical part that we wish to focus on is the treatment of raw forecasts and the resulting portfolio decisions. We can summarize the gist of the flow as follows:

Action	Actors
Generating macro and micro forecasts	Forecasters
Adjusting raw forecasts for forecaster's ability	EA experts
Generating portfolio based on adjusted forecasts	Portfolio managers
Analyzing portfolio forecasts	EA experts
Analyzing portfolio realizations	EA experts

All of this is in pursuit of maximizing the Sharpe measure of the complete portfolio. Now consider the following:

1. Suppose a certain forecaster issues a forecast for the alpha value of a stock. Assuming this forecast is properly adjusted for the forecaster's ability, it will be unbiased. The subsequent realization will include a forecasting error with zero mean.

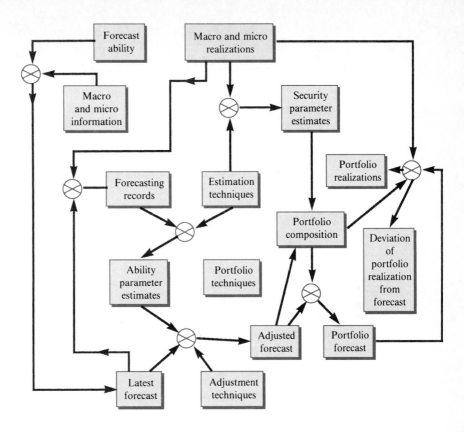

2. The assessment of the forecaster's ability also yields the variance of the forecasting error, which is the remaining risk if we use the forecaster's service.

3. Suppose we use a team of security analysts who submit raw forecasts. If we properly adjust all the forecasts for the ability of the forecasters, the adjusted risk estimates can be used to generate the optimal active portfolio *plus* an unbiased forecast for the portfolio return and risk.

4. As a corollary to (3), if the investment management organization adjusts the forecasts properly, then evaluation of portfolio forecasts, rather than realizations, will capture the value and contribution of the macro and micro forecasters, as well as the overall contribution of the portfolio managers. Analysis of portfolio return *realizations* (compared to forecasts) is relevant only for assessment of the quality of the *forecast adjustment* process.

The basis for these arguments is statistical, and the proof is technical. The implications are quite far-reaching, however, and deserve some discussion at each level of the organization.

1. *Evaluation at the individual forecaster level*

The contribution of an individual forecaster is measured in two ways:

    a. Forecast accuracy

b. Contribution to the performance value of the portfolio

The measurement of the forecast accuracy is a straightforward application of statistics to recover the bias and efficiency (variance of forecasting error) from the forecaster's track record. The contribution of the forecaster to the active portfolio is measured by the contribution of the forecaster to the improvement in the Sharpe measure that the active portfolio brings about.

From the Treynor-Black model we know that the marginal contribution of an individual security to the Sharpe measure of the risky portfolio is given by its appraisal ratio, equal to the ratio of its alpha to the residual standard deviation. Note that this ratio must use the adjusted forecast and its standard error.

2. *Evaluation at the active portfolio level*

The contribution of the entire active portfolio (when optimized) to the Sharpe measure of the overall risky portfolio, again, equals the appraisal ratio. In this case too, the forecasting ability is accounted for, because the active portfolio alpha comes out of the adjusted alpha forecasts for the individual securities and its risk from the adjusted residual variances.

The performance of the active portfolio must be evaluated over an extended interval, to avoid effects of a particular nonrepresentative holding period. It is best measured by the average of the appraisal ratio, to which the contribution of a single stock is just the average of its own appraisal ratio.

3. *Evaluation at the complete portfolio level*

The complete portfolio is simply the overall risky portfolio mixed with the safe asset portfolio. Thus, theoretically, the Sharpe measure of the complete portfolio is identical to that of the overall risky portfolio. In reality, however, it will occasionally turn out that the optimal complete portfolio, embodying all forecasts and estimates, violates some of the policy constraints. In that case the optimal theoretical solution will be replaced by a compromised solution. The forecast for the Sharpe measure of the complete portfolio should be evaluated, period by period. The average difference between the constrained and the unconstrained complete portfolios provides the cost of the policy constraints.

Concept Check

Question 6. Given the forecast and portfolio positions from question 1 and questions 3 to 5, what limited evaluation and attribution can you make?

---

4. *Evaluation of the adjustment process*

The forecast adjustment process is the wild card in performance evaluation and attribution. It disengages ex ante performance evaluation from ex post realized returns. The quality of the adjustment process is critical to the operational decentralization and overall success of the investment management organization.

Beginning at the individual forecast level, consider the track record of a security analyst that consists of a sequence of alpha forecasts and subsequent realizations (of the stock residual). The objective of the adjustment expert is to identify any form of bias that is revealed by the track record. When this is done, future forecasts will be first corrected for bias. Next, the series of paired bias-corrected forecasts and subsequent realizations is used to determine the ability parameter, that is, the squared correlation between the corrected forecast and realizations. A complication arises from the fact that the bias coefficient and ability parameters are subject to estimation error. Adapting the adjustment process to this problem is what makes it technically complex. Regardless of how the adjustment expert does the job, the task of gauging the success of the adjustment is quite simple. All we need is the time series of the *adjusted* forecasts and subsequent realizations to test whether the adjusted forecasting error is zero-mean noise. For that reason, part of the adjustment expert's task is to monitor this relationship. The moment that the adjusted forecasting error begins to exhibit some predictable pattern, the adjuster knows that something has gone wrong. Thus the evaluation of the time series of forecasting errors provides the adjuster's feedback mechanism.

As far as the success of the organization is concerned, anytime that a forecast adjustment goes wrong the portfolio decision deviates from the optimal.

FIGURE 26.7

Organization chart of the Evaluation and Attribution Group.

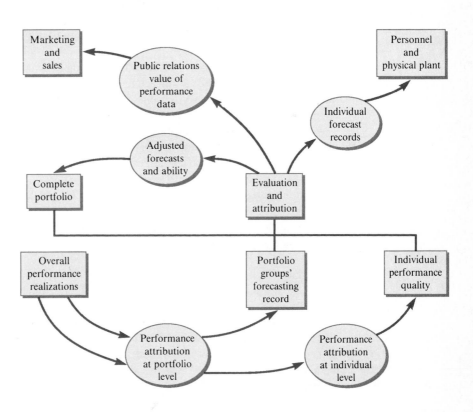

The organization chart of the EA unit is shown in Figure 26.7. The external communication lines connect the unit with the logistics units of the organization. Specifically, the Marketing and Sales unit is expected to make use of the performance measures of the complete portfolio to make the organization attractive to investors. The attributed performance reports are also useful for the personnel resource allocation function, to determine adequate compensation at the various levels of the organization.

26.8   *Logistics*

The investment management organization depends on proper logistics. Of course, what is defined as logistics may depend on the nature of the organization. For the investment management operation, clearing, marketing, financial control, and personnel functions can be grouped as the logistics units.

The cost of engaging in active strategy is significant. To operate a passive (index) fund, as far as line units go, all you have to do is maintain an index portfolio. No analysts or forecasts are needed. There is no need at all for staff units. Finally, the logistics are less complicated and less costly. The one logistics function that is required in both operations is accounting and financial control to maintain client accounts. To justify the cost, the active strategy has to beat the passive alternative by a sufficient margin.

An interesting question is whether economies of scale can diminish the impact of expenses on the desirability of the active strategy. Unfortunately, the issue of economies of scale cuts both ways. On the one hand, there are substantial fixed costs in operating an active strategy, as our description of the organization clearly shows. Therefore, given a fixed-sized organization, the more money under management, the lower the cost per dollar of money managed.

On the other hand, as the amount of money under management grows, there is an acute need to expand the breadth of the active strategy (cover more stocks). The problem is that investment of a lot of money in one mispriced security will drive the price up. Thus, as an investment budget grows, the only effective way to manage it is to spread the funds over a broader active portfolio. This, of course, requires hiring more security analysts who are way above average—yet the pool of such analysts is limited.

The expenditures of the active strategy organization are composed of three parts:
1. Fixed cost
2. Cost that varies with the dollar size of the portfolio
3. Cost that varies with the size of the operation

The role of top management is to analyze these expenditures to determine optimal strategy and structure. We can expect the dollar size of the portfolio to vary more frequently and more widely than the ideal size of the operation. Analysis of the dependence of cost on portfolio size therefore is a tactical issue that requires constant reevaluation.

An important component in variable cost is transaction expenses, that is, brokerage and commissions. Sustaining extra transaction costs is one clear disadvantage of the active strategy, although this item may be easily overstated in today's environment.

To begin with, consider that one "round-trip" commission (the cost of buying and selling one share of stock) for a large money management organization is about 5 cents per share. The dollar value of an average share of stock of the type that large institutions concentrate on is about $25. Thus round-trip commissions account for approximately 20 basis points per round-trip. Hence, to incur a 1% differential against a perfectly passive strategy, the active investment manager can buy and sell each stock in his portfolio five times a year. This is of course true for large organizations, but then again excellent analysts can produce large profits for their clients, against which any transaction costs will pale. Clients obviously profit from reduced transaction costs. So do managers, because more money flows into active accounts.

Transaction costs to large institutions can be even lower if we consider **soft dollars;** that is, brokers produce research that they provide "free of charge" to customers in exchange for their business. The cost of producing this research is covered by brokerage fees charged to the institution. Thus the already-low transaction costs cover research as well.

In good capitalistic fashion the soft-dollar business enhances research quality. A typical example shows how. The organization's investment committee (a group of senior portfolio managers and analysts) meets periodically to discuss the quality of the research output that brokers have made available to the organization since the last meeting. At the end of the discussion the members vote on the allocation of trading volume to the various brokers over the next period. The consequent allocation of research responsibility to brokerage houses eliminates duplication of effort among a multitude of money managers. To get business, brokers compete in producing and communicating high-quality research to client investment managers.

Although deregulation of brokerage commissions in 1975 resulted in widespread reduction in commissions, actually it was a reduction in the production cost of brokerage services that opened the floodgates. Reduced costs are attributable to factors much the same as those affecting products such as computers, namely:

1. Increase in the volume of transactions (consider that average NYSE daily volume went from 30 million shares to 200 million shares in just a few years)
2. Automation and computerization of back-office functions

Portfolio decisions are made by the line units and expressed in terms of the proportions of the funds under management to allocate to various assets. The decision that the Complete Portfolio Group feeds to the Clearing and Transactions unit takes the following form (all in investment proportions):

1. Composition of active portfolio
2. Composition of index portfolio
3. Proportion of active and index portfolios in the risky portfolio
4. Composition of the safe asset portfolio
5. Proportions of the risky and safe portfolios in the complete portfolio

The Clearing and Transactions unit has to translate this barrage into the following chain:

1. The net proportion of funds in each asset
2. The dollar position in each asset that is implied by the desired net proportion
3. The desired change in dollar holding of each asset from the current portfolio
4. The number of shares of stocks or face value of bonds to be bought, sold, or sold short

This is an impressive task that calls for sophisticated computerization and management.

Accounting and Financial Control

The accounting function of the investment organization can be broken down into two parts:

1. External: client accounts
2. Internal: the organization's managerial and financial accounting

As far as client accounting goes, there is no inherent difference between passive and active investment management organizations, although client accounting issues will vary between a pension fund and a mutual fund, for example.

The internal managerial and financial accounting function of the active organization, however, is far more complicated than that of the passive organization. Beyond the production of standard financial statements, the role of the accounting system is to provide adequate input into the management information system (MIS) that will serve to identify the fixed and variable cost functions. These are essential ingredients in strategic planning and tactical decision-making. The profitability of the organization, as well as the welfare of its clients, depends on these features.

Marketing and Sales

Savvy business people understand that the marketing and sales function represents the "home stretch." One extreme view is that good marketing will sell anything. The opposite extreme is that a good product will sell itself and that good marketing ends at the end of the production line. There are examples of both schools in the world today. Most professionals take the view that the truth lies somewhere in between.

What makes the marketing of an active management organization problematic is the difficulty of communicating the quality of the product. There are no television commercials celebrating a firm's Sharpe measure, but there seem to be some advances in getting the message across.

Consider, for example, the explosion in the growth of defined-benefit pension plans, funds that corporations accumulate to pay for employees' pension benefits. These funds are controlled by corporate financial officers who parcel them out to investment managers. Professionals of this sort are becoming financially educated enough to respond to an appropriate marketing pitch, and such a trend should continue.

The real challenge in managing this function is personnel. The physical plant component is no different from that found in any standard service organization.

The real wealth in the investment management organization is in its human capital. To say that the active investment management industry is labor intensive would be the understatement of the decade. The overall function of personnel management has three components:

1. Search for new talent
2. Evaluation, compensation, and retention of existing talent
3. Allocation of effort of existing talent with the organization

For relevant criteria and information the Personnel unit depends critically on the line and staff units.

Search for new talent

Athletic scouting is a cinch compared with scouting for investment management talent. It requires in-house data to distinguish the true performance of any individual from aggregate organizational success. Our discussion in Chapter 24 shows that assessing even aggregate performance from publicly available data is extremely difficult.

A natural approach to developing new talent is to create the organization's own "farm system." Hire the young while they are still unproven and inexpensive, spend some capital on training, and—most of all—close evaluation and attribution.

Evaluation, compensation, and retention

We have put forth a blueprint for performance evaluation and attribution of individuals within a firm. It is logical that compensation ought to be directly related to the outcomes from this elaborate process. The general layout of determining compensation to security analysts may be as follows:

Level	Item
Individual	1. Accuracy of individual forecasts
	2. Attribution of portfolio group performance to individual forecasters
Active Portfolio Group	3. Accuracy of active portfolio forecasts
	4. Attribution of risky portfolio performance to active portfolio performance
Organization	5. Overall performance

A similar approach should be taken for all actors in the organization.

Allocation of efforts of existing talent within the organization

Beware of the "Peter principle." A great security analyst may turn out to be no better at managing an active portfolio than a great defensive back at managing a football team. In many active investment management organizations, however, a natural career path takes a recruit from "gofer" to security analyst, to portfolio manager, to member of the board. To identify the area that best fits the particular talent of a fledgling analyst, training will require rotation through the various functions of the organization for some time.

Summary

This chapter has provided a broad-brush image of what it would take to run an investment management organization in a spirit that accords with financial theory. There are countless difficulties that we do not explore because of space constraints.

In comparison, consider the luxuriously simple way traditional managers operate:
1. Analysts are assigned to specific parts of the security universe, usually by industry groups.
2. Analyst output is in the following form of recommendation:
   a. Strong sell
   b. Sell
   c. Hold
   d. Buy
   e. Strong buy

   plus some price range for the horizon of the recommendation, usually 1 to 3 months.
3. Portfolio managers translate analysts' output to portfolio proportions using mostly intuition.
4. Daily investment committees coordinate and review policy.

   Compared with an elaborate optimization process, this is like a day in the park. It would be fun (alas not for investors) if this could last. However, times are "a'changing," and investment managers have to move the process of change along.

Key Terms

Adjusting forecasts
Term premium
Soft dollars

Selected Readings

The pioneering article on active portfolio management includes a discussion on adjusting forecasts:
Treynor, Jack L., and Black, Fischer, "How to Use Security Analysis to Improve Portfolio Selection," *Journal of Business,* January 1973.

Please read the appendix to this chapter before solving the following problems.

Problems

The files of the Data, Resources, and Estimation Group reveal the following records:

Macro Forecasts

Quarter	Money Rate	Market Portfolio* Forecast	Market Portfolio* Actual
1	3.84	70.00	18.98
2	6.93	−15.00	−14.66
3	8.00	30.00	26.47
4	5.80	25.00	37.20
5	5.08	−25.00	23.84
6	5.12	−30.00	−7.18
7	7.18	0.00	6.56
8	10.38	60.00	18.44
9	11.24	60.00	32.42
10	14.71	10.00	−4.91

*Annual rates compounded quarterly. The forecasts are for 1 quarter.

Micro Forecasts

Quarter	Stock A† Forecast	Stock A† Actual	Stock B† Forecast	Stock B† Actual
0		45.125		24.75
1	40.00	46.25	20.00	22.50
2	33.00	38.625	30.00	19.375
3	16.00	21.125	33.00	12.625
4	27.00	18.50	22.00	21.875
5	33.00	27.25	31.00	26.75
6	22.00	34.875	14.00	17.25
7	25.00	23.00	23.00	22.875
8	25.00	17.625	40.00	44.00
9	27.00	19.75	27.00	32.625
10	18.00	20.50	46.00	38.625

†Prices are adjusted for dividends, and the forecasts are 1 quarter ahead.

1. Use the 10-quarter market portfolio and money rate data to compute the long-run mean excess return and unconditional standard deviation (that is, deviations from the long-run mean) of the market rate of return.

2. Convert the market returns and macro forecasts to deviations from the long-run mean.

3. Compute the stock residuals.

4. Convert the micro forecasts to forecasts of abnormal returns.

5. Use the first 5 quarters as the initial data base. For quarters 6 to 10 estimate the regressions of the forecasts on residuals, and record the bias adjustments and ability parameters.

6. Compute the adjusted forecasts for quarters 6 to 10 and the ability-adjusted risk parameters.

7. Construct the optimal active and risky portfolios for quarters 6 to 10 with the following constraints:
   a. No short positions
   b. The position in any individual stock cannot exceed 25%

8. Construct the optimal complete portfolio for quarters 6 to 10 with the response coefficient $A_m = 1.5$, subject to the constraint that the position in the risky portfolio is between 50% and 90%.

9. Evaluate the performance record for quarters 6 to 10 at the individual level.

10. Evaluate performance at the active portfolio level.

11. Evaluate performance at the complete portfolio level.

12. Compute the deviation of the active, risky, and complete portfolio from their forecasts, and evaluate the adjustment process.

13. Use the ability parameters and the macro forecasts to compute the values of P_1 and P_2 of the macro forecaster for each of the quarters 6 to 10. Using the constraints of 50% to 90% in stocks, what is the value of the macro forecaster?

Appendix

Adjusting Macro Forecasts

The excess return on the market portfolio can be written as

$$E(r_M) - r_f = \pi_M + e_M$$

where π is the long-run historical mean. It is the uninformed prior, and e is the period-by-period deviation from it. The macro forecast is an attempt to forecast that deviation. We can always obtain the forecast, s, of the deviation, e, by subtracting the long-run average excess return from the macro forecast for $r_M - r_f$.

To obtain the "discounted" forecast, we apply an ability parameter to the raw forecast:

$$s_M^* = \rho_M^2 s_M$$

Active Portfolio Management

The adjustment rationale is this: the forecast, s_M, contains a forecasting error, ϵ_M, so that

$$s_M = e_M + \epsilon_M$$

where ϵ_M is zero-mean noise. We measure the ability of the forecaster from the square of the correlation coefficient, ρ_M, between forecasts and realizations, as follows:

$$\rho_M^2 = \frac{\sigma^2(e_M)}{\sigma^2(s_M)}$$

$$= \frac{\sigma^2(e_M)}{\sigma^2(e_M) + \sigma^2(\epsilon_M)}$$

To obtain an unbiased forecast, it is necessary to multiply the raw forecast, s, by the square of the correlation coefficient, ρ. Perfect forecasting will yield $\rho = 1$, and the forecasts will be taken at face value. Useless forecasters will have $\rho = 0$, and their forecasts will be ignored.

Forecasting risk of a variable whose uncertainty is measured by its variance, $\sigma^2(e_M)$, is effectively reduced in proportion to the forecaster's ability. The uncertainty of the *adjusted* forecast, $\sigma_\rho^2(e_M)$, is given by

$$\sigma_\rho^2(e_M) = (1 - \rho_M^2)\sigma^2(e_M)$$

With perfect ability there will be no forecasting risk at all, whereas with no ability risk remains at $\sigma^2(e_M)$.

Using an adjusted forecast, the index portfolio expected return is

$$E(r_M) - r_f = \pi_M + s_M^*$$

with variance

$$\sigma_\rho^2(e_M) = (1 - \rho_M^2)\sigma^2(e_M)$$

Maintaining an Efficient Index Portfolio

Denote the positions in the n stocks in portfolio M by w_i. Then the excess rate of return on M is given by

$$r_M - r_f = \Sigma\, w_i(r_i - r_f)$$

Superimposing the relationship between each security, i, and the market portfolio, M^*,

$$r_i - r_f = \beta_i(r_{M}^* - r_f) + e_i$$

on $r_M - r_f$, we have for the index portfolio, M,

$$r_M - r_f = \Sigma\, w_i[\beta_i(r_M{}^* - r_f) + e_i]$$
$$= (r_M{}^* - r_f)\Sigma w_i\beta_i + \Sigma w_i e_i$$

As we already know, the weighted average, $\Sigma w_i\beta_i$, is just the beta of M on M^*, β_M. If we denote the index portfolio's nonsystematic component, $\Sigma w_i e_i$, by e_M, we have

$$r_M - r_f = \beta_M(r_M{}^* - r_f) + e_M$$

with the covariance between M and M^* being

$$\text{Cov}(r_M, r_M{}^*) = \beta_M\sigma_M^2{}^*$$

and the nonsystematic risk of M,

$$\sigma^2(e_M) = \Sigma w_i^2\sigma^2(e_i)$$

The objective is then to construct M, choosing the weights, w_i, so as to minimize $\sigma^2(e_M)$ subject to the portfolio beta being one.

In addition, the weights must sum to one to satisfy the feasibility constraint. In sum, once we decide on a subset of, for example, $n = 100$ stocks, we solve for

$$\underset{w_i}{\text{Min}}\ \sigma^2(e_M) = \Sigma w_i^2\sigma^2(e_i)$$

such that

$$\beta_M = \Sigma w_i\beta_i = 1$$
$$\Sigma w_i = 1$$

Deciding the number of stocks and which ones is not easy, however. To make this decision, we construct a data base that includes the following:

1. Daily rates of return on the market portfolio, M^*, for the past year
2. Daily rates of return for the past year on all the stocks in M^* that the prospectus and policy allow us to hold
3. Different values for n to be tried; for example, $n = 50, 60, 70, 80, 90, 100$
4. For each value of n, a number of (for example, $m = 20$) random samples[a] of stocks from M^* as candidates for inclusion in M

From steps 3 and 4 we have six different sizes for n, and for each of these we try 20 samples, so we are going to select M from 120 candidate optimal index portfolios.

We demonstrate the procedure for $n = 50$. We first generate 20 randomly selected lists of stocks with 50 stocks in each. For each of these 50 stocks in each of the 20 samples we estimate, from the data base, the following parameters:

$$\beta_{ik},\ \sigma(e_{ik}) \qquad \begin{aligned} i &= 1, \ldots, 50 \\ k &= 1, \ldots, 20 \end{aligned}$$

---

[a]It is possible to select m in a statistically efficient way rather than randomly. This is a technical issue, however.

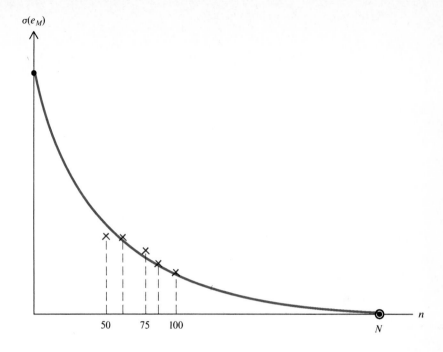

FIGURE 26A.1

The trade-off between the size of the market-index proxy and its nonsystematic risk.

For each of the 20 samples we now solve the optimization program, generating 20 candidates (50 stocks each) for the optimal index portfolio. For each $k = 1, \ldots,$ 20 of these candidate portfolios, the optimization procedure yields the weights of stocks in it (w_{ik}) and the resulting nonsystematic risk, $\sigma(e_{Mk})$. We then choose the one portfolio with the lowest $\sigma(e_{Mk})$.

Repeating this procedure for all the designated sizes of n, we can graph the trade-off between n and $\sigma(e_M)$, which is displayed in Figure 26A.1. The points show the hypothetical 20 estimates for the various levels of n.

Note that, when n is as large as the number (N) of stocks in the ideal M^* portfolio, then by definition, $\sigma(e_M) = 0$. The larger n is, the smaller $\sigma(e_M)$. But the $\sigma(e_M)$ drops at a decreasing rate, so the manager will want to weigh the cost of holding a larger n against $\sigma(e_M)$ before deciding on the optimal level.

Another trade-off in the selection process is the number of selected samples, m, to be examined. The more samples attempted for any size portfolio, the greater the chance of coming close to the best possible portfolio of size n in the universe of N stocks in M^*, that is, the one with the smallest $\sigma(e_M)$ for its size. Increasing m will improve the efficiency of the decision.

Given the following *adjusted* forecasts,

$$\text{Macro:} \quad E(r_M) - r_f, \; \sigma_M \equiv \sigma_\rho(e_M)$$
$$\text{Micro:} \quad s_A, \; \sigma_\rho(e_A), \; \beta_A$$

the position in the active portfolio before adjusting for beta is

$$w_0 = \frac{s_A / \sigma_\rho^2(e_A)}{(r_M - r_f)/\sigma_M^2}$$

Adjusting for β_A,

$$w = \frac{w_0}{1 + (1 - \beta_A)w_0}$$

The forecast for the optimized portfolio is then

1. *Mean*

$$E(r_P) = r_f + w[E(r_A) - r_f] + (1 - w)[E(r_M) - r_f]$$
$$= r_f + ws_A + [1 + w(\beta_A - 1)][E(r_M) - r_f]$$
$$= r_f + s_P + \beta_P[E(r_M) - r_f]$$

where the risky portfolio forecast of the abnormal return is

$$s_P = ws_A$$

and its beta

$$\beta_P = 1 + w(\beta_A - 1)$$

2. *Variance*

$$\sigma_P^2 = \sigma_\rho^2(e_P) + \beta_P^2 \sigma_\rho^2(e_M)$$
$$= w^2 \sigma_\rho^2(e_A) + \sigma_M^2[1 + w(\beta_A - 1)]^2$$

where the portfolio residual risk is $\sigma^2(e_P) = w^2\sigma_\rho^2(e_A)$. Finally, using A_m, the position, y_m, in this portfolio is

$$y_m = \frac{E(r_P) - r_f}{A_m \sigma_P^2}$$

PART VIII

Players and Strategies

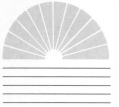

CHAPTER 27

Principles of Portfolio Management

There are many possible ways to approach formulating policy on portfolio management. In this chapter we follow a framework advocated by the Institute of Chartered
Financial Analysts.[1] It has three basic steps, which are outlined in Table 27.1. The
first two columns require specification of the investor's objectives and constraints.
The third is actual determination of portfolio policies that will achieve the stated objectives while satisfying the constraints identified.

For purposes of this chapter we divide individual and institutional investors into
seven major classes. Each has different objectives, constraints, and policies. First we
discuss the objectives of each group, and then we turn to constraints and policy.

27.1 *Objectives*

We can look at objectives as having two components: a return requirement and an
attitude toward risk. Table 27.2 lists factors governing return requirements and risk
attitudes for each of the seven major investor categories discussed.

TABLE 27.1   Determination of Portfolio Policies

Objectives	*Constraints*	*Policies*
Return requirements	Liquidity	Asset allocation
Risk tolerance	Horizon	Diversification
	Regulations	Risk positioning
	Taxes	Tax positioning
	Unique needs	Income generation

---

[1]This exposition is based on Part II of Maginn, John L., and Tuttle, Donald L. (editors), *Managing Investment Portfolios*,
Boston: Warren, Gorham, & Lamont, 1983, which is required reading for the ICFA qualifying examinations.

TABLE 27.2   Matrix of Objectives

Type of Investor	Return Requirement	Risk Tolerance
Individual and personal trusts	Life cycle (education, children, retirement)	Life cycle (younger are more risk tolerant)
Mutual funds	Variable	Variable
Pension funds	Assumed actuarial rate	Depends on proximity of payouts
Endowment funds	Determined by current income needs and need for asset growth to maintain real value	Generally conservative
Life insurance companies	Should exceed new money rate by sufficient margin to meet expenses and profit objectives; also actuarial rates important	Conservative
Nonlife insurance companies	No minimum	Conservative
Banks	Interest spread	Variable

Individual Investors

Individual investors are simply households. The basic factors affecting individual investor return requirements and risk tolerance are life-cycle stage and individual preferences. We will have much more to say about individual investor objectives in Chapter 28.

Personal Trusts

Personal trusts are established when an individual confers legal title to property to another person or institution (the trustee) to manage that property for one or more beneficiaries. Beneficiaries customarily are divided into **income beneficiaries,** who receive the interest and dividend income from the trust during their lifetimes, and **remaindermen,** who receive the principal of the trust when the income beneficiary dies and the trust is dissolved. The trustee is usually a bank, a savings and loan association, a lawyer, or an investment professional. Investment of a trust is subject to state trust laws, as well as "prudent man" rules that limit the types of allowable trust investment to those that a prudent man would select.

Objectives in the case of personal trusts normally are more limited in scope than those of the individual investor. Because of their fiduciary responsibility, personal trust managers typically are more risk averse than are individual investors. Certain asset classes such as options and futures contracts, for example, and strategies such as short-selling or buying on margin are ruled out.

When there are both income beneficiaries and remaindermen, the trustee faces a built-in conflict between the interests of the two sets of beneficiaries because greater current income inherently entails a sacrifice of future capital gain. For the typical case where the life beneficiary has substantial income requirements, there is pressure on the trustee to invest heavily in fixed-income securities or high dividend–yielding common stocks.

Mutual Funds

Mutual funds are firms that manage pools of investors' money. They invest it in ways specified in their prospectuses and issue shares to investors entitling them to a pro rata portion of the income generated by the funds. The objectives of a mutual fund are spelled out in its prospectus. We discuss mutual funds in detail in Chapter 3.

Pension Funds

Pension fund objectives depend on the type of pension plan. There are two basic types: **defined contribution plans** and **defined benefit plans.** Defined contribution plans are in effect tax-deferred retirement savings accounts established by the firm in trust for its employees, with the employee bearing all the risk and receiving all the return from the plan's assets.

The largest pension funds, however, are defined benefit plans. In these plans the assets serve as collateral for the liabilities that the firm sponsoring the plan owes to the plan beneficiaries. The liabilities are life annuities, earned during the employee's working years, that start at the plan participant's retirement. The sponsoring firm's pension actuary makes an assumption about the rate of return that will be earned on the plan's assets and uses this assumed rate to compute the amount that the firm must contribute regularly to fund the plan's liabilities.

If the pension fund's actual rate of return exceeds the actuarial assumed rate, then the firm's shareholders experience an unanticipated gain, since the excess can be used to reduce future contributions. If the plan's actual rate of return falls short of the assumed rate, the firm eventually will have to increase future contributions. Thus it is the sponsoring firm's shareholders who bear the risk in a defined benefit pension plan, so it is natural to assume that a main objective of the plan will be to reward the shareholders for bearing this risk.

Many firms try to match the risk of the pension assets with the risk of their pension liabilities. Often a distinction is made between the firm's liability to already-retired participants, which is a known flow of money, fixed in nominal amount, and its liability to active participants, which is tied to the employee's final wage or salary under most benefit formulas. The firm can hedge its known liability to retired workers by investing in fixed-income securities, but it cannot completely hedge the pension benefits it owes to active workers because this liability is effectively linked directly to future wages, which are not known in advance.[2]

Many pension plans view their assumed actuarial rate of return as their target rate of return and consider their tolerance for earning less than that rate to be quite low. We discuss pension plans more fully in Chapter 28.

---

[2]This statement is not entirely correct because a pension fund can transfer all of its pension liabilities to a life insurance company. In such a case the plan is called an insured pension plan.

Endowment Funds

Endowment funds are organizations chartered to use their money for specific nonprofit purposes. They are financed by gifts from one or more sponsors and are typically managed by educational, cultural, and charitable organizations or by independent foundations established solely to carry out the fund's specific purposes. Generally, the investment objectives of an endowment fund are to produce a steady flow of income subject to only a moderate degree of risk. Trustees of an endowment fund, however, can specify other objectives as dictated by the circumstances of the particular endowment fund.

Life Insurance Companies

Life insurance companies generally try to invest so as to hedge their liabilities, which are defined by the policies they write. Thus there are as many objectives as there are distinct types of policies. Until a decade or so ago there were only two types of life insurance policies available for individuals: whole-life and term.

A **whole-life insurance policy** combines a death benefit with a kind of savings plan that provides for a gradual buildup of cash value that the policyholder can withdraw at a later point in life, usually at age 65. **Term insurance,** on the other hand, provides death benefits only, with no buildup of cash value.

The interest rate that is imbedded in the schedule of cash value accumulation promised under a whole-life policy is a fixed rate, and life insurance companies try to hedge this liability by investing in long-term bonds. Often the insured individual has the right to borrow at a prespecified fixed interest rate against the cash value of the policy.

During the inflationary years of the 1970s and early 1980s, when many older whole-life policies carried contractual borrowing rates as low as 4% or 5% per year, policyholders borrowed heavily against the cash value to invest in money market mutual funds paying double-digit yields. Other actual and potential policyholders abandoned whole-life policies and took out term insurance, investing the difference in the premiums on their own. By 1981, term insurance accounted for more than half the volume of new sales of individual life policies.

In response to these developments the insurance industry came up with two new policy types: **variable life** and **universal life.** Under a variable life policy the insured's premium buys a fixed death benefit plus a cash value that can be invested in a variety of mutual funds from which the policyholder can choose. With a universal life policy, policyholders can increase or reduce the premium or death benefit according to their changing needs. Furthermore, the interest rate on the cash value component changes with market interest rates.

The great advantage of variable and universal life insurance policies is that earnings on the cash value are not taxed until the money is withdrawn. Since the Tax Reform Act of 1986 these policies are one of the few tax-advantaged investments left.

The life insurance industry also provides products for pension plans. The two major products are **insured defined benefit pensions** and **guaranteed insurance contracts** (GICs).

In the case of insured defined benefit pensions, the firm sponsoring the pension plan enters into a contractual agreement by which the life insurance company assumes all liability for the benefits accrued under the plan. The insurance company provides this service in return for an annual premium based on the benefit formula, and the number and characteristics of the employees covered by the plan. In the case of GICs the insurance company sells to a pension plan a contract promising a stated nominal interest rate over some specified period of time, usually several years. A GIC is in effect a zero-coupon bond issued by an insurance company. With respect to both types of product the insurance company usually pursues an investment policy designed to hedge the associated risk.

Life insurance companies may be organized as either mutual companies or stock companies. In principle, the organizational form should affect the investment objectives of the company. Mutual companies are supposed to be run solely for the benefit of their policyholders, whereas stock companies have as their objective the maximization of shareholder value.

In actuality, it is hard to discern from its investment policies which organizational form a particular insurance company has. Some examples of mutual insurance companies are Prudential and Mutual of Omaha. Examples of stock companies are Travelers and Aetna.

Nonlife Insurance Companies

Nonlife insurance companies such as property and casualty insurers have investable funds primarily because they pay claims *after* they collect policy premiums. Typically, they are conservative in their attitude toward risk. As with life insurers, nonlife insurance companies can be either stock companies or mutual companies.

Banks

The defining characteristic of banks is that most of their investments are loans to businesses and consumers and most of their liabilities are accounts of depositors. As investors, the objective of banks is to try to match the risk of assets to liabilities while earning a profitable spread between the lending and borrowing rates.

27.2 Constraints

Constraints may be divided into four categories: liquidity, time horizon, legal and regulatory, and tax status. For our purposes liquidity should be taken to mean the ability to turn assets into cash immediately at a fair and predictable price. According to this definition, cash and money market instruments would be the most liquid assets and real estate the least liquid. Table 27.3 presents a matrix summarizing the main constraints in each category for each of the seven types of investors.

TABLE 27.3   Matrix of Constraints

Type of Investor	Liquidity	Horizon	Regulatory	Taxes
Individuals and personal trusts	Variable	Life cycle	None	Variable
Mutual funds	Low	Short	Little	None
Pension funds	Young, low; mature, high	Long	ERISA	None
Endowment funds	Little	Long	Little	None
Life insurance companies	Low	Long	Complex	Yes
Nonlife insurance companies	High	Short	Little	Yes
Banks	Low	Short	Changing	Yes

Rather than discussing each constraint for each class of investor, let us explore the four constraint categories, illustrating how they may vary for different types of investors. In this way we can show how the general framework helps to organize the process of formulating portfolio policy. Although liquidity needs can vary a great deal depending on the specific circumstances of the individual or institution, generally speaking, endowment funds, life insurance companies, and pension funds of young companies have low liquidity requirements and long time horizons. On the other hand, nonlife insurance companies, banks, and pension funds of mature companies with many retired workers who are drawing benefits typically have short time horizons and high liquidity requirements. A young household with income exceeding its consumption spending will have low liquidity requirements and a long time horizon, whereas a family paying college tuition for one or more children might have high liquidity needs and a short time horizon.

Legal and regulatory constraints, which are virtually absent in the case of individual investors, can be quite complex for institutions such as banks and defined benefit pension plans. One example is the Employee Retirement Income Security Act (ERISA) of 1974, which sets minimum funding and investment standards for private defined benefit pension plans and establishes federal insurance for them, financed by a flat premium per covered employee.

Tax considerations are sometimes dominant in individual investor portfolio decisions. We examine this factor in some detail in Chapter 28. Tax status varies from the extremes of tax exemption for endowment and pension funds to full corporate taxation of the investment income of insurance companies and banks.

27.3   *Asset Allocation*

Consideration of their objectives and constraints leads investors to a set of investment policies. By far the most important part of policy determination is asset allocation, that is, deciding how much of the portfolio to invest in each major asset category.

We can view the process of asset allocation as consisting of the following steps:

1. Specify asset classes to be included in the portfolio. The major classes usually considered are the following:

   a. Money market instruments (usually called cash)

   b. Fixed-income securities (usually called bonds)

   c. Stocks

   d. Real estate

   e. Precious metals

   f. Other

Institutional investors will rarely invest in more than the first four categories, whereas individual investors frequently will include precious metals and other more exotic types of investments in their portfolios.

2. Specify capital market expectations. This step consists of using both historical data and economic analysis to determine your expectations of future rates of return over the relevant holding period on the assets to be considered for inclusion in the portfolio.

3. Derive the efficient portfolio frontier. This step consists of finding portfolios that achieve the maximum expected return for any given degree of risk.

4. Find the optimal asset mix. This step consists of selecting the efficient portfolio that best meets your risk and return objectives while satisfying the constraints you face.

Let us illustrate how the process works by considering a simple example. We start the process by initially restricting our portfolio to cash, bonds, and stocks. Later we will consider how much of an improvement we can achieve by adding real estate and other asset classes.

Specifying Capital Market Expectations

Having decided to restrict ourselves to cash, bonds, and stocks, we must specify our expectations of the holding period returns on these asset classes over the period until our next planned revision in the asset mix. Although professional investors usually revise their asset mix every 3 months when they receive new information about the state of the economy, market developments may cause us to revise more frequently.[3] In our example we will express all rates of return in annualized terms, but the holding period should be thought of as 3 months.

The set of capital market expectations must be in a form that allows assessment of both expected rates of return and risk. Sometimes investors will make only point forecasts of holding period returns on assets. These may serve as measures of expected rates of return, but they do not allow assessment of risks.

There are two sources of information relevant to forming capital market expectations: historical data on capital market rates and economic forecasts. The investment

---

[3] The Department of Commerce, for example, releases its figures on the Gross National Product quarterly.

professional must exercise considerable judgment when deciding how much to rely on each of these two sources.

For example, suppose that based entirely on economic forecasts derived from careful analysis of all the information we can assemble, we have determined the probability distribution of holding period returns exhibited in Table 27.4.

Our assessment of the HPR on bonds comes from a consideration of a 30-year U.S. Treasury bond with a 9% coupon. If there is normal growth, then we expect interest rates to remain at their current level and we will experience neither capital gains nor losses on the bond. Our HPR will simply equal the coupon rate of 9%.

If there is a boom, then we think interest rates will rise and the price of the bond will fall. The amount by which interest rates will fall depends on whether there is a low or a high rate of inflation. With low inflation interest rates will rise a little bit, causing a capital loss of only 5% on bonds, for a net HPR of 4%. However, if inflation is high, interest rates will rise a lot, causing a capital loss of 19%, for a net HPR of −10% on bonds.

If there is a recession, then we think that the direction of interest rates will depend on inflation. If there is low inflation interest rates will fall, but if there is high inflation they will rise despite the recession. In the low inflation recessionary scenario bonds will do very well, with an HPR of 35%. But in the high inflation recessionary scenario, the bond price will fall by 9%, leaving an HPR of 0.

The assessment of the rates of return on stocks for each scenario is evident from Table 27.4. Stocks are expected to do best in a noninflationary boom and worst in an inflationary recession.

To the extent that these parameter estimates—either the means, the standard deviations, or the correlation coefficient—differ from what they have been in the past, we may want to adjust their values so that they conform more to historical experience. In the rest of our example, however, we will use the unadjusted numbers calculated in Table 27.4.

TABLE 27.4 Probability Distribution of HPR on Stocks, Bonds, and Cash

State of Economy	Probability	Holding Period Return		
		Stocks (%)	Bonds (%)	Cash (%)
Boom with low inflation	.1	74	4	6
Boom with high inflation	.2	20	−10	6
Normal growth	.4	14	9	6
Recession with low inflation	.2	0	35	6
Recession with high inflation	.1	−30	0	6
Expected return	$E(r)$	14.0	9.0	6
Standard deviation	σ	24.5	14.8	0

Correlation coefficient between stocks and bonds is −.2372.

Concept Check

Question 1. Suppose that you revised your assessment of the probabilities of each of the five economic scenarios in Table 27.4 as follows:

State of Economy	Probability	Holding Period Return		
		Stocks %	Bonds %	Cash %
Boom with low inflation	.05	74	4	6
Boom with high inflation	.2	20	-10	6
Normal growth	.5	14	9	6
Recession with low inflation	.2	0	35	6
Recession with high inflation	.05	-30	0	6

What are your new estimates of expected returns, standard deviations, and correlations?

Deriving the Efficient Portfolio Frontier

Given the probability distribution of holding period returns in Table 27.4, what is the efficient portfolio frontier? Since we are considering only two risky assets for inclusion in the portfolio, we can use the formula presented in Chapter 7 to find the optimal combination of stocks and bonds to be combined with the risk-free asset.

The formula is reproduced here as equation 27.1:

$$w^* = \frac{[E(r_s) - r_f]\sigma_b^2 - [E(r_b) - r_f]\text{cov}(r_s, r_b)}{[E(r_s) - r_f]\sigma_b^2 + [E(r_b) - r_f]\sigma_s^2 - [E(r_s) - r_f + E(r_b) - r_f]\text{cov}} \quad (27.1)$$

where w^* is the proportion of stocks and $1 - w^*$ is the proportion of bonds.

Substituting in this equation we find that $w^* = .45$:

$$w^* = \frac{(14 - 6) \times 218 - (9 - 6) \times (-86)}{8 \times 218 + 3 \times 600 - (8 + 3)(-86)} = .45$$

Thus the optimal stock-bond portfolio to be combined with cash is 45% stocks and 55% bonds.

Its expected HPR, $E(r^*)$, and standard deviation, σ^*, are

FIGURE 27.1

The risk-reward
trade-off for portfolios
of stocks, bonds, and
cash.

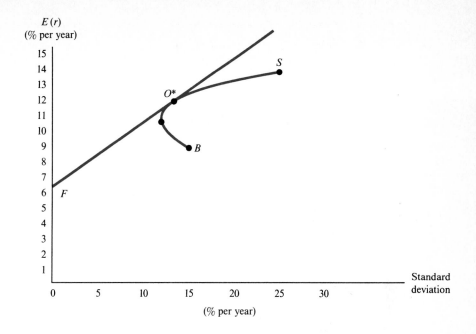

$$E(r^*) = w^*E(r_s) + (1 - w^*)E(r_b)$$
$$= .45 \times 14\% + .55 \times 9\%$$
$$= 11.25\%$$
$$\sigma^{*2} = w^{*2}\sigma_s^2 + (1 - w^*)^2\sigma_b^2 + 2\,w^*(1 - w^*)\text{cov}(r_s, r_b)$$
$$= .45^2 \times 600 + .55^2 \times 218 + 2 \times .45 \times .55 \times (-86)$$
$$= 144.875$$
$$\sigma^* = 12.0\%$$

Figure 27.1 displays the efficient portfolio frontier.

Point F represents 100% invested in cash, point B 100% in bonds, and point S 100% in stocks. Point O^* is the optimal combination of stocks and bonds (45% stocks and 55% bonds) to be combined with cash to form the investor's final portfolio. All efficient portfolios lie along the straight line connecting points F and O^*. The slope of this efficient frontier, the reward to variability ratio, is:

$$S^* = \frac{E(r^*) - r_f}{\sigma^*}$$
$$= \frac{11.25\% - 6\%}{12.0}$$
$$= .4375$$

The fact that we have drawn the segment of the efficient frontier to the right of O^* with the same slope as to the left reflects the assumption that we can borrow at a risk-free rate of 6% per year to buy the O^* portfolio on margin. If the borrowing rate is higher than 6% per year, then the slope to the right of point O^* will be lower than to the left.

If we rule out buying the O^* portfolio on margin altogether, then the segment of the efficient frontier to the right of O^* will be the curve linking points O^* and S. This indicates that, to achieve an expected HPR higher than $E(r^*)$ in the absence of borrowing, we would have to increase the proportion of our portfolio invested in stocks and reduce the proportion in bonds relative to their proportions in O^*. The maximum expected HPR under these circumstances would be the expected HPR on stocks, achieved by investing 100% in stocks.

Concept Check

Question 2. What is the O^* portfolio for the set of revised capital market parameters you derived in question 1?

The Optimal Mix

Our choice of where to be on the efficient frontier will depend on our degree of risk aversion, as shown in Chapters 5 through 7. We reproduce here as equation 27.2 the formula for the optimal proportion to invest in portfolio O^*:

$$y^* = \frac{E(r^*) - r_f}{A\sigma^{*2}} \tag{27.2}$$

where A is our coefficient of risk aversion.

For example, we might wonder how risk averse we need to be to want to hold the portfolio O^* itself, with nothing invested in cash. To find the answer, we set y^* equal to 1 and solve for A. The answer is $A = 3.65$.

Diversifying Into Different Asset Classes

Diversification is a good thing in asset allocation. But can there be too much of a good thing? After all, there are many different asset categories. Should you have some of each in your portfolio: stocks, bonds, real estate, precious metals, art, collectibles, and so on? And if so, how much?

The basic principle of efficient diversification suggests that you can never be made worse off by broadening the set of assets included in your portfolio. However, when we quantify the improvement in portfolio efficiency resulting from including additional assets, we often find that it is not large enough to justify the additional time, trouble, and other transaction costs associated with implementing it.

For example, let us consider whether we should add real estate to our portfolio in the example above. The first thing we need is the mean, standard deviation, and the correlations of the HPR on real estate with the returns on stocks and bonds. One way to derive them is from an expansion of the scenario analysis presented earlier in this chapter. Another way is by looking at past data.

TABLE 27.5   Capital Market Expectations: Stocks, Bonds, and Real Estate

	Stocks	Bonds	Real Estate	Cash
Expected HPR $E(r)$	14.0%	9.0%	10.0%	6%
Standard deviation σ	24.5%	14.8%	20.0%	0
Correlation Coefficients				
Stocks	1.0	−.24	0	
Bonds		1.0	0	
Real estate			1.0	

Data on real estate holding period returns is not as readily available as data on stock and bond returns. One feasible approach, however, is to gather data on a few publicly traded REITs[4] and treat them as representative of real estate as a whole. The advantage of doing so is that we can then invest in the shares of those same REITs when it comes time to implement our investment policy.

Let us assume that we have used one or more of these methods to derive the following set of capital market parameters for real estate:

$$E(r_r) = 10\% \text{ per year}$$
$$\sigma_r = 20\%$$
$$\rho_{RE,s} = 0 \text{ (correlation between real estate and stock returns)}$$
$$\rho_{RE,b} = 0 \text{ (correlation between real estate and bond returns)}$$

In addition, let us use the parameters for stocks, bonds, and cash as we did in Table 27.4:

$$r_f = 6\%$$
$$E(r_s) = 14\% \ \sigma_s = 24.5\%$$
$$E(r_b) = 9\% \ \sigma_b = 14.8\%$$
$$\rho_{sb} = -.24 \text{ (correlation between stock and bond returns)}$$

Table 27.5 presents a convenient summary of these capital market assumptions.

We use a computer-based optimization program to find the optimal combination of risky assets to combine with cash.[5] Table 27.6 shows the new O^* portfolio composition and characteristics, as well as the old.

Thus the reward-to-variability ratio that we face is .480, compared with .438 in the case without real esate. The optimal portfolio for an investor whose coefficient of

---

[4]REITs (real estate investment trusts) are discussed in Chapter 3. They are investment companies that invest either directly in real estate or in debt instruments secured by real estate.

[5]The software diskette provided with this text contains such a program.

TABLE 27.6 The Optimal Combination of Risky Assets ($O*$) With and Without Real Estate

	New	Old
Portfolio Proportions		
Stocks	35%	45%
Bonds	43%	55%
Real estate	22%	
Parameters of $O*$ Portfolio		
Expected HPR $E(r*)$	11.0%	11.25%
Standard deviation $\sigma*$	10.4%	12.0%
Reward-to-variability ratio $S*$	.480	.438

risk aversion is 3.65 and who previously would have chosen to hold the old $O*$ portfolio with no cash would be:

$$y* = \frac{E(r*) - r_f}{A\sigma^2}$$
$$= \frac{.11 - .06}{3.65 \times .0108}$$
$$= 1.27$$

Thus, if this were you and if you had $100,000 of your own money to invest, you should invest $127,000 in the $O*$ mutual fund, borrowing the other $27,000 at an interest rate of 6% per year.

The mean and standard deviation of your optimal portfolio would be

$$E(r) = r_f + 1.27[E(r*) - r_f]$$
$$= 6\% + 1.27(11\% - 6\%)$$
$$= 12.35\%$$
$$\sigma = 1.27\sigma*$$
$$= 1.27 \times 10.4\%$$
$$= 13.21\%$$

And your certainty-equivalent HPR would be

$$U = E(r) - \tfrac{1}{2}A\sigma^2$$
$$= .1235 - .5 \times 3.65 \times .0175$$
$$= .092$$
$$= 9.2\% \text{ per year}$$

This is .6% per year higher than the comparable certainty-equivalent HPR of 8.6% per year that you would have if you excluded real estate from your portfolio.

What can we conclude from all of this about the value of adding real estate to

TABLE 27.7 Capital Market Expectations: Stocks, Bonds, Real Estate, and Gold

	Stocks	Bonds	Real Estate	Gold	Cash
Expected HPR $E(r)$	14.0%	9.0%	10.0%	7.0%	6%
Standard deviation σ	24.5%	14.8%	20.0%	20.0%	0
Correlation Coefficients					
Stocks	1.0	−.24	0	0	
Bonds		1.0	0	0	
Real estate			1.0	0	
Gold				1.0	

stocks, bonds, and cash in creating your investment portfolio? Is it worth the effort?

The first thing to point out is that the specific results we got are very sensitive to the specific assumptions that we made about the parameters of the probability distribution of the HPR on real estate. In our example the reward-to-variability ratio goes up from .438 to .480, but had we assumed different numbers for the means, standard deviations, and correlation coefficients, the results could have been very different.

For example, had we assumed a higher value for the expected HPR on real estate, the optimization program would have indicated that we should invest much more heavily in it. The resultant increase in the reward-to-variability ratio would have been higher too. By experimenting with the optimization program that accompanies this text, you can gain a feel for the contribution that real estate would make to improving the efficiency of your portfolio under a variety of assumptions about the relevant parameter values.

Whenever we add an asset class, the process is identical to the one described for real estate. We first must specify the mean and standard deviation of the HPR and its correlation with the other asset classes. Our optimization program then tells us what the optimal proportions of all risky assets are in the O^* portfolio. We then can compute $E(r^*)$, σ^*, and S^*, and decide which combination of the risk-free asset and the new, expanded O^* mutual fund is optimal for us.

For example, suppose we are thinking of adding gold to our portfolio. Suppose that we think that its $E(r)$ is 7%, its σ is 20%, and its correlation with the other three risky assets is zero. Table 27.7 summarizes our capital market assumptions. What is the composition of the new O^* portfolio, and how much do we gain by diversifying into gold?

Our portfolio optimization program tells us that the new O^* has the following portfolio proportions:

Stocks	33%
Bonds	41%
Real estate	21%
Gold	5%

The expected return and risk of this new O^* portfolio are

$$E(r^*) = 10.76\%$$
$$\sigma^* = 9.87\%$$

and the new reward-to-variability ratio is

$$S^* = .482$$

This compares with a reward-to-variability ratio of .480 for the previous case without gold. It would appear that the gain from adding gold to the portfolio is slight.

In general it seems to be true that, unless you can identify an additional asset that has a high expected HPR, the gain from further diversification will be slight. You can explore the gains from additional diversification, using your own capital market assumptions, with the aid of the portfolio optimization program provided with this book.

If you are willing to rely on the judgment of others regarding both capital market expectations and your risk-return preferences, then as the nearby box describes, you can select a mutual fund that will do asset allocation for you.

Hedging Against Inflation

As we pointed out in the introductory chapter, what is of concern to the individual investor is *real* as opposed to *nominal* rates of return. A portfolio is therefore efficient if it offers the minimum variance of real rate of return for any given mean real rate of return.

Most textbook expositions of portfolio selection theory, however, and indeed most real-world applications of that theory, are cast in nominal terms. Typically, Treasury bills are taken as the risk-free asset, and the optimal combination of risky assets is constructed on the basis of the covariance matrix of nominal returns. All efficient portfolios are combinations of cash and the optimal nominally risky portfolio.

Since January 1988, however, investors in the United States have had available to them the possibility of investing in virtually risk-free securities linked to the U.S. consumer price level. The new securities were issued by the Franklin Savings Association of Ottawa, Kansas, in two different forms. The first is certificates of deposit, called Inflation-Plus CDs, insured by the Federal Savings and Loan Insurance Corporation (FSLIC), and paying an interest rate tied to the Bureau of Labor Statistics' Consumer Price Index (CPI). Interest is paid monthly and is equal to a stated real rate plus the proportional increase in the CPI during the previous month. As of July 1988 the real rate ranged from 3% per year for a 1-year maturity CD to 3.3% per year for a 10-year maturity.

The second form is 20-year noncallable collateralized bonds, called Real Yield Securities, or REALs. These offer a floating coupon rate of 3% per year plus the previous year's proportional change in the CPI, adjusted and payable quarterly.

Although it is still too early to say how many other issuers, if any, will follow the lead of Franklin Savings, this is still a milestone in the history of the financial markets in the United States. For many years prominent economists from across the ideo-

New Funds Broaden Investment Base

Asset Allocation Approach Aims to Spread Risk Between Stocks, Bonds, Metals, Others

Talk about market timing.

In 1986 and early 1987, a handful of mutual fund companies introduced funds whose managers were permitted to apportion assets among stocks, bonds, cash, and sometimes precious metals and foreign securities, as market conditions warranted.

Then the stock market collapsed last October. Ever since, some sponsors of these so-called asset allocation funds have advertised them as havens for shell-shocked investors who don't want to be fully invested in stocks at all times, but lack the time or expertise to make market-timing decisions.

What constitutes an asset allocation fund is still being debated in the mutual fund industry, but many fund managers and industry observers agree that such funds come in two basic varieties: flexible and fixed. In the more common flexible funds, the portfolio manager can apportion assets among various investments as he or she sees fit, within broad parameters spelled out in the fund's prospectus. In fixed funds, assets are allocated among stocks, bonds, money-market instruments and other investments in unchanging proportions.

Though asset allocation funds seem similar to old-fashioned balanced funds, there are significant differences. Says Henry Shilling, a vice president with Lipper Analytical Securities Corp., a New York City investment advisory firm: "Balanced funds maintain a specified balance between equities and fixed-income securities—on average, 60 percent equities and 40 percent fixed income. But the managers of some asset allocation funds can place as much as 100 percent of their assets in a single sector."

Fixed asset allocation funds differ from balanced funds in that assets are split among more types of investments than the standard trio of stocks, bonds and cash.

Are asset allocation funds a worthy investment alternative? It's hard to say because most have only been in business for a year or two. Says Bert Berry, publisher of *NoLoad Fund*X*, a San Francisco-based investment advisory newsletter: "If these guys are smart enough to be in the right sectors at the right time, it's

A sampling of asset allocation funds
(Performance for year ending March 31)

Fund	Year-to-date Performance
Alliance Balanced Shares	−1.58%
Blanchard Strategic Growth Fund	0.68
Claremont Fund	−2.59
Cornerstone Fund	−5.63
Dreyfus Strategic Investing	4.69
Dreyfus Strategic Aggressive Invest.	65.70
Morison Asset Allocation Fund	−6.14
Oppenheimer Asset Allocation Fund	2.98
Permanent Portfolio	5.01
Primary Trend Fund	5.44
Shearson Lehman Special Equity Portfolios Strategic Investors	−1.85
Strong Total Return Fund	−3.07
Standard & Poor's 500	−11.25

Source: Lipper Analytical Services.

wonderful. But most of these funds haven't been around long enough to prove whether that kind of market timing can be done well."

Berry is downright dubious about a fund's chances for long-term success if asset allocations are static. "You're in a self-canceling situation unless most of the sectors are favorable," he says. "If equities are up 50 percent, but bonds are down 50 percent, where have you gone?"

The following descriptions of 15 asset allocation funds illustrate the diversity of their investment philosophies.

• **Alliance Balanced Shares** (sold by brokers; 5.5 percent load; minimum initial and subsequent investments: $250, $50) is the 55-year-old granddaddy of asset allocation funds. No less than 25 percent of the fund's assets must be invested in debt securities, pre-

Continued.

ferred stocks and convertible debt securities. Portfolio manager J. Andrew Richey now has 63 percent in stocks and convertibles, 35 percent in bonds and 2 percent in cash. Says he: "We have a very aggressive portfolio assuming a good stock market and a reasonably solid economy for the next 12 to 18 months. We have no forecast for recession."

• **Blanchard Strategic Growth Fund** (800-922-7771; $125 account start-up fee; minimum initial and subsequent investments: $3,000, $500) employs five investment advisers: Four manage investments in US stocks, foreign securities, precious metals and US and foreign fixed-income securities, and a fifth oversees the investment mix. The fund can invest 5 percent to 35 percent of its assets in fixed-income securities and 10 percent to 50 percent in the other three categories. "We're not market timers," says fund president Michael Freedman. "On average, we make allocation changes every three to four weeks, but we don't make dramatic, radical shifts. We try to read long-term economic trends and make gradual changes." Freedman is now 30 percent in cash, 25 percent in foreign stocks, 18 percent in US stocks, 15 percent in US and foreign fixed-income securities and 12 percent in precious metals.

Blanchard spawned a clone last year that's sold by brokers: **National Strategic Allocation Fund** (7.75% load; minimum initial and subsequent investments: $1,000, $250).

• **The Claremont Fund** (sold by brokers; 4.75 percent load; minimum initial and subsequent investments: $500, $100) gives three investment advisers fairly free rein in allocating assets among stocks, bonds and cash. According to shareholder services representative Steve Daiken, the fund is now 51 percent in stock, 28 percent in bonds and 21 percent in cash.

• **Cornerstone Fund** (800-531-8000; no load; minimum initial and subsequent investments: $1,000, $100) is managed by USAA Investment Management Co., a Texas firm that started out selling auto and home insurance to military officers. Eighteen to 22 percent of assets is invested in each of five investment groups: US and foreign gold stocks, foreign stocks, US real estate stocks, US government securities and undervalued US stocks.

• Dreyfus boasts a trio of asset allocation funds:

Strategic Investing, Strategic Aggressive Investing and **Strategic World Investing** (sold by brokers; 3 percent load; minimum initial and subsequent investments: $2,500, $500). Asset allocations change frequently because fund manager Stanley F. Druckenmiller employs sophisticated trading and hedging techniques, including short selling. Strategic Investing takes a six- to 12-month view of the market, while the other two funds shoot for short-term gains. All three can invest in foreign securities, but Strategic World Investing is required to put 65 percent of its assets in securities that aren't traded in the US.

• **Morison Asset Allocation Fund** (sold by brokers: 7.25 percent load; minimum initial and subsequent investments: $500, $50) is managed by economist Thomas J. Morison who invests in stocks, government bonds and cash depending upon the availability of securities that meet his investment criteria. Says he: "This isn't market timing. I think that's a low probability." Morison is now 35 percent in stocks, 10 percent in cash, 25 percent in long-term bonds and 30 percent in bonds with maturities of less than three years.

• **Oppenheimer Asset Allocation Fund** (sold by brokers; 4.7 percent load; minimum initial and subsequent investments: $1,000, $25) is less than a year old. According to executive vice president Bridget Macaskill, the fund is now 45 percent in stocks, 11 percent in foreign securities, 39 percent in bonds and 5 percent in cash.

• **PaineWebber Asset Allocation Fund** (sold by brokers, 5 percent maximum back-end load; minimum initial and subsequent investments: $1,000, $100) changes its investment mix monthly to reflect shifts in Paine-Webber's asset allocation model. According to vice-president Ellen Harris, the fund is 36 percent in stocks, 51 percent in bonds and 13 percent in cash. Performance: Up 4.38 percent.

• **The Permanent Portfolio** (800-531-5142; $35 account startup plus $18 annual maintenance fee; minimum initial and subsequent investments: $1,000, $100) always keeps 20 percent of its assets in gold, 5 percent in silver, 10 percent in Swiss franc assets, 15 percent in US and foreign real estate and natural resource stocks, 15 percent in common stocks and warrants and 35 percent in US Treasury bills, bonds and other dollar assets.

Continued.

- **The Primary Trend Fund** (800-443-6544; no load, minimum initial and subsequent investments: $5,000, $100) apportions assets among undervalued stocks, government and corporate bonds and cash. According to fund secretary Roger Stafford, about 50 percent of the fund's assets were in cash during most of last year, but the manager loaded up on equities after the market crash and is now fully invested.

- **Shearson Lehman Special Equity Portfolios Strategic Investors Portfolio** (sold by brokers; 5 percent maximum back-end load; minimum initial and subsequent investments: $500, $200) invests in stocks, bonds, cash and gold securities. Up to 25 percent of the fund's assets may be invested in gold securities; up to 10 percent may be in foreign stocks and bonds. Currently, the fund is 60 percent in equities, 35 percent in bonds and 5 percent in cash.

- **The Strong Total Return Fund** (sold by brokers; 1 percent load; minimum initial and subsequent investments: $250, $200) has taken a conservative turn: 45 percent of its assets are in cash, 30 percent in stocks and 25 percent in bonds. Says chairman and portfolio manager Richard S. Strong: "The stock market is up five, working on six, years. Relative to history, the financial markets and economy are overextended as far as this economic recovery goes."

TABLE 27.8 Probability Distribution of Inflation and the Nominal HPR on Stocks and Bonds

State of Economy	Probability	Holding Period Return		
		Stocks	Bonds	Inflation
Boom with low inflation	.1	74%	4%	1%
Boom with high inflation	.2	20%	−10%	9%
Normal growth	.4	14%	9%	5%
Recession with low inflation	.2	0	35%	1%
Recession with high inflation	.1	−30	0	9%
Expected return	$E(r)$	14.0%	9.0%	5.0%
Standard deviation	σ	24.49%	14.76%	3.1%
Correlation				
Stocks			−.238	

logical spectrum have been arguing in favor of the U.S. Treasury's issuing such securities, and scholars have speculated about why private markets for them have not developed.

The purpose of this section is to analyze the gain to investors from having this new investment alternative. We first analyze the difference between portfolio optimization using nominal rates of return and real rates of return and measure the loss in portfolio efficiency from failing to take account of inflation risk. We then show how introduction of bonds offering a real risk-free rate of interest can improve portfolio efficiency.

Let us first consider the probability distribution of inflation and the distribution of

TABLE 27.9   Probability Distribution of the Real HPR on Stocks and Bonds and Cash

State of Economy	Probability	Holding Period Return		
		Stocks	Bonds	Cash
Boom with low inflation	.1	73%	3%	5%
Boom with high inflation	.2	11%	−19%	−3%
Normal growth	.4	9%	4%	1%
Recession with low inflation	.2	−1%	34%	5%
Recession with high inflation	.1	−39%	−9%	−3%
Expected return	E(r)	9.0%	4.0%	1.0%
Standard deviation	σ	25.71%	17.40%	3.10%
Correlation Coefficient				
Stocks			−.0295	.442
Bonds				.875

nominal HPRs presented in Table 27.8. When we do the portfolio optimization in nominal terms using a risk-free rate of 6%, we find that the $O*$ portfolio consists of 45% stocks and 55% bonds.

Now let us consider the portfolio optimization in real terms. Table 27.9 shows the probability distribution of real holding period returns implied by Table 27.8. The real HPR is defined in this case as the nominal HPR minus the rate of inflation.

Table 27.10 compares the parameters of the nominally efficient portfolios with those of the real efficient portfolios derived under the assumption that short sales and buying securities on margin are not permitted. Table 27.10 shows that the asset mixes that were efficient in nominal terms are not efficient in real terms, but the differences are not large. In fact, they are so small that optimization in nominal terms appears to be a satisfactory substitute for optimization in real terms.

For a portfolio with a mean real holding period return of 2%, for example, the standard deviation of the efficient portfolio (12% stocks, 4% bonds, and 84% cash) is 5.14%, whereas that of the nominally efficient portfolio is 5.34%, a difference of only 20 basis points. And this is the largest difference reported in the table.

The restriction on short sales means that for portfolios with a mean real HPR greater than 6.5% the real and nominal efficient portfolios are the same, and consist only of stocks and bonds. It also means that the minimum risk portfolio is 100% cash. If short sales were permitted, this portfolio would be −7.1% stocks, −20.1% bonds, and 127.2% cash, and it would have a mean of −.17% and a σ of .49%.

Figure 27.2 shows the risk-return trade-off in real terms graphically.

When we add a real risk-free asset offering a real interest rate of 3% to the other assets, it completely displaces cash. The optimal combination of risky assets ($O**$) is 71.2% stocks and 28.8% bonds. The mean real HPR of this portfolio is 7.56% per

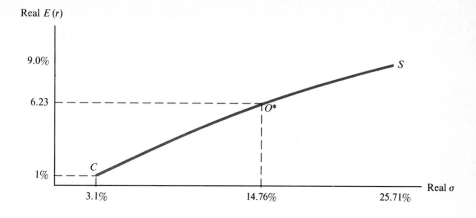

FIGURE 27.2

The efficient frontier in real terms, no real risk-free asset, and no short selling or borrowing.

TABLE 27.10   Real vs. Nominal Efficient Portfolios*

| | | Real Efficient Portfolios | | | | Nominal Efficient Portfolios | | |
| | | Portfolio Weights | | | | Portfolio Weights | | |
Mean (%)	σ (%)	Stocks	Bonds	Cash (%)	σ (%)	Stocks	Bonds	Cash (%)
1.0	3.10	0	0	100.0	3.10	0	0	100.0
2.0	5.14	11.9	3.6	84.5	5.34	9.1	11.1	79.8
4.0	9.58	28.4	24.2	47.4	9.68	25.7	31.4	42.9
5.0	12.06	37.7	35.6	26.7	12.13	35.0	42.7	22.3
6.0	14.27	45.9	45.8	8.3	14.34	43.3	52.9	3.8
6.23	14.67	47.4	47.7	4.9	14.76	44.6	55.4	0
6.5	15.31	50.0	50.0	0	15.31	50.0	50.0	0
7.0	16.74	60.0	40.0	0	16.74	60.0	40.0	0
9.0	25.71	100.0	0	0	25.71	100.0	0	0

*No real risk-free asset and no short selling or borrowing.

year, and the standard deviation 18.84%. There is a substantial gain in portfolio efficiency for portfolios with means below that of O^{**}. The lower the mean, the greater the gain.

The situation is best described with the help of Figure 27.3 and Table 27.11, which show the efficient frontier in real terms and compare it to points corresponding to the previous efficient frontier in the absence of a real risk-free asset.

Note that a risk-averse investor, who would hold a portfolio with a mean real HPR of 3% per year, stands to gain the most from holding the real risk-free asset. Using stocks, bonds, and cash, the σ of the portfolio would be 7.43% per year (point D in Figure 27.3), as opposed to zero risk using the real risk-free asset. The less risk averse the investor, that is, the smaller the proportion invested in cash in the absence of a real risk-free asset, the smaller the gain from adding CPI-linked bonds to the menu of assets.

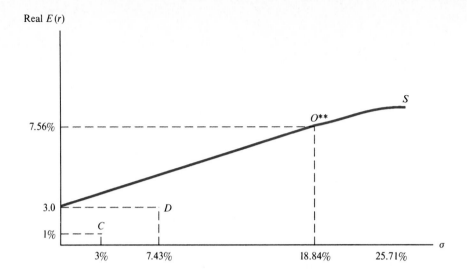

FIGURE 27.3
Real efficient trade-off line with real risk-free asset.

TABLE 27.11   Real Efficient Portfolios With and Without a Real Risk-Free Asset*

| | | Without Risk-Free Asset | | | | With Risk-Free Asset | | |
| | | Portfolio Weights | | | | Portfolio Weights | | |
Mean	σ (%)	Stocks	Bonds	Cash (%)	σ (%)	Stocks	Bonds	Riskless Asset (%)
1.0	3.10	0	0	100.0	—	—	—	—
2.0	5.14	11.9	3.6	84.5	—	—	—	—
3.0	7.43	20.4	14.2	65.4	0	0	0	100
4.0	9.58	28.4	24.2	47.4	4.13	15.6	6.3	78.1
5.0	12.06	37.7	35.6	26.7	8.26	31.2	12.6	56.1
6.0	14.27	45.9	45.8	8.3	12.40	46.8	18.9	34.2
6.5	15.31	50.0	50.0	0	14.46	54.6	22.1	23.2
7.0	16.74	60.0	40.0	0	16.53	62.5	25.3	12.3
7.56	18.84	71.2	28.8	0	18.84	71.2	28.8	0
9.0	25.71	100.0	0	0	25.71	100.0	0	0

*No short selling and no borrowing.

Taxes and Asset Allocation

Until this point we have completely ignored the issue of income taxes in discussing asset allocation. Of course, to the extent that you are a tax-exempt investor such as a pension fund, or if all of your investment portfolio is in a tax-sheltered account such as an individual retirement account (IRA), then taxes are irrelevant to your portfolio decisions.

But let us say that at least some of your investment income is subject to income taxes at a rate of 38.5%, the highest rate under current law. You are interested in the after-tax HPR on your portfolio. At first glance it might appear to be a simple matter to figure out what the after-tax HPRs on stocks, bonds, and cash are if you know what they are before taxes. However, there are several complicating factors.

The first is the fact that you can choose between tax-exempt and taxable bonds. We discuss this issue in Chapter 2 and conclude there that you will choose to invest in tax-exempt bonds (that is, Munis) if your personal tax rate is such that the after-tax rate of interest on taxable bonds is less than the interest rate on Munis.

Since we are assuming that you are in the highest tax bracket, it is fair to assume that you will prefer to invest in Munis for both the short maturities (cash) and the long maturities (bonds). As a practical matter, this means that cash for you will probably be a tax-exempt money market fund.

The second complication is not quite so easy to deal with. It arises from the fact that part of your HPR is in the form of a capital gain or loss. Under the current tax system you pay income taxes on a capital gain only if you *realize* it by selling the asset during the holding period. This applies to bonds, as well as stocks, and makes the after-tax HPR a function of whether the security will actually be sold at the end of the holding period. Sophisticated investors time the realization of their sales of securities to maximize their tax advantage. This often calls for selling securities that are losing money at the end of the tax year and holding on to those that are making money.

Furthermore, since cash dividends on stocks are fully taxable and capital gains taxes can be deferred by not selling stocks that appreciate in value, the after-tax HPR on stocks will depend on the dividend payout policy of the corporations that issued the stock.

These tax complications make the process of portfolio selection for a taxable investor a lot harder than for the tax-exempt investor. There is a whole branch of the money management industry that deals with ways to avoid paying taxes through special investment strategies. Unfortunately, many of these strategies contradict the principles of efficient diversification.

We will discuss these and related issues in greater detail in Chapter 28.

Summary

1. When discussing the principles of portfolio management, it is useful to distinguish among seven classes of investors:
   a. Individual investors and personal trusts
   b. Mutual funds
   c. Pension funds
   d. Endowment funds
   e. Life insurance companies
   f. Nonlife insurance companies
   g. Banks
In general, these groups have somewhat different investment objectives, constraints, and portfolio policies.

2. To some extent, most institutional investors seek to match the risk-and-return characteristics of their investment portfolios to the characteristics of their liabilities.

Thus a pension fund of a mature company with a large number of retired employees receiving dollar-fixed annuities may seek to hold an immunized portfolio of fixed-income securities. On the other hand, the pension fund of a young company whose plan participants are far from retirement may choose to invest heavily in equities.

3. The process of asset allocation consists of the following steps:
    a. Specification of the asset classes to be included
    b. Specification of capital market expectations
    c. Finding the efficient portfolio frontier
    d. Determining the optimal mix

4. For investors concerned about risk and return in real as opposed to nominal terms, there can be substantial gains from including a real risk-free asset in the portfolio mix. The gains are greatest for the most risk-averse investors.

5. For investors who must pay taxes on their investment income, the process of asset allocation is complicated by the fact that they pay income taxes only on certain kinds of investment income. Interest income on Munis is exempt from tax, and high tax-bracket investors will prefer to hold them rather than short- and long-term taxable bonds. However, the really difficult part of the tax effect to deal with is the fact that capital gains are taxable only if realized through the sale of an asset during the holding period. Investment strategies designed to avoid taxes may contradict the principles of efficient diversification.

Key Terms

Personal trusts	Whole-life insurance policy
Income beneficiaries	Term insurance
Remaindermen	Variable life
Defined contribution plans	Universal life
Defined benefit plans	Insured defined benefit pensions
Endowment funds	Guaranteed insurance contracts

Selected Readings

For a collection of essays presenting the Institute of Chartered Financial Analysts approach to portfolio management see:
Maginn, John L., and Tuttle, Donald L. (editors), *Managing Investment Portfolios,* Boston: Warren, Gorham, & Lamont, 1983.
A good discussion of asset allocation in practice is:
Brinson, G.P., Diermeier, J.J., and Schlarbaum, G.G., "A Composite Portfolio Benchmark for Pension Plans," *Financial Analysts Journal,* March-April, 1986.

Problems

1. (1988 CFA Examination, Level I)
    Several discussion meetings have provided the following information about one of your firm's new advisory clients, a charitable endowment fund recently created by means of a one-time $10,000,000 gift:

Objectives

Return requirement. Planning is based on a minimum total return of 8% per year, including an initial current income component of $500,000 (5% on beginning capital). Realizing this current income target is the endowment fund's primary return goal. (See "Unique needs" following.)

Constraints

Time horizon. Perpetuity, except for requirement to make an $8,500,000 cash distribution on June 30, 1998. (See "Unique needs.")

Liquidity needs. None of a day-to-day nature until 1998. Income is distributed annually after year-end. (See "Unique needs" below.)

Tax considerations. None; this endowment fund is exempt from taxes.

Legal and regulatory considerations. Minimal, but the prudent man rule applies to all investment actions.

Unique needs, circumstances, and preferences. The endowment fund must pay out to another tax-exempt entity the sum of $8,500,000 in cash on June 30, 1998. The assets remaining after this distribution will be retained by the fund in perpetuity. The endowment fund has adopted a "spending rule" requiring a first year current income payout of $500,000; thereafter the annual payout is to rise by 3% in real terms. Until 1998 annual income in excess of that required by the spending rule is to be reinvested. After 1998 the spending rate will be reset at 5% of the then-existing capital.

With this information and information found in this chapter, do the following:

a. Formulate an appropriate investment policy statement for the endowment fund.

b. Identify and briefly explain three major ways in which your firm's initial asset allocation decisions for the endowment fund will be affected by the circumstances of the account.

2. (1988 CFA Examination, Level I)

Your client says, "With the unrealized gains in my portfolio, I have almost saved enough money for my daughter to go to college in 8 years, but educational costs keep going up." Based on this statement alone, which one of the following appears to be least important to your client's investment policy?

a. Time horizon
b. Purchasing power risk
c. Liquidity
d. Taxes

3. (1988 CFA Examination, Level I)

The common stock investments of the defined contribution plan of a corporation are being managed by the trust department of a national bank. The risk of investment loss is borne by the

a. Pension Benefit Guarantee Corporation
b. Employees
c. Corporation
d. Federal Deposit Insurance Corporation

4. (1988 CFA Examination, Level I)

The aspect least likely to be included in the portfolio management process is

a. Identifying an investor's objectives, constraints, and preferences

b. Organizing the management process itself

c. Implementing strategies regarding the choice of assets to be used

d. Monitoring market conditions, relative values, and investor circumstances

5. (1988 CFA Examination, Level I)

Investors in high marginal tax brackets probably would be least interested in a

a. Portfolio of diversified stocks

b. Tax-free bond fund

c. Commodity pool

d. High-income bond fund

6. (1988 CFA Examination, Level II)

Sam Short, CFA, has recently joined the investment management firm of Green, Spence, and Smith (GSS). For several years, GSS has worked for a broad array of clients, including employee benefit plans, wealthy individuals, and charitable organizations. Also, the firm expresses expertise in managing stocks, bonds, cash reserves, real estate, venture capital, and international securities. To date, the firm has not utilized a formal asset allocation process but instead has relied on the individual wishes of clients or the particular preferences of its portfolio managers. Short recommends to GSS management that a formal asset allocation process would be beneficial and emphasizes that a large part of a portfolio's ultimate return depends on asset allocation. He is asked to take his conviction an additional step by making a proposal to executive management.

a. Recommend and justify an approach to asset allocation that could be used by GSS.

b. Apply the approach to a middle-aged, wealthy individual characterized as a fairly conservative investor (sometimes referred to as a "Guardian Investor").

7. (1987 CFA Examination, Level II)

John Oliver, formerly a senior partner of a large management consulting firm, has been elected president of Mid-South Trucking Company. He has contacted you, a portfolio manager for a large investment advisory firm, to discuss the company's defined benefit pension plan. Upon assuming his duties, Oliver learned that Mid-South's pension plan was 100% in bonds, with a maximum ma-

TABLE 27P.1 Current Portfolio

	Cost	Market Value	Current Yield	Yield to Maturity
Short-term reserves	$ 10,000,000	$ 10,000,000	5.8%	5.8%
Notes, 90 days to 1 year	25,000,000	25,500,000	6.5	6.4
Notes, 1 to 5 years	110,000,000	115,000,000	8.0	7.8
Bonds, 5 to 10 years	115,000,000	127,500,000	8.8	8.5
TOTAL	**$260,000,000**	**$278,000,000**	**8.1%**	**7.9%**

turity of 10 years. He believes that "a pension plan should be managed so as to maximize return within well-defined risk parameters," and "anyone can buy bonds and sit on them." Mr. Oliver has suggested that he meet with you, as an objective advisor, and the plan's actuary to discuss possible changes in plan asset mix. To aid you in preparing for the meeting, Mr. Oliver has provided the current portfolio (Table 27P.1). He also has provided the following information about the company and its pension plan.

Company

Mid-South is the eighth largest domestic trucking company, with annual revenues of $500 million. Revenues have grown about 8% per year over the past 5 years, with 1 down year. The company employs about 7,000 people, compared with 6,500 5 years ago. The annual payroll is about $300 million. The average age of the workforce is 43 years. Company profits last year were $20 million, compared with $12 million 5 years ago.

Pension plan

Mid-South's pension plan is a defined benefit plan that was established in 1965. The company annually contributes 7% of payroll to fund the plan. During the past 5 years portfolio income has been used to meet payments for retirees, while company contributions have been available for investment. Although the plan is adequately funded on a current basis, unfunded past service liabilities are equal to 40% of plan assets. This liability is to be funded over the next 35 years. Plan assets are valued annually on a rolling 4-year average for actuarial purposes.

Whereas FASB No. 87 requires an annual reassessment of the assumed rate of return, for purposes of this analysis Mid-South's management, in consultation with the actuary, has decided to use an assumed annual rate of 7%. This compares with actual plan results that have averaged 10% per year over the past 20 years. Wages and salaries are assumed to increase 5% per year, identical with past company experience.

Before the meeting, you review your firm's investment projections, dated March 31, 1987. Your firm believes that continued prosperity is the most likely outlook for the next 3 to 5 years but has allowed for two alternatives: first, a return to high inflation; or second, a move into deflation/depression. The details of the projections are shown in Table 27P.2.

a. Based on this information, create an investment policy statement for the Mid-South Trucking Company's pension plan. Based upon your policy statement and the expectations shown recommend an appropriate asset allocation strategy for Mid-South Trucking Company's pension plan limited to the same asset classes shown. Justify your changes, if any, from the current portfolio. Your allocation must sum to 100%.

b. At the meeting, the actuary suggests that Mid-South consider terminating the defined benefit plan, purchasing annuities for retirees and vested employees with the proceeds, and establishing a defined contribution plan. The company would continue to contribute 7% of payroll to the defined contribution plan.

TABLE 27P.2   Investment Projections

Scenarios	Expected Annual Total Return (%)
Continued Prosperity (60% Probability)	
Short-term reserves (Treasury bills)	6.0
Stocks (S&P 500 index)	12.0
Bonds (S&P high-grade bond index)	8.0
High-Inflation Scenario (25% Probability)	
Short-term reserves (Treasury bills)	10.0
Stocks (S&P 500 index)	15.0
Bonds (S&P high-grade bond index)	3.0
Deflation/Depression Scenario (15% Probability)	
Short-term reserves (Treasury bills)	2.0
Stocks (S&P 500 index)	−6.0
Bonds (S&P high-grade bond index)	12.0

Compare the key features of a defined benefit plan and a defined contribution plan. Assuming Mid-South were to adopt and retain responsibility for a defined contribution plan, briefly explain any revisions to your asset allocation strategy developed in part (a) above. Again, your allocation must sum to 100% and be limited to the same asset classes shown.

8. (1981 CFA Examination, Level II)

You are a portfolio manager and senior executive vice president of Advisory Securities Selection, Inc. Your firm has been invited to meet with the Trustees of the Wood Museum Endowment Funds. Wood Museum is a privately endowed charitable institution that is dependent on the investment return from a $25 million endowment fund to balance the budget. The treasurer of the Museum has recently completed the budget that indicates a need for cash flow of $3 million in 1982, $3.2 million in 1983, and $3.5 million in 1984 from the endowment fund to balance the budget in those years. At the present time the entire endowment portfolio is invested in Treasury bills and money market funds because the Trustees fear a financial crisis. The Trustees do not anticipate any further capital contributions to the Fund.

The Trustees are all successful business people, and they have been critical of the Fund's previous investment advisors because they did not follow a logical decision-making process. In fact, several previous managers have been dismissed because of their inability to communicate with the Trustees and their preoccupation with the Fund's relative performance rather than the cash flow needs.

Advisory Securities Selection, Inc. has been contacted by the Trustees because of its reputation for understanding and relating to the client's needs. The Trustees have asked you, as a prospective portfolio manager for the Wood Museum Endowment Fund, to prepare a written report in response to the following questions. Your report will be circulated to the Trustees before the initial interview on June 15, 1981.

Explain in detail how each of the following relates to the determination of either investor objectives or investor constraints that can be used to determine the portfolio policies for this 3-year period for the Wood Museum Endowment Fund.

a. Liquidity requirements
b. Return requirements
c. Risk tolerance
d. Time horizon
e. Tax considerations
f. Regulatory and legal considerations
g. Unique needs and circumstances

9. (1985 CFA Examination, Level III)

Mrs. Mary Atkins, age 66, has been your firm's client for 5 years, since the death of her husband, Dr. Charles Atkins. Dr. Atkins had built a successful newspaper business that he sold 2 years before his death to Merit Enterprises, a publishing and broadcasting conglomerate, in exchange for Merit common stock. The Atkinses had no children, and their wills provide that upon their deaths the remaining assets shall be used to create a fund for the benefit of Good Samaritan Hospital, to be called the Atkins Endowment Fund.

Good Samaritan is a 180-bed, not-for-profit hospital with an annual operating budget of $12.5 million. In the past the hospital's operating revenues have often been sufficient to meet operating expenses and occasionally even generate a small surplus. In recent years, however, rising costs and declining occupancy rates have caused Good Samaritan to run a deficit. The operating deficit has averaged $300,000 to $400,000 annually over the last several years. Existing endowment assets (that is, excluding the Atkins' estate) of $7.5 million currently generate approximately $375,000 of annual income, up from less than $200,000 5 years ago. This increased income has been the result of somewhat higher interest rates, as well as a shift in asset mix toward more bonds. To offset operating deficits, the Good Samaritan Board of Governors has determined that the endowment's current income should be increased to approximately 6% of total assets (up from 5% currently). The hospital has not received any significant additions to its endowment assets in the past 5 years.

Identify and describe an appropriate set of investment objectives and constraints for the Atkins Endowment Fund to be created after Mrs. Atkins's death.

10. (1982 CFA Examination, Level III)

You have been named as investment advisor to a foundation established by Dr. Walter Jones with an original contribution consisting entirely of the common stock of Jomedco, Inc. Founded by Dr. Jones, Jomedco manufactures and markets medical devices invented by the doctor and collects royalties on other patented innovations.

All of the shares that made up the initial contribution to the Foundation were sold at a public offering of Jomedco common stock, and the $5 million proceeds

TABLE 27P.3   Capital Market Expectations: Stocks, Bonds, and Real Estate

	Stocks	Bonds	Real Estate	Cash
Expected HPR $E(r)$	14%	9%	11%	6%
Standard deviation σ	24.5%	14.8%	20.0%	0
Correlation Coefficients				
Stocks	1.0	$-.24$	0	
Bonds		1.0	0	
Real estate			1.0	

will be delivered to the Foundation within the next week. At the same time, Mrs. Jones will receive $5 million in proceeds from the sale of her stock in Jomedco.

Dr. Jones's purpose in establishing the Jones Foundation was to "offset the effect of inflation on Medical School tuition for the maximum number of worthy students."

You are preparing for a meeting with the Foundation Trustees to discuss investment policy and asset allocation.

a. Define and give examples that show the differences between an investment objective, an investment constraint, and investment policy.

b. Identify and describe an appropriate set of investment objectives and investment constraints for the Jones Foundation.

c. Based on the investment objectives and investment constraints identified in part (b), prepare a comprehensive investment policy statement for the Jones Foundation to be recommended for adoption by the Trustees.

11. (Use the computer-based portfolio optimization program to do this problem.)

Assume the set of capital market expectations regarding stocks, bonds, real estate and cash given in the Table 27P.3. What is the composition of the O^* portfolio, its mean, standard deviation, and the reward-to-variability ratio?

CHAPTER 28

Individual Investors and Pension Funds

The overriding consideration in individual investor goal-setting is one's stage in the life cycle. Most young people start their adult lives with only one asset—their earning power. In this early stage of the life cycle an individual may not have much interest in investing in stocks and bonds. The needs for liquidity and preserving safety of principal dictate a conservative policy of putting savings in a bank or a money market fund. If and when a person gets married, the purchase of life and disability insurance will be required to protect the value of human capital.

When a married couple's labor income grows to the point at which insurance and housing needs are met, the couple may start to save for their children's college education and their own retirement, especially if the government provides tax incentives for retirement savings. Retirement savings typically constitute a family's first pool of investable funds. This is money that can be invested in stocks, bonds, and real estate (other than the primary home). It is the issue of how to allocate these investable funds that we address in the first part of this chapter.

First, we examine in some detail the retirement income planning issue. We discuss the magnitude of the savings required for this purpose and consider how these savings should be invested. Next, we consider ways to shelter investment income from taxation.

We then examine pitfalls of two pieces of conventional investment wisdom. The first is the notion that common stocks are less risky in the long run than in the short run. The second is the idea that it is important to distinguish between securities on the basis of how much of their return is in the form of current income and how much in the form of price appreciation.

The final part of this chapter is devoted to pension fund investment policy.

28.1 The Life Cycle Approach

It is commonly believed that investors' degree of risk aversion increases as they age. Table 28.1 lends some support to this view, at least toward the older end of the

TABLE 28.1   Amount of Risk That Investors Said They Were Willing to Take by Age

	Under 35	35-54	55 and Over
No risk	54%	57%	71%
A little risk	30	30	21
Some risk	14	18	8
A lot of risk	2	1	1

From Market Facts, Inc., Chicago, Ill.

spectrum. Although there seems to be no significant difference in risk-taking attitudes between investors under age 35 and those between 35 and 54, those over age 55 are clearly more risk averse.

One widely believed explanation for this pattern is that as the age of retirement approaches, investors cannot rely as much as before on labor income to recoup possible losses on their investment portfolios. If they want to maintain a stable level of consumption spending throughout their retirement, they must invest in assets that will produce a predictable and stable flow of returns.

The Consumption-Retirement Savings Decision

To illustrate how an individual accumulates a pool of investable funds in anticipation of retirement, let us offer the following simple example: you are currently 35 years old, expect to retire in 30 years at age 65, and then to live for 15 more years until age 80.

Assuming that your current labor income is $30,000 per year, that you have no accumulated assets, and that you expect a Social Security benefit of $10,000 per year of today's purchasing power starting at age 65, what constant level of consumption spending can you sustain from now through age 80? How much of your income must you save between now and retirement?

Let us simplify the example by ignoring taxes and assuming that the real rate of return on any invested funds is zero. Also, let us assume that your real labor income remains at $30,000 per year until age 65.

Let C denote the level of real consumption spending that you are looking for. Then $30,000 minus C is the amount saved each year from age 35 to 65. At age 65 the total accumulation will be $30 \times (30,000 - C)$. The amount withdrawn from the retirement account each year after age 65 to supplement Social Security will be $C - 10,000$. Since you will live only another 15 years, the total amount required will be $15 \times (C - 10,000)$.

To find C we set the two amounts equal to each other:

TABLE 28.2   Consumption and Savings as a Function of the Real Interest Rate

Real Interest Rate r (%)	Consumption (C)	Saving (S)
0	23,333	6,667
1	24,300	5,700
2	25,189	4,811
4	26,691	3,309
6	27,812	2,188
8	28,595	1,405
10	29,116	884

$$30(30,000 - C) = 15(C - 10,000)$$
$$60,000 - 2C = C - 10,000$$
$$C = \frac{70,000}{3}$$
$$= \$23,333 \text{ per year}$$

Thus the level of consumption spending is $23,333 per year. Annual savings in the preretirement years must therefore be $6,667 per year, and the amount withdrawn after age 65 must be $13,333 per year. The total accumulation at age 65 will be $200,000 in today's purchasing power.

More generally, we can show that C is such that the present value of C per year for 45 years equals the present value of $30,000 of labor income per year for 30 years plus the present value of $10,000 of Social Security income per year for 15 years starting 30 years from now. Algebraically, we have this equation:

$$C \sum_{t=1}^{45} \frac{1}{(1+r)^t} = 30,000 \sum_{t=1}^{30} \frac{1}{(1+r)^t} + 10,000 \sum_{t=31}^{45} \frac{1}{(1+r)^t}$$

where r is the real interest rate earned on the funds in the retirement account.

Table 28.2 shows what consumption and saving will be as a function of the real interest rate. Notice that higher real rates allow investment to grow more rapidly and thus allow a greater stream of consumption expenditures.

Concept Check

Question 1. Suppose Suzanne wants to start a retirement savings plan. She is currently 30 years old, and plans to retire at age 65 and to live to age 85. Her labor income is $25,000 per year, and her expected Social Security benefit is $8,000 per year. She intends to maintain a constant level of real consumption spending over the next 55 years. Assuming no taxes, no growth in real labor income, and a real interest rate of 3% per year, how much must she save in real terms each year until retirement?

Human Capital Risk and Insurance

The major asset of most persons during their early working years is their earning power, or human capital. The risk to their total wealth, human and nonhuman, stemming from the possibility of illness or injury is far greater than the risk associated with the assets in their portfolio of stocks, bonds, and other securities.

The most direct way of hedging human capital risk is to purchase disability insurance. If we think of insurance as a security, then the combination of this security with one's labor income has lower risk than the labor income itself. Considering a family as an individual investor, the purchase of life insurance is a hedge against loss of income because of death of any of the family's income earners.

Home Ownership as a Hedge

The first major asset that many people acquire is their own house. Normally, an alternative is to rent rather than buy one's place of residence. The decision to buy is therefore an investment decision.

An important consideration in assessing the risk-and-return aspects of this investment is the value of a house as a hedge against two kinds of risk. The first kind is the risk of increases in house rental rates. If you own a house, any increase in rental rates increases your return on your investment and your implicit rental expense by the same amount, thus leaving you unaffected.

The second kind of risk is that the particular house or apartment where you live may not always be available to you. By buying, you guarantee its availability in the future.

Discounted Cash Flow Analysis of the Buy vs. Rent Decision

The most appropriate way to analyze the decision to buy a house (or apartment) is to apply discounted cash flow concepts, just as you do in deciding whether to buy a particular stock. The major difficulty is finding the correct discount rate.

In the case of common stock, you would typically use the security market line relationship and the stock's beta (as shown in Chapter 8) on the assumption that the simple CAPM is approximately correct. But the simple CAPM is inadequate for evaluating the house you live in because it ignores the hedging value of home ownership. A more general multifactor model such as the APT would be required for this purpose. In general, the correct discount rate appears to be less than the one that would be derived using the CAPM.

Let us take a numerical example with a two-stage analysis. First we will consider the house as an unleveraged investment; that is, we will assume the buyer does not need or want to borrow to finance the purchase. Then we will examine the effect of mortgage financing on the desirability of the purchase.

R.E. Agent is currently renting a house for $800 per month (utilities not included) and now has an option to buy it for $100,000. Property taxes are deductible for income tax purposes, and Agent is in a 28% tax bracket. The maintenance, insurance, and property taxes are estimated to be as follows:

Maintenance	$150 per month
Insurance	50
Taxes	200
TOTAL	**$400**

Agent assumes that the rent his family would have to pay in the future if they did not buy the house now would increase at the same rate as the general level of consumer prices. He also assumes that maintenance, insurance, and property taxes will do the same. What is the internal rate of return on the investment?

No date for eventually selling the house has been specified, so we will assume for simplicity that Agent has an infinite horizon, perhaps because he intends to leave the house in a bequest to future generations.

The expected monthly after-tax cash flow will consist of the monthly rent less the monthly expenses net of the income tax savings from deductibility of the property taxes:

$$\text{Cash flow} = \$800 - \$400 + .28 \times 200$$
$$= \$456 \text{ per month}$$

On an investment of $100,000, the income flow provides a return of .456% per month, or 5.472% per year. Since the nominal cash flow is expected to increase at the rate of inflation, this is a real rate of return.

Considering its value as a hedge, Agent thinks that a real after-tax discount rate of 4% per year (.333% per month) is appropriate for this investment. The net present value of the investment, using the valuation formula for a level perpetuity, is therefore

$$\text{NPV} = \frac{\$456}{.00333} - 100,000$$
$$= \$136,800 - 100,000$$
$$= \$36,800$$

Under these circumstances our analysis shows that Agent should buy the house.

Now let us assume that buying the house makes it possible for Agent to get an $80,000 mortgage loan. Assuming that Agent does not have to borrow to buy the house, should he take the loan?

Without getting into a detailed computation of the NPVs of various mortgage contracts, such as conventional fixed-rate vs. adjustable rate, we can specify the principle to use in evaluating this decision. It will pay Agent to take the loan only if one of the following is true:

1. The mortgage makes it possible to do tax arbitrage; that is, the mortgage loan frees up funds that may be invested in tax-exempt bonds earning a higher interest rate than the after-tax rate that Agent will have to pay on the mortgage.
2. Agent wants to borrow to diversify his asset portfolio into assets other than his house, and a mortgage loan is the cheapest source of credit.

Returning to the retirement saving issue, consider that in effect as you age and accumulate financial assets you are using up your human capital and converting part of it into nonhuman capital. In principle, in early stages of life an individual might like to diversify some of the risk of labor income by trading some human capital for nonhuman capital. However, there is no market mechanism for accomplishing this type of risk reduction.

The fact that most people can increase their labor income in the event that their portfolio of nonhuman assets performs badly implies a possible negative correlation between labor income and the return of nonhuman assets. In general, this makes it possible for younger investors to tolerate a riskier portfolio of securities than older investors.

The theory of lifetime portfolio selection suggests that in the absence of this effect an individual investor's optimal asset allocation might very well remain the same, regardless of age and wealth level, as long as the parameters of the distribution of security returns remain unchanged.

In a famous article, Paul A. Samuelson developed a model of lifetime portfolio selection showing that under some standard assumptions about preferences an investor would not alter the composition of the investment portfolio over the life cycle.[1] The proportion invested in risky assets would be inversely proportional to the investor's degree of risk aversion (as shown in Chapter 5) and would not be changed as age and wealth level changed. His model proves that investing for many periods does not *in itself* introduce extra tolerance for riskiness at early, or any, stages of life.

The Samuelson model, however, does not allow for labor income. As we have seen, it may be the labor income effect that allows greater tolerance for risk at early stages of life. In the real world older individuals do exhibit greater risk aversion, as you saw in Table 28.1.

The task of life cycle financial planning is a formidable one for most individuals. Therefore it is not surprising that a whole industry has grown in recent years to provide personal financial advice. As the article in the accompanying box points out, the main problem for the client is to be able to sort out the good from the bad advice.

28.2   *Tax Sheltering*

In this section we explain three important tax sheltering options that can radically affect optimal asset allocation for individual investors. The first is the tax-deferral option, which arises from the fact that you do not have to pay tax on a capital gain until you choose to realize the gain. The second is tax-deferred retirement plans such as Individual Retirement Accounts, and the third is tax-deferred annuities offered by

---

[1]Samuelson, Paul A., "Lifetime Portfolio Selection by Dynamic Stochastic Programming," *Review of Economics and Statistics, 51,* 1969.

Time for a Heart-to-Heart With a Planner?

You've been meaning to sit down and put your finances in order, but it takes something drastic to stir you to action. Well, you have it in the great Wall Street wipeout. A calming step might be to see a financial planner—a self-styled financial physician who examines your earnings, assets, and expenses and prescribes strategies to manage them. "Most people come in because they're fed up with saving and investing on an ad hoc basis," says Joel Isaacson at Weber Lipshie, a New York accounting-and-planning firm.

Many insurance companies, brokerage houses, banks, and accounting firms are now establishing "financial advisory" units or will recommend consultants. So will friends, who might be more objective. In any case, there's a critical first question: Is this consultant in your financial class? "You have to match the financial planner to your income level," says Gary Greenbaum, a West Orange (N.J.) planner. Second, determine if you fit his or her clientele. A planner who specializes in, say, self-employed professionals may not be too hot on corporate stock options.

Ask to examine some actual reports the planner has prepared for clients (names will be blanked out, of course). If the reports seem too canned, back off. Most plans have three basic parts: a profile of your current assets, an analysis that projects future income and expenses, and recommendations. A comprehensive plan covering tax, estate, and retirement strategies can range from 30 to 80 pages, but don't assume thicker is better. The proposals should be tailor-made and trim, not padded with boilerplate on medicare and estate-tax rules. " 'Planning by the pound' is one of my pet peeves," says Larry Carroll, chairman of the International Association of Financial Planners.

Pin down the planner's compensation method. Some work on a fee-only basis, charging either an hourly rate or a percentage of total assets, often 1%. At Asset Management Group, an Englewood (Colo.) firm that works mainly with senior management executives, clients pay an average of $250 an hour—typically some $15,000 a year.

Your Financial Physician May Not Have a License

Financial planning is an unregulated industry. The International Association for Financial Planning estimates that some 250,000 people now claim to be "financial consultants." Of those, about 30,000 use the titles certified financial planner (CFP) or chartered financial consultant (ChFC). But these designations are educational degrees conferred by industry groups or colleges—unlike a CPA, which signifies a state license. Many planners are also qualified as CPAs, stockbrokers, or insurance agents.

The IAFP (800 241-2148) publishes a directory of independent firms ranging in size from 1 to 100 planners. Those listed have been in practice at least two years and have passed advanced exams. Members maintain their good standing by doing 30 hours of classroom work annually.

Big Commissions

Other planners work on a fee-and-commission basis: They charge a flat sum for the plan and collect commissions for selling financial products. Although some services advertise fees as low as $200, a customized plan usually starts at $1,000. If your income is $75,000 to $200,000, a $5,000 fee would be at the high end.

Fee-and-commission planners' bills often run less than those of their fee-only colleagues. That's because their income derives primarily from the products they sell. "There's no money in just counseling," says David Cohen, a Metairie (La.) planner. But there is in commissions, which can be as much as 8% for mutual funds, 10% for real estate partnerships, and 130% of first-year insurance-policy premiums—and, yes, a lot of planners started out in insurance sales.

Continued.

life insurance companies. Not treated here at all is the possibility of investing in the tax-exempt instruments discussed in Chapter 2.

The Tax-Deferral Option

A fundamental feature of the U.S. Internal Revenue Code is that tax on a capital gain on an asset is payable only when the asset is sold[2]; this is its **tax-deferral option.** The investor therefore can control the timing of the tax payment. From a tax perspective this option makes stocks in general preferable to fixed-income securities.

To see this, compare IBM stock with an IBM bond. Both offer an expected total return of 15% this year. The stock has a dividend yield of 5% and an expected appreciation in price of 10%, whereas the bond has an interest rate of 15%. The bond investor must pay tax on the bond's interest in the year it is earned, whereas the IBM stockholder pays tax only on the dividend and defers paying tax on the capital gain until the stock is sold.

---

[2]The only exception to this rule occurs in futures investing, where the IRS treats a gain as taxable in the year it occurs regardless of whether the investor closes his or her position.

Suppose the investor is investing $5,000 for 5 years and is in a 28% tax bracket. An investment in the bond will earn an after-tax return of 10.8% per year ($.72 \times 15\%$). The yield after taxes at the end of 5 years is:

$$\$1,000 \times 1.108^5 = \$1,669.93$$

For the stock, dividend yield after taxes will be 3.6% per year ($.72 \times 5\%$). Because no taxes are paid on the capital gain until year 5, the return before paying the capital gains tax is

$$\$1,000 \times (1 + .036 + .10)^5 = 1,000(1.136)^5$$
$$= \$1,891.87$$

In year 5 the capital gain is

$$\$1,891.87 - \$1,000(1.036)^5 = 1,891.87 - 1,193.44$$
$$= \$698.43$$

Taxes due are $195.56, leaving $1,696.31, which is $26.38 more than the bond investment yields. Deferral of the capital gains tax allows the investment to compound at a faster rate until the tax is actually paid.

Note that the more of one's total return that is in the form of price appreciation, the greater the value of the tax-deferral option.

Tax-Deferred Retirement Plans

Recent years have seen establishment of **tax-deferred retirement plans** in which investors can choose how to allocate assets. Such plans would include IRAs, Keogh plans, and employer-sponsored "tax-qualified" defined contribution plans. A feature they all have in common is that contributions and earnings are not subject to federal income tax until the individual withdraws them as benefits.

Typically an individual may have some investment in the form of such qualified retirement accounts and some in the form of ordinary taxable accounts. The basic investment principle that applies is to hold whatever bonds you want to hold in the retirement account while holding equities in the ordinary account. You maximize the tax advantage of the retirement account by holding it in the security that is the least tax advantaged.

To see this point, consider the following example. Suppose Eloise has $200,000 of wealth, $100,000 of it in a tax-qualified retirement account. She has decided to invest half of her wealth in bonds and half in stocks, so she allocates half of her retirement account and half of her nonretirement funds to each. By doing this, Eloise is not maximizing her after-tax returns. She could reduce her tax bill with no change in before-tax returns by simply shifting her bonds into the retirement account and holding all her stocks outside the retirement account.

Deferred Annuities

Deferred annuities are essentially tax-sheltered accounts offered by life insurance companies. They combine the same kind of deferral of taxes available on IRAs with the option of withdrawing one's funds in the form of a life annuity. Variable annuity contracts offer the additional advantage of mutual fund investing. One major difference between an IRA and a variable annuity contract is that, whereas the amount one can contribute to an IRA is tax-deductible and extremely limited as to maximum amount, the amount one can contribute to a deferred annuity is unlimited, but not tax-deductible.

The defining characteristic of a life annuity is that its payments continue as long as the recipient is alive, although virtually all deferred annuity contracts have several withdrawal options, including a lump sum of cash paid out at any time. You need not worry about running out of money before you die. Like Social Security, therefore, life annuities offer longevity insurance and therefore would seem to be an ideal asset for someone in the retirement years. Indeed, theory suggests that where there are no bequest motives, it would be optimal for people to invest heavily in actuarially fair life annuities.[3]

There are two types of life annuities, **fixed annuities** and **variable annuities.** A fixed annuity pays a fixed nominal sum of money per period (usually each month), whereas a variable annuity pays a periodic amount linked to the investment performance of some underlying portfolio.

In pricing annuities, insurance companies use **mortality tables** that show the probabilities that individuals of various ages will die within a year. These tables enable the insurer to compute with reasonable accuracy how many of a large number of people in a given age-group will die in each future year. If it sells life annuities to a large group, the insurance company can estimate fairly accurately the amount of money it will have to pay in each future year to meet its obligations.

Variable annuities are structured so that the investment risk of the underlying asset portfolio is passed through to the recipient, much as shareholders bear the risk of a mutual fund. There are two stages in a variable annuity contract: an accumulation phase and a payout phase. During the *accumulation* phase, the investor contributes money periodically to one or more open-end mutual funds and accumulates shares.

---

[3]For an elaboration of this point see Kotlikoff, Laurence J., and Spivak, Avia, "The Family as an Incomplete Annuities Market," *Journal of Political Economy, 89*, April 1981.

The second, or *payout*, stage usually starts at retirement, when the investor typically has several options, including the following:

1. Taking the market value of the shares in a lump sum payment
2. Receiving a fixed annuity until death
3. Receiving a variable amount of money each period that is computed according to a certain procedure

This procedure is best explained by the following example. Assume that at retirement John Shortlife has $100,000 accumulated in a variable annuity contract. The initial annuity payment is determined by setting an assumed investment return (AIR), 4% per year in this example, and an assumption about mortality probabilities. In Shortlife's case we assume he will live for only 3 years after retirement and will receive three annual payments starting 1 year from now.

The benefit payment in each year, B_t, is given by the recursive formula:

$$B_t = B_{t-1} \frac{1 + R_t}{1 + \text{AIR}} \tag{28.1}$$

where R_t is the actual holding period return on the underlying portfolio in year t. In other words, each year the amount Shortlife receives equals the previous year's benefit multiplied by a factor that reflects the actual investment return compared with the assumed investment return. In our example, if the actual return equals 4%, the factor will be one, and this year's benefit will equal last year's. If R_t is greater than 4%, the benefit will increase, and if R_t is less than 4%, the benefit will decrease.

The starting benefit is found by computing a hypothetical constant payment with a present value of $100,000 using the 4% AIR to discount future values and multiplying it by the first year's performance factor. In our example the hypothetical constant payment is $36,035.

The box on p. 848 summarizes the computation and shows what the payment will be in each of 3 years if R_t is 6%, then 2% and 4%. The last column shows the balance in the fund after each payment.

This method guarantees that the initial $100,000 will be sufficient to pay all benefits due regardless of what actual holding period returns turn out to be. In this way the variable annuity contract passes all portfolio risk through to the annuitant.

By selecting an appropriate mix of underlying assets, such as stocks, bonds, and cash, an investor can create a stream of variable annuity payments with a wide variety of risk-return combinations. Naturally, the investor wants to select a combination on the efficient frontier, that is, a combination that offers the highest expected level of payments for any specified level of risk.[4]

---

[4]For an elaboration on possible combinations see Bodie, Zvi, "An Innovation for Stable Real Retirement Income," *Journal of Portfolio Management,* fall 1980, and Bodie, Zvi, and Pesando, James E., "Retirement Annuity Design in an Inflationary Climate," Chap. 11 in Bodie, Zvi, and Shoven, J.B. (editors), *Financial Aspects of The United States Pension Systems,* Chicago: University of Chicago Press, 1983.

ILLUSTRATION OF A VARIABLE ANNUITY

Starting accumulation = $100,000

R_t = Rate of return on underlying portfolio in year t

Assumed investment return (AIR) = 4% per year

B_t = Benefit received at end of year $t = B_{t-1} \dfrac{1 + R_t}{1 + \text{AIR}}$

B_0 = $36,035. This is the hypothetical constant payment, which has a present value of $100,000, using a discount rate of 4% per year.

A_t = Remaining balance after B_t is withdrawn

t	R_t	B_t	Remaining balance = $A_t = A_{t-1} \times (1 + R_t) - B_t$
0			$100,000
1	6%	36,728	69,272
2	2%	36,022	34,635
3	4%	36,022	0

Concept Check

Question 3. Assume Victor is now 75 years old and is expected to live until age 80. He has $100,000 in a variable annuity account. If the assumed investment return is 4% per year, what is the initial annuity payment? Suppose the annuity's asset base is the S&P 500 equity portfolio and its holding period return for the next 5 years is each of the following: 4%, 10%, −8%, 25%, and 0. How much would Victor receive each year? Verify that the insurance company would wind up using exactly $100,000 to fund Victor's benefits.

Variable and Universal Life Insurance

Variable life insurance is another tax-deferred investment vehicle offered by the life insurance industry. A variable life insurance policy combines life insurance with the tax-deferred annuities described earlier.

To invest in this product, you pay either a single premium or a series of premiums. In each case there is a stated death benefit, and the policyholder can allocate the money invested to several portfolios, which generally include a money market fund, a bond fund, and at least one common stock fund. The allocation can be changed at any time.

A variable life policy has a cash surrender value equal to the investment base minus any surrender charges. Typically, there is a surrender charge (about 6% of the purchase payments) if you surrender the policy during the first several years, but not thereafter. At policy surrender income taxes become due on all investment gains.

Variable life insurance policies offer a death benefit that is the greater of the stated face value or the market value of the investment base. In other words, the death benefit may rise with favorable investment performance, but it will not go below the guaranteed face value. Furthermore, the surviving beneficiary is not subject to income tax on the death benefit.

The policyholder can choose from a number of income options to convert the policy into a stream of income, either on surrender of the contract or as a partial withdrawal. In all cases income taxes are payable on the part of any distribution representing investment gains.

The insured can gain access to the investment without having to pay income tax by borrowing against the cash surrender value. Policy loans of up to 90% of the cash value are available at any time at a contractually specified interest rate.

A universal life insurance policy is similar to a variable life policy except that, instead of having a choice of portfolios to invest in, the policyholder earns a rate of interest that is set by the insurance company and changed periodically as market conditions change. The disadvantage of universal life insurance is that the company controls the rate of return to the policyholder, and, although companies may change the rate in response to competitive pressures, changes are not automatic. Different companies offer different rates, so it often pays to shop around for the best.

Since the passage of the Tax Reform Act of 1986, the investment products offered by the life insurance industry—tax-deferred annuities, variable and universal life insurance—are among the most attractive of the remaining tax-advantaged opportunities.

28.3 *A Critical Examination of Some Conventional Wisdom*

Risk in the Long Run

One of the standard pieces of conventional investment wisdom is that common stocks are risky in the short run, but that for long holding periods they are relatively safe. This point is often "demonstrated" by focusing on simulations of the probability distribution of the compound annual average rate of return on a stock portfolio as the holding period gets very long.

Figure 28.1 shows the typical picture that results from such simulations. As the length of the holding period grows, the variance of the compound annual average rate of return for stocks falls. It becomes a short step to the conclusion that for retirement savings, the optimal asset mix should be heavily weighted toward stocks.

This conclusion, however, is faulty. Although the uncertainty of the average compound rate of return drops, the uncertainty of terminal wealth increases as the investment horizon lengthens, as demonstrated in Figure 28.2. Thus it is not true that investing for the long run by itself lessens risk.[5]

---

[5]For further discussion of this point, see Merton, R.C., and Samuelson, Paul A., "Fallacy of the Log-Normal Approximation to Optimal Portfolio Decision-Making Over Many Periods," in Friend, I., and Bicksler, J., (editors), *Risk and Return in Finance,* Volume I, Cambridge, Mass.: Ballinger Publishing Co., 1977.

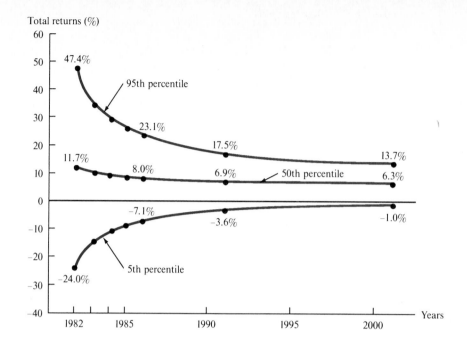

FIGURE 28.1

Projections of inflation-adjusted geometric mean returns for common stocks for the period 1982 to 2001.

(From Ibbotson, Roger G., and Rex A. Sinquefield, "Stocks, Bonds, Bills, and Inflation (SBBI), 1982, updated in *SBBI Yearbook*, Ibbotson Associates, Chicago.)

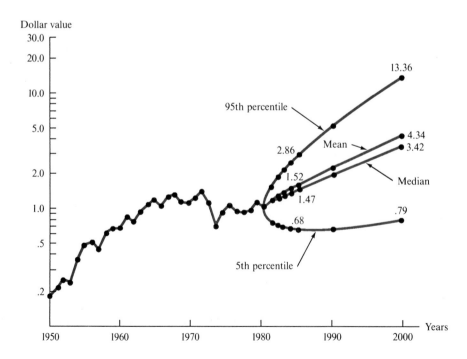

FIGURE 28.2

Projections of inflation-adjusted common stock wealth index values for the period 1982 to 2001; year-end 1981 equals 1.00.

(From Ibbotson, Roger G., and Rex A. Sinquefield, "Stocks, Bonds, Bills, and Inflation (SBBI), 1982, updated in *SBBI Yearbook*, Ibbotson Associates, Chicago.)

Growth vs. Income

There is a strong tendency in the popular investments literature to talk as if the investor must use only dividend and interest income for current consumption spending and reserve appreciation in security prices (that is, growth) for future spending. The only sensible justification behind such a policy would be the existence of significant transaction costs for selling securities, because in fact expenses can be met by selling securities just as easily as by collecting and dispensing the cash from dividends or interest.

For example, suppose you have $100,000 in assets and expect to spend $8,000 this year. You are trying to decide between two mutual funds that have the same expected return and risk. Income Fund offers an expected dividend yield of 8% and zero expected capital gains, while Growth Fund offers a dividend yield of 5% and expected capital gains of 3%. You can meet your planned $8,000 current expenditure in two ways:

	Invest in Income Fund	Invest in Growth Fund
Expected rate of return	8%	8%
Dividends	$8,000	$5,000
Sale of shares	0	$3,000
TOTAL	**$8,000**	**$8,000**
Portfolio value		
Before sale of shares	$100,000	$103,000
Sale of shares	0	−$ 3,000
End-of-year value	**$100,000**	**$100,000**

Note that in both cases the $8,000 for current spending is derived from portfolio returns and the end-of-year portfolio is worth the same $100,000. Whether the $8,000 comes from dividends or capital gains is irrelevant.

The classification of stocks into income vs. growth stocks really represents an implicit assessment about risk. Mutual funds termed "income funds" tend to have lower risk and lower expected returns than so-called growth funds. The choice between income and growth funds really should be viewed in terms of the risk-return trade-off. The purpose to which investment returns will be applied is irrelevant.

28.4 Pension Funds

Defined Contribution vs. Defined Benefit Plans

Although employer pension programs vary in design, they are usually classified into two broad types: defined contribution and defined benefit. These two categories are distinguished in the law under the Employee Retirement Income Security Act (ERISA). Under a defined contribution (DC) plan, each employee has an account into which the employer and the employee (in a contributory plan) make regular contributions. Benefit levels depend on the total contributions and investment earnings of the accumulation in the account. Defined contribution plans are in effect tax-deferred savings accounts held in trust for the employees.

In a defined benefit (DB) plan, the employee's pension benefit entitlement is determined by a formula that takes into account years of service for the employer and, in most cases, wage or salary. Many defined benefit formulas also take into account the Social Security benefit to which an employee is entitled. These are called "integrated" plans.

Defined Contribution Plans

The DC arrangement is conceptually simpler. The employer, and sometimes also the employee, make regular contributions into the employee's retirement account. The contributions usually are specified as a predetermined fraction of salary, although that fraction need not be constant over the course of a career.

Contributions from both parties are tax-deductible, and investment income accrues tax-free. Often, the employee has some choice as to how the account is to be invested. In principle, contributions may be invested in any security, although in practice most plans limit investment options to various bond, stock, and money market funds. At retirement, the employee typically receives an annuity whose size depends on the accumulated value of the funds in the retirement account. The employee bears all the investment risk; the retirement account is by definition fully funded, and the firm has no obligation beyond making its periodic contribution.

Defined Benefit Plans

A typical DB plan determines the employee's benefit as a function of both years of service and wage history. As a representative plan, consider one in which the employee receives retirement income equal to 1% of final salary multiplied by the number of years of service. Thus an employee retiring after 40 years of service with a final salary of $15,000 per year would receive a retirement benefit of 40% of $15,000, or $6,000 per year.

The annuity promised to the employee is the employer's liability. The present value of this liability represents the amount of money that the employer must set aside today to fund the deferred annuity that commences upon the employee's retirement.

Concept Check

Question 4. An employee is 40 years old and has been working for the firm for 15 years. If normal retirement age is 65, the interest rate is 8%, and the employee's life expectancy is 80, what is the present value of the accrued pension benefit?

Players and Strategies

Alternative perspectives on DB plans

Defined benefit pension funds are pools of assets that serve as collateral for firms' pension liabilities. Traditionally, these funds have been viewed as separate from the corporation. Funding and asset allocation decisions are supposed to be made in the beneficiaries' best interests, regardless of the financial condition of the sponsoring corporation.

Beneficiaries presumably want corporate pension plans to be as well funded as possible. Their preferences with regard to asset allocation policy, however, are less clear. If beneficiaries could not share in any windfall gains—if the defined benefit liabilities were really fixed in nominal terms—rationally, they would prefer that the funds be invested in the least risky assets. If beneficiaries had a claim on surplus assets, however, the optimal asset allocation could in principle include virtually any mix of stocks and bonds.

Another way to view the pension fund investment decision is as an integral part of overall corporate financial policy. Seen in this perspective, defined benefit liabilities are part and parcel of the firm's other fixed financial liabilities, and pension assets are part of the firm's assets. From this point of view, any plan surplus or deficit belongs to the firm's shareholders. The firm thus manages an extended balance sheet, which includes both its normal assets and liabilities and its pension assets and liabilities, in the best interests of *shareholders*.

Asset allocation in DB pension plans

The practitioner literature seems to view a firm's pension liabilities as divided into two parts—retired and active. Benefits owed to retired participants are nominal, and benefits accruing to active participants are real. The nominal benefits can be immunized by investing in fixed-income securities with the same duration or even exactly the same pattern of cash flows as the pension annuities. Accruing benefits, on the other hand, call for a very different investment policy.

The essence of that policy can be summarized as follows. In estimating the liabilities to active participants, the firm's actuaries make an "actuarial interest rate" assumption that should become the target rate for the pension asset portfolio. The pension fund should view the possibility of receiving a rate of return below the actuarial assumption as having a greater negative weight than the positive weight associated with a return above the actuarial assumption. This factor will affect the asset allocation decision.

Portfolio insurance is a new investment strategy that has developed recently in response to this view. It calls for maintaining an asset portfolio with a truncated and positively skewed probability distribution of returns. The probability of getting returns below the actuarial rate is zero, whereas the probabilities of returns above the actuarial rate are positive.

Portfolio insurance can be provided in a number of ways. The most direct method is to invest in common stocks and buy protective puts on them, which eliminates downside risk while maintaining upside potential. Of course, the guaranteed minimum return on such a policy will always be lower than the risk-free rate. Another method is to invest in T-bills and buy call options.

The third way of providing portfolio insurance is to pursue a dynamic hedging strategy with stocks and T-bills. The strategy involves continuous portfolio revision to replicate the payoff structure of the two previous strategies. It involves selling stocks when their price falls and buying them when their price rises.[6]

Recent changes in accounting rules may have a profound effect on the investment policies of pension funds. The accompanying box explains the issues involved.

The Black-Dewhurst Proposal

In 1981 Fischer Black and Moray Dewhurst created a stir among pension plan finance specialists by making a proposal that carried to a logical extreme the notion that a pension plan is a way to shelter investment income from corporate income taxes.[7] They claimed that, to maximize the value of a firm to its shareholders, a firm should fully fund its pension plan and invest the entire amount in bonds.

They propose the firm arbitrage taxes by substituting bonds for stocks in the pension fund. The simple form of the plan consists of four operations carried out at the same time:

1. Sell all equities, X, in the pension fund
2. Purchase on pension account X of bonds of the same risk as the firm's own bonds
3. Issue new debt in an amount equal to X
4. Invest X in equities on corporate account

The net effect of these operations will be that the firm will have more debt outstanding owed on corporate account and more bonds owned on pension account. The market value of the firm's own shares should thereby go up by as much as the corporate tax rate multiplied by the amount of new debt taken on in the maneuver.

The plan adds value because the firm earns close to the pretax rate of return on the bonds in the fund while paying the after-tax rate on the debt issued to support the procedure. Because only 15% of the dividends from the common stock are taxable and the tax on the capital gains can be deferred indefinitely by not selling appreciated stock, the effective tax rate on the equities held on corporate account will be very low. Thus the after-tax return on the equities will not fall significantly if they are switched from pension account to corporate account. If all value accrues to the firm's shareholders, if the effective corporate tax rate on equities were zero, and if the stocks held on corporate account are equivalent to the stocks previously held by the pension fund, the gain to shareholders has a present value of TX, where T is the marginal corporate income tax rate faced by the firm.

To clarify this proposal, let us take a specific example. The Hi-Tek Corporation is a relatively new company with a young workforce and a fully funded defined benefit pension plan. Hi-Tek's total corporate assets are worth $50 million, and its capital

---

[6]For a more complete discussion of dynamic hedging see Chapter 20. In addition, see Rubinstein, Mark, "Alternative Paths to Portfolio Insurance," *Financial Analysts Journal*, July/August 1985.

[7]See Black, Fischer, and Dewhurst, M.P., "A New Investment Strategy for Pension Funds," *Journal of Portfolio Management*, summer 1981.

Pension Funds Are Fat—
So Why the Long Faces?

New Rules and a Flagging Dow Have Companies Spooked

The Dow Jones industrial average is down 10% from its August peak. Yields in the government bond market are hovering around a nerve-wracking 10%. And corporate pension-fund managers are worried. From here on, "the consensus is that there's more likelihood of a drop in value than a substantial runup," says Eugene M. McQuade, a senior vice-president at Manufacturers Hanover Trust Co. So, he adds, many fund managers "are thinking of strategies to protect values where they are now."

What they are out to preserve is a treasure trove of assets: overfunded pension plans. The surplus of corporate pension-fund assets over liabilities has grown by at least $300 billion so far in 1987. "The 1980s have been the golden age for pension funds," says Irwin Tepper, head of his own Boston-based pension consulting firm. They offer "a once-in-a-lifetime experience," agrees John Carroll, president of GTE Investment Management Corp. The prosperity has come largely from a five-year stock market surge that everyone agrees can't be repeated in the next five.

Equal Billing

The pressure to lock in gains is greater than ever. Pension-fund performance may be peaking just when it is becoming highly visible to employees and investors. The reason is accounting rule changes being phased in by the Financial Accounting Standards Board. In next spring's crop of 1987 annual reports, most companies will have to show pension-fund performance right on the balance sheet, or give it equal billing elsewhere in the annual report.

Basically, the FASB rules "recognize that pension assets or liabilities are corporate assets and liabilities," says Richard Roll, a vice-president at Goldman, Sachs & Co. Companies with pension surpluses can capture those extra assets for their own corporate use, such as paying off debt, funding acquisitions, or making them-

WHERE PENSION PLANS ARE MOST OVERFUNDED

Company	Pension Surplus* Millions of Dollars
General Motors	$1,933
Southwestern Bell	1,882
United Technologies	1,407
Sears Roebuck	1,165
Unisys	898
Tenneco	853
Chevron	795
Allied Signal	745

Data from Compustat Services Inc.
*Funds in excess of pension liabilities.

selves less tempting to a corporate raider. An underfunded plan, on the contrary, is an onerous corporate liability. The unfunded liability of the six biggest steel companies totals nearly $6 billion.

For some pension sponsors, however, the new accounting rules are a pleasure—as long as the pensions remain overfunded. The complex calculations required by the FASB end up benefiting a company with a growing pension surplus. In fact, a company that wins in the pension-fund investment game can end up with "pension income." Moreover, the pension-fund bonanza will beef up corporate earnings dramatically. Many corporate pension-fund sponsors will be removed from any obligation to add new money to their already healthy funds. According to Salomon Brothers, the effect will be to increase pretax corporate profits by $25 billion, or almost 10%, in 1988 alone.

What's worrying senior management is the uncertainty of investment returns. If a falling Dow pummels their pension funds, the drop in assets will now show up on the balance sheet. Before, any unfunded liability was simply an annual report footnote. In the worst case, unfunded pension liabilities now can cut into a

Continued.

company's net worth. A potentially wild swing factor has been introduced into corporate financial statements.

If that weren't daunting enough, companies will be required to calculate their pension liabilities using a current bond-market interest rate. The result: big changes from year to year in how much money a company has to kick into its fund. Before, it was widely believed that pension assets had grown steadily year after year from an underfunded position in 1980 to an overfunded status this year. The neat lock-step trick was achieved by basing interest calculations on very conservative estimates offered by accountants and pension-fund consultants.

Yet, to take just one example, pension funds were reported as being slightly underfunded in 1980 using the actuarial rate of 7.3%. If the bond-market rate then, 13.4%, had been used to value liabilities, as the new FASB rules require, pension funds were in a healthy surplus. Market interest rates, which shift abruptly, can have a drastic effect on funding levels.

Only the Best

So companies are moving swiftly to take advantage of today's surpluses. One tactic is to capture a portion of a company's pension bonanza without taking the controversial route of terminating the whole pension plan. Citicorp, for example, boosted its third quarter pretax earnings by $300 million ($160 million aftertax) by capturing a portion of its funding surplus through the revised FASB rules. It did so by buying a $400 million annuity from Metropolitan Life Insurance Co. that covered part of its overall pension obligation.

Manufacturers Hanover pioneered this kind of transaction. It has enjoyed a total pension earnings gain of $127 million in three similar annuity purchases. Its latest maneuver helped out third-quarter earnings to the tune of $55 million pretax or $30 million aftertax. And Manny Hanny still has a $700 million pension surplus. Interest in buying annuities is widely expected to grow with today's rising interest rates. Annuities are cheaper to buy when rates are high since the same amount of principal provides income for more plan participants. They also allow plan sponsors to lock in today's lucrative stock market profits while satisfying any future pension obligations.

A related strategy is to sell stocks and buy bonds. "Now is a good time to switch to bonds because stocks are overvalued relative to bonds," says a corporate pension executive overseeing a fund of nearly $1 billion. Pension consultant Tepper agrees. He argues that buying bonds, with maturities matched to employees' retirement schedules, is a way to protect the balance sheet from any future pension liability hit. Pension-fund surpluses will inevitably decline, Tepper stresses, as stock prices fall while companies are free from any requirement to add new money to the plan.

Not everyone agrees with the "buy bonds" reasoning. "Making significant investment decisions based on accounting needs is a mistake," says GTE's Carroll. Shifting assets wholesale into bonds is "self-defeating if you believe it's the long-term plan to minimize corporate contributions." The reason: Equities have outperformed bonds over the decades and a pension fund is a long-term investment.

Sitting Pretty

But there's no doubt in the pension-fund field that many pension sponsors are buying bonds and selling stock—including Carroll. The stock market runup earlier this year pushed equities to more than 75% of his $10 billion pension-fund portfolio. He prefers keeping 65% to 75% of his assets in stocks. So even he's working to bring the ratio down. Many fund managers are in similiar straits since the preferred asset allocation is 60% stocks and 40% bonds.

Most companies are sitting pretty—for now. Many have a new source of visible wealth. But now that pension-fund performance is so visible to everyone, top executives will have to keep a closer eye on it themselves.

TABLE 28.3   Hi-Tek Corp. Balance Sheets Before Black-Dewhurst Maneuver

Assets		Liabilities and Owners' Equity	
A. Corporate Balance Sheet			
Current assets	$ 2 million	Debt	$10 million
Property plant & equipment	48	Owners' equity	$40 million
Total assets	**$50**		
B. Pension Fund Balance Sheet			
Stocks	$10 million	PV of accrued benefits	$10 million
		Fund balance	0

structure is 20% debt and 80% equity. Its pension assets consist entirely of a well-diversified portfolio of common stocks indexed to the S&P 500 and worth $10 million. The present value of its pension liabilities is $10 million. The corporate balance sheet is presented in Table 28.3, part *A,* and the pension fund's balance sheet in Table 28.3, part *B*.

Hi-Tek's treasurer, who is in charge of the pension fund, reads the Black-Dewhurst article and decides to implement the proposal. The pension fund sells its entire $10 million stock portfolio to the corporation and invests the proceeds in corporate bonds issued by other high-technology companies. The corporation pays for the stock by issuing $10 million of new bonds. The resulting new balance sheets are presented in Table 28.4.

According to Black and Dewhurst, the result of these transactions should be an increase in the market value of owners' equity of as much as $10 million multiplied by the corporate tax rate, currently 34%. In other words, the market value of the outstanding shares of Hi-Tek's common stock should increase by $3.4 million.[8]

To see why, let r be the interest rate on the debt. As a result of the previous four operations, the company will now be earning $r \times$ $10 million per year in interest on the bonds it bought on pension account and paying from its after-tax cash flow $(1 - T)r \times$ $10 million per year on the debt it issued on corporate account. The net cash flow to the firm will be $.34r \times$ $10 million per year, the tax saving on the interest. The present value of this saving in perpetuity is $3.4 million:

$$\frac{(.34r \times \$10 \text{ million})}{r} = \$3.4 \text{ million}$$

Note that, even though Hi-Tek's debt ratio has increased from .2 to .3, the overall risk of the firm has not changed. If we accept the theory that the pension fund assets and liabilities belong to the shareholders, the risk of the assets does not change when the $10 million of stock in the pension fund is, in effect, transferred to corporate account.

---

[8]If the corporate tax rate on equities is greater than zero, the gain in shareholders' equity will be smaller than $3.4 million.

TABLE 28.4   Hi-Tek Corp. Balance Sheets After Black-Dewhurst Maneuver

Assets		Liabilities and Owners' Equity	
A. Corporate Balance Sheet ($ Million)			
Current assets	$ 2	Debt	$20
Property plant and equipment	48	Owners' equity	40
Stocks	10		
Total assets	**60**		
B. Pension Fund Balance Sheet ($ Million)			
Bonds	$10	PV of accrued benefits	$10
		Fund balance	0

This plan implies that the company should increase its contributions to the pension fund up to the limits allowed by the IRS. This is because for every dollar of assets added to the pension fund, invested in bonds, and supported by issuing new bonds, the tax saving increases by rT per year and the PV of shareholders' equity increases by $\$T$. Thus, if T is .34, shareholders' equity rises by $.34 for every dollar added to pension assets or for every dollar switched out of stocks into bonds.

Summary

1. The life cycle approach to the management of an individual's investment portfolio views the individual as passing through a series of stages, becoming more risk averse in later years. The rationale underlying this approach is that as we age, we use up our human capital and have less time remaining to recoup possible portfolio losses through increased labor supply.

2. Saving is in large part motivated by a desire to smooth consumption spending over the life cycle. Part of our income in the early years is transferred to the later years to supplement Social Security benefits. Retirement savings often constitute an individual's first pool of investable funds.

3. People buy life and disability insurance during their prime earning years to hedge against the risk associated with loss of their human capital, that is, their future earning power.

4. A major investment for most people is the purchase of a house. Home ownership provides a hedge against unanticipated increases in the cost of shelter, so the discount rate to use in a discounted cash flow analysis should be lower than would normally be the case.

5. There are three ways to shelter investment income from federal income taxes besides investing in tax-exempt bonds. The first is by investing in assets whose returns take the form of appreciation in value, such as common stocks or real estate. As long as capital gains taxes are not paid until the asset is sold, the tax can be deferred indefinitely.

The second way of tax sheltering is through investing in tax-deferred retirement plans such as IRAs. The general investment rule is to hold the least tax-advantaged assets in the plan and the most tax-advantaged assets outside of it.

The third way of sheltering is to invest in the tax-advantaged products offered by the life insurance industry—tax-deferred annuities and variable and universal life insurance. They combine the flexibility of mutual fund investing with the tax advantages of tax deferral.

6. Long-run compound average rates of return can be very misleading in making asset allocation decisions.

7. Distinguishing between income and growth in investment returns is justified only to the extent that transaction costs of selling assets are significant.

8. Pension plans are either defined contribution plans or defined benefit plans. Defined contribution plans are in effect retirement funds held in trust for the employee by the employer. The employees in such plans bear all the risk of the plan's assets and often have some choice in the allocation of those assets. Defined benefit plans give the employees a claim to a money-fixed annuity at retirement. The annuity level is determined by a formula that takes into account years of service and the employee's wage or salary history.

9. A popular new investment strategy employed by managers of defined benefit funds is portfolio insurance, which is designed to guarantee downside protection while maintaining upside potential.

10. Black and Dewhurst have proposed a strategy that allows a firm with a defined benefit pension plan to exploit the tax arbitrage opportunity provided by the tax-exempt status of the plan's assets. A firm should shift all the stocks in its pension fund to corporate account and replace them with an equal amount of bonds financed by issuing new corporate debt. By doing so, the firm can earn the before-tax interest rate on the bonds while paying the after-tax rate of interest. The market value of the firm's common stock should increase substantially as a result.

Key Terms

Tax-deferral option	Variable annuities
Tax-deferred retirement plans	Mortality tables
Deferred annuities	Portfolio insurance
Fixed annuities	

Selected Readings

For a further discussion of the theory and evidence regarding the investment policies of corporate defined benefit pension plans see:

Bodie, Z., Light, J., Morck, R., and Taggart, R.A., "Corporate Pension Policy: An Empirical Investigation," *Financial Analysts Journal, 41:*5 September/October 1985.

Problems

1. Your neighbor has heard that you have just successfully completed a course in investments and has come to seek your advice. She and her husband are both 50 years old. They have just finished making their last payments for their condomin-

ium and their children's college education and are planning for retirement. Until now they have not been able to set aside any savings for retirement and so have not participated in their employer's voluntary tax-sheltered savings plan, nor have they opened IRAs. Both of them work, and their combined after-tax income last year was $50,000. They are in the 28% marginal tax bracket. They plan to retire at age 65 and would like to maintain the same standard of living in retirement as they had before.

a. Devise a simple plan for them on the assumption of a combined Social Security income of $10,000 per year. How much should they start saving? (Assume they will live to age 80, can shelter as much retirement savings as they want from tax, and will earn a zero real rate of return.)

b. Redo (a) with the following changes:
   i. The real interest rate is assumed to be 3% per year.
   ii. Your neighbors are 40 years old instead of 50.
   iii. The tax bracket after retirement drops to 15%.

c. What advice on investing their retirement savings would you give them? If they are very risk averse, what would you advise?

2. You are considering investing in real estate and have spotted a house with three rental units. You already own your own house and are not thinking of moving into the three-unit house.

The property would cost $120,000 and a bank would provide a conventional mortgage loan of $100,000 for 25 years at an interest rate of 12% per year. The other $20,000 would be your down payment. Mortgage payments will be once a year. Maintenance, property taxes, and insurance will be $4,000 in the first year and are expected to increase at the rate of inflation, 8% per year. Utilities will be paid by the tenants. You intend to depreciate the house over 15 years using the straight-line method. Although the property costs $120,000, $30,000 of that is the value of the land, and only the other $90,000 can be depreciated. You assume the nominal value of the property will appreciate at 8% per year and are planning to sell it in 4 years. You anticipate gross rental revenue of $20,000 from all three units combined in the first year and expect this to increase at the inflation rate.

a. If you are in a 28% tax bracket, what are the expected net after-tax cash flows to you from this investment? (Remember the capital gains tax in year 4.)

b. If your required nominal after-tax rate of return is 10% per year, what is the NPV of the investment?

3. (Based on the 1982 CFA Examination, Level I)

C.B. Snow, recently deceased president of Highway Cartage Company, left a net estate of $300,000. Under his will, a trust of $300,000 was created for his surviving spouse, with Peninsular Trust Company named trustee. A daughter is the remainderman of her mother's trust. The widow's trust is composed of the following assets:

	Proportion of Portfolio	Amount at Market	Current Yield (%)
Money market fund	25%	$ 75,000	14.7
Tax-exempt municipal bonds	35%	105,000	8.0[a]
Highway Cartage Co. common stock	40%	120,000	7.9
	100%	$ 300,000	

[a] Yield to maturity equals 12.0%

As a portfolio manager with Peninsular, you have just attended a meeting with the widow and learned the following:

She is 65 and in good health (mortality tables indicate an expected life span of 18 years). As a retirement benefit, she is eligible for Highway's generous group medical insurance plan for the remainder of her life.

Her estimated household and other expenses last year, adjusted to allow for inflation this year, are $19,600. In the absence of her husband's salary, her tax bracket will decline substantially to 30%. Next week she will be eligible to receive Social Security payments of $600 per month. (See following Note on the taxation of Social Security benefits.)

She plans to purchase a $60,000 condominium as a vacation residence within the next 6 months, using $15,000 in deferred compensation (after taxes) due her husband as a down payment. Conventional mortgage financing is available for 75% of the cost at 17.5% for 30 years. She anticipates that any tax savings from the credit for mortgage interest payments will be consumed by maintenance fees charged to the owner. She also intends to join an adjacent golf club where dues are $125 per month.

She wishes to retain all of the Highway common stock because, "It's the only stock C.B. ever owned and he had such great confidence in the company's future. Also, the yield is very generous, I think, despite the dividend reduction last year when the economy sagged."

At the conclusion of the meeting, Mrs. Snow requested that the assets in her trust be left intact, if possible. Mrs. Snow is co-trustee of her trust and can veto any of your recommendations.

a. Calculate Mrs. Snow's income sources and expenses, assuming her request is honored, and state whether her income requirements can be met.
b. Identify and discuss the investment objectives and constraints that appear applicable to Mrs. Snow's situation.
c. Recommend and justify changes in her present trust portfolio that are consistent with the objectives and constraints in part (b). (Use the information in Table 28P.1.)

Note on the taxation of Social Security benefits:

If the sum of all income (including interest on municipal bonds) plus one half of Social Security benefits is greater than $32,000 (for a couple filing jointly; $25,000 for an individual) then either one half of the Social Security benefit or the excess of total income over $32,000 is taxable as ordinary income.

TABLE 28P.1   Market Data

Category	Beta Coefficient	Implied Total Return	Current Yield
Fixed-Income Securities			
Money market funds			14.7%
Government bonds:			
Intermediate-term			14.4
Long-term			14.0
Corporate bonds (A-rated):			
Intermediate-term			15.1
Long-term			16.0
Tax-exempt municipals:			
Intermediate-term			10.2
Long-term			11.1
Common Stocks			
Industrials	1.0	17.0%	5.2%
Trucking	1.1	14.8%	4.0%
Highway Cartage Co.	1.3	14.8%	7.9%
Consumer Price Index (Average Annual Index)			
8.9% projected current year	8.0% projected next year	5%-15% range next 5 years	7%-10% most probable next 5 years

4. (Based on the 1985 CFA Examination, Level II)

You are Faye Trotter, assistant treasurer of Ednam Products Company, a firm that recently terminated its defined benefit (pension) retirement plan in favor of a new defined contribution (profit-sharing) retirement plan. Termination proceeds were used to purchase an annuity for each employee, with normal retirement at age 65. Before termination, Ednam had also sponsored a generous savings plan under which many employees have accumulated sizeable participations. These accumulations have been incorporated into the employees' individual accounts as an integral part of the new Plan, which is fully qualified under ERISA and meets all requirements for protecting employee tax benefits that are part of this arrangement.

Each employee is now responsible for investment decisions in his or her own personal Plan account. This includes selection of the vehicles of implementation, current disposition of the accumulated monies now awaiting investment, and ongoing monitoring and adjustment of account exposure, as well as disposition of future company profit-sharing contributions. This decision-making requirement is a totally new experience for most employees and is one about which many concerns have been expressed to Ednam management.

Responding to these concerns, the company has made five investment alternatives available under the Plan and has designated you as a resource person for interested employees.

Your role is to provide information about the Plan and its investment alternatives, about the no-load mutual funds selected by the company as investment vehicles, about consensus capital market expectations, and about the fundamentals of investing. Although Ednam management realizes that this response falls short of being a complete counseling program, they believe that the combination of a wide range of investment vehicles and continuing access to an objective and experienced person should enable employees to make intelligent investment choices. Moreover, the Plan provides that allocations to any or all of the five investment vehicles may be changed at 6-month intervals. Employees have been told that investing is a process that requires their continuing participation, with particular attention to adjustment of market exposures as personal and external conditions change through time. Overall, employee reactions have been enthusiastic and three individuals already have requested appointments with you. The following background information on the three individuals has been made available to you:

- Tom Davis, sales manager, age 58; he intends to retire at age 62; married; no children; wife employed. Owns $150,000 house (no mortgage) and $100,000 portfolio of growth stocks. No family health problems; no major indebtedness. Accumulated in Plan investment account: $160,000.
- Margaret Custer, assistant director of Market Research, age 30, single; excellent health; buying condominium (heavily mortgaged) and car. Accumulated in Plan investment account: $40,000.
- Glenn Abbott, plant supervisor, age 42, widower, two children, ages 14 and 10; buying $130,000 house ($80,000 mortgage). No other indebtedness except regular heavy use of credit cards. Accumulated in Plan investment account: $110,000.

You expect that each of these individuals will want to discuss allocation of their account accumulations, as well as details of the Plan and the no-load mutual fund investment vehicles described here:

- Money market fund. Average maturity typically is 30 days.
- High-grade bond fund. Average duration maintained at 15 years.
- Index stock fund. An S&P 500 proxy. Beta of 1.00.
- Growth stock fund. Portfolio beta maintained at 1.30.
- Real estate equity fund. Owns diversified portfolio of commercial properties. Holds no mortgages; not a tax-shelter fund.

As part of your preparation, you have determined that consensus risk and return expectations for the various asset classes over the next several years are in line with average historical experience, accompanied by modest inflation levels.

Utilizing this information and your own assessment of the risk-bearing capacities of Tom, Margaret, and Glenn, do the following:

a. Identify and discuss the differences in investor life cycle position and in investment objectives and constraints that exist among the three individuals. Frame the identification part of your answer in the matrix format shown below:

Investment Considerations	Tom	Margaret	Glenn

  b. Prepare a normal, long-term allocation of the accumulated monies in each of the three individual accounts and justify the resulting asset mix. Your allocations should sum to 100% in each case and be based on your part (a) conclusions. Do not base your answer on any qualitative considerations related to current or expected market considerations as you perceive them.

5. George More is a participant in a defined contribution pension plan that offers a fixed-income fund and a common stock fund as investment choices. He is 40 years old and has an accumulation of $100,00 in each of the funds. He currently contributes $1,500 per year to each. He plans to retire at age 65, and his life expectancy is age 80.

  a. Assuming a 3% per year real earnings rate for the fixed-income fund and 6% per year for common stocks, what will be George's expected accumulation in each account at age 65?

  b. What will be the expected real retirement annuity from each account, assuming these same real earnings rates?

  c. If George wanted a retirement annuity of $30,000 per year from the fixed-income fund, by how much would he have to increase his annual contributions?

6. A firm has a defined benefit pension plan that pays an annual retirement benefit of 1.5% of final salary per year of service. Joe Loyal is 60 years old and has been working for the firm for the last 35 years. His current salary is $40,000 per year.

  a. If normal retirement age is 65, the interest rate is 8%, and Joe's life expectancy is 80, what is the present value of his accrued pension benefit?

  b. If Joe wanted to retire now, what would be an actuarially fair annual pension benefit? (Assume the first payment would be made 1 year from now.)

7. Unlimited Horizons, Inc. (UH) has corporate assets of $100 million and conventional debt of $40 million. Its defined benefit pension plan has assets (50% stocks and 50% bonds) with a current market value of $10 million, and the present value of accrued benefits is $12 million. UH is in the 34% tax bracket.

  a. What do its corporate and pension fund balance sheets look like? What is the net worth on corporate account, and what is its net worth, including its pension plan?

b. According to Black and Dewhurst, what could the firm do to increase the value of shareholders' equity?

c. What would its corporate and pension fund balance sheets look like after implementation of the Black and Dewhurst plan?

8. (Adapted from the 1983 CFA Examination, Level III)

You are Mr. R.J. Certain, a retired C.F.A., who formerly was the chief investment officer of a major investment management organization. Although you have over 30 years of experience in the investment business, you have kept up with the literature and developed a reputation for your knowledge and ability to blend modern portfolio theory and traditional portfolio methods.

The chairman of the board of Morgan Industries has asked you to serve as a consultant to him and the other members of the Board of Trustees of the company's pension fund. Since you are interested in developing a consulting practice and in keeping actively involved in the investment management business, you welcome the opportunity to develop a portfolio management decision-making process for Morgan Industries that you could apply to all types of investment portfolios.

Morgan Industries is a company in transition. Its long established business, dating back to the early years of the century, is the production of steel. Since the 1960s, however, Morgan has gradually built a highly profitable stake in the domestic production of oil and gas.

Most of the company's 1982 sales of $4 billion were still derived from steel operations. Because Morgan occupies a relatively stable niche in a specialized segment of the steel industry, its losses on steel during the 1982 recession were moderate compared to industry experience. At the same time, profit margins for Morgan's oil and gas business remained satisfactory despite all the problems in the world oil market. This segment of the company's operations accounted for the entire 1982 net profit of $150 million. Even when steel operations recover, oil and gas operations are expected to contribute, on average, over half of Morgan's annual profits.

Based on the combination of the two segments of the company's operations, the overall cyclicality of company earnings appears to be approximately the same as that of the S&P 500. Several well-regarded security analysts, citing the outlook for recovery in steel operations, as well as further gains in the oil and gas production, project earnings progress for Morgan over the next 5 years at about the same rate as for the S&P 500. Debt comprises about 35% of the long-term capital structure, and the beta (market risk) for the company's common stock is also about the same as for the S&P 500.

Morgan's defined benefit pension plan covers 25,000 active employees, vested and unvested, and 15,000 retired employees, with the latter projected to exceed 20,000 in 5 years. The burden of pension liabilities is large because the steel industry has long been labor intensive and the company's current labor force in this area of operations is not as large as it was some years ago. The oil and gas operations, although growing at a significant rate, account for only 10% of the active plan participants and for even less of the retired beneficiaries.

Pension assets amounted to $1 billion of market value at the end of 1982. For the purpose of planning investment policy, the present value of the unfunded pension liability is calculated at $500 million. Although the company's outstanding debt is $600 million, it is clear that the unfunded pension liability adds significantly to the leverage in the capital structure.

Pension expenses charged to company income—and reflected in company contributions to the pension trust—were $80 million in 1982. The level of expenses, which are projected to rise with payroll, reflects current assumptions concerning inflation, the rate of return on pension assets, wage and salary increases, and benefits changes. If these assumptions were to prove completely correct, the current method of funding would amortize the unfunded pension liability over 20 years. Since assumptions are subject to change in the light of new information, they must be reviewed periodically. Revision by one percentage point in the assumed rate of investment return, for example, would require a current change in the level of pension expenses by $15 million before taxes, or about $7 million after taxes. The current actuarially assumed rate of return is 8.5%.

Pension investment policy, through its influence on pension expenses, unfunded pension liability, and the company's earnings progress, is a critical issue of Morgan management. The chairman is strongly committed to the corporate goal of achieving a total investment return for shareholders superior to that of other large industrial companies. He recognizes that a more aggressive pension investment policy—if successful—would facilitate attainment of the corporate goal through a significant reduction in pension expenses and unfunded pension liability. He also worries, however, that a significant drop in the market value of the company's pension fund—now $1 billion—could result in a major setback in the company's growth strategy. Current pension investment policy is based on an asset mix of approximately 50% common stocks and 50% fixed-income securities.

The chairman is concerned about the overall investment management and direction of the pension fund and is very interested in your informed and objective evaluation.

What recommendations would you make to the chairman and why?

Appendix

Quantitative Review

Students in management and investment courses typically come from a variety of backgrounds. Some, who have had strong quantitative training, may feel perfectly comfortable with formal mathematical presentation of material. Others, who have had less technical training, may easily be overwhelmed by mathematical formalism.

Most students, however, will benefit from some coaching to make the study of investments easier and more efficient. If you had a good introductory quantitative methods course, and liked the text that was used, you may want to refer to it whenever you feel in need of a refresher. If you feel uncomfortable with standard quantitative texts, this reference is for you. Our aim is to present the essential quantitative concepts and methods in a self-contained, nontechnical, and intuitive way. Our approach is considered structured in line with requirements for the CFA program. The material included is relevant to investment management by the ICFA, the Institute of Chartered Financial Analysts. We hope you find this appendix helpful. Use it to make your venture into investments more enjoyable.

Note: If you do not already have a financial calculator, we strongly advise you get one. Most financial calculators have a statistical mode that allows you to compute expected values, standard deviations, and regressions with ease. Actually, working through the user manual is a helpful exercise by itself. If you are interested in investments, you should look at a financial calculator as a good initial investment.

A.1 *Probability Distributions*

Statisticians talk about "experiments," or "trials," and refer to possible outcomes as "events." In a roll of a die, for example, the "elementary events" are the numbers 1 through 6. Turning up one side represents the most disaggregate *mutually exclusive* outcome. Other events are *compound,* that is, they consist of more than one elementary event, such as the result "odd number" or "less than 4." In this case "odd" and "less than 4" are not mutually exclusive. Compound events can be mutually exclusive outcomes, however, such as "less than 4" and "equal to or greater than 4."

In decision making, "experiments" are circumstances in which you contemplate a decision that will affect the set of possible events (outcomes) and their likelihood (probabilities). Decision theory calls for you to identify optimal decisions under various sets of circumstances (experiments), which you may do by determining losses from departures from optimal decisions.

When the outcome of a decision (experiment) can be quantified, that is, when a numerical value can be assigned to each elementary event, the decision outcome is called a *random variable*. In the context of investment decision making, the random variable (the payoff to the investment decision), is denominated either in dollars or as a percentage rate of return.

The set or list of all possible values of a random variable, *with* their associated probabilities, is called the *probability distribution* of the random variable. Values that are impossible for the random variable to take on are sometimes listed with probabilities of zero. All possible elementary events are assigned values and probabilities, and thus the probabilities have to sum to 1.0.

Sometimes the values of a random variable are *uncountable,* meaning that you cannot make a list of all possible values. For example, suppose you roll a ball on a line and report the distance it rolls before it comes to a rest. Any distance is possible, and the precision of the report will depend on the need of the roller and/or the quality of the measuring device. Another uncountable random variable is one that describes the weight of a newborn baby. Any positive weight (with some upper bound) is possible.

We call uncountable probability distributions "continuous," for the obvious reason that, at least within a range, the possible outcomes (those with positive probabilities) lie anywhere on a continuum of values. Because there is an infinite number of possible values for the random variable in any continuous distribution, such a probability distribution has to be described by a formula that relates the values of the random variable and their associated probabilities, instead of by a simple list of outcomes and probabilities. We discuss continuous distributions later in this section.

Even countable probability distributions can be complicated. For example, on the New York Stock Exchange stock prices are quoted in eighths. This means the price of a stock at some future date is a *countable* random variable. Probability distributions of countable random variables are called *discrete distributions.* Although a stock price cannot dip below zero, it has no upper bound. Therefore a stock price is a random variable that can take on infinitely many values, even though they are countable, and its discrete probability distribution will have to be given by a formula just like a continuous distribution.

There are random variables that are both discrete and finite. When the probability distribution of the relevant random variable is countable and finite, decision making is tractable and relatively easy to analyze. One example is the decision to call a coin toss "heads" or "tails," with a payoff of zero for guessing wrong and 1 for guessing right. The random variable of the decision to guess "heads" has a discrete, finite probability distribution. It can be written as

Event	Value	Probability
Heads	1	.5
Tails	0	.5

This type of analysis usually is referred to as "scenario analysis." Because scenario analysis is relatively simple, it is used sometimes even when the actual random variable is infinite and uncountable. You can do this by specifying values and probabilities for a set of compound, yet exhaustive and mutually exclusive, events. Because it is simple and has important uses, we handle this case first.

Here is a problem from the 1988 CFA examination.

Mr. Arnold, an Investment Committee member, has confidence in the forecasting ability of the analysts in the firm's research department. However, he is concerned that analysts may not appreciate risk as an important investment consideration. This is especially true in an increasingly volatile investment environment. In addition, he is conservative and risk averse. He asks for your risk analysis for Anheuser-Busch stock.

1. Using Table A.1, calculate the following measures of dispersion of returns for Anheuser-Busch stock under each of the three outcomes displayed. Show calculations.
   a. Range
   b. Variance: $\Sigma \operatorname{Pr}(i)[r_i - E(r)]^2$
   c. Standard Deviation
   d. Coefficient of variation: $\mathrm{CV} = \dfrac{\sigma}{E(r)}$
2. Discuss the usefulness of each of the four measures listed in quantifying risk.

The examination questions require very specific answers. We use the questions as a framework for exposition of scenario analysis.

Table A.1 specifies a three-scenario decision problem. The random variable is the rate of return on investing in Anheuser-Busch stock. However, the third column that specifies the value of the random variable does not say simply "Return"—it says "Expected Return." This tells us that the scenario description is a compound event consisting of many elementary events, as is almost always the case. We streamline or simplify reality in order to gain tractability.

TABLE A.1   Anheuser-Busch Companies, Inc., Dispersion of Potential Returns

Outcome	Probability	Expected Return*
Number 1	.20	20%
Number 2	.50	30%
Number 3	.30	50%

*Assume for the moment that the expected return in each scenario will be realized with certainty. This is the way returns were expressed in the original question.

Analysts who prepare input lists must decide on the number of scenarios with which to describe the entire probability distribution, as well as the rates of return to allocate to each one. This process calls for determining the probability of occurrence of each scenario, *and* the expected rate of return *within* (conditional on) each scenario, which governs the outcome of each scenario. Once you become familiar with scenario analysis, you will be able to build a simple scenario description from any probability distribution.

Expected returns

The expected value of a random variable is the answer to the question, "What would be the value of the variable if the 'experiment' (the circumstances and the decision) were repeated infinitely?" In the case of an investment decision, your answer is meant to describe the reward from making the decision.

Note that the question is hypothetical and abstract. It is hypothetical because, practically, the exact circumstances of a decision (the "experiment") often cannot be repeated even once, much less infinitely. It is abstract because, even if the experiment were to be repeated many times (short of infinitely), the *average* rate of return may not be one of the possible outcomes. To demonstrate, suppose that the probability distribution of the rate of return on a proposed investment project is +20% or −20%, with equal probabilities of .5. Intuition indicates that repeating this investment decision will get us ever closer to an average rate of return of zero. But a one-time investment cannot produce a rate of return of zero. Is the "expected" return still a useful concept when the proposed investment represents a one-time decision?

One argument for using expected return to measure the reward from making investment decisions is that, although a specific investment decision may be made only once, the decision maker will be making many (though different) investment decisions over time. Over time, then, the average rate of return will come close to the average of the expected values of all the individual decisions. Another reason for using the expected value is that admittedly we lack a better measure.[1]

The probabilities of the scenarios in Table A.1 predict the relative frequencies of the outcomes. If the current investment in Anheuser-Busch could be replicated many times, a 20% return would occur 20% of the time, a 30% return would occur 50% of the time, and a 50% return would occur the remaining 30% of the time. This notion of probabilities and the definition of the expected return tells us how to calculate the expected return[2]:

$$E(r) = .20 \times .20 + .50 \times .30 + .30 \times .50 = .34 \text{ (or 34\%)}$$

---

[1] Another case where we use a less-than-ideal measure is the case of yield to maturity on a bond. The YTM measures the rate of return from investing in a bond *if* it is held to maturity and *if* the coupons can be reinvested at the same yield to maturity over the life of the bond.

[2] We will consistently perform calculations in decimal fractions to avoid confusion.

Labeling each scenario $i = 1,2,3$, and using the summation sign, Σ, we can write the formula for the expected return:

$$E(r) = \Pr(1)r_1 + \Pr(2)r_2 + \Pr(3)r_3 \qquad (A.1)$$

$$= \sum_{i=1}^{3} \Pr(i)r_i.$$

The definition of the expectation in equation A.1 reveals two important properties of random variables. First, if you add a constant to a random variable, its expectation is also increased by the same constant. If, for example, the return in each scenario in Table A.1 were increased by 5%, the expectation would increase to 39%. Try this, using equation A.1. If a random variable is multiplied by a constant, its expectation will change by that same proportion. If you multiply the return in each scenario by 1.5, $E(r)$ would change to $1.5 \times .34 = .51$ (or 51%).

Second, the deviation of a random variable from its expected value is itself a random variable. Take any rate of return r_i in Table A.1 and define its deviation from the expected value by

$$d_i = r_i - E(r)$$

What is the expected value of d? $E(d)$ is the expected deviation from the expected value, and by equation A.1 it is necessarily zero because

$$E(d) = \Sigma \Pr(i)d_i = \Sigma \Pr(i)[r_i - E(r)]$$
$$= \Sigma \Pr(i)r_i - E(r)\Sigma \Pr(i)$$
$$= E(r) - E(r) = 0$$

Measures of dispersion: the range

Assume for a moment that the expected return for each scenario in Table A.1 will be realized with certainty in the event that scenario occurs. Then the set of possible return outcomes is unambiguously 20%, 30%, and 50%. The *range* is the difference between the maximum and the minimum values of the random variable, 50% − 20% = 30% in this case. Range is clearly a crude measure of dispersion. Here it is particularly inappropriate because the scenario returns themselves are given as expected values, and therefore the true range is unknown. There is a variant of the range, the *interquartile range,* that we explain in the discussion of descriptive statistics.

Measures of dispersion: the variance

One interpretation of variance is that it measures the "expected surprise." Although that may sound like a contradiction in terms, it really is not. First, think of a surprise as a deviation from expectation. The surprise is not in the *fact* that expectation has not been realized, but rather in the *direction* and *magnitude* of the deviation.

In our example Table A.1 leads us to *expect* a rate of return of 34% from investing in Anheuser-Busch stock. A second look at the scenario returns, however, tells us that we should stand ready to be surprised because the probability of earning exactly

34% is zero. Being sure that our expectation will not be realized does not mean that we can be sure what the realization is going to be. The element of surprise lies in the direction and magnitude of the deviation of the actual return from expectation, and that is the relevant random variable for the measurement of uncertainty. Its probability distribution adds to our understanding of the nature of the uncertainty that we are facing.

We measure the reward by the expected return. Intuition suggests that we measure uncertainty by the expected *deviation* of the rate of return from expectation. We showed in the previous section, however, that the expected deviation from expectation must be zero. Positive deviations, when weighted by probabilities, are exactly offset by negative deviations. To get around this problem, we replace the random variable "deviation from expectations" (denoted earlier by d) with its square, which must be positive even if d itself is negative.

We define the *variance,* our measure of surprise or dispersion, by the *expected squared deviation of the rate of return from its expectation.* With the Greek letter sigma square denoting variance, the formal definition is

$$\sigma^2(r) = E(d^2) = E[r_i - E(r)]^2 = \sum \Pr(i)[r_i - E(r)]^2 \qquad (A.2)$$

Squaring each deviation eliminates the sign, which eliminates the offsetting effects of positive and negative deviations.

In the case of Anheuser-Busch, the variance of the rate of return on the stock is

$$\sigma^2(r) = .2(.20 - .34)^2 + .5(.30 - .34)^2 + .3(.50 - .34)^2 = .0124$$

Remember that if you add a constant to a random variable, the variance does not change at all. This is because the expectation also changes by the same constant, and hence deviations from expectation remain unchanged. You can test this by using the data from Table A.1.

Multiplying the random variable by a constant, however, *will* change the variance. Suppose that each return is multiplied by the factor k. The new random variable, kr, has expectation of $E(kr) = kE(r)$. Therefore the deviation of kr from its expectation is

$$d(kr) = kr - E(kr) = kr - kE(r) = k[r - E(r)] = kd(r)$$

If each deviation is multiplied by k, the squared deviations are multiplied by the square of k:

$$\sigma^2(kr) = k^2\sigma^2(r)$$

To summarize, adding a constant to a random variable does not affect the variance. Multiplying a random variable by a constant, though, will cause the variance to be multiplied by the square of that constant.

Measures of dispersion: the standard deviation

A closer look at the variance will reveal that its dimension is different from that of the expected return. Recall that we squared deviations from the expected return in order to make all values positive. This alters the *dimension* (units of measure) of the variance to "square percents." To transform the variance into terms of percentage return, we simply take the square root of the variance. This measure is the *standard deviation*. In the case of Anheuser-Busch's stock return, the standard deviation is

$$\sigma = (\sigma^2)^{1/2} = \sqrt{.0124} = .1114 \text{ (or } 11.14\%) \tag{A.3}$$

Note that you always need to calculate the variance first before you can get the standard deviation. The standard deviation conveys the same information as the variance but in a different form.

We know already that adding a constant to r will not affect its variance, and it will not affect the standard deviation either. We also know that multiplying a random variable by a constant multiplies the variance by the square of that constant. From the definition of the standard deviation in equation (A.3), it should be clear that multiplying a random variable by a constant will multiply the standard deviation by the (absolute value of this) constant. The absolute value is needed because the sign of the constant is lost through squaring the deviations in the computation of the variance. Formally,

$$\sigma(kr) = \text{Abs}(k)\ \sigma(r)$$

Try a transformation of your choice using the data in Table A.1.

Measures of dispersion: the coefficient of variation

To evaluate the magnitude of dispersion of a random variable, it is useful to compare it to the expected value. The ratio of the standard deviation to the expectation is called the *coefficient of variation*. In the case of returns on Anheuser-Busch stock, it is

$$\text{CV} = \frac{\sigma}{E(r)} = \frac{.1114}{.3400} = .3275 \tag{A.4}$$

This standard deviation of the Anheuser-Busch return is about one third of the expected return (reward). Whether this value for the coefficient of variation represents a big risk depends on what can be obtained with alternative investments.

The coefficient of variation is far from an ideal measure of dispersion. Suppose that a plausible expected value for a random variable is zero. In this case, regardless of the magnitude of the standard deviation, the coefficient of variation will be infinite. Clearly, this measure is not applicable in all cases. Generally, the analyst must choose a measure of dispersion that fits the particular decision at hand. In finance, the standard deviation is the measure of choice in most cases where overall risk is concerned. (For individual assets, the measure β, explained in the text, is the measure used.)

Skewness

So far, we have described the measures of dispersion as indicating the size of the average surprise, loosely speaking. The standard deviation is not exactly equal to the average surprise though, because squaring deviations, and then taking the square root of the average square deviation, results in greater weight (emphasis) placed on larger deviations. Other than that, it is simply a measure that tells us how big a deviation from expectation can be expected.

Most decision makers agree that the expected value and standard deviation of a random variable are the most important statistics. However, once we calculate them another question about risk (the nature of the random variable describing deviations from expectations) is pertinent: are the larger deviations (surprises) more likely to be positive? Risk-averse decision makers worry about bad surprises, and the standard deviation does not distinguish good from bad ones. Most risk avoiders are believed to prefer random variables with likely *small negative surprises* and *less* likely *large positive surprises,* to the reverse, likely *small good surprises* and *less* likely *large bad surprises*. More than anything, risk is really defined by the possibility of disaster (large bad surprises).

One measure that distinguishes between the likelihood of large good-vs.-bad surprises is the "third moment." It builds on the behavior of deviations from the expectation, the random variable we have denoted by d. Denoting the *third moment* by M_3, we define it:

$$M_3 = E(d^3) = E[r_i - E(r)]^3 = \Sigma \Pr(i)[r_i - E(r)]^3 \qquad (A.5)$$

Cubing each value of d (taking it to the third power) magnifies larger deviations more than smaller ones. Raising values to an odd power causes them to retain their sign. Recall that the sum of all deviations multiplied by their probabilities is zero because positive deviations weighted by their probabilities exactly offset the negative. When *cubed* deviations are multiplied by their probabilities and then added up, however, large deviations will dominate. The sign will tell us in this case whether *large positive* deviations dominate (positive M_3) or whether *large negative* deviations dominate (negative M_3).

Incidentally, it is obvious why this measure of skewness is called the third moment; it refers to cubing. Similarly, the variance is often referred to as the second moment, because it requires squaring.

Returning to the investment decision described in Table A.1, with the expected value of 34%, the third moment is

$$M_3 = .2(.20 - .34)^3 + .5(.30 - .34)^3 + .3(.50 - .34)^3 = .000648$$

The sign of the third moment tells us that larger *positive* surprises dominate in this case. You might have guessed this by looking at the deviations from expectation and their probabilities; that is, the most likely event is a return of 30%, which makes for a small negative surprise. The other negative surprise (20% − 34% = −14%) is smaller in magnitude than the positive surprise (50% − 34% = 16%) *and* is also *less* likely (probability .20) relative to the positive surprise, 50% (probability .30). The difference appears small, however, and we do not know whether the third moment may be an important issue for the decision to invest in Anheuser-Busch.

It is difficult to judge the importance of the third moment, here .000648, without a benchmark. Following the same reasoning we applied to the standard deviation, we can take the *third root* of M_3 (which we denote m_3) and compare it to the standard deviation. This yields $m_3 = .0865 = 8.65\%$, which is not trivial compared with the standard deviation (11.14%).

Another example: options on Anheuser-Busch stock

Suppose that the current price of Anheuser-Busch stock is $30. A call option on the stock is selling for 60 cents, and a put is selling for $4. Both have an exercise price of $42 and maturity date to match the scenarios in Table A.1.

The call option allows you to buy the stock at the exercise price. You will choose to do so if the call ends up "in the money," that is, the stock price is above the exercise price. The profit in this case is the difference between the stock price and the exercise price, less the cost of the call. Even if you exercise the call, your profit may still be negative if the cash flow from the exercise of the call does not cover the initial cost of the call. If the call ends up "out of the money," that is, the stock price is below the exercise price, you will let the call expire worthless and suffer a loss equal to the cost of the call.

The put option allows you to sell the stock at the exercise price. You will choose to do so if the put ends up "in the money," that is, the stock price is below the exercise price. Your profit is then the difference between the exercise price and the stock price, less the initial cost of the put. Here, again, if the cash flow is not sufficient to cover the cost of the put, the investment will show a loss. If the put ends up "out of the money," you again let it expire worthless, taking a loss equal to the initial cost of the put.

The scenario analysis of these alternative investments is described in Table A.2.

The expected rates of return on the call and put are

$$E(r_{call}) = .2(-1) + .5(-1) + .3(4) = .5 \text{ (or 50\%)}$$
$$E(r_{put}) = .2(.5) + .5(-.25) + .3(-1) = -.325 \text{ (or } -32.5\%)$$

The negative expected return on the put may be justified by the fact that it is a hedge asset, in this case an insurance policy against losses from holding Anheuser-Busch stock. The variance and standard deviation of the two investments are

$$\sigma_{call}^2 = .2(-1 - .5)^2 + .5(-1 - .5)^2 + .3(4 - .5)^2 = 5.25$$

$$\sigma_{put}^2 = .2[.5 - (-.325)]^2 + .5[-.25 - (-.325)]^2 + .3[-1 - (-.325)]^2 = .2756$$

$$\sigma_{call} = \sqrt{5.25} = 2.2913 \text{ (or 229.13\%)}$$
$$\sigma_{put} = \sqrt{.2756} = .525 \text{ (or 52.5\%)}$$

These are very large standard deviations. Comparing the standard deviation of the call's return to its expected value, we get the coefficient of variation:

$$CV_{call} = \frac{2.2913}{.5} = 4.5826$$

TABLE A.2   Scenario Analysis for Investment in Options
on Anheuser-Busch Stock

	Scenario 1	Scenario 2	Scenario 3
Probability	.20	.50	.30
Event			
1. Return on stock	20%	30%	50%
Stock price	$36.00	$39.00	$45.00
(initial price = $30)			
2. Cash flow from call	0	0	$3.00
(exercise price = $42)			
Call profit	−$.60	−$.60	$2.40
(initial price = $.60)			
3. Call rate of return	−100%	−100%	400%
Cash flow from put	$6.00	$3.00	0
(exercise price = $42)			
Put profit	$2.00	−$1.00	−$4.00
(initial price = $4)			
Put rate of return	50%	−25%	−100%

Refer back to the coefficient of variation for the stock itself, .3275, and it is clear that these instruments have high standard deviations. This is quite common for stock options. The negative expected return of the put illustrates again the problem in interpreting the magnitude of the "surprise" indicated by the coefficient of variation.

Moving to the third moments of the two probability distributions:

$$M_3(\text{call}) = .2(-1 - .5)^3 + .5(-1 - .5)^3 + .3(4 - .5)^3 = 10.5$$
$$M_3(\text{put}) = .2[.5 - (-.325)]^3 + .5[-.25 - (-.325)]^3 + .3[-1 - (-.325)]^3$$
$$= .02025$$

Both instruments are positively skewed, which is typical of options and one part of their attractiveness. In this particular circumstance the call is more skewed than the put. To establish this fact, note the third root of the third moment:

$$m_3(\text{call}) = M_3(\text{call})^{1/3} = 2.1898 \text{ (or } 218.98\%)$$
$$m_3(\text{put}) = .02^{1/3} = .2725 \text{ (or } 27.25\%)$$

Compare these figures to the standard deviations, 229.13% for the call and 52.5% for the put, and you can see that a large part of the standard deviation of the option is driven by the possibility of large good surprises instead of by the more likely, yet smaller, bad surprises.[3]

---

[3]Note that the expected return of the put is −32.5%; hence the worst surprise is −67.5%, and the best is 82.5%. The middle scenario is also a positive deviation of 7.5% (with a high probability of .50). These two elements explain the positive skewness of the put.

So far we have described discrete probability distributions using scenario analysis. We shall come back to decision making in a scenario analysis framework in Section A.3 on multivariate statistics.

Continuous Distributions: Normal and Lognormal Distributions

When a compact scenario analysis is possible and acceptable, decisions may be quite simple. Often, however, so many relevant scenarios must be specified that scenario analysis is impossible for practical reasons. Even in the case of Anheuser-Busch, as we were careful to specify, the individual scenarios considered actually represented compound events.

When many possible values of the rate of return have to be considered, we must use a formula that describes the probability distribution (relates values to probabilities). As we noted earlier, there are two types of probability distributions: discrete and continuous. Scenario analysis involves a discrete distribution. However, the two most useful distributions in investments, the normal and lognormal, are continuous. At the same time they are often used to approximate variables with distributions that are known to be discrete, such as stock prices. The probability distribution of future prices and returns is discrete—prices are quoted in eighths. Yet the industry norm is to approximate these distributions by the normal or lognormal distribution.

Standard normal distribution

The normal distribution, also known as Gaussian (after the mathematician Gauss) or bell-shaped, describes random variables with the following properties and is shown in Figure A.1:

- The expected value is the mode (the most frequent elementary event) and also the median (the middle value in the sense that half the elementary events are greater and half smaller). Note that the expected value, unlike the median or mode, requires weighting by probabilities to produce the concept of central value.
- The normal probability distribution is symmetric around the expected value. In other words, the likelihood of equal absolute-positive and negative deviations from

FIGURE A.1
Probabilities under the normal density.

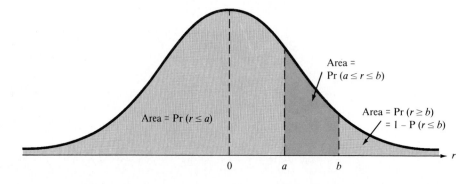

expectation is equal. Larger deviations from the expected value are less likely than are smaller deviations. In fact, the essence of the normal distribution is that the probability of deviations decreases exponentially with the magnitude of the deviation (positive and negative alike).

- A normal distribution is identified completely by two parameters, the expected value and the standard deviation. The property of the normal distribution that makes it most convenient for portfolio analysis is that any weighted sum of normally distributed random variables produces a random variable that also is normally distributed. This property is called stability. It is also true that if you add a constant to a "normal" random variable (meaning a random variable with a normal probability distribution) or multiply it by a constant, then the transformed random variable also will be normally distributed.

Suppose that n is any random variable (not necessarily normal), with expectation μ and standard deviation σ. As we showed earlier, if you add a constant c to n, the standard deviation is not affected at all, but the mean will change to $\mu + c$. If you multiply n by a constant b, its mean and standard deviation will change by the same proportion to $b\mu$ and $b\sigma$. If n is normal, the transformed variable also will be normal.

Stability, together with the property that a normal variable is completely characterized by its expectation and standard deviation, implies that if we know one normal probability distribution with a given expectation and standard deviation, we know them all.

Thus the *standard normal distribution* has an expectation of zero, and both variance and standard deviation equal to 1.0. Formally, the relationship between the value of the standard normal random variable, z, and its probability, f, is given by

$$f(z) = \frac{1}{\sqrt{2\pi}} \exp\left(\frac{-z^2}{2}\right) \qquad (A.6)$$

where "exp" is the quantity e to the power of the expression in the brackets. The quantity e is an important number just like the well-known π that also appears in the function. It is important enough to earn a place on the keyboard of your financial calculator, mostly because it is used also in continuous compounding.

Probability functions of continuous distributions are called *densities* and denoted by f, rather than by the "Pr" of scenario analysis. The reason is that the probability of any of the infinitely many possible values of z is infinitesimally small. Density is a function that allows us to obtain the probability of a *range of values* by integrating it over a desired range. In other words, whenever we want the probability that a standard normal variate (a random variable) will fall in the range from $z = a$ to $z = b$, we have to add up the density values, $f(z)$ for all zs from a to b. There are infinitely many zs in that range, regardless how close a is to b. *Integration* is the mathematical operation that achieves this task.

Consider first the probability that a standard normal variate will take on a value less than or equal to a, that is, z is in the range $[-\infty, a]$. We have to integrate the density from ∞ to a. The result is called the *cumulative (normal) distribution,* and denoted by $N(a)$. When a approaches infinity, any value is allowed for z; hence the probability that z will end up in that range approaches 1.0. It is a property of any density that when it is integrated over the entire range of the random variable, the cumulative distribution is 1.0.

In the same way, the probability that a standard normal variate will take on a value less than or equal to b is $N(b)$. The probability that a standard normal variate will take on a value in the range $[a,b]$ is just the difference between $N(b)$ and $N(a)$. Formally,

$$\Pr(a \leqq z \leqq b) = N(b) - N(a)$$

These concepts are illustrated in Figure A.1. The graph shows the normal density. It demonstrates the symmetry of the normal density around the expected value (zero for the standard normal variate, which is also the mode and the median), and the smaller likelihood of larger deviations from expectation. As is true for any density, the entire area under the density graph adds up to 1.0. The values a and b are chosen to be positive, so they are to the right of the expected value. The left-most shaded area is the proportion of the area under the density for which the value of z is less than or equal to a. Thus this area yields the cumulative distribution for a, the probability that z will be smaller than or equal to a. The right-most shaded area is the area under the density graph between a and b. If we add that area to the cumulative distribution of a, we get the entire area up to b, that is, the probability that z will be anywhere to the right of b. Thus the area between a and b has to be the probability that z will fall between a and b.

Applying the same logic, we find the probability that z will take on a value greater than b. We know already that the probability that z will be smaller than or equal to b is $N(b)$. The compound events "smaller than or equal to b" and "greater than b" are mutually exclusive *and* "exhaustive," meaning that they include all possible outcomes. Thus their probabilities sum to 1.0, and the probability that z is greater than b is simply equal to one minus the probability that z is less than or equal to b. Formally, $\Pr(z > b) = 1 - N(b)$.

Look again at Figure A.1. The area under the density graph between b and infinity is just the difference between the entire area under the graph (equal to 1.0), and the area between minus infinity and b, that is, $N(b)$.

The normal density is sufficiently complex that its cumulative distribution, its integral, does not have an exact formulaic closed-form solution. It must be obtained by numerical (approximation) methods. These values are produced in tables that give the value $N(z)$ for any z, such as Table 19.7 of this text.

To illustrate, let us find the following probabilities for a standard normal variate:

$\Pr(z \leqq - .36) = N(-.36) =$ Probability that z is less than or equal to .36
$\Pr(z \leqq .94) = N(.94) =$ Probability that z is less than or equal to .94
$\Pr(-.36 \leqq z \leqq .94) = N(.94) - N(-.36) =$ Probability that z will be
in the range $[-.36, .94]$
$\Pr(z > .94) = 1 - N(.94) =$ Probability that z is greater than .94

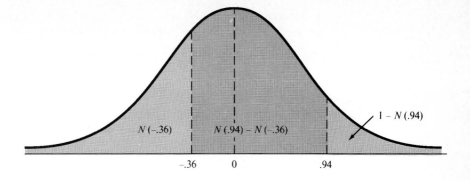

$N(-.36)$ $N(.94) - N(-.36)$ $1 - N(.94)$

$-.36$ 0 $.94$

Use Table 19.7 of the cumulative standard normal (sometimes called the area under the normal density) and Figure A.2. The table shows that

$$N(-.36) = .3594$$
$$N(.94) = .8264$$

In Figure A.2 the area under the graph between $-.36$ and $.94$ is the probability that z will fall between $-.36$ and $.94$. Hence,

$$Pr(-.36 \leq z \leq .94) = N(.94) - N(-.36) = .8264 - .3594 = .4670$$

The probability that z is greater than $.94$ is the area under the graph in Figure A.2, between $.94$ and infinity. Thus it is equal to the entire area (1.0) less the area from minus infinity to $.94$. Hence,

$$Pr(z > .94) = 1 - N(.94) = 1 - .8264 = .1736$$

Finally, one can ask, "what is the value, a, so that z will be smaller than or equal to a with probability P?" The notation for the function that yields the desired value of a is $\Phi(P)$ so that

$$\text{If } \Phi(P) = a, \text{ then } P = N(a) \tag{A.7}$$

For instance, suppose the question is, "which value has a cumulative density of $.50$?" A glance at Figure A.2 reminds us that the area between minus infinity and zero (the expected value) is $.5$. Thus we can write

$$\Phi(.5) = 0, \text{ because } N(0) = .5$$

Similarly,

$$\Phi(.8264) = .94 \text{ because } N(.94) = .8264$$

and

$$\Phi(.3594) = -.36$$

For practice, confirm with Table 19.7 that $\Phi(.6554) = .40$, meaning that the value of z with a cumulative distribution of .6554 is $z = .40$.

Nonstandard normal distributions

Suppose that the monthly rate of return on a stock is closely approximated by a normal distribution with a mean of .015 (1.5% per month), and standard deviation of .127 (12.7% per month). What is the probability that the rate of return will fall below zero in a given month? Recall that because the rate is a normal variate, its cumulative density has to be computed by numerical methods. The standard normal table can be used for any normal variate.

Any random variable, x, may be transformed into a new standardized variable, x^*, by the following rule:

$$x^* = \frac{x - E(x)}{\sigma(x)} \tag{A.8}$$

Note that all that we have done to x was (1) *subtract* its expectation and (2) *multiply* by one over its standard deviation, $1/[\sigma(x)]$. According to our earlier discussion, the effect of transforming a random variable by adding and multiplying by a constant is such that the expectation and standard deviation of the transformed variable are

$$E(x^*) = \frac{E(x) - E(x)}{\sigma(x)} = 0; \; \sigma(x^*) = \frac{\sigma(x)}{\sigma(x)} = 1 \tag{A.9}$$

From the stability property of the normal distribution we also know that if x is normal, so is x^*. A normal variate is characterized completely by two parameters: its expectation and standard deviation. For x^*, these are zero and 1.0, respectively. When we subtract the expectation and then divide a normal variate by its standard deviation, we standardize it; that is, we transform it to a standard normal variate. This trick is used extensively in working with normal (and approximately normal) random variables.

Returning to our stock, we have learned that if we subtract .15 and then divide the monthly returns by .127, the resultant random variable will be standard normal. We can now determine the probability that the rate of return will be zero or less in a given month. We know that

$$z = \frac{r - .015}{.127}$$

where z is standard normal and r the return on our stock. Thus if r is zero, z has to be

$$z(r = 0) = \frac{0 - .015}{.127} = -.1181$$

For r to be zero, the corresponding standard normal has to be -11.81%, a negative number. The event "r will be zero or less" is identical to the event "z will be $-.1181$ or less." Calculating the probability of the latter will solve our problem. That probability is simply $N(-.1181)$. Visit the standard normal table and find that

$$N(-.1181) = \Pr(r \leq 0) = .5 - .047 = .453$$

The answer makes sense. Recall that the expectation of r is 1.5%. Thus, whereas the probability that r will be 1.5% or less is .5, the probability that it will be *zero* or less has to be close, but somewhat less.

Confidence intervals

Given the large standard deviation of our stock, it is logical to be concerned about the likelihood of extreme values for the monthly rate of return. One way to quantify this concern is to ask: "What is the interval (range) within which the stock return will fall in a given month, with a probability of .95?" Such an interval is called the *95% confidence interval*.

Logic dictates that this interval be centered on the expected value, .015, because r is a normal variate (has a normal distribution), which is symmetric around the expectation. Denote the desired interval by

$$[E(r) - a, E(r) + a] = [.015 - a, .015 + a]$$

which has a length of $2a$. The probability that r will fall within this interval is described by the following expression:

$$\Pr(.015 - a \leq r \leq .015 + a) = .95$$

To find this probability, we start with a simpler problem, involving the standard normal variate, that is, a normal with expectation of zero and standard deviation of 1.0.

What is the 95% confidence interval for the standard normal variate, z? The variable will be centered on zero, so the expression is

$$\Pr(-a^* \leq z \leq a^*) = N(a^*) - N(-a^*) = .95$$

FIGURE A.3
Confidence intervals and the standard normal density.

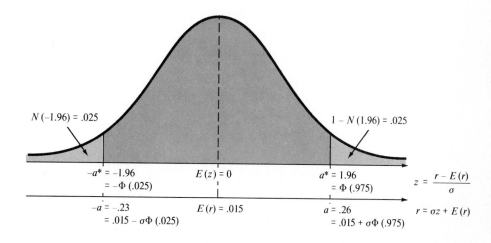

Quantitative Review

A17

You might best understand the substitution of the difference of the appropriate cumulative distributions for the probability with the aid of Figure A.3. The probability of falling outside of the interval is $1 - .95 = .05$. By the symmetry of the normal distribution, z will be equal to or less than $-a^*$ with probability of .025, and with probability .025, z will be greater than a^*. Thus we solve for a^* using

$$-a^* = \Phi(.025) \text{ which is equivalent to } N(-a^*) = .025$$

We can summarize the chain that we have pursued so far as follows. If we seek a $P = .95$ level confidence interval, we define α as the probability to fall outside the confidence interval. Because of the symmetry, α will be split so that half of it is the probability of falling to the right of the confidence interval, while the other half of α is the probability of falling to the left of the confidence interval. Therefore the relation between α and P is

$$\alpha = 1 - P = .05; \quad \frac{\alpha}{2} = \frac{1 - P}{2} = .025$$

We use $\alpha/2$ to indicate that the area that is excluded for r is equally divided between the tails of the distributions. Each tail that is excluded for r has an area of $\alpha/2$. The value, $\alpha = 1 - P$, represents the entire value that is excluded for r.

To find $z = \Phi(\alpha/2)$, which is the lower boundary of the confidence interval for the standard normal variate, we have to locate the z value for which the standard normal cumulative distribution is .025, finding $z = -1.96$. Thus we conclude that $-a^* = -1.96$ and $a^* = 1.96$. The confidence interval for z is

$$[E(z) - \Phi(\alpha/2), E(z) + \Phi(\alpha/2)] = [-\Phi(.025), \Phi(.025)]$$
$$= [-1.96, 1.96]$$

To get the interval boundaries for the nonstandard normal variate r, we transform the boundaries for z by the usual relationship, $r = z\sigma(r) + E(r) = \Phi(\alpha/2)\sigma(r) + E(r)$. Note that all we are doing is setting the expectation at the center of the confidence interval and extending it by a number of standard deviations. The number of standard deviations is determined by the probability that we allow for falling outside the confidence interval (α), or equivalently, the probability of falling in it (P). Using minus and plus 1.96 for $z = \pm\Phi(0.25)$, the distance on each side of the expectation is $\pm 1.96 \times .127 = .249$. Thus we obtain the confidence interval

$$[E(r) - \sigma(r)\Phi(\alpha/2), E(r) + \sigma(r)\Phi(\alpha/2)] = [E(r) - .249, E(r) + .249]$$
$$= [-.234, .264]$$

so that

$$P = 1 - \alpha = \Pr[E(r) - \sigma(r)\Phi(\alpha/2) \leqq r \leqq E(r) + \sigma(r)\Phi(\alpha/2)]$$

which, for our stock (with expectation .015 and standard deviation .127) amounts to

$$\Pr[-.234 \leqq r \leqq .264] = .95$$

Note that, because of the large standard deviation of the rate of return on the stock, the 95% confidence interval is 49% wide.

To reiterate with a variation on this example, suppose we seek a 90% confidence interval for the annual rate of return on a portfolio, r_p, with a monthly expected return of 1.2% and standard deviation of 5.2%.

The solution is simply

$$\Pr\left[E(r) - \sigma(r)\Phi\left(\frac{1-P}{2}\right) \leq r_p \leq E(r) + \sigma(r)\Phi\left(\frac{1-P}{2}\right)\right]$$
$$= \Pr[.012 - .052 \times 1.645) \leq r_p \leq .012 + .052 \times 1.645)]$$
$$= \Pr[-.0735 \leq r_p \leq .0975] = .90$$

Since the portfolio is of low risk this time (and we allow a 90% rather than a 95% probability of falling within the interval), the 90% confidence interval is only 2.4% wide.

The Lognormal distribution

The normal distribution is not adequate to describe stock prices and returns for two reasons. First, whereas the normal distribution admits any value, including negative values, actual stock prices cannot be negative. Second, the normal distribution does not account for compounding. The lognormal distribution addresses these two problems.

The lognormal distribution describes a random variable that grows, *every instant*, by a rate that is a normal random variable. Thus the progression of a lognormal random variable reflects continuous compounding.

Suppose that the *annual continuously compounded* (ACC) rate of return on a stock is normally distributed with expectation $\mu = .12$ and standard deviation $\sigma = .42$. The stock price at the beginning of the year is $P_0 = \$10$. With continuous compounding (see appendix to Chapter 4), if the ACC rate of return, r_C, turns out to be .23, then the end-of-year price will be

$$P_1 = P_0 \exp(r_C) = 10e^{.23} = \$12.586$$

representing an effective annual rate of return of

$$r = \frac{P_1 - P_0}{P_0} = e^{r_C} - 1 = .2586 \text{ (or 25.86\%)}$$

This is the practical meaning of r, the annual rate on the stock, being lognormally distributed. Note that however negative the ACC rate of return (r_C) is, the price, P_1, cannot become negative.

Two properties of lognormally distributed financial assets are important: their expected return and the allowance for changes in measurement period.

Expected return of a lognormally distributed asset

The expected annual rate of return of a lognormally distributed stock (as in our example) is

$$E(r) = \exp(\mu + \tfrac{1}{2}\sigma^2) - 1 = \exp(.12 + \tfrac{1}{2} \times .42^2) - 1 = e^{.2082} - 1$$

$$= .2315 \text{ (or 23.15\%)}$$

This is just a statistical property of the distribution. For this reason, a useful statistic is

$$\mu^* = \mu + \tfrac{1}{2}\sigma^2 = .2082$$

Often, when analysts refer to the expected ACC return on a lognormal asset, they are really referring to μ^*. Often, the asset is said to have a normal distribution of the ACC return with expectation μ^* and standard deviation σ.

Change of frequency of measured returns

The lognormal distribution allows for easy change of the holding period of returns. Suppose that we want to calculate returns monthly instead of annually. We use the parameter t to indicate the fraction of the year that is desired, in the case of monthly periods $t = 1/12$. To transform the annual distribution to a t-period (monthly) distribution, it is necessary merely to multiply the expectation and variance of the ACC return by t (in this case, 1/12).

The monthly continuously compounded return on the stock in our example has the expectation and standard deviation of

$$\mu(\text{monthly}) = .12/12 = .01 \text{ (1\% per month)}$$
$$\sigma(\text{monthly}) = .42/\sqrt{12} = .1212 \text{ (or 12.12\% per month)}$$
$$\mu^*(\text{monthly}) = .2082/12 = .01735 \text{ (or 1.735\% per month)}$$

Note that we divide variance by 12 when changing from annual to monthly frequency; the standard deviation therefore is divided by the square root of 12.

Similarly, we can convert a non-annual distribution to an annual distribution by following the same routine. For example, suppose that the weekly continuously compounded rate of return on a stock is normally distributed with $\alpha = .003$ and $\sigma = .07$. Then the ACC return is distributed with

$$\mu^* = 52 \times .003 = .156 \text{ (or 15.6\% per year)}$$
$$\sigma = \sqrt{52} \times .07 = .5048 \text{ (or 50.48\% per year)}$$

In practice, to obtain normally distributed, continuously compounded returns, R, we take the log of 1.0 plus the raw returns:

$$r_C = \log(1 + r)$$

For short intervals, raw returns are small, and the continuously compounded returns, R, will be practically identical to the raw returns, r. The rule of thumb is that this conversion is not necessary for periods of 1 month or less. That is, approximating stock returns as normal will be accurate enough. For longer intervals, however, the transformation may be necessary.

A.2 Descriptive Statistics

Our analysis so far has been forward looking, or, as economists like to say, ex ante. We have been concerned with probabilities, expected values, and surprises. We made our analysis more tractable by assuming that decision outcomes are distributed according to relatively simple formulas, and that we know the parameters of these distributions.

Investment managers must satisfy themselves that these assumptions are reasonable, which they do by constantly analyzing observations from relevant random variables that accumulate over time. Distribution of past rates of return on a stock is one element they need to know in order to make optimal decisions. True, the distribution of the rate of return itself changes over time. However, a sample that is not too old does yield information relevant to the next period probability distribution and its parameters. In this section we explain descriptive statistics, or the organization and analysis of such historic samples.

Histograms, Boxplots, and Time Series Plots

Table A.3 shows the annual excess returns (over the T-bill rate) for two major classes of assets, the S&P 500 index and a portfolio of long-term government bonds, for the period 1926 to 1987.

TABLE A.3 Excess Return (Risk Premiums) on Stocks and Long-Term Treasury Bonds (Maturity Premiums)

Date	Equity Risk Premium	Maturity Premium
1926	0.0835	0.045
1927	0.3437	0.0581
1928	0.4037	−0.0314
1929	−0.1317	−0.0133
1930	−0.2731	0.0225
1931	−0.4441	−0.0638
1932	−0.0915	0.1588
1933	0.5369	−0.0038
1934	−0.016	0.0986
1935	0.475	0.0481
1936	0.3374	0.0733
1937	−0.3534	−0.0008
1938	0.3114	0.0555
1939	−0.0043	0.0592
1940	−0.0978	0.0609
1941	−0.1165	0.0087
1942	0.2007	0.0295
1943	0.2555	0.0173
1944	0.1942	0.0248

Continued.

TABLE A.3 Excess Return (Risk Premiums) on Stocks and Long-Term Treasury Bonds (Maturity Premiums)—cont'd

Date	Equity Risk Premium	Maturity Premium
1945	0.3611	0.104
1946	−0.0842	−0.0045
1947	0.0521	−0.0313
1948	0.0469	0.0259
1949	0.1769	0.0535
1950	0.3051	−0.0114
1951	0.2253	−0.0543
1952	0.1671	−0.005
1953	−0.0281	0.0181
1954	0.5176	0.0633
1955	0.2999	−0.0287
1956	0.041	−0.0805
1957	−0.1392	0.0431
1958	0.4182	−0.0764
1959	0.0901	−0.0521
1960	−0.0219	0.1112
1961	0.2476	−0.0116
1962	−0.1146	0.0416
1963	0.1968	−0.0191
1964	0.1294	−0.0003
1965	0.0852	−0.0322
1966	−0.1482	−0.0111
1967	0.1977	−0.134
1968	0.0585	−0.0547
1969	−0.1508	−0.1166
1970	−0.0252	0.0557
1971	0.0992	0.0884
1972	0.1514	0.0184
1973	−0.2159	−0.0804
1974	−0.3447	−0.0365
1975	0.314	0.0339
1976	0.1876	0.1167
1977	−0.123	−0.0579
1978	−0.0062	−0.0834
1979	0.0806	−0.116
1980	0.2118	−0.1519
1981	−0.1962	−0.1286
1982	0.1087	0.2981
1983	0.1371	−0.0812
1984	−0.0358	0.0558
1985	0.2444	0.2325
1986	0.1231	0.1828
1987	−0.0024	−0.0816
Average	0.0833	0.0106
Standard deviation	0.2106	0.0798
Minimum	−0.4441	−0.1519
Maximum	0.5369	0.2981

Data from the Center for Research of Security Prices, University of Chicago, Chicago, Illinois.

One way to understand the data is to present it graphically, commonly in a *histo-gram* or frequency distribution. Histograms of the 62 observations in Table A.3 are shown in Figure A.4. We construct a histogram according to the following principles:

- The range (of values) of the random variable is divided into a relatively small number of equal-sized intervals. The number of intervals that makes sense depends on the number of available observations. The data in Table A.3 provide 62 observa-

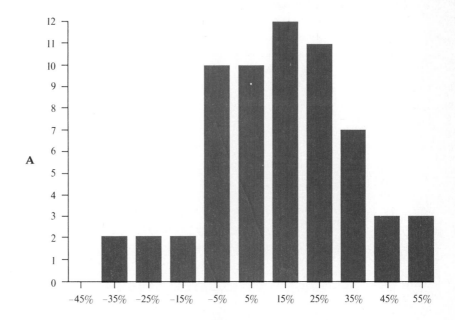

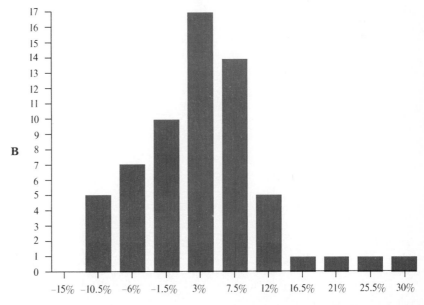

tions, and thus deciles (10 intervals) seem adequate.

- A rectangle is drawn over each interval. The height of the rectangle represents the frequency of observations for each interval.
- If the observations are concentrated in one part of the range, the range may be divided to unequal intervals. In that case the rectangles are scaled so that their *area* represents the frequency of the observations for each interval. (This is not the case in our samples, however.)
- If the sample is representative, the shape of the histogram will reveal the probability distribution of the random variable. In our case 62 observations are not a large sample, but a look at the histogram does suggest that the returns may be reasonably approximated by a normal or lognormal distribution.

FIGURE A.5
Boxplots of annual equity risk premium and long-term bond (maturity) risk premium (1926-1987).

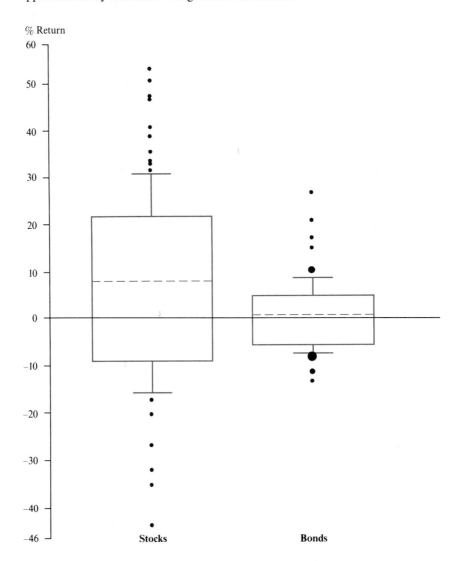

Another way to represent sample information graphically is by *boxplots*. Figure A.5 is an example that uses the same data as in Table A.3. Boxplots are most useful to show the dispersion of the sample distribution. A commonly used measure of dispersion is the *interquartile range*. Recall that the range, a crude measure of dispersion, is defined as the distance between the largest and smallest observations. By its nature, this measure is unreliable because it will be determined by the two most extreme outliers of the sample.

The interquartile range, a more satisfactory variant of the simple range, is defined as the difference between the lower and upper quartiles. Below the *lower* quartile lies 25% of the sample; similarly, above the *upper* quartile lies 25% of the sample. The interquartile range therefore is confined to the central 50% of the sample. The greater the dispersion of a sample, the greater the distance between these two values.

In the boxplot the horizontal broken line represents the median, the box the interquartile range, and the vertical lines extending from the box the range. The vertical lines representing the range often are restricted (if necessary) to extend only to 1.5 times the interquartile range, so that the more extreme observations can be shown separately (by points) as outliers.

As a concept check, verify from Table A.3 that the points on the boxplot of Figure A.5 correspond to the following list:

	Equity Risk Premium	Bond (Maturity) Risk Premium
Lowest extreme points	−43.94	−13.66
	−35.23	−12.85
	−31.92	−11.21
	−26.66	−10.94
	−20.19	−10.50
	−17.10	−7.85
		−7.74
		−7.52
		−7.52
		−7.46
Lowest quartile	−8.39	−5.06
Median	8.15	1.30
Highest quartile	22.19	5.29
Highest extreme points	31.14	9.85
	33.32	10.37
	33.68	10.82
	35.99	11.11
	39.10	15.73
	41.19	17.22
	47.19	21.58
	47.42	26.96
	51.31	
	53.53	

Continued.

	Equity Risk Premium	Bond (Maturity) Risk Premium
Interquartile range	30.58	10.35
1.5 times the interquartile range	45.87	15.53
From:	−14.79	−6.46
To:	31.09	9.06

Finally, a third form of graphing is time series plots, which are used to convey the behavior of economic variables over time. Figure A.6 shows a time series plot of the excess returns on stocks and bonds from Table A.3. Even though the human eye is apt to see patterns in randomly generated time series, examining time series evolution over a long period does yield some information. Sometimes, such examination can be as revealing as that provided by formal statistical analysis.

Sample Statistics

Suppose we can assume that the probability distribution of stock returns has not changed over the past 62 years. We wish to draw inferences about the probability distribution of stock returns from the sample of 62 observations of annual stock excess returns in Table A.3.

A central question is whether given observations represent independent observations from the underlying distribution. If they are, statistical analysis is quite straightforward. Our analysis assumes that this is indeed the case. Empiricism in financial markets tends to confirm this assumption in most cases.

Estimating expected returns from the sample average

The definition of expected returns suggests that the sample average be used as an estimate of the expected value. Indeed, one definition of the expected return is the average of a sample when the number of observations tends to infinity.

Denoting the sample returns in Table A.3 by R_t, $t = 1, \ldots, T = 62$, the estimate of the annual expected excess rate of return is

$$\bar{r} = \frac{1}{T} \Sigma R_t = 8.33\%$$

The bar over the r is a common notation for an estimate of the expectation. Intuition suggests that the larger the sample the greater the reliability of the sample average, and the larger the standard deviation of the measured random variable, the less reliable the average. We discuss this property more fully later.

Estimating higher moments

The principle of estimating expected values from sample averages applies to higher moments as well. Recall that higher moments are defined as expectations of some power of the deviation from expectation. For example, the variance (second

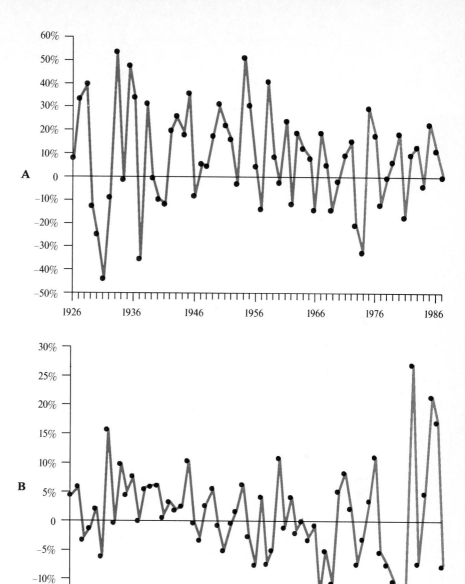

FIGURE A.6

A, Equity risk premium, 1926-1987.
B, Bond maturity premium, 1926-1987.

moment) is the expectation of the squared deviation from expectation. Accordingly, the sample average of the squared deviation from the average will serve as the estimate of the variance, denoted by s^2:

$$s^2 = \frac{1}{T-1} \Sigma(R_t - \overline{R}^2 = \frac{1}{61} \Sigma(R_t - .0833)^2 = .04436 \; (s = 21.06\%)$$

where $\overline{R}$ is the estimate of the sample average. The average of the squared deviation is taken over $T - 1 = 61$ observations for a technical reason. If we were to divide by T, the estimate of the variance will be downward-biased by the factor $(T - 1)/T$. Here too, the estimate is more reliable the larger the sample and the smaller the true standard deviation.

A.3 *Multivariate Statistics*

Building portfolios requires combining random variables. The rate of return on a portfolio is the weighted average of the individual returns. Hence understanding and quantifying the interdependence of random variables is essential to portfolio analysis. In the first part of this section we return to scenario analysis. Later we return to making inferences from samples.

The Basic Measure of Association: Covariance

Table A.4 summarizes what we have developed so far for the scenario returns on Anheuser-Busch stock and options. We know already what happens when we add a constant to one of these return variables, or multiply by a constant. But what if we combine any two of them? Suppose that we add the return on the stock to the return on the call. We create a new random variable that we denote by $r(s + c) = r(s) + r(c)$, where $r(s)$ is the return on the stock and $r(c)$ is the return on the call.

From the definition, the expected value of the combination variable is

$$E[r(s + c)] = \Sigma Pr(i)r_i(s + c) \tag{A.10}$$

Substituting the definition of $r(s + c)$ into equation A.10 we have

$$E[r(s + c)] = \Sigma Pr(i)[r_i(s) + r_i(c)] = \Sigma Pr(i)r_i(s) + \Sigma Pr(i)r_i(c) \tag{A.11}$$
$$= E[r(s)] + E[r(c)]$$

TABLE A.4 Probability Distribution of Anheuser-Busch Stock and Options

	Scenario 1	Scenario 2	Scenario 3
Probability	.20	.50	.30
Rates of Return(%)			
Stock	20	30	50
Call option	−100	−100	400
Put option	50	−25	−100
	E(r)	σ	σ²
Stock	.34	.1114	.0124
Call option	.50	2.2913	5.25
Put option	−.325	.5250	.2756

In words, the expectation of the sum of two random variables is just the sum of the expectations of the component random variables. Can the same be true about the variance? The answer is "no," which is, perhaps, the most important fact in portfolio theory. The reason lies in the statistical association between the combined random variables.

As a first step, we introduce the *covariance,* the basic measure of association. Although the expressions that follow may look intimidating, they are merely squares of sums; that is, $(a + b)^2 = a^2 + b^2 + 2ab$, and $(a - b)^2 = a^2 + b^2 - 2ab$, where the *a*s and *b*s might stand for random variables, their expectations, or their deviations from expectations. From the definition of the variance

$$\sigma_{s+c}^2 = E[r_{s+c} - E(r_{s+c})]^2 \qquad (A.12)$$

To make equations A.12 through A.20 easier to read, we will identify the variables by subscripts *s* and *c* and drop the subscript *i* for scenarios. Substitute the definition of $r(s + c)$ and its expectation into equation A.12:

$$\sigma_{s+c}^2 = E[r_s + r_c - E(r_s) - E(r_c)]^2 \qquad (A.13)$$

Changing the order of variables within the brackets in equation A.13.

$$\sigma_{s+c}^2 = E[r_s - E(r_s) + r_c - E(r_c)]^2$$

Within the square brackets we have the sum of the deviations from expectations of the two variables, which we denote by *d*. Writing this out,

$$\sigma_{s+c}^2 = E[(d_s + d_c)^2] \qquad (A.14)$$

Equation A.14 is the expectation of a complete square. Taking the square we find

$$\sigma_{s+c}^2 = E(d_s^2 + d_c^2 + 2d_s d_c) \qquad (A.15)$$

The term in the brackets in equation A.15 is the summation of three random variables. Since the expectation of a sum is the sum of the expectations, we can write equation A.15 as

$$\sigma_{s+c}^2 = E(d_s^2) + E(d_c^2) + 2E(d_s d_c) \qquad (A.16)$$

In equation A.16 the first two terms are the variance of the stock (the expectation of its squared deviation from expectation) plus the variance of the call. The third term is twice the expression that is the definition of the covariance discussed in equation A.17. (Note that the expectation is multiplied by 2 because expectation of twice a variable is twice the variable's expectation.)

In other words, the variance of a sum of random variables is the sum of the variances, *plus* twice the covariance, which we denote by $Cov(r_s, r_c)$, or the covariance between the return on *s* and the return on *c*. Specifically,

$$Cov(r_s, r_c) = E(d_s d_c) = E\{[r_s - E(r_s)][r_c - E(r_c)]\} \qquad (A.17)$$

The sequence of the variables in the expression for the covariance is of no consequence. Since the order of multiplication makes no difference, the definition of the covariance in equation A.17 shows that it will not affect the covariance either.

We use the data in Table A.4 to set up the input table for the calculation of the covariance, as shown in Table A.5.

First, we analyze the covariance between the stock and the call. In scenarios 1 and 2, both assets show *negative* deviations from expectation. This is an indication of *positive co-movement*. When these two negative deviations are multiplied, the product, which eventually contributes to the covariance between the returns, is positive. Multiplying deviations leads to positive covariance when the variables move in the same direction, and negative covariance when they move in the opposite direction. In scenario 3 both assets show *positive* deviations, reinforcing the inference that the co-movement is positive. The magnitude of the products of the deviations, weighted by the probability of each scenario, when added up, results in a covariance that shows not only the direction of the co-movement (by its sign) but also the degree of the co-movement.

The covariance is a variance-like statistic. Whereas the variance shows the degree of the movement of a random variable about its expectation, the covariance shows the degree of the co-movement of two variables about their expectations. It is important for portfolio analysis that the covariance of a variable with itself is equal to its variance. You can see this by substituting the appropriate deviations in equation A.17; the result is the expectation of the variable's squared deviation from expectation.

The first three values in the last column of Table A.5 are the familiar variances of the three assets, the stock, the call, and the put. The last three are the covariances; two of them are negative. Examine the covariance between the stock and the put, for example. In the first two scenarios the stock realizes negative deviations, while the put realizes positive deviations. When we multiply such deviations, the sign becomes negative. The same happens in the third scenario, except that the stock realizes a positive deviation and the put a negative one. Again, the product is negative, adding to the inference of negative co-movement.

TABLE A.5 Deviations, Squared Deviations, and Weighted Products of Deviations From Expectations of Anheuser-Busch Stock and Options

	Scenario 1	Scenario 2	Scenario 3	Probability-Weighted Sum
Probability	.20	.50	.30	
Deviation of stock	−.14	−.04	.16	
Squared deviation	.0196	.0016	.0256	.0124
Deviation of call	−1.50	−1.50	3.50	
Squared deviation	2.25	2.25	12.25	5.25
Deviation of put	.825	.075	−.675	
Squared deviation	.680625	.005625	.455635	.275628
Product of deviations $(d_s d_c)$	.21	.06	.56	.24
Product of deviations $(d_s d_p)$	−.1155	−.003	−.108	−.057
Product of deviations $(d_c d_p)$	−1.2375	−.1125	−2.3625	−1.0125

With other assets and scenarios the product of the deviations can be negative in some scenarios, in others positive. The *magnitude* of the products, when *weighted* by the probabilities, determines which co-movements dominate. However, whenever the sign of the products varies from scenario to scenario, the results will offset one another, contributing to a small, close-to-zero covariance. In such cases we may conclude that the returns have either a small, or no, average co-movement.

Covariance between transformed variables

Since the covariance is the expectation of the product of deviations from expectation of two variables, analyzing the effect of transformations on deviations from expectation will show the effect of the transformation on the covariance.

Suppose that we add a constant to one of the variables. We know already that the expectation of the variable increases by that constant; so deviations from expectation will remain unchanged. Just as adding a constant to a random variable does not affect its variance, it also will not affect its covariance with other variables.

Multiplying a random variable by a constant also multiplies its expectation, as well as its deviation from expectation. Therefore the covariance with any other variable will also be multiplied by that constant. Using the definition of the covariance, check that this summation of the foregoing discussion is true:

$$\text{Cov}[a_1 + b_1 r_s, a_2 + b_2 r_c] = b_1 b_2 \text{Cov}(r_s, r_c) \tag{A.18}$$

The covariance allows us to calculate the variance of sums of random variables, and eventually the variance of portfolio returns.

A Pure Measure of Association: The Correlation Coefficient

If we tell you that the covariance between the rates of return of the stock and the call is .24 (see Table A.5), what have you learned? Because the sign is positive, you know that the returns generally move in the same direction. However, the number .24 adds nothing to your knowledge of the degree of co-movement of the stock and the call.

To obtain a measure of association that conveys the degree of intensity of the co-movement, we relate the covariance to the standard deviations of the two variables. Each standard deviation is the square root of the variance. Thus the product of the standard deviations has the dimension of the variance that is also shared by the covariance. Therefore we can define the correlation coefficient, denoted by ρ, as

$$\rho_{sc} = \frac{\text{Cov}(r_s, r_c)}{\sigma_s \sigma_c} \tag{A.19}$$

where the subscripts on ρ identify the two variables involved. Since the order of the variables in the expression of the covariance is of no consequence, equation A.19 shows that the order does not affect the correlation coefficient either.

We use the covariances from Table A.5 to show the *correlation matrix* for the three variables:

	Stock	Call	Put
Stock	1.0	.94	−.97
Call	.94	1.0	−.84
Put	−.97	−.84	1.0

The highest (in absolute value) correlation coefficient is between the stock and the put, −.97, although the absolute value of the covariance between them is the lowest by far. The reason is attributable to the effect of the standard deviations. The following properties of the correlation coefficient are important:

- Because the correlation coefficient, just as the covariance, measures only the degree of association, it tells us nothing about causality. The direction of causality has to come from theory and be supported by specialized tests.
- The correlation coefficient is determined completely by deviations from expectations, as are the components in equation A.19. We expect, therefore, that it is not affected by adding constants to the associated random variables. However, the correlation coefficient is invariant also to multiplying the variables by constants. You can verify this property by referring to the effect of multiplication by a constant on the covariance and standard deviation.
- The correlation coefficient can vary from −1.0, perfect negative correlation, to 1.0, perfect positive correlation. This can be seen by calculating the correlation coefficient of a variable with itself. You expect it to be 1.0. Recalling that the covariance of a variable with itself is its own variance, you can verify this using equation A.19. The more ambitious can verify that the correlation between a variable and the negative of itself is equal to −1.0. First, find from equation A.17 that the covariance between a variable and its negative equals the negative of the variance. Then check equation A.19.

Since the correlation between x and y is the same as the correlation between y and x, the *correlation matrix is symmetric about the diagonal*. The diagonal consists of 1.0s because it represents the correlation of the returns with themselves. Therefore it is customary to present only the lower triangle of the correlation matrix.

Reexamine equation A.16. You can invert it so that the covariance is presented in terms of the correlation coefficient and the standard deviations as in equation A.20:

$$\text{Cov}(r_s, r_c) = \rho_{sc}\sigma_s\sigma_c \qquad (A.20)$$

This formulation can be useful, because many think in terms of correlations rather than covariances.

Estimating correlation coefficients from sample returns

Assuming that a sample consists of independent observations, we assign equal weights to all observations and use simple averages to estimate expectations. When estimating variances and covariances, we get an average by dividing by the number of observations minus one.

Suppose that you are interested in estimating the correlation between stocks and long-term default-free (government) bonds. Assume that the sample of 62 annual excess returns for the period 1926 to 1987 in Table A.3 is representative.

Using the definition for the correlation coefficient in equation A.19, you estimate the following statistics (using the subscripts s for stocks, b for bonds, and t for time):

$$\bar{R}_s = \frac{1}{62}\sum_{t=1}^{62}R_{s,t} = .08334;\ \bar{R}_b = \frac{1}{62}\sum R_{b,t} = .01058$$

$$\sigma_s = \left[\frac{1}{61}\sum(R_{s,t} - \bar{R}_s)^2\right]^{1/2} = .21064$$

$$\sigma_b = \left[\frac{1}{61}\sum(R_{b,t} - \bar{R}_b)^2\right]^{1/2} = .07977$$

$$\mathrm{Cov}(R_s,R_b) = \frac{1}{61}\sum[(R_{s,t} - \bar{R}_s)(R_{b,t} - \bar{R}_b)] = .00257$$

$$\rho_{sb} = \frac{\mathrm{Cov}(R_s,R_b)}{\sigma_s\sigma_b} = .15295$$

Here is one example of how problematic estimation can be. Recall that we predicate our use of the sample on the assumption that the probability distributions have not changed over the sample period. To see the problem with this assumption, suppose that we reestimate the correlation between stocks and bonds over a more recent period—for example, beginning in 1965, about the time of onset of government debt financing of both the war in Vietnam and the Great Society programs.

Repeating the previous calculations for the period 1965 to 1987, we find:

$$\bar{R}_s = .0312;\quad \bar{R}_b = -.00317$$
$$\sigma_s = .15565;\quad \sigma_b = .11217$$
$$\mathrm{Cov}(R_s,R_b) = .0057;\quad \rho_{sb} = .32647$$

A comparison of the two sets of numbers suggests that it is likely, but by no means certain, that the underlying probability distributions have changed. The variance in the rates of return and the size of the samples are why we cannot be sure. We shall return to the issue of testing the sample statistics shortly.

Regression Analysis

We will use a problem from the CFA examination (Level I, 1986) to represent the degree of understanding of regression analysis that is required for the ground level. However, first let us develop some background.

In analyzing measures of association so far, we have ignored the question of causality, identifying simply *independent* and *dependent* variables. Suppose that theory (in its most basic form) tells us that all asset excess returns are driven by the same economic force, whose movements are captured by a broad-based market index, such as excess return on the S&P 500 stock index.

Suppose further that our theory predicts a simple, linear relationship between the excess return of any asset and the market index. A linear relationship, one that can be described by a straight line, takes on this form:

$$R_{j,\,t} = a_j + b_j R_{M,t} + e_{j,\,t} \qquad (A.21)$$

where the subscript j represents any asset, M represents the market index (the S&P 500), and t represents variables that change over time. (In the following discussion we omit subscripts when possible.) On the left-hand side of equation A.21 is the dependent variable, the excess return on asset j. The right-hand side has two parts, the explained and unexplained (by the relationship) components of the dependent variable.

The explained component of R_j is the $a + b R_M$ part. It is plotted in Figure A.7. The quantity a, also called the intercept, gives the value of R_j when the *independent* variable is zero. This relationship assumes that it is a constant. The second term in the explained part of the return represents the driving force, R_M, times the sensitivity coefficient, b, that transmits movements in R_M to movements in R_j. The term b is also assumed to be constant. Figure A.7 shows that b is the slope of the regression line.

The unexplained component of R_j is represented by the *disturbance* term, e_j. The disturbance is assumed to be uncorrelated with the explanatory variable, R_M, and of zero expectation. Such a variable is also called a noise variable, because it contributes to the variance but not to the expectation of the dependent variable, R_j.

FIGURE A.7

Simple regression estimates and residuals. The intercept and slope are chosen so as to minimize the sum of the squared deviations from the regression line.

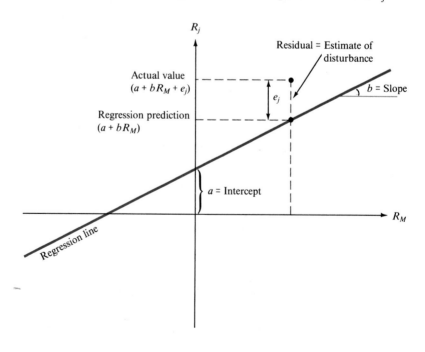

A relationship such as that shown in equation A.21 applied to data, with coefficients estimated, is called a *regression equation*. A relationship including only one explanatory variable is called *simple regression*. The parameters a and b are called (simple) *regression coefficients*. Since every value of R_j is explained by the regression, the expectation and variance of R_j are also determined by it. Suppose we use the expectation of the expression in equation A.21:

$$E(R_j) = a + bE(R_M) \qquad (A.22)$$

The constant a has no effect on the variance of R_j. Because the variables r_M and e_j are uncorrelated, the variance of the sum, $bR_M + e$, is the sum of the variances. Accounting for the parameter b multiplying R_M, the variance of R_j will be

$$\sigma_j^2 = b^2\sigma_M^2 + \sigma_e^2 \qquad (A.23)$$

Equation A.23 tells us that the contribution of the variance of R_M to that of R_j depends on the regression (slope) coefficient b. The term $(b\sigma_M)^2$ is called the *explained variance*. The variance of the disturbance makes up the *unexplained* variance.

The covariance between R_j and R_M is also given by the regression equation. Setting up the expression, we have

$$\begin{aligned} \text{Cov}(R_j, R_M) &= \text{Cov}(a + bR_M + e, R_M) \\ &= \text{Cov}(bR_M, R_M) = b\text{Cov}(R_M, R_M) = b\sigma_M^2 \end{aligned} \qquad (A.24)$$

The intercept, a, is dropped because a constant added to a random variable does not affect the covariance with any other variable. The disturbance term e is dropped because it is, by assumption, uncorrelated with the market return.

Equation A.24 shows that the slope coefficient of the regression, b, is equal to

$$b = \frac{\text{Cov}(R_j, R_M)}{\sigma_M^2}$$

The slope thereby measures the co-movement of j and M as a fraction of the movement of the driving force, the explanatory variable.

One way to measure the explanatory power of the regression is by the fraction of the variance of R_j that it explains. This fraction is called the *coefficient of determination*, and denoted by ρ^2.

$$\rho_{jM}^2 = \frac{b^2\sigma_M^2}{\sigma_j^2} = \frac{b^2\sigma_M^2}{b_M^2\sigma_M^2 + \sigma_e^2} \qquad (A.25)$$

Note that the unexplained variance, σ_e^2, has to make up the difference between the coefficient of determination and 1.0. Therefore another way to represent the coefficient of determination is by

$$\rho_{jM}^2 = 1 - \frac{\sigma_e^2}{\sigma_j^2}$$

Some algebra shows that the coefficient of determination is the square of the correlation coefficient. Finally, squaring the correlation coefficient tells us what proportion of the variance of the dependent variable is explained by the independent (the explanatory) variable.

Estimation of the regression coefficients a and b is based on minimizing the sum of the square deviation of the observations from the estimated regression line (see Figure A.7). Your calculator, as well as any spreadsheet program, can compute regression estimates.

The CFA 1986 examination for Level I included this question:

Question.

Pension plan sponsors place a great deal of emphasis on universe rankings when evaluating money managers. In fact, it appears that sponsors assume implicitly that managers who rank in the top quartile of a representative sample of peer managers are more likely to generate superior relative performance in the future than managers who rank in the bottom quartile.

The validity of this assumption can be tested by regressing percentile rankings of managers in one period on their percentile rankings from the prior period.

1. Given that the implicit assumption of plan sponsors is true to the extent that there is perfect correlation in percentile rankings from one period to the next, list the numerical values you would expect to observe for the slope of the regression, and the R-squared of the regression.
2. Given that there is no correlation in percentile rankings from period to period, list the numerical values you would expect to observe for the intercept of the regression, the slope of the regression, and the R-squared of the regression.
3. Upon performing such a regression, you observe an intercept of .51, a slope of $-.05$, and an R-squared of .01. Based on this regression, state your best estimate of a manager's percentile ranking next period if his percentile ranking this period were .15.
4. Some pension plan sponsors have agreed that a good practice is to terminate managers who are in the top quartile and to hire those who are in the bottom quartile. State what those who advocate such a practice expect implicitly about the correlation and slope from a regression of the managers' subsequent ranking on their current ranking.

Answer.

1. Intercept = 0
   Slope = 1
   R-squared = 1
2. Intercept = .50
   Slope = 0.0
   R-squared = 0.0
3. 50th percentile, derived as follows:
   $y = a + bx$
   $= .51 - 0.05(.15)$
   $= .51 - .0075$
   $= .5025$

   Given the very low R-squared, it would be difficult to estimate what the manager's rank would be.
4. Sponsors who advocate firing top-performing managers and hiring the poorest implicitly expect that both the correlation and slope would be significantly negative.

In many cases, theory suggests that a number of independent, explanatory variables drive a dependent variable. This concept becomes clear enough when demonstrated by a two-variable case. A real estate analyst offers the following regression equation to explain the return on a nationally diversified real estate portfolio:

$$RE_t = a + b_1RE_{t-1} + b_2NVR_t + e_t \qquad (A.26)$$

The dependent variable is the period t real estate portfolio return, RE_t. The model specifies that the explained part of that return is driven by two independent variables. The first is the previous period return, RE_{t-1} representing persistence or momentum. The second explanatory variable is the current national vacancy rate (NVR_t).

As in the simple regression, a is the intercept, representing the value that RE is expected to take when the explanatory variables are zero. The (slope) regression coefficients, b_1 and b_2, represent the *marginal* effect of the explanatory variables.

The coefficient of determination is defined exactly as before. The ratio of the variance of the disturbance, e, to the total variance of RE is 1.0 *minus* the coefficient of determination. The regression coefficients are estimated here, too, by finding coefficients that minimize the sum of squared deviations of the observations from the prediction of the regression.

A.4 *Hypothesis Testing*

The central hypothesis of investment theory is that nondiversifiable (systematic) risk is rewarded by a higher *expected* return. But do the data support the theory? Consider the data on the excess return on stocks in Table A.3. The estimate of the expected excess return (the sample average) is 8.33%. This appears to be a hefty risk premium, but so is the risk—the estimate of the standard deviation for the same sample is 21.06%. Could it be that the positive average is just the luck of the draw? Hypothesis testing supplies probabilistic answers to such concerns.

The first step in hypothesis testing is to state the claim that is to be tested. This is called the *null hypothesis* (or the null for short), denoted by H_0. Against the null, an alternative claim (hypothesis) is stated, which is denoted by H_1. The objective of hypothesis testing is to decide whether to reject the null in favor of the alternative, while identifying the probabilities of the possible errors in the determination.

A hypothesis is *specified* if it assigns a value to a variable. A claim that the risk premium on stocks is zero is one example of a specified hypothesis. Often, however, a hypothesis is general. A claim that the risk premium on stocks is not zero would be a completely general alternative against the specified hypothesis that the risk premium is zero. It amounts to "anything but the null." The alternative that the risk premium is *positive*, while not completely general, is still unspecified. Although it is sometimes desirable to test two unspecified hypotheses (for instance, the claim that the risk premium is zero or negative, against the claim that it is positive), unspecified hypotheses complicate the task of determining the probabilities of errors in judgment.

What are the possible errors? There are two, called type I and type II errors. Type I is the event that we will *reject* the null when it is *true*. The probability of type I error is called the *significance level*. Type II is the event that we will *accept* the null when it is *false*.

Suppose we set a criterion for acceptance of H_0 that is so lax that we know for certain we will accept the null. In doing so we will drive the significance level to zero (which is good). If we will never reject the null, we will also never reject it when it is true. At the same time the probability of type II error will become 1 (which is bad). If we will accept the null for certain, we must also do so when it is false.

The reverse is to set a criterion for acceptance of the null that is so stringent that we know for certain that we will reject it. This drives the probability of type II error to zero (which is good). By never accepting the null, we avoid accepting it when it is false. Now, however, the significance level will go to 1 (which is bad). If we always reject the null, we will reject it even when it is true.

To compromise between the two evils, hypothesis testing fixes the significance level; that is, it limits the probability of type I error. Then, subject to this preset constraint, the ideal test will minimize the probability of type II error. If we *avoid* type II error (accepting the null when it is false) we actually *reject* the null when it is indeed *false*. The probability of doing so is *one minus the probability of type II error,* which is called the *power of the test.* Minimizing the probability of type II error maximizes the power of the test.

Testing the claim that stocks earn a risk premium, we set the hypotheses as

$$H_0: \quad E(R) = 0 \quad \text{The expected excess return is zero.}$$
$$H_1: \quad E(R) > 0 \quad \text{The expected excess return is positive.}$$

H_1 is an *unspecified alternative*. When a null is tested against a completely general alternative, it is called a *two-tailed test* because you may reject the null in favor of both greater or smaller values.

When both hypotheses are unspecified, the test is difficult because the calculation of the probabilities of type I and II errors is complicated. Usually, at least one hypothesis is simple (specified) and set as the null. In that case it is relatively easy to calculate the significance level of the test. Calculating the power of the test that assumes the *unspecified* alternative is true remains complicated; often it is left unsolved.

As we will show, setting the hypothesis that we wish to reject, $E(R) = 0$ as the null (the "straw man"), makes it harder to accept the alternative that we favor, our theoretical bias, which is appropriate.

In testing $E(R) = 0$, suppose we fix the significance level at 5%. This means that we will reject the null (and accept that there is a positive premium) *only* when the data suggest that the probability the null is true is 5% or less. To do so, we must find a critical value, denoted z_α (or critical values in the case of two-tailed tests) that corresponds to $\alpha = .05$, which will create two regions, an acceptance region and a rejection region. Look at Figure A.8 as an illustration.

Under the null
hypothesis the sample
average excess return
should be distributed
around zero. If the
actual average exceeds
z_α, we conclude that
the null hypothesis is
false.

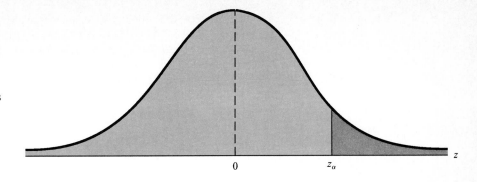

If the sample average is to the right of the critical value (in the rejection region), the null is rejected; otherwise, it is accepted. In the latter case it is too likely (that is, the probability is greater than 5%) that the sample average is positive simply because of sampling error. If the sample average is greater than the critical value, we will reject the null in favor of the alternative. The probability that the positive value of the sample average results from sampling error is 5% or less.

If the alternative is one-sided (one-tailed), as in our case, the acceptance region covers the entire area from minus infinity to a positive value, above which lies 5% of the distribution (see Figure A.8). The critical value is z_α in Figure A.8. When the alternative is two-tailed, the area of 5% lies at both extremes of the distribution and is equally divided between them, 25% on each side. A two-tailed test is more stringent (it is harder to reject the null). In a one-tailed test the fact that our theory predicts the direction in which the average will deviate from the value under the null is weighted in favor of the alternative. The upshot is that for a significance level of 5%, with a one-tailed test, we use a confidence interval of $\alpha = .05$, instead of $\alpha/2 = .025$ as with a two-tailed test.

Hypothesis testing requires assessment of the probabilities of the test statistics, such as the sample average and variance. Therefore it calls for some assumption about the probability distribution of the underlying variable. Such an assumption becomes an integral part of the null hypothesis, often an implicit one.

In this case we assume that the stock portfolio excess return is normally distributed. The distribution of the test statistic is derived from its mathematical definition and the assumption of the underlying distribution for the random variable. In our case the test statistic is the sample average.

The sample average is obtained by summing all observations ($T = 62$), and then multiplying by $1/T = 1/62$. Each observation is a random variable, drawn independently from the same underlying distribution, with an unknown expectation μ and standard deviation σ. The expectation of the sum of all observations is the sum of the T expectations (all equal to μ) divided by T, therefore equal to the population expectation. The result is 8.33%, which is equal to the true expectation *plus* sampling errors. Under the null hypothesis, the expectation is zero, and the entire 8.33% constitutes sampling errors.

To calculate the variance of the sample average, recall that we assume d observations were independent, or uncorrelated. Hence the variance of the sum is the sum of the variances, that is, T times the population variance. However, we also transform the sum, multiplying it by $1/T$; therefore we have to divide the variance of the sum $T\sigma^2$ by T^2. We end up with the variance of the sample average as the population variance divided by T. The standard deviation of the sample average, which is called the *standard error*, is

$$\sigma(\text{average}) = \left(\frac{1}{T^2}\Sigma\sigma^2\right)^{1/2} = \left(\frac{1}{T^2}T\sigma^2\right)^{1/2} = \frac{\sigma}{\sqrt{T}} = \frac{.21064}{\sqrt{62}} = .02675 \quad \text{(A.27)}$$

Our test statistic has a standard error of 2.675%. It makes sense that the more the number of observations, the *smaller* the *standard error* of the estimate of the expectation. However, note that it is the variance that goes down by the proportion $T = 62$. The standard error goes down by a much smaller proportion, $\sqrt{T} = 7.87$.

Now that we have the sample mean, 8.33%, its standard deviation, 2.675%, and know that the distribution under the null is normal, we are ready to perform the test. We want to determine whether 8.33% is significantly positive. We achieve this by standardizing our statistic, which means that we subtract from its expected value under the null hypothesis and divide by its standard deviation. This standardized statistic can now be compared to z values from the standard normal tables. We ask whether

$$\frac{\bar{R} - E(R)}{\sigma} > z_\alpha$$

We would be finished except for another caveat. The assumption of normality is all right in that the test statistic is a weighted sum of normals (according to our assumption about returns). Therefore it is also normally distributed. However, the analysis also requires that we *know* the variance. Here we are using a sample variance that is only an *estimate* of the true variance.

The solution to this problem turns out to be quite simple. The normal distribution is replaced with the *student-t* (or *t*, for short) *distribution*. Like the normal, the t distribution is symmetric. It depends on degrees of freedom, that is, the number of observations less one. Thus, here we replace z_α with $t_{\alpha,T-1}$.

The test is then

$$\frac{\bar{R} - E(R)}{s} > t_{\alpha,T-1}$$

When we substitute in sample results, the left-hand side is a standardized statistic and the right-hand side is a *t*-value derived from *t* tables for $\alpha = .05$ and $T - 1 = 62 - 1 = 61$. We ask whether the inequality holds. If it does, we *reject* the null hypothesis with a 5% significance level; if it does not we *cannot reject* the null hypothesis. Proceeding, we find that

Appendix

$$\frac{.0833 - 0}{.02675} = .3114 > 1.671$$

In our sample the inequality holds, and we reject the null hypothesis in favor of the alternative that the risk premium is positive.

A repeat of the test of this hypothesis for the 1965-to-1987 period may make a skeptic out of you. For that period the sample average is 3.12%, the sample standard deviation is 15.57%, and there are $23 - 1 = 22$ degrees of freedom. Does that give you second thoughts?

The t-Test of Regression Coefficients

Suppose that we apply the simple regression model (equation A.21), to the relationship between the long-term government bond portfolio and the stock market index, using the sample in Table A.3. The estimation result (percent per year) is

$$a = .5668, \ b = .0589, \ R\text{-squared} = .0242$$

We interpret these coefficients as follows. For periods when the excess return on the market index is zero, we expect the bonds to earn an excess return of 56.68 basis points. This is the role of the intercept. As for the slope, for each percentage return of the stock portfolio in any year, the bond portfolio is expected to earn, *additionally*, 5.89 basis points. With the average equity risk premium for the sample period of 8.33%, the sample average for bonds is $.5668 + .0589 \times 8.33 = 1.058\%$. From the squared correlation coefficient you know that the variation in stocks explains 2.42% of the variation in bonds.

Can we rely on these statistics? One way to find out is to set up a hypothesis test, presented here for the regression coefficient b.

H_0: $b = 0$ The regression slope coefficient is zero, meaning that changes in the independent variable do not explain changes in the dependent variable.

H_1: $b > 0$ The dependent variable is sensitive to changes in the independent variable (with a *positive* covariance).

Any decent regression software supplies the statistics to test this hypothesis. The regression customarily assumes that the dependent variable and the disturbance are normally distributed, with an unknown variance that is estimated from the sample. Thus the regression coefficient b is normally distributed. Because once again the null is that $b = 0$, all we need is an estimate of the standard error of this statistic.

The estimated standard error of the regression coefficient is computed from the estimated standard deviation of the disturbance and the standard deviation of the explanatory variable. For the regression at hand, that estimate is, $s(b) = .0479$. Just as in the previous exercise, the critical value of the test is

$$s(b)t_{\alpha, T - 1}$$

Compare this value to the value of the estimated coefficient b. We will reject the null in favor of $b > 0$ if

$$b > s(b)t_{\alpha,T-1}$$

which, because the standard deviation $s(b)$ is positive, is equivalent to the following condition:

$$\frac{b}{s(b)} > t_{\alpha,T-1}$$

The t-test reports the ratio of the estimated coefficient to its estimated standard deviation. Armed with this t-ratio, the number of observations, T, and a table of the student-t distribution, you can perform the test at the desired significance level.

The t-ratio for our example is $.0589/.0479 = 1.2305$. The t-table for 61 degrees of freedom shows we cannot reject the null at a significance level of 5%, for which the critical value is 1.671.

A question from the CFA 1987 level exam calls for understanding of regression analysis and hypothesis testing.

Question.

An academic suggests to you that the returns on common stocks differ based on a company's market capitalization, its historical earnings growth, the stock's current yield, and whether or not the company's employees are unionized. You are skeptical that there are any attributes other than market exposure as measured by beta that explain differences in returns across a sample of securities.

Nonetheless, you decide to test whether or not these other attributes account for the differences in returns. You select the S&P 500 stocks as your sample, and regress their returns each month for the past 5 years against the company's market capitalization at the beginning of each month, the company's growth in earnings throughout the previous 12 months, the prior year's dividend divided by the stock price at the beginning of each month, and a dummy variable that has a value of 1 if employees are unionized and 0 if not.

1. The average R-squared from the regressions is .15, and it varies very little from month-to-month. Discuss the significance of this result.
2. You note that all of the coefficients of the attributes have t-statistics greater than 2 in most of the months in which the regressions were run. Discuss the significance of these attributes in terms of explaining differences in common stock returns.
3. You observe in most of the regressions that the coefficient of the dummy variable is $-.14$, and that the t-statistic is -4.74. Discuss the implication of the coefficient regarding the relationship between unionization and the return on a company's common stock.

Answer.

1. Differences in the attributes' values together explain about 15% of the differences in return among the stocks in the S&P 500 index. The remaining unexplained differences in return may be attributable to omitted attributes, industry affiliations, or stock-specific factors. This information by itself is not sufficient to form any qualitative conclusions. The fact that the R-squared varied little from month to month implies that the relationship is stable and the observed results are not sample specific.

2. Given a *t*-statistic greater than 2 in most of the months, one would regard the attribute co-efficients as statistically significant. If the attribute coefficients were not significantly different from zero, one would expect *t*-statistics greater than 2 in fewer than 5% of the regressions for each attribute coefficient. Since the *t*-statistics are greater than 2 much more frequently, one should conclude that they are definitely significant in terms of explaining differences in stock returns.

3. Since the coefficient for the dummy variable representing unionization has persistently been negative and since it persistently has been statistically significant, one would conclude that disregarding all other factors, unionization lowers a company's common stock return. That is, everything else being equal, non-unionized companies will have higher returns than companies whose employees are unionized. Of course, one would want to test the model further to see if there are omitted variables or other problems that might account for this apparent relationship.

Solutions to Concept Checks

I *Introduction*

Chapter 1 — The Investment Environment

1. The real assets are patents, customer relations, and the college education. These assets enable individuals or firms to produce goods or services that yield profits or income. Lease obligations are simply claims to pay or receive income and do not in themselves create new wealth. Similarly, the $5 bill is only a paper claim on the government and does not produce wealth.

2. The car loan is a primitive security. Payments on the loan depend only on the solvency of the borrower.

3. The borrower has a financial liability, the loan owed to the bank. The bank treats the loan as a financial asset.

4. a. Used cars trade in direct search markets when individuals advertise in local newspapers, and in dealer markets at used-car lots or automobile dealers.

   b. Paintings trade in broker markets when clients commission brokers to buy or sell art for them, in dealer markets at art galleries, and in auction markets.

   c. Rare coins trade mostly in dealer markets in coin shops, but they also trade in auctions and in direct search markets when individuals advertise they want to buy or sell coins.

5. Creative unbundling can separate interest or dividend from capital gains income. Dual funds do just this. In tax regimes where capital gains are taxed at lower rates than other income, or where gains can be deferred, such unbundling may be a way to attract different tax clienteles to a security.

Chapter 2 — Markets and Instruments

1. The discount yield at bid is 6.08. Therefore
$$P = 10,000 \ [1 - .0608 \times (61/360)] = \$9,896.978$$

2. If the bond is selling below par, it is unlikely that the government will find it op-

timal to call the bond at par, when it can instead buy the bond in the secondary market for less than par. Therefore it makes sense to assume that the bond will remain alive until its maturity date. In contrast, premium bonds are vulnerable to call because the government can acquire them by paying only par value. Hence it is likely that the bonds will repay principal at the first call date, and the yield to first call is the statistic of interest.

3. Tax rates were reduced substantially in the 1980s. The reduction in these rates would be expected to reduce the tax advantage of municipal bonds. As a result, munis would need to offer higher yields relative to taxable bonds, and the yield ratio would be expected to rise.

4. a. You are entitled to a prorated share of IBM's dividend payments and to vote in any of IBM's stockholder meetings.

   b. Your potential gain is unlimited because IBM's stock price has no upper bound.

   c. Your outlay was $50 \times 100 = \$5,000$. Because of limited liability, this is the most you can lose.

5. The price-weighted index increases from 62.5 $[(100 + 25)/2]$ to 65 $[(110 + 20)/2]$, a gain of 4%. An investment of one share in each company requires an outlay of $125 that would increase in value to $130, for a return of 4% (5/125), which equals the return to the price-weighted index.

6. The market value–weighted index return is calculated by computing the increase in value of the stock portfolio. The portfolio of the two stocks starts with an initial value of $100 million + $500 million = $600 million and falls in value to $110 million + $400 million = $510 million, a loss of 90/600 = .15 or 15%. The index portfolio return is a weighted average of the returns on each stock with weights of $\frac{1}{6}$ on XYZ and $\frac{5}{6}$ on ABC, (weights proportional to relative investments). Because the return on XYZ is 10%, while that on ABC is -20%, the index portfolio return is $\frac{1}{6} \times 10\% + \frac{5}{6} \times (-20\%) = -15\%$, equal to the return on the market value–weighted index.

7. The payoff to the option is $3 per share at maturity. The option cost $.75 share. The dollar profit is therefore $2.25. The put option expires worthless. Therefore the investor's loss is the cost of the put, or $.625.

Chapter 3 — How Securities Are Traded

1. $$\frac{100P - \$4,000}{100P} = .4$$
    $$100P - \$4,000 = 40P$$
    $$60P = \$4,000$$
    $$P = \$66.67 \text{ per share}$$

2. The investor will purchase 150 shares, with a rate of return as follows:

Year-End Change in Price	Year-End Value of Shares	Repayment of Principal and Interest	Investor's Rate of Return
30%	19,500	$5,450	40.5%
No change	15,000	5,450	−4.5%
− 30%	10,500	5,450	−49.5%

3. $\dfrac{\$150,000 - 1,000P}{1,000P} = .4$

$\$150,000 - 1,000P = 400P$

$1,400P = \$150,000$

$P = \$107.14$ per share

Chapter 4—Concepts and Issues

1. a. $1 + r = (1 + R)(1 + i)$
   $= (1.03)(1.08)$
   $= 1.1124$
   $r = 11.24\%$

   b. $1 + r = (1.03)(1.10)$
   $= 1.133$
   $r = 13.3\%$

2. $R = (.12 - .13)/.13$
   $= -.00885$ or $-.885\%$

   When the inflation rate exceeds the nominal interest rate, the real rate of return is negative.

II Portfolio Theory

Chapter 5—Risk and Risk Aversion

1. The expected rate of return on the risky portfolio is $22,000/$100,000 = .22, or 22%. The T-bill rate is 5%. The risk premium therefore is 22% − 5% = 17%.

2. The investor is taking on exchange rate risk by investing in a pound-denominated asset. If the exchange rate moves in the investor's favor, the investor will benefit and will earn more from the U.K. bill than the U.S. bill. For example, if both the U.S. and U.K. interest rates are 5%, and the current exchange rate is $1.50 per pound, a $1.50 investment today can buy one pound, which can be invested in England at a certain rate of 5%, for a year-end value of 1.05 pounds. If the year-end exchange rate is $1.60 per pound, the 1.05 pounds can be exchanged for $1.05 \times \$1.6 = \$1.68$ for a rate of return in dollars of $1 + r = \$1.68/\$1.50 = 1.12$, or 12%, more than is available from U.S. bills. Therefore, if the investor

expects favorable exchange rate movements, the U.K. bill is a speculative investment. Otherwise, it is a gamble.

3. For the $A = 4$ investor the utility of the risky portfolio is
$$U = .20 - \tfrac{1}{2} \times 4 \times .2^2$$
$$= .12$$
while the utility of bills is
$$U = .07 - \tfrac{1}{2} \times 4 \times 0$$
$$= .07$$
The investor will prefer the risky portfolio to bills. (Of course, a mixture of bills and the portfolio might be even better, but that is not a choice here.)

For the $A = 8$ investor, the utility of the risky portfolio is
$$U = .20 - \tfrac{1}{2} \times 8 \times .2^2$$
$$= .04$$
while the utility of bills is again .07. The more risk-averse investor therefore prefers the risk-free alternative.

4. The less risk-averse investor has a shallower indifference curve. An increase in risk requires less increase in expected return to restore utility to the original level.

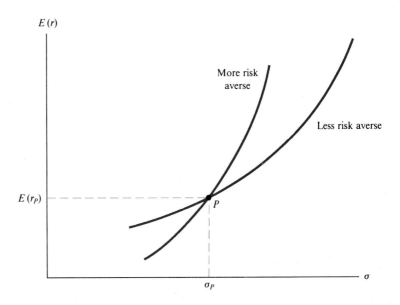

5. Despite the fact that gold investments *in isolation* seem dominated by the stock market, gold still might play a useful role in a diversified portfolio. Because gold and stock market returns have very low correlation, stock investors can reduce their portfolio risk by placing part of their portfolios in gold.

6. a. With the given distribution for SugarKane, the scenario analysis looks as follows:

	Normal Year for Sugar		Abnormal Year
	Bullish Stock Market	Bearish Stock Market	Sugar Crisis
Probability	.5	.3	.2

	Rate of Return (%)		
Best Candy	.25	.10	−.25
SugarKane	.07	−.05	.20
T-bills	.05	.05	.05

The expected return and standard deviation of SugarKane is now

$$E(r_{\text{SugarKane}}) = .5 \times .07 + .3(-.05) + .2 \times .20$$
$$= .06$$
$$\sigma_{\text{SugarKane}} = [.5(.07 - .06)^2 + .3(-.05 - .06)^2 + .2(.20 - .06)^2]^{1/2}$$
$$= .0872$$

The covariance between the returns of Best and SugarKane is

$$\text{Cov(SugarKane, Best)} = .5(.07 - .06)(.25 - .105)$$
$$+ .3(-.05 - .06)(.10 - .105) + .2(.20 - .06)(-.25 - .105) = -.00905$$

and the correlation coefficient is

$$\rho_{\text{(SugarKane, Best)}} = \frac{\text{Cov(SugarKane, Best)}}{\sigma_{\text{(SugarKane)}}\sigma_{\text{(Best)}}}$$
$$= \frac{-.00905}{.0872 \times .1890}$$
$$= -.55$$

The correlation is negative, but less than before (−.55 instead of −.86) so we expect that SugarKane will now be a less powerful hedge than before. Investing 50% in SugarKane and 50% in Best will result in a portfolio probability distribution of

Probability	.5	.3	.2
Portfolio return	.16	.025	−.025

resulting in a mean and standard deviation of

$$E(r_{\text{Hedged portfolio}}) = .5 \times .16 + .3 \times .025 + .2(-.025)$$
$$= .0825$$
$$\sigma_{\text{Hedged portfolio}} = [.5(.16 - .0825)^2 + .3(.025 - .0825)^2 + .2(-.025 - .0825)^2]^{1/2}$$
$$= .0794.$$

b. It is obvious that even under these circumstances the hedging strategy dominates the risk-reducing strategy that uses T-bills (which results in $E(r) = 7.75\%$, $\sigma = 9.45\%$). At the same time, the standard deviation of the hedged position (7.94%) is not as low it was using the original data.

c, d. Using Rule 5 for portfolio variance, we would find that

$$\sigma^2 = .5^2 \times \sigma^2_{Best} + .5^2 \times \sigma^2_{Kane} + 2 \times .5 \times .5 \times \text{Cov(SugarKane, Best)}$$
$$= .5^2 \times .189^2 + .5^2 \times .0872^2 + 2 \times .5 \times .5 \times (-.00905)$$
$$= .006306$$

which implies that $\sigma = .0794$, precisely the same result that we obtained by analyzing the scenarios directly.

A.1. Investors appear to be more sensitive to extreme outcomes relative to moderate outcomes than variance and higher *even* moments can explain. Casual evidence suggests that investors are eager to insure extreme losses and express great enthusiasm for highly, positively skewed lotteries. This hypothesis is, however, extremely difficult to prove with properly controlled experiments.

A.2. The better diversified the portfolio, the smaller is its standard deviation, as the sample standard deviations of Table 5A.1, p. 151, confirm. When we draw from distributions with smaller standard deviations, the probability of extreme values shrinks. Thus the expected smallest and largest values from a sample get closer to the expected value as the standard deviation gets smaller. This expectation is confirmed by the samples of Table 1 for both the sample maximum and minimum annual rate.

B.1. a. $U(W) = \sqrt{W}$
$U(50,000) = \sqrt{50,000}$
$\qquad\qquad = 223.61$
$U(150,000) = 387.30$

b. $E(U) = .5 \times 223.61 + .5 \times 387.30$
$\qquad\quad = 305.45$

c. We must find W_{CE} that has utility level 305.45. Therefore
$W_{CE} = 305.45$
$W_{CE} = 305.45^2$
$\qquad = \$93,301$

d. Yes. The certainty equivalent of the risky venture is less than the expected outcome of $100,000.

e. The certainty equivalent of the risky venture to this investor is greater than it was for the log utility investor considered in the text. Hence this utility function displays less risk aversion.

Chapter 6—Capital Allocation Between the Risky Asset and the Risk-Free Asset

1. Holding 50% of your invested capital in Ready Assets means that your investment proportion in the risky portfolio is reduced from 70% to 50%.

Your risky portfolio is constructed to invest 54% in IBM and 46% in GM. Thus the proportion of IBM in your overall portfolio is $.5 \times .54 = 27\%$, and the dollar value of your position in IBM is $300,000 \times .27 = \$81,000$.

2. In the expected return-standard deviation plane all portfolios that are constructed from the same risky and risk-free funds (with various proportions) lie on a line from the risk-free rate through the risky fund. The slope of this CAL (capital allocation line) is the same everywhere; hence the reward-to-variability ratio is the same for all of these portfolios. Formally, if you invest a proportion, y, in a risky fund with expected return, $E(r_P)$, and standard deviation, σ_P, and the remainder, $1 - y$, in a risk-free asset with a sure rate, r_f, then the portfolio's expected return and standard deviation are

$$E(r_C) = r_f + y[E(r_P) - r_f]$$
$$\sigma_C = y\sigma_P$$

and therefore the reward-to-variability ratio of this portfolio is

$$S_C = \frac{E(r_C) - r_f}{\sigma_C} = \frac{y[E(r_P) - r_f]}{y\sigma_P} = \frac{E(r_P) - r_f}{\sigma_P}$$

which is independent of the proportion, y.

3. The lending and borrowing rates are unchanged at: $r_f = 7\%$, $r_f^B = 9\%$. The standard deviation of the risky portfolio is still 22%, but its expected rate of return shifts from 15% to 17%.

The slope of the two-part CAL is

$$\frac{E(r_P) - r_f}{\sigma_P} \quad \text{for the lending range}$$

$$\frac{E(r_P) - r_f^B}{\sigma_P} \quad \text{for the borrowing range}$$

Thus in both cases the slope increases: from 8/22 to 10/22 for the lending range, and from 6/22 to 8/22 for the borrowing range.

4. a. The parameters are: $r_f = .07$, $E(r_P) = .15$, $\sigma_P = .22$. With these parameters an investor with a degree of risk aversion, A, will choose a proportion, y, in the risky portfolio of

$$y = \frac{E(r_P) - r_f}{A\sigma_P^2}$$

With $A = 3$ we find that

$$y = \frac{.15 - .07}{3 \times .0484} = .55$$

When the degree of risk aversion decreases from the original value of four to the new value of three, investment in the risky portfolio increases from 41% to 55%. Accordingly, the expected return and standard deviation of the optimal portfolio increase.

$$E(r_C) = .07 + .55 \times .08 = .114 \quad \text{(before: .1028)}$$
$$\sigma_C = .55 \times .22 = .121 \quad \text{(before: .0902)}$$

b. All investors whose degree of risk aversion is such that they would hold the risky portfolio in a proportion equal to 100% or less ($y < 1.00$) are lending rather than borrowing, and so are unaffected by the borrowing rate. The least risk-averse of these investors hold 100% in the risky portfolio ($y = 1$). We can solve for the degree of risk aversion of these "cut off" investors, from the parameters of the investment opportunities:

$$y = 1 = \frac{E(r_P) - r_f}{A\sigma_P^2} = \frac{.08}{.0484A}$$

which implies

$$A = \frac{.08}{.0484} = 1.65$$

Any investor who is more risk tolerant (that is, with A less than 1.65) would borrow if the borrowing rate were 7%. For borrowers,

$$y = \frac{E(r_P) - r_f^B}{A\sigma_P^2}$$

Suppose, for example, an investor has an A of 1.1. When $r_f = r_f^B = 7\%$, this investor chooses to invest in the risky portfolio.

$$y = \frac{.08}{1.1 \times .0484} = 1.50$$

which means that the investor will borrow 50% of the total investment capital. Raise the borrowing rate, in this case to $r_f^B = 9\%$, and the investor will invest less in the risky asset. In that case,

$$y = \frac{.06}{1.1 \times .0484} = 1.13$$

and "only" 13% of his or her investment capital will be borrowed. Graphically, the line from r_f to the risky portfolio shows the CAL for lenders. The dashed part *would* be relevant if the borrowing rate equaled the lending rate. When the borrowing rate exceeds the lending rate, the CAL is kinked at the point corresponding to the risky portfolio.

The following figure shows indifference curves of two investors. The steeper indifference curve portrays the more risk-averse investor, who chooses portfolio C_0, which involves lending. This investor's choice is unaffected by the borrowing rate.

The more risk-tolerant investor is portrayed by the shallower-sloped indifference curves. If the lending rate equaled the borrowing rate, this investor would choose portfolio C_1 on the dashed part of the CAL. When the borrowing rate goes up, this investor chooses portfolio C_2 (in the borrowing range of the kinked CAL), which involves less borrowing than before. This investor is hurt by the increase in the borrowing rate.

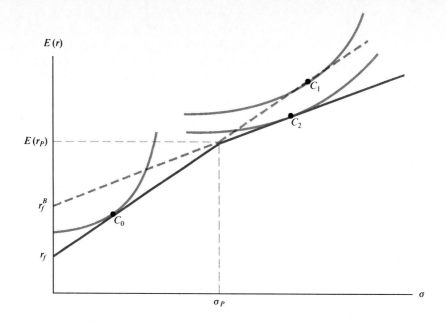

5. If all the investment parameters remain unchanged, the only reason for an investor to decrease the investment proportion in the risky asset is an increase in the degree of risk aversion. If you think that this is unlikely, than you have to reconsider your faith in your assumptions. Perhaps the S&P 500 is not a good proxy for the optimal risky portfolio. Perhaps investors expect a higher real rate on T-bills (inflation is ignored in this model).

Chapter 7—Optimal Risky Portfolios

1. a. The first term will be $w_D \times w_D \times \sigma_D^2$, since this is the element in the top corner of the matrix (σ_D^2) times the term on the column border (w_D) times the term on the row border (w_D). Applying this rule to each term of the covariance matrix results in the sum $w_D^2 \sigma_D^2 + w_D w_E \text{Cov}(r_E, r_D) + w_E w_D \text{Cov}(r_D, r_E) + w_E^2 \sigma_E^2$, which is the same as equation 7.2, since $\text{Cov}(r_E, r_D) = \text{Cov}(r_D, r_E)$.

   b. The bordered covariance matrix is

	w_X	w_Y	w_Z
w_X	σ_X^2	$\text{Cov}(r_X, r_Y)$	$\text{Cov}(r_X, r_Z)$
w_Y	$\text{Cov}(r_Y, r_X)$	σ_Y^2	$\text{Cov}(r_Y, r_Z)$
w_Z	$\text{Cov}(r_Z, r_X)$	$\text{Cov}(r_Z, r_Y)$	σ_Z^2

There are nine terms in the covariance matrix. Portfolio variance is calculated, from these nine terms:

$$\sigma_P^2 = w_X^2\sigma_X^2 + w_Y^2\sigma_Y^2 + w_Z^2\sigma_Z^2$$
$$+ w_Xw_Y \, \text{Cov}(r_X,r_Y) + w_Yw_X \, \text{Cov}(r_Y,r_X)$$
$$+ w_Xw_Z \, \text{Cov}(r_X,r_Z) + w_Zw_X \, \text{Cov}(r_Z,r_X)$$
$$+ w_Yw_Z \, \text{Cov}(r_Y,r_Z) + w_Zw_Y \, \text{Cov}(r_Z,r_Y)$$
$$= w_X^2\sigma_X^2 + w_Y^2\sigma_Y^2 + w_Z^2\sigma_Z^2$$
$$+ 2w_Xw_Y \, \text{Cov}(r_X,r_Y) + 2w_Xw_Z \, \text{Cov}(r_X,r_Z) + 2w_Yw_Z \, \text{Cov}(r_Y,r_Z)$$

2. The parameters of the opportunity set are $E(r_D) = .20$, $E(r_E) = .15$, $\sigma_D = .45$, $\sigma_E = .32$, and $\rho(D,E) = .25$. From the standard deviations and the correlation coefficient we generate the covariance matrix:

Stock	D	E
D	.2025	.0360
E	.0360	.1024

The *global minimum-variance* portfolio is constructed so that

$$w_D = [\sigma_E^2 - \text{Cov}(r_D,r_E)] \div [\sigma_D^2 + \sigma_E^2 - 2 \, \text{Cov}(r_D,r_E)]$$
$$= (.1024 - .0360) \div (.2205 + .1024 - 2 \times .0360) = .2851$$
$$w_E = 1 - w_D = .7149.$$

Its expected return and standard deviation are

$$E(r_P) = .2851 \times .20 + .7149 \times .15 = .1643$$
$$\sigma_P = [w_D^2\sigma_D^2 + w_E^2\sigma_E^2 + 2w_Dw_E \, \text{Cov}(r_D,r_E)]^{1/2}$$
$$= [.2851^2 \times .2025 + .7149^2 \times .1024 + 2 \times .2851 \times .7149 \times .0360]^{1/2}$$
$$= .2889$$

For the other points we simply increase w_D from .10 to .90 in increments of .10; accordingly, w_E ranges from .90 to .10 in the same increments. We substitute these portfolio proportions in the formulas for expected return and standard deviation. Note that for w_D or w_E equal to 1.0, the portfolio parameters equal those of the stock.

We then generate the following table:

w_D	w_E	$E(r)$	σ
.00	1.00	.1500	.3200
.10	.90	.1550	.3024
.20	.80	.1600	.2918
.2851	.7149	.1643	.2889(min)
.30	.70	.1650	.2890
.40	.60	.1700	.2942
.50	.50	.1750	.3070

w_D	w_E	$E(r)$	σ
.60	.40	.1800	.3264
.70	.30	.1850	.3515
.80	.20	.1900	.3811
.90	.10	.1950	.4142
1.00	.00	.2000	.4500

You can now draw your graph.

3. a. The computations of the opportunity set of the stock and risky bond funds are like those of Question 2 and will not be shown here. You should perform these computations, however, in order to give a graphical solution to part a. Note that the covariance between the funds is

$$\text{Cov}(r_A, r_B) = \rho(A,B) \times \sigma_A \times \sigma_B$$
$$= -.2 \times .20 \times .60 = -.0240$$

b. The proportions in the optimal risky portfolio are given by

$$w_A = \frac{(.10 - .05).60^2 - (.30 - .05)(-.0240)}{(.10 - .05).60^2 + (.30 - .05).20^2 - .30(-.0240)}$$
$$= .6818$$
$$w_B = 1 - w_A = .3182$$

The expected return and standard deviation of the optimal risky portfolio are

$$E(r_P) = .6818 \times .10 + .3182 \times .30 = .1636$$
$$\sigma_P = [.6818^2 \times .20^2 + .3182^2 \times .60^2 + 2 \times .6818 \times .3182(-.0240)]^{1/2}$$
$$= .2113$$

Note that in this case the standard deviation of the optimal risky portfolio is smaller than the standard deviation of stock A. Note also that portfolio P is not the global minimum variance portfolio. The proportions of the latter are given by

$$w_A = [.60^2 - (-.0240)] \div [.60^2 + .20^2 - 2(-.0240)] = .8571$$
$$w_B = 1 - w_A = .1429$$

With these proportions, the standard deviation of the minimum variance portfolio is

$$\sigma(\text{min}) = [.8571^2 \times .20^2 + .1429^2 \times .60^2 + 2 \times .8571 \times .1429 \times (-.0240)]^{1/2}$$
$$= .1757$$

which is smaller than that of the optimal risky portfolio.

c. The CAL is the line from the risk-free rate through the optimal risky portfolio.

This line represents all efficient portfolios that combine T-bills with the optimal risky portfolio. The slope of the CAL is

$$S = [E(r_P) - r_f]/\sigma_P$$
$$= (.1636 - .05)/.2113 = .5376$$

d. Given a degree of risk aversion, A, an investor will choose a proportion, y, in the optimal risky portfolio of

$$y = [E(r_P) - r_f]/(A\sigma_P^2)$$
$$= (.1636 - .05)/(5 \times .2113^2) = .5089$$

This means that the optimal risky portfolio, with the given data, is attractive enough for an investor with $A = 5$ to invest 50.89% of his or her wealth in it. Since stock A makes up 68.18% of the risky portfolio and stock B 31.82%, the investment proportions for this investor are

Stock *A*:   .5089 × 68.18 = 34.70%
Stock *B*:   .5089 × 31.82 = 16.19%
                              TOTAL   50.89%

4. Efficient frontiers derived by portfolio managers depend on forecasts of the rates of return on various securities and estimates of risk, that is, the covariance matrix. The forecasts themselves do not control outcomes. Thus preferring managers with rosier forecasts (northwesterly frontiers) is tantamount to rewarding the bearers of good news and punishing the bearers of bad news. What we should do is reward bearers of *accurate* news. Thus, if you get a glimpse of the frontiers (forecasts) of portfolio managers on a regular basis, what you want to do is develop the track record of their forecasting accuracy and steer your advisees toward the more accurate forecaster. Their portfolio choices will, in the long run, outperform the field.

5. Portfolios that lie on the CAL are combinations of the tangency (risky) portfolio and the risk-free asset. Hence they are just as dependent on the accuracy of the efficient frontier as portfolios that are on the frontier itself. If we judge forecasting accuracy by the accuracy of the reward-to-volatility ratio, then all portfolios on a CAL will be exactly as accurate as the tangency portfolio.

A.1 The parameters are $E(r) = .15$, $\sigma = .60$, and the correlation between any pair of stocks is $\rho = .5$.

a. The portfolio expected return is invariant to the size of the portfolio because all stocks have identical expected returns. The standard deviation of a portfolio with $n = 25$ stocks is

$$\sigma_P = [\sigma^2(1/n) + \rho \times \sigma^2(n - 1)/n]^{1/2}$$
$$= [.60^2/25 + .5 \times .60^2 \times 24/25]^{1/2} = .4327$$

b. Because the stocks are identical, efficient portfolios are equally weighted. To obtain a standard deviation of 43%, we need to solve for *n*:

$$.43^2 = .60^2/n + .5 \times .60^2(n-1)/n$$
$$.1849n = .3600 + .1800n - .1800$$
$$n = \frac{.1800}{.0049} = 36.73$$

Thus we need 37 stocks and will come in slightly under the target.

c. As n gets very large, the variance of an efficient (equally weighted) portfolio diminishes, leaving only the variance that comes from the covariances among stocks, that is

$$\sigma_P = \sqrt{\rho \times \sigma^2} = \sqrt{.5 \times .60^2} = .4243$$

Note that with 25 stocks we came within 84 basis points of the systematic risk, that is, the nonsystematic risk of a portfolio of 25 stocks is 84 basis points. With 37 stocks the standard deviation is .4300, of which nonsystematic risk is 57 basis points.

d. If the risk-free is 10%, then the risk premium on any size portfolio is $15 - 10 = 5\%$. The standard deviation of a well-diversified portfolio is (practically) 42.43%, hence the slope of the CAL is

$$S = 5/42.43 = .1178$$

III *Equilibrium in Capital Markets*

Chapter 8—The Capital Asset Pricing Model

1. We can characterize the entire population by two representative investors. One is the "uninformed" investor, who does not engage in security analysis and holds the market portfolio, whereas the other optimizes using the Markowitz algorithm with input from security analysis. The uninformed investor does not know what input the informed investor uses to make portfolio purchases. The uninformed investor knows, however, that if the other investor is informed the market portfolio proportions will be optimal. Therefore to depart from these proportions would constitute an uninformed bet, which will, on average, reduce the efficiency of diversification with no compensating improvement in expected returns.

2. a. Substituting the historical mean and standard deviation in equation 8.2 yields a coefficient of risk aversion of

$$\overline{A} = \frac{E(r_M) - r_f}{\sigma_M^2} = \frac{.085}{.21^2} = 1.93$$

b. This relationship also tells us that for the historical standard deviation and a coefficient of risk aversion of 3.5 the risk premium would be

$$E(r_M) - r_f = \overline{A}\sigma_M^2 = 3.5 \times .21^2 = .154 \ (15.4\%)$$

3. $\beta_{Ford} = \beta_{GM} = 1.15$. Therefore, whatever the investment proportions, w_{Ford}, w_{GM}, the portfolio β, which is

$$\beta_P = w_{Ford}\beta_{Ford} + w_{GM}\beta_{GM}$$

will equal 1.15.

As the market risk premium, $E(r_M) - r_f$, is .08, the portfolio risk premium will be

$$E(r_P) - r_f = \beta_P[E(r_M) - r_f]$$
$$= 1.15 \times .08 = .092$$

4. The alpha of a stock is its expected return in excess of that required by the CAPM.

$$\alpha = E(r) - [r_f + \beta[E(r_M) - r_f]]$$
$$\alpha_{XYZ} = .12 - [.05 + 1.0(.11-.05)] = .01$$
$$\alpha_{ABC} = .13 - [.05 + 1.5(.11-.05)] = -.01$$

ABC plots below the SML, while *XYZ* plots above.

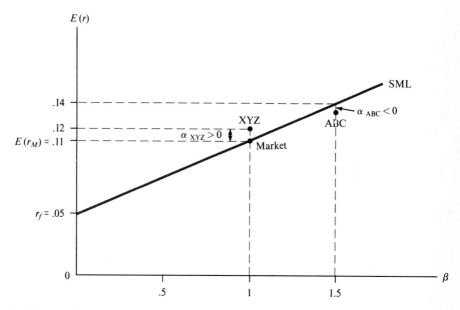

5. The project-specific required expected return is determined by the project beta coupled with the market risk premium and the risk-free rate. The CAPM tells us that an acceptable expected rate of return for the project is

$$E(r_f) + \beta[E(r_M) - r_f] = 8 + 1.3(16 - 8) = 18.4\%$$

which becomes the project's hurdle rate. If the IRR of the project is 19%, than it is desirable. Any project with an IRR equal to or less than 18.4% should be rejected.

6. If the basic CAPM holds, any zero-beta asset must be expected to earn on average the risk-free rate. Hence the posited performance of the zero-beta portfolio violates the simple CAPM. It does not, however, violate the zero-beta CAPM. Since we know that borrowing restrictions do exist, we expect the zero-beta version of the model is more likely to hold, with the zero-beta rate differing from the virtually risk-free T-bill rate.

Chapter 9 — Index Models

1. The variance of each stock is $\beta^2 \sigma_M^2 + \sigma^2(e)$.
   For stock A, we obtain

$$\sigma_A^2 = .9^2(.20)^2 + .3^2 = .1224$$
$$\sigma_A = .35$$

For stock B,

$$\sigma_B^2 = 1.1^2 (.20)^2 + .1^2 = .0584$$
$$\sigma_B = .24$$

The covariance is

$$\beta_A \beta_B \sigma_M^2 = .9 \times 1.1 \times .2^2 = .0396$$

2. $\sigma^2(e_P) = (1/2)^2[\sigma^2(e_A) + \sigma^2(e_B)]$
   $= 1/4(.3^2 + .1^2)$
   $= 1/4(.09 + .01)$
   $= .025$

Therefore

$\sigma(e_P) = .158$

3. a. Total market capitalization is $3000 + 1940 + 1360 = 6300$. Therefore the mean excess return of the index portfolio is

$$\frac{3000}{6300} \times .10 + \frac{1940}{6300} \times .02 + \frac{1360}{6300} \times .17 = .10$$

   b. The covariance between stock A and the index portfolio equals,

$$\text{Cov}(R_A, R_M) = \beta_A \sigma_M^2 = .1 \times .25^2 = .0125$$

   c. The variance of B equals

$$\sigma_B^2 = \text{Var}(\beta_B R_M + e_B) = \beta_B^2 \sigma_M^2 + \sigma^2(e_B)$$

Thus, the firm specific variance of B equals

$$\sigma_B^2 - \beta_B^2 \sigma_M^2 = .30^2 - .2^2 \times .25^2 = .0875$$

4. The CAPM is a model that relates expected rates of return to risk. It results in the expected return-beta relationship where the expected excess return on any asset is

proportional to the expected excess return on the market portfolio with beta as the proportionality constant. As such the model is impractical for two reasons: (i) expectations are unobservable, and (ii) the theoretical market portfolio includes every publicly traded risky asset and is in practice unobservable. The next three models incorporate assumptions that overcome these problems.

The single factor model assumes that one economic factor, denoted F, exerts the only common influence on security returns. Beyond it, security returns are driven by independent, firm-specific factors. Thus, for any security i,

$$r_i = a_i + b_i F + e_i$$

The single index model assumes that in the single factor model, the factor, F, is perfectly correlated with and therefore can be replaced by a broad-based index of securities that can proxy for the CAPM's theoretical market portfolio.

At this point it should be said that many interchange the meaning of the index and market models. The concept of the market model is that rate of return surprises on a stock are proportional to corresponding surprises on the market index portfolio, again with proportionality constant β.

5. Merrill Lynch's alpha is related to the CAPM alpha by

$$\alpha_{\text{Merrill}} = \alpha_{\text{CAPM}} + (1 - \beta) r_f$$

For GM, $\alpha_{\text{Merrill}} = .12\%$, $\beta = .83$, and we are told that r_f was .6%. Thus

$$\alpha_{\text{CAPM}} = .12 - (1 - .83).6$$
$$= .018\%$$

GM still performed well relative to the market and the index model. It beat its "benchmark" return by an average of .018% per month.

6. The industries with positive adjustment factors are most sensitive to the economy. Their betas would be expected to be higher because the business risk of the firms is higher. In contrast, the industries with negative adjustment factors are in business fields with a lower sensitivity to the economy. Therefore, for any given financial profile, their betas are lower.

Chapter 10—Arbitrage Pricing Theory

1. The least profitable scenario currently yields a profit of $10,000 and gross proceeds from the equally weighted portfolio of $700,000. As the price of Dreck falls, less of the equally weighted portfolio can be purchased from the proceeds of the short sale. When Dreck's price falls by more than a factor of 10,000/700,000, arbitrage no longer will be feasible, because the profits in the worst state will be driven below zero.

To see this, suppose that Dreck's price falls to $10 \times (1 - 1/70)$. The short sale of 300,000 shares now yields $2,957,142, which allows dollar investments of only $985,714 in each of the other shares. In the high real interest rate–low inflation scenario, profits will be driven to zero:

Stock	Dollar Investment	Rate of Return	Dollar Return
Apex	$985,714	.20	197,143
Bull	985,714	.70	690,000
Crush	985,714	−.20	−197,143
Dreck	−2,957,142	.23	−690,000
TOTAL	0		0

At any price for Dreck stock *below* $10 × (1 − 1/70) = $9.857, profits are negative, which means this arbitrage opportunity is eliminated. *Note:* $9.857 is not the equilibrium price of Dreck. It is simply the upper bound on Dreck's price that rules out the simple arbitrage opportunity.

2. $\sigma(e_P) = \sqrt{\sigma^2(e_i)/n}$

   a. $\sqrt{30/10} = 1.732\%$

   b. $\sqrt{30/100} = .548\%$

   c. $\sqrt{30/1,000} = .173\%$

   d. $\sqrt{30/10,000} = .055\%$

We conclude that nonsystematic volatility can be driven to arbitrarily low levels in well-diversified portfolios.

3. A portfolio consisting of two thirds of portfolio A and one third of the risk-free asset will have the same beta as portfolio E, but an expected return of (⅓ × 4 + ⅔ × 10) = 8%, less than that of portfolio E. Therefore one can earn arbitrage profits by shorting the combination of portfolio A and the safe asset, and buying portfolio E.

4. a. For portfolio P,

$$K = \frac{E(r_P) - r_f}{\beta_P} = \frac{.10 - .05}{.5} = .10$$

   For portfolio Q,

$$K = \frac{.15 - .05}{1} = .10$$

   b. The equally weighted portfolio has an expected return of 12.5% and a beta of .75. $K = (.125 - .05)/.75 = .10$.

5. Using equation 10.6, the expected return is

$$.04 + .2(.06) + 1.4(.08) = .164$$

Chapter 11—Equilibrium With Multiple Sources of Risk: The Multifactor CAPM

1. In George's original position, the portfolio is divided equally between risky portfolio P [with $E(r_P) = .15$, $\sigma = .25$] and T-bills (with $r_f = .07$). The complete portfolio has expected return and standard deviation:

$$E(r) = .50 \times .15 + .50 \times .07 = .11$$
$$\sigma = .50 \times .25 = .125$$

In the hedging strategy, energy price risk is offset by holdings of Oilex stock. Of the portfolio, 50% remains in the risky portfolio P, 13.64% is placed in Oilex (which is assumed to be uncorrelated with P and has expected return .07), and 36.36% is left in bills. Therefore

$$E(r) = .50 \times .15 + .1364 \times .07 + .3636 \times .07 = .11$$
$$\sigma^2 = .50^2 \times .25^2 + .1364^2 \times .22^2 = .0165$$
$$\sigma = .1286$$

George's hedge strategy portfolio has the same expected return as the original portfolio, but a higher standard deviation. Hence it cannot be mean-variance efficient with respect to portfolio rates of return. Nevertheless, the hedge strategy is an improvement over the original position because more than rate of return is important here. George cares about energy prices as well as about his portfolio value, and he must hedge both sources of risk.

2. Since the beta of the one-factor CAPM measures the sensitivity of portfolio returns to the market return, and ignores other hedging motives, it will be inadequate as a complete description of security risk in this more general context.

3. The security will be held *short* in the hedge portfolio. The extra hedge demand therefore will drive down demand for the security and will drive up its expected rate of return relative to the simple CAPM.

4. a. For Louisiana residents, the stock is not a hedge. When their economy does poorly (low oil prices) the stock also does poorly, thereby aggravating their problems.

   b. For Boston residents, the stock is a hedge. When energy prices increase, the stock will provide greater wealth with which to purchase energy.

   c. If energy consumers (who are willing to bid up the price of the stock for its hedge value) dominate the economy, then high oil–beta stocks will have low expected rates of return.

5. Although people will want to hedge this source of risk, the lack of correlation between security returns and the risk factor will make such hedging impossible. Because security returns are uncorrelated with the risk factor, the securities cannot serve to offset the uncertainty surrounding that factor. Hence there is no reason for investors to tilt their portfolios toward or away from any security for hedging in connection with the factor.

6. a. The industry factor is a statistically useful means to describe returns because it helps to explain movement in a nontrivial group of stocks. It is a common fac-

tor for all machine tool producers. However, there is no compelling reason to identify this industry return with a significant extramarket hedge factor. Investors can diversify away "industry-specific" risk if each industry is sufficiently small. On this score, a machine-tool factor would not be expected to appear in connection with the multifactor CAPM.

b. One would not expect the factor to command a risk premium. In the jargon of the APT, it would be a nonpriced factor. The industry factor would not be expected to command a risk premium by the usual principles of the CAPM, since industry-specific risk presumably can be diversified away. Neither does it seem that the machine tool–industry portfolio is a natural hedge for any significant source of extramarket risk. More generally, the APT allows for many factors (such as industry co-movements) that help to describe returns of various subsets of securities, but that do not serve to hedge a meaningful source of systematic risk.

Chapter 12—Empirical Evidence on Security Returns

1. The SCL is estimated for each stock; hence we need to estimate 100 equations. Our sample consists of 60 monthly rates of return for each of the 100 stocks and for the market index. Thus each regression is estimated with 60 observations. Equation 12.1 in the text shows that when stated in excess return form, the SCL should pass through the origin, that is, have a zero intercept.

2. When the SML has a positive intercept and its slope is less than the mean excess return on the market portfolio, it is flatter than predicted by the CAPM. Low beta stocks therefore have yielded returns that, on average, were more than they should have been on the basis of their beta. Conversely, high beta stocks were found to have yielded, on average, less than they should have on the basis of their betas.

3. The intercept of the SML was .00359 (36 basis points) instead of zero as it should have been according to the simple CAPM. Equation 12.5 in the text shows that if the zero-beta version of the CAPM is valid because of restrictions on borrowing, and the SCL and SML are estimated from excess returns over the risk-free rate (rather than over the zero-beta rate), then the intercept will be the difference between the zero-beta rate and the risk-free rate. Thus, if BJS had found that the average risk premium of the zero-beta portfolio was 36 basis points (per month), the zero-beta version of the CAPM would have been supported. Similarly, the slope of the estimated SML should equal the difference between the market mean return and that of the zero-beta portfolio. The market index risk premium averaged 1.42% per month, and the slope of the SML was estimated as 1.08%. Here, a risk premium of 34 basis points would have supported the zero-beta version of the CAPM.

4. A positive coefficient on beta-squared would indicate that the relationship between risk and return is nonlinear. High beta securities would provide expected returns more than proportional to risk. A positive coefficient on $\sigma(e)$ would indicate that firm-specific risk affects expected return, a direct contradiction of the CAPM and APT.

5. It is very difficult to identify the portfolios that serve to hedge systematic sources of risk to future consumption opportunities. Both lines of research explore the data in search of such portfolios. Factor analysis techniques indicate the portfolios that may be providing hedge services. Researchers can then try to figure out what the source of risk is and show how important it is. The second line of attack attempts to use theoretical arguments to guess at the identity of economic variables that may be correlated with consumption risk and then determines whether these variables do indeed explain rates of return.

Chapter 13—Market Efficiency

1. The information sets that pertain to the weak, semistrong, and strong form of the EMH can be described by the following illustration:

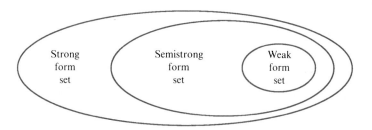

The weak-form information set includes only the history of prices and volumes. The semistrong form set includes the weak form set *plus* all publicly available information. In turn, the strong-form set includes the semistrong set *plus* insiders' information. It is illegal to act on the incremental information (insiders' private information). The direction of *valid* implication is

Strong-form EMH $\Rightarrow$ Semistrong-form EMH $\Rightarrow$ Weak-form EMH

The reverse direction implication is *not* valid. For example, stock prices may reflect all past price data (weak-form efficiency) but may not reflect relevant fundamental data (semistrong-form inefficiency).

2. The point we made in the preceding discussion is that the very fact that we observe stock prices near so-called resistance levels belies the assumption that the price can be a resistance level. If a stock is observed to sell *at any price,* then investors must believe that a fair rate of return can be earned if the stock is purchased at that price. It is logically impossible for a stock to have a resistance level *and* offer a fair rate of return at prices just below the resistance level. If we accept that prices are appropriate, we must reject any presumption concerning resistance levels.

3. If *everyone* follows a passive strategy, sooner or later prices will fail to reflect new information. At this point there are profit opportunities for active investors who uncover mispriced securities. As they buy and sell these assets, prices again will be driven to fair levels.

4. Predictably declining CARs do violate the EMH. If one can predict such a phenomenon, a profit opportunity emerges: sell (or short sell) the affected stocks on an event date just before their prices are predicted to fall.

5. The answer depends on your prior beliefs about market efficiency. Magellan's record has been incredibly strong. On the other hand, with so many funds in existence, it is less surprising that *some* fund would appear to be consistently superior after the fact. The answer really depends more on faith than inference.

6. If profit opportunities can be made, one would expect mutual funds specializing in small stocks to spring into existence. Moreover, one wonders why buyers of small stocks do not compete for those stocks in December and bid up their prices before the January rise.

7. Concern over the deficit was an ongoing issue in 1987. No significant *new* information concerning the deficit was released on October 19. Hence this explanation for the crash is not consistent with the EMH.

IV Fixed-Income Securities

Chapter 14—Bond Prices and Yields

1. At a semiannual interest rate of 3%, the bond is worth $40 \times PA(3\%, 60) + \$1,000 \times PF(3\%, 60) = \$1,276.75$, which results in a capital gain of $276.75. This exceeds the capital loss of $189.29 ($1,000 − $810.71) when the interest rate increased to 5%.

2. Yield to maturity exceeds current yield, which exceeds coupon rate. An example is the 8% coupon bond with a yield to maturity of 10% per year (5% per half year). Its price is $810.71, and therefore its current yield is $80/810.77 = .0987$ or 9.87%, which is higher than the coupon rate but lower than the yield to maturity.

3. Price $= \$35 \times PA(4\%, 4) + \$1,000 \times PF(4\%, 4) = \$981.85$

$$\text{Rate of return to investor} = \frac{\$35 + (\$981.85 - \$977.74)}{\$977.74} = .040 \text{ or } 4.0\%$$

4. It should receive a negative coefficient. A high ratio of liabilities to assets is a poor omen for a firm that should lower its credit rating.

5. The bond with the 6% coupon rate currently sells for $30 \times PA(3.5\%, 20) + 1,000 \times PF(3.5\%, 20) = \$928.94$. If the interest rate immediately drops to 6% (3% per half year), the bond price will rise to $1,000, for a capital gain of $71.06, or 7.65%. The 8% coupon bond currently sells for $1,071.06. If the interest rate falls to 6%, the present value of the *scheduled* payments increases to $1,148.77. However, the bond will be called at $1,100, for a capital gain of only $28.94, or 2.70%.

6. The premium bond should offer a higher promised yield in compensation for its greater susceptibility to being called.

1. The bond sells today for $683.18 (from Table 15.2). Next year, it will sell for $1,000 ÷ [(1.10)(1.11)(1.11)] = $737.84, for a return $1 + r$ = 737.84/683.18 = 1.08, or 8%.

2. The data pertaining to the T-bill imply that the 6-month interest rate is $300/$9,700 = .03093, or 3.093%. To obtain the forward rate, we look at the 1-year T-bond: The pricing formula

$$1,000 = \frac{40}{1.03093} + \frac{1040}{(1.03093)(1 + f)}$$

implies that f = .04952, or 4.952%.

3. 9%.

4. The risk premium will be zero.

5. If issuers wish to issue long-term bonds, they will be willing to accept higher expected interest costs on long bonds over short bonds. This willingness combines with investors' demands for higher rates on long-term bonds to reinforce the tendency toward a positive liquidity premium.

6. If r_4 equaled 9.66%, then the 4-year bond would sell for $1,000/[(1.08)(1.10)(1.11)(1.0966)] = $691.53. The yield to maturity would satisfy the equation $691.53(1 + y_4)^4$ = 1,000, or y_4 = 9.66%. At a lower value of r_4, the bond would sell for a higher price and offer a lower yield. At a higher value of r_4, the yield would be greater.

7.

Time	Cash Flow	Discount Factor	Present Value
1	120	1.08	111.11
2	120	(1.08)(1.10)	101.01
3	1,120	(1.08)(1.10)(1.11)	849.33
			1,061.45

The bond will sell for $1061.45, and so offer a conventional yield to maturity satisfying:

$$\$1061.45 = \$120 \times PA(y, 3) + 1000 \times PF(y, 3)$$

or y = 9.55%. The realized compound yield is determined from the accumulated future value of all reinvested coupons

Time	Cash Flow	Growth Factor	Future Value
1	120	(1.10)(1.11)	146.52
2	120	(1.11)	133.20
3	1,120	1	1,120.00
			1,399.72

The realized compound yield is the solution to

$$1061.45 \times (1 + y)^3 = 1399.72$$

so that $y = 9.66\%$.

Chapter 16: Fixed-Income Portfolio Management

1. The duration of a level perpetuity is $(1 + y)/y$ or $1 + 1/y$, which clearly falls as y increases. Tabulating duration as a function of r we get

y	D
.01	101 years
.02	51
.05	21
.10	11
.20	6
.25	5
.40	3.5

2. Potential gains and losses are proportional to both duration *and* portfolio size. The dollar loss on a fixed-income portfolio resulting from an increase in the portfolio's yield to maturity is, from equation 16.2, $D \times P \times \Delta y/(1 + y)$, where P is the initial market value of the portfolio. Hence $D \times P$ must be equated for immunization.

3. The perpetuity's duration now would be $1.08/.08 = 13.5$. We need to solve the following equation for w:

$$w \times 2 + (1 - w) \times 13.5 = 6$$

   Therefore $w = .6522$

4. Dedication would be more attractive. Cash flow matching eliminates the need for rebalancing and thus saves transaction costs.

5. The 30-year 8% coupon bond will provide a stream of coupons of $40 per half-year, which invested at the assumed rate of 4% per half-year will accumulate to $480.24. The bond will sell in 5 years at a price equal to $40 × PA(4.25%, 50) + $1,000 × PF(4.25%, 50), or $948.52, for a capital gain of $51.71. The total 5-year income is $51.71 + $480.24 = $531.95, for a 5-year return of $531.95/ $896.81 = .5932, or 59.32%. Based on this scenario, the 20-year 10% coupon bond offers a higher return for a 5-year horizon.

6. The trigger point is $10M/(1.12)^3 = \$7.118M$.

7. The fund has long-term liabilities and short-term assets. If interest rates fall, it will suffer, as the value of the liabilities will rise by more than the value of the assets. To offset this duration mismatch, the fund should swap an obligation to make variable rate payments in return for receipt of fixed cash flows. The swap gives the fund a long-term asset and a short-term liability.

V *Equities*

Chapter 17: Equity Valuation

1. a. Dividend yield = $2.15/50 = 4.3\%$
      Capital gains yield = $(59.77 - 50)/50 = 19.54\%$
      Total return = $4.3\% + 19.54\% = 23.84\%$
   b. $k = 6\% + 1.15 (14\% - 6\%) = 15.2\%$
   c. $V_0 = (\$2.15 + \$59.77)/1.152 = \$53.75$, which exceeds the market price. This would indicate a "buy" opportunity.

2. a. $E(D_1)/(k - g) = \$2.15/(.152 - .112) = \$53.75$
   b. $E(P_1) = P_0(1 + g) = \$53.75(1.112) = \$59.77$
   c. The expected capital gain equals $\$59.77 - \$53.75 = \$6.02$, for a percentage gain of 11.2\%. The dividend yield is $E(D_1)/P_0 = \$2.15/53.75 = 4\%$, for an HPR of $4\% + 11.2\% = 15.2\%$.

3. a. IBX plowback ratio is $1 - .3$ or $.7$, and its expected growth rate is $.7 \times 16\% = 11.2\%$ per year.
   b. $V_0 = D_1/(k - g) = .3 \times \$7.17/(.152 - .112) = \$53.75$
   c. i. $E(r) = E(D_1)/P_0 + g = \$2.15/50 + 11.2\% = 4.3\% + 11.2\% = 15.5\%$
      ii. $E(r) = \dfrac{E(D_1)}{P_0} + \dfrac{E(P_1) - P_0}{P_0} = \dfrac{2.15}{50} + \dfrac{59.77 - 50}{50}$
      $= 4.3\% + 19.54\% = 23.84\%$

4. a. ROE = 12\%
      $b = \$.50/\$2 = .25$
      $g = \text{ROE} \times b = 12\% \times .25 = 3\%$
      $P_0 = D_1/(k - g) = \$1.50/(.10 - .03) = \$21.43$
      $P_0/E(E_1) = \$21.43/\$2 = 10.71$
   b. If $b = .4$, then $.4 \times \$2 = \$.80$ would be reinvested and the remainder of earnings, or $1.20, paid as dividends.

      $$g = 12\% \times .4 = 4.8\%$$
      $$P_0 = E(D_1)/(k - g) = \$1.20/(.10 - .048) = \$23.08$$
      $$P_0/E(E_1) = \$23.08/\$2.00 = 11.54$$

5. a. The cash flow diagram is:

t	0	1	2	3	4 . . .
	.	.	.	.	.
D_t	\$2.00	\$2.20	\$2.42	\$2.662	\$2.76848 . . .

The estimated price at $t = 3$ is:

$$P_3 = \frac{D_4}{k - g} = \frac{\$2.76848}{.12 - .04} = \$34.606$$

The current price should be the PV of dividends in years 1 through 3 plus the PV of P_3.

$$P_0 = \frac{\$2.20}{1.12} + \frac{\$2.42}{1.12^2} + \frac{\$2.662 + 34.606}{1.12^3} = \$30.42$$

b. The expected price 1 year from now is the PV of dividends in years 2 and 3 plus the PV of P_3:

$$P_1 = \frac{\$2.42}{1.12} + \frac{\$2.662 + 34.606}{1.12^2} = \$31.87$$

c. The expected dividend yield is $\$2.20/\$30.42 = .0723$, or 7.23%. The expected rate of capital appreciation is $\dfrac{\$31.87 - 30.42}{\$30.42} = .0477$ or 4.77%. Note that they sum to k, or 12%.

6. a. $V_0 = \dfrac{D_0(1 + g_n)}{k - g_n} + \dfrac{D_0 H(g_a - g_n)}{k - g_n}$

$= \dfrac{2(1.06)}{.12 - .06} + \dfrac{2 \times 10(.35 - .06)}{.12 - .06}$

$= 35.333 + 96.667$

$= \$132$

b. $y = \dfrac{D_0}{P_0}[(1 + g_n) + H(g_a - g_n)] + g_n$

$= \dfrac{2}{100}[(1.06) + 10(.35 - .06)] + .06$

$= .1392$, or 13.92% per year

7. a. $P_0 = \dfrac{(1 - b)E(E_1)}{k - g} = \dfrac{.6 \times \$1}{.1 - .04} = \$10$

b. $\dfrac{E(D_1^*)}{P_0} = \dfrac{(1 - b)E(E_1^*)}{P_0} = \dfrac{(1 - .4) \times \$1}{\$10} = .06$, or 6% per year

The rate of price appreciation $= g^* = b^* \times \text{ROE}^* = 4\%$ per year

c. i. $g = (1.04)(1.06) - 1 = .1024$, or 10.24%;

ii. $\dfrac{E(D_1)}{P_0} = \dfrac{E(D_1^*)(1 + i)}{P_0} = .06 \times 1.06 = .0636$, or 6.36%

iii. ROE $= 16.6\%$

iv. $b = \dfrac{g}{\text{ROE}} = \dfrac{.1024}{.166} = .6169$

1. A debt/equity ratio of 1 implies that Mordett will have $50 million of debt and $50 million of equity. Interest expense will be .09 × $50 million, or $4.5 million per year. Mordett's net profits and ROE over the business cycle will therefore be

		Nodett		Mordett	
Scenario	**EBIT**	**Net profits**	**ROE**	**Net profits**[a]	**ROE**[b]
Bad year	$5M	$3 million	3%	$.3 million	.6%
Normal year	10M	6	6%	3.3	6.6%
Good year	15M	9	9%	6.3	12.6%

[a]Mordett's after-tax profits are given by: .6(EBIT − $4.5 million).
[b]Mordett's equity is only $50 million.

2.

Ratio Decomposition Analysis for Mordett Corporation

		(1) Net profit / Pretax profit	(2) Pretax profit / EBIT	(3) EBIT / Sales	(4) Sales / Assets	(5) Assets / Equity	(6) Combined leverage factor
	ROE			**(ROS)**	**(ATO)**		**(2) × (5)**
a. *Bad year*							
Nodett	.030	.6	1.000	.0625	.800	1.000	1.000
Somdett	.018	.6	.360	.0625	.800	1.667	.600
Mordett	.006	.6	.100	.0625	.800	2.000	.200
b. *Normal year*							
Nodett	.060	.6	1.000	.100	1.000	1.000	1.000
Somdett	.068	.6	.680	.100	1.000	1.667	1.134
Mordett	.066	.6	.550	.100	1.000	2.000	1.100
c. *Good year*							
Nodett	.090	.6	1.000	.125	1.200	1.000	1.000
Somdett	.118	.6	.787	.125	1.200	1.667	1.311
Mordett	.126	.6	.700	.125	1.200	2.000	1.400

3. GI's ROE in 19X3 was 3.03% computed as follows:

$$\text{ROE} = \frac{\$5,285}{.5(\$171,843 + 177,128)} = .303, \text{ or } 3.03\%$$

Its P/E ratio was $4 = \dfrac{\$21}{\$5.285}$

and its P/B ratio was $.12 = \dfrac{\$21}{\$177}$

Its earnings yield was 25% compared with an industry average of 12.5%.

Note that in our calculations the earnings yield will not equal ROE/(P/B) because we have computed ROE with average shareholders' equity in the denominator and P/B with end-of-year shareholders' equity in the denominator.

4.

Honeywell Ratio Analysis

		(1) Net profit / Pretax profit	(2) Pretax profit / EBIT	(3) EBIT / Sales	(4) Sales / Assets	(5) Assets / Equity	(6) Combined leverage factor	(7) ROA
Year	ROE			(ROS)	(ATO)		(2) × (5)	(3) × (4)
1987	11.4%	.616	.796	7.75%	1.375	2.175	1.731	10.65%
1984	10.2%	.636	.932	8.88%	1.311	1.474	1.374	11.65%

ROE went up despite a decline in operating margin and a decline in the tax burden ratio because of increased leverage and turnover. Note that ROA declined from 11.65% in 1984 to 10.65% in 1987.

5. LIFO accounting results in lower reported earnings than does FIFO. Fewer assets to depreciate results in lower reported earnings because there is less bias associated with the use of historic cost. More debt results in lower reported earnings because the inflation premium in the interest rate is treated as part of interest expense and not as repayment of principal. If ABC has the same reported earnings as XYZ despite these three sources of downward bias, its real earnings must be greater.

VI Derivative Assets: Options and Futures

Chapter 19: An Introduction to Options Markets

1. Before the split, profits would have been $100 \times (\$120 - \$110) = \$1,000$. After the split, profits are $1,000 \times (\$12 - \$11) = \$1,000$. Profits are unaffected.

2. a. Payoff to put writer $= \begin{cases} 0 & \text{if } S_T > X \\ -(X - S_T) & \text{if } S_T \leq X \end{cases}$

   b. Profit = Initial premium realized + Ultimate payoff

   $= \begin{cases} P & \text{if } S_T > X \\ P - (X - S_T) & \text{if } S_T \leq X \end{cases}$

c. Put written

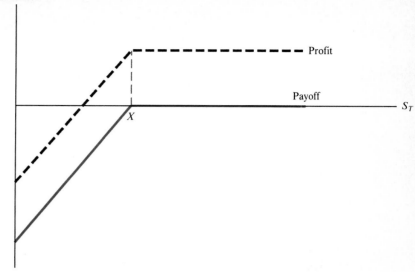

d. Put writers do well when the stock price increases and poorly when it falls.

3.

Payoff to a Strip

	$S_T \leq X$	$S_T > X$
2 Puts	$2(X - S_T)$	0
1 Call	0	$S_T - X$

Payoff and
profit

Strip

Slope = −2

Payoff

Slope = 1

Profit

S_T

X

Payoff to a Strap

	$S_T < X$	$S_T > X$
1 Put	$X - S_T$	0
2 Calls	0	$2(S_T - X)$

Strap

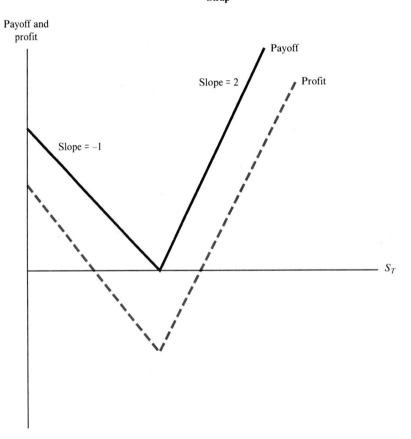

4. Yes. Consider the same scenarios as for the call:

Stock price	$10	$20	$30	$40	$50
Put payoff	$20	$10	$ 0	$ 0	$ 0

Stock price	$20	$25	$30	$35	$40
Put payoff	$10	$ 5	$ 0	$ 0	$ 0

The low volatility scenario yields a lower expected payoff.

5. Puts should be more valuable for higher dividend policies. These policies reduce future stock prices, which will increase the expected payout from the put.

6. Implied volatility exceeds .5. Given a standard deviation of .5, the option value is $13.70. A higher volatility is needed to justify the actual $15 price.

7. The depositor's implicit cost per dollar invested is now only ($.03 − $.005) per 6-month period. Calls cost $10/$250 = $.04 per dollar invested in the index. The multipler falls to .025/.04 = .625.

Chapter 20: Options Markets: A Closer Look

1. The parity relationship assumes that all options are held until expiration and that there are no cash flows until expiration. These assumptions are valid only in the special case of European options on nondividend-paying stocks. If the stock pays no dividends, the American and European calls are equally valuable, whereas the American put is worth more than the European put. Therefore, although the parity theorem for European options states that

$$P = C + S_0 - PV(X)$$

in fact, P will be *greater* than this value if the put is American.

2. A $1 increase in stock price is a percentage increase of $1/122 = .82\%$. The put option will fall by $(.4 \times \$1) = \$.40$, a percentage decrease of $\$.40/\$4 = 10\%$. Elasticity is $-10/.82 = -12.2$.

3. The covered call strategy would consist of a straight bond with a call written on the bond. The value of the strategy at option expiration as a function of the value of the straight bond is given in the following figure, which is virtually identical to Figure 20.7.

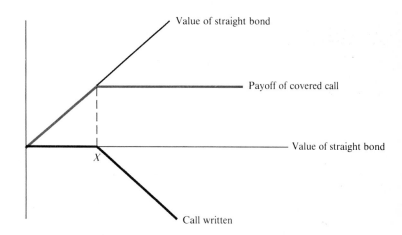

4. The call option is worth less as call protection is expanded. Therefore the coupon rate need not be as high.

5. Lower. Investors will accept a lower coupon rate in return for the conversion option.

6. Higher. For deep out-of-the-money options, an increase in the stock price still leaves the option unlikely to be exercised. Its value increases only fractionally.

For deep in-the-money options, exercise is likely, and option holders benefit by a full dollar for each dollar increase in the stock, as though they already own the stock.

Chapter 21—Futures and Forward Markets: General Principles

1.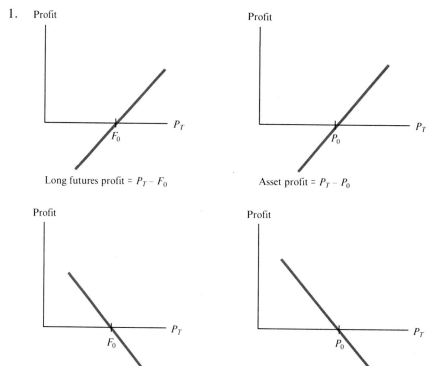

   Long futures profit = $P_T - F_0$

   Asset profit = $P_T - P_0$

   Short futures profit = $F_0 - P_T$

   Short sale profit = $P_0 - P_T$

2. The futures price is the agreed-upon price for deferred delivery of the asset. If that price is fair, then the *value* of the agreement ought to be zero; that is, the contract will be a zero-NPV agreement for each trader.

3. Because long positions equal short positions, futures trading *must* entail a "canceling out" of bets on the asset. Moreover, no cash is transacted at the inception of futures trading. Thus, there should be minimal impact on the spot market for the asset, and futures trading should not be expected to reduce capital available for other uses.

4. The clearinghouse has a zero net position in all contracts. Its long and short positions are offsetting, so that net cash flow from marking to market must be zero.

5. Zero. Zero.

6. The risk would be that aluminum and bauxite prices do not move perfectly together. Thus basis risk involving the spread between the futures price and bauxite

spot prices could persist even if the aluminum futures price were set perfectly relative to aluminum itself.

7.

Action	Initial CF	Time-T CF
Lend S_0	$-S_0$	$+S_0(1 + r_f)^T$
Short stock	S_0	$-S_T$
Long futures	0	$S_T - F_0$
	0	$S_0(1 + r_f)^T - F_0$

8. It must have zero beta. If the futures price is an unbiased estimator, then we infer that it has a zero risk premium, which means that beta must be zero.

Chapter 22 — Futures Markets: A Closer Look

1. As the payoffs to the two strategies are identical, so should be the costs of establishing them. The synthetic stock strategy costs $F_0/(1 + r_f)^T$ to establish, this being the present value of the futures price. The stock index purchased directly costs S_0. Therefore we conclude that $S_0 = F_0/(1 + r_f)^T$, or, $F_0 = S_0(1 + r_f)^T$, which is the parity relationship.

2. If the futures price is above the parity level, investors would sell futures and buy stocks. Short selling would not be necessary. Therefore the top of the no-arbitrage band would be unaffected by the use of the proceeds. If the futures price is too low, investors would want to short sell stocks and buy futures. Now the costs of short selling are important. If proceeds from the short sale become available, short selling becomes less costly and the bottom of the band will move up.

3. According to interest rate parity, F_0 should be $1.817. Since the futures price is too high, we should reverse the arbitrage strategy just considered.

	CF Now ($)	CF in 1 Year
1. Borrow $1.80 in the U.S. Convert to one pound.	+1.80	−1.80(1.06)
2. Lend the one pound in the U.K.	−1.80	1.05 E_1
3. Enter a contract to sell 1.05 pounds at a futures price of 1.83.	0	$(1.05)(1.83 - E_1)$
TOTAL	0	.0135

4. Stocks offer a total return (capital gain plus dividends) large enough to compensate investors for the time value of the money tied up in the stock. Wheat prices do not necessarily increase over time. In fact, across a harvest, wheat prices will fall. The returns necessary to make storage economically attractive are lacking.

5. If systematic risk were higher, the appropriate discount rate, k, would increase. Referring to equation 22.5, we conclude that F_0 would fall. Intuitively, the claim to 1 pound of orange juice is worth less today if its expected price is unchanged, but the risk associated with the value of the claim increases. Therefore, the amount investors are willing to pay today for future delivery is lower.

Chapter 23—The Theory of Active Portfolio Management

1. We show the answer for the annual compounded rate of return for each strategy and leave you to compute the monthly rate.

Beginning-of-period fund:

$$F_0 = \$1,000$$

End-of-period fund for each strategy:

$$F_1 = \begin{cases} 3{,}600 & \text{Strategy} = \text{Bills only} \\ 67{,}500 & \text{Strategy} = \text{Market only} \\ 5{,}360{,}000{,}000 & \text{Strategy} = \text{Perfect timing} \end{cases}$$

Number of periods: $N = 52$ years
Annual compounded rate:

$$[1 + r_A]^N = \frac{F_1}{F_0}$$

$$r_A = \left(\frac{F_1}{F_0}\right)^{1/N} - 1$$

$$r_A = \begin{cases} 2.49\% & \text{Strategy} = \text{Bills only} \\ 8.44\% & \text{Strategy} = \text{Market only} \\ 34.71\% & \text{Strategy} = \text{Perfect timing} \end{cases}$$

2. The timer will guess bear or bull markets completely randomly. One half of all bull markets will be preceded by a correct forecast, and similarly for bear markets. Hence, $P_1 + P_2 - 1 = \frac{1}{2} + \frac{1}{2} - 1 = 0$.

3. a. When short positions are prohibited, the analysis is identical except that negative alpha stocks are dropped from the list. In that case the sum of the ratios of alpha to residual variance for the remaining two stocks is .7895. This leads to the new composition of the active portfolio:

$$x_1 = .3457/.7895 = .4379$$
$$x_2 = .4438/.7895 = .5621$$

The alpha, beta, and residual standard deviation of the active portfolio are now:

$$\alpha_A = .4379 \times .07 + .5621 \times .03 = .0475$$
$$\beta_A = .4379 \times 1.6 + .5621 \times .5 = .9817$$
$$\sigma(e_A) = [.4379^2 \times .45^2 + .5621^2 \times .26^2]^{1/2} = .2453$$

The cost of the short sale restriction is already apparent. The alpha has shrunk from 20.56% to 4.75%, while the reduction in the residual risk is more moderate, from 82.62% to 24.53%. In fact, a negative alpha stock is potentially more attractive than a positive alpha one: since most stocks are positively correlated, the negative position that is required for the negative alpha stock creates a better diversified active portfolio.

The optimal allocation of the new active portfolio is:

$$w_0 = \frac{.0475/.6019}{.08/.04} = .3946$$

$$w^* = \frac{.3946}{1 + (1 - .9817) \times .3946} = .3918$$

Here, too, the beta correction is essentially irrelevant because the portfolio beta is so close to 1.0.

Finally, the performance of the overall risky portfolio is estimated at

$$S_P^2 = .16 + \left[\frac{.0475}{.2453}\right]^2 = .1975; \; S_P = .44$$

It is clear that in this we have lost about half of the original improvement in the Sharpe measure. Note, however, that this is an artifact of the small coverage of the security analysis division. When more stocks are covered, then a good number of positive alpha stocks will keep the residual risk of the active portfolio low. This is the key to extracting large gains from the active strategy.

b. When the forecast for the market index portfolio is more optimistic, the position in the active portfolio will be smaller and the contribution of the active portfolio to the Sharpe measure of the risky portfolio will be of a smaller magnitude. In the original example the allocation to the active portfolio would be

$$w_0 = \frac{.2056/.6826}{.12/.04} = .1004$$

$$w^* = \frac{.1004}{1 + (1 - .9519) \times .1004} = .0999$$

Although the Sharpe measure of the market is now better, the improvement derived from security analysis is smaller:

$$S_P^2 = \left(\frac{.12}{.20}\right)^2 + \left(\frac{.2056}{.8262}\right)^2 = .4219$$

$$S_P = .65; \; S_M = .60$$

Chapter 24—Portfolio Performance Evaluation

1.	Time	Action	Cash Flow
	0	Buy two shares	−40
	1	Collect dividends; then sell one of the shares	4 + 22
	2	Collect dividend on remaining share, then sell it	2 + 19

a. Dollar-weighted return:

$$-40 + \frac{26}{1 + r} + \frac{21}{(1 + r)^2} = 0$$

$$r = .1191 = 11.91\%$$

b. Time-weighted return:

The rates of return on the stock in the 2 years were

$$r_1 = \frac{2 + (22 - 20)}{20} = .20$$

$$r_2 = \frac{2 + (19 - 22)}{22} = -.045$$

$$(r_1 + r_2)/2 = .077, \text{ or } 7.7\%$$

2. a. $E(r_A) = [.15 + (-.05)]/2 = .05$

$E(r_G) = [(1.15)(.95)]^{\frac{1}{2}} - 1 = .045$

b. The expected stock price is $(115 + 95)/2 = 105$

c. The expected rate of return on the stock is 5%, equal to r_A.

3. Sharpe: $(\bar{r} - \bar{r}_f)/\sigma$

$$S_P = (.35 - .06)/.42 = .69$$

$$S_M = (.28 - .06)/.30 = .733$$

Alpha: $\bar{r} - [r_f + \beta(\bar{r}_M - \bar{r}_f)]$

$$\alpha_P = .35 - [.06 + 1.2(.28 - .06)] = .026$$

$$\alpha_M = 0$$

Treynor: $(\bar{r} - \bar{r}_f)/\beta$

$$T_P = (.35 - .06)/1.2 = .242$$

$$T_M = (.28 - .06)/1.0 = .22$$

Appraisal ratio: $\alpha/\sigma(e)$

$$A_P = .026/.18 = .144$$

$$A_M = 0$$

4. The t-statistic on α is $.2/2 = .1$. The probability that a manager with a true alpha of zero could obtain a sample period alpha with a t-statistic of .1 or better by pure luck can be calculated approximately from a table of the normal distribution. The probability is 46%.

Chapter 25—International and Extended Diversification

1. The graph would asymptote to a lower level, as shown in the following figure, reflecting the improved opportunities for diversification. However, there still would remain a positive level of nondiversifiable risk.

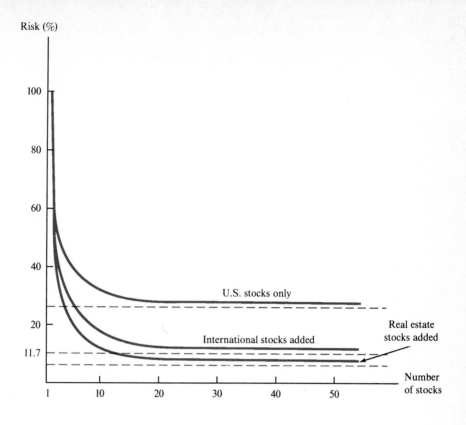

Risk (%)

U.S. stocks only

Real estate
stocks added

International stocks added

11.7

Number
of stocks

2. $1 + r(US) = [(1 + r_f(UK)] \times (E_1/E_0)$
  a. $1 + r(US) = 1.1 \times 1.0 = 1.10$ $r(US) = 10\%$
  b. $1 + r(US) = 1.1 \times 1.1 = 1.21$ $r(US) = 21\%$

3. You must sell forward the number of pounds that you will end up with at the end of the year. However, this value cannot be known with certainty unless the rate of return of the pound-denominated investment is known.
  a. $10,000 \times 1.20 = 12,000$ pounds
  b. $10,000 \times 1.30 = 13,000$ pounds

4. *Country selection:*

$$(.40 \times .10) + (.20 \times .05) + (.40 \times .15) = .11$$

This is a loss of .015 (1.5%) relative to the EAFE passive benchmark.
Currency selection:

$$(.40 \times 1.10) + (.20 \times .9) + (.40 \times 1.30) = 1.14$$

This is a loss of 6% relative to the EAFE benchmark.

1. The first step is to obtain the ability parameter of the analyst by regressing the forecasts on subsequent realizations. The square of the correlation coefficient that is implied by the forecaster's record is $\rho^2 = .32$. The forecast itself implies

$$s_M = E(r_M) - \pi_M = 15 - 9 = 6\%$$

and hence the adjusted forecast is

$$s_M^* = \rho_M^2 s_M = .32 \times 6 = 1.92\%$$

The adjusted forecast for the market excess return is

$$r_M^* = \pi_M + s_M^* = 9 + 1.92 = 10.92\%$$

2. Applying the constant-dividend growth model to these data, we calculate the fair price for the stock at

$$P_0^* = \frac{D_1}{r_\beta - g_Q} = \frac{.60}{.045 - .015} = \$20.00$$

The stock is currently mispriced by $P_0^* - P_0 = 20 - 18.50 = \$1.50$. This dollar difference will translate into an abnormal return according to how fast the stock price will approach its true value.

Consider two examples. In one the analyst predicts that the difference will be fully amortized within half a year, in the other over an amortization period of 3 years. With a half-year amortization, the stock will sell at its fair price when the forthcoming dividend, D_3, is forecast to reach the following level:

$$D_3 = D_1(1 + g_Q)^2 = .6 \times 1.015^2 = \$.618$$

Therefore the fair stock price (which will equal the actual stock price) two quarters hence will be

$$P_2 = \frac{D_3}{r_\beta - g_Q} = \frac{.618}{.045 - .015} = \$20.60$$

The cash flows from purchasing the stock under this assumption are shown in the following figure

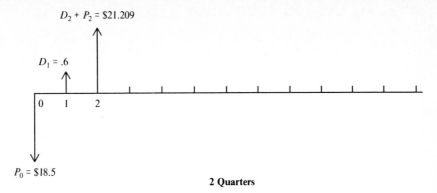

2 Quarters

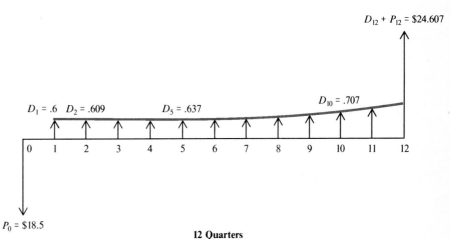

12 Quarters

The internal rate of return (IRR) per quarter of this investment "project" will solve the following equation:

$$P_0 = 18.5 = \frac{D_1}{1 + IRR_Q} + \frac{D_2 + P_2}{(1 + IRR_Q)^2}$$

$$= \frac{6}{1 + IRR_Q} + \frac{.609 + 20.60}{(1 + IRR_Q)^2}$$

with the solution, $IRR_Q = 8.71\%$. Subtracting the required rate of return of 4.5%, we get a hefty alpha value of 4.21%, implying an annual abnormal return of 18%.

The alpha value is so high because we assumed a fast rate of amortization. The market is expected to catch on to its error within 6 months. Of course, if the stock price were to jump to its current fair value of $20 the instant we bought it for $18.50, the IRR (as well as the alpha value) of the investment "project" would be infinite. But one can hardly expect this to happen. It may take a few quarters for investors to recognize that they have misforecast the dividend growth rate.

If it were to take 3 years (12 quarters) for the market to catch on, then at that time the consensus forecast will be that the next dividend is

$$D_{13} = D_1(1 + g_Q)^{12} = .6 \times 1.015^{12} = \$.717$$

and the price (fair and actual) at that time would be

$$P_{12} = \frac{D_{13}}{r_\beta - g_Q} = \frac{.717}{.045 - .015} = \$23.90$$

The cash flow of the investment "project" under this assumption is shown in the figure. The quarterly IRR in this case is "only" 5.3%, implying an annual abnormal return of 3.2%. At the minimum, it will take forever for the market to realize its mistake. In this case we obtain the alpha value by simply computing the actual rate of return from holding the stock forever. This is done by inverting the constant dividend growth model formula to compute

$$E(r) = \frac{D_1}{P_0} + g = \frac{.6}{18.5} + .015 = 4.74\%$$

and obtaining alpha by

$$\alpha = E(r) - r_\beta = .0474 - .045 = .0024 = .24\%$$

resulting in a modest annual alpha value of 24 basis points.

This extreme case is no more realistic than the infinite rate case. Because if dividends grow at 6% forever, why should not other analysts adjust *their* forecasts, currently implicit in stock XYZ's price at

$$g_\beta = r_\beta - \frac{D_1}{P_0} = .045 - \frac{.6}{18.5} = .0126 = 1.26\%$$

rather than our analyst's 1.5%. The effect of the length of the amortization period of a mispriced security on its alpha value is shown in the following figure. The graph in this figure shows that the alpha value declines at a decreasing rate as the amortization time increases. Obviously, the accuracy of the length of the amortization period, whenever it is relatively short, is as important as the forecast of the dollar mispricing of the stock.

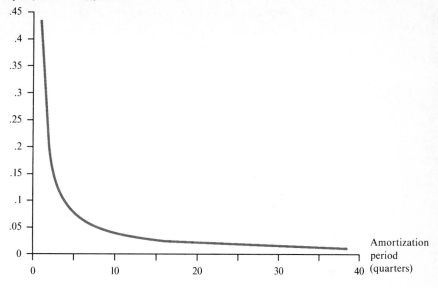

Alpha (annual rate %)

Amortization period (quarters)

3. We need to generate the track record of David's alpha forecasts (s). To this end we compute David's projected quarterly rates of return (IRR) and subtract from them the required rate of return implied by the market forecasts and the stock beta. For the first period we have

$$\text{IRR} = \frac{\text{Projected price}}{\text{Current price}} - 1 = \frac{7}{5.375} - 1 = 30.23\%$$

$$r_\beta = r_f + \beta_Z(\pi_M + s_M^*) = 1.75 + 1.65(-7.5 - 1.75) = -13.51\%$$

$$s_Z = \text{IRR} - r_\beta = 30.23 - (-13.51) = 43.74\%$$

To match David's forecasts we need the ex-post residuals. First, we compute the actual rate of return from holding the stock. The residual is then obtained by subtracting the expected rate on the stock, given what the actual rate on the market was (just as the abnormal return would be calculated in an event study). For the first period we have

$$r_Z = \frac{\text{End price}}{\text{Current price}} - 1 = \frac{6.50}{5.375} - 1 = 20.93\%$$

$$e_Z = r_Z - [r_f + \beta_Z(r_M - r_f)] = 20.93 - [1.75 + 1.65(-.15 - 1.75)]$$
$$= 22.32\%$$

Computing these statistics for the rest of David's forecasting history produces the following record:

Period	IRR	Residual forecast (s)	Actual returns (r)	Actual residual (e)
1	30.23	43.74	20.93	22.32
2	38.46	60.00	17.31	23.09
3	-8.20	-19.31	-11.48	-19.26
4	27.78	20.86	85.19	11.34

The square of the correlation coefficient in the regression of David's forecasts on the subsequent realization is $\rho^2 = .19$. His current forecast can now be analyzed:

$$IRR = \frac{15}{12.50} - 1 = 20\%$$

$$r_\beta = 1.5 + 1.65(5 - 1.5) = 7.275\%$$

$$s_Z = 20 - 7.275 = 12.725\%$$

$$s_Z^* = \rho_Z^2 s_Z = .19 \times 12.725 = 2.33\%$$

The assumed estimate for the residual risk of Z is $\sigma(e_Z) = 35\%$. Using the current ability parameter we have $\sigma_\rho(e_Z) = [(1 - \rho^2)\sigma^2(e_Z)]^{1/2} = [(1 - .19).35^2]^{1/2} = 31.5\%$.

4. From question 1 the macro forecast ability parameter is $\rho^2 = .32$. The data also suggest that the annual standard deviation is approximately 20%, and hence the variance of the quarterly adjusted macro forecast is

$$\sigma_\rho^2(e_M) = (1 - \rho_M^2)\sigma^2(e_M) = (1 - .32).20^2/4 = .0068$$

Equating Z with the active portfolio, A, the forecast data can be summarized by

$$s_A^* = 2.33\%; \quad \sigma_\rho(e_A) = 31.50\%; \quad \beta_A = 1.65$$

$$\pi_M + s_M^* = 3.5\%; \quad \sigma_\rho(e_M) = 8.25\%$$

With this data, the optimal position in $A = Z$ and the market index portfolio is

$$w_0 = \frac{s_A^*/\sigma_\rho^2(e_A)}{(\pi_M + s_M^*)/\sigma_\rho^2(e_M)} = \frac{.0233/.09925}{.035/.0068} = .0456$$

$$w = \frac{w_0}{1 + (1 - \beta_A)w_0} = \frac{.0456}{1 + (1 - 1.65).0456} = .047$$

The results tell us that over the next quarter the macro forecasters are relatively more optimistic and more reliable than is David. The resultant optimal risky portfolio is only about 4.7% in Z; the balance will be invested in the market index.

5. Investing 4.7% of our funds in stock Z and 95.3% in the market index portfolio results in a risky portfolio, P, with a beta, alpha, and rate of return forecast for the next quarter of:

$$\beta_P = [1 + w(\beta_A - 1)] = 1 + .047 \times .65 = 1.031$$

$$E(r_P) - r_f = ws_A^* + \beta_P(\pi_M + s_M^*) = .047 \times .0233 + 1.031 \times .035 = .0372$$

$$\sigma_P = [w^2\sigma_\rho(e_A) + \beta_P^2\sigma_\rho^2(e_M)]^{\frac{1}{2}}$$

$$= [.047^2 \times .315^2 + 1.031^2 \times .0825^2]^{\frac{1}{2}} = .0863$$

With $A = 2.0$ the complete portfolio invests in portfolio P

$$w_P = .0372/(2 \times .0863^2) = 2.5$$

which means that management will invest in a risky portfolio as much as the prospectus and the prudent man allows. Assuming 100% in the risky portfolio, its alpha is then

$$\alpha_P = .047 \times 2.33 = .11\% \text{ (or 11 basis points)}$$

and its quarterly Sharpe measure is

$$S_P = .0372/.0863 = .431$$

6. a. *Evaluation at the individual forecaster level*
  i. *Macro forecaster*
  Regressing the forecasts, s_M, on the realizations, e_M, we find

$$s_M = a + be_M + \epsilon_M = .52 + .97e_M + \epsilon_M$$

  The coefficient a is not significantly different from zero and b is not significantly different from 1. There is no need to correct the forecast for bias.
  The correlation coefficient between the forecast and realization is .57. This amounts to outstanding performance. The computation of the value of the accuracy of the macro forecast is beyond our scope here.
  ii. *Micro forecaster*
  The regression of forecasts on realizations yields

$$s_Z = 12.1 + .47e_Z + \epsilon_Z$$

The data suggests the possibility of some bias. Correcting for this type of bias is a technical problem. The correlation coefficient between forecast and realization is .43, which is very valuable.
  In this example stock Z makes up the entire active portfolio; hence the discussion of the contribution of the micro forecaster to the active portfolio is identical to that of the contribution of the active portfolio to the complete portfolio.
  b. *Evaluation at the active portfolio level*
  The decomposition of the Sharpe measure of the risky portfolio with our data:

$$S_P^2 = \left[\frac{\pi_M + s_M^*}{\sigma_\rho(e_M)}\right]^2 + \left[\frac{s_A^*}{\sigma_\rho(e_A)}\right]^2 = \left[\frac{3.5}{8.25}\right]^2 + \left[\frac{2.33}{31.50}\right]^2$$

$$= .18 + .0055 = .1855$$

This contribution raises the Sharpe measure for the period from .424 to .431. It should be noted that this contribution (which is not small) is not larger because the active portfolio is limited to one security.

  c. *Evaluation at the complete portfolio level*

    Since there are no effective constraints on the complete portfolio and (evaluated by the Sharpe measure) there is no active safe asset management, the performance of the complete portfolio is identical to that of the active portfolio.

VIII   *Players and Strategies*

Chapter 27—Principles of Portfolio Management

1. The new estimates are as follows:

State of Economy	Probability	Holding Period Return		
		Stocks	Bonds	Cash
Boom with low inflation	.05	74%	4%	6%
Boom with high inflation	.2	20%	−10%	6%
Normal growth	.5	14%	9%	6%
Recession with low inflation	.2	0	35%	6%
Recession with high inflation	.05	−30%	0	6%
Expected return	$E(r)$	13.2%	9.7%	6%
Standard deviation	σ	17.96%	14.57%	0

    Correlation coefficient between stocks and bonds is −.3449.

2. To find the composition of the optimal combination of stocks and bonds to be combined with cash we use the following formula:

$$w^* = \frac{[E(r_s) - r_f]\sigma_b^2 - [E(r_b) - r_f]\text{Cov}(r_b, r_s)}{[E(r_s) - r_f]\sigma_b^2 + [E(r_b) - r_f]\sigma_s^2 - [E(r_s) - r_f + E(r_b) - r_f]\text{Cov}(r_b, r_s)}$$

where w^* is the proportion of stocks in portfolio O^* and $1 - w^*$ is the proportion of bonds. Substituting in the formula we get

$$w^* = \frac{(13.2 - 6)212.2849 - (9.7 - 6)(90.2525)}{7.2 \times 212.2849 + 3.7 \times 322.5616 + (7.2 + 3.7)90.2525}$$

$$= \frac{1194.5}{1738.2} = .687$$

So the proportion of stocks in the O^* portfolio changes from 45% to 69%.

Chapter 28—Individual Investors and Pension Funds

1. The relevant formula is

$$C \sum_{t=1}^{55} \frac{1}{1.03^t} = 25,000 \sum_{t=1}^{35} \frac{1}{1.03^t} + 8,000 \sum_{t=36}^{55} \frac{1}{1.03^t}$$

$$26.7744C = 25,000 \times 21.4872 + 8,000 \times 5.2873 = 537,180.50 + 42,297.66$$

$$C = \frac{577,478.16}{26.7744} = \$21,643 \text{ per year}$$

Saving is: $S = 25,000 - C = 25,000 - 21,643 = \$3,357$ per year

2. If Eloise keeps her present asset allocation, she will have the following amounts to spend after taxes 5 years from now:

Tax-qualified account

Bonds:	$\$50,000 (1.1)^5 \times .72$	$= \$ 57,978.36$
Stocks:	$\$50,000 (1.15)^5 \times .72$	$= \$ 72,408.86$
	Subtotal	**$130,387.22**

Nonretirement account

Bonds:	$\$50,000 (1.072)^5$	$= \$ 70,785.44$
Stocks:	$\$50,000 (1.15)^5 - .28 \times [50,000(1.15)^5 - 50,000]$	$= \$ 86,408.86$
	Subtotal	**$157,194.30**
	TOTAL	**$287,581.52**

If Eloise shifts all of the bonds into the retirement account and all of the stock into the nonretirement account she will have the following amounts to spend after taxes 5 years from now:

Tax-qualified account:

Bonds:	$\$100,000 (1.1)^5 \times .72$	$= \$115,957$

Nonretirement account:

Stocks:	$\$100,000 (1.15)^5 - .28[100,000(1.15)^5 - 100,000]$	$= \$172,817.72$
	TOTAL	$= \mathbf{\$288,774.72}$

Her spending budget will increase by $1,193.20.

3. $B_0 \times \text{PA}(4\%, 5 \text{ years}) = 100,000$ implies that $B_0 = \$22,462.71$.

t	R_t	B_t	A_t
0			$100,000.00
1	4%	$22,462.71	$ 81,537.29
2	10%	$23,758.64	$ 65,923.38
3	−8%	$21,017.26	$ 39,640.53
4	25%	$25,261.12	$ 24,289.54
5	0	$24,289.54	0

4. He has accrued an annuity of $.01 \times 15 \times 15,000 = \$2,250$ per year for 15 years, starting in 25 years. The PV of this annuity is $2,812.13. PV = 2,250 PA (8%, 15) × PF (8%, 25).

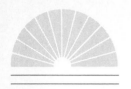

Glossary

Abnormal return. Return on a stock beyond what would be predicted by market movements alone. Cumulative abnormal return (CAR) is the total abnormal return for the period surrounding an announcement or the release of information.

Accounting earnings. Earnings of a firm as reported on its income statement.

Acid test ratio. See Quick ratio.

Active management. Attempts to achieve portfolio returns more than commensurate with risk, either by forecasting broad market trends or by identifying particular mispriced sectors of a market or securities in a market.

Active portfolio. In the context of the Treynor-Black model, the portfolio formed by mixing analyzed stocks of perceived non-zero alpha values. This portfolio is ultimately mixed with the passive market index portfolio.

Adjustable-rate mortgage. A mortgage whose interest rate varies according to some specified measure of the current market interest rate.

Adjusted forecast. A (micro or macro) forecast that has been adjusted for the imprecision of the forecast.

Agency problem. Conflicts of interest among stockholders, bondholders, and managers.

Alpha. The abnormal rate of return on a security in excess of what would be predicted by an equilibrium model like the CAPM or APT.

American option, European option. An American option can be exercised before and up to its expiration date. Compare with a *European option,* which can be exercised only on the expiration date.

Announcement date. Date on which particular news concerning a given company is announced to the public. Used in *event studies,* which researchers use to evaluate the economic impact of events of interest.

Appraisal ratio. The signal-to-noise ratio of an analyst's forecasts. The ratio of alpha to residual standard deviation.

Arbitrage. A zero-risk, zero-net investment strategy that still generates profits.

Arbitrage pricing theory. An asset pricing theory that is derived from a factor model, using diversification and arbitrage arguments. The theory describes the relationship between expected returns on securities, given that there are no opportunities to create wealth through risk-free arbitrage investments.

Asked price. The price at which a dealer will sell a security.

A88

Asset allocation decision. Choosing among broad asset classes such as stocks vs. bonds.

Asset turnover (ATO). The annual sales generated by each dollar of assets (sales/assets).

Auction market. A market where all traders in a good meet at one place to buy or sell an asset. The NYSE is an example.

Average collection period, or days' receivables. The ratio of accounts receivable to sales, or the total amount of credit extended per dollar of daily sales (average AR/sales × 365).

Bank discount yield. An annualized interest rate assuming simple interest, a 360-day year, and using the face value of the security rather than purchase price to compute return per dollar invested.

Banker's acceptance. A money market asset consisting of an order to a bank by a customer to pay a sum of money at a future date.

Basis. The difference between the futures price and the spot price.

Basis risk. Risk attributable to uncertain movements in the spread between a futures price and a spot price.

Benchmark error. Use of an inappropriate proxy for the true market portfolio.

Beta. The measure of the systematic risk of a security. The tendency of a security's returns to respond to swings in the broad market.

Bid price. The price at which a dealer is willing to purchase a security.

Bid-asked spread. The difference between a dealer's bid and asked price.

Binomial model. An option valuation model predicated on the assumption that stock prices can move to only two values over any short time period.

Black-Scholes formula. An equation to value a call option that uses the stock price, the exercise price, the risk-free interest rate, the time to maturity, and the standard deviation of the stock return.

Block house. Brokerage firms that help to find potential buyers or sellers of large block trades.

Block sale. A transaction of more than 10,000 shares of stock.

Block transactions. Large transactions in which at least 10,000 shares of stock are bought or sold. Brokers or "block houses" often search directly for other large traders rather than bringing the trade to the stock exchange.

Bogey. The return an investment manager is compared to for performance evaluation.

Bond. A security issued by a borrower that obligates the issuer to make specified payments to the holder over a specific period. A *coupon bond* obligates the issuer to make interest payments called coupon payments over the life of the bond, then to repay the *principal* at maturity.

Bond equivalent yield. Bond yield calculated on an annual percentage rate method. Differs from effective annual yield.

Book value. An accounting measure describing the net worth of common equity according to a firm's balance sheet.

Brokered market. A market where an intermediary (a broker) offers search services to buyers and sellers.

Bull CD, bear CD. A *bull CD* pays its holder a specified percentage of the increase in return on a specified market index while guaranteeing a minimum rate of return. A *bear CD* pays the holder a fraction of any fall in a given market index.

Bullish, bearish. Words used to describe investor attitudes. *Bullish* means optimistic; *bearish* means pessimistic. Also used in bull market and bear market.

Bundling, Unbundling. A trend allowing creation of securities either by combining primitive and derivative securities into one composite hybrid or by separating returns on an asset into classes.

Call option. The right to buy an asset at a specified exercise price on or before a specified expiration date.

Call protection. An initial period during which a callable bond may not be called.

Callable bond. A bond that the issuer may repurchase at a given price in some specified period.

Capital allocation line (CAL). A graph showing all feasible risk-return combinations of a risky and risk-free asset.

Capital gains. The amount by which the sale price of a security exceeds the purchase price.

Capital market line (CML). A capital allocation line provided by the market index portfolio.

Capital markets. Includes longer-term, relatively riskier securities.

Cash delivery. The provision of some futures contracts that requires not delivery of the underlying assets (as in agricultural futures) but settlement according to the cash value of the asset.

Cash equivalents. Short-term money-market securities.

Cash flow matching. A form of immunization, matching cash flows from a bond with an obligation.

Cash/bond selection. Asset allocation in which the choice is between short-term cash equivalents and longer-term bonds.

Certainty equivalent. The certain return providing the same utility as a risky portfolio.

Certificate of deposit. A bank time deposit.

Clearinghouse. Established by exchanges to facilitate transfer of securities resulting from trades. For options and futures contracts, the clearinghouse may interpose itself as a middleman between two traders.

Closed-end (mutual) fund. A fund whose shares are traded through brokers at market prices; the fund will not redeem shares at their net asset value. The market price of the fund can differ from the net asset value.

Collateral. A specific asset pledged against possible default on a bond. *Mortgage* bonds are backed by claims on property. *Collateral trust bonds* are backed by claims on other securities. *Equipment obligation bonds* are backed by claims on equipment.

Collateralized mortgage obligation (CMO). A mortgage pass-through security that partitions cash flows from underlying mortgages into successive maturity groups, called *tranches,* that receive principal payments according to different maturities.

Commercial paper. Short-term unsecured debt issued by large corporations.

Commission broker. A broker on the floor of the exchange who executes orders for other members.

Common stock. Equities, or equity securities, issued as ownership shares in a publicly held corporation. Shareholders have voting rights and may receive dividends based on their proportionate ownership.

Comparison universe. The collection of money managers of similar investment style used for assessing relative performance of a portfolio manager.

Complete portfolio. The entire portfolio, including risky and risk-free assets.

Constant growth model. A form of the dividend discount model that assumes dividends will grow at a constant rate.

Contango theory. Holds that the futures price must exceed the expected future spot price.

Contingent claim. Claim whose value is directly dependent on or is contingent on the value of some underlying assets.

Contingent immunization. A mixed passive-active strategy that immunizes a portfolio if necessary to guarantee a minimum acceptable return but otherwise allows active management.

Convergence property. The convergence of futures prices and spot prices at the maturity of the futures contract.

Convertible bond. A bond with an option allowing the bondholder to exchange the bond for a specified number of shares of common stock in the firm. A *conversion ratio* specifies the number of shares. The *market conversion price* is the current value of the shares for which the bond may be exchanged. The *conversion premium* is the excess of the bond's value over the conversion price.

Corporate bonds. Long-term debt issued by private corporations typically paying semiannual coupons and returning the face value of the bond at maturity.

Correlation coefficient. A statistic that scales the covariance to a value between minus one (perfect negative correlation) and plus one (perfect positive correlation).

Cost-of-carry relationship. See spot-futures parity theorem.

Country selection. A type of active international management that measures the contribution to performance attributable to investing in the better-performing stock markets of the world.

Coupon rate. A bond's interest payments per dollar of par value.

Covariance. A measure of the degree to which returns on two risky assets move in tandem. A positive covariance means that asset returns move together. A negative covariance means they vary inversely.

Covered call. A combination of selling a call on a stock together with buying the stock.

Covered interest arbitrage relationship. See interest-rate parity theorem.

Credit enhancement. Purchase of the financial guarantee of a large insurance company to raise funds.

Cross hedge. Hedging a position in one asset using futures on another commodity.

Cumulative abnormal return. See abnormal returns.

Currency selection. Asset allocation in which the investor chooses among investments denominated in different currencies.

Current ratio. A ratio representing the ability of the firm to pay off its current liabilities by liquidating current assets (current assets/current liabilities).

Current yield. A bond's annual coupon payment divided by its price. Differs from yield to maturity.

Day order. A buy order or a sell order expiring at the close of the trading day.

Day's receivables. See average collection period.

Dealer market. A market where traders specializing in particular commodities buy and sell assets for their own accounts. The OTC market is an example.

Debenture or unsecured bond. A bond not backed by specific collateral.

Dedication strategy. Refers to multiperiod cash flow matching.

Default premium. A differential in promised yield that compensates the investor for the risk inherent in purchasing a corporate bond that entails some risk of default.

Deferred annuities. Tax-advantaged life insurance product. Deferred annuities offer deferral of taxes with the option of withdrawing one's funds in the form of a life annuity.

Defined benefit plans. Pension plans in which retirement benefits are set according to a fixed formula.

Defined contribution plans. Pension plans in which the corporation is committed to making contributions according to a fixed formula.

Delta (of option). See hedge ratio.

Derivative asset/Contingent claim. Securities providing payoffs that depend on or are contingent on the values of other assets such as commodity prices, bond and stock prices, or market index values. Examples are futures and options.

Derivative security. See primitive security.

Detachable warrant. A warrant entitles the holder to buy a given number of shares of stock at a stipulated price. A detachable warrant is one that may be sold separately from the package it may have originally been issued with (usually a bond).

Direct search market. Buyers and sellers seek each other directly and transact directly.

Discount function. The discounted value of $1 as a function of time until payment.

Discounted dividend model (DDM). A formula to estimate the intrinsic value of a firm by figuring the present value of all expected future dividends.

Discretionary account. An account of a customer who gives a broker the authority to make buy and sell decisions on the customer's behalf.

Diversifiable risk. Risk attributable to firm-specific risk, or nonmarket risk. Nondiversifiable risk refers to systematic or market risk.

Diversification. Spreading a portfolio over many investments to avoid excessive exposure to any one source of risk.

Dividend payout ratio. Percentage of earnings paid out as dividends.

Dollar-weighted return. The internal rate of return on an investment.

Doubling option. A sinking fund provision that may allow repurchase of twice the required number of bonds at the sinking fund call price.

Dual funds. Funds in which income and capital shares on a portfolio of stocks are sold separately.

Duration. A measure of the average life of a bond, defined as the weighted average of the times until each payment is made, with weights proportional to the present value of the payment.

Dynamic hedging. Constant updating of hedge positions as market conditions change.

EAFE index. The European, Australian, Far East index, computed by Morgan, Stanley, is a widely used index of non-U.S. stocks.

Earnings retention ratio. Plowback ratio.

Earnings yield. The ratio of earnings to price, E/P.

Economic earnings. The real flow of cash that a firm could pay out forever in the absence of any change in the firm's productive capacity.

Effective annual yield. Annualized interest rate on a security computed using compound interest techniques.

Efficient diversification. The organizing principle of modern portfolio theory, which maintains that any risk-averse investor will search for the highest expected return for any level of portfolio risk.

Efficient frontier. Graph representing a set of portfolios that maximize expected return at each level of portfolio risk.

Efficient market hypothesis. The prices of securities fully reflect available information. Investors buying securities in an efficient market should expect to obtain an equilibrium rate of return. Weak-form EMH asserts that stock prices already reflect all information contained in the history of past prices. The semistrong-form hypothesis asserts that stock prices already reflect all publicly available information. The strong-form hypothesis asserts that stock prices reflect all relevant information including insider information.

Elasticity (of an option). Percentage change in the value of an option accompanying a 1% change in the value of a stock.

Endowment funds. Organizations chartered to invest money for specific purposes.

Equivalent taxable yield. The pretax yield on a taxable bond providing an after-tax yield equal to the rate on a tax-exempt municipal bond.

Eurodollars. Dollar-denominated deposits at foreign banks or foreign branches of American banks.

European option. A European option can be exercised only on the expiration date. Compare with an American option, which can be exercised before, up to, and including its expiration date.

Event study. Research methodology designed to measure the impact of an event of interest on stock returns.

Exchange rate. Price of a unit of one country's currency in terms of another country's currency.

Exchanges. National or regional auction markets providing a facility for members to trade securities. A seat is a membership on an exchange.

Exercise or strike price. Price set for calling (buying) an asset or putting (selling) an asset.

Expectations hypothesis (of interest rates). Theory that forward interest rates are unbiased estimates of expected future interest rates.

Expected return. The probability weighted average of the possible outcomes.

Expected return-beta relationship. Implication of the CAPM that security risk premiums (expected excess returns) will be proportional to beta.

Factor model. A way of decomposing the factors that influence a security's rate of return into common and firm-specific influences.

Factor portfolio. A well-diversified portfolio constructed to have a beta of 1.0 on one factor and a beta of zero on any other factor.

Fair game. An investment prospect that has a zero risk premium.

FIFO. The first-in first-out accounting method of inventory valuation.

Filter rule. A technical analysis technique stated as a rule for buying or selling stock according to past price movements.

Financial assets. Financial assets such as stocks and bonds are claims to the income generated by real assets or claims on income from the government.

Financial intermediary. An institution such as a bank, mutual fund, investment company, or insurance company that serves to connect the household and business sectors so households can invest and businesses can finance production.

Firm-specific risk. See diversifiable risk.

First-pass regression. A time series regression to estimate the betas of securities or portfolios.

Fixed annuities. Annuity contracts in which the insurance company pays a fixed dollar amount of money per period.

Fixed-charge coverage ratio. Ratio of earnings to all fixed cash obligations, including lease payments and sinking fund payments.

Fixed-income security. A security such as a bond that pays a specified cash flow over a specific period.

Flight to quality. Describes the tendency of investors to require larger default premiums on investments under uncertain economic conditions.

Floating-rate bond. A bond whose interest rate is reset periodically according to a specified market rate.

Floor broker. A member of the exchange who can execute orders for commission brokers.

Flower bond. Special Treasury bond (no longer issued) that may be used to settle federal estate taxes at par value under certain conditions.

Forced conversion. Use of a firm's call option on a callable convertible bond when the firm knows that bondholders will exercise their option to convert.

Foreign exchange market. An informal network of banks and brokers that allows customers to enter forward contracts to purchase or sell currencies in the future at a rate of exchange agreed upon now.

Forward contract. An arrangement calling for future delivery of an asset at an agreed-upon price. Also see futures contract.

Forward interest rate. Rate of interest for a future period that would equate the total return of a long-term bond with that of a strategy of rolling over shorter-term bonds. The forward rate is inferred from the term structure.

Fourth market. Direct trading in exchange-listed securities between one investor and another without the benefit of a broker.

Fully diluted earnings per share. Earnings per share expressed as if all outstanding convertible securities and warrants have been exercised.

Fundamental analysis. Research to predict stock value that focuses on such determinants as earnings and dividends prospects, expectations for future interest rates, and risk evaluation of the firm.

Futures contract. Obliges traders to purchase or sell an asset at an agreed-upon price on a specified future date. The long position is held by the trader who commits to purchase. The short position is held by the trader who commits to sell. Futures differ from forward contracts in their standardization, exchange trading, margin requirements, and daily settling (marking to market).

Futures option. The right to enter a specified futures contract at a futures price equal to the stipulated exercise price.

Geometric average. The nth root of the product of n numbers. It is used to measure the compound rate of return over time.

Globalization. Tendency toward a world-wide investment environment, and the integration of national capital markets.

Guaranteed insurance contract. A contract promising a stated nominal rate of interest over some specific time period, usually several years.

Hedge ratio (for an option). The number of stocks required to hedge against the price risk of holding one option. Also called the option's delta.

Hedging. Investing in an asset to reduce the overall risk of a portfolio.

Hedging demands. Demands for securities to hedge particular sources of consumption risk, beyond the usual mean-variance diversification motivation.

Holding period return. The rate of return over a given period.

Homogenous expectations. The assumption that all investors use the same expected returns and covariance matrix of security returns as inputs in security analysis.

Horizon analysis. Interest rate forecasting that uses a forecast yield curve to predict bond prices.

Immunization. A strategy that matches durations of assets and liabilities so as to make net worth unaffected by interest rate movements.

Implied volatility. The standard deviation of stock returns that is consistent with an option's market value.

In the money. In the money describes an option whose exercise would produce profits. Out of the money describes an option where exercise would not be profitable.

Income beneficiary. One who receives income from a trust.

Income fund. A mutual fund providing for liberal current income from investments.

Indenture. The document defining the contract between the bond issuer and the bondholder.

Index arbitrage. An investment strategy that exploits divergences between actual futures prices and their theoretically correct parity values to make a profit.

Index fund. A mutual fund holding shares in proportion to their representation in a market index such as the S&P 500.

Index model. A model of stock returns using a market index such as the S&P 500 to represent common or systematic risk factors.

Index option. A call or put option based on a stock market index.

Indifference curve. A curve connecting all portfolios with the same utility according to their means and standard deviations.

Initial public offering. Stock issued to the public for the first time by a formerly privately owned company.

Inside information. Nonpublic knowledge about a corporation possessed by corporate officers, major owners, or other individuals with privileged access to information about a firm.

Insider trading. Trading by officers, directors, major stockholders, or others who hold private inside information allowing them to benefit from buying or selling stock.

Insurance principle. The law of averages. The average outcome for many independent trials of an experiment will approach the expected value of the experiment.

Interest coverage ratio, or times interest earned. A financial leverage measure (EBIT divided by interest expense).

Interest rate. The number of dollars earned per dollar invested per period.

Interest rate parity theorem. The spot-futures exchange rate relationship that prevails in well-functioning markets.

Interest rate swaps. A method to manage interest rate risk where parties trade the cash flows corresponding to different securities without actually exchanging securities directly.

Intermarket spread swap. Switching from one segment of the bond market to another (from Treasuries to corporates, for example).

Intrinsic value (of a firm). The present value of a firm's expected future net cash flows discounted by the required rate of return.

Intrinsic value of an option. Stock price minus exercise price, or the profit that could be attained by immediate exercise of an in-the-money option.

Investment bankers. Firms specializing in the sale of new securities to the public, typically by underwriting the issue.

Investment company. Firm managing funds for investors. An investment company may manage several mutual funds.

Investment portfolio. Set of securities chosen by an investor.

Investment grade bond. Bond rated BBB and above or Baa and above. Lower-rated bonds are classified as speculative-grade or junk bonds.

Jensen's measure. The alpha of an investment.

Junk bond. See speculative grade bond.

Law of one price. The rule stipulating that equivalent securities or bundles of securities must sell at equal prices to preclude arbitrage opportunities.

Leakage. Release of information to some persons before official public announcement.

Leverage ratio. Measure of debt to total capitalization of a firm.

LIFO. The last-in first-out accounting method of valuing inventories.

Limit order. An order specifying a price at which an investor is willing to buy or sell a security.

Limited liability. The fact that shareholders have no personal liability to the creditors of the corporation in the event of failure.

Liquidation value. Net amount that could be realized by selling the assets of a firm after paying the debt.

Liquidity preference theory. Theory that the forward rate exceeds expected future interest rates.

Liquidity premium. Forward rate minus expected future short interest rate.

Load fund. A mutual fund with a sales commission, or load.

London Interbank Offered Rate (LIBOR). Rate that most creditworthy banks charge one another for large loans of Eurodollars in the London market.

Long position or long hedge. Protecting the future cost of a purchase by taking a long futures position to protect against changes in the price of the asset.

Maintenance, or variation, margin. An established value below which a trader's margin cannot fall. Reaching the maintenance margin triggers a margin call.

Margin. Describes securities purchased with money borrowed from a broker. Current maximum margin is 50%.

Market capitalization rate. The market-consensus estimate of the appropriate discount rate for a firm's cash flows.

Market model. Another version of the index model that breaks down return uncertainty into systematic and nonsystematic components.

Market or systematic risk, firm-specific risk. Market risk is risk attributable to common macroeconomic factors. Firm-specific risk reflects risk peculiar to an individual firm that is independent of market risk.

Market order. A buy or sell order to be executed immediately at current market prices.

Market portfolio. The portfolio for which each security is held in proportion to its market value.

Market price of risk. A measure of the extra return, or risk premium, that investors demand to bear risk. The reward-to-risk ratio of the market portfolio.

Market segmentation or preferred habitat theory. The theory that long- and short-maturity bonds are traded in essentially distinct or segmented markers and that prices in one market do not affect those in the other.

Market timer. An investor who speculates on broad market moves rather than on specific securities.

Market timing. Asset allocation in which the investment in the market is increased if one forecasts that the market will outperform T-bills.

Market value–weighted index. An index of a group of securities computed by calculating a weighted average of the returns of each security in the index, with weights proportional to outstanding market value.

Market-book ratio. Market price of a share divided by book value per share.

Marking to market. Describes the daily settlement of obligations on futures positions.

Mean-variance analysis. Evaluation of risky prospects based on the expected value and variance of possible outcomes.

Mean-variance criterion. The selection of portfolios based on the means and variances of their returns. The choice of the higher expected return portfolio for a given level of variance or the lower variance portfolio for a given expected return.

Measurement error. Errors in measuring an explanatory variable in a regression that lead to biases in estimated parameters.

Membership or seat on an exchange. A limited number of exchange positions that enable the holder to trade for the holder's own accounts and charge clients for the execution of trades for their accounts.

Minimum variance frontier. Graph of the lowest possible portfolio variance that is attainable for a given portfolio expected return.

Minimum variance portfolio. The portfolio of risky assets with lowest variance.

Modern portfolio theory (MPT). Principles underlying analysis and evaluation of rational portfolio choices based on risk-return trade-offs and efficient diversification.

Money market. Includes short-term, highly liquid, and relatively low-risk debt instruments.

Mortality tables. Tables of probabilities that individuals of various ages will die within a year.

Mortgage-backed security. Ownership claim in a pool of mortgages or an obligation that is secured by such a pool. Also called a *pass-through*, because payments are passed along from the mortgage originator to the purchaser of the mortgage-backed security.

Multifactor CAPM. Generalization of the basic CAPM that accounts for extra-market hedging demands.

Municipal bonds. Tax-exempt bonds issued by state and local governments, generally to finance capital improvement projects. General obligation bonds are backed by the general taxing power of the issuer. Revenue bonds are backed by the proceeds from the project or agency they are issued to finance.

Mutual fund. A firm pooling and managing funds of investors.

Mutual fund theorem. A result associated with the CAPM, asserting that investors will choose to invest their entire risky portfolio in a market-index mutual fund.

Naked option writing. Writing an option without an offsetting stock position.

NASDAQ. The automated quotation system for the OTC market, showing current bid-asked prices for thousands of stocks.

Neglected-firm effect. That investments in stock of less well-known firms have generated abnormal returns.

Nonsystematic risk. Nonmarket or firm-specific risk factors that can be eliminated by diversification. Also called unique risk or diversifiable risk. Systematic risk refers to risk factors common to the entire economy.

Normal backwardation theory. Holds that the futures price will be bid down to a level below the expected spot price.

Open (good-till-canceled) order. A buy or sell order remaining in force for up to 6 months unless canceled.

Open interest. The number of futures contracts outstanding.

Open-end (mutual) fund. A fund that issues or redeems its own shares at their net asset value (NAV).

Optimal risky portfolio. An investor's best combination of risky assets to be mixed with safe assets to form the complete portfolio.

Option elasticity. The percentage increase in an option's value given a 1% change in the value of the underlying security.

Original issue discount bond. A bond issued with a low coupon rate that sells at a discount from par value.

Out of the money. Out of the money describes an option where exercise would not be profitable. In the money describes an option where exercise would produce profits.

Over-the-counter market. An informal network of brokers and dealers who negotiate sales of securities (not a formal exchange).

Par value. The face value of the bond.

Pass-through security. Pools of loans (such as home mortgage loans) sold in one package. Owners of pass-throughs receive all principal and interest payments made by the borrowers.

Passive investment strategy. See passive management.

Passive management. Buying a well-diversified portfolio to represent a broad-based market index without attempting to search out mispriced securities.

Passive strategy. See passive management.

Passive portfolio. A market index portfolio.

P/E effect. That portfolios of low P/E stocks have exhibited higher average risk-adjusted returns than high P/E stocks.

Personal trust. An interest in an asset held by a trustee for the benefit of another person.

Plowback ratio. The proportion of the firm's earnings that is reinvested in the business (and not paid out as dividends). The plowback ratio equals 1 minus the dividend payout ratio.

Political risk. Possibility of the expropriation of assets, changes in tax policy, restrictions on the exchange of foreign currency for domestic currency, or other changes in the business climate of a country.

Portfolio insurance. The practice of using options or dynamic hedge strategies to provide protection against investment losses while maintaining upside potential.

Portfolio management. Process of combining securities in a portfolio tailored to the investor's preferences and needs, monitoring that portfolio, and evaluating its performance.

Portfolio opportunity set. The possible expected return-standard deviation pairs of all portfolios that can be constructed from a given set of assets.

Preferred habitat theory. Holds that investors prefer specific maturity ranges but can be induced to switch if premiums are sufficient.

Preferred stock. Nonvoting shares in a corporation, paying a fixed or variable stream of dividends.

Premium. The purchase price of an option.

Price-earnings multiple. See Price-earnings ratio.

Price-earnings ratio. The ratio of a stock's price to its earnings per share. Also referred to as the P/E multiple.

Primary market. New issues of securities are offered to the public here.

Primitive security, derivative security. A *primitive security* is an instrument such as a stock or bond for which payments depend only on the financial status of its issuer. A *derivative security* is created from the set of primitive securities to yield returns that depend on factors beyond the characteristics of the issuer and that may be related to prices of other assets.

Principal. The outstanding balance on a loan.

Profit margin. See Return on sales.

Program trading. Coordinated buy orders and sell orders of entire portfolios, usually with the aid of computers, often to achieve index arbitrage objectives.

Prospectus. A final and approved registration statement including the price at which the security issue is offered.

Protective covenant. A provision specifying requirements of collateral, sinking fund, dividend policy, etc., designed to protect the interests of bondholders.

Protective put. Purchase of stock combined with a put option that guarantees minimum proceeds equal to the put's exercise price.

Proxy. An instrument empowering an agent to vote in the name of the shareholder.

Public offering, private placement. A *public offering* consists of bonds sold in the primary market to the general public; a *private placement* is sold directly to a limited number of institutional investors.

Pure yield pickup swap. Moving to higher yield bonds.

Put bond. A bond that the holder may choose either to exchange for par value at some date or to extend for a given number of years.

Put option. The right to sell an asset at a specified exercise price on or before a specified expiration date.

Put-call parity theorem. An equation representing the proper relationship between put and call prices. Violation of parity allows arbitrage opportunities.

Quick ratio. A measure of liquidity similar to the current ratio except for exclusion of inventories (cash plus receivables divided by current liabilities).

Random walk. Describes the notion that stock price changes are random and unpredictable.

Rate anticipation swap. A switch made in response to forecasts of interest rates.

Real assets, financial assets. *Real assets* are land, buildings, and equipment that are used to produce goods and services. *Financial assets* are claims such as securities to the income generated by real assets.

Real interest rate. The excess of the interest rate over the inflation rate. The growth rate of purchasing power derived from an investment.

Realized compound yield. Yield assuming that coupon payments are invested at the going market interest rate at the time of their receipt and rolled over until the bond matures.

Rebalancing. Realigning the proportions of assets in a portfolio as needed.

Registered bond. A bond whose issuer records ownership and interest payments. Differs from a bearer bond, which is traded without record of ownership and whose possession is its only evidence of ownership.

Registered trader. A member of the exchange who executes frequent trades for his or her own account.

Registration statement. Required to be filed with the SEC to describe the issue of a new security.

Regression equation. An equation that describes the average relationship between a dependent variable and a set of explanatory variables.

REIT. Real estate investment trust, which is similar to a closed-end mutual fund. REITs invest in real estate or loans secured by real estate and issue shares in such investments.

Remainderman. One who receives the principal of a trust when it is dissolved.

Replacement cost. Cost to replace a firm's assets. "Reproduction" cost.

Repurchase agreements (repos). Short-term, often overnight, sales of government securities with an agreement to repurchase the securities at a slightly higher price. A *reverse repo* is a purchase with an agreement to resell at a specified price on a future date.

Residual claim. Refers to the fact that shareholders are at the bottom of the list of claimants to assets of a corporation in the event of failure or bankruptcy.

Residuals. Parts of stock returns not explained by the explanatory variable (the market-index return). They measure the impact of firm-specific events during a particular period.

Resistance level. A price level above which it is supposedly difficult for a stock or stock index to rise.

Return on assets (ROA). A profitability ratio; earnings before interest and taxes divided by total assets.

Return on equity (ROE). An accounting ratio of net profits divided by equity.

Return on sales (ROS), or profit margin. The ratio of operating profits per dollar of sales (EBIT divided by sales).

Reversing trade. Entering the opposite side of a currently held futures position to close out the position.

Reward-to-volatility ratio. Ratio of excess return to portfolio standard deviation.

Riding the yield curve. Buying long-term bonds in anticipation of capital gains as yields fall with the declining maturity of the bonds.

Risk arbitrage. Speculation on perceived mispriced securities, usually in connection with merger and acquisition targets.

Risk-averse, risk-neutral, risk-lover. A *risk-averse* investor will consider risky portfolios only if they provide compensation for risk via a risk premium. A *risk-neutral* investor finds the level of risk irrelevant and considers only the expected return of risk prospects. A *risk-lover* is willing to accept lower expected returns on prospects with higher amounts of risk.

Risk-free asset. An asset with a certain rate of return; often taken to be short-term T-bills.

Risk-free rate. The interest rate that can be earned with certainty.

Risk lover. See risk averse.

Risk neutral. See risk averse.

Risk premium. An expected return in excess of that on risk-free securities. The premium provides compensation for the risk of an investment.

Risk-return trade-off. If an investor is willing to take on risk, there is the reward of higher expected returns.

Risky asset. An asset with an uncertain rate of return.

Seasoned new issue. Stock issued by companies that already have stock on the market.

Second-pass regression. A cross-sectional regression of portfolio returns on betas. The estimated slope is the measurement of the reward for bearing systematic risk during the period.

Secondary market. Already-existing securities are bought and sold on the exchanges or in the OTC market.

Securitization. Pooling loans for various purposes into standardized securities backed by those loans, which can then be traded like any other security.

Security market line. Graphical representation of the expected return-beta relationship of the CAPM.

Security analysis. Determining correct value of a security in the marketplace.

Security characteristic line.. A plot of the expected excess return on a security over the risk-free rate as a function of the excess return on the market.

Security selection. See security selection decision.

Security selection decision. Choosing the particular securities to include in a portfolio.

Semistrong-form EMH. See Efficient market hypothesis.

Separation property. The property that portfolio choice can be separated into two independent tasks: (1) determination of the optimal risky portfolio, which is a purely technical problem, and (2) the personal choice of the best mix of the risky portfolio and the risk-free asset.

Serial bond issue. An issue of bonds with staggered maturity dates that spreads out the principal repayment burden over time.

Sharpe's measure. Reward-to-volatility ratio; ratio of portfolio excess return to standard deviation.

Shelf registration. Advance registration of securities with the SEC for sale up to 2 years following initial registration.

Short interest rate. A one-period interest rate.

Short position or hedge. Protecting the value of an asset held by taking a short position in a futures contract.

Short sale. The sale of shares not owned by the investor but borrowed through a broker and later repurchased to replace the loan. Profit comes from initial sale at a higher price than the repurchase price.

Simple prospect. An investment opportunity where a certain initial wealth is placed at risk and only two outcomes are possible.

Single-factor model. A model of security returns that acknowledges only one common factor. See factor model.

Single index model. A model of stock returns that decomposes influences on returns into a systematic factor, as measured by the return on a broad market index, and firm-specific factors.

Sinking fund. A procedure that allows for the repayment of principal at maturity by calling for the bond issuer to repurchase some proportion of the outstanding bonds either in the open market or at a special call price associated with the sinking fund provision.

Skip-day settlement. A convention for calculating yield that assumes a T-bill sale is not settled until 2 days after quotation of the T-bill price.

Small-firm effect. That investments in stocks of small firms appear to have earned abnormal returns.

Soft dollars. The value of research services that brokerage houses supply to investment managers "free of charge" in exchange for the investment managers' business.

Specialist. A trader who makes a market in the shares of one or more firms and who maintains a "fair and orderly market" by dealing personally in the stock.

Speculation. Undertaking a risky investment with the objective of earning a positive profit compared with investment in a risk-free alternative (a risk premium)

Speculative grade bond. Bond rated Ba or lower by Moody's, or BB or lower by Standard & Poor's, or an unrated bond.

Spot rate. The current interest rate appropriate for discounting a cash flow of some given maturity.

Spot-futures parity theorem, or cost-of-carry relationship. Describes the theoretically correct relationship between spot and futures prices. Violation of the parity relationship gives rise to arbitrage opportunities.

Spread (futures). Taking a long position in a futures contract of one maturity and a short position in a contract of different maturity, both on the same commodity.

Spread (options). A combination of two or more call options or put options on the same stock with differing exercise prices or times to expiration. A vertical or money spread refers to a spread with different exercise price; a horizontal or time spread refers to differing expiration date.

Squeeze. The possibility that enough long positions hold their contracts to maturity that supplies of the commodity are not adequate to cover all contracts. A *short squeeze* describes the reverse: short positions threaten to deliver an expensive-to-store commodity.

Standard deviation. Square root of the variance.

Stock exchanges. Secondary markets where already-issued securities are bought and sold by members.

Stock selection. An active portfolio management technique that focuses on advantageous selection of particular stocks rather than on broad asset allocation choices.

Stock split. Issue by a corporation of a given number of shares in exchange for the current number of shares held by stockholders. Splits may go in either direction, either increasing or decreasing the number of shares outstanding. A *reverse split* decreases the number outstanding.

Stop-loss order. A sell order to be executed if the price of the stock falls below a stipulated level.

Straddle. A combination of buying both a call and a put, each with the same exercise price and expiration date. The purpose is to profit from expected volatility in either direction.

Straight bond. A bond with no option features such as callability or convertibility.

Street name. Describes securities held by a broker on behalf of a client but registered in the name of the firm.

Strike price. See Exercise price.

Strip, strap. Variants of a straddle. A *strip* is two puts and one call on a stock; a *strap* is two calls and one put, both with the same exercise price and expiration date.

Stripped of coupons. Describes the practice of some investment banks that sell "synthetic" zero coupon bonds by marketing the rights to a single payment backed by a coupon-paying Treasury bond.

Strong-form EMH. See Efficient market hypothesis.

Subordination clause. A provision in a bond indenture that restricts the issuer's future borrowing by subordinating the new leaders' claims on the firm to those of the existing bond holders. Claims of *subordinated* or *junior* debtholders are not paid until the prior debt is paid.

Substitution swap. Exchange of one bond for a bond with similar attributes but more attractively priced.

Support level. A price level below which it is supposedly difficult for a stock or stock index to fall.

Systematic risk. Risk factors common to the whole economy, for example nondiversifiable risk; see market risk.

Tax anticipation notes. Short-term municipal debt to raise funds to pay for expenses before actual collection of taxes.

Tax swap. Swapping two similar bonds to receive a tax benefit.

Tax deferral option. The feature of the U.S. Internal Revenue Code that the capital gains tax on an asset is payable only when the gain is realized by selling the asset.

Tax-deferred retirement plans. Employer-sponsored and other plans that allow contributions and earnings to be made and accumulate tax free until they are paid out as benefits.

Tax-timing option. Describes the investor's ability to shift the realization of investment gains or losses and their tax implications from one period to another.

Technical analysis. Research to identify mispriced securities that focuses on recurrent and predictable stock price patterns and on proxies for buy or sell pressure in the market.

Tender offer. An offer from an outside investor to shareholders of a company to purchase their shares at a stipulated price, usually substantially above the market price, so that the investor may amass enough shares to obtain control of the company.

Term insurance. Provides a death benefit only, no build-up of cash value.

Term premiums. Excess of the yields to maturity on long-term bonds over those of short-term bonds.

Term structure of interest rates. The pattern of interest rates appropriate for discounting cash flows of various maturities.

Third market. Trading of exchange-listed securities on the OTC market.

Time value (of an option). The part of the value of an option that is due to its positive time to expiration. Not to be confused with present value or the time value of money.

Time-weighted return. An average of the period-by-period holding period returns of an investment.

Times interest earned. See interest coverage ratio.

Tobin's *q*. Ratio of market value of the firm to replacement cost.

Tranche. See collateralized mortgage obligation.

Treasury bill. Short-term, highly liquid government securities issued at a discount from the face value and returning the face amount at maturity.

Treasury bond or note. Debt obligations of the federal government that make semiannual coupon payments and are sold at or near par value in denominations of $1,000 or more.

Treynor's measure. Ratio of excess return to beta.

Triple-witching hour. The four times a year that the S&P 500 futures contract expires at the same time as the S&P 100 index option contract and option contracts on individual stocks.

Unbundling. See Bundling.

Underwriting, underwriting syndicate. Underwriters (investment bankers) purchase securities from the issuing company and resell them. Usually a syndicate of investment bankers is organized behind a lead firm.

Unique risk. See Diversifiable risk.

Unit investment trust. Money invested in a portfolio whose composition is fixed for the life of the fund. Shares in a unit trust are called redeemable trust certificates, and they are sold at a premium above NAV.

Universal life policy. An insurance policy that allows for a varying death benefit and premium level over the term of the policy, with an interest rate on the cash value that changes with market interest rates.

Uptick, or zero-plus tick. A trade resulting in a positive change in a stock price, or a trade at a constant price following a preceding price increase.

Utility value. The welfare a given investor assigns to an investment with a particular return and risk.

Utility. The measure of the welfare or satisfaction of an investor.

Variable annuities. Annuity contracts in which the insurance company pays a periodic amount linked to the investment performance of an underlying portfolio.

Variable life policy. An insurance policy that provides a fixed death benefit plus a cash value that can be invested in a variety of funds from which the policyholder can choose.

Variance. A measure of the dispersion of a random variable. Equals the expected value of the squared deviation from the mean.

Variation margin. See Maintenance margin.

Warrant. An option issued by the firm to purchase shares of the firm's stock.

Weak-form EMH. See Efficient market hypothesis.

Weekend effect. The common recurrent negative average return from Friday to Monday in the stock market.

Well-diversified portfolio. A portfolio spread out over many securities in such a way that the weight in any security is close to zero.

Whole-life insurance policy. Provides a death benefit and a kind of savings plan that builds up cash value for possible future withdrawal.

Workout period. Realignment period of a temporary misaligned yield relationship.

World investable wealth. The part of world wealth that is traded and is therefore accessible to investors.

Writing a call. Selling a call option.

Yield curve. A graph of yield to maturity as a function of time to maturity.

Yield to maturity. A measure of the average rate of return that will be earned on a bond if held to maturity.

Zero-beta portfolio. The minimum-variance portfolio uncorrelated with a chosen efficient portfolio.

Zero coupon bond. A bond paying no coupons that sells at a discount and provides payment of the principal only at maturity.

Zero-investment portfolio. A portfolio of zero net value, established by buying and shorting component securities, usually in the context of an arbitrage strategy.

Name Index

Subject Index

Constant growth rate model, 474-477
Constraint
  borrowing restriction and, 210
  portfolio management and, 812-813
  program, 204
Consumer Price Index
  contract based on, 683-686
  risk-free securities and, 822, 826-828
Consumption-retirement savings,
    838-839
Contango, 649-650
Contingent claim, 68, 547
  pricing of, 502
Contingent immunization, 458
Continuity, price, 84
Continuous compounding, 126-128,
    152
Contract
  consumer price index, 683-686
  dollar index, 686
  existing, 630-632
  forward, 626
  futures, 70-72, 627-632
    stock index, 655-657
  insurance, 138
  option, 550
Contribution plan, 810
Convergence of price to intrinsic value,
    477-478
Conversion premium, 406
Conversion ratio, 406
Convertible bond, 406
  corporate, 54
Convertible security, 608-611
Cornerstone Fund, 824
Corporate bond, 53-54
  price of, 381-382, 392-407
  risk and, 383
Corporation
  common stocks and, 56
  finance and, 489-491
Correlation coefficient, 143
Cost
  of factor model, 256
  replacement, 471
  storage, 678-679
  of trading, 95-97
Cost-of-carry relationship, 645
Coupon bond
  after-tax return and, 391-392
  maturity and duration and, 444-445
  price and, 379-380, 387-390
Covariance, 142, 256
  asset risk and, 235

Covariance—cont'd
  security returns and, 254
Covariance matrix, 202
Covenant, protective, 402
Coverage ratio, 525-526
  bond safety and, 400
Covered call, 570-572
Covered interest arbitrage relationship,
    673
Covering short position, 89
CPI; see Consumer Price Index
Crash, stock market
  October 19, 1987
    efficient market hypothesis and,
      366
    naked puts and, 561-563
    portfolio insurance and, 604-606
    specialist system and, 84-85
  recession and, 496-498
Credit enhancement, 29
Credit union, 18
Cross hedging, 640
CRSP; see Center for Research in
    Security Prices
Cumulative abnormal return, 352-354,
    513
Currency
  foreign, 669-674
  option and, 553
Current vs. future performance,
    342
Current ratio, 525
  bond safety and, 400
Current yield, 54
Curve
  indifference, 137
  yield
    bond and, 415
    riding of, 457-458
    term structure and, 428
    zero coupon bond and, 419

D

DARTS, 385
Data base, 18, 788-791
Data, Resources, and Estimation
    Group, 788-791
Date, announcement, 352-354
Day-of-the-week effect, 363-365
DB; see Defined benefit plan
DC; see Defined contribution plan
DDM; see Discounted dividend model
Dealer market, 23
  over-the-counter and, 86

Debenture
  bond, 404
  corporate, 54
Debt
  federal agency, 48-49
  leveraged equity and risky, 614
Debtholder, 403
December effect, 361
Decomposition of return on equity,
    520-523
Dedication strategy, 453
Default premium, 394
Default risk, 383-384
Default-free bond, 166
  coupon, 387
Defensive investor, 211
Deferred annuity, 846-848
Deferred callable bond, 405
Defined benefit plan
  defined contribution vs., 851-852
  pension funds and, 810, 812
Defined contribution plan, 810,
    851-852
Delivery, futures and, 635-637
Delta, 599
Delta Airlines, 231
Demand
  clientele, 16-22
  hedging, 303-309
Demand curve, 110
Depository Institutions Deregulation
    and Monetary Control Act, 16
Depreciation, 533
Depression, Great, 496-498
Derivative market, 68-72
Derivative security, 3, 20, 547
  bundling and, 29
Detachable warrant, 611
Developmental bond, 50
Deviation; see Standard deviation
Direct search market, 22
Discount, original issue, 384, 386-387
Discount bond, 384
Discount broker, 95
Discount function, 420-421
Discount yield, 39-41
Discounted cash flow analysis
  buy vs. rent decision and, 840-841
  commodity futures and, 679-683
Discounted dividend model, 473-487
  constant growth rate model and,
    474-477
  convergence of price to intrinsic
    value and, 477-478

In-house performance evaluation and attribution, 792-795
Initial public offering, 76, 78
Inside information, 91-94, 365-366
Institute of Chartered Financial Analysts' Code of Ethics and Professional Conduct, 91
Institutional investor, 570-572
Instrument, money market, 37-45
Insurance
  hedging and, 138
  human capital risk and, 840
  life
    objectives of, 811-812
    variable and universal, 848-849
  nonlife, 812
  portfolio, 5
    Black-Scholes formula and, 601-606
    defined benefit pension plans and, 853-854
  principle and, 184, 220-222
Insurance company
  commingled funds and, 104
  credit enhancement and, 29
  as financial intermediary, 18
  immunization strategies and, 448
Insured defined benefit pension, 812
Interest, open, 632-633
Interest rate
  bond and, 8
    after-tax return on, 392
    callable, 404-405
    coupon, 380, 389-390
  determinants of, 109-113
  forward, 417-418
  inflation and, 533-534
  pension fund and, 448
  risk and, 438-447
  swap, 461-463
  term structure of, 413-437
    certainty and, 413-418
    forward rates and, 422-424
    interpreting of, 428-431
    measuring of, 418-422
    realized compound yield to maturity and, 432-433
    theories of, 424-428
Interest rate futures, 674-677
  Consumer Price Index, 685
Interest rate option, 553
Interest rate parity, 671-674
Intermarket spread swap, 455
Internal Revenue Service, 386-387

International and extended diversification, 753-773
  investments and, 753-768
    passive and active, 763-765
    precious metals and, 769-770
    real estate and, 768-769
International capital market, 766-768
In-the-money option, 547, 575
Intrinsic value
  convergence of price to, 477-478
  in-the-money option and, 575
  market price vs., 472-473
Inventory valuation, 532-533
Investing, value, 535
Investment
  environment of, 10-36; see also Investment environment
  international, 753-768
  opportunity set and, 169
    capital allocation line and, 196
  options vs. stock, 558-563
  pension fund and; see Pension fund
  policy, mutual fund and, 100-103
  pool and, 104
  portfolio of, 2
  return on, 718-723
Investment banking, 19
  issuing of securities and, 76-77
Investment company, 18
Investment environment, 10-36
  client demands and, 16-22
    financial system and, 12-16
  households and businesses and, 32-33
  markets and, 22-23
  real assets vs. financial assets and, 10-12
  recent trends and, 23-31
Investment-grade bond, 396
IPO; see Initial public offering

J

January effect, 360-362
Jensen's measure, 725
Junior debtholder, 403
Junk bond, 396, 399-400

K

Kennedy correction, 498

L

Labor income, 306-307
Last-in first-out system, 532-533
Legal constraint, 813

Leverage ratio, 522-523
  bond safety and, 400
Leveraged equity and risky debt, 614
Liability
  bank, 447
  common stock and, 56-57
LIBOR; see London Interbank Offered Rate
Life cycle approach, 837-842
Life insurance
  objectives of, 811-812
  variable and universal, 848-849
Lifetime consumption, 247
Lifetime portfolio selection, 842
LIFO; see Last-in first-out system
Limit order, 82
Limited liability, 56-57
Line
  capital market, 230
  security characteristic, 260, 315
  security market; see Security market line
Liquidation value, 471
Liquidity, 525-526
  as constraint, 813
Liquidity preference, 424-426
Liquidity premium, 434
  bond and, 423, 429
Liquidity ratio, bond safety and, 400
Listing, stock market, 57-59; see also Exchange
Load fund, 98
Loan
  collateralized-automobile receivable and, 24, 27
  margin and, 86-88
  mortgage; see Mortgage
Logistics, 796-800
Lognormal distribution, 151-153
London Interbank Offered Rate, 44-45
  interest rate swap and, 462
Long position
  futures and, 70, 627-628
  hedging and, 639-640
Long-term bond
  deep discount, 21
  interest rate and, 440
  liquidity preference and, 424-426
  market segmentation theory and, 427-428
  safety and, 423
Low-volatility scenario, 577-578
Lucky event, 355-357
LYON, 385

Price change, random walk and, 342-343
Price continuity, 84
Price/earnings effect, 359
Price/earnings multiple, 481-482
Price/earnings ratio, 59, 526-527
  inflation and, 493
Price-weighted average, 60
Pricing model
  capital asset; *see* Capital asset pricing model
  option, 602
Pricing theory, arbitrage; *see* Arbitrage pricing theory
Primary market, 22-23, 76
Primary Trend Fund, 825
Primitive security, 20
  bundling and, 29
Principal, bond and, 379
Private placement, 76
Private purpose bond, 51
Probability distribution, 147-151
Profit
  active bond management and, 454-456
  arbitrage and, 280-283
  futures contract and, 635
  paper, 516
  protective put vs. stock investment, 568-569
Profit margin, 521
Profitability ratio, 400
Program
  buy, 8
  constraint, 204
Program trading, 662
Promised yield vs. expected yield, 394-399
Property, separation, 208
Proportion
  investment, 189-190
  optimal overall portfolio, 199
Prospect, simple, 131
Prospectus, 77
Protection, call, 405
Protective covenant, 402
Protective put, 566-569
  portfolio insurance and, 601
Proxy
  market, 326
  vote by, 56
Proxy fight, 33
Pseudo-American formula, 621
Public offering, 76, 78

Pure yield curve, 419
Pure yield pickup swap, 455-456
Put
  bond, 406
  option, 68, 547, 557-558
    American, 598
    collateralized loans and, 612
    portfolio insurance and, 601-602
    protective, 566-569
    valuation of, 584, 598
Put-call parity theorem, 564-566

Q

Quant, 7
Quick ratio, 525-526
  bond safety and, 400

R

Random variable, 147
Random walk, 342-343 violations of, 358
Rate
  certainty equivalent, 135
  coupon, 379
  exchange, 760-763
  forward, 422-424
  interest; *see* Interest rate
  market capitalization, 473
  reinvestment, 450-451
  of return; *see* Return
  risk-free, 205
  spot, 415
    expected future, 429-430
  utility, 242
Rate anticipation swap, 455
Rate of return
  arbitrage and, 281
  continuously compounded annual, 152
  risk-sharing vs. risk-pooling and, 220-222
  time diversification and, 222-226
  yield to maturity and, 382-383
Rating, bond, 397-399
Ratio
  acid test, 525-526
  appraisal, 725
  asset utilization, 523-525
  bond safety and, 400
  conversion, 406
  coverage, 525-526
  current, 525
  dividend payout, 479

Ratio—cont'd
  future investment opportunity and, 481-482
  leverage, 522-523
  market-to-book value, 526
  plowback, 478-482
    inflation and, 493
  price/earnings, 59, 526-527
  quick, 525-526
  reward-to-variability, 170, 194
Ratio analysis, 520-530
Rational portfolio management, 349-350
Real asset, 34
  financial asset vs., 10-12
Real estate
  diversification and, 818-822
    international and extended, 768-769
  investment trust and, 14, 104
Real risk vs. nominal risk, 119
Real Yield Securities, 822
Realized compound yield, 432-433
Realized return, 264-266
  expected vs., 734-735
REALs; *see* Real Yield Securities
Rebalancing immunized portfolio, 452
Receivable, collateralized-automobile, 24, 27
Recession, 498-499
  Roosevelt, 497
Red herring, 77
Redeemable stock, 59
Redeemable trust certificate, 103-104
Refunding, bond and, 404
Regional exchange, 79
Registered trader, 82
Registration statement, 77
Regression, 268
  first- and second-pass, 315-320
Regulation
  client demand and, 21
  futures markets and, 637, 638
  government, 15-16
  Q, 16
    taxation and, 21-22
  of securities markets, 90-92
Regulatory constraint, 813
Reinvestment rate risk, 450-451
REIT; *see* Real estate, investment trust and
Relative strength approach, 345
Remainderman, 809
Rent vs. buy decision, 840-841

Useful Formulas

Measures of Risk

Variance of returns: $\sigma^2 = E[r - E(r)]^2$

Standard deviation: $\sqrt{\sigma^2}$

Covariance between returns: $\text{Cov}(r_i, r_j) = E\{[r_i - E(r_i)][r_j - E(r_j)]\}$

Beta of security i: $\beta_i = \dfrac{\text{Cov}(r_i, r_M)}{\text{Var}(r_M)}$

Portfolio Theory

Expected rate of return on a portfolio with weights w_i in each security:

$$E(r_p) = \sum_{i=1}^{n} w_i E(r_i)$$

Variance of portfolio rate of return: $\sigma_p^2 = \sum_{j=1}^{n} \sum_{i=1}^{n} w_j w_i \, \text{Cov}(r_i, r_j)$

Optimal fraction of the complete portfolio to place in the optimal risky portfolio: $y = \dfrac{E(r_p) - r_f}{A\sigma_P^2}$

Market Equilibrium

The security market line: $E(r_i) = r_f + \beta_i[E(r_M) - r_f]$

Fixed-Income Analysis

Present value of $1

Discrete period compounding: $\text{PV} = 1/(1 + r)^T$

Continuous compounding: $\text{PV} = e^{-rT}$

Forward rate of interest for period T: $f_T = \dfrac{(1 + y_T)^T}{(1 + y_{T-1})^{T-1}}$

Real interest rate: $R = \dfrac{1 + r}{1 + i} - 1$

where r is the nominal interest rate
and i is the inflation rate

Duration of a security: $D = \sum_{t=1}^{T} t \times \dfrac{CF_t}{(1 + y)^t} / \text{Price}$